Introduction to Contemporary Civilization in the West A SOURCE BOOK

PREPARED BY THE CONTEMPORARY CIVILIZATION

STAFF OF COLUMBIA COLLEGE, COLUMBIA UNIVERSITY

VOLUME II · THIRD EDITION · 1961

Columbia University Press

NEW YORK AND LONDON

PREFACE TO THE FIRST EDITION

VOLUME TWO of this *Source Book*, though designed for the latter part of the first year course in Contemporary Civilization at Columbia, may be used independently, and may be adapted to other and very different needs.

Of the introductions to the individual selections in these volumes, many written by the collaborators on the 1941–43 fascicle edition have been retained and revised, and many have been written by the present editorial committee for the new selections chosen. Introductions for new selections in Volume Two have also been contributed by Frederick de W. Bolman, Jr., J. Bartlet Brebner, Alan W. Brown, George Crothers, Ernest Nagel, John H. Randall, Jr., John A. Scott, Richard C. Snyder, Boris M. Stanfield, and Morton G. White.

The numerous translations made especially for these volumes are the work of the earlier and present committees, and of others whose services were solicited by Columbia College.

The committee wishes to express thanks to Lore L. Kapp, Paul O. Kristeller, and Benjamin N. Nelson, who have contributed aid on special problems; and to Matilda L. Berg and Eugenia Porter of Columbia University Press, who have expedited the production of the book.

The conclusion of this enterprise would not be complete without a reference to those who founded or shaped the course from which the *Source Book* derives. It is impossible to mention all of them, but perhaps they can be represented by the name of the late John J. Coss, who was central in the conception and furtherance of the Contemporary Civilization idea.

In the most literal sense, these volumes have been made possible by the energetic sponsorship of the Dean of Columbia College, Harry J. Carman.

JUSTUS BUCHLER
K. WILLIAM KAPP
ROBERT S. LOPEZ

Columbia College, Columbia University
June, 1946

PREFACE TO THE SECOND EDITION

THE SECOND volume of the *Source Book* contains readings in the civilization of the Western world since the French Revolution. Its chapter headings correspond to those of the companion book of background readings, Volume Two of *Chapters in Western Civilization*.

In addition to the general re-editing specified in the Preface to the second edition of Volume One, Volume Two of the *Source Book* has undergone the following changes:

1. New source-readings have been introduced,
   (a) from authors and documents hitherto unrepresented: Debates on the Corn Laws (The Free Trade Controversy), Bentham, *The Economist* (Owen), Bakunin, De Tocqueville, Buckle, Green, Rathenau, Rhodes, Gide, Shaw (Fabianism), Sorel, Jaurès, The Atomic Bomb;
   (b) from authors already represented: Disraeli, Santayana.

2. Certain existing source-readings have been amplified, contracted or re-edited for one reason or another—*e.g.,* greater fullness, greater conciseness, better continuity, the insertion of significant passages: Burke, Hegel, M'Culloch, Owen, Carlyle, Duke of Wellington, Comte, Spencer, Pius XI, The Oxford Conference, Fascism in Action.

3. Certain authors and movements represented by selections that did not prove useful in the classroom have been omitted: Von Liebig, Considérant, Bagehot, Hobson, Protectionism, Cole, National Minorities.

None of the new pieces has been introduced merely for its intellectual modishness or journalistic contemporaneity. Some, however, notably the Bakunin, De Tocqueville, Sorel, and concluding Santayana selections, are inserted so that certain ironies and ambivalences of Western mind and society in the nineteenth and twentieth centuries may be more clearly drawn out.

In Volume One the committee has already acknowledged the counsel and assistance of many persons in connection with its work, as well as the kindness of publishers who allowed the use of copyrighted material. For Volume Two new introductions have been written and many old ones revised by Harold Barger, Jacques Barzun, J. Bartlet Brebner, Irwin Edman, Charles

Frankel, Horace L. Friess, Henry L. Roberts, and Paul Seabury, as well as by members of the committee.

Editorial Committee
JOSEPH L. BLAU
RALPH H. BOWEN
PETER J. GAY
SIDNEY GELBER
GEORGE T. MATTHEWS
RICHARD M. MORSE, *Chairman*
STEPHEN W. ROUSSEAS

Columbia University
October, 1953

PREFACE TO THE THIRD EDITION

THIS THIRD edition represents a considerable reworking of the second half of the first year of the Contemporary Civilization course in Columbia College. Basically, the course and this volume now cover aspects of Western life and thought in the nineteenth century including the period of the French Revolution to the eve of the First World War. So much of the second edition has been recast that comparison of the contents of this new edition with the old would take almost as much space as the table of contents. Two notable general changes, however, are the introduction of more material on the religious quarrels of the nineteenth century and a significant increase in the documents on imperialism after 1870. Most of the introductions have been rewritten and shortened, in keeping with the policy stated in the Preface to the recently revised first volume of readings. The introductions do not give a précis of the document but provide only essential historical or biographical background.

Besides those colleagues and assistants thanked at the end of Volume One we would like to express gratitude to Elinor Stoneman and William W. Ryding for translations, and to Barry Augenbraun, Thomas Vargish, and Morton Paley for editorial assistance. Benjamin Bennett, Dennis Flynn, Allan N. Galpern, and John Galton helped with the proof.

Editorial Committee
MARVIN HARRIS
SIDNEY MORGENBESSER
JOSEPH ROTHSCHILD
BERNARD WISHY, *Chairman*

Columbia College
Columbia University
October, 1960

CONTENTS

I THE FRENCH REVOLUTION

ARTHUR YOUNG

T̲H̲E̲ *Travels in France during 1787, 1788, and 1789* (published in 1792–94) by Arthur Young (1741–1820) are today a primary source for the student of the economic condition of France immediately before the Revolution. Young was concerned in all his travels to show that agriculture, rather than commerce and industry, was fundamental. Neither this objective, however, nor his preconception in favor of the British Constitution prevented his being a shrewd observer of the revolutionary situation.

Young's greatest importance was as a pioneer in the practice and propagation of scientific farming, and he was one of the principals in the progress of British agriculture in this respect. His written works advocating such measures as rotation of crops, the abolition of fallows, the use of artificial grasses, together with his reports of his wide travels, won him during his lifetime an international reputation.

TRAVELS IN FRANCE, 1787–90

OCTOBER, 1787

. . . [PARIS.] Dined to-day with a party, whose conversation was entirely political. Mons. de Calonne's *Requête au Roi* [1] is come over, and all the world are reading and disputing on it. It seems, however, generally agreed that, without exonerating himself from the charge of the agiotage, he has thrown no inconsiderable load on the shoulders of the archbishop of Toulouze, the present premier, who will be puzzled to get rid of the attack. But both these ministers were condemned on all hands in the lump; as being absolutely unequal to the difficulties of so arduous a period. One opinion pervaded the whole company, that they are on the eve of some great revolution in the government: that everything points to it: the confusion in the finances great; with a *deficit* impossible to provide for without the states-general of the kingdom, yet no ideas formed of what would be the consequence of their meeting: no minister existing, or to be looked to in or out of power, with such decisive talents as to promise any other remedy than palliative ones: a prince on the throne, with excellent dispositions, but without the resources of a mind that could govern in such a moment without ministers: a court buried in pleasure and dissipation; and adding to the distress, instead of endeavouring to be

---

[1] [*Petition to the King.*]

placed in a more independent situation: a great ferment amongst all ranks of men, who are eager for some change, without knowing what to look to, or to hope for: and a strong leaven of liberty, increasing every hour since the American revolution; altogether form a combination of circumstances that promise e'er long to ferment into motion, if some master hand, of very superior talents, and inflexible courage, is not found at the helm to guide events, instead of being driven by them. It is very remarkable, that such conversation never occurs, but a bankruptcy is a topic: the curious question on which is, *would a bankruptcy occasion a civil war, and a total overthrow of the government?* The answers that I have received to this question, appear to be just: such a measure, conducted by a man of abilities, vigour and firmness, would certainly not occasion either one or the other. But the same measure, attempted by a man of a different character, might possibly do both. All agree, that the states of the kingdom cannot assemble without more liberty being the consequence; but I meet with so few men that have any just ideas of freedom, that I question much the species of this new liberty that is to arise. They know not how to value the privileges of THE PEOPLE: as to the nobility and the clergy, if a revolution added any thing to their scale, I think it would do more mischief than good.

SEPTEMBER, 1788

The 2d. Rennes is well built, and it has two good squares; that particularly of Louis XV. where is his statue. The parliament being in exile, the house is not to be seen. The Benedictines garden, called the *Tabour,* is worth viewing. But the object at Rennes most remarkable at present is a camp, with a marshal of France (de Stainville), and four regiments of infantry, and two of dragoons, close to the gates. The discontents of the people have been double, first on account of the high price of bread, and secondly for the banishment of the parliament. The former cause is natural enough, but why the people should love their parliament was what I could not understand, since the members, as well as of the states, are all noble, and the distinction between the *noblesse* and *roturiers* [2] no where stronger, more offensive, or more abominable than in Bretagne. They assure me, however, that the populace have been blown up to violence by every art of deception, and even by money distributed for that purpose. The commotions rose to such a height before the camp was established, that the troops here were utterly unable to keep the peace. Mons. Argentaise, to whom I had brought letters, had the goodness, during the four days I was here, to shew and explain every thing to be seen. I find Rennes very cheap; and it appears the more so to me just come from Normandy, where

[2] [*The common people.*]

every thing is extravagantly dear. The table d'hôte, at the *grand maison*, is well served; they give two courses, containing plenty of good things, and a very ample regular dessert: the supper one good course, with a large joint of mutton, and another good dessert; each meal, with the common wine, 40s. and for 20 more you have very good wine, instead of the ordinary sort: 30s. for the horse: thus, with good wine, it is no more than 6 liv. 10s. a day, or 5s. 10d. Yet a camp which they complain has raised prices enormously.

The 5th. To Montauban. The poor people seem poor indeed; the children terribly ragged, if possible worse clad than if with no cloaths at all; as to shoes and stockings they are luxuries. A beautiful girl of six or seven years playing with a stick, and smiling under such a bundle of rags as made my heart ache to see her: they did not beg, and when I gave them any thing seemed more surprised than obliged. One third of what I have seen of this province seems uncultivated, and nearly all of it in misery. What have kings, and ministers, and parliaments, and states, to answer for their prejudices, seeing millions of hands that would be industrious, idle and starving, through the execrable maxims of despotism, or the equally detestable prejudices of a feudal nobility. Sleep at the *lion d'or,* at Montauban, an abominable hole.—20 miles.

The 6th. The same inclosed country to Brooms; but near that town improves to the eye, from being more hilly. At the little town of Lamballe, there are above fifty families of noblesse that live in winter, who reside on their estates in the summer. There is probably as much foppery and nonsense in their circles, and for what I know as much happiness, as in those of Paris. Both would be better employed in cultivating their lands, and rendering the poor industrious.—30 miles. . . .

The 24th. . . . Nantes is an *enflammé* in the cause of liberty, as any town in France can be; the conversations I witnessed here, prove how great a change is effected in the minds of the French, nor do I believe it will be possible for the present government to last half a century longer, unless the clearest and most decided talents are at the helm. The American revolution has laid the foundation of another in France, if government does not take care of itself. The 23d one of the twelve prisoners from the Bastile arrived here —he was the most violent of them all—and his imprisonment has been far enough from silencing him.

JUNE, 1789

The 8th. To my friend Lazowski, to know where were the lodgings I had written him to hire me, but my good dutchess d'Estissac would not allow him to execute my commission. I found an apartment in her hotel prepared for me. Paris is at present in such a ferment about the States General, now holding at Versailles, that conversation is absolutely absorbed by them. Not a word of any thing else talked of. Every thing is considered, and justly so, as important in such a crisis of the fate of four-and-twenty millions of people. It is now a serious contention whether the representatives are to be called the *Commons* or *Tiers Etat;* they call themselves steadily the former, while the court and the great lords reject the term with a species of apprehension, as if it involved a meaning not easily to be fathomed. But this point is of little consequence, compared with another, that has kept the states for sometime in inactivity, the verification of their power separately or in common. The nobility and the clergy demand the former, but the Commons steadily refuse it; the reason why a circumstance, apparently of no great consequence, is thus tenaciously regarded, is that it may decide their sitting for the future in separate houses or in one. Those who are warm for the interest of the people declare that it will be impossible to reform some of the grossest abuses in the state, if the nobility, by sitting in a separate chamber, shall have a negative on the wishes of the people: and that to give such a *veto* to the clergy would be still more preposterous; if therefore, by the verification of their powers in one chamber, they shall once come together, the popular party hope that there will remain, no power afterwards to separate. The nobility and clergy foresee the same result, and will not therefore agree to it. In this dilemma it is curious to remark the *feelings* of the moment. It is not my business to write memories of what passes, but I am intent to catch, as well as I can, the opinions of the day most prevalent. While I remain at Paris, I shall see people of all descriptions, from the coffee-house politicians to the leaders in the states; and the chief object of such rapid notes as I throw on paper, will be to catch the ideas of the moment; to compare them afterwards with the actual events that shall happen, will afford amusement at least. The most prominent feature that appears at present is, that an idea of common interest and common danger does not seem to unite those, who, if not united, may find themselves too weak to oppose the common danger that must arise from the people being sensible of a strength the result of *their* weakness. The king, court, nobility, clergy, army, and parliament, are nearly in the same situation. All these consider, with equal dread, the ideas of liberty, now afloat; except the first, who, for reasons obvious to those who know his character, troubles himself little, even with circumstances that concern his power the most intimately. Among the rest, the feeling of danger is common, and they would unite, were there a head to render it easy, in order to do without the states at all. That the commons themselves look for some such hostile union as more than probable, appears from an idea which gains ground, that they will find it necessary should the other two orders continue [not] to unite with them in one chamber, to declare themselves boldly the representatives of the kingdom at large, calling on the nobility and clergy to take their places—and to enter upon deliberations of business without them, should they refuse it. All conversation at present is on this topic, but opinions are more divided than I should have expected. There seem to be many who hate the clergy so cordially, that rather than permit them to form a distinct chamber would venture on a new system, dangerous as it might prove.

The 9th. The business going forward at present in the pamphlet shops of Paris is incredible. I went to the Palais Royal to see what new things were published, and to procure a catalogue of all. Every hour produces something new. Thirteen came out to-day, sixteen yesterday, and ninety-two last week. We think sometimes that Debrett's or Stockdale's shops at London are crouded, but they are mere deserts, compared to Desein's, and some others here, in which one can scarcely squeeze from the door to the counter. The price of printing two years ago was from 27 liv. to 30 liv. per sheet, but now it is from 60 liv. to 80 liv. This spirit of reading political tracts, they say, spreads into the provinces, so that all the presses of France are equally employed. Nineteen-twentieths of these productions are in favour of liberty, and commonly violent against the clergy and nobility; I have to-day bespoke many of this description, that have reputation; but enquiring for such as had appeared on the other side of the question, to my astonishment I find there are but two or three that have merit enough to be known. Is it not wonderful, that while the press teems with the most levelling and even seditious principles, that if put in execution would overturn the monarchy, nothing in reply appears, and not the least step is taken by the court to restrain this extreme licentiousness of publication. It is easy to conceive the spirit that must thus be raised among the people. But the coffee-houses in the Palais Royal present yet more singular and astonishing spectacles; they are not only crouded within, but other expectant crouds are at the doors and windows, listening *a gorge deployé* [3] to certain orators, who from chairs or tables harangue each his little audience: the eagerness with which they are heard, and the thunder of applause they receive for every sentiment of more than common hardiness or violence against the present government, cannot easily be imagined. I am all amazement at the ministry permitting such nests and hotbeds of sedition and revolt, which disseminate amongst the people, every hour, principles that by and by must be opposed with vigour, and therefore it seems little short of madness to allow the propagation at present.

The 10th. Every thing conspires to render the present period in France critical: the want of bread is terrible: accounts arrive every moment from the

---

[3] [*With wholehearted response.*]

provinces of riots and disturbances, and calling in the military, to preserve the peace of the markets. The prices reported are the same as I found at Abbeville and Amiens 5s. (2½.) a pound for white bread, and 3½s. to 4s. for the common sort, eaten by the poor: these rates are beyond their faculties, and occasion great misery. . . .

The 15th. This has been a rich day, and such an one as ten years ago none could believe would ever arrive in France; a very important debate being expected on what, in our house of commons, would be termed the state of the nation. My friend Mons. Lazowski and myself were at Versailles by eight in the morning. We went immediately to the hall of the states to secure good seats in the gallery; we found some deputies already there, and a pretty numerous audience collected. The room is too large; none but stentorian lungs, or the finest clearest voices can be heard; however the very size of the apartment, which admits 2000 people, gave a dignity to the scene. It was indeed an interesting one. The spectacle of the representatives of twenty-five millions of people, just emerging from the evils of 200 years of arbitrary power, and rising to the blessings of a freer constitution, assembled with open doors under the eye of the public, was framed to call into animated feelings every latent spark, every emotion of a liberal bosom. To banish whatever ideas might intrude of their being a people too often hostile to my own country,—and to dwell with pleasure on the glorious idea of happiness to a great nation—of felicity to millions yet unborn. Mons. l'Abbé Syeyes opened the debate. He is one of the most zealous sticklers for the popular cause; carries his ideas not to a regulation of the present government, which he thinks too bad to be regulated at all, but wishes to see it absolutely overturned; being in fact a violent republican: this is the character he commonly bears and in his pamphlets he seems pretty much to justify such an idea. . . .

The 18th. Yesterday the commons decreed themselves, in consequence of the Abbé Syeyes's amended motion, the title of *Assemblée Nationale;* and also, considering themselves then in activity, the illegality of all taxes; but granted them during the session, declaring that they would, without delay, deliberate on the consolidating of the debt; and on the relief of the misery of the people. These steps give great spirits to the violent partizans of a new constitution, but amongst more sober minds, I see evidently an apprehension that it will prove a precipitate measure. It is a violent step, which may be taken hold of by the court, and converted very much to the people's disadvantage. The reasoning of Mons. de Mirabeau against it was forcible and just. . . .

The 23d. The important day is over: in the morning Versailles seemed filled with troops: the streets, about ten o'clock, were lined with the French guards, and some Swiss regiments, &c.: the hall of the states was surrounded, and centinels fixed in all the passages, and at the doors; and none but deputies admitted. This military preparation was ill-judged, for it seemed admitting the impropriety and unpopularity of the intended measure, and the expectation, perhaps fear of popular commotions. They pronounced, before the king left the chateau, that his plan was adverse to the people, from the military parade with which it was ushered in. The contrary, however, proved to be the fact; the propositions are known to all the world: the plan was a good one; much was granted to the people in great and essential points; and as it was granted before they had provided for these public necessities of finance, which occasioned the states being called together; and consequently left them at full power in future to procure for the people all that opportunity might present, they apparently ought to accept them, provided some security is given for the future meetings of the states, without which all the rest would be insecure; but as a little negociation may easily secure this, I apprehend the deputies will accept them conditionally: the use of soldiers, and some imprudencies in the manner of forcing the king's system, relative to the interior constitution, and assembling of the deputies, as well as the ill-blood which had had time to brood for three days past in their minds, prevented the commons from receiving the king with any expressions of applause; the clergy, and some of the nobility, cried *vive le Roi!* but treble the number of mouths being silent, took off all effect. It seems they had previously determined to submit to no violence: when the king was gone, and the clergy and nobility retired, the marquis de Brézé waiting a moment to see if they meant to obey the king's express orders, to retire also to another chamber prepared for them, and perceiving that no one moved, addressed them,—*Messieurs, vous connoissez les intentions du Roi.*[4] A dead silence ensued; and then it was that superior talents bore the sway, that overpowers in critical moments all other considerations. The eyes of the whole assembly were turned on the count de Mirabeau, who instantly replied to the marquis de Brézé—*Oui, Monsieur, nous avons entendu les intentions qu'on a suggéreés au Roi, & vous qui ne sauriez être son organe auprès des etats généraux, vous qui n'avez ici ni place, ni voix, ni droit de parler, vous n'étes pas fait pour nous rapeller son discours. Cependant pour eviter toute equivoque, & tout delai, je vous declare que si l'on vous a chargé de nous faire sortir d'ici, vous devez demander des ordres pour employer la force, car nous ne quitterons nos places que par la puissance de la baionette.*[5]—On which there was a general cry of—*Tel est le vœu de l'As-*

---

[4] [*Gentlemen, you are aware of the King's intentions.*]

[5] [*Yes, sir, we have heard the intentions that have been suggested to the King, and you who are present in the Estates General merely as his instrument, who have here neither place nor vote nor right of speech, you are not the person to remind us of his word. Nevertheless, to re-*

semblee.[6] They then immediately passed a confirmation of their preceding arrets; and, on the motion of the count de Mirabeau, a declaration that their persons, individually and collectively, were sacred; and that all who made any attempts against them should be deemed infamous traitors to their country.

The 24th. The ferment at Paris is beyond conception; 10,000 people have been all this day in the Palais Royal; a full detail of yesterday's proceedings was brought this morning, and read by many apparent leaders of little parties, with comments, to the people. To my surprise, the king's propositions are received with universal disgust. He said nothing explicit on the periodical meeting of the states; he declared all the old feudal rights to be retained as property. These, and the change in the balance of representation in the provincial assemblies, are the articles that give the greatest offence. But instead of looking to, or hoping for further concessions on these points, in order to make them more consonant to the general wishes; the people seem, with a sort of phrenzy, to reject all idea of compromise, and to insist on the necessity of the orders uniting, that full power may consequently reside in the commons, to effect what they call the regeneration of the kingdom, a favourite term, to which they affix no precise idea, but add the indefinite explanation of the general reform of all abuses. They are also full of suspicions at M. Necker's offering to resign, to which circumstance they seem to look more than to much more essential points. It is plain to me, from many conversations and harangues I have been witness to, that the constant meetings at the Palais Royal, which are carried to a degree of licentiousness and fury of liberty, that is scarcely credible, united with the innumerable inflammatory publications that have been hourly appearing since the assembly of the states, have so heated the people's expectations, and given them the idea of such total changes, that nothing the king or court could do, would now satisfy them; consequently it would be idleness itself to make concessions that are not steadily adhered to, not only to be observed by the king, but to be enforced on the people, and good order at the same time restored. But the stumbling-block to this and every plan that can be devised, as the people know and declare in every corner, is the situation of the finances, which cannot possibly be restored but by liberal grants of the states on one hand, or by a bankruptcy on the other. It is well known, that this point has been warmly debated in the council: Mons. Necker has proved to them, that a bankruptcy is inevitable, if they break with the states before the finances are restored; and the dread and terror of taking such a step, which no minister would at present dare to venture on, has been the

---

move all possibilities of misunderstanding, and to avoid delay, I tell you that if you have been assigned to remove us from here, you had better ask for orders to use force, because we shall leave our places only under pressure of the bayonet.]

[6] [Such is the vote of the Assembly.]

great difficulty that opposed itself to the projects of the Queen and the count
d'Artois. The measure they have taken is a middle one, from which they hope
to gain a party among the people, and render the deputies unpopular enough
to get rid of them: an expectation, however, in which they will infallibly be
mistaken. If, on the side of the people it is urged, that the vices of the old
government make a new system necessary, and that it can only be by the firmest
measures that the people can be put in possession of the blessings of a free
government; it is to be replied, on the other hand, that the personal character
of the king is a just foundation for relying that no measures of actual violence
can be seriously feared: that the state of the finances, under any possible regimen, whether of faith or bankruptcy, must secure their existence, at least for
time sufficient to secure by negociation, what may be hazarded by violence:
that by driving things to extremities, they risque an union between all the
other orders of the state, with the parliaments, army, and a great body even
of the people, who must disapprove of all extremities; and when to this is
added the possibility of involving the kingdom in a civil war, now so familiarly
talked of, that it is upon the lips of all the world, we must confess, that the
commons, if they steadily refuse what is now held out to them, put immense
and certain benefits to the chance of fortune, to that hazard which may make
posterity curse, instead of bless, their memories as real patriots, who had nothing in view but the happiness of their country. . . .

The 27th. The whole business now seems over, and the revolution complete.
The king has been frightened by the mobs into overturning his own act of
the *seance royale,*[7] by writing to the presidents of the orders of the nobility and
clergy, requiring them to join the commons,—full in the teeth of what he
had ordained before. It was represented to him, that the want of bread was
so great in every part of the kingdom, that there was no extremity to which
the people might not be driven: that they were nearly starving, and consequently ready to listen to any suggestions, and on the *qui vive*[8] for all sorts
of mischief: that Paris and Versailles would inevitably be burnt; and in a
word, that all sorts of misery and confusion would follow his adherence to
the system announced in the *seance royale.* His apprehensions got the better
of the party, who had for some days guided him; and he was thus induced to
take this step, which is of such importance, that he will never more know
where to stop, or what to refuse; or rather he will find, that in the future arrangement of the kingdom, his situation will be very nearly that of Charles I.
a spectator, without power, of the effective resolutions of a long parliament.
The joy this step occasioned was infinite: the assembly, uniting with the
people, all hurried to the chateau. *Vive le Roi* might have been heard at Marly:

[7] [*Royal session.*]   [8] [On the *alert.*]

the king and queen appeared in the balcony, and were received with the loudest shouts of applause; the leaders, who governed these motions, knew the value of the concession much better than those who made it. I have to-day had conversation with many persons on this business; and, to my amazement, there is an idea, and even among many of the nobility, that this union of the orders is only for the verification of their powers, and for *making the constitution,* which is a new term they have adopted; and which they use as if a constitution was a pudding to be made by a receipt. In vain I have asked, where is the power that can separate them hereafter, if the commons insist on remaining together, which may be supposed, as such an arrangement will leave all the power in their own hands? And in vain I appeal to the evidence of the pamphlets written by the leaders of that assembly, in which they hold the English constitution cheap, because the people have not power enough, owing to that of the crown and the house of lords. The event now appears so clear, as not to be difficult to predict: all real power will be henceforward in the commons, having so much inflamed the people in the exercise of it, they will find themselves unable to use it temperately; the court cannot sit to have their hands behind them; the clergy, nobility, parliaments, and army, will, when they find themselves all in danger of annihilation, unite in their mutual defence; but as such an union will demand time, will find the people armed, and a bloody civil war must be the result. I have more than once declared this as my opinion, but do not find that others unite in it. At all events, however, the tide now runs so strongly in favour of the people, and the conduct of the court seems to be so weak, divided, and blind, that little can happen that will not clearly date from the present moment. Vigour and abilities would have turned every thing on the side of the court; for the great mass of nobility in the kingdom, the higher clergy, the parliaments, and the army, were with the crown; but this desertion of the conduct, that was necessary to secure its power, at a moment so critical, must lead to all sorts of pretensions. At night the fire-works, and illuminations, and mob, and noise, at the Palais Royal increased; the expence must be enormous; and yet nobody knows with certainty from whence it arises: shops there are, however, that for 12*s.* give as many squibs and serpents as would cost five livres. There is no doubt of it being the duc d'Orleans' money: the people are thus kept in a continual ferment, are for ever assembled, and ready to be in the last degree of commotion whenever called on by the men they have confidence in. Lately a company of Swiss would have crushed all this; a regiment would do it now if led with firmness; but, let it last a fortnight longer, and an army will be wanting. . . . I shall leave Paris, however, truly rejoiced that the representatives of the people have it undoubtedly in their power so to improve the constitution of their country, as to render all great abuses in future, if not impossible, at least exceedingly difficult, and consequently will establish to all useful purposes an undoubted political liberty; and if they effect this, it cannot be doubted that they will have a thousand opportunities to secure to their fellow-subjects the invaluable blessing of civil liberty also. The state of the finances is such, that the government may easily be kept virtually dependent on the states, and their periodical existence absolutely secured. Such benefits will confer happiness on 25 millions of people; a noble and animating idea, that ought to fill the mind of every citizen of the world, whatever be his country, religion, or pursuit. I will not allow myself to believe for a moment, that the representatives of the people can ever so far forget their duty to the French nation, to humanity, and their own fame, as to suffer any inordinate and impracticable views,—any visionary or theoretic systems,—any frivolous ideas of speculative perfection: much less any ambitious private views, to impede their progress, or turn aside their exertions, from that security which is in their hands, to place on the chance and hazard of public commotion and civil war, the invaluable blessings which are certainly in their power. I will not conceive it possible, that men who have eternal fame within their grasp, will place the rich inheritance on the cast of a die, and, losing the venture, be damned among the worst and most profligate adventurers that ever disgraced humanity.—The duc de Liancourt having made an immense collection of pamphlets, buying every thing that has a relation to the present period; and, among the rest, the cahiers of all the districts and towns of France of the three orders; it was a great object with me to read these, as I was sure of finding in them a representation of the grievances of the three orders, and an explanation of the improvements wished for in the government and administration. These cahiers being instructions given to their deputies, I have now gone through them all, with a pen in hand, to make extracts, and shall therefore leave Paris tomorrow.

JULY, 1789

The 20th. . . . On arriving at the inn, hear the interesting news of the revolt of Paris.—The *Guardes Françoises* joining the people; the little dependence on the rest of the troops; the taking the Bastile; and the institution of the *milice bourgeoise;* [9] in a word, of the absolute overthrow of the old government. Every thing being now decided, and the kingdom absolutely in the hands of the assembly, they have the power to make a new constitution, such as they think proper; and it will be a great spectacle for the world to view, in this enlightened age, the representatives of twenty-five millions of people

[9] [*Citizen militia.*]

sitting on the construction of a new and better order and fabric of liberty, than Europe has yet offered. It will now be seen, whether they will copy the constitution of England, freed from its faults, or attempt, from theory, to frame something absolutely speculative: in the former case, they will prove a blessing to their country; in the latter they will probably involve it in inextricable confusions and civil wars, perhaps not in the present period, but certainly at some future one. I hear nothing of their removing from Versailles; if they stay there under the controul of an armed mob, they must make a government that will please the mob; but they will, I suppose, be wise enough to move to some central town Tours, Blois, or Orleans, where their deliberations may be free. But the Parisian spirit of commotion spreads quickly; it is here; the troops that were near breaking my neck, are employed to keep an eye on the people who shew signs of an intended revolt. They have broken the windows of some magistrates that are no favourites; and a great mob of them is at this moment assembled demanding clamourously to have meat at 5s. a pound. They have a cry among them that will conduct them to good lengths,—*Point d'impôt & vivent les états.* . . .[10]

The 27th. To Besançon; the country mountain, rock, and wood, above the river; some scenes are fine. I had not arrived an hour before I saw a peasant pass the inn on horseback, followed by an officer of the *guard bourgeois,* of which there are 1200 here, and 200 under arms, and his party-coloured detachment, and these by some infantry and cavalry. I asked, why the militia took the *pas* of the king's troops? *For a very good reason,* they replied, *the troops would be attacked and knocked on the head, but the populace will not resist the milice.* This peasant, who is a rich proprietor, applied for a guard to protect his house, in a village where there is much plundering and burning. The mischiefs which have been perpetrated in the country, towards the mountains and Vesoul, are numerous and shocking. Many chateaus have been burnt, others plundered, the seigneurs hunted down like wild beasts, their wives and daughters ravished, their papers and titles burnt, and all their property destroyed: and these abominations not inflicted on marked persons, who were odious for their former conduct or principles, but an indiscriminating blind rage for the love of plunder. Robbers, galley-slaves, and villains of all denominations, have collected and instigated the peasants to commit all sorts of outrages. Some gentlemen at the table d'hôte informed me, that letters were received from the Maconois, the Lyonois, Auvergne, Dauphiné, &c. and that similar commotions and mischiefs were perpetrating every where; and that it was expected they would pervade the whole kingdom. The backwardness of France is beyond credibility in every thing that pertains to intelligence.

[10] [*No taxation and long live the Assembly.*]

From Strasbourg hither, I have not been able to see a newspaper. Here I asked for the *Cabinet Literaire?* None. The gazettes? At the coffee-house. Very easily replied; but not so easily found. Nothing but the *Gazette de France;* for which at this period, a man of common sense would not give one *sol*. To four other coffee-houses; at some no paper at all, not even the *Mercure;* at the *Café Militaire*, the *Courier de l'Europe* a fortnight old; and well dressed people are now talking of the news of two or three weeks past, and plainly by their discourse know nothing of what is passing. The whole town of Besançon has not been able to afford me a sight of the *Journal de Paris*, nor of any paper that gives a detail of the transactions of the states; yet it is the capital of a province, large as half a dozen English counties, and containing 25,000 souls,—with strange to say! the post coming in but three times a week. At this eventful moment, with no licence, nor even the least restraint on the press, not one paper established at Paris for circulation in the provinces, with the necessary steps taken by *affiche*, or *placard*,[11] to inform the people in all the towns of its establishment. For what the country knows to the contrary, their deputies are in the Bastile, instead of the Bastile being razed; so the mob plunder, burn, and destroy, in complete ignorance: and yet, with all these shades of darkness, these clouds of tenebrity, this universal mass of ignorance, there are men every day in the states, who are puffing themselves off for the FIRST NATION IN EUROPE! the GREATEST PEOPLE IN THE UNIVERSE! as if the political juntas, or literary circles of a capital constituted a people; instead of the universal illumination of knowledge, acting by rapid intelligence on minds prepared by habitual energy of reasoning to receive, combine, and comprehend it. That this dreadful ignorance of the mass of the people, of the events that most intimately concern them, is owing to the old government, no one can doubt; it is however curious to remark, that if the nobility of other provinces are hunted like those of Franche Compté, of which there is little reason to doubt, that whole order of men undergo a proscription, suffer like sheep, without making the least effort to resist the attack. . . .

JANUARY, 1790

The 6th, 7th, and 8th. The duke of Liancourt having an intention of taking a farm into his own hands, to be conducted on improved principles after the English manner, he desired me to accompany him, and my friend Lazowski, to Liancourt, to give my opinion of the lands, and of the best means towards executing the project, which I very readily complied with. I was here witness to a scene which made me smile: at no great distance from the *chateau* of Liancourt, is a piece of waste land, close to the road, and belonging to the

[11] [*Posted notice.*]

duke. I saw some men very busily at work upon it, hedging it in, in small divisions; levelling, and digging, and bestowing much labour for so poor a spot. I asked the steward if he thought that land worth such an expence? he replied, that the poor people in the town, upon the revolution taking place, declared, that the poor were the nation; that the waste belonged to the nation; and, proceeding from theory to practice, took possession, without any further authority, and began to cultivate; the duke not viewing their industry with any displeasure, would offer no opposition to it. This circumstance shews the universal spirit that is gone forth; and proves, that were it pushed a little farther, it might prove a serious matter for all the property in the kingdom. In this case, however, I cannot but commend it; for if there be one public nuisance greater than another, it is a man preserving the possession of waste land, which he will neither cultivate himself, nor let others cultivate. The miserable people die for want of bread, in sight of wastes that would feed thousands. I think them wise and rational, and philosophical, in seizing such tracts: and I heartily wish there was a law in England for making this action of the French peasants a legal one with us.—72 miles.

CAHIERS

THE GROWTH OF new economic conditions, ideas, and social ambitions within the resistant shell of France's old regime piled up discontents and led to a widespread urge for reform. When Louis XVI's government, faced with bankruptcy, finally summoned the long-neglected Estates-General, the people's hopes found expression in the *cahiers de doléances,* addresses to the crown which their deputies carried with them to Versailles. These documents, prepared by the clergy, nobles, and commoners in every section of France, furnish a unique historical record of conditions and opinions on the eve of the Revolution.

The writing of the *cahiers* paralleled the election of the deputies who were to present them to the king. Procedure varied somewhat from place to place, but in general it may be said that France was divided into electoral constituencies, in each of which the clergy, nobles, and third estate met separately to draw up their respective addresses to the crown and to choose their respective deputies to the Estates-General. But whereas most clergymen (first estate) and nobles (second estate) attended personally the meetings of their constituencies, commoners belonging to the third estate were required to use a form of indirect election: in subdivisions of each constituency primary assemblies were held, which drew up "particular" *cahiers* and chose electors; the electors for the constituency as a whole then met together, chose deputies for the Estates-General, and agreed upon incorporation of the demands of the "particular" *cahiers* into a "general" *cahier* corresponding to that of the nobles or clergy. Thus of the more than twenty thousand *cahiers* written in 1789 some six hundred were "general" and the rest "particular."

In such a vast attempt to examine public opinion—amounting to virtual manhood suffrage, since there was only a small property qualification for commoners wishing to take part in preliminary assemblies—some flaws were inevitable. Like the indirect electoral machinery, the process of summarizing the views of preliminary *cahiers* gave middle-class members of the third estate, particularly merchants and lawyers, an influence out of all proportion to their numbers. In many cases the "particular" *cahiers* themselves show signs of a natural tendency to be guided by prominent individuals and by the abundant pamphlet literature of the day. Taken as a whole, however, the *cahiers de doléances* of 1789 are a reliable and indispensable source for the study of the French Revolution. Taken individually, they must be used with care lest unrepresentative opinions be given undue weight. With this consideration in mind, the following *cahier* of the third estate of Dourdan, near Orléans in the Loire valley, has been chosen. The translation from the French is that given in John Hall Stewart, *A Documentary Survey of the French Revolution* (copyright 1951 by the Macmillan Company, New York), reprinted here by permission of the publisher.

CAHIER OF THE THIRD ESTATE OF
DOURDAN—29 MARCH, 1789

THE ORDER of the third estate of the City, *Bailliage*,[1] and County of Dourdan, imbued with gratitude prompted by the paternal kindness of the King, who deigns to restore its former rights and its former constitution, forgets at this moment its misfortunes and impotence, to harken only to its foremost sentiment and its foremost duty, that of sacrificing everything to the glory of the *Patrie* and the service of His Majesty. It supplicates him to accept the grievances, complaints, and remonstrances which it is permitted to bring to the foot of the throne, and to see therein only the expression of its zeal and the homage of its obedience.

It wishes:

1. That his subjects of the third estate, equal by such status to all other citizens, present themselves before the common father without other distinction which might degrade them.

2. That all the orders, already united by duty and a common desire to contribute equally to the needs of the State, also deliberate in common concerning its needs.

3. That no citizen lose his liberty except according to law; that, consequently, no one be arrested by virtue of special orders, or, if imperative circumstances necessitate such orders, that the prisoner be handed over to the regular courts of justice within forty-eight hours at the latest.

4. That no letters or writings intercepted in the post be the cause of the detention of any citizen, or be produced in court against him, except in case of conspiracy or undertaking against the State.

5. That the property of all citizens be inviolable, and that no one be required to make sacrifice thereof for the public welfare, except upon assurance of indemnification based upon the statement of freely selected appraisers.

6. That, since the maintenance of the commonwealth necessitates an effective revenue, all taxes established since 1614, the year of the last meeting of the Estates General, be confirmed provisionally by His Majesty on the request of the Estates General, and the collection thereof ordered during a limited period of time, not to exceed one year, despite the fact that, owing to lack of consent of the nation, such taxes may be regarded as illegal.

7. That the customary and ordinary charges of the State be regulated; that the expenditure of every department [of the Government], the appointment

---

[1] [*Bailiwick.*]

of all who are employed therein, and the retirement pensions of same be established invariably.

8. That the taxes on land and on all real or nominal property, the domains of the Crown, and other branches of revenue deriving from establishments useful to the public, such as postal and messenger service, etc., be preferably assigned to the aforementioned primarily necessary charges.

9. That the national debt be verified; that the payment of arrears of said debt be assured by such indirect taxes as may not be injurious to the husbandry, industry, commerce, liberty, or tranquillity of the citizens.

10. That an annual reimbursement fund be established to liquidate the capital of the debt.

11. That as one part of the debt is liquidated, a corresponding part of the indirect tax also be liquidated.

12. That every tax, direct or indirect, be granted only for a limited time, and that every collection beyond such term be regarded as peculation, and punished as such.

13. That no loan be contracted, under any pretext or any security whatsoever, without the consent of the Estates General.

14. That every anticipation and every issuance of treasurer's notes or others on the account of the State, without public sanction, be regarded as a violation of public faith, and that the administrators ordering or authorizing them be punished.

15. That every personal tax be abolished; that thus the *capitation* [2] and the *taille* [3] and its accessories be merged with the *vingtièmes* [4] in a tax on land and real or nominal property.

16. That such tax be borne equally, without distinction, by all classes of citizens and by all kinds of property, even feudal and contingent rights.

17. That the tax substituted for the *corvée* [5] be borne by all classes of citizens equally and without distinction. That said tax, at present beyond the capacity of those who pay it and the needs to which it is destined, be reduced by at least one-half.

18. That provincial Estates, subordinate to the Estates General, be established and charged with the assessment and levying of subsidies, with their deposit in the national treasury, with the administration of all public works, and with the examination of all projects conducive to the prosperity of lands situated within the limits of their jurisdiction.

19. That such Estates be composed of freely elected deputies of the three orders from the cities, boroughs, and parishes subject to their administration,

[2] [*Poll tax.*]   [3] [*Personal tax.*]   [4] [Taxes on income.]
[5] [A tax in the form of compulsory labor service.]

and in the proportion established for the next session of the Estates General.

20. That district bureaux under said Estates be established in the chief towns of the *bailliages;* and that such jurisdictions be created for said bureaux that there may be prompt and convenient correspondence between the chief town and all points accountable thereto.

21. That in case of the death or retirement of deputies of the order of the third estate in the Estates General, or of any one among them, during the course of the next session, the present electors be authorized to reassemble to elect others in their place.

JUSTICE

1. That the administration of justice be reformed, either by restoring strict execution of ordinances, or by reforming the sections thereof that are contrary to the dispatch and welfare of justice.

2. That every royal *bailliage* have such jurisdiction that persons be not more than three or four leagues distant from their judges, and that these pass judgment in the last resort up to the value of 300 *livres*.

3. That seigneurial courts of justice created by purely gratuitous right be suppressed.

4. That seigneurial courts of justice separated from the jurisdiction of royal *bailliages* . . . be returned thereto.

5. That seigneurial courts of justice, the creation of which has not been gratuitous, or usurpation of which is not proved, be suppressed with reimbursement. . . .

7. That venality of offices be suppressed by successive reimbursement in proportion to their disestablishment; that, accordingly, a fund be constituted forthwith to effect such reimbursement.

8. That the excessive number of offices in the necessary courts be reduced in just measure, and that no one be given an office of magistracy if he is not at least twenty-five years of age, and until after a substantial public examination has verified his morality, integrity, and ability.

9. That all exceptional jurisdictions, . . . salt stores, and financial bureaux be suppressed as useless and productive of law-suits and jurisdictional conflicts; that their competence be returned to the jurisdiction within which they are situated, and the officials composing them either incorporated into such *bailliages* or reimbursed out of their finances.

10. That the study of law be reformed; that it be directed in a manner analogous to our legislation, and that candidates for degrees be subjected to rigorous tests which may not be evaded; that no dispensation of age or time be granted.

11. That a body of general customary law be drafted of all articles common to all the customs of the several provinces and *bailliages,* and that the customs of said several provinces and *bailliages* thereafter contain only articles which are in exception to the general custom.

12. That deliberations of courts and companies of magistracy which tend to prevent entry of the third estate thereto be rescinded and annulled as injurious to the citizens of that order, in contempt of the authority of the King, whose choice they limit, and contrary to the welfare of justice, the administration of which would become the patrimony of those of noble birth instead of being entrusted to merit, enlightenment, and virtue.

13. That military ordinances which restrict entrance to the service to those possessing nobility be reformed.

That naval ordinances establishing a degrading distinction between officers born into the order of nobility and those born into that of the third estate be revoked, as thoroughly injurious to an order of citizens and destructive of the competition so necessary to the glory and prosperity of the State.

FINANCES

1. That if the Estates General considers it necessary to preserve the fees of *aides,*[6] such fees be made uniform throughout the entire kingdom and reduced to a single denomination; that, accordingly, all ordinances and declarations in force be revoked. . . .

2. That the tax of the *gabelle*[7] be eliminated if possible, or that it be regulated among the several provinces of the kingdom . . .

3. That the taxes on hides, which have totally destroyed that branch of commerce and caused it to go abroad, be suppressed forever. . . .

7. That the fee for registration of documents be established universally and uniformly, and that, accordingly, all exemptions, subscriptions, and alienations in favor of individual officials or provinces be revoked.

8. That an explicit and exact tariff establish the quota of such fee in an invariable manner; that in said tariff the contract of marriage be treated with the favor it merits; . . . that whatever agreements said act include, it never be subject to more than one fee . . . ; that notes and receipts . . . be taxed as moderately as possible . . . ; finally, that every act not included in the categories established by the tariff be placed in the most analogous category and the one most favorable to the taxpayer; that such classification . . . be determined by the royal judges . . . ; that the draft of said tariff be published one year before its execution, in order that the provincial Estates and all orders of citizens may express their opinions thereon . . .

[6] [*Excises.*]　　　　　　　　　　[7] [*Salt monopoly.*]

9. That the fees of *franc-fief*,[8] established without motives since fiefs are no longer subject to military service, be suppressed entirely, or that, if the needs of the State necessitate their further preservation, the collection thereof be made only every twenty years, whatever change take place during such interval; that said fee not exceed one year's actual revenue, and that it not be burdened with any additional tax. . . .

AGRICULTURE

1. That exchange fees, disastrous to husbandry, . . . be suppressed.

2. That the letters patent of 26 August, 1786, establishing the fees of land commissioners at triple and quadruple their former compensation be revoked; that such fees be reduced to just limits, and that the *terrier* [9] be renewed only after forty years and by new letters patent.

3. That the privilege of hunting be restricted within its just limits; that the decrees of the *parlement* [10] of the years 1778 and 1779, which tend rather to obstruct the claims of the cultivator than to effect his indemnification, be rescinded and annulled; that after having declared the excessive amount of game and summoned the seigneur to provide therefor, the landowner and the cultivator be authorized to destroy said game on their own lands and in their own woods—without permission, however, to use firearms, the carrying of which is forbidden by ordinances; that, moreover, a simple and easy method be established whereby every cultivator may have the damage verified and obtain compensation therefor.

4. That the right to hunt may never affect the property of the citizen; that, accordingly, he may at all times travel over his lands, have injurious herbs uprooted, and cut [hay] . . . and other produce whenever it suits him; and that stubble may be freely raked immediately after the harvest.

5. That, in conformity with former ordinances, gamekeepers be forbidden to carry arms, even in the retinue of their masters.

6. That hunting offences be punished only by pecuniary fines.

7. That His Majesty be supplicated to have enclosed the parks and forests which are reserved for his enjoyment; also to authorize elsewhere the destruction of wild beasts which ruin the rural districts, and particularly that bordering on this forest of Dourdan.

8. That every individual who, without title or valid occupancy, has dovecotes or aviaries, be required to destroy them; that those who have title or valid occupancy be required to confine their pigeons at seedtime and harvest.

9. That all leases on tithes, lands, and revenues belonging to ecclesiastics

---

[8] [Fees on conveyance of noble land to or among commoners.]
[9] [*Fee and rent roll.*]   [10] [One of the several high or "sovereign" courts.]

and persons in *mainmorte* [11] be made before royal judges . . . ; and that, accordingly, leases thus made remain valid even after the death of the titular incumbents, and that said leases be made for not fewer than nine years.

10. That no cultivator be permitted . . . several farms or farmings, if the total thereof necessitates the use of more than two ploughs.

11. That the rights of *champart* [12] and others of similar nature be converted into payment, either in grain or in money, according to a high and favorable estimate, for landowners designated by the King on the request of the Estates General; and that transportation outside the parish of straw from *champarts* and tithes be forbidden henceforth.

That individuals as well as communities be permitted to free themselves from the rights of *banalité* [13] and *corvée,* by payments in money or in kind, at a rate likewise established by His Majesty on the basis of the deliberations of the Estates General.

12. That the corporal domains of the crown be rented in grain in perpetuity. . . .

15. That the militia, which devastates the country, takes workers away from husbandry, produces premature and ill-matched marriages, and imposes secret and arbitrary taxes upon those who are subject thereto, be suppressed and replaced by voluntary enlistment at the expense of the provinces.

16. That individuals and communities be permitted to free themselves from the *rentes* which they owe to persons in *mainmorte,* by paying the principal at a rate to be established, upon condition that the persons in *mainmorte* invest such principal in loans authorized guaranteed by the King and the nation.

17. That the ordinance and regulation concerning woods and forests be reformed so as to preserve property rights, encourage plantings, and prevent deforestation.

That the administration of forests and woods belonging to persons in *mainmorte* be subject to the provincial Estates and subordinate to the district bureaux, and that new laws be established to assure the preservation thereof and to punish offences pertaining thereto.

19. That seigneurs who are inspectors of highways may not plant or appropriate trees planted on property bordering the highways; that, on the contrary, such trees be designated as the property of the owners of the estates, who shall be reimbursed for the cost of the planting.

20. That the width of highways and connecting and rural roads be established uniformly and unalterably.

---

[11] [A vestigial form of servile tenure.]
[12] [A fee on peasant tenures consisting of part of the crop.]
[13] [A fee for use of the seigneur's mill, oven, wine press.]

21. That penalties be imposed upon whosoever cultivate connecting and rural roads.

COMMERCE

1. That every regulation which tends to impede the business of citizens be revoked.

2. That the exportation and circulation of grain be directed by the provincial Estates, which shall correspond among themselves in order to prevent sudden and artificial increases in the price of provisions.

3. That when wheat reaches the price of twenty-five *livres* per *septier* in the markets, all day laborers be forbidden to buy any, unless it be for their sustenance.

4. That if circumstances necessitate the revenue from certificates and letters of mastership in the arts and crafts, no member be admitted into corporations except upon condition of residing in the place of his establishment; that widows may carry on the profession of their husbands without new letters; that their children be admitted thereto at a moderate price; that all persons without an established and recognized domicile be forbidden to peddle.

5. That fraudulent bankruptcy be considered a public crime; that the public prosecutor be enjoined to prosecute it as such, and that privileged positions no longer serve as a refuge for bankrupts.

6. That all toll rights and other similar ones be suppressed throughout the interior of the kingdom, that customhouses be moved back to the frontiers, and that rights of *traite* [14] be entirely abolished.

7. That, within a given time, weights and measures be rendered uniform throughout the entire kingdom.

MORALS

1. That in the chief town of every *bailliage* a public school be established, where young citizens may be brought up in the principles of religion and provided with the necessary education by methods authorized by His Majesty on the request of the nation.

2. That in cities and villages schools be established where the poor will be admitted without cost, and instructed in whatever is necessary for them concerning either morals or their individual interests.

3. That livings and benefices for the care of souls henceforth be granted only by competitive examination.

4. That prelates and *curés* be subject to perpetual residence, under penalty of loss of the fruits of their benefices.

[14] [Right to collect internal customs duties.]

5. That, under the same penalty, beneficiaries without a charge be bound to residence during most of the year in the chief town of their benefice, if they have an annual income of 1,000 *livres* or more.

6. That no ecclesiastic hold more than one benefice if such benefice is worth 3,000 *livres* revenue or over; that those in excess of such revenue be declared vacant.

7. That every lottery, the effect of which is to corrupt public morals, every loan involving the element of chance, the effect of which is to encourage speculation and divert funds destined for agriculture and commerce, be proscribed forever.

8. That every community be required to provide for the maintenance of its invalid poor; that, accordingly, all private alms be strictly forbidden; that in every district a charity workshop be established, the funds for which shall be composed of voluntary contributions of individuals and sums which the provincial Estates shall designate therefor, in order to assure constant work for the able-bodied poor.

9. That within the limits of every principal administration a house of correction be established for the confinement of beggars and vagabonds.

10. That all charlatans, and those who have not completed the necessary studies and passed the required examinations, be forbidden to sell drugs or medicines or to practise medicine or surgery, and that the granting of any certificate, permission, or exemption for such purpose be forbidden.

11. That no woman may practise the art of midwifery until she has taken a course in it, has obtained a certificate of competence from a college of surgery, and has been received into the *bailliage*.

12. That the *maréchaussées* [15] be enjoined to obey the orders of the officials of the *bailliages* for the maintenance of public order; and that the municipalities of the several parishes be authorized to have internal police power therein, except in special cases which are to be reported to the public prosecutor of the *bailliage*.

13. That the sacraments be administered gratuitously, and contingent fees suppressed.

[15] [A corps of policemen.]

JOSEPH EMMANUEL SIEYÈS

THE ABBÉ SIEYÈS (1748–1836) was not by choice a priest but a *philosophe* and reformer. His power during the years from 1789 to 1799 stemmed originally from his activities as a pamphleteer. *What Is the Third Estate?* is one of the most forceful tracts for the time that has been written. Through identifying the unprivileged third estate with the nation, it fused the diverse discontents of revolutionary France into what seemed to be a systematically developed program for righting existing wrongs. One report is that this pamphlet sold 30,000 copies in the three weeks following its publication early in January, 1789, and it succeeded in creating for Sieyès a host of admirers.

Sieyès liked to consider himself an original thinker, and only rarely does he mention other writers. Principal among those for whom he does express admiration are Locke and Condillac. Nevertheless, *What Is the Third Estate?* gives forceful indication of the intellectual influence on the Revolution exerted by the *philosophes* of the Enlightenment. In a simple and lucid fashion Sieyès puts to political use the Physiocrat emphasis upon laissez faire and the basic value of the land; he uses, and mixes, the philosophies of natural rights and utilitarianism; and although Sieyès denied Rousseau any part in establishing the "principles of the social art," he agreed with Rousseau's account of the foundation of society, and the central part of his political philosophy rests on the notion of the general will. Sieyès's chief addition to the theory of government of *The Social Contract* is a greater emphasis upon representative government.

It was natural that it should have been Sieyès who, with Mirabeau, led the commoners of the third estate in their proclamation of a National Assembly, committed to the formulation of a new constitution for France. As the Revolution gathered force he occupied a moderate position, opposing both the radical Jacobins and the federalism of the Girondists, and advocating policies which he hoped would unify the French state. In pursuit of this nationalist objective he urged universal military training, reorganization of France in order to break down sectionalism, and control of religion and education by the state.

Although his power waned after the triumph of the Jacobins, Sieyès was one of the few early leaders of the Revolution who was almost continuously in public office during the ten years after 1789. His moderate position as a representative of the "Plain," as well as his capacity to submerge his own personality, enabled him to survive the thrusts and counterthrusts within the revolutionary movement, and as a member of the Directory in 1799 he was in a position to conspire with Napoleon Bonaparte and to contribute to the latter's *coup d'état*. Sieyès was one of the three consuls empowered by Napoleon's Constitution of the Year VIII, and although the personality of the First Consul thoroughly eclipsed his own, he maintained a position as one of the Empire's most honored citizens. With the Restoration, Sieyès was forced into exile but returned to Paris after the Revolution of 1830, where he lived for six years in obscurity.

୨

WHAT IS THE THIRD ESTATE?

THE PLAN of this work is quite simple. We have three questions to consider:

(1) What is the third estate? Everything.

(2) What has it been in the political order up to the present? Nothing.

(3) What does it demand? To become something. . . .

THE THIRD ESTATE IS A COMPLETE NATION

What is necessary for the subsistence and prosperity of a nation? *Particular* labors and *public* functions.

Particular labors can be divided into four classes: 1) The soil and water furnish the primary materials for the satisfaction of human needs, and the first class in this order will be that of all the families attached to the work of the field. 2) From the first sale of materials until their consumption or use, a new handiwork, more or less multifarious, adds to these materials a secondary value more or less compound. Human industry succeeds in perfecting the goods of nature and multiplies their value as raw materials twofold, tenfold, a hundredfold. Such are the works of the second class. 3) Between production and consumption, and also between the various stages of production there is a multitude of intermediary agents, useful as much to the producers as to the consumers: these are the merchants. . . . This useful group makes up the third class. 4) In addition to these three classes of productive citizens who are busy with the *objects* of consumption and use, society requires a group of special works and services *directly* useful or pleasing to the *person*. This fourth class embraces everything from the most liberal and distinguished scientific professions to the least esteemed domestic services. Such are the works which maintain society. Who supports them? The third estate.

Public functions may similarly, in the existing state, be arranged under the four recognized denominations, the Sword, the Robe, the Church and the Administration. It would be superfluous to run through them in detail, in order to show how the third estate is nineteen-twentieths of these, with this difference, that it is responsible for all that is truly laborious, all the services that the privileged order refuses to perform. The lucrative and titulary positions are occupied by members of the privileged order. Should we give them credit for that? It would be justifiable if the third estate either refused to fill these positions or if it were not so capable of performing their functions. The truth of the matter is known; yet they have dared to place the third estate under interdiction. They have said to it: "Whatever your services, whatever your talents, you shall go just so far; you shall not pass beyond. It is not a good thing for you to be honored." . . . If this exclusion is a social crime against the third estate, might one at least be able to say that it serves the public interest? Well, are not the effects of monopoly known? If it discourages those whom it excludes, does it not also render unskilled those whom it favors? Isn't it known that every work removed from free competition will be at once more expensive and less well done?

WHAT HAS THE THIRD ESTATE BEEN UP TO THE PRESENT? NOTHING

We shall not examine the state of servitude in which the people has groaned for so long, no more than the state of constraint and humiliation in which it is still held. Its civil condition has changed; it ought to change more: it is quite impossible that the body of the nation or even that any particular order should become free if the third estate is not free. Privileges do not make one free, but rather the rights that belong to everyone.

If the aristocrats should attempt, even at the cost of this liberty of which they have shown themselves unworthy, to keep the people oppressed, it is fair to ask by what right. If the answer is by the right of conquest, then, it must be agreed, the matter must be pushed a bit farther. The third estate need not fear going back to the past in this way. For it will go back to the year preceding the conquest; and since it is today strong enough not to allow itself to be conquered, its opposition will be more effective. Why should not all these families that maintain the foolish pretention that they are descended from the conquerors and are the inheritors of their rights return to the forests of Franconie?

The nation, thus purged, will be able to console itself, I think, with being reduced to regard itself as made up of only the descendants of the Gauls and the Romans. In truth, if one insists upon making distinctions based on birth, might it not be revealed to our poor compatriots that those that are descended from the Gauls and the Romans are at least worthy as those that come from the Sicambres, the Welches and other savages come out of the woods and swamps of ancient Germany? Yes, it will be said; but the conquest has upset all relationships, and nobility of birth has passed to the side of the conquerors. Well! then it must change sides again, and the third estate will get back its nobility by becoming the conqueror in its turn. . . .

Let us continue. By the third estate must be understood the mass of citizens who belong to the common order. Everyone who is privileged by law, in whatever manner, departs from the common order, is an exception to the common law, and, consequently, does not belong to the third estate. We have said that a common law and a common representation are what make *one* nation. It is only too true that one is *nothing* in France, when one is only under the protection of the common law; if one does not hold some privilege he must make up his mind to endure scorn, insult and vexations of all kinds. In order to prevent his being completely crushed the only resource of the unfortunate unprivileged person is to attach himself by all sorts of sordid tricks to some dignitary; only at this price does he buy the power, on occasions, to call himself *somebody*.

But it is less in its civil estate than in its relations to the constitution that we have to consider the third estate here. Let us study it with respect to the Estates General.

Who have been its pretended representatives? Either the newly ennobled or the temporarily privileged. These false deputies have not even always been freely chosen in a popular election. Sometimes in the Estates General, and almost always in the provincial estates, the representation of the people is looked upon as the peculiar right of certain positions or offices.

The old nobility cannot stand the new nobles; it only permits them to sit with it when they can claim, as is said, four generations and a hundred years. So it thrusts them back into the third estate to which they obviously no longer belong. However, in the eyes of the law all nobles are equal, those of yesterday and those who succeed greatly or very little in hiding their origin or their usurpation. All have the same privileges. Only opinion distinguishes between them. But if the third estate is compelled to support a prejudice sanctioned by the law there is hardly any reason for its submitting to a prejudice which is against the text of the law.

No matter who is made a noble it is certain that from the moment that a citizen acquires privileges contrary to the common right he is no longer a member of the common order. His new interest is opposed to the general interest; he is incapacitated from voting for the people. . . .

Is separating from the third estate not only the hereditarily privileged, but also those who are enjoying privileges only temporarily, . . . is this an attempt to weaken this order by depriving it of its most enlightened, most courageous and most respected members?

. . . The third estate is always identified in my mind with the idea of a nation. Whatever our motive may be, can we make the truth not the truth? Because an army has had the misfortune of seeing its best troops desert it, does it follow that it must depend upon them to defend it? All privilege, it cannot be repeated too much, is opposed to the common right; therefore all the privileged, without distinction, form a class that is different from and opposed to the third estate. At the same time, this truth ought to contain nothing that will alarm the friends of the people. On the contrary, it serves the national interest, by making forcefully apparent the necessity of immediately suppressing all temporary privileges, which divide the third estate and would appear to condemn this order to placing its destinies in the hands of its enemies. Besides, this observation must not be separated from the one that follows: the abolition of privileges in the third estate is not the loss of exemptions which a few of its members enjoy. These exemptions are nothing but the common right. It has been supremely unjust to deprive the generality of people of them. So I demand not the loss of a right but its restitution; and if it is objected that by making some of these privileges common, like, that of not being drafted for the militia, the means of filling a social need is prevented, I answer that every public need ought to be the responsibility of everybody, and not of a particular class of citizens, and that one must be as much a stranger to all reflection as to all justice not to find a more national means of completing and maintaining such military establishment as one wishes to have. . . .

Let one read history with the intention of examining whether the facts are in conformity with or contrary to this assertion, and he will be assured, I have had the experience, that it is a great error to believe that France is subject to a monarchical regime.

It is enough at this point to have made it apparent that the pretended utility of a privileged order for the public service is only a chimera; that without it, everything that is laborious in this service is discharged by the third estate; that without it the superior places would be infinitely better filled; that they ought to be the natural portion and reward of recognized talents and services; and that if the privileged have succeeded in usurping every lucrative and titulary post, it is at once an odious crime against the generality of citizens and a betrayal of the public interest.

Who would dare to say, therefore, that the third estate does not contain in itself all that is necessary to constitute a complete nation? It is like a strong and robust man whose arms are still in chains. If the privileged order were removed the nation would not be something less but something more. So, what is the third estate? Everything, but an "everything" shackled and oppressed. What would it be without the privileged order? Everything, but an "everything" free and flourishing. Nothing can get along without it, everything will get along infinitely better without the others. Nor is the whole case stated when it is shown that the privileged, far from being useful to the nation, can only weaken it and harm it; further, it must be proved that the nobility does not enter into the social order; that it can well be a *burden* on the nation, but that it is not capable of being a part of it.

First, it is impossible to know where to place the nobles among the various elements in the nation. I know that there are many individuals, indeed too many, in whom infirmity, incompetence, incurable laziness, or the force of bad habits, operate to make them strangers to the work of society. Everywhere the exception and the abuse is side by side with the rule, especially in a vast empire. But at least it will be agreed that the fewer these abuses the better the State is regulated. The worst regulated of all will be that State in which not only are there particular persons isolated, but an entire class of citizens finds its glory in remaining inactive in the midst of general activity and is able to consume the best part of the produce without having helped in any way to bring it into existence. Such a class is surely foreign to the nation in its *sloth*.

The noble order is foreign among us not less because of its civil and public prerogatives.

What is a nation? A body of associates living under a *common* law and represented by the same *legislature*.

Is it not all too certain that the noble order has privileges, exemptions, and even rights separated from the rights of the great body of citizens? It departs in this respect from the common order, from the common law. Its civil rights make it already a people apart in the nation at large. It is truly *imperium in imperio*.[1]

With regard to its *political* rights, it also exists apart. It has representatives of its own, who are not responsible in any way for acting on behalf of the people. The body of its deputies sits apart; and when it assembles in the same room with the deputies of simple citizens it is no less true that its representation is essentially distinct and separate: it is foreign to the nation in its principle, since its commission does not come from the people, and in its object, since it consists in defending not the general interest, but a particular one.

The third estate therefore includes everything that belongs to the nation; and everything that is not the third estate cannot be regarded as being of the nation. What is the third estate? Everything.

Remove from our annals a few years of Louis XI, of Richelieu, and a few moments of Louis XIV, where one sees only pure despotism, and you would believe that you were reading the history of an *aulic*[2] aristocracy. It is the court which has reigned and not the monarch. It is the court which makes and unmakes, which calls and recalls the ministers, which creates and distributes positions, etc. And what is the court, if not the head of that immense aristocracy which covers every part of France, which, through its members, attains to everything and exercizes everywhere what is essential to every part of the public interest? Thus the people has accustomed itself to separate in its grumblings the monarch from the powers behind the throne. It has always

---

[1] [*A sovereignty within a sovereignty.*]   [2] [*Court.*]

regarded the king as a man so surely deceived and so without protection in the middle of an active and all-powerful court, that it has never thought to blame him for all the evil that is done in his name.

To sum up: the third estate has not had up to the present true representatives in the Estates General. Therefore its political rights are nought.

WHAT DOES THE THIRD ESTATE DEMAND? TO BECOME SOMETHING

It is not necessary to judge its demands on the basis of the isolated observations of a few authors more or less informed about the rights of man. The third estate is still very backward in this respect, not only with regard to the insights of those who have studied the social order, but also with regard to that mass of common ideas which constitutes public opinion. The true petitions of this estate cannot be appreciated except in terms of the authentic protests which the great municipalities of the kingdom have addressed to the government. What do these show? That the people want to be *something,* and in truth the least possible. It wants to have genuine representatives in the Estates General, that is to say, deputies *drawn from its own ranks,* who are capable of being the interpreters of its desire and the protectors of its interests. But of what use is it to this estate to be present in the Estates General if the interest contrary to its own predominates there! It would only serve to give sanction by its presence to the oppression of which it is the eternal victim. Therefore it is quite certain that it cannot come to vote at the Estates General if it ought not to have there *an influence which is at least equal to that of the privileged classes,* and it demands a number of representatives equal to the number of the two other orders together. Finally, this equality of representation would become completely illusory if every chamber had its separate voice. The third estate demands therefore that the votes be taken *by heads and not by order.* These protests which have created such alarm in the circles of the privileged amount to this, because it is only from this that the reform of abuses would follow. The true intention of the third estate is to have in the Estates General an influence *equal* to that of the privileged. I repeat, can it ask less? And is it not clear that if its influence there is not equal, one cannot hope that it will leave its state of political nullity and become *something?* . . .

THE DECLARATION OF THE
RIGHTS OF MAN
AND OF THE CITIZEN

T HE Declaration of the Rights of Man and of the Citizen drew heavily on
Rousseau and the Declaration of Independence of the United States, as
well as on the various bills of rights that had been worked out for individual American colonies. The document was the work of a committee made
up of more than twenty leaders of the National Assembly. In addition to its
proclamation of individual rights which have since served as watchwords for
liberals and radicals of many ideologies and economic interests, it expressed the
commitment of the then dominant group in the Revolutior. to the rights of property. The Jacobins alone of the major parties dissented in this respect. Robespierre
said: "You have . . . afford[ed] the largest possible latitude to the right to one's
property, and yet you have not added a word in limitation of this right, with
the result that your *Declaration of the Rights of Man* might make the impression
of having been created not for the poor, but for the rich, the speculators, for the
stock exchange jobbers." However much rooted it was in the interests of the
middle classes, the Declaration was soon taken as a universal invitation to liberty.

The Declaration was promulgated in 1789 and attached to the Constitution of
1793. Throughout the nineteenth century it served as a symbol of revolutionary
effort against the Old Regime in Europe and as a model for liberal constitutions. Its
influence, furthermore, was wielded in circles far outside the propertied classes. The
following translation from the French appears in Thomas Paine's *Rights of Man*
(1790).

DECLARATION OF THE RIGHTS OF MAN AND
OF THE CITIZEN

THE REPRESENTATIVES of the people of France, formed into a National Assembly, considering that ignorance, neglect, or contempt of human rights, are
the sole causes of public misfortunes and corruptions of Government, have
resolved to set forth in a solemn declaration, these natural, imprescriptible,
and inalienable rights: that this declaration being constantly present to the
minds of the members of the body social, they may be for ever kept attentive
to their rights and their duties; that the acts of the legislative and executive
powers of government, being capable of being every moment compared with
the end of political institutions, may be more respected; and also, that the

future claims of the citizens, being directed by simple and incontestable principles, may always tend to the maintenance of the Constitution, and the general happiness.

For these reasons, the National Assembly doth recognize and declare, in the presence of the Supreme Being, and with the hope of his blessing and favour, the following *sacred* rights of men and of citizens:

I. Men are born, and always continue, free and equal in respect of their rights. Civil distinctions, therefore, can be founded only on public utility.

II. The end of all political associations, is the preservation of the natural and imprescriptible rights of man; and these rights are liberty, property, security, and resistance of oppression.

III. The nation is essentially the source of all sovereignty; nor can any individual, or any body of men, be entitled to any authority which is not expressly derived from it.

IV. Political liberty consists in the power of doing whatever does not injure another. The exercise of the natural rights of every man, has no other limits than those which are necessary to secure to every *other* man the free exercise of the same rights; and these limits are determinable only by the law.

V. The law ought to prohibit only actions hurtful to society. What is not prohibited by the law, should not be hindered; nor should any one be compelled to that which the law does not require.

VI. The law is an expression of the will of the community. All citizens have a right to concur, either personally, or by their representatives, in its formation. It should be the same to all, whether it protects or punishes; and all being equal in its sight, are equally eligible to all honours, places, and employments, according to their different abilities, without any other distinction than that created by their virtues and talents.

EQUALITY before the law.

VII. No man should be accused, arrested, or held in confinement, except in cases determined by the law, and according to the forms which it has prescribed. All who promote, solicit, execute, or cause to be executed, arbitrary orders, ought to be punished, and every citizen called upon, or apprehended by virtue of the law, ought immediately to obey, and renders himself culpable by resistance.

No lettres de cachet

VIII. The law ought to impose no other penalties but such as are absolutely and evidently necessary; and no one ought to be punished, but in virtue of a law promulgated before the offence, and legally applied.

IX. Every man being presumed innocent till he has been convicted, whenever his detention becomes indispensable, all rigour to him, more than is necessary to secure his person, ought to be provided against by the law.

religious toleration

X. No man ought to be molested on account of his opinions, not even on account of his *religious* opinions, provided his avowal of them does not disturb the public order established by the law.

XI. The unrestrained communication of thoughts and opinions being one *Freedom of speech & press* of the most precious rights of man, every citizen may speak, write, and publish freely, provided he is responsible for the abuse of this liberty, in cases determined by the law.

XII. A public force being necessary to give security to the rights of men and of citizens, that *Army* force is instituted for the benefit of the community and not for the particular benefit of the persons to whom it is intrusted.

XIII. A common contribution being necessary for the support of the public *proportionate* force, and for defraying the other expenses of government, it ought to be *taxation* divided equally among the members of the community, according to their abilities.

XIV. Every citizen has a right, either by himself or his representative, to a free voice in determining the necessity of public contributions, the appropriation of them, and their amount, mode of assessment, and duration.

XV. Every community has had a right to demand of all its agents an account of their conduct.

XVI. Every community in which a separation of powers and a security of rights is not provided for, wants a constitution.

XVII. The right to property being inviolable and sacred, no one ought to be deprived of it, except in cases of evident public necessity, legally ascertained, and on condition of a previous just indemnity.

THE CIVIL CONSTITUTION
OF THE CLERGY

THE Civil Constitution of the Clergy was drafted by the Comité Ecclésiastique of the National Assembly, and was approved on July 12, 1790. It abolished the old dioceses and established new ones to coincide with the new administrative *départements;* it provided for the election of bishops by the electoral assembly in each *département,* and the election of parish priests by the electoral assembly in each district. The pope lost all jurisdiction in France; newly elected bishops and priests were simply to notify him of their election. Members of the clergy received the status of civil servants and were to be paid by the state.

Although Louis XVI sought the counsel of Pope Pius VI through his ambassador at Rome, the National Assembly itself never negotiated directly with the pope over the new religious code. On November 27, 1790, the Assembly decided to exact from all civil servants an oath of fidelity to the new constitution; it determined to begin with the election of new priests if the old ones refused to take the oath.

In a brief of March 10, 1791, Pope Pius finally condemned the principles of the Revolution and the Civil Constitution of the Clergy. Orthodox Catholics were forced to choose between abandoning either the Revolution or their faith. More than half of the French clergy refused to take the oath and resigned from their posts. With the assistance of Talleyrand, bishop of Autun, the government consecrated new bishops, but these "constitutional priests" were in many places rejected by their parishioners, especially the women. Because of its vigorous persecution of the "refractory priests," the government alienated many of its supporters in the rural areas. It was not until Napoleon's Concordat of 1801 redefined the official position of the Church that the religious problem was settled.

The following selections from the speeches of supporters of the Civil Constitution have been translated by Barry Augenbraun from the *Procès-Verbal de l'Assemblée Nationale,* Vol. 21 (Paris, 1790). The selections from the speeches of the opposition have been translated by William W. Ryding from B. J. B. Buchez and P. C. Roux, *Histoire Parlementaire de la Révolution Française, Journal des Assemblées Nationales depuis 1789 jusqu'en 1815,* Vol. VI (1790; Paris, 1834).

EXTRACTS FROM THE PROCEEDINGS OF
THE NATIONAL ASSEMBLY, MAY 1790

REMARKS OF THE ARCHBISHOP OF AIX, MAY 29, 1790

DOES THE ecclesiastical committee know how useful is the influence of religion on our citizens? It is the brake that holds back the wicked; it is the encouragement of the virtuous. Religion is the seal on the declaration that guarantees man's rights and liberties: it is inalterable in its dogmas; its ethical views cannot change; its doctrines will remain forever the same. The committee wishes to call the churchmen back to the original purity of the early church. All well and good. The bishops, who are the successors of the Apostles, and the pastors responsible for preaching the Gospel, cannot protest against such a procedure. But since the committee members choose to remind us of our duties, they will permit us to remind them of our rights, and of the sacred principles of ecclesiastical power. We must remind them of the indispensable authority of the Church, for it is a question of the truths of religion: I mean to set forth those truths with all the firmness and conviction suitable to ministers of the Lord. Jesus Christ, for the salvation of the faithful, entrusted his mission to the Apostles and their successors. He did not confide that mission to magistrates and kings; for this is an order of things where kings and magistrates must obey. The mission we have received by way of ordination dates back to the time of the Apostles. Today, you are being asked to destroy part of the ministries, to divide a jurisdiction established and defined by the Apostles. No human power has such a right. (*Murmurs*)

I must point out that this is a matter of purely spiritual jurisdiction. Abuses have indeed occurred within it, and I, no less than another, am deeply troubled that it should be so. But the spirit of the early church is always there to repress them. It is not the abuses but the canons and traditions of the Church we claim as our own: church councils alone can dismember ecclesiastical provinces. Observe that I speak only of the spiritual order; there, only the Church can govern; she alone can determine relationships. A bishop cannot exercise his jurisdiction in a foreign bishopric: to suppress even a part of this organization is to destroy for the faithful the entire administration of the Church. The jurisdiction of the curates is limited by the bishops; they can make no changes except by virtue of their orders. Today the State wishes to extend its power over the objects of ecclesiastical discipline. We are stunned indeed to see the holy canons and titles of the Church disappear in such a way. . . . It is possible to conceive of certain powers being transferred away from the Church; but she must first be consulted; it were sacrilege to take her administration from her. Doubtless abuses must be corrected and a new order of things inaugurated. We believe that the ecclesiastical power must do its utmost to reconcile your interests with those of religion; but we are deeply pained to witness the existence of a sinful plot to destroy ecclesiastical power.

If you do not choose to have recourse to the authority of the Church in these matters you do not rightly understand the Catholic unity that forms the constitution of the Empire. We cannot in any case abandon forms prescribed by church councils, for in them resides the power that must safeguard the depository of faith; it is within church councils that, duly instructed in our duties and in your desires, we shall reconcile the interests of the people and those of religion. We are here to present to you a declaration of our feelings. We respectfully beseech the King and the National Assembly to permit our calling a national council. If this way is not adopted, we regretfully declare that we can no longer participate in the deliberations of this body.

REMARKS OF M. LE CURÉ LE CLERC

IF THE committee had been satisfied to propose to you the reform of abuses in ecclesiastical administration; if it had asked you to protect the regulations of the Church, we should all have applauded its work; but it has presented only a program of suppression and destruction. Already some religious houses have ceased to exist; there is no asylum left for fervent piety. The bishoprics, the archbishoprics, the collegiate churches, and the cathedrals are threatened with proscription in a kingdom that professes the Catholic religion. No one has yet thought of abolishing houses of debauchery and prostitution, those tombs that gobble up the lives and fortunes of our citizens; it is to them that our reformers ought to have applied their severity; but it appears that financial ends direct this assembly. . . .

The powers of the Church are inalienable and indefeasible; their essence is divine: she can therefore exercise them in complete independence. St. Athanasius asks what is the canon that authorizes the invasion of the churches and the seizure of ecclesiastical administration. Such was the heresy of the Arians. . . . The Church received, along with the right to teach, all the rights of ecclesiastical government; that of legislation, for the general good; that of coercion, to prevent infractions of the law; and that of institution, to institute pastors. . . . The Church has an external jurisdiction manifested in public acts; she has the right to make canons and establish ecclesiastical discipline; she must also have the strength necessary to enforce those canons and maintain that discipline. We read in the Gospels that the Church must punish incorrigible sinners; the church fathers acknowledge such a jurisdiction; they acknowledge that bishops may receive accusations, hear witnesses, and judge. In ecclesiastical crimes, says Justinian, it is the bishops' responsibility to examine and punish. To direct and govern churches, to regulate discipline, to make laws, to institute priests, such is the ecclesiastical jurisdiction. Now such a jurisdiction can only come from Jesus Christ; therefore it is independent of social institutions. To invade this jurisdiction is to go against the intentions of the Church and its founder. Princes, the protectors of the rights of the Church, now wish to usurp rather than maintain those rights. God forbid, says Fénelon, that the protector govern; let him humbly wait until his protection is asked for; let him obey.

Charlemagne, as protector of canon law, saw to the execution of what the bishops had determined. Louis the Pious, in imitation of Charlemagne, also remained within the prescribed limits of his authority. He took, not the title of legislator, but that of *monitor* of ecclesiastical laws. Princes, therefore, do not regulate the churches, nor do they make laws; they add to the authority of the Church that which God has put in their hands. Thus the sovereign, in his capacity as protector of the Church, must limit himself to making the laws necessary to implement the laws of the Church, the laws solicited by the Church, those that protect her and which the Church adopts and validates by open or tacit consent. . . . The national assembly has not shown itself any less determined than our kings in enforcing and implementing ecclesiastical laws. Since the origins of the Church, there has been not one bishopric instituted by a temporal power, nor has any ever been suppressed, for only that power that creates can destroy. Secular power is therefore always incompetent to change the constitution of the Church. And the Church, furthermore, does not govern by financial speculations. . . . I shall not mention the numerous bishops who cannot legitimately be deposed, since they have committed no crime. Nor shall I mention the much admired curates who would nonetheless be banished and deprived of their offices. The spiritual power alone can legitimately appoint clergymen to benefices, judge of their capacities and the validity of their titles. Popular election would be a usurpation and perhaps even a form of simony. In the first centuries of the Christian era, elections were by the people, but because of the numerous irregularities and difficulties that arose, the elections were given over to the bishops. And since then, kings have taken over this right. . . .

I do not see this affair as a political question; I speak only in accordance with the ideas of hierarchy consecrated by the Council of Trent. By assimilating the curates to the seventy-two disciples rather than by indicating them as the successors of the Apostles, we do not abnegate principles. I shall be faithful to those principles, because they are matters of faith. We severely denounce a doctrine that would lead to presbyterianism. If we did not openly declare our opposition, the bishops, on judgment day, would be within their rights in asking us to account for our cowardice. I therefore support the declaration of the Archbishop of Aix. I subscribe to it not only in my own name but also in the name of the churches I represent.

REMARKS OF M. TREILHARD, MAY 30, 1790

GENTLEMEN: The vices of the French government have corrupted all classes of citizens; and the clergy, notwithstanding the virtues of many of its members, has not been able to resist the fatal influence of a bad constitution.

Institutions without purpose or utility, bishoprics and parishes grossly overextended or extremely small, positions assigned without discernment or selection, wastrels drawing large salaries, diligent men neglected and falling into poverty: this is the picture which the present organization of the clergy presents; it is the remedy for these evils which the nation expects to receive from you.

The plan which the Committee has presented involves three things: the reduction of the number of benefices to those which are useful or necessary, the manner of appointment to these benefices, and the fixing of the salaries attached to them.

Are the changes which have been proposed useful? Have you the right to order them? It is to these two questions that I shall limit this discussion. . . .

When you fix your attention on two parishes, one of them ten leagues in circumference, the other not containing ten hearths; when you leave a bishopric which encompasses some 1500 parishes to enter another which does not have 20; when you see the pastor of a huge territory reduced to a salary of 700 livres, forced, as a consequence, to abandon without aid a father enfeebled by old age, poverty and disease, or to assist him by depriving himself of his own every-day needs; when in this same parish there stands a magnificent edifice, the center of a useless benefice, its incumbent combining in his hands the wealth of a hundred useful clergymen, and not at home to anyone except the tax-farmers who support him; may not one be permitted to believe that only blind chance has devised such a system, and that it is only necessary to recognize this disorder to rectify it?

Yes, gentlemen, this disorder exists, it has existed for many generations, and has found, to this day, supporters and advocates; for there are people for whom ancient usage has the power to legitimize anything, and slavery itself has not lacked for defenders.

But the time has come when all abuses ought to be reformed. . . .

In the first article of the plan of the Committee, there is proposed the reduction of the number of bishoprics and parishes, and the suppression of all useless benefices.

Certainly no one will disagree with the principle that any benefice, bishopric or parish, ought to be large enough to provide for its incumbent, but not so great as to overburden him; if the benefice is too large, it is poorly served; if it is far too small, the incumbent, falling prey to idleness and all its consequences, is almost always a discredit to himself and to others; fortunate, moreover, if he is not an object of scandal!

A new apportionment of benefices, then, will obviously be valuable: valuable to the pastor, who is faced with a burden not beyond his strength; valuable to the faithful, who are assured a more equal and ready distribution of spiritual comfort; valuable to the state, which must not be overtaxed by an excessive multiplication of tithes; valuable to religion itself, finally, since vain and frivolous spirits only too often point to the abuses of ecclesiastical institutions. . . .

There are too many bishoprics and too many parishes; there are bishoprics and parishes which are too large; there are more yet which are not large enough: the necessity for a reorganization, during this age of regeneration, cannot be denied.

It is no less necessary to abolish benefices without functions. Why? . . . they are useless.

Purchasable benefices, with no requirement of residence for their holders, are so oppressive and so opposed to the spirit of the Church, that doubtless no one will take it upon himself to defend them. It is also understood that, in principle, priests should be ordained only in that number which is actually needed, and that each ought to have his individual responsibility; it is only in times of moral laxity and degradation that the parasitic benefices are formed, benefices which intelligent people have never ceased deploring and which the public will today demand that we abolish. . . .

Yes, gentlemen, you have the right to order the changes proposed by the Committee; when you do order them, far from striking a blow at religion, you will be offering to it the greatest possible homage.

Those who are able to think an action which consists solely of suppressing useless benefices, and thus only the dangerous ones; of assuring to the faithful ministers of the highest integrity and virtue, men most worthy of the confidence of the people; of allotting to these ministers a burden commensurate with their strength: those people, I say, who believe that you cannot decree such an action without wounding the cause of religion, have formed a very strange and false view of that religion.

As for me, gentlemen, I assume that the most fatal enemy to religion will be he who, discounting completely the general interest of the Church when it is in opposition to his particular advantage, dares to try to defeat a reform manifestly useful, because it concerns certain abuses from which he profits.

There is the man who could destroy religion if it were not indeed completely divine, if it were not the faith *against which the gates of hell cannot prevail,* and if your own wisdom could not distinguish between the minister and his divine charge.

But I need not linger over that general and striking observation that a Sovereign cannot even be suspected of offering an affront to religion when he commands nothing but that which is truly in its best interests. . . .

Jesus Christ, after his resurrection, said to the Apostles: *Arise, instruct the Gentiles and baptize them, teaching them to observe all that I have commanded you.* . . . Again, he said to them: *As my Father has sent me so I send you; receive the Holy Spirit, those whose sins you shall remit, will be remitted.*

There you find the only claims of the spiritual jurisdiction of the Church: the power transmitted to the Apostles consists of no more than this: *instruction, administering of the sacraments.* . . .

It is already a great step forward, gentlemen, to have understood the limits which J[esus] C[hrist] fixed to the spiritual jurisdiction, *the propagation of the doctrine, the administering of the sacraments.* It is important not to lose sight of these things; for religion came perfect from the hands of its Founder; its doctrine is one, immutable, and can never change.

All the concessions which earthly monarchs have been able to make to the Church and its ministers, are not essential to the religion which existed in glory before their coming and which, consequently, can again live in glory after their passing. . . .

You can judge whether, as a matter of fact, the manner of appointing to benefices is not purely one of discipline, and whether it has anything to do with dogma or faith. The present apportionment of dioceses no longer suffices; but these are simply questions of administration, and administration always varies according to needs and circumstances: it can thus change again without the religion being changed; on the contrary, religion can only gain from changes which bring it into greater harmony with its original institutions.

But if all these changes are purely ones of administration and discipline, if they do not at all involve dogma and faith, how is it possible that the temporal power has not the right to order them? How can the ecclesiastical jurisdiction—limited by its own Founder to that which is purely spiritual —have the right to oppose these changes?

Let us distinguish between two very different things, the confusion of which has produced much disorder.

It is a principle of faith that the Apostles must have successors; it is a principle of faith that the Apostles should ordain and install those who succeed them; it is a principle of faith that the sacraments ought to be administered by the Apostles: all this is spiritual and consequently under the jurisdiction of the Church. But it is not a principle of faith that an Apostle ought to be installed in this or that place; it is not a principle of faith that a diocese ought to be larger or smaller; it is not a principle of faith that an Apostle should reside in one town rather than another; it is not a principle of faith that he be appointed or chosen in this or that manner: all these things are concerned only with external and temporal discipline, and the sovereign, consequently, has the right to regulate them.

By what calamity has the spiritual jurisdiction—which should be concerned only with dogma and faith—found itself in opposition with the temporal authority, when the latter is concerned neither with faith nor doctrine? Such conflicts could not have arisen during the first age of Christianity, because the Apostles were too close to their first institution to have forgotten its limits: why have these conflicts arisen today? Here is the reason.

The successors of the Apostles became temporal lords; on this basis they became members of assemblages in which they regulated the principal affairs of the state: before long they acquired there that influence which endowed them with the double quality of Princes of the Church and of the Empire. I do not know whether they acquired by this change many civic virtues, but it cannot be denied that they lost certain of their apostolic virtues. . . .

The piety of Emperors and Kings, perhaps their weakness, has given to the priests, or allowed them to assume, a jurisdiction which they certainly do not hold from J[esus] C[hrist]. They have often been consulted on affairs concerned solely with the administration and external discipline of the Church, they have been accorded functions in this manner which I am far from belittling; but is it not evident that all that the Church holds by the concession of the sovereign is foreign to religion, which remains always complete as long as the jurisdiction which J[esus] C[hrist] gave it is not affected? Is it not evident that all which is not comprised in that original concession the Church can hold only as a secondary concession, on the expressed or tacit consent of the sovereigns?

Must it protect itself with these concessions, and with those which followed in the wake of the earlier ones, in order to establish its rights? It is thus that the clergy defends its alleged property, thus that the nobles defend their abusive privileges, the magistrates their right to concur in the formation of the law: what facts, what precedents, what laws do they not cite! But what can facts and rules of discipline effect against the eternal authority of natural right and reason.

In a word, it is always necessary to return to the principle and source of the spiritual jurisdiction, it comprises only the faith, the mysteries, and the doctrine: there you have what is spiritual.

All that relates to the temporal, pertains to the temporal jurisdiction. . . .

This is the doctrine and morality of the Church: *all that we are commanded* (says St. Augustine) *ought to be observed for the sake of the common peace, as long as it is not contrary to the Faith and to good morals. . . .*

In order to decide whether a question falls under the competence of the Church or the sovereign, it is necessary then to determine whether it deals purely and solely with faith and doctrine; every question that does not directly, immediately, and uniquely concern faith and doctrine is necessarily submitted to the temporal authority, and it is the latter alone that has the power to decide. Is it a question of ordaining a priest? The Church alone can have this right. Is it a question of installing and consecrating a Bishop? It is for the Church to do this. Is it a question of administering a sacrament? The temporal magistrate has no right.

But is it a question of proscribing a particular institution, a religious order or anything of that nature? The sovereign has the right to declare that he does not wish this institution. Is it a question of disposing of the property attached to it? The sovereign has the power to do it. Is it a question of providing a more useful arrangement of bishoprics and parishes? Again, it is the prerogative of the sovereign. Is it a question of regulating the manner of appointment to benefices? It is likewise the sovereign who is empowered to act. . . .

A state can admit or not admit a religion; it can, with the greatest justification, declare that it does not wish this or that particular institution, without which the religion still survives; it can, with the greatest justification, declare that it wishes these institutions to exist in this or that place; it can, with the greatest justification, declare that it wishes these institutions to be administered in this or that manner: nothing is more foreign to dogma and faith, nothing, consequently, is of less importance to religion. . . .

You say that religion is attacked by the changes which are being proposed; but, think upon this; let us suppose that the nation had already decreed that there should be no more than 83 bishoprics and that the number of parishes should be reduced and set up according to a given proportion; let us suppose further that the people, by the authority of these decrees, had already elected its pastors. Tell us if we would cease to be Christians. What do you answer: "We will not ordain priests, we will not establish Parishes, we will not consecrate Bishops, and the people will be without ministers."

We will always be Christians, and you will not ordain our priests, you will not establish our parishes, you will not consecrate our bishops? You would, then, have the shocking audacity to leave the faithful without pastors; you would interrupt, insofar as it was in your power, that perpetual accession of Apostles which is a principle of the faith; and *cloaking private interests and passions under the sacred name of religion,*[1] abusing that sacred character which was entrusted to you solely for the public utility, you would employ your ministry only to defend certain temporal possessions, at the risk of destroying both the Church and the state! . . .

Let there be no doubt in our minds, the Church . . . will hasten to ordain priests, to install bishops and parish priests wherever necessary. This is the object of its ministry; this the exercise of that completely spiritual jurisdiction which it holds from J[esus] C[hrist] which it ought always to exercise for the greatest well-being of the state, and which you have certainly never wished to contest.

Your decrees, far from constituting an attack on this religion, will restore it to its original purity; you will then become in fact Christians of the Gospels; you will be Christians like the Apostles and their first disciples. . . .

It is then, gentlemen, then that the regeneration will in fact be consummated, when there will really exist no more privileges and distinctions; when there will be found among us none but Frenchmen, brothers, when we will all have but one heart, one soul, one will; the will to establish the public welfare on unshakeable foundations; and that day, which I make bold to say is not far off, that day will for all true citizens be the happiest of their lives.

REMARKS OF M. CAMUS, MAY 31, 1790

. . . . .

WHAT IS the meaning, then, of the procedure which up to now has existed in France of resorting to the Pope for the erection of bishoprics, the division of ecclesiastical provinces, the disposition of sees? The custom has

[1] Proclamation of the King, May 29.

taken root, because the French nation does not exercise its rights. The moment it once again assumes the exercise of its rights, the customs which were founded on its inaction and silence should disappear.

It is the Church, it is said, which invests the bishop with the exercise of his spiritual jurisdiction over such or such an extent of territory: the Church alone is able to remove that which it granted; and the bishop who comes to exercise jurisdiction over a territory that the Church has assigned to another bishop, and from which it has not removed him, would be a usurper.

This entire point of view rests on a fallacy: the belief that it was the Church which determined the territory of the dioceses. I well understand that it was the Pope who defined the boundaries of the Diocese of Blois in 1697; but the Pope is not the Church. He acts, I am told, in the name of and as representative of the Church; but I doubt that this power of representation can be found in any legitimate document emanating from the Church. I well know that the Popes have proclaimed this right as their own; but it seems to me that this claim is itself invalid. I point to the pernicious titular claims of the Popes in the Decretals, generally recognized as false; and when, turning to the period before the dismal epoch of the False Decretals, I examine the conduct the Church has followed, I see that the bishoprics have been distributed according to the structure of the civil provinces; I understand the Fathers of the Council of Chalcedony ordered that the ecclesiastic disposition of provinces should follow the dispositions made by the civil power: I conclude that the conduct which was followed then ought to be followed today; that it is for the nation to designate those towns which ought to be the chief towns of a diocese; and the Church is not able to establish or to preserve a distribution of provinces opposed to that which the public power has established. . . .

Why does the Church, which is part of the state, rise up against a disposition which has been made by the state? Is it not undeniably true that a nation has the power to admit such or such a religion? It abuses its power if it refuses to receive the true religion, if it admits a false one: but, in the final analysis, that is within its power. Doubtless, a nation cannot, while admitting a religion, refuse to allow it to enjoy those rights which are essential to that religion: it is impossible to wish a thing without wishing that which is part of its essence. But for all those things which are only accessory, the nation is free; it can make its own conditions which must be accepted.

The French nation is today making a constitution; it is assembled in the National Convention; it would render itself guilty of a horrible crime if, after recognizing the truth and sanctity of the Catholic religion—as far as it has the good fortune to recognize it—it would reject it; it would lapse into a senseless absurdity if, while admitting the Catholic religion, it would not wish to admit bishops and priests, essential ministers of its faith and its ritual: but why is it not authorized to say to the leaders of this religion: "you need episcopal towns: let us give you 83 towns, and we do not think it good for the civil and political order of the state that there be more"? This condition, impossible to reject at the moment when a National Convention was first admitting the Catholic religion, appears to us equally impossible to reject at the moment when a National Convention is preserving, as is its right, the religion of our fathers, the true religion. . . .

The question of appeals forms the fourth principal object of the constitution proposed by the Committee on Ecclesiastical Problems. I have taken note, gentlemen, that your Committee would suppress appeals to Rome; and on this point it is again necessary to agree that the Committee has recalled the very maxims of the ancient and pure discipline of the Church.

God forbid that I should fail to recognize either the primacy of the successors of St. Peter, or the indispensable necessity for all the churches of the world to communicate with the Church of Rome as with the center of Catholic unity. But it does not follow that the central body must have jurisdiction over all the churches. The primacy of Peter was one of surveillance and exhortation; it was not a primacy of jurisdiction. . . .

It is time that such appeals be finally prohibited; that the Church of France, always jealous of its liberties, but not always strong enough to maintain them to their rightful extent, be delivered from the servitude of seeing its judgments subject to annulment by a foreign power; it is time that cases be judged in the same territory where they arose, for that is the only means by which the parties can avoid ruinous expenses, the only means of making available all the evidence necessary to guarantee just and enlightened decisions. . . .

Fears are expressed lest the civil power wish to exercise the prerogative of granting powers which the Church alone is able to transmit. The powers attached to the priesthood and the circumscription of the limits of a territory are two things, distinct and not to be confused. The civil power will never have the desire, the more so since it has not the right, to grant the power to administer the sacraments. The bishops and priests receive this power from God; they can receive it only from God, they receive it in the sacrament of ordination which the Church confers upon them. But in what territory shall they exercise their power? In those towns which have been built by men, and of which the temporal society determines the boundaries and the limits. The Church consecrates a priest for Paris; when he has been consecrated, it is in the civil laws, not in the ecclesiastical laws, that he must search for the boundaries of the territory of Paris. . . .

It is important never to confuse the power or the source of power with the determination of the greater or lesser extent of the territory, or the greater or lesser number of persons, over whom this power, legitimately held elsewhere, will be exercised.

MAXIMILIEN ROBESPIERRE

THE EPITHET "incorruptible" has traditionally been attached to the name of Maximilien Robespierre (1758–1794). It has stood for a number of things. Unsympathetic or conservative historians have represented Robespierre as the very model of that kind of political dogmatist whose unflinching devotion to an ideal makes him peculiarly insensible to the urgencies of the immediate moment. On the other hand, friendlier observers have insisted that Robespierre was a practical politician who was "incorruptible" only in his devotion to the cause of the Parisian populace, and that the democratic revolution in France ended, for the time, with his execution.

A fairly successful lawyer in Arras, Robespierre championed democratic egalitarianism and universal suffrage when he was elected deputy to the Estates General. In 1792 he became a member of the Paris Commune, and thenceforth was one of the more influential spokesmen of the Jacobins, leading their struggle against the more moderate Girondists.

Robespierre was the moving spirit in the second Committee of Public Safety which was established after the revolution of 1793. He was the leading defender of this government before the National Convention, and he consequently came to be regarded as its head. Indeed, after his execution during the reaction against the "reign of terror" he was often accused of having seized dictatorial power.

Robespierre's ultimate program was the establishment of a republic of small independent producers, and he intended to turn the machinery of the state to the consummation of this project. There was no one during the Revolution who matched his devotion to the philosophy of Rousseau. It was, also, largely through Robespierre's doing that the rationalist cult of the Supreme Being was established as the official state religion. And, thoroughly convinced as he was that the situation required the strong measures he adopted, Robespierre was consistent in identifying the "general will" of the French nation with the activities of the Jacobins.

IN FAVOR OF AN ARMED PEOPLE, OF A WAR AGAINST THE VENDÉE

MAY 8, 1793

THE ARMIES of the Vendée, the armies of Brittany and of Coblenz are marching against Paris.

Parisians! The feudal masters are arming themselves because you are the vanguard of humanity. All the great powers of Europe are equipping themselves against you and all the base and depraved persons in France support them.

We now know the entire plan of our enemies, and have means for our defense in our hands. I am not stating secrets to you, I am merely repeating the speech I delivered this morning in the Convention. I declared this morning in the Convention that the Parisians will march to La Vendée, and that on all the roads and in all the cities on our journey we shall gather friends and brothers, and that we must extinguish in a single blow all of them, all the rebels. All the friends of the Republic must rise in order to annihilate all the aristocrats in La Vendée.

This morning in the Convention I said that the rascals in La Vendée have allies in the very heart of Paris, and I demanded emphatically that the Parisian fighters who have borne the terrible burden of the Revolution for five years, a portion of whom will now take the field—that these republicans must not lose their wives and children during their absence, at the murderous hands of the counter-revolution. And no one to-day dared in the Convention to dispute the necessity of these measures.

Parisians! Let us hasten to meet the bandits of La Vendée!

Do you know why La Vendée is becoming a danger to us? La Vendée is a danger because great precautions have been taken to disarm a section of the population. But we shall create new republican legions and we shall not hand over our wives and children to the daggers of the counter-revolution.

This morning, in the Convention, I demanded the destruction of the rebels from La Vendée, and I also demanded that all aristocrats and moderates should at once be excluded from the Paris sections, and I also demanded that these suspected persons should be jailed.

We do not regard a person as a suspect merely because he was once a nobleman, a farmer general or a trader. Those persons are suspects who have not proved their quality as citizens, and they shall remain in our prisons until such time as the war may be terminated victoriously.

I asked money this morning in the Convention for the *sans-culottes,* for we must deliberate in the sections, and the workingman cannot deliberate and work at home at the same time. But he must receive pay for his task of guarding the city. I have asked millions for the *sans-culottes* of Paris. . . . I have asked that people cease calumniating in the Convention the people of Paris and that the newspaper writers who desire to contaminate public opinion have their mouths stopped for them.

I demanded this morning in the Convention, and I demand it here again— and neither in the Convention nor here do I hear any contrary voices—that an army be held in readiness in Paris, an army not like that of Dumouriez, but an army consisting of *sans-culottes* and workingmen. And this army must investigate Paris, must keep the moderates in check, must occupy all posts and inspire all enemies with terror.

¹ [Supporters of republicanism, so-called because they wore long trousers instead of knee breeches (*culottes*).]

I asked in the Convention that the forges in all public squares be set to work in order to forge weapons, weapons, and again weapons, and I asked that the Council of Ministers should supervise this production of arms.

The tyrants of this earth have made their plans. The defenders of the Republic are to be their sacrifices. Very well—in this most grave of all moments, we shall save freedom by the severest measures, we shall not consent to be murdered one by one.

Citizens! Certain representatives of the people have attempted to play off the Parisians against the Departments, the Departments against Paris, the Convention against the provinces, and the people in the galleries against the masses of the Parisians. They will not succeed. I have informed these gentlemen to this effect, and if the entire people of France could hear me, the entire people of France would be on my side.

Citizens! Do not be dismayed. We are told of immeasurably large foreign armies, of their connections with La Vendée, of their connections with Paris. Very well! What will all their efforts avail them against millions of *sans-culottes?*

We have an immense people of strong *sans-culottes* at our disposal, who cannot be permitted to drop their work. Let the rich pay! We have a Convention; perhaps not all its members are poor and resolute, but the corrupt section will for all that not be able to prevent us from fighting. Do you believe that the Mountain has not enough forces to defeat the adherents of Dumouriez, Orléans and Coburg combined? Parisians, the fate of all France, of all Europe, and all humanity is in your hands. The Mountain needs the People. The people needs the Mountain. And I brand the reports that the provinces are turning their arms against the Jacobins as fabrications on the part of our enemies.

In conclusion, I demand what I demanded in the Convention this morning, namely, that the Parisians shall be the revolutionary nucleus of the army, strong enough to drag the *sans-culottes* with them, that an army should remain in Paris in order to keep our enemies in check, that all enemies who are caught shall be placed under arrest, and that money must be confiscated from the rich in order to enable the poor to continue the struggle.

REPORT ON THE PRINCIPLES OF A REVO-LUTIONARY GOVERNMENT

DECEMBER 25, 1793

CITIZENS, members of the Convention! Success induces the weak to sleep, but fills the strong with even more powers of resistance.

Let us leave to Europe and to history the task of lauding the marvels of Toulon, and let us arm for new victories of liberty!

The defenders of the Republic will be guided by Cæsar's maxim, and believe that nothing has been accomplished so long as anything remains to be accomplished.

To judge by the power and the will of our republican soldiers, it will be easy to defeat the English and the traitors. But we have another task of no less importance, but unfortunately of greater difficulty. This task is the task of frustrating, by an uninterrupted excess of energy, the eternal intrigues of all enemies of freedom within the country, and of paving the way for the victory of the principles on which the general weal depends.

These are the big tasks that you have imposed upon your Committee of Public Safety.

Let us first demonstrate the principles and the necessity of a revolutionary government, after which we shall describe those factors that aim to paralyze the birth of such a government.

The theory of the revolutionary government is as new as the Revolution itself, from which this government was born. This theory may not be found in the books of the political writers who were unable to predict the Revolution, nor in the law books of the tyrants. The revolutionary government is the cause of the fear of the aristocracy, or the pretext for its calumnies. For the tyrants this government is a scandal, for most people it is a miracle. It must be explained to all, so that at least all good citizens may be rallied around the principles of the general weal. . . .

The goal of a constitutional government is the protection of the Republic; that of a revolutionary government is the establishment of the Republic.

The Revolution is the war waged by liberty against its foes—but the Constitution is the régime of victorious and peaceful freedom.

The Revolutionary Government will need to put forth extraordinary activity, because it is at war. It is subject to no constant laws, since the circumstances under which it prevails are those of a storm, and change with every moment. This government is obliged unceasingly to disclose new sources of energy to oppose the rapidly changing face of danger.

Under constitutional rule, it is sufficient to protect individuals against the encroachments of the state power. Under a revolutionary régime, the state power itself must protect itself against all that attack it.

The revolutionary government owes a national protection to good citizens; to its foes it owes only death. . . .

Is the revolutionary government, by reason of the greater rapidity of its course and the greater freedom of its movements than are characteristic of an ordinary government, therefore less just and less legitimate? No, it is based on the most sacred of all laws, on the general weal and on the ironclad law of necessity!

This government has nothing in common with anarchy or with disorder; on the contrary, its goal requires the destruction of anarchy and disorder in order to realize a dominion of law. It has nothing in common with autocracy, for it is not inspired by personal passions.

The measure of its strength is the stubbornness and perfidy of its enemies; the more cruelly it proceeds against its enemies, the closer is its intimacy with the republicans; the greater the severities required from it by circumstances, the more must it recoil from unnecessary violations of private interests, unless the latter are demanded by the public necessity. . . .

If we were permitted a choice between an excess of patriotism and a base deficiency in public spirit, or even a morass of moderation, our choice should soon be made. A healthy body, tormented by an excess of strength, has better prospects than a corpse.

Let us beware of slaying patriotism in the delusion that we are healing and moderating it.

By its very nature, patriotism is energetic and enthusiastic. Who can love his country coldly and moderately? Patriotism is the quality of common men who are not always capable of measuring the consequences of all their acts, and where is the patriot to be found who is so enlightened as never to err? If we admit the existence of moderates and cowards who act in good faith, why should there not also exist patriots in good faith, who sometimes err by excess of zeal? If, therefore, we are to regard all those as criminals who have exceeded the limits of caution in the revolutionary movement, we should be obliged to condemn equally the bad citizens, the enemies of the republic, as well as its enthusiastic friends, and should thus destroy the stoutest props of the Republic. There could be no other outcome than that the emissaries of tyranny would be our public prosecutors.

In indicating the duties of the revolutionary government we have also pointed out the spots in which it is endangered. But the greater its power, the freer and swifter its actions, the more must they be subjected to the test of good faith. The day on which such a government falls into unclean and perfidious hands is the day of the death of the Republic. Its name will become the pretext, the excuse of counter-revolution; its strength will be the strength of venom.

The establishment of the French Revolution was no child's play; it cannot be the work of caprice and carelessness, nor can it be the accidental product of the coalition of all the individual demands and of the revolutionary elements.

Wisdom and power created the universe. In assigning to men from your own midst the terrible task of watching over the destinies of our country, you have placed at their disposal your abilities and your confidence. If the revolutionary government is not supported by the intelligence and the patriotism and by the benevolence of all the representatives of the people, where else should it draw the strength enabling it to face the efforts of a united Europe on an equal plane? The authority of the Constituent Assembly must be respected by all Europe. The tyrants are exhausting the resources of their politics, and sacrificing their treasures, in order to degrade this authority and destroy it. The National Assembly, however, prefers its government to the cabinets of London and all the other courts of Europe. Either we shall rule, or the tyrants will rule us. What are the resources of our enemies in this war of treachery and corruption waged by them against the Republic? All the vices fight for them; the Republic has all the virtues on its side. The virtues are simple, poor, often ignorant, sometimes brutal. They are the heritage of the unhappy, the possession of the people. Vice is surrounded by all the treasures, armed with all the charms of voluptuousness, with all the enticements of perfidy; it is escorted by all the dangerous talents that have placed their services at the disposal of crime.

Great skill is shown by the tyrants in turning against us—not to mention our passions and our weaknesses—even our patriotism! No doubt the germs of disunion which they sow among us would be capable of rapid dissemination if we should not hasten to stifle them.

By virtue of five years of treason, by virtue of feeble precautions, and by virtue of our gullibility, Austria, England, Russia and Italy have had time to set up, as it were, a secret government in France, a government that competes with the French government. They have their secret committees, their treasures, their agents, they absorb men from us and appropriate them to themselves, they have the unity that we lack, they have the policy that we have often neglected, they have the consistency which we have so often failed to show.

Foreign courts have for some time been spewing out on French soil their well-paid criminals. Their agents still infect our armies, as even our victory at Toulon will show. All the bravery of our soldiers, all the devotion of our generals, and all the heroism of the members of this Assembly had to be put forth to defeat treason. These gentlemen still speak in our administrative bodies, in the various sections; they secure admission to the clubs; they sometimes may be found sitting among us; they lead the counter-revolution; they lurk about us, they eavesdrop on our secrets; they flatter our passions and seek even to influence our opinions and to turn our own decisions against us. When you are weak, they praise our caution. When you are cautious, they accuse us of weakness. Your courage they designate as audacity, your justice as cruelty. If we spare them, they will conspire publicly; if we threaten them, they will conspire secretly or under the mask of patriotism. Yesterday they murdered the defenders of liberty; to-day they mingle in the procession of mourners and weep for their own victims. Blood has flowed all over the country on their account, but we need this blood in the struggle against the tyrants of Europe. The foreigners have set themselves up as the arbitrators of public peace; they have sought to do their work with money; at their behest, the people found bread; when they willed it otherwise, the bread was not available; they succeeded in inaugurating gatherings in front of the bakeshops and in securing the leadership of bands of famished men. We are surrounded by their hired assassins and their spies. We know this, we witness it ourselves, and yet they live! The perfidious emissaries who address us, who flatter us—these are the brothers, the accomplices, the bodyguard of those who destroy our crops, who threaten our cities, massacre our brothers, cut down our prisoners. They are all looking for a leader, even among us. Their chief interest is to incite us to enmity among ourselves. If they succeed in this, this will mean a new lease of life for the aristocracy, the hour of the rebirth of the Federalist plans. They would punish the faction of the Girondistes for the obstacles that have been placed in their way. They would avenge themselves on the Mountain for its splendid spirit of self-sacrifice, for their attacks are aimed at the Convention. We shall continue to make war, war against England, against the Austrians, against all their allies. Our only possible answer to their pamphlets and lies is to destroy them. And we shall know how to hate the enemies of our country.

It is not in the hearts of the poor and the patriots that the fear of terror must dwell, but there in the midst of the camp of the foreign brigands, who would bargain for our skin, who would drink the blood of the French people.

The Committee of Public Safety has recognized that the law does not punish the great criminals with the necessary swiftness. Foreigners, well-known agents of the allied kings, generals besmirched with the blood of Frenchmen, former accomplices of Dumouriez and Custine and Lamarlières have long been in custody and are yet not executed.

The conspirators are very numerous. It is far less necessary to punish a hundred unknown, obscure wretches, than to seize and put to death a single leader of the conspirators.

The members of the Revolutionary Tribunal, whose patriotism and rectitude can for the most part only be praised, have called the attention even of the members of the Committee of Public Safety to the deficiencies in the laws. We propose to you that the Committee of Public Safety be entrusted with the task of introducing a number of innovations in this connection, with the purpose of strengthening and accelerating the hand of justice in its procedure against intrigues. You have already commissioned the Committee, in a decree, to this effect. We propose that you create the means by which its judgments may be accelerated against foreigners and against generals conspiring with the tyrants.

It is not enough to terrify the enemies of our country; we must also aid its defenders.

We ask that favorable conditions be created for the soldiers who are fighting and dying for liberty.

The French army is not only a terror to the tyrants, it is the glory of humanity and of the nation. In their march to victory, our victorious warriors shout, "Long live the Republic!" They die under the swords of the foe, with the shout, "Long live the Republic!" on their lips; their last words are pæans to liberty, their last gasps are exclamations of homage to their country. If the leaders of the army were as valiant as our soldiers, Europe would have been defeated long ago.

Any measure adopted in favor of the army is an act of national gratitude.

What we have done thus far for the defenders of our country and for their families seems far too little. We should increase the allowances one-third. The immense resources of the Republic permit it; our country demands it. We have also ascertained that the invalids, as well as the widows and children of those who have died for their country, are often injured by the formalities of the law, and by the indifference and ill-favor of subaltern officers. We demand that they be aided by official advocates, who will assist them in attaining their rights. For all these reasons, I ask that the Convention adopt the following measures:

I. The public prosecutor assigned to the revolutionary tribunal shall at once draw up articles of indictment against Dietrich Custine, the son of the general condemned by law, Desbrullis, Biron, Barthélemy, and all the other generals and officers who were connected with Dumouriez, Custine, Lamarlières and Houchard. The public prosecutor shall also indict foreigners, bankers, and all other individuals having any communications with the kings allied against the Republic.

II. The Committee of Public Safety shall report at the earliest possible moment on the appropriate means for securing an improvement in the organization of the Revolutionary Tribunal.

III. Allowances and aids, as paid hitherto to veterans or their dependents, shall be increased one-third.

IV. A commission shall be appointed entrusted with the task of defending the rights of veterans and their dependents.

V. The members of this Commission shall be appointed by the Convention and shall be nominated by the Committee of Public Safety.

CONSPIRACY OF THE EQUALS

I T IS A TRUISM that the French Revolution has meant many things to many men, both at the time of its occurrence and ever since. Yet the full significance of this great social movement must be sought not only in what its forerunners and participants thought and did but also in its relation to subsequent ideas and institutions—for example, to political democracy, nationalism, and socialism in the nineteenth and twentieth centuries. Some understanding of what the Revolution was capable of becoming once its slogans and ideals were reevaluated in later social movements may, however, be achieved by the study of men and aims that played a small part in the Revolution itself but foreshadowed important later tendencies. Such a movement was the "Conspiracy of the Equals" associated with the name of "Gracchus" Babeuf.

François Noel Babeuf (1760–97) was a former keeper of feudal records who had helped draw up his neighborhood *cahier* in 1789 and had filled several minor posts when the Revolution swung leftward into the "reign of terror." When in 1794 the pendulum moved the other way with Robespierre's downfall and the coming of the Thermidorean reaction, Babeuf began to publish his conviction that the Revolution, short of socialism, was incomplete. His newspaper (*Journal de la liberté de la presse,* later *Le Tribun du peuple*) was suppressed, and Babeuf was sent to prison, but upon his release he became, in 1795, the central figure in a movement aiming at economic and political equality. With its ranks swollen by radical Jacobins and sufferers from the inflation and with Babeuf's revived *Tribun du peuple* serving as its mouthpiece, this so-called Pantheon Society was successful enough in the winter of 1795–96 to arouse the fears of the Directory. Police spies worked their way into the organization, and late in February, 1796, it was dissolved, the order being carried out by young General Bonaparte. Babeuf and the other leaders of the movement then made elaborate plans for an insurrection which was to overthrow the Directory, socialize property, and give France "liberty, equality, and the Constitution of 1793." The expectation of winning over to their cause large sections of the populace and army was never put to the test, for the government, at all times aware of their plans, arrested the leaders before they were ready to strike the first blow (May, 1796). After a lengthy trial Babeuf and a colleague were executed. Others of the conspirators were deported.

Even if it be granted that the Conspiracy of the Equals might with better luck have overthrown the Directory, there can be no doubt that France was far from ready for their socialist interpretation of the ideals of 1789. A minority foredoomed to failure, they nevertheless serve to highlight—especially for the student of today—important "bourgeois" characteristics of the French Revolution. The following manifesto, written by Babeuf's friend Sylvain Maréchal and distributed after the dissolution of the Pantheon Society, is a trustworthy, brief expression of their social criticism. It is taken, in translation from the French, from Ernest Belfort Bax's *The Last Episode of the French Revolution* (London, Grant Richards, 1911).

ॐ

MANIFESTO OF THE EQUALS

PEOPLE OF FRANCE! During fifteen centuries you have lived as slaves, and in consequence unhappily. It is scarcely six years that you have begun to breathe, in the expectation of independence, happiness, equality! The first demand of nature, the first need of man, and the chief knot binding together all legitimate association! People of France! you have not been more favoured than other nations who vegetate on this unfortunate growth! Always and everywhere the poor human race, delivered over to more or less adroit cannibals, has served as a plaything for all ambitions, as a pasture for all tyrannies. Always and everywhere men have been lulled by fine words; never and nowhere have they obtained the thing with the word. From time immemorial it has been repeated, with hypocrisy, that *men are equal;* and from time immemorial the most degrading and the most monstrous inequality ceaselessly weighs on the human race. Since the dawn of civil society this noblest appanage of man has been recognised without contradiction, but has on no single occasion been realised; equality has never been anything but a beautiful and sterile fiction of the law. To-day, when it is demanded with a stronger voice, they reply to us: "Be silent, wretches! Equality of fact is nought but a chimera; be contented with conditional equality; you are all equal before the law. Canaille, what do you want more?" What do we want more? Legislators, governors, rich proprietors, listen, in your turn! We are all equal, are we not? This principle remains uncontested. For, unless attacked by madness, no one could seriously say that it was night when it was day.

Well! we demand henceforth to live and to die equal, as we have been born equal. We demand real equality or death; that is what we want.

And we shall have it, this real equality, it matters not at what price! Woe betide those who place themselves between us and it! Woe betide him who offers resistance to a vow thus pronounced!

The French Revolution is but the precursor of another, and a greater and more solemn revolution, and which will be the last!

The People has marched over the bodies of kings and priests who coalesced against it: it will be the same with the new tyrants, with the new political hypocrites, seated in the place of the old ones! What do we want more than equality of rights? We want not only the equality transcribed in the declaration of the Rights of Man and the citizens; we will have it in the midst of us, under the roof of our houses. We consent to everything for its sake; to make a clear board, that we may hold to it alone. Perish, if it must be, all the arts, provided real equality be left us! [1] Legislators and governors, who have neither genius nor good faith; rich proprietors without bowels of compassion, you will try in vain to neutralise our holy enterprise by saying that it does no more than reproduce that agrarian law already demanded more than once before! Calumniators! be silent in your turn, and, in the silence of confusion, listen to our demands, dictated by nature and based upon justice!

The agrarian law, or the partition of lands, was the immediate aim of certain soldiers without principles, of certain peoples moved by their instinct rather than by reason. We aim at something more sublime and more equitable —the common good, or the community of goods. No more individual property in land; the land belongs to no one. We demand, we would have, the communal enjoyment of the fruits of the earth, fruits which are for everyone!

We declare that we can no longer suffer, with the enormous majority of men, labour and sweat in the service and for the good pleasure of a small minority! Enough and too long have less than a million of individuals disposed of that which belongs to more than twenty millions of their kind!

Let this great scandal, that our grandchildren will hardly be willing to believe in, cease!

Let disappear, once for all, the revolting distinction of rich and poor, of great and small, of masters and valets, of governors and governed! [2]

Let there be no other difference between human beings than those of age and sex. Since all have the same needs and the same faculties, let there be one education for all, one food for all. We are contented with one sun and one air for all. Why should the same portion and the same quality of nourishment not suffice for each of us? But already the enemies of an order of things the most natural that can be imagined, declaim against us. Disorganisers and factious persons, say they, you only seek massacre and plunder. People of France! we shall not waste our time in replying to them, but we shall tell you: the holy enterprise which we organise has no other aim than to put an end to civil dissensions and to the public misery.

Never has a vaster design been conceived or put into execution. From time to time some men of genius, some sages, have spoken of it in a low and trembling voice. Not one of them has had the courage to tell the whole truth.

The moment for great measures has come. The evil is at its height. It covers the face of the earth. Chaos, under the name of politics, reigns there throughout too many centuries. Let everything return once more to order, and reassume its just place!

---

[1] This was one of the sentences objected to by other members of the committee.

[2] The idea of the abolition of governors and governed was also, as we are informed by Buonarroti, objected to by some of his colleagues.

At the voice of equality, let the elements of justice and well-being organise themselves. The moment has arrived for founding the Republic of the Equals, that grand refuge open for all men. The days of general restitution have come. Families groaning in misery, come and seat yourselves at the common table prepared by nature for all her children! People of France! the purest form of all glory has been reserved for thee! Yes, it is you who may first offer to the world this touching spectacle!

Ancient customs, antiquated conventions, would anew raise an obstacle to the establishment of the Republic of the Equals. The organisation of real equality, the only kind that answers all needs without making victims, without costing sacrifices, will not perhaps please everybody at first. The egoist, the ambitious man, will tremble with rage. Those who possess unjustly will cry aloud against its injustice. Exclusive enjoyments, solitary pleasures, personal ease, will cause sharp regrets on the part of individuals who have fattened on the labour of others. The lovers of absolute power, the vile supporters of arbitrary authority, will scarcely bend their arrogant chiefs to the level of real equality. Their narrow view will penetrate with difficulty, it may be, the near future of common well-being. But what can a few thousand malcontents do against a mass of men, all of them happy, and surprised to have sought so long for a happiness which they had beneath their hand?

The day after this veritable revolution they will say, with astonishment, What? the common well-being was to be had for so little? We had only to will it. Ah! why did we not will it sooner? Why had we to be told about it so many times? Yes, doubtless, with one man on earth richer, more powerful than his neighbours, than his equals, the equilibrium is broken, crime and misery are already in the world. People of France! by what sign ought you henceforward to recognise the excellence of a constitution? That which rests entirely on an equality of fact is the only one that can benefit you and satisfy all your wants.

The aristocratic charters of 1791 to 1795 have only riveted your bonds instead of rending them. That of 1793 was a great step indeed towards real equality, and never before had it been approached so closely; but yet, it did not achieve the aim and did not touch the common well-being, of which, nevertheless, it solemnly consecrated the great principle.

People of France! open your eyes and your heart to the fullness of happiness. Recognise and proclaim with us the "Republic of the Equals"!

NAPOLEON BONAPARTE

NAPOLEON BONAPARTE was born in Corsica in 1769, just one year after it became French territory. Although his parents were Italian, and members of the lower nobility, he received an excellent military education at Brienne and at Paris, accepting a commission as an artillery officer in September, 1785.

During the Revolution he distinguished himself in the capture of Toulon from the British in 1793; for his service in this action he was promoted by the Committee of Public Safety to the rank of Brigadier-General. His support of Robespierre's party led to his imprisonment as a suspect after the latter's fall from power on 9 Thermidor. A personal letter to the Convention avowing his loyalty secured his release. He demonstrated this loyalty by putting down the insurrection of 1795 with the famed "whiff of grapeshot," and was rewarded with the command of the Army of Italy (March, 1796).

With the First Italian Campaign Napoleon's rapid rise to power began. Within a few months he gained control of Northern Italy and negotiated the Treaty of Campo-Formio on his own initiative (October, 1797). Although his subsequent campaign in Egypt (1798–99) was far less successful, his growing influence among both the military and political forces of the Directorate enabled him to seize power in the *coup d'état* of 18 Brumaire (November 9, 1799). One month later, the Constitution of the Year VIII proclaimed him First Consul; in 1802 he became Consul for life; in 1804, Emperor.

For fifteen years Napoleon fought off a series of European coalitions. Victories at Austerlitz (1805), Jena and Auerstadt (1806), and Wagram (1809) enabled him to change the map of Europe. The boundaries of territorial France were extended by annexations on the Rhine and in Sardinia and Italy, the Holy Roman Empire was abolished, and Austria and Prussia were reduced to second-rate powers. New kingdoms were formed in Italy, Naples, Holland (until 1810) and Westphalia, and were turned over to his brothers Joseph, Jerome, and Louis, and to his stepson, Eugène de Beauharnais. These satellite states, along with his dominance of the Confederation of the Rhine (created in 1806), clearly established Napoleon's hegemony in western and central Europe.

Within France, Napoleon maintained the essential economic and social changes of the Revolution, embodying them in the Civil Code of 1804. The Concordat of 1801 with Pope Pius VII gave implicit legitimacy to his rule, while his reorganization and centralization of the administrative system set the pattern for French government which has continued to this day. Endowed with prodigious energy and great determination, Napoleon ruled France as a monarch in fact as well as in name; no subject was too great or too small for the consideration of the Emperor.

With the opening of the War in Spain in 1808, the Napoleonic System suffered its first shock. The catastrophe of the Russian Campaign of 1812 reinforced the rise of national sentiment in Germany and Spain and resulted in a new coalition of European powers. Napoleon was defeated and exiled to Elba in 1814. His dramatic return during "The Hundred Days" (March–June, 1815) was no more than an epilogue to his career. On June 18, 1815, Napoleon was defeated at Waterloo; he was banished to St. Helena, where he died in 1821.

The selections that follow present Napoleon in various ways. The first is Napoleon's own account of his *coup d'état* taken from the 2d edition of *Memoirs of the History of France during the Reign of Napoleon* (London, 1823). His advice on local and imperial administration comes from J. M. Thompson's edition of *Letters of Napoleon* (Oxford: Basil Blackwell, 1934). Napoleon's reflections in the third person on the Battle of Austerlitz are taken from *The Mind of Napoleon,* ed. by J. Christopher Herold (New York: Columbia University Press, 1955).

ॐ

NAPOLEON ON THE EIGHTEENTH BRUMAIRE

THE Council of Ancients met on the 18th of Brumaire, at two o'clock, in the great gallery of the Chateau of Saint-Cloud. At four, General Bonaparte was introduced, and having received from the President permission to address the Council, he spoke as follows:

"REPRESENTATIVES OF THE PEOPLE. You do not now meet under common circumstances, you are upon a volcano. Permit me to address you with the freedom of a soldier, the candour of a citizen zealous for the welfare of his country; and to intreat you to suspend your judgment till you have heard the whole of what I am about to say.

"I was residing in tranquillity at Paris, when I received the decree of the Council of Ancients, which declared to me the dangers of the Council and of the Republic. I instantly summoned around me my brethren in arms, and we came to afford you our support, to offer you the arms of the nation, because you are its head. Our intentions were pure and disinterested; but in return for the devotedness which we evinced yesterday, we are to-day overwhelmed with calumnies. Some talk of a second Caesar, some of another Cromwell: it is reported that I wish to establish a military government.

"Had I wished, Representatives, to overthrow the liberties of my country —had I aimed at usurping the sovereign authority, I should not have obeyed the orders you gave me; I should not have had occasion to receive that authority from the Senate. More than once, and under the most favourable circumstances, I have been called upon to assume it. After our triumphs in Italy, I was invited to it by the voices of my comrades, by those of the soldiers who have been so ill used since I ceased to command them, and who, in the deserts of the west, are at this time compelled to carry on a horrible war, which prudence and a recurrence to principles had appeased, but which imbecility or treason has rekindled.

"I swear, Representatives, that the nation possesses no defender more zealous than myself; I devote myself without reserve to the execution of your orders; but the welfare of the nation depends on you alone, for there is now no Directory: four of the members who composed that body have given in their resignation, and the fifth has been placed under superintendence for his own safety. Danger presses, and disasters are increasing: the Minister of Police has just informed me that several fortified places in La Vendée have fallen into the hands of the Chouans. Representatives of the people, the Council of the Ancients is invested with great powers, but the wisdom which inspires it is still greater. Consult only that wisdom, and the imminence of our dangers. Save the state from being torn to pieces; save us from the loss of what we have sacrificed so much to obtain, Liberty and Equality!"

(Here, being interrupted by a member, who reminded him of the Constitution, Bonaparte resumed thus):

"The Constitution! You violated it on the 18th of Fructidor; you violated it on the 22d of Floreal; you violated it on the 30th of Prairial. The Constitution! all factions invoke it, and they infringe its laws; it is despised by them all. It can no longer be a source of protection to us, for it is not respected by any one. Representatives of the people, you see in me no wretched intriguer, covered by the mask of hypocrisy. I have given proofs of my devotion to my country, and dissimulation would to me be unavailing. I hold this language to you only because I am desirous that the reward of such mighty sacrifices may not be lost. The constitution and the rights of the people have been repeatedly violated; and since it is no longer permitted to us to pay that constitution the respect which it ought to command, let us save the foundations on which it rests. Let us preserve equality and liberty; let us find means of securing to every one the liberty which is his right, and in which the constitution has proved inadequate to protect him. I declare to you that as soon as the dangers which have caused extraordinary powers to be confided to me are over, I will abdicate those powers. With respect to the Magistracy to which you may appoint me, I only wish to be the arm to support it, and to execute your commands."

(A member required General Bonaparte to furnish proofs of the existence of the dangers he alluded to.)

"If a full explanation is required, if individuals must be named, I will name them. I say the Directors Barras and Moulins have proposed to me to put myself at the head of a party tending to the ruin of all men of liberal ideas."

(A discussion now took place, whether Bonaparte should continue his address in public, or whether the assembly should resolve itself into a secret committee. It was decided that he should be heard in public.)

"Once more, Representatives of the people, I repeat that the Constitution, thrice violated, no longer affords any security to the citizens: it cannot maintain harmony, for it commands no respect. I repeat that I do not hold this language for the sake of possessing myself of power, after the fall of existing authorities; yet that power has been offered to me continually since my return to Paris. All the different factions have knocked at my door, but I have paid no attention to them, because I belong to no cabal; I am of no party but that of the French people.

"Several members of the Council of Ancients know that I have discoursed with them on the proposals that have been made; and I have only accepted the authority which you have confided to me for the purpose of sustaining the cause of the Republic. I will not conceal from you, Representatives, that in taking the command, I relied only on the Council of the Ancients. I did not reckon on the Council of Five Hundred, which is divided; and which contains men who would restore conventions, revolutionary committees, and scaffolds. I did not rely on the Council of Five Hundred, in which the heads of that party have just taken their seats;—on that Council whence emissaries are even now proceeding with instructions to instigate and organize a tumult in Paris.

"Fear not, Representatives, these criminal projects. Surrounded by my brethren in arms, I shall find means to protect you from them. Your courage will enable me to fulfil my promise, brave comrades, to whom I am represented as hostile to liberty; grenadiers, whose caps I observe; brave soldiers, armed with those bayonets which I have so often directed to the humiliation of kings—which have aided me to found Republics. Should some orator, in foreign pay, talk of outlawing me, let him beware lest he draw down that condemnation upon himself. Should he talk of outlawing me, I would appeal to you, my brave companions in arms, to you, valiant soldiers, whom I have so often led to victory; to you, intrepid defenders of the Republic, with whom I have shared so many dangers to establish liberty and equality. I would in that case rely on you, my friends, and on my own good fortune.

"I call upon you, Representatives of the people, to resolve yourselves into a general committee, and therein to take the salutary measures which the urgency of our danger imperiously requires. You shall always find my arm ready to carry your resolutions into effect."

(The President, in the name of the Council, invited the General to develop, fully, the plot with which the Republic was threatened.)

"I have already had the honour to state to the Council that the Constitution is incapable of preserving the country, and that such an order of things must be created as will enable us to raise her out of the abyss in which she is plunged. The former part of what I have just repeated, was stated to me by the two Directors whom I have named to you, and who, had they done nothing more than give utterance to a truth known to all the nation, would not be more guilty than many other Frenchmen. Since it is allowed that the Constitution is insufficient to preserve the Republic, hasten then to take the means of withdrawing it from danger, if you wish to escape the bitter and eternal reproaches of the French people, of your families, and of your own hearts."

NOTE DICTATED TO LUCIEN BONAPARTE, MINISTER FOR HOME AFFAIRS

Paris, December 25, 1799

IF I had not to go to war, I should initiate the prosperity of France through the local authorities. If one is to regenerate a nation, it is much simpler to deal with its inhabitants a thousand at a time than to pursue the romantic ideal of individual welfare. Each local body in France represents 1,000 inhabitants. If you work for the prosperity of 36 thousand communities you will be working for that of 36 million inhabitants, whilst simplifying the issue, and reducing the difficulties arising out of the difference in scale between thousands and millions. That was what Henri IV had in mind when he talked about providing everyone with a fowl for his stock-pot: it would have been a stupid remark otherwise.

The Minister for Home Affairs should pay special attention to the following ideas:

Before the Revolution every village belonged to its landlord, and to its priest. The tenant and the parishioner had no roads to travel by; there were no byres where their cows or sheep could shelter, no meadows where they could go to grass. But since 1790, when this common right of moving and grazing cattle was suddenly and quite properly taken out of the hands of the feudal landlord, each municipality has become a real *person*, under the protection of common law, with the right of possessing, acquiring, and buying property, and of performing, for the benefit of the municipal family, every act contemplated in our codes. Thanks to this great national conception, France found herself suddenly divided into 36 thousand personalities, each of which was faced with the responsibilities of *ownership* —anxious to extend its property, improve its produce, increase its income, and so forth.

In that change lay the germ of French prosperity. Why has further development been impossible? Because, whilst an individual owner, with a personal interest in his property, is always wide awake, and brings his plans to fruition, communal interest is inherently sleepy and unproductive; because individual enterprise is a matter of instinct, and communal enterprise a matter of public spirit—and that is rare.

Consequently, since 1790, the 36 thousand local bodies have been like 36 thousand orphan girls. Heiresses to the old feudal rights, they have been neglected or defrauded for the past ten years by the municipal trustees of the Convention or of the Directory. A new set of mayors, assessors, or municipal councillors has generally meant nothing more than a fresh form of robbery: they have stolen the by-road, stolen the foot-path, stolen the timber, robbed the church, and filched the property of the commune; and this looting is still going on under the slack municipal system of the Year VIII.

If this system were to last another ten years, what would become of the local bodies? They would inherit nothing but debts, and be so bankrupt that they would be asking charity of the inhabitants, instead of giving them the help and protection that is their due. Like the family prodigal, they would have sold or pawned their last stick of furniture, and be unable to borrow a penny to live on. No one would venture to settle down in a community so heavily in debt that he would have nothing to look forward to but fees and taxes of all kinds—charitable contributions, donations, subscriptions, special collections, and so forth. The existence of a local authority ought to attract population: under these conditions it would repel it.

It is the first duty of a Home Secretary to arrest a disease which would carry infection into the 36 thousand limbs of the great body of society. And the first thing to do, towards this end, is to form a clear notion of the seriousness of the disease and of its symptoms. The Minister will therefore begin by having a general inventory made of the 36 thousand *communes*— this has always been wanting. . . . Local bodies will be divided into three classes: those which are in debt, those which just pay their way, and those which show a surplus. The second and third classes are in a minority, and there need be no hurry to deal with them. The point is to restore solvency to those which are in debt. . . . Once this inventory is drawn up, the Prefects and Sub-prefects will be warned to bring the whole force of the administration to bear upon the insolvent municipalities, and to get rid at once of any mayors or assessors who do not see eye to eye with them as to local improvement and regeneration. It will be the duty of the Prefect to visit these bodies at least twice a year, and of the Sub-prefect four times a year, under penalty of dismissal. He will make a monthly report to the Minister about each municipality, stating the results of what he has tried to do, and what still remains to be done.

I should like proposals for a prize for those mayors who have got their municipalities out of debt within 2 years: whereas, in the case of any municipality which is not solvent at the end of 5 years, the Government will nominate a special commission to take over its administration. (This will involve the drafting of a law.)

Thus at the end of 5 years France will have only two classes of local bodies left—those that are working at a profit, and those which make both ends meet. We shall have expunged from the map of France the insolvent municipalities, whose property is falling to pieces, and becoming a burden on the inhabitants.

This first levelling-up accomplished, the efforts of the Minister and of the municipalities will be devoted to securing that, by the end of a further period, the solvent *communes* rise into the class of those which show a surplus; so that, in 10 years' time, this may be the only class left.

When this is done, the movement towards national prosperity initiated by the efforts of 36 million individuals will be multiplied by the regenerative power of 36 thousand communal personalities, all working, under the supreme direction of the Government, towards the goal of progressive perfectibility.

Every year the 50 mayors who have done most to rid their community of debt, or to manage it at a profit, will be summoned to Paris, at the expense of the State, and formally presented to the three Consuls.

A column put up at the expense of the Government, at the main entrance of the village or town, will perpetuate the name of its mayor; and posterity will read these words:—

"To the Guardian of the Community; from his grateful Country."

TO PRINCE EUGÈNE, VICEROY OF ITALY

Milan, June 5, 1805

BY entrusting you with the government of Our Kingdom of Italy, We have
given you proof of the respect your conduct has inspired in Us. But you
are still at an age when one does not realise the perversity of men's hearts;
I cannot therefore too strongly recommend to you prudence and circumspection. Our Italian subjects are more deceitful by nature than the citizens
of France. The only way in which you can keep their respect, and serve
their happiness, is by letting no one have your complete confidence, and
by never telling anyone what you really think of the ministers and high
officials of your court. Dissimulation, which comes naturally at a maturer
age, has to be emphasised and inculcated at yours. If you ever find yourself
speaking unnecessarily, and from the heart, say to yourself, "I have made a
mistake," and don't do it again. Show respect for the nation you govern,
and show it all the more as you discover less grounds for it. You will come
to see in time that there is little difference between one nation and another.
The aim of your administration is the happiness of my Italian peoples; and
the first sacrifice you will have to make will be to fall in with certain of
their customs which you detest. In any position but that of Viceroy of Italy
you may boast of being a Frenchman: but here you must forget it, and
count yourself a failure unless the Italians believe that you love them. They
know there is no love without respect. Learn their language; frequent
their society; single them out for special attention at public functions; like
what they like, and approve what they approve.

The less you talk, the better: you aren't well enough educated, and you
haven't enough knowledge, to take part in informal debates. Learn to listen,
and remember that silence is often as effective as a display of knowledge.
Don't be ashamed to ask questions. Though a Viceroy, you are only 23;
and however much people flatter you, in reality they all know your limitations, and honour you less for what they believe you to be than for what
they hope you will become.

Don't imitate me in every respect; you need more reserve.

Don't preside often over the State Council; you have too little experience
to do it successfully—though I see no objection to your attending it, whilst
an Assessor acts as president, from his ordinary seat. Your ignorance of
Italian, and of legislation too, for that matter, is an excellent excuse for

staying away. Anyhow, never make a speech there: they would listen to you, and would not answer you back; but they would see at once that you aren't competent to discuss business. So long as a prince holds his tongue, his power is incalculable; he should never talk, unless he knows he is the ablest man in the room.

Don't trust spies. They are more trouble than they are worth. There is never enough unrest at Milan to bother about, and I expect it is the same elsewhere. Your military police make sure of the army, and that is all you want.

The army is the one thing you can deal with personally, and from your own knowledge.

Work with your ministers twice a week—once with each of them separately, and once with them all together in Council. Half the battle will be won when your ministers and councillors realise that your only object in consulting them is to listen to reason, and to prevent yourself being taken by surprise.

At public functions, and at fêtes, whenever you have Frenchmen and foreigners together, arrange beforehand where they are to be, and what you are to do. It is better never to form a following; and you must take the greatest care not to expose yourself to any sort of affront. If anything of the kind occurs, don't stand for it. Prince, ambassador, minister, general—whoever it may be, even if it is the Austrian or Russian ambassador, have him arrested on the spot. On the other hand, such incidents are always a nuisance; and what matters little in my case might have troublesome results in yours.

Nothing is so advisable as to treat the Italians well, and to get to know all their names and families. Don't show too much attention to foreigners: there is nothing to be gained by it. An ambassador will never speak well of you, because it is his business to speak ill. Ministers of foreign countries are, in plain words, accredited spies. It is as well to keep them at arm's length. They always think better of those they seldom see than of their professed friends and benefactors.

There is only one man here at Milan who really matters—the Minister of Finance: he is a hard worker, and knows his job well.

Although they know I am behind you, I have no doubt they are trying to gauge your character. See that your orders are carried out, particularly in the army: never allow them to be disobeyed.

The public decree that I have signed defines the powers I am delegating to you. I am reserving for myself the most important of all—the power of directing your operations. Send me an account of your doings every day. It is only by degrees that you will come to understand how I look at everything.

Don't show my letters to a single soul, under any pretext whatsoever. It ought not to be known what I write to you, or even that I write at all. Keep one room to which no one is admitted—not even your private secretaries.

You will find M. Méjan useful, if he doesn't try to make money; and he won't do that if he knows that you are watching him, and that a single act of this kind will ruin him in my eyes as well as yours. He ought to be well paid, and to have good prospects of promotion. But in that case he must be available at all hours: he will be useless to you if he gets into the way of working only at certain hours, and amusing himself the rest of the day. And you will have to rebuke him for a tendency he shares with all Frenchmen to deprecate this country—all the more so as it is accompanied by melancholia. Frenchmen are never happy out of France.

Keep my household and stables in order, and make up all my accounts at least once a week; this is all the more necessary as they have no idea how to manage things here.

Hold a review at Milan every month.

Cultivate the young Italians, rather than the old; the latter are good for nothing. . . .

You have an important position, and will find it pretty hard work. Try to get to know the history of all the towns in my kingdom of Italy; visit the fortresses, and all the famous battlefields. It is likely enough that you will see fighting before you are thirty, and it is a tremendous asset to know the lie of the land.

One last word. Punish dishonesty ruthlessly. The exposure of a dishonest accountant is a victory for the government. And don't allow any smuggling in the French Army.

NAPOLEON'S VIEWS ON AUSTERLITZ

[*Austerlitz, December 3, 1805*] On December 1 the Emperor, from the height of his bivouac, observed with indescribable joy that the Russian army, almost within artillery range from his outposts, was beginning a flanking movement intended to turn his right. He could see then to what extent presumptuousness and ignorance of the art of war had misled the councils of that brave army. He said several times, "Before tomorrow night this army will be mine. . . ."

At nightfall, the Emperor wished to visit all the bivouacs, on foot and incognito, but no sooner had he walked a few steps than he was recognized. It would be impossible to describe the soldiers' enthusiasm when they saw him. Instantly, straw torches were tied to thousands of poles, and eighty thousand men turned to the Emperor, greeting him with cheers—some in order to celebrate the anniversary of his coronation [December 2, 1804], some shouting that the army would present its bouquet to him on the morrow. One of the oldest grenadiers stepped up to him and said, "Sire, you won't have to take any chances with your person. I promise you in the name of the grenadiers of the army that you won't have to fight with anything except your eyes and that we'll bring you the flags and the guns of the Russian army to celebrate the anniversary of your coronation tomorrow."

Returning to his bivouac, which consisted of a ramshackle and roofless hut built for him out of straw by the grenadiers, the Emperor said: "This is the finest evening of my life. But I am sorry at the thought that I shall lose a good many of those brave people. By the sadness this causes me I can feel that they are indeed my children—and, to tell the truth, I sometimes blame myself for this feeling, for I fear that it will end up by spoiling me for war. . . ."

On December 2, dawn came at last. The sun rose radiant, and that anniversary of the Emperor's coronation, on which one of the most glorious feats of the century was to take place, was one of the finest autumn days.

This battle, which the soldiers persist in calling the Three Emperors' Battle, which others call the Battle of the Anniversary, and which the Emperor has named the Battle of Austerlitz, will be forever memorable in the annals of our great nation.

Passing in front of several regiments in battle array, the Emperor said, "Soldiers! We must end this battle with a thunderclap that will confound the arrogance of our enemies"; and instantly their hats waving at the ends of their bayonets and shouts of *Vive l'Empereur!* gave the actual signal for the battle to begin. A second later, gunfire could be heard from the extreme right, which had already been by-passed by the enemy vanguard. But their unforeseen encounter with Marshal Davout stopped the enemy short, and the fighting began. . . .

A terrible artillery duel began along the whole line. The noise of two hundred guns and nearly two hundred thousand men was terrifying. It was a true battle of giants. The fighting had lasted less than an hour when the entire enemy left had been cut off. . . . The cavalry of the Russian imperial guards charged and overran a battalion of our fourth regiment of the line; but the Emperor was not far; he noticed their maneuver, he ordered Marshal Bessières to come to the aid of the right with his invincibles, and soon the two guards were locked in combat.

The issue could not be in doubt: after a short time the Russian guard was routed. Their colonel, their artillery, their standards, everything was captured. The regiment of Grand Duke Constantine was crushed; he himself owed his escape only to the speed of his horse.

From the heights of Austerlitz, the two emperors were watching the defeat of the Russian guards. . . .

At one o'clock in the afternoon the victory was decided. It had never been in doubt for a moment. Not a single soldier of the reserve had been needed, and none had been used. The cannonade continued only on our right. The enemy corps which had been surrounded and dislodged from all the heights was now in a depression, with its back against a lake. The Emperor attacked it with twenty artillery pieces. This corps was hunted from position to position, and a horrible spectacle could be seen . . . : twenty thousand men throwing themselves into the water and drowning in the lake! . . .

Never did a battlefield look more horrible. From the middle of the immense lake, the screams of thousands of men could be heard, but there was no way of coming to their aid. It will take three days before all the enemy wounded can be evacuated to Brünn; one's heart bleeds. May all this bloodshed, may all these miseries be avenged at last on the perfidious islanders who are responsible. May the cowardly oligarchs in London be visited with punishment for so much suffering!

HEINRICH HEINE

Heinrich Heine was born in Düsseldorf of Jewish parents on December 13, 1797. He was educated at private schools and then at the local Lyceum. He was more attracted to literature and history than to the family banking business, and in 1820 he traveled to Göttingen and then to Berlin.

At Berlin, Heine entered easily into fashionable literary circles, contributing poems to Berlin magazines and, in December, 1821, he published his first volume, *Gedichte*. In 1824 he returned to Göttingen to complete his degree, and there he formally embraced Christianity. *Die Harzreise,* based on his journey through the Hartz mountains, was published in May, 1826; its sensitive lyrics and original wit made it an immediate success. It was followed in 1827 by perhaps the most famous of Heine's works, his *Buch der Lieder*. He spent the next three years traveling abroad. Heine became an editor of a political journal in 1828, but gave it up within a year. He hailed the news of the July Revolution in Paris as the beginning of a new era of freedom, and, deciding to act on an old plan of settling in Paris, he left Germany in May, 1831.

Heine scored a great success in Paris, becoming intimate with many French celebrities and literary figures. A position as correspondent for several German newspapers assured him of a comfortable livelihood, until a literary feud resulted in a ban against Heine's writings in Germany. He applied to the French government, and was awarded an annual stipend of 4,800 francs, which he received from 1837 through 1848, giving rise to the accusation that he had entered into the pay of the French government in return for his vilification of Germany. From 1848 to his death in 1856, Heine was condemned to a "mattress grave" by a serious spinal disease. That his intellect was not dimmed, however, he demonstrated in the publication of his most passionate and intense lyrics.

It was as a brilliant wit and satirist in such works as *The Romantic School* (1836) and *Germany, A Winter's Journey* (1844) that Heine became best known in his own lifetime. Although he was associated with the German romantics early in his career, he later denounced them bitterly. A liberal in his convictions and his politics, Heine had nothing but scorn for the "Teutomanes" who made a cult of mysticism and medievalism. He regarded them as agents of political reaction, and supporters of a corrupt and demoralizing regime. His bitter denunciation of the "Teutomanes" cost him many of his friends and much of his financial support. He died in Paris on February 17, 1856, and was buried in Montmartre.

The following famous memoir of Napoleon has been taken from "The Emperor and the Drummer," in *Ideen: Das Buch Le Grand* (1826), translated by E. B. Ashton in Heinrich Heine, *Works of Prose,* ed. by Hermann Kesten (New York, 1943).

THE EMPEROR AND THE DRUMMER

THE TOWN of Düsseldorf is very beautiful, and if you think of it abroad and happen to have been born there, you get into a strange mood. I was born there, and I feel as if I had to go home right away. And when I say, "go home," I mean Bolker Street and the house in which I was born. This house will be very notable some day, and I have sent word to the old woman who owns it that she should not sell the house at any price. . . .

As yet, however, my fame sleeps in the marble quarries of Carrara; the paper laurels with which my brow is wreathed have not yet spread their fragrance throughout the world; and when the green-veiled, noble English-women come to Düsseldorf now, they leave the famous house unvisited and go straight to the Marktplatz and look at the black, colossal equestrian statue in the middle of it. It is supposed to represent the Elector Jan Wilhelm. He wears black armor and a flowing full-bottomed wig. As a boy, I heard a tale that the artist who made the statue had noticed with dismay, while casting, that his metal would not suffice, and then the citizens of the town had come running and brought him their silver spoons, to fill the mold. . . .

He is supposed to have been a nice gentleman, very art-loving and very skillful himself. He founded the picture gallery in Düsseldorf, and in the observatory there they still show an extremely artful set of tumblers fitting into each other which he carved in his hours of leisure, of which he had twenty-four each day.

At that time, princes were not yet the troubled folk they are now, and their crowns were grown fast to their heads; and at night they pulled night-caps over them; and at their feet in quiet slumber lay the peoples; and when they woke up in the morning, they said, "Good morning, father!" and the princes replied, "Good morning, dear children!"

But there came a sudden change. One morning, when we awoke in Düsseldorf and wanted to say, "Good morning, father!" our father had left and in the whole town there was nothing but dull dismay; a sort of funereal mood reigned everywhere, and people silently sneaked to the Marktplatz and read the long paper placard on the town hall door. The weather was bleak; but, regardless, the thin tailor Kilian stood there in his Nanking jacket that he wore only at home, and his blue wool stockings hung down so that his bare little legs peered out sadly, and his thin lips quivered as he murmured the text of the placard to himself. An old disabled soldier from the Palatinate read somewhat more loudly, and at some words a clear tear trickled down into his white, honest mustache. I stood next to him and wept, too, and asked him: why were we crying? And he replied: "The Elector's getting his thanks."

And then he read again, and at the words, "<u>for proven subjects' fidelity,</u>" an<u>d, "release you from your allegiance," he wept still more.</u> It is a strange sight when such an old man in a faded uniform and with a scarred soldier's face suddenly cries so much. And while we read, the Electoral coat-of-arms was taken down from the town hall; everything became frighteningly dismal, as if one were awaiting an eclipse of the sun; the gentlemen of the town council went about in a slow, abdicated manner; even the all-powerful bailiff looked as if he no longer had orders to give and stood there with such a peaceful indifference—although Mad Aloysius was standing on one leg again and was chattering off the names of the French generals with a crazy grimace, while soused Crooked Gumpertz wallowed in the gutter singing, "*Ça ira, ça ira!*"

I, however, went home, weeping and wailing: "The Elector's getting his thanks." My mother had a hard time with me: I knew what I knew and did not let anyone tell me otherwise; I went to bed weeping, and in the night I dreamed: the world had come to an end—the lovely flower gardens and green meadows were taken from the ground and rolled up like rugs; the bailiff climbed up a high ladder and took the sun down from the sky; the tailor Kilian stood by talking to himself, "I must go home and dress neatly, because I am dead and am to be buried today"—it grew even darker; a few stars shimmered faintly above, and these too fell down like yellow leaves in autumn; gradually the people vanished and I, poor child, roamed anxiously and finally stood before the willow fence of a desolate farmhouse and there saw a man digging up the earth with a spade, and beside him an ugly, sneering woman who held in her apron something like a severed human head; and that was the moon, and she laid it anxiously carefully into the open pit—and behind me stood the disabled soldier from the Palatinate and sobbed and spelled: "The Elector's getting his thanks."

When I awoke, the sun shone through the window again, as usual; on the street a drum was beaten, and when I stepped into our living-room and bade my father who sat in his white dressing-gown a good morning, I heard the light-footed barber telling him in minutest detail during the hairdressing: that in the town hall today homage would be paid to the new Grand Duke Joachim; that he came from a very good family and was to get the Emperor Napoleon's sister to wife and really was of fine presence and wore his beautiful black hair in curls and shortly would make his entry and certainly please all the women. Meanwhile the drumming in the street continued, and I stepped before the door and looked at the French troops marching in, the gay race of glory who with song and play moved through the world, the gaily serious grenadier faces, the bear-skin caps, the tri-colored cockades, the glistening bayonets, the *voltigeurs*—full of cheer and *point d'honneur*—and the gigantic, silver-embroidered drum-major who could throw his baton with the gilded point as high as the second floor, and his eyes as high as the third where pretty girls sat at the window. I was glad that soldiers would be quartered in our house—my mother was not glad—and I hurried to the Marktplatz. It looked quite different now. It was as if the world had been freshly painted. On the town hall hung a new coat-of-arms; the iron balustrade on the balcony was hung with embroidered velvet drapes; French grenadiers stood guard; the old gentlemen of the town council had donned new faces along with their Sunday coats, and they looked at each other in French and said, "bon jour"; ladies were peering from every window; curious citizens and neat soldiers filled the square, and I, with some other boys, climbed on the Elector's big horse and from there looked down on the bright market bustle. . . .

Long Short told us that there was no school today because of the cele-bration. We had to wait a long time for it to start. In the end the town hall balcony was filled with brightly-dressed gentlemen, flags and trumpets, and our burgomaster in his famous red coat made a speech which stretched out somewhat like India-rubber, or like a knitted night-cap into which you throw a stone—not, however, the philosopher's stone—and I could distinctly hear a few of the phrases; for instance, that they wanted to make us happy—and at the last word the trumpets sounded and the flags were waved and the drums beaten and *Viva!* was yelled—and when I myself cried *Viva!* I clutched the old Elector. And there was need for that, for I was getting quite dizzy. I thought the people were standing on their heads because the world had turned over; the Electoral head with the full-bottomed wig nodded and whispered, "Hold on to me!"—and not until the cannonade started on the wall did I grow sober again and slowly climb down from the Elector's horse.

Going home, I saw Mad Aloysius dancing again on one leg while he chattered off the names of the French generals, and Crooked Gumpertz wallowing drunkenly in the gutter roaring, "*Ça ira, ça ira,*" and I told my mother: "They want to make us happy, and that is why there is no school today. . . ."

Parbleu! how much do I not owe to the French drummer who was so long quartered in our house, and who looked like the devil and was as kind of heart as an angel and drummed so very excellently.

He was a little, agile figure with a fearful black mustache, beneath which red lips bulged defiantly while his fiery eyes darted about. I, a little boy, stuck to him like a burr, and helped him rub his buttons mirror-bright and whiten his vest with chalk—for M. Le Grand liked to look well—and I followed him to the watch, to the roll-call, to the parade—there was nothing but the gleam of arms and merriment—*les jours de fête sont passés!* M. Le Grand knew but a little broken German, only the main phrases—bread, kiss, honor—but on the drum he could make himself very well understood; for instance, if I did not know what the word *liberté* meant he drummed the Marseillaise—and I understood him. If I did not know the meaning of *egalité* he drummed the march, "*Ça ira, ça ira—les aristocrats á la lanterne!*—and I understood him. If I did not know what *bêtise* was he drummed the Dessauer March, which we Germans, as Goethe also reports, drummed in Champagne—and I understood. Once he wanted to explain the word *L'Allemagne* to me, and he drummed that all too simple basic melody which on market-days is often played to dancing dogs—*dum -dum–dum;* it made me angry but, still, I understood him.

In a similar manner he taught me modern history. I did not understand a word he spoke, but as he constantly drummed while speaking I knew what he meant to say. This is fundamentally the best method. We cannot rightly grasp the history of the storming of the Bastille, of the Tuileries, etc., until we know what was drummed on such occasions. In our school compendiums we merely read: "Their Excellencies the Barons and Counts and their most noble spouses were decapitated; Their Highnesses the Dukes and Princes and their most noble spouses were decapitated; His Majesty the King and his most illustrious spouse were decapitated"—but not until you hear the red guillotine march drummed do you grasp that fully, and see the why and the how. Madame, that is an odd march! I shivered in marrow and bone when I first heard it, and was glad that I forgot it. We forget such things as we grow older; a young man has so much other knowledge to keep in his head nowadays—whist, Boston, genealogical registers, parliamentary resolutions, dramaturgy, liturgy, carving—and in fact, no matter how I racked my brain, for a long time I could not recall that mighty tune. But think of it, Madame—not long ago I was sitting at table with a whole menagerie of counts, princes, princesses, chamberlains, court-marshalesses, seneschals, lord masters of ceremonies, ladies of the lord keepers of the plate and the lord masters of the hunt, and whatever else these aristocratic domestics may be called, and their sub-domestics ran about behind their chairs and shoved the full plates under their mouths—but I, who was passed by and neglected, sat idly without any occupation for my jaws and kneaded bread-balls and drummed with my fingers from boredom, and to my horror, I suddenly drummed the red, long-forgotten guillotine march.

"And what happened?"

Madame, these people do not allow themselves to be disturbed while eating; nor do they know that other people when they have nothing to eat suddenly start drumming—and very queer marches too which long were believed forgotten.

Now, whether drumming was an inborn talent or early developed by me—enough, it sits in my limbs, hands and feet, and often comes out involuntarily. Once I sat in Berlin in the lecture-room of Privy Councillor Schmalz, a man who had saved the state by his book on the "Red and Black Coat of Danger." You may remember from Pausanias, Madame, that an equally dangerous plot was once discovered by the braying of an ass; you know from Livy, or from Becker's *World History,* that geese saved the Capitol, and you know certainly from Sallust that it was through a loquacious *putaine,* Madam Fulvia, that the terrible conspiracy of Catiline came to light. However, to return to our aforesaid mutton, I was listening to Herr Privy Councillor Schmalz's lecture on international law, and it was a dull summer afternoon and I sat on the bench and heard less and less—my head had gone to sleep—and all at once I awoke from the sound of my own feet. They had not gone to sleep, and probably had heard just the contrary of international law expounded there and constitutional tendencies being reviled, and my feet, which with their little corns see more of the world's doing than the Privy Councillor with his big Juno eyes— these poor dumb feet, unable to express their humble opinion in words, sought to make themselves understood by drumming and drummed so loudly that I nearly got into trouble.

Those damned unthinking feet! They once played a similar prank on me in Göttingen, when I sat in one of Professor Saalfeld's lectures, and as he jumped about on the platform with his stiff movements, and got good and hot so as to be able properly to abuse the Emperor Napoleon—no, poor feet, I cannot blame you for drumming then; nor should I have blamed you if in your mute naïveté you had expressed yourselves still more kick-explicitly. How could I, Le Grand's pupil, hear the Emperor reviled? The Emperor! the Emperor! the great Emperor!

When I think of the great Emperor, my memory turns quite summer-green and golden again, a long linden avenue emerges in full bloom, nightingales sing on leafy twigs, the waterfall rustles, flowers stand in round beds and dreamily move their fair heads—and I stood in a wondrous intercourse with them; painted tulips greeted me with beggar-proud condescension, nerve-sick lilies nodded with sad tenderness, drunkenly red roses laughed at me from afar and sweet violets sighed—with myrtle and laurel I was not yet acquainted at the time, for they did not entice with radiant blossoms; but with the mignonette, now on such bad terms with me, I was particularly intimate. I speak of the Hofgarten in Düsseldorf, where I often lay on the lawn and devoutly listened to M. Le Grand telling me of the great Emperor's warlike feats and in accompaniment beating the marches drummed during those deeds, so that I vividly saw and heard it all. I saw the march over the Simplon—the Emperor at the head, and his brave grenadiers climbing behind him while frightened birds screamed and the glaciers thundered in the distance—I saw the Emperor, flag in hand, on the bridge of Lodi—I saw the Emperor in his grey cloak at Marengo—I saw the Emperor on horseback, in the battle of the Pyramids —nothing but powder-smoke and Mamelukes—I saw the Emperor in the battle of Austerlitz—whew! how the bullets whistled there over the smooth, icy road! I saw, I heard the battle of Jena—*dum, dum, dum*—I saw, I heard the battles of Eylau, of Wagram—no, I could hardly stand it! M. Le Grand drummed so that it nearly burst my own ear-drums.

But what were my feelings when first I saw him in person, with my own highly blest eyes—him, Hosannah! the Emperor.

It was in the same avenue of the Düsseldorf Hofgarten. Pushing through the gaping crowd, I thought of the deeds and battles M. Le Grand had drummed to me; my heart beat the general march—and yet, I thought at the same time of the police order that no one must ride through the avenue, under penalty of five thalers. And the Emperor with his retinue was riding straight down the avenue; the trembling trees bent forward wherever he passed, the sun-rays quivered through the green leaves in timid curiosity, and in the blue sky above swam visibly a golden star. The Emperor wore his simple, green uniform and the world-historic little hat. He rode a little white horse, and it moved with such calm pride, so surely, with such distinction that had I been Crown Prince of Prussia then I would have envied that horse. The Emperor sat nonchalantly, almost slackly; one hand held the rein high, the other good-naturedly patted the little horse's neck. It was a sunny, marble hand, a mighty hand, one of the pair which had tamed the many-headed monster of anarchy and brought order into the strife of nations—and it good-naturedly patted the horse's neck. Even the face had that hue we find in marble busts, Greek and Roman; its features, too, were nobly proportioned as those of the antiques and on that face was written, "Thou shalt have no gods before me." A smile warming and calming all hearts played about his lips—and yet all knew that those lips had but to whistle *et la Prusse n'existait plus;* those lips had but to whistle and the entire clergy had tinkled its last; those lips had but to whistle for the whole Holy Roman Empire to dance. And those lips were smiling, and the eye too was smiling. It was an eye clear as the sky; it could read the hearts of men; it saw all things in this world at a glance, while we others see them only one after another, and see only colored shadows. The brow was not so clear; the spectres of future battles were nesting there; and at times flashes crossed that brow and they were the creative thoughts, the great seven-league-boots ideas with which the Emperor's spirit invisibly strode over the world—and I think that each of these thoughts would have provided a German author with material to write about the rest of his life.

The Emperor calmly rode straight down the avenue; no policeman stopped him; behind him, on proud, snorting horses and loaded with gold and decorations, rode his retinue; the trumpets pealed; near me, the Mad Aloysius spun round and rattled off the names of his generals; not far away, the drunken Gumpert roared and the people, with a thousand voices, cried: "Long live the Emperor!"

The Emperor is dead. His lonely grave is on a desolate island in the Atlantic, and he for whom the world was too narrow lies quietly under a little hill, where five weeping willows hang their green heads in grief and a pious little brook ripples by, sadly lamenting. There is no inscription on his tomb; but Clio, with the just pen, wrote invisible words on it that will sound like spectral tones through thousands of years.

It was a clear, frosty fall day when a young man who looked like a student walked slowly down the avenue of the Düsseldorf Hofgarten, sometimes as in childish fun pushing up the leaves on the ground with his feet, but sometimes also looking sadly at the bare trees on which only a few golden leaves still hung. When he looked up like this, he thought of the words of Glaucus:

> Like the leaves in the forest, e'en so are the races of mortals;
> Leaves are blown down to the earth by the wind, while others are driven
> Away by the green budding wood, when fresh up-liveth the springtide;
> So the races of man—this grows and the other departeth.

. . . . But while I sat on the old bench in the Hofgarten and dreamed back into the past, I heard behind me confused human voices lamenting the fate of the poor Frenchmen who in the Russian War had been dragged to Siberia as prisoners and held there for several long years although there was peace; they had not returned until now. I looked up, and really saw those orphaned children of glory: through the gaps in their ragged uniforms lurked naked misery; in their weather-beaten faces lay deep, plaintive eyes; though maimed, weary, and mostly lame, they still retained a kind of military step, and—strange enough!—a drummer with a drum was swaying at their head. And with an inner shudder I was seized by the memory of the saga of the soldiers who fell in battle and rise at night from the field where they lie, and with the drummer at their head march to their home-towns, and of whom the old ballad sings:

> The drum is beaten up and down;
> They march to quarters in the town,
>   They're halting right before—
>   Tralarie, tralarei, tralara—
>   They halt at true love's door.
>
> There in the morning stand the bones
> In serried ranks like burial stones,
>   The drum before the line—
>   Tralarie, tralarei, tralara—
> So she can see him fine.

Truly, the poor French drummer seemed to have risen from the grave, half decayed; he was only a small shadow in a dirty torn grey capote, a deceased yellow face with a big mustache hanging sorrowfully over the faded lips; the eyes were like burned-out tinder in which only a few sparks still gleam—and yet, by a single one of these sparks I knew M. Le Grand.

He knew me too, and drew me down on the grass, and there we sat as before when he taught me French and modern history on the drum. It was still the well-known old drum, and I could not marvel enough how he had guarded it from Russian greed. He drummed again as before, but he did not speak with it. But even though his lips were uncannily tight, his eyes talked all the more and lighted up triumphantly as he drummed the old marches. The poplars near us trembled when he let the red guillotine march thunder again. The old fights for freedom, the old battles, the deeds of the Emperor, he drummed them all as before and it seemed as if the drum itself was a living creature and glad to be able to speak its inner joy. I heard the roar of the cannon again, the whistling of the balls, the noise of the battle; I saw again the death-defying valor of the Guards, I saw again the flying flags, I saw again the Emperor on horseback—but gradually a dark tone sneaked into those joyous whirls; sounds issued from the drum in which the wildest jubilation and the most frightful grief were eerily mingled, it seemed a victory march and a death march at the same time; Le Grand's eyes opened wide, ghost-like, and in them I saw nothing but a wide, white icy plain, covered with dead—it was the Battle of the Moskwa.

I should never have thought that the old, hard drum could emit such painful sounds as M. Le Grand now managed to elicit from it. They were drummed tears, and they sounded ever more softly, and like a dull echo deep sighs broke from Le Grand's breast. He became ever more weary and ghostly, his thin hands trembled with cold; he sat as if dreaming and moved only the air with his drumsticks and listened as for distant voices, and finally he looked at me with a deep, unfathomably deep, imploring glance—I understood it—and then his head sank down upon the drum.

M. Le Grand never drummed again in his life. His drum never issued another sound, either. It was to serve no enemy of freedom for a servile taps. I had well understood Le Grand's last imploring glance, and I drew the sword from my cane and pierced the drumhead.

II THE RECONSTRUCTION OF EUROPEAN SOCIETY

EDMUND BURKE

EDMUND BURKE (1729–97) was born in Dublin. In 1765 he became secretary to the Marquis of Rockingham, leader of the Whig party, and during the same year he entered Parliament. He was for a generation the most eloquent spokesman of the Whigs.

Burke's general principles were developed in his *Reflections on the Revolution in France* (1790), from which selections follow. On the whole, however, he distrusted abstract inquiries into political questions. His spiritual father was Montesquieu, and his conservatism rested upon his conviction that society was too massively complex an organism to be subjected to merely rational control. "One sure symptom of an ill-conducted state is the propensity of the people to theories. . . . No rational man ever did govern himself by abstractions and universals."

That this philosopher of conservatism was a Whig is not so strange as it may seem. His opinions on specifically English questions were those of one who looked back to the days of a forceful Whig nobility, and he was concerned, consequently, to save the Constitution of 1689 from the subversive influence of France and from attack at the hands of George III. It was as a Whig that he defended the colonies in the American Revolution, and it was as a Whig that he attacked the abuses of government in India and fought the wealthy "nabobs" whose purchase of English pocket boroughs threatened the continuing balance of power (that is, the power of the gentry).

REFLECTIONS ON THE REVOLUTION IN FRANCE

IT APPEARS TO ME as if I were in a great crisis, not of the affairs of France alone, but of all Europe, perhaps of more than Europe. All circumstances taken together, the French Revolution is the most astonishing that has hitherto happened in the world. The most wonderful things are brought about in many instances by means the most absurd and ridiculous; in the most ridiculous modes; and, apparently, by the most contemptible instruments. Everything seems out of nature in this strange chaos of levity and ferocity, and of all sorts of crimes jumbled together with all sorts of follies. In viewing this monstrous tragic-comic scene, the most opposite passions necessarily succeed, and sometimes mix with each other in the mind; alternate contempt and indignation; alternate laughter and tears; alternate scorn and horror.

It cannot, however, be denied, that to some this strange scene appeared in quite another point of view. Into them it inspired no other sentiments than those of exultation and rapture. They saw nothing in what has been done in France, but a firm and temperate exertion of freedom: so consistent, on the whole, with morals and with piety as to make it deserving not only of the secular applause of dashing Machiavelian politicians, but to render it a fit theme for all the devout effusions of sacred eloquence.

On the forenoon of the 4th of November last, Doctor Richard Price, a non-conforming minister of eminence, preached at the dissenting meeting-house of the Old Jewry, to his club or society, a very extraordinary miscellaneous sermon, in which there are some good moral and religious sentiments, and not ill expressed, mixed up in a sort of porridge of various political opinions and reflections; but the Revolution in France is the grand ingredient in the cauldron. . . . His doctrines affect our constitution in its vital parts. He tells the Revolution Society in this political sermon, that his Majesty "is almost the *only* lawful king in the world, because the *only* one who owes his crown to the *choice of his people."* . . .

This doctrine, as applied to the prince now on the British throne, either is nonsense, and therefore neither true nor false, or it affirms a most unfounded, dangerous, illegal, and unconstitutional position. According to this spiritual doctor of politics, if his Majesty does not owe his crown to the choice of his people, he is no *lawful king*. Now nothing can be more untrue than that the crown of this kingdom is so held by his Majesty. Therefore if you follow their rule, the king of Great Britain, who most certainly does not owe his high office to any form of popular election, is in no respect better than the rest of the gang of usurpers, who reign, or rather rob, all over the face of this our miserable world, without any sort of right or title to the allegiance of their people. . . . If you admit this interpretation, how does their idea of election differ from our idea of inheritance? And how does the settlement of the crown in the Brunswick line derived from James the First come to legalize our monarchy, rather than that of any of the neighbouring countries? At some time or other, to be sure, all the beginners of dynasties were chosen by those who called them to govern. There is ground enough for the opinion that all the kingdoms of Europe were, at a remote period, elective, with more or fewer limitations in the objects of choice. But whatever kings might have been here, or elsewhere, a thousand years ago, or in whatever manner the ruling dynasties of England or France may have begun, the king of Great Britain is, at this day, king by a fixed rule of succession, according to the laws of his country; and whilst the legal conditions

of the compact of sovereignty are performed by him (as they are performed),
he holds his crown in contempt of the choice of the Revolution Society, who
have not a single vote for a king amongst them, either individually or collectively; though I make no doubt they would soon erect themselves into an
electoral college, if things were ripe to give effect to their claim. His Majesty's
heirs and successors, each in his time and order, will come to the crown
with the same contempt of their choice with which his Majesty has succeeded
to that he wears.

Whatever may be the success of evasion in explaining away the gross
error of *fact*, which supposes that his Majesty (though he holds it in concurrence with the wishes) owes his crown to the choice of his people; yet
nothing can evade their full explicit declaration, concerning the principle of
a right in the people to choose; which right is directly maintained, and
tenaciously adhered to. All the oblique insinuations concerning election
bottom in this proposition, and are referable to it. Lest the foundation of the
king's exclusive legal title should pass for a mere rant of adulatory freedom,
the political divine proceeds dogmatically to assert, that, by the principles
of the Revolution, the people of England have acquired three fundamental
rights, all which, with him, compose one system, and lie together in one
short sentence; namely, that we have acquired a right,

1. "To choose our own governors."
2. "To cashier them for misconduct."
3. "To frame a government for ourselves."

This new, and hitherto unheard-of, bill of rights, though made in the name
of the whole people, belongs to those gentlemen and their faction only. The
body of the people of England have no share in it. They utterly disclaim it.
They will resist the practical assertion of it with their lives and fortunes.
They are bound to do so by the laws of their country, made at the time of
that very Revolution which is appealed to in favour of the fictitious rights
claimed by the society which abuses its name.

These gentlemen of the Old Jewry, in all their reasonings on the Revolution of 1688, have a Revolution which happened in England about forty
years before, and the late French Revolution, so much before their eyes, and
in their hearts, that they are constantly confounding all the three together.
It is necessary that we should separate what they confound. We must recall
their erring fancies to the *acts* of the Revolution which we revere, for the
discovery of its true *principles*. If the *principles* of the Revolution of 1688
are anywhere to be found, it is in the statute called the *Declaration of Right*.
In that most wise, sober, and considerate declaration, drawn up by great
lawyers and great statesmen, and not by warm and inexperienced enthusiasts,

not one word is said, nor one suggestion made, of a general right "to choose our own *governors;* to cashier them for misconduct; and to *form* a government for *ourselves.*" . . .

You will observe, that from Magna Charta to the Declaration of Right, it has been the uniform policy of our constitution to claim and assert our liberties, as an *entailed inheritance* derived to us from our forefathers, and to be transmitted to our posterity; as an estate specially belonging to the people of this kingdom, without any reference whatever to any other more general or prior right. By this means our constitution preserves a unity in so great a diversity of its parts. We have an inheritable crown; an inheritable peerage; and a House of Commons and a people inheriting privileges, franchises, and liberties, from a long line of ancestors.

This policy appears to me to be the result of profound reflection; or rather the happy effect of following nature, which is wisdom without reflection, and above it. A spirit of innovation is generally the result of a selfish temper and confined views. People will not look forward to posterity, who never look backward to their ancestors. Besides, the people of England well know, that the idea of inheritance furnishes a sure principle of conservation and a sure principle of transmission; without at all excluding a principle of improvement. It leaves acquisition free; but it secures what it acquires. Whatever advantages are obtained by a state proceeding on these maxims, are locked fast as in a sort of family settlement; grasped as in a kind of mortmain for ever. By a constitutional policy, working after the pattern of nature, we receive, we hold, we transmit our government and our privileges, in the same manner in which we enjoy and transmit our property and our lives. The institutions of policy, the goods of fortune, the gifts of providence, are handed down to us, and from us, in the same course and order. Our political system is placed in a just correspondence and symmetry with the order of the world, and with the mode of existence decreed to a permanent body composed of transitory parts; wherein, by the disposition of a stupendous wisdom, moulding together the great mysterious incorporation of the human race, the whole, at one time, is never old, or middle-aged, or young, but, in a condition of unchangeable constancy, moves on through the varied tenor of perpetual decay, fall, renovation, and progression. Thus, by preserving the method of nature in the conduct of the state, in what we improve, we are never wholly new; in what we retain, we are never wholly obsolete. By adhering in this manner and on those principles to our forefathers, we are guided not by the superstition of antiquarians, but by the spirit of philosophic analogy. In this choice of inheritance we have given to our frame of polity the image of a relation in blood; binding up the constitution of our country with our dearest domestic ties; adopting our fundamental laws into the bosom of our family affections; keeping inseparable, and cherishing with the warmth of all their combined and mutually reflected charities, our state, our hearths, our sepulchres, and our altars.

Through the same plan of a conformity to nature in our artificial institutions, and by calling in the aid of her unerring and powerful instincts, to fortify the fallible and feeble contrivances of our reason, we have derived several other, and those no small benefits, from considering our liberties in the light of an inheritance. Always acting as if in the presence of canonized forefathers, the spirit of freedom, leading in itself to misrule and excess, is tempered with an awful gravity. This idea of a liberal descent inspires us with a sense of habitual native dignity, which prevents that upstart insolence almost inevitably adhering to and disgracing those who are the first acquirers of any distinction. By this means our liberty becomes a noble freedom. It carries an imposing and majestic aspect. It has a pedigree and illustrious ancestors. It has its bearings, and its ensigns armorial. It has its gallery of portraits; its monumental inscriptions; its records, evidences, and titles. We procure reverence to our civil institutions on the principle upon which nature teaches us to revere individual men; on account of their age, and on account of those from whom they are descended. All your sophisters cannot produce anything better adapted to preserve a rational and manly freedom than the course that we have pursued, who have chosen our nature rather than our speculations, our breasts rather than our inventions, for the great conservatories and magazines of our rights and privileges.

You might, if you pleased, have profited of our example, and have given to your recovered freedom a correspondent dignity. Your privileges, though discontinued, were not lost to memory. Your constitution, it is true, whilst you were out of possession, suffered waste and dilapidation; but you possessed in some parts the walls, and, in all, the foundations, of a noble and venerable castle. You might have repaired those walls; you might have built on those old foundations. Your constitution was suspended before it was perfected; but you had the elements of a constitution very nearly as good as could be wished. In your old states you possessed that variety of parts corresponding with the various descriptions of which your community was happily composed; you had all that combination, and all that opposition of interests, you had that action and counteraction, which, in the natural and in the political world, from the reciprocal struggle of discordant powers, draws out the harmony of the universe. These opposed and conflicting interests, which you considered as so great a blemish in your old and in our present constitution, interpose a salutary check to all precipitate resolutions. They render deliberation a matter not of choice, but of necessity; they make all change a subject of *compromise,* which naturally begets moderation; they produce *temperaments* preventing the sore evil of harsh, crude, unqualified reformations; and rendering all the headlong exertions of arbitrary power, in the few or in the many, for ever impracticable. Through that diversity of members and interests, general liberty had as many securities as there were separate views in the several orders; whilst by pressing down the whole by the weight of a real monarchy, the separate parts would have been prevented from warping, and starting from their allotted places.

You had all these advantages in your ancient states; but you chose to act as if you had never been moulded into civil society, and had everything to begin anew. You began ill, because you began by despising everything that belonged to you. You set up your trade without a capital. If the last generations of your country appeared without much lustre in your eyes, you might have passed them by, and derived your claims from a more early race of ancestors. Under a pious predilection for those ancestors, your imaginations would have realized in them a standard of virtue and wisdom, beyond the vulgar practice of the hour: and you would have risen with the example to whose imitation you aspired. Respecting your forefathers, you would have been taught to respect yourselves. You would not have chosen to consider the French as a people of yesterday, as a nation of low-born servile wretches until the emancipating year of 1789. . . .

Compute your gains: see what is got by those extravagant and presumptuous speculations which have taught your leaders to despise all their predecessors, and all their contemporaries, and even to despise themselves, until the moment in which they became truly despicable. By following those false lights, France has bought undisguised calamities at a higher price than any nation has purchased the most unequivocal blessings! France has bought poverty by crime! France has not sacrificed her virtue to her interest, but she has abandoned her interest, that she might prostitute her virtue. All other nations have begun the fabric of a new government, or the reformation of an old, by establishing originally, or by enforcing with greater exactness, some rites or other of religion. All other people have laid the foundations of civil freedom in severer manners, and a system of a more austere and masculine morality. France, when she let loose the reins of regal authority, doubled the licence of a ferocious dissoluteness in manners, and of an insolent irreligion in opinions and practices; and has extended through all ranks of life, as if she were communicating some privilege, or laying open some secluded benefit, all the unhappy corruptions that usually were the disease of wealth and power. This is one of the new principles of equality in France. . . .

Believe me, Sir, those who attempt to level, never equalise. In all societies, consisting of various descriptions of citizens, some description must be upper-most. The levellers therefore only change and pervert the natural order of things; they load the edifice of society, by setting up in the air what the solidity of the structure requires to be on the ground. The associations of tailors and carpenters, of which the republic (of Paris, for instance) is com-posed, cannot be equal to the situation, into which, by the worst of usurpa-tions, an usurpation on the prerogatives of nature, you attempt to force them.

The Chancellor of France at the opening of the States, said, in a tone of oratorical flourish, that all occupations were honourable. If he meant only, that no honest employment was disgraceful, he would not have gone beyond the truth. But in asserting that anything is honourable, we imply some dis-tinction in its favour. The occupation of a hair-dresser, or of a working tallow-chandler, cannot be a matter of honour to any person—to say nothing of a number of other more servile employments. Such descriptions of men ought not to suffer oppression from the state; but the state suffers oppression, if such as they, either individually or collectively, are permitted to rule. In this you think you are combating prejudice, but you are at war with nature.

I do not, my dear Sir, conceive you to be of that sophistical, captious spirit, or of that uncandid dulness, as to require, for every general observation or sentiment, an explicit detail of the correctives and exceptions, which reason will presume to be included in all the general propositions which come from reasonable men. You do not imagine, that I wish to confine power, authority, and distinction to blood, and names, and titles. No, Sir. There is no qualifica-tion for government but virtue and wisdom, actual or presumptive. Wherever they are actually found, they have, in whatever state, condition, profession or trade, the passport of Heaven to human place and honour. Woe to the coun-try which would madly and impiously reject the service of the talents and virtues, civil, military, or religious, that are given to grace and to serve it; and would condemn to obscurity everything formed to diffuse lustre and glory around a state! Woe to that country too, that, passing into the opposite extreme, considers a low education, a mean contracted view of things, a sordid, mercenary occupation, as a preferable title to command! Everything ought to be open; but not indifferently to every man. No rotation; no appointment by lot; no mode of election operating in the spirit of sortition, or rotation, can be generally good in a government conversant in extensive objects. Be-cause they have no tendency, direct or indirect, to select the man with a view to the duty, or to accommodate the one to the other. I do not hesitate to say, that the road to eminence and power from obscure condition, ought not to be made too easy, nor a thing too much of course. If rare merit be the rarest of all rare things, it ought to pass through some sort of probation. The temple of honour ought to be seated on an eminence. If it be opened through virtue, let it be remembered too, that virtue is never tried but by some difficulty and some struggle.

Nothing is a due and adequate representation of a state, that does not represent its ability, as well as its property. But as ability is a vigorous and active principle, and as property is sluggish, inert, and timid, it never can be safe from the invasions of ability, unless it be, out of all proportion, predominant in the representation. It must be represented too in great masses of accumulation, or it is not rightly protected. The characteristic essence of property, formed out of the combined principles of its acquisition and conservation, is to be *unequal*. The great masses therefore which excite envy, and tempt rapacity, must be put out of the possibility of danger. Then they form a natural rampart about the lesser properties in all their gradations. The same quantity of property, which is by the natural course of things divided among many, has not the same operation. Its defensive power is weakened as it is diffused. In this diffusion each man's portion is less than what, in the eagerness of his desires, he may flatter himself to obtain by dissipating the accumulations of others. The plunder of the few would indeed give but a share inconceivably small in the distribution to the many. But the many are not capable of making this calculation; and those who lead them to rapine never intend this distribution. . . .

It is said, that twenty-four millions ought to prevail over two hundred thousand. True; if the constitution of a kingdom be a problem of arithmetic. This sort of discourse does well enough with the lamp-post for its second: to men who *may* reason calmly, it is ridiculous. The will of the many and their interest must very often differ; and great will be the difference when they make an evil choice. A government of five hundred country attorneys and obscure curates is not good for twenty-four millions of men, though it were chosen by eight-and-forty millions; nor is it the better for being guided by a dozen of persons of quality, who have betrayed their trust in order to obtain that power. At present, you seem in everything to have strayed out of the high road of nature. The property of France does not govern it. Of course property is destroyed, and rational liberty has no existence. All you have got for the present is a paper circulation and a stock-jobbing constitution: and, as to the future, do you seriously think that the territory of France, upon the republican system of eighty-three independent municipalities (to say nothing of the parts that compose them), can ever be governed as one body, or can ever be set in motion by the impulse of one mind? When the National Assembly has completed its work, it will have accomplished its ruin. These commonwealths will not long bear a state of subjection to the republic of Paris. They will not bear that this one body should monopolize the captivity of the king, and the dominion over the Assembly calling itself national. Each will keep its own portion of the spoil of the church to itself; and it will not suffer either that spoil, or the more just fruits of their industry, or the natural produce of their soil, to be sent to swell the insolence, or pamper the luxury, of the mechanics of Paris. In this they will see none of the equality, under the pretence of which they have been tempted to throw off their allegiance to their sovereign, as well as the ancient constitution of their country. There can be no capital city in such a constitution as they have lately made. They have forgot, that when they framed democratic governments, they had virtually dismembered their country. The person, whom they persevere in calling king, has not power left to him by the hundredth part sufficient to hold together this collection of republics. The republic of Paris will endeavour indeed to complete the debauchery of the army, and illegally to perpetuate the Assembly, without resort to its constituents, as the means of continuing its despotism. It will make efforts, by becoming the heart of a boundless paper circulation, to draw everything to itself; but in vain. All this policy in the end will appear as feeble as it is now violent. . . .

Far am I from denying in theory, full as far is my heart from withholding in practice (if I were of power to give or to withhold), the *real* rights of men. In denying their false claims of right, I do not mean to injure those which are real, and are such as their pretended rights would totally destroy. If civil society be made for the advantage of man, all the advantages for which it is made become his right. It is an institution of beneficence; and law itself is only beneficence acting by a rule. Men have a right to live by that rule; they have a right to do justice, as between their fellows, whether their fellows are in public function or in ordinary occupation. They have a right to the fruits of their industry; and to the means of making their industry fruitful. They have a right to the acquisitions of their parents; to the nourishment and improvement of their offspring; to instruction in life, and to consolation in death. Whatever each man can separately do, without trespassing upon others, he has a right to do for himself; and he has a right to a fair portion of all which society, with all its combinations of skill and force, can do in his favour. In this partnership all men have equal rights; but not to equal things. He that has but five shillings in the partnership, has as good a right to it, as he that has five hundred pounds has to his larger proportion. But he has not a right to an equal dividend in the product of the joint stock; and as to the share of power, authority, and direction which each individual ought to have in the management of the state, that I must deny to be amongst the direct original rights of man in civil society; for I have in my contemplation the civil social man, and no other. It is a thing to be settled by convention.

If civil society be the offspring of convention, that convention must be its law. That convention must limit and modify all the descriptions of constitution which are formed under it. Every sort of legislative, judicial, or executory power are its creatures. They can have no being in any other state of things; and how can any man claim under the conventions of civil society, rights which do not so much as suppose its existence? rights which are absolutely repugnant to it? One of the first motives to civil society, and which becomes one of its fundamental rules, is, *that no man should be judge in his own cause.* By this each person has at once divested himself of the first fundamental right of uncovenanted man, that is, to judge for himself, and to assert his own cause. He abdicates all right to be his own governor. He inclusively, in a great measure, abandons the right of self-defence, the first law of nature. Men cannot enjoy the rights of an uncivil and of a civil state together. That he may obtain justice, he gives up his right of determining what it is in points the most essential to him. That he may secure some liberty, he makes a surrender in trust of the whole of it.

Government is not made in virtue of natural rights, which may and do exist in total independence of it; and exist in much greater clearness, and in a much greater degree of abstract perfection: but their abstract perfection is their practical defect. By having a right to everything they want everything. Government is a contrivance of human wisdom to provide for human *wants*. Men have a right that these wants should be provided for by this wisdom. Among these wants is to be reckoned the want, out of civil society, of a sufficient restraint upon their passions. Society requires not only that the passions of individuals should be subjected, but that even in the mass and body, as well as in the individuals, the inclinations of men should frequently be thwarted, their will controlled, and their passions brought into subjection. This can only be done *by a power out of themselves;* and not, in the exercise of its function, subject to that will and to those passions which it is its office to bridle and subdue. In this sense the restraints on men, as well as their liberties, are to be reckoned among their rights. But as the liberties and the restrictions vary with times and circumstances, and admit of infinite modifications, they cannot be settled upon any abstract rule; and nothing is so foolish as to discuss them upon that principle.

The moment you abate anything from the full rights of men, each to govern himself, and suffer any artificial, positive limitation upon those rights, from that moment the whole organization of government becomes a consideration of convenience. This it is which makes the constitution of a state, and the due distribution of its powers, a matter of the most delicate and complicated skill. It requires a deep knowledge of human nature and human necessities, and of the things which facilitate or obstruct the various ends, which are to be pursued by the mechanism of civil institutions. The state is to have recruits to its strength, and remedies to its distempers. What is the use of discussing a man's abstract right to food or medicine? The question is upon the method of procuring and administering them. In that deliberation I shall always advise to call in the aid of the farmer and the physician, rather than the professor of metaphysics.

The science of constructing a commonwealth, or renovating it, or reforming it, is, like every other experimental science, not to be taught *à priori*. Nor is it a short experience that can instruct us in that practical science; because the real effects of moral causes are not always immediate; but that which in the first instance is prejudicial may be excellent in its remoter operation; and its excellence may arise even from the ill effects it produces in the beginning. The reverse also happens: and very plausible schemes, with very pleasing commencements, have often shameful and lamentable conclusions. In states there are often some obscure and almost latent causes, things which appear at first view of little moment, on which a very great part of its prosperity or adversity may most essentially depend. The science of government being therefore so practical in itself, and intended for such practical purposes, a matter which requires experience, and even more experience than any person can gain in his whole life, however sagacious and observing he may be, it is with infinite caution that any man ought to venture upon pulling down an edifice, which has answered in any tolerable degree for ages the common purposes of society, or on building it up again, without having models and patterns of approved utility before his eyes.

These metaphysic rights entering into common life, like rays of light which pierce into a dense medium, are, by the laws of nature, refracted from their straight line. Indeed in the gross and complicated mass of human passions and concerns, the primitive rights of men undergo such a variety of refractions and reflections, that it becomes absurd to talk of them as if they continued in the simplicity of their original direction. The nature of man is intricate; the objects of society are of the greatest possible complexity: and therefore no simple disposition or direction of power can be suitable either to man's nature, or to the quality of his affairs. When I hear the simplicity of contrivance aimed at and boasted of in any new political constitutions, I am at no loss to decide that the artificers are grossly ignorant of their trade, or totally negligent of their duty. The simple governments are fundamentally defective, to say no worse of them. If you were to contemplate society in but one point of view, all these simple modes of polity are infinitely captivating. In effect each would answer its single end much more perfectly than the more complex is able to attain all its complex purposes. But it is better that the whole should be imperfectly and anomalously answered, than that, while some parts are provided for with great exactness, others might be totally neglected, or perhaps materially injured, by the overcare of a favourite member.

The pretended rights of these theorists are all extremes: and in proportion as they are metaphysically true, they are morally and politically false. The rights of men are in a sort of *middle,* incapable of definition, but not impossible to be discerned. The rights of men in governments are their advantages; and these are often in balances between differences of good; in compromises sometimes between good and evil, and sometimes between evil and evil. Political reason is a computing principle; adding, subtracting, multiplying, and dividing, morally and not metaphysically, or mathematically, true moral denominations.

By these theorists the right of the people is almost always sophistically confounded with their power. The body of the community, whenever it can come to act, can meet with no effectual resistance; but till power and right are the same, the whole body of them has no right inconsistent with virtue, and the first of all virtues, prudence. Men have no right to what is not reasonable, and to what is not for their benefit. . . .

History will record, that on the morning of the 6th of October, 1789, the king and queen of France, after a day of confusion, alarm, dismay, and slaughter, lay down, under the pledged security of public faith, to indulge nature in a few hours of respite, and troubled, melancholy repose. From this sleep the queen was first startled by the voice of the sentinel at her door, who cried out to her to save herself by flight—that this was the last proof of fidelity he could give—that they were upon him, and he was dead. Instantly he was cut down. A band of cruel ruffians and assassins, reeking with his blood, rushed into the chamber of the queen, and pierced with a hundred strokes of bayonets and poniards the bed, from whence this persecuted woman had but just time to fly almost naked, and, through ways unknown to the murderers, had escaped to seek refuge at the feet of a king and husband, not secure of his own life for a moment.

This king, to say no more of him, and this queen, and their infant children (who once would have been the pride and hope of a great and generous people), were then forced to abandon the sanctuary of the most splendid palace in the world, which they left swimming in blood, polluted by massacre, and strewed with scattered limbs and mutilated carcases. Thence they were conducted into the capital of their kingdom. Two had been selected from the unprovoked, unresisted, promiscuous slaughter, which was made of the gentlemen of birth and family who composed the king's body guard. These two gentlemen, with all the parade of an execution of justice, were cruelly and publicly dragged to the block, and beheaded in the great court of the palace. Their heads were stuck upon spears, and led the procession; whilst the royal captives who followed in the train were slowly moved along, amidst the horrid yells, and shrilling screams, and frantic dances, and infamous contumelies, and all the unutterable abominations of the furies of hell, in the abused shape of the vilest of women. After they had been made to taste, drop by drop, more than the bitterness of death, in the slow torture of a journey of twelve miles, protracted to six hours, they were, under a guard, composed of those very soldiers who had thus conducted them through this famous triumph, lodged in one of the old palaces of Paris, now converted into a bastile for kings. . . .

It is now sixteen or seventeen years since I saw the queen of France, then the dauphiness, at Versailles; and surely never lighted on this orb, which she hardly seemed to touch, a more delightful vision. I saw her just above the horizon, decorating and cheering the elevated sphere she just began to move in,—glittering like the morning-star, full of life, and splendour, and joy. Oh! what a revolution! and what a heart must I have to contemplate without emotion that elevation and that fall! Little did I dream when she added titles of veneration to those of enthusiastic, distant, respectful love, that she should ever be obliged to carry the sharp antidote against disgrace concealed in that bosom; little did I dream that I should have lived to see such disasters fallen upon her in a nation of gallant men, in a nation of men of honour, and of cavaliers. I thought ten thousand swords must have leaped from their scabbards to avenge even a look that threatened her with insult. But the age of chivalry is gone. That of sophisters, economists, and calculators, has succeeded; and the glory of Europe is extinguished for ever. Never, never more shall we behold that generous loyalty to rank and sex, that proud submission, that dignified obedience, that subordination of the heart, which kept alive, even in servitude itself, the spirit of an exalted freedom. The unbought grace of life, the cheap defence of nations, the nurse of manly sentiment and heroic enterprise, is gone! It is gone, that sensibility of principle, that chastity of honour, which felt a stain like a wound, which inspired courage whilst it mitigated ferocity, which ennobled whatever it touched, and under which vice itself lost half its evil, by losing all its grossness.

This mixed system of opinion and sentiment had its origin in the ancient chivalry; and the principle, though varied in its appearance by the varying state of human affairs, subsisted and influenced through a long succession of generations, even to the time we live in. If it should ever be totally extinguished, the loss I fear will be great. It is this which has given its character to modern Europe. It is this which has distinguished it under all its forms of government, and distinguished it to its advantage, from the states of Asia, and possibly from those states which flourished in the most brilliant periods of the antique world. It was this, which, without confounding ranks, had produced a noble equality, and handed it down through all the gradations of social life. It was this opinion which mitigated kings into companions, and raised private men to be fellows with kings. Without force or opposition, it subdued the fierceness of pride and power; it obliged sovereigns to submit to the soft collar of social esteem, compelled stern authority to submit to elegance, and gave a dominating vanquisher of laws to be subdued by manners.

But now all is to be changed. All the pleasing illusions, which made power gentle and obedience liberal, which harmonized the different shades of life, and which, by a bland assimilation, incorporated into politics the sentiments which beautify and soften private society, are to be dissolved by this new conquering empire of light and reason. All the decent drapery of life is to be rudely torn off. All the superadded ideas, furnished from the wardrobe of a moral imagination, which the heart owns, and the understanding ratifies, as necessary to cover the defects of our naked, shivering nature, and to raise it to dignity in our own estimation, are to be exploded as a ridiculous, absurd, and antiquated fashion.

On this scheme of things, a king is but a man, a queen is but a woman; a woman is but an animal, and an animal not of the highest order. All homage paid to the sex in general as such, and without distinct views, is to be regarded as romance and folly. Regicide, and parricide, and sacrilege, are but fictions of superstition, corrupting jurisprudence by destroying its simplicity. The murder of a king, or a queen, or a bishop, or a father, are only common homicide; and if the people are by any chance, or in any way, gainers by it, a sort of homicide much the most pardonable, and into which we ought not to make too severe a scrutiny.

On the scheme of this barbarous philosophy, which is the offspring of cold hearts and muddy understandings, and which is as void of solid wisdom as it is destitute of all taste and elegance, laws are to be supported only by their own terrors, and by the concern which each individual may find in them from his own private speculations, or can spare to them from his own private interests. In the groves of *their* academy, at the end of every vista, you see nothing but the gallows. Nothing is left which engages the affections on the part of the commonwealth. On the principles of this mechanic philosophy, our institutions can never be embodied, if I may use the expression, in persons; so as to create in us love, veneration, admiration, or attachment. But that sort of reason which banishes the affections is incapable of filling their place. These public affections, combined with manners, are required sometimes as supplements, sometimes as correctives, always as aids to law. . .   When the old feudal and chivalrous spirit of *fealty,* which, by freeing kings from fear, freed both kings and subjects from the precautions of tyranny, shall be extinct in the minds of men, plots and assassinations will be anticipated by preventive murder and preventive confiscation, and that long roll of grim and bloody maxims, which form the political code of all power, not standing on its own honour, and the honour of those who are to obey it. Kings will be tyrants from policy, when subjects are rebels from principle.

When ancient opinions and rules of life are taken away, the loss cannot possibly be estimated. From that moment we have no compass to govern us; nor can we know distinctly to what port we steer. Europe, undoubtedly, taken in a mass, was in a flourishing condition the day on which your revolution was completed. How much of that prosperous state was owing to the spirit of our old manners and opinions is not easy to say; but as such causes cannot be indifferent in their operation, we must presume, that, on the whole, their operation was beneficial.

We are but too apt to consider things in the state in which we find them, without sufficiently adverting to the causes by which they have been produced, and possibly may be upheld. Nothing is more certain, than that our manners, our civilization, and all the good things which are connected with manners and with civilization, have, in this European world of ours, depended for ages upon two principles; and were indeed the result of both combined; I mean the spirit of a gentleman, and the spirit of religion. The nobility and the clergy, the one by profession, the other by patronage, kept learning in existence, even in the midst of arms and confusions, and whilst governments were rather in their causes, than formed. Learning paid back what it received to nobility and to priesthood; and paid it with usury, by enlarging their ideas, and by furnishing their minds. Happy if they had all continued to know their indissoluble union, and their proper place! Happy if learning, not debauched by ambition, had been satisfied to continue the instructor, and not aspired to be the master! Along with its natural protectors and guardians, learning will be cast into the mire, and trodden down under the hoofs of a swinish multitude. . . .

I hear it is sometimes given out in France, that what is doing among you is after the example of England. I beg leave to affirm, that scarcely anything done with you has originated from the practice or the prevalent opinions of this people, either in the act or in the spirit of the proceeding. Let me add, that we are as unwilling to learn these lessons from France, as we are sure that we never taught them to that nation. The cabals here, who take a sort of share in your transactions, as yet consist of but a handful of people. . . .

The whole [frame of our constitution] has been done under the auspices, and is confirmed by the sanctions, of religion and piety. The whole has emanated from the simplicity of our national character, and from a sort of native plainness and directness of understanding, which for a long time characterized those men who have successively obtained authority amongst us. This disposition still remains; at least in the great body of the people.

We know, and what is better, we feel inwardly, that religion is the basis of civil society, and the source of all good and of all comfort. In England we are so convinced of this, that there is no rust of superstition, with which the accumulated absurdity of the human mind might have crusted it over in the course of ages, that ninety-nine in a hundred of the people of England would not prefer to impiety. We shall never be such fools as to call in an enemy to the substance of any system to remove its corruptions, to supply its defects, or to perfect its construction. If our religious tenets should ever want a further elucidation, we shall not call on atheism to explain them. We shall not light up our temple from that unhallowed fire. It will be illuminated with other lights. It will be perfumed with other incense, than the infectious stuff which is imported by the smugglers of adulterated metaphysics. If our ecclesiastical establishment should want a revision, it is not avarice or rapacity, public or private, that we shall employ for the audit, or receipt, or application of its consecrated revenue. Violently condemning neither the Greek nor the Armenian, nor, since heats are subsided, the Roman system of religion, we prefer the Protestant; not because we think it has less of the Christian religion in it, but because, in our judgment, it has more. We are Protestants, not from indifference, but from zeal.

We know, and it is our pride to know, that man is by his constitution a religious animal; that atheism is against, not only our reason, but our instincts; and that it cannot prevail long. But if, in the moment of riot, and in a drunken delirium from the hot spirit drawn out of the alembic of hell, which in France is now so furiously boiling, we should uncover our nakedness, by throwing off that Christian religion which has hitherto been our boast and comfort, and one great source of civilization amongst us, and amongst many other nations, we are apprehensive (being well aware that the mind will not endure a void) that some uncouth, pernicious, and degrading superstition might take place of it.

For that reason, before we take from our establishment the natural, human means of estimation, and give it up to contempt, as you have done, and in doing it have incurred the penalties you well deserve to suffer, we desire that some other may be presented to us in the place of it. We shall then form our judgment.

On these ideas, instead of quarrelling with establishments, as some do, who have made a philosophy and a religion of their hostility to such institutions, we cleave closely to them. We are resolved to keep an established church, an established monarchy, an established aristocracy, and an established democracy, each in the degree it exists, and in no greater. . . .

Society is indeed a contract. Subordinate contracts for objects of mere occasional interest may be dissolved at pleasure—but the state ought not to be considered as nothing better than a partnership agreement in a trade of pepper and coffee, calico or tobacco, or some other such low concern, to be taken up for a little temporary interest, and to be dissolved by the fancy of the parties. It is to be looked on with other reverence; because it is not a partnership in things subservient only to the gross animal existence of a temporary and perishable nature. It is a partnership in all science; a partnership in all art; a partnership in every virtue, and in all perfection. As the ends of such a partnership cannot be obtained in many generations, it becomes a partnership not only between those who are living, but between those who are living, those who are dead, and those who are to be born. Each contract of each particular state is but a clause in the great primæval contract of eternal society, linking the lower with the higher natures, connecting the visible and invisible world, according to a fixed compact sanctioned by the inviolable oath which holds all physical and all moral natures, each in their appointed place. This law is not subject to the will of those, who by an obligation above them, and infinitely superior, are bound to submit their will to that law. The municipal corporations of that universal kingdom are not morally at liberty at their pleasure, and on their speculations of a contingent improvement, wholly to separate and tear asunder the bands of their subordinate community, and to dissolve it into an unsocial, uncivil, unconnected chaos of elementary principles. It is the first and supreme necessity only, a necessity that is not chosen, but chooses, a necessity paramount to deliberation, that admits no discussion, and demands no evidence, which alone can justify a resort to anarchy. This necessity is no exception to the rule; because this necessity itself is a part too of that moral and physical disposition of things, to which man must be obedient by consent or force: but if that which is only submission to necessity should be made the object of choice, the law is broken, nature is disobeyed, and the rebellious are outlawed, cast forth, and exiled, from this world of reason, and order, and peace, and virtue, and fruitful penitence, into the antagonist world of madness, discord, vice, confusion, and unavailing sorrow. . . .

When all the frauds, impostures, violences, rapines, burnings, murders, confiscations, compulsory paper currencies, and every description of tyranny and cruelty employed to bring about and to uphold this Revolution, have their natural effect, that is, to shock the moral sentiments of all virtuous and sober minds, the abettors of this philosophic system immediately strain their throats in a declamation against the old monarchial government of France. . . . Have these gentlemen never heard, in the whole circle of the worlds of theory and practice, of anything between the despotism of the monarch and the despotism of the multitude? Have they never heard of a monarchy directed by laws, controlled and balanced by the great hereditary wealth and hereditary dignity of a nation; and both again controlled by a judicious check from the reason and feeling of the people at large, acting by a suitable and permanent organ? Is it then impossible that a man may be found, who, without criminal ill intention, or pitiable absurdity, shall prefer such a mixed and tempered government to either of the extremes; and who may repute that nation to be destitute of all wisdom and of all virtue, which, having in its choice to obtain such a government with ease, *or rather to confirm it when actually possessed,* thought proper to commit a thousand crimes, and to subject their country to a thousand evils, in order to avoid it? Is it then a truth so universally acknowledged, that a pure democracy is the only tolerable form into which human society can be thrown, that a man is not permitted to hesitate about its merits, without the suspicion of being a friend to tyranny, that is, of being a foe to mankind?

I do not know under what description to class the present ruling authority in France. It affects to be a pure democracy, though I think it in a direct train of becoming shortly a mischievous and ignoble oligarchy. But for the present I admit it to be a contrivance of the nature and effect of what it pretends to. I reprobate no form of government merely upon abstract principles. There may be situations in which the purely democratic form will become necessary. There may be some (very few, and very particularly circumstanced) where it would be clearly desirable. This I do not take to be the case of France, or of any other great country. Until now, we have seen no examples of considerable democracies. The ancients were better acquainted with them. Not being wholly unread in the authors, who had seen the most of those constitutions, and who best understood them, I cannot help concurring with their opinion, that an absolute democracy, no more than absolute monarchy, is to be reckoned among the legitimate forms of government. They think it rather the corruption and degeneracy, than the sound constitution of a republic. If I recollect rightly, Aristotle observes, that a democracy has many striking points of resemblance with a tyranny. Of this I am certain, that in a democracy, the majority of the citizens is capable of exercising the most cruel oppressions upon the minority, whenever strong divisions prevail in that kind of polity, as they often must; and that oppression of the minority will extend to far greater numbers, and will be carried on with much greater fury, than can almost ever be apprehended from the dominion of a single sceptre. In such a popular persecution, individual sufferers are in a much more deplorable condition than in any other. Under a cruel prince they have the balmy compassion of mankind to assuage the smart of their wounds; they have the plaudits of the people to animate their generous constancy under their sufferings: but those who are subjected to wrong under multitudes, are deprived of all external consolation. They seem deserted by mankind, overpowered by a conspiracy of their whole species. . . .

Corporate bodies are immortal for the good of the members, but not for their punishment. Nations themselves are such corporations. As well might we in England think of waging inexpiable war upon all Frenchmen for the evils which they have brought upon us in the several periods of our mutual hostilities. You might, on your part, think yourselves justified in falling upon all Englishmen on account of the unparalleled calamities brought on the people of France by the unjust invasions of our Henrys and our Edwards. Indeed we should be mutually justified in this exterminatory war upon each other, full as much as you are in the unprovoked persecution of your present countrymen, on account of the conduct of men of the same name in other times.

We do not draw the moral lessons we might from history. On the contrary, without care it may be used to vitiate our minds and to destroy our happiness. In history a great volume is unrolled for our instruction, drawing the materials of future wisdom from the past errors and infirmities of mankind. It may, in the perversion, serve for a magazine, furnishing offensive and defensive weapons for parties in church and state, and supplying the means of keeping alive, or reviving, dissensions and animosities, and adding fuel to civil fury. History consists, for the greater part, of the miseries brought upon the world by pride, ambition, avarice, revenge, lust, sedition, hypocrisy, ungoverned zeal, and all the train of disorderly appetites, which shake the public with the same

> troublous storms that toss
> The private state, and render life unsweet. . . .

Your citizens of Paris formerly had lent themselves as the ready instruments to slaughter the followers of Calvin, at the infamous massacre of St. Bartholomew. What should we say to those who could think of retaliating on the Parisians of this day the abominations and horrors of that time? They are indeed brought to abhor *that* massacre. Ferocious as they are, it is not difficult to make them dislike it; because the politicians and fashionable teachers have no interest in giving their passions exactly the same direction. Still, however, they find it their interest to keep the same savage dispositions alive. It was but the other day that they caused this very massacre to be acted on the stage for the diversion of the descendants of those who committed it. In this tragic farce they produced the cardinal of Lorraine in his robes of function, ordering general slaughter. Was this spectacle intended to make the Parisians abhor persecution, and loathe the effusion of blood?—No; it was to teach them to persecute their own pastors; it was to excite them, by raising a disgust and horror of their clergy, to an alacrity in hunting down to destruction an order, which, if it ought to exist at all, ought to exist not only in safety, but in reverence. It was to stimulate their cannibal appetites (which one would think had been gorged sufficiently) by variety and seasoning; and to quicken them to an alertness in new murders and massacres, if it should suit the purpose of the Guises of the day. An Assembly, in which sat a multitude of priests and prelates, was obliged to suffer this indignity at its door. The author was not sent to the galleys, nor the players to the house of correction. Not long after this exhibition, those players came forward to the Assembly to claim the rites of that very religion which they had dared to expose, and to show their prostituted faces in the senate, whilst the archbishop of Paris, whose function was known to his people only by his prayers and benedictions, and his wealth only by his alms, is forced to abandon his house, and to fly from his flock (as from ravenous wolves), because, truly, in the sixteenth century, the cardinal of Lorraine was a rebel and a murderer.

Such is the effect of the perversion of history, by those, who, for the same nefarious purposes, have perverted every other part of learning. But those who will stand upon that elevation of reason, which places centuries under our eye, and brings things to the true point of comparison, which obscures

little names, and effaces the colours of little parties, and to which nothing
can ascend but the spirit and moral quality of human actions, will say to
the teachers of the Palais Royal,—The cardinal of Lorraine was the murderer
of the sixteenth century, you have the glory of being the murderers in the
eighteenth; and this is the only difference between you. But history in the
nineteenth century, better understood, and better employed, will, I trust,
teach a civilized posterity to abhor the misdeeds of both these barbarous
ages. It will teach future priests and magistrates not to retaliate upon the
speculative and inactive atheists of future times, the enormities committed
by the present practical zealots and furious fanatics of that wretched error,
which, in its quiescent state, is more than punished, whenever it is embraced. It will teach posterity not to make war upon either religion or philosophy, for the abuse which the hypocrites of both have made of the two
most valuable blessings conferred upon us by the bounty of the universal
Patron, who in all things eminently favours and protects the race of man.

JOSEPH DE MAISTRE

As THE SON of a president of the Senate of Savoy, Joseph de Maistre (1753–1821) was expected to play a role in public life. After receiving his preliminary education from the Jesuits, he was sent to Turin to study law. A bright minor future seemed in store for him: he entered the magistracy in 1774, was made fiscal advocate-general six years later, and became a senator at the age of thirty-five. All this was disrupted, however, when French troops occupied Savoy in September, 1792. As a loyal supporter of the king of Sardinia, Maistre had to begin what was to be only his first period of exile.

In the service of his king, Maistre spent four years in Lausanne, Switzerland. He wrote a number of royalist tracts there, but his principles did not prevent him from frequenting the society of Madame de Staël and her father, M. Necker. In 1797 the influence of the Directory forced him to leave Lausanne for Venice; there he spent two difficult years before being able to return to his own country. In 1802 he was abroad again, this time as Sardinia's envoy extraordinary to the court of Russia. The tsar appreciated Maistre's abilities, but his own sovereign apparently did not: he had little real authority and was subject to privation and humiliation. During his fifteen years in Russia he wrote his major works, but most of these were not published until much later. Maistre returned to Savoy in 1817. He was given the title of Minister of State and assumed charge of the kingdom's judicial affairs. He died in February, 1821, several days before Austrian troops occupied Piedmont.

Maistre's first book of importance was his *Considerations* on France, written in 1789 but not published until 1797. Here he expressed his conviction that France had a divine role to play in the world, even her errors being part of a providential plan. The leaders of the Revolution, for example, were "tools of God" designed to scourge the country's ruling class for having embraced the ideas of the *philosophes*. Despite his hatred of the Revolution, Maistre had no wish to see France dismembered by her enemies: it was now up to the Jacobin armies, he said, to preserve "the most beautiful kingdom after that of heaven."

The only political work which Maistre published while in Russia was the *Essay on the Generative Principles of Political Constitutions* (1810). The generative principles were divinely selected historical forces which use men for the purposes of Providence. Maistre believed that men alone cannot hope to create a successful constitution, as the Jacobins attempted to do. In contrast, Maistre writes, historical circumstances produced in England "the most beautiful balance of political force that has ever been seen in the world."

In 1819 *On the Papacy,* written in Russia, was finally published at Lyons. In it Maistre undertook to defend papal sovereignty in matters both spiritual and temporal; he also prognosticated the lapse into atheism of Protestant schismatics. As a postscript to this discussion he published *The Relations of the Gallican Church with the Papacy* (1821). According to the *Catholic Encyclopedia,* "He dealt Gallicanism such decisive blows that it never rose again." *Evenings in St. Petersburg* appeared shortly after its author's death in 1821.

The selection below is from that work, in which Maistre expresses his belief that only the miraculous can maintain civil order. The translation is by William W. Ryding.

ॐ

EVENINGS IN ST. PETERSBURG

The Senator: I am delighted that a sally by M. le Chevalier gave you the idea of a philosophical symposium. The subject we shall treat could not be more interesting: the happiness of the wicked, the unhappiness of the just! This is the great scandal of human reason. Could we use our evening better than in devoting it to the examination of this mystery of divine metaphysics? We shall be led to explore, in so far as it is permitted to human frailty, the whole question of the ways of Providence in the government of the moral world.

The Count: For a long time, Gentlemen, people have complained of the way Providence distributes good and evil; but I confess to you that these difficulties have never succeeded in making the slightest impression on my mind. I see with an intuitive certainty—for which I humbly thank this same Providence—that on this point man is *mistaken,* in the fullest sense of the word.

I should like to be able to say with Montaigne that man is deceived, for that is the right word. Yes, undoubtedly man is deceived; but he is deceived by himself; he takes the fallacies of his naturally rebellious heart (alas, nothing is more certain!) for real doubts arising in his understanding. If sometimes superstitious people *believe that they believe,* an accusation often made against them, it happens still more often that the proud man *believes he does not believe.* In either case, it is man who deceives himself, but in the second case the deception is worse.

In any event, Gentlemen, there is no subject on which I feel more strongly than on that of the temporal government of Providence; it is therefore with complete conviction that I shall impart to two people I tenderly love a few of the useful thoughts I have gathered together on the road, already long, of a life devoted entirely to serious study.

The Chevalier: I shall listen with the greatest pleasure, and I do not doubt that our mutual friend will accord you the same attention as I; but permit me, I pray you, to quarrel with you before you start; and do not accuse me of answering your silence, for it is as if you had already

spoken. I know very well what you are going to say. You are, without
the slightest doubt, about to begin where the preachers end, with *eternal
life:* "The wicked are happy in this world, but they shall be tormented
in the other; the just, on the contrary, suffer in this world, but they shall
know bliss in the other." That is what everyone says. Why should I conceal my feeling that this cogent answer does not fully satisfy me? I hope
you will not suspect me of seeking to destroy or weaken this great proof;
but it seems to me that it would do no harm to buttress it with others.

The Count: Gentlemen, have you ever heard a soldier complain that
in war the blows fall only on the good men, and that if one wishes to be
invulnerable one need only be enough of a scoundrel? I am sure you
have not, because in fact everyone knows that bullets do not choose their
victims. I should be perfectly justified in establishing at the very least
a parallel between the evils of war with regard to soldiers, and the evils
of life in general with regard to all men; and this parallel, presumably exact,
would alone suffice to remove a difficulty based on an obvious falsehood;
for it is not only false, it is *obviously* false, that crime leads in general to
happiness, and virtue to unhappiness in this world: it is, on the contrary,
perfectly clear that good and evil are a sort of lottery in which each man,
without distinction, may draw a black or a white ball. We ought therefore
to rephrase the question and ask *why, in the temporal order, the just man
is not exempt from the evils that afflict the guilty; and why the wicked are
not deprived of the goods that the just enjoy. . . .*

I return to my comparison: a good man is killed in battle; is that unjust?
No, it is unfortunate. If he has the gout, or kidney stones; if his friend
betrays him; if he is crushed by a falling building, etc., it is still unfortunate and nothing more, since all men are subject to the same kind of
misfortune. Never lose sight of this simple truth: *A general law, if it is not
unjust for all, cannot be unjust for the individual.* You did not have this
or that illness, but you could have had it. You have it, but you could just
as well not. He who died in battle might have escaped, he who came
back might have remained. All did not die, but all were there to die. From
that point on, there is no longer a question of injustice; the just law is
not one that has its effect on everyone, but one that is made for everyone;
the effect on one or another individual is an accident and nothing more.
To find anything difficult in this order of things, one must love difficulties.
Unfortunately, man loves them and looks for them: the human heart,
in continual revolt against the authority that restricts it, tells tales to the
mind that willingly believes; we accuse Providence to avoid having to
accuse ourselves, we raise against Providence objections that we should

blush to raise against a sovereign or a simple administrator whose wisdom we admire. Strange indeed that we should find it easier to be fair toward men than toward God! . . . .

There is yet another reason why we are often mistaken in such matters: we cannot prevent ourselves from attributing to God, without even noticing it, the ideas that we ourselves have about the dignity and importance of men. Where we are concerned, these ideas are perfectly reasonable, since we all live within an established social order, but when we transpose those same ideas into the general order, we are like that queen who used to say: *When it is a matter of damning people of our quality, believe me, God thinks about it more than once.* Elisabeth of France climbs onto the scaffold, a moment later it is Robespierre. The angel and the monster, upon entering this world, were subject to all the general laws that govern it. No words can describe the crime of those scoundrels who shed the purest and noblest blood in the universe; and yet, with reference to the general order, there is no injustice; it is only a misfortune indissolubly linked to the human condition and nothing more. Any man, *qua* man, is subject to all the misfortunes of mankind: the law is general; therefore it is not unjust. To claim that the dignity or dignities of a given man ought to exempt him from the action of an iniquitous or mistaken court is the same as to wish that his dignity exempt him from apoplexy, for example, or death.

Notice, however, that in spite of these general and necessary laws, it is far from true that the alleged equality on which I have so far insisted is in fact the case. I have supposed so, as I told you, to make the problem more difficult; but nothing is more false, as you will see.

Let us begin by setting aside all consideration of the individual. The general law, the visible and visibly just law is *that by far the greater share of happiness, even temporal happiness, goes not to the virtuous man, but to virtue.* If it were otherwise, there would be neither vice, nor virtue, nor merit, nor demerit, and consequently no moral order. Suppose that every virtuous action were *paid for,* as it were, with some temporal advantage; the act, no longer related to the supernatural order, could no longer deserve a reward of that order. Suppose, on the other hand, that by virtue of a divine law, the hand of a thief were to fall off at the moment he committed a crime; then people would abstain from stealing as they abstain from laying their hands under a butcher's cleaver; the moral order would completely disappear. In order to harmonize the moral order (the only one possible for intelligent beings) with the laws of earthly justice, virtue has to be rewarded and vice punished, even temporally, but not always, and not immediately; the incomparably greater share of temporal happiness must go to the virtuous, and a proportional share of unhappiness to the wicked, but the individual must never be sure of anything. And that is, in fact, the case. Imagine any other hypothesis; it will lead you inevitably to the destruction of the moral order or to the creation of another world.

Getting down to matters of detail, let us begin with human justice. God, having desired that men should govern themselves, at least externally, put into the hands of sovereigns the eminent prerogative of the punishment of crimes, and it is in that above all that they are His representatives. . . . From this fearful prerogative there results the necessary existence of a man destined to inflict on criminals the punishments prescribed by human justice; and this man is in fact to be found everywhere, without there being any way of explaining why; for reason cannot discover in the nature of man any motive sufficient to determine the choice of this profession. You are both so accustomed to serious reflection that it must often have occurred to you to think about the executioner. What is this inexplicable being who prefers to all the pleasant, lucrative, honest and even honorable professions which offer themselves to human strength and dexterity, that of putting his fellow men to death? Are his head and heart like ours? Do they not contain something strange, something foreign to our nature? For myself, I cannot begin to doubt it. He is like us externally; he is born like us, but he is extraordinary, and for him to exist in the human family a special decree is necessary, a FIAT of the creative power. He is created like a world. See what he is in the opinion of men and understand, if you can, how he can be unaware of that opinion or how he can face it. No sooner has his dwelling been officially designated, no sooner has he begun to live there, than the other habitations begin to move away until they are out of sight of his. In the midst of this solitude, this sort of vacuum formed around him, he lives alone with his female and his offspring, who alone permit him to know the sound of the human voice. Were it not for them, he would hear only groans. . . . A lugubrious signal is given; an abject minister of justice knocks at his door to notify him that he is needed; he leaves; he arrives at the public square surging with an eager and palpitating crowd. He is given a poisoner, a parricide, a committer of sacrilege: he seizes him, stretches him out, ties him to a horizontal cross, raises his arm: a horrible hush comes over the crowd; then there is nothing but the cry of bone shattered under his iron bar and the howling of the victim. He unties him, carries him onto the rack, binds his broken limbs to the spokes; the head hangs, the hair stands on end, and the mouth, like an open fur-

nace, exhales only a few bloody words that beg for death. The executioner's
job is done; his heart beats, but it is with joy; he congratulates himself
and says in his heart: *Nobody racks better than I do.* He steps down, holds
out a blood-smeared hand, and from a suitable distance, justice tosses him
a few pieces of gold that he carries through a double row of men spread
apart by horror. He sits at table, and he eats; and so to bed, and he sleeps.
The next day, upon awakening, he thinks of things unrelated to what he
did the day before. Is this a man? Yes, God receives him in his temples
and permits him to pray. He is not a criminal, and yet no language con-
sents to say, for example, *that he is a good man, that he is virtuous, that
he is worthy,* etc. No moral praise is suitable, for such praise presupposes
relations with other men, and he has none at all.

And yet, all greatness, all power, and all subordination depend on the
executioner: he is the horror and the bond of human association. Take from
the world this incomprehensible agent, and in that very instant order gives
way to chaos; thrones collapse, and society disappears. God, the author of
sovereignty, is also the author of punishment: He has cast our Earth on
these twin poles: *For Jehovah is master of the two poles and on them he
makes the world turn.*[1]

There is therefore in the temporal circle a divine and visible law for
the punishment of crime; and that law, as stable as the society whose continuance it guarantees, has been enforced without variation since the beginning of time: evil is among us, it acts unremittingly; and as a necessary
consequence it must be unremittingly repressed by punishment; and in
fact we see over the entire surface of the globe a constant action on the
part of all governments to prevent or punish crime. The sword of justice has
no scabbard; it must always menace or strike. What then can people mean
when they speak of the *impunity of crime?* For whom are the knout, the
gallows, the rack, the stake? For criminals, obviously. The mistakes of
particular courts are exceptions that cannot disturb the general rule. I
have, moreover, several thoughts to offer you on this point. In the first
place, these fatal errors are much less frequent than people suppose; public
opinion tending always against restrictive authority, the public ear greedily
absorbs the slightest rumors of a judicial murder. A thousand individual
passions add themselves to this general tendency, but I call upon your
long experience as testimony, Senator, that only very rarely does a court
commit murder, either through passion or error. When an innocent man
is punished, it is a misfortune like any other; that is, it is common to all
mankind. When a guilty man escapes punishment, it is another exception

[1] Song of Anna, I Kings 2–13.

of the same kind. But it remains true that in general there is on Earth a universal and visible order for the temporal punishment of crime. . . .

From the corporal punishments that justice inflicts, let us pass on to sickness. You anticipate already the drift of my argument. If we were to take from the world all kinds of intemperance, we should eliminate most, if not all, sickness. Everyone can understand this in a rough, general way, but we should examine the matter more closely. . . . No doubt there are sicknesses that are no more than the accidental results of a general law: the most righteous of men must die; and of two men who race violently, one to save his fellow man, the other to murder him, either one might die of pleurisy. But what a fearful number of sicknesses, both general and particular, are due only to our vices! I recall Bossuet preaching before Louis XIV and all his court, citing medical testimony to show the disastrous consequences of debauchery. He was perfectly right in pointing out what was strikingly obvious and of immediate concern; but he would also have been justified in generalizing his observation; for myself, I cannot deny that I agree with a recent apologist who holds that all sicknesses have their source in some vice forbidden by the Gospels; that this holy law contains the true medicines of the body, as well as those of the spirit, such that, if a society of just men were to make use of it, death would be no more than the inevitable end of a healthy and robust old age; this is an idea that I believe Origen upheld. What deceives us in this matter is that when the effect is not immediate we no longer perceive it; but it is nonetheless real. Sicknesses, once established, multiply, mix and amalgamate through their fatal affinity for one another. And so we carry with us today physical pains deriving from excesses committed perhaps as much as a century ago.

The Chevalier: Permit me to interrupt you and to be a little impolite, if necessary, to force you to clarify your statement. You say that perhaps we suffer today for excesses committed a century ago; now, it seems to me that we ought not to answer for such crimes in the same way that we must for the sin of our first parents. I cannot believe that faith extends so far. Unless I am mistaken, one original sin is enough, since that sin alone subjects us to all the miseries of this life. It seems to me, therefore, that physical illness that comes to us hereditarily has nothing to do with the temporal government of Providence. . . .

The Count: If I have spoken indiscriminately of sicknesses we owe to our personal crimes and those we inherit from our ancestors, the fault is minimal; since, as I told you a while ago, they are all, in reality, punishments for a crime. It is only this idea of heredity that shocks human reason at the outset. But without going into unnecessary detail, let us be satisfied with the general rule: *Every being that reproduces can only produce another like himself.* It is here, Senator, that I invoke your intellectual conscience: if a man gives himself over to such crimes that they are capable of corrupting the moral principle in him, you understand that this degradation is transmissible just as you understand the hereditary transmission of scrofula and syphilis. Furthermore, I have no need of these hereditary ills. Consider what I have so far said as a parenthesis in our conversation; everything remains intact. Putting together all the considerations I have set before you, there can be no further doubt, I hope, that the innocent man, when he suffers, never suffers except in his quality as a man; and that the immense majority of misfortune is visited upon crime.

What does it matter what words we use? Man is bad, horribly bad. Did God create him so? Undoubtedly he did not, and Plato himself hastens to tell us *that the good neither wish nor do evil to anyone.* We are therefore degraded. But how? That corruption that Plato saw in himself was clearly not particular to his person, and surely he did not think of himself as worse than his fellows. Therefore, he said essentially that same thing David did: *My mother conceived me in iniquity;* and if this expression had been available to him, he could have adopted it without difficulty. Now, since all degradation must be in the nature of a penalty, and since all penalties presuppose a crime, we are led by reason alone to the idea of original sin; for our fatal penchant toward evil, being a truth of experience and feeling proclaimed by all men in all periods of history, and this inclination, more or less victorious over conscience and law, never having ceased to produce on earth transgressions of all kinds, mankind has never been able to recognize and deplore this sad state without in that very act admitting the lamentable dogma I am discussing with you. For he cannot be wicked without being bad, nor bad without being degraded, nor degraded without being punished, nor punished without being guilty.

JOHANN WOLFGANG VON GOETHE

LIKE his own *Faust,* Goethe (1749–1832), through the extraordinary fullness of his life and the universality of his mind, has always been an outstanding symbol of romanticism. From his much loved city of Weimar, whose chief ornament he became, Goethe's ideas spread throughout Europe and brought him, in return, recognition as one of the great men of Europe. His largeness made his outlook essentially cosmopolitan, as different from the positive world views of German romanticists like Fichte and Hegel as it is similar to their impatience with the Enlightenment.

After producing, while still quite young, lyrics and prose narratives that marked an epoch in German literature, Goethe gave himself over for some years to the study of art, philosophy, and science. In his mind met all the great currents of ancient and modern thought—eighteenth-century skepticism, Greek epicureanism, medieval and modern mysticism, natural science. For a time even his unusually strong temperament was swamped with conflicting doctrines, and he emerged with a deep distrust of systems. What he found in Spinoza was the notion of an infinite Nature, which man's mind cannot exhaust, but which man's will drives him to investigate in order to achieve the calm and peace of natural knowledge.

As a poet, Goethe was not only a thinker and moralist but—like Wordsworth and Hugo—a great visualizer, an observer and recorder of factual detail. This propensity, combined with his philosophic inclination, serves to explain why his scientific work was done in the fields of botany, comparative anatomy, and optics. His theory of color, to which he attached the utmost importance, contains some interesting observations but is in the main discredited. His discovery of the inter-maxillary bone in man was, however, a real contribution to anatomy, as was his insistence on the vertebral origin of the skull. This last idea reflects his ever-present and characteristically romantic sense of the constant transformation of things. He successfully applied the concept of becoming, development, and evolution of forms to plants. With his recorded researches and experiments went jottings, essays, and introductory remarks on the nature of science and the meaning of organic life. An excerpt from the *Fragments on Natural Science* is a good illustration of the half-poetical, half-philosophical character of some of Goethe's speculation:

"Nature! We are embraced and enclosed by her—powerless to leave her bonds, powerless to go deeper into her realm. Unasked and unwarned, we are seized and thrown into the whirl of her dance. . . . She seems to have no other goal but Individuality, and yet individuals are nothing to her. She builds continually and destroys continually, and her workshop is inaccessible. . . . She is the only artist, creating all from the simplest bit of matter to the most complex forms, without sign of effort reaching the greatest perfection. . . . She is playing a comedy; but whether she herself sees it, we do not know, and yet she plays it for us who are standing in the corner. . . . She is, however, fixed: her steps are measured, her exceptions rare, her laws immutable."

It has often been said of Goethe that his life, rich in the fundamental human experiences of friendship and love, statesmanship, art, and thought, is his greatest work. Throughout all of his life Goethe strove to achieve a balance between the romantic impulse toward passionate experience and the claims of order. This is apparent in his persistent preoccupation with the power of unconscious, so-called "daemonic" forces in the life of the artist and the actions of men. This concern with the subrational springs in human conduct reappears in subsequent thinkers, notably in Freud. The following selections, from books that exhibit the interplay of his living and thinking, are from the autobiography *Poetry and Truth* (translated from the German by Minna Steele Smith; London, George Bell and Sons, 1908); and from Johann Peter Eckermann's *Conversations of Goethe with Eckermann* (translated from the German by John Oxenford, 1850). The former work was published between 1811 and 1833, the latter in 1836 and 1848.

POETRY AND TRUTH

. . . VOLTAIRE, the wonder of his time, had grown old, along with the literature of which, for nearly a century, he had been the animating and ruling spirit. By his side there still existed many *littérateurs,* vegetating in a more or less active and happy old age, and then disappearing in their turn one by one. The influence of society upon authors increased more and more; for the best society, consisting of persons of birth, rank, and property, chose literature as one of their chief recreations, making it entirely social and genteel in tone. Persons of rank and literary men mutually cultivated and of necessity mutually perverted one another; for the genteel is naturally exclusive; that is what French criticism became, negative, detracting, and fault-finding. The upper classes applied this kind of criticism to authors; the authors, with somewhat less decorum, used the same procedure towards each other, and even towards their patrons. If the public was not to be awed, they endeavoured to take it by surprise, or to persuade it by humility; and thus—apart from the movements which shook church and state to their inmost core—there arose such a literary ferment, that Voltaire himself had to strain to the utmost all the resources of his activity, and of his literary dictatorship, to keep himself afloat above the torrent of universal censure. As it was, he was openly called an old self-willed child; his indefatigable endeavours were regarded as the vain efforts of decrepit age; those principles, for which he had stood all his life, and to the spread of which he had devoted his days, were no longer held in honour or esteem: nay, that very Deity he acknowledged, and so continued to declare himself free from atheism, was discredited; and thus he

himself, the venerable patriarch, was forced, like his youngest competitor, to
watch the present moment, to sue for fresh favours—to show too much love
to his friends, too much hate to his enemies; and under the appearance of a
passionate striving after truth, to act deceitfully and falsely. Was it worth
while to have led such a great and active life, if it was to end in greater dependence than it had begun? His high spirit, his delicate sensitiveness, felt
only too keenly the galling nature of such a position. He often relieved himself by swift onslaughts, gave the reins to his humour, and exceeded all bounds,
—at which both friends and enemies showed themselves indignant; for everyone thought himself capable of gauging him, though none could equal him.
A public which hears only the judgment of old men, becomes over-wise too
soon; and nothing is more unsatisfactory than a mature judgment adopted
by an immature mind.

We young men, with our German love of truth and nature, considered
honesty towards ourselves and others as the best guide in life and art; hence
Voltaire's factious dishonesty and his consonant perversion of noble subjects
became more and more distasteful to us, and our aversion to him grew daily.
He seemed never to have done with degrading religion and the Holy Scriptures on which it rests, for the sake of injuring priestcraft, as they called it,
and had thereby awakened in me feelings of irritation. But when I now
learned that, to weaken the tradition of a deluge, he had denied the existence of all fossilized shells, and admitted them only as *lusus naturæ*,[1] he entirely lost my confidence; for my own eyes had shown me on the Bastberg,
plainly enough, that I stood on what had been the floor of an ancient sea,
among the *exuviæ* [2] of its original inhabitants. These mountains had certainly
been once covered with waves, whether before or during the deluge did not
concern me; it was enough that the valley of the Rhine had been one vast
lake, a bay extending further than eye could see; no amount of talk could
shake me in this conviction. I hoped, rather, to extend my knowledge of
lands and mountains, let the result be what it would. . . .

What I have here tried to state connectedly and in a few words was, at the
time I speak of, the cry of the moment, a perpetual discord in our ears, unconnected and uninstructive. Nothing was heard but the praise of those who
had gone before. The demand was continually for something good and new;
yet the newest never found favour. . . .

If we heard the encyclopedists mentioned, or opened a volume of their
colossal work, we felt as if we were moving amidst the innumerable whirling
spools and looms of a great factory, where, what with the mere creaking and
rattling—what with all the mechanism, bewildering both to eyes and brain

---

[1] [*A joke on Nature's part.*]   [2] [*Remains.*]

—what with the mere impossibility of understanding how the various parts fit in and work with one another—what with the contemplation of all that is necessary to prepare a single piece of cloth, we felt disgusted with the very coat we wore upon our backs.

Diderot was sufficiently akin to us, as, indeed, in all the points for which the French blame him, he is a true German. But even his point of view was too lofty, his range of vision too wide for us to be able to rise to his height and place ourselves at his side. Yet the children of nature he continued to produce and to ennoble by his great rhetorical art delighted us: we were enchanted with his brave poachers and smugglers; and this rabble throve later only too well on the German Parnassus. He, too, like Rousseau, by diffusing a disgust of social life, unobtrusively paved the way for those monstrous world-wide changes, in which all that had hitherto existed seemed to be swallowed up.

However, we should now put aside these considerations, and observe what influence these two men have had upon art. Here, too, they pointed to nature and urged us to turn from art and follow her.

The highest problem of all art is to produce by illusion the semblance of a higher reality. But it is a false endeavour to push the realization of the illusion so far that at last only a commonplace reality remains. . . .

We had neither desire nor inclination to be enlightened or advanced by the aid of philosophy; on religious subjects we thought we had sufficiently enlightened ourselves, and therefore looked on with comparative indifference at the violent contest between the French philosophers and the priesthood. Prohibited books condemned to the flames, of which so much was heard at the time, produced no effect upon us. I mention as a typical instance, the *Système de la Nature* [of Holbach] which we looked into out of curiosity. We did not understand how such a book could be dangerous. It seemed to us so gloomy, so Cimmerian, so deathlike, that we found it difficult to endure its presence, and shuddered at it as at a spectre. The author fancies he is giving his book a great recommendation, when he declares in his preface, that as a decrepit old man, just sinking into the grave, he is anxious to announce the truth to his contemporaries and to posterity.

We laughed at him; for we thought we had observed that old people are incapable of appreciating whatever is good and loveable in the world. "Old churches have dark windows.—To know how cherries and berries taste, we must ask children and sparrows." These were our gibes and maxims; and so that book, as the very quintessence of senility, seemed to us insipid, or even offensive. "All had of necessity to be," so said the book, "and therefore there was no God." But could not God also exist of necessity? we asked. We did indeed admit, at the same time, that we could not escape from the necessities of day and

night, the seasons, the influence of climate, and from physical and animal conditions; but nevertheless we felt within us something that seemed like perfect
freedom of will, and again something which sought to counterbalance this
freedom.

We could not give up the hope of becoming more and more rational, of
making ourselves more and more independent of external things, and even
of ourselves. The word freedom has so fair a sound, that we cannot dispense
with it, even though it designates an error.

None of us had read the book through; for it had disappointed the expectation with which we opened it. It had announced a system of nature; and we
had, therefore, hoped really to learn something of nature—of this idol of ours.
Physics and chemistry, descriptions of heaven and earth, natural history and
anatomy, with much besides, had now for years, and up to this very moment,
constantly pointed us to the great world and its wealth of beauty; and we
would fain have heard more, both in particular and in general, of suns and
stars, planets and moons, mountains, valleys, rivers and seas, with all that live
and move in them. That in the course of such an exposition much must occur
which would appear to the common man as pernicious, to the clergy as
dangerous, and to the state as inadmissible, we had no doubt; and we hoped
that the small volume had not unworthily undergone the fiery ordeal. But how
hollow and empty did we feel this melancholy, atheistic half-night to be,
where earth vanished with all its creatures, heaven with all its stars. Matter
was supposed to have existed and to have been in motion from all eternity,
and to this motion, to right and to left and in every direction, were attributed
the infinite phenomena of existence. We might have allowed even so much
to pass, if the author, out of his matter in motion, had really built up the
world before our eyes. But he seemed to know as little about nature as we
did; for, after simply propounding some general ideas, he forthwith disre-
gards them in order to change what seems above nature, or a higher nature
within nature, into matter with weight and motion but without aim or shape
—and by this he fancies he has gained much.

If this book did us any harm at all, it was in giving us a hearty and lasting
dislike to all philosophy, and especially to metaphysics; while, on the other
hand, we threw ourselves into living knowledge, experience, action, and
poetry, with all the more zeal and ardour.

Thus, on the very borders of France, we had at one blow got rid of everything French about us. The French way of life was too definite and too
genteel for us, their poetry cold, their criticism annihilating, their philosophy
abstruse, and yet unsatisfying. . . .

In the course of this biography we have shown in detail how the child, the boy, the youth, sought by various ways to approach the supernatural; first, looking with strong inclination to a religion of nature; then, clinging with love to a positive one; and, finally, concentrating himself in the trial of his own powers and joyfully giving himself up to a general faith. Whilst he wandered to and fro, seeking and looking about him, in the intervals which lay between these several phases, he met with much that would not fit into any of them, and he seemed to realize more and more clearly the desirability of turning his thoughts away from the immense and incomprehensible.

He thought he could detect in nature—both animate and inanimate, with soul and without soul—something which manifested itself only in contradictions, and which, therefore, could not be comprehended under any idea, still less under one word. It was not godlike, for it seemed without reason; nor human, for it had no understanding; nor devilish, for it was beneficent; nor angelic, for it often betrayed a malicious pleasure. It resembled chance, for it evinced no succession; it was like Providence, for it hinted at connection. It seemed to penetrate all that limits us; it seemed to deal arbitrarily with the necessary elements of our existence; it contracted time and expanded space. In the impossible alone did it appear to find pleasure, while it rejected the possible with contempt.

To this principle, which seemed to come in between all other principles and separate them, and yet link them together, I gave the name of Daemonic, after the example of the ancients and others with similar experiences. I sought to escape from this terrible principle, by taking refuge, according to my wont, in a creation of the imagination.

Among the parts of history which I had particularly studied, were the events that made the countries which subsequently became the United Netherlands so famous. I had diligently examined the original sources, and had endeavoured, as far as possible, to get my facts at first hand, and to bring the whole period vividly before me. The situations it presented appeared to me to be in the highest degree dramatic, while Count Egmont, whose greatness as a man and a hero most captivated me, seemed to me a suitable central figure round whom the others might be grouped with happiest effect.

But for my purpose it was necessary to convert him into a character marked by such peculiarities as would grace a youth better than a man in years, and an unmarried man better than the father of a family; a man leading an independent life, rather than one, who, however free in thought, is nevertheless restrained by the various relations of life.

Having then, in my conception of Egmont's character, made him youthful, and freed him from all fettering restraints, I gave him unlimited love of life, boundless self-reliance, a gift of attracting all men, enabling him to win the favour of the people, the unspoken attachment of a princess, the avowed passion of a child of nature, the sympathy of a shrewd politician, and even the loving admiration of the son of his greatest adversary.

The personal courage which distinguishes the hero is the foundation upon which his whole character rests, the ground whence it springs. He knows no danger, and is blind to the greatest peril when it confronts him. When surrounded by enemies, we may, at need, cut our way through them; the meshes of state policy are harder to break. The Daemonic element, which plays a part on both sides, in conflict with which what is loveable falls while what is hated triumphs; further the prospect that out of this conflict will spring a third element, and fulfil the wishes of all men;—this perhaps is what has gained for the piece (not, indeed, on its first appearance, but later and in due time), the favour which it still enjoys. Here, therefore, for the sake of many dear readers, I will forestall myself, and as I do not know when I shall have another opportunity, will express a conviction, which did not become clear to me till a later date.

Although this Daemonic element manifests itself in all corporeal and incorporeal things, and even expresses itself most distinctly in animals, yet it is primarily in its relation to man that we observe its mysterious workings, which represent a force, if not antagonistic to the moral order, yet running counter to it, so that the one may be regarded as the warp, and the other as the woof.

For the phenomena which result there are innumerable names; for all philosophies and religions have sought in prose and poetry to solve this enigma and to read once for all the riddle; and may they still continue to seek.

But the most fearful manifestation of the Daemonic is when it is seen predominating in some individual character. During my life I have observed several instances, either closely or at a distance. Such persons are not always the most eminent men, either in intellect or special gifts, and they are seldom distinguished by goodness of heart; a tremendous energy seems to emanate from them, and they exercise a wonderful power over all creatures, and even over the elements; and, indeed, who shall say how much further such influence may extend? All the moral powers combined are of no avail against them; in vain does the more enlightened portion of mankind attempt to throw suspicion upon them as dupes or as deceivers—the masses are attracted by them. Seldom if ever do they find their equals among their contemporaries; nothing can vanquish them but the universe itself, with which they have begun the fray.

CONVERSATIONS WITH ECKERMANN

March 2, 1831

I dined with Goethe to-day; and, the conversation soon turning again on the Daemonic, he added remarks to define it more closely.

"The Daemonic is that which cannot be explained by Reason or Understanding; it lies not in my nature, but I am subject to it."

"Napoleon," said I, "seems to have been of the daemonic sort."

"He was so, thoroughly and in the highest degree, so that scarce anyone is to be compared with him. Our late Grand Duke, too, was a daemonic nature, full of unlimited power of action and unrest; so that his own dominion was too little for him, and the greatest would have been too little. Daemonic beings of such sort the Greeks reckoned among their demigods."

"Is not the Daemonic," said I, "perceptible in events also?"

"Particularly, and indeed in all that we cannot explain by Reason and Understanding. It manifests itself in the most varied manner throughout nature—in the invisible as in the visible. Many creatures are of a purely daemonic kind; in many, parts of it are effective."

"Has not Mephistopheles," said I, "daemonic traits, too?"

"No, Mephistopheles is much too negative a being. The Daemonic manifests itself in a thoroughly active power. Among artists it is found more among musicians—less among painters. In Paganini, it shows itself in a high degree; and it is thus he produces such great effects." . . .

March 8, 1831

"In poetry," said Goethe, "especially in what is unconscious, before which reason and understanding fall short, and which therefore produces effects far surpassing all conception, there is always something daemonic.

"So it is with music, in the highest degree; for it stands so high that no understanding can reach it, and an influence flows from it which masters all, and for which none can account. Hence, religious worship cannot dispense with it; it is one of the chief means of working upon men miraculously. Thus the Daemonic loves to throw itself into significant individuals, especially when they are in high places, like Frederick and Peter the Great.

"Our late Grand Duke had it to such a degree, that nobody could resist him. He had an attractive influence upon men by his mere tranquil presence, without needing even to show himself good-humoured and friendly. All that I undertook by his advice succeeded; so that, in cases where my own understanding and reason were insufficient, I needed only to ask him what was to be done; he gave me an answer instinctively, and I could always be sure of happy results.

"He would have been enviable indeed if he could have possessed himself of my ideas and higher strivings; for when the daemonic spirit forsook him, and only the human was left, he knew not how to set to work, and was much troubled at it.

"In Byron, also, this element was probably active in a high degree; so that he possessed great powers of attraction, and women especially could not resist him."

"Into the idea of the Divine," said I, by way of experiment, "this active power which we name the Daemonic would not seem to enter."

"My good friend," said Goethe, "what do we know of the idea of the Divine? and what can our narrow ideas tell of the Highest Being? Should I, like a Turk, name it with a hundred names, I should still fall short, and, in comparison with such boundless attributes, have said nothing." . . .

March, 1832

We talked of the tragic idea of Destiny among the Greeks.

"It no longer suits our way of thinking," said Goethe; "it is obsolete, and is also in contradiction with our religious views. If a modern poet introduces such antique ideas into a drama, it always has an air of affectation. It is a costume long since out of fashion; which, like the Roman toga, no longer suits us.

"It is better for us moderns to say with Napoleon, 'Politics are Destiny.' But let us beware of saying, with our latest *literati,* that politics are poetry, or a suitable subject for the poet. The English poet Thomson wrote a very good poem on the Seasons, but a very bad one on Liberty; and that not from want of poetry in the poet, but from want of poetry in the subject.

"If a poet would work politically, he must give himself up to a party; and so soon as he does that, he is lost as a poet—he must bid farewell to his free spirit, his unbiased view, and draw over his ears the cap of bigotry and blind hatred.

"The poet, as a man and citizen, will love his native land; but the native land of his *poetic* powers and poetic action is the good, noble, and beautiful, which is confined to no particular province or country, and which he seizes upon and forms wherever he finds it. Therein is he like the eagle, which hovers with free gaze over whole countries, and to whom it is of no consequence whether the hare on which he pounces is running in Prussia or in Saxony.

"And, then, what is meant by love of one's country? what is meant by patriotic deeds? If the poet has employed a life in battling with pernicious prejudices, in setting aside narrow views, in enlightening the minds, purifying the tastes, ennobling the feelings and thoughts of his countrymen, what better could he have done? how could he have acted more patriotically?

"To make such ungrateful and unsuitable demands upon a poet is just as if we required the captain of a regiment to show himself a patriot by taking part in political innovations and thus neglecting his proper calling. The captain's country is his regiment; and he will show himself an excellent patriot by troubling himself about political matters only so far as they concern him, and bestowing all his mind and all his care on the battalions under him, trying so to train and discipline them that they may do their duty if ever their native land should be in peril.

"I hate all bungling like sin; but, most of all, bungling in state affairs, which produces nothing but mischief to thousands and millions.

"You know that, on the whole, I care little what is written about me; but yet it comes to my ears, and I know well enough that, hard as I have toiled all my life, all my labours are as nothing in the eyes of certain people, just because I have disdained to mingle in political parties. To please such people I must have become a member of a Jacobin club, and preached bloodshed and murder. However, not a word more upon this wretched subject, lest I become unwise in railing against folly."

In the same manner he blamed the political course, so much praised by others, of Uhland.

"Mind," said he, "the politician will devour the poet. To be a member of the States, and to live amid daily jostlings and excitements, is not for the delicate nature of a poet. His song will cease, and that is in some sort to be lamented. Swabia has plenty of men, sufficiently well educated, well meaning, able, and eloquent, to be members of the States; but only one poet of Uhland's class."

GEORG WILHELM FRIEDRICH HEGEL

HEGEL (1770–1831), for many years the "court philosopher" of Prussian Germany, was the reigning philosophic genius of his time. He was, during most of his life, professor in the universities of Jena, Heidelberg, and Berlin, and it was especially at the last of these institutions that he made his greatest reputation.

Hegel was the most outstanding of those who argued that the mechanistic thought of the eighteenth century was inadequate for dealing with facts of change and development. However, he continued the dominant interest of the Enlightenment in tracing the career of human reason. He felt it was possible to explain this career in such a way as to show the unbroken and continuous unfolding of reason in history. The central fact of the universe was this growth of reason, but it was necessary to explicate its laws in such a way as to explain the seemingly contradictory and confusing process of universal development. In other words, the laws of history must be "dialectical": history progresses by bringing contraries into a new unity, whose fate is to be undone in turn by the rise of new ideas and interests, the process continuing until the ultimate unity is reached in Absolute Mind.

Hegel's program, liberal for its time, stood for the modernizing and nationalizing of Germany. Nevertheless, the idea that the World Spirit far transcends the understanding of any individual, and that history has a predetermined goal, lent itself easily to becoming an argument on behalf of the conservative predisposition to allow events to take their "natural" course. The ease with which Hegel's dialectic could, however, also be used for revolutionary ends is demonstrated by its influence on the work of Karl Marx. And Hegel's view that freedom realizes itself through the history of civilization embodies one of the major themes in recent Western thought—the ideal of man as a distinctive individual who refuses to be content with an identity established by traditional cultural norms.

The selection that follows is from Hegel's introduction to his *Philosophy of History,* posthumously edited from students' lecture notes in 1837, and translated by J. Sibree in 1857. The translation from the German has been slightly altered in a few places.

INTRODUCTION TO THE PHILOSOPHY OF HISTORY

THE HISTORY of the world is none other than the progress of the consciousness of Freedom; a progress whose development according to the necessity of its nature, it is our business to investigate. . . .

The destiny of the spiritual World, and,—since this is the *substantial World,* while the physical remains subordinate to it, or, in the language of speculation, has no truth, as *against* the spiritual,—*the final cause of the World at large,* we allege to be the *consciousness* of its own freedom on the part of Spirit, and *ipso facto,* the *reality* of that freedom. But that this term "Freedom," without further qualification, is an indefinite, and incalculable ambiguous term; and that while that which it represents is the *ne plus ultra* of attainment, it is liable to an infinity of misunderstandings, confusions and errors, and to become the occasion for all imaginable excesses,—has never been more clearly known and felt than in modern times. Yet, for the present, we must content ourselves with the term itself without farther definition. Attention was also directed to the importance of that infinite difference between a principle in the abstract, and its realisation in the concrete. In the process before us, the essential nature of freedom—which involves in it absolute necessity,—is to be displayed as coming to a consciousness of itself (for it is in its very nature, self-consciousness) and thereby realising its existence. Itself is its own object of attainment, and the sole aim of Spirit. This result it is, at which the process of the World's History has been continually aiming; and to which the sacrifices that have ever and anon been laid on the vast altar of the earth, through the long lapse of ages, have been offered. This is the only aim that sees itself realised and fulfilled; the only pole of repose amid the ceaseless change of events and conditions, and the sole efficient principle that pervades them. This final aim is God's purpose with the world; but God is the absolutely perfect Being, and can, therefore, will nothing other than himself—his own Will. The Nature of His Will—that is, His Nature itself—is what we here call the Idea of Freedom; translating the language of Religion into that of Thought. The question, then, which we may next put, is: What means does this principle of Freedom use for its realisation? . . .

The question of the *means* by which Freedom develops itself to a World, conducts us to the phenomenon of History itself. Although Freedom is, primarily, an undeveloped idea, the means it uses are external and phenomenal; presenting themselves in History to our sensuous vision. The first glance at history convinces us that the actions of men proceed from their needs, their passions, their interests, their characters, and talents; and impresses us with the belief that such needs, passions and interests are the sole springs of action—the efficient agents in this scene of activity. Among these may, perhaps, be found aims of a liberal or universal kind

—benevolence it may be, or noble patriotism; but such virtues and general views are but insignificant as compared with the world and its doings. We may perhaps see the ideal of Reason actualized in those who adopt such aims, and within the spheres of their influence; but they bear only a trifling proportion to the mass of the human race; and the extent of that influence is limited accordingly. Passions, private aims, and the satisfaction of selfish desires, are on the other hand, most effective springs of action. Their power lies in the fact that they respect none of the limitations which justice and morality would impose on them; and that these natural impulses have a more direct influence over man than the artificial and tedious discipline that tends to order and self-restraint, law and morality. When we look at this display of passions, and the consequences of their violence; the unreason which is associated not only with them, but even (rather we might say *especially*) with *good* designs and righteous aims; when we see the evil, the vice, the ruin that has befallen the most flourishing kingdoms which the mind of man ever created, we can scarce avoid being filled with sorrow at this universal taint of corruption: and, since this decay is not the work of mere nature, but of the human will—a moral embitterment—a revolt of the good spirit (if it have a place within us) may well be the result of our reflections. Without rhetorical exaggeration, a simply truthful combination of the miseries that have overwhelmed the noblest of nations and polities, and the finest exemplars of private virtue,—forms a picture of most fearful aspect, and excites emotions of the profoundest and most hopeless sadness, counter-balanced by no consolatory result. We endure in beholding it a mental torture, allowing no defence or escape but the consideration that what has happened could not be otherwise; that it is a fatality which no intervention could alter. And at last we draw back from the intolerable disgust with which these sorrowful reflections threaten us, into the more agreeable environment of our individual life—the present formed by our private aims and interests. In short we retreat into the selfishness that stands on the quiet shore, and thence enjoy in safety the distant spectacle of "wrecks confusedly hurled." But even regarding history as the slaughter-bench at which the happiness of peoples, the wisdom of states, and the virtue of individuals have been victimised—the question involuntarily arises —to what principle, to what final aim these enormous sacrifices have been offered. From this point the investigation usually proceeds to that which we have made the general commencement of our enquiry. Starting from this we pointed out those events which made up a picture so suggestive of gloomy emotions and thoughtful reflections—as *the very field* which we, for our part, regard as exhibiting only the means for realising what we assert to be the essential destiny—the absolute aim, or—which comes to the same thing—the true *result* of the world's history. We have all along purposely eschewed "moral reflections" as a method of rising from the scene of particular historical events to the general principles which they embody. Besides, it is not the interest of such sentimentalities, really to rise above those depressing emotions; and to solve the enigmas of providence which the considerations that occasioned them, present. It is essential to their character to find a gloomy satisfaction in the empty and fruitless sublimities of that negative result. We return then to the point of view which we have adopted; observing that the successive steps (*Momente*) of the analysis to which it will lead us, will also evolve the conditions requisite for answering the enquiries suggested by the panorama of sin and suffering that history unfolds. . . .

We assert then that nothing has been accomplished without interest on the part of the actors; and—if interest be called passion, inasmuch as the whole individuality, to the neglect of all other actual or possible interests and aims, is devoted to an object with every fibre of volition, concentrating all its desires and powers upon it—we may affirm absolutely that *nothing great* in *the world* has been accomplished without *passion*. Two elements, therefore, enter into the object of our investigation; the first the Idea, the second the complex of human passions; the one the warp, the other the woof of the vast tapestry of universal history. The concrete mean and union of the two is liberty, under the conditions of morality in a state. We have spoken of the idea of freedom as the nature of Spirit, and the absolute goal of history. Passion is regarded as a thing of sinister aspect, as more or less immoral. Man is required to have no passions. Passion, it is true, is not quite the suitable word for what I wish to express. I mean here nothing more than human activity as resulting from private interests—special, or if you will, self-seeking designs—with this qualification, that the whole energy of will and character is devoted to their attainment; that other interests (which would in themselves constitute attractive aims), or rather all things else, are sacrificed to them. The object in question is so bound up with the man's will, that it entirely and alone determines the "hue of resolution," and is inseparable from it. It has become the very essence of his volition. For a person is a specific existence; not man in general (a term to which no real existence corresponds), but a particular human being. The term "character" likewise expresses this idiosyncrasy of will and intelligence. But *character* comprehends all peculiarities whatever; the way in which a person conducts himself in private relations, &c., and is not limited to his idiosyncrasy in its practical and active phase. I shall, therefore, use the term "passion"; understanding thereby the particular bent of character, as far as the peculiarities of volition are not limited to private interest, but supply the impelling and actuating force for accomplishing deeds shared in by the community at large. Passion is in the first instance the *subjective,* and therefore the *formal* side of energy, will, and activity—leaving the object or aim still undetermined. And there is a similar relation of formality to reality in merely individual conviction, individual views, individual conscience. It is always a question, of essential importance, what is the purport of my conviction, what the object of my passion, in deciding whether the one or the other is of a true and substantial nature. Conversely, if it is so, it will inevitably attain actual existence—be actualized.

From this comment on the second essential element in the historical embodiment of an aim, we infer—glancing at the institution of the state in passing—that a state is then well constituted and internally powerful, when the private interest of its citizens is one with the common interest of the state; when the one finds its gratification and realisation in the other,—a proposition in itself very important. But in a state many institutions must be adopted, much political machinery invented, accompanied by appropriate political arrangements,—necessitating long struggles of the understanding before what is really appropriate can be discovered,—involving, moreover, contentions with private interest and passions, and a tedious discipline of these latter, in order to bring about the desired harmony. The epoch when a state attains this harmonious condition, marks the period of its bloom, its virtue, its vigour, and its prosperity. But the history of mankind does not begin with a *conscious* aim of any kind, as it is the case with the particular circles into which men form themselves of set purpose. The mere social instinct implies a conscious purpose of security for life and property; and when society has been constituted, this purpose becomes more comprehensive. The history of the world begins with its general aim—the realisation of the idea of Spirit—only in an *implicit* form (*an sich*) that is, as nature; an inmost, unconscious instinct; and the whole process of history (as already observed), is directed to rendering this unconscious impulse a conscious one. Thus appearing in the form of merely natural existence, natural will—that which has been called the subjective side,—physical craving, instinct, passion, private interest, as also opinion and subjective conception,—spontaneously present themselves at the very commencement. This vast congeries of volitions, interests and activities, constitute the instruments and means of the world-spirit for attaining its object; bringing it to consciousness, and realising it. And this aim is none other than finding itself —coming to itself—and contemplating itself in concrete actuality. But that those manifestations of vitality on the part of individuals and peoples, in which they seek and satisfy their own purposes, are, at the same time, the means and instruments of a higher and broader purpose of which they know nothing,—which they realise unconsciously,—might be made a matter of question; rather has been questioned, and in every variety of form negatived, decried and contemned as mere dreaming and "philosophy." But on this point I announced my view at the very outset, and asserted our hypothesis,—which, however, will appear in the sequel, in the form of a legitimate inference,—and our belief, that Reason governs the world, and has consequently governed its history. In relation to this independently universal and substantial existence—all else is subordinate, subservient to it, and the means for its development. But moreover this Reason is immanent in historical existence and attains to its own perfection in and through that existence. The union of universal abstract existence generally with the individual,—the subjective—that this alone is truth, belongs to the department of speculation, and is treated in this general form in logic.—But in the process of the world's history itself,—as still incomplete,—the abstract final aim of history is not yet made the distinct object of desire and interest. While these limited sentiments are still unconscious of the purpose they are fulfilling, the universal principle is implicit in them, and is realising itself through them. The question also assumes the form of the union of *freedom and necessity;* the latent abstract process of Spirit being regarded as *necessity,* while that which exhibits itself in the conscious will of men, as their interest, belongs to the domain of *freedom.* . . .

I will endeavour to make what has been said more vivid and clear by examples.

The building of a house is, in the first instance, a subjective aim and design. On the other hand we have, as means, the several substances required for the work,—iron, wood, stones. The elements are made use of in working up this material: fire to melt the iron, wind to blow the fire, water to set wheels in motion, in order to cut the wood, &c. The result is, that the wind, which has helped to build the house, is shut out by the house; so also are the violence of rains and floods, and the destructive powers of fire, so far as the house is made fire-proof. The stones and beams obey the law of gravity,—press downwards,—and so high walls are carried up. Thus the elements are made use of in accordance with their nature, and yet co-operate for a product, by which their operation is limited. Thus the passions of men are gratified; they develop themselves and their aims in accordance with their natural tendencies, and build up the edifice of human society; thus fortifying a position for right and order *against themselves.*

The connection of events above indicated, involves also the fact, that in history an additional result is commonly produced by human actions beyond that which they aim at and obtain—that which they immediately recognise and desire. They gratify their own interest; but something farther is thereby accomplished, latent in the actions in question, though not present to their consciousness, and not included in their design. An analogous example is offered in the case of a man who, from a feeling of revenge,—perhaps not an unjust one, but produced by injury on the other's part,—burns that other man's house. A connection is immediately established between the deed itself and a train of circumstances not directly included in it, taken abstractedly. In itself it consisted in merely presenting a small flame to a small portion of a beam. Events not involved in that simple act follow of themselves. The part of the beam which was set fire to is connected with its remote portions; the beam itself is united with the woodwork of the house generally, and this with other houses; so that a wide conflagration ensues, which destroys the goods and chattels of many other persons besides his against whom the act of revenge was first directed; perhaps even costs not a few men their lives. This lay neither in the deed abstractedly, nor in the design of the man who committed it. But the action has a further general bearing. In the design of the doer it was only revenge executed against an individual in the destruction of his property, but it is moreover a crime, and that involves punishment also. This may not have been present to the mind of the perpetrator, still less in his intention; but his deed itself, the general principles it calls into play, its substantial content entails it. By this example I wish only to impress on you the consideration, that in a simple act, something further may be implicated than lies in the intention and consciousness of the agent. The example before us involves, however, this additional consideration, that the substance of the act, consequently we may say the act itself, recoils upon the perpetrator,—reacts upon him with destructive tendency. This union of the two extremes—the embodiment of a general idea in the form of direct actuality, and the elevation of a particularity into connection with universal truth—is brought to pass, at first sight, under the conditions of an utter diversity of nature between the two, and an indifference of the one extreme towards the other. The aims which the agents set before them are limited and special; but it must be remarked that the agents themselves are intelligent thinking beings. The purport of their aims is interwoven with *general, essential* considerations of justice, good, duty, &c.; for mere desire —volition in its rough and savage forms—falls not within the scene and sphere of universal history. Those general considerations, which form at the same time a norm for directing aims and actions, have a determinate purport; for such an abstraction as "good for its own sake," has no place in living actuality. If men are to act, they must not only intend the good, but must have decided for themselves whether this or that particular thing is a good. What special course of action, however, is good or not, is determined, as regards the ordinary contingencies of private life, by the laws and customs of a state; and here no great difficulty is presented. Each individual has his position; he knows on the whole what a just, honourable course of conduct is. As to ordinary, private relations, the assertion that it is difficult to choose the right and good,—the regarding it as the mark of an exalted morality to find difficulties and raise scruples on that score,—may be set down to an evil or perverse will, which seeks to evade duties not in themselves of a perplexing nature; or, at any rate, to an idly reflective habit of mind—where a feeble will affords no sufficient exercise to the faculties,—leaving them therefore to find occupation within themselves, and to expend themselves on moral self-adulation.

It is quite otherwise with the comprehensive relations that history has to do with. In this sphere are presented those momentous collisions between existing, acknowledged duties, laws, and rights, and those contingencies which are adverse to this fixed system; which assail and even destroy its foundations and existence; whose tenor may nevertheless seem good,—on the large scale advantageous,—yes, even indispensable and necessary. These contingencies realise themselves in history: they involve a general principle of a different order from that on which depends the *permanence* of a people or a state. This principle is an essential phase in the development of the *creating* Idea, of truth striving and urging towards (consciousness of) itself. Historical men—*world-historical individuals*—are those in whose aims such a general principle lies.

Caesar, in danger of losing a position, not perhaps at that time of superiority, yet at least of equality with the others who were at the head of the state, and of succumbing to those who were just on the point of becoming his enemies,—belongs essentially to this category. These enemies—who were at the same time pursuing *their* personal aims—had the form of the constitution, and the power conferred by an appearance of justice, on their side. Caesar was contending for the maintenance of his position, honour, and safety; and, since the power of his opponents included the sovereignty over the provinces of the Roman Empire, his victory secured for him the conquest of that entire empire; and he thus became—though leaving the form of the constitution—the autocrat of the state. That which secured for him the execution of a design, which in the first instance was of negative import—the autocracy of Rome,—was, however, at the same time an independently necessary feature in the history of Rome and of the world. It was not, then, his private gain merely, but an unconscious impulse that occasioned the accomplishment of that for which the time was ripe. Such are all great historical men,—whose own particular aims involve those large issues which are the will of the world-spirit. They may be called heroes, inasmuch as they have derived their purposes and their vocation, not from the calm, regular course of things, sanctioned by the existing order; but from a concealed fount—one which has not attained to phenomenal, present existence,—from that inner Spirit, still hidden beneath the surface, which, impinging on the outer world as on a shell, bursts it in pieces, because it is another kernel than that which belonged to the shell in question. They are men, therefore, who appear to draw the impulse of their life from themselves; and whose deeds have produced a condition of things and a complex of historical relations which appear to be only *their* interest, and *their* work.

Such individuals had no consciousness of the general Idea they were unfolding, while prosecuting those aims of theirs; on the contrary, they were practical, political men. But at the same time they were thinking men, who had an insight into the requirements of the time—*what was ripe for development*. This was the very truth for their age, for their world; the species next in order, so to speak, and which was already formed in the womb of time. It was theirs to know this nascent principle; the necessary, directly sequent step in progress, which their world was to take; to make this their aim, and to expend their energy in promoting it. World-historical men—the heroes of an epoch—must, therefore, be recognised as its clear-sighted ones; *their* deeds, *their* words are the best of that time. Great men have formed purposes to satisfy themselves, not others. Whatever prudent designs and counsels they might have learned from others, would be the more limited and inconsistent features in their career; for it was they who best understood affairs; from whom *others* learned, and approved, or at least acquiesced in—their policy. For that Spirit which had taken this fresh step in history is the inmost soul of all individuals; but in a state of unconsciousness which the great men in question aroused. Their fellows, therefore, follow these soul-leaders; for they feel the irresistible power of their own inner spirit thus embodied. If we go on to cast a look at the fate of these world-historical persons, whose vocation it was to be the agents of the world-spirit,—we shall find it to have been no happy one. They attained no calm enjoyment; their whole life was labour and trouble; their whole nature was nought else but their master-passion. When their object is attained they fall off like empty hulls from the kernel. They die early, like Alexander; they are murdered, like Caesar; transported to St. Helena, like

Napoleon. This fearful consolation—that historical men have not enjoyed what is called happiness, and of which only private life (and this may be passed under very various external circumstances) is capable,—this consolation those may draw from history, who stand in need of it; and it is craved by envy—vexed at what is great and transcendent,—striving, therefore, to depreciate it, and to find some flaw in it. Thus in modern times it has been demonstrated *ad nauseam* that princes are generally unhappy on their thrones; in consideration of which the possession of a throne is tolerated, and men acquiesce in the fact that not themselves but the personages in question are its occupants. The free man, we may observe, is not envious, but gladly recognises what is great and exalted, and rejoices that it exists. . . .

A world-historical individual is not so unwise as to indulge a variety of wishes to divide his regards. He is devoted to the one aim, regardless of all else. It is even possible that such men may treat other great, even sacred interests, inconsiderately; conduct which is indeed obnoxious to moral reprehension. But so mighty a form must trample down many an innocent flower—crush to pieces many an object in its path. . . .

But though we might tolerate the idea that individuals, their desires and the gratification of them, are thus sacrificed, and their happiness given up to the empire of chance, to which it belongs; and that as a general rule, individuals come under the category of means to an ulterior end,—there is one aspect of human individuality which we should hesitate to regard in that subordinate light, even in relation to the highest; since it is absolutely no subordinate element, but exists in those individuals as inherently eternal and divine. I mean *morality, ethics, religion.* Even when speaking of the realisation of the great ideal aim by means of individuals, the *subjective* element in them—their interest and that of their cravings and impulses, their views and judgments, though exhibited as the merely formal side of their existence,—was spoken of as having an infinite right to be consulted. The first idea that presents itself in speaking of *means* is that of something external to the object, and having no share in the object itself. But merely natural things—even the commonest lifeless objects—used as means, must be of such a kind as adapts them to their purpose; they must possess something in common with it. Human beings least of all, sustain the bare external relation of mere means to the great ideal aim. Not only do they in the very act of realising it, make it the occasion of satisfying personal desires, whose purport is diverse from that aim—but they share in that ideal aim itself; and are for that very reason objects of their own existence; not *formally* merely, as the world of living beings generally is—whose individual life is essentially subordinate to that of man, and is properly used *up* as an instrument. Men, on the contrary, are objects of existence to them-selves, as regards the intrinsic import of the aim in question. To this order belongs that in them which we would exclude from the category of mere means,—morality, ethics, religion. That is to say, man is an object of exist-ence in himself only in virtue of the divine that is in him,—that which was designated at the outset as *Reason;* which, in view of its activity and power of self-determination, was called *freedom.* And we affirm—without entering at present on the proof of the assertion—that religion, morality, &c. have their foundation and source in that principle, and so are essentially elevated above all alien necessity and chance. And here we must remark that in-dividuals, to the extent of their freedom, are responsible for the depravation and enfeeblement of morals and religion. This is the seal of the absolute and sublime destiny of man—that he knows what is good and what is evil; that his destiny *is* his very ability to will either good or evil,—in one word, that he is the subject of moral imputation, imputation not only of evil, but of good; and not only concerning this or that particular matter, and all that happens *ab extrâ,* but *also* the good and evil attaching to his individual freedom. The brute alone is simply innocent. It would, however, demand an extensive explanation—as extensive as the analysis of moral freedom itself—to preclude or obviate all the misunderstandings which the statement that what is called innocent imports the entire unconsciousness of evil— is wont to occasion.

In contemplating the fate which virtue, morality, even piety experience in history, we must not fall into the litany of lamentations, that the good and pious often—or for the most part—fare ill in the world, while the evil-disposed and wicked prosper. The term *prosperity* is used in a variety of meanings—riches, outward honour, and the like. But in speaking of some-thing which in and for itself constitutes an aim of existence, that so-called well or ill-faring of these or those isolated individuals cannot be regarded as an essential element in the rational order of the universe. With more justice than happiness,—or a fortunate environment for individuals,—it is de-manded of the grand aim of the world's existence, that it should foster, nay involve the execution and ratification of good, moral, righteous purposes. What makes men morally discontented (a discontent, by the by, on which they somewhat pride themselves), is that they do not find the present adapted to the realisation of aims which they hold to be right and just (more especially in modern times, ideals of political constitutions); they contrast unfavourably things as they *are,* with their idea of things as they *ought* to be. In this case it is not private interest nor passion that desires gratification, but reason, justice, liberty; and equipped with this title, the demand in question assumes a lofty bearing, and readily adopts a position not merely of discontent, but of open revolt against the actual condition of the world. To estimate such a feeling and such views aright, the demands insisted upon, and the very dogmatic opinions asserted, must be examined. At no time so much as in our own, have such general principles and notions been advanced, or with greater assurance. If in days gone by, history seems to present itself as a struggle of passions; in our time—though displays of passion are not wanting—it exhibits partly a predominance of the struggle of notions assuming the authority of principles; partly that of passions and interests essentially subjective, but under the mask of such higher sanctions. The pretensions thus contended for as legitimate in the name of that which has been stated as the ultimate aim of Reason, pass accordingly, for absolute aims,—to the same extent as religion, morals, ethics. Nothing, as before remarked, is now more common than the complaint that the *ideals* which imagination sets up are not realised—that these glorious dreams are destroyed by cold actuality. These ideals—which in the voyage of life founder on the rocks of hard reality—may be in the first instance only subjective, and belong to the idiosyncrasy of the individual, imagining himself the highest and wisest. Such do not properly belong to this category. For the fancies which the individual in his isolation indulges, cannot be the model for universal reality; just as *universal* law is not designed for the units of the mass. These as such may, in fact, find their interests decidedly thrust into the background. But by the term "Ideal," we also understand the ideal of reason, of the good, of the true. Poets, as *e.g.* Schiller, have painted such ideals touchingly and with strong emotion, and with the deeply melancholy conviction that they could not be realised. In affirming, on the contrary, that the universal Reason *does* realise itself, we have indeed nothing to do with the individual empirically regarded. That admits of degrees of better and worse, since here chance and particularity have received authority from the Idea to exercise their monstrous power. Much, therefore, in particular aspects of the grand phenomenon might be found fault with. This subjective fault-finding,—which, however, only keeps in view the individual and its deficiency, without taking notice of Reason pervading the whole,—is easy; and inasmuch as it asserts an excellent intention with regard to the good of the whole, and seems to result from a kindly heart, it feels authorized to give itself airs and assume great consequence. It is easier to discover a deficiency in individuals, in states, and in providence, than to see their real import and value. For in this merely negative fault-finding a proud position is taken,—one which overlooks the object, without having entered into it,—without having comprehended its positive aspect. Age generally makes men more tolerant; youth is always discontented. The tolerance of age is the result of the ripeness of a judgment which, not merely as the result of indifference, is satisfied even with what is inferior; but, more deeply taught by the grave experience of life, has been led to perceive the substantial, solid worth of the object in question. The insight then to which—in contradistinction from those ideals—philosophy is to lead us, is, that the actual world is as it ought to be—that the truly good—the universal divine reason—is not a mere abstraction, but a vital principle capable of realising itself. This *good,* this *Reason,* in its most concrete form, is God. God governs the world; the actual working of his government—the carrying out of his plan—is the history of the world. This plan philosophy strives to comprehend; for only that which has been developed as the result of it, possesses *bonâ fide* reality. That which does not accord with it, is negative, worthless existence. Before the pure light of this divine Idea—which is no mere ideal—the phantom of a world whose events are an incoherent concourse of fortuitous circumstances, utterly vanishes. Philosophy wishes to discover the substantial purport, the actual side of the divine idea, and to justify the so much despised actuality of things; for Reason is the comprehension of the divine work. But as to what concerns the perversion, corruption, and ruin of religious, ethical and moral purposes, and states of society generally, it must be affirmed, that in their *essence* these are infinite and eternal; but that the forms they assume may be of a limited order, and consequently belong to the domain of mere nature, and be subject to the sway of chance. They are therefore perishable, and exposed to decay and corruption. Religion and morality—in the same way as inherently universal essences—have the peculiarity of being present in the individual soul, in the full extent of their Idea, and therefore truly and really; although they may not manifest themselves in it *in extenso,* and are not applied to fully developed relations. The religion, the morality of a limited sphere of life— that of a shepherd or a peasant, *e.g.*—in its intensive concentration and limitation to a few perfectly simple relations of life,—has infinite worth; the same worth as the religion and morality of extensive knowledge, and of an existence rich in the compass of its relations and actions. This inner focus —this simple region of the claims of subjective freedom,—the home of volition, resolution, and action,—the abstract sphere of conscience,—that which comprises the responsibility and moral value of the individual, remains untouched; and is quite shut out from the noisy din of the world's history— including not merely external and temporal changes, but also those entailed by the absolute necessity inseparable from the realisation of the Idea of freedom itself. But as a general truth this must be regarded as settled, that whatever in the world possesses claims as noble and glorious, has nevertheless a higher existence above it. The claim of the world-spirit rises above all special claims. . . .

What is the material in which the ideal of Reason is wrought out? The primary answer would be,—personality itself—human desires—subjectivity generally. In human knowledge and volition, as its material element, Reason attains positive existence. We have considered subjective volition where it has an object which is the truth and essence of a reality, viz. where it constitutes a great world-historical passion. As a subjective will, occupied with limited passions, it is dependent, and can gratify its desires only within the limits of this dependence. But the subjective will has also a substantial life— a reality,—in which it moves in the region of *essential* being and has the essential itself as the object of its existence. This essential being is the union of the *subjective* with the *rational* will: it is the moral whole, the state, which is that form of actuality in which the individual has and enjoys his freedom; but on the condition of his recognising, believing in and willing that which is common to the whole. And this must not be understood as if the subjective will of the social unit attained its gratification and enjoyment through that common Will; as if this were a means provided for its benefit; as if the individual, in his relations to other individuals, thus limited his freedom, in order that this universal limitation—the mutual constraint of all—might secure a small space of liberty for each. Rather, we affirm, are law, morality, government, and they alone, the positive fact and completion of freedom. Freedom of a low and limited order, is mere caprice; which finds its exercise in the sphere of particular and limited desires.

Subjective volition—passion—is that which sets men in activity, that which effects "practical" actualisation. The Idea is the inner spring of action; the state is the actually existing, realised moral life. For it is the unity of the universal, essential will, with that of the individual; and this is "morality." The individual living in this unity has a moral life; possesses a value that consists in this substantiality alone. Sophocles in his Antigone, says, "The divine commands are not of yesterday, nor of today; no, they have an infinite existence, and no one could say whence they came." The laws of morality are not accidental, but are the essentially rational. It is the very object of the state that what is essential in the practical activity of men, and in their dispositions, should be duly recognised; that it should have a manifest existence, and maintain its position. It is the absolute interest of Reason that this moral whole should exist; and herein lies the justification and merit of heroes who have founded states,—however rude these may have been. In the history of the world, only those peoples can come under our notice which form a state. For it must be understood that this latter is the realisation of freedom, *i.e.* of the absolute final aim, and that it exists for its own sake. It must further be understood that all the worth which the human being possesses—all spiritual actuality, he possesses only through the state. For his spiritual actuality consists in this, that his own essence—Reason—is objectively present to him, that it possesses objective immediate existence for him. Thus only is he fully conscious; thus only is he a partaker of morality —of a just and moral social and political life. For truth is the unity of the universal and subjective will; and the universal is to be found in the state, in its laws, its universal and rational arrangements. The state is the divine Idea as it exists on earth. We have in it, therefore, the object of history in a more definite shape than before; that in which freedom obtains objectivity, and lives in the enjoyment of this objectivity. For law is the objectivity of spirit; volition in its true form. Only that will which obeys law, is free; for it obeys itself—it is independent and so free. When the state or our country constitutes a community of existence; when the subjective will of man submits to laws,—the contradiction between liberty and necessity vanishes. The rational has necessary existence, as being the reality and substance of things, and we are free in recognising it as law, and following it as the substance of our own being. The objective and the subjective will are then reconciled, and present one identical homogeneous whole. For the morality (*Sittlichkeit*) of the state is not of that ethical (*moralische*) reflective kind, in which one's own conviction bears sway; this latter is rather the peculiarity of the modern time, while the true antique morality is based on the principle of abiding by one's duty (to the state at large). An Athenian citizen did what was required of him, as it were from instinct; but if I reflect on the object of my activity, I must have the consciousness that my will has been called into exercise. But morality is duty—substantial right—a *"second* nature" as it has been justly called; for the *first* nature of man is his primary merely animal existence.

The development *in extenso* of the Idea of the state belongs to the philosophy of jurisprudence; but it must be observed that in the theories of our time various errors are current respecting it, which pass for established truths, and have become fixed prejudices. We will mention only a few of them, giving prominence to such as have a reference to the object of our history.

The error which first meets us is the direct contradictory of our principle that the state presents the realisation of freedom; the opinion, viz., that man is free by *nature,* but that in *society,* in the state—to which nevertheless he is irresistibly impelled—he must limit this natural freedom. That man is free by nature is quite correct in one sense; viz., that he is so according to the idea of humanity; but we imply thereby that he is such only in virtue of his destiny—that he has an undeveloped power to become such; for the "nature" of an object is exactly synonymous with its "Idea." But the view in question imports more than this. When man is spoken of as "free by nature," the mode of his existence as well as his destiny is implied. His merely natural and primary condition is intended. In this sense a "state of nature" is assumed in which mankind at large are in the possession of their natural rights with the unconstrained exercise and enjoyment of their freedom. This assumption is not indeed raised to the dignity of the historical fact; it would indeed be difficult, were the attempt seriously made, to point out any such condition as actually existing, or as having ever occurred. Examples of a savage state of life can be pointed out, but they are marked by brutal passions and deeds of violence; while, however rude and simple their conditions, they involve social arrangements which (to use the common phrase) *restrain* freedom. That assumption is one of those nebulous images which theory produces; an idea which it cannot avoid originating, but which it fathers upon real existence, without sufficient historical justification.

What we find such a state of nature to be in actual experience, answers exactly to the idea of a *merely* natural condition. Freedom as the *ideal* of that which is original and natural, does not exist *as original and natural*. Rather must it be first sought out and won; and that by an incalculable medial discipline of the intellectual and moral powers. The state of nature is, therefore, predominantly that of injustice and violence, of untamed natural impulses, of inhuman deeds and feelings. Limitation is certainly produced by society and the state, but it is a limitation of the mere brute emotions and rude instincts; as also, in a more advanced stage of culture, of the premeditated self-will of caprice and passion. This kind of constraint is part of the instrumentality by which only the consciousness of freedom and the desire for its attainment, in its true—that is rational and ideal form—can be obtained. To the notion of freedom, law and morality are indispensably requisite; and they are in and for themselves, universal existences, objects and aims; which are discovered only by the activity of thought, separating itself from the merely sensuous, and developing itself, in opposition thereto; and which must on the other hand, be introduced into and incorporated with the originally sensuous will, and that contrarily to its natural inclination. The perpetually recurring misapprehension of freedom consists in regarding that term only in its *formal,* subjective sense, abstracted from its essential objects and aims; thus a constraint put upon impulse, desire, passion—pertaining to the particular individual as such—a limitation of caprice and self-will is regarded as a fettering of freedom. We should on the contrary look upon such limitation as the indispensable proviso of emancipation. Society and the state are the very conditions in which freedom is realised. . . .

We have considered two aspects of freedom,—the objective and the subjective; if, therefore, freedom is asserted to consist in the individuals of a state all agreeing in its arrangements, it is evident that only the subjective aspect is regarded. The natural inference from this principle is, that no law can be valid without the approval of all. This difficulty is attempted to be obviated by the decision that the minority must yield to the majority; the majority therefore bear the sway. But long ago J. J. Rousseau remarked, that in that case there would be no longer freedom, for the will of the *minority* would cease to be respected. At the Polish Diet each single member had to give his consent before any political step could be taken; and this kind of freedom it was that ruined the state. Besides, it is a dangerous and false prejudice, that the people *alone* have reason and insight, and know what justice is; for each popular faction may represent itself as the people, and the question as to what constitutes the state is one of advanced science, and not of popular decision.

If the principle of regard for the individual will is recognised as the only basis of political liberty, viz., that nothing should be done by or for the state to which all the members of the body politic have not given their sanction, we have, properly speaking, no *constitution*. The only arrangement that would be necessary, would be, first, a centre having no *will* of its own, but which should take into consideration what appeared to be the necessities of the state; and, secondly, a contrivance for calling the members of the state together, for taking the votes, and for performing the arithmetical operations of reckoning and comparing the number of votes for the different propositions, and thereby deciding upon them. The state is an *abstraction,* having its generic existence in its citizens; but it is an actuality, and its simple generic existence must embody itself in individual will and activity. The want of government and political administration in general is felt; this necessitates the selection and separation from the rest of those who have to take the helm in political affairs, to decide concerning them, and to give orders to other citizens, with a view to the execution of their plans. If, *e.g.*, even the people in a democracy resolve on a war, a general must head the army. It is only by a constitution that the *abstraction*—the state—attains life and actuality; but this involves the distinction between those who command and those who obey.—Yet obedience seems inconsistent with liberty, and those who command appear to do the very opposite of that which the fundamental notion of the state, viz., that of freedom, requires. It is, however, urged that,—though the distinction between commanding and obeying is absolutely necessary, because affairs could not go on without it—and indeed this seems only a compulsory limitation, external to and even contravening freedom in the abstract—the constitution should be at least so framed, that the citizens may obey as little as possible, and the smallest modicum of free volition be left to the commands of the superiors;—that the substance of that for which subordination is necessary, even in its most important bearings, should be decided and resolved on by the people—by the will of many or of all the citizens; though it is supposed to be thereby provided that the state should be possessed of vigour and strength as an actuality—an individual unity.—The primary consideration is, then, the distinction between the governing and the governed, and political constitutions in the abstract have been rightly divided into monarchy, aristocracy, and democracy; which gives occasion, however, to the remark that monarchy itself must be further divided into despotism and monarchy proper; that in all the divisions to which the leading notion gives rise, only the generic character is to be made prominent,—it being not intended thereby that the particular category under review should be exhausted as a form, order, or kind in its *concrete* development. But especially it must be observed, that the above-mentioned divisions admit of a multitude of particular modifications,—not only such as lie within the limits of those classes themselves,—but also such as are mixtures of several of these essentially distinct classes, and which are consequently misshapen, unstable, and inconsistent forms. In such a collision, the concerning question is, what is the *best constitution;* that is, by what arrangement, organisation, or mechanism of the power of the state its object can be most surely attained. This object may indeed be variously understood; for instance, as the calm enjoyment of life on the part of the citizens, or as universal happiness. Such aims have suggested the so-called ideals of constitutions, and,—as a particular branch of the subject,—ideals of the education of princes (Fénelon), or of the governing body—the aristocracy at large (Plato); for the chief point they treat of is the condition of those subjects who stand at the head of affairs; and in these ideals the concrete details of political organisation are not at all considered. The enquiry into the best constitution is frequently treated as if not only the theory were an affair of subjective independent conviction, but as if the introduction of a constitution recognised as the best, —or as superior to others,—could be the result of a resolve adopted in this theoretical manner; as if the form of a constitution were a matter of free choice, determined by nothing else but reflection. Of this artless fashion was that deliberation,—not indeed of the Persian *people*, but of the Persian *grandees*, who had conspired to overthrow the pseudo-Smerdis and the Magi, after their undertaking had succeeded, and when there was no scion of the royal family living,—as to what constitution they should introduce into Persia; and Herodotus gives an equally naïve account of this deliberation.

In the present day, the constitution of a country and people is not represented as so entirely dependent on free and deliberate choice. The fundamental but abstractly (and therefore imperfectly) entertained conception of freedom, has resulted in the republic being very generally regarded—in *theory*—as the only just and true political constitution. Many even, who occupy elevated official positions under monarchical constitutions—so far from being opposed to this idea—are actually its supporters; only they see that such a constitution, though the best, cannot be realised under all circumstances; and that—while men are what they are—we must be satisfied with less freedom; the monarchical constitution—under the given circumstances, and the present moral condition of the people—being even regarded as the most advantageous. In this view also, the necessity of a particular constitution is made to depend on the condition of the people in such a way as if the latter were non-essential and accidental. This representation is founded on the distinction which the reflective understanding makes between a notion and the corresponding reality; holding to an abstract and consequently untrue notion; not grasping it in its completeness, or—which is virtually, though not in point of form, the same—not taking a concrete view of a people and a state. We shall have to shew further on, that the constitution adopted by a people makes one substance—one spirit—with its religion, its art and philosophy, or, at least, with its conceptions and thoughts —its culture generally; not to expatiate upon the additional influences, *ab extrâ,* of climate, of neighbours, of its place in the world. A state is an individual totality, of which you cannot select any particular side, although a supremely important one, such as its political constitution; and deliberate and decide respecting it in that isolated form. Not only is that constitution most intimately connected with and dependent on those other spiritual forces; but the form of the entire moral and intellectual individuality— comprising all the forces it embodies—is only a step in the development of the grand whole,—with its place preappointed in the process; a fact which gives the highest sanction to the constitution in question, and establishes its absolute necessity.—The origin of a state involves imperious lordship on the one hand, instinctive submission on the other. But even obedience—lordly power, and the fear inspired by a ruler—in itself implies some degree of voluntary connection. Even in barbarous states this is the case; it is not the isolated will of individuals that prevails; individual pretensions are relinquished, and the general will is the essential bond of political union. This unity of the general and the particular is the Idea itself, manifesting itself as a *state,* and which subsequently undergoes further development within itself. The abstract yet necessitated process in the development of truly independent states is as follows:—They begin with regal power, whether of patriarchal or military origin. In the next phase, particularity and individuality assert themselves in the form of aristocracy and democracy. Lastly, we have the subjection of these separate interests to a single power; but which can be absolutely none other than one outside of which those spheres have an independent position, viz., the monarchical. Two phases of royalty, therefore, must be distinguished,—a primary and a secondary one. This process is necessitated, so that the form of government assigned to a particular stage of development *must* present itself: it is therefore no matter of choice, but is that form which is adapted to the spirit of the people.

In a constitution the main feature of interest is the self-development of the *rational,* that is, the *political* condition of a people; the setting free of the successive elements of the Idea: so that the several powers in the state manifest themselves as separate,—attain their appropriate and special perfection,—and yet in this independent condition, work together for one object, and are held together by it—*i.e.,* form an organic whole. The state is thus the embodiment of rational freedom, realising and recognising itself in an objective form. For its objective consists in this,—that its successive stages are not merely ideal, but are present in an appropriate reality; and that in their separate and several working, they are absolutely merged in that agency by which the totality—the soul—the individual unity—is produced, and of which it is the result.

The state is the idea of Spirit in the external manifestation of human will and its freedom. It is to the state, therefore, that change in the aspect of history indissolubly attaches itself; and the successive phases of the Idea manifest themselves in it as distinct political *principles.* The constitutions under which world-historical peoples have reached their culmination, are peculiar to them; and therefore do not present a generally applicable political basis. . . . The ancient and the modern have not their essential principle in common. Abstract definitions and dogmas respecting just government,—importing that intelligence and virtue ought to bear sway—are, indeed, common to both. But nothing is so absurd as to look to Greeks,

Romans, or Orientals, for models for the political arrangements of our time. From the East may be derived beautiful pictures of a patriarchal condition, of paternal government, and of devotion to it on the part of peoples; from Greeks and Romans, descriptions of popular liberty. Among the latter we find the idea of a free constitution admitting all the citizens to a share in deliberations and resolves respecting the affairs and laws of the commonwealth. In our times, too, this is its general acceptation; only with this modification, that—since our states are so large, and there are so many of "the many," the latter,—direct action being impossible,—should by the indirect method of elective substitution express their concurrence with resolves affecting the common weal; that is, that for legislative purposes generally, the people should be represented by deputies. The so-called representative constitution is that form of government with which we connect the idea of a free constitution, and this notion has become a rooted prejudice. On this theory people and government are separated. But there is a perversity in this antithesis; an ill-intentioned *ruse* designed to insinuate that the people are the totality of the state. Besides, the basis of this view is the principle of isolated individuality—the absolute validity of the subjective will—a dogma which we have already investigated. The great point is, that freedom in its ideal conception has not subjective will and caprice for its principle, but the recognition of the universal will; and that the process by which freedom is realised is the free development of its successive stages. The subjective will is a merely formal determination—a *carte blanche*—not including what it is that is willed. Only the *rational* will is that universal principle which independently determines and unfolds its own being, and develops its successive elemental phases as organic members. Of this Gothic-cathedral architecture the ancients knew nothing. . . .

Summing up what has been said of the state, we find that we have been led to call its vital principle, as actuating the individuals who compose it, —morality. The state, its laws, its arrangements, constitute the rights of its members; its natural features, its mountains, air, and waters, are *their* country, their fatherland, their outward material property; the history of this state, *their* deeds; what their ancestors have produced, belongs to them and lives in their memory. All is their possession, just as they are possessed by it; for it constitutes their existence, their being.

Their imagination is occupied with the ideas thus presented, while the adoption of these laws, and of a fatherland so conditioned, is the expression of their will. It is this matured totality which thus constitutes *one* being, the spirit of *one* people. To it the individual members belong; each unit is the son of his nation, and at the same time—in as far as the state to which he belongs is undergoing development—the son of his age. None remains behind it, still less advances beyond it. This spiritual being (the spirit of his time) is his; he is a representative of it; it is that in which he originated, and in which he lives. Among the Athenians the word Athens had a double import; suggesting primarily, a complex of political institutions, but no less, in the second place, that goddess who represented the spirit of the people and its unity.

This spirit of a people is a *determinate* and particular spirit, and is, as just stated, further modified by the degree of its historical development. This spirit, then, constitutes the basis and substance of those other forms of a nation's consciousness, which have been noticed. For Spirit in its self-consciousness must become an object of contemplation to itself, and objectivity involves, in the first instance, the rise of differences which make up a total of distinct spheres of objective spirit; in the same way as the soul exists only as the complex of its faculties, which in their form of concentration in a simple unity produce that soul. It is thus *One Individuality* which, presented in its essence as God, is honoured and enjoyed in *religion;* which is exhibited as an object of sensuous contemplation in *art;* and is apprehended as an intellectual conception, in *philosophy*. In virtue of the original identity of their essence, purport, and object, these various forms are inseparably united with the spirit of the state. Only in connection with this particular religion, can this particular political constitution exist; just as in such or such a state, such or such a philosophy or order of art.

The remark next in order is, that each particular national genius is to be treated as only one individual in the process of universal history. For that history is the exhibition of the divine, absolute development of Spirit in its highest forms,—that gradation by which it attains its truth and consciousness of itself. The forms which these grades of progress assume are the characteristic "national spirits" of history; the peculiar tenor of their moral life, of their government, their art, religion, and science. To realise these grades is the boundless impulse of the World-Spirit—the goal of its irresistible urging; for this division into organic members, and the full development of each, is its Idea.—Universal history is exclusively occupied with shewing how Spirit comes to a recognition and adoption of the truth: the dawn of knowledge appears; it begins to discover salient principles, and at last it arrives at full consciousness. . . .

The very essence of Spirit is activity; it actualizes its potentiality—makes itself its own deed, its own work—and thus becomes an object to itself; contemplates itself as an objective existence. Thus is it with the Spirit of a people: it is a Spirit having strictly defined characteristics, which erects itself into an objective world, that exists and persists in a particular religious form of worship, customs, constitution and political laws,—in the whole complex of its institutions,—in the events and transactions that make up its history. That is its work—that is what this particular nation *is*. Nations are what their deeds are. Every Englishman will say: We are the men who navigate the ocean, and have the commerce of the world; to whom the East Indies belong and their riches; who have a parliament, juries, &c. —The relation of the individual to that Spirit is that he appropriates to himself this substantial existence; that it becomes his character and capability, enabling him to have a definite place in the world—to be *something*. For he finds the being of the people to which he belongs an already established, firm world—objectively present to him—with which he has to incorporate himself. In this its work, therefore—its world—the spirit of the people enjoys its existence and finds its satisfaction.—A nation is moral—virtuous— vigorous—while it is engaged in realising its grand objects, and defends its work against external violence during the process of giving to its purposes an objective existence. The contradiction between its potential, subjective being—its inner aim and life—and its *actual* being is removed; it has attained full actuality, has itself objectively present to it. But this having been attained, the activity displayed by the Spirit of the people in question is no longer needed; it has its desire. The nation can still accomplish much in war and peace at home and abroad; but the living substantial soul itself may be said to have ceased its activity. The essential, supreme interest has consequently vanished from its life, for interest is present only where there is opposition. The nation lives the same kind of life as the individual when passing from maturity to old age,—in the enjoyment of itself,—in the satisfaction of being exactly what it desired and was able to attain. Although its imagination might have transcended that limit, it nevertheless abandoned any such aspirations as objects of *actual endeavour*, if the real world was less than favourable to their attainment—and restricted its aim by the conditions thus imposed. This mere *customary life* (the watch wound up and going on of itself) is that which brings on natural death. Custom is activity without opposition, for which there remains only a formal duration; in which the fulness and zest that originally characterised the aim of life is out of the question,—a merely external sensuous existence which has ceased to throw itself enthusiastically into its object. Thus perish individuals, thus perish peoples by a natural death; and though the latter may continue in being, it is an existence without intellect or vitality; having no need of its institutions, because the need for them is satisfied,—a political nullity and tedium. In order that a truly universal interest may arise, the spirit of a people must advance to the adoption of some new purpose: but whence can this new purpose originate? It would be a higher, more comprehensive conception of itself—a transcending of its principle—but this very act would involve a principle of a new order, a new national spirit.

Such a new principle does in fact enter into the spirit of a people that has arrived at full development and self-realisation; it dies not a simply natural death,—for it is not a mere single individual, but a spiritual, generic life; in its case natural death appears to imply destruction through its own agency. The reason of this difference from the single natural individual, is that the spirit of a people exists as a *genus,* and consequently carries within it its own negation, in the very generality which characterises it. A people can only die a violent death when it has become naturally dead in itself, as *e.g.,* the German imperial cities, the German imperial constitution.

It is not of the nature of the all-pervading Spirit to die this merely natural death; it does not simply sink into the senile life of mere custom, but—as being a national spirit belonging to universal history—attains to the consciousness of what its work is; it attains to a conception of itself. In fact, it is world-historical only in so far as a *universal principle* has lain in its fundamental element,—in its grand aims: only so far is the work which such a spirit produces, a moral, political organization. If it be mere desires that impel nations to activity, such deeds pass over without leaving a trace; or their traces are only ruin and destruction.

JOHANN GOTTLIEB FICHTE

FICHTE (1762–1814) was the son of a ribbon weaver and received an education as a result of the patronage of a neighboring nobleman. He fell under the influence of Kant and an early work, written in 1792, *Critique of All Revelation,* sounded so much like the great philosopher's that Fichte's future was assured. On the strength of it and other writings he was summoned to the chair of philosophy at Jena in 1794.

In his *Addresses to the German Nation,* delivered to an aroused public of German intellectuals during the winter of 1807–8, after the humiliating Treaty of Tilsit, Fichte pleaded for the establishment of a national system of education as the immediate means of unifying the German people. The system of education which he championed was intended to change the character of the Germans by habituating them to love and by creating the freedom and unity of the "fatherland." Fichte argued that the Germans alone among European peoples were capable of creating an integrated free culture for Europe. He transformed the doctrines and ideals of the Enlightenment into romantic nationalism, teaching the Germans to believe that they alone could achieve "perfect" freedom and unity.

Freedom, to Fichte, is the consciousness of one's true vocation, which consists in the struggle for perfection. By identifying his will with that of a greater personality, the Nation, man can lay hold of something infinite and eternal; for a nation is a reflection of the Divine Will. Hence the importance of Fichte's emphasis (in the selections that follow) on "the devouring flame of higher patriotism, which embraces the nation as the vestures of the eternal." A nation or people is to be distinguished from a government: governments, not peoples, change and are conquered. The flavor of Fichte's romanticism emerges vividly in *The Vocation of Man,* and in almost any of its passages: "To stand, cold and unmoved, amid the current of events, a passive mirror of fugitive and passing phenomena,—this existence is insupportable to me; I scorn and detest it. I will love:—I will lose myself in sympathy;—I will know the joy and the grief of life. . . . I will rejoice when I have done right, I will grieve when I have done wrong; and even this sorrow shall be sweet to me, for it is a chord of sympathy,—a pledge of future amendment. In love only there is life; without it is death and annihilation."

The passages reprinted are from the *Addresses,* translated from the German by R. F. Jones and G. H. Turnbull (Chicago, Open Court Publishing Company, 1922).

ADDRESSES TO THE GERMAN NATION

GERMAN CHARACTERISTICS

THE ATTEMPT at complete emancipation from all belief in external authority was the right objective of the strife raging in foreign countries, and this attempt acted as a fresh stimulus to the Germans, from whom it had first proceeded by means of the reformation of the Church. It is true that second-rate and unoriginal minds among us simply repeated this foreign doctrine —better the foreign doctrine, it seems, than the doctrine of their fellow-countrymen, though this was to be had just as easily; the reason being that they took the former to be more distinguished—and these minds tried to convince themselves about it, so far as that was possible. But where the independent German spirit was astir, the sensuous was not enough, and there arose the problem of discovering the supersensuous (which is, of course, not to be believed in on external authority) in the reason itself, and thus of creating for the first time true philosophy by making free thought the source of independent truth, as it should be. To that end Leibniz strove in his conflict with that foreign philosophy; and the end was attained by the true founder of modern German philosophy,[1] not without a confession of having been aroused to it by the utterance of a foreigner, which had, however, been taken more profoundly than it had been intended. Since that time the problem has been completely solved among us, and philosophy has been perfected. One must be content for the present with stating this as a fact, until an age comes which comprehends it. . . .

We have seen how the inhabitants of a foreign country [2] took up lightly, and with fervent daring, another problem of reason and philosophy for the modern world—the establishment of the perfect State. But, shortly afterwards, they abandoned this task so completely that they are compelled by their present condition to condemn the very thought of the problem as a crime, and they had to use every means to delete, if possible, those efforts from the annals of their history. The reason for this result is as clear as day; the State in accordance with reason cannot be built up by artificial measures from whatever material may be at hand; on the contrary, the nation must first be trained and educated up to it. Only the nation which has first solved in actual practice the problem of educating perfect men will then solve also the problem of the perfect State. . . .

[1] [Kant, who confessed to having been roused from his "dogmatic slumber" by Hume.]
[2] [The reference is to the French Revolution.]

In what has been said you have a clear conspectus of the whole history of culture in the modern world, and of the never-varying relationship of the different parts of the modern world to the world of antiquity. True religion, in the form of Christianity, was the germ of the modern world; and the task of the latter may be summed up as follows: to make this religion permeate the previous culture of antiquity and thereby to spiritualize and hallow it. The first step on this path was to rid this religion of the external respect of form which robbed it of freedom, and to introduce into it also the free-thinking of antiquity. Foreign countries provided the stimulus to this step; the German took the step. The second step, which is really the continuation and completion of the first, namely, to discover in our own selves this religion, and with it all wisdom—this, too, was prepared by foreign countries and completed by the German. The next step forward that we have to make in the plan of eternity is to educate the nation to perfect manhood. Without this, the philosophy that has been won will never be widely comprehended, much less will it be generally applicable in life. On the other hand, and in the same way, the art of education will never attain complete clearness in itself without philosophy. Hence, there is an interaction between the two, and either without the other is incomplete and unserviceable. If only because the German has hitherto brought to completion all the steps of culture and has been preserved in the modern world for that special purpose, it will be his work, too, in respect of education. But, when education has once been set in order, the same will follow easily with the other concerns of humanity.

This, then, is the actual relationship in which the German nation has hitherto stood with regard to the development of the human race in the modern age. We have still to throw more light upon an observation, which has already been made twice, as to the natural course of development which events have taken with our nation, viz., that in Germany all culture has proceeded from the people. That the reformation of the Church was first brought before the people, and that it succeeded only because it became their affair, we have already seen. But we have further to show that this single case was not an exception; it has, on the contrary, been the rule.

The Germans who remained in the motherland had retained all the virtues of which their country had formerly been the home—loyalty, uprightness, honor, and simplicity; but of training to a higher and intellectual life they had received no more than could be brought by the Christianity of that period and its teachers to men whose dwellings were scattered. This was but little: hence, they were not so advanced as their racial kinsmen who had emigrated. They were in fact good and honest, it is true, but none the less semi-barbarians. There arose among them, however, cities erected by members of the people. In these cities every branch of culture quickly developed into the fairest bloom. In them arose civic constitutions and organizations which, though but on a small scale, were none the less of high excellence; and, proceeding from them, a picture of order and a love of it spread throughout the rest of the country. Their extensive commerce helped to discover the world. Their league was feared by kings. The monuments of their architecture are standing at the present day and have defied the ravages of centuries; before them posterity stands in admiration and confesses its own impotence.

It is not my intention to compare these burghers of the German imperial cities in the Middle Ages with the other estates of the same period, nor to ask what was being done at that time by the nobles and the princes. But, in comparison with the other Teutonic nations—leaving out of account some districts of Italy, and in the fine arts the Germans did not lag behind even these, whereas in the useful arts they surpassed them and became their teachers —leaving these out of account, I say that the German burghers were the civilized people, and the others the barbarians. The history of Germany, of German might, German enterprise and inventions, of German monuments and the German spirit—the history of all these things during that period is nothing but the history of those cities; and everything else, for example the mortgaging of petty territories and their subsequent redemption and so on, is unworthy of mention. Moreover, this period is the only one in German history in which this nation is famous and brilliant, and holds the rank to which, as the parent stock, it is entitled. As soon as its bloom is destroyed by the avarice and tyranny of princes, and as soon as its freedom is trodden underfoot, the whole nation gradually sinks lower and lower, until the condition is reached in which we are at present. But, as Germany sinks, the rest of Europe is seen to sink with it, if we regard, not the mere external appearance, but the soul.

The decisive influence of this burgher class, which was in fact the ruling power, upon the development of the German imperial constitution, upon the reformation of the Church, and upon everything that ever characterized the German nation and thence took its way abroad, is everywhere unmistakable; and it can be proved that everything which is still worthy of honor among the Germans has arisen in its midst.

In what spirit did this German burgher class bring forth and enjoy this period of bloom? In the spirit of piety, of honor, of modesty, and of the sense of community. For themselves they needed little; for public enterprises they set no limits to their expenditure. Seldom does the name of an individual stand out or distinguish itself, for they were all of like mind and alike in sacrifice for the common weal. Under precisely the same external conditions as in

Germany, free cities had arisen in Italy also. Compare the histories of both; contrast the continual disorders, the internal conflicts, nay, even wars, the constant change of constitutions and rulers in the latter with the peaceful unity and concord in the former. How could it be more clearly demonstrated that there must have been an inward difference in the disposition of the two nations? The German nation is the only one among the neo-European nations that has shown in practice, by the example of its burgher class for centuries, that it is capable of enduring a republican constitution.

Of the separate and special means of once more raising the German spirit a very powerful one would be in our hands if we had a soul-stirring history of the Germans in that period—one that would become a book for the nation and for the people, just as the Bible and the hymn-book are now, until the time came when we ourselves had again achieved something worthy of record. But such a history should not set forth deeds and events after the fashion of a chronicle; it should transport us by its fascinating power, without any effort or clear consciousness on our part, into the very midst of the life of that time, so that we ourselves should seem to be walking and standing and deciding and acting with them. This it should do, not by means of childish and trumpery fabrications, as so many historical novels have done, but by the truth; and it should make those deeds and events visible manifestations of the life of that time. Such a work, indeed, could only be the fruit of extensive knowledge and of investigations that have perhaps, never yet been made; but the author should spare us the exhibition of this knowledge and these investigations, and simply lay the ripened fruit before us in the language of the present day and in a manner that every German without exception could understand. In addition to this historical knowledge, such a work would command a high degree of philosophical spirit, which should display itself just as little, and above all things a faithful and loving disposition.

That age was the nation's youthful dream, within a narrow sphere, of its future deeds and conflicts and victories, and the prophecy of what it would be once it had perfected its strength. Evil associations and the seductive power of vanity have swept the growing nation into spheres which are not its own; and, because it there sought glory too, it stands to-day covered with shame and fighting for its very life. But has it indeed grown old and feeble? Has not the well of original life continued to flow for it, as for no other nation, since then and until to-day? Can those prophecies of its youthful nations and by the plan of civilization for all humanity—can they remain unfulfilled? Impossible! O, that someone would bring back this nation from its false path, and in the mirror of its youthful dreams show it its true disposition and its true vocation! There let it stand and ponder, until it develops the power to take up its vocation with a mighty hand. May this challenge be of some avail in bringing out right soon a German man equipped to perform this preliminary task! . . .

PEOPLE AND FATHERLAND

People and fatherland in this sense, as a support and guarantee of eternity on earth and as that which can be eternal here below, far transcend the State in the ordinary sense of the word, viz., the social order as comprehended by mere intellectual conception and as established and maintained under the guidance of this conception. The aim of the State is positive law, internal peace, and a condition of affairs in which everyone may by diligence earn his daily bread and satisfy the needs of his material existence, so long as God permits him to live. All this is only a means, a condition, and a framework for what love of fatherland really wants, viz., that the eternal and the divine may blossom in the world and never cease to become more and more pure, perfect, and excellent. That is why this love of fatherland must itself govern the State and be the supreme, final, and absolute authority. Its first exercise of this be to limit the State's choice of means to secure its immediate object —internal peace. To attain this object, the natural freedom of the individual must, of course, be limited in many ways. If the only consideration and intention in regard to individuals were to secure internal peace, it would be well to limit that liberty as much as possible, to bring all their activities under a uniform rule, and to keep them under unceasing supervision. Even supposing such strictness were unnecessary, it could at any rate do no harm, if this were the sole object. It is only the higher view of the human race and of peoples which extends this narrow calculation. Freedom, including freedom in the activities of external life, is the soil in which higher culture germinates; a legislation which keeps the higher culture in view will allow to freedom as wide a field as possible, even at the risk of securing a smaller degree of uniform peace and quietness, and of making the work of government a little harder and more troublesome.

To illustrate this by an example. It has happened that nations have been told to their face that they do not need so much freedom as many other nations do. It may even be that the form in which the opinion is expressed is considerate and mild, if what is really meant is that the particular nation would be quite unable to stand so much freedom, and that nothing but extreme severity could prevent its members from destroying each other. But when the words are taken as meaning what they say, they are true only on the supposition that such a nation is thoroughly incapable of hav-

ing original life or even the impulse towards it. Such a nation—if a nation
could exist in which there were not even a few men of noble mind to make
an exception to the general rule—would in fact need no freedom at all,
for this is needed only for the higher purposes that transcend the State. It
needs only to be tamed and trained, so that the individuals may live peaceably with each other and that the whole may be made into an efficient instrument for arbitrary purposes in which the nation as such has no part.
Whether this can be said with truth of any nation at all we may leave
undecided; this much is clear, that an original people needs freedom, that
this is the security for its continuance as an original people, and that, as it
goes on, it is able to stand an ever-increasing degree of freedom without
the slightest danger. This is the first matter in respect of which love of
fatherland must govern the State itself.

Then, too, it must be love of fatherland that governs the State by placing
before it a higher object than the usual one of maintaining internal peace,
property, personal freedom, and the life and well-being of all. For this
higher object alone, and with no other intention, does the State assemble
an armed force. When the question arises of making use of this, when the
call comes to stake everything that the State, in the narrow conception of
the word, sets before itself as object, viz., property, personal freedom, life,
and well-being, nay, even the continued existence of the State itself; when
the call comes to make an original decision with responsibility to God
alone, and without a clear and reasonable idea that what is intended will
surely be attained—for this is never possible in such matters—then, and
then only, does there live at the helm of the State a truly original and
primary life, and at this point, and not before, the true sovereign rights of
government enter, like God, to hazard the lower life for the sake of the
higher. In the maintenance of the traditional constitution, the laws, and
civil prosperity there is absolutely no real true life and no original decision.
Conditions and circumstances, and legislators perhaps long since dead, have
created these things; succeeding ages go on faithfully in the paths marked
out, and so in fact they have no public life of their own; they merely repeat
a life that once existed. In such times there is no need of any real government. But, when this regular course is endangered, and it is a question of
making decisions in new and unprecedented cases, then there is need of a
life that lives of itself. What spirit is it that in such cases may place itself
at the helm, that can make its own decisions with sureness and certainty,
untroubled by any hesitation? What spirit has an undisputed right to
summon and to order everyone concerned, whether he himself be willing
or not, and to compel anyone who resists, to risk everything including his

life? Not the spirit of the peaceful citizen's love for the constitution and the laws, but the devouring flame of higher patriotism, which embraces the nation as the vestures of the eternal, for which the noble-minded man joyfully sacrifices himself, and the ignoble man, who only exists for the sake of the other, must likewise sacrifice himself. It is not that love of the citizen for the constitution; that love is quite unable to achieve this, so long as it remains on the level of the understanding. . . .

In this belief our earliest common forefathers, the original stock of the new culture, the Germans, as the Romans called them, bravely resisted the on-coming world-dominion of the Romans. Did they not have before their eyes the greater brilliance of the Roman provinces next to them and the more refined enjoyments in those provinces, to say nothing of laws and judges' seats and lictors' axes and rods in superfluity? Were not the Romans willing enough to let them share in all these blessings? In the case of several of their own princes, who did no more than intimate that war against such benefactors of mankind was rebellion, did they not experience proofs of the belauded Roman clemency? To those who submitted the Romans gave marks of distinction in the form of kingly titles, high commands in their armies, and Roman fillets; and if they were driven out by their countrymen, did not the Romans provide for them a place of refuge and a means of subsistence in their colonies? Had they no appreciation of the advantages of Roman civilization, e.g., of the superior organization of their armies, in which even an Arminius did not disdain to learn the trade of war? They cannot be charged with ignorance or lack of consideration of any one of these things. Their descendants, as soon as they could do so without losing their freedom, even assimilated Roman culture, so far as this was possible without losing their individuality. Why, then, did they fight for several generations in bloody wars, that broke out again and again with ever renewed force? A Roman writer puts the following expression into the mouth of their leaders: "What was left for them to do, except to maintain their freedom or else to die before they became slaves." Freedom to them meant just this: remaining Germans and continuing to settle their own affairs independently and in accordance with the original spirit of their race, going on with their development in accordance with the same spirit, and propagating this independence in their posterity. All those blessings which the Romans offered them meant slavery to them, because then they would have to become something that was not German, they would have to become half Roman. They assumed as a matter of course that every man would rather die than become half a Roman, and that a true German could only want to live in order to be, and to remain, just a German and to bring up his children as Germans. . . .

THE PRESERVATION OF THE GERMAN PEOPLE

The notorious doctrine of a balance of power was artificially maintained among European states. If Christian Europe had remained one, as it ought to be and as it originally was, there would never have been any occasion to think of such a thing. That which is one rests upon itself and supports itself, and does not split up into conflicting forces which must be brought to an equilibrium. Only when Europe became divided and without a law did the thought of a balance acquire a meaning from necessity. To this Europe, divided and without a law, Germany did not belong. If only Germany at any rate had remained one, it would have rested on itself in the centre of the civilized world like the sun in the centre of the universe; it would have kept itself at peace, and with itself the adjacent countries; and without any artificial measures it would have kept everything in equilibrium by the mere fact of its natural existence. It was only the deceit of foreign countries that dragged Germany into their own lawlessness and their own disputes; it was they who taught Germany the treacherous notion of the balance of power, for they knew it to be one of the most effective means of deluding Germany as to its own true advantage and of keeping it in that state of delusion. This aim is now sufficiently attained, and the result that was intended is now complete before our eyes. Even if we cannot do away with this result, why should we not at any rate extirpate the source of it in our own understanding, which is now almost the only thing over which we still have sovereign power? Why should the old dream still be placed before our eyes, now that disaster has awakened us from sleep? Why should we not now at any rate see the truth and perceive the only means that could have saved us? Perhaps our descendants may do what we see ought to be done, just as we now suffer because our fathers dreamed. Let us understand that the conception of an equilibrium to be artificially maintained might have been a consoling dream for foreign countries amid the guilt and evil that oppressed them; but that this conception, being an entirely foreign product, ought never to have taken root in the mind of a German, and that the Germans ought never to have been so situated that it could take root among them. Let us understand that now at any rate we must perceive the utter worthlessness of such a conception, and must see that the salvation of all is to be found, not in it, but solely in the unity of the Germans among themselves.

Just as foreign to the German is the freedom of the seas, which is so frequently preached in our days, whether what is intended be real freedom or merely the power to exclude everyone else from it. Throughout the course of centuries, while all other nations were in rivalry, the German showed little desire to participate in this freedom to any great extent, and he will never do so. Moreover, he is not in need of it. The abundant supplies of his own land, together with his own diligence, afford him all that is needed in the life of a civilized man; nor does he lack skill in the art of making his resources serve that purpose. As for acquiring the only true advantage that world-trade brings in its train, viz., the increase in scientific knowledge of the earth and its inhabitants, his own scientific spirit will not let him lack a means of exchange. O, if only his kindly fortune had preserved the German from indirect participation in the booty of other worlds, as it preserved him from direct participation! If only we had not been led by our credulity, and by the craving for a life as fine and as distinguished as that of other peoples, to make necessaries of the wares produced in foreign parts which we could do without; if only we had made conditions tolerable for our free fellow-citizen in regard to the wares we can less easily do without, instead of wishing to draw a profit from the sweat and blood of a poor slave across the seas! Then, at any rate, we should not ourselves have furnished the pretext for our present fate; war would not have been waged against us as purchasers, nor would we have been ruined because we are a market-place. Almost ten years ago, before anyone could foresee what has since happened, the Germans were advised [3] to make themselves independent of world-trade, and to turn themselves into a closed commercial State. This proposal ran counter to our habits, and especially to our idolatrous veneration of coined metals; it was passionately attacked and thrust aside. Since then we have been learning, in dishonor and under the compulsion of a foreign power, to do without those things, and far more than those things, which we then protested we could not do without, though we might have done so then in freedom and with the greatest honor to ourselves. O, that we might seize this opportunity, since enjoyment at least is not corrupting us, to correct our ideas once for all! O, that we might at last see that all those swindling theories about world-trade and manufacturing for the world-market, though they suit the foreigner and form part of the weapons with which he has always made war on us, have no application to the Germans; and that, next to the unity of the Germans among themselves, their internal autonomy and commercial independence form the second means for their salvation, and through them for the salvation of Europe!

[3] [In 1800 by Fichte himself, in *Der geschlossene Handelsstaat* (The Closed Commercial State).]

THE JEWS IN REVOLUTIONARY FRANCE

O N August 27, 1789, the revolutionary National Assembly promulgated the *Declaration of the Rights of Man and of the Citizen*. For the first time in European history, the conception of the citizen was to become civic and secular, divorced from theological overtones or religious commitments. The first group to be favorably affected by this change was the Jews.

For centuries the Jews had been regarded as aliens in every country in which they settled. They formed independent communities, self-sufficient and self-governing, and paid heavy taxes and fines to gain protection from persecution and oppression—frequently to no avail. Nowhere did they enjoy formal rights and the concomitant responsibilities of citizenship, although nations like the Netherlands and Cromwell's England were distinguished for their more humane and tolerant treatment of the Jews. When the National Assembly enfranchised the Jews on September 28, 1791, according them complete rights of citizenship, they found themselves faced with the necessity of defining their relationship to the modern state and unburdening themselves of the heritage of centuries of persecution, inferior status, and isolation.

The successful advance of the revolutionary armies heralded the advance of the new doctrines of religious freedom. Among the German states in particular, the conquests of Napoleon assisted the Jews in their struggle for religious toleration and political rights which had been begun in the previous generation. After his assumption of the Imperial title, however, Napoleon's policy toward the Jews became less consistent.

Napoleon's first pronouncement concerning the Jews came over the problem of Jewish creditors in Alsace and their relationship to their Gentile debtors. On April 30, 1806, Napoleon issued an anti-Semitic statement, asserting the danger of permitting so great a number of Jews—who formed a state within a state —to live so close to the borders of the enemy. Within a week he had retreated from this view, however, and, after issuing a mild statement in which he declared a year's moratorium on all debts to Jews on the Rhine, he affirmed his opposition to any persecution of the Jews. On May 30 he issued a decree summoning an Assembly of Jewish Notables to convene in Paris.

The first session of the Assembly was called by the Emperor for July 26, 1806 —a Saturday, and consequently a day on which religious Jews are forbidden to undertake business ventures or new activities of any sort. Nevertheless, the meeting was held and discussion begun immediately on the twelve questions submitted by the Emperor for review by the Assembly. The answers were agreed upon unanimously by the group, which tried consistently to affirm its patriotism to France and loyalty to the Emperor. The Emperor's Commissioner, Molé, expressed his satisfaction with the answers submitted and the spirit in which the discussions were conducted. In order to invest these answers with sanctity and binding force for the Jewish community, however, the Emperor determined to convene a "Grand Sanhedrin." Modeled upon the ancient tribunal of the Jews in Jerusalem in pre-Christian times, the French Sanhedrin was to be made up of seventy-one members, two thirds of them rabbis, one third lay leaders. The members of the Sanhedrin were elected by the Assembly, which was also instructed to invite delegates from all Jewish communities in Europe.

The Sanhedrin was convened on February 9, 1807, under the presidency of Rabbi David Sinzheim of Strasbourg. In addition to the elected members, there were delegates from congregations in Italy, Amsterdam, and the Confederation of the Rhine. The meetings were conducted partly in French and partly in Hebrew, and the answers of the Assembly of Notables to the Emperor's questions were passed as "laws" without dissent. The Sanhedrin was dissolved on March 9, and the Assembly dissolved a month later, after submitting its report to the Emperor.

On March 17, 1808, Napoleon issued a decree providing for Jewish "consistories": Jewish communities were to be organized as corporate bodies on a legal basis, with a defined hierarchical system, under the Emperor's aegis. This arrangement provided for the same centralized organization of religion under his own control which Napoleon had prescribed for French Catholics and Protestants. Despite his assertions of tolerance and generosity, and his acceptance of the answers of the Assembly, Napoleon issued a second decree on that day which restricted the legal rights of the Jews, excluded them from certain businesses, and limited the size of Jewish settlements in Germany.

The following passages, illustrating the difficulty of reconciling a traditional corporate identity with the new conception of loyalty to a nation, has been taken from the 1807 translation by M. Diogene Taina of the *Transactions of the Parisian Sanhedrin*.

๛

TRANSACTIONS OF THE PARISIAN SANHEDRIM

FROM A LETTER OF M. BERR-ISAAC-BERR TO HIS BRETHREN, IN 1791,

ON THE RIGHTS OF ACTIVE CITIZENS BEING GRANTED TO THE JEWS

We must then, dear brethren, strongly bear this truth in our minds, that till such a time as we work a change in our manners, in our habits, in short; in our whole education, we cannot expect to be placed by the esteem of our fellow citizens in any of those situations in which we can give signal proofs of that glowing patriotism so long cherished in our bosoms. God forbid that I should mean anything derogatory to our professed religion, or to our established form of worship; far from me the idea of proposing any innovation in them. I should consider as monsters those among us, who, from the prospect of some advantages, they might expect from the new constitution, would presume to alter the dogmas of their religion. If, during our tribulations, we have derived some consolation from our strict adherence to our religion, how much more are we bound to remain firmly attached to it now, when we are reaping the fruits of our perseverance and of our attachment to our religious worship, when we behold that of all ancient nations we are the only one who has been able to withstand the heavy tides of misfortune, succeeding each other for centuries! And now, expressedly chosen by the French constitution, should we, at the first dawn of liberty, prove refractory to our laws, after having remained faithful to them, during eighteen centuries of persecution? No; I shall not believe any of my brethren capable of this. I shall not therefore address you on this head, not doubting but we all perfectly agree on the fundamental point. But I cannot too often repeat to you how absolutely necessary it is for us to divest ourselves entirely of the narrow spirit, of *Corporation* and *Congregation*, in all civil and political matters, not immediately connected with our spiritual laws; in these things we must absolutely appear simply as individuals, as Frenchmen, guided only by a true patriotism and by the general good of the nation; to know how to risk our lives and fortunes for the defence of the country, to make ourselves useful to our fellow citizens, to deserve their esteem and their friendship, to join our efforts to theirs in maintaining public tranquility, on which that of individuals depends; such ought to be the principal aim of our daily employment; and as we are not yet able to fulfil those noble functions ourselves, we must turn our minds to the means necessary to be acquired, and, above all, in our attention on our children, and procure for them all the necessary instructions. . . .

We had the privilege of forming a distinct body of people and a separate community; but this carried with it the exclusion from all other corporations, and the submission to particular taxes, much above our means and our resources, and arbitrarily imposed. If a member of that community was accused of any misdemeanors whatever, the reproaches and the humiliation fell on the whole, we were exempt from militia and from public works, but it was because we were deemed unworthy of it; and to palliate the injustice of such proceedings, we were exempted, on condition of paying in money three times the value of such services, &c. It is certainly no hard matter to give up such privileges. . . .

The first of our parental cares must be, no doubt, to see that our children, in preference to all things, learn the holy Bible in the very language in which it was penned by the divine hand, and transmitted to us by Moses our lawgiver; let them, then, know perfectly the Hebrew language, which notwithstanding its penury, is the key of all other languages, and must be, for us in particular, the first object of our studies. But to this day do we really understand it? Have we masters able to explain it to us, and to give us its true meaning in a faithful translation? Before we possessed a real treasure in *the translation of the Bible in German by Mendelshon,* our children learnt Hebrew from masters who explained it in a dialect which neither the tutor nor the pupil could understand. Each master had his method of translating and his manner of speaking, according to the country he came from; hardly could we have met three children, having learnt from three different masters, who would have explained in the same manner, in the same language, or with the same pronunciation the clearest passage of the holy writings.

Even now that we possess the sublime translation of Mendelshon, we have but very few teachers who are truly masters of the two languages into which the Bible is written and translated. We see now and then some scholars from Berlin, who come to this country, they are are too few and too expensive to allow many of us to avail themselves of their instructions. It is however indispensable that, while we are getting our children instructed in the principles of their religion in the original language, we should procure for them an explanation in the ordinary language, which they hear and speak from their infancy.

It appears to me that were it possible to get our children taught the holy Bible by a French version, instead of a German one, provided such a version should be as faithful as that of the immortal Mendelshon, a great and material advantage would result from the change: they would have only two languages to learn at the same time, Hebrew and French; whereas now they are obliged to learn three at the same time, Hebrew, German, and French. Accordingly, this last, which ought to be their mother tongue, since they are reared with and among Frenchmen, has always been the language in which they have made the least proficiency, and which very often they scarcely understand. It is only when compelled by necessity to speak and to be understood by their neighbours that they begin to blunder some inarticulate words; from hence proceeds this other inconveniency, that those among us who have felt early enough the usefulness of the French language, and have acquired the habit of speaking it with facility, cannot, however, get rid of a German or other foreign accents. Their phrases, too, are generally incorrect. I even must say myself, that while I am thus addressing you in French, I feel my want of experience and of proficiency in that language, which I have however chosen in preference, to prove to you, that Jews may commune together and confer with one another in that language, on all topics even on religious matters, and that it is entirely in our power to avoid encumbering the minds of our youth with the useless study of foreign languages. Have we not the ex- ample of the Jews of Asia, the most devout and the most scrupulous of our brethren, who read and write only Hebrew and the language of their country? Why should we continue to bear the name of German or Polish Jews, while we are happily French Jews? . . . .

Moreover, dear brethren, when we have fulfilled our first duty towards our children; when once they are thoroughly initiated in the principles and spirit of our religion, we may, without apprehension of danger, avail our- selves of the resources offered to us by our generous countrymen, by send- ing them to share the advantages of national education in the public schools, certainly they will not be thwarted in their religious opinions; and once easy on that score, they soon will become beloved among their comrades, by sharing their emulation and their wishes of deserving the approbation of their superiors. By means of that union in schools, our children, like those of our fellow-citizens, will remark from their tender youth that neither opinions, nor difference of religion, are a bar to fraternal love; and that every one naturally embracing and following the religion of his fathers, all may, in fulfilling their religious duties, fulfil also those of citizenship; from that, all aversion, all hatred, all antipathy between them will be done away. In proportion as they increase in years, those ties of friendship and of fraternity will be drawn closer, in whatever is of social and political nature, not contrary to the dogmas of religion. . . .

IMPERIAL DECREE, GIVEN AT THE PALACE OF ST. CLOUD, MAY 30, 1806

Napoleon, Emperor of the French, King of Italy.

On the report which has been made to us, that in many of the northern departments of our empire, certain Jews, following no other profession than that of usurers, have, by the accumulation of the most enormous interests, reduced many husbandmen of these districts to the greatest dis- tress:

We have thought it incumbent on us to lend our assistance to those of our subjects whom rapacity may have reduced to these hard extremities.

These circumstances have, at the same time, pointed out to us the urgent necessity of reviving, among individuals of the Jewish persuasion residing in our dominions, sentiments of civil morality, which, unfortunately, have been stifled in many of them by the abject state in which they have long languished, and which it is not our intention either to maintain, or to renew.

To carry this design into execution, we have determined to call together an assembly of the principal Jews, and to make our intentions known to them by commissioners whom we shall name for that purpose, and who shall, at the same time, collect their opinions as to the means they deem the fittest, to reestablish among the brethren the exercise of mechanical arts and useful professions, in order to replace, by an honest industry, the shameful resources to which many of them resorted, from generation to generation, these many centuries. . . .

QUESTIONS PROPOSED TO THE ASSEMBLY OF THE JEWS BY THE COM-
MISSIONERS NAMED BY HIS MAJESTY THE EMPEROR AND KING, TO
TRANSACT WHATEVER CONCERNS THEM

1st. Is it lawful for Jews to marry more than one wife?

2nd. Is divorce allowed by the Jewish religion?

Is divorce valid, although not pronounced by courts of Justice, and by virtue of laws in contradiction with the French code?

3d. Can a Jewess marry a Christian, or a Jew a Christian woman?

Or has the law ordered that the Jews should only intermarry among themselves?

4th. In the eyes of Jews are Frenchmen considered as brethren or as strangers?

5th. In either case what conduct does their law prescribe towards Frenchmen not of their religion?

6th. Do the Jews born in France, and treated by the law as French citizens, acknowledge France as their country?

Are they bound to defend it?

Are they bound to obey the laws, and to follow the directions of the civil code?

7th. What kind of Police-jurisdiction have the Rabbis among the Jews?

What judicial power do they exercise among them?

9th. Are the forms of the elections of the Rabbis and their police-ju-risdiction, regulated by the law, or are they only sanctioned by custom?

10th. Are there professions from which the Jews are excluded by their law?

11th. Does the law forbid the Jews from taking usury from their own brethren?

12th. Does it forbid or does it allow usury towards strangers?

During the reading of these questions, the assembly manifested by unan-imous and spontaneous emotions, how deeply it was affected by the doubt which the questions seemed to convey, as to the attachment of Frenchmen, following the law of Moses, for their fellow citizens, and for their country, and as to their sense of the duty by which they are bound to defend it.

The assembly was not able to conceal the emotions caused by the sixth question, in which it is asked of Jews born in France and treated by the law as French citizens, to acknowledge France as their country, and if they are bound to defend it. The whole assembly unanimously exclaimed,— *Even to death.* . . .

FROM A SPEECH BY M. MARG FOY, SEN[IOR] DEPUTY OF THE DEPARTMENT OF THE LOWER PYRENEES

. . . How sad would our situation be, if it were thought possible that France could be indifferent to us; or that a country which, in return for manifold benefits, has received our oaths of fidelity and love, could, for an instant, doubt our sincerity; that the French people could, in short, consider us as forming a particular body within the state! No, such a doubt cannot exist; or if it has existed, but for one moment, it must have been done away, when; by an energetic and spontaneous impulse, we all together manifested before the Commissioners of His Imperial and Royal Majesty, how dear and sacred France and Frenchmen were to our hearts. . . .

We will then say to His Majesty, "Yes, Sire, we can, according to religious principles, consider France as our country; share the rights of citizens of your empire; follow the dispositions of the civil code; and obey, in every thing, the will of the prince. Our duty is to defend the territory of France, to pay our share of the burthens of the state, and to use all the means in our power for the prosperity of the empire. The law of God commands whatever is just and good; it never can raise an obstacle to the obedience due to the laws; for although we have a different mode of worship, we are nevertheless, bound to fulfil all the honourable duties which constitute good citizens. . . .

FROM A DISCOURSE READ BY M. MOLÉ, ONE OF THE COMMISSIONERS OF HIS MAJESTY

His Majesty's intention is, that no plea shall be left to those who may refuse to become citizens; the free exercise of your religious worship and the full enjoyment of your political rights, are secured to you. But, in return for his gracious protection, His Majesty requires a religious pledge for the strict adherence to the principles contained in your answers. This assembly, constituted as it is now, could not of itself give such a security. Its answers, converted into decisions by another assembly, of a nature still more dignified and more religious, must find a place near the Talmud, and thus acquire, in the eyes of the Jews of all countries and of all ages, the greatest possible authority. It is also the only means left to you to meet the grand and generous views of His Majesty, and to impart, to all of your persuasion, the blessings of this new era.

The purity of your law has, no doubt, been altered by the crowd of commentators, and the diversity of their opinions must have thrown doubts in the minds of those who read them. It will be then a most important service, conferred on the whole Jewish community, to fix their belief on those points which have been submitted to you. To find, in the history of Israel, an assembly capable of attaining the object now in view, we must go back to the Great Sanhedrim, and it is the Great Sanhedrim, which His Majesty this day intends to convene. This senate, destroyed together with the temple, will rise again to enlighten the people it formerly governed; although dispersed throughout the whole world, it will bring back the Jews to the true meaning of the law, by giving interpretations, which shall set aside the corrupted glosses of commentators; it will teach them to love and to defend the country they inhabit; it will convince them that the land, where, for the first time since their dispersion, they have been able to raise their voice, is intitled to all those sentiments which rendered their ancient country so dear to them. . . .

Plan

Art. I. A Synagogue and a Consistory shall be established in every department which contains two thousand individuals professing the religion of Moses.

II. In case a department should not contain two thousand Israelites, the jurisdiction of the Consistorial Synagogue shall extend over as many of the adjoining departments as shall make up the said number. The seat of the Synagogue shall always be in the most populous city.

III. In no case can there be more than one Consistorial Synagogue for each department.

IV. No particular Synagogue can be established, but after being proposed by the Consistorial Synagogue, to the competent authority. Each particular Synagogue shall be superintended by a Rabbi and two elders, who shall be named by the competent authorities.

V. There shall be a Grand Rabbi in each Consistorial Synagogue.

VI. The Consistories shall be composed, as much as possible, of a grand Rabbi, and of three other Israelites, two of whom shall be chosen among the inhabitants of the town which is the Seat of the Consistory.

VII. The oldest member shall be President of the Consistory. He shall take the title of *Elder of the Consistory.*

VIII. In each Consistorial district the competent authority shall name twenty-five *Notables* among the Israelites who pay the largest contributions.

IX. The *Notables* shall name the members of the Consistory, who must be approved by the competent authority.

X. No one can be a member of the Consistory if he is not thirty years of age, if he has been a bankrupt, unless he honourably paid afterwards, or if he is known to be a usurer.

XI. Every Israelite, wishing to settle in France or in the kingdom of Italy, shall give notice of his intention, within three months after his arrival, to the Consistory nearest his place of residence.

XII. The functions of the Consistory shall be—

1st. To see that the Rabbis do not, either in public or in private, give any instructions or explanations of the law, in contradiction to the answers of the assembly confirmed by the decisions of the GREAT SANHEDRIM.

2nd. To maintain order in the interior of Synagogues, to inspect the administration of particular Synagogues, to settle the assessment, and to regulate the use of the sums necessary for the maintenance of the Mosaic worship, and to see that for cause or under the pretence of religion, no praying assembly be formed without being expressly authorized.

3rd. To encourage, by all possible means, the Israelites of the Consistorial district to follow useful professions, and to report to government the names of those who cannot render a satisfactory account of their means of subsistence.

4th. To give annually to government the number of the Israelitish conscripts within the district.

XIII. There shall be formed in Paris a Central Consistory, composed of three Rabbis and two other Israelites.

XIV. The Rabbis of the Central Consistory shall be selected from the Grand Rabbis, and the rules contained in the tenth article shall apply to all others.

XV. A member of the Central Consistory shall go out every year, but he may always be re-elected.

XVI. The vacant place shall be filled by the remaining members. The member elect shall not take his place till his election is approved by government.

XVII. The functions of the Central Consistory are,

1st. To correspond with the Consistories.

2nd. To watch over the execution of every article of the present regulations.

3rd. To denounce to the competent authority all infractions of these said regulations, either through negligence or through design.

4th. To confirm the nomination of Rabbis, and to propose to the competent authority, when necessary, the removal of Rabbis and of members of Consistories.

XVIII. The Grand Rabbi shall be named by the twenty-five *Notables,* mentioned in the eighth article.

XIX. The new Grand Rabbi elect shall not enter into his functions till he has been approved by the Central Consistory.

XX. No Rabbi can be elected—

1st. If he is not a native of France or of Italy, or if he has not been naturalized.

2nd. If he does not produce a certificate of his abilities, signed by three Frenchmen, if he is a Frenchman, and by three Italians, if he is an Italian: and from the year 1820, if he does not understand the French language in France, and the Italian in the kingdom of Italy. The candidate who joins some proficiency in Greek or Latin to the knowledge of the Hebrew language, will be preferred, all things besides being equal.

XXI. The functions of the Rabbis are—

1st. To teach religion.

2nd. To inculcate the doctrines contained in the decisions of the GREAT SANHEDRIM.

3rd. To preach obedience to the laws, and more particularly to those which relate to the defence of the country; to dwell especially on this point every year, at the epoch of the conscription, from the moment government shall first call upon the people till the law is fully executed.

4th. To represent military service to the Israelites as a sacred duty, and to declare to them, that, while they are engaged in it, the law exempts them from the practices which might be found imcompatible with it.

5th. To preach in the Synagogues, to recite the prayers which are publicly made for the EMPEROR and the *Imperial Family.*

6th. To celebrate marriages and to pronounce divorces, without, on any pretence, acting in either case, till the parties who require their ministry have produced due proofs of the act having been sanctioned by the civil authority. . . .

CONGRESS OF VIENNA

NAPOLEON'S DEFEAT in March, 1814, was confirmed by his abdication and the return of Louis XVIII as Bourbon monarch of France. The Allied powers were now faced with the responsibility for reorganizing Europe after fifteen years of French hegemony. In the Treaty of Chaumont (March, 1814), Austria, Prussia, Russia, and Great Britain pledged themselves to close cooperation in the task that lay before them. Plans were made for a European Congress to convene at Vienna in September, and on September 22 the delegates of the four great powers assembled. Austria was represented by Prince Metternich, principal minister of Austria since 1809, and chairman of the Congress. Prince von Hardenburg represented Frederick III of Prussia, while Lord Castlereagh (creator of the Alliance of Chaumont) appeared on behalf of Britain. Tsar Alexander I himself appeared as Russia's representative.

From the first, the Congress was beset with problems of organization. No precedent existed for conducting a conference on so grand a scale, and the Allies were determined not to allow control of the settlement to slip from their hands. It was agreed, therefore, that the ministers of the "Four" were to provide the "initiative," and submit the results of their deliberations to the assembled Congress for ratification. The French delegate to the Congress, Talleyrand, arrived on September 24 and refused to accede to this procedure. The formal opening of the Congress was therefore postponed twice, as informal discussions continued among the great powers.

The wily Talleyrand profited from the dissension which now plagued the Allies, and he succeeded in winning for France a place in their councils, transforming the "Four" into the "Five." Prussia's threat of war over this turn of events was countered by a secret defensive alliance between France, Britain, and Austria, and the "Five" now turned their attention to reorganizing territorial boundaries north of the Alps and preparing the basis for an Italian settlement. The representatives of the other nations of Europe, organized as the "Eight," dealt with more general matters in their deliberations; the Congress—as a body representative of all Europe—never formally met. The final treaty embodying the complicated territorial settlements were signed on June 9, 1815, by the "Eight" (except Spain), and acceded to by all Europe.

Charles Maurice de Talleyrand-Perigord, French delegate to Vienna, had pursued a brilliant, if erratic career. As bishop of Autun and representative to the Estates-General in 1789, he opposed the merging of the clergy into the National Assembly. He later became associated with the left in the Assembly, and was the first bishop to accede to the Civil Constitution of the Clergy, consecrating new "Constitutional bishops" to maintain the succession. For this action, he was placed under the ban of the Church in 1791 by Pope Pius VI. After serving as unofficial ambassador to Britain, Talleyrand fled to America upon receiving word of the execution of Louis XVI (January, 1793). He returned to France under the Directory, becoming foreign minister in 1797, and was instrumental in organizing the coup that brought Napoleon to power. He served as Napoleon's foreign minister from 1799 to 1807 Upon the surrender of Paris to the Allies (March, 1814), Alexander I took up lodgings with Talleyrand, who convinced him that the restoration of the Bourbons was a prerequisite to the peace and stability of Europe. On April 1, Talleyrand convened the French Senate and proclaimed that Napoleon had forfeited the crown. Talleyrand was French representative to Vienna and served briefly as foreign minister to Louis XVIII. He died in 1838.

Clemens Wenzel Lothar Metternich-Winneburg (1773–1859) had served as Austrian ambassador at Berlin in 1803, and at Moscow in 1806. He was made Minister of State and Minister of Foreign Affairs in 1809; from that time until 1848 he served as Austrian Prime Minister, and became the most important director of Austrian policy. The Revolution of 1848 forced him to flee Vienna in disguise, and he settled in England. He returned to Austria in 1851, and died eight years later.

The following letter about the divisive issues of Poland and Saxony was sent by Talleyrand to Metternich at Vienna on December 12, 1814. It is taken from the *Memoirs of Prince Metternich (1773–1815)*, edited by Prince Richard Metternich and translated by Mrs. Alexander Napier (New York, 1880).

LETTER FROM TALLEYRAND TO METTERNICH

Vienna, 12th December, 1814

MY PRINCE, I am anxious to fulfil the intentions of his Imperial and Royal Apostolic Majesty, expressed in the letter which your Highness has done me the honour to write to me, and I have brought to the cognisance of his Most Christian Majesty the confidential note which you addressed on the 10th of this month to the Chancellor of State, Prince Hardenberg, and which you officially communicated to me.

It is sufficient reply to the satisfaction which the declared determinations in that note gave the King, to compare them with the orders which his Majesty has given to his ambassadors at the Congress.

⌈France had there no object of ambition or personal interest. Replaced in her ancient boundaries, she does not wish to extend them⌋ like the sea which never overflows its banks except when tempests stir it up, her armies, full of glory, no longer aspire to new conquests. Delivered from that oppression of which she had been much less the instrument than the victim, happy at having recovered her legitimate princes, and with them the repose which she was afraid she had lost for ever, she had no claims to make, no pretensions to bring forward. She had raised none; she will raise none. But it remains for her to desire that the work of restoration should be accomplished for the whole of Europe as well as for her, that everywhere and for ever the spirit of revolution should cease, that all legitimate rights should be considered sacred, and that all ambition, or unjust enterprise, should find condemnation and a perpetual obstacle in an explicit recognition and formal guarantee of these same principles, of which the Revolution has only been one long and terrible oblivion. The desire of France must be that of every European State which does not blind itself. Till such an order of things is established, none can be a single moment certain of its future.

Never was a more noble aim offered to the governments of Europe; never was a result so necessary, and never could there have been so much hope of obtaining it, as at a period when the whole of Christendom was for the first time called upon to form a Congress. Perhaps it would already have been completely obtained if, as the King had hoped, the Congress had, when first assembled, laid down the principles, determined its object, and marked out the only road which could lead to it. Doubtless we should not have then seen the Powers making a pretext to destroy what it could only have been meant to preserve. Truly, when the treaty of May 30 proposed that the ultimate result of the operations of the Congress should be a real and durable equilibrium, it did not mean to sacrifice to the establishment of that equilibrium the rights which it should guarantee. It did not mean to confound, in one and the same mass, all territories and all people, to divide them again according to certain proportions; it wished that every legitimate dynasty should be either preserved or reestablished, that every legitimate right should be respected, and that the vacant territories, that is to say, without a sovereign, should be distributed conformably to principles of political equilibrium, or, which is the same thing, to principles conservative of the rights of every one, and the repose of all. It would be, besides, a very great error to consider, as the sole elements of equilibrium, those quantities which political arithmeticians enumerate. "Athens," says Montesquieu, "had in her breast the same strength, when she ruled with so much glory, and when she served with so much shame. She had twenty thousand citizens when she defended the Greeks against the Persians, when she disputed the empire at Lacedemonia, and when she attacked Sicily; she had twenty thousand when Demetrius of Phalera numbered them, as one counts slaves in a market." The equilibrium would not be then but an empty work if one made an abstraction, not of that ephemeral and deceitful strength which the passions produce, but of the true moral strength which consists in virtue. Now, in the relations of people to people, the first virtue is justice.

Penetrated with these principles, the King has prescribed as an invariable rule to his Ambassadors to seek before all that which is just, not to swerve from it in any case or for any consideration; not to subscribe or acquiesce in anything which would be contradictory to it, and, in the course of legitimate combinations, to attach themselves in preference to those which can the most efficaciously contribute to the establishment, and the maintenance, of a true equilibrium.

In all the questions which must be considered at the Congress, the King would have considered as the first, the greatest, the most eminently European, beyond all comparison, that of Poland, if it had been possible for him to hope, as much as he would desire, that a people so worthy of the interest of all the others by its antiquity, valour, the services which it formerly rendered to Europe, and by its misfortune, could be restored to its ancient and complete independence. The division which erased it from the number of the nations was the prelude, partly the cause, and perhaps, up to a certain point, the excuse for the revolutions to which Europe has been a prey. But when the force of circumstances, prevailing over even the noblest and most generous dispositions of the Sovereigns to whom the former Polish provinces are subject, had reduced the question of Poland to a simple affair of division and boundaries, which the three interested Powers discussed among themselves, and to which their former treaties had rendered France a stranger, there only remained to the latter, after having offered, which she has done, to support the most equitable pretensions, the desire that you should be satisfied, and she is so, if you are. The question of Poland could then hardly have, not only for France, but for Europe and herself even, that pre-eminence which it would have had in the above-mentioned supposition, and the question of Saxony has become the most important and the first of all, because there is no other at this moment where the two principles of legitimacy and equilibrium would be compromised at once and to such an extent as they are by the disposition which it is intended to make of this Kingdom.

To recognise this disposition as legitimate, it would be necessary to admit —that Kings can be judged, that they can be so by those who covet and can deprive them of their possessions; that they can be condemned without being heard, without being able to defend themselves; that in their condemnation are necessarily involved their families and relations; that confiscation, banished from the codes of enlightened nations, should be, in the nineteenth century, consecrated by the general agreement of Europe, the confiscation of a Kingdom being doubtless less odious than that of a simple cottage; that these people should have no distinct rights with those of their

Sovereigns, and can be assimilated like the cattle on a farm; that Sovereignty is lost and acquired by the single fact of conquest; that the nations of Europe are not united among themselves by any other moral ties than those which unite them to the islanders of the Australian Ocean, that they only live together by the pure law of Nature, and that what is called the public law of Europe does not exist; that, although civil societies in all the world are entirely or in part governed by customs, which are to them laws, the customs which are established among the nations of Europe, and which they have universally, constantly, and reciprocally observed for three centuries, are not a law for them; in one word, that everything is legitimate to the strongest. But Europe, to whom these doctrines have caused so many evils, to whom they have cost so many tears and so much blood, has only bought the right of detesting and cursing them. They inspire equal horror at Vienna, St. Petersburg, London, Paris, Madrid, and Lisbon.

The disposition which they wished to make of the Kingdom of Saxony, pernicious as an example, will be still more so by its influence on the general equilibrium of Europe, an equilibrium which consists in a reciprocal agreement between the forces of aggression and resistance in the different political bodies; and these it will injure in two ways, both very serious.

1st. By creating a very strong aggressive force against Bohemia, and thus threatening the safety of the whole of Austria. For the special force of resistance of Bohemia must be proportionally increased, and this can only be at the expense of the general force of resistance of the Austrian Monarchy. Now, the safety of Austria is of too great importance to Europe, not to excite the particular solicitude of the King.

2nd. By creating in the midst of the Germanic body, and for (one of its members,) PRUSSIA an aggressive force out of proportion to the others, putting the latter in danger, and forcing them to seek support from without and thus render void the strength of resistance which, in the system of a general equilibrium in Europe, the whole body must offer, and which it can only have by the intimate union of its members.

France can say with truth, like Austria, that she entertains no feeling of jealousy or animosity against Prussia, and it is precisely because she is really interested in her, that she does not wish to see her obtain apparent advantages, which, acquired by injustice and dangerous for Europe, must become sooner or later fatal to herself. Let Prussia acquire all she can legitimately; and not only will France not oppose her, but she will be the first to applaud her. Let it be no question of what the King of Prussia will cede of Saxony to the King of Saxony; that would be a confusion of all ideas of justice and reason. But if it is a question of what the King of

Saxony will cede of Saxony to the King of Prussia, and if it is to restore more completely to Prussia an existence such as she had in 1805, then cessions on the part of the King of Saxony are necessary, and the King of France will be the first to induce that Prince to make such as are in the interest of Austria and the interest of Germany, which on this occasion means the general interest of Europe. Your Highness seems to me to have indicated the right measure in the tables which were enclosed in your note.

His most Christian Majesty invariably decided not to sanction, even by his silence, the execution of projects formed against the King and the Kingdom of Saxony, but, wishing to believe that these projects are the fruit of some error or illusion, which a more attentive examination will cause to disappear; full of confidence in the personal uprightness and the sentiments of his Majesty the King of Prussia, who has also known misfortune; knowing all the influence of his Majesty the Emperor of All the Russias, and all which he has a right to expect from the noble qualities which distinguish him; persuaded, in short, that he should never despair of a just cause, has not despaired of that of Saxony. He will be still further from despair on learning that his Majesty the Emperor of Austria, by a determination worthy of him, has boldly taken up the defence, and declared that he will never abandon it.

THE HOLY ALLIANCE

To the idea of the Divine Right of Kings, the French Revolution opposed the idea of the sovereignty of the nation; to the idea of the hereditary government of a dynasty, it opposed the idea of the temporary, conditional rule of the people's elected servants. The French Revolution did not merely threaten crowns; sweeping away the old order of life in France, it threatened traditionalist society everywhere in Europe. Napoleon's armies brought about drastic changes in age-old institutions, particularly in Germany and Italy. The force of French example made itself felt in Prussia and Spain.

It may be said that Napoleon's bid for European hegemony was doomed almost from its very start. Destroying in radical fashion the balance of power, the dictator raised up against himself strong enemies in the form of Russia, Prussia, Austria, and England; and the peoples of many countries, fired by national ardor, rallied to the coalition in its effort to overthrow the French tyranny. This determination was embodied in the Treaty of Chaumont, March, 1814, when a declaration was made that the Allies would never lay down their arms until Napoleon was finally vanquished. It was agreed that the Quadruple Alliance thus brought into being should last for twenty years.

On the basis thus established the crowned heads of Europe—that is, the heads of Austria, Prussia, Russia, and England—created a Quadruple Alliance, formalized in November, 1815, which set about the task of repairing the breaches made by the Revolution in the walls of the old society. This, however, was not sufficient for the Tsar Alexander I. The Tsar, who in his youth had toyed with liberal ideas, had developed with the passage of time into a rigorous champion of conservatism. He required that the alliance of the Crowns against the Revolution be cemented in the spirit of a reactionary mysticism that invoked God as guide and sanction. The Holy Alliance, as this new agreement was called, was signed by the Emperor of Austria and the King of Prussia—and, in fact, by all the rulers of Europe save the Pope, the Sultan, and the King of England—in September, 1815. A vast review of Russian troops gave point to the occasion.

The alliance of the Crowns was not long in being put to the test. Revolutions against restored sovereigns broke out in 1820 in Naples, Spain, Portugal, and France. Meeting at Troppau, the Quadruple Alliance established the principle, from which England's Castlereagh dissented, that the *status quo* should be maintained by force if necessary; and the reasons believed to justify intervention in the internal affairs of States were set down.

The following selections are taken from the University of Pennsylvania series, "Translations and Reprints," Vol. I (1896); and W. P. Cressom, *The Holy Alliance* (New York, Oxford University Press, 1922).

TEXT OF THE HOLY ALLIANCE, 1815

THEIR MAJESTIES, the Emperor of Austria, the King of Prussia and the Emperor of Russia, in view of the great events which the last three years have brought to pass in Europe and in view especially of the benefits which it has pleased Divine Providence to confer upon those states whose governments have placed their confidence and their hope in Him alone, having reached the profound conviction that the policy of the powers, in their mutual relations, ought to be guided by the sublime truths taught by the eternal religion of God our Saviour, solemnly declare that the present act has no other aim than to manifest to the world their unchangeable determination to adopt no other rule of conduct, either in the government of their respective countries or in their political relations with other governments, than the precepts of that holy religion, the precepts of justice, charity and peace. These, far from being applicable exclusively to private life, ought on the contrary directly to control the resolutions of princes and to guide their steps as the sole means of establishing human institutions and of remedying their imperfections. Hence their majesties have agreed upon the following articles:

Article I. Conformably to the words of Holy Scripture which command all men to look upon each other as brothers, the three contracting monarchs will continue united by the bonds of a true and indissoluble fraternity and, regarding themselves as compatriots, they shall lend aid and assistance to each other on all occasions and in all places, viewing themselves, in their relations to their subjects and to their armies, as fathers of families, they shall direct them in the same spirit of fraternity by which they are animated for the protection of religion, peace and justice.

Article II. Hence the sole principle of conduct, be it between the said government or their subjects, shall be that of rendering mutual service, and testifying by unceasing good-will, the mutual affection with which they should be animated. Considering themselves all as members of one great Christian nation, the three allied princes look upon themselves as delegates of Providence called upon to govern three branches of the same family, viz: Austria, Russia and Prussia. They thus confess that the Christian nation, of which they and their people form a part, has in reality no other sovereign than He alone to whom belongs by right the power, for in Him alone are to be found all the treasures of love, of knowledge and of infinite wisdom, that is to say God, our Divine Saviour Jesus Christ, the word of the Most High, the word of life. Their majesties recommend, therefore, to their peoples, as the sole means of enjoying that peace which springs from a good conscience and is alone enduring, to fortify themselves each day in the principles and practice of those duties which the Divine Saviour has taught to men.

Article III. All those powers who wish solemnly to make avowal of the sacred principles which have dictated the present act, and who would recognize how important it is to the happiness of nations, too long agitated, that these truths should hereafter exercise upon human destiny all the influence belonging to them, shall be received into this Holy Alliance with as much cordiality as affection.

Engrossed in three copies and signed at Paris, year of grace, 1815, September 14/26.

> Francis,
> *Signed*   Frederick William,
> Alexander. . . .

DECLARATION OF TROPPAU, 1820

ANY STATE forming part of the European Alliance which may change its form of interior government through revolutionary means, and which might thus become a menace to other states, will automatically cease to form a part of the Alliance, and will remain excluded from its council until its situation gives every guarantee of order and stability.

The Allied Powers not only formally declare the above to be their unalterable policy, but, faithful to the principles which they have proclaimed concerning the authority of legitimate governments, they further agree to refuse to recognize any changes brought about by other than legal means. In the case of states where such changes have already taken place and such action has thereby given cause for apprehension to neighboring states (if it lies within the ability of the powers to take such useful and beneficent action) they will employ every means to bring the offenders once more within the sphere of the Alliance. Friendly negotiations will be the first means resorted to, and if this fails, coercion will be employed, should this be necessary.

CIRCULAR NOTE FROM TROPPAU, 1820

HAVING BEEN INFORMED of the false and exaggerated rumors which have been circulated by ill-intentioned and credulous persons in regard to the results of the conferences at Troppau, the allied courts deem it necessary to transmit authentic explanations to their representatives at foreign courts, in order to enable them to refute the erroneous ideas to which these rumors have given rise. The brief report here annexed will enable them to do this, and although it is not proposed to make this the subject of a formal communication the contents may be imparted in a confidential manner. They shall arrange the measures to be taken in this matter with the ministers of the two other allied powers. . . .

The events which took place in Spain, March 8, at Naples, July 2, as well as the catastrophe in Portugal, could not but arouse a feeling of the deepest indignation, apprehension and sorrow in those who are called upon to guard the tranquillity of the nations and at the same time, emphasize the necessity of uniting in order to determine in common the means of checking the misfortunes which threaten to envelop Europe. It was but natural that these sentiments should leave a deep impression upon those powers which had but lately stifled revolution and who now beheld it once more raise its head. Nor was it less natural that these powers, in encountering revolution for the third time, should have recourse to the same methods which they had employed with so much success in the memorable struggle which freed Europe from a yoke she had borne for twenty years. Everything encouraged the hope that that alliance formed in the most critical circumstances, crowned with the most brilliant success and strengthened by the conventions of 1814, 1815 and 1818, as it had prepared the way for, established and assured the peace of the world and delivered the European Continent from the military representatives of Revolution, so it would be able to check a new form of oppression, not less tyrannical and fearful, that of revolt and crime.

Such were the motives and the aim of the meeting at Troppau. The motives are too obvious to need further explanation. The aim is so honorable and justifiable that the best wishes of all right minded persons will doubtless accompany the allied courts into the noble arena they are about to enter. This undertaking which is imposed upon them by their most sacred engagements is a grave and difficult one. But an encouraging presentiment leads them to hope that, by invariably maintaining the spirit of the treaties to which Europe is indebted for the peace and union which reigns amongst its various states, they will attain their end.

The Powers are exercising an incontestable right in taking common measures in respect to those states in which the overthrow of the government through a revolt, even if it be considered simply as a dangerous example, may result in a hostile attitude toward all constitutions and legitimate governments. The exercise of this right becomes an urgent necessity when those who have placed themselves in this situation seek to extend to their neighbors the ills which they have brought upon themselves and to promote revolt and confusion around them.

A situation of this kind and such conduct is an obvious infraction of the arrangement which guarantees to all European governments, in addition to the inviolability of their territory, the enjoyment of peaceful relations, which excludes all reciprocal encroachment upon their rights.

This is the incontestable fact which the allied courts have made their point of departure. Hence the ministers, who might be furnished at Troppau even with positive instructions on the part of their monarchs, came to an agreement upon the plan of action to be followed in regard to those states where the governments had been overturned by violence, and upon the pacific or coercive measures which might bring these states once more into the European alliance, in case the allies could succeed in exercising a distinct, salutary influence. The results of their deliberations were transmitted to the courts of Paris and London, in order that these might take them into consideration.

Nothing could menace more directly the tranquillity of the neighboring states than the revolution at Naples, gaining ground as it did daily. In view of the fact that the allied courts could not be attacked so promptly and immediately as these, it was deemed expedient to proceed in regard to the Kingdom of the Two Sicilies according to the principles above enunciated.

In order to prepare conciliatory measures toward this end, the monarchs, convened at Troppau, resolved to ask the King of the Two Sicilies to meet them at Laibach, with the single aim of freeing his majesty from all external compulsion and placing this monarch in the position of mediator between his erring people and the states whose tranquillity they threaten. The monarchs, having resolved in no case to recognize governments set up by a revolt, can only negotiate with the king in person, and their ministers and agents in Naples have been instructed to this effect.

France and England have been requested to co-operate in these measures and it is to be anticipated that they will not refuse since the principle upon which the request is based is completely in accord with the treaties which they have entered into, and affords moreover a guarantee of the fairest and most peaceful intentions.

The system pursued in concert by Prussia, Austria and Russia is in no way new. It is based upon the same principles as those upon which the conventions rested which created the alliance of the European states. The intimate union among the courts which form the nucleus of this Confederation, can only gain hereby in strength and permanence. The alliance will be consolidated by the same means which the powers, to whom it owes its origin, used in its formation, and which have caused the system to be adopted by all the other powers, convinced of its advantages which are more incontestable than ever.

Moreover, it is needless to prove that the resolutions taken by the Powers are in no way to be attributed to the idea of conquest, nor to any intention of interfering with the independence of other governments in their internal administration, nor lastly, to the purpose of preventing wise improvements freely carried out and in harmony with the true interest of the people. Their only desire is to preserve and maintain peace, to deliver Europe from the scourge of revolutions and to obviate or lessen the ills which arise from the violation of the precepts of order and morality.

On such terms, these Powers believe that they may, as a reward for their solicitude and exertions, count upon the unanimous approval of the world.

THE CARLSBAD DECREES

In post-Napoleonic Germany, liberalism was an intellectual rather than a political movement. It was particularly popular among the members of the General Youth Society or Students' League (*Burschenschaften*), branches of which had been organized in the universities during the last years of the struggle against Napoleon.

Seizing upon the occasions of a national meeting of the *Burschenshaften* at the Wartburg in October, 1817 (where certain symbols of oppression were burned in a bonfire), and the murder of a reactionary poet-historian by a demented student of theology shortly thereafter, Metternich invited the more important princes of Germany who were convened at Carlsbad in Bohemia in August, 1819, to consider ways of dealing with the "restless disposition of men's minds."

In order to "restore peace and order, respect for law, the general welfare, and the undisturbed possession of property," the Austrian chancellor proposed the adoption of certain resolutions. The conference agreed. The resolutions were then presented to the Assembly of the Confederation (the Diet) on September 20, 1819, and adopted. The resolutions were kept on the books for nearly twenty years, and during this time liberalism was silenced everywhere in Germany.

There were four decrees. The first dealt with the technique of enforcing these and other resolutions of the Assembly in the territories of states who were not in sympathy with them, and it provided for the use of military force to be authorized by the Assembly. The other three decrees follow. They have been translated from the *Protokolle der deutschen Bundesversammlung,* Vol. VIII.

RESOLUTION CONCERNING MEASURES TO BE ADOPTED IN REGARD TO THE UNIVERSITIES

Article 1. A special governmental representative, endowed with proper instructions and extensive powers, shall be appointed to each university, and he shall reside in the locality of the university. He may be the existing Curator or any other man whom the government may deem qualified.

The functions of this plenipotentiary shall be: to see to the strictest enforcement of the existing laws and disciplinary regulations, to observe carefully the spirit in which the instructors conduct their public and class-room lectures, to give this spirit salutary guidance with a view to the future attitude of the students, without, however, interfering directly in matters of scholarship or methods of instruction, and finally, to devote unceasing attention to everything that might contribute to the promotion of morality, good order, and propriety among the students.

The relations between these extraordinary agents and the University Senates, as well as all matters pertaining to the definition of their spheres of action and methods of procedure, shall be stipulated as precisely as possible in the instructions which they shall receive from the heads of their governments, and which shall be drawn up with regard to the circumstances that have necessitated their appointment.

Article 2. The Confederated Governments mutually pledge themselves to remove from Universities and other such institutions of learning all university instructors and other public teachers who have shown themselves obviously unfit for the administration of the important office entrusted to them, either by demonstrable deviation from duty or by exceeding the bounds of their profession, by abuse of their legitimate influence upon the minds of youth, or by disseminating pernicious ideas which are dangerous to the public peace and order or are subversive of the basis of existing governmental institutions; saving that, until definitive regulation of this matter shall be decided upon, and as long as the present resolution is in effect, these obligations may not constitute any impediment to the various governments. Moreover, no measure of this sort may be undertaken except upon the fully documented proposal of the appointed governmental representative to the university or upon the basis of a report previously demanded of them.

A teacher who has been expelled in this fashion may not be appointed again to any public institution of learning in any other state of the Confederation.

Article 3. The laws which have existed for some time against secret and unauthorized societies in the universities shall remain in full force and severity; and especially they shall all the more definitely apply to the association established some years since under the name of *Allgemeine Burschenschaft* [1] since this society is based upon the utterly inadmissible conception of lasting fellowship and communication between the universities. In considering this matter the governmental agents shall be obligated to exercise especial vigilance.

The governments agree that no individual who shall be proved to have entered into, or remained in, any such secret or unauthorized association after the publication of the present resolution, may be admitted to any public office.

Article 4. No student who is expelled from a university by a decision of the University Senate which has been approved or proposed by the governmental agent, and no student who leaves the university in order to escape such action, may be admitted to another university; furthermore, no student may be accepted in another university without a certificate of good behavior from the university he has left.

[1] [Literally, *General Fellowship*.]

RESOLUTION CONCERNING PRESS LAW

Article 1. As long as the present resolution remains in force, publications which appear in the form of daily newspapers or as periodicals, similarly publications which do not exceed twenty pages of print, may not be sent to press in any state of the German Confederation without the foreknowledge and previous approval of the government officials.

Publications which do not belong to one of the categories here mentioned shall henceforth be treated according to laws already proclaimed or to be proclaimed in the separate Confederated States. If any such publication, however, should give any Confederated State cause for complaint, action shall be taken against the author or publisher of the publication in question, in the name of the government to which the complaint was directed and according to the practice prevailing in the separate states of the Confederation.

Article 2. Precise designation of the measures and provisions required for the enforcement of this resolution is left up to the individual governments. These measures must be of such a nature, however, as to satisfy completely the meaning and purpose of the main provisions of Article 1.

Article 3. Since the present resolution is occasioned by the need for preventative measures against the abuse of the press, which need is recognized by the Confederated Governments under the existing circumstances, the press laws, which apply to classes of publications listed in Article 1, and which provide for the judicial prosecution and punishment of abuses and offenses already committed, cannot be regarded as adequate in any of the Confederated States as long as the present resolution remains in force.

Article 4. For publications appearing within its jurisdiction, and consequently for those included under the provisions of Article 1, in so far as they may injure the honor or safety of another Confederated State or attack its constitution or administration, each State of the Confederation is responsible not only to the offended party itself, but to the entire Confederation.

Article 5. In order that this mutual responsibility, which is basic to the nature of the German Confederation and inseparable from its existence, may not cause any disturbance of the existing friendly relations between the Confederated Governments, all members of the German Confederation mutually accept the solemn obligation to proceed earnestly and vigilantly to the supervision of the newspapers, magazines, and pamphlets published within their jurisdiction and to manage this supervision so as to obviate in every way possible mutual recriminations and unpleasant incidents.

Article 6. In order, however, that the collective and mutual guarantee of inviolability both of the Confederation as a whole and of the individual members (which is the concern of this resolution) may not be endangered in a single respect, the government of a Confederated State which believes itself to have been injured by any publication appearing within the jurisdiction of another of the Confederated States, and is unable to obtain complete satisfaction and redress by friendly discussion or diplomatic correspondence, shall in any such case have the privilege of complaining of such publications before the Assembly of the Confederation. The latter, thereupon, shall be obliged to provide a commission to investigate the complaints presented and, if these are found to be justified, to provide by a definitive verdict for the immediate suppression of the publication in question as well as further issues of the same if it should belong to the category of periodicals.

The Confederate Assembly shall have the right, moreover, to suppress upon its own authority, without being petitioned, publications included in the provisions of Article 1, in whatever German State they may appear, if, in the opinion of a committee appointed by it, they run counter to the honor of the Confederation, the safety of individual states, or the maintenance of peace and tranquillity in Germany. There shall be no appeal from such decisions, and the governments involved are bound to see that they are put into execution.

Article 7. If a newspaper or periodical is suppressed by order of the Confederate Assembly, the editor thereof may not, within five years, be admitted to the editorship of a similar publication in any state of the Confederation.

The authors, publishers, and dealers of publications included under the provisions of Article 1 shall remain in other respects free of all further responsibility if they have complied with the requirements of this resolution; and the decisions of the Assembly of the Confederation provided for in Article 6 shall be directed exclusively against publications, never against persons.

Article 8. All members of the Confederation undertake to inform the Assembly of the Confederation, within a period of two months, of the decrees and regulations by which they propose to discharge their obligations under Article 1 of this resolution.

Article 9. All publications appearing in Germany, whether or not they are among those designated in this resolution, must be provided with the name of the publisher, and, in so far as they belong to the category of newspapers or periodicals, also with the name of the editor. Publications in which this regulation is not observed may not be put into circulation in any state of the Confederation and, if distributed clandestinely, they must be seized upon their appearance and the distributor of the same must be punished by an appropriate fine or imprisonment, according to the nature of the circumstances.

Article 10. The present provisional resolution shall remain in force for five years from this day. Before the expiration of this time, the Assembly shall study thoroughly the manner in which the uniform regulations mentioned in Article 18 of the Act of Confederation concerning the freedom of the press may best be provided, and thereupon bring to pass a final resolution concerning the proper limits of the freedom of the press in Germany.

RESOLUTION FOR THE ESTABLISHMENT OF A CENTRAL COMMISSION TO INVESTIGATE THE REVOLUTIONARY ACTIVITIES DISCOVERED IN SEVERAL STATES OF THE CONFEDERATION

Article 1. Within fourteen days, reckoned from the adoption of the present resolution, a Central Investigation Commission, appointed by the Confederation and consisting of seven members including the chairman, shall meet in the city and federal fortress of Mainz.

Article 2. The purpose of the Commission shall be to investigate jointly, and as thoroughly and extensively as possible, and to establish the facts concerning the origin and manifold ramifications of the revolutionary activity and demagogic associations directed against the existing Constitution and the domestic peace of the entire Confederation as well as of the individual Confederated States, direct or indirect evidence of which is already at hand or may come to light in the course of the investigation.

Article 3. The Assembly of the Confederation shall choose, by a majority vote in the Assembly, the seven members of the Confederation who are to name the members of the Central Investigating Commission.

The seven commissioners, appointed by the members of the Confederation, shall, upon having established themselves as the Central Investigating Commission, elect a chairman from their midst.

Article 4. Only government officials, who hold or have held a judicial office in the state which appoints them, or who have already undertaken important investigations, may be appointed members of the Central Investigating Commission.

Each commissioner shall be provided by his government with an official actuary or secretary who collectively shall form the personnel of the Commission.

The chairman shall apportion the business to be done among the individual members.

After a preliminary report, decisions shall be made by majority vote.

Article 5. In order to achieve their purpose, the Central Investigating Commission shall assume direction of local investigations which have been or may in the future be undertaken in the various Confederated States.

Officials who have hitherto conducted such investigations or may hereafter conduct them, shall be instructed by their governments to forward reports of proceedings which have taken place under their direction to the Central Investigating Commission, either in the original or in copies and as soon as possible. They shall further be ordered to carry out promptly and fully all instructions which they may receive from the said Federal Commission, and to proceed with the necessary investigations with the greatest possible thoroughness and expedition, and to cause the arrest of the accused persons.

Moreover, the local officials shall be ordered by the chiefs of their governments to maintain constant communication with the Central Investigating Commission, as well as with themselves, and to support one another in accordance with Article 2 of the Act of Confederation.

Article 6. All members of the Confederation within whose jurisdiction investigations have already been introduced, pledge themselves to notify the Central Investigating Commission, immediately upon its establishment, of the local officials or commissioners whom they have entrusted with the investigation.

The members of the Confederation, in whose states investigations of this sort have not yet been initiated, but which nonetheless may yet become necessary, are obliged to institute an investigation immediately upon receipt of a request of this import from the Central Investigating Commission, and to signify to the Central Commission the officials who have been assigned to the undertaking.

Article 7. The Central Federal Commission is authorized to examine individuals itself, when it deems this necessary. In order to summon these individuals, it shall apply to the superior state authorities, or to the authorities which have been indicated to them in accordance with Article 6. In cases where the Central Commission believes it to be unavoidably necessary, and upon the demand of the Central Commission directed, as provided above, to the superior state authorities or the local officials already designated, these persons shall be arrested and sent under secure guard to Mainz.

Article 8. The necessary provisions shall be made for the safekeeping of individuals transported to the seat of the Commission.

The expenses of the Commission as well as of the investigation itself, shall be borne by the Confederation.

Article 9. The Central Investigating Commission shall rely upon the present resolutions of the Confederation instead of special instructions.

In all instances where difficulties arise, especially if the Central Investigating Commission feels obliged to obtain additional administrative orders, the Commission shall report to the Assembly of the Confederation, which shall then appoint a commission of three from among its own members to initiate discussion of a resolution and make a report.

Article 10. Moreover, the Central Investigating Commission shall, from time to time, report to the Assembly of the Confederation upon the results of the investigation, which is to be carried out as speedily as possible.

The Assembly of the Confederation shall decide to institute legal proceedings according to individual results or to the outcome of the entire deliberations whenever they shall have been completed.

FRANÇOIS RENÉ DE CHATEAUBRIAND

FRANÇOIS RENÉ DE CHATEAUBRIAND was born at Saint-Malo in Brittany; or, in his own words, his mother "inflicted life" upon him there. His childhood was a solitary one. At eighteen Chateaubriand became a lieutenant in the army. In 1791 he sailed for America, ostensibly in search of the Northwest Passage. What he found instead was material for the Indian romances that were later to make him a literary sensation.

Returning to France in 1792, Chateaubriand fought in the monarchist army against the Revolution, was wounded, and followed the émigrés into exile in London. There he lived for seven years in embittered poverty, producing in 1797 his first book, the pessimistic *Essai historique, politique, et moral sur les révolutions.* Upon the deaths of his mother and one of his sisters, in 1798, he underwent a religious crisis. "I wept and I believed," he later wrote in explanation.

In 1801, Chateaubriand became famous with the publication of *Atala, or The Loves of Two Savages in the Desert. René,* originally intended as another part of this work, was included in *Le Génie du christianisme* (1802), Chateaubriand's defense of Christianity upon emotional and esthetic grounds. The author of the *Génie* was rewarded with an embassy post at Rome, but he soon began to oppose Napoleon and, in fact, became the leading publicist of the Bourbon faction; his *De Buonaparte et des Bourbons* (1814) was, said Louis XVIII, worth an army.

With the restoration of the Bourbons, Chateaubriand returned to diplomatic activity, first as an ambassador, then as Foreign Minister. It was in the latter capacity that he supported the French intervention in Spain for the purpose of reenthroning Ferdinand VII. Though this venture was successful, Chateaubriand's political fortunes darkened in 1824 and he was deprived of his post. Idealistic in his conservatism and occasionally stubbornly liberal (he defended the freedom of the press in 1827), he was ill suited to serve under the Restoration ministry. Chateaubriand wrote of himself: "I am *Bourbonien* by honor, royalist by inclination, republican by taste and by character."

He spent most of his remaining years after 1830 in retirement with his companion, Madame Récamier. Among the several books which he produced in this period was his *Mémoires d'outre-tombe.* He had worked on this book from 1811 to 1841 and had intended it only for posthumous publication, but it was printed without his consent shortly before his death in 1848.

The following address on the French intervention in Spain in 1823 has been translated by William W. Ryding from the *Archives Parliamentaires de 1787 à 1860,* Vol. XXXVIII (Paris, 1878).

ON FRENCH INTERVENTION IN SPAIN

GENTLEMEN, I shall first set aside my personal objections. My private concerns have no place here. I have no answer to make to those abominable pieces printed by who knows what means in the foreign press. I began my career as Minister during the Hundred Days with the honorable speaker who preceded me today. We both had interim appointments, I at Ghent, he at Paris. I was writing a novel at the time; he was busy with history; I still choose to limit myself to novels.

I shall survey the series of objections presented at this tribunal. They are numerous and diverse; so as not to lose my way in so vast a subject, I shall classify the objections under separate headings.

The speakers who had the floor at the time of the vote on the address had their speeches printed. Yesterday, in public session, some of the honorable deputies referred their opinions to those same speeches. Today some speakers have brought up pieces of the argument that occurred in secret committee. I shall therefore try to respond to what has been said, printed, and repeated, in order to provide a truly comprehensive view of the matter.

Following in order the objections raised by those who sit among the opposition, I shall examine: 1) the right to intervention, because it is basic to our argument; 2) the right to speak of institutions that might be useful to Spain; and 3) the right of alliance, and the proceedings at Verona; and finally a few other objections.

Let us first examine the question of intervention.

Does a government have the right to intervene in the internal affairs of another government?

This great question has been resolved in two different ways.

Those who consider it a natural right, like Bacon, Puffendorf, Grotius, and the ancients, thought it permissible to take up arms in the name of human society against those who violate the principles on which the general order is based, in the same way that a State punishes within its boundaries those who disturb the public peace.

Those who see the question as a matter of civil right hold, on the contrary, that a government has no right to intervene in the affairs of another government.

Thus the first group place the right of intervention among the duties of man, and the second place it among his interests.

I, Gentlemen, adopt the principle emanating from civil right. I side with the modern political thinkers who say: No government has the right to interfere in the internal affairs of another government.

Indeed, if this principle were not allowed, particularly by people who enjoy the advantages of a free constitution, no nation could feel secure within its borders. The corruption of a minister or the ambition of a king would suffice to precipitate an attack on any State that sought to improve its lot. To the various causes of war you would add a perpetual principle of hostility; a principle of which any man in power would be the judge, since he could always say to his neighbors: "I do not like your institutions; change them or I shall declare war on you."

I hope my honorable adversaries will agree that I speak plainly.

But if I am present at this tribunal to uphold the justice of our intervention in the affairs of Spain, how shall I be exempted from the principle I have myself clearly enunciated? You will see, Gentlemen.

When modern statesmen rejected the right of intervention, shifting from a position of natural right to one of civil right, they found themselves in an embarrassing situation. Cases arose in which it was impossible to abstain from intervention without endangering the State. At the beginning of the Revolution, they had said: "Let the colonies perish rather than a principle"; and the colonies perished. Should they also have said: "Let the social order perish rather than a principle"? So as not to break the very rule that they had established, they had recourse to an exception, returning to natural right and saying: No government has the right to intervene in the internal affairs of another nation except when the immediate security and essential interests of that government are compromised. I shall soon cite the authority for these words.

The exception, Gentlemen, seems to me no more contestable than the rule: No nation can permit its essential interests to perish without danger of perishing itself as a State. Now that we have arrived at this point in the question, everything changes place. We are transported onto new ground; I need no longer fight victoriously against the rule; I need only prove that the exceptional case has arisen for France.

Before giving the reasons that justify our intervention in Spain's affairs, I must first, Gentlemen, support my argument with the authority of examples.

In the rest of my speech I shall often have occasion to speak of England, since my honorable adversaries use her example against us at every moment, in their spoken, written and printed discourses.

It was Great Britain who, alone at Verona, defended principles; it is she who rises up today against the right of intervention; it is she who is ready to take up arms in the cause of a free people; it is she who condemns an impious war, an infringement of the rights of mankind, a war that a bigoted and servile faction wishes to undertake, planning to return and burn the French Charter after tearing up the Spanish constitution. Is it not so, Gentlemen? We shall come back to all these points. Let us speak first of intervention.

I fear that my honorable adversaries have poorly chosen their authority. England, they say, affords us a great example by protecting the independence of nations.

That England, secure amid her fleets and defended by old institutions; that England, having endured neither the disasters of two invasions nor the disorders of thirty years of revolution, should think she has nothing to fear from Spain and should not wish to intervene in her affairs, is perfectly natural; but does it follow that France enjoys the same security or is in the same position? When, in other circumstances, the essential interests of Great Britain were compromised, was it not she who, for her own safety, and no doubt quite justly, acted contrarily to the principle invoked in her name today?

England, upon entering into war against France, issued in November, 1793 the famous Whitehall declaration. Permit me, Gentlemen, to read you a passage from it. The declaration begins by recalling the evils of the Revolution, then adds:

"This state of affairs cannot go on in France without involving in common danger the powers that border her, without giving them the right, without imposing upon them the duty of stopping the progress of an evil thing that exists only by successively violating all laws and all properties, and by the subversion of the fundamental principles that bind men together in human society. His Majesty does not wish to contest France's right to reform her laws; he would never have desired by external force to influence the manner of government in an independent State. He desires to do so now only in so far as it has become necessary to the peace and security of other powers. In these circumstances he asks France, and asks her with due right, finally to put an end to an anarchic system whose force is only for evil; incapable of fulfilling for the French people the primary responsibility of governments: to repress disorders, to punish the crimes that multiply daily within the country; but arbitrarily disposing of their property and blood to disrupt the tranquillity of other nations and to make of all Europe the theatre of similar crimes and calamities. He asks her to establish a legitimate and stable govenment, founded on the recognized principles of universal justice, suitable for maintaining relations with other countries in peace and unity. . . .

"The King promises in advance and in his name: the suspension of hostilities, friendship, and (as far as eventualities will permit, over which the human will has no dominion) security and protection for all those who, by declaring themselves for a monarchic government, repudiate the despotism of a bloody anarchy, an anarchy that has broken the most sacred bonds of society, shattered all the relations of civil life, violated all rights, confounded all duties, using the name of liberty to exercise the cruellest tyranny, to demolish property and seize fortunes, basing its power on the alleged consent of the people, reducing whole provinces to blood and flame because they asked for the return of their laws, their religion, and their legitimate sovereign."

Well, Gentlemen, what do you think of that declaration? Did you not think you were hearing the very speech made by the King at the opening of the present session? That same speech, but developed, interpreted and commented upon with as much strength as eloquence? England says that she acts in concert with her allies; and yet it would be a crime for us to have allies. England promises protection to the French royalists; and yet it would be wrong for us to protect Spanish royalists. England holds that she has the right to intervene to save herself and Europe from the evils that ravage France; and yet we are forbidden to defend ourselves against the Spanish contagion. England rejects the supposed consent of the French people; she imposes on France, as a condition of peace, the establishing of a government founded on the principles of justice and suitable for maintaining natural relations with other States; and yet we would be obliged to recognize the alleged sovereignty of the people, the legality of a consitution established by a military revolt; and we presumably have no right to ask Spain, in the interest of our security, for institutions legitimated by the liberty of Ferdinand.

And yet we must be fair: When England published this famous declaration, Marie Antoinette and Louis XVI were no more. I agree that Marie-Josephine was as yet only a captive and had been made to shed only her tears; Ferdinand is now only a prisoner in his palace, as was Louis XVI before going to the Temple and from there to the scaffold. I do not wish to calumniate the Spaniards; but neither do I wish to esteem them more highly than my countrymen. Revolutionary France gave birth to a Convention, why should not revolutionary Spain produce hers? The judge who condemned Don Carlos to the galleys was a worthy member of that court. Did not the Spanish take our Revolution as a model? Do they not copy ours slavishly? Do they not proclaim the same principles? Have they not already despoiled the altars, assassinated the priests in their prisons, wrought instruments of torture, decreed confiscations and exiles? Can we, who have had this terrible sickness, mistake the symptoms and not fear for the life of Ferdinand? Dare we say that in hastening the moment of intervention we make the position of that monarch more perilous? But did England save Louis XVI by postponing her declaration? Is not the intervention that prevents an evil more useful than one that avenges it? Spain had a diplomatic agent in Paris at the time of the bloody catastrophe, and his prayers were of no avail. What was that family witness doing there? Certainly his presence was not necessary to verify a death known to Heaven and Earth. Gentlemen, the trials of Charles I and of Louis XVI are still too much with us. Another judicial assassination and we shall establish, by the authority of *precedents,* a kind of right to crime, and a body of jurisprudence for the use of the people against their king.

But perhaps England, although admitting an exception in her own interests, refuses exception to others? No, Gentlemen, England's political principles are not so narrow and personal; she recognizes for others the same rights she claims for herself. Her essential interests were not compromised in the Neapolitan revolution and she did not feel duty-bound to intervene; but she decided that the case of Austria was different, and it was in connection with this situation that Lord Castelreagh explained himself so clearly in his circular of 19 January, 1821. He first attacks the principle of intervention, which he finds set forth too generally by Russia, Prussia, and Austria in the Laybach circular; then he adds: *"It must be clearly understood that no government can be more disposed than that of the British to maintain the right of any nation or nations to intervene when its immediate security or essential interests are seriously compromised by the domestic affairs of another State."* Nothing more formal than this declaration, and Great Britain's Minister of the Interior, the honorable Mr. Peel, was not afraid to say, in one of the recent sessions of the House of Commons, that Austria had the right to interfere in the affairs of Naples. Certainly if Austria had the right to go to Naples to destroy the Spanish constitution, there can be no objection to our combatting that constitution in Spain itself when France is imperilled.

I hope, Gentlemen, that the opinion and example of England will no longer be cited against us on the subject of intervention, since I have refuted these objections by the very example and opinion of England; it must now be proved that we are in a legal case of exception and that our essential interests are endangered.

First, our essential interests are endangered by the state of suffering in which the Spanish revolution holds a part of our commerce. We are forced to maintain warships in the American seas, infested by pirates born of the Spanish anarchy. Many of our merchant ships have been pillaged, and unlike England we have not the maritime strength to force the Cortes [the Spanish legislature] to indemnify our losses.

Furthermore, our provinces bordering on Spain have the most pressing need to see order re-established on the other side of the Pyrenees. As early as June 1820 (and then there was no question of war) an honorable deputy said in this tribunal that the Spanish revolution, by interrupting communications with France, had diminished by half the value of land in the department of the Landes. Only the trade in mules was of any considerable value. The peasants of Rouergue, of Haute-Auvergne, of Haut-Limousin, and of Poitou, often paid their land-taxes with the money obtained from the sale of mules. As far as Dauphiné, there was hardly a man who did not participate in this profitable traffic. Our southern grains used also to flow into Spain, where they were paid for in piastres, the negotiation of which brought new gains. Our cloths used to find a vast market in the ports of the Spanish peninsula; the troubles that followed upon the military insurrection in the island of Léon have considerably cut down these exchanges. Any government that allows an entire population to be ruined without offering protection is guilty indeed. May we hope that the civil wars will soon cease and leave the field open for our commerce? Do not count on it; nothing ends by itself in Spain, neither passions nor virtues.

Our consuls personally threatened, our ships driven from the Spanish ports, our territory thrice violated—have we here a compromise of our essential interests? An honorable deputy once thought that it was only a question of the little valley of Andorra, recognized as neutral by treaties. True, this valley has also been overrun by the soldiers of Mina; but French soil has not been respected either. Our territory violated! How and why? To go and slit the throats of a few miserable wounded who thought they might die in peace in the vicinity and, as it were, in the shade of our generous country. Their cries were heard by our peasants who in their thatched cottages blessed the King to whom they owe the happiness of deliverance from revolution.

Our essential interests are again compromised by the simple fact that we must keep up an army of observation on the frontiers of Spain. How many days, months, years must we maintain this army? This state of half-hostility has all the inconveniences of war and none of the advantages; it weighs heavily on our finances, it disturbs the public mind, it exposes soldiers too long inactive to all the corruptions of the agents of discord. Do the partisans of peace at any price wish us to obey the demands of M. de San Miguel that we withdraw our army of observation? Well then, let us flee before them, and may the memory of our weakness on the occasion of this first military act of the Restoration be united forever with the memory of the return to legitimacy.

But why have we established an army of observation? Why did we not let Spain consume herself privately? What neutrality is this? If we were so sure that we were safe from the calamities that ravage our neighbors, we would look on undisturbed while they slit one another's throats without trying to extend our generous hand! And if we were not sure of being respected, should we have allowed the Spaniards, through our own lack of foresight, to settle their quarrel in our midst, burning our villages and pillaging the lands of our peasants? Would not the violation of our territory suffice to justify the establishment of a security cordon? England herself approved the wisdom of this measure. In an official note from His Grace, the Duke of Wellington, presented to the Verona Congress, we find this passage:

Considering that civil war has broken out along the entire length of the frontiers separating the two countries, that active armies are operating at every point along this frontier on the French side, and that there is not a city or village located on the French side that does not risk disturbance or insult, no one could disapprove of the precautions taken by his Most Catholic Majesty in forming an observation corps to protect his frontiers and the tranquillity of his people.

A note addressed the 11th of January last to the chargé d'affaires [envoy] of his Most Catholic Majesty in London by the principal Secretary of State of his British Majesty contains these words:

The Duke of Wellington has raised no objections in the name of the King his master, against the measures of precaution taken by France on her own frontiers, because these measures were obviously authorized by her right to defend herself, not only against the dangers to public health which were the origin of these measures, and the only motive alleged up to the month of September to maintain them, but also against the disturbances that might arise in France from the civil disorders of a country separated from her solely by a conventional demarcation; against the moral contagion of political intrigues; finally against the violation of French territory by fortuitous military excursions.

The moral contagion. Gentlemen, it is not I who said it. But I act on this admission: I agree that the moral contagion is the most terrible of all.

It above all compromises our essential interests. Who does not know that the Spanish revolutionaries are in touch with ours? Have there not been public provocations seeking to incite our soldiers to revolt? Have we not heard threats that the tricolor will descend from the peaks of the Pyrenees to bring back the son of Napoleon? Do we not know the schemes, the conspiracies and the names of guilty men escaped from justice who claim they will return in brave uniforms that so ill become traitors? A revolution that quickens in us so many dormant passions and memories would not compromise our essential interests? This revolution, they say, is isolated, firmly enclosed within the peninsula, whence it cannot move out. As if in the present state of civilization there were in Europe countries foreign to one another! What happened not long ago at Naples and Turin is sufficient proof that moral contagion can cross the Pyrenees. Was it not for the constitution of the Cortes that there was an attempt to overthrow the governments of those countries? And let it not be said that the people wanted that constitution because of its excellence: people knew so little about it that when it was adopted a commission was appointed to translate it. (*Laughter, right*) And so it passed away like everything that is not national, like everything that is foreign to the ways of a people. Born in ridicule, it died in scorn between a carbonaro and an Austrian corporal.

With regard to external politics, our essential interests are no less compromised. The President of the Council has already said as much to the Chamber of Peers. We pretend in Spain neither to particular advantages, nor to the re-establishment of treaties that time has destroyed, but we must desire an equality that leaves us nothing to fear: If the constitution of Cadiz were to remain such as it is now, it would lead Spain ineluctably to a republican government. Then we should see alliances formed and relations created that in future wars would considerably diminish our strength. Before the Revolution France had but one frontier to defend. She was guarded in the south by the Mediterranean, in the west by Spain, in the north by the Ocean, in the east by Switzerland. There remained only a rather short line between the north and east, a line bristling with fortresses and on which we could concentrate all our armed strength. Change this state of affairs: be forced to survey the eastern and western fronts, and on the instant your divided armies oblige you, in order to protect the north, to make efforts that exhaust the State. From this position the worst calamities could result. Yes, Gentlemen, the worst calamities. And I know whereof I speak. Let experience instruct us: Where did the armies that have invaded our territory come from? From Switzerland and Spain; from Switzerland and Spain, detached from our alliance by the insane ambition and erroneous politics of one man. Let us not short-sightedly suppose that the innovations in Spain have nothing to do with us, nor expose our posterity to the consequences of our faults.

I come, Gentlemen, to the great question of the alliance and the congresses. The alliance was conceived for the servitude of the world; tyrants got together to conspire against the people. At Verona France begged Europe to help her destroy liberty; at Verona our plenipotentiaries compromised honor and sold the independence of their country; at Verona the military occupation of France and Spain was decided upon. And the Cossacks poured out from the depths of their caves to execute the high deeds of kings; they forced France to enter a hateful war, as the ancients sometimes made their slaves march into combat. (*Laughter, right*)

It is here, Gentlemen, that I must make an effort to control myself, to put into my response the moderation and restraint that maintain dignity of character. It is difficult, I agree, to hear without being deeply moved, such strange accusations made against a former minister who commands the respect of all who approach him. I have only one regret, and it is sincere, that you cannot hear from the very mouth of my predecessor explanations to which his virtues would give a weight I cannot flatter myself to provide. (*Interruptions, left*)

He has been called at this tribunal the *Duke of Verona*: if it is because of the esteem he has inspired in all the sovereigns of Europe, he deserves to be so named: it is a new title of nobility added to all those already possessed by the Montmorencies. (*Bravos, right*)

As for my noble colleagues at the Verona Congress, to defend them were to insult them: a companion in exile to the King, a friend of the Duke of Berri, are above suspicion of having betrayed the interests of their country.

There remains only myself: the Chamber has no need of my apologies; but I will dare to say that among so many honorable deputies, there is not one that I concede to be a better Frenchman than I. (*Great commotion*)

I do not wish to make recriminations; however, I ask your permission to lay stress for a moment upon a particular observation.

In reading the papers whose opinion is opposed to mine, I see the incessant praise, much merited, moreover, of the English. Good Frenchmen suggest that there would be no great misfortune were the British to break neutrality and take up arms against our country in the cause of liberty: they forget the insults they lavished upon this same England not a year ago, the caricatures with which they covered our Boulevards, the brochures with which they flooded Paris, and the patriotism they thought they displayed so brilliantly by insulting in the crudest way the poor artists of London. In their love of revolution, they appear to have forgotten their hatred toward the soldiers who were victorious at Waterloo: little they care now what happened then, provided that they find a means of upholding against a Bourbon the revolutionaries of Spain.

What is more, those continental allies from whom they sought approval, have become the object of their recent animadversions. Why did they not complain of the loss of our independence when the foreigners were exercising so great an influence on our fate, when they were consulting the ambassadors on the very laws being drafted in the two Chambers? "Europe," they told us then, "applauds the decree of the 5th of September (*Laughter, right*); Europe approves of the treatment the royalists are subjected to; Europe, in public acts, has just declared her satisfaction with the system; and out of consideration for this system she reduces indemnities." Who then, Gentlemen, protested against the abandonment of the dignity of France? Perhaps those very persons who supposedly went to Verona to abase that dignity? In that case, it would be only fair to hear them out before condemning them, before hastening to the conclusion that they changed their interests and principles because others did.

Gentlemen, I must make a confession to you. I arrived at the Congress with prejudices which were hardly favorable to it; I still remember the mistakes of Europe; as a sincere friend of public liberties and of the independence of nations, I had been not a little disturbed by the calumnies we still hear repeated every day; what was I forced to see at Verona? princes full of moderation and justice, good, honest kings whom their subjects would like to have as friends if they did not have them as masters. I put into writing, Gentlemen, the words I heard from the mouth of a prince whose magnanimity my honorable adversaries lauded and whose favor they eagerly sought in another epoch.

"I am pleased," the Emperor Alexander said to me one day, "that you have come to Verona to bear witness to the truth. Would you have believed, as our enemies say, that alliance is a word that serves only to conceal ambition? Perhaps that may have been true in earlier days; but now it is a question of especial interest, since the civilized world is in peril! There can no longer be English, French, Russian, Prussian, and Austrian politics. There is but one general political system which must for the safety of all be admitted in common by peoples and kings. It is my responsibility to take the lead, showing myself to be the first convinced of the principles on which I based the alliance. An opportunity arose, the uprising in Greece. Probably nothing appeared to be more in my interests and those of my people, than a religious war against Turkey. But I thought I discerned in the Peloponnesian disturbances the signs of revolution. From that moment I abstained from interfering. (*Laughter, left*) What have our enemies not done in order to break up the alliance? They have sought in turn to wound my pride, and accuse me of prejudice. They did not know me very well if they thought that my principles would not withstand petty assaults on my self-respect or that those principles would yield before the sting of resentment. No, I shall never separate from those monarchs to whom I am united. Kings must be permitted to have public alliances to protect themselves from secret societies. What could tempt me? What need have I to expand my empire? Providence did not place 800,000 men at my disposal that I might satisfy my ambitions, but rather that I might protect religion, morality and justice, and inaugurate the reign of those principles of order on which society is based."

(*Voice left: Answer in one year!* . . . .)

(*President calls for silence. Voices left: These are personal opinions. President: Be quiet anyway.*)

Such words, Gentlemen, in the mouth of such a sovereign, deserve to be remembered, and I take pleasure in transmitting them to you, sure that they will kindle in your hearts feelings of admiration similar to mine. Could a prince who expresses himself in such language belie himself an instant later by proposing anything that might compromise the independence and honor of France? Moderation is the dominant trait of Alexander's character: Do you think he might have wanted war at any price, by virtue of who knows what divine right; and out of hatred for popular liberty? That, Gentlemen, is a gross error. At Verona, everything proceeded from the principle of peace; at Verona the allied powers never spoke of a war they might wage against Spain; but they did feel that France's position was different from theirs, and that she might be forced into such a war; did there result from this conviction the birth of treaties onerous and dishonorable for France? No. Was there any question of allowing the passage of foreign troops into French territory? Never. Then what happened? It happened that France is one of the five great powers that make up the alliance; that she will remain unshakably attached to it; that in consequence of this alliance, now in its eighth year, she will find in already foreseen and clearly defined circumstances, a support which, far from compromising her dignity, will testify to the high rank she occupies in Europe. (*Bravos, right*)

The error of my honorable adversaries is that they confuse independence and isolation. Does a nation cease to be free because she signs treaties? Are her movements constrained? Does she bear a shameful yoke because she has relations with powers of equal strength and subject to the conditions of a perfect reciprocity? What nation was ever without alliances? Is there a single example in all of history? Would you make of the French a kind of Jewish people, separated from mankind? Think what other and more serious reproaches the government would invite had it foreseen nothing, prepared nothing, and if, in the case of a possible war, it had not so much as known what course other countries might take!

When we had no army, when we counted for nothing among the States of the continent, when the petty princes of Germany invaded our villages with impunity and we dared not complain, nobody said that we were slaves. Today our military resurrection astonishes Europe; today in the councils of kings our voice is heard, today new conventions obliterate the memory of treaties by which we were made to expiate our victories; and yet today, they say we bear the yoke of humiliation! Cast your eyes upon Italy and see another effect of the Verona Congress: Piedmont whose evacuation will be completed in October; the Kingdom of Naples, from which 17,000 men are to be withdrawn, whose military contribution has been reduced, and which would now be totally evacuated if it had not re-established an army; yet did not Austria aspire to the domination of all Italy? Did not the Laybach Congress deliver to her this beautiful country? and in general are not all congresses conceived to extend oppression and suffocate the liberties of the people under long military occupations? And yet, Gentlemen, scarcely one year has passed and we see ambitious Austria begin to give back to their legitimate sovereigns the States that she has saved from revolution! (*Murmurs left; lively support right*)

I am undisturbed today about the fate of my country. It is not at the moment when France rediscovers the armies that fought so gloriously in defense of her independence that I tremble for her liberty.

I proceed now, Gentlemen, to a few objections of detail.

This sentence in the speech of the Crown has been criticized: *Let Ferdinand be free to give to his people the institutions that they can hold only from him.*

The same objection was raised against the word *granted* (*octroyé*) placed in the Charter, and it proceeds from the same principle. The critics will not allow that the source of sovereignty proceeds from the sovereign. We were free to speak or not to speak of the institutions we might give to Spain: had we said nothing about them, the critics would have cried out on the instant that we wished war with Spain in order to re-establish the absolute monarch and the Inquisition; but because it was just, generous and politic to speak of institutions, was it therefore necessary to submit to two principles that upset all social order: the sovereignty of the people and military insurrection? Is that formless mass, the constitution of the Cortes, even worth looking at? France was therefore able to wish Spain in 1823, as England did France in 1793, institutions better suited to make her happy and prosperous. But France, they say, has recognized for five years the constitution of the Cortes, why should she no longer wish to recognize it today? Great European powers also had ambassadors in Paris from 1789 to 1793. They watched with great anxiety the beginnings of the Revolution; but they hoped that sooner or later, reasonable men would make their voices heard; when their hope was deceived, when their essential interests were seriously compromised by the growing Revolution, they had to withdraw and seek in the fortunes of war a security that they could not find in peace.

France has no intention, Gentlemen, of imposing institutions on Spain. Enough national liberties repose in the laws of the former Cortes of Aragon and Castille to permit the Spaniards to find a simultaneous remedy against anarchy and despotism. We should, however, agree among ourselves and not suffer the reproach on the one hand of intending to uphold despotism in Spain, and on the other, of intending to naturalize our Charter in their country. We cannot simultaneously desire slavery and liberty. Gentlemen, I will put it bluntly: It is for the Spaniards to decide what is best for their civilization; but I wish this great people liberties commensurate with their mores, institutions that will protect their virtues from the inconstancy of fortune and the caprices of men. Spaniards, it is not your enemy who speaks, it is one who proclaims the return of your noble destinies when you appeared to have passed forever from the stage of the world. You have surpassed my predictions. You snatched Europe from the yoke that the most powerful empires could not break; you owe to France your misery and your glory. She sent to you her two scourges, Bonaparte and the Revolution. (*Keen agreement, right*) Deliver yourselves from the second just as you repulsed the first.

May I be permitted, Gentlemen, to draw anew the comparison that has been adduced between the invasion of Bonaparte and the one that we are compelled to make today, between a Bourbon who marches to save a Bourbon, and the usurper who went to seize the crown of a Bourbon after laying hold of his person through a treason without precedent; between a conqueror who marched to destroy the altars, killing monks, deporting priests, and overthrowing the institutions of the country, and a grandson of Saint Louis who comes to protect what is sacred among men, and who, although himself proscribed long ago, comes to make proscriptions cease. Bonaparte might not have met friends among the subjects of a Bourbon and the descendants of the heroes of Castille, but we have neither assassinated the last of the Condés nor exhumed the Cid, and the armed strength that fought against Napoleon will fight for us.

France does not abandon pacifism by choice, but by necessity. If she is forced to resort to arms, it is for her own security and not, whatever they may say, to re-establish despotism and the Inquisition. She does not intend to impose theories or fight other theories with cannonballs. She does not declare war on institutions: those institutions declare war on her; it is her old enemy in a Spanish cloak that provokes her; it is revolution, which, dogging the footsteps of the Bourbons, seeks a second victim.

We shall not let ourselves be dismayed by declamations and threats. If the only men who rose up against this war were men of honorable opinion, we might perhaps hesitate; but when all the revolutionaries of Europe vociferate about peace as with one voice, they must feel that they are threatened in Spain. They fear they will be ousted from their last stronghold. If a man be moved to pity at the thought of the evils this war will bring, he fears our successes more than our defeats.

FRANÇOIS GUIZOT

FRANÇOIS PIERRE GUILLAUME GUIZOT was born in Nîmes on October 4, 1787, of Protestant parents. His father was executed during the height of the Revolutionary Terror (April 8, 1794), and he was brought up by his mother in Calvinist Geneva. In 1805 he began the study of law in Paris, but under the Napoleonic Empire devoted himself almost exclusively to literary activity. One of his ventures during this period was the publication of a critical edition of Gibbon's *Decline and Fall of the Roman Empire*.

In 1812 Guizot was appointed to the chair of modern history at the Sorbonne. He came into close touch with many political figures of liberal convictions in Paris, especially Royer-Collard (1763–1845), who secured for him the post of secretary-general of the Ministry of Interior under the first Restoration. During the "Hundred Days," Guizot visited Louis XVIII at Ghent and advised him that only a liberal policy would establish his rule on a secure foundation; his advice was ill received and resented by the Court.

From 1815 to 1816 Guizot held the post of secretary-general of the Ministry of Justice, and from 1819 to 1820 he was director of the Ministry of Interior. He was one of the acknowledged leaders of the *Doctrinaires*—the political party that sought strict adherence to the Charter, or constitution, and worked for a reconciliation between monarchical principles and popular representation. With the fall of the moderate Décazes ministry in 1820, Guizot was deprived of office, and from 1822 to 1828 his lectures were interdicted. He now found himself at the head of the liberal opposition to the reactionary Charles X.

Despite his great political activity during this period, the years 1820 to 1830 were also the time of Guizot's most fruitful literary efforts. The *Histoire des origins du gouvernement représentatif* was published in 1821–22, the *Histoire de la révolution d'Angleterre depuis Charles Ier à Charles II* in 1826–27, the *Histoire de la civilisation en Europe* in 1828, and the *Histoire de la civilisation en France* in 1830. Guizot also published two great collections of sources for English and French history during this period, as well as a revised translation of Shakespeare and a series of essays and pamphlets.

In January, 1830, Guizot was elected to the Chamber of Deputies from Lisieux, a seat which he retained for the rest of his political life. Although sincerely committed to the principles of hereditary monarchy and legitimate succession, he was persuaded to support Louis-Philippe when the cause of the Bourbons seemed irrevocably lost. Guizot now took his place at the head of the conservative supporters of the regime; for the next eighteen years he opposed democratic agitation and championed a system of "monarchy limited by a limited number of bourgeois." He played an important role in the reform of the educational system, and organized research into medieval chronicles and diplomatic papers for the Société de l'Histoire de France, which he was instrumental in founding. Guizot served a brief term as ambassador to England, and from 1840 to 1848 headed the last government under the Orleans monarchy; he succeeded in holding together the

Conservative party under extremely trying conditions. During the Revolution of 1848 he fled to England, where he wrote a number of important studies of the Puritan Revolution and Cromwell. From 1858 to 1868 Guizot published the nine volumes of his *Mémoires pour servir à l'Histoire de mon temps.* His last years were devoted to literature and historical research. Guizot died on September 12, 1874.

The following selection from *French Government since the Restoration and the Present Ministry* (Paris, 1820) has been translated by William W. Ryding.

ON THE PRESENT FRENCH MINISTRY

WHAT HAS HAPPENED since 1815 shows us, as the most elementary reasoning indicated, that there are two ways of governing France: with the new interests and to their advantage, or with the old interests and under their influence.

I assume, as I must, that both interests have the same goal, that both mean to establish constitutional order and maintain the legitimate throne. Therefore the question may be put in these terms: to reach this twofold goal, which is the better instrument, revolution or counter-revolution? Or, if you will: which would be the easier undertaking, to persuade the revolution to accept the throne, or the counter-revolution to accept the charter? I shall go even further, to make my position quite clear: of these two undertakings, which is the only one possible?

It is obvious, on the one hand, that before 1820 every ministry tried to reconcile the throne and the charter by taking the new France as its ally and support; and, on the other hand, that the present ministry seeks its allies and support in the old regime.

Is it true that the revolution cannot be governed to the throne's advantage? Or that the counter-revolution can be governed to the charter's advantage? There lies the core of the debate between the ministers and the men who share my opinion.

Before answering, let us examine, in their contacts and relations with one another, the revolution and the counter-revolution, and legitimacy. Let us try to understand what they really are.

The Revolution. I said it when I began. The revolution was a war; that war led to a triumph, the triumph of equality over privilege, of the third estate over the nobility and the clergy, who had for a long time dominated both France and the third estate itself.

The theorists of the revolution were either mistaken or lying when they alleged the sovereignty of the people. At bottom, it was not a question of the sovereignty of the people, although at the time everybody said it was, and even believed it. It was purely and simply the victory of one portion of the people over another portion, of some of the people over the rest of the people.

And because the victors made up an overwhelming numerical majority, the sovereignty of the people was invoked as doctrine and as strength, since even superior strength must have its doctrine, so great is man's need to believe, and make others believe, that he is right.

The revolution, in fact, was right, both in principle and in tendency. Considered in these terms, it proposed to introduce justice, that is, the empire of moral law, into the relations among the citizens, and into the relations between the government and the citizens. That is what makes the revolution invincible.

Considered in terms of its acts, as an event enclosed between two dates, as a thing that began one day and on some other must irrevocably come to a close, the revolution was an act of vengeance, the triumph of the long-oppressed majority over the long-dominant minority.

Anyone who fails to see these two aspects of the revolution cannot understand it. They alone explain its hopes and disappointments, its truths and errors, its virtues and crimes, its successes and failures, the enthusiasm and fear it inspired, what it had that was sublime, and what it offered that was hideous.

To be able to understand the revolution, to be able, I will not say to subject it to rule, but only to deal with it, we must realize, on the one hand, that it sought justice and does so still, and on the other hand, that it waged war and still seeks victory.

The justice it seeks is for everyone, but the war is against some. That is inevitable.

The revolution will not rest, therefore, until its conquests have been assured; that is its immediate need. Justice in the future; that is its goal.

Does it know already? Has it succeeded in understanding its needs and its true nature? If so, it can be governed; it is even in ideal circumstances for securing and maintaining good government.

To ask the question, I had to say what the revolution was. To answer it, let us see what it is today.

Let us speak first of France in general, of the great mass of citizens who have no desire to rule, who are absorbed in their personal feelings and private interests, who wish only to live in an atmosphere where they can breathe easily and prosper.

What is it that all parties, and the government itself, find so praiseworthy about the charter? They say that in it are realized all the hopes of France, that it gives everything the people wanted in 1789. It must be true, because we hear it repeated on all sides. The liberals say so when they demand *the whole charter*. Their adversaries say so when they demand *nothing but the charter*. It is what the people cry for when they feel threatened; it is the refuge of the government when it feels endangered. Whether in attack or defense, in fear or in hope, it is the charter that is invoked. *France wants only the charter,* shout the various parties and the government in turn; *we want the charter,* France answers to all.

But the charter is here; it has been given to us; we possess it. This is a strangely intractable people who seek only what they already have, what has been promised and delivered for ever and ever. Then what is the problem? Government by the charter, according to the charter. Apparently that is enough; everyone seems to agree. Then why is it not enough? Is it possible that the ministers are not governing according to the charter, that all our troubles stem from the simple fact that they do not know how to go about their business?

The charter is a vague word, they say; the revolution is not a simple homogeneous thing; France is scattered and broken up. Furthermore, there are in France certain classes, and in the revolution certain forces, that favor anarchy and the destruction of the established order. That is where the danger lies.

Obviously the problems cannot originate from any of the interests that the charter guarantees and recognizes as legitimate. Let us therefore set aside equal rights, religious liberty, national properties, and the votes and opinions expressed in the course of our difficulties. If those interests are disturbed, if they aspire to the destruction of the present regime, then it cannot be the charter that governs us. They cannot be dissatisfied with the charter, because it promises their security and proclaims their triumph; clearly it was neither pure whimsy nor the pleasure of incurring danger that prompted certain positive interests to solicit this painful change. "The revolutions that occur in great states," says Sully, "are not the result of chance or of popular caprice." I repeat: if some constitutional interest feels uneasy, then constitutional government does not exist; the ministers do not for a moment contest the fact that these things are our due.

Therefore we shall have to seek outside these sacred walls for the enemy interests and anarchic forces that the revolution still opposes to the establishment of orderly government.

Yes, there are such interests, there are forces of this kind. I cannot deny it. Certainly no ministry ever dreamed that a country, torn from its foundations and seeking new ones to settle on, would find them effortlessly and alone, or that it would calmly place itself in new hands and turn over to the government the mild task of reaping what it did not sow, of settling down under a roof it did not build. The revolution did not labor in France and in Europe merely to rest in the lap of a sleeping ministry. Certainly their heritage is not free of encumbrances; certainly the revolution left obstacles and enemies that the most able government would have found trouble dealing with. But I fear that our ministers see difficulties where they do not exist and go clumsily about attacking them where they are. . . .

I must say at the outset that I do not deny the dangers. I think that in the present situation there are many, both for the throne and for the nation. But to my mind, the system of the ministers makes the dangers immensely greater. The counter-revolution is poisoning the revolution.

As for Jacobins, I am not one of those who deny their existence. Counted individually, I doubt that there are very many of them; however, I do believe that there are some. It would be surprising indeed if the revolution that produced so many of them should have left none at all. Buonaparte did not deport them all. It is not possible that after five or six years of frantic license and furious passion, after so much local tyranny, after so much petty and violent oppression, there should not have survived a certain number of the men who then wrought havoc. Such men are unquestionably declared enemies of the established order and are eager to destroy it. They plant seeds of hatred and encourage distrust; they neither believe in tranquillity nor desire it. They ruled through anarchy; anarchy alone gives them opportunity; anarchy alone attracts them.

And yet I do not think it is their number that is disturbing; it is their influence. No doubt of it, the Jacobins are not now in a position to rise up and become dangerous in themselves. All their former allies who have assumed important places in society have broken off relations with them and abandoned the old slogans. Where then does their influence come from? We have seen a day when they had scarcely any; they were despised, rejected, and even unjustly treated; and no one protested, no one seemed to be distressed about their fate. The Jacobins, you will agree, whether they abjured or resisted, set few obstacles in the way of the establishment of imperial despotism and had little success against it. Why should they find more favor today? Could it be that France has developed a taste for anarchy, or that, fearing counter-revolution, she welcomes all its enemies?

If this last reason be put forward, I can only repeat what I said earlier. Since the object of the charter is to prevent counter-revolution, it would be strange indeed if the charter government were the one to provoke that fear. If there is a fear of counter-revolution, then, it must be because the charter does not actually govern, unless it be claimed that 29 million Frenchmen are blind and insane enough to believe that they are living in 1788 when they are quite obviously and certainly living in 1820. If the charter is governing, if the ministry is really a constitutional ministry, then the situation of the Jacobins is unfavorable; they cannot have any real influence.

Has France herself changed? Has the madness of 1793 struck again? It has been both affirmed and denied. Does the ministry wish to alert us to the danger? Anarchy is at the door, democratic theories contaminate the people's minds, and all disordered passions rise up before us. Does the ministry need to exaggerate the danger? All France wants peace and order; she rejects with disgust and indignation every revolutionary attempt; she laughs at the utopias of the dreamers. When are we to believe the ministry, in its panicky or its arrogant mood? When does it see clearly, when it trembles or when it brags?

To my mind, it sees clearly in neither case. France is neither disposed to anarchy nor ready to endure tyranny to avoid anarchy. She has no faith in utopias, but she has even less faith in the old regime. She does not call for a republic, but she rejects counter-revolution. Her profound distrust of counter-revolution is the yeast that makes her ferment in spite of herself, against her will. Remove this source of fear, and only the legitimate fears for liberty will remain.

Let us therefore not worry about the Jacobins, since we ourselves are responsible for what power they have. Let us not feel threatened by their reappearance, since we seem to have set ourselves the task of reviving them. They are not all dead; all evil passions are not stilled; all minds are not healed of their sickness. France has not lived long enough under free and lawful rule to get rid of all her anarchic prejudices and disorderly habits, to be able always to recognize and reject them. They are still among us, deceiving us, and spreading confusion. But the things that really determine the character of a country are its natural instincts and tendencies; that is where the government must find its strength. Our instincts lead us only toward order, law, and constitutional liberty. They are what we sought in the midst of so many crimes and evils; they are what we still pursue. They are what we have been promised.

The Buonapartists are, in my opinion, much more formidable than the Jacobins. They are a younger party and know more precisely what they want; since they know more precisely, they can more clearly impress their views on the masses and more easily win them over. Crude and simple agitation is not for them; they need a sharply determined goal. Finally, whereas the Jacobins have lost all faith in their former doctrines and have endured long humiliation, the Buonapartists still believe in Buonaparte; for them, he fell in the fullness of his glory; they attribute his fall to chance and to treason; they still respect the man and his system. Under his rule they saw order established and France triumphant. The great harm he did us is a deep and interior hurt that many fail to see. He filled hungry imaginations, absorbed lives in activity. He exercised men while he corrupted them, for that was the most effective means of seduction. And so he lives on, and his name still acts on the multitude. He is a religion, a legitimacy, an almost inexhaustible source of prejudice, of emotion, of regret and of nostalgia. The material interests of the revolution lived securely under his power. Vanities were not offended. No wonder he fills the thoughts of a certain number of individuals, holds a very real sway over certain classes.

That this evil should be deplored, I can readily understand; that we should defend ourselves against it, I find absolutely necessary. But there is nothing here that need surprise us, nothing that need reduce the country to despair. A nation that has lasted this long does not perish overnight. The Jacobins plagued England for a long time with conspiracies and civil wars. But the national party fought and won. Obviously, the Buonapartists are not, for us, the national party. They take on all masks, I know. They remind those who deplore the present weakness of France that France was powerful under the imperial regime; they promise those who are alarmed on behalf of the new interests that they will know uncontested security. But if the authority of the government were firm and sure, if the charter were to rule with a strength and assurance, then the Buonapartists would have nothing to offer. Like the spirit of anarchy, they draw their strength from the terrors of counter-revolution. We must combat Buonapartism by allying ourselves with the new interests; with the aid of the national party, we can defeat it. Today there are only two things that make the imperial faction strong. It gave security to private interests, and it infused new life into many dull existences. Search out other means of security and other principles of life within the constitutional system. They are there, and they are only there. In all periods, and especially in our own, people have needed both repose and activity, both confidence and hope. A quiet and otiose peace is not enough; people need guarantees to reassure them and movement to enliven them. Open up new careers for these lives, for these active minds that seek matter to work on. War is not the only means of stimulating men's imaginations and absorbing their strength. But inactivity and boredom are dangerous after the intoxications of war. Only the principles and interests of liberty can now erase the memory of those terrible games. You are right to deplore the adventurous spirit that agitates us; but to defend ourselves from it, repression will scarcely do; we must turn that spirit from its course and force it into new channels. As long as France is anxious and inactive, Buonapartism will have a foothold; but obviously boredom and anxiety are not the essence of the constitutional government. Cease then to say that the revolution cannot be governed. You have at your disposal, within the government that you say is yours, all the means necessary to govern it.

The revolution can be governed; that much is clear. But it can be governed only on certain conditions. There lies the difficulty. Either these conditions are misunderstood, or else it is not clear how they are to be satisfied. Even after carefully collecting and examining the seeds of anarchy and disorder that afflict the present regime, nothing will have been explained or accomplished. It will be easy to destroy the effects of the fear. It will be possible, without great mental effort, to refute arguments or to put cause for reassurance beside causes for concern. Everywhere the instruments of government lie behind the phantoms of fear, resources are ready to hand near the obstacles, remedies lie but a few steps from the ills. By what strange reversal of all the laws of reason, by what absurd denial of the experience of the ages does it happen that a country in a period of development and strength, not one of degradation and decadence, a country that has known all disorders, endured all tyrannies, and felt all their pains, should be unruly in the hands of a government that offers liberty and peace? Such things do not happen. Peoples who have gone through similar crises have always come to rest in the bosom of the government they originally sought; and once they possessed it, they learned to live under its laws and defend it against its enemies. Surely we are not especially designated to suffer a more cruel fate. We have not fought long and gloriously simply to end, in an example as fatal as it is unheard of, by disgusting the world forever with the quest for liberty and by drying up at their source the noblest hopes of mankind.

The question remains. The new France can be governed; the only matter to be decided is under what conditions. Remember that the revolution was fought in order that France might be governed only on condition: the charter is that condition, necessary and absolute. Any power that, voluntarily or

involuntarily, through evil intent or through clumsiness, by not accepting
or by not understanding the charter, refuses to avail itself of the means of
action, influence, and stability that it offers, will be incapable of governing
France. France may suffer the consequences, but she will not take the blame.
She knows that evil forces lurk within her breast; she detests them even
though in her anguish she seems to accept them. She would joyfully see them
defeated by an authoritative power able to win her confidence, able to
persuade her that it belongs to her and that it will never abandon her. But
when she is disturbed and restless, when she lives in uncertainty and danger,
when the ministers who direct her destiny admit that they are incompetent
to govern by and through her, deserting her alliance to side with the party
she fears the most, then indeed she must reject them; and, I repeat, the King
gave her the charter that it might be so.

Will the counter-revolution offer the ministers more manageable weapons,
better instruments to attain the goal we all pursue?

The Counter-Revolution. . . . What does the counter-revolution want?
Where would it like to stop? What would it like to be? Nobody knows,
including the counter-revolution itself. Its need, its work today, is only to
destroy. It must, before all else and at any price, demolish the revolution. It
is often claimed that the revolution produced nothing but a *tabula rasa,* that
it destroyed everything and offered nothing in replacement. Arrogant and
absurd pretentions of the vanquished! Interests succumb only to other interests; ideas yield only to other ideas, forces give way only to other forces.
An entire system of opinions, institutions and habits does not crumble beneath the blows of a system that harbors in its bosom nothing powerful or
real. Has French soil lain fallow because it has changed owners? Have we
lacked armies because it is no longer necessary to be well-born to become an
officer? Has the population wasted away because of the absence of monastic
orders? Have families disappeared since substitutions were abolished? Has
national wealth dwindled under the empire of equal taxation? Has the suppression of masters and wardenships been fatal to the development of industry? Has the civil code increased the number of lawsuits? Has education
been less general, have minds been less active, have the sciences flourished
less than in 1788? If none of those things has happened, and we may boldly
assert that none of them has; if the movement of lives, of souls, and of society
as a whole has accelerated rather than slackened, then unquestionably the
revolution is fertile and life-giving, it has done more than destroy, and it has
at its disposal all the materials necessary for new constructions.

The counter-revolution knows all this perfectly well, although it says the
opposite. Therefore, in its effort to destroy, it attacks especially the more

positive and productive aspects of the new order. It is much more ill-disposed toward the ideas and forces that sustain the revolution and assure its future than toward the means it used to demolish the past. It finds religious liberty much more odious than impiety; the sovereignty of law infuriates it much more than the so-called sovereignty of the people. Equal shares in inheritances displease it much more than the agrarian laws. And every time the new ideas find their support in moral principle—the only lasting standard—every time the principles of liberty are translated into effective laws, the counter-revolution will become doubly restive and work doubly hard to prevent the new order from raising up solid constructions on the ruins that the counter-revolution uses as grounds for accusation.

Judging from such symptoms, who could fail to recognize that the essential characteristic of the counter-revolution is its passion to destroy? Destruction is also its primary need. It must tear down what is being built up, it must dig out the nascent seeds in order to seize the land and try to build its own edifices. The same fatal necessity that forced the revolution to tear down everything that was, today forces the counter-revolution to tear down everything that is. The situation is strictly analogous. The necessity is equally fatal.

But the world knows from experience that the only ungovernable forces are the ones that need to destroy. The revolution itself has just proved it. As long as occupied terrain lay before it, as long as there was someone to dispossess or something to strike down, it shook off all laws, refused all curbs, rejected all orderly procedures. It accepted no yoke, submitted to no order whatever until the day when its work of destruction seemed finished. Only then could it settle down and wish to be regulated.

The counter-revolution, now engaged in the same kind of attempt, is condemned to the same fate. Aggression, violence, scorn for human rights, indifference as to means, and the spirit of disorder are its inevitable lot. It is useless for it to promise, to struggle, even to tremble for its weakness, it cannot escape its nature, the law of its existence.

And this law is all the more powerful and irrevocable because the destruction the counter-revolution aspires to is itself impossible. In social conflicts, when a system that dominates society is over-thrown and held down for a period of thirty years, it does not ultimately triumph. Only new systems can resist defeat and await the day of success. The old regime ruled, ruled for a long time; it perished because it was old and worn-out. Its fall did not make it any younger or stronger. The counter-revolution is therefore at an immense disadvantage in pitting its weakness against the strength that conquered it. Everything works against its purposes, time, patience, even success. The revolution has undertaken more than it can accomplish. And the more it undertakes the impossible, the more it will be forced to accept help in any form, the more it will be forced to reject no possible means of success. Iniquity, falsehood, violence, and disorder are all the more necessary because the chances of success are so slight, because the energy to resist is in such short supply. True enough, the forces that seek destruction are ungovernable, but when they are weak, they are much more so.

What then would happen if this party, whose destiny impels it toward destruction, toward a destruction it cannot accomplish, were chosen, called upon to conserve, indeed to complete and perfect . . . what? . . . the very work it must destroy? And yet this is exactly what the ministers have done in allying themselves with the counter-revolution in their effort to found a constitutional monarchy.

In truth, I cannot help feeling some embarrassment when I insist on the glaring absurdity of such a hope. Has the light of reason gone out in the minds of those involved in this unfortunate situation? The old regime, which for thirty years fought against France's right to the charter and lost the throne in the struggle, has now suddenly become the only force capable of maintaining the throne and the charter! The old regime is declared to be the only instrument suitable to a government it did not want, to the exclusion of the new France, which both wanted it and worked to obtain it!

Let us enter into the factual details and try to decide whether alliance with the counter-revolution can be of any real help, or offer any hope of success. . . .

The elements that still militate in favor of the old regime when analyzed reduce to a total of four, whose combined action provides its strength, and whose collective membership, in its best days, constituted its party. Those elements are: the court, the provincial nobility, the clergy, and finally the timid people whom the excesses of the revolution, rightly or wrongly, alienated from its cause. Are there in this group any who can be expected to complete, or even to contribute to, the work of simultaneously establishing the legitimate throne and constitutional order? . . . . It is commonly assumed that the men of the counter-revolution are and always will be ignorant, incompetent, and incapable of exercising firm and intelligent power. It is imagined that they all stem from the same decrepit breed, all equally devoid of courage and talent. What a strange blindness party spirit inflicts! Just let the struggle that perturbs our nation go on, with all its uncertainties; let it continue to call forth all the strength of the old regime and offer it opportunities. Then we would see their party produce or win over able and daring men, eager to try their fortune, lacking neither courage nor skill. The national party in England also boasted that they had all the active minds and robust hearts. They were proud of their victories, of all the energy and political skill they displayed and acquired; but when the party of the court had got its breath again and found new hopes, it no longer lacked either talent or audacity. Serious politicians, great orators, and enterprising men appeared and rallied their forces. The Shaftsburys, the Arlingtons, the Danbys, and the Buckinghams were not mediocre men, and the ministry of the Cabal, so fatal to its country, was perhaps one of those that showed the most spirit, obstinacy and shrewdness in handling the people's affairs. The men of the old regime have already made considerable progress of the same kind right here. Already they show evidence of sound tactics, of caution, of firm direction; already they have learned to dissemble, to wait, to recruit allies, to veil their weaknesses, to use their experience and strength fruitfully. I am therefore far from sharing the common opinion in this matter. I am not blessed with the capacity to count on the eternal debility and incorrigible incompetence of our adversaries; but neither do I share the hope of those who expect from this quarter a more religious and moral political order. On the contrary, I think, and the facts are with me, that the parties of the past, devoted to retrograde systems, eager to re-establish despotism and privilege, can only give birth to the most immoral and perverse of governments. Permit me to cite the example of England. The more one studies her history, the more one discovers important truths. There too, many righteous men, disgusted with revolutionary excesses, the corruption of the Long Parliament and of Cromwell's men, deceived themselves into thinking that the Tories would bring back order, right, and everything sacred. The Tories, once in power, provided their country with the most depraved and licentious of ministries. They persecuted nonconformists in the name of the national church, while they themselves were profoundly impious. They boasted interminably of England's ancient ways, of the high moral seriousness of old England, while their own disgusting immorality betrayed their hypocrisy. The national spirit was against them, and so to combat it they gave to parliamentary corruption an amplitude and regularity it had never known before. Clarendon himself accused them, and Robert Walpole did no more than follow in the path marked out by the Count of Danby. Why? Because it is the essence of a party whose center is the court and the old aristocracy to press more than any other for a perverse and licentious political order. They take advantage of the opportunities presented by revolutionary excesses; they praise virtue and urge the need for stability; they exploit the ideas of *order, religion* and *morality*. But such ideas are to them only auxiliary forces and circumstantial necessities; reverting to their true character, they disdain, disregard and outrage those same ideas, but they never cease solemnly to invoke them. Thus they offer a mixture of depravation and hypocrisy, the most deadly of examples, the most shameful of burdens.

When I hear pious men, virtuous citizens, and sincere friends of all that is honest and pure place their trust in the present political direction for a return of the feelings, ideas and habits they so rightly cherish, I confess that I feel overwhelmed with pain and anguish, for there is nothing so disheartening as a noble expectation that is doomed to disappointment.

I know perfectly well what that expectation is based on today. The present ministers are worthy men to whom what I have just said cannot apply; I sincerely believe it; it is not they whom I accuse. I accuse the system that conceals all those things within its bosom. If that system prevails, if it has time to run its course, all that it conceals will be brought to light. We shall see other ministers much more deeply committed to the counter-revolution; they will pursue its interests more directly, and its spirit and tendencies will show themselves more boldly. Finally the day will come when ministers profess beliefs they scorn, solemnly proclaim principles they laugh at, and supplement their strength with cunning and violence; ministers unable to depend on elections will assiduously corrupt them; unsure of public opinion, they will try to enslave it; finally, I sincerely hope, they will count among their adversaries the same desires and hopes that today seem to promise an altogether different future. But from now until then, how much time will be wasted, how much evil done! . . .

In every way, the old regime seems to me the most disastrous of allies, the least appropriate and most dangerous instrument that a ministry not wishing a return to the old regime could adopt. How then does it happen that such consequences are obvious only to the old regime and its avowed defenders? The counter-revolution in itself cannot be governed; it certainly cannot be governed to the charter's advantage. Is it possible that the revolution, which can be governed in itself, cannot be governed to the advantage of legitimacy?

Legitimacy. I would like to avoid all metaphysical discussion. I believe neither in divine right nor in the sovereignty of the people. I see in both of them only usurpations of power. I believe only in the sovereignty of reason, justice, and right. They are the legitimate sovereign the world seeks now and always will; for reason, truth and justice reside nowhere totally and infallibly. No man, no group of men possesses them or can possess them entirely and limitlessly. The best forms of government are those that place us most securely and make us advance most rapidly under the empire of their holy law. That is the virtue of representative government.

When one man claimed to be the image of God on earth and on this basis demanded passive obedience, he created tyranny. When people counted their heads and proclaimed the omnipotence of number, they created tyranny. Of the two usurpations, the first is the more insolent, the second the more brutal. . . .

It is not enough for a society that the principle of right reside in the citizenry; it must also reside in the government. It does not mean very much to say that a man possesses or claims his liberties as a legitimate right if the power that commands men does not also exercise a legitimate right in their eyes. If right belongs only to government, then society has disappeared; if government has no right, if right is scattered and dispersed among isolated individuals, then society is dissolved. The idea of right necessarily implies a relation; rights must be reciprocal in order to be based on and limited by one another. Where reciprocity is lacking, right, in its sole possessor, degenerates inevitably into tyranny. On the contrary, where reciprocity exists, rights subsist together and soon attach themselves to the superior principle from which they both derive, the idea and the sense of duty. Therefore let right and legitimacy be everywhere, only then is society stable and power regulated.

The heredity of thrones has no other object than to place right on the throne in order that it will be everywhere. This is the only sense in which heredity is legitimate, but it is also in this sense that it becomes a true legitimacy; and from this principle, which gives it strength, result also all its advantages.

Those advantages must be very great indeed, since all governments and all parties ardently seek them. I do not know what the future holds; no doubt it has many secrets impossible to guess at; but until the present time, in all societies that have lasted long and where legitimacy has struck its roots, it has been impossible to abolish it; it has changed place, condition and name; it has survived all these changes. The periods that saw its ruin also saw its resurrection; the men who destroyed it also re-established it; the powers that it condemned ultimately adopted it; it gives to social life, in past and future, the extension, the perpetuity that is one of the most profound needs of our nature. As a superstition, legitimacy had to perish; as an institution it remains strong and precious.

But institutions, whatever they are, are not simply improvised. It is no easier to make a king legitimate than it is to make a people free. The idea and the sense of right, which are the basic principles of all institutions and the source of their strength, do not take root and grow in a single day. In the beginning, everything is more or less the product of brute force, and that force denatures it in the very moment of its creation. The seed of right is dirtied and adulterated by the passions and disorders of force. Time must ultimately take over, purifying and nurturing, and finally making right emerge from the crude mixture in which violence and error originally enveloped it. Legitimacy has always and everywhere begun with an act of usurpation, just as liberty has always begun with anarchy. But at the beginning, they were neither legitimacy nor liberty.

When, therefore, a true legitimacy exists, purified by time, and, although suspended for a while, not yet destroyed, which was and is capable of becoming again the institution that I have just described, it would be singularly absurd not to receive it with open arms, not to do our utmost to profit from its advantages. We must undertake to give new life to what exists, to re-create in the face of myriad perils, and only for the future, what can be conserved and adapted to the present. A young man, M. Thierry, now seriously engaged in studies worthy of his distinguished talents, seeks to find in our history all the debris, all the monuments, all the proofs of our ancient liberties. He believes that he is doing the new liberty a great service by relating it to the past, by calling it back to its cradle, by extending our institutions and rights back to their origin: and he is right. Liberty is strong because it has lived; it is fortified by its memories, and society, in order to believe in itself, needs to believe in its past. What M. Thierry deems useful to the cause of liberty, is equally useful to all institutions, to all the elements of the social order; it is good for them not to feel that they are just now being born, or rather it is only when they have lasted, when time has tested them, that institutions are what they ought to be.

Thus, firmly persuaded that the legitimacy of thrones is an excellent institution, I wonder by what fatal error the revolution could misjudge or reject such a good thing.

To begin with, it is obvious that, considered apart from circumstances, legitimacy is a neutral institution, it is not indissolubly linked to any particular form of government or state of society. In Constantinople it coexisted with despotism, in France with the feudal regime, in England with representative government. It adapts itself to times, necessities and situations. We have seen it lend its strength to the communes as well as to the aristocracy, to the infallibility of the Pope as well as to the national church. Its nature has no other need than recognition and existence. Whatever the political laws or interior condition of a state may be, if the state and the laws can produce and sustain a regular government, then legitimacy can easily assume its place and play its role, while conferring its advantages. It has been adopted by all the peoples of Europe, in the most diverse situations, the most distant epochs, even after complete upsets in which it saw itself engulfed and which effected the most radical changes.

The obstacles that it faces here today are not therefore the necessary result of its nature. The fears it stirs up do not relate necessarily to its essence. The fears we feel on its behalf are not legitimately based in the new social order. And yet there are real obstacles, and there is a legitimate basis for fear. These are truths we must face.

To my mind, these are the facts.

The revolution and the counter-revolution are now at odds over legitimacy. The first would adopt it without repugnance and even with joy, if it were sure that legitimacy was its property, its conquest. The second, which would perish without its support, is trying desperately to hold on to it, to chain it to its own destiny. If legitimacy offers a safe harbor to the revolution, it will enter at full sail. For the counter-revolution, that would mean hopeless shipwreck.

It is easy to understand that in this dispute the revolution should appear more fearful, the counter-revolution more ardent. By a fatal error, when the struggle began, legitimacy was unable to sever its ties with the old regime. It let itself be involved in a cause that was not its own; the revolution, then in full attack, bent on destruction, struck blows that crushed the old regime. It was a great misfortune both for the revolution and for legitimacy. The misfortune is still with us. Memories of the old regime are kept alive by the presence of the Bourbons. The people fear them. The old regime boasts of them. Civil war and absence have nourished reciprocal prejudices. Influential and powerful factions abroad work to exploit those sources of irritation. They play, with respect to the nation, the same role that the counter-revolution plays with respect to legitimacy. They try to persuade the nation that they uphold its cause, and that its cause is bound up with theirs. Which explains the uneasiness of the people, their credulity, their animosity, and their obstinacy. Which in turn explains the uncertainty of so many honest citizens who wish France well, who are strangers to hatred, who are not blind to the advantages of legitimacy, but who cannot give themselves into its hands until they see positive indications of its dedication to the interests of France. Simply to have received the charter is not sufficient; the charter must be received continuously, at every moment, in the spirit of the government, in its acts and in its language. The King has taken his position in favor of the charter. That is the right position, the national position; but a position, once assumed, must still be maintained, and not only maintained but strengthened and enlarged, always winning new ground and extending itself further.

Today the revolution and legitimacy have one fundamental trait in common, the urgent need to preserve both themselves and the established order. Neither one needs to destroy; whereas the counter-revolution, which has lost everything, must seek to regain everything at the expense of the revolution and of legitimacy. That in itself should be enough to teach legitimacy and the revolution that their alliance is both natural and necessary, the only profitable alliance for either one. Every action that draws them closer to the counter-revolution is hurtful equally to both. Only the counter-revolution can gain from reconciliation.

Then who are the true defenders of legitimacy, those who call upon it in the name of the new order, or those who wish to put it back at the head of the old regime? Which of the two tendencies has experience and reason on its side? Was the position taken by the throne during the revolution more secure than the constitutional position? The present ministers would give the throne back to the allies who lost it in 1791, losing themselves in the process. We ask, on the contrary, that the throne remain with the conquerors. Not only in our common interest, but also because it has been promised, because it has been given to us. The charter is more than a peace treaty. It is an alliance. The new France could not have received the charter without putting herself in its hands. To keep the charter, she must first possess it. The representative government is not, like legitimacy, neutral and impartial in its nature. It belongs to those who fought for and won it. It is an instrument of triumph, a stronghold. If this instrument falls into enemy hands, if this stronghold is handed over to murderers, then everything changes; what was a source of protection becomes a danger. Let me speak with complete frankness. I have been and still am one of those who consider the complete quinquennial renewal of the chamber of deputies a very desirable institution, one that promises both liberty and stability. But if, through irregularities and falsifications in the electoral system, the counter-revolution were to succeed in extorting from France a counter-revolutionary chamber, and if the complete renewal were to be momentarily turned to the advantage of the old regime, if it were to give it for a time the power it is so close to seizing now, I would unhesitatingly change my attitude and conduct, without, for all that, changing my principles. I would demand frequent and partial elections to break a dangerous majority and to frustrate an evil system of government. Institutions are nothing in themselves; it is not for themselves that they are desired; they serve a particular end; they have a practical use; they are means of attack and defense; and when the government, which is the center of all institutions, is invaded by its adversaries, then there is but one course of action; reconquest. . . .

Perhaps the error committed in 1819 by the men who sincerely meant to develop our institutions was their premature belief that the old regime was done for, and that the new order was in full control. They wished to permit the good and regular enjoyment of the benefits of the new order; they thought that since the revolution was triumphant, it should cease to behave in revolutionary ways; and in that they were right. But perhaps the fundamental condition of such progress had not yet been fulfilled, perhaps the point of departure was not yet sure enough. Perhaps they ought to have foreseen that a well-struck blow would suffice to knock down the constitutional order and open the door to lurking counter-revolutionary forces. I do not think that the actions I spoke of determined in any sense the events that have occurred. Those events had anterior causes that were much more powerful, that brought them about independently of any constitutional advantage. But the old regime is not sufficiently beaten down to let slip the opportunities provided by the elections of 1819 and by the deplorable attack of February 13. Now it has made its move. If the elections that now draw near strike the right blow against them, they may not give up entirely, but there will be few opportunities left for them, and we shall have many to strengthen our grip on what legitimately belongs to France, to the throne, and to liberty.

ALFRED DE MUSSET

Louis Charles Alfred de Musset was born in Paris in 1810. His parents were members of the lesser aristocracy, and shared an intense interest in literature, which they imparted to their children. At the age of seventeen, Musset won second prize at the Collège Henri IV for an essay on *The Origin of the Feelings*. Although he took up both law and medicine, he found himself unable to continue either study.

Musset was still a youth when he was introduced into the salon of Victor Hugo, where he associated with some of the leading figures in French literary life, including Alfred de Vigny, Prosper Mérimée, and Sainte-Beuve. His first published work was a free translation of De Quincey's *Opium Eater* (*L'Anglais mangeur d'opium*, 1828), and his first original work, *Tales of Spain and Italy*, appeared a year later. It attracted some notoriety because of its parody of romantic verse, which—to Musset's amusement—was taken seriously by many.

Musset's career as a playwright began at the age of twenty—with a failure. Deeply hurt, he turned from the stage and published his plays for "armchair consumption" instead of producing them. In 1833 he published three works, one of which, *Les caprices de Marianne*, has remained a part of the repertory of the Théâtre Français for over one hundred years.

In the same year, 1833, Musset became involved in the fateful romance with George Sand which so influenced his life and work. He traveled with her to Italy, where they parted; after a partial reconciliation, they were permanently separated in 1835. The *Revue des deux mondes* published seven of Musset's major works that year, among them *The Confession of a Child of the Century*, a fictional account of his relationship with George Sand, from which the following excerpt, descriptive of the post-Napoleonic generation, is taken.

Musset is generally regarded—along with Hugo, Lamartine, and Vigny—as one of the great figures of French romanticism. Although he published a number of lyrics that are highly musical and intensely passionate, it is for his dramatic works that he is chiefly remembered, especially his *proverbs*, witty and graceful comedies to illustrate proverbial sayings. He also published a number of *nouvelles*.

Musset's last years were devoted to journalism and poetry. In 1848, however, his plays began to win wider audiences, and for the next three years his work enjoyed some vogue in Paris, although he never achieved the popularity which he felt he deserved. In 1852, Musset was elected to the Académie Français, not without strong opposition. He died in 1857.

This selection is taken from *The Confession of a Child of the Century*, Vol. VIII, in K. Warren's translation, *The Complete Writings of Alfred De Musset*, 10 vols. (New York: E. C. Hill, 1905).

THE CONFESSION OF A CHILD
OF THE CENTURY

DURING the wars of the Empire, while the husbands and brothers were in Germany, the anxious mothers brought forth an ardent, pale, nervous generation. Conceived between two battles, educated amidst the noises of war, thousands of children looked about them with a somber eye while testing their puny muscles. From time to time their blood-stained fathers would appear, raise them on their gold-laced bosoms, then place them on the ground and remount their horses.

The life of Europe was centered in one man; all were trying to fill their lungs with the air which he had breathed. Every year France presented that man with three hundred thousand of her youth; it was the tax paid to Caesar, and, without that troop behind him, he could not follow his fortune. It was the escort he needed that he might traverse the world, and then perish in a little valley in a deserted island, under the weeping willow.

Never had there been so many sleepless nights as in the time of that man; never had there been seen, hanging over the ramparts of the cities, such a nation of desolate mothers; never was there such a silence about those who spoke of death. And yet there was never such joy, such life, such fanfares of war, in all hearts. Never was there such pure sunlight as that which dried all this blood. God made the sun for this man, they said, and they called it the Sun of Austerlitz. But he made this sunlight himself with his ever-thundering cannons which dispelled all clouds but those which succeed the day of battle.

It was this air of the spotless sky, where shone so much glory, where glistened so many swords, that the youth of the time breathed. They well knew that they were destined to the hecatomb; but they regarded Murat as invulnerable, and the emperor had been seen to cross a bridge where so many bullets whistled that they wondered if he could die. And even if one must die, what did it matter? Death itself was so beautiful, so noble, so illustrious, in his battle-scarred purple! It borrowed the color of hope, it reaped so many ripening harvests that it became young, and there was no more old age. All the cradles of France, as all its tombs, were armed with shield and buckler; there were no more old men, there were corpses or demi-gods.

Nevertheless, the immortal emperor stood one day on a hill watching seven nations engaged in mutual slaughter; as he did not know whether he would be master of all the world or only half, Azrael passed along, touched him with the tip of his wing, and pushed him into the Ocean. At the noise of his fall, the dying powers sat up in their beds of pain; and stealthily advancing with furtive tread, all the royal spiders made the partition of Europe, and the purple of Caesar became the frock of Harlequin.

Just as the traveler, sure of his way, hastens night and day through rain and sunlight, regardless of vigils or of dangers; but when he has reached his home and seated himself before the fire, he is seized upon by a feeling of extreme lassitude and can hardly drag himself to his bed: thus France, the widow of Caesar, suddenly felt her wound. She fell through sheer exhaustion, and lapsed into a sleep so profound that her old kings, believing her dead, wrapped about her a white shroud. The old army, its hair whitened in service, returned exhausted with fatigue, and the hearths of deserted castles sadly flickered into life.

Then the men of the Empire, who had been through so much, who had lived in such carnage, kissed their emaciated wives and spoke of their first love; they looked into the fountains of their natal prairies and found themselves so old, so mutilated, that they bethought themselves of their sons, in order that they might close their eyes in peace. They asked where they were; the children came from the schools, and seeing neither sabers, nor cuirasses, neither infantry nor cavalry, they asked in turn where were their fathers. They were told that the war was ended, that Caesar was dead, and that the portraits of Wellington and of Blücher were suspended in the antechambers of the consulates and the embassies, with these two words beneath: Salvatoribus mundi.[1]

Then there seated itself on a world in ruins an anxious youth. All the children were drops of burning blood which had inundated the earth; they were born in the bosom of war, for war. For fifteen years they had dreamed of the snows of Moscow and of the sun of the pyramids. They had not gone beyond their native towns; but they were told that through each gate of these towns lay the road to a capital of Europe. They had in their heads all the world; they beheld the earth, the sky, the streets and the highways; all these were empty, and the bells of parish churches resounded faintly in the distance.

Pale phantoms shrouded in black robes, slowly traversed the country; others knocked at the doors of houses, and when admitted, drew from their pockets large well-worn documents with which they drove out the tenants. From every direction came men still trembling with the fear which had seized them when they fled twenty years before. All began to urge their

[1] [To the saviors of the world.]

claims, disputing loudly and crying for help; it was strange that a single death should attract so many crows.

The king of France was on his throne, looking here and there to see if he could perchance find a bee [2] in the royal tapestry. Some held out their hats, and he gave them money; others showed him a crucifix, and he kissed it; others contented themselves with pronouncing in his ear great names of powerful families, and he replied to these by inviting them into his "grand salle," where the echoes were more sonorous; still others showed him their old cloaks, when they had carefully effaced the bees, and to these he gave new apparel.

The children saw all this, thinking that the spirit of Caesar would soon land at Cannes and breathe upon this larva; but the silence was unbroken and they saw floating in the sky only the paleness of the lily. When these children spoke of glory, they were answered: "Become priests"; when they spoke of hope, of love, of power, of life: "Become priests."

And yet there mounted the rostrum a man who held in his hand a contract between the king and the people; he began by saying that glory was a beautiful thing, and ambition and war as well; but there was something still more beautiful, and it was called liberty.

The children raised their heads and remembered that their grandfathers had spoken thus. They remembered having seen in certain obscure corners of the paternal home mysterious marble busts with long hair and a Latin inscription; they remembered seeing their grandsires shake their heads and speak of a stream of blood more terrible than that of the emperor. There was something in that word liberty that made their hearts beat with the memory of a terrible past and the hope of a glorious future.

They trembled at the word; but returning to their homes they encountered on the street three panniers [3] which were being borne to Clamart; there were, within, three young men who had pronounced that word liberty too distinctly.

A strange smile hovered on their lips at that sad sight; but other speakers, mounted on the rostrum, began publicly to estimate what ambition had cost and how very dear was glory; they pointed out the horror of war and called the hecatombs butcheries. And they spoke so often and so long that all human illusions, like the trees in autumn, fell leaf by leaf about them, and those who listened passed their hands over their foreheads as though awakened from a feverish dream.

Some said: "The emperor has fallen because the people wished no more of him"; others added: "The people wished the king; no, liberty; no, reason; no,

[2] [Symbol of the Emperor.]   [3] [Baskets.]

religion; no, the English constitution; no, absolutism"; and the last one said: "No, none of these things, but repose."

Three elements entered into the life which offered itself to these children: behind them a past forever destroyed, moving uneasily on its ruins with all the fossils of centuries of absolutism; before them the aurora of an immense horizon, the first gleams of the future; and between these two worlds—something like the Ocean which separates the old world from Young America, something vague and floating, a troubled sea filled with wreckage, traversed from time to time by some distant sail or some ship breathing out heavy vapor; the present, in a word, which separates the past from the future, which is neither the one nor the other, which resembles both, and where one can not know whether, at each step, one is treading on a seed or a piece of refuse.

It was in this chaos that choice must be made; this was the aspect presented to children full of spirit and of audacity, sons of the Empire and grandsons of the Revolution.

As for the past, they would none of it, they had no faith in it; the future, they loved it, but how? As Pygmalion loved Galatea: it was for them a lover in marble and they waited for the breath of life to animate that breast, for the blood to color those veins.

There remained then, the present, the spirit of the time, angel of the dawn who is neither night nor day; they found him seated on a lime sack filled with bones, clad in the mantle of egoism, and shivering in terrible cold. The anguish of death entered into the soul at the sight of that specter, half mummy and half fetus; they approached it as the traveler who is shown at Strasbourg the daughter of an old count of Sarvenden, embalmed in her bride's dress: that childish skeleton makes one shudder, for her slender and livid hand wears the wedding-ring and her head falls into dust in the midst of orange blossoms.

As upon the approach of a tempest there passes through the forests a terrible sound which makes all the trees shudder, to which profound silence succeeds, thus had Napoleon, in passing, shaken the world; kings felt their crowns tremble in the storm and, raising their hands to steady them, they found only their hair, bristling with terror. The pope had traveled three hundred leagues to bless him in the name of God and to crown him with the diadem; but Napoleon had taken it from his hands. Thus everything trembled in that dismal forest of old Europe; then silence succeeded.

It is said that when you meet a mad dog if you keep quietly on your way without turning, the dog will merely follow you a short distance growling and showing his teeth; but if you allow yourself to be frightened into a movement of terror, if you but make a sudden step, he will leap at your throat and devour you; when the first bite has been taken there is no escaping him.

In European history it has often happened that a sovereign has made that movement of terror and his people have devoured him; but if one had done it, all had not done it at the same time, that is to say, one king had disappeared, but not all royal majesty. Before the sword of Napoleon majesty made this movement, this gesture which loses everything, and not only majesty, but religion, nobility, all power both human and divine.

Napoleon dead, human and divine power were re-established, but belief in them no longer existed. A terrible danger lurks in the knowledge of what is possible, for the mind always goes farther. It is one thing to say: "That may be" and another thing to say: "That has been"; it is the first bite of the dog.

The deposition of Napoleon was the last flicker of the lamp of despotism; it destroyed and it parodied kings as Voltaire the Holy Scripture. And after him was heard a great noise: it was the stone of St. Helena which had just fallen on the ancient world. Immediately there appeared in the heavens the cold star of reason, and its rays, like those of the goddess of the night, shedding light without heat, enveloped the world in a livid shroud.

There had been those who hated the nobles, who cried out against priests, who conspired against kings; abuses and prejudices had been attacked; but all that was not so great a novelty as to see a smiling people. If a noble or a priest or a sovereign passed, the peasants who had made war possible began to shake their heads and say: "Ah! when we saw this man at such a time and place he wore a different face." And when the throne and altar were mentioned, they replied: "They are made of four planks of wood; we have nailed them together and torn them apart." And when some one said: "People, you have recovered from the errors which led you astray; you have recalled your kings and your priests," they replied: "We have nothing to do with those prattlers." And when some one said: "People, forget the past, work and obey," they arose from their seats and a dull rumbling could be heard. It was the rusty and notched saber in the corner of the cottage chimney. Then they hastened to add: "Then keep quiet, at least; if no one harms you, do not seek to harm." Alas! they were content with that.

But youth was not content. It is certain that there are in man two occult powers engaged in a death struggle: the one, clear-sighted and cold, is concerned with reality, calculation, weight, and judges the past; the other is thirsty for the future and eager for the unknown. When passion sways man, reason follows him weeping and warning him of his danger; but when man listens to the voice of reason, when he stops at her request and says: "What a fool I am; where am I going?" passion calls to him: "And must I die?"

A feeling of extreme uneasiness began to ferment in all young hearts. Condemned to inaction by the powers which governed the world, delivered to vulgar pedants of every kind, to idleness and to ennui, the youth saw the foaming billows which they had prepared to meet, subside. All these gladiators, glistening with oil, felt in the bottom of their souls an insupportable wretchedness. The richest became libertines; those of moderate fortune followed some profession and resigned themselves to the sword or to the robe. The poorest gave themselves up with cold enthusiasm to great thoughts, plunged into the frightful sea of aimless effort. As human weakness seeks association and as men are herds by nature, politics became mingled with it. There were struggles with the *garde du corps* on the steps of the legislative assembly; at the theater, Talma wore a peruke which made him resemble Caesar; every one flocked to the burial of a liberal deputy.

But of the members of the two parties there was not one who, upon returning home, did not bitterly realize the emptiness of his life and the feebleness of his hands.

While life outside was so colorless and so mean, the interior life of society assumed a somber aspect of silence; hypocrisy ruled in all departments of conduct; English ideas of devotion, gaiety even, had disappeared. Perhaps Providence was already preparing new ways, perhaps the herald angel of future society was already sowing in the hearts of women the seeds of human independence. But it is certain that a strange thing suddenly happened: in all the salons of Paris the men passed to one side and the women to the other; and thus, the one clad in white like a bride and the other in black like an orphan began to take measurements with the eye.

Let us not be deceived: that vestment of black which the men of our time wear is a terrible symbol; before coming to this, the armor must have fallen piece by piece and the embroidery flower by flower. Human reason has overthrown all illusions; but it bears in itself sorrow, in order that it may be consoled.

The customs of students and artists, those customs so free, so beautiful, so full of youth, began to experience the universal change. Men in taking leave of women whispered the word which wounds to the death: contempt. They plunged into the dissipation of wine and courtesans. Students and artists did the same; love was treated as glory and religion; it was an old illusion. The grisette, that class so dreamy, so romantic, so tender, and so sweet in love, abandoned herself to the counting-house and to the shop. She was poor and no one loved her; she wanted dresses and hats and she sold herself. O, misery! the young man who ought to love her, whom she loved, who used to take her to the woods of Verrieres and Romainville, to the dances on the lawn, to the suppers under the trees; he who used to talk with her as she sat near the lamp in the rear of the shop on the long winter evenings; he who shared her crust of bread moistened with the sweat of her brow, and her love at once sublime and poor; he, that same man, after having abandoned her, finds her after a night of orgy, pale and leaden, forever lost, with hunger on her lips and prostitution in her heart.

About this time two poets, whose genius was second only to that of Napoleon, consecrated their lives to the work of collecting all the elements of anguish and of grief scattered over the universe. Goethe, the patriarch of a new literature, after having painted in "Werther" the passion which leads to suicide, traced in his "Faust" the most somber human character which has ever represented evil and unhappiness. His writings began to pass from Germany into France. From his studio, surrounded by pictures and statues, rich, happy and at ease, he watched with a paternal smile, his gloomy creations marching in dismal procession across the frontiers of France. Byron replied to him by a cry of grief which made Greece tremble, and suspended "Manfred" over the abyss as if nothingness had been the answer of the hideous enigma with which he enveloped him.

When English and German ideas passed thus over our heads there ensued disgust and mournful silence, followed by a terrible convulsion. For to formulate general ideas is to change saltpeter into powder, and the Homeric brain of the great Goethe had sucked up, as an alembic, all the juice of the forbidden fruit. Those who did not read him did not believe it, knew nothing of it. Poor creatures! The explosion carried them away like grains of dust into the abyss of universal doubt.

It was a degeneration of all things of heaven and of earth that might be termed disenchantment, or if you preferred, despair; as if humanity in lethargy had been pronounced dead by those who held its place. Like a soldier who was asked: "In what do you believe?" and who replied: "In myself." Thus the youth of France, hearing that question, replied: "In nothing."

Then they formed into two camps: on one side the exalted spirits, sufferers, all the expansive souls who had need of the infinite, bowed their heads and wept; they wrapt themselves in unhealthy dreams and there could be seen nothing but broken reeds on an ocean of bitterness. On the other side the men of flesh remained standing, inflexible in the midst of positive joys, and cared for nothing except to count the money they had acquired. It was only a sob and a burst of laughter, the one coming from the soul, the other from the body.

This is what the soul said:

"Alas! Alas! religion has departed; the clouds of heaven fall in rain; we have no longer either hope or expectation, not even two little pieces of black wood in the shape of a cross before which to clasp our hands. The star of the future is loath to rise; it can not get above the horizon; it is enveloped in clouds, like the sun in winter its disk is the color of blood, as in '93. There is no more love, no more glory. What heavy darkness over all the earth! And we shall be dead when the day breaks."

This is what the body said:

"Man is here below to satisfy his senses, he has more or less of white or yellow metal to which he owes more or less esteem. To eat, to drink and to sleep, that is life. As for the bonds which exist between men, friendship consists in loaning money; but one rarely has a friend whom he loves enough for that. Kinship determines inheritance; love is an exercise of the body; the only intellectual joy is vanity."

Like the Asiatic plague exhaled from the vapors of the Ganges, frightful despair stalked over the earth. Already Chateaubriand, prince of poesy, wrapping the horrible idol in his pilgrim's mantle, had placed it on a marble altar in the midst of perfumes and holy incense. Already the children were tightening their idle hands and drinking in their bitter cup the poisoned brewage of doubt. Already things were drifting toward the abyss, when the jackals suddenly emerged from the earth. A cadaverous and infected literature which had no form but that of ugliness, began to sprinkle with fetid blood all the monsters of nature.

Who will dare to recount what was passing in the colleges? Men doubted everything: the young men denied everything. The poets sung of despair; the youth came from the schools with serene brow, their faces glowing with health and blasphemy in their mouths. Moreover, the French character, being by nature gay and open, readily assimiliated English and German ideas; but hearts too light to struggle and to suffer withered like crushed flowers. Thus the principle of death descended slowly and without shock from the head to the bowels. Instead of having the enthusiasm of evil we had only the negation of the good; instead of despair, insensibility. Children of fifteen seated listlessly under flowering shrubs, conversed for pastime on subjects which would have made shudder with terror the motionless groves of Versailles. The Communion of Christ, the host, those wafers that stand as the eternal symbol of divine love, were used to seal letters; the children spit upon the bread of God.

Happy they who escaped those times! Happy they who passed over the abyss while looking up to Heaven. There are such, doubtless, and they will pity us.

The rich said: "There is nothing real but riches, all else is a dream; let us enjoy and then let us die." Those of moderate fortune said: "There is nothing real but oblivion, all else is a dream; let us forget and let us die." And the poor said: "There is nothing real but unhappiness, all else is a dream; let us blaspheme and die."

This is too black? It is exaggerated? What do you think of it? Am I a misanthrope? Allow me to make a reflection.

In reading the history of the fall of the Roman Empire, it is impossible to overlook the evil that the Christians, so admirable in the desert, did the state when they were in power. "When I think," said Montesquieu, "of the profound ignorance into which the Greek clergy plunged the laity, I am obliged to compare them to the Scythians of whom Herodotus speaks, who put out the eyes of their slaves in order that nothing might distract their attention from their work. . . . No affair of state, no peace, no truce, no negotiation, no marriage could be transacted by any one but the clergy. The evils of this system were beyond belief."

Montesquieu might have added: Christianity destroyed the emperors but it saved the people. It opened to the barbarians the palaces of Constantinople, but it opened the doors of cottages to the ministering angels of Christ. It had much to do with the great ones of earth. And what is more interesting than the death-rattle of an empire corrupt to the very marrow of its bones, than the somber galvanism under the influence of which the skeleton of tyranny danced upon the tombs of Heliogabalus and Caracalla! What a beautiful thing that mummy of Rome, embalmed in the perfumes of Nero and swathed in the shroud of Tiberius! It had to do, messieurs the politicians, with finding the poor and giving them life and peace; it had to do with allowing the worms and tumors to destroy the monuments of shame, while drawing from the ribs of this mummy a virgin as beautiful as the mother of the Redeemer, hope, the friend of the oppressed.

That is what Christianity did; and now, after many years, what have they who destroyed it done? They saw that the poor allowed themselves to be oppressed by the rich, the feeble by the strong, because of that saying: "The rich and the strong will oppress me on earth; but when they wish to enter paradise, I shall be at the door and I will accuse them before the tribunal of God." And so, alas! they were patient.

The antagonists of Christ therefore said to the poor: "You wait patiently for the day of justice: there is no justice; you wait for the life eternal to achieve your vengeance: there is no life eternal; you gather up your tears and those of your family, the cries of children and the sobs of women, to place them at the feet of God at the hour of death: there is no God."

Then it is certain that the poor man dried his tears, that he told his wife to check her sobs, his children to come with him, and that he stood upon the earth with the power of a bull. He said to the rich: "Thou who oppressest me, thou art only man"; and to the priest: "Thou who hast consoled me, thou hast lied." That was just what the antagonists of Christ desired. Perhaps they thought this was the way to achieve man's happiness, sending him out to the conquest of liberty.

But, if the poor man, once satisfied that the priests deceive him, that the rich rob him, that all men have rights, that all good is of this world, and that misery is impiety; the poor man, believing in himself and in his two arms, says to himself some fine day: "War on the rich! for me, happiness here in this life, since there is no other! for me, the earth, since heaven is empty! for me and for all, since all are equal." Oh! reasoners sublime who have led him to this, what will you say to him if he is conquered?

Doubtless you are philanthropists, doubtless you are right about the future, and the day will come when you will be blessed; but thus far, we have not blessed you. When the oppressor said: "This world for me!" the oppressed replied: "Heaven for me!" Now what can he say?

All the evils of the present come from two causes: the people who have passed through 1793 and 1814, nurse wounds in their hearts. That which was is no more; what will be, is not yet. Do not seek elsewhere the cause of our malady.

Here is a man whose house falls in ruins; he has torn it down in order to build another. The rubbish encumbers the spot, and he waits for fresh materials for his new home. At the moment he has prepared to cut the stone and mix the cement, while standing, pick in hand, with sleeves rolled up, he is informed that there is no more stone, and is advised to whiten the old material and make the best possible use of that. What can you expect this man to do who is unwilling to build his nest out of ruins? The quarry is deep, the tools too weak to hew out the stones. "Wait!" they say to him, "we will draw out the stones one by one; hope, work, advance, withdraw." What do they not tell him? And in the meantime he has lost his old house, and has not yet built the new; he does not know where to protect himself from the rain, or how to prepare his evening meal, nor where to work, nor where to sleep, nor where to die; and his children are newly born.

I am much deceived if we do not resemble that man. O, people of the future! when on a warm summer day you bend over your plows in the green fields of your native land; when you see, in the pure sunlight under a spotless sky, the earth, your fruitful mother, smiling in her matutinal robe on the workman, her well-beloved child; when drying on your brow the holy baptism of sweat, you cast your eye over the vast horizon, when there will not be one blade higher than another in the human harvest, but only violets and marguerites in the midst of ripening sheaves. Oh! free men! when you thank God that you were born for that harvest, think of those who are no more, tell yourself that we have dearly purchased the repose which you enjoy; pity us more than all your fathers, for we have suffered the evil which entitled them to pity and we have lost that which consoled them.

III THE ADVANCE OF INDUSTRIALIZATION

ENCLOSURES

FROM 1714 to 1801 about six million acres of English land were parceled out anew through 2,183 enclosure acts. Each member of a community received an area equal in size, but not necessarily in quality, to that of his open-field strips, plus a proportional addition in lieu of his undivided right to the commons. Obviously if he was a small landowner the additional area he received was trifling, while the great landowners received the lion's share. The cottagers received no addition at all. Migration to the cities now took on larger proportions and spilled over into what became the British Dominions and the United States. Both agriculture and industry ultimately benefited from this painful trek. The former witnessed a rapid technical progress, and the latter was fed by a steady supply of cheap manpower. As a result, the general standard of living improved, though by 1800 landlords, tenant farmers, and wage labor had come to characterize the rural pattern. Towards the end of the nineteenth century there were attempts to revive the small farms. Some progress in this direction was achieved during both World Wars, but it fell far short of creating an agriculture of moderate-sized, owner-worked farms.

The selection that follows is taken from the *General Report of the Agricultural State, and Political Circumstances of Scotland* (1814) drawn up under the direction of Sir John Sinclair for the British Board of Agriculture and Internal Improvement. Obviously the Board reflected the views of the ruling class of Great Britain as the latter was constituted before the Victorian Compromise.

GENERAL REPORT OF THE AGRICULTURAL STATE, AND POLITICAL CIRCUMSTANCES, OF SCOTLAND

INTRODUCTION

. . . THE TERM *Inclosure* has very different meanings in the rural and legal languages of Scotland and England. In England, the conversion of lands held in common, either for pasturage or cultivation, into severalty, or exclusive individual property, must in general be accomplished by a separate act of Parliament, which has obtained the name of an *Inclosure Bill,* because the commissioners, appointed for dividing and allocating the lands subjected to their authority, among those having interest, have power to inclose, as well as to divide or apportion them; and hence they are termed Commissioners of Inclosure.

This matter is far otherwise managed in Scotland, where so expensive an expedient has not been found necessary. The Legislature of this country, above an hundred years ago, provided a general law for that purpose, which has been so universally acted upon, that common-field lands, and common wastes or pastures, have both become very rare in Scotland. In Scotland, common-field lands used to be known by the name of run-rig or run-dale, because the alternate lands or ridges belonging to different proprietors or occupants run alongside of each other; while the term common was restricted to wastes or pastures not occupied in severalty. These are indeed still to be found in various parts of Scotland; but the run-rig or common-field lands have almost entirely disappeared, except in places where the crown has an interest, or in such as belong to royal burghs, which were exempted from the operation of this most salutary law. . . .

GENERAL VIEW OF THE ADVANTAGES OF INCLOSURES

In considering the advantages to be derived from proposed inclosures, a landed proprietor has occasion for the exercise of much attentive observation, and sagacious reflection, before he determines upon any specific plan. In most cases, he ought to take counsel with himself and others, to enable him to ascertain what benefits are most wanted by his lands, and how these are most likely to be effected by inclosures, and then to form his plan upon a mature consideration of all the circumstances combined. It is not enough that he be offered a percentage for the outlay, or a larger money rent in consequence of inclosure, unless convinced that the specific plan is good, and embraces at least the most important advantages that can be effected by inclosures. When this fundamental point is settled, he will next reflect upon the means of its accomplishment, and on the best plan of economy, for saving unnecessary expence, both in the first instance and in future, and for securing the permanence of the fences. When all these have been successively and duly considered, he may enter into engagements for their execution, but not sooner. The advantages of inclosures ought to be considered as connected with climate, soil, and occupancy.

1. A climate that is naturally warm or mild, will hardly require artificial shelter; but if cold, and backward for the production of crops, and hazardous or injurious to live-stock, shelter ought to be one of the first and most important objects held in view.

2. A dry and kindly soil gives encouragement for plans of improvement

by cultivation, and the fences and inclosures ought to be adapted for that purpose, not forgetting what may be necessary in regard to climate. If the soil be wet, a large proportion of the fences ought also to be planned and constructed for the additional purpose of drainage.

3. If the lands to be inclosed are to be occupied in pasture, the plan must be adapted to that end, taking into consideration the particular kind of stock with which it is to be occupied. The same kind of fence that may sufficiently confine cattle, does not answer for sheep; and various breeds of sheep require different kinds of fences. The general objects of consideration on this head are, to save expence in herding and attendance, to arrange the stock, to enable them to pasture quietly, undisturbed by dogs or other violence, and to shelter them, as effectually as may be, from cold and storms.

4. If the lands are to be chiefly occupied under grain, or other cultivated crops, the great objects of inclosure must be, a good arrangement of the fields for easy and correct access and cultivation, and for the effectual protection of the crops from trespass and depredation.

5. When a mixed mode of occupancy is in view, embracing both cultivation and pasturage, a combination of the foregoing considerations must form the basis for a proper plan of inclosure.

ADVANTAGES OF INCLOSURE TO PROPRIETORS

Under many defects in the plan still usually pursued, and in the modes of execution, inclosures are considered so necessary and useful by all practical farmers, that, in consideration of having their land properly inclosed and fenced, they readily agree to pay a liberal percentage to the landlord for the expence, and to uphold the fences at their own charges during the occupancy, providing they have a reasonable time allowed them for reaping the consequent advantages.

Even the appearance of inclosures indicates comfort and security; and landlords never fail to draw very advanced rents from well-inclosed lands, which generally let from 20 to 50, and in some cases, even 70 *per cent*. higher than open lands of the same description in the neighbourhood; the value or rate of rent continuing to advance, as the inclosed soil goes on to improve. By means likewise of inclosure, the landlord often has an opportunity to appropriate many waste spots, and otherwise useless corners, for plantations; to the great embellishment of his property, and the solid emolument of himself or his successors. These patches are of very little value to the occupier, and pay scarcely any rent to the proprietor; and the ultimate value of the plantations may therefore be considered as clear gain after the expences of inclosing and planting are defrayed. Indeed, instead of diminishing the rental, the plantations, after a few years, will render the contiguous farms more valuable, and capable of paying a higher rent than before, when these spots were attached to them. It is the universal and equitable practice in Scotland, that no charge is made upon the farmer for so much of the fencing as is necessary to the protection of young plantations, and these fences are always upheld afterwards by the landlord.

ADVANTAGES OF INCLOSURES TO FARMERS

Farmers derive many important advantages from judiciously disposed and well constructed inclosures. Their value, however, materially differs, under particular circumstances;—owing to errors in the original plan, defects in the formation and upholding of the fences, or improper management of the inclosed live-stock or growing crops; by means of which defects, all inclosures may be rendered comparatively worthless. If, however, the abuse of any thing were to become an argument against its usefulness, no circumstance whatever, in the economy of any country, could escape this mode of objection. It is from the aggregate of all the advantages derivable from judiciously planned, well constructed, and well managed inclosures and fences, that farmers are enabled, at the same time, to pay more liberal rents, to advance the value of their live-stocks and crops, and finally to augment their own individual profits. Of these advantages we propose to take a rapid view, in their order.

In the pasturage of live-stock, the farmer is relieved, by means of inclosures, from the very considerable expence of herding and attendance; which is materially diminished in the management of sheep, and almost entirely saved in that of cattle, when the fences are all good. The farmer has it in his power to arrange his live-stock, according to their age, condition, and other circumstances, by means of his inclosures, without which his management cannot be correct. This arrangement, especially in sheep-stocks, is often absolutely necessary for the preservation of a part, and is almost always important for the prosperity and improvement of the whole. By means of inclosures, the pasturing stock is protected from being perpetually teazed, harassed, and interrupted in feeding, by dogs or other violence, and is allowed in peace to eat up the food upon the pastures to its utmost limits; and thus it improves much better and faster on the same extent of land, and of course returns more ample profit to the farmer.

The mere prevention of poaching in wet weather, by the trampling of cattle when chased by dogs, is an advantage of no small importance derived from inclosures or fence divisions. Even the warmth derived from inclosures to the live-stock, in cold and stormy weather, is stated by one intelligent observer, as running from five to eight degrees of the thermometer above that of bleak unsheltered lands in the same neighbourhood. It is of the utmost importance, to the comfort and consequent thriving of live-stock, that, in inclosures, they can always have a sheltered place in which to sleep or ruminate: and it is well known, that the grass is both earlier and more abundant in inclosures, than in bleak exposed open lands, of similar soils, and in the same neighbourhood.

In the management of his arable lands, the farmer derives other solid advantages from inclosures. The important idea of security against trespass, from his own live-stock and those of his neighbours, gives a stimulus to his exertions towards improvement, enabling him to adopt a correct rotation of crops, to proceed with vigour in their cultivation, and to reap their fruits in safety. The case is widely different on open lands; in which wheat, sown grasses, turnips, and other crops, are constantly exposed to trespass in winter, and cannot therefore be cultivated to advantage.

In addition to the foregoing important advantages, a judiciously planned and well executed fence, often operates as a most useful drain to the land in its neighbourhood. Were the entire advantages, derivable by farmers from good inclosures, capable of being correctly estimated in contrast with uninclosed land, it would probably appear, that an acre of inclosed pasture land, is worth twice as much as an acre of the same kind of land, and in the same climate, if not inclosed. When the whole of a farm is under tillage rotations, as is the case in the Carse of Gowrie, and on the best land of East Lothian, subdivision fences, though still very advantageous, cannot indeed be supposed to add so much to the value of the soil.

ADVANTAGES TO THE LABOURERS

Labourers find a great source of employment, in the first instance, in the execution of plans of inclosure, and afterwards in upholding them; besides which, there is a great extension of work provided for them, in consequence of the various improvements required upon inclosed land, far beyond what is called for in open lands; for the same waste that afforded only the miserable wages and bare subsistence of a herd-boy, and that only for a portion of the year, becomes capable, when inclosed, cultivated, and improved, to give employment and bread to many.

Even from the division of commons in Scotland, there is no injury to be dreaded by the labouring class, as their cottages give no right to keep cows on these wastes; and, where they have a right of fuel, that is always guarded in a process of division. Wherever extensive inclosures are forming, there is always a very considerable source of employment and subsistence for industrious labourers; and the prospective advantages, afforded by the future improvements on the land when inclosed, are still more considerable and encouraging.

ADVANTAGES OF INCLOSURES TO THE PUBLIC

In regard to the public, the advantages arising from inclosures, are numerous and important. By means of them, the country is, at the same time, partly drained, and considerably sheltered, which latter improvement upon the climate is rendered more extensive and more remarkable, when plantations of trees are formed along with inclosures. No person acquainted with the naturally bleak, moist and ungenial climate of Scotland, can refuse to acknowledge the great improvement it has received from plantations.

Although all inclosures do not add to the ornamental or picturesque appearance of a country; yet all that are judiciously planned and well conducted ought to have this effect, more especially in a country so much diversified with hill and dale. Accordingly, and with few exceptions, inclosures have added much to the ornament of Scotland; and particularly such of them as have been conjoined with plantations. By the latter also, as connected with inclosures, which they always necessarily require to a certain extent, weedings of young trees are procured for various useful purposes, and timber may be furnished hereafter for our wooden walls and commercial ships, together with oak bark for the purposes of the tanner.

From what has been already stated, respecting the wages and subsistence, afforded by means of inclosures, to a numerous set of labourers, and the subsequent great increase of food for mankind, which the inclosed land afterwards produces, it necessarily follows, that the population of the kingdom must be proportionally encouraged, increased, and supported, and that a numerous and hardy peasantry will thereby be trained up in the most productive and most valuable species of labour. As the physical strength of the nation evidently depends on the numbers of its hardy peasantry, every thing that tends to increase their numbers, and to contribute towards their comfortable subsistence, is deserving of the utmost encouragement.

ANDREW URE

THE RAPID GROWTH of the factory system in England in the first half of the nineteenth century brought with it manifold problems. Critics attacked its consequences from many different points of view, while apologists enthusiastically pointed to the economic progress achieved and defended the factory as the benefactor of humanity. Prominent among the latter was Andrew Ure (1778–1857), a Scottish chemist who turned his talents to the study of industry and to its defense. Ure is chiefly remembered today for his glowing descriptions of the healthful working conditions of the factory operatives, and for his praise of child labor. He wrote, of child workers, that

"They seemed to be always cheerful and alert, taking pleasure in the light play of their muscles—enjoying the mobility natural to their age. The scene of industry, so far from exciting sad emotions in my mind, was always exhilarating. It was delightful to observe the nimbleness with which they pieced the broken ends, as the mule-carriage began to recede from the fixed roller-beam, and to see them at leisure, after a few seconds' exercise of their tiny fingers, to amuse themselves in any attitude they chose, till the stretch and winding-on were once more completed. The work of these lively elves seemed to resemble a sport, in which habit gave them a pleasing dexterity. Conscious of their skill, they were delighted to show it off to any stranger. As to exhaustion by the day's work, they evinced no trace of it on emerging from the mill in the evening; for they immediately began to skip about any neighbouring playground, and to commence their little amusements with the same alacrity as boys issuing from a school. . . ."

And again,

"Of all the common prejudices that exist with regard to factory labour, there is none more unfounded than that which ascribes to it excessive tedium and irksomeness above other occupations, owing to its being carried on in conjunction with the 'unceasing motion of the steam-engine.' . . . Of all manufacturing employments, those are by far the most irksome and incessant in which steam-engines are not employed, as in lace-running and stocking-weaving; and the way to prevent an employment from being incessant, is to introduce a steam-engine into it. These remarks certainly apply more especially to the labour of children in factories. Three-fourths of the children so employed are engaged in piecing at the mules. 'When the carriages of these have receded a foot and a half or two feet from the rollers,' says Mr. Tufnell [Supplementary Report of Factory Commissioners] 'nothing is to be done, not even attention is required from either spinner or piecer.' Both of them stand idle for a time, and in fine spinning particularly, for three-quarters of a minute, or more. Consequently, if a child remains at this business twelve hours daily, he has nine hours of inaction. And though he attend two mules, he has still six hours of non-exertion. Spinners sometimes dedicate these intervals to the perusal of books."

Ure's writings are of interest from another standpoint. They bring to us the reflections of a thoughtful contemporary on the nature and course of industrial development in the first half of the nineteenth century, and valuable observations on industrial processes. The following selection, like those above, is taken from his *The Philosophy of Manufactures* (1835). This book may be considered a rejoinder to the first effective Factory Act (1833), by which, after a generation of vain effort, the central government laid down and enforced regulations governing the labor of children.

♋

THE PHILOSOPHY OF MANUFACTURES

[Book I]

CHAPTER I: GENERAL VIEW OF MANUFACTURING INDUSTRY

. . . THE TERM *Factory System,* in technology, designates the combined operation of many orders of work-people, adult and young, in tending with assiduous skill a series of productive machines continuously impelled by a central power. This definition includes such organizations as cotton-mills, flax-mills, silk-mills, woollen-mills, and certain engineering works; but it excludes those in which the mechanisms do not form a connected series, nor are dependent on one prime mover. Of the latter class, examples occur in iron-works, dye-works, soap-works, brass-foundries, &c. Some authors, indeed, have comprehended under the title *factory,* all extensive establishments wherein a number of people co-operate towards a common purpose of art; and would therefore rank breweries, distilleries, as well as the workshops of carpenters, turners, coopers, &c., under the factory system. But I conceive that this title, in its strictest sense, involves the idea of a vast automaton, composed of various mechanical and intellectual organs, acting in uninterrupted concert for the production of a common object, all of them being subordinated to a self-regulated moving force. If the marshalling of human beings in systematic order for the execution of any technical enterprise were allowed to constitute a factory, this term might embrace every department of civil and military engineering—a latitude of application quite inadmissible.

In its precise acceptation, the Factory system is of recent origin, and may claim England for its birthplace. The mills for throwing silk, or making organzine, which were mounted centuries ago in several of the Italian states, and furtively transferred to this country by Sir Thomas Lombe in 1718, contained indeed certain elements of a factory, and probably suggested some hints of those grander and more complex combinations of self-acting machines, which were first embodied half a century later in our cotton manufacture by Richard Arkwright, assisted by gentlemen of Derby, well acquainted with its celebrated silk establishment. But the spinning of an entangled flock of fibres into a smooth thread, which constitutes the main operation with cotton, is in silk superfluous; being already performed by the unerring instinct of a worm, which leaves to human art the simple task of doubling and twisting its regular filaments. The apparatus requisite for this purpose is more elementary, and calls for few of those gradations of machinery which are needed in the carding, drawing, roving, and spinning processes of a cotton-mill.

When the first water-frames for spinning cotton were erected at Cromford, in the romantic valley of the Derwent, about sixty years ago, mankind were little aware of the mighty revolution which the new system of labour was destined by Providence to achieve, not only in the structure of British society, but in the fortunes of the world at large. Arkwright alone had the sagacity to discern, and the boldness to predict in glowing language, how vastly productive human industry would become, when no longer proportioned in its results to muscular effort, which is by its nature fitful and capricious, but when made to consist in the task of guiding the work of mechanical fingers and arms, regularly impelled with great velocity by some indefatigable physical power. What his judgment so clearly led him to perceive, his energy of will enabled him to realize with such rapidity and success, as would have done honour to the most influential individuals, but were truly wonderful in that obscure and indigent artisan.

The main difficulty did not, to my apprehension, lie so much in the invention of a proper self-acting mechanism for drawing out and twisting cotton into a continuous thread, as in the distribution of the different members of the apparatus into one co-operative body, in impelling each organ with its appropriate delicacy and speed, and above all, in training human beings to renounce their desultory habits of work, and to identify themselves with the unvarying regularity of the complex automaton. To devise and administer a successful code of factory discipline, suited to the necessities of factory diligence, was the Herculean enterprise, the noble achievement of Arkwright. Even at the present day, when the system is perfectly organized, and its labour lightened to the utmost, it is found nearly impossible to convert persons past the age of puberty, whether drawn from rural or from handicraft occupations, into useful factory hands. After struggling for a while to conquer their listless or restive habits, they either renounce the employment spontaneously, or are dismissed by the overlookers on account of inattention.

If the factory Briareus could have been created by mechanical genius alone, it should have come into being thirty years sooner; for upwards of ninety years have now elapsed since John Wyatt, of Birmingham, not only invented the series of fluted rollers, (the spinning fingers usually ascribed to Arkwright,) but obtained a patent for the invention, and erected "a spinning engine without hands" in his native town. The details of this remarkable circumstance, recently snatched from oblivion, will be given in our Treatise on the Cotton Manufactures. Wyatt was a man of good education, in a respectable walk of life, much esteemed by his superiors, and therefore favourably placed, in a mechanical point of view, for maturing his admirable scheme. But he was of a gentle and passive spirit, little qualified to cope with the hardships of a new manufacturing enterprise. It required, in fact, a man of a Napoleon nerve and ambition to subdue the refractory tempers of work-people accustomed to irregular paroxysms of diligence, and to urge on his multifarious and intricate constructions in the face of prejudice, passion, and envy. Such was Arkwright, who, suffering nothing to stay or turn aside his progress, arrived gloriously at the goal, and has for ever affixed his name to a great era in the annals of mankind,—an era which has laid open unbounded prospects of wealth and comfort to the industrious, however much they may have been occasionally clouded by ignorance and folly.

Prior to this period, manufactures were everywhere feeble and fluctuating in their development; shooting forth luxuriantly for a season, and again withering almost to the roots, like annual plants. Their perennial growth now began in England, and attracted capital in copious streams to irrigate the rich domains of industry. When this new career commenced, about the year 1770, the annual consumption of cotton in British manufactures was under four millions of pounds weight, and that of the whole of Christendom was probably not more than ten millions. Last year the consumption in Great Britain and Ireland was about two hundred and seventy millions of pounds, and that of Europe and the United States together four hundred and eighty millions. This prodigious increase is, without doubt, almost entirely due to the factory system founded and upreared by the intrepid native of Preston. If, then, this system be not merely an inevitable step in the social progression of the world, but the one which gives a commanding station and influence to the people who most resolutely take it, it does not become any man, far less a denizen of this favoured land, to vilify the author of a benefaction, which, wisely administered, may become the best temporal gift of Providence to the poor,—a blessing destined to mitigate, and in some measure to repeal, the primeval curse pronounced on the labour of man, "in the sweat of thy face shalt thou eat bread." Arkwright well deserves to live in honoured remembrance among those ancient master-spirits, who persuaded their roaming companions to exchange the precarious toils of the chase, for the settled comforts of agriculture.

In my recent tour, continued during several months, through the manufacturing districts, I have seen tens of thousands of old, young, and middle-aged of both sexes, many of them too feeble to get their daily bread by any of the former modes of industry, earning abundant food, raiment, and domestic accommodation, without perspiring at a single pore, screened meanwhile from the summer's sun and the winter's frost, in apartments more airy and salubrious than those of the metropolis in which our legislative and fashionable aristocracies assemble. In those spacious halls the benignant power of steam summons around him his myriads of willing menials, and assigns to each the regulated task, substituting for painful muscular effort on their part, the energies of his own gigantic arm, and demanding in return only attention and dexterity to correct such little aberrations as casually occur in his workmanship. The gentle docility of this moving force qualifies it for impelling the tiny bobbins of the lace-machine with a precision and speed inimitable by the most dexterous hands, directed by the sharpest eyes. Hence, under its auspices, and in obedience to Arkwright's polity, magnificent edifices, surpassing far in number, value, usefulness, and ingenuity of construction, the boasted monuments of Asiatic, Egyptian, and Roman despotism, have, within the short period of fifty years, risen up in this kingdom, to show to what extent capital, industry, and science may augment the resources of a state, while they meliorate the condition of its citizens. Such is the factory system, replete with prodigies in mechanics and political economy, which promises in its future growth to become the great minister of civilization to the terraqueous globe, enabling this country, as its heart, to diffuse along with its commerce the life-blood of science and religion to myriads of people still lying "in the region and shadow of death."

When Adam Smith wrote his immortal elements of economics, automatic machinery being hardly known, he was properly led to regard the division of labour as the grand principle of manufacturing improvement; and he showed, in the example of pin-making, how each handicraftsman, being thereby enabled to perfect himself by practice in one point, became a quicker and cheaper workman. In each branch of manufacture he saw that some parts were, on that principle, of easy execution, like the cutting of pin wires into uniform lengths, and some were comparatively difficult, like the formation and fixation of their heads; and therefore he concluded that to each a workman of appropriate value and cost was naturally assigned. This appropriation forms the very essence of the division of labour, and has been constantly made since the origin of society. The ploughman, with powerful hand and skilful eye, has been always hired at high wages to form the furrow, and the ploughboy at low wages, to lead the team. But what was in Dr. Smith's time a topic of useful illustration, cannot now be used without risk of misleading the public mind as to the right principle of manufacturing industry. In fact, the division, or rather adaptation of labour to the different talents of men, is little thought of in factory employment. On the contrary, wherever a process requires peculiar dexterity and steadiness of hand, it is withdrawn as soon as possible from the *cunning* workman, who is prone to irregularities of many kinds, and it is placed in charge of a peculiar mechanism, so self-regulating, that a child may superintend it. Thus,—to take an example from the spinning of cotton—the first operation in delicacy and importance, is that of laying the fibres truly parallel in the spongy slivers, and the next is that of drawing these out into slender spongy cords, called rovings, with the least possible twist; both being perfectly uniform throughout their total length. To execute either of these processes tolerably by a hand-wheel would require a degree of skill not to be met with in one artisan out of a hundred. But fine yarn could not be made in factory-spinning except by taking these steps, nor was it ever made by machinery till Arkwright's sagacity contrived them. Moderately good yarn may be spun indeed on the *hand-wheel* without any drawings at all, and with even indifferent rovings, because the thread, under the twofold action of twisting and extension, has a tendency to equalize itself.

The principle of the factory system then is, to substitute mechanical science for hand skill, and the partition of a process into its essential constituents, for the division or graduation of labour among artisans. On the handicraft plan, labour more or less skilled was usually the most expensive element of production—*Materiem superabat opus;* but on the automatic plan, skilled labour gets progressively superseded, and will, eventually, be replaced by mere overlookers of machines.

By the infirmity of human nature it happens, that the more skilful the workman, the more self-willed and intractable he is apt to become, and, of course, the less fit a component of a mechanical system, in which, by occasional irregularities, he may do great damage to the whole. The grand object therefore of the modern manufacturer is, through the union of capital and science, to reduce the task of his work-people to the exercise of vigilance and dexterity,—faculties, when concentred to one process, speedily brought to perfection in the young. In the infancy of mechanical engineering, a machine-factory displayed the division of labour in manifold gradations—the file, the drill, the lathe, having each its different workmen in the order of skill: but the dextrous hands of the filer and driller are now superseded by the planing, the key-groove cutting, and the drilling-machines; and those of the iron and brass turners, by the self-acting slide-lathe. Mr. Anthony Strutt, who conducts the mechanical department of the great cotton factories of Belper and Milford, has so thoroughly departed from the old routine of the schools, that he will employ no man who has learned his craft by regular apprentice-ship; but in contempt, as it were, of the division of labour principle, he sets a ploughboy to turn a shaft of perhaps several tons weight, and never has rea-son to repent his preference, because he infuses into the turning apparatus a precision of action, equal, if not superior, to the skill of the most experienced journeyman.

An eminent mechanician in Manchester told me, that he does not choose to make any steam-engines at present, because, with his existing means, he would need to resort to the old principle of the division of labour, so fruitful of jealousies and strikes among workmen; but he intends to prosecute that branch of business whenever he has prepared suitable arrangements on the equalization of labour, or automatic plan. On the graduation system, a man must serve an apprenticeship of many years before his hand and eye become skilled enough for certain mechanical feats; but on the system of decomposing a process into its constituents, and embodying each part in an automatic ma-chine, a person of common care and capacity may be intrusted with any of the said elementary parts after a short probation, and may be transferred from one to another, on any emergency, at the discretion of the master. Such translations are utterly at variance with the old practice of the division of la-bour, which fixed one man to shaping the head of a pin, and another to sharpening its point, with most irksome and spirit-wasting uniformity, for a whole life.

It was indeed a subject of regret to observe how frequently the work-man's eminence, in any craft, had to be purchased by the sacrifice of his health and comfort. To one unvaried operation, which required unremitting dexterity and diligence, his hand and eye were constantly on the strain, or if they were suffered to swerve from their task for a time, considerable loss ensued, either to the employer, or the operative, according as the work was done by the day or by the piece. But on the equalization plan of self-acting machines, the operative needs to call his faculties only into agreeable exer-cise; he is seldom harassed with anxiety or fatigue, and may find many leisure moments for either amusement or meditation, without detriment to his master's interests or his own. As his business consists in tending the work of a well-regulated mechanism, he can learn it in a short period; and when he transfers his services from one machine to another, he varies his task, and enlarges his views, by thinking on those general combinations which result from his and his companions' labours. Thus, that cramping of the faculties, that narrowing of the mind, that stunting of the frame, which were ascribed and not unjustly, by moral writers, to the division of labour, cannot, in com-mon circumstances, occur under the equable distribution of industry. How superior in vigour and intelligence are the factory mechanics in Lancashire, where the latter system of labour prevails, to the handicraft artisans of London, who, to a great extent, continue slaves to the former! The one set is familiar with almost every physico-mechanical combination, while the other seldom knows anything beyond the pin-head sphere of his daily task.

It is, in fact, the constant aim and tendency of every improvement in machinery to supersede human labour altogether, or to diminish its cost, by substituting the industry of women and children for that of men; or that of ordinary labourers for trained artisans. In most of the water-twist, or throstle cotton-mills, the spinning is entirely managed by females of sixteen years and upwards. The effect of substituting the self-acting mule for the common mule, is to discharge the greater part of the men spinners, and to retain adolescents and children. The proprietor of a factory near Stockport states, in evidence to the commissioners, that, by such substitution, he would save 50*l.* a week in wages, in consequence of dispensing with nearly forty male spinners, at about 25*s.* of wages each. This tendency to employ merely children with watchful eyes and nimble fingers, instead of journeymen of long experience, shows how the scholastic dogma of the division of labour into degrees of skill has been exploded by our enlightened manufacturers.

[Book II]

CHAPTER II: NATURE, &C. OF A COTTON FACTORY

The art of spinning may be traced to the most remote antiquity, especially that by the distaff; and it is claimed as an honourable discovery by many nations. The Egyptians ascribe it to Isis, the Chinese to their emperor Yao, the Lydians to Arachne, the Greeks to Minerva, the Peruvians to Mamacella, the wife of Manco Capac their first sovereign. The Greek and Roman authors attribute to their own nations respectively the invention of the spindle, as well as the art of weaving. Many writers of different countries give the honour of spinning to the fair sex; and the ancients, in particular, regarded this occupation as unworthy of men. It was under the infatuation of love that Hercules degraded himself by spinning at the feet of Omphale. Modern opinions have undergone a complete revolution with regard to this species of industry. A man is no longer deemed to be deserving of contempt for exercising the functions of a spinner; but what a superior result does he produce to that produced by Hercules! The Grecian demi-god, with all his talent, spun but a single thread at a time, while a Manchester operative spins nearly 2000. This art consists, philosophically speaking, in forming a flexible cylinder of greater or less diameter, and of indeterminate length, out of fine fibrils of vegetable or animal origin, arranged as equally as possible, alongside and at the ends of each other, so that when twisted together, they may form an uniform continuous thread. Hence with very short filaments, like those of wool, cotton, and cachemire, a thread of the greatest length may be formed by torsion, possessed of nearly the sum of the cohesive forces of its elementary parts. Its size, or number, is measured by the area of the section perpendicular to its length; and this size is known to be variable or untrue, when equal lengths have different weights. Persons accustomed to deal in yarn can discover defects of this kind by mere inspection; but for accurate purposes they generally weigh a certain length of it. Its strength is easily estimated by the weight sustained by it; and this, as already stated, does not depend on the length of the specimen tried.

There is nothing in the history of commerce which can be compared with the wonderful progression of our cotton trade. Fifty years ago, the manufacture of woollens was the great staple of the country. In the year 1780, the whole export of manufactured cotton goods, of every description, amounted in value to only 355,000*l.* In 1785, two years after the American war, and when the commerce of this country had in some measure recovered from the difficulties under which it necessarily laboured during that conflict, the whole extent of our cotton exports, of every description, amounted to no more than 864,000*l.*; whilst, at the same period, the exports of woollen manufactured goods amounted to considerably more than four millions: the proportion between the two commodities being at that time as one to five. From the last year up to 1822, incredible as it may almost appear, the exports alone of manufactured cotton goods rose, by the official estimate, to the enormous amount of 33,337,000*l.*, being forty times greater than it was in the year 1785. But with respect to the woollen, the great staple trade of the country in former times, the exports in 1822 did not amount to more than 6,000,000*l.*, being not so much as one-fifth of those of cotton. Here we see what pre-eminent advantages arise from the principle of allowing capital to run in an open and unrestrained channel. The official value is no doubt higher than the real, but it is equally so for both branches. Mr. Huskisson stated in the House of Commons, on March 8, 1824, that according to the best information he had been able to obtain on the subject—and he said he had taken some pains to acquire it—he believed he was not overstating the fact, when he affirmed that the real value of cotton goods consumed at home within the last year amounted to 32,000,000*l.* sterling. Of these thirty-two millions worth of goods, not more than six millions were invested in the raw material; and the remaining twenty-six millions went to the profits of the capitalist, and the income of the persons employed in the manufacture.

A great truth is here taught to the rulers of mankind. When they remove the restrictions and burdens from any particular branch of industry, they afford relief not only to the amount of the tax remitted, but lay the foundation for commercial enterprise, to an extent of benefit impossible to foresee. We may ask any man who has attentively considered the resources of this country, whether, if the restrictions had not been removed from the manufacture of cotton, this country could possibly have made the gigantic exertions which it put forth during the late long war with the world, or could now pay the interest of the debt contracted in carrying on that war? We may also ask, whether the number of persons employed in this manufacture, to the amount probably of a million and a half, whose wants are supplied in return for their labour, does not afford more real encouragement to the agriculture of the country, than any regulation for keeping up artificial prices could possibly effect? It is to the increasing wealth of the manufacturing population, and the progress of creative industry, and not to artificial regulations for creating high prices, that this country must look not only for relief from her present burdens, but for the power of making fresh exertions whenever her position may demand them. The relief claimed for agriculture, by the landed aristocracy, cannot be given by any artificial measures, either to it or any other mode of occupation. It can flow only from the undisturbed and increasing industry of the people.

The most remarkable feature in the history of the cotton manufacture is the impetus which it has given to invention, the numerous valuable discoveries which it has brought forth, the ingenuity which it has called into action, the lights it has reflected, and the aids it has lent to the woollen, linen, and silk trades: the tendency and effect of all which have been to produce British goods at the lowest possible rate, and of a quality suited to every market, domestic and foreign. Each of these improvements, each corporeal transformation, so to speak, was attended at the time with some inconvenience to those engaged in the business, who were not in harmony with the movement; but the result has been, that not only has much more capital been beneficially invested in buildings and machinery, but a greater number of hands has been employed to occupy them, in proportion as the prospects of fresh resources were laid open to the manufacturer.

The details of the cotton trade, including a proper analysis of its operations, demand much ampler space than the limits of this volume allow; but such an outline of them may be given as will fill up our general view of the factory system. The perspective picture which fronts the title-page represents a cotton factory, recently erected at Stockport on the most improved plan, and

it will serve perfectly to illustrate the arrangement of the machines and concatenation of the processes.

The building consists of a main body, and two lateral wings; the former
being three hundred feet long, and fifty feet wide; the latter projecting fifty-
eight feet in front of the body. There are seven stories, including the attics.
The moving power consists of two eighty-horse steam-engines, working rec-
tangularly together, which are mounted with their great geering-wheels on
the ground floor, at the end of the body opposite the spectator's right hand,
and are separated by a strong wall from the rest of the building. This wall is
perforated for the passage of the main horizontal shaft, which, by means of
great bevil wheels, turns the main upright shaft, supported at its lower end in
an immense pier of masonry, of which the largest stone weighs nearly five
tons. The velocity of the piston in each of these unison engines is two hundred and forty feet per minute; which, by the balance beam, and main wheel,
is made to give to the first horizontal shaft 44.3 revolutions, and to the main
upright shaft 58.84 revolutions per minute. As the one engine works with
its maximum force, when the other works with its minimum, the two together
cause an uniformity of impulsive power to pervade every arm throughout
the factory, devoid of those vibratory alternations so injurious to delicate
and finely-poised mechanisms. The engines make sixteen strokes per minute,
of seven feet and six-tenths each, and perform their task with chronometric
ease and punctuality.

The boilers for supplying steam to the engines, and to the warming-pipes
of the building, are erected in an exterior building at the right-hand end of
the mill; and transmit the smoke of their furnaces through a subterraneous
tunnel to the monumental-looking chimney on the picturesque knoll, shown
in the drawing. By this means, a powerful furnace draught is obtained,
corresponding to a height of fully three hundred feet.

As this mill spins warp yarn by throstles, weft yarn by mules, and weaves
up both by power-looms, it exhibits in the collocation of its members an instructive specimen of the *philosophy of manufactures*. Both systems of spinning, namely, the continuous or by throstles, and the discontinuous or by
mules, require the cotton to be prepared on the same system of machines;
and therefore they must be both arranged subordinately to the *preparation
rooms*. This arrangement has been considered in the true spirit of manufacturing economy by the engineer.

As the looms require the utmost stability, and an atmosphere rather humid
than dry, they are placed on the ground-floor of the body of the building, as
also in a shed behind it, to the number of about one thousand. The throstle-

frames occupy the first and second stories of the main building; the mules, the fourth and fifth stories; each of these four apartments forming a noble gallery, three hundred feet long by fifty wide, and twelve feet high. The third story is the preparation gallery, intermediate between the throstles and mules, as it is destined to supply both with materials. Towards one end of this floor are distributed the carding-engines; towards the middle, the drawing-machines for arranging the cotton fibres in parallel lines, and forming them into uniform slivers, or soft narrow ribands; and towards the other end, the bobbin and fly-frames, or roving-machines, for converting the said slivers into slender porous cords, called rovings. These rovings are carried downstairs to be spun into warp-yarn on the throstles, and upstairs to be spun into weft (or sometimes warp) yarn on the mules.

The engine occupies an elevation of three stories at the right hand end of the mill. The stories immediately over it are devoted to the cleaning and lapping the cotton for the cards. Here are, 1. The willows for winnowing out the coarser impurities; 2. the blowing-machine for thoroughly opening out the cotton into clean individual fibres; and 3. the lapping-machine, for converting these fibres into a broad soft fleece-like wadding, and coiling the fleece into cylindrical rolls. These laps are carried to the continuous carding-engines, and applied to their feed-aprons. The winding-machines, and a few mules, occupy the remaining apartments in the right wing. The attic story of the main building is appropriated to the machines for warping and dressing the yarn for the power-looms. The other wing of the mill is occupied with the counting-house, store-rooms, and apartments for winding the cotton on the large bobbins used for the warping-frame.

A staircase is placed in the corner of each wing, which has a horse-shoe shape, in order to furnish, in its interior, the tunnel space of the teagle or hoist apparatus, for raising and lowering the work-people and the goods from one floor to another.

The plan and sections of this finished model of mill architecture are replete with the finest lessons of practical mechanics. They will be represented in accurate engravings, and explained with suitable details in our treatise on the cotton trade.

It will not be inexpedient, however, to describe here the American saw-gin, the ingenious invention of Whitney, which has had so great a share in reducing the price of cotton wool, as also the processes of carding and drawing in some measure common to all the textile manufactures. The saw-gin has never, to my knowledge, been fully figured or explained in any work in our language, though if rightly made and applied, it would prove highly useful to our commerce in cleaning the cottons of Hindostan. The attempts made with it there have hitherto proved abortive from want of knowledge and skill.

The French Minister of Marine, with the view of encouraging the growth of cotton in Senegal, caused experiments to be made in Paris with a Carolina saw-gin imported from New York. In the first experiment twenty-eight pounds of Senegal seed-cotton, in its native state, were used. The filaments of this species adhere loosely to the seeds. The machine was set in motion, first by one man, and then by two men, for three-quarters of an hour, and it yielded a product of eight pounds of picked cotton, and nineteen pounds and a half of seeds. Half a pound of cotton fibres seem to have been dispersed through the apartment, causing an apparent waste, which would not be felt on the great scale. The second experiment was made on a Georgian cotton, which sticks strongly to the seeds. Two workmen cleared out, in a quarter of an hour, seven pounds of native cotton, and obtained five pounds of seeds, and nearly two pounds of cotton wool. The cotton, as it left the machine, appeared in a sound state, and so well opened, that it might have been carded without previous blowing or batting. The commissioners thought, however, that the saw-teeth of the gin, in tearing the fibres from the seeds, broke several of them, and thus injured the staple. The experienced American ginner avoids this evil.

From these experiments, it would appear, that two men, working ten hours a day, would obtain one hundred and six pounds of wool from the first kind of seed-cotton, and only ninety from the second. It may be remarked, also, that while one workman turns the machine, another can feed in the crude cotton, and gather the ginned wool into bags. The commissioners, thinking favourably of this machine, recommended its introduction into the French colonies.

THE LUDDITES

THE problem of technological unemployment, the elimination of types of employment by the introduction of machinery, became a major one only with the advent of large-scale industrialization in the nineteenth century. It led to resistance on the part of laborers to the introduction of the machinery that threatened their jobs, and in England this took a violent form in the Luddite riots. In 1811 and 1812 workers banded together in variously armed groups and destroyed or tried to destroy their machine enemies, agricultural as well as industrial equipment. They were dealt with severely by a government and society dedicated to the development of industry, and the problem they tried thus crudely and hopelessly to dramatize reappeared with every new major advance in technology. With industrialization also came cyclical depressions in trade which reduced the displaced worker's chance of finding employment elsewhere; during "hard times," for this reason, feeling against the new machines was especially acute.

The following selection, designed to show the attitudes of the state and the middle class on the one hand, and of the laborers on the other, is taken from the *Proceedings at York Special Commission, January, 1813.*

PROCEEDINGS HELD AT THE CASTLE OF YORK, JANUARY, 1813

MR. BARON THOMSON . . . delivered the following Charge: *Gentlemen of the Grand Inquest,* we are assembled, by virtue of His Majesty's Commission, to exercise the criminal judicature in this county, at this unusual season of the year for the occurrence of such solemnities. None of us, however, can be insensible of the necessity which exists for a speedy investigation of the charges against the very numerous class of prisoners in your calendar. You will perceive I allude to those persons, who are accused of having participated (and several of them in repeated instances) in those daring acts of tumultuous outrage, violence and rapine, by which the public tranquillity has been disturbed throughout that great manufacturing district in the West Riding of this county, for a period comprising, with little intermission, almost the whole of the year which has just elapsed.

Those mischievous Associations, dangerous to the public peace, as well as destructive of the property of individual subjects, and in some instances of their lives, seem to have originated in a neighbouring county, and at first to have had for their object merely the destruction of machinery invented for the purpose of saving manual labour in manufactures: a notion, probably suggested by evil designing persons, to captivate the working manufacturer, and engage him in tumult and crimes, by persuading him that the use of machinery occasions a decrease of the demand for personal labour, and a consequent decrease of wages, or total want of work. A more fallacious and unfounded argument cannot be made use of. It is to the excellence of our Machinery that the existence probably, certainly the excellence and flourishing state, of our manufactures are owing. Whatever diminishes expense, increases consumption, and the demand for the article both in the home and foreign market; and were the use of machinery entirely to be abolished, the cessation of the manufacture itself would soon follow, inasmuch as other countries, to which the machinery would be banished, would be enabled to undersell us.

The spirit of insubordination and tumult, thus originating, has spread itself into other manufacturing districts; and when large bodies of men are once assembled to act against law, the transition unhappily is too easy from one irregular act to another, even to the highest of crimes against society. And thus we find that the destruction of tools has been succeeded by destroying the houses and the workshops of the manufacturers; it has led to the violent robbery of arms, to protect the tumultuous in their illegal practices, and to enable them to resist or to attack successfully; and from the robbery of arms they have proceeded to the general plunder of property of every description, and even to the murder, the deliberate assassination, of such as were supposed to be hostile to their measures. A temporary impunity (for the law, though sure, is slow) has led on these deluded persons from one atrocious act to another; from the breaking of shears to the stealing of arms, to nightly robberies, to the destruction of property, and of life itself.

The peaceful and industrious inhabitants of the country, where these enormous practices have been committed, have had the misfortune to suffer in their persons and property, from the acts of men confederated against society, and executing the purposes of their association under circumstances carrying with them the utmost terror and dismay. Armed bodies of these men, in some instances several hundred in number, apparently organized under the command of leaders, and generally with their faces blacked or otherwise disguised, have attacked the mills, shops, and houses of manufacturers and others, by day as well as by night, destroyed tools worked by machinery, and in some instances shot at the persons whose property they have thus attacked. But the worst of these misdeeds is yet behind, a most foul Assassination. While such outrages as those mentioned were carrying on in that part of the country, a person in a respectable station of life, returning from Huddersfield to his residence at Marsden, was fired at and shot from behind the wall of an inclosure near the road, receiving several wounds, of which he died shortly after. . . .

With regard to the guilt, which persons may incur by engaging in any riotous assembly, the Statute of 1 George I. commonly called the Riot Act, has enacted, That if any persons, to the number of twelve or more, who shall be unlawfully, riotously, and tumultuously assembled together, to the disturbance of the public peace, shall not disperse, but continue in that state for the space of an hour after such proclamation made as is directed in the Act, they shall be guilty of Felony without benefit of Clergy. And by the same Statute, if any persons, so unlawfully, riotously, and tumultuously assembled together, to the disturbance of the public peace, shall unlawfully and with force demolish or pull down any dwelling house or other buildings therein mentioned, they shall also be guilty of Felony without benefit of Clergy.

So also by the Statute of 9 George III. it is made a capital Felony, for persons, being riotously and tumultuously assembled, to pull down or demolish, or to begin to pull down or demolish, any wind saw-mill or other windmill, or any watermill or other mill, or to set fire to the same. In addition to which, the Act of 43 George III. cap. 58. has provided against the maliciously setting fire (among other things) to any mill, warehouse or shop, with intent to injure or defraud any of the King's subjects, by subjecting the offenders, their counsellors, aiders and abettors, to a capital punishment. . . .

The prisoners having been arraigned, and severally pleaded Not Guilty, the Indictment was opened by Mr. Richardson.

Mr. Park.—May it please your Lordships; Gentlemen of the Jury, We are now assembled to try a different species of offence, from either that of yesterday, or those of the preceding days. Gentlemen, this case is one of those, to which allusion has been made; it is connected with the system that has been prevailing in the country, and is one almost of the first of the desperate attacks that were made in this country, before that unfortunate event which deprived Mr. Horsfall of life. And you will find in the course of this, as indeed appeared in the course of that trial, that the irritation produced in the minds of the unfortunate persons who have suffered death for that offence, by what passed at Mr. Cartwright's mill, probably led to that lamentable event. The day that is material for your consideration here, is Saturday the eleventh of April 1812.

The Act of Parliament upon which the prisoners stand indicted, I will first state to you. It was one passed in the 9th year of His present Majesty's reign,

cap. 29. intituled, "An Act for the more effectual punishment of such persons
as shall demolish or pull down, burn, or otherwise destroy or spoil any mill
or mills." I need not trouble you with any further statement of the title of it.
It goes on to enact, "That if any person or persons, unlawfully riotously
and tumultuously assembled together, to the disturbance of the public peace,
shall unlawfully and with force demolish or pull down or begin to demolish
or pull down any wind-saw-mill or other wind-mill, or any water-mill or other
mill, which shall have been or shall be erected, or any of the works thereto
respectively belonging, that then every such demolishing or pulling down, or
beginning to demolish or pull down, shall be adjudged felony without benefit
of clergy." This is the law upon which these men stand indicted.

It is well known, that in the manufacturing part of the West Riding of
this county, there have been various implements of machinery introduced,
and wisely introduced, for the purpose of expediting our manufactures, and
bringing them into better use. The advantages to the labourers themselves,
if they would have given themselves the patience to understand the thing,
would have convinced them of the great utility of such machinery; but unfortunately they took a different course, and would not stay to consider the
great mischiefs they would bring on themselves, not only if punishment followed, but the absolute poverty, misery and distress which the destruction
of those mills, where such machinery was used, must bring on all the unfortunate persons who were occupied in them. If they had so considered, I
think that common prudence, independently of moral obligation, would have
prevented their doing what has been done. For if only this devastation, which
was intended for Mr. Cartwright's mill, had been effected, a number of families must have been thereby thrown out of bread, at least for a considerable
time, till he could erect new works. It must therefore have produced dreadful distress. But that argument did not prevail with these misguided persons;
and for a considerable period of time, these deluded, foolish, ignorant, and
wicked men, were going round the country, destroying all the obnoxious
machinery, and stealing arms; so that previously to the 11th of April, they
had collected a considerable quantity of gunpowder, guns, pistols and other
weapons.

Mr. Cartwright, whose mill, called Rawfolds mill, was so attacked on the
11th of April, had had previous notice, that among those people he had been
denounced, on account of his employing the most improved machinery. In
consequence of which notice, this gentleman slept in his mill for upwards of
six weeks before the 11th of April, deserting his family (for his dwelling-
house was elsewhere); and not only that, but he had beds prepared for five
military, and four of his own workmen. He prepared for his defence, as

every prudent man should do; and I have only to lament, that the same spirit Mr. Cartwright displayed, was not displayed by other gentlemen, whose property was threatened. Probably if that spirit had been manifested, their Lordships and you would not have been troubled on the present occasion. I will not go through all that he did with his mill. It seemed almost impossible for any, but a most active military force, to destroy the works he erected there. But there is one thing I must mention, because it affords almost decisive evidence against one of the unfortunate men now at the bar. It seems the different floors (I think there were three above the ground floor) were laid with flags of a considerable size, in a row, which were raised obliquely, so as to make loop-holes; so that if any man should attack the lower windows of the manufactory with hatchets and hammers, those within might fire down upon them; and Mr. Cartwright furnished himself with muskets and gunpowder for that purpose.

On the 11th of April (for I will now state the facts, applying them afterwards to the men at the bar) Mr. Cartwright will state, that he had retired to bed soon after twelve, having previously ascertained that his watchmen were on their posts; two of whom were set on the outside, to give notice of the approach of an enemy; but, like many more of our watchmen, they were surprised, and were actually seized, before any alarm could be given by them. About twenty-five minutes before one, as well as he could ascertain the time, a large dog, which was chained on the ground floor, began to bark furiously. This gentleman, whose feelings were all alive, immediately jumped out of bed, and flew to the stairs; but while he was doing so, being still in his shirt, he was astonished by an immediate heavy fire of musketry poured into his upper windows, and violent hammering at the door next to the road; for you will find by the description, that this mill had a pond on one side, so that it was to a certain degree protected. Mr. Cartwright and his men had piled their arms the night before; he immediately rushed towards them, and met his own men and the soldiers, without any covering but their shirts, having just jumped out of bed. By his orders they commenced a heavy firing from within the mill, and this they continued, as will be proved to you, upwards of twenty minutes. The mob, during that time kept up their fire also; and you will find that it consisted of more than an hundred persons. They broke all the windows, many of the window frames, and one of the doors, calling out, with the most horrible imprecations (which I shall not repeat) "Bang up, lads!—Are you within, lads?—Damn them, keep close." Mr. Cartwright had placed an alarm-bell at the top of his building; this was rung with considerable force, till the bell-rope broke. The mob, upon hearing it ring, called out, "Damn it, silence that bell." But two of Cartwright's men went up, and rang the bell, by turn firing and ringing. At length, the firing still continuing from within, and probably the ammunition of the mob running short, the assailants began to slacken fire, and at last it entirely ceased, except that one man fired a single shot at the close. Mr. Cartwright heard the people go off towards Huddersfield, and, when their clamour subsided, was able to hear the groans of some who were left behind wounded, but he was afraid of going out, lest it should be said that he had murdered them. It was so dark that nothing could be distinguished by sight. But when assistance came, Mr. Cartwright and his men went out, and found a great number of malls, hammers, muskets and so on, left on the road to Huddersfield. They also found two men, who were too badly wounded to escape, and who afterwards unfortunately died, upon whom the Coroner's Jury sat, and found a verdict (as they were bound to do) of justifiable homicide. . . .

The prisoners capitally convicted being . . . put to the bar, and asked what they had to say, why Sentence of Death should not be passed on them, prayed that their lives might be spared.

Mr. Baron Thomson:

John Swallow, John Batley, Joseph Fisher, John Lumb, Job Hey, John Hill, William Hartley, James Hey, Joseph Crowther, Nathan Hoyle, James Haigh, Jonathan Dean, John Ogden, Thomas Brook, John Walker, you, unhappy prisoners at the bar, stand convicted of various offences, for which your lives are justly forfeited to the injured laws of your Country. You have formed a part of that desperate association of men, who, for a great length of time, have disturbed the peace and tranquillity of the West Riding of this county. You have formed yourselves into bodies; you have proceeded to the most serious extremities against the property of many individuals. The cause of your so associating appears to have been a strange delusion, which you entertained, that the use of machinery in the woollen manufacture was a detriment to the hands that were employed in another way in it; a grosser delusion never could be entertained, proceeding probably from the misrepresentations of artful and designing men, who have turned it to the very worst purpose which riot and sedition could produce. You have proceeded to great extremities. The first object, perhaps, seems to have been that of your procuring arms, in order to carry on your nefarious designs. With that view, it seems that some of you went about inquiring for such arms at different houses, and getting them wherever you could find them.

But not stopping there, and not contenting yourselves with getting what arms you could lay your hands upon, you proceeded to plunder the habitations with a great degree of force, and took from them property of every description, which you could find in those houses. An offence of that nature is brought home, and sufficiently established against you the prisoners *John Swallow, John Batley, Joseph Fisher, John Lumb, Job Hey, John Hill, William Hartley, James Hey, Joseph Crowther,* and *Nathan Hoyle.*

You the prisoners, *Job Hey, John Hill,* and *William Hartley,* did upon the occasion, when you went to the house of your prosecutor, carrying away certainly nothing but arms, but you carried them away with great terror, and under circumstances which were sufficient unquestionably to make him deliver what he had. The other prisoners, whose names I have last recited, have been concerned in breaking a dwelling-house in the night time, some of them getting notes, money, and other things; and the last prisoners, *James Hey, Joseph Crowther,* and *Nathan Hoyle,* for robbing a person in his dwelling-house.

The evidence, that has been given against you all, was too clear to admit of any doubt; and you have all been convicted of these offences upon the most satisfactory evidence.

You, the other prisoners, *James Haigh, Jonathan Dean, John Ogden, Thomas Brook,* and *John Walker,* have been guilty of one of the greatest outrages that ever was committed in a civilized country. You had been long armed and organized, you had assembled upon this night, when the mill of Mr. Cartwright was attacked; you had assembled at the dead hour of night in great numbers; you had formed yourselves into companies under the command of different leaders; you were armed with different instruments of offence, with guns, with pistols, with axes, and with other weapons; you marched in military order and array to the mill, which was afterwards in part pulled down; you began there your attack with firearms, discharged into that mill, and kept up a most dreadful fire, and at the same time applied the instruments, which you had brought there, of a description calculated to do the worst of mischief, in beginning to demolish the mill, intending, as it is obvious, to do also mischief to and to demolish the machinery which that mill contained. The cries and exclamations that proceeded from this riotous tumultuous mob thus assembled, of which you formed a very powerful part, were such as were enough to alarm a man of less firmness than that man possessed, who was the owner of the mill so attacked. Your cry was, "Get in, get in, kill them all"; and there is but little doubt, it is to be feared, that if you had made good your entry into that mill, these threats would have been put into execution, and that the mischief done would hardly have been confined to the machinery which was there. The courage and resolution, however, which that individual displayed, had the effect of making you desist at that time from the attack, and two of your wretched companions paid the forfeit of their lives on that occasion. . . .

In the awful situation in which you, prisoners, stand, let me seriously exhort you to set about the great work of repentance, and to spend the very short time that you must be allowed to remain in this world, in endeavouring to make your peace with your God, and to reconcile him by deep repentance. A full confession of your crime is the only atonement you can make for that which you have committed. Give yourselves up to the pious admonitions of the reverend Clergyman, whose office it will be to prepare you for your awful change; and God grant, that, worthily lamenting your sins, and acknowledging your wretchedness, you may obtain of the God of all mercy perfect remission and forgiveness.

Hear the sentence which the Laws of man pronounce upon your crimes. The sentence of the Law is, and this Court doth adjudge, That you, the several Prisoners at the bar, be taken from hence to the place from whence you came, and from thence to the place of execution, where you shall be severally hanged by the neck until you are dead. The Lord have mercy upon your souls.

HONORÉ DE BALZAC

HONORÉ BALZAC was born in Tours, France, on May 20, 1799. His father was a prosperous merchant who had risen to success under Napoleon and had served as director of commissariat to one of Napoleon's divisions. Balzac studied at the Collège des Oratoriens in Vendôme, at Paris. He hated school, finding it "brutalizing," and was unpopular with his teachers and fellow students.

In 1816 Balzac entered the University of Paris to study jurisprudence. He gave up his studies in 1819, although threatened with lack of suport by his parents, and became an author. For years he worked in a small garret, beneath a picture of Napoleon on which he had written, "What Napoleon could not do with the sword, I shall accomplish with the pen." He wrote desperately, turning out a prodigious stream of works in order to secure a livelihood. During this period he collaborated on a series of insignificant novels, and involved himself in a passionate love affair with a woman whose daughter was older than Balzac himself. From 1826 to 1828, he speculated in three business ventures which failed, leaving him 90,000 francs in debt and forcing him to abscond.

Balzac attained his first fame with his *Scenes from Private Life,* in 1830. He added a "de" to his name, and began living in a grand manner. Three years later he met Madame de Hanska, whom he courted for eighteen years before she became his wife. He also flirted with politics, and ran unsuccessfully for deputy. His erratic literary habits and complicated finances involved him in many legal actions.

In 1833, Balzac published *The Thirteen,* which met with great popularity. It was expanded in 1834, and in the next year the story from which the following excerpt is taken, *The Girl with the Golden Eyes,* was added. Other important works during this period were *Eugénie Grandet* (1834), *Père Goriot* (1838), and a series of short stories, *Droll Tales* (1832).

Balzac attempted to reproduce a complete catalogue of human passions and character types in his works. With this in mind, he set about reorganizing his writings into a magnum opus, *La Comédie Humaine.* The first three volumes in the series appeared in 1842, and four years later the first edition of sixteen volumes was completed. Two of his greatest works, *Cousin Bette* and *Cousin Pons* were published in 1846 and 1847.

Balzac died in Paris on August 18, 1850, just a few months after his wedding. The eulogy at his funeral was delivered by Victor Hugo, and his pallbearers included Hugo, Dumas, and Sainte-Beuve.

The following selection has been taken from *The Thirteen,* translated by Ellen Marriage (Boston, Dana Estes and Co., 1901).

THE GIRL WITH THE GOLDEN EYES

To Eugène Delacroix, Painter

ONE of those sights in which most horror is to be encountered is, surely, the general aspect of the Parisian populace—a people fearful to behold, gaunt, yellow, tawny. Is not Paris a vast field in perpetual turmoil from a storm of interests beneath which are whirled along a crop of human beings, who are, more often than not, reaped by death, only to be born again as pinched as ever, men whose twisted and contorted faces give out at every pore the instinct, the desire, the poisons with which their brains are pregnant; not faces so much as masks; masks of weakness, masks of strength, masks of misery, masks of joy, masks of hypocrisy; all alike worn and stamped with the indelible signs of a panting cupidity? What is it they want? Gold or pleasure? A few observations upon the soul of Paris may explain the causes of its cadaverous physiognomy, which has but two ages—youth and decay: youth, wan and colorless; decay, painted to seem young. In looking at this excavated people, foreigners, who are not prone to reflection, experience at first a movement of disgust towards the capital, that vast workshop of delights, from which, in a short time, they cannot even extricate themselves, and where they stay willingly to be corrupted. A few words will suffice to justify physiologically the almost infernal hue of Parisian faces, for it is not in mere sport that Paris has been called a hell. Take the phrase for truth. There all is smoke and fire, everything gleams, crackles, flames, evaporates, dies out, then lights up again, with shooting sparks, and is consumed. In no other country has life ever been more ardent or acute. The social nature, even in fusion, seems to say after each completed work: "Pass on to another!" Just as Nature says herself. Like Nature herself, this social nature is busied with insects and flowers of a day—ephemeral trifles; and so, too, it throws up fire and flame from its eternal crater. Perhaps, before analyzing the causes which lend a special physiognomy to each tribe of this intelligent and mobile nation, the general cause should be pointed out which bleaches and discolors, tints with blue or brown individuals in more or less degree.

By dint of taking interest in everything, the Parisian ends by being interested in nothing. No emotion dominating his face, which friction has rubbed away, it turns gray like the faces of those houses upon which all kinds of dust and smoke have blown. In effect, the Parisian, with his indifference on the day for what the morrow will bring forth, lives like a child, whatever may be his age. He grumbles at everything, consoles himself for everything, jests at everything, forgets, desires, and tastes everything, seizes all with passion, quits all with indifference—his kings, his conquests, his glory, his idols of bronze or glass—as he throws away his stockings, his hats, and his fortune. In Paris no sentiment can withstand the drift of things, and their current compels a struggle in which the passions are relaxed: there love is a desire, and hatred a whim; there's no true kinsman but the thousand-franc note, no better friend than the pawnbroker. This universal toleration bears its fruits, and in the salon, as in the street, there is no one *de trop,* there is no one absolutely useful, or absolutely harmful—knaves or fools, men of wit or integrity. There everything is tolerated: the government and the guillotine, religion and the cholera. You are always acceptable to this world, you will never be missed by it. What, then, is the dominating impulse in this country without morals, without faith, without any sentiment, wherein, however, every sentiment, belief, and moral has its origin and end? It is gold and pleasure. Take those two words for a lantern, and explore that great stucco cage, that hive with its black gutters, and follow the windings of that thought which agitates, sustains, and occupies it! Consider! And, in the first place, examine the world which possesses nothing.

The artisan, the man of the proletariat, who uses his hands, his tongue, his back, his right arm, his five fingers, to live—well, this very man, who should be the first to economize his vital principle, outruns his strength, yokes his wife to some machine, wears out his child, and ties him to the wheel. The manufacturer—or I know not what secondary thread which sets in motion all these folk who with their foul hands mould and gild porcelain, sew coats and dresses, beat out iron, turn wood and steel, weave hemp, festoon crystal, imitate flowers, work woolen things, break in horses, dress harness, carve in copper, paint carriages, blow glass, corrode the diamond, polish metals, turn marble into leaves, labor on pebbles, deck out thought, tinge, bleach, or blacken everything—well, this middleman has come to that world of sweat and good-will, of study and patience, with promises of lavish wages, either in the names of the town's caprices or with the voice of the monster dubbed speculation. Thus, these *quadrumanes* set themselves to watch, work, and suffer, to fast, sweat, and bestir them. Then, careless of the future, greedy of pleasure, counting on their right arm as the painter on his palette, lords for one day, they throw their money on Mondays to the *cabarets* which gird the town like a belt of mud, haunts of the most shameless of the daughters of Venus, in which the periodical money of this people, as ferocious in their pleasures as they are calm at work, is squandered as it had been at play. For five days, then, there is no repose for this laborious portion of Paris! It is given up to actions which make it warped and rough, lean and pale, gush forth with a thousand fits of creative energy. And then its pleasure, its repose, are an exhausting debauch, swarthy and black with blows, white with intoxication, or yellow with indigestion. It lasts but two days, but it steals to-morrow's bread, the week's soup, the wife's dress, the child's wretched rags. Men, born doubtless to be beautiful—for all creatures have a relative beauty—are enrolled from their childhood beneath the yoke of force, beneath the rule of the hammer, the chisel, the loom, and have been promptly vulcanized. Is not Vulcan, with his hideousness and his strength, the emblem of this strong and hideous nation—sublime in its mechanical intelligence, patient in its season, and once in a century terrible, inflammable as gunpowder, and ripe with brandy for the madness of revolution, with wits enough, in fine, to take fire at a captious word, which signifies to it always Gold and Pleasure! If we comprise in it all those who hold out their hands for an alms, for lawful wages, or the five francs that are granted to every kind of Parisian prostitution, in short, for all money well or ill earned, this people numbers three hundred thousand individuals. Were it not for the *cabarets,* would not the Government be overturned every Tuesday? Happily, by Tuesday, this people is gutted, sleeps off its pleasure, is penniless, and returns to its labor, to dry bread, stimulated by a need of material procreation, which has become a habit to it. None the less, this people has its phenomenal virtues, its complete men, unknown Napoleons, who are the type of its strength carried to its highest expression, and sum up its social capacity in an existence wherein thought and movement combine less to bring joy into it than to neutralize the action of sorrow.

Chance has made an artisan economical, chance has favored him with forethought, he has been able to look forward, has met with a wife and found himself a father, and, after some years of hard privation, he embarks in some little draper's business, hires a shop. If neither sickness nor vice blocks his way—if he has prospered—there is the sketch of this normal life.

And, in the first place, hail to that king of Parisian activity, to whom time and space give way. Yes, hail to that being, composed of saltpetre and gas, who makes children for France during his laborious nights, and in the day multiplies his personality for the service, glory, and pleasure of his fellow-citizens. This man solves the problem of sufficing at once to his amiable wife, to his hearth, to the *Constitutionnel,* to his office, to the opera, and to God; but, only in order that the *Constitutionnel,* his wife, and God may be changed into coin. In fine, hail to an irreproachable pluralist. Up every day at five o'clock, he traverses like a bird the space which separates his dwelling from the Rue Montmartre. Let it blow or thunder, rain or snow, he is at the *Constitutionnel,* and waits there for the load of newspapers which he has undertaken to distribute. He receives this political bread with eagerness, takes it, bears it away. At nine o'clock he is in the bosom of his family, flings a jest to his wife, snatches a loud kiss from her, gulps down a cup of coffee, or scolds his children. At a quarter to ten he puts in an appearance at the *Mairie.* There, stuck upon a stool, like a parrot on its perch, warmed by Paris town, he registers until four o'clock, with never a tear or a smile, the deaths and births of an entire district. The sorrow, the happiness, of the parish flow beneath his pen—as the essence of the *Constitutionnel* traveled before upon his shoulders. Nothing weighs upon him! He goes always straight before him, takes his patriotism ready made from the newspaper, contradicts no one, shouts or applauds with the world, and lives like a bird. Two yards from his parish, in the event of an important ceremony, he can yield his place to an assistant, and betake himself to chant a requiem from a stall in the church of which on Sundays he is the fairest ornament, where his is the most imposing voice, where he distorts his huge mouth with energy to thunder out a joyous *Amen.* So is he chorister. At four o'clock, freed from his official servitude, he reappears to shed joy and gaiety upon the most famous shop in the city. Happy is his wife, he has no time to be jealous: he is a man of action rather than of sentiment. His mere arrival spurs the young ladies at the counter; their bright eyes storm the customers; he expands in the midst of all the finery, the lace and muslin kerchiefs, that their cunning hands have wrought. Or, again, more often still, before his dinner he waits on a client, copies the page of a newspaper, or carries to the doorkeeper some goods that have been delayed. Every other day, at six, he is faithful to his post. A permanent bass for the chorus, he betakes himself to the opera, prepared to become a soldier or an Arab, prisoner, savage, peasant, spirit, camel's leg or lion, a devil or a genie, a slave or a eunuch, black or white; always ready to feign joy or sorrow, pity or astonishment, to utter cries that never vary, to hold his tongue, to hunt, or fight for Rome or Egypt, but always at heart—a huckster still.

At midnight he returns—a man, the good husband, the tender father; he slips into the conjugal bed, his imagination still afire with the illusive forms of the operatic nymphs, and so turns to the profit of conjugal love the world's depravities, the voluptuous curves of Taglioni's leg. And, finally, if he sleeps, he sleeps apace, and hurries through this slumber as he does his life.

This man sums up all things—history, literature, politics, government, religion, military science. Is he not a living encyclopaedia, a grotesque Atlas; ceaselessly in motion, like Paris itself, and knowing not repose? He is all legs. No physiognomy could preserve its purity amid such toils. Perhaps the artisan who dies at thirty, an old man, his stomach tanned by repeated doses of brandy, will be held, according to certain leisured philosophers, to be happier than the huckster is. The one perishes in a breath, and the other by degrees. From his eight industries, from the labor of his shoulders, his throat, his hands, from his wife and his business, the one derives—as from so many farms—children, some thousands of francs, and the most laborious happiness that has ever diverted the heart of man. This fortune and these children, or the children who sum up everything for him, become the prey of the world above, to which he brings his ducats and his daughter or his son, reared at college, who, with more education than his father, raises higher his ambitious gaze. Often the son of a retail tradesman would fain be something in the State.

Ambition of that sort carries on our thought to the second Parisian sphere. Go up one story, then, and descend to the *entresol:* or climb down from the attic and remain on the fourth floor; in fine, penetrate into the world which has possessions: the same result! Wholesale merchants, and their men—people with small banking accounts and much integrity—rogues and catspaws, clerks old and young, sheriffs' clerks, barristers' clerks, solicitors' clerks; in fine, all the working, thinking, and speculating members of that lower middle class which honeycombs the interests of Paris and watches over its granary, accumulates the coin, stores and products that the proletariat have made, preserves the fruits of the South, the fishes, the wine from every sun-flavored hill; which stretches its hands over the Orient, and takes from it the shawls that the Russ and Turk despise; which harvests even from the Indies; crouches down in expectation of a sale, greedy of profit; which discounts bills, turns over and collects all kinds of securities, holds all Paris in its hand, watches over the fantasies of children, spies out the caprices and the vices of mature age, sucks money out of disease. Even so, if they drink no brandy, like the artisan, nor wallow in the mire of debauch, all equally abuse their strength, immeasurably strain their bodies and their minds alike, are burned away with desires, devastated with the swiftness of the pace. In their case the physical distortion is accomplished beneath the whip of interests, beneath the scourge of ambitions which torture the educated portion of this monstrous city, just as in the case of the proletariat it is brought about by the cruel see-saw of the material elaborations perpetually required from the despotism of the aristocratic "*I will.*" Here, too, then, in order to obey that universal master, pleasure or gold, they must devour time, hasten time, find more than four-and-twenty hours in the day and night, waste themselves, slay themselves, and purchase two years of unhealthy repose with thirty years of old age. Only, the working-man dies in hospital when the last term of his stunted growth expires; whereas the man of the middle class is set upon living, and lives on, but in a state of idiocy. You will meet him, with his worn, flat old face, with no light in his eyes, with no strength in his limbs, dragging himself with a dazed air along the boulevard—the belt of his Venus, of his beloved city. What was his want? The sabre of the National Guard, a permanent stock-pot, a decent plot in Père Lachaise, and, for his old age, a little gold honestly earned. *His* Monday is on Sunday, his rest a drive in a hired carriage—a country excursion during which his wife and children glut themselves merrily with dust or bask in the sun; his dissipation is at the restaurateur's whose poisonous dinner has won renown, or at some family ball, where he suffocates till midnight. Some fools are surprised at the phantasmagoria of the monads which they see with the aid of the microscope in a drop of water; but what would Rabelais' Gargantua—that misunderstood figure of an audacity so sublime—what would that giant say, fallen from the celestial spheres, if he amused himself by contemplating the motions of this secondary life of Paris, of which here is one of the formulae? Have you seen one of those little constructions—cold in summer, and with no other warmth than a small stove in winter—placed beneath the vast copper dome which crowns the Halle-aublé? Madame is there by morning. She is engaged at the markets, and makes by this occupation twelve thousand francs a year, people say. Monsieur, when Madame is up, passes into a gloomy office, where he lends money till the week-end to the tradesmen of his district. By nine o'clock he is at the passport office, of which he is one of the minor officials. By evening he is at the box-office of the Théâtre Italien, or of any other theatre you like. The children are put out to nurse, and only return to be sent to college or to boarding-school. Monsieur and Madame live on the third floor, have but one cook, give dances in a salon twelve foot by eight, lit by argand lamps; but they give a hundred and fifty thousand francs to their daughter, and retire at the age of fifty, an age when they begin to show themselves on the balcony of the opera, in a *fiacre* at Longchamps; or, on sunny days, in faded clothes on the boulevards—the fruit of all this sowing. Respected by their neighbors, in good odor with the government, connected with the upper middle classes,

Monsieur obtains at sixty-five the Cross of the Legion of Honor, and his daughter's father-in-law, a parochial mayor, invites him to his evenings. These life-long labors, then, are for the good of the children, whom these lower middle classes are inevitably driven to exalt. Thus each sphere directs all its efforts towards the sphere above it. The son of the rich grocer becomes a notary, the son of the timber merchant becomes a magistrate. No link is wanting in the chain, and everything stimulates the upward march of money.

Thus we are brought to the third circle of this hell, which, perhaps, will some day find its Dante. In this third social circle, a sort of Parisian belly, in which the interests of the town are digested, and where they are condensed into the form known as *business,* there moves and agitates, as by some acrid and bitter intestinal process, the crowd of lawyers, doctors, notaries, councillors, business men, bankers, big merchants, speculators, and magistrates. Here are to be found even more causes of moral and physical destruction than elsewhere. These people—almost all of them— live in unhealthy offices, in fetid ante-chambers, in little barred dens, and spend their days bowed down beneath the weight of affairs; they rise at dawn to be in time, not to be left behind, to gain all or not to lose, to over-reach a man or his money, to open or wind up some business, to take advantage of some fleeting opportunity, to get a man hanged or set him free. They infect their horses, they overdrive and age and break them, like their own legs, before their time. Time is their tyrant: it fails them, it escapes them; they can neither expand it nor cut it short. What soul can remain great, pure, moral, and generous, and, consequently, what face can retain its beauty in this depraving practice of a calling which compels one to bear the weight of the public sorrows, to analyze them, to weigh them, estimate them, and mark them out by rule? Where do these folk put aside their hearts? . . . I do not know; but they leave them somewhere or other, when they have any, before they descend each morning into the abyss of the misery which puts families on the rack. For them there is no such thing as mystery; they see the reverse side of society, whose confessors they are, and despise it. Then, whatever they do, owing to their contact with corruption, they either are horrified at it and grow gloomy, or else, out of lassitude, or some secret compromise, espouse it. In fine, they necessarily become callous to every sentiment, since man, his laws and his institutions, make them steal, like jackals, from corpses that are still warm. At all hours the financier is trampling on the living, the attorney on the dead, the pleader on the conscience. Forced to be speaking without a rest, they substitute words for ideas, phrases for feelings, and their soul becomes a larynx. Neither the great merchant, nor the judge, nor the pleader preserves his sense of right; they feel no more, they apply set rules that leave cases out of count. Borne along by their headlong course, they are neither husbands nor fathers nor lovers; they glide on sledges over the facts of life, and live at all times at the high pressure conduced by business and the vast city. When they return to their homes they are required to go to a ball, to the opera, into society, where they can make clients, acquaintances, protectors. They all eat to excess, play and keep vigil, and their faces become bloated, flushed, and emaciated.

To this terrific expenditure of intellectual strength, to such multifold moral contradictions, they oppose—not, indeed, pleasure, it would be too pale a contrast—but debauchery, a debauchery both secret and alarming, for they have all means at their disposal, and fix the morality of society. Their genuine stupidity lies hid beneath their specialism. They know their business, but are ignorant of everything which is outside it. So that to preserve their self-conceit they question everything, are crudely and crookedly critical. They appear to be sceptics and are in reality simpletons; they swamp their wits in interminable arguments. Almost all conveniently adopt social, literary, or political prejudices, to do away with the need of having opinions, just as they adapt their conscience to the standard of the Code or the Tribunal of Commerce. Having started early to become men of note, they turn into mediocrities, and crawl over the high places of the world. So, too, their faces present the harsh pallor, the deceitful coloring, those dull, tarnished eyes, and garrulous, sensual mouths, in which the observer recognizes the symptoms of the degeneracy of the thought and its rotation in the circle of a special idea which destroys the creative faculties of the brain and the gift of seeing in large, of generalizing and deducing. No man who has allowed himself to be caught in the revolutions of the gear of these huge machines can ever become great. If he is a doctor, either he has practised little or he is an exception—a Bichat who dies young. If a great merchant, something remains—he is almost Jacques Coeur. Did Robespierre practise? Danton was an idler who waited. But who, moreover, has ever felt envious of the figures of Danton and Robespierre, however lofty they were? These men of affairs, *par excellence,* attract money to them, and hoard it in order to ally themselves with aristocratic families. If the ambition of the working-man is that of the small tradesman, here, too, are the same passions. In Paris vanity sums up all the passions. The type of this class might be either an ambitious *bourgeois,* who after a life of privation and continual scheming, passes into the Council of State as an ant passes through a chink; or some newspaper editor, jaded with intrigue, whom the king makes a peer of France—perhaps to revenge himself on the nobility; or some notary become mayor of his parish: all people crushed with business, who, if they attain their end, are literally *killed* in its attainment. In France the usage is to glorify wigs. Napoleon, Louis XVI, the great rulers, alone have always wished for young men to fulfil their projects.

Above this sphere the artist world exists. But here, too, the faces stamped with the seal of originality are worn, nobly indeed, but worn, fatigued, nervous. Harassed by a need of production, outrun by their costly fantasies, worn out by devouring genius, hungry for pleasure, the artists of Paris would regain by excessive labor what they have lost by idleness, and vainly seek to reconcile the world and glory, money and art. To begin with, the artist is ceaselessly panting under his creditors; his necessities beget his debts, and his debts require of him his nights. After his labor, his pleasure. The comedian plays until midnight, studies in the morning, rehearses at noon; the sculptor is bent before his statue; the journalist is a marching thought, like the soldier when at war; the painter who is the fashion is crushed with work, the painter with no occupation, if he feels himself to be a man of genius, gnaws his entrails. Competition, rivalry, calumny assail talent. Some, in desperation, plunge into the abyss of vice, others die young and unknown because they have discounted their future too soon. Few of these figures, originally sublime, remain beautiful. On the other hand, the flagrant beauty of their heads is not understood. An artist's face is always exhorbitant, it is always above or below the conventional lines of what fools call the *beau-idéal*. What power is it that destroys them? Passion. Every passion in Paris resolves into two terms: gold and pleasure. Now, do you not breathe again? Do you not feel air and space purified? Here is neither labor nor suffering. The soaring arch of gold has reached the summit. From the lowest gutters, where its stream commences, from the little shops where it is stopped by puny coffer-dams, from the heart of the counting-houses and great workshops, where its volume is that of ingots—gold, in the shape of dowries and inheritances, guided by the hands of young girls or the bony fingers of age, courses towards the aristocracy, where it will become a blazing, expansive stream. But, before leaving the four territories upon which the utmost wealth of Paris is based, it is fitting, having cited the moral causes, to deduce those which are physical, and to call attention to a pestilence, latent, as it were, which incessantly acts upon the faces of the porter, the artisan, the small shopkeeper; to point out a deleterious influence the corruption of which equals that of the Parisian administrators who allow it so complacently to exist!

If the air of the houses in which the greater proportion of the middle classes live is noxious, if the atmosphere of the streets belches out cruel miasmas into stuffy back-kitchens where there is little air, realize that, apart from this pestilence, the forty thousand houses of this great city have their foundations in filth, which the powers that be have not yet seriously attempted to enclose with mortar walls solid enough to prevent even the most fetid mud from filtering through the soil, poisoning the wells, and maintaining subterraneously to Lutetia the tradition of her celebrated name. Half of Paris sleeps amidst the putrid exhalations of courts and streets and sewers. But let us turn to the vast salons, gilded and airy; the hotels in their gardens, the rich, indolent, happy, moneyed world. There the faces are lined and scarred with vanity. There nothing is real. To seek for pleasure is not to find *ennui?* People in society have at an early age warped their nature. Having no occupation other than to wallow in pleasure, they have speedily misused their sense, as the artisan has misused brandy. Pleasure is of the nature of certain medical substances: in order to obtain constantly the same effects the doses must be doubled, and death or degradation is contained in the last. All the lower classes are on their knees before the wealthy, and watch their tastes in order to turn them into vices and exploit them. Thus you see in these folk at an early age tastes instead of passions, romantic fantasies and lukewarm loves. There impotence reigns; there ideas have ceased—they have evaporated together with energy amongst the affectations of the boudoir and the cajolements of women. There are fledglings of forty, old doctors of sixty years. The wealthy obtain in Paris readymade wit and science—formulated opinions which save them from the need of having wit, science, or opinion of their own. The irrationality of this world is equaled by its weakness and its licentiousness. It is greedy of time to the point of wasting it. Seek in it for affection as little as for ideas. Its kisses conceal a profound indifference, its urbanity a perpetual contempt. It has no other fashion of love. Flashes of wit without profundity, a wealth of indiscretion, scandal, and above all, commonplace. Such is the sum of its speech; but these happy fortunates pretend that they do not meet to make and repeat maxims in the manner of La Rochefoucauld as though there did not exist a mean, invented by the eighteenth century, between a superfluity and absolute blank. If a few men of character indulge in witticism, at once subtle and refined, they are misunderstood; soon, tired of giving without receiving, they remain at home, and leave fools to reign over their territory. This hollow life, this perpetual expectation of a pleasure which never comes, this permanent *ennui* and emptiness of soul, heart, and mind, the lassitude of the upper Parisian world, is reproduced on its

features, and stamps its parchment faces, its premature wrinkles, that
physiognomy of the wealthy upon which impotence has set its grimace,
in which gold is mirrored, and whence intelligence has fled.

Such a view of moral Paris proves that physical Paris could not be other
than it is. This coroneted town is like a queen, who, being always with child,
has desires of irresistible fury. Paris is the crown of the world, a brain
which perishes of genius and leads human civilization; it is a great man,
a perpetually creative artist, a politician with second-sight who must of
necessity have wrinkles on his forehead, the vices of the great man, the
fantasies of the artist, and the politician's disillusions. Its physiognomy
suggests the evolution of good and evil, battle and victory; the moral combat of '89, the clarion calls of which still re-echo in every corner of the
world; and also the downfall of 1814. Thus this city can no more be moral,
or cordial, or clean, than the engines which impel those proud leviathans
which you admire when they cleave the waves! Is not Paris a sublime
vessel laden with intelligence? Yes, her arms are one of those oracles which
fatality sometimes allows. The *City of Paris* has her great mast, all of
bronze, carved with victories, and for watchman—Napoleon. The barque
may roll and pitch, but she cleaves the world, illuminates it through the
hundred mouths of her tribunes, ploughs the seas of science, rides with
full sail, cries from the height of her tops, with the voice of her scientists
and artists: "Onward, advance! Follow me!" She carries a huge crew,
which delights in adorning her with fresh streamers. Boys and urchins
laughing in the rigging; ballast of heavy *bourgeoisie;* working-men and
sailor-men touched with tar; in her cabin the lucky passengers; elegant
midshipmen smoke their cigars leaning over the bulwarks; then, on the
deck, her soldiers, innovators or ambitious, would accost every fresh shore,
and shooting out their bright lights upon it, ask for glory which is pleasure, or for love which needs gold.

Thus the exorbitant movement of the proletariat, the corrupting influence
of the interests which consume the two middle classes, the cruelties of the
artist's thought, and the excessive pleasure which is sought for incessantly
by the great, explain the normal ugliness of the Parisian physiognomy.
It is only in the Orient that the human race presents a magnificent figure,
but that is an effect of the constant calm affected by those profound philosophers with their long pipes, their short legs, their square contour,
who despise and hold activity in horror, whilst in Paris the little and the
great and the mediocre run and leap and drive, whipped on by an inexorable goddess, Necessity—the necessity for money, glory, and amusement.
Thus, any face which is fresh and graceful and reposeful, any really young

face, is in Paris the most extraordinary of exceptions; it is met with rarely. Should you see one there, be sure it belongs either to a young and ardent ecclesiastic or to some good abbé of forty with three chins; to a young girl of pure life such as is brought up in certain middle-class families; to a mother of twenty, still full of illusions, as she suckles her first-born; to a young man newly embarked from the provinces, and intrusted to the care of some devout dowager who keeps him without a sou; or, perhaps, to some shop assistant who goes to bed at midnight wearied out with folding and unfolding calico, and rises at seven o'clock to arrange the window; often again to some man of science or poetry, who lives monastically in the embrace of a fine idea, who remains sober, patient, and chaste; else to some self-contented fool, feeding himself on folly, reeking of health, in a perpetual state of absorption with his own smile; or to the soft and happy race of loungers, the only folk really happy in Paris, which unfolds for them hour by hour its moving poetry.

ROBERT VAUGHAN

R OBERT VAUGHAN was born in the west of England on October 14, 1795. His parents, of Welsh descent, were poor and could offer him few advantages of education. He studied for the ministry under the tutelage of William Thorp (1771–1833), an independent minister at Castle Green, Bristol. While still a student he was called to serve as minister of an independent congregation in Worcester. His dramatic oratorical style and powerful rhetoric made him a popular preacher, and in March, 1825, he accepted a position at Kensington.

Vaughan gained considerable repute as an historian with the publication of his *Life and Opinions of John de Wycliffe* (1828) and *Memorials of the Stuart Dynasty* (1831), and in 1834 he was appointed to the chair of history at the University of London. In this position he came into close touch with important Whig leaders, and he increased his popularity as a preacher, now attracting many of the upper classes to his sermons. In 1836, he received the Doctor of Divinity degree from Glasgow University.

In 1843, Vaughan was appointed president of Lancashire Independent College and professor of theology. His inaugural discourse on *Protestant Nonconformity* was published that same year. He founded the *British Quarterly* in 1845—an organ of nonconformist Protestantism that attained a considerable circulation because of its discriminating scholarship and wide range of interests. Vaughan edited the magazine for the next twenty years, and his own contributions to it were collected in *Essays on History, Philosophy and Theology* (1849).

Vaughan was an important figure among British nonconformists. He was a vigorous pamphleteer and debater, and frequently led the counterattack against critics of nonconformism. He died at Torquay on June 15, 1868.

The following selection, taken from Vaughan's *The Age of Great Cities* (London, 1843), was an exceptional defense of the possibilities of city life and presents a marked contrast to the usual views of his time.

THE AGE OF GREAT CITIES

CHAPTER IV: ON GREAT CITIES IN THEIR RELATION TO SCIENCE, ART, AND LITERATURE

Section 1.—On Great Cities in Their Relation to the Designs of Providence.

It is a poet of our own who has said—"God made the country; man made the town." In this saying there is a portion of truth, but it does not contain the whole truth. As commonly understood, its effect is to substitute error in the place of truth.

Even the country, in the greater part, is no longer seen as it would appear if wholly devoid of the agency of man. In the absence of what man has done upon it, the surface of the earth must have remained barren, or have degenerated into a monstrous wilderness. No visible hand beside could have prevented it from becoming the home of every rank production, and of every unclean thing.

Nor should it be forgotten, that it was as much a part of the purpose of the Creator with regard to man, that he should build towns, as that he should till the land. If the history of cities, and of their influence on their respective territories, be deducted from the history of humanity, the narrative remaining would be, as we suspect of no very attractive description. In such case, the kind of picture which human society must everywhere have presented, would be such as we see in the condition, from the earliest time, of the wandering hordes of Mongolians and Tartars, spread over the vast flats of central Asia. In those regions, scarcely anything has been "made" by man. But his most happy circumstance, as it seems to be accounted—this total absence of anything reminding you of human skill and industry, has never been found to realize our poetic ideas of pastoral beauty and innocence. It has called forth enough of the squalid and the ferocious, but little of the refined, the powerful, or the generous.

Thus the manifest tendency of the half-truth contained in the saying adverted to, is not to convey a true impression so much as a false one—and how large a portion of the error in the world may be traced in this manner, to partial announcements of truth! If this saying has any meaning, it must mean, that man in the city, is in a less favourable condition for the development of his nature, than man in the field; that in prosecuting the higher arts which flourish in cities, he is not so much in his place as in attending to the more limited arts which relate to pasturage and cattle. But where is the man of sense that would not as soon think of reasoning to the first quadruped he should meet upon the village road, as to the head that could really mean to insinuate such a notion?

If anything be certain, it would seem to be certain, that man is constituted to realize his destiny from his association with man, more than from any contact with places. The great agency in calling forth his capabilities, whether for good or for evil, is that of his fellows. The picturesque, accordingly, may be with the country, but the intellectual, speaking generally, must be with the town. Agriculture may possess its science, and the farmer, as well as the landowner, may not be devoid of intelligence; but in such connexions, science and intelligence, in common with the nourishment of the soil, must be derived, in the main, from the studies prosecuted in cities, and from the wealth realized in the traffic of cities. If pasturage is followed by tillage, and if tillage is made to partake of the nature of a study and a science, these signs of improvement are peculiar to lands in which cities make their appearance, and they become progressive only as cities become opulent and powerful. In this sense we might venture to change the language of our poet a little and say, "Man makes the country, where art makes the town." In so saying we should make a much nearer approach toward the truth. . . .

Section II.—On Great Cities in Their Relation to Physical Science.

Regarding great cities in their relation to physical science, we may safely speak of this branch of intelligence as deriving all its higher culture, if not its existence, from the ingenuities which are natural to men in such associations. Cities are at once the great effect, and the great cause, of progress in this department of knowledge. The monuments of Thebes and Persepolis, of Athens and Rome, are as so many mutilated treatises on the science of the ancients. Next to the memorials of mind transmitted to us in the literature of an ancient city, are those present in its monuments. In the latter we trace the developments of thought, reasoning, imagination, and taste, no less certainly than in the former; and in consequence of the peculiar visibility which attaches to them, they bring a susceptible spirit into the nearest possible fellowship with the spirits of remote times. Cities which can hardly be said to have had a literature at all, have risen to extraordinary magnificence purely as the effect of science; and in our time, the mouldering fragments which bespeak their scientific skill, furnish almost the only direct testimony to their power and character, and in some cases to their existence.

Every region that has become the home of such cities has become the home of an improved agriculture. This has resulted in part from the wealth of cities; but still more from their mechanical and scientific skill. In this manner it has often been reserved to cities to convert the desert into a garden, and to give to the richer soils of the earth the aspect of a paradise. The science extended to agriculture by the Babylonians and Egyptians, by the Carthaginians, and by the Moslems of Spain, was hardly less conspicuous than the wonders which adorned the capitals of their respective territories. The owners of land, accordingly, have always had a deep interest in the prosperity of cities; and when such persons begin to regard cities with jealousy, and become employed in defaming them, in cramping their resources, and in endeavouring to reduce them to a state of weakness and passiveness, they become chargeable with the baseness of ingratitude, or with the madness of self-destruction. Lands which bring forth a hundred-fold in the place of thirty-fold, they owe to the science of cities; and sales which give them a high price for their produce in place of a low one, they owe to the wealth of cities.

But while science is in this manner the parent and the offspring of cities, first creating them, and then nourished by them, it is often alleged against the character of society when made up in a great degree of commercial men, that it is sure to become imbued with a mercenary temper, inconsistent with an enlightened patronage of science, considered in its higher purposes. Nor will it be pretended, we presume, by any man, that there is no danger of this kind in such connexions.

It may be accounted probable, and indeed certain, that a body of citizens, however comparatively enlightened, will be disposed to look on science in its relation to the immediate and the practical, so as rarely to make it an object of much encouragement, viewed in its remoter principles and tendencies. The great occupation of such persons is in production and traffic: and it is to be presumed, that, in general, the man will be most secure of their applause and bounty, whose discoveries bear most immediately on practical processes, and so upon the matter of gain. Your philosopher, disposed to indulge in lofty speculations, may possess many claims to admiration; but the large body of busy traders in a great city, will be in danger of forming their estimate concerning the value of such speculations according to their relation in respect to the market. Hence what philosophy does in giving a homely and useful application to its principles, and does often only as something by the way, rather than as its great object, is in danger of being regarded as the only thing it has ever done that was worth doing.

It is admitted, then, that high theoretic attainment in such pursuits, must always depend in a great measure upon leisure, seclusion, and meditation; and that to such habits the ceaseless action pervading great cities is by no means favourable. In the complex interests, pursuits, and relations of a large city community, we perceive much tending to secure society against great and sudden changes. It is a piece of machinery which has not been suddenly put together, and which cannot be suddenly taken to pieces. It is not the production of a single cause, and it will not be annihilated by a single cause. Nevertheless, in a state of society, so constituted, particularly where affairs, extended and mixed as they have become, are still left subject to a good deal of influence from the spirit of freedom,—in all such communities there is a constant vibration and movement, a ceaseless occurrence of the distracting and exciting, which must be admitted to be very unfriendly to the prosecution of works demanding the exercise of silent, continuous, and profound thought. Minds which do their sincere worship to truth, and which find the happiness and charm of existence in its service, can have little congeniality with the crowded places where the working-day multitude of men do all things after their own pleasure, and often with an inconsiderateness, dogmatism, and violence natural to their imperfect mental and moral training. In some of these respects there is an obvious advantage in a more aristocratic state of society.

But if it be an error to regard philosophy as valueless except as it is applied to the immediately practical and useful, the spirit which would divorce it from such applications, or which may be disposed to look upon it as almost degraded when so applied, is not at all less censurable. It may be well that minds of the higher order should be allowed to fix themselves intently on their favourite speculations, as in a region apart; but if the mood in which minds of that class give themselves up to such pursuits shall be such as to dispose them to account it a trivial or mean thing to be useful in respect to the common affairs of men, the men engaged in such affairs owe it to themselves to discountenance such a temper in every way within their power. The worship of the beautiful, in common with the worship of the useful, may be pushed to extremes, until it becomes, in a moral sense, a homage rendered to deformity. To err in that form was the fault of many among the ancient philosophers: and the tendency to counteract extravagance of that sort which belongs to the character of society in great cities, is, for the most part, wholesome in its operation. We have no wish to see such men as Plato and Aristotle wholly superseded by such men as Arkwright and Watt. We would retain both: our civilization has its spaces for both: and either would be the better for that modification from the other which modern society has done much to realize.

It is, of course, better that science should obtain patronage from men intent only on practical objects, than that it should be without patronage of any kind; and this is the alternative awaiting it, as having its place among the people who built cities, or among the people who do not build them. Nor is this all—it is possible that the patronage of the many, though bestowed with a view to such limited objects only, may do more toward the advancement of real science than the patronage of the few, though taking in a much wider range. The quantity of patronage may do much to make up for some deficiencies in the quality. We have observed that some of our most valuable discoveries have risen up unsought, as a kind of happy ac-

cidents, in the path of investigation. Now whenever men are widely occupied in inquiry and experiment, such accidents may be expected to occur
frequently. All things in nature have relations which seem to promise
such results—the particular with the general, the practical with the theoretic.
Men who labour much on the confines of the known, will be sure to make
frequent incursions into the regions of the unknown. Where many things
are done, also, some things will be sure to be done well. Mediocrity will rise
into excellence, and the fresh consciousness of power to make progress, will
naturally lead to progression.

When we look, moreover, on the distracting or absorbing effect of the
ceaseless action pervading great cities, it must be remembered that the end
of this action is accumulation, and that the effect of accumulation is not only
to raise classes above the crowd, but to raise certain minds capable of excelling
in abstract studies, and others capable of sympathizing with them, into positions favourable to the indulgence of their higher preferences. Nor should
it be overlooked, that if the habit of thought among such a people is not
immediately congenial with this more elevated feeling, it is thought of a
kind likely to prove strongly hostile to false pretension. It may undervalue
the severe and retired labour which is so necessary to all real greatness; but
its propensity to judge for itself, its little reverence for precedents or great
names, the importance which it attaches to fact, experiment, and the testimony of the senses, its very conceit, which prompts it to conclude that it
can understand everything and do everything,—all serve as a check on the
presumption and on the arts of the superficial, and open a fair field on which
to display the superiority of real science.

It may be that the United States will be appealed to, as affording striking
evidence of the low mechanical routine to which all science is reduced, in
proportion as the elements of society become more and more democratic. It
should be a sufficient answer to such persons, to remind them that the
republican institutions of Athens, so far from being incompatible with a
high state of civic refinement, have contributed to render that city the
model of all cities in respect to such cultivation. In the history of the United
States, the useful has hitherto very naturally taken a marked precedence of
the ornamental, partly from the youth of the States themselves, and partly
from the fact that England is, in this respect, only as another province to
North America, everything new in British discovery being at the service
of the Anglo-American people so soon as it becomes known among ourselves.
Down to this time it has been enough that the people of the United States
should apply the stores of knowledge placed continually at their disposal.
Of America, we may say, her age of invention is to come. But come it will,

though her danger, in common with all states in which the commercial spirit becomes predominant, will continue to be on the side of looking to science too much in its relation to mechanism and profit, and too little in relation to its less obvious and wider results. The great check upon this tendency will be found in the general intelligence of her people; in the necessary increase of wealth with certain classes among them; and in the national pride, which will always be much affected by the consciousness of this deficiency so long as it exists.

It appears, then, that apart from the influence of great cities, the higher developments of the intellect in relation to science would not be realized at all; and that when cities become so far governed by a commercial spirit, as to be in danger of falling under a mercenary influence in relation to such objects, there are many causes, inseparable from such a state of society, which are of a nature strongly to counteract the proneness to that particular form of deterioration. It would be easy to show that the affairs of a large commercial state necessarily prefer a strong demand on all the capabilities even of the highest order of intellect. The merchant and the capitalist are fully as likely to be men of large views as the country gentleman, or as the noble who can trace his blood to the times of the Conquest, or to those of Charlemagne. The minds of such men need be familiar with all countries and with all people. It is their direct interest to acquire a knowledge of the natural and the artificial in all lands. It behoves them, also, to weigh carefully all the knowledge of which they become possessed, in order that their schemes, involving the gravest responsibilities, may be conducted with certainty. Large fortunes are seen to be realized by means of such knowledge skilfully applied, while ruin is seen as often to ensue from the want of such information and discretion. Hence the extraordinary capacity displayed by the statesmen who have grown up in the midst of such cities as Venice, Florence and Amsterdam.

The web of social policy never becomes so intricate as when wrought up from the thread-work of commerce; and the causes which serve to elicit a peculiar genius in the ministers of commercial states, serve to generate a keen, a comprehensive, and a robust, if not a highly refined intelligence, among the leading men in such states. The intricate becomes familiar to such minds, and practice gives them a mastery over it. In such communities the power of making the difficult plain, in matters of policy, is of great price. The few, in such connexions, cannot act without the many, nor, in consequence, without becoming able teachers of the many. Even the mass of the people, in a great commercial city, are made to feel in a much greater degree than any other people, as citizens of the world. They see that their interests depend, not on themselves, nor upon their nearest neighbours, but upon relations which subsist between them and the ends of the earth. It is only in proportion as commercial states have been capable of looking thus abroad, that they have become great. The fear, accordingly, in such a state of society, is not so much that there will be a want of boldness and expansion of thought, as that men will learn to trust with too much confidence to the powers of their own understanding, and be carried away by an ill-regulated passion for novelty, as the effect of their constant familiarity with progression and change.

Section III.—On Great Cities in Their Relation to the History of Political Science.

If the influence of great cities on the progress of natural science is thus manifest, their tendency to foster just and enlightened views in relation to political science is no less obvious. Every municipal body must have its local regulations, and its local functionaries to carry them into effect. As those regulations have respect to the common interest, it is natural that they should be the result of something like common deliberation, and common consent. If it be reasonable that laws relating to the common interest should seem to emanate from the common will, it is further reasonable that the common will should reserve to itself the power of choosing its own executive.

In this manner a popular character naturally attaches to municipal law and municipal authority. Every such community is constantly under influences which dispose it to imbibe the spirit, and to take up the forms of a commonwealth. In proportion as a nation becomes a nation of towns and cities, this spirit, and these forms, are likely to become more prevalent and more fixed. Cities are states upon a small scale, and are of necessity schools in relation to the policy most in harmony with the genius of a people. Political knowledge never diffuses itself more wholesomely among a people, than when it results, in this manner, slowly and steadily, from circumstances and experience; and when its principles are to be brought out upon a large scale, by men who have worked them successfully on a smaller scale. . . .

With regard to this connexion between commerce on a large scale, and general liberty, the history of the United Provinces, and of Great Britain, are pregnant examples. In the English House of Commons we see a power which has become strong on the side of just laws and equal liberty, in proportion to the increase of the population, the wealth, and the power of the boroughs and cities which it has represented. In the capability of that house to replenish the treasury of the crown, we may trace the secret of its power in rescinding bad laws and enacting good ones, during nearly the whole period of its history. On some occasions the upper house has shown itself less fanatical or less corrupt than the lower; but, in general, the people have given the impression of their sentiments to the commons, and the commons have acted in the same manner upon the lords. In our recent history, the house which is the greatest authority in relation to money bills, has been virtually the great authority in all things; so as to make it certain, that we should speak more correctly, if not more eloquently—to use the language of a distinguished living writer—were we to describe our liberties as purchased, not so much by the blood of our ancestors, as by their money.

In this manner, then, the principles of self-government have ascended from the borough to the senate, from the councilmen of the city to the councilmen of the nation. Such is the natural course of things. The more the principles of self-government are acted upon in the parish, the town, the great city, and the district, the more will men be interested in the affairs of their country generally, the more competent will they be to judge of the manner in which the business of their country should be conducted, and the more probable will it be that statesmen will regulate their course by principles that will abide the severest scrutiny. Let a nation advance in intelligence and social virtue, and its rulers must be obedient to this propulsive power, and advance proportionately in the same qualities. Let the spirit and forms of constitutional liberty be thus localized through a country, and you possess in that fact the best guarantee for their being centralized in its supreme councils. In so doing, you provide for the rational exercise of popular power, and give the best security to the power itself. Rulers of an arbitrary temper have not been insensible to this truth, and have made it a great object of their policy to crush muncipal independence in all cases when not deterred by a sense of weakness, or by other selfish considerations. . . .

CHAPTER V: ON THE AGE OF GREAT CITIES IN RELATION TO POPULAR INTELLIGENCE

Section 1.—On the Effect of Association in Great Cities with Regard to Popular Intelligence.

. . . . Cities, then, are the natural centres of association. Of course the advantages derived from association are there realized in an eminent degree. Men live there in the nearest neighbourhood. Their faculties, in place of becoming dull from inaction, are constantly sharpened by collision. They have their prejudices, but all are liable to be assailed. Manufactures, commerce, politics, religion, all become subjects of discussion. All these are looked upon from more points, talked about more variously, and judged of more correctly, as being matters in which a great number of minds are interested, and on which those minds are not only accustomed to form conclusions, but to form them with a view to utterance and action. It may be the lot of very few to possess much vigour of thought, but each man stimulates his fellow, and the result is a greater general intelligence. The shop, the factory, or the market-place; the local association, the news-room, or the religious meeting, all facilitate this invigorating contact of mind with mind. The more ignorant come into constant intercourse with the more knowing. Stationariness of thought is hardly possible, and if its movements are not always wise, the errors of today are as lessons of experience for tomorrow. Such, indeed, is often the astuteness acquired in the exercise of this greatest of free schools, that the smith of Sheffield, or the weaver of Manchester, would frequently prove, on any common ground, more than a match for many a college graduate. But does your man of technical education ever apprehend any such rencontre with the village ploughman? Or has it ever occurred to him to reckon the plough-man's assistant as superior in shrewdness to the city apprentice? In short, noth-ing can be more plain, than that the unavoidable intercourse of townsmen must always involve a system of education; and that while instruction reaches, in such connexions, to a much lower level than elsewhere, minds of better capac-ity naturally make the common intelligence about them the starting-point in their own race of superiority.

It has been intimated that in towns there are greater facilities than in the country for conducting education in its more direct and technical form. These facilities are greater in towns, partly on account of their greater wealth, and their greater freedom from prejudice; and partly in consequence of their more general sympathy with popular improvement, and their comparative freedom from the discountenance or control of powerful individuals or classes. Towns are not like villages, subject, it may be, to the oversight and guidance of a sin-gle family, or of a single clergyman. They possess greater means and greater liberty, and, in general, a stronger disposition to use both in favour of edu-cation, even in behalf of the children of the poorest.

In towns also, where numbers may be more easily collected, masters find a better return for their toil, and the practice of teaching on a larger scale brings with it a greater proficiency in the art of teaching. In the one case, too, the public reap the benefit of competition; in the other it is hardly admissible. In the populous town, a field is open to different labourers. Every man has space in which to make trial of his favourite method. The observers are many, and the stimulus is proportionate. But in the rural district, it is probable that the schoolmaster will enter upon the duties of his office with no great aptness for the discharge of them; and when it is remembered that the number he will be required to teach will generally be small, that the instruction he will be expected to impart will be very limited, and that in imparting it he will know nothing of competition, and be subject in general to very imperfect oversight, it will be seen that the natural course of things, both as respects the character of the teacher and the result of his labours, is in nearly all points the reverse of that which may be reasonably expected in a city population.

With regard to mechanics' institutes and literary institutions, it is obvious that the benefit to be derived from them must be restricted almost entirely to the people of towns and cities. In most of the towns of Great Britain such associations exist. In the larger cities they are numerous, and their advantages are made accessible to almost every grade of the community. Of course the knowledge communicated by such institutions must always be elementary and popular, rather than comprehensive or profound. But the natural effect of such associations is to strengthen the taste for improvement where it exists, and often to create it where it is not. They serve to bring something more of the intellectual into alliance with the commercial. By such means the mind is taken, in some degree, from the groove of its daily occupation, and glimpses are opened to it, showing the manner in which the closer exercises of thought have conducted to wealth, and power, and greatness. The library, the reading-room, the debating class, and the lecture theatre, all contribute to this result. Where this effect is produced, leisure ceases to be a burden. Much is done to redeem it from the bait of sensuality. The mental and moral habits of many thousands among our young men have been thus affected by such means. . . .

CHAPTER VI: ON GREAT CITIES IN THEIR RELATION TO MORALS

Section VIII.—On the Connexion Between the State of Society in Great Cities, and the Morality of Law, Order and Liberty.

Nor are we accustomed to look on this course of things with apprehension, considered in its bearing on morals. It may be very true that offences against property are more numerous in manufacturing districts, and in large cities, than in rural parishes. But this is saying no more, than that offences against property are most frequent, where property is most abundant; and that men become the victims of temptation the most, where there is the greater number to be tempted, and where the temptation itself is the strongest. Side by side, also, with the infirmity which yields to temptation, is the virtue which resists it; and the stronger the test to which virtue is exposed, the higher must be its quality if it shall come forth unscathed. In all such cases, accordingly, it becomes us not merely to look to the positive amount of convicted delinquency, but to the no less positive, and far greater amount, of fairly accredited principle. It is only as men become themselves civilized, that they are found capable of withstanding the temptations to wrong doing which are opened and multiplied in the relations of civilized life.

It is obvious, that with the first notion of property must come the notion of a right in it as such, and of usage or law as the means of upholding that right. With the increase of wealth, must come the complex social relations natural to it, and a familiarity of mind with all the complex moral questions which these relations involve. To ascertain the just, with regard to such questions, and to secure its enforcement in the best manner, must then be one of the great objects of human sagacity. As some fixed notion on this subject is necessary to the existence of society in its rudest state, so much elaborate thought in relation to it becomes necessary when society has passed from its state of rudeness to refinement. Protection against wrong, in relation to person and property, is then felt to be the great want; and the power of thought and invention directed toward that object, is in proportion to the promptings of the strong law of necessity with regard to it. Hence as society is nowhere so much dependent on the prevalence of enlightened sentiments in respect to all matters of social justice as in great cities, so the intellect, and the passions, in regard to that subject, are nowhere else so disciplined and powerful.

Commercial credit, from its humblest to its very highest form, is based on moral confidence—confidence, not so much perhaps in what the individual trusted might probably do if left to himself, as in what he will be constrained to do rather than brave the resentment with which the moral feelings of society would be prepared to visit the unjust or dishonourable. If much should be wanting in the principle of the individual, much will be supplied by the principle of society: and if the man should wholly fail in this respect, the community will not. With every step in social advancement, this system of credit widens, and becomes more intricate, and in the greatness of its compass, and in the delicacy of its details, we perceive that as men become more opulent and civilized, they learn to place increasing confidence in each other, manifestly regarding each other as more trustworthy—more moral. In all these respects, the morality of law is the public morality embodied. We may add, that order, punctuality, promptitude, courage, all are more or less necessary to mercantile success, and all are in the same degree necessary as elements of moral habit. Nor can it be less obvious, that the constant and earnest occupation which so effectually precludes idleness, must do much to preclude vice.

We have seen already, that causes which contribute in this manner to the dominion of ascertained law, contribute necessarily to establish general liberty. But civil freedom is not more the natural offspring of cities, than the natural parent of morality. It owes its origin, indeed, to moral feeling as much as to intellectual attainment, but it reacts upon both as with usury. It is natural that despotism should generate suspicion, concealment, treachery, falsehood, objectness. It may carry with it some of the appearances of virtue, but only in such degree as may be necessary to perpetuate its peculiar vices. It may be in some degree benignant, but only in such measure as may be necessary in order that social existence may be possible. In general, the virtues allied with such governments exist in spite of them, rather than as proceeding from them, or as nourished by them.

It does not, indeed, necessarily follow, that the more a people diverge from the line of despotism, the more virtuous they become. But the probability lies strongly in that direction. If they know how to halt within the limits of freedom, without plunging into anarchy, or substituting the despotism of a popular, in place of the despotism of a monarchical power, we may be assured that high moral intelligence has been in action to produce such effects, and that further moral results will not be wanting. The people who possess a freedom of this nature, give evidence in that fact of being distinguished in no inconsiderable degree by their mental cultivation and social virtue, inasmuch as such freedom cannot be expected to come into existence except in alliance with such qualities, and inasmuch as it cannot be expected to continue except as these qualities shall continue. It vests men with a new power to do wrong, which must always be an element of mischief, except as placed in the hands of a people whose prevailing disposition is to do right.

Every such system must conduce to the cause of virtue, in so far as it provides that no man shall be made to suffer as the penalty of virtue. It tends to the suppression of vice, by depriving it of its most plausible excuses, and by connecting it with its merited disgrace. Fear, concealment, deception—all may be accounted comparatively innocent, in the case of the man who sees in the power above him a huge machinery of suspicion, fraud, and tyranny, from the pressure of which, should he once be deemed an offender, there can be no way of escape. Widely different are the circumstances of the man who can demand to meet his accusers face to face, who can insist on his right, not only to invoke the protection of law, but to sift evidence to the utmost in his own defence, and who, encircling himself thus with the immunities of the free, can set the passions even of the most powerful at defiance. If such a man shall be found wanting in a regard to truth, justice, or humanity, he is thus wanting without excuse. He cannot plead that these vices are the last refuge left by a bad government to the weak. He must know, that, in his case, they are the needless and the chosen vices of the strong. With the free, the law is generally as a terror to evil-doers, and as a praise to those who do well; but with the victim of despotism it is often the reverse; and thus while in the latter case there must commonly be much temptation on the side of vice, in the former case there is always strong inducement on the side of its opposite.

It may be true that a feeling of self-interest has much to do with putting the dispositions of men upon a track of this nature. Men may discountenance wrong generally, in order to protect their own persons, or their own property, against aggression in that form. Much also of the general industry, which by contributing to increase the wealth and intelligence of society, contributes to its moral improvement, may have been carried on without any reference to such a result, and purely with a view to particular or individual interests. Even the men who labour more directly with a view to social improvement, as public men and authors may have their personal feelings to gratify, and their personal interests to serve by such efforts.

But if the spirit of trade and manufactures is to be accounted as unfavourable to morality, because liable to such mixtures of feeling, the agriculture must be regarded as in the same predicament, inasmuch as it can hardly be pretended that farmers are less liable to the influence of narrow selfish passions than merchants. Such moral infirmities are attendant on the cultivation of the soil, in at least as great a degree as on the processes of manufactures. Nor should it be forgotten, that there is a regard to our personal interest which belongs to the virtuous rather than the immoral. It is easy to give bad names to secondary motives—to see in the love of esteem, nothing beside covetousness; but that is not the Christian, nor the philosophical, nor even the honest mode of looking at human nature. Admitting the excess of the selfish in most men, we must bear in mind that those who work consciously with a view to human improvement, and those who work toward that end unconsciously, have their place alike in the system of Divine Providence, and are laid under contribution alike toward the accomplishment of its purposes; and that it behoves us to look to the good which is attendant on improved social relations, and always to place it over against the particular forms of evil which may be found to be also attendant upon them.

Section X.—On the Less Permanent Nature of the Social Relation in Modern Society, and on Its Moral Influence.

The tendency of the great facts which characterize modern civilization in regard to the social relations, is an extended subject. In some views, the moral results proceeding from this cause may not be pleasing. But we must look to the feeling which this change has served to generate, as well as to that which it has tended to efface or impair. The relation subsisting between master and servant, landlord and tenant, employer and employed, are no longer the same, either in fact or feeling. The permanence attaching to these relations in more feudal times is hardly discoverable in these later days. Every such connexion seems to partake of the uncertain and the transient, and is wanting accordingly in the feeling which could not fail to result from old recollections, and from a stronger sense of mutual service, interest, and expectation.

But this change is the natural effect of that greater degree of social independence, and of that nearer approach toward equality, which characterizes modern society, and which brings its good along with its evil. In proportion as society is graduated into classes, men think more about their class than about the community. Protection, and favour, and even sympathy, may descend from those who are above to those who are beneath, but it is still as from the high to the low. It is not the more full, manly, and moral sentiment which has place between equals. No man can have been an observant reader of history, without perceiving that the majority of historians have been men of this defective sympathy; and that in general they have commended themselves to persons of the same temperament. Plebeian wrong and suffering have met with sorry treatment at their hand, plainly because they knew that such things had never met with much consideration from the hands of the classes above plebeians, and because, in the greatness of their wisdom, they had learnt to conclude, that as it has been in this respect, so it must continue to be. . . .

We account it one of the most benignant aspects of modern society that it tends strongly to diminish the immoral in this form, by abating the power of the causes from which it has proceeded. If the chivalrous devotion induced by the conventionalism of feudal times is gone, something of the sense of moral obligation proper to much wiser times has come. If we are bound less strongly to the men immediately about us, we are bound more strongly to man as everywhere. If we make little pretension to occasional acts of heroic generosity, we know how to value the moral habit which causes a man to abstain from doing wrong, to uphold the right and to compassionate the suffering. If the humanity of chivalry was an advance on the preceding barbarism, the humanity of modern civilization is a further advance in the same direction. If the rudiments of the moral sentiments in feudalism were sufficient to render it an institute of great social value in its time, it is just the wider expansion, and the more varied application of these rudiments, which has given to the institutes of modern society their distinctive character. Under this new influence, men will be less governed by passion, but they will be more obedient to principle. They may not be devoid of coarseness, but neither will they be devoid of humanity. They may not be forward to do great things in behalf of each other, but it will be their habit to do a multitude of little things, which, taken together, will prove to be of much greater worth. Nothing daring or brilliant may be contemplated by them, but the place of such things may be well supplied by the honest, the orderly, the laborious, the useful.

In all these respects, our social state is one of great admixture. The new has come into the place of the old, but only in such measure as to bring the opposite elements into almost ceaseless conflict. In no connexion do we feel this change more immediately or strongly than in the relations between master and servant. This has come to be a relationship in which the slightest tokens of sympathy are too often wanting on both sides. On the one side there is little power to command, on the other a restless disinclination to obey. It is plain from this fact, that the very frame-work of society is changing, and that the lower portions of it are approaching more nearly toward the level of the higher.

Still, we are not certain that the moralist should see much to deplore in a fact of this nature. It clearly shows that a new sense of right has taken possession of the class required to serve. But a better sense of right in regard to what is due to themselves, will hardly be separable from a better sense of what is due to others. The present tendencies of society are not toward putting an end to the distinction between the serving and the served—a point which no stage of democracy can reach—but to require that the relation between these parties should be on another footing than formerly, on a footing involving much more considerateness and humanity toward the dependent and the necessitous. We must confess, that we see little to regret in the circumstances which promise to constrain even the most reluctant to cultivate the bearing, if not the spirit of humanity. . . .

The causes which have served to diminish the power of the master, have served to diminish that of the parent. In all countries where the government is despotic or aristocratic, the fathers of families are vested with somewhat of a patriarchal authority. In such countries it is not usual to move in anything by the process of many wills, and the same obtains in the family. The father, accordingly, is a kind of sovereign in his household, somewhat after the model of the sovereignty in the state. His dignity, moreover, is hereditary, and those ancestral recollections, to which an aristocratic imagination clings with so much fondness, have in him their centre and chronicler. But where manufactures and commerce make their appearance, augmenting population, and diffusing equality, the scene becomes greatly altered in these respects. Parental authority then ceases at an early period. The young assume independence at an early age. . . .

It generally happens that the character of the government among such a people facilitates this kind of change. If based on popular institutions, it looks to men, less as members of families, than as subjects of the state. It distinguishes between the father and the son, but as the former may be the man of most years and of the largest possessions. It looks on men, not as to be idlers at home, but as to be abroad and active wherever occasion may require. It loosens the ties which bind men artificially to their family, but it strengthens all that is natural in the domestic relations, while binding them by new obligations to society at large. Such is the social bearing of a popular form of government, as distinguished from the aristocratic and the arbitrary. It connects a sense of honour with the feeling of individual responsibility, more than with those passions which take the form of the passive.

In some respects the moral influence of these circumstances cannot be regarded as favourable. It cannot be good that the young should often be exposed to the full force of temptation at a season when least capable of meeting it. But it should be remembered, that though parental authority may cease with childhood, parental influence does not; and that there is good reason to believe, that what is taken away from the arbitrary or capricious in the parental relation by this means, is more than made up by the connexion into which it is brought with the affectionate and confiding. Among a people whose ideas and impressions are derived from popular institutions, filial affection, if evinced with less of stately observance, may be more genuine, as the effect of having respect to a relationship which has become more free, familiar, and inviting. Parents are not likely to be less considerate or kind toward their children, from knowing that considerateness and kindness are their only means of influence. . . .

On the whole, it does not necessarily follow, that the relation between the manufacturer and the artisan will be less humane than the relation between the great landlord and the peasant. The history of trade-unions, of strikes, and of machine-breaking, shews plainly that the relation between master and man in the system of manufactures, may become characterized by a lamentable degree of selfishness and malignity. But, on the other hand, a similar inference is suggested concerning the relation between the farmer and the labourer by the history of rick-burning, and by the frequent migrating of our rural population into the manufacturing districts. Nor will it be doubted, by any person competent to judge on such a matter, that the cases are very common in which fully as much of mutual good feeling subsists between the mill-owner and his workman, as between the superior and inferior in any other connexion. The reason is plain; capitalists, whether their property be embarked in a farm or in a mill, subject themselves by such speculations to about the same measure of dependence on the skill and labour of other men, and on that law of Providence which secures a considerable identity of interest between the men who supply skill and labour, and the men who pay for such supplies.

The relations, then, of lord and vassal, of proprietor and serf, have no place in modern society. Hence, uncertainty, with regard to social relationship, is more or less everywhere. But the evil resulting from this change is in great part counteracted by the good which it brings along with it. Men change masters more frequently than in feudal times, but the moral feeling which bound them to one man, or to one household, now binds them to their class or to society. The change is not so much that the heart has lost its moral affection, as that the object of that affection is no longer strictly the same.

It has been alleged by a distinguished writer on subjects of this nature, that the tendency of our manufacturing system, as now carried on increasingly by means of machinery, by division of labour, and by large capital, must be, not only to create a new species of aristocracy in the persons of our large manufacturers, but to lower the operative, both in intelligence and station, in precisely the same ratio,—the man becoming nothing, in proportion as the machine, and the money power commanding it, become everything. But this is one of the many points on which experience is against speculation.

Machinery has been improved and extended beyond all precedent during the last forty years; but the British artisan, in place of becoming—as this theory would lead us to expect—a mere automaton, has increased in general intelligence, and in the feeling of independence, in a manner no less unprecedented. It is in the natural course of things that the ingenuity which gives a man a better machine to work with, should give him a more intelligent and a better moral atmosphere to dwell in. Invention makes a less demand upon his skill in some forms, but it renders him more familiar with the exhibitions of skill in other forms, and thus supplies with one hand more than it subtracts with the other. Education comes not from the structure of a loom, but from the texture of society. Hence the sort of skill which is lost to man as an artisan in such case, is more than repaid by the relation into which he is brought with an improved state of society. The lesser order of ingenuity has thus given place to the greater, that in its train might come a greater wealth, and with greater wealth a larger measure of general improvement. Thus, while the machine abridges instruction in the factory, it augments the sources of instruction everywhere else. In this manner does Providence often counterbalance the elements of social progress, placing new tendencies toward good, side by side with new tendencies toward evil, and shewing the folly of such predictions concerning the future as are founded on a partial attention to the present.

THOMAS ROBERT MALTHUS

THOMAS ROBERT MALTHUS (1766–1835) was the second son of Daniel Malthus, a cultivated English country gentleman. It was partly owing to the influence of Rousseau's theories (expressed in *Émile*) that Malthus's education in his early years came to be entrusted to private tutors. Malthus subsequently attended Jesus College at Cambridge. After graduating he was ordained as an Anglican clergyman in 1788.

Malthus's earliest interest in population theory can be traced to his unpublished work, written in 1796, entitled "The Crisis, a View of the Recent Interesting State of Great Britain by a Friend of the Constitution." In 1798, at the age of thirty-two, he published anonymously *An Essay on the Principle of Population, as it Affects the Future Improvement of Society: With Remarks on the Speculations of Mr. Godwin, M. Condorcet, and other writers.*

There is more than a little irony in the fact that Malthus's writings changed political economy from a cheerful to a "dismal science," for such was not his intention. Nor should he be made responsible for many of the propagandistic uses to which his ideas were put. For Malthus was a generous, warm-hearted humanitarian whose foremost concerns were the alleviation of poverty and the betterment of human society. He was a pessimist only in the sense that he doubted the adequacy of theories which assumed the inevitability of social progress, or which taught that it would occur "automatically" in consequence of a supposed "pre-established harmony" of egoistic interests guided only by an "invisible hand."

To many of his contemporaries, however, it seemed that Malthus's most significant achievement had been to prove that no one was so directly responsible for the existence of poverty as the poor themselves—that their misery was solely caused by the "improvidence" that led working men to marry early and have large families, thus glutting the labor market and driving wages down. This argument was decisively invoked in 1834 when a draconian Poor Law was enacted by Parliament on the plea that the harshest possible treatment of the poor was actually the most merciful. It is true that the Malthusian argument today demands a far more subtle and complex formulation than was once the case. But the passion with which its originator's name is still invoked, by disciples and critics alike, indicates a vitality and economic insight which many of Malthus's more popular contemporaries seem in retrospect not to have possessed.

More than twenty years after the publication of the *Essay on Population* Malthus published his *Principles of Political Economy* (1820) in which the old skeptic questioned not only the validity of Say's denial of overproduction, which he considered "utterly unfounded," but also the general belief in the beneficial effects of parsimony or thrift. Malthus thus became one of the first English economists who questioned, at least by implication, the classical faith in the self-equilibrating tendencies of the capitalist economy.

However, Malthus's views met with no agreement. An extended and famous controversy on the subject with Ricardo led to no result. Ricardo remained adamant, and the successors of the classical economists tended, as J. M. Keynes says, "to dismiss the problem from the corpus of economics not by solving it but by not mentioning it." Ricardo's *Notes on Malthus's Principles of Political Economy,* published posthumously in 1928, contains the following significant passage, which indicates clearly the practical implications of Malthus's theories to which he objected: "We are it seems a nation of producers and have few consumers amongst us, and the evil has at last become of that magnitude that we shall be irretrievably miserable if the Parliament or the ministers do not immediately adopt an efficient plan of expenditure." That these were, indeed, the practical implications of Malthus's dissent as he himself understood them, may be seen from the following extracts from the concluding section of Malthus's *Principles:*

"It is of importance to know that, in our endeavours to assist the working classes in a period like the present, it is desirable to employ them in those kinds of labor, the results of which do not come for sale into the market, such as roads, and public works. The objection to employing a large sum in this way, raised by taxes, would not be its tendency to diminish the capital employed in productive labor; because this to a certain extent, is exactly what is wanted; but it might, perhaps, have the effect of concealing too much the failure of the national demand for labor, and prevent the population from gradually accommodating itself to a reduced demand. This however might be, in a considerable degree, corrected by the wages given. And altogether I should say that the employment of the poor in roads and public works, and a tendency among landlords and persons of property to build, to improve and beautify their grounds, and to employ workmen and menial servants, are the means most within our power and most directly calculated to remedy the evils arising from that disturbance in the balance of produce and consumption, which has been occasioned by the sudden conversion of soldiers, sailors and various other classes which the war employed, into productive labourers."

A second edition of the *Essay on Population* appeared in 1803. It was an extensive revision of the first and contained a great mass of historical evidence in support of his original thesis. With the exception of the first chapter, the following selections are taken from the seventh edition of the *Essay* (1872). The initial chapter has been taken from the first edition because it contains the most forthright and concise statement of Malthus's leading principles.

The selections from *Principles* serve not only to illustrate Malthus's general refutation of the "law of markets" on the grounds of the possibility of excessive savings, but also to indicate the manner in which his doctrine of population had been integrated into the general body of classical economic theory. The selections are from the second edition (1836) of the *Principles.*

AN ESSAY ON POPULATION

[Book I]

CHAPTER I: . . . OUTLINE OF THE PRINCIPAL ARGUMENT OF THE ESSAY

THE GREAT and unlooked for discoveries that have taken place of late years in natural philosophy; the increasing diffusion of general knowledge from the extension of the art of printing; the ardent and unshackled spirit of inquiry that prevails throughout the lettered, and even unlettered world; the new and extraordinary lights that have been thrown on political subjects, which dazzle and astonish the understanding; and particularly that tremendous phenomenon in the political horizon the French Revolution, which, like a blazing comet, seems destined either to inspire with fresh life and vigour, or to scorch up and destroy the thinking inhabitants of the earth, have all concurred to lead able men into the opinion, that we were touching upon a period big with the most important changes, changes that would in some measure be decisive of the future fate of mankind.

It has been said, that the great question is now at issue, whether man shall henceforth start forwards with accelerated velocity towards illimitable, and hitherto unconceived improvement; or be condemned to a perpetual oscillation between happiness and misery, and after every effort remain still at an immeasurable distance from the wished-for goal.

Yet, anxiously as every friend of mankind must look forwards to the termination of this painful suspense; and, eagerly as the inquiring mind would hail every ray of light that might assist its view into futurity, it is much to be lamented, that the writers on each side of this momentous question still keep far aloof from each other. Their mutual arguments do not meet with a candid examination. The question is not brought to rest on fewer points; and even in theory scarcely seems to be approaching to a decision.

The advocate for the present order of things, is apt to treat the sect of speculative philosophers, either as a set of artful and designing knaves, who preach up ardent benevolence, and draw captivating pictures of a happier state of society, only the better to enable them to destroy the present establishments, and to forward their own deep-laid schemes of ambition: or, as wild and mad-headed enthusiasts, whose silly speculations, and absurd paradoxes, are not worthy the attention of any reasonable man.

The advocate for the perfectibility of man, and of society, retorts on the defender of establishments a more than equal contempt. He brands him as the slave of the most miserable, and narrow prejudices; or, as the defender of the abuses of civil society, only because he profits by them. He paints him either as a character who prostitutes his understanding to his interest; or as one whose powers of mind are not of a size to grasp anything great and noble; who cannot see above five yards before him; and who must therefore be utterly unable to take in the views of the enlightened benefactor of mankind.

In this unamicable contest, the cause of truth cannot but suffer. The really good arguments on each side of the question are not allowed to have their proper weight. Each pursues his own theory, little solicitous to correct, or improve it, by an attention to what is advanced by his opponents.

The friend of the present order of things condemns all political speculations in the gross. He will not even condescend to examine the grounds from which the perfectibility of society is inferred. Much less will he give himself the trouble in a fair and candid manner to attempt an exposition of their fallacy.

The speculative philosopher equally offends against the cause of truth. With eyes fixed on a happier state of society, the blessings of which he paints in the most captivating colours, he allows himself to indulge in the most bitter invectives against every present establishment, without applying his talents to consider the best and safest means of removing abuses, and without seeming to be aware of the tremendous obstacles that threaten, even in theory, to oppose the progress of man towards perfection.

It is an acknowledged truth in philosophy, that a just theory will always be confirmed by experiment. Yet so much friction, and so many minute circumstances occur in practice, which it is next to impossible for the most enlarged and penetrating mind to foresee, that on few subjects can any theory be pronounced just, that has not stood the test of experience. But an untried theory cannot be advanced as probable, much less as just, till all the arguments against it have been maturely weighed, and clearly and consistently confuted.

I have read some of the speculations on the perfectibility of man and of society with great pleasure. I have been warmed and delighted with the enchanting picture which they hold forth. I ardently wish for such happy improvements. But I see great, and, to my understanding, unconquerable difficulties in the way to them. These difficulties it is my present purpose to state; declaring, at the same time, that so far from exulting in them, as a cause of triumphing over the friends of innovation, nothing would give me greater pleasure than to see them completely removed.

The most important argument that I shall adduce is certainly not new. The principles on which it depends have been explained in part by Hume, and more at large by Dr. Adam Smith. It has been advanced and applied to the present subject, though not with its proper weight, or in the most forcible point of view, by Mr. Wallace: [1] and it may probably have been stated by many writers that I have never met with. I should certainly, therefore, not think of advancing it again, though I mean to place it in a point of view in some degree different from any that I have hitherto seen, if it had ever been fairly and satisfactorily answered.

The cause of this neglect on the part of the advocates for the perfectibility of mankind is not easily accounted for. I cannot doubt the talents of such men as Godwin and Condorcet. I am unwilling to doubt their candour. To my understanding, and probably to that of most others, the difficulty appears insurmountable. Yet these men of acknowledged ability and penetration, scarcely deign to notice it, and hold on their course in such speculations, with unabated ardour and undiminished confidence. I have certainly no right to say that they purposely shut their eyes to such arguments. I ought rather to doubt the validity of them, when neglected by such men, however forcibly their truth may strike my own mind. Yet in this respect it must be acknowledged that we are all of us too prone to err. If I saw a glass of wine repeatedly presented to a man, and he took no notice of it, I should be apt to think that he was blind or uncivil. A juster philosophy might teach me rather to think that my eyes deceived me, and that the offer was not really what I conceived it to be.

In entering upon the argument I must premise that I put out of the question, at present, all mere conjectures; that is, all suppositions, the probable realization of which cannot be inferred upon any just philosophical grounds. A writer may tell me that he thinks man will ultimately become an ostrich. I cannot properly contradict him. But before he can expect to bring any reasonable person over to his opinion, he ought to show that the necks of mankind have been gradually elongating; that the lips have grown harder, and more prominent; that the legs and feet are daily altering their shape; and that the hair is beginning to change into stubs of feathers. And till the probability of so wonderful a conversion can be shown, it is surely lost time and lost eloquence to expatiate on the happiness of man in such a state; to describe his powers, both of running and flying; to paint him in a condition where all narrow luxuries would be contemned; where he would be employed, only in collecting the necessaries of life; and where, consequently, each man's share of labour would be light, and his portion of leisure ample.

I think I may fairly make two postulata.

First, That food is necessary to the existence of man.

[1] [Robert Wallace (1697–1771) a minister, wrote various books on the question of population. A passage in his *Various Prospects of Mankind, Nature, and Providence* (1761) is believed to have stimulated Malthus.]

Secondly, That the passion between the sexes is necessary, and will remain nearly in its present state.

These two laws ever since we have had any knowledge of mankind, appear to have been fixed laws of our nature; and, as we have not hitherto seen any alteration in them, we have no right to conclude that they will ever cease to be what they are now, without an immediate act of power in that Being who first arranged the system of the universe; and for the advantage of his creatures, still executes, according to fixed laws, all its various operations.

I do not know that any writer has supposed that on this earth man will ultimately be able to live without food. But Mr. Godwin has conjectured that the passion between the sexes may in time be extinguished. As, however, he calls this part of his work, a deviation into the land of conjecture, I will not dwell longer upon it at present, than to say, that the best arguments for the perfectibility of man are drawn from a contemplation of the great progress that he has already made from the savage state, and the difficulty of saying where he is to stop. But towards the extinction of the passion between the sexes, no progress whatever has hitherto been made. It appears to exist in as much force at present as it did two thousand, or four thousand years ago. There are individual exceptions now as there always have been. But, as these exceptions do not appear to increase in number, it would surely be a very unphilosophical mode of arguing, to infer merely from the existence of an exception, that the exception would, in time, become the rule, and the rule the exception.

Assuming, then, my postulata as granted, I say, that the power of population is indefinitely greater than the power in the earth to produce subsistence for man.

Population, when unchecked, increases in a geometrical ratio. Subsistence only increases in an arithmetical ratio. A slight acquaintance with numbers will show the immensity of the first power in comparison of the second.

By that law of our nature which makes food necessary to the life of man, the effects of these two unequal powers must be kept equal.

This implies a strong and constantly operating check on population from the difficulty of subsistence. This difficulty must fall some where; and must necessarily be severely felt by a large portion of mankind.

Through the animal and vegetable kingdoms, nature has scattered the seeds of life abroad with the most profuse and liberal hand. She has been comparatively sparing in the room, and the nourishment necessary to rear them. The germs of existence contained in this spot of earth, with ample food, and ample room to expand it, would fill millions of worlds in the course of a few thousand years. Necessity, that imperious, all-pervading law of nature, restrains them within the prescribed bounds. The race of plants, and the race of animals shrink under this great restrictive law. And the race of man cannot, by any efforts of reason, escape from it. Among plants and animals its effects are waste of seed, sickness, and premature death. Among mankind, misery and vice. The former, misery, is an absolutely necessary consequence of it. Vice is a highly probable consequence, and we therefore see it abundantly prevail; but it ought not, perhaps, to be called an absolutely necessary consequence. The ordeal of virtue is to resist all temptation to evil.

This natural inequality of the two powers of population, and of production in the earth, and that great law of our nature which must constantly keep their effects equal, form the great difficulty that to me appears insurmountable in the way to perfectibility of society. All other arguments are of slight and subordinate consideration in comparison of this. I see no way by which man can escape from the weight of this law which pervades all animated nature. No fancied equality, no agrarian regulations in their utmost extent, could remove the pressure of it even for a single century. And it appears, therefore, to be decisive against the possible existence of a society, all the members of which should live in ease, happiness, and comparative leisure; and feel no anxiety about providing the means of subsistence for themselves and families.

Consequently, if the premises are just, the argument is conclusive against the perfectibility of the mass of mankind.

I have thus sketched the general outline of the argument; but I will examine it more particularly; and I think it will be found that experience, the true source and foundation of all knowledge, invariably confirms its truth.

CHAPTER II: OF THE GENERAL CHECKS TO POPULATION, AND THE MODE OF THEIR OPERATION

The ultimate check to population appears then to be a want of food, arising necessarily from the different ratios according to which population and food increase. But this ultimate check is never the immediate check, except in cases of actual famine.

The immediate check may be stated to consist in all those customs, and all those diseases, which seem to be generated by a scarcity of the means of subsistence; and all those causes, independent of this scarcity, whether of a moral or physical nature, which tend prematurely to weaken and destroy the human frame.

These checks to population, which are constantly operating with more or less force in every society, and keep down the number to the level of the means of subsistence, may be classed under two general heads—the preventive and the positive checks.

The preventive check, as far as it is voluntary, is peculiar to man, and arises from that distinctive superiority in his reasoning faculties which enables him to calculate distant consequences. The checks to the indefinite increase of plants and irrational animals are all either positive, or, if preventive, involuntary. But man cannot look around him and see the distress which frequently presses upon those who have large families; he cannot contemplate his present possessions or earnings, which he now nearly consumes himself, and calculate the amount of each share, when with very little addition they must be divided, perhaps, among seven or eight, without feeling a doubt whether, if he follow the bent of his inclinations, he may be able to support the offspring which he will probably bring into the world. In a state of equality, if such can exist, this would be the simple question. In the present state of society other considerations occur. Will he not lower his rank in life, and be obliged to give up in great measure his former habits? Does any mode of employment present itself by which he may reasonably hope to maintain a family? Will he not at any rate subject himself to greater difficulties, and more severe labour, than in his single state? Will he not be unable to transmit to his children the same advantages of education and improvement that he had himself possessed? Does he even feel secure that, should he have a large family, his utmost exertions can save them from rags and squalid poverty, and their consequent degradation in the community? And may he not be reduced to the grating necessity of forfeiting his independence, and of being obliged to the sparing hand of Charity for support?

These considerations are calculated to prevent, and certainly do prevent, a great number of persons in all civilised nations from pursuing the dictate of nature in an early attachment to one woman.

If this restraint do not produce vice, it is undoubtedly the least evil that can arise from the principle of population. Considered as a restraint on a strong natural inclination, it must be allowed to produce a certain degree of temporary unhappiness; but evidently slight, compared with the evils which result from any of the other checks to population; and merely of the same nature as many other sacrifices of temporary to permanent gratification, which it is the business of a moral agent continually to make.

When this restraint produces vice, the evils which follow are but too conspicuous. A promiscuous intercourse to such a degree as to prevent the birth of children seems to lower, in the most marked manner, the dignity of human nature. It cannot be without its effect on men, and nothing can be more obvious than its tendency to degrade the female character, and to destroy all its most amiable and distinguishing characteristics. Add to which, that among those unfortunate females, with which all great towns abound, more real distress and aggravated misery are, perhaps, to be found than in any other department of human life.

When a general corruption of morals, with regard to the sex, pervades all the classes of society, its effects must necessarily be to poison the springs of domestic happiness, to weaken conjugal and parental affection, and to lessen the united exertions and ardour of parents in the care and education of their children—effects which cannot take place without a decided diminution of the general happiness and virtue of the society; particularly as the necessity of art in the accomplishment and conduct of intrigues, and in the concealment of their consequences, necessarily leads to many other vices.

The positive checks to population are extremely various, and include every cause, whether arising from vice or misery, which in any degree contributes to shorten the natural duration of human life. Under this head, therefore, may be enumerated all unwholesome occupations, severe labour and exposure to the seasons, extreme poverty, bad nursing of children, great towns, excesses of all kinds, the whole train of common diseases and epidemics, wars, plague, and famine.

On examining these obstacles to the increase of population which I have classed under the heads of preventive and positive checks, it will appear that they are all resolvable into moral restraint, vice, and misery.

Of the preventive checks, the restraint from marriage which is not followed by irregular gratifications may properly be termed moral restraint.

Promiscuous intercourse, unnatural passions, violations of the marriage bed, and improper arts to conceal the consequences of irregular connections, are preventive checks that clearly come under the head of vice.

Of the positive checks, those which appear to arise unavoidably from the laws of nature, may be called exclusively misery; and those which we obviously bring upon ourselves, such as wars, excesses, and many others which it would be in our power to avoid, are of a mixed nature. They are brought upon us by vice, and their consequences are misery.

The sum of all these preventive and positive checks, taken together, forms the immediate check to population; and it is evident that, in every country where the whole of the procreative power cannot be called into action, the preventive and the positive checks must vary inversely as each other; that is, in countries either naturally unhealthy, or subject to a great mortality, from whatever cause it may arise, the preventive check will prevail very little. In those countries, on the contrary, which are naturally healthy, and where the preventive check is found to prevail with considerable force, the positive check will prevail very little, or the mortality be very small.

In every country some of these checks are, with more or less force, in con-stant operation; yet, notwithstanding their general prevalence, there are few states in which there is not a constant effort in the population to increase beyond the means of subsistence. This constant effort as constantly tends to subject the lower classes of society to distress, and to prevent any great permanent melioration of their condition.

These effects, in the present state of society, seem to be produced in the following manner. We will suppose the means of subsistence in any country just equal to the easy support of its inhabitants. The constant effort towards population, which is found to act even in the most vicious societies, increases the number of people before the means of subsistence are increased. The food, therefore, which before supported eleven millions, must now be divided among eleven millions and a half. The poor consequently must live much worse, and many of them be reduced to severe distress. The number of labourers also being above the proportion of work in the market, the price of labour must tend to fall, while the price of provisions would at the same time tend to rise. The labourer therefore must do more work to earn the same as he did before. During this season of distress, the discouragements to marriage and the difficulty of rearing a family are so great that the progress of popula-tion is retarded. In the meantime, the cheapness of labour, the plenty of la-bourers, and the necessity of an increased industry among them, encourage cultivators to employ more labour upon their land, to turn up fresh soil, and to manure and improve more completely what is already in tillage, till ulti-mately the means of subsistence may become in the same proportion to the population as at the period from which we set out. The situation of the la-bourer being then again tolerably comfortable, the restraints to population are in some degree loosened; and, after a short period, the same retrograde and progressive movements, with respect to happiness, are repeated.

This sort of oscillation will not probably be obvious to common view; and it may be difficult even for the most attentive observer to calculate its periods. Yet that, in the generality of old states, some alternation of this kind does exist though in a much less marked, and in a much more irregular manner, than I have described it, no reflecting man, who considers the subject deeply, can well doubt.

One principal reason why this oscillation has been less remarked, and less decidedly confirmed by experience than might naturally be expected, is, that the histories of mankind which we possess are, in general, histories only of the higher classes. We have not many accounts that can be depended upon of the manners and customs of that part of mankind where these retrograde and progressive movements chiefly take place. A satisfactory history of this kind, of one people and of one period, would require the constant and minute attention of many observing minds in local and general remarks on the state of the lower classes of society, and the causes that influenced it; and to draw accurate inferences upon this subject, a succession of such historians for some centuries would be necessary. This branch of statistical knowledge has, of late years, been attended to in some countries, and we may promise ourselves a clearer insight into the internal structure of human society from the progress of these inquiries. But the science may be said yet to be in its infancy, and many of the objects, on which it would be desirable to have information, have been either omitted or not stated with sufficient accuracy. Among these, perhaps, may be reckoned the proportion of the number of adults to the number of marriages; the extent to which vicious customs have prevailed in consequence of the restraints upon matrimony; the comparative mortality among the children of the most distressed part of the community and of those who live rather more at their ease; the variations in the real price of labour; the observable differences in the state of the lower classes of society, with respect to ease and happiness, at different times during a certain period; and very accurate registers of births, deaths, and marriages, which are of the utmost importance in this subject.

A faithful history, including such particulars, would tend greatly to elucidate the manner in which the constant check upon population acts; and would probably prove the existence of the retrograde and progressive movements that have been mentioned; though the times of their vibration must necessarily be rendered irregular from the operation of many interrupting causes; such as, the introduction or failure of certain manufactures; a greater or less prevalent spirit of agricultural enterprise; years of plenty or years of scarcity; wars, sickly seasons, poor laws, emigrations, and other causes of a similar nature.

A circumstance which has, perhaps more than any other, contributed to conceal this oscillation from common view is the difference between the nominal and real price of labour. It very rarely happens that the nominal price of labour universally falls; but we well know that it frequently remains the same while the nominal price of provisions has been gradually rising. This, indeed, will generally be the case if the increase of manufactures and commerce be sufficient to employ the new labourers that are thrown into the market, and to prevent the increased supply from lowering the money-price. But an increased number of labourers receiving the same money-wages will necessarily, by their competition, increase the money-price of corn. This is, in fact, a real fall in the price of labour; and, during this period, the condition of the lower classes of the community must be gradually growing worse. But the farmers and capitalists are growing rich from the real cheapness of labour. Their increasing capitals enable them to employ a greater number of men; and, as the population had probably suffered some check from the greater difficulty of supporting a family, the demand for labour, after a certain period, would be great in proportion to the supply, and its price would of course rise, if left to find its natural level; and thus the wages of labour, and consequently the condition of the lower classes of society, might have progressive and retrograde movements, though the price of labour might never nominally fall.

In savage life, where there is no regular price of labour, it is little to be doubted that similar oscillations took place. When population has increased nearly to the utmost limits of the food, all the preventive and the positive checks will naturally operate with increased force. Vicious habits with respect to the sex will be more general, the exposing of children more frequent, and both the probability and fatality of wars and epidemics will be considerably greater; and these causes will probably continue their operation till the population is sunk below the level of the food; and then the return to comparative plenty will again produce an increase, and, after a certain period, its further progress will again be checked by the same causes.

But without attempting to establish these progressive and retrograde movements in different countries, which would evidently require more minute histories than we possess, and which the progress of civilization naturally tends to counteract, the following propositions are intended to be proved:—

1. Population is necessarily limited by the means of subsistence.

2. Population invariably increases where the means of subsistence increase, unless prevented by some very powerful and obvious checks.

3. These checks, and the checks which repress the superior power of population, and keep its effects on a level with the means of subsistence, are all resolvable into moral restraint, vice, and misery.

The first of these propositions scarcely needs illustration. The second and third will sufficiently be established by a review of the immediate checks to population in the past and present state of society.

[Book IV]

CHAPTER III: OF THE ONLY EFFECTUAL MODE OF IMPROVING THE
CONDITION OF THE POOR

He who publishes a moral code, or system of duties, however firmly he
may be convinced of the strong obligation on each individual strictly to
conform to it, has never the folly to imagine that it will be universally or
even generally practised. But this is no valid objection against the publication of the code. If it were, the same objection would always have applied;
we should be totally without general rules; and to the vices of mankind arising from temptation would be added a much longer list than we have at
present of vices from ignorance.

Judging merely from the light of nature, if we feel convinced of the misery
arising from a redundant population on the one hand, and of the evils and
unhappiness, particularly to the female sex, arising from promiscuous intercourse, on the other, I do not see how it is possible for any person who acknowledges the principle of utility as the great criterion of moral rules to
escape the conclusion that moral restraint, or the abstaining from marriage
till we are in a condition to support a family, with a perfectly moral conduct
during that period, is the strict line of duty; and when revelation is taken
into the question, this duty undoubtedly receives very powerful confirmation.
At the same time I believe that few of my readers can be less sanguine than I
am in their expectations of any sudden and great change in the general
conduct of man on this subject: and the chief reason why in the last chapter
I allowed myself to suppose the universal prevalence of this virtue was, that I
might endeavour to remove any imputation on the goodness of the Deity, by
showing that the evils arising from the principle of population were exactly of
the same nature as the generality of other evils which excite fewer complaints:
that they were increased by human ignorance and indolence, and diminished
by human knowledge and virtue; and on the supposition that each individual
strictly fulfilled his duty would be almost totally removed; and this without
any general diminution of those sources of pleasure, arising from the regulated indulgence of the passions, which have been justly considered as the
principal ingredients of human happiness.

If it will answer any purpose of illustration, I see no harm in drawing the
picture of a society in which each individual is supposed strictly to fulfil his
duties; nor does a writer appear to be justly liable to the imputation of being
visionary unless he make such universal or general obedience necessary to

the practical utility of his system, and to that degree of moderate and partial improvement, which is all that can rationally be expected from the most complete knowledge of our duties.

But in this respect there is an essential difference between that improved state of society, which I have supposed in the last chapter, and most of the other speculations on this subject. The improvement there supposed, if we ever should make approaches towards it, is to be effected in the way in which we have been in the habit of seeing all the greatest improvements effected, by a direct application to the interest and happiness of each individual. It is not required of us to act from motives to which we are unaccustomed; to pursue a general good which we may not distinctly comprehend, or the effect of which may be weakened by distance and diffusion. The happiness of the whole is to be the result of the happiness of individuals, and to begin first with them. No co-operation is required. Every step tells. He who performs his duty faithfully will reap the full fruits of it, whatever may be the number of others who fail. This duty is intelligible to the humblest capacity. It is merely that he is not to bring beings into the world for whom he cannot find the means of support. When once this subject is cleared from the obscurity thrown over it by parochial laws and private benevolence, every man must feel the strongest conviction of such an obligation. If he cannot support his children they must starve; and if he marry in the face of a fair probability that he shall not be able to support his children, he is guilty of all the evils which he thus brings upon himself, his wife, and his offspring. It is clearly his interest, and will tend greatly to promote his happiness, to defer marrying till by industry and economy he is in a capacity to support the children that he may reasonably expect from his marriage; and as he cannot in the meantime gratify his passions without violating an express command of God, and running a great risk of injuring himself, or some of his fellow-creatures, considerations of his own interest and happiness will dictate to him the strong obligation to a moral conduct while he remains unmarried.

However powerful may be the impulses of passion, they are generally in some degree modified by reason. And it does not seem entirely visionary to suppose that, if the true and permanent cause of poverty were clearly explained and forcibly brought home to each man's bosom, it would have some, and perhaps not an inconsiderable influence on his conduct; at least the experiment has never yet been fairly tried. Almost everything that has been hitherto done for the poor has tended, as if with solicitous care, to throw a veil of obscurity over this subject, and to hide from them the true cause of their poverty. When the wages of labour are hardly sufficient to maintain two children, a man marries and has five or six; he of course finds

himself miserably distressed. He accuses the insufficiency of the price of labour to maintain a family. He accuses his parish for their tardy and sparing
fulfilment of their obligation to assist him. He accuses the avarice of the rich,
who suffer him to want what they can so well spare. He accuses the partial
and unjust institutions of society, which have awarded him an inadequate
share of the produce of the earth. He accuses perhaps the dispensations of
Providence, which have assigned to him a place in society so beset with unavoidable distress and dependence. In searching for objects of accusation, he
never adverts to the quarter from which his misfortunes originate. The last
person that he would think of accusing is himself, on whom in fact the
principal blame lies, except so far as he has been deceived by the higher
classes of society. He may perhaps wish that he had not married, because he
now feels the inconveniences of it; but it never enters into his head that he
can have done anything wrong. He has always been told that to raise up subjects for his king and country is a very meritorious act. He has done this, and
yet is suffering for it; and it cannot but strike him as most extremely unjust
and cruel in his king and country to allow him thus to suffer, in return for
giving them what they are continually declaring that they particularly want.

Till these erroneous ideas have been corrected, and the language of nature
and reason has been generally heard on the subject of population, instead of
the language of error and prejudice, it cannot be said that any fair experiment has been made with the understandings of the common people; and we
cannot justly accuse them of improvidence and want of industry till they act
as they do now after it has been brought home to their comprehensions that
they are themselves the cause of their own poverty; that the means of redress
are in their own hands, and in the hands of no other persons whatever; that
the society in which they live and the government which presides over it are
without any *direct* power in this respect; and that however ardently they may
desire to relieve them, and whatever attempts they may make to do so, they
are really and truly unable to execute what they benevolently wish, but unjustly promise; that, when the wages of labour will not maintain a family, it
is an incontrovertible sign that their king and country do not want more
subjects, or at least that they cannot support them; that, if they marry in this
case, so far from fulfilling a duty to society, they are throwing a useless burden
on it, at the same time that they are plunging themselves into distress; and
that they are acting directly contrary to the will of God, and bringing down
upon themselves various diseases, which might all, or the greater part, have
been avoided if they had attended to the repeated admonitions which he gives
by the general laws of nature to every being capable of reason.

Paley, in his Moral Philosophy, observes that in countries "in which subsistence is become scarce, it behoves the state to watch over the public morals with increased solicitude; for nothing but the instinct of nature, under the restraint of chastity, will induce men to undertake the labour, or consent to the sacrifice of personal liberty and indulgence, which the support of a family in such circumstances requires." That it is always the duty of a state to use every exertion likely to be effectual in discouraging vice and promoting virtue, and that no temporary circumstances ought to cause any relaxation in these exertions, is certainly true. The means therefore proposed are always good; but the particular end in view in this case appears to be absolutely criminal. We wish to force people into marriage when from the acknowledged scarcity of subsistence they will have little chance of being able to support their children. We might as well force people into the water who are unable to swim. In both cases we rashly tempt Providence. Nor have we more reason to believe that a miracle will be worked to save us from the misery and mortality resulting from our conduct in the one case than in the other.

The object of those who really wish to better the condition of the lower classes of society must be to raise the relative proportion between the price of labour and the price of provisions, so as to enable the labourer to command a larger share of the necessaries and comforts of life. We have hitherto principally attempted to attain this end by encouraging the married poor, and consequently increasing the number of labourers, and overstocking the market with a commodity which we still say that we wish to be dear. It would seem to have required no great spirit of divination to foretell the certain failure of such a plan of proceeding. There is nothing however like experience. It has been tried in many different countries, and for many hundred years, and the success has always been answerable to the nature of the scheme. It is really time now to try something else.

When it was found that oxygen, or pure vital air, would not cure consumptives as was expected, but rather aggravated their symptoms, trial was made of an air of the most opposite kind. I wish we had acted with the same philosophical spirit in our attempts to cure the disease of poverty; and having found that the pouring in of fresh supplies of labour only tended to aggravate the symptoms, had tried what would be the effect of withholding a little these supplies.

In all old and fully-peopled states it is from this method, and this alone, that we can rationally expect any essential and permanent melioration in the condition of the labouring classes of the people.

In an endeavour to raise the proportion of the quantity of provisions to the number of consumers in any country, our attention would naturally be first directed to the increasing of the absolute quantity of provisions; but finding that, as fast as we did this, the number of consumers more than kept pace with it, and that with all our exertions we were still as far as ever behind, we should be convinced that our efforts directed only in this way would never succeed. It would appear to be setting the tortoise to catch the hare. Finding, therefore, that from the laws of nature we could not proportion the food to the population, our next attempt should naturally be to proportion the population to the food. If we can persuade the hare to go to sleep, the tortoise may have some chance of overtaking her.

We are not, however, to relax our efforts in increasing the quantity of provisions, but to combine another effort with it; that of keeping the population, when once it has been overtaken, at such a distance behind as to effect the relative proportion which we desire; and thus unite the two grand *desiderata,* a great actual population and a state of society in which abject poverty and dependence are comparatively but little known; two objects which are far from being incompatible.

If we be really serious in what appears to be the object of such general research, the mode of essentially and permanently bettering the condition of the poor, we must explain to them the true nature of their situation, and show them that the withholding of the supplies of labour is the only possible way of really raising its price, and that they themselves, being the possessors of this commodity, have alone the power to do this.

I cannot but consider this mode of diminishing poverty as so perfectly clear in theory, and so invariably confirmed by the analogy of every other commodity which is brought to market, that nothing but its being shown to be calculated to produce greater evils than it proposes to remedy can justify us in not making the attempt to put it into execution.

CHAPTER V: OF THE CONSEQUENCES OF PURSUING THE OPPOSITE MODE

It is an evident truth that, whatever may be the rate of increase in the means of subsistence, the increase of population must be limited by it, at least after the food has once been divided into the smallest shares that will support life. All the children born beyond what would be required to keep up the population to this level must necessarily perish, unless room be made for them by the deaths of grown persons. It has appeared indeed clearly in the course of this work that in all old states the marriages and births depend principally upon the deaths, and that there is no encouragement to early unions so powerful as a great mortality. To act consistently, therefore, we should facilitate, instead of foolishly and vainly endeavouring to impede, the operations of nature in producing this mortality; and if we dread the too frequent visitation of the horrid form of famine, we should sedulously encourage the other forms of destruction which we compel nature to use. Instead of recommending cleanliness to the poor, we should encourage contrary habits. In our towns we should make the streets narrower, crowd more people into the houses, and court the return of the plague. In the country, we should build our villages near stagnant pools, and particularly encourage settlements in all marshy and unwholesome situations. But above all, we should reprobate specific remedies for ravaging diseases; and those benevolent, but much mistaken men, who have thought they were doing a service to mankind by projecting schemes for the total extirpation of particular disorders. If by these and similar means the annual mortality were increased from 1 in 36 or 40, to 1 in 18 or 20, we might probably every one of us marry at the age of puberty, and yet few be absolutely starved.

If, however, we all marry at this age, and yet still continue our exertions to impede the operations of nature, we may rest assured that all our efforts will be vain. Nature will not, nor cannot, be defeated in her purposes. The necessary mortality must come in some form or other; and the extirpation of one disease will only be the signal for the birth of another perhaps more fatal. We cannot lower the waters of misery by pressing them down in different places, which must necessarily make them rise somewhere else; the only way in which we can hope to effect our purpose is by drawing them off. To this course nature is constantly directing our attention by the chastisements which await a contrary conduct. These chastisements are more or less severe in proportion to the degree in which her admonitions produce their intended effect. In this country at present these admonitions are by no means entirely neglected. The preventive check to population prevails to a considerable degree, and her chastisements are in consequence moderate; but if we were all to marry at the age of puberty they would be severe indeed. Political evils would probably be added to physical. A people goaded by constant distress, and visited by frequent returns of famine, could not be kept down but by a cruel despotism. We should approach to the state of the people in Egypt or Abyssinia; and I would ask whether in that case it is probable that we should be more virtuous?

Physicians have long remarked the great changes which take place in diseases; and that, while some appear to yield to the efforts of human care and skill, others seem to become in proportion more malignant and fatal. Dr. William Heberden published, not long since, some valuable observations on this subject deduced from the London bills of mortality. In his preface, speaking of these bills, he says, "the gradual changes they exhibit in particular diseases correspond to the alterations which in time are known to take place in the channels through which the great stream of mortality is constantly flowing." In the body of his work, afterwards, speaking of some particular diseases, he observes with that candour which always distinguishes true science; "It is not easy to give a satisfactory reason for all the changes which may be observed to take place in the history of diseases. Nor is it any disgrace to physicians, if their causes are often so gradual in their operation, or so subtle, as to elude investigation."

I hope I shall not be accused of presumption in venturing to suggest that, under certain circumstances, such changes must take place; and perhaps without any alteration in those proximate causes which are usually looked to on these occasions. If this should appear to be true, it will not seem extraordinary that the most skilful and scientific physicians, whose business it is principally to investigate proximate causes, should sometimes search for these causes in vain.

In the country which keeps its population at a certain standard, if the average number of marriages and births be given, it is evident that the average number of deaths will also be given; and, to use Dr. Heberden's metaphor, the channels through which the great stream of mortality is constantly flowing will always convey off a given quantity. Now if we stop up any of these channels it is perfectly clear that the stream of mortality must run with greater force through some of the other channels; that is, if we eradicate some diseases, others will become proportionally more fatal. In this case the only distinguishable cause is the damming up a necessary outlet of mortality. Nature, in the attainment of her great purposes, seems always to seize upon the weakest part. If this part be made strong by human skill, she seizes upon the next weakest part, and so on in succession; not like a capricious deity, with an intention to sport with our sufferings and constantly to defeat our labours; but like a kind, though sometimes severe instructor, with the intention of teaching us to make all parts strong, and to chase vice and misery from the earth. In avoiding one fault we are too apt to run into some other; but we always find Nature faithful to her great object, at every false step we commit ready to admonish us of our errors by the infliction of some physical or moral evil. If the prevalence of the preventive check to population in a sufficient degree were to remove many of those diseases which now afflict us, yet be accompanied by a considerable increase of the vice of promiscuous intercourse, it is probable that the disorders and unhappiness, the physical and moral evils arising from this vice, would increase in strength and degree; and, admonishing us severely of our error, would point to the only line of conduct approved by nature, reason, and religion, abstinence from marriage till we can support our children and chastity till that period arrives.

In the case just stated, in which the population and the number of marriages are supposed to be fixed, the necessity of a change in the mortality of some diseases, from the diminution or extinction of others, is capable of mathematical demonstration. The only obscurity which can possibly involve this subject arises from taking into consideration the effect that might be produced by a diminution of mortality in increasing the population, or in decreasing the number of marriages. That the removal of any of the particular causes of mortality can have no further effect upon population than the means of subsistence will allow, and that it has no certain and necessary influence on these means of subsistence, are facts of which the reader must be already convinced. Of its operation in tending to prevent marriage, by diminishing the demand for fresh supplies of children, I have no doubt; and there is reason to think that it had this effect in no inconsiderable degree on the extinction of the plague, which had so long and so dreadfully ravaged this country. Dr. Heberden draws a striking picture of the favourable change observed in the health of the people of England since this period; and justly attributes it to the improvements which have gradually taken place, not only in London but in all great towns; and in the manner of living throughout the kingdom, particularly with respect to cleanliness and ventilation. But these causes would not have produced the effect observed if they had not been accompanied by an increase of the preventive check; and probably the spirit of cleanliness, and better mode of living, which then began to prevail, by spreading more generally a decent and useful pride, principally contributed to this increase. The diminution in the number of marriages, however, was not sufficient to make up for the great decrease of mortality from the extinction of the plague, and the striking reduction of the deaths in the dysentery. While these and some other disorders became almost evanescent, consumption, palsy, apoplexy, gout, lunacy, and small-pox became more mortal. The widening of these drains was necessary to carry off the population which still remained redundant, notwithstanding the increased operation of the preventive check, and the part which was annually disposed of and enabled to subsist by the increase of agriculture.

Dr. Haygarth, in the Sketch of his benevolent plan for the extermination of the casual small-pox, draws a frightful picture of the mortality which has been occasioned by this distemper, attributes to it the slow progress of population, and makes some curious calculations on the favourable effects which would be produced in this respect by its extermination. His conclusions, however, I fear, would not follow from his premises. I am far from doubting that millions and millions of human beings have been destroyed by the small-pox. But were its devastations, as Dr. Haygarth supposes, many thousand degrees greater than the plague, I should still doubt whether the average population of the earth had been diminished by them. The small-pox is certainly one of the channels, and a very broad one, which nature has opened for the last thousand years to keep down the population to the level of the means of subsistence; but had this been closed, others would have become wider, or new ones would have been formed. In ancient times the mortality from war and the plague was incomparably greater than in modern. On the gradual diminution of this stream of mortality, the generation and almost universal prevalence of the small-pox is a great and striking instance of one of those changes in the channels of mortality which ought to awaken our attention and animate us to patient and persevering investigation. For my own part I feel not the slightest doubt that, if the introduction of the cow-pox should extirpate the small-pox, and yet the number of marriages continue the same, we shall find a very perceptible difference in the increased mortality of some other diseases. Nothing could prevent this effect but a sudden start in our agriculture; and if this should take place, it will not be so much owing to the number of children saved from death by the cow-pox inoculation, as to the alarms occasioned among the people of property by the late scarcities, and to the increased gains of farmers, which have been so absurdly reprobated. I am strongly however inclined to believe that the number of marriages will not, in this case, remain the same; but that the gradual light which may be expected to be thrown on this interesting topic of human inquiry will teach us how to make the extinction of a mortal disorder a real blessing to us, a real improvement in the general health and happiness of the society.

If, on contemplating the increase of vice which might contingently follow an attempt to inculcate the duty of moral restraint, and the increase of misery that must necessarily follow the attempts to encourage marriage and population, we come to the conclusion not to interfere in any respect, but to leave every man to his own free choice, and responsible only to God for the evil which he does in either way; this is all I contend for; I would on no account do more; but I contend that at present we are very far from doing this.

Among the lower classes of society, where the point is of the greatest importance, the poor-laws afford a direct, constant, and systematical encouragement to marriage, by removing from each individual that heavy responsibility, which he would incur by the laws of nature, for bringing beings into the world which he could not support. Our private benevolence has the same direction as the poor-laws, and almost invariably tends to encourage marriage, and to equalise as much as possible the circumstances of married and single men.

Among the higher classes of people, the superior distinctions which married women receive, and the marked inattentions to which single women of advanced age are exposed, enable many men, who are agreeable neither in mind nor person, and are besides in the wane of life, to choose a partner among the young and fair, instead of being confined, as nature seems to dictate, to persons of nearly their own age and accomplishments. It is scarcely to be doubted that the fear of being an old maid, and of that silly and unjust ridicule, which folly sometimes attaches to this name, drives many women into the marriage union with men whom they dislike, or at best to whom they are perfectly indifferent. Such marriages must to every delicate mind appear little better than legal prostitutions; and they often burden the earth with unnecessary children, without compensating for it by an accession of happiness and virtue to the parties themselves.

Throughout all the ranks of society the prevailing opinions respecting the duty and obligation of marriage cannot but have a very powerful influence. The man who thinks that, in going out of the world without leaving representatives behind him, he shall have failed in an important duty to society, will be disposed to force rather than to repress his inclinations on this subject; and when his reason represents to him the difficulties attending a family, he will endeavour not to attend to these suggestions, will still determine to venture, and will hope that, in the discharge of what he conceives to be his duty, he shall not be deserted by Providence.

In a civilised country, such as England, where a taste for the decencies and comforts of life prevails among a very large class of people, it is not possible that the encouragements to marriage from positive institutions and prevailing opinions should entirely obscure the light of nature and reason on this subject; but still they contribute to make it comparatively weak and indistinct. And till this obscurity is removed, and the poor are undeceived with respect to the principal cause of their poverty, and taught to know that their happiness or misery must depend chiefly upon themselves, it cannot be said that, with regard to the great question of marriage, we leave every man to his own free and fair choice.

PRINCIPLES OF POLITICAL ECONOMY

[Book II]

CHAPTER I: ON THE PROGRESS OF WEALTH

Section 1.—Statement of the particular Object of Inquiry

THERE IS scarcely any inquiry more curious, or, from its importance, more worthy of attention, than that which traces the causes which practically check the progress of wealth in different countries, and stop it, or make it proceed very slowly, while the power of production remains comparatively undiminished, or at least would furnish the means of a great and abundant increase of produce and population.

In a former work [1] I endeavoured to trace the causes which practically keep down the population of a country to the level of its actual supplies. It is now my object to shew what are the causes which chiefly influence these supplies, or call the powers of production forth into the shape of increasing wealth.

Among the primary and most important causes which influence the wealth of nations, must unquestionably be placed, those which come under the head of politics and morals. Security of property, without a certain degree of which, there can be no encouragement to individual industry, depends mainly upon the political constitution of a country, the excellence of its laws and the manner in which they are administered. And those habits which are the most favourable to regular exertions as well as to general rectitude of character, and are consequently most favourable to the production and maintenance of wealth, depend chiefly upon the same causes, combined with moral and religious instruction. It is not however my intention at present to enter fully into these causes, important and effective as they are; but to confine myself chiefly to the more immediate and proximate causes of increasing wealth, whether they may have their origin in these political and moral sources, or in any others more specifically and directly within the province of political economy.

It is obviously true that there are many countries, not essentially different either in the degree of security which they afford to property, or in the moral and religious instruction received by the people, which yet, with nearly equal natural capabilities, make a very different progress in wealth. It is the principal object of the present inquiry to explain this; and to furnish some solution of certain phenomena frequently obtruded upon our attention, whenever we take a view of the different states of Europe, or of the world; namely, coun-

[1] Essay on the Principle of Population.

tries with great powers of production comparatively poor, and countries with small powers of production comparatively rich.

If the actual riches of a country not subject to repeated violences and a frequent destruction of produce, be not after a certain period in some degree proportioned to its power of producing riches, this deficiency must have arisen from the want of an adequate stimulus to continued production. The practical question then for our consideration is, what are the most immediate and effective stimulants to the continued creation and progress of wealth.

Section II.—Of the Increase of Population considered as a Stimulus to the continued Increase of Wealth

Many writers have been of opinion that an increase of population is the sole stimulus necessary to the increase of wealth, because population, being the great source of consumption, must in their opinion necessarily keep up the demand for an increase of produce, which will naturally be followed by a continued increase of supply.

That a continued increase of population is a powerful and necessary element of increasing demand, will be most readily allowed; but that the increase of population alone, or, more properly speaking, the pressure of the population hard against the limits of subsistence, does not furnish an effective stimulus to the continued increase of wealth, is not only evident in theory, but is confirmed by universal experience. If want alone, or the desire of the labouring classes to possess the necessaries and conveniences of life, were a sufficient stimulus to production, there is no state in Europe, or in the world, which would have found any other practical limit to its wealth than its power to produce; and the earth would probably before this period have contained, at the very least, ten times as many inhabitants as are supported on its surface at present.

But those who are acquainted with the nature of effectual demand, will be fully aware that, where the right of private property is established, and the wants of society are supplied by industry and barter, the desire of any individual to possess the necessaries, conveniences and luxuries of life, however intense, will avail nothing towards their production, if there be no where a reciprocal demand for something which he possesses. . . .

It will be said perhaps that the increase of population will lower wages, and, by thus diminishing the costs of production, will increase the profits of the capitalists and the encouragement to produce. Some temporary effect of this kind may no doubt take place, but it is evidently very strictly limited. The fall of real wages cannot go on beyond a certain point without not only stopping the progress of the population but making it even retrograde; and before this point is reached, the increase of produce occasioned by the labour of the additional number of persons will have so lowered its value, and reduced profits, as to determine the capitalist to employ less labour. Though the producers of necessaries might certainly be able in this case to obtain the funds required for the support of a greater number of labourers; yet if the effectual demand for necessaries were fully supplied, and an adequate taste for unproductive consumption, or personal services had not been established, no motive of interest could induce the producers to make an effectual demand for this greater number of labourers.

It is obvious then in theory that an increase of population, when an additional quantity of labour is not required, will soon be checked by want of employment and the scanty support of those employed, and will not furnish the required stimulus to an increase of wealth proportioned to the power of production.

But, if any doubts should remain with respect to the *theory* on the subject, they will surely be dissipated by a reference to *experience*. It is scarcely possible to cast our eyes on any nation of the world without seeing a striking confirmation of what has been advanced. Almost universally, the actual wealth of all the states with which we are acquainted is very far short of their powers of production; and among those states, the slowest progress in wealth is often made where the stimulus arising from population alone is the greatest, that is, where the population presses the hardest against the actual limits of subsistence. It is quite evident that the only fair way, indeed the only way, by which we can judge of the practical effect of population alone as a stimulus to wealth, is to refer to those countries where, from the excess of population above the funds applied to the maintenance of labour, the stimulus of want is the greatest. And if in these countries, which still have great powers of production, the progress of wealth is very slow, we have certainly all the evidence which experience can possibly give us, that population alone cannot create an effective demand for wealth.

To suppose a great and continued increase of population is to beg the question. We may as well suppose at once an increase of wealth; because such an increase of population cannot take place without a proportionate or nearly proportionate increase of wealth. The question really is, whether encouragements to population, or even the natural tendency of population to increase beyond the funds destined for its maintenance, will, or will not, alone furnish an adequate stimulus to the increase of wealth. And this question, Spain, Portugal, Poland, Hungary, Turkey, and many other countries in Europe, together with nearly the whole of Asia and Africa, and the greatest part of America, distinctly answer in the negative.

Section III.—Of Accumulation, or the Saving from Revenue to add to Capital, considered as a Stimulus to the Increase of Wealth

Those who reject mere population as an adequate stimulus to the increase of wealth, are generally disposed to make everything depend upon accumulation. It is certainly true that no permanent and continued increase of wealth can take place without a continued increase of capital; and I cannot agree with Lord Lauderdale in thinking that this increase can be effected in any other way than by saving from the stock which might have been destined for immediate consumption, and adding it to that which is to yield a profit; or in other words, by the conversion of revenue into capital.

But we have yet to inquire what is the state of things which generally disposes a nation to accumulate; and further, what is the state of things which tends to make that accumulation the most effective, and lead to a further and continued increase of capital and wealth. . . .

It has been thought by some very able writers, that although there may easily be a glut of particular commodities, there cannot possibly be a glut of commodities in general; because, according to their view of the subject, commodities being always exchanged for commodities, one half will furnish a market for the other half, and production being thus the sole source of demand, an excess in the supply of one article merely proves a deficiency in the supply of some other, and a general excess is impossible. M. Say, in his distinguished work on political economy, has indeed gone so far as to state that the consumption of a commodity by taking it out of the market diminishes demand, and the production of a commodity proportionably increases it.

This doctrine, however, as generally applied, appears to me to be utterly unfounded, and completely to contradict the great principles which regulate supply and demand.

It is by no means true, as a matter of fact, that commodities are always exchanged for commodities. An immense mass of commodities is exchanged directly, either for productive labour, or personal services: and it is quite obvious, that this mass of commodities, compared with the labour with which it is to be exchanged, may fall in value from a glut just as any one commodity falls in value from an excess of supply, compared either with labour or money. . . .

M. Say, Mr. Mill, and Mr. Ricardo, the principal authors of these new doctrines, appear to me to have fallen into some fundamental errors in the view which they have taken of this subject.

In the first place, they have considered commodities as if they were so many mathematical figures, or arithmetical characters, the relations of which were to be compared, instead of articles of consumption, which must of course be referred to the numbers and wants of the consumers.

If commodities were only to be compared and exchanged with each other, then indeed it would be true that, if they were all increased in their proper proportions to any extent, they would continue to bear among themselves the same relative value; but, if we compare them, as we certainly ought to do, with the means of producing them, and with the numbers and wants of the consumers, then a great increase of produce with comparatively stationary numbers or with wants diminished by parsimony, must necessarily occasion a great fall of value estimated in labour, so that the same produce, though it might have *cost* the same quantity of labour as before, would no longer *command* the same quantity; and both the power of accumulation and the motive to accumulate would be strongly checked.

It is asserted that effectual demand is nothing more than the offering of one commodity in exchange for another which has cost the same quantity of labour. But is this all that is necessary to effectual demand? Though each commodity may have cost the same quantity of labour in its production, and they may be exactly equivalent to each other in exchange, yet why may not both be so plentiful as not to command more labour, than they have cost, that is, to yield no profit, and in this case, would the demand for them be effectual? Would it be such as to encourage their continued production? Unquestionably not. Their relation to each other may not have changed; but their relation to the wants of the society, and their relation to labour, may have experienced a most important change. . . .

Another fundamental error into which the writers above-mentioned and their followers appear to have fallen is, the not taking into consideration the influence of so general and important a principle in human nature, as indolence or love of ease.

It has been supposed that, if a certain number of farmers and a certain number of manufacturers had been exchanging their surplus food and clothing with each other, and their powers of production were suddenly so increased that both parties could, with the same labour, produce luxuries in addition to what they had before obtained, there could be no sort of difficulty with regard to demand, as part of the luxuries which the farmer produced would be exchanged against part of the luxuries produced by the manufacturer; and the only result would be, the happy one of both parties being better supplied and having more enjoyments.

But in this intercourse of mutual gratifications, two things are taken for granted, which are the very points in dispute. It is taken for granted that luxuries are always preferred to indolence, and that an adequate proportion of the profits of each party is consumed as revenue. What would be the effect of a desire to save under such circumstances, shall be considered presently. The effect of a preference of indolence to luxuries would evidently be to occasion a want of demand for the returns of the increased powers of production supposed, and to throw labourers out of employment. The cultivator, being now enabled to obtain the necessaries and conveniences to which he had been accustomed, with less toil and trouble, and his tastes for ribands, lace and velvet not being fully formed, might be very likely to indulge himself in indolence, and employ less labour on the land; while the manufacturer, finding his velvets rather heavy of sale, would be led to discontinue their manufacture, and to fall almost necessarily into the same indolent system as the farmer. That an efficient taste for luxuries and conveniences, that is, such a taste as will properly stimulate industry, instead of being ready to appear at the moment it is required, is a plant of slow growth, the history of human society sufficiently shows; and that it is a most important error to take for granted, that mankind will produce and consume all that they have the power to produce and consume, and will never prefer indolence to the rewards of industry, will sufficiently appear from a slight review of some of the nations with which we are acquainted. . . .

It has also been said, that there is never an indisposition to consume, that the indisposition is to produce. Yet, what is the disposition of those master manufacturers, and merchants who produce very largely and consume sparingly? Is their will to purchase commodities for their consumption proportioned to their power? Does not the use which they make of their capital clearly show that their will is to produce, not to consume? and in fact, if there were not in every country some who were indisposed to consume to the value of what they produced, how could the national capital ever be increased?

A third very serious error of the writers above referred to, and practically the most important of the three, consists in supposing that accumulation ensures demand; or that the consumption of the labourers employed by those whose object is to save, will create such an effectual demand for commodities as to encourage a continued increase of produce.

Mr. Ricardo observes, that "If £10,000 were given to a man having £100,000 per annum, he would not lock it up in a chest, but would either increase his expenses by £10,000, employ it himself productively, or lend it to some other person for that purpose; in either case demand would be increased, although it would be for different objects. If he increased his expenses, his effectual demand might probably be for buildings, furniture, or some such enjoyment. If he employed his £10,000 productively, his effectual demand would be for food, clothing, and raw materials, which might set new labourers to work. But still it would be *demand*."

Upon this principle it is supposed that if the richer portion of society were to forego their accustomed conveniences and luxuries with a view to accumulation, the only effect would be a direction of nearly the whole capital of the country to the production of necessaries, which would lead to a great increase of cultivation and population. But this is precisely the case in which Mr. Ricardo distinctly allows that there might be a universal glut; for there would undoubtedly be more necessaries produced than would be sufficient for the existing demand. This state of things could not, however, continue; since, owing to the fall which would take place, cultivation would be checked, and accumulation be arrested in its progress. . . .

If, in the process of saving, all that was lost by the capitalist was gained by the labourer, the check to the progress of wealth would be but temporary, as stated by Mr. Ricardo; and the consequences need not be apprehended. But if the conversion of revenue into capital pushed beyond a certain point must, by diminishing the effectual demand for produce, throw the labouring classes out of employment, it is obvious that the adoption of parsimonious habits beyond a certain point, may be accompanied by the most distressing effects at first, and by a marked depression of wealth and population afterwards.

It is not, of course, meant to be stated that parsimony, or even a temporary diminution of consumption,[2] is not often in the highest degree useful, and sometimes absolutely necessary to the progress of wealth. A state may certainly be ruined by extravagance; and a diminution of the actual expenditure may not only be necessary on this account, but when the capital of a country is deficient, compared with the demand for its products, a temporary economy of consumption is required, in order to provide that supply of capital which can alone furnish the means of an increased consumption in future. All that is contended for is, that no nation can *possibly* grow rich by an accumulation of capital, arising from a permanent diminution of consumption; because such accumulation being beyond what is wanted in order to supply the effectual demand for produce, a part of it would very soon lose both its use and its value, and cease to possess the character of wealth. . . .

Though it may be allowed therefore that the laws which regulate the increase of capital are not quite so distinct as those which regulate the increase of population, yet they are certainly just of the same kind; and it is equally vain, with a view to the permanent increase of wealth, to continue converting

[2] Parsimony, or the conversion of revenue into capital, may take place without any diminution of consumption, if the revenue increases first.

revenue into capital, when there is no adequate demand for the products of such capital, as to continue encouraging marriage and the birth of children without a demand for labour and an increase of the funds for its maintenance. . . .

Section X.—Application of some of the preceding Principles to the Distresses of the Labouring Classes since 1815, *with General Observations.*

It has been said that the distresses of the labouring classes since 1815 are owing to a deficient capital, which is evidently unable to employ all that are in want of work.

That the capital of the country does not bear an adequate proportion to the population; that the capital and revenue together do not bear so great a proportion as they did before 1815; and that such a disproportion will at once account for very great distress among the labouring classes, I am most ready to allow. But it is a very different thing to allow that the capital is deficient compared with the population; and to allow that it is deficient compared with the demand for it, and the demand for the commodities procured by it. The two cases are very frequently confounded, because they both produce distress among the labouring classes; but they are essentially distinct. They are attended with some very different symptoms, and require to be treated in a very different manner.

If one fourth of the capital of a country were suddenly destroyed, or entirely transferred to a different part of the world, without any other cause occurring of a diminished demand for commodities, this scantiness of capital would certainly occasion great inconvenience to consumers, and great distress among the working classes; but it would be attended with great advantages to the remaining capitalists. Commodities, in general, would be scarce, and bear a high price on account of the deficiency in the means of producing them. Nothing would be so easy as to find a profitable employment for capital; but it would by no means be easy to find capital for the number of employments in which it was deficient; and consequently the rate of profits would be very high. In this state of things there would be an immediate and pressing demand for capital, on account of there being an immediate and pressing demand for commodities; and the obvious remedy would be, the supply of the demand in the only way in which it could take place, namely, by saving from revenue to add to capital. This supply of capital would, as I have before stated, take place just upon the same principle as a supply of population would follow a great destruction of people on the supposition of there being an immediate and pressing want of labour evinced by the high real wages given to the labourer.

On the other hand, if the capital of the country were diminished by the failure of demand in some large branches of trade, which had before been very prosperous, and absorbed a great quantity of stock; or even if, while capital were suddenly destroyed, the revenue of the landlords was diminished in a greater proportion owing to peculiar circumstances, the state of things, with the exception of the distresses of the poor, would be almost exactly reversed. The remaining capitalists would be in no respect benefited by events which had diminished demand in a still greater proportion than they had diminished the supply. Commodities would be everywhere cheap. Capital would be seeking employment, but would not easily find it; and the profits of stock would be low. There would be no pressing and immediate demand for capital, because there would be no pressing and immediate demand for commodities; and, under these circumstances, the saving from revenue to add to capital, instead of affording the remedy required, would only aggravate the distresses of the capitalists, and fill the stream of capital which was flowing out of the country. The distresses of the capitalists would be aggravated, just upon the same principle as the distresses of the labouring classes would be aggravated if they were encouraged to marry and increase, after a considerable destruction of people, although accompanied by a still greater destruction of capital which had kept the wages of labour very low. There might certainly be a great deficiency of population, compared with the territory and powers of the country, and it might be very desirable that it should be greater; but if the wages of labour were still low, notwithstanding the diminution of people, to encourage the birth of more children would be to encourage misery and mortality rather than population.

Now I would ask, to which of these two suppositions does the present state of this country [3] bear the nearest resemblance? Surely to the latter. That a great loss of capital has lately been sustained, is unquestionable. During nearly the whole of the war, owing to the union of great powers of production with a great effectual consumption and demand, the prodigious destruction of capital by the government was much more than recovered. To doubt this would be to shut our eyes to the comparative state of the country in 1792 and 1813. The two last years of the war were, however, years of extraordinary expense, and being followed immediately by a period marked by a very unusual stagnation of effectual demand, the destruction of capital which took place in those years was not probably recovered. But this stagnation itself was much more disastrous in its effects upon the national capital, and still more upon the national revenue, than any previous destruction of stock. It commenced certainly with the extraordinary fall in the value of the raw produce

[3] This was written in 1820.

of the land, to the amount, it has been supposed, of nearly one third. When this fall had diminished the capitals of the farmers, and still more the revenues both of landlords and farmers, and of all those who were otherwise connected with the land, their power of purchasing manufactures and foreign products was of necessity greatly diminished. The failure of home demand filled the warehouses of the manufacturers with unsold goods, which urged them to export more largely at all risks. But this excessive exportation glutted all the foreign markets, and prevented the merchants from receiving adequate returns; while, from the diminution of the home revenues, aggravated by a sudden and extraordinary contraction of the currency, even the comparatively scanty returns obtained from abroad found a very insufficient domestic demand, and the profits and consequent expenditure of merchants and manufacturers were proportionably lowered. . . . For the four or five years since the war, on account of the change in the distribution of the national produce, and the want of effectual consumption and demand occasioned by it, a check has been given to the rate of production, and the population, under its former impulse, has increased, not only faster than the demand for labour, but faster than the actual produce; yet this produce, though deficient, compared with the population, is redundant, compared with the effectual demand for it and the revenue which is to purchase it. Though labour is cheap, there is neither the power nor the will to employ it all; because not only has the capital of the country diminished, compared with the number of labourers, but, owing to the diminished revenues of the country, the commodities which those labourers would produce are not in such request as to ensure tolerable profits to the reduced capital.

But when profits are low and uncertain, when capitalists are quite at a loss where they can safely employ their capitals, and when on these accounts capital is flowing out of the country; in short, when all the evidence which the nature of the subject admits, distinctly proves that there is no effective demand for capital at home, is it not contrary to the general principles of political economy, is it not a vain and fruitless opposition to that first, greatest, and most universal of all its principles, the principle of supply and demand, to recommend saving, and the conversion of more revenue into capital? Is it not just the same sort of thing as to recommend marriage when people are starving and emigrating?

I am fully aware that the low profits of stock, and the difficulty of finding employment for it, which I consider as an unequivocal proof that the immediate want of the country is not capital, has been attributed to other causes; but to whatever causes they may be attributed, an increase in the proportion of capital to revenue must aggravate them. With regard to these causes, such as the cultivation of our poor soils, our restrictions upon commerce, and our weight of taxation, I find it very difficult to admit a theory of our distresses so inconsistent with the theory of our comparative prosperity. While the greatest quantity of our poor lands were in cultivation; while there were more than usual restrictions upon our commerce, and very little corn was imported; and while taxation was at its height, the country confessedly increased in wealth with a rapidity never known before. Since some of our poorest lands have been thrown out of cultivation; since the peace has removed many of the restrictions upon our commerce, and, notwithstanding our corn laws, we have imported a great quantity of corn; and since seventeen millions of taxes have been taken off from the people, we have experienced the greatest degree of distress, both among capitalists and labourers.

I am very far indeed from meaning to infer from these striking facts that restrictions upon commerce and heavy taxation are beneficial to a country. But the facts certainly show that, whatever may be the future effect of the causes above alluded to in checking the progress of our wealth, we must look elsewhere for the immediate sources of our present distresses. How far our artificial system, and particularly the changes in the value of our currency operating upon a large national debt, may have aggravated the evils we have experienced, it would be extremely difficult to say. But I feel perfectly convinced that a very considerable portion of these evils might be experienced by a nation without poor land in cultivation, without taxes, and without any fresh restrictions on trade.

If a large country, of considerable fertility, and sufficient inland communications, were surrounded by an impassable wall, we all agree that it might be tolerably rich, though not so rich as if it enjoyed the benefit of foreign commerce. Now, supposing such a country gradually to indulge in a considerable consumption, to call forth and employ a great quantity of ingenuity in production, and to save only yearly that portion of its revenue which it could most advantageously add to its capital, expending the rest in consumable commodities and personal services, it might evidently, under such a balance of produce and consumption, be increasing in wealth and population with considerable rapidity. But if, upon the principle laid down by M. Say, that the consumption of a commodity is a diminution of demand, the society were greatly and generally to slacken their consumption, and add to their capitals, there cannot be the least doubt, on the principle of demand and supply, that the profits of capitalists would soon be greatly reduced, though there were no poor land in cultivation; and the population would be thrown out of work and would be starving, although without a single tax, or any restrictions on trade.

The state of Europe and America may perhaps be said, in some points, to resemble the case here supposed; and the stagnation which has been so generally felt and complained of since the war, appears to me inexplicable upon the principles of those who think that the power of production is the only element of wealth, and, who consequently infer that if the means of production be increased, wealth will certainly increase in proportion. Now it is unquestionable that the means of production were increased by the cessation of war, and that more people and more capital were ready to be employed in productive labour; but notwithstanding this obvious increase in the means of production, we hear everywhere of difficulties and distresses, instead of ease and plenty. In the United States of America in particular, a country of extraordinary physical resources, the difficulties which have been experienced are very striking, and such certainly as could hardly have been expected. These difficulties, at least, cannot be attributed to the cultivation of poor land, restrictions upon commerce, and excess of taxation. Altogether the state of the commercial world, since the war, clearly shows that something else is necessary to the continued increase of wealth besides an increase in the means of producing.

That the transition from war to peace, of which so much has been said, is a main cause of the effects observed, will be readily allowed, but not as the operation is usually explained. It is generally said that there has not been time to transfer capital from the employments where it is redundant to those where it is deficient, and thus to restore the proper equilibrium. But such a transfer could hardly require so much time as has now elapsed since the war; and I would ask, where are the under-stocked employments, which, according to this theory, ought to be numerous, and fully capable of absorbing all the redundant capital, which is confessedly glutting the markets of Europe in so many different branches of trade? It is well known by the owners of floating capital, that none such are now to be found; and if the transition in question is to account for what has happened, it must have produced some other effects besides that which arises from the difficulty of moving capital. This I conceive to be a diminution of the demand compared with the supply of produce. The necessary changes in the channels of trade would be effected in a year or two; but the general diminution of demand, compared with the supply occasioned by the transition from such a war to a peace, may last for a very considerable time. The returned taxes, and the excess of individual gains above expenditure, which were so largely used as revenue during the war, are now in part, and probably in no inconsiderable part, saved. I cannot doubt, for instance, that in our own country very many persons have taken the opportunity of saving a part of their returned property-tax, particularly those who have only life-incomes, and who, contrary to the principles of just taxation, had been assessed at the same rate with those whose incomes were derived from realized property. This saving is quite natural and proper, and forms no just argument against the removal of the tax; but still it contributes to explain the cause of the diminished demand for commodities, compared with their supply since the war. If some of the principal governments concerned spent the taxes which they raised in a manner to create a greater and more certain demand for labour and commodities, particularly the former, than the present owners of them, and if this difference of expenditure be of a nature to last for some time, we cannot be surprised at the duration of the effects arising from the transition from war to peace.

FRÉDÉRIC BASTIAT

RÉDÉRIC BASTIAT was born in Bayonne, France, on June 29, 1801. He became
a young man of importance in his native *département* of Landes; he was
appointed a magistrate in 1831 and member of the *conseil général* of Landes
in 1832, where he gained some repute as an agriculturist and writer.

Bastiat became interested in the anti-protectionist agitation waged in England
by Cobden, and in 1844 he published a celebrated essay, "De l'influence des
tarifs français et anglais sur l'avenir des deux peuples," in the *Journal des
Économistes*. In 1845 he published *Cobden et la ligue*. He sought to reproduce
the success of the English Anti-Corn Law League by organizing a series of
"Associations pour la Liberté des Echanges," and became secretary of the Paris
Association. Bastiat's reputation was enhanced by his *Sophismes économiques*
and *Petits pamphlets*—popular essays attacking protectionism and other forms of
economic privilege—in which he displayed unusual wit and satirical power.
These works were extremely popular in France, and English translations of the
polemical pamphlets were later used for anti-protectionist propaganda in the
United States.

Bastiat was elected to the Assembly in 1849, just after the Revolution had given
widespread circulation to socialist ideas and programs. In rapid succession, he
produced a series of pamphlets and brilliant essays in which he denounced
socialism and communism as new and dangerous forms of protectionism. Encouraged by the success of these essays, he began to work on a systematic exposition of his economic doctrines, *Les Harmonies Économiques,* the first volume of
which appeared in 1850.

Bastiat was among the most ardent and uncompromising of the continental
advocates of economic liberalism. His views on value and rent marked a departure from the classical system of Ricardo. By viewing rent as a reward for
income expended in making land more productive, instead of simply an unearned income which accrues to the landowner as more land is called into cultivation, Bastiat hoped to meet the attacks of socialists upon the inequity of rent and
the injustice of the landowner's wealth. Nevertheless, it is not as an original
theorist that he is remembered, but rather as a popularizer of the doctrines of
economic liberalism.

In the autumn of 1850, ill health drove Bastiat to Rome, where he died on
December 24, 1850.

The following selection is taken from *The Harmonies of Political Economy,*
translated by P. J. Stirling (London, 1860).

TO THE YOUTH OF FRANCE

LOVE OF STUDY, and lack of fixed opinions,—a mind free from prejudice, a heart devoid of hate, zeal for the propagation of truth,—ardent sympathies, disinterestedness, devotion, candour,—enthusiasm for all that is good and fair, simple and great, honest and religious,—such are the precious attributes of youth. It is for this reason that I dedicate my work to you. And the seed must have in it no principle of life if it fail to take root in a soil so generous.

I had thought to offer you a picture, and all I have given you is a sketch; but you will pardon me; for who, in times like the present, can sit down to finish a grave and important work? My hope is that some one among you, on seeing it, will be led to exclaim, with the great artist, *Anch' io son pittore!* and, seizing the pencil, impart to my rude canvass colour and flesh, light and shade, sentiment and life.

You may think the title of the work somewhat ambitious; and assuredly I make no pretension to reveal the designs of Providence in the social order, and to explain the mechanism of all the forces with which God has endowed man for the realization of progress. All that I have aimed at is to put you on the right track, and make you acquainted with the truth, that *all legitimate interests are in harmony*. That is the predominant idea of my work, and it is impossible not to recognise its importance.

For some time it has been the fashion to laugh at what has been called the *social problem;* and no doubt some of the solutions which have been proposed afford but too much ground for raillery. But in the problem itself there is nothing laughable. It is the ghost of Banquo at the feast of Macbeth —and no dumb ghost either; for in formidable accents it calls out to terror-stricken society—a solution or death!

Now this solution, you will at once see, must be different according as men's interests are held to be naturally harmonious or naturally antagonistic.

In the one case, we must seek for the solution in Liberty—in the other, in Constraint. In the one case, we have only to be passive—in the other, we must necessarily offer opposition.

But Liberty assumes only one shape. Once convinced that each of the molecules which compose a fluid possesses in itself the force by which the general level is produced, we conclude that there is no surer or simpler way of seeing that level realized than not to interfere with it. All, then, who set out with this fundamental principle, that *men's interests are harmonious,* will agree as to the practical solution of the social problem,—to abstain from displacing or thwarting these interests.

Constraint, on the other hand, may assume a thousand shapes, according to the views which we take of it, and which are infinitely varied. Those schools which set out with the principle, that *men's interests are antagonistic,* have done nothing yet towards the solution of the problem, unless it be that they have thrust aside Liberty. Among the infinite forms of Constraint, they have still to choose the one which they consider good, if indeed any of them be so. And then, as a crowning difficulty, they have to obtain universal acceptance, among men who are free agents, for the particular form of Constraint to which they have awarded the preference.

But, on this hypothesis, if human interests are, by their very nature, urged into fatal collision, and if this shock can be avoided only by the accidental invention of an artificial social order, the destiny of the human race becomes very hazardous, and we ask in terror,

1st, If any man is to be found who has discovered a satisfactory form of Constraint?

2d, Can this man bring to his way of thinking the innumerable schools who give the preference to other forms?

3d, Will mankind give in to that particular form which, by hypothesis, runs counter to all individual interests?

4th, Assuming that men will allow themselves to be rigged out in this new attire, what will happen if another inventor presents himself, with a coat of a different and improved cut? Are we to persevere in a vicious organization, knowing it to be vicious; or must we resolve to change that organization every morning according as the caprices of fashion and the fertility of inventors' brains may dictate?

5th, Would not all the inventors whose plans have been rejected unite together against the particular organization which had been selected, and would not their success in disturbing society be in exact proportion to the degree in which that particular form of organization ran counter to all existing interests?

6th, And, last of all, it may be asked, Does there exist any human force capable of overcoming an antagonism which we presuppose to be itself the very essence of human force?

I might multiply such questions *ad infinitum,* and propose, for example, this difficulty:

If individual interest is opposed to the general interest, where are we to place the active principle of Constraint? Where is the fulcrum of the lever to be placed? Beyond the limits of human society? It must be so if we are to escape the consequences of your law. If we are to intrust some men with arbitrary power, prove first of all that these men are formed of a different clay from other mortals; that they in their turn will not be acted upon by the fatal principle of self-interest; and that, placed in a situation which excludes the idea of any curb, any effective opposition, their judgments will be exempt from error, their hands from rapacity, and their hearts from covetousness.

The radical difference between the various Socialist schools (I mean here, those which seek the solution of the social problem in an artificial organization) and the Economist school, does not consist in certain views of detail or of governmental combination. We encounter that difference at the starting point, in the preliminary and pressing question—Are human interests, when left to themselves, antagonistic or harmonious?

It is evident that the Socialists have set out in quest of an artificial organization only because they judge the natural organization of society bad or insufficient; and they have judged the latter bad and insufficient only because they think they see in men's interests a radical antagonism, for otherwise they would not have had recourse to Constraint. It is not necessary to constrain into harmony what is in itself harmonious.

Thus they have discovered antagonism everywhere:
> Between the proprietor and the *prolétaire;*
> Between capital and labour;
> Between the masses and the *bourgeoisie;*
> Between agriculture and manufactures;
> Between the rustic and the burgess;
> Between the native and the foreigner;
> Between the producer and the consumer;
> Between civilisation and organization;
> > In a word,
> Between Liberty and Harmony.

And this explains why it happens that, although a certain kind of sentimental philanthropy finds a place in their hearts, gall and bitterness flow continually from their lips. Each reserves all his love for the new state of society he has dreamt of; but as regards the society in which we actually live and move, it cannot, in their opinion, be too soon crushed and overthrown, to make room for the New Jerusalem they are to rear upon its ruins.

I have said that the *Economist* school, setting out with the natural harmony of interests, is the advocate of Liberty.

And yet I must allow that if Economists in general stand up for Liberty, it is unfortunately not equally true that their principles establish solidly the foundation on which they build—the harmony of interests.

Before proceeding further, and to forewarn you against the conclusions which will no doubt be drawn from this avowal, I must say a word on the situations which Socialism and Political Economy respectively occupy.

It would be folly in me to assert that Socialism has never lighted upon a truth, and that Political Economy has never fallen into an error.

What separates, radically and profoundly, the two schools is their difference of methods. The one school, like the astrologer and the alchemist, proceeds on hypothesis; the other, like the astronomer and the chemist, proceeds on observation.

Two astronomers, observing the same fact, may not be able to arrive at the same result.

In spite of this transient disagreement, they feel themselves united by the common process which sooner or later will cause that disagreement to disappear. They recognise each other as of the same communion. But between the astronomer, who observes, and the astrologer, who imagines, the gulf is impassable, although accidentally they may sometimes approximate.

The same thing holds of Political Economy and Socialism.

The Economists observe man, the laws of his organization, and the social relations which result from those laws. The Socialists conjure up an imaginary society, and then create a human heart to suit that society.

Now, if philosophy never errs, philosophers often do. I deny not that Economists may make false observations; I will add, that they must necessarily begin by doing so.

But, then, what happens? If men's interests are harmonious, it follows that every incorrect observation will lead logically to antagonism. What, then, are the Socialist tactics? They gather from the works of Economists certain incorrect observations, follow them out to their consequences, and show those consequences to be disastrous. Thus far they are right. Then they set to work upon the observer, whom we may assume to be Malthus or Ricardo. Still they have right on their side. But they do not stop there. They turn against the science of Political Economy itself, accusing it of being heartless, and leading to evil. Here they do violence to reason and justice, inasmuch as science is not responsible for incorrect observation. At length they proceed another step. They lay the blame on society itself:—they threaten to overthrow it for the purpose of reconstructing the edifice:—and why? Because, say they, it is proved by science that society as now constituted is urged onwards to destruction. In this they outrage good sense—for either science is not mistaken, and then why attack it?—or it is mistaken, and in that case they should leave society in repose, since society is not menaced.

But these tactics, illogical as they are, have not been the less fatal to economic science, especially when the cultivators of that science have had the misfortune, from a chivalrous and not unnatural feeling, to render themselves liable, *singuli in solidum,* for their predecessors and for one another. Science is a queen whose gait should be frank and free:—the atmosphere of the *coterie* stifles her.

I have already said that in Political Economy every erroneous proposition must lead ultimately to antagonism. On the other hand, it is impossible that the voluminous works of even the most eminent economists should not include some erroneous propositions. It is ours to mark and to rectify them in the interest of science and of society. If we persist in maintaining them for the honour of the fraternity, we shall not only expose ourselves, which is of little consequence, but we shall expose truth itself, which is a serious affair, to the attacks of Socialism.

To return: the conclusion of the Economists is for Liberty. But in order that this conclusion should take hold of men's minds and hearts, it must be solidly based on this fundamental principle, that interests, left to themselves, tend to harmonious combinations, and to the progressive preponderance of the general good.

Now many Economists, some of them writers of authority, have advanced propositions, which, step by step, lead logically to *absolute evil,* necessary injustice, fatal and progressive inequality, and inevitable pauperism, &c.

Thus, there are very few of them who, so far as I know, have not attributed *value* to natural agents, to the gifts which God has vouchsafed *gratuitously* to his creatures. The word *value* implies that we do not give away the portion of it which we possess except for an equivalent consideration. Here, then, we have men, especially proprietors of land, bartering for effective labour the gifts of God, and receiving recompense for utilities in the creation of which their labour has had no share—an evident, but a necessary, injustice, say these writers.

Then comes the famous theory of Ricardo, which may be summed up in a few words: The price of the necessaries of life depends on the labour required to produce them on the least productive land in cultivation. Then the increase of population obliges us to have recourse to soils of lower and lower fertility. Consequently mankind at large (all except the landowners) are forced to give a larger and larger amount of labour for the same amount of subsistence; or, what comes to the same thing, to receive a less and less amount of subsistence for the same amount of labour,—whilst the landowners see their rental swelling by every new descent to soils of an inferior quality. Conclusion: Progressive opulence of men of leisure—progressive poverty of men of labour; in other words, fatal inequality.

Finally, we have the still more celebrated theory of Malthus, that population has a tendency to increase more rapidly than the means of subsistence, and that at every given moment of the life of man. Now, men cannot be happy, or live in peace, if they have not the means of support; and there are but two obstacles to this increase of population which is always threatening us, namely, a diminished number of births, or an increase of mortality in all its dreadful forms. Moral restraint, to be efficacious, must be universal, and no one expects that. There remains, then, only the repressive obstacles—vice, poverty, war, pestilence, famine; in other words, pauperism and death.

I forbear to mention other systems of a less general bearing, which tend in the same way to bring us to a dead-stand. Monsieur de Tocqueville, for example, and many others, tell us, if we admit the right of primogeniture, we arrive at the most concentrated aristocracy—if we do not admit it, we arrive at ruin and sterility.

And it is worthy of remark, that these four melancholy theories do not in the least degree run foul of each other. If they did, we might console ourselves with the reflection that they are alike false, since they refute each other. But no,—they are in unison, and make part of one and the same general theory, which, supported by numerous and specious facts, would seem to explain the spasmodic state of modern society, and, fortified by the assent of many masters in the science, presents itself with frightful authority to the mind of the confused and discouraged inquirer.

We have still to discover how the authors of this melancholy theory have been able to lay down, as their principle, the *harmony of interests,* and, as their conclusion, Liberty.

For if mankind are indeed urged on by the laws of Value towards Injustice,—by the laws of Rent towards Inequality,—by the laws of Population towards Poverty,—by the laws of Inheritance towards Sterility,—we can no longer affirm that God has made the moral as he has made the natural world—a harmonious work; we must bow the head, and confess that it has pleased Him to base it on revolting and irremediable dissonance.

You must not suppose, young men, that the socialists have refuted and repudiated what, in order to wound no one's susceptibilities, I shall call the theory of dissonances. No; let them say as they will, they have assumed the truth of that theory, and it is just because they have assumed its truth that they propose to substitute Constraint for Liberty, artificial for natural organization, their own inventions for the work of God. They say to their opponents (and in this, perhaps, they are more consistent than the latter),—if, as you have told us, human interests when left to themselves tend to harmonious combination, we cannot do better than welcome and magnify Liberty as you do. But you have demonstrated unanswerably that those interests, if allowed to develop themselves freely, urge mankind towards injustice, inequality, pauperism, and sterility. Your theory, then, provokes reaction precisely because it is true. We desire to break up the existing fabric of society just because it is subject to the fatal laws which you have described; we wish to make trial of our own powers, seeing that the power of God has miscarried.

Thus they are agreed as regards the premises, and differ only on the conclusion.

The Economists to whom I have alluded say that *the great providential laws urge on society to evil;* but that we must take care not to disturb the action of those laws, because such action is happily impeded by the secondary laws which retard the final catastrophe; and arbitrary intervention can only enfeeble the embankment, without stopping the fatal rising of the flood.

The Socialists say that *the great providential laws urge on society to evil;* we must therefore abolish them, and select others from our inexhaustible storehouse.

The Catholics say that *the great providential laws urge on society to evil;* we must therefore escape from them by renouncing worldly interests, and taking refuge in abnegation, sacrifice, asceticism, and resignation.

It is in the midst of this tumult, of these cries of anguish and distress, of these exhortations to subversion, or to resignation and despair, that I endeavour to obtain a hearing for this assertion, in presence of which, if it be correct, all difference of opinion must disappear—*it is not true that the great providential laws urge on society to evil.*

It is with reference to the conclusions to be deduced from their common premises that the various schools are divided and combat each other. I deny those premises, and I ask, Is not that the best way of putting an end to these disputes?

The leading idea of this work, the harmony of interests, is *simple.* Is simplicity not the touchstone of truth? The laws of light, of sound, of motion, appear to us to be all the truer for being simple—Why should it be otherwise with the law of interests?

This idea is *conciliatory.* What is more fitted to reconcile parties than to demonstrate the harmony of the various branches of industry: the harmony of classes, of nations, even of doctrines?

It is *consoling,* seeing that it points out what is false in those systems which adopt, as their conclusion, progressive evil.

It is *religious,* for it assures us that it is not only the celestial but the social mechanism which reveals the wisdom of God, and declares His glory.

It is *practical,* for one can scarcely conceive anything more easily reduced to practice than this,—to allow men to labour, to exchange, to learn, to associate, to act and react on each other,—for, according to the laws of Providence, nothing can result from their intelligent spontaneity but order, harmony, progress, good, and better still; better *ad infinitum*.

Bravo, you will say; here we have the optimism of the Economists with a vengeance! These Economists are so much the slaves of their own systems that they shut their eyes to facts for fear of seeing them. In the face of all the poverty, all the injustice, all the oppressions which desolate humanity, they coolly deny the existence of evil. The smell of revolutionary gunpowder does not reach their blunted senses—the pavement of the barricades has no voice for them; and were society to crumble to pieces before their eyes, they would still keep repeating, "All is for the best in the best of worlds."

No indeed,—we do not think that all is for the best; but I have faith in the wisdom of the laws of Providence, and for the same reason I have faith in Liberty.

The question is, Have we Liberty?

The question is, Do these laws act in their plenitude, or is their action not profoundly troubled by the countervailing action of human institutions?

Deny evil! deny suffering! Who can? We must forget that our subject is man. We must forget that we are ourselves men. The laws of Providence may be regarded as harmonious without their necessarily excluding evil. Enough that evil has its explanation and its mission, that it checks and limits itself, that it destroys itself by its own action, and that each suffering prevents a greater suffering by repressing the cause of suffering.

Society has for its element man, who is a *free* agent; and since man is free, he may choose,—since he may choose, he may be mistaken,—since he may be mistaken, he may suffer.

I go further. I say he must be mistaken and suffer—for he begins his journey in ignorance, and for ignorance there are endless and unknown roads, all of which, except one, lead to error.

Now, every Error engenders suffering; but either suffering reacts upon the man who errs, and then it brings Responsibility into play,—or, if it affects others who are free from error, it sets in motion the marvellous reactionary machinery of Solidarity.

The action of these laws, combined with the faculty which has been vouchsafed to us of connecting effects with their causes, must bring us back, by means of this very suffering, into the way of what is good and true.

Thus, not only do we not deny the existence of evil, but we acknowledge that it has a mission in the social, as it has in the material world.

But, in order that it should fulfil this mission, we must not stretch

Solidarity artificially, so as to destroy Responsibility,—in other words, we must respect Liberty.

Should human institutions step in to oppose in this respect the divine laws, evil would not the less flow from error, only it would shift its position. It would strike those whom it ought not to strike. It would be no longer a warning and a monitor. It would no longer have the tendency to diminish and die away by its own proper action. Its action would be continued, and increase, as would happen in the physiological world if the imprudences and excesses of the men of one hemisphere were felt in their unhappy effects only by the inhabitants of the opposite hemisphere.

Now this is precisely the tendency not only of most of our governmental institutions, but likewise, and above all, of those which we seek to establish as remedies for the evils which we suffer. Under the philanthropical pretext of developing among men a factitious Solidarity, we render Responsibility more and more inert and inefficacious. By an improper application of the public force, we alter the relation of labour to its remuneration, we disturb the laws of industry and of exchange, we offer violence to the natural development of education, we give a wrong direction to capital and labour, we twist and invert men's ideas, we inflame absurd pretensions, we dazzle with chimerical hopes, we occasion a strange loss of human power, we change the centres of population, we render experience itself useless,—in a word, we give to all interests artificial foundations, we set them by the ears, and then we exclaim that—Interests are antagonistic: Liberty has done all the evil,— let us denounce and stifle Liberty.

And yet, as this sacred word has still power to stir men's hearts and make them palpitate, we despoil Liberty of its *prestige* by depriving it of its name; and it is under the title of *Competition* that the unhappy victim is led to the sacrificial altar, amid the applause of a mob stretching forth their hands to receive the shackles of servitude.

It is not enough, then, to exhibit, in their majestic harmony, the natural laws of the social order; we must also explain the disturbing causes which paralyze their action; and this is what I have endeavoured to do in the second part of this work.

I have striven to avoid controversy; and, in doing so, I have no doubt lost an opportunity of giving to the principles which I desire to disseminate the stability which results from a thorough and searching discussion. And yet, might not the attention of the reader, seduced by digressions, have been diverted from the argument taken as a whole? If I exhibit the edifice as it stands, what matters it in what light it has been regarded by others, even by those who first taught me to look at it?

And now I would appeal with confidence to men of all schools, who prefer truth, justice, and the public good to their own systems.

Economists! like you, I am the advocate of LIBERTY; and if I succeed in shaking some of those premises which sadden your generous hearts, perhaps you will see in this an additional incentive to love and to serve our sacred cause.

Socialists! you have faith in ASSOCIATION. I conjure you, after having read this book, to say whether society as it is now constituted, apart from its abuses and shackles, that is to say, under the condition of Liberty, is not the most beautiful, the most complete, the most durable, the most universal, the most equitable, of all Associations.

Egalitaires! you admit but one principle, the MUTUALITY OF SERVICES. Let human transactions be free, and I assert that they are not and cannot be anything else than a reciprocal exchange of *services,*—services always diminishing in *value,* always increasing in *utility.*

Communists! you desire that men, become brothers, should enjoy in common the goods which Providence has lavished on them. My aim is to demonstrate that society as it exists has only to acquire freedom in order to realize and surpass your wishes and your hopes. For all things are common to all, on the single condition that each man takes the trouble to gather what God has given, which is very natural; or remunerate freely those who take that trouble for him, which is very just.

Christians of all communions! unless you stand alone in casting doubt on the divine wisdom, manifested in the most magnificent of all God's works which have come within the range of our knowledge, you will find in this book no expression which can shock the severest morals, or the most mysterious dogmas of your faith.

Proprietors! whatever be the extent of your possessions, if I establish that your rights, now so much contested, are limited, like those of the most ordinary workman, to the receiving of services in exchange for real and substantial services which have been actually rendered by you, or by your forefathers, those rights will henceforth repose on a basis which cannot be shaken.

Prolétaires! men who live by wages! I undertake to demonstrate that you obtain the fruits of the land of which you are not the owners with less pain and effort than if you were obliged to raise those fruits by your own direct labour,—with less than if that land had been given to you in its primitive state, and before being prepared for cultivation by labour.

Capitalists and labourers! I believe myself in a position to establish the law that, in proportion as capital is accumulated, the *absolute* share of the total product falling to the capitalist increases, and his *proportional* share is diminished; while both the *absolute* and *relative* share of the product falling to the labourer is augmented,—the reverse effects being produced when capital is lessened or dissipated. If this law is established, the obvious deduction is, a harmony of interests between labourers and those who employ them.

Disciples of Malthus! sincere and calumniated philanthropists, whose only fault has been in warning mankind against the effects of a law which you believe to be fatal, I shall have to submit to you another law more reassuring: "—*Coeteris paribus,* increasing density of population is equivalent to increasing facility of production." And if it be so, I am certain it will not be you who will grieve to see a stumbling-block removed from the threshold of our favourite science.

Men of spoliation! you who, by force or fraud, by law or in spite of law, batten on the people's substance; you who live by the errors you propagate, by the ignorance you cherish, by the wars you light up, by the trammels with which you hamper trade; you who tax labour after having rendered it unproductive, making it lose a sheaf for every handful you yourselves pluck from it; you who cause yourselves to be paid for creating obstacles, in order to get afterwards paid for partially removing those obstacles; incarnations of egotism in its worst sense; parasitical excrescences of a vicious policy, prepare for the sharpest and most unsparing criticism. To you, alone, I make no appeal, for the design of this book is to sacrifice you, or rather to sacrifice your unjust pretensions. In vain we cherish conciliation. There are two principles which can never be reconciled—Liberty and Constraint.

If the laws of Providence are harmonious, it is when they act with freedom, without which there is no harmony. Whenever, then, we remark an absence of harmony, we may be sure that it proceeds from an absence of liberty, an absence of justice. Oppressors, spoliators, contemners of justice, you can have no part in the universal harmony, for it is you who disturb it.

Do I mean to say that the effect of this work may be to enfeeble power, to shake its stability, to diminish its authority? My design is just the opposite. But let me not be misunderstood.

It is the business of political science to distinguish between what ought and what ought not to fall under State control; and in making this important distinction we must not forget that the State always acts through the intervention of Force. The services which it renders us, and the services which it exacts from us in return, are alike imposed upon us under the name of contributions.

The question then comes back to this: What are the things which men have a right to impose upon each other *by force?* Now I know but one thing in this situation, and that is *Justice.* I have no right to *force* any one whatever to be religious, charitable, well educated, or industrious; but I have a right to *force* him to be *just,*—this is a case of legitimate defence.

Now, individuals in the aggregate can possess no right which did not preexist in individuals as such. If, then, the employment of individual force is justified only by legitimate defence, the fact that the action of government is always manifested by Force should lead us to conclude that it is essentially limited to the maintenance of order, security, and justice.

All action of governments beyond this limit is a usurpation upon conscience, upon intelligence, upon industry; in a word, upon human Liberty.

This being granted, we ought to set ourselves unceasingly and without compunction to emancipate the entire domain of private enterprise from the encroachments of power. Without this we shall not have gained Freedom, or the free play of those laws of harmony which God has provided for the development and progress of the human race.

Will Power by this means be enfeebled? Will it have lost in stability because it has lost in extent? Will it have less authority because it has fewer functions to discharge? Will it attract to itself less respect because it calls forth fewer complaints? Will it be more the sport of factions, when it has reduced those enormous budgets and that coveted influence which are the baits and allurements of faction? Will it encounter greater danger when it has less responsibility?

To me it seems evident, that to confine public force to its one, essential, undisputed, beneficent mission,—a mission desired and accepted by all,—would be the surest way of securing to it respect and universal support. In that case, I see not whence could proceed systematic opposition, parliamentary struggles, street insurrections, revolutions, sudden changes of fortune, factions, illusions, the pretensions of all to govern under all forms, those dangerous and absurd systems which teach the people to look to government for everything, that compromising diplomacy, those wars which are always in perspective, or armed truces which are nearly as fatal, those crushing taxes which it is impossible to levy on any equitable principle, that absorbing and unnatural mixing up of politics with everything, those great artificial displacements of capital and labour, which are the source of fruitless heartburnings, fluctuations, stoppages, and commercial crises. All those causes of trouble, of irritation, of disaffection, of covetousness, and of disorder, and a thousand others, would no longer have any foundation, and the depositaries of power, instead of disturbing, would contribute to the universal harmony, —a harmony which does not indeed exclude evil, but which leaves less and less room for those ills which are inseparable from the ignorance and perversity of our feeble nature, and whose mission it is to prevent or chastise that ignorance and perversity.

Young men! in these days in which a grievous Scepticism would seem to be at once the effect and the punishment of the anarchy of ideas which prevails, I shall esteem myself happy if this work, as you proceed in its perusal, should bring to your lips the consoling words, I BELIEVE,—words of a sweet-smelling savour, which are at once a refuge and a force, which are said to remove mountains, and stand at the head of the Christian's creed—I believe. "I believe, not with a blind and submissive faith, for we are not concerned here with the mysteries of revelation, but with a rational and scientific faith, befitting things which are left to man's investigation.—I believe that He who has arranged the material universe has not witheld His regards from the arrangements of the social world.—I believe that He has combined, and caused to move in harmony, free agents as well as inert molecules.—I believe that His over-ruling Providence shines forth as strikingly, if not more so, in the laws to which He has subjected men's interests and men's wills, as in the laws which He has imposed on weight and velocity.—I believe that everything in human society, even what is apparently injurious, is the cause of improvement and of progress.—I believe that Evil tends to Good, and calls it forth, whilst Good cannot tend to Evil; whence it follows that Good must in the end predominate.—I believe that the invincible social tendency is a constant approximation of men towards a common moral, intellectual, and physical level, with, at the same time, a progressive and indefinite elevation of that level.—I believe that all that is necessary to the gradual and peaceful development of humanity is that its tendencies should not be disturbed, but have the liberty of their movements restored. —I believe these things, not because I desire them, not because they satisfy my heart, but because my judgment accords to them a deliberate assent."

Ah! whenever you come to pronounce these words, I BELIEVE, you will be anxious to propagate your creed, and the social problem will soon be resolved, for let them say what they will it is not of difficult solution. Men's interests are harmonious,—the solution then lies entirely in this one word—LIBERTY.

DAVID RICARDO

DAVID RICARDO was born in London on April 19, 1772, the third child of a large family. His father, an orthodox Jew from Holland, settled in England and became a successful and respected member of the stock exchange. David went to school in England and in Holland. At fourteen he entered his father's business, and at twenty-one he was married.

About this time, David abandoned Judaism, thereby causing some discord, but no rupture, with his father.

When the younger Ricardo entered business for himself in the 1790's, England was experiencing unprecedented financial disturbances. He took advantage of every opportunity and quickly made a fortune. Like his father, he was generally admired and respected, but the details of business could not satisfy him intellectually. The new advances in science intrigued him, and he became a member of the Geological Society when it was founded in 1807. Ricardo's chief interest, however, was the study of political economy. He first read Adam Smith's *Wealth of Nations* in 1799. From 1809 to 1819 he published letters and pamphlets on the state of the currency, on the corn laws, and on the value of bank notes, as well as his brilliant full length economic treatises.

Ricardo became a member of Parliament in 1819 and was reelected the following year. He held his seat until his death in 1823. Although an independent thinker, he agreed almost entirely with the policies of the radical party seeking to reform England's oligarchic and corrupt government. But when, in 1819, he served on a committee to examine the schemes of Robert Owen, he proved unsympathetic to Owen's socialism and refused to share his objections to machinery. Ricardo voted for Parliamentary reform and for extension of the ballot, attacked the corn laws, and generally opposed every kind of government restriction or bounty. In April, 1822, he claimed that he had voted for every reduction of taxes proposed during that session. He considered taxes as leading to surpluses, and surpluses as temptations for expenditure. Ricardo was a favorite with the utilitarian followers of Jeremy Bentham and became an original member of the Political Economy Club at its founding in 1821.

After the publication of *Principles of Political Economy and Taxation* in 1817, Ricardo wrote little. He lived happily with his family in the country, far from London; his kindness, bountiful charities, and good humor won him many friends. He died in 1823, leaving his wife and seven children.

Ricardo's early reputation as an authority on economics brought him into touch with Malthus and James Mill, with whom he formed warm friendships. It was they who urged him to provide a more systematic exposition of his theories. *The Principles of Political Economy,* from which the following selection is taken, has been regarded as the "orthodox manifesto" of classical political economy. It won for him a reputation as the founder of that school. Among many ideas he used, the "labor theory of value" and the so-called "iron law of wages" were expounded by McCulloch and James Mill, and they greatly influenced the social and economic theory of John Stuart Mill and Karl Marx.

THE PRINCIPLES OF POLITICAL ECONOMY AND TAXATION

CHAPTER I: ON VALUE

Section 1.—The value of a commodity, or the quantity of any other commodity for which it will exchange, depends on the relative quantity of labour which is necessary for its production, and not on the greater or less compensation which is paid for that labour.

It has been observed by Adam Smith that "the word Value has two different meanings, and sometimes expresses the utility of some particular object, and sometimes the power of purchasing other goods which the possession of that object conveys. The one may be called *value in use;* the other *value in exchange.*" "The things," he continues, "which have the greatest value in use, have frequently little or no value in exchange; and, on the contrary, those which have the greatest value in exchange, have little or no value in use." Water and air are abundantly useful; they are indeed indispensable to existence, yet, under ordinary circumstances, nothing can be obtained in exchange for them. Gold, on the contrary, though of little use compared with air and water, will exchange for a great quantity of other goods.

Utility then is not the measure of exchangeable value, although it is absolutely essential to it. If a commodity were in no way useful—in other words, if it could in no way contribute to our gratification—it would be destitute of exchangeable value, however scarce it might be, whatever quantity of labour might be necessary to procure it.

Possessing utility, commodities derive their exchangeable value from two sources; from their scarcity, and from the quantity of labour required to obtain them.

There are some commodities, the value of which is determined by their scarcity alone. No labour can increase the quantity of such goods, and therefore their value cannot be lowered by an increased supply. Some rare statues and pictures, scarce books and coins, wines of a peculiar quality, which can be made only from grapes grown on a particular soil, of which there is a very limited quantity, are all of this description. Their value is wholly independent of the quantity of labour originally necessary to produce them, and varies with the varying wealth and inclinations of those who are desirous to possess them.

These commodities, however, form a very small part of the mass of commodities daily exchanged in the market. By far the greatest part of those goods which are the objects of desire are procured by labour; and they may be multiplied, not in one country alone, but in many, almost without any assignable limit, if we are disposed to bestow the labour necessary to obtain them.

In speaking, then, of commodities, of their exchangeable value, and of the laws which regulate their relative prices, we mean always such commodities only as can be increased in quantity by the exertion of human industry, and on the production of which competition operates without restraint.

In the early stages of society, the exchangeable value of these commodities, or the rule which determines how much of one shall be given in exchange for another, depends almost exclusively on the comparative quantity of labour expended on each.

"The real price of everything," says Adam Smith,

What everything really costs to the man who wants to acquire it, is the toil and trouble of acquiring it. What everything is really worth to the man who has acquired it, and who wants to dispose of it, or exchange it for something else, is the toil and trouble which it can save to himself, and which it can impose upon other people. Labour was the first price—the original purchase-money that was paid for all things.

Again,

in that early and rude state of society which precedes both the accumulation of stock and the appropriation of land, the proportion between the quantities of labour necessary for acquiring different objects seems to be the only circumstance which can afford any rule for exchanging them for one another. If, among a nation of hunters, for example, it usually cost twice the labour to kill a beaver which it does to kill a deer, one beaver should naturally exchange for, or be worth, two deer. It is natural that what is usually the produce of two days' or two hours' labour should be worth double of what is usually the produce of one day's or one hour's labour.

That this is really the foundation of the exchangeable value of all things, excepting those which cannot be increased by human industry, is a doctrine of the utmost importance in political economy; for from no source do so many errors, and so much difference of opinion in that science proceed, as from the vague ideas which are attached to the word value.

If the quantity of labour realised in commodities regulate their exchangeable value, every increase of the quantity of labour must augment the value of that commodity on which it is exercised, as every diminution must lower it.

Adam Smith, who so accurately defined the original source of exchangeable value, and who was bound in consistency to maintain that all things became more or less valuable in proportion as more or less labour was bestowed on their production, has himself erected another standard measure of value, and speaks of things being more or less valuable in proportion as they will exchange for more or less of this standard measure. Sometimes he speaks of corn, at other times of labour, as a standard measure; not the quantity of labour bestowed on the production of any object, but the quantity which it can command in the market; as if these were two equivalent expressions, and as if, because a man's labour had become doubly efficient, and he could therefore produce twice the quantity of a commodity, he would necessarily receive twice the former quantity in exchange for it. . . .

CHAPTER IV: ON NATURAL AND MARKET PRICE

In making labour the foundation of the value of commodities, and the comparative quantity of labour which is necessary to their production, the rule which determines the respective quantities of goods which shall be given in exchange for each other, we must not be supposed to deny the accidental and temporary deviations of the actual or market price of commodities from this, their primary and natural price.

In the ordinary course of events, there is no commodity which continues for any length of time to be supplied precisely in that degree of abundance which the wants and wishes of mankind require, and therefore there is none which is not subject to accidental and temporary variations of price.

It is only in consequence of such variations that capital is apportioned precisely, in the requisite abundance and no more, to the production of the different commodities which happen to be in demand. With the rise or fall of price, profits are elevated above, or depressed below, their general level; and capital is either encouraged to enter into, or is warned to depart from, the particular employment in which the variation has taken place.

Whilst every man is free to employ his capital where he pleases, he will naturally seek for it that employment which is most advantageous; he will naturally be dissatisfied with a profit of 10 per cent, if by removing his capital he can obtain a profit of 15 per cent. This restless desire on the part of all the employers of stock to quit a less profitable for a more advantageous business has a strong tendency to equalise the rate of profits of all, or to fix them in such proportions as may, in the estimation of the parties, compensate for any advantage which one may have, or may appear to have, over the other. It is perhaps very difficult to trace the steps by which this change is effected; it is probably effected by a manufacturer not absolutely changing his employment, but only lessening the quantity of capital he has in that employment. In all rich countries there is a number of men forming what is called the moneyed class; these men are engaged in no trade, but live on the interest of their money, which is employed in discounting bills, or in loans to the more industrious part of the community. The bankers too employ a large capital on the same objects. The capital so employed forms a circulating capital of a large amount, and is employed, in larger or smaller proportions, by all the different trades of a country. There is perhaps no manufacturer, however rich, who limits his business to the extent that his own funds alone will allow: he has always some portion of this floating capital, increasing or diminishing according to the activity of the demand for his commodities. When the demand for silk increases, and that for cloth diminishes, the clothier does not remove with his capital to the silk trade, but he dismisses some of his workmen, he discontinues his demand for the loan from bankers and moneyed men; while the case of the silk manufacturer is the reverse: he wishes to employ more workmen, and thus his motive for borrowing is increased; he borrows more, and thus capital is transferred from one employment to another without the necessity of a manufacturer discontinuing his usual occupation. When we look to the markets of a large town, and observe how regularly they are supplied both with home and foreign commodities, in the quantity in which they are required, under all the circumstances of varying demand, arising from the caprice of taste, or a change in the amount of population, without often producing either the effects of a glut from a too abundant supply, or an enormously high price from the supply being unequal to the demand, we must confess that the principle which apportions capital to each trade in the precise amount that it is required is more active than is generally supposed.

A capitalist, in seeking profitable employment for his funds, will naturally take into consideration all the advantages which one occupation possesses over another. He may therefore be willing to forego a part of his money profit in consideration of the security, cleanliness, ease, or any other real or fancied advantage which one employment may possess over another.

If from a consideration of these circumstances the profits of stock should be so adjusted that in one trade they were 20, in another 25, and in another 30 per cent they would probably continue permanently with that relative difference, and with that difference only; for if any cause should elevate the profits of one of these trades 10 per cent, either these profits would be temporary, and would soon again fall back to their usual station, or the profits of the others would be elevated in the same proportion.

The present time appears to be one of the exceptions to the justness of this remark. The termination of the war has so deranged the division which before existed of employments in Europe, that every capitalist has not yet found his place in the new division which has now become necessary.

Let us suppose that all commodities are at their natural price, and consequently that the profits of capital in all employments are exactly at the same rate, or differ only so much as, in the estimation of the parties, is equivalent to any real or fancied advantage which they possess or forego. Suppose now that a change of fashion should increase the demand for silks and lessen that for woollens; their natural price, the quantity of labour necessary to their production, would continue unaltered, but the market price of silks would rise and that of woollens would fall; and consequently the profits of the silk manufacturer would be above, whilst those of the woollen manufacturer would be below, the general and adjusted rate of profits. Not only the profits, but the wages of the workmen, would be affected in these employments. This increased demand for silks would, however, soon be supplied by the transference of capital and labour from the woollen to the silk manufacture; when the market prices of silks and woollens would again approach their natural prices, and then the usual profits would be obtained by the respective manufacturers of those commodities.

It is then the desire, which every capitalist has, of diverting his funds from a less to a more profitable employment that prevents the market price of commodities from continuing for any length of time either much above or much below their natural price. It is this competition which so adjusts the changeable value of commodities that, after paying the wages for the labour necessary to their production, and all other expenses required to put the capital employed in its original state of efficiency, the remaining value or overplus will in each trade be in proportion to the value of the capital employed.

In the seventh chapter of the *Wealth of Nations,* all that concerns this question is most ably treated. Having fully acknowledged the temporary effects which, in particular employments of capital, may be produced on the prices of commodities, as well as on the wages of labour, and the profits of stock, by accidental causes, without influencing the general price of commodities, wages, or profits, since these effects are equally operative in all stages of society, we will leave them entirely out of our consideration whilst we are treating of the laws which regulate natural prices, natural wages, and natural profits, effects totally independent of these accidental causes. In speaking, then, of the exchangeable value of commodities, or the power of purchasing possessed by any one commodity, I mean always that power which it would possess if not disturbed by any temporary or accidental cause, and which is its natural price.

CHAPTER V: ON WAGES

Labour, like all other things which are purchased and sold, and which may be increased or diminished in quantity, has its natural and its market price. The natural price of labour is that price which is necessary to enable the labourers, one with another, to subsist and to perpetuate their race, without either increase or diminution.

The power of the labourer to support himself, and the family which may be necessary to keep up the number of labourers, does not depend on the quantity of money which he may receive for wages, but on the quantity of food, necessaries, and conveniences become essential to him from habit which that money will purchase. The natural price of labour, therefore, depends on the price of the food, necessaries, and conveniences required for the support of the labourer and his family. With a rise in the price of food and necessaries, the natural price of labour will rise; with the fall in their price, the natural price of labour will fall.

With the progress of society the natural price of labour has always a tendency to rise, because one of the principal commodities by which its natural price is regulated has a tendency to become dearer from the greater difficulty of producing it. As, however, the improvements in agriculture, the discovery of new markets, whence provisions may be imported, may for a time counteract the tendency to a rise in the price of necessaries, and may even occasion their natural price to fall, so will the same causes produce the correspondent effects on the natural price of labour.

The natural price of all commodities, excepting raw produce and labour, has a tendency to fall in the progress of wealth and population; for though, on one hand, they are enhanced in real value, from the rise in the natural price of the raw material of which they are made, this is more than counterbalanced by the improvements in machinery, by the better division and distribution of labour, and by the increasing skill, both in science and art, of the producers.

The market price of labour is the price which is really paid for it, from the natural operation of the proportion of the supply to the demand; labour is dear when it is scarce and cheap when it is plentiful. However much the market price of labour may deviate from its natural price, it has, like commodities, a tendency to conform to it.

It is when the market price of labour exceeds its natural price that the condition of the labourer is flourishing and happy, that he has it in his power to command a greater proportion of the necessaries and enjoyments of life, and therefore to rear a healthy and numerous family. When, however, by the encouragement which high wages give to the increase of population, the number of labourers is increased, wages again fall to their natural price, and indeed from a reaction sometimes fall below it.

When the market price of labour is below its natural price, the condition of the labourer is most wretched; then poverty deprives them of those comforts which custom renders absolute necessaries. It is only after their privations have reduced their number, or the demand for labour has increased, that the market price of labour will rise to its natural price, and that the labourer will have the moderate comforts which the natural rate of wages will afford.

Notwithstanding the tendency of wages to conform to their natural rate, their market rate may, in an improving society, for an indefinite period, be constantly above it; for no sooner may the impulse which an increased capital gives to a new demand for labour be obeyed, than another increase of capital may produce the same effect; and thus, if the increase of capital be gradual and constant, the demand for labour may give a continued stimulus to an increase of people.

Capital is that part of the wealth of a country which is employed in production, and consists of food, clothing, tools, raw materials, machinery, etc., necessary to give effect to labour.

Capital may increase in quantity at the same time that its value rises. An addition may be made to the food and clothing of a country at the same time that more labour may be required to produce the additional quantity than before; in that case not only the quantity but the value of capital will rise.

Or capital may increase without its value increasing, and even while its value is actually diminishing; not only may an addition be made to the food and clothing of a country, but the addition may be made by the aid of machinery, without any increase, and even with an absolute diminution in the proportional quantity of labour required to produce them. The quantity of capital may increase, while neither the whole together, nor any part of it singly, will have a greater value than before, but may actually have a less.

In the first case, the natural price of labour, which always depends on the price of food, clothing, and other necessaries, will rise; in the second, it will remain stationary or fall; but in both cases the market rate of wages will rise, for in proportion to the increase of capital will be the increase in the demand for labour; in proportion to the work to be done will be the demand for those who are to do it.

In both cases, too, the market price of labour will rise above its natural price; and in both cases it will have a tendency to conform to its natural price, but in the first case this agreement will be most speedily effected. The situation of the labourer will be improved, but not much improved; for the increased price of food and necessaries will absorb a large portion of his increased wages; consequently a small supply of labour, or a trifling increase in the population, will soon reduce the market price to the then increased natural price of labour.

In the second case, the condition of the labourer will be very greatly improved; he will receive increased money wages without having to pay any increased price, and perhaps even a diminished price for the commodities which he and his family consume; and it will not be till after a great addition has been made to the population that the market price of labour will again sink to its then low and reduced natural price.

Thus, then, with every improvement of society, with every increase in its capital, the market wages of labour will rise; but the permanence of their rise will depend on the question whether the natural price of labour has also risen; and this again will depend on the rise in the natural price of those necessaries on which the wages of labour are expended.

It is not to be understood that the natural price of labour estimated even in food and necessaries, is absolutely fixed and constant. It varies at different times in the same country, and very materially differs in different countries. It essentially depends on the habits and customs of the people. An English labourer would consider his wages under their natural rate, and too scanty to support a family, if they enabled him to purchase no other food than potatoes, and to live in no better habitation than a mud cabin; yet these moderate demands of nature are often deemed sufficient in countries where "man's life is cheap" and his wants easily satisfied. Many of the conveniences now enjoyed in an English cottage, would have been thought luxuries at an earlier period of our history.

From manufactured commodities always falling and raw produce always rising, with the progress of society, such a disproportion in their relative value is at length created, that in rich countries a labourer, by the sacrifice of a very small quantity only of his food, is able to provide liberally for all his other wants.

Independently of the variations in the value of money, which necessarily affect money wages, but which we have here supposed to have no operation, as we have considered money to be uniformly of the same value, it appears then that wages are subject to a rise or fall from two causes:—

First, the supply and demand of labourers.

Secondly, the price of the commodities on which the wages of labour are expended.

In different stages of society, the accumulation of capital, or of the means of employing labour, is more or less rapid, and must in all cases depend on the productive powers of labour. The productive powers of labour are generally greatest when there is an abundance of fertile land; at such periods accumulation is often so rapid that labourers cannot be supplied with the same rapidity as capital.

It has been calculated that under favourable circumstances population may be doubled in twenty-five years; but under the same favourable circumstances the whole capital of a country might possibly be doubled in a shorter period. In that case, wages during the whole period would have a tendency to rise, because the demand for labour would increase still faster than the supply.

In new settlements, where the arts and knowledge of countries far advanced in refinement are introduced, it is probable that capital has a tendency to increase faster than mankind; and if the deficiency of labourers were not supplied by more populous countries, this tendency would very much raise the price of labour. In proportion as these countries become populous, and land of a worse quality is taken into cultivation, the tendency to increase of capital diminishes; for the surplus produce remaining, after satisfying the wants of the existing population, must necessarily be in proportion to the facility of production, viz. to the smaller number of persons employed in production. Although, then, it is probable that, under the most favourable circumstances, the power of production is still greater than that of population, it will not long continue so; for the land being limited in quantity, and differing in quality, with every increased portion of capital employed on it there will be a decreased rate of production, whilst the power of population continues always the same.

In those countries where there is abundance of fertile land, but where, from the ignorance, indolence, and barbarism of the inhabitants, they are exposed to all the evils of want and famine, and where it has been said that population presses against the means of subsistence, a very different remedy should be applied from that which is necessary in long settled countries, where, from the diminishing rate of the supply of raw produce, all the evils of a crowded population are experienced. In the one case, the evil proceeds from bad government, from the insecurity of property, and from a want of education in all ranks of the people. To be made happier they require only to be better governed and instructed, as the augmentation of capital, beyond the augmentation of people, would be the inevitable result. No increase in the population can be too great, as the powers of production are still greater. In the other case, the population increases faster than the fund required for its support. Every exertion of industry, unless accompanied by a diminished rate of increase in the population, will add to the evil, for production cannot keep pace with it.

With a population pressing against the means of subsistence, the only remedies are either a reduction of people or a more rapid accumulation of capital. In rich countries, where all the fertile land is already cultivated, the latter remedy is neither very practicable nor very desirable, because its effort would be, if pushed very far, to render all classes equally poor. But in poor countries, where there are abundant means of production in store, from fertile land not yet brought into cultivation, it is the only safe and efficacious means of removing the evil, particularly as its effect would be to elevate all classes of the people.

The friends of humanity cannot but wish that in all countries the labouring classes should have a taste for comforts and enjoyments and that they should be stimulated by all legal means in their exertions to procure them. There cannot be a better security against a superabundant population. In those countries where the labouring classes have the fewest wants, and are contented with the cheapest food, the people are exposed to the greatest vicissitudes and miseries. They have no place of refuge from calamity; they cannot seek safety in a lower station; they are already so low that they can fall no lower. On any deficiency of the chief article of their subsistence there are few substitutes of which they can avail themselves and dearth to them is attended with almost all the evils of famine.

In the natural advance of society, the wages of labour will have a tendency to fall, as far as they are regulated by supply and demand; for the supply of labourers will continue to increase at the same rate, whilst the demand for them will increase at a slower rate. If, for instance, wages were regulated by a yearly increase of capital at the rate of 2 per cent, they would fall when it accumulated only at the rate of 1½ per cent. They would fall still lower when it increased only at the rate of 1 or ½ per cent, and would continue to do so until the capital became stationary, when wages also would become stationary, and be only sufficient to keep up the numbers of the actual population. I say that, under these circumstances, wages would fall if they were regulated only by the supply and demand of labourers; but we must not forget that wages are also regulated by the prices of the commodities on which they are expended.

As population increases, these necessaries will be constantly rising in price, because more labour will be necessary to produce them. If, then, the money wages of labour should fall, whilst every commodity on which the wages of labour were expended rose, the labourer would be doubly affected, and would be soon totally deprived of subsistence. Instead, therefore, of the money wages of labour falling, they would rise; but they would not rise sufficiently to enable the labourer to purchase as many comforts and necessaries as he did before the rise in the price of those commodities. If his annual wages were before £24, or six quarters of corn when the price was £4 per quarter, he would probably receive only the value of five quarters when corn rose to £5 per quarter. But five quarters would cost £25; he would, therefore, receive an addition in his money wages, though with that addition he would be unable to furnish himself with the same quantity of corn and other commodities which he had before consumed in his family.

Notwithstanding, then, that the labourer would be really worse paid, yet this increase in his wages would necessarily diminish the profits of the manufacturer; for his goods would sell at no higher price, and yet the expense of producing them would be increased. This, however, will be considered in our examination into the principles which regulate profits.

It appears, then, that the same cause which raises rent, namely, the increasing difficulty of providing an additional quantity of food with the same proportional quantity of labour, will also raise wages; and therefore, if money be of an unvarying value, both rent and wages will have a tendency to rise with the progress of wealth and population.

But there is this essential difference between the rise of rent and the rise of wages. The rise in the money value of rent is accompanied by an increased share of the produce; not only is the landlord's money rent greater, but his corn rent also; he will have more corn, and each defined measure of that corn will exchange for a greater quantity of all other goods which have not been raised in value. The fate of the labourer will be less happy; he will receive more money wages, it is true, but his corn wages will be reduced; and not only his command of corn, but his general condition will be deteriorated, by his finding it more difficult to maintain the market rate of wages above their natural rate. While the price of corn rises 10 per cent, wages will always rise less than 10 per cent, but rent will always rise more; the condition of the labourer will generally decline, and that of the landlord will always be improved.

JEAN-BAPTISTE SAY

J EAN-BAPTISTE SAY was born in Lyons on January 5, 1767. He came from an old Protestant family who fled France after the revocation of the Edict of Nantes (1685) and returned in the eighteenth century. Say planned for a commercial career, and he served an apprenticeship in the house of an English merchant. Under the influence of Adam Smith's *The Wealth of Nations* (1776), he devoted himself to the study of economics, publishing his first pamphlet in 1789. In 1803 his principal work appeared—the *Treatise on Political Economy*.

Say became the leading advocate of economic liberalism on the Continent. Although his work consisted, for the most part, of a popularization of Smith's doctrines, his logical exposition and lucid writing gave the *Treatise* great popularity and wide circulation. His tripartite division of questions of political economy into questions of production, distribution, and consumption was followed by writers throughout the nineteenth century. With his famous "law of gluts," Say tried to demonstrate that in a truly free market overproduction was impossible. If gluts did occur (and Say recognized that they did), he told how they could be avoided in the future.

Because Say's free trade views were displeasing to Napoleon, he was dismissed from the post of Tribune to which he had been elected in 1799. He built a spinning mill and retired from public life to devote himself to industry and to the revision of his *Treatise*, the second edition of which appeared in 1814. He was sent by Napoleon's government to study economic conditions in England that same year, and returned to publish his tract, *England and the English*. In 1819 a chair of industrial economy was founded for him at the Conservatoire des Arts et Métiers, and in 1830 he was appointed professor of political economy at the Collège de France. During this period (1828–30) he published his *Complete Course in Political Economy*. Say's writings and lectures served to popularize the cause of economic liberalism in England as well as on the Continent; James Mill had the greatest respect for his work and John Stuart Mill praises him warmly in his *Autobiography*.

Say died in Paris on November 15, 1832.

The famous passages on the "law of gluts" printed below are taken from the American edition of *A Treatise on Political Economy* (Philadelphia, 1848).

A TREATISE ON POLITICAL ECONOMY

CHAPTER XV: OF THE DEMAND OR MARKET FOR PRODUCTS

It is common to hear adventurers in the different channels of industry assert, that their difficulty lies not in the production, but in the disposal of commodities; that products would always be abundant, if there were but a ready demand, or market for them. When the demand for their commodities is slow, difficult, and productive of little advantage, they pronounce money to be scarce; the grand object of their desire is, a consumption brisk enough to quicken sales and keep up prices. But ask them what peculiar causes and circumstances facilitate the demand for their products, and you will soon perceive that most of them have extremely vague notions of these matters; that their observation of facts is imperfect, and their explanation still more so; that they treat doubtful points as matter of certainty, often pray for what is directly opposite to their interests, and importunately solicit from authority a protection of the most mischievous tendency.

To enable us to form clear and correct practical notions in regard to markets for the products of industry, we must carefully analyse the best established and most certain facts, and apply to them the inferences we have already deduced from a similar way of proceeding; and thus perhaps we may arrive at new and important truths, that may serve to enlighten the views of the agents of industry, and to give confidence to the measures of governments anxious to afford them encouragement.

A man who applies his labour to the investing of objects with value by the creation of utility of some sort, cannot expect such a value to be appreciated and paid for, unless where other men have the means of purchasing it. Now, of what do these means consist? Of other values of other products, likewise the fruits of industry, capital, and land. Which leads us to a conclusion that may at first sight appear paradoxical, namely, that it is production which opens a demand for products.

Should a tradesman say, "I do not want other products for my woollens, I want money," there could be little difficulty in convincing him that his customers could not pay him in money, without having first procured it by the sale of some other commodities of their own. "Yonder farmer," he may be told, "will buy your woollens, if his crops be good, and will buy more or less according to their abundance or scantiness; he can buy none at all, if his crops fail altogether. Neither can you buy his wool nor his corn yourself, unless you contrive to get woollens or some other article to buy withal. You say, you only want money; I say, you want other commodities, and not money. For what, in point of fact, do you want the money? Is it not for the purchase of raw materials or stock for your trade, or victuals for your support?[1] Wherefore, it is products that you want,

---

[1] Even when money is obtained with a view to hoard or bury it, the ultimate object is always to employ it in a purchase of some kind. The heir of the lucky finder uses it in that way, if the miser does not; for money has no other use than to buy with.

and not money. The silver coin you will have received on the sale of your own products, and given in the purchase of those of other people, will the next moment execute the same office between other contracting parties, and so from one to another to infinity; just as a public vehicle successively transports objects one after another. If you cannot find a ready sale for your commodity, will you say, it is merely for want of a vehicle to transport it? For, after all, money is but the agent of the transfer of values. Its whole utility has consisted in conveying to your hands the value of the commodities, which your customer has sold, for the purpose of buying again from you; and the very next purchase you make, it will again convey to a third person the value of the products you may have sold to others. So that you will have bought, and everybody must buy, the objects of want or desire, each with the value of his respective products transformed into money for the moment only. Otherwise, how could it be possible that there should now be bought and sold in France five or six times as many commodities, as in the miserable reign of Charles VI? Is it not obvious, that five or six times as many commodities must have been produced, and that they must have served to purchase one or the other?

Thus, to say that sales are dull, owing to the scarcity of money, is to mistake the means for the cause; an error that proceeds from the circumstance, that almost all produce is in the first instance exchanged for money before it is ultimately converted into other produce: and the commodity, which recurs so repeatedly in use, appears to vulgar apprehensions the most important of commodities, and the end and object of all transactions, whereas it is only the medium. Sales cannot be said to be dull because money is scarce, but because other products are so. There is always money enough to conduct the circulation and mutual interchange of other values, when those values really exist. Should the increase of traffic require more money to facilitate it, the want is easily supplied, and is a strong indication of prosperity—a proof that a great abundance of values has been created, which it is wished to exchange for other values. In such cases, merchants know well enough how to find substitutes for the product serving as the medium of exchange or money: and money itself soon pours in, for this reason, that all produce naturally gravitates to that place where it is most in demand. It is a good sign when the business is too great for the money; just in the same way as it is a good sign when the goods are too plentiful for the warehouses.

When a superabundant article can find no vent, the scarcity of money has so little to do with the obstruction of its sale, that the sellers would gladly receive its value in goods for their own consumption at the current price of the day: they would not ask for money, or have any occasion for that product, since the only use they could make of it would be to convert it forthwith into articles of their own consumption.[2]

This observation is applicable to all cases, where there is a supply of commodities or of services in the market. They will universally find the most extensive demand in those places, where the most of values are produced; because in no other places are the sole means of purchase created, that is, values. Money performs but a momentary function in this double exchange; and when the transaction is finally closed, it will always be found, that one kind of commodity has been exchanged for another.

It is worth while to remark, that a product is no sooner created, than it, from that instant, affords a market for other products to the full extent of its own value. When the producer has put the finishing hand to his product, he is most anxious to sell it immediately, lest its value should diminish in his hands. Nor is he less anxious to dispose of the money he may get for it; for the value of money is also perishable. But the only way of getting rid of money is in the purchase of some product or other. Thus, the mere circumstance of the creation of one product immediately opens a vent for other products.

For this reason, a good harvest is favourable, not only to the agriculturist, but likewise to the dealers in all commodities generally. The greater the crop, the larger are the purchases of the growers. A bad harvest, on the contrary, hurts the sale of commodities at large. And so it is also with the products of manufacture and commerce. The success of one branch of commerce supplies more ample means of purchase, and consequently opens a market for the products of all the other branches; on the other hand the stagnation of one channel of manufacture, or of commerce, is felt in all the rest.

But it may be asked, if this be so, how does it happen, that there is at times so great a glut of commodities in the market, and so much difficulty in finding a vent for them? Why cannot one of these superabundant commodities be exchanged for another? I answer that the glut of a particular commodity arises from its having outrun the total demand for it in one or two ways; either because it has been produced in excessive abundance, or because the production of other commodities has fallen short.

---

[2] I speak here of their aggregate consumption, whether unproductive and designed to satisfy the personal wants of themselves and their families, or expended in the sustenance of reproductive industry. The woollen or cotten manufacturer operates a two-fold consumption of wool and cotton: 1. For his personal wear. 2. For the supply of his manufacture; but, be the purpose of his consumption what it may, whether personal gratification or reproduction, he must needs buy what he consumes with what he produces.

It is because the production of some commodities has declined, that other commodities are superabundant. To use a more hackneyed phrase, people have bought less, because they have made less profit; and they have made less profit for one or two causes; either they have found difficulties in the employment of their productive means, or these means have themselves been deficient.

It is observable, moreover, that precisely at the same time that one commodity makes a loss, another commodity is making excessive profit. And, since such profits must operate as a powerful stimulus to the cultivation of that particular kind of products, there must needs be some violent means, or some extraordinary cause, a political or natural convulsion, or the avarice or ignorance of authority, to perpetuate this scarcity on the one hand, and consequent glut on the other. No sooner is the cause of this political disease removed, than the means of production feel a natural impulse towards the vacant channels, the replenishment of which restores activity to all the others. One kind of production would seldom outstrip every other, and its products be disproportionately cheapened, were production left entirely free.[3]

[3] These considerations have hitherto been almost wholly overlooked, though forming the basis of correct conclusions in matters of commerce, and of its regulation by the national authority. The right course where it has, by good luck, been pursued, appears to have been selected by accident, or, at most, by a confused idea of its propriety, without either self-conviction, or the ability to convince other people.

Sismondi, who seems not to have very well understood the principles laid down in this and the three first chapters of Book II, of this work, instances the immense quantity of manufactured products with which England has of late inundated the markets of other nations, as a proof, that it is impossible for industry to be too productive. (*Nouv. Prin.* liv, iv, c, 4.) But the glut thus occasioned proves nothing more than the feebleness of production in those countries that have been thus glutted with English manufactures. Did Brazil produce wherewithal to purchase the English goods exported thither, those goods would not glut her market. Were England to admit the import of the products of the United States, she would find a better market for her own in those States. The English government, by the exorbitance of its taxation upon import and consumption, virtually interdicts to its subjects many kinds of importation, thus obliging the merchant to offer to foreign countries a higher price for those articles, whose import is practicable, as sugar, coffee, gold, silver, &c. for the price of the precious metals to them is enhanced by the low price of their commodities, which accounts for the ruinous returns of their commerce.

I would not be understood to maintain in this chapter, that one product cannot be raised in too great abundance, in relation to all others; but merely that nothing is more favourable to the demand of one product, than the supply of another; that the import of English manufactures into Brazil would cease to be excessive and be rapidly absorbed, did Brazil produce on her side returns sufficiently ample; to which end it would be necessary that the legislative bodies of either country should consent, the one to free production, the other to free importation. In Brazil, every thing is grasped by monopoly, and property is not exempt from the invasion of the government. In England, the heavy duties are a serious obstruction to the foreign commerce of the nation, inasmuch as they circumscribe the choice of returns. I happen myself to know of a most valuable and scientific collection of natural history, which could not be imported from Brazil into England by reason of the exorbitant duties.

Should a producer imagine, that many other classes, yielding no material products, are his customers and consumers equally with the classes that raise themselves a product of their own; as, for example, public functionaries, physicians, lawyers, churchmen, &c., and thence infer, that there is a class of demand other than that of the actual producers, he would but expose the shallowness and superficiality of his ideas. A priest goes to a shop to buy a gown or a surplice; he takes the value, that is to make the purchase, in the form of money. Whence had he that money? From some tax-gatherer who has taken it from a tax-payer. But whence did this latter derive it? From the value he has himself produced. This value, first produced by the tax-payer, and afterwards turned into money, and given to the priest for his salary, has enabled him to make the purchase. The priest stands in the place of the producer, who might himself have laid the value of his product on his own account, in the purchase, perhaps, not of a gown or surplice, but of some other more serviceable product. The consumption of the particular product, the gown or surplice, has but supplanted that of some other product. It is quite impossible that the purchase of one product can be affected, otherwise than by the value of another.[4]

From this important truth may be deduced the following important conclusions:—

1. That, in every community the more numerous are the producers, and the more various their productions, the more prompt, numerous, and extensive are the markets for those productions; and, by a natural consequence, the more profitable are they to the producers; for price rises with the demand. But this advantage is to be derived from real production alone, and not from a forced circulation of products; for a value once created is not augmented in its passage from one hand to another, nor by being seized and expended by the government, instead of by an individual. The man, that lives upon the productions of other people, originates no demand for those productions; he merely puts himself in the place of the producer, to the great injury of production, as we shall presently see.

2. That each individual is interested in the general prosperity of all, and that the success of one branch of industry promotes that of all the others. In fact, whatever profession or line of business a man may devote himself to, he is the better paid and the more readily finds employment,

---

[4] The capitalist, in spending the interest of his capital, spends his portion of the products raised by the employment of that capital. . . . Should he ever spend the principal, still he consumes products only; for capital consists of products, devoted indeed to reproductive, but susceptible of unproductive consumption; to which it is in fact consigned whenever it is wasted or dilapidated.

in proportion as he sees others thriving equally around him. A man of talent, that scarcely vegetates in a retrograde state of society, would find a thousand ways of turning his faculties to account in a thriving community that could afford to employ and reward his ability. A merchant established in a rich and populous town, sells to a much larger amount than one who sets up in a poor district, with a population sunk in indolence and apathy. What could an active manufacturer, or an intelligent merchant, do in a small deserted and semibarbarous town in a remote corner of Poland or Westphalia? Though in no fear of a competitor, he could sell but little, because little was produced; whilst at Paris, Amsterdam, or London, in spite of the competition of a hundred dealers in his own line, he might do business on the largest scale. The reason is obvious: he is surrounded with people who produce largely in an infinity of ways, and who make purchases, each with his respective products, that is to say, with the money arising from the sale of what he may have produced.

This is the true source of the gains made by the towns' people out of the country people, and again by the latter out of the former; both of them have wherewith to buy more largely, the more amply they themselves produce. A city, standing in the centre of a rich surrounding country, feels no want of rich and numerous customers; and on the other hand, the vicinity of an opulent city gives additional value to the produce of the country. The division of nations into agricultural, manufacturing, and commercial, is idle enough. For the success of a people in agriculture is a stimulus to its manufacturing and commercial prosperity; and the flourishing condition of its manufacture and commerce reflects a benefit upon its agriculture also.

The position of a nation, in respect of its neighbours, is analogous to the relation of one of its provinces to the others, or of the country to the town; it has an interest in their prosperity, being sure to profit by their opulence. The government of the United States, therefore, acted most wisely, in their attempt, about the year 1802, to civilize their savage neighbours, the Creek Indians. The design was to introduce habits of industry amongst them, and make them producers capable of carrying on a barter trade with the States of the Union; for there is nothing to be got by dealing with a people that have nothing to pay. It is useful and honourable to mankind, that one nation among so many should conduct itself uniformly upon liberal principles. The brilliant results of this enlightened policy will demonstrate, that the systems and theories really destructive and fallacious, are the exclusive and jealous maxims acted upon by the old European governments, and by them most impudently styled *practical truths,* for no other reason, as it would seem, than because they have the misfortune to put them in practice. The United States will have the honour of proving experimentally, that true policy goes hand-in-hand with moderation and humanity.

3. From this fruitful principle, we may draw this further conclusion, that it is no injury to the internal or national industry and production to buy and import commodities from abroad; for nothing can be bought from strangers, except with native products, which find a vent in the external traffic. Should it be objected, that this foreign produce may have been bought with specie, I answer, specie is not always a native product, but must have been bought itself with the products of native industry; so that, whether the foreign articles be paid for in specie or in home products, the vent for national industry is the same in both cases.

4. The same principle leads to the conclusion, that the encouragement of mere consumption is no benefit to commerce; for the difficulty lies in supplying the means, not in stimulating the desire of consumption; and we have seen that production alone, furnishes those means. Thus, it is the aim of good government to stimulate production, of bad government to encourage consumption.

For the same reason that the creation of a new product is the opening of a new market for other products, the consumption or destruction of a product is the stoppage of a vent for them. This is no evil where the end of the product has been answered by its destruction, which end is the satisfying of some human want, or the creation of some new product designed for such a satisfaction. Indeed, if the nation be in a thriving condition, the gross national re-production exceeds the gross consumption. The consumed products have fulfilled their office, as it is natural and fitting they should; the consumption, however, has not opened a new market, but just the reverse.[5]

Having once arrived at the clear conviction, that the general demand for products is brisk in proportion to the activity of production, we need not trouble ourselves much to inquire towards what channel of industry production may be most advantageously directed. The products created give rise to various degrees of demand, according to the wants, the manners, the comparative capital, industry, and natural resources of each country; the article most in request, owing to the competition of buyers, yields the

---

[5] If the barren consumption of a product be of itself adverse to reproduction, and a diminution *pro tanto* of the existing demand or vent for produce, how shall we designate that degree of insanity, which would induce a government deliberately to burn and destroy the imports of foreign products, and thus to annihilate the sole advantage accruing from unproductive consumption, that is to say the gratification of the wants of the consumer?

best interest of money to the capitalist, the largest profits to the adventurer, and the best wages to the labourer; and the agency of their respective services is naturally attracted by these advantages towards those particular channels.

In a community, city, province, or nation, that produces abundantly, and adds every moment to the sum of its products, almost all the branches of commerce, manufacture, and generally of industry, yield handsome profits, because the demand is great, and because there is always a large quantity of products in the market, ready to bid for new productive services. And, *vice versa,* wherever, by reason of the blunders of the nation or its government, production is stationary, or does not keep pace with consumption, the demand gradually declines, the value of the product is less than the charges of its production; no productive exertion is properly rewarded; profits and wages decrease; the employment of capital becomes less advantageous and more hazardous; it is consumed piecemeal, not through extravagance, but through necessity, and because the sources of profit are dried up.[6] The labouring classes experience a want of work; families before in tolerable circumstances, are more cramped and confined; and those before in difficulties are left altogether destitute. Depopulation, misery, and returning barbarism, occupy the place of abundance and happiness.

Such are the concomitants of declining production, which are only to be remedied by frugality, intelligence, activity, and freedom.

[6] Consumption of this kind gives no encouragement to future production, but devours products already in existence. No additional demand can be created until there be new products raised; there is only an exchange of one product for another. Neither can one branch of industry suffer without affecting the rest.

THE FREE TRADE CONTROVERSY

As soon as the war with Napoleon was over, British merchants looked to see in what foreign markets they could sell the products of the new factories. The continent of Europe could once again buy British goods; and the revolt of the Spanish colonies opened trade with South America. Yet if foreigners were to buy, they must also be allowed to sell in Britain. The Navigation Acts and the import restrictions, and even prohibitions, that had been the occasion for the loss of the American colonies were still in effect. Because they traded with foreign parts and were therefore more directly irked by the restrictions than was any other group, the merchants of London were the first to demand the freeing of imports. On May 8, 1820, they presented a *Petition* to Parliament at a time when the agricultural interests were asking even higher protection for "corn" (that is, wheat and other cereals). The *Petition* was tabled after David Ricardo (1772–1823) advised the gradual adoption of its principles, once capital invested in the protected industries had had sufficient time to find new channels. In 1825 William Huskisson (1770–1830), as President of the Board of Trade, liberalized both the Navigation Acts and the tariff on almost everything but corn. Unfortunately Huskisson was run down at the opening of the Liverpool and Manchester railway, and further progress had to be left to others.

The movement for free trade initiated by the London merchants was soon taken up by the manufacturers and by urban workingmen—indeed by almost everybody except the farmers. After 1825 the agitation centered on the duties paid by imported corn. The controversy was for long conducted more or less on party lines. Whigs urged a low duty or none at all; Tories defended the existing tariff as necessary to the farmer. But the Whigs were not finally converted to repeal until after the foundation of the Anti-Corn Law League (1839). By pamphlets, petitions, and great public meetings, partly financed by factory owners but enlisting many idealists, the League fought steadily for seven years. Among other results, the controversy produced widespread discussion and reexamination of economic and political doctrine.

Beginning in 1838 Charles Villiers made it an annual practice to move in the House of Commons the total repeal of the duties on imported grain. On February 18, 1842, he moved his customary motion in the speech printed below. Sir Robert Peel (1788–1850) the Tory Prime Minister of the day of course resisted, and as expected the motion was defeated 393 to 90, on February 24. Four years later the situation had changed sharply. In October, 1845, the failure of the Irish potato crop compelled Peel to suspend the duties on wheat for Ireland, which in practice meant free grain for England also. Peel was convinced it would be politically impossible to restore the duties, and decided to ask the House of Commons for their formal repeal. In doing so he split the Tory party. The main issue was fought out in the Commons during February, 1846, on a technical motion "that the House go into Committee to consider the Corn Laws," and when this was carried 337 to 240 on February 27 all knew that agricultural protection was doomed. Repeal reached the statute book June 26, 1846.

The *Petition of the Merchants of London* was drawn up by Thomas Tooke (1774-1858), a follower of Ricardo and Huskisson who later acquired a degree of note with his lengthy *History of Prices* (1838). The extracts from the debates of 1842 and 1846 that follow are taken from Hansard's *Parliamentary Debates,* 3d series, Vols. LX and LXXXIII.

༒

PETITION OF THE MERCHANTS OF LONDON (*1820*)

THAT FOREIGN COMMERCE is eminently conducive to the wealth and prosperity of a country, by enabling it to import the commodities for the production of which the soil, climate, capital, and industry of other countries are best calculated, and to export in payment those articles for which its own situation is better adapted.

That freedom from restraint is calculated to give the utmost extension to foreign trade, and the best direction to the capital and industry of the country.

That the maxim of buying in the cheapest market and selling in the dearest, which regulates every merchant in his individual dealings, is strictly applicable as the best rule for the trade of the whole nation.

That a policy founded on these principles would render the commerce of the world an interchange of mutual advantages, and diffuse an increase of wealth and enjoyments among the inhabitants of each state.

That, unfortunately, a policy the very reverse of this has been, and is, more or less, adopted and acted upon by the government of this and of every other country, each trying to exclude the productions of other countries, with the specious and well-meant design of encouraging its own productions; thus inflicting on the bulk of its subjects, who are consumers, the necessity of submitting to privations in the quantity or quality of commodities; and thus rendering what ought to be the source of mutual benefit and harmony among states, a constantly-recurring occasion of jealousy and hostility.

That the prevailing prejudices in favour of the protective or restrictive system may be traced to the erroneous supposition that every importation of foreign commodities occasions a diminution of our own productions to the same extent: whereas it may be clearly shown that, although the particular description of production which could not stand against unrestrained foreign competition would be discouraged, yet as no importation could be continued for any length of time without a corresponding exportation, direct or indirect, there would be an encouragement, for the purpose of that exportation, of some other production to which our situation might be better suited; thus affording at least an equal, and probably a greater, and certainly a more beneficial employment to our own capital and labour.

That, of the numerous protective and prohibitory duties of our commercial code, it may be proved, that, while all operate as a very heavy tax on the community at large, very few are of any ultimate benefit to the classes in whose favour they were originally instituted, and none to the extent of the loss occasioned by them to other classes.

That, among the other evils of the restrictive or protective system, not the least is, that the artificial protection of one branch of industry, or source of protection, against foreign competition, is set up as a ground of claim by other branches for similar protection; so that, if the reasoning upon which these restrictive or prohibitory regulations are founded were followed out consistently, it would not stop short of excluding us from all foreign commerce whatsoever. And the same train of argument, which with corresponding prohibitions and protective duties should exclude us from foreign trade, might be brought forward to justify the re-enactment of restrictions upon the interchange of productions (unconnected with public revenue) among the kingdoms composing the union, or among the counties of the same kingdom.

That an investigation of the effects of the restrictive system, at this time, is peculiarly called for, as it may, in the opinion of your petitioners, lead to a strong presumption that the distress which now so generally prevails is considerably aggravated by that system, and that some relief may be obtained by the earliest practicable removal of such of the restraints as may be shown to be the most injurious to the capital and industry of the community, and to be attended with no compensating benefit to the public revenue.

That a declaration against the anti-commercial principles of our restrictive system is of the more importance at the present juncture, inasmuch as, in several instances of recent occurrence, the merchants and manufacturers in foreign states have assailed their respective governments with applications for further protective or prohibitory duties and regulations, urging the example and authority of this country, against which they are almost exclusively directed, as a sanction for the policy of such measures. And certainly, if the reasoning upon which our restrictions have been defended is worth anything, it will apply in behalf of the regulations of foreign states against us. They insist upon our superiority in capital and machinery, as we do upon their comparative exemption from taxation, and with equal foundation.

That nothing would more tend to counteract the commercial hostility of foreign states than the adoption of a more enlightened and more conciliatory policy on the part of this country.

That although, as a matter of mere diplomacy, it may sometimes answer to hold out the removal of particular prohibitions or high duties, as depending upon corresponding concessions by other states in our favour, it does not follow that we should maintain our restrictions, in cases where the desired concession on their part cannot be obtained. Our restrictions would not be the less prejudicial to our own capital and industry, because other governments persisted in preserving impolitic regulations.

That, upon the whole, the most liberal would prove to be the most politic course on such occasions.

That, independent of the direct benefit to be derived by this country on every occasion of such concession or relaxation, a great incidental object would be gained by the recognition of a sound principle or standard, to which all subsequent arrangements might be referred, and by the salutary influence which a promulgation of such just views by the legislature, and by the nation at large, could not fail to have on the policy of other states.

That in thus declaring, as your petitioners do, their conviction of the impolicy and injustice of the restrictive system, and in desiring every practicable relaxation of it, they have in view only such parts of it as are not connected, or are only subordinately so, with the public revenue. As long as the necessity for the present amount of revenue subsists, your petitioners cannot expect so important a branch of it as the customs to be given up, nor to be materially diminished, unless some substitute, less objectionable, be suggested. But it is against every restrictive regulation of trade not essential to the revenue—against all duties merely protective from foreign competition—and against the excess of such duties as are partly for the purpose of revenue, and partly for that of protection—that the prayer of the present petition is respectfully submitted to the wisdom of parliament.

The petitioners therefore humbly pray that the House will be pleased to take the subject into consideration, and to adopt such measures as may be calculated to give greater freedom to foreign commerce, and thereby to increase the resources of the state.

DEBATES ON THE CORN LAWS (1842, 1846)

HOUSE OF COMMONS, FEBRUARY 18 TO 24, 1842

Mr. *Villiers* [Whig: Wolverhampton] rose and said, he wished to read a petition signed by the chairman of a conference, lately held in London, consisting of delegates from all parts of England, Scotland, and Wales. The petition was as follows:—

"To the Honourable the Commons of Great Britain and Ireland, in Parliament assembled.

"The Petition of the undersigned Peter Alfred Taylor, of the City of London,

"Humbly sheweth, that your petitioner was chairman of a conference held at the Crown and Anchor tavern, Strand, on the 8th, 9th, 10th, 11th, and 12th days of February, 1842, of 720 delegates from all parts of England, Scotland, and Wales, appointed by large numbers of their fellow-subjects, to consider of the total and immediate repeal of the corn and provision laws.

"That the delegates at that meeting were appointed from large towns and extensive districts in which all the principal staple manufactures of the country were carried on—viz. cotton, linen, cloth, hosiery, hardware, cutlery, flax, &c.

"That at that conference the following resolution, expressing a desire to forego all protection for their several manufactures, was unanimously passed:—

"That the deputies present connected with the staple manufactures of the country, whilst they demand the removal of all restrictions upon the importation of corn and provisions, declare their willingness to aid in the abolition of all duties imposed for their own protection.

"That this resolution was not passed without previous thought and deep consideration, the same resolution having been passed at large meetings held in the immediate towns and districts where the several branches of manufacture are extensively in operation, viz., at Manchester, at a meeting of those engaged in the cotton trade of Lancashire; at Leeds, by those engaged in the clothing trade of Yorkshire; at Bath, for the West of England clothing trade; at Derby, for the hosiery and other manufactures of the midland counties; at Birmingham, for the hardware of Staffordshire and Warwickshire; at Sheffield, for cutlery and plated ware; at Dundee, for the flax and linen trade.

"That as all the principal branches of manufacturing industrial employment and capital have thus expressed their desire to give up all legislative protection whatever, your petitioner prays your honourable House that all classes of her Majesty's subjects be placed upon the same footing, and that the trade in corn and provisions be left free and open, as well as in all the productions of manufacturing industry.

"P. A. TAYLOR."

After reading the petition, Mr. *Villiers* said, that he trusted that that petition would be considered as no inappropriate introduction to the motion of which he had given notice—a motion also which, whatever had been said with respect to the illogical order in which it was now submitted to the House, was brought forward at a moment that he could only consider as favourable to it, following as it did the discussion in which the greatest ability and ingenuity had been displayed on both sides of the House, in manifesting the evils and difficulties which belonged both to the project proposed by the present Government, and that which was proposed by their predecessors, thus rendering the motion he was about to submit, somewhat in place, for whatever arguments might be urged against it, it was clear of those difficulties and those objections which had been urged against the other measures; he therefore now rose, in pursuance of his notice, to ask the House to condemn *in toto,* and to abolish for ever that law which they were then in committee to consider—a law which had for its avowed purpose to raise the price by limiting the amount of human subsistence —a law which, by the admission of a distinguished Member of the Government, had the effect of raising the price of food, of raising the rate of rent, but not of raising the wages of labour, a law which he must consider, inasmuch as it had those purposes and objects in view, under whatever impression it might have been passed, erroneous if they pleased, or designedly bad as many thought—could only exist in gross and open violation of every principle that ought to regulate the economy and policy of any state, and he would not yet despair of persuading that House of the prudence and importance of abolishing, never to re-enact, such a law.

The Marquess of *Granby* [1] [Tory; Stamford] said it was impossible for an Englishman to consider the distress which prevailed in the manufacturing districts, without most fully and deeply sympathising with it, but he did think, that in proportion to the extent and depth of that sympathy, it was the duty of the House to take care, that by repealing the Corn-laws, they did not increase that distress, by driving the agriculturist to seek for the means of a scanty support in the great manufacturing towns. It had been said, that in the repeal of the Corn-laws, the remedy for that distress would be found. He did not think so. The natural consequence of cheaper food would be a fall in the rate of wages. In all the countries of Europe cheap wages were the consequences of cheap food. Mr. M'Culloch stated, that in Bengal, where the wages of labour were governed by the cost of the food consumed by the labourer, and the labourer was able to subsist on the merest trifle, the consequence was, that the rate of wages in common employments was $2\frac{1}{2}d$. a day. He thought that this was sufficient evidence that cheap food was not synonymous with plenty of it. He thought therefore, that the repeal of the Corn-laws would not produce the good effects which hon. Gentlemen opposite seemed to expect.

[1] [Eldest surviving son of the 5th Duke of Rutland, to whose title he succeeded in 1857 as 6th Duke.]

Mr. *Escott* [Tory; Winchester] said . . . that man must be a madman, or something worse, who would attack the principle of a law which has not only answered its purpose better than any other principle which has ever been tried, but under which the owners and occupiers of lands have been taught by this House and the Legislature to believe themselves safe and secure. Six Parliaments have maintained this principle. Talk of public faith indeed! here is the faith of Parliament pledged to the landed property of England—pledged not indeed to particular enactments and clerical details of scales and figures— who could imagine such a folly?—but pledged to the principle of protection— protection without prohibition; but still protection to the home grower. And under this solemn sanction and security, and relying on this faith of Parliament, have they purchased, taken leases, made devises and settlements, laid out vast sums in improvements and expensive systems; married, made plans in life, educated and provided for children in business, and whom they fondly thought were safe under the shelter of that protection beneath which their fathers rested. Is the hon. Gentleman prepared for a system of treachery and confiscation? I know he is not; but I know also that his motion, if carried, would be equivalent to such a system. . . .

Mr. *Cobden* [Whig; Stockport]: . . . I want to know what you will do with the hard-working classes of the community, the labouring artisans, if the price of bread is to be kept up by Act of Parliament. Will you give them a law to keep up the rate of their wages? You will say that you cannot keep up the rate of wages; but that is no reason you should pass a law to mulct the working man one third of the loaf he earns. I know well the way in which the petitions of the hand-loom weavers were received in this House. "Poor, ignorant men," you said, "they know not what they ask, they are not political economists, they do not know that the price of labour, like other commodities, finds its own level by the ordinary law of supply and demand. We can do nothing for them." But I ask, then, why do you pass a law to keep up the price of corn, and at the same time say you cannot pass a law to keep up the price of the poor man's labour? . . . Having patiently waited for twenty-five years, I think we are entitled at last to a clear explanation of the pretext upon which you tax the food of the people for the acknowledged benefit of the landowners. The right hon. Baronet [Sir Robert Peel] tells us we must not be dependent upon foreigners for our supply, or that that dependence must be supplementary, that certain years produce enough of corn for the demand, and that we must legislate for the introduction of corn only when it is wanted. Granted. On that point the right hon. Baronet and I are perfectly agreed. Let us only legislate, if you please, for the introduction of corn, when it is wanted. Exclude it as much as you please when it is not wanted. But all I supplicate for on the part of the starving people is, that they and not you, shall be the judges of when corn is wanted. By what right do they pretend to gauge the appetites and admeasure the wants of millions of people? Why, there is no despotism that ever dreamed of doing any thing so monstrous as this; yet you sit here, and presume to judge when people want food, dole out your supply when you condescend to think they want it, and stop it when you choose to consider that they have had enough. Are you in a position to judge of the wants of artisans, of hand-loom weavers? you, who never knew the want of a meal in your lives, do you presume to know when the people want bread? . . . It is not merely an extension of the pension list to the landed proprietors, as was said by the *Times* some years ago, when that paper stigmatised the Corn-laws as an extension of the pension list to the whole of the landed aristocracy; it is the worst kind of pauperism; it is the aristocracy submitting to be fed at the expense of the poorest of the poor. If this is to be so, if we are to bow our necks to a landed oligarchy, let things be as they were in ancient Venice; let the nobles inscribe their names in a golden book, and draw their money direct from the Exchequer. It would be better for the people than to suffer the aristocracy to circumscribe our trade, destroy our manufactures, and draw the money from the pockets of the poor by indirect and insidious means. Such a course would be more easy for us, and more honest for you. But have the hon. Gentlemen who maintain a system like this, considered that the people of this country are beginning to understand it a little better than they did? And do they think that the people, with a better understanding of the subject, will allow one class not only to tax the rest of the community for their own exclusive advantage, but to be living in a state of splendour upon means obtained by indirect taxation from the pockets of the poor? . . .

HOUSE OF COMMONS, FEBRUARY 9 TO 27, 1846

Sir *Robert Peel* [Tory; Tamworth; Prime Minister]: . . . This night is to decide between the policy of continued relaxation of restriction, or the return to restraint and prohibition. This night you will select the motto which is to indicate the commercial policy of England. Shall it be "advance" or "recede"? Which is the fitter motto for this great Empire? Survey our position, consider the advantage which God and nature have given us, and the destiny for which we are intended. We stand on the confines of Western Europe, the chief connecting link between the old world and the new. The discoveries of science, the improvement of navigation, have brought us within ten days of St. Petersburgh, and will soon bring us within ten days of New York. We have an extent of coast greater in proportion to our population and the area of our land than any other great nation, securing to us maritime strength and superiority. Iron and coal, the sinews of manufacture, give us advantages over every rival in the great competition of industry. Our capital far exceeds that which they can command. In ingenuity—in skill—in energy—we are inferior to none. Our national character, the free institutions under which we live, the liberty of thought and action, an unshackled press, spreading the knowledge of every discovery and of every advance in science—combine with our natural and physical advantages to place us at the head of those nations which profit by the free interchange of their products. And is this the country to shrink from competition? Is this the country to adopt a retrograde policy? Is this the country which can only flourish in the sickly artificial atmosphere of prohibition? Is this the country to stand shivering on the brink of exposure to the healthful breezes of competition?

Choose your motto. "Advance" or "Recede." Many countries are watching with anxiety the selection you may make. Determine for "Advance," and it will be the watchword which will animate and encourage in every state the friends of liberal commercial policy. Sardinia has taken the lead. Naples is relaxing her protective duties and favouring British produce. Prussia is shaken in her adherence to restriction. The Government of France will be strengthened; and, backed by the intelligence of the reflecting, and by conviction of the real welfare of the great body of the community, will perhaps ultimately prevail over the self-interest of the commercial and manufacturing aristocracy which now predominates in her Chambers. Can you doubt that the United States will soon relax her hostile Tariff, and that the friends of a freer commercial intercourse—the friends of peace between the two countries—will hail with satisfaction the example of England?

This night, then—if on this night the debate shall close—you will have to decide what are the principles by which your commercial policy is to be regulated. Most earnestly, from a deep conviction, founded not upon the limited experience of three years alone, but upon the experience of the results of every relaxation of restriction and prohibition, I counsel you to set the example of liberality to other countries. Act thus, and it will be in perfect consistency with the course you have hitherto taken. Act thus, and you will provide an additional guarantee for the continued contentment, and happiness, and well-being of the great body of the people. Act thus, and you will have done whatever human sagacity can do for the promotion of commercial prosperity.

You may fail. Your precautions may be unavailing. They may give no certain assurance that mercantile and manufacturing prosperity will continue without interruption. It seems to be incident to great prosperity that there shall be a reverse—that the time of depression shall follow the season of excitement and success. That time of depression must perhaps return; and its return may be coincident with scarcity caused by unfavourable seasons. Gloomy winters, like those of 1841 and 1842, may again set in. Are those winters effaced from your memory? From mine they never can be. Surely you cannot have forgotten with what earnestness and sincerity you re-echoed the deep feelings of a gracious Queen, when at the opening and at the close of each Session, She expressed the warmest sympathy with the sufferings of Her people, and the warmest admiration of their heroic fortitude.

These sad times may recur. "The years of plenteousness may have ended," and "the years of dearth may have come;" and again you may have to offer the unavailing expressions of sympathy, and the urgent exhortations to patient resignation.

Commune with your own hearts and answer me this question: will your assurances of sympathy be less consolatory—will your exhortations to patience be less impressive—if, with your willing consent, the Corn Laws shall have then ceased to exist? Will it be no satisfaction to you to reflect, that by your own act, you have been relieved from the grievous responsibility of regulating the supply of food? Will you not then cherish with delight the reflection that, in this the present hour of comparative prosperity, yielding to no clamour, impelled by no fear—except, indeed, that provident fear, which is the mother of safety—you had anticipated the evil day, and, long before its advent, had trampled on every impediment to the free circulation of the Creator's bounty?

When you are again exhorting a suffering people to fortitude under their privations, when you are telling them, "These are the chastenings of an all-wise and merciful Providence, sent for some inscrutable but just and beneficent purpose—it may be, to humble our pride, or to punish our unfaithfulness, or to impress us with the sense of our own nothingness and dependence on His mercy;" when you are thus addressing your suffering fellow subjects, and encouraging them to bear without repining the dispensations of Providence, may God grant that by your decision of this night you may have laid in store for yourselves the consolation of reflecting that such calamities are, in truth, the dispensations of Providence—that they have not been caused, they have not been aggravated by laws of man restricting, in the hour of scarcity, the supply of food!

Mr. *Stafford O'Brien* [Tory; Northamptonshire, North] said that, even if he admitted the truth of all the doctrines upon which political economists were agreed they must prove far more before he could assent to the proposed measure of the Government. Hon. Gentlemen opposite were too apt—nay, indeed, the literature of the day, and the habits of thought which prevailed among them all—were too apt to confound political economy with the science of legislation. He had always understood political economy to be the science which treated of the amassing and of the distribution of wealth. Now, if the accumulation and the distribution of wealth constituted the whole science of legislation, the terms would be—and might be fairly used as—synonymous. But the accumulation and distribution of wealth was one amongst the many elements of which the science of legislation consisted. And if hon. Gentlemen opposite, or the Government, could prove that wealth—in the modern sense of the word, in which it meant money—not in the old sense, in which it meant prosperity—would surely follow from a certain course, they would have established, not the whole, but not even a half of the case they were now setting up. He would take the case of protection to British industry generally. It was said that "labour was the property of the poor man." That was the dogma given out by the political economists, and supported by the right hon. Baronet [Sir Robert Peel] and Her Majesty's Government. But, addressing such language to the poor labourers of England, unless he sadly misunderstood the consequences of such teaching, they must not stop there. They must not tell the poor man that his property was not to be protected. If they did tell the poor man so, would he not consider this—that whilst they were blessed with leisure, possessed of wealth, and armed with power, the property of the poor man must protect itself? He would not say that such would be the reflection or consideration of all; but that would be the effect upon the country at large. This question of protection, too, came most unfortunately from a country which boasted of employing the labour of children from seven or eight years old. Having found, however, that interference with labour was difficult, were they prepared to abandon their labouring fellow countrymen, and watch in passive silence whether the Englishmen or the foreigner triumphed? He did not speak of the shopkeeper or the person who did possess some property. His interest was soon to become a convert to that favourite maxim of buying in the cheapest and selling in the dearest market; but he would take the case of certain of the duties proposed to be reduced by the measure of the right hon. Baronet. They would not better illustrate his argument than any other case of a similar character, but they would be fresh in the remembrance of the House. Supposing, then, that acting upon that axiom of buying in the cheapest and selling in the dearest market, he, a wealthy man in England, furnished his house with paper-hangings from Paris. Supposing that he travelled in a continental carriage, that he purchased all his hardware from Germany; supposing all this, when he looked out of the window of his gaudy house, or his foreign-built carriage, what would he see? A vast multitude of unemployed starving

Englishmen. And what would they say to him? "We are poor English paper-stainers; we are Birmingham hardwaremen; our trade has been taken away from us—what are we to do?" And what could be his reply? "My good fellows, I have done the best I could to make you idle—to take all employment out of your hands—to leave you starving; but, believe me, I did it not from a bad motive." What consolation would it afford them to be told, that all this happened; because, on the 27th of January, 1846, Sir R. Peel propounded a doctrine in which all political economists were agreed, that labour might protect itself, and that we must buy in the cheapest market and sell in the dearest; and that the Legislature in abolishing protection was actuated by no consideration of self-interest, but solely with a desire that the great truths of political economy should have fair play? Would any one venture to say, that the feelings in the hearts of these poor people would be the feelings of love, reverence, or attachment to our institutions, or that they could feel that they were living under a paternal government? But it was not only the widespread poverty which such a measure would produce which they had to consider. Let them not forget the amount of alienation and disaffection which would be the result. Equal neglect was not impartial kindness; and instead of propounding this hard clumsy dogma that the property of the poor might be left to protect itself, there never was a time when it behoved them more to reflect on the course pursued by their ancestors, sometimes wisely and sometimes unwisely, but always with the view of doing their best to protect the property of the poor from foreign competition, from domestic tyranny, from the oppression of the rich, and from their own madness.

Mr. *Scrope* [Whig; Stroud]: . . . I take the speech of the hon. Member for Northamptonshire [Mr. O'Brien], who may be considered to represent the pure protectionists, from whom, therefore, if from any one, as the ablest speaker of that class, we might expect to hear the best defence that can be urged of the principle of the law. Now what was the real argument contained in that speech, under cover, I own, of very able and feeling oratory? I appeal to the recollection of the House if the main point of that speech was not an attack on what the hon. Member called a stern dogma of a cold and hard political economy, viz., that "we should buy as cheap and sell as dear as we can"—a maxim which I would venture to call, not a dogma of political economy, but the very first principle of all commerce, the A B C of trade. But perhaps the hon. Member despises trade and its shopkeeping maxims. Perhaps he thinks a trading community should act on the opposite principle of selling cheap and buying dear. But I am much mistaken if his friends and clients, the tenant-farmers, act on any other than this vulgar and cruel mercantile principle themselves. I have always understood that they were tolerably hard bargainers, at fair and market, for a profit, if any could be made, on their sales and purchases. They would not like to be compelled to act on the opposite principle of buying dear and selling cheap. No; what they really mean, and the hon. Member, too, in railing against the principle of buying cheap and selling dear, is, that the manufacturers should sell cheap to them, the farmers, while they sell dear to the manufacturers; and *vice versa,* that the manufacturers should buy dear of the farmers, and the farmers buy cheap of the manufacturers; and this is in fact the object aimed at by the Corn Laws. But the hon. Member illustrated the cruelty of this flagitious dogma of a cold political economy by pathetic pictures, which were not without their effect on the feelings of the House. The first was that of a crowd of paper-stainers and silk weavers, thrown out of employment by the unpatriotic and antinational preference of French silks and paper-hangings to those of British manufacture. Every picture has its reverse: and to the hon. Member's picture of an ideal scene resulting from the operation of our mercantile principle, I will oppose a picture of the result of his protective principle, not drawn from the imagination, but one of the real scenes which did occur, in hundreds of instances, but a few years ago, in Paisley, in Stockport, in Manchester, and other places. Let the hon. Member imagine a manufacturer at that time, his warehouses choked with goods which he could not dispose of, his foreign correspondents writing to him that the foreign market was equally glutted; imagine that, after putting his workpeople first on low wages, next on half work, he finally finds himself obliged to discharge them altogether, and to shut up his mill. They crowd in hundreds round him—a melancholy spectacle—men, women, and children, imploring him for work and food. What is his answer? "My friends, my heart bleeds for you. I employed you so long as I possessed the means of doing so; but those means can only be furnished by the sale of the produce of your labour. All my capital lies locked up in yonder warehouses, and I have exhausted my credit likewise. The foreigner can buy no more of the goods you make, because our laws prohibit his paying for them in the only thing he has to sell—his corn, the very food you want; nay, at this moment, while you are starving, there lie hundreds of thousands of quarters of corn in the Queen's warehouses a few miles off, consignments from foreign merchants, who would be glad to take any goods in exchange for it if the law did not interfere. This law, enacted by landowners for their own supposed interest, prevents your feeding on corn that you do not buy of them. Therefore you must starve, and I must be ruined by this unjust landlords' law." I ask the hon. Member what does he think would be, nay, what are the feelings of crowds of starving men, to whom this language—that of truth, be it observed—is necessarily addressed? The hon. Member does not seem to be aware of the fact that to buy anything from the foreigner we must sell to him something of equal value—that for every quarter of foreign corn, or every piece of foreign silk imported, we must expect to pay for it an equal value of goods the produce of our own manufactures,—and that British or native industry is just as much employed in the one case as in the other; the only difference being (and a great difference it is) that by the free exchange we get more of what we want, or of a better quality, in return for our native industry, than if we attempted to produce it at home. And this is just the benefit which commerce confers. The hon. Member does not seem to be aware that the principle he declaims against as a cold dogma of a stern political economy is the one sole vivifying principle of all commerce—the stimulus to all improvement—the mainspring of civilization—the principle, namely, of obtaining the largest and the best result at the least cost—in other words, to get the most you can of what you want for your money or your labour. . . .

I have placed before the House one form of this argument, and to me a convincing one, to show that whether Corn Laws raise the price of Corn or do not, they are an unjustifiable interference with the freedom of industry. Nor has there been, in my opinion, a single argument of the slightest weight produced in the course of this debate to show that we can be warranted in such interference by any considerations. The onus of proof, if proof there can be, rests upon you who would restrict and fetter the industry of the people. I call on you then no longer to maintain these laws—laws odious in character and questionable in motive. I call on you no longer to interfere between the people and their spontaneous supplies of food—no longer by unwise and unjust laws to prevent the industrious classes of this country from availing themselves of the ample means which God and nature have placed at their disposal for obtaining, by the exercise of their unrivalled skill and energy, an abundant supply of the first necessaries of life.

Mr. *Disraeli* [Tory; Shrewsbury]: . . . I say that it is the first duty of the Minister, and the first interest of the State, to maintain a balance between the two great branches of national industry; that is a principle which has been recognised by all great Ministers for the last two hundred years; and the reasons upon which it rests are so obvious, that it can hardly be necessary to mention them. Why we should maintain that balance between the two great branches of national industry, involves political considerations—social considerations, affecting the happiness, prosperity, and morality of the people, as well as the stability of the State. But I go further; I say that in England we are bound to do more—I repeat what I have repeated before, that in this country there are special reasons why we should not only maintain the balance between the two branches of our national industry, but why we should give a preponderance . . . to the agricultural branch; and the reason is, because in England we have a territorial Constitution. We have thrown upon the land the revenues of the Church, the administration of justice, and the estate of the poor; and this has been done, not to gratify the pride, or pamper the luxury of the proprietors of the land, but because, in a territorial Constitution, you, and those whom you have succeeded, have found the only security for self-government—the only barrier against that centralising system which has taken root in other countries. I have always maintained these opinions: my constituents are not landlords; they are not aristocrats; they are not great capitalists; they are the children of industry and toil; and they believe, first, that their material interests are involved in a system which favours native industry, by insuring at the same time real competition; but they believe also that their social and political interests are involved in a system by which their rights and liberties have been guaranteed; and I agreed with them—I have these old-fashioned notions. I know that we have been told, and by one who on this subject should be the highest authority, that we shall derive from this great struggle, not merely the repeal of the Corn Laws, but the transfer of power from one class to another—to one distinguished for its intelligence and wealth, the manufacturers of England. My conscience assures me that I have not been slow in doing justice to the intelligence of that class; certain I am, that I am not one of those who envy them their wide and deserved prosperity; but I must confess my deep mortification, that in an age of political regeneration, when all social evils are ascribed to the operation of class interests, it should be suggested that we are to be rescued from the alleged power of one class only to sink under the avowed dominion of another. I, for one, if this is to be the end of all our struggles—if this is to be the great result of this enlightened age—I, for one, protest against the ignominious catastrophe. I believe that the monarchy of England, its sovereignty mitigated by the acknowledged authority of the estates of the realm, has its root in the hearts of the people, and is capable of securing the happiness of the nation and the power of the State. But, Sir, if this be a worn-out dream—if, indeed, there is to be a change, I, for one, anxious as I am to maintain the present polity of this country, ready to make as many sacrifices as any man for that object—if there is to be this great change, I, for one, hope, that the foundations of it may be deep, the scheme comprehensive, and that instead of falling under such a thraldom, under the thraldom of Capital—under the thraldom of those, who, while they boast of their intelligence, are more proud of their wealth—if we must find a new force to maintain the ancient throne and immemorial monarchy of England, I, for one, hope, that we may find that novel power in the invigorating energies of an educated and enfranchised people.

FRIEDRICH LIST

THE CLASSICAL DOCTRINE of free trade was an application of the arguments in favor of a free division of labor in the domestic economy to the field of international economic relations. Just as a policy of *laissez faire* within the national economy could be relied upon to bring about the most efficient specialization, so would freedom of international trade lead to an optimum division of labor yielding a maximum of output at a minimum of costs. The foundations for the theory of free trade had been laid by the Physiocrats and Adam Smith. The arguments for free trade found their classical formulation in the famous seventh chapter of Ricardo's *Principles of Political Economy and Taxation,* just before the *Petition of the Merchants of London* translated these arguments into popular language when it pointed out: "that foreign commerce is eminently conducive to the wealth and prosperity of a country, by enabling it to import the commodities for the production of which the soil, climate, capital, and industry of other countries are best calculated and to export in payment those articles for which its own situation is better adapted."

Friedrich List's *The National System of Political Economy* (1841–44) did not undertake to refute the general validity of the classical arguments. List objected only to what he considered the unhistorical and non-political approach of the classical school to the problem of international trade. He felt that by disregarding the political factors of international relations and especially by denying the reality of international conflicts the classical school had vitiated its main conclusions in favor of a system of international trade which no responsible statesman could be expected to put into practice. More specifically, List argued that only the English could afford the luxury of free trade; indeed, at the stage of development England had attained free trade was not a luxury at all, but a policy that was markedly beneficial so far as the English alone were concerned. At the same time, however, it was a policy that made it impossible for the other nations of the world, including America, to develop their productive forces and especially the power to produce manufactured goods. The development of manufacturing in the less advanced countries depended, according to List, upon the adoption of a policy of protectionism designed to insure "infant industries" against competition by low cost imports from Great Britain. He also felt that since the present highly imperfect state of union among the nations of the world can be shattered by war or, as he said, "by the selfish action of individual nations," it would be dangerous to ignore national and political requirements in the formulation of international economic policies. But the policy of protectionism which List advocated did not preclude the possibility of "a final alliance of nations under the rule of law . . . in the form of a confederation."

As part of this general program List campaigned for a German commercial union (*Zollverein*) that would make a single economic unit out of the various petty German states that survived the Napoleonic wars. It was his advocacy of this latter policy that brought him into conflict with the authorities, and in

1825 he was finally forced to flee from his native Württemberg to the United States. In America also he threw himself into the struggle for economic protectionism when the tariff controversy then going on between Great Britain and the United States gave him an opportunity to air his views, and in 1827 there appeared his *Outlines of American Political Economy.*

List played a not unimportant part in the development of an American philosophy of economic nationalism, and he was among the first to apply the experience of the New World to European conditions. The only chapter that was ever published of his projected major work, "The American Economist," he sent to Andrew Jackson, whose friend he was and whom he had supported in the presidential campaign of 1828. List wanted Jackson to send him to a diplomatic post in France from which he believed he could attack English monopoly and promote Franco-American commerce. He received only an unpaid consulship at Leipzig in 1832, which, however, gave him the chance to remain on the Continent and continue his struggle. By 1844 he found German officialdom far more favorably disposed toward his views than it once had been, and the last years of his life were spent in campaigning for a German policy that would combat England's repeal of the Corn Laws. His constant labors undermined his health, however, and he died by his own hand in 1846.

The selection from the Introduction to the *National System* is taken from M. E. Hirst, *The Life of Friedrich List and Selections from His Writings* (New York, Charles Scribner's Sons, 1909.) The selections from the *National System* are taken from the Sampson S. Lloyd translation which appeared in 1885.

THE NATIONAL SYSTEM OF POLITICAL ECONOMY

Introduction

IN NO BRANCH of political economy is there such a divergence of opinions between theorists and practical men as in regard to international commerce and commercial policy. At the same time, there is no question within the scope of this science which is of so much importance, not only for the prosperity and civilization of nations, but also for their independence, power, and continued existence. Poor, weak, and barbarous countries have become, mainly as a result of wise commercial policy, empires abounding in wealth and power, while other countries, for opposite reasons, have sunk from a high level of national importance into insignificance. Nay, in some instances nations have forfeited their independence and political existence mainly on account of a commercial policy which was unfavourable to the development and encouragement of their nationality. In our own days, more than ever before, these questions have awakened an interest far greater than that felt in any other economic problems. For the more rapid the growth of a spirit of industrial invention and improvement, of social and political reform, the wider becomes the gap between stationary and progressive nations, and the more dangerous it is to remain on the further side. If in the past centuries were required for Great Britain to succeed in monopolizing the most important manufacture of those days, the wool industry, later decades were sufficient in the case of the far more important cotton industry, and in our own time a few years' start enabled her to annex the whole linen industry of the Continent.

And at no former date has the world seen a manufacturing and commercial supremacy like that which in our own day, endowed with such immense power, has followed so systematic a policy, and has striven so hard to monopolize all manufactures, all commerce, all shipping, all the chief colonies, all the ocean, and to make the rest of the world, like the Hindus, its serfs in all industrial and commercial relations.

Alarmed at the effects of this policy, nay, rather forced by the convulsions which it produced, we have lately seen a country whose civilization seemed little adapted for manufacturing, we have seen Russia seek her salvation in the system of prohibition so much abhorred by orthodox theory. What has been the result? National prosperity.

On the other hand, North America, which was attaining a high position under protection, was attracted by the promises of the theory, and induced to open her ports again to English goods. What was the fruit of free competition? Convulsion and ruin.

Such experiences are well fitted to awake doubts whether the theory is so infallible as it pretends to be; whether the common practice is so insane as it is depicted by the theory; to arouse fears lest our nationality might be in danger of perishing at last from an error in the theory, like the patient who followed a printed prescription and died of a misprint; and to produce a suspicion that this much-praised theory may be built like the old Greek horse, with vast womb and lofty sides, only to conceal men and weapons and to induce us to pull down our walls of defence with our own hands.

This much at least is certain, that although the great questions of commercial policy have been discussed by the keenest brains of all nations in books and legislative assemblies, yet the gulf between theory and practice which has existed since the time of Quesnay and Smith is not only not filled up, but gapes wider and wider each year. And of what use is a science to us, if it throws no light on the path which practice ought to follow. Is it rational to suppose that the intellect of the one party is so immeasurably great that it can apprehend the nature of things perfectly in all cases, while that of the other party is so weak that it is unable to grasp the truths which its opponents have discovered and brought to light, so that through whole generations it considers manifest errors as truths? Should we not rather suppose that practical men, even if they are as a rule too much inclined to keep to the beaten track, still could not oppose the theory so long and so stubbornly if the theory were not opposed to the nature of things?

In fact, we believe that we can prove the responsibility for the divergence between the theory and practice of commercial policy to rest as much with the theorists as with the practical men. In questions of international trade, political economy must derive its teaching from experience, must adapt its measures to the needs of the present and to the particular circumstances of each nation, without neglecting the claims of the future and of mankind as a whole. Accordingly it founds itself upon philosophy, politics, and history.

Philosophy demands, in the interests of the future and of mankind, an even closer friendship among nations, avoidance of war as far as possible, the establishment and development of international law, the change of what we call the law of nations into the law of federated states, freedom of international intercourse, both in intellectual and material things; and, finally, the alliance of all nations under the rule of law—that is, a universal union.

But politics demands, in the interests of each separate nation, guarantees for its independence and continued existence, special regulations to help its progress in culture, prosperity, and power, to build its society into a perfectly complete and harmoniously developed body politic, self-contained and independent. History, for its part, speaks unmistakably in favour of the claims of the future, since it teaches how the material and moral welfare of mankind has grown at all times with the growth of their political and commercial unity. But it also supports the claims of the present and of nationality when it teaches how nations which have not kept in view primarily the furtherance of their own culture and power have gone to ruin; how unrestricted trade with more advanced nations is certainly an advantage to every nation in the early stages of its development, but how each reaches a point when it can only attain to higher development and an equality with more advanced nationalities through certain restrictions on its international trade. Thus history points out the middle course between the extreme claims of philosophy and politics.

But the practice and theory of political economy in their present forms each takes sides with a faction, the one supporting the special claims of nationality, the other the one-sided demands of cosmopolitanism.

Practice, or, in other words, the so-called mercantile system, commits the great error of maintaining the absolute and universal advantage and necessity of restriction, because it has been advantageous and beneficial to certain nations at certain periods of their development. It does not see that restriction is only the means, and freedom is the end. Looking only at the nation, never at the individual, only at the present, never at the future, it is exclusively political and national in thought, and is devoid of philosophical outlook or cosmopolitan feeling. The ruling theory, on the contrary, founded by Adam Smith on the dreams of Quesnay, has in view only the cosmopolitan claims of the future, indeed of the most distant future. Universal union and absolute freedom of international trade, which at the present time are a cosmopolitan dream only to be realized perhaps after the lapse of centuries, can (according to the theory) be realized at the present time. It does not understand the needs of the present and the meaning of nationality—in fact, it ignores national existence, and with it the principle of national independence. In its exclusive cosmopolitanism, it considers mankind only as a whole, and the welfare of the whole race, not caring for the nation or national welfare, it shudders at the teachings of politics, and condemns theory and practice as mere worthless routine. It only pays attention to history when the latter agrees with its own one-sided view, but ignores or distorts its teaching when it conflicts with the system. Indeed, it is forced even to deny the influence of the English Navigation Acts, the Methuen Treaty, and English commercial policy in general, and to maintain a view entirely contrary to truth—that England has reached wealth and power not by means, but in spite of, its commercial policy.

When we realize the one-sided nature of each system we can no longer wonder that the practice, in spite of serious errors, was unwilling and unable to be reformed by the theory. We understand why the theory did not wish to learn anything from history or experience, from politics or nationality. If this baseless theory is preached in every alley and from every house-top, and with the greatest fervour among those nations whose national existence it most endangers, the reason is to be found in the prevailing tendency of the age towards philanthropic experiments and the solution of philosophical problems.

But for nations as for individuals, there are two efficacious remedies against the illusions of ideology—experience and necessity. If we are not mistaken, all those states which have recently hoped to find their salvation in free trade with the ruling commercial and manufacturing power, are on the point of learning valuable truths by experience.

It is a sheer impossibility that the free states of North America can attain even a mediocre economic position by the maintenance of existing commercial conditions. It is absolutely necessary that they should revert to their earlier tariff. Even if the slave states resist and are supported by the party in power, the force of circumstances must be stronger than party politics. Nay, we fear that cannons will sooner or later cut the gordian knot which the legislature has been unable to untie. America will pay her debt to England in powder and shot, the effective prohibition of war will correct the errors of American tariff legislation, and the conquest of Canada will put a stop for ever to the vast system of contraband foretold by Huskisson.

May we be mistaken! But in case our prophecy should be fulfilled, we wish to lay on the free trade theory the responsibility of this war. Strange irony of Fate, that a theory based on the great idea of perpetual peace should kindle a war between two Powers which, according to the theorists, are absolutely fitted for reciprocal trade! Almost as strange as the result of the philanthropic abolition of the slave trade, in consequence of which thousands of negroes have been sunk in the depths of the sea.

France, in the course of the past fifty years (or, rather, of the past twenty-five years, for the times of the Revolution and the Napoleonic War can hardly be reckoned), in spite of all mistakes, excrescences, and exaggerations, has made a great experiment in the restrictive system. Its success must strike every unbiassed observer. Consistency, however, demands that the theory should deny this success. Since it has already been capable of uttering the desperate assertion (and convincing the world of its truth), that England did not become rich and powerful by means, but in spite of her commercial policy, why should it hesitate to make the less startling statement that the manufactures of France without protection would have been much more flourishing than they are now? . . .

We thus see of what great practical importance the question of international free trade is at present, and how necessary it is that a thorough and unbiassed inquiry should at last be undertaken to see whether and how far theory and practice are guilty of error in this matter. Thus the problem of harmonizing the two might be solved, or, at least, a serious attempt made to solve it. In very truth the author must explain (not from mock modesty, but from a real and deep-rooted mistrust of his powers) that it is only after a mental struggle of many years' standing, after he has a hundred times questioned the correctness of his views and a hundred times found them true, only after he has a hundred times tested the views and principles opposed to his own and a hundred times realized their error, that he has determined to venture the solution of this problem. This is no vain attempt to contradict ancient authorities and to found new theories. If he had been an Englishman he would scarcely have doubted the main principles of Adam Smith's system.

It was the state of his own country which more than twenty years ago roused in him the first doubts in its infallibility. It has been the state of his own country which has induced him since then, in many unsigned articles, and, finally, in longer essays under his own name, to develop views opposed to the prevailing theory. And to-day it is still mainly the interests of Germany which have emboldened him to come forward with this book, although he cannot deny that a personal consideration has also influenced him. This is, the obligation he feels to make clear through a work of some length that he is not entirely unqualified to speak a word on questions of political economy. In direct antagonism to the theory, the author first seeks the lessons of history, deduces from them his fundamental principles, develops them, subjects previous systems to a critical examination, and finally (since his aim throughout is practical) explains the present position of commercial policy. For the sake of clearness, here follows an outline of the main results of his researches and reflections.

Union of individual faculties in pursuit of a common end is the most effective means of obtaining individual happiness. Alone and apart from his fellows the individual is weak and helpless. The greater the number of those to whom he is socially united and the more complete the union, the greater and more complete is the resulting moral and physical welfare of the individual members.

The highest union of individuals realized up to the present under the rule of law is in the State and the nation. The highest imaginable is the union of all mankind. Just as in the State and nation the individual can attain his special end to a much higher extent than when he is isolated, so all nations would attain their ends to a much greater extent if they were united by the rule of law, perpetual peace, and free intercourse. Nature herself gradually urges nations to this highest union, since through varieties of climate, soil, and products she forces them to barter, and through excess of population, capital, and talent to emigrate and found colonies. International trade is one of the mightiest levers of civilization and prosperity, for by the awakening of new wants it incites men to activity and exertion and passes on new ideas, inventions, and faculties from one nation to another.

But at present the union of nations which arises from international trade is still very imperfect, since it can be shattered, or at least weakened, by war, or by the selfish action of individual nations. By war a nation can be robbed of its independence, property, freedom, laws, and constitution, its national character, and, still worse, of the culture and well-being to which it has attained. It can, in a word, be reduced to a state of servitude. By the selfish measures of foreign countries a nation can be hindered or impaired in the completeness of its economic development.

Maintenance, development, and perfecting of national spirit at present is, and must be, a chief object of national endeavour. It is no wrong and selfish aim, but a rational one, in perfect harmony with the true interests of mankind in general. It leads naturally to a final alliance of nations under the rule of law, the universal union, which can only contribute to the well-being of the human race if it is realized in the form of a confederation. A union proceeding from the overwhelming political strength and wealth of a single nation, and thus basing itself upon the subjection and dependence of all other nations, would, on the contrary, result in the destruction of all national characteristics and all international emulation; it is opposed both to the interest and sentiment of nations, since they all feel themselves destined to independence and the attainment of a high level of wealth and political importance. Such a union would only be a repetition of the former attempt by Rome, carried out indeed by means of manufactures and commerce instead of by cold steel as in former times, but none the less leading back to barbarism. The civilization, political development, and strength of nations are mainly dependent on their economic circumstances; and the converse is also true. The more its economy is developed and perfected, the more civilized and powerful is the nation; the higher the level of its civilization and power, the higher the level of its economic development.

In national economic development we must distinguish the following stages: the savage, the pastoral, the agricultural, the agricultural and manufacturing, the agricultural, manufacturing, and commercial. Obviously the nation which, possessing an extensive territory endowed with many natural resources, combines with a large population, agriculture, manufactures, shipping, and home and foreign trade, is incomparably more civilized, politically advanced and powerful than a merely agricultural state. Manufactures are the basis of internal and external trade, of shipping, of improvements in agriculture, and consequently of civilization and political power. Any nation must of necessity attain to universal dominion which succeeded in monopolizing the whole manufacturing power of the world, and in keeping other nations at such a point of economic development that they produced only food and raw materials and carried on merely the most necessary local industries.

Every nation, which attaches any value to its independence and continued existence, must strive to pass with all speed from a lower stage of culture to a higher, and to combine within its own territory agriculture, manufactures, shipping, and commerce. The transition from savagery to the pastoral state, and from the latter to the agricultural state, are best effected by free trade with civilized, that is, manufacturing and commercial nations. The transition from an agricultural community into the class of agricultural, commercial, and manufacturing nations could only take place under free trade if the same process of development occurred simultaneously in all nations destined to manufactures, if nations put no hindrance in the way of one another's economic development, if they did not check one another's progress through war and tariffs. But since individual nations, through specially favourable circumstances, gained an advantage over others in manufactures, trade, and shipping, and since they early understood the best means of getting and maintaining through these advantages political ascendency, they have accordingly invented a policy which aimed, and still aims, at obtaining a monopoly in manufactures and trade, and at checking the progress of less advanced nations. The combination of the details of this policy (prohibition of imports, import duties, restrictions on shipping, bounties on exports) is known as the tariff system.

Less advanced nations were forced by the earlier progress of other nations, by foreign tariff systems, and by war, to seek in themselves the means by which they could effect the transition from agriculture to manufactures, and to restrict the trade with more advanced countries aiming at a manufacturing monopoly (in so far as this trade was a hindrance to the transition) by the help of a customs tariff. Customs tariffs, then, are not, as is asserted, the invention of some theorist, they are the natural result of a nation's endeavours to secure its existence and well-being, or to obtain supreme power. But this endeavour is only legitimate and rational when it is not a hindrance but a help to the nation which pursues it and is not in opposition to the higher aim of mankind, the future federation of the world. Just as human society can be regarded from two points of view—the cosmopolitan, which considers mankind as a whole; and the political, which pays attention to particular national interests and conditions, so both the economy of the individual and of society can be regarded from two main aspects, as we look at the personal, social, and material forces by which wealth is produced, or the exchange value of material goods.

Hence there is a cosmopolitan and a political economy, a theory of exchange values and a theory of productive powers, two doctrines which are essentially distinct and which must be developed independently. The productive powers of a nation are not only limited by the industry, thrift, morality, and intelligence of its individual members, and by its natural resources or material capital, but also by its social, political, and municipal laws and institutions, and especially by the securities for the continued existence, independence, and power of the nationality. However industrious, thrifty, enterprising, moral, and intelligent the individuals may be, without national unity, national division of labour, and national co-operation of productive powers the nation will never reach a high level of prosperity and power, or ensure to itself the lasting possession of its intellectual, social, and material goods. The principle of division of labour has not been fully grasped up to the present. Productivity depends not only on the division of various manufacturing operations among many individuals, but still more on the moral and physical co-operation of these individuals for a common end.

Thus the principle is applicable not merely to single factories or estates, but to the whole agricultural, manufacturing, and commercial forces of a nation. Division of labour and co-operation of productive powers exist where the intellectual activity of a nation bears a proper ratio to its material production, where agriculture, industry, and trade are equally and harmoniously developed.

In a purely agricultural nation, even when it enjoys free trade with manufacturing and commercial nations, a great part of its productive powers and natural resources lies idle and unused. Its intellectual and political development and its powers of defence are hampered. It can have no shipping of importance, no extensive trade. All its prosperity, so far as it results from international trade, can be interrupted, injured, or ruined by foreign regulations or by war.

Manufacturing power, on the contrary, promotes science, art, and political development, increases the well-being of the people, the population, national revenue, and national power, provides the country with the means of extending its commerce to all quarters of the world and of founding colonies, and nourishes the fishing industry, shipping and the navy. Through it alone can home agriculture be raised to a high pitch of development. Agriculture and manufactures in one and the same nation, united, that is, under one political authority, live in perpetual peace. Their mutual relations cannot be disturbed by war or foreign measures, consequently they ensure to the nation continued advance in well-being, civilization, and power. Nature lays down certain conditions for the existence of agriculture and manufactures, but these conditions are not always the same.

As far as natural resources are concerned the lands of the temperate zone are peculiarly fitted for the development of a manufacturing power, since a temperate climate is the natural home of physical and mental effort. Yet although the lands of the tropics are ill-suited for manufactures, they possess a natural monopoly of valuable agricultural products which are much in request by the inhabitants of temperate countries. In the exchange of the manufactures of the temperate zone for the products of the tropics ("colonial goods") we find the best example of cosmopolitan division of labour and co-operation of powers, of international trade on a large scale.

Any attempt to found a native manufacturing power would be most injurious to the tropics. Unfitted by nature for such a course, they will make far greater advances in national wealth and civilization if they continue to exchange their products for the manufactures of temperate countries. This policy, of course, leaves the tropics in a state of dependence. But this dependence will be harmless, indeed it will disappear, when more of the nations of the temperate zone are upon an equality in manufactures, commerce, shipping, and political power; when it is both advantageous and possible for several manufacturing countries to prevent any of their number from misusing their power over the weaker nations of the tropics. Such power would only be dangerous and harmful if all manufactures, commerce, shipping, and sea-power were monopolized by one country.

Then take the case of nations in the temperate zone possessing large territories full of natural resources. They would neglect one of the richest springs of prosperity, civilization, and power if they did not, as soon as they gained the necessary economic, intellectual, and social resources, attempt to realize on a national scale division of labour and co-operation of productive powers.

By economic resources we mean a fairly advanced state of agriculture which cannot be helped appreciably by any further export of its products. By intellectual resources we mean a good system of education. By social resources we mean laws and institutions which secure to the citizen safety for his person and property and free scope for his intellectual and physical powers. We include also well-managed facilities for transport, and the absence of all institutions, such as the feudal system, which are destructive of industry, freedom, intelligence, and morality.

It is the interest of such a nation, first of all, to endeavour to provide its own market with its own manufactured goods, and then to come more and more into direct intercourse with tropical countries, so that it can export manufactured goods to them in its own ships and take from them their own products in return. In comparison with this intercourse between the manufacturing countries of the temperate zone and the agricultural countries of the tropics, all other international trade, with the exception of a few articles, such as wine, is of little importance.

For great nations of the temperate zone the production of raw materials and food stuffs is only of importance as far as their internal trade is concerned. Through the export of corn, wine, flax, hemp, or wool, a rude and poor country gets a great initial impulse towards agriculture, but a great nation has never attained riches, civilization, and power through such a course.

We may lay it down as a general principle, that a nation is rich and powerful in the proportion in which it exports manufactures, imports raw materials, and consumes tropical products.

To manufacturing nations tropical products are not merely food or the raw materials of industry, but before all things incentives to the cultivation of agriculture and manufactures. We shall always find that among the nations which consume the greatest quantity of tropical products a correspondingly large quantity of their own manufactures and raw material is produced and consumed.

Four distinct periods can be recognized in the economic development of nations by means of international trade. In the first, home agriculture is fostered by the importation of foreign manufactured goods and the export of agricultural products and raw materials. In the second, home manufactures arise by the side of foreign imports. In the third, home manufactures supply the greater part of the home-market. In the fourth, large quantities of home-manufactured goods are exported and raw materials and agricultural products imported from abroad.

The tariff system, as a means of advancing the economic development of the nation by regulation of its foreign trade, must constantly follow the principle of national industrial *education*.

It is madness to attempt to help home agriculture by protection, since home agriculture can only be advanced on economic principles by the development of home manufactures, and the exclusion of foreign raw materials and agricultural products can only depress home manufactures.

The economic betterment of a nation which is at a low level of intelligence and culture, or in which the population is small in relation to the extent and productivity of its territory, is best accomplished through free trade with highly cultivated, rich, and industrious nations. In the case of such a country every restriction of trade, intended to plant manufacturing industry within its borders, is premature and injurious, not only to the welfare of mankind in general, but to the progress of the nation itself. Only when the intellectual, political, and economic education of the nation has so far advanced as a result of free trade that its further progress would be checked and hindered by the import of foreign manufactures and the lack of a sufficient market for its own goods, can protective measures be justified.

The territory of some nations is not of great extent nor supplied with many natural resources, the mouths of its rivers are not within its boundaries, and it does not form a homogeneous whole. Such a nation cannot apply the protective system at all, or only with imperfect success until it has first supplied its deficiencies by conquest or treaty.

Manufacturing power embraces so many branches of science and knowledge, and presupposes so much experience, skill, and practice, that national industrial development can only be gradual. Any exaggeration or hastening of protection punishes itself by diminished national prosperity. The most injurious and objectionable course is the sudden and complete isolation of the country by prohibition. Yet even this can be justified if, separated from other countries by a long war, it has suffered from an involuntary prohibition of foreign manufactures, and has been forced to supply itself. In this case a gradual transition from prohibition to protection should be effected by deciding beforehand upon a system of gradually diminishing duties. But a nation which desires to pass from a non-protective policy to protection must, on the contrary, begin with low taxes, which increase gradually upon a pre-determined scale. Taxes pre-determined in this way must be maintained intact by statesmen. They must not lower the taxes before the time, though they may raise them if they seem insufficient.

Excessively high import duties, which entirely cut off foreign competition, injure the country which imposes them, since its manufacturers are not forced to compete with foreigners, and indolence is fostered. If home manufactures do not prosper under moderate and gradually increasing duties, this is a proof that the country has not the necessary qualifications for the development of its own manufacturing system. Duties in a branch of industry that is already protected should not fall so low, that the existence of the industry is endangered by foreign competition. Support of existing manufactures, and protection for the essentials of national industry must be unalterable principles. Foreign competition, accordingly, can be allowed only a share in the yearly increase of consumption. The duties must be raised as soon as the foreigner gains the greater part or the whole of the yearly increase.

A nation like England, whose manufacturing power has a long start of all other countries, best maintains and extends its industrial and commercial supremacy by the freest possible trade. In its case cosmopolitan and political principles are identical. This explains the preference of distinguished English statesmen for absolute free trade and the unwillingness of wise financiers in other countries to apply this principle under the existing conditions of the world. For the last quarter of a century the system of prohibition and protection has worked to the disadvantage of England and the advantage of her rivals. Most disadvantageous of all are its restrictions on the importation of foreign raw materials and food stuffs.

Commercial unions and commercial treaties are the most effective means of facilitating intercourse between different nations. But commercial treaties are only legitimate and valuable when they involve mutual benefits. They are injurious and illegitimate when the development of a manufacturing power in one country is sacrificed in order to gain concessions for the exports of its agricultural products to another country. . . . All the offers which England has made since then to France and other countries are of the same character.

Even if protection temporarily enhances prices, yet it ensures cheapness in the future as a result of home competition. For a perfectly developed industry can fix a much lower price for its products than the cost of transport and of trader's profits allow when raw materials and food must be exported and manufactures imported.

The loss which a nation incurs by protection is only one of *values*, but it gains *powers* by which it is enabled to go on producing permanently inestimable amounts of value. This loss in value should be regarded merely as the price paid for the industrial education of the nation.

Protection to manufactures does not injure the agriculturists of the protected nation. Through the growth of a home manufacturing power, wealth, population, and with them the demand for agricultural products will vastly increase. Consequently there will be a considerable rise in the rents and selling prices of landed property, while as time goes by the manufactured products required by agriculturists will fall in price. These gains will outweigh the losses sustained by the agriculturists through the temporary rise in the prices of manufactured goods.

Similarly, both home and foreign trade gain from protection, since both are of importance only in the case of countries which can supply their own markets with manufactures, consume their own agricultural products, and exchange their own manufacturing surplus for foreign raw materials and food stuffs. Merely agricultural nations of the temperate zone have an insignificant home and foreign trade; foreign trade in such cases is generally in the hands of the manufacturing and commercial nations who hold intercourse with them.

Moderate protection does not grant a monopoly to home manufactures, only a guarantee against loss for those individuals who have devoted their capital, talent, and labour to new and untried industries. There can be no monopoly since home competition takes the place of foreign, and it is open to each member of the state to share in the benefits it offers to individuals. There is merely a monopoly for the inhabitants of one country against those of foreign countries, who themselves possess at home a similar monopoly. But this monopoly is useful, not only because it wakes productive forces lying idle and dormant in the nation, but because it attracts to the country foreign productive forces (material and intellectual capital, *entrepreneurs,* skilled and unskilled workmen).

In the case of many nations of long standing culture the export of raw materials and agricultural products, and the import of foreign manufactures, can no longer benefit their powers of production. Such nations suffer many serious evils if they do not foster their own manufactures. Their agriculture must necessarily be crippled, since, if important home manufacturers arose, the increased population would find employment there, and the consequent great demand for agricultural products would make agriculture on a large scale very profitable and favour its development. But in the case supposed the surplus population could only be employed in agriculture. The result would be a subdivision of land and increase of small cultivators which would be most injurious to the power, civilization, and wealth of the nation.

An agricultural population consisting for the most part of peasant proprietors can neither contribute large quantities of products to the home trade nor exercise an important demand for manufacturers. In such a case the consumption of each individual is limited for the most part to what he himself produces. Under these conditions the nation can never develop any satisfactory system of transport, and can never possess the incalculable advantages arising from such a system. The inevitable result is national weakness, moral and material, individual and political. These consequences are the more dangerous when neighbouring nations pursue the opposite course, when they advance as we fall back, when yonder the hope of better things to come increases the courage, power, and enterprise of the citizens, while here courage and spirit are more and more depressed by the outlook into a hopeless future. History affords striking examples of whole nations falling into ruin because they did not know how to undertake at the right moment the great task of planting their own manufactures, and a powerful industry and commerce, by which they could insure to themselves intellectual, economic, and political independence.

[Book II]

CHAPTER XIV: PRIVATE ECONOMY AND NATIONAL ECONOMY

We have proved historically that the unity of the nation forms the fundamental condition of lasting national prosperity; and we have shown that only where the interest of individuals has been subordinated to those of the nation, and where successive generations have striven for one and the same object, the nations have been brought to harmonious development of their productive powers, and how little private industry can prosper without the united efforts both of the individuals who are living at the time, and of successive generations directed to one common object. We have further tried to prove in the last chapter how the law of union of powers exhibits its beneficial operation in the individual manufactory, and how it acts with equal power on the industry of whole nations. In the present chapter we have now to demonstrate how the popular school has concealed its misunderstanding of the national interests and of the effects of national union of powers, by confounding the principles of private economy with those of national economy.

"What is prudence in the conduct of every private family," says Adam Smith, "can scarce be folly in that of a great kingdom." Every individual in pursuing his own interests necessarily promotes thereby also the interests of the community. It is evident that every individual, inasmuch as he knows his own local circumstances best and pays most attention to his occupation, is far better able to judge than the statesman or legislator how his capital can most profitably be invested. He who would venture to give advice to the people how to invest their capital would not merely take upon himself a useless task, but would also assume to himself an authority which belongs solely to the producer, and which can be entrusted to those persons least of all who consider themselves equal to so difficult a task. Adam Smith concludes this: "Restrictions on trade imposed on the behalf of the internal industry of a country, are mere folly; every nation, like every individual, ought to buy articles where they can be procured the cheapest; in order to attain to the highest degree of national prosperity, we have simply to follow the maxim of letting things alone (*laisser faire et laisser aller*)." Smith and Say compare a nation which seeks to promote its industry by protective duties, to a tailor who wants to make his own boots, and to a bootmaker who would impose a toll on those who enter his door, in order to promote his prosperity. As in all errors of the popular school, so also in this one does Thomas Cooper go to extremes in his book which is directed against the American system of protection. "Political economy," he alleges, "is almost synonymous with the private economy of all individuals; *politics* are no essential ingredient of *political economy;* it is folly to suppose that the community is something quite different from the individuals of whom it is composed. Every individual knows best how to invest his labour and his capital. The wealth of the community is nothing else than the aggregate of the wealth of all its individual members; and if every individual can provide best for himself, that nation must be the richest in which every individual is most left to himself." The adherents of the American system of protection had opposed themselves to this argument, which had formerly been adduced by importing merchants in favour of free trade; the American navigation laws had greatly increased the carrying trade, the foreign commerce, and fisheries of the United States; and for the mere protection of their mercantile marine millions had been annually expended on their fleet; according to his theory those laws and this expense also would be as reprehensible as protective duties. "In any case," exclaims Mr. Cooper, "no commerce by sea is worth a naval war; the merchants may be left to protect themselves."

Thus the popular school, which had begun by ignoring the principles of nationality and national interests, finally comes to the point of altogether denying their existence, and of leaving individuals to defend them as they may solely by their own individual powers.

How? Is the wisdom of private economy, also wisdom in national economy? Is it in the nature of individuals to take into consideration the wants of future centuries, as those concern the nature of the nation and the State? Let us consider only the first beginning of an American town; every individual left to himself would care merely for his own wants, or at the most for those of his nearest successors, whereas all individuals united in one community provide for the convenience and the wants of the most distant generations; they subject the present generation for this object to privations and sacrifices which no reasonable person could expect from individuals. Can the individual further take into consideration in promoting his private economy, the defence of the country, public security, and the thousand other objects which can only be attained by the aid of the whole community? Does not the State require individuals to limit their private liberty according to what these objects require? Does it not even require that they should sacrifice for these some part of their earnings, of their mental and bodily labour, nay, even their own life? We must first root out, as Cooper does, the very ideas of "State" and "nation" before this opinion can be entertained.

No; that may be wisdom in national economy which would be folly in private economy, and *vice versa;* and owing to the very simple reason, that a tailor is no nation and a nation no tailor, that one family is something very different from a community of millions of families, that one house is something very different from a large national territory. Nor does the individual merely by understanding his own interests best, and by striving to further them, if left to his own devices, always further the interests of the community. We ask those who occupy the benches of justice, whether they do not frequently have to send individuals to the tread-mill on account of their excess of inventive power, and of their all too great industry. Robbers, thieves, smugglers, and cheats know their own local and personal circumstances and conditions extremely well, and pay the most active attention to their business; but it by no means follows therefrom, that society is in the best condition where such individuals are least restrained in the exercise of their private industry.

In a thousand cases the power of the State is compelled to impose restrictions on private industry. It prevents the shipowner from taking on board slaves on the west coast of Africa, and taking them over to America. It imposes regulations as to the building of steamers and the rules of navigation at sea, in order that passengers and sailors may not be sacrificed to the avarice and caprice of the captains. In England certain rules have recently been enacted with regard to shipbuilding, because an infernal union between assurance companies and shipowners has been brought to light, whereby yearly thousands of human lives and millions in value were sacrificed to the avarice of a few persons. In North America millers are bound under a penalty to pack into each cask not less than 198 lbs. of good flour, and for all market goods market inspectors are appointed, although in no other country is individual liberty more highly prized. Everywhere does the State consider it to be its duty to guard the public against danger and loss, as in the sale of necessaries of life, so also in the sale of medicines, &c.

But the cases which we have mentioned (the school will reply) concern unlawful damages to property and to the person, not the honourable exchange of useful objects, not the harmless and useful industry of private individuals; to impose restrictions on these latter the State has no right whatever. Of course not, so long as they remain harmless and useful; that which, however, is harmless and useful in itself, in general commerce with the world, can become dangerous and injurious in national internal commerce, and *vice versa*. In time of peace, and considered from a cosmopolitan point of view, privateering is an injurious profession; in time of war, Governments favour it. The deliberate killing of a human being is a crime in time of peace, in war it becomes a duty. Trading in gunpowder, lead, and arms in time of peace is allowed; but whoever provides the enemy with them in time of war, is punished as a traitor.

For similar reasons the State is not merely justified in imposing, but bound to impose, certain regulations and restrictions on commerce (which is in itself harmless) for the best interests of the nation. By prohibitions and protective duties it does not give directions to individuals how to employ their productive powers and capital (as the popular school sophistically alleges); it does not tell the one, "You must invest your money in the building of a ship, or in the erection of a manufactory"; or the other, "You must be a naval captain or a civil engineer"; it leaves it to the judgment of every individual how and where to invest his capital, or to what vocation he will devote himself. It merely says, "It is to the advantage of our nation that we manufacture these or the other goods ourselves; but as by free competition with foreign countries we can never obtain possession of this advantage, we have imposed restrictions on that competition, so far as in our opinion is necessary, to give those among us who invest their capital in these new branches of industry, and those who devote their bodily and mental powers to them, the requisite guarantees that they shall not lose their capital and shall not miss their vocation in life; and further to stimulate foreigners to come over to our side with their productive powers. In this manner, it does not in the least degree restrain private industry; on the contrary, it secures to the personal, natural, and moneyed powers of the nation a greater and wider field of activity. It does not thereby do something which its individual citizens could understand better and do better than it; on the contrary, it does something which the individuals, even if they understood it, would not be able to do for themselves."

The allegation of the school, that the system of protection occasions unjust and anti-economical encroachments by the power of the State against the employment of the capital and industry of private individuals, appears in the least favourable light if we consider that it is the *foreign* commercial regulations which allow such encroachments on *our* private industry to take place, and that only by the aid of the system of protection are we enabled to counteract those injurious operations of the foreign commercial policy. If the English shut out our corn from their markets, what else are they doing than compelling our agriculturists to grow so much less corn than they would have sent out to England under systems of free importation? If they put such heavy duties on our wool, our wines, or our timber, that our export trade to England wholly or in great measure ceases, what else is thereby effected than that the power of the English nation restricts proportionately our branches of production? In these cases a direction is evidently given by *foreign legislation* to *our* capital and *our* personal productive powers, which but for the regulations made by it they would scarcely have followed. It follows from this, that were we to disown giving, by means of *our* own legislation, a direction to our own national industry in accordance with our own national interests, we could not prevent foreign nations from regulating our national industry after a fashion which corresponds with their own real or presumed advantage, and which in any case operates disadvantageously to the development of our own productive powers. But can it possibly be wiser on our part, and more to the advantage of those who nationally belong to us, for us to allow our private industry to be regulated by a foreign national Legislature, in accordance with foreign national interests, rather than regulate it by means of our own Legislature and in accordance with our own interests? Does the German or American agriculturist feel himself less restricted if he has to study every year the English Acts of

Parliament, in order to ascertain whether that body deems it advantageous to encourage or to impose restrictions on his production of corn or wool, than if his own Legislature imposes certain restrictions on him in respect of foreign manufactured goods, but at the same time insures him a market for all his products, of which he can never again be deprived by foreign legislation?

If the school maintains that protective duties secure to the home manufacturers a monopoly to the disadvantage of the home consumers, in so doing it makes use of a weak argument. For as every individual in the nation is free to share in the profits of the home market which is thus secured to native industry, this is in no respect a private monopoly, but a privilege, secured to all those who belong to our nation, as against those who nationally belong to foreign nations, and which is the more righteous and just inasmuch as those who nationally belong to foreign nations possess themselves the very same monopoly, and those who belong to us are merely thereby put on the same footing with them. It is neither a privilege to the exclusive advantage of the producers, nor to the exclusive disadvantage of the consumers; for if the producers at first obtain higher prices, they run great risks, and have to contend against those considerable losses and sacrifices which are always connected with all beginnings in manufacturing industry. But the consumers have ample security that these extraordinary profits shall not reach unreasonable limits, or become perpetual, by means of the competition at home which follows later on, and which, as a rule, always lowers prices further than the level at which they had steadfastly ranged under the free competition of the foreigner. If the agriculturists, who are the most important consumers to the manufacturers, must also pay higher prices, this disadvantage will be amply repaid to them by increased demands for agricultural products, and by increased prices obtained for the latter.

It is a further sophism, arrived at by confounding the theory of mere values with that of the powers of production, when the popular school infers from the doctrine, *"that the wealth of the nation is merely the aggregate of the wealth of all individuals in it, and that the private interest of every individual is better able than all State regulations to incite to production and accumulation of wealth,"* the conclusion that the national industry would prosper best if only every individual were left undisturbed in the occupation of accumulating wealth. That doctrine can be conceded without the conclusion resulting from it at which the school desires thus to arrive; for the point in question is not (as we have shown in a previous chapter) that of immediately increasing by commercial restrictions the amount of *the values of exchange* in the nation, but of increasing *the amount of its productive powers*. But that the aggregate of the productive powers of the nation is not synonymous with the aggregate of the productive powers of all individuals, each considered separately—that the total amount of these powers depends chiefly on social and political conditions, but especially on the degree in which the nation has rendered effectual the division of labour and the confederation of the powers of production within itself—we believe we have sufficiently demonstrated in the preceding chapters. . . .

The school recognises no distinction between nations which have attained a higher degree of economical development, and those which occupy a lower stage. Everywhere it seeks to exclude the action of the power of the State; everywhere, according to it, will the individual be so much better able to produce, the less the power of the State concerns itself for him. In fact, according to this doctrine savage nations ought to be the most productive and wealthy of the earth, for nowhere is the individual left more to himself than in the savage state, nowhere is the action of the power of the State less perceptible. . . .

CHAPTER XV: NATIONALITY AND THE ECONOMY OF THE NATION

The system of the school suffers, as we have already shown in the preceding chapters, from three main defects: firstly, from boundless *cosmopolitanism*, which neither recognises the principle of nationality, nor takes into consideration the satisfaction of its interests; secondly, from a dead *materialism*, which everywhere regards chiefly the mere exchangeable value of things without taking into consideration the mental and political, the present and the future interests, and the productive powers of the nation; thirdly, from a *disorganising particularism* and *individualism*, which, ignoring the nature and character of social labour and the operation of the union of powers in their higher consequences, considers private industry only as it would develop itself under a state of free interchange with society (i.e. with the whole human race) were that race not divided into separate national societies.

Between each individual and entire humanity, however, stands THE NATION, with its special language and literature, with its peculiar origin and history, with its special manners and customs, laws and institutions, with the claims of all these for existence, independence, perfection, and continuance for the future, and with its separate territory; a society which, united by a thousand ties of mind and of interests, combines itself into one independent whole, which recognises the law of right for and within itself, and in its united character is still opposed to other societies of a similar kind in their national liberty, and consequently can only under existing conditions of the world maintain self-existence and independence by its own power and resources. As the individual chiefly obtains by means of the nation and in the nation mental culture, power of production, security, and prosperity, so is the civilisation of the human race only conceivable and possible by means of the civilisation and development of the individual nations.

Meanwhile, however, an infinite difference exists in the condition and circumstances of the various nations: we observe among them giants and dwarfs, well-formed bodies and cripples, civilised, half-civilised, and barbarous nations; but in all of them, as in the individual human being, exists the impulse of self-preservation, the striving for improvement which is implanted by nature. It is the task of politics to civilise the barbarous nationalities, to make the small and weak ones great and strong, but, above all, to secure to them existence and continuance. It is the task of national economy to accomplish *the economical development of the nation,* and to prepare it for admission into the universal society of the future.

A nation in its normal state possesses one common language and literature, a territory endowed with manifold natural resources, extensive, and with convenient frontiers and a numerous population. Agriculture, manufactures, commerce, and navigation must be all developed in it proportionately; arts and sciences, educational establishments, and universal cultivation must stand in it on an equal footing with material production. Its constitution, laws, and institutions must afford to those who belong to it a high degree of security and liberty, and must promote religion, morality, and prosperity; in a word, must have the well-being of its citizens as their object. It must possess sufficient power on land and at sea to defend its independence and to protect its foreign commerce. It will possess the power of beneficially affecting the civilisation of less advanced nations, and by means of its own surplus population and of their mental and material capital to found colonies and beget new nations.

A large population, and an extensive territory endowed with manifold national resources, are essential requirements of the normal nationality; they are the fundamental conditions of mental cultivation as well as of material development and political power. A nation restricted in the number of its population and in territory, especially if it has a separate language, can only possess a crippled literature, crippled institutions for promoting art and science. A small State can never bring to complete perfection within its territory the various branches of production. In it all protection becomes mere private monopoly. Only through alliances with more powerful nations, by partly sacrificing the advantages of nationality, and by excessive energy, can it maintain with difficulty its independence.

A nation which possesses no coasts, mercantile marine, or naval power, or has not under its dominion and control the mouths of its rivers, is in its foreign commerce dependent on other countries; it can neither establish colonies of its own nor form new nations; all surplus population, mental and material means, which flows from such a nation to uncultivated countries, is lost to its own literature, civilisation and industry, and goes to the benefit of other nationalities.

A nation not bounded by seas and chains of mountains lies open to the attacks of foreign nations, and can only by great sacrifices, and in any case only very imperfectly, establish and maintain a separate tariff system of its own.

Territorial deficiencies of the nation can be remedied either by means of hereditary succession, as in the case of England and Scotland; or by purchase, as in the case of Florida and Louisiana; or by conquests, as in the case of Great Britain and Ireland.

In modern times a fourth means has been adopted, which leads to this object in a manner much more in accordance with justice and with the prosperity of nations than conquest, and which is not so dependent on accidents as hereditary succession, namely, the union of the interests of various States by means of conventions.

By its Zollverein, the German nation first obtained one of the most important attributes of its nationality. But this measure cannot be considered complete so long as it does not extend over the whole coast, from the mouth of the Rhine to the frontier of Poland, including *Holland* and *Denmark*. A natural consequence of this union must be the admission of both these countries into the German Bund, and consequently into the German nationality, whereby the latter will at once obtain what it is now in need of, namely, fisheries and naval power, maritime commerce and colonies. Besides, both these nations belong, as respects their descent and whole character, to the German nationality. The burden of debt with which they are oppressed is merely a consequence of their unnatural endeavours to maintain themselves as independent nationalities, and it is in the nature of things that this evil should rise to a point when it will become intolerable to those two nations themselves, and when incorporation with a larger nationality must seem desirable and necessary to them.

Belgium can only remedy by means of confederation with a neighbouring larger nation her needs which are inseparable from her restricted territory and population. *The United States* and *Canada,* the more their population increases, and the more the protective system of the United States is developed, so much the more will they feel themselves drawn towards one another, and the less will it be possible for England to prevent a union between them.

DEBATE ON THE FACTORY BILL

ABOMINABLE working conditions in English factories caused a persistent agitation for the passage of factory acts. The first bill attempting to regulate labor in factories was carried through by the elder Peel in 1802. The act applied to the labor of "apprentices"—pauper children bound out to the cotton mills—and attempted to limit their labor to twelve hours a day and to abolish night work. But the act had no teeth in it, and it was outmoded by the further progress of technology. In 1815, Peel proposed to meet the new conditions created by the movement of factories to towns. He succeeded in having enacted in 1819 an emasculated set of provisions, applying only to cotton mills, abolishing the employment of children under nine and setting a twelve-hour limit for those under sixteen. After twelve years of intermittent efforts another act was passed, which also applied only to the cotton industry and limited to twelve hours a day the labor of all persons under eighteen. The report of the Parliamentary Committee on Factory Children's Labour, 1831–32, shocked the public conscience with its account of conditions, and another factory act was enacted in 1833. It prohibited the employment in textile factories of children under nine and set a forty-eight-hour week for those ten to thirteen and a sixty-nine-hour week for all those thirteen to eighteen.

The climactic victory for the agitators for factory reform came with the Ten-Hour Law of 1847, which summarily restricted the work of women and children in textile factories to ten hours a day. The battle for these reforms set up strange divisions. The Factory Act of 1847 was the product, on the one hand, of years of agitation on the part of the working class, especially in Yorkshire and Lancashire, and, on the other, of the leadership of philanthropic manufacturers such as John Fielden (1784–1849) and benevolent Tory reformers, especially Michael Sadler (1780–1835) and Anthony Ashley Cooper, known as Lord Ashley, who later became the seventh Earl of Shaftesbury (1801–85). The most prominent opponent of the Factory Acts was John Bright. The following debate took place on March 15, 1844. In 1843 a proposal for reform had met with severe criticism and widespread protest from nonconformists, because it included provisions for compulsory education for factory children under the direction of the Established Church. Accordingly, in 1844, the government of Peel and Graham proposed another measure, with the unpopular provisions stricken out. The hours of labor for children were limited to twelve. Shaftesbury was initially successful in getting a ten-hour-day amendment accepted, but he was outmaneuvered by the government, which finally succeeded in passing a bill of its own formulation, although it was somewhat different from the first. The working hours of children were reduced to six and one-half per day, and a twelve-hour day was provided for women and young persons. It was this act which was responsible for the difficulty of administering effectively the Factory Act of 1847. This latter act was passed simply in the form of an amendment to the first, but the complicated wording of the first allowed an interpretation by which mill owners, while they could not actually work young persons for more than ten hours each day, could nevertheless keep them within the confines of the mill and subject to call during the hours that it was open.

The debate is reported in Hansard's *Parliamentary Debates* for 1844.

ॐ

DEBATE ON THE FACTORY BILL

HOUSE OF COMMONS, MARCH 15, 1844

LORD ASHLEY [Tory; Dorsetshire]: Nearly eleven years have now elapsed since I first made the proposition [limiting hours of work] to the House which I shall renew this night. Never, at any time, have I felt greater apprehension or even anxiety; not through any fear of personal defeat, for disappointment is "the badge of all our tribe"; but because I know well the hostility that I have aroused, and the certain issues of indiscretion on my part affecting the welfare of those who have so long confided their hopes and interests to my charge. And here let me anticipate the constant, but unjust accusation that I am animated by a peculiar hostility against factory masters, and I have always selected them as exclusive objects of attack. I must assert that the charge, though specious, is altogether untrue. I began, I admit, this public movement by an effort to improve the condition of the factories; but this I did, not because I ascribed to that department of industry a monopoly of all that was pernicious and cruel, but because it was then before the public eye, comprised the wealthiest and most responsible proprietors, and presented the greatest facilities for legislation. As soon as I had the power, I showed my impartiality by moving the House for the Children's Employment Commission. The curious in human suffering may decide on the respective merits of the several reports; but factory labour has no longer an unquestionable pre-eminence of ill fame; and we are called upon to give relief, not because it is the worst system, but because it is oppressive, and yet capable of alleviation. Sir, I confess that ten years of experience have taught me that avarice and cruelty are not the peculiar and inherent qualities of any one class or occupation—they will ever be found where the means of profit are combined with great, and, virtually, irresponsible power—they will be found wherever interest and selfishness have a purpose to serve, and a favourable opportunity. We are all alike, I fully believe, in the town and in the country, in manufactures and in agriculture—though we have not all of us the same temptations, or the same means of rendering our propensities a source of profit; and oftentimes, what we will not do ourselves, we connive at in others, if it add in any way to our convenience or pleasure. . . .

And here it is just to state, that if I can recite many examples of unprincipled and griping tyranny, I can quote many also of generous and parental care, and of willing and profuse expenditure for the benefit of the people. If there are prominent instances of bad, there are also prominent instances of good men. I will suppose for the sake of argument, that all are the victims, rather than the causes of the system; but whatever the cause, the condition inflicts a great amount of physical and moral suffering. I know I am arousing a fierce spirit of reply; be it so—"Strike me, but hear me." I shall altogether leave to others that part of the question which belongs to trade and commerce. I am neither unwilling, nor perhaps, unable, to handle it; but I desire to keep myself within the bounds that I have always hitherto observed in the discussion of this matter, and touch only the consideration of the moral and physical effects, produced by the system, on the great body of the work-people. I am spared too the necessity of arguing the propriety or impropriety of interfering to regulate the hours of labour for persons under certain ages; the principle has long been conceded, and acted on by Parliament: our controversy can relate only to the degree in which it shall be carried out. I have never omitted an opportunity of asserting the claim I ventured to put forward nearly eleven years ago; and I return, therefore, this evening, to my original proposition. Sir, I assume as one ground of the argument, that, apart from considerations of humanity, which, nevertheless, should be paramount, the State has an interest and a right to watch over, and provide for the moral and physical well-being of her people: the principle is beyond question; it is recognised and enforced under every form of civilised Government. . . . If foreign powers consider it a matter both of duty and policy thus to interpose on behalf of their people, we, surely, should much more be animated by feelings such as theirs, when we take into our account the vast and progressively increasing numbers who are employed in these departments of industry. See how it stands: in 1818, the total number of all ages, and both sexes, employed in all the cotton factories, was 57,323. In 1835, the number employed in the five departments—cotton, woolen, worsted, flax, and silk, was 354,684. In 1839, the number in the same five departments was 419,500: the total number of both sexes under eighteen years of age, in the same year, was 192,887. Simultaneously, however, with the increase of numbers has been the increase of toil. The labour performed by those engaged in the process of manufacture, is three times as great as in the beginning of such operations. Machinery has executed, no doubt, the work that would demand the sinews of millions of men; but it has also prodigiously multiplied the labour of those who are governed by its fearful movements. I hope the House will allow me to go through several details connected with this portion of the subject; they are technical, it is true; but, nevertheless, of sufficient importance to be brought under your attention. In 1815, the labour of following a pair of mules spinning cotton yarn of Nos. 40, reckoning twelve hours to the working day, involved a necessity for walking eight miles; that is to say, the piecer, who was employed in going from one thread to another in a day of twelve hours, performed a journey of eight miles. In 1832, the distance travelled in following a pair of mules spinning cotton yarn of the same numbers was twenty miles, and frequently more. But the amount of labour performed by those following the mules, is not confined merely to the distance walked. There is far more to be done. In 1835, the spinner put up daily on each of these mules 820 stretches; making a total of 1,640 stretches in the course of the day. In 1832, the spinner put upon each mule 2,200 stretches, making a total of 4,400. In 1844, according to a return furnished by a practised operative spinner, the person working puts up in the same period 2,400 stretches on each mule, making a total of 4,800 stretches in the course of the day; and in some cases, the amount of labour required is even still greater. . . .

Now, Sir, it is no difficult transition from such a statement of daily toil, passed as it is, in crowded rooms, heated atmospheres, noxious gases, and injurious agencies of various kinds, to the following statement of physical mischiefs to the workers employed. Since 1816, eighty surgeons and physicians, and three medical commissioners in 1833 (one of whom, Doctor Bisset Hawkins, declared that he had the authority of a large majority of the medical men of Lancashire) have asserted the prodigious evil of the system. . . .

There is one more fact to which I wish to call the attention of the House. Those honourable Gentlemen who have been in the habit of perusing the melancholy details of mill accidents, should know that a large proportion of those accidents—particularly those which may be denominated the minor class, such as loss of fingers, and the like, occur in the last hours of the evening, when the people become so tired that they absolutely get reckless of the danger. I state this on the authority of several practical spinners. Hence arise many serious evils to the working classes; none greater than the early prostration of their strength, their premature superannuation, and utter incapacity to sustain their families by the labour of their hands. I will prove my assertions by . . . [a table] from which you will observe that at the very period of life at which in many other departments of industry, men are regarded as in the prime of their strength, those employed in the cotton manufacture are superannuated and set aside, as incapable of earning their livelihood by factory labour. The ages above forty are seldom found in this employment. . . . In 1839, the returns from certain mills in Stockport and Manchester, showed that the number of hands employed in these mills were 22,094— Now of all that immense multitude, how many does the House suppose were above forty-five years of age? Why, only 143 persons; and of these, sixteen were retained by special favour, and one was doing boy's work. . . .

Now, let this condition of things be contrasted with the condition of agricultural life; and let us see how much longer is the duration of the working powers in that class of labour. In June, 1841, on an estate in Worcestershire . . . of 341 labourers, 180 were above forty years of age. Contrast the condition of these people with that of a multitude of 22,000, of whom only 143 were above the age of forty-five. . . . It will be borne in mind that the present system has prevailed so long, and is of such a nature as completely to have destroyed every idea of thrift and economy. The education both of males and females is such that domestic economy is almost wholly unknown to them; and it very rarely happens that they have the foresight to accumulate savings during the period at which they can work to subsist upon in the days of their old age. It will also be remembered that their strength is so wholly exhausted that they are unable to enter into any different active occupation when discharged from the mill; and that thereafter they sink down into employments, of the nature of which I will give a specimen to the House. In June, 1841, from a return which was presented to me, it appeared that in 11 auction rooms in Manchester, out of 11 common jobbers, as they are called, 9 were discharged factory hands. Of 37 hawkers of nuts and oranges, 32 were factory hands; of 9 sellers of sand, 8 were factory hands; of 28 hawkers of boiled sheeps' feet, 22 belonged to the same class; of 14 hawkers of brushes, 11 were factory hands; of 25 sellers of coal, 16 were factory hands—thus out of 113 persons pursuing these miserable occupations, 89 were discharged factory hands. I may add that upon a further examination being made, it was found that of 341 discharged factory hands, 217 were maintained entirely by the earnings of their children. . . . With reference to these men I asked the question, how many may expect to be taken up on a revival of trade? The answer was, scarcely one; that the masters required young hands and unexhausted strength, and that they would rather take men of twenty-five than of thirty-five years of age. . . .

The tendency of the various improvements in machinery is to supersede the employment of adult males, and substitute in its place, the labour of children and females. What will be the effect on future generations, if their tender frames be subjected, without limitation or control, to such destructive agencies? Consider this; in 1835, the numbers stood thus; the females in the five departments of industry, 196,383; in 1839, females, 242,296; of these, the females under eighteen, 112,192. The proportions in each department stood, females in cotton, 56¼ per cent.; ditto worsted, 69½ ditto: ditto silk, 70½ ditto; ditto flax, 70½ ditto. Thus while the total amount of both sexes and all ages, in the cotton manufacture, in 1818, were equal only to 57,323, the females alone in that branch, in 1839, were 146,331. Now the following is an extract of a letter from a great mill-owner in 1842:—

The village of —— two miles distant, sends down daily to the mills in this town, at least a thousand females, single and married, who have to keep strictly the present long hours of labour. Seven years ago, these persons were employed at their own homes; but now, instead of the men working at the power-looms, none but girls or women are allowed to have it.

But, Sir, look at the physical effect of this system on the women. See its influence on the delicate constitutions and tender forms of the female sex. Let it be recollected that the age at which the "prolonged labour," as it is called, commences, is at the age of thirteen. That age, according to the testimony of medical men, is the tenderest period of female life. Observe the appalling progress of female labour; and remember that the necessity for particular protection to females against overwork is attested by the most eminent surgeons and physicians. . . .

Where, Sir, under this condition, are the possibilities of domestic life? how can its obligations be fulfilled? Regard the woman as wife or mother, how can she accomplish any portion of her calling? And if she cannot do that which Providence has assigned her, what must be the effect on the whole surface of society? . . .

Many females state, that the labour induces "an intolerable thirst; they can drink, but not eat." I do not doubt that several of the statements I have read, will create surprise in the minds of many hon. Members; but if they were to converse with operatives who are acquainted with the practical effects of the system, they would cease to wonder at the facts I have detailed. I might detain the House by enumerating the evils which result from the long working of males and females together in the same room. I could show the many and painful effects to which females are exposed, and the manner in which they lament and shrink from the inconveniences of their situation. I have letters from Stockport and Manchester, from various individuals, dwelling on the mischievous consequences which arise from the practice of modest women working so many hours together with men, and not being able to avail themselves of those opportunities which would suggest themselves to every one's mind without particular mention. . . .

But listen to another fact, and one deserving of serious attention; that the females not only perform the labour, but occupy the places of men; they are forming various clubs and associations, and gradually acquiring all those privileges which are held to be the proper portion of the male sex. These female clubs are thus described:—Fifty or sixty females, married and single, form themselves into clubs, ostensibly for protection; but, in fact, they meet together, to drink, sing, and smoke; they use, it is stated, the lowest, most brutal, and most disgusting language imaginable. . . .

This will conclude the statement that I have to make to the House—and now, Sir, who will assert that these things should be permitted to exist? Who will hesitate to apply the axe to the root of the tree, or, at least, endeavour to lop off some of its deadliest branches? What arguments from general principles will they adduce against my proposition? What, drawn from peculiar circumstances? They cannot urge that particular causes in England give rise to particular results; the same cause prevails in various countries; and wherever it is found, it produces the same effects. I have already stated its operation in France, in Russia, in Switzerland, in Austria, and in Prussia; I may add also in America; for I perceive by the papers of the 1st of February, that a Bill has been proposed in the Legislature of Pennsylvania, to place all persons under the age of sixteen, within the protection of the "ten hours" limit. I never thought that we should have learned justice from the City of Philadelphia. . . . Let me remind, too, the House, of the mighty change which has taken place among the opponents to this question. When I first brought it forward in 1833, I could scarcely number a dozen masters on my side, I now count them by hundreds. We have had, from the West Riding of Yorkshire, a petition signed by 300 millowners, praying for a limitation of labour to ten hours in the day. Some of the best names in Lancashire openly support me. I have letters from others who secretly wish me well, but hesitate to proclaim their adherence; and even among the members of the Anti-Corn-Law League, I may boast of many firm and efficient friends. Sir, under all the aspects in which it can be viewed, this system of things must be abrogated or restrained—it affects the internal tranquillity of those vast provinces, and all relations between employer and employed—it forms a perpetual grievance and ever comes uppermost among their complaints in all times of difficulty and discontent. It disturbs the order of nature, and the rights of the labouring men, by ejecting the males from the workshop, and filling their places by females, who are thus withdrawn from all their domestic duties, and exposed to insufferable toil at half the wages that would be assigned to males, for the support of their families. It affects—nay, more, it absolutely annihilates, all the arrangements and provisions of domestic economy—thrift and management are altogether impossible; had they twice the amount of their present wages, they would be but slightly benefited—everything runs to waste; the house and children are deserted; the wife can do nothing for her husband and family; she can neither cook, wash, repair clothes, or take charge of the infants; all must be paid for out of her scanty earnings, and, after all, most imperfectly done. Dirt, discomfort, ignorance, recklessness, are the portion of such households; the wife has no time for learning in her youth, and none for practice in her riper age; the females are most unequal to the duties of the men in the factories; and all things go to rack and ruin, because the men can discharge at home no one of the especial duties that Providence has assigned to the females. . . .

Whose experience is so confined that it does not extend to a knowledge and an appreciation of the maternal influence over every grade and department of society? It matters not whether it be prince or peasant, all that is best, all that is lasting in the character of a man, he has learnt at his mother's knees. Search the records, examine the opening years of those who have been distinguished for ability and virtue, and you will ascribe, with but few exceptions, the early culture of their minds, and above all, the first discipline of the heart, to the intelligence and affection of the mother, or at least of some pious woman, who with the self-denial and tenderness of her sex, has entered as a substitute, on the sacred office. . . . Are you reasonable to impute to me a settled desire, a single purpose, to exalt the landed, and humiliate the commercial aristocracy? Most solemnly do I deny the accusation; if you think me wicked enough, do you think me fool enough, for such a hateful policy? Can any man in his senses now hesitate to believe that the permanent prosperity of the manufacturing body, in all its several aspects, physical, moral, and commercial, is essential, not only to the welfare, but absolutely to the existence of the British Empire? No, we fear not the increase of your political power, nor envy your stupendous riches; "peace be within your walls, and plenteousness within your palaces!" We ask but a slight relaxation of toil, a time to live, and a time to die; a time for those comforts that sweeten life, and a time for those duties that adorn it; and, therefore, with a fervent prayer to Almighty God that it may please him to turn the hearts of all who hear me to thoughts of justice and of mercy, I now finally commit the issue to the judgment and humanity of Parliament.

Sir *J. Graham* [Independent; Dorchester; Home Secretary in Sir Robert Peel's ministry]: . . . There never was a greater subject, as it appears to me, considered in this House—the comfort, the happiness, the physical and moral condition, as my noble Friend has justly put it, of a large portion of the working classes, come under our notice this evening. Their wrongs are entitled to redress, if we can redress them; their feelings are entitled to indulgent consideration, even though we may be unable to redress their wrongs. . . . On the other hand justice compels me to say, the question of the commercial prosperity and manufacturing industry of this country is to-night materially involved in the question upon which we are deliberating. It was with some astonishment, therefore, that I heard my noble Friend declare, that he would discard all commercial views on this occasion, and treat the question as one purely of morals and of religious obligation. Nay, my noble Friend must excuse me for saying that when I listened to his eloquent appeal, and to his statement of facts as bearing on infantine and female labour, I will not say I thought there was exaggeration—but I could almost have believed that the necessary consequence of that appeal and of that statement of facts must have been to lead to the conclusion at which he arrived with respect to mines and collieries, namely, that females and infants should no longer be employed in factory labour. Now, allow me to beg of the Committee to consider. I have said the matter is most important; but still allow me to recall to the attention of the Committee how narrow comparatively is the question we are called upon to discuss. It is not whether females shall cease to be employed in factories, nor whether children shall cease to labour there—it is whether females shall be employed ten or twelve hours in factories, and whether the period of infantile labour shall be eight hours in each day, or something shorter. . . . It is not, as my noble Friend in the earlier part of his speech justly remarked, a question of principle that we are now called upon to discuss, it is one of degree. I think it clearly unnecessary on the present occasion to enter at length into the principle. It was certainly a violation of principle that the Legislature should interfere in a case of this kind at all. . . .

My noble Friend has dwelt very much upon the improvements which have taken place in machinery, and the consequent increase of labour to the parties so employed. Allow me just to remark, in passing, that although the intention of the Factory Act was humane, and its operation has been partially such, yet I have no doubt whatever its practical effect has been to stimulate in the highest degree the improvement of machinery with a view to the displacement of manual labour. . . . Mark, then, it is as clear as possible, if you reduce the hours of labour by one-eleventh or one-sixth, the machinery will be accelerated to counteract the reduction of the hours of work, and in point of fact the labour will be more intense and severe. My noble Friend refers to early superannuation. Now, in the first place, I decidedly admit, that there was an excess of infantine and female labour injurious to health, and until the Act of 1833 passed there was no legislative restriction. But there are now stringent regulations, and I am not disposed to call upon the House of Commons to increase them, because I believe they are quite sufficient. Just in proportion as by improvement in machinery you increase the speed of that machinery, so you do make a call for increased strength on the part of those you employ, even to the displacement of the labour of aged persons, younger and more active persons being required to perform the duties. . . . My noble Friend drew a comparison between agricultural and manufacturing labourers, and he did not, I am sure, draw that comparison invidiously. I must, however, express some doubt as to the physical fact stated by my noble Friend. I believe, when you take into consideration the exposure to the inclemency of the weather, and other disadvantageous circumstances which fall upon the agricultural labourer, that it may very fairly be doubted, whether on account of the vicissitudes he encounters, the chances are not, upon the whole, against the agricultural labourer, on the score of health, as compared with the manufacturer. But the House will consider whether it be of any practical advantage to discuss that point now. We have arrived at a state of society when without commerce and manufactures this great community cannot be maintained. Let us, as far as we can, mitigate the evils arising out of this highly artificial state of society; but let us take care to adopt no step that may be fatal to commerce and manufactures. . . .

My noble Friend stated that he would not enter into the commercial part of the question; but if I can show that the inevitable result of the abridgement of time will be the diminution of wages to the employed, then I say, with reference to the interests of the working classes themselves, there never was a more doubtful question before Parliament than this. The House will remember that the branches of manufacture affected by this Bill are dependent upon machinery. Such is the rapidity with which improvements are made, that no machinery can last more than twelve or thirteen years without alterations; and master-manufacturers have been obliged to pull down machinery that was perfectly sound and good to make the necessary alterations which competition forces upon them. Well, then, it is necessary to replace machinery in the course of twelve or thirteen years. You are now discussing whether you shall abridge by one-sixth the period of time in which capital is to be replaced, all interest upon it paid, and the original outlay restored. Such an abridgement would render it impossible that capital with interest should be restored. Then in the close race of competition which our manufacturers are now running with foreign competitors, it must be considered what effect this reduction of one-sixth of the hours of labour would have upon them. The question in its bearing upon competition must be carefully considered; and I have been informed that in that respect such a step would be fatal to many of our manufacturers; a feather would turn the scale: an extra pound weight would lose the race. But that would not be the first effect. The first effect would fall upon the operative. It is notorious that a great part of the power of the mill-owners, a power which alone justifies such legislation as this, arises from the redundant supply of labour. It follows that when a master is pressed upon by your legislation, he will compensate himself by forcing upon those in his employ a decrease of wages. . . . Though I am most anxious to take every precaution with regard to infant labour—though I am as firmly resolved as my noble Friend to urge upon the House to put a limit upon female labour, still, upon the whole, I cannot recommend the House to adopt an enactment which limits the labour of young persons to a shorter period than twelve hours. My noble Friend has referred to foreign countries, but in these countries, if I am not mistaken, there is no limitation, direct or indirect, of adult labour. My noble Friend spoke in decisive terms upon the failure of health in the manufacturing districts, and offered most important considerations to the House bearing upon that part of the subject. But if I am not misinformed, it will be found when there is full work, even to some excess, on the part of adults—when there is full work and good wages, that health in the manufacturing districts is in a satisfactory condition. On the other hand, when there is short time—shorter time than is proposed by my noble Friend—short time caused by the failure of the demand for manufactured articles, and reduced to eight instead of ten hours as occurred about two years ago, then disease is rife in the manufacturing districts; then is the time when immoral habits are generated, and disease is their inevitable result. . . . I believe, moreover, so far from being advantageous to the working classes, my noble Friend's proposition would be ruinous to their interests, and fatal to our commercial prosperity, and though my feelings and wishes are with him, my sense of duty never more clearly pointed out the course I ought to take, in reluctantly, but firmly, resisting his proposition.

Mr. *Milner Gibson* [Whig; Manchester] said that, . . . With regard to the proposition of the noble Lord, he could not say it was within his knowledge approved of by either masters or operatives. He had made it his business to ascertain to the best of his ability the state of feeling among the labouring people themselves upon this proposition of short hours of labour, and he had been told by many of the most intelligent and thinking operatives—men calculated to have influence with their class, and they considered that it would be an interference with the only property they had to dispose of, namely, their labour, and they could not agree to the proposition, whatever might be the urgency and necessity of working hard to earn a living, that they should be prevented from working twelve hours in a factory, if they found it fit and advantageous so to do. It might be thought that by preventing young persons, and women of all ages, from working more than ten hours, the labour of male adults was not interfered with. But that was not so. To enact that no young persons or women of any age should work more than ten hours was, in point of fact, to enact that no factory engines should be kept in operation more than ten hours. It was not simply dealing with the labour of women and young persons, but it was an interference with the labour of adults, and an interference also with that fixed capital so eloquently dwelt upon by the right hon. Baronet, the Secretary of State for the Home Department [Sir J. Graham]. What was the cure? They were diminishing in that manner the effective production of all the great staple articles of manufacture no less than 20 per cent. If they destroyed the profit of a manufacture by cutting off two hours of labour, they, in effect, deprived the labourer of the means of earning his subsistence; so that, acting from the most benevolent motives, they might be inflicting the greatest of all possible evils upon the very class they sought to benefit. . . .

He (Mr. Gibson) was for increasing the field of employment, so that the labouring population might be able to take care of themselves, and not be driven to the necessity of working for such protracted hours. That appeared to him to be the right way in which the evil complained of by the noble Lord should be cured. He confessed, when he found hon. Members coming forward in that House, and expressing such great sympathy for the labouring classes, he was not quite ready to give them credit for sincerity on finding them, at the same time, so reluctant in making the least sacrifices on their own parts, in order to afford the people the enjoyment and advantage of a free market for their labour. Nothing was so easy as to sympathise and be generous at the expense of others. If the landed gentry really wished to gain credit for the welfare of the people, and for a desire to place the labourer in a better condition than he was in at present, they should come forward in a truly liberal spirit, and at once consent to a repeal of the Corn Laws. They should do their utmost to give full scope to the exertions of industry by widening the field of manual employment. . . .

Mr. *H. G. Ward* [Whig; Sheffield]: No man in this House has listened with deeper attention to the noble Lord than myself; and certainly I am bound to say, that all my feelings and all my sympathies have been in favour of the course which he has proposed. But when I come to weigh the consequences of that course—when I come to look not only to the interest of the one class whose cause the noble Lord is advocating, but to the interests of the many classes which this measure would materially affect—I feel that I cannot adopt the principle of interference advocated by the noble Lord—above all, to the extent he would carry it, without incurring the greatest possible responsibility as regarded the general welfare of the country, and, more especially, as regarded the whole manufacturing interests of the Kingdom. It is impossible to have listened to the argument of the noble Lord, and especially to the description he gave of the state of degradation and misery which existed among the labouring classes in the manufacturing districts, without wishing that it was in the power of Parliament to apply an efficient remedy. But will anybody say, that this House can apply a remedy? Will anybody deny that we may most seriously aggravate the evils by attempting to cure them? The argument of the noble Lord, if legitimately carried out, goes against the system of manufactures by human labour altogether. It is not merely a question between a twelve hours' Bill and a ten hours' Bill, but it is in principle an argument to get rid of the whole system of factory labour. . . . I can show among my own constituents that there are descriptions of labour which are inevitably fatal to those engaged in them within a certain limited period; yet there are persons who feel themselves forced into it, and who incur all the danger, for the sake of the immediate advantages it brings with it, of death being its almost certain result. . . . What is the cause which obliges the people to labour to this excess? There is no inborn love of work within them. No man, except from necessity would devote himself to toil. Their lot, as it happens to be cast in the different ranks of society, does not necessarily deprive them of the love of enjoyment and of leisure. I believe that there is as much natural affection and as much desire to retain the woman in her own proper domestic circle among the working classes, as there exists among ourselves. No, it is not from a difference of nature that men and women and children toil during a long period of hours, but it is necessity that compels them to do so. Such is the pressure of that necessity upon the working classes, more especially, that you find men driven to do things, which, when we come to reflect on the consequences, strikes us as almost criminal, and as casting a blot on the social system; and then it is that we are induced to look to legislation as the means of affording some remedy for the evil. Poverty is enacted by the law, and then other enactments are necessary against the consequences which poverty compels men to resort to! If it be said, as it has been said, that no allusion ought to be made to the Corn Laws, the answer is, that by the admission of all parties they materially affect the demand for labour. It is upon the permanent demand for labour that the wages and the comforts of the operative classes depend. . . .

We may suppose such a state of affairs in a most prosperous community, where a man at the end of his moderate day's labour shall be able to repair to his family circle and spend the evening in the company of his wife and in the education of his children; but I do not know in what part of the world such a condition of society exists, and I am quite sure that it has never existed in any part of the history of this country. . . . I oppose the Bill from a strong desire to benefit the operative classes, and from a perfect conviction that inter-ference of this kind will be utterly fruitless. No manufacturer can carry on his trade unless he can obtain a remunerative return for his capital; and ad-mitting the truth of what was said by the right hon. Baronet, that a well-regulated self-interest is the great moving principle with the world, you can-not expect manufacturers to neglect it. I believe that the House could not enter upon a task more fraught with danger than to make an attempt unduly to restrict the hours of labour, since it is founded upon a false principle of humanity, which in the end is certain to defeat itself.

Lord *Francis Egerton* [Independent; Lancashire, South; younger son of the Marquis of Stafford]: I shall preface the few observations I intend to make by an avowal that I mean to vote for the Motion of my noble Friend. . . .

My hon. Friend, the Member for Sheffield, says, that if we pass this Bill, it will be necessary to apply a remedy to the evils of other employments more injurious to health than factories. I think we should do so when we can; and the principal reason for a Factory Regulation Bill has been, that you are able to carry it into effect. . . .

My right hon. Friend the Secretary for the Home Department has opposed the Motion with great ability, and upon strong grounds. He has stated what I believe will most probably be the effect of the measure—the diminution of wages. . . . I was prepared to believe that this consideration had been a good deal overlooked by some of the parties who desired the Bill, and I am bound to say that as far as my communications have gone, I have been undeceived upon that point. I never met with more rational or reasonable men than some of those I have seen upon this subject. They admit at once the probability of a reduction of wages; but they had balanced the probabilities, considered the evil, and were prepared to meet the consequences. It is partly upon that ground that I am disposed to consider the question in the light I view it. . . .

At all events, I am not of opinion that it can be said that factory labourers invariably have the advantage: on the contrary, a man in a good position on agricultural property, seems to me to have a better chance of permanent employment than a factory labourer. As to the great question incidentally introduced, I do not wish at all to dwell upon it, though I admit the right of hon. Members, if they think fit, to make this another Corn Law Debate. I do not, however, apprehend that the discussion of this Bill will derive any benefit from the introduction of so wide a question, but with the opinions held by the hon. Members for Manchester and Sheffield, it would certainly be too much to expect that they should not advert to it. They must act upon their own opinions with respect to the Corn Laws, and I must act upon mine, differing as I do materially from them as to the advantages of Corn Law Repeal. I am not aware that it is necessary for me to say more in explanation of the vote I shall give, and I know that it will be received with great dissatisfaction by some Gentlemen in the part of the country where I live, from whom I differ with great regret; and without undue egotism, I may be allowed to observe that I am not liable to the reproach of being a landed gentleman, standing up to deal with other interests but his own. If a diminution of wages be the consequence of this measure, I believe that nobody will be more directly sensible of the change than I shall be; even in an agricultural point of view, as far as I possess land, I am entirely dependent upon the manufacturing market. I have therefore felt, and shall feel again, any decrease of consumption. I have only indulged in this reference in order to rescue myself from the imputation of being opposed to interests because they are not my own. . . .

Mr. *Bright* [Whig; Durham City] said: . . . I am not one who will venture to say that the manufacturing districts of this country are a paradise; I believe there are in those districts evils great and serious; but whatever evils do there exist are referable to other causes than to the existence of factories and long chimnies. Most of the statements which the noble Lord has read, would be just as applicable to Birmingham, or to this metropolis, as to the northern districts; and as he read them over, with respect to the ignorance and intemperance of the people, the disobedience of children to their parents, the sufferings of mothers, and the privations which the children endure, I felt that there was scarcely a complaint which has been made against the manufacturing districts of the north of England, which might not be urged with at least as much force against the poorest portion of the population of every large city in Great Britain and Ireland. But among the population of Lancashire and Yorkshire, where towns are so numerous as almost to touch each other, these evils are more observable than in a population less densely crowded together. I can prove, however, and I do not wish to be as one-sided as the noble Lord, I can prove from authorities, which are at least as worthy of attention as his, the very reverse in many respects of what he has stated as the true state of those districts. Now the Committee will bear in mind that a large portion of the documents which the noble Lord has quoted, have neither dates nor names. I can give dates and names, . . . and I believe that the authorities I shall cite are worthy of the deepest attention. I must go over the grounds of complaint which the noble Lord has urged, and although I may run the risk of being a little tedious, yet considering that for two hours or more I have listened to the charges which he has made, I do think that, connected as I am most intimately with the population and the district to which the noble Lord has alluded, I have a right to an audience for the counter-statement which I have to make. Now, with respect to the health of the persons employed: . . .

In conclusion, then, it is proved, by a preponderance of seventy-two witnesses against seventeen, that the health of those employed in cotton mills is nowise inferior to that in other occupations; and, secondly, it is proved by tables drawn up by the secretary of a sick club, and by the more extensive tables of a London actuary, that the health of the factory children is decidedly superior to that of the labouring poor otherwise employed.

. . . I admit there are evils, serious evils, and much distress in the manufacturing districts; many are still out of employment, and in many branches of trade wages are low. We have violent fluctuations in trade, and periods when multitudes endure great suffering and it becomes this House to inquire why do these fluctuations occur, and what is the great cause of their suffering. I attribute much of this to the mistaken and unjust policy pursued by this House, with respect to the trade and industry of the country. Hitherto manufacturers have had no fair chance: you have interfered with their natural progress, you have crippled them by your restrictions, you have at times almost destroyed them by monopolies, you have made them the sources of your public revenue, and the upholders of your rents, but at your hands they have never to this moment received justice and fair dealing. I do not charge the noble Lord with dishonesty, but I am confident if he had looked at this question with as anxious a desire to discover truth, as he has to find materials for his case, he would have found many subjects of congratulation to counterbalance every one which he would have had reason to deplore. The noble Lord and hon. Gentlemen opposite, when they view from their distant eminence the state of the manufacturing districts, look through the right end of the telescope; what they see is thus brought near to them, and is greatly magnified; but when they are asked to look at the rural districts, they reverse the telescope and then everything is thrown to the greatest possible distance and is diminished as much as possible. That great hardships were once practised in the manufactories of this country cannot be denied, but a most gratifying change and improvement has taken place since the time when the respected father of the right hon. Baronet (Sir R. Peel) was so largely connected with them. But this change has not arisen from legislation in this House; it has sprung from that general improvement which is observable throughout all classes of the community. The treatment of children in schools is now rational and humane,—formerly it was irrational and cruel; the treatment of lunatics in our asylums was once a disgrace to humanity,—now, how great is the change; the prisoners in our gaols feel the influence of this growing sentiment in favour of gentler treatment; and the spread of civilization and consideration for each other among the people has done infinitely more for the weak and helpless than all the laws which this House has ever passed. I do not charge the noble Lord with being actuated by feelings of malice in his conduct towards the manufacturers of this country, but I do believe him to have been, and to be now, grossly imposed upon by the persons upon whose information he relies. . . .

The labourers employed in the cotton trade are more steadily employed and better paid than in any other trade in this country. I admit this people have suffered severely, but they have struggled manfully with the adversity which has overtaken them, whilst we have been foolish enough to permit the existence of monopolies and injustice, enough to have destroyed for ever the energies and the prosperity of an ordinary people. In addition to these monopolies, we have taxes most oppressive and unequal. The tax on raw cotton alone amounts to 50*l.* to 100*l.* per week on many manufacturing establishments; that with which I am connected being thus burthened to the amount of 75*l.* per week; and as four-fifths of all these manufactures are exported, and compete with foreign manufacturers who pay no such tax, the whole amount of it must come out of the profits and the wages of those engaged in the cotton trade. The noble Lord, the Member for Liverpool, says, he is most anxious to improve the condition of the working classes; he points to more education, a higher state of morals, better food and better clothing, as the result of the adoption of the proposition now before the House. But there is one thing that noble Lord has failed to prove; he has failed to show how working only ten hours will give the people more sugar. The noble Lord is the representative of the sugar monopolists of Liverpool, and, after voting to deprive the people of sugar, he is perfectly consistent in denying them the liberty even to work. The people ask for freedom for their industry, for the removal of the shackles on their trade; you deny it to them, and then forbid them to labour, as if working less would give them more food, whilst your monopoly laws make food scarce and dear. Give them liberty to work, give them the market of the world for their produce, give them the power to live comfortably, and increasing means and increasing intelligence will speedily render them independent enough and wise enough to bring the duration of labour to that point at which life shall be passed with less of irksome toil of every kind, and more of recreation and enjoyment. It is because I am convinced this project is now impracticable, and that under our present oppressive Legislation, it would make all past injustice only more intolerable, that I shall vote against the proposition [limiting hours of work] which the noble Lord, the Member for Dorset, has submitted to the House.

THOMAS CARLYLE

ANYONE WHO READS the Parliamentary debates at the time of the passing of the Ten Hour Factory Act will notice that they express a growing concern with welfare at the expense of wealth. Not the least of those who contributed to changing the climate of opinion was Thomas Carlyle (1795–1881). The son of a Scottish stonemason, Carlyle had originally been intended for the Calvinist ministry, but his early reading of the French rationalists, and then of Gibbon, convinced him "that Christianity was not true." He abandoned the ministry, but not Calvinism. The conclusions of rationalism seemed to be unavoidable, but he felt them inadequate without a religious support. Reading in the works of the Germans—Schiller, Goethe, Kant, and Fichte—revived his belief in a moral order. Skepticism he now considered to be the consequence of an uncritically exclusive dependence upon "understanding," rather than upon the higher faculty of "reason," which alone could pronounce "the Everlasting Yea."

It was characteristic of Carlyle to refer social ills to the deep-lying moral error of his times—its thoroughgoing "mechanism." Political activity that went on within parliamentary halls without any regard for the deeply social and moral forces on which it was based seemed to him to be frivolous; Chartism was for him merely a symptom, a tremendously significant one, the function of which was to point to a more fundamental issue—"the Condition-of-England question." This fundamental social problem revolved for Carlyle around the growing division between the working classes on the one hand and the privileged and propertied classes on the other. His *French Revolution* was, at least in part, the attempt to teach the historical lesson that an irresponsible ruling class could expect only to be swept under in the revolutionary uprising of the masses—a revolution that would be purely negative.

Carlyle saw the cure for this disease in the "gospel of work." The notion of a place for every man and every man in his place was one that was obviously similar to the functionally organized medieval society. And in *Past and Present,* the most developed expression of his social philosophy, Carlyle criticized the materialism, the egoism, and the irreligion of his age in the light of a society which had been founded on the opposite ideals. Like Saint-Simon, he recognized the similarity of the industrial factory to the centralized and disciplined medieval group life; but he recognized that without the gospel of work the individual worker could get no sense of participation in the common mission of society, and that without the spirit of chivalry the new masters of society, the "Captains of Industry," could exercise only coercive authority. In more positive terms, the ideal society delineated by Carlyle was one in which those naturally superior would rule righteously. His belief in Providence led him to feel that such men were providentially sent when the need arose.

Although Carlyle was radical in his antagonism to what James Mill called "the Sinister Interest of Privilege," he thus differed from the utilitarians in his disregard for the forms of politics and his disaffection for democracy. "Benthamee

Radicalism" seemed to him to epitomize the spirit of the age—its egoism, its leveling downward, its "mammonism." The attempt of the multitude, through universal suffrage, to be ruled by the multitude seemed to him to contravene the basic law of nature which sets men in a hierarchy of leaders and led. In place of an appeal for the pursuit of happiness such as Bentham's, his appeal was for a higher sense of justice. His influence permeated the thought of many thinkers of his generation and those following. In his emphasis upon the functional organization of society there is one of the roots of later Fabianism; in his emphasis upon immaterial values and upon the worker's active participation in society we find the background of Ruskin's *Political Economy of Art* and the elements of the "welfare economics" of men like J. A. Hobson; and in his cult of the Hero we find background for present-day anti-democratic tendencies and the contemporary deification of the Leader.

The following selections are taken from *Past and Present* (1843).

PAST AND PRESENT

Proem

MIDAS

THE CONDITION of England, on which many pamphlets are now in the course of publication, and many thoughts unpublished are going on in every reflective head, is justly regarded as one of the most ominous, and withal one of the strangest, ever seen in this world. England is full of wealth, of multifarious produce, supply for human want in every kind; yet England is dying of inanition. With unabated bounty the land of England blooms and grows; waving with yellow harvests; thick-studded with workshops, industrial implements, with fifteen millions of workers, understood to be the strongest, the cunningest and the willingest our Earth ever had; these men are here; the work they have done, the fruit they have realized is here, abundant, exuberant on every hand of us: and behold, some baleful fiat as of Enchantment has gone forth, saying, "Touch it not, ye workers, ye master-workers, ye master-idlers; none of you can touch it, no man of you shall be the better for it; this is enchanted fruit!" On the poor workers such fiat falls first, in its rudest shape; but on the rich master-workers too it falls; neither can the rich master-idlers, nor any richest or highest man escape, but all are like to be brought low with it, and made "poor" enough, in the money sense or a far fataler one.

Of these successful skilful workers some two millions, it is now counted, sit in Workhouses, Poor-law Prisons; or have "out-door relief" flung over the wall to them,—the workhouse Bastille being filled to bursting, and the strong Poor-law broken asunder by a stronger. They sit there, these many months now; their hope of deliverance as yet small. In workhouses, pleasantly so-named, because work cannot be done in them. Twelve-hundred-thousand workers in England alone; their cunning right-hand lamed, lying idle in their sorrowful bosom; their hopes, outlooks, share of this fair world, shut-in by narrow walls. They sit there, pent up, as in a kind of horrid enchantment; glad to be imprisoned and enchanted, that they may not perish starved. The picturesque Tourist, in a sunny autumn day, through this bounteous realm of England, descries the Union Workhouse on his path.

Passing by the Workhouse of St. Ives in Huntingdonshire, on a bright day last autumn [says the picturesque Tourist], I saw sitting on wooden benches, in front of their Bastille and within their ring-wall and its railings, some half-hundred or more of these men. Tall robust figures, young mostly or of middle age; of honest countenance, many of them thoughtful and even intelligent-looking men. They sat there, near by one another; but in a kind of torpor, especially in a silence, which was very striking. In silence: for, alas, what word was to be said? An Earth all lying round, crying, Come and till me, come and reap me;—yet we here sit enchanted! In the eyes and brows of these men hung the gloomiest expression, not of anger, but of grief and shame and manifold inarticulate distress and weariness; they returned my glance with a glance that seemed to say, "Do not look at us. We sit enchanted here, we know not why. The Sun shines and the Earth calls; and, by the governing Powers and Impotences of this England, we are forbidden to obey. It is impossible, they tell us!" There was something that reminded me of Dante's Hell in the look of all this; and I rode swiftly away. . . .

HERO-WORSHIP

To the present editor, not less than to Bobus, a Government of the Wisest, what Bobus calls an Aristocracy of Talent, seems the one healing remedy: but he is not so sanguine as Bobus with respect to the means of realizing it. He thinks that we have at once missed realizing it, and come to need it so pressingly, by departing far from the inner eternal Laws, and taking-up with the temporary outer semblances of Laws. He thinks that "enlightened Egoism," never so luminous, is not the rule by which man's life can be led. That "Laissez-faire," "Supply-and-demand," "Cash-payment for the sole nexus," and so forth, were not, are not and will never be, a practicable Law of Union for a Society of Men. That Poor and Rich, that Governed and Governing, cannot long live together on any such Law of Union. Alas, he thinks that man has a soul in him, *different* from the stomach in any sense of this word; that if said soul be asphyxied, and lie quietly forgotten, the man and his affairs are in a bad way. He thinks that said soul will have to be resuscitated from its asphyxia; that if it prove irresuscitable, the man is not long for this world. In brief, that Midas-eared Mammonism, double-barrelled Dilettantism, and their thousand adjuncts and corollaries, are *not* the Law by which God Almighty has appointed this His Universe to go. That, once for all, these are not the Law: and then farther that we shall have to return to what *is* the Law,—not by smooth flowery paths, it is like, and with "tremendous cheers" in our throat; but over steep untrodden places, through stormclad chasms, waste oceans, and the bosom of tornadoes; thank Heaven, if not through very Chaos and the Abyss! The resuscitating of a soul that has gone to asphyxia is no momentary or pleasant process, but a long and terrible one.

To the present Editor, "Hero-worship," as he has elsewhere named it, means much more than an elected Parliament, or stated Aristocracy, of the Wisest; for in his dialect it is the summary, ultimate essence, and supreme practical perfection of all manner of "worship," and true worthships and noblenesses whatsoever. Such blessed Parliament and, were it once in perfection, blessed Aristocracy of the Wisest, god-honored and man-honored, he does look for, more and more perfected,—as the topmost blessed practical apex of a whole world reformed from sham-worship, informed anew with worship, with truth and blessedness! He thinks that Hero-worship, done differently in every different epoch of the world, is the soul of all social business among men; that the doing of it well, or the doing of it ill, measures accurately what degree of well-being or of ill-being there is in the world's affairs. . . .

"Hero-worship," if you will,—yes, friends; but, first of all, by being ourselves of heroic mind. A whole world of Heroes; a world not of Flunkies, where no Hero-King *can* reign: that is what we aim at! We, for our share, will put away all Flunkyism, Baseness, Unveracity from us; we shall then hope to have Noblenesses and Veracities set over us; never till then. Let Bobus and Company sneer, "That is your Reform!" Yes, Bobus, that is our Reform; and except in that, and what will follow out of that, we have no hope at all. Reform, like Charity, O Bobus, must begin at home. Once well at home, how will it radiate outwards, irrepressible, into all that we touch and handle, speak and work; kindling ever new light, by incalculable contagion, spreading in geometric ratio, far and wide,—doing good only, wheresoever it spreads, and not evil.

By Reform Bills, Anti-Corn-Law Bills, and thousand other bills and methods, we will demand of our Governors, with emphasis, and for the first time not without effect, that they cease to be quacks, or else depart; that they set no quackeries and blockheadisms anywhere to rule over us, that they utter or act no cant to us,—it will be better if they do not. For we shall now know quacks when we see them; cant, when we hear it, shall be horrible to us! . . .

Yes friends: Hero-kings, and a whole world not unheroic,—there lies the port and happy haven, towards which, through all these stormtost seas, French Revolutions, Chartisms, Manchester Insurrections, that make the heart sick in these bad days, the Supreme Powers are driving us. On the whole, blessed be the Supreme Powers, stern as they are! Towards that haven will we, O friends; let all true men, with what of faculty is in them, bend valiantly, incessantly, with thousand-fold endeavor, thither, thither! There, or else in the Ocean-abysses, it is very clear to me, we shall arrive. . . .

The Modern Worker

GOSPEL OF MAMMONISM

True, it must be owned, we for the present, with our Mammon-Gospel, have come to strange conclusions. We call it a Society; and go about professing openly the totalest separation, isolation. Our life is not a mutual helpfulness; but rather, cloaked under the due laws-of-war, named "fair competition" and so forth, it is a mutual hostility. We have profoundly forgotten everywhere that *Cash-payment* is not the sole relation of human beings; we think, nothing doubting, that *it* absolves and liquidates all engagements of man. "My starving workers?" answers the rich mill-owner: "Did not I hire them fairly in the market? Did I not pay them, to the last sixpence, the sum covenanted for? What have I to do with them more?"—Verily Mammon-worship is a melancholy creed. When Cain, for his own behoof, had killed Abel, and was questioned, "Where is thy brother?" he too made answer, "Am I my brother's keeper?" Did I not pay my brother *his* wages, the thing he had merited from me?

O sumptuous Merchant-Prince, illustrious game-preserving Duke, is there no way of "killing" thy brother but Cain's rude way! . . .

One of Dr. Alison's Scotch facts struck us much. A poor Irish Widow, her husband having died in one of the Lanes of Edinburgh, went forth with her three children, bare of all resource, to solicit help from the Charitable Establishments of that City. At this Charitable Establishment and then at that she was refused; referred from one to the other, helped by none;—till she had exhausted them all; till her strength and heart failed her: she sank down in typhus-fever; died, and infected her Lane with fever, so that "seventeen other persons" died of fever there in consequence. The humane Physician asks thereupon, as with a heart too full for speaking, Would it not have been *economy* to help this poor Widow? She took typhus-fever, and killed seventeen of you!—

Very curious. The forlorn Irish Widow applies to her fellow-creatures, as if saying, "Behold I am sinking, bare of help: ye must help me! I am your sister, bone of your bone; one God made us: ye must help me!" They answer, "No, impossible; thou art no sister of ours." But she proves her sisterhood; her typhus-fever kills *them:* they actually were her brothers, though denying it! Had human creature ever to go lower for a proof? . . .

HAPPY

Does not the whole wretchedness, the whole *Atheism* as I call it, of man's ways, in these generations, shadow itself for us in that unspeakable Life-philosophy of his: The pretension to be what he calls "happy"? . . .

We construct our theory of Human Duties, not on any Greatest-Nobleness Principle, never so mistaken; no, but on a Greatest-Happiness Principle. "The word *Soul* with us, as in some Slavonic dialects, seems to be synonymous with *Stomach.*" We plead and speak, in our Parliaments and elsewhere, not as from the Soul, but from the Stomach;—wherefore indeed our pleadings are so slow to profit. We plead not for God's Justice; we are not ashamed to stand clamoring and pleading for our own "interests," our own rents and trade-profits; we say, They are the "interests" of so many; there is such an intense desire in us for them! We demand Free-Trade, with much just vociferation and benevolence, That the poorer classes, who are terribly ill-off at present, may have cheaper New-Orleans bacon. Men ask on Free-trade platforms, How can the indomitable spirit of Englishmen be kept up without plenty of bacon? We shall become a ruined Nation!—Surely, my friends, plenty of bacon is good and indispensable: but, I doubt, you will never get even bacon by aiming only at that. You are men, not animals of prey, well-used or ill-used! Your Greatest-Happiness Principle seems to me fast becoming a rather unhappy one. . .

The only happiness a brave man ever troubled himself with asking much about was, happiness enough to get his work done. Not "I can't eat!" but "I can't work!" that was the burden of all wise complaining among men. It is, after all, the one unhappiness of a man, That he cannot work; that he cannot get his destiny as a man fulfilled. Behold, the day is passing swiftly over, our life is passing swiftly over; and the night cometh, wherein no man can work. The night once come, our happiness, our unhappiness,—it is all abolished, vanished, clean gone; a thing that has been: "not of the slightest consequence" . . . ! Brief brawling Day, with its noisy phantasms, its poor paper-crowns tinsel-gilt, is gone; and divine everlasting Night, with her star-diadems, with her silences and her veracities, is come! What hast thou done, and how? Happiness, unhappiness: all that was but the *wages* thou hadst; thou hast spent all that, in sustaining thyself hitherward; not a coin of it remains with thee, it is all spent, eaten: and now thy work, where is thy work? Swift, out with it; let us see thy work!

Of a truth, if man were not a poor hungry dastard, and even much of a blockhead withal, he would cease criticising his victuals to such extent; and criticise himself rather, what he does with his victuals!

THE ENGLISH

And yet, with all thy theoretic platitudes, what a depth of practical sense in thee, great England! A depth of sense, of justice, and courage; in which, under all emergencies and world-bewilderments, and under this most complex of emergencies we now live in, there is still hope, there is still assurance! . . .

Bull is a born Conservative; for this too I inexpressibly honor him. All great Peoples are conservatives; slow to believe in novelties; patient of much error in actualities; deeply and forever certain of the greatness that is in Law, in Custom once solemnly established, and now long recognized as just and final.—True, O Radical Reformer, there is no Custom that can, properly speaking, be final; none. And yet thou seest *Customs* which, in all civilized countries, are accounted final; nay, under the Old-Roman name of *Mores,* are accounted *Morality,* Virtue, Laws of God Himself. Such, I assure thee, not a few of them are; such almost all of them once were. And greatly do I respect the solid character,—a blockhead, thou wilt say; yes, but a well-conditioned blockhead, and the best-conditioned,—who esteems all "Customs once solemnly acknowledged" to be ultimate, divine, and the rule for a man to walk by, nothing doubting, not inquiring farther. . . .

O my Conservative friends, who still specially name and struggle to approve yourselves "Conservative," would to Heaven I could persuade you of this world-old fact, than which Fate is not surer, That Truth and Justice alone are *capable* of being "conserved" and preserved! The thing which is unjust, which is *not* according to God's Law, will you, in a God's Universe, try to conserve that? It is so old, say you. Yes, and the hotter haste ought *you,* of all others, to be in, to let it grow no older! If but the faintest whisper in your hearts intimate to you that it is not fair,—hasten, for the sake of Conservatism itself, to probe it rigorously, to cast it forth at once and forever if guilty. How will or can you preserve *it,* the thing that is not fair? "Impossibility" a thousandfold is marked on that. And ye call yourselves Conservatives, Aristocracies:—ought not honor and nobleness of mind, if they had departed from all the Earth elsewhere, to find their last refuge with you? Ye unfortunate! . . .

If I were the Conservative Party of England (which is another bold figure of speech), I would not for a hundred thousand pounds an hour allow those

Corn-Laws to continue! Potosi and Golconda put together would not purchase my assent to them. Do you count what treasuries of bitter indignation they are laying up for you in every just English heart? Do you know what questions, not as to Corn-prices and Sliding-scales alone, they are *forcing* every reflective Englishman to ask himself? Questions insoluble, or hitherto unsolved; deeper than any of our Logic-plummets hitherto will sound: questions deep enough,—which it were better that we did not name even in thought! You are forcing us to think of them, to begin uttering them. The utterance of them is begun; and where will it be ended, think you? When two millions of one's brother-men sit in Workhouses, and five millions, as is insolently said, "rejoice in potatoes," there are various things that must be begun, let them end where they can.

UNWORKING ARISTOCRACY

. . . What looks maddest, miserablest in these mad and miserable Corn-Laws is independent altogether of their "effect on wages," their effect on "increase of trade," or any other such effect: it is the continual maddening proof they protrude into the faces of all men, that our Governing Class, called by God and Nature and the inflexible law of Fact, either to do something toward government, or to die and be abolished,—have not yet learned even to sit still and do no mischief! For no Anti-Corn-Law League yet asks more of them than this;—Nature and Fact, very imperatively, asking so much more of them. Anti-Corn-Law League asks not, Do something; but, Cease your destructive misdoing, Do ye nothing!

Nature's message will have itself obeyed: messages of mere Free-Trade, Anti-Corn-Law League and Laissez-faire, will then need small obeying!— Ye fools, in name of Heaven, work, work, at the Ark of Deliverance for yourselves and us, while hours are still granted you! No: instead of working at the Ark, they say, "We cannot get our hands kept rightly warm"; and *sit obstinately burning the planks*. No madder spectacle at present exhibits itself under this Sun.

The Working Aristocracy; Mill-owners, Manufacturers, Commanders of Working Men: alas, against them also much shall be brought in accusation; much,—and the freest Trade in Corn, total abolition of Tariffs, and uttermost "Increase of Manufactures" and "Prosperity of Commerce," will permanently mend no jot of it. The Working Aristocracy must strike into a new path; must understand that money alone is *not* the representative either of man's success in the world, or of man's duties to man; and reform their own selves from top to bottom, if they wish England reformed. England will not be habitable long, unreformed.

The Working Aristocracy— Yes, but on the threshold of all this, it is again and again to be asked, What of the Idle Aristocracy? Again and again, What shall we say of the Idle Aristocracy, the Owners of the Soil of England; whose recognized function is that of handsomely consuming the rents of England, shooting the partridges of England, and as an agreeable amusement (if the purchase-money and other conveniences serve), dilettante-ing in Parliament and Quarter-Sessions for England? We will say mournfully, in the presence of Heaven and Earth,—that we stand speechless, stupent, and know not what to say! That a class of men entitled to live sumptuously on the marrow of the earth; permitted simply, nay entreated, and as yet entreated in vain, to do nothing at all in return, was never heretofore seen on the face of this Planet. That such a class is transitory, exceptional, and, unless Nature's Laws fall dead, cannot continue. That it has continued now a moderate while; has, for the last fifty years, been rapidly attaining its state of perfection. That it will have to find its duties and do them; or else that it must and will cease to be seen on the face of this Planet, which is a Working one, not an Idle one.

Alas, alas, the Working Aristocracy, admonished by Trades-unions, Chartist conflagrations, above all by their own shrewd sense kept in perpetual communion with the fact of things, will assuredly reform themselves, and a working world will still be possible:—but the fate of the Idle Aristocracy, as one reads its horoscope hitherto in Corn-Laws and suchlike, is an abyss that fills one with despair. Yes, my rosy fox-hunting brothers, a terrible *Hippocratic look* reveals itself (God knows, not to my joy) through those fresh buxom countenances of yours. Through your Corn-Law Majorities, Sliding-Scales, Protecting-Duties, Bribery-Elections, and triumphant Kentish-fire, a thinking eye discerns ghastly images of ruin, too ghastly for words; a handwriting as of MENE, MENE. Men and brothers, on your Sliding-Scale you seem sliding, and to have slid,—you little know whither! Good God! did not a French Donothing Aristocracy, hardly above half a century ago, declare in like manner, and in its featherbed believe in like manner, "We cannot exist, and continue to dress and parade ourselves, on the just rent of the soil of France; but we must have farther payment than rent of the soil, we must be exempted from taxes too,"—we must have a Corn-Law to extend our rent? This was in 1789: in four years more— Did you look into the Tanneries of Meudon, and the long-naked making for themselves breeches of human skins! May the merciful Heavens avert the omen; may we be wiser, that so we be less wretched. . . .

REWARD

All true work is sacred; in all true work, were it but true hand-labor, there is something of divineness. Labor, wide as the Earth, has its summit in Heaven. Sweat of the brow; and up from that to sweat of the brain, sweat of the heart; which includes all Kepler calculations, Newton meditations, all Sciences, all spoken Epics, all acted Heroisms, Martyrdoms,—up to that "Agony of bloody sweat," which all men have called divine! O brother, if this is not "worship," then I say, the more pity for worship; for this is the noblest thing yet discovered under God's sky. Who art thou that complainest of thy life of toil? Complain not. Look up, my wearied brother; see thy fellow Workmen there, in God's Eternity; surviving there, they alone surviving: sacred Band of the Immortals, celestial Bodyguard of the Empire of Mankind. Even in the weak Human Memory they survive so long, as saints, as heroes, as gods; they alone surviving; peopling, they alone, the unmeasured solitudes of Time! To thee Heaven, though severe, is *not* unkind; Heaven is kind,—as a noble Mother; as that Spartan Mother, saying while she gave her son his shield, "With it, my son, or upon it!" Thou too shalt return *home* in honor; to thy far-distant Home, in honor; doubt it not,—if in the battle thou keep thy shield! Thou, in the Eternities and deepest Death-kingdoms, are not an alien; thou everywhere art a denizen! Complain not; the very Spartans did not *complain*. . . .

On the whole, we do entirely agree with those old Monks, *Laborare est Orare*. In a thousand senses, from one end of it to the other, true Work *is* Worship. He that works, whatsoever be his work, he bodies forth the form of Things Unseen; a small Poet every Worker is. The idea, were it but of his poor Delf Platter, how much more of his Epic Poem, is as yet "seen," half-seen, only by himself; to all others it is a thing unseen, impossible; to Nature herself it is a thing unseen, a thing which never hitherto was;—very "impossible," for it is as yet a No-thing! The Unseen Powers had need to watch over such a man; he works in and for the Unseen. Alas, if he look to the Seen Powers only, he may as well quit the business; his No-thing will never rightly issue as a Thing, but as a Deceptivity, a Sham-thing,—which it had better not do! . . .

Horoscope

CAPTAINS OF INDUSTRY

The leaders of industry, if Industry is ever to be led, are virtually the Captains of the World! if there be no nobleness in them, there will never be an Aristocracy more. But let the Captains of Industry consider: once again, are they born of other clay than the old Captains of Slaughter; doomed forever to be no Chivalry, but a mere gold-plated *Doggery,*—what the French well name *Canaille,* "Doggery" with more or less gold carrion at its disposal? Captains of Industry are the true Fighters, henceforth recognizable as the only true ones: Fighters against Chaos, Necessity and the Devil and Jötuns; and lead on Mankind in that great, and alone true, and universal warfare; the stars in their courses fighting for them, and all Heaven and all Earth saying audibly, Well done! Let the Captains of Industry retire into their own hearts, and ask solemnly, If there is nothing but vulturous hunger, for fine wines, valet reputation and gilt carriages, discoverable there? Of hearts made by the Almighty God I will not believe such a thing. Deep-hidden under wretchedest god-forgetting Cants, Epicurisms, Dead-Sea Apisms; forgotten as under foulest fat Lethe mud and weeds, there is yet, in all hearts born into this God's-World, a spark of the Godlike slumbering. Awake, O nightmare sleepers; awake, arise, or be forever fallen! This is not playhouse poetry; it is sober fact. Our England, our world cannot live as it is. It will connect itself with a God again, or go down with nameless throes and fire-consummation to the Devils. Thou who feelest aught of such a Godlike stirring in thee, any faintest intimation of it as through heavy-laden dreams, follow *it,* I conjure thee. Arise, save thyself, be one of those that save thy country. . . .

Love of men cannot be bought by cash-payment; and without love men cannot endure to be together. You cannot lead a Fighting World without having it regimented, chivalried: the thing, in a day, becomes impossible; all men in it, the highest at first, the very lowest at last, discern consciously, or by a noble instinct, this necessity. And can you any more continue to lead a Working World unregimented, anarchic? I answer, and the Heavens and Earth are now answering, No! The thing becomes not "in a day" impossible; but in some two generations it does. Yes, when fathers and mothers, in Stockport hunger-cellars, begin to eat their children, and Irish widows have to prove their relationship by dying of typhus-fever; and amid Governing "Corporations of the Best and Bravest," busy to preserve their game by "bushing," dark millions of God's human creatures start up in mad Chartisms, impracticable Sacred-Months, and Manchester Insurrections;—and there is a virtual Industrial Aristocracy as yet only half-alive, spell-bound amid money-bags and ledgers; and an actual Idle Aristocracy seemingly near dead in somnolent delusions, in trespasses and double-barrels; "sliding," as on inclined-planes, which every new year they *soap* with new Hansard's-jargon under God's sky, and so are "sliding," ever faster, toward a "scale" and balance-scale whereon is written *Thou art found Wanting:*—in such days, after a generation or two, I say, it does become, even to the low and simple, very palpably impossible! . . .

PERMANENCE

Standing on the threshold, nay as yet outside the threshold, of a "Chivalry of Labor," and an immeasurable Future which it is to fill with fruitfulness and verdant shade; where so much has not yet come even to the rudimental state, and all speech of positive enactments were hazardous in those who know this business only by the eye,—let us here hint at simply one widest universal principle, as the basis from which all organization hitherto has grown up among men, and all henceforth will have to grow: The principle of Permanent Contract instead of Temporary. . . .

A question arises here: Whether, in some ulterior, perhaps some not far-distant stage of this "Chivalry of Labor," your Master-Worker may not find it possible, and needful, to grant his Workers permanent *interest* in his enterprise and theirs? So that it become, in practical result, what in essential fact and justice it ever is, a joint enterprise; all men, from the Chief Master down to the lowest Overseer and Operative, economically as well as loyally concerned for it?—Which question I do not answer. The answer, near or else far, is perhaps, Yes;—and yet one knows the difficulties, despotism is essential in most enterprises; I am told, they do not tolerate "freedom of debate" on board a Seventy-four! Republican senate and *plebiscita* would not answer well in Cotton-Mills. And yet observe there too: Freedom, not nomad's or ape's Freedom, but man's Freedom; this is indispensable. We must have it, and will have it! To reconcile Despotism with Freedom:—well, is that such a mystery? Do you not already know the way? It is to make your Despotism *just*. Rigorous as Destiny; but just too, as Destiny and its Laws. The Laws of God: all men obey these, and have no "Freedom" at all but in obeying them. The way is already known, part of the way;—and courage and some qualities are needed for walking on it!

IV PROGRAMS FOR REFORM

JEREMY BENTHAM

THE LIFE of the indefatigable Jeremy Bentham (1748–1832) spanned the era between the publication of Rousseau's *Discourse on the Arts and Sciences* and England's first Reform Bill. The influence of Hume, Joseph Priestley, and Helvétius, all in their various ways precursors of the utilitarianism of Bentham, is apparent in his earlier writings. But Bentham, not a slave to any intellectual tradition, converted these inspirations into his own distinctive contribution to moral philosophy and social reform. His lifework represents an achievement impressive not only for its scope and quantity but also for its suggestive power. Bentham's writings covered such subjects as civil law, criminal law, constitutional law, international law, political economy, colonialism, legal procedure and evidence, moral philosophy, language, and religion. All of his work was done in self-imposed seclusion and isolation from the active social world of his admirers.

Because it emphasizes the actual consequences of human conduct rather than debatable motives, Bentham's moral theory was a particularly suitable basis for social action. His later works on legal and social reform carried forward Bentham's initial assault upon moral complacency and self-contentment. The development of his moral philosophy eventually became subservient to the needs for the reconstruction and reform of English society. Bentham's works on legal reform had influence in France, Russia, the Latin American republics, Portugal, Spain, and Germany; he maintained an interest in the United States, and even turned his attentions to possible reforms for India, Egypt, and Poland.

Disappointed with the Tories as reformers, Bentham came into closer association with James Mill and his circle of "philosophical radicals" and inspired them to a more decisive and articulate campaign for English reform. In 1824 Bentham founded the *Westminster Review,* a magazine for the promotion and publication of the views of this group. They held up to effective criticism cumbersome and outmoded political and legal institutions, and they set before the public the standard of a democratic and economical government. Their program won major victories in the passage of the Reform Bill of 1832 and in a wide variety of subsequent reforms. G. M. Young, in *Victorian England, Portrait of An Age* (1936), made this estimate of the Benthamite contribution: "The Philosophical Radicals . . . came into a world where medieval prejudice, Tudor Law, Stuart Economics, and Hanoverian patronage still luxuriated in wild confusion, and by the straight and narrow paths they cut we are walking still. . . . It would be hard to find any corner of our public life where the spirit of Bentham is not working today." Bentham's effect upon modern English society can hardly be overstated.

The readings that follow are from Bentham's "Principles of Legislation" in *The Theory of Legislation* (New York: Harcourt, Brace, 1931). This work first appeared in Etienne Dumont's French version (*Traités de legislation civile et penale,* 1802) and was translated into English by Richard Hildreth in 1864. Prior to

Hildreth's translation there were German, Russian, Spanish, and Hungarian renditions of the *Traités*. It has also been translated into Polish and Portuguese.

ઌ

PRINCIPLES OF LEGISLATION

CHAPTER I: THE PRINCIPLE OF UTILITY

THE PUBLIC GOOD ought to be the object of the legislator; GENERAL UTILITY ought to be the foundation of his reasonings. To know the true good of the community is what constitutes the science of legislation; the art consists in finding the means to realize that good.

The principle of *utility*, vaguely announced, is seldom contradicted; it is even looked upon as a sort of commonplace in politics and morals. But this almost universal assent is only apparent. The same ideas are not attached to this principle; the same value is not given to it; no uniform and logical manner of reasoning results from it.

To give it all the efficacy which it ought to have, that is, to make it the foundation of a system of reasonings, three conditions are necessary.

First,—To attach clear and precise ideas to the word *utility*, exactly the same with all who employ it.

Second,—To establish the unity and the sovereignty of this principle, by rigorously excluding every other. It is nothing to subscribe to it in general; it must be admitted without any exception.

Third,—To find the processes of a moral arithmetic by which uniform results may be arrived at.

The causes of dissent from the doctrine of utility may all be referred to two false principles, which exercise an influence, sometimes open and sometimes secret, upon the judgments of men. If these can be pointed out and excluded, the true principle will remain in purity and strength.

These three principles are like three roads which often cross each other, but of which only one leads to the wished-for destination. The traveller turns often from one into another, and loses in these wanderings more than half his time and strength. The true route is however the easiest; it has mile-stones which cannot be shifted, it has inscriptions, in a universal language, which cannot be effaced; while the two false routes have only contradictory directions in enigmatical characters. But without abusing the language of allegory, let us seek to give a clear idea of the true principle, and of its two adversaries.

Nature has placed man under the empire of *pleasure* and of *pain*. We owe

to them all our ideas; we refer to them all our judgments, and all the determinations of our life. He who pretends to withdraw himself from this subjection knows not what he says. His only object is to seek pleasure and to shun
pain, even at the very instant that he rejects the greatest pleasures or embraces
pains the most acute. These eternal and irresistible sentiments ought to be the
great study of the moralist and the legislator. The *principle of utility* subjects
everything to these two motives.

Utility is an abstract term. It expresses the property or tendency of a thing
to prevent some evil or to procure some good. *Evil* is pain, or the cause of
pain. *Good* is pleasure, or the cause of pleasure. That which is conformable to
the utility, or the interest of an individual, is what tends to augment the total
sum of his happiness. That which is conformable to the utility, or the interest
of a community, is what tends to augment the total sum of the happiness of
the individuals that compose it.

A *principle* is a first idea, which is made the beginning or basis of a system
of reasonings. To illustrate it by a sensible image, it is a fixed point to which the
first link of a chain is attached. Such a principle must be clearly evident—to
illustrate and to explain it must secure its acknowledgment. Such are the
axioms of mathematics; they are not proved directly; it is enough to show
that they cannot be rejected without falling into absurdity.

The *logic of utility* consists in setting out, in all the operations of the judgment, from the calculation or comparison of pains and pleasures, and in not
allowing the interference of any other idea.

I am a partisan of the *principle of utility* when I measure my approbation
or disapprobation of a public or private act by its tendency to produce pleasure
or pain; when I employ the words *just, unjust, moral, immoral, good, bad,*
simply as collective terms including the ideas of certain pains or pleasures;
it being always understood that I use the words *pain* and *pleasure* in their
ordinary signification, without inventing any arbitrary definition for the sake
of excluding certain pleasures or denying the existence of certain pains. In
this matter we want no refinement, no metaphysics. It is not necessary to consult Plato, nor Aristotle. *Pain* and *pleasure* are what everybody feels to be
such—the peasant and the prince, the unlearned as well as the philosopher.

He who adopts the *principle of utility,* esteems virtue to be a good only
on account of the pleasures which result from it; he regards vice as an evil
only because of the pains which it produces. Moral good is *good* only by its
tendency to produce physical good. Moral evil is *evil* only by its tendency to
produce physical evil; but when I say *physical,* I mean the pains and pleasures
of the soul as well as the pains and pleasures of sense. I have in view man,
such as he is, in his actual constitution.

If the partisan of the *principle of utility* finds in the common list of virtues an action from which there results more pain than pleasure, he does not hesitate to regard that pretended virtue as a vice; he will not suffer himself to be imposed upon by the general error; he will not lightly believe in the policy of employing false virtues to maintain the true.

If he finds in the common list of offences some indifferent action, some innocent pleasure, he will not hesitate to transport this pretended offence into the class of lawful actions; he will pity the pretended criminals, and will reserve his indignation for their persecutors.

CHAPTER II: THE ASCETIC PRINCIPLE [1]

This principle is exactly the rival, the antagonist of that which we have just been examining. Those who follow it have a horror of pleasures. Everything which gratifies the senses, in their view, is odious and criminal. They found morality upon privations, and virtue upon the renouncement of one's self. In one word, the reverse of the partisans of utility, they approve everything which tends to diminish enjoyment, they blame everything which tends to augment it.

This principle has been more or less followed by two classes of men, who in other respects have scarce any resemblance, and who even affect a mutual contempt. The one class are philosophers, the other, devotees. The ascetic philosophers, animated by the hope of applause, have flattered themselves with the idea of seeming to rise above humanity, by despising vulgar pleasures. They expect to be paid in reputation and in glory, for all the sacrifices which they seem to make to the severity of their maxims. The ascetic devotees are foolish people, tormented by vain terrors. Man, in their eyes, is but a degenerate being, who ought to punish himself without ceasing for the crime of being born, and never to turn off his thoughts from that gulf of eternal misery which is ready to open beneath his feet. Still, the martyrs to these absurd opinions have, like all others, a fund of hope. Independent of the worldly pleasures attached to the reputation of sanctity, these atrabilious pietists flatter themselves that every instant of voluntary pain here below will procure them an age of happiness in another life. Thus, even the ascetic principle reposes upon some false idea of utility. It acquired its ascendancy only through mistake.[2]

---

[1] Ascetic, by its etymology, signifies *one who exercises.* It was applied to the monks, to indicate their favorite practices of devotion and penitence.

[2] This mistake consists in representing the Deity in words, as a being of infinite benevolence, yet ascribing to him prohibitions and threats which are the attributes of an implacable being, who uses his power only to satisfy his malevolence.

We might ask these ascetic theologians what life is good for, if not for the pleasures it procures us?—and what pledge we have for the goodness of God in another life. if he has forbidden the enjoyment of this?

The devotees have carried the ascetic principle much further than the philosophers. The philosophical party has confined itself to censuring pleasures; the religious sects have turned the infliction of pain into a duty. The stoics said that pain was not an evil; the Jansenists maintained that it was actually a good. The philosophical party never reproved pleasures in the mass, but only those which it called gross and sensual, while it exalted the pleasures of sentiment and understanding. It was rather a preference for the one class, than a total exclusion of the other. Always despised, or disparaged under its true name, pleasure was received and applauded when it took the titles of *honour, glory, reputation, decorum,* or *self-esteem.*

Not to be accused of exaggerating the absurdity of the ascetics, I shall mention the least unreasonable origin which can be assigned to their system.

It was early perceived that the attraction of pleasure might seduce into pernicious acts; that is, acts of which the good was not equivalent to the evil. To forbid these pleasures, in consideration of their bad effects, is the object of sound morals and good laws. But the ascetics have made a mistake, for they have attacked pleasure itself; they have condemned it in general; they have made it the object of a universal prohibition, the sign of a reprobate nature; and it is only out of regard for human weakness that they have had the indulgence to grant some particular exemptions.

CHAPTER III: THE ARBITRARY PRINCIPLE; OR THE PRINCIPLE OF SYMPATHY AND ANTIPATHY

This principle consists in approving or blaming by sentiment, without giving any other reason for the decision except the decision itself. *I love, I hate;* such is the pivot on which this principle turns. An action is judged to be good or bad, not because it is conformable, or on the contrary, to the interest of those whom it affects, but because it pleases or displeases him who judges. He pronounces sovereignly; he admits no appeal; he does not think himself obliged to justify his opinion by any consideration relative to the good of society. "It is my interior persuasion; it is my intimate conviction; I feel it; sentiment consults nobody; the worse for him who does not agree with me—he is not a man, he is a monster in human shape." Such is the despotic tone of these decisions.

But, it may be asked, are there men so unreasonable as to dictate their particular sentiments as laws, and to arrogate to themselves the privilege of infallibility? What you call the *principle of sympathy and antipathy* is not a principle of reasoning; it is rather the negation, the annihilation of all principle. A true anarchy of ideas results from it; since every man having an equal right to give *his* sentiments as a universal rule, there will no longer be any common measure, no ultimate tribunal to which we can appeal.

Without doubt the absurdity of this principle is sufficiently manifest. No man, therefore, is bold enough to say openly, "I wish you to think as I do, without giving me the trouble to reason with you." Every one would revolt against a pretension so absurd. Therefore, recourse is had to diverse inventions of disguise. Despotism is veiled under some ingenious phrase. Of this the greater part of philosophical systems are a proof.

One man tells you that he has in himself something which has been given him to teach what is good and what is evil; and this he calls either his *conscience* or his *moral sense.* Then, working at his ease, he decides such a thing to be good, such another to be bad. Why? Because my moral sense tells me so; because my conscience approves or disapproves it.

Another comes and the phrase changes. It is no longer the moral sense,—it is *common sense* which tells him what is good and what is bad. This common sense is a sense, he says, which belongs to everybody; but then he takes good care in speaking of everybody to make no account of those who do not think as he does.

Another tells you that this moral sense and this common sense are but dreams; that the *understanding* determines what is good and what is bad. His understanding tells him so and so; all good and wise men have just such an understanding as he has. As to those who do not think in the same way, it is a clear proof that their understandings are defective or corrupt.

Another tells you that he has an *eternal and immutable rule of right,* which rule commands this and forbids that; then he retails to you his own particular sentiments, which you are obliged to receive as so many branches of the eternal rule of right.

You hear a multitude of professors, of jurists, of magistrates, of philosophers, who make the *law of nature* echo in your ears. They all dispute, it is true, upon every point of their system; but no matter—each one proceeds with the same confident intrepidity, and utters his opinions as so many chapters of the *law of nature.* The phrase is sometimes modified, and we find in its place, *natural right, natural equity, the rights of man, etc.*

One philosopher undertakes to build a moral system upon what he calls *truth;* according to him, the only evil in the world is lying. If you kill your father, you commit a crime, because it is a particular fashion of saying that he is not your father. Everything which this philosopher does not like, he disapproves under the pretext that it is a sort of falsehood—since it amounts to asserting that we ought to do what ought not to be done. . . .

To sum up;—the *ascetic principle* attacks utility in front. The *principle of sympathy* neither rejects it nor admits it; it pays no attention to it; it floats at hazard between good and evil. The ascetic principle is so unreasonable, that its most senseless followers have never attempted to carry it out. The principle of sympathy and antipathy does not prevent its partisans from having recourse to the principle of utility. This last alone neither asks nor admits any exceptions. *Qui non sub me contra me;* that which is not under me is against me; such is its motto. According to this principle, to legislate is an affair of observation and calculation; according to the ascetics, it is an affair of fanaticism; according to the principle of sympathy and antipathy, it is a matter of humour, of imagination, of taste. The first method is adapted to philosophers; the second to monks; the third is the favourite of wits, of ordinary moralists, of men of the world, of the multitude.

CHAPTER IV: OPERATION OF THESE PRINCIPLES UPON LEGISLATION

. . . The principle which has exercised the greatest influence upon governments, is that of sympathy and antipathy. In fact, we must refer to that principle all those specious objects which governments pursue, without having the general good for a single and independent aim; such as good morals, equality, liberty, justice, power, commerce, religion; objects respectable in themselves, and which ought to enter into the views of the legislator; but which too often lead him astray, because he regards them as ends, not as means. He substitutes them for public happiness, instead of making them subordinate to it.

Thus, a government, entirely occupied with wealth and commerce, looks upon society as a workshop, regards men only as productive machines, and cares little how much it torments them, provided it makes them rich. The customs, the exchanges, the stocks, absorb all its thoughts. It looks with indifference upon a multitude of evils which it might easily cure. It wishes only for a great production of the means of enjoyment, while it is constantly putting new obstacles in the way of enjoying.

Other governments esteem power and glory as the sole means of public good. Full of disdain for those states which are able to be happy in a peaceful security, they must have intrigues, negotiations, wars and conquests. They do not consider of what misfortunes this glory is composed, and how many victims these bloody triumphs require. The *éclat* of victory, the acquisition of a province, conceal from them the desolation of their country, and make them mistake the true end of government.

Many persons do not inquire if a state be well administered; if the laws protect property and persons; if the people are happy. What they require, without giving attention to anything else, is political liberty—that is, the most equal distribution which can be imagined of political power. Wherever they do not see the form of government to which they are attached, they see nothing but slaves; and if these pretended slaves are well satisfied with their condition, if they do not desire to change it, they despise and insult them. In their fanaticism they are always ready to stake all the happiness of a nation upon a civil war, for the sake of transporting power into the hands of those whom an invincible ignorance will not permit to use it, except for their own destruction. . . .

CHAPTER VII: PAINS AND PLEASURES CONSIDERED AS SANCTIONS

The will cannot be influenced except by motives; but when we speak of *motives,* we speak of *pleasures* or *pains.* A being whom we could not effect either by painful or pleasurable emotions would be completely independent of us.

The pain or pleasure which is attached to a law form what is called its sanction. The laws of one state are not laws in another because they have no sanction there, no obligatory force.

Pleasures and pains may be distinguished into four classes:

     1st. Physical.
     2nd. Moral.
     3rd. Political.
     4th. Religious.

Consequently, when we come to consider pains and pleasures under the character of punishments and rewards, attached to certain rules of conduct, we may distinguish four sanctions.

1st. Those pleasures and pains which may be expected from the ordinary course of nature, acting by itself, without human intervention, compose the *natural or physical sanction.*

2nd. The pleasures or pains which may be expected from the action of our fellow-men, in virtue of their friendship or hatred, of their esteem or their contempt—in one word, of their spontaneous disposition towards us, compose the *moral sanction;* or it may be called the *popular sanction, sanction of public opinion, sanction of honour, sanction of the pains and pleasures of sympathy.*

3rd. The pleasures or pains which may be expected from the action of the magistrate, in virtue of the laws, compose the *political sanction;* it may also be called the *legal sanction.*

4th. The pleasures or pains which may be expected in virtue of the threats or promises of religion, compose the *religious sanction.*

A man's house is destroyed by fire. Is it in consequence of his imprudence?— It is a pain of the natural sanction. Is it by the sentence of a judge?—It is a pain of the political sanction. Is it by the malice of his neighbours?—It is a pain of the popular sanction. Is it supposed to be the immediate act of an offended Divinity?—In such a case it would be a pain of the religious sanction, or vulgarly speaking, a judgment of God.

It is evident from this example that the same sort of pains belong to all the sanctions. The only difference is in the circumstances which produce them.

This classification will be very useful in the course of this work. It is an easy and uniform nomenclature, absolutely necessary to distinguish and describe the different kinds of moral powers, those intellectual levers which constitute the machinery of the human heart.

These four sanctions do not act upon all men in the same manner, nor with the same degree of force. They are sometimes rivals, sometimes allies, and sometimes enemies. When they agree, they operate with an irresistible power; when they are in opposition, they mutually enfeeble each other; when they are rivals, they produce uncertainties and contradictions in the conduct of men.

Four bodies of laws may be imagined, corresponding to these four sanctions. The highest point of perfection would be reached if these four codes constituted but one. This perfection, however, is as yet far distant, though it may not be impossible to attain it. But the legislator ought always to recollect that he can operate directly only by means of the political sanction. The three others must necessarily be its rivals or its allies, its antagonists or its ministers. If he neglects them in his calculations, he will be deceived in his results; but if he makes them subservient to his views, he will gain an immense power. There is no chance of uniting them, except under the standard of utility.

The natural sanction is the only one which always acts; the only one which works of itself; the only one which is unchangeable in its principal characteristics. It insensibly draws all the others to it, corrects their deviations, and produces whatever uniformity there is in the sentiments and the judgments of men.

The popular sanction and the religious sanction are more variable, more dependent upon human caprices. Of the two, the popular sanction is more equal, more steady, and more constantly in accordance with the principle of utility. The force of the religious sanction is more unequal, more apt to change with times and individuals, more subject to dangerous deviations. It grows weak by repose, but revives by opposition.

In some respects the political sanction has the advantage of both. It acts upon all men with a more equal force; it is clearer and more precise in its precepts; it is surer and more exemplary in its operations; finally, it is more susceptible of being carried to perfection. Its progress has an immediate influence upon the progress of the other two; but it embraces only actions of a certain kind; it has not a sufficient hold upon the private conduct of individuals; it cannot proceed except upon proofs which it is often impossible to obtain; and secrecy, force, or stratagem are able to escape it. It thus appears, from considering what each of these sanctions can effect, and what they cannot, that neither ought to be rejected, but that all should be employed and directed towards the same end. They are like magnets, of which the virtue is destroyed when they are presented to each other by their contrary poles, while their power is doubled when they are united by the poles which correspond.

It may be observed, in passing, that the systems which have most divided men have been founded upon an exclusive preference given to one or the other of these sanctions. Each has had its partisans, who have wished to exalt it above the others. Each has had its enemies, who have sought to degrade it by showing its weak side, exposing its errors, and developing all the evils which have resulted from it, without making any mention of its good effects. Such is the true theory of all those paradoxes which elevate nature against society, politics against religion, religion against nature and government, and so on.

Each of these sanctions is susceptible of error, that is to say, of some applications contrary to the principle of utility. But by applying the nomenclature above explained, it is easy to indicate by a single word the seat of the evil. Thus, for example, the reproach which after the punishment of a criminal falls upon an innocent family is an error of the popular sanction. The offence of usury, that is, of receiving interest above the legal interest, is an error of the political sanction. Heresy and magic are errors of the religious sanction. Certain sympathies and antipathies are errors of the natural sanction. The first germ of mistake exists in some single sanction, whence it commonly spreads into the others. It is necessary, in all these cases, to discover the origin of the evil before we can select or apply the remedy.

CHAPTER VIII: THE MEASURE OF PLEASURES AND PAINS

The sole object of the legislator is to increase pleasures and to prevent pains; and for this purpose he ought to be well acquainted with their respective values. As pleasures and pains are the only instruments which he employs, he ought carefully to study their power.

If we examine the *value* of a pleasure, considered in itself, and in relation to a single individual, we shall find that it depends upon four circumstances,—

1st. *Its intensity.*

2nd. *Its duration.*

3rd. *Its certainty.*

4th. *Its proximity.*

The value of a pain depends upon the same circumstances.

But it is not enough to examine the value of pleasures and pains as if they were isolated and independent. Pains and pleasures may have other pains and pleasures as their consequences. Therefore, if we wish to calculate the *tendency* of an act from which there results an immediate pain or pleasure, we must take two additional circumstances into the account, viz.—

5th. *Its productiveness.*

6th. *Its purity.*

A *productive pleasure* is one which is likely to be followed by other pleasures of the same kind.

A *productive pain* is one which is likely to be followed by other pains of the same kind.

A *pure pleasure* is one which is not likely to produce pains.

A *pure pain* is one which is not likely to produce pleasures.

When the calculation is to be made in relation to a collection of individuals, yet another element is necessary,—

7th. *Its extent.*

That is, the number of persons who are likely to find themselves affected by this pain or pleasure.

When we wish to value an action, we must follow in detail all the operations above indicated. These are the elements of moral calculation; and legislation thus becomes a matter of arithmetic. The *evil* produced is the outgo, the *good* which results is the income. The rules of this calculation are like those of any other. This is a slow method, but a sure one; while what is called sentiment is a prompt estimate, but apt to be deceptive. It is not necessary to recommence this calculation upon every occasion. When one has become familiar with the process; when he has acquired the justness of estimate which results from it; he can compare the sum of good and of evil with so much promptitude as scarcely to be conscious of the steps of the calculation. It is thus that we perform many arithmetical calculations, almost without knowing it. The analytical method, in all its details, becomes essential, only when some new or complicated matter arises; when it is necessary to clear up some disputed point, or to demonstrate a truth to those who are yet unacquainted with it.

This theory of moral calculation, though never clearly explained, has always been followed in practice; at least, in every case where men have had clear ideas of their interest. What is it, for example, that makes up the value of a landed estate? Is it not the amount of pleasure to be derived from it? and does not this value vary according to the length of time for which the estate is to be enjoyed; according to the nearness or the distance of the moment when the possession is to begin; according to the certainty or uncertainty of its being retained?

Errors, whether in legislation or the moral conduct of men, may be always accounted for by a mistake, a forgetfulness, or a false estimate of some one of these elements, in the calculation of good and evil.

CHAPTER IX: CIRCUMSTANCES WHICH AFFECT SENSIBILITY

All causes of pleasure do not give the same pleasure to all; all causes of pain do not always produce the same pain. It is in this that *difference of sensibility* consists. This difference is in degree, or in kind: in degree, when the impression of a given cause upon many individuals is uniform, but unequal; in kind, when the same cause produces opposite sensations in different individuals.

This difference of sensibility depends upon certain circumstances which influence the physical or moral condition of individuals, and which, being changed, produce a corresponding change in their feelings. This is an experimental fact. Things do not affect us in the same manner in sickness and in health, in plenty and in poverty, in infancy and old age. But a view so general is not sufficient; it is necessary to go deeper into the human heart. Lyonet wrote a quarto volume upon the anatomy of the caterpillar; morals are in need of an investigator as patient and philosophical. I have not courage to imitate Lyonet. I shall think it sufficient if I open a new point of view—if I suggest a surer method to those who wish to pursue this subject.

The foundation of the whole is *temperament,* or the original constitution. By this word I understand that radical and primitive disposition which attends us from our birth, and which depends upon physical organization, and the nature of the soul.

But although this radical constitution is the basis of all the rest, this basis lies so concealed that it is very difficult to get at it, so as to distinguish those varieties of sensibility which it produces from those which belong to other causes.

It is the business of the physiologist to distinguish these temperaments; to follow out their mixtures; and to trace their effects. But these grounds are as yet too little known to justify the moralist or legislator in founding anything upon them. . . .

CHAPTER X: ANALYSIS OF POLITICAL GOOD AND EVIL.—HOW THEY ARE DIFFUSED THROUGH SOCIETY

It is with government as with medicine; its only business is the choice of evils. Every law is an evil, for every law is an infraction of liberty. Government,

I repeat it, has but the choice of evils. In making that choice, what ought to be the object of the legislator? He ought to be certain of two things: 1st, that in every case, the acts which he undertakes to prevent are really evils; and, 2nd, that these evils are greater than those which he employs to prevent them.

He has then two things to note—the evil of the offence, and the evil of the law; the evil of the malady, and the evil of the remedy.

An evil seldom comes alone. A portion of evil can hardly fall upon an individual, without spreading on every side, as from a centre. As it spreads, it takes different forms. We see an evil of one kind coming out of an evil of another kind; we even see evil coming out of good, and good out of evil. . . .

The propagation of good is less rapid and less sensible than that of evil. The seed of good is not so productive in hopes as the seed of evil is fruitful in alarms. But this difference is abundantly made up, for good is a necessary result of natural causes which operate always; while evil is produced only by accident, and at intervals.

Society is so constituted that, in labouring for our particular good, we labour also for the good of the whole. We cannot augment our own means of enjoyment without augmenting also the means of others. Two nations, like two individuals, grow rich by a mutual commerce; and all exchange is founded upon reciprocal advantages.

It is fortunate also that the effects of evil are not always evil. They often assume the contrary quality. Thus, juridical punishments applied to offences, although they produce an evil of the first order, are not generally regarded as evils, because they produce a good of the second order. They produce alarm and danger,—but for whom? Only for a class of evil-doers, who are voluntary sufferers. Let them obey the laws, and they will be exposed neither to danger nor alarm.

We should never be able to subjugate, however imperfectly, the vast empire of evil, had we not learned the method of combatting one evil by another. It has been necessary to enlist auxiliaries among pains, to oppose other pains which attack us on every side. So, in the art of curing pains of another sort, poisons well applied have proved to be remedies.

CHAPTER XII: THE LIMITS WHICH SEPARATE MORALS FROM LEGISLATION

Morality in general is the art of directing the actions of men in such a way as to produce the greatest possible sum of good.

Legislation ought to have precisely the same object.

But although these two arts, or rather sciences, have the same end they differ greatly in extent. All actions, whether public or private, fall under the jurisdiction of morals. It is a guide which leads the individual, as it were, by the hand through all the details of his life, all his relations with his fellows. Legislation cannot do this; and, if it could, it ought not to exercise a continual interference and dictation over the conduct of men.

Morality commands each individual to do all that is advantageous to the community, his own personal advantages included. But there are many acts useful to the community which legislation ought not to command. There are also many injurious actions which it ought not to forbid, although morality does so. In a word, legislation has the same centre with morals, but it has not the same circumference.

There are two reasons for this difference: 1st. Legislation can have no direct influence upon the conduct of men, except by punishments. Now these punishments are so many evils, which are not justifiable, except so far as there results from them a greater sum of good. But, in many cases in which we might desire to strengthen a moral precept by a punishment, the evil of the punishment would be greater than the evil of the offence. The means necessary to carry the law into execution would be of a nature to spread through society a degree of alarm more injurious than the evil intended to be prevented.

2nd. Legislation is often arrested by the danger of overwhelming the innocent in seeking to punish the guilty. Whence comes this danger? From the difficulty of defining an offence, and giving a clear and precise idea of it. For example, hardheartedness, ingratitude, perfidy, and other vices which the popular sanction punishes, cannot come under the power of the law, unless they are defined as exactly as theft, homicide, or perjury.

But, the better to distinguish the true limits of morals and legislation, it will be well to refer to the common classification of moral duties.

Private morality regulates the actions of men, either in that part of their conduct in which they alone are interested, or in that which may affect the interests of others. The actions which affect a man's individual interest compose a class called, perhaps improperly, *duties to ourselves;* and the quality or disposition manifested in the accomplishment of those duties receives the name of *prudence.* That part of conduct which relates to others composes a class of actions called *duties to others.* Now there are two ways of consulting the happiness of others: the one negative, abstaining from diminishing it; the other positive, labouring to augment it. The first constitutes *probity;* the second is *beneficence.*

Morality upon these three points needs the aid of the law; but not in the same degree, nor in the same manner.

I. The rules of prudence are almost always sufficient of themselves. If a man fails in what regards his particular private interest, it is not his will which is in fault, it is his understanding. If he does wrong, it can only be through mistake. The fear of hurting himself is a motive of repression sufficiently strong; it would be useless to add to it the fear of an artificial pain.

Does any one object, that facts show the contrary? That excesses of play, those of intemperance, the illicit intercourse between the sexes, attended so often by the greatest dangers, are enough to prove that individuals have not always sufficient prudence to abstain from what hurts them?

Confining myself to a general reply, I answer, in the first place, that, in the greater part of these cases, punishment would be so easily eluded, that it would be inefficacious; secondly, that the evil produced by the penal law would be much beyond the evil of the offence.

Suppose, for example, that a legislator should feel himself authorized to undertake the extirpation of drunkenness and fornication by direct laws. He would have to begin by a multitude of regulations. The first inconvenience would therefore be a complexity of laws. The easier it is to conceal these vices, the more necessary it would be to resort to severity of punishment, in order to destroy by the terror of examples the constantly recurring hope of impunity. This excessive rigour of laws forms a second inconvenience not less grave than the first. The difficulty of procuring proofs would be such that it would be necessary to encourage informers, and to entertain an army of spies. This necessity forms a third inconvenience, greater than either of the others. Let us compare the results of good and evil. Offences of this nature, if that name can be properly given to imprudences, produce no alarm; but the pretended remedy would spread a universal terror; innocent or guilty, every one would fear for himself or his connexions; suspicions and accusations would render society dangerous; we should fly from it; we should involve ourselves in mystery and concealment; we should shun all the disclosures of confidence. Instead of suppressing one vice, the laws would produce other vices, new and more dangerous.

It is true that example may render certain excesses contagious; and that an evil which would be almost imperceptible, if it acted only upon a small number of individuals, may become important by its extent. All that the legislator can do in reference to offences of this kind is, to submit them to some slight punishment in cases of scandalous notoriety. This will be sufficient to give them a taint of illegality, which will excite the popular sanction against them.

It is in cases of this kind that legislators have governed too much. Instead of trusting to the prudence of individuals, they have treated them like children, or slaves. They have suffered themselves to be carried away by the same passion which has influenced the founders of religious orders, who, to signalize their authority, and through a littleness of spirit, have held their subjects in the most abject dependence, and have traced for them, day by day, and moment by moment, their occupations, their food, their rising up, their lying down, and all the petty details of their life. There are celebrated codes, in which are found a multitude of clogs of this sort; there are useless restraints upon marriage; punishments decreed against celibacy; sumptuary laws regulating the fashion of dress, the expense of festivals, the furniture of houses, and the ornaments of women; there are numberless details about aliments, permitted or forbidden; about ablutions of such or such a kind; about the purifications which health or cleanliness require; and a thousand similar puerilities, which add, to all the inconveniences of useless restraint, that of besotting the people, by covering these absurdities with a veil of mystery, to disguise their folly.

Yet more unhappy are the States in which it is attempted to maintain by penal laws a uniformity of religious opinions. The choice of their religion ought to be referred entirely to the prudence of individuals. If they are persuaded that their eternal happiness depends upon a certain form of worship or a certain belief, what can a legislator oppose to an interest so great? It is not necessary to insist upon this truth—it is generally acknowledged; but, in tracing the boundaries of legislation, I cannot forget those which it is the most important not to overstep.

As a general rule, the greatest possible latitude should be left to individuals, in all cases in which they can injure none but themselves, for they are the best judges of their own interests. If they deceive themselves, it is to be supposed that the moment they discover their error they will alter their conduct. The power of the law need interfere only to prevent them from injuring each other. It is there that restraint is necessary; it is there that the application of punishments is truly useful, because the rigour exercised upon an individual becomes in such a case the security of all.

II. It is true that there is a natural connection between prudence and probity; for our own interest, well understood, will never leave us without motives to abstain from injuring our fellows. . . .

A man enlightened as to his own interest will not indulge himself in a secret offence through fear of contracting a shameful habit, which sooner or later will betray him; and because the having secrets to conceal from the prying curiosity of mankind leaves in the heart a sediment of disquiet, which corrupts every pleasure. All he can acquire at the expense of security cannot make up for the loss of that; and, if he desires a good reputation, the best guarantee he can have for it is his own esteem.

But, in order that an individual should perceive this connection between the interests of others and his own, he needs an enlightened spirit and a heart free from seductive passions. The greater part of men have neither sufficient light, sufficient strength of mind, nor sufficient moral sensibility to place their honesty above the aid of the laws. The legislator must supply the feebleness of this natural interest by adding to it an artificial interest, more steady and more easily perceived.

More yet. In many cases morality derives its existence from the law; that is, to decide whether the action is morally good or bad, it is necessary to know whether the laws permit or forbid it. It is so of what concerns property. A manner of selling or acquiring, esteemed dishonest in one country, would be irreproachable in another. It is the same with offences against the state. The state exists only by law, and it is impossible to say what conduct in this behalf morality requires of us before knowing what the legislator has decreed. There are countries where it is an offence to enlist into the service of a foreign power, and others in which such a service is lawful and honourable.[3]

III. As to beneficence some distinctions are necessary. The law may be extended to general objects, such as the care of the poor; but, for details, it is necessary to depend upon private morality. Beneficence has its mysteries, and loves best to employ itself upon evils so unforeseen or so secret that the law cannot reach them. Besides, it is to individual free-will that benevolence owes its energy. If the same acts were commanded, they would no longer be benefits, they would lose their attractions and their essence. It is morality and especially religion, which here form the necessary complement to legislation, and the sweetest tie of humanity.

However, instead of having done too much in this respect, legislators have not done enough. They ought to erect into an offence the refusal or the omission of a service to humanity when it would be easy to render it, and when some distinct ill clearly results from the refusal; such, for example, as abandoning a wounded man in a solitary road without seeking any assistance for him; not giving information to a man who is ignorantly meddling with poisons; not reaching out the hand to one who has fallen into a ditch from which he cannot extricate himself; in these, and other similar cases, could any fault be found with a punishment, exposing the delinquent to a certain degree of shame, or subjecting him to a pecuniary responsibility for the evil which he might have prevented? . . .

[3] Here we touch upon one of the most difficult of questions. If the law is not what it ought to be; if it openly combats the principle of utility; ought we to obey it? Ought we to violate it? Ought we to remain neuter between the law which commands an evil, and morality which forbids it? The solution of this question involves considerations both of prudence and benevolence. We ought to examine if it is more dangerous to violate the law than to obey it; we ought to consider whether the probable evils of obedience are less or greater than the probable evils of disobedience.

CHAPTER XIII: FALSE METHODS OF REASONING ON THE SUBJECT OF LEG-
ISLATION

It has been the object of this introduction to give a clear idea of the principle of utility, and of the method of reasoning conformable to that principle.
There results from it a legislative logic, which can be summed up in a few
words. What is it to offer a *good reason* with respect to a law? It is to allege
the good or evil which the law tends to produce: so much good, so many
arguments in its favour; so much evil, so many arguments against it; remembering all the time that good and evil are nothing else than pleasure and
pain.

What is it to offer a *false reason?* It is the alleging for or against a law
something else than its good or evil effects.

Nothing can be more simple, yet nothing is more new. It is not the principle of utility which is new; on the contrary, that principle is necessarily as
old as the human race. All the truth there is in morality, all the good there
is in the laws, emanate from it; but utility has often been followed by instinct,
while it has been combatted by argument. If in books of legislation it throws
out some sparks here and there, they are quickly extinguished in the surrounding smoke. BECCARIA is the only writer who deserves to be noted as an
exception; yet even in his work there is some reasoning drawn from false
sources.

It is upwards of two thousand years since Aristotle undertook to form, under
the title of *Sophisms,* a complete catalogue of the different kinds of false reasoning. This catalogue, improved by the information which so long an interval
might furnish, would here have its place and its use. But such an undertaking
would carry me too far. I shall be content with presenting some heads of error
on the subject of legislation. By means of such a contrast, the principle of
utility will be put into a clearer light.

1. *Antiquity Is Not a Reason.* The antiquity of a law may create a prejudice
in its favour; but in itself, it is not a reason. If the law in question has contributed to the public good, the older it is, the easier it will be to enumerate its
good effects, and to prove its utility by a direct process.

2. *The Authority of Religion Is Not a Reason.* Of late, this method of reasoning has gone much out of fashion, but till recently its use was very extensive.
The work of Algernon Sidney is full of citations from the *Old Testament;*
and he finds there the foundation of a system of Democracy, as Bossuet had
found the principle of absolute power. Sidney wished to combat the partisans
of divine right and passive obedience with their own weapons.

If we suppose that a law emanates from the Deity, we suppose that it emanates from supreme wisdom, and supreme bounty. Such a law, then, can only have for its object the most eminent utility; and this utility, put into a clear light, will always be an ample justification of the law.

3. *Reproach of Innovation Is Not a Reason.* To reject innovation is to reject progress; in what condition should we be, if that principle had been always followed? All which exists had had a beginning; all which is established has been innovation. Those very persons who approve a law to-day because it is ancient, would have opposed it as new when it was first introduced.

4. *An Arbitrary Definition Is Not a Reason.* Nothing is more common, among jurists and political writers, than to base their reasonings, and even to write long works, upon a foundation of purely arbitrary definitions. This artifice consists in taking a word in a particular sense, foreign from its common usage; in employing that word as no one ever employed it before; and in puzzling the reader by an appearance of profoundness and of mystery.

Montesquieu himself has fallen into this fault in the very beginning of his work. Wishing to give a definition of law, he proceeds from metaphor to metaphor; he brings together the most discordant objects—the Divinity, the material world, superior intelligences, beasts and men. We learn, at last, that *laws are relations; and eternal relations.* Thus the definition is more obscure than the thing to be defined. The word *law,* in its proper sense, excites in every mind a tolerably clear idea, the word *relation* excites no idea at all. The word *law,* in its figurative sense, produces nothing but equivocations; and Montesquieu, who ought to have dissipated the darkness has only increased it. . . .

5. *Metaphors Are Not Reasons.* I mean either metaphor properly so called, or allegory, used at first for illustration or ornament, but afterwards made the basis of an argument.

Blackstone, so great an enemy of all reform, that he has gone so far as to find fault with the introduction of the English language into the reports of cases decided by the courts, has neglected no means of inspiring his readers with the same prejudice. He represents the law as a castle, as a fortress, which cannot be altered without being weakened. I allow that he does not advance this metaphor as an argument; but why does he employ it? To gain possession of the imagination; to prejudice his readers against every idea of reform; to excite in them an artificial fear of all innovation in the laws. There remains in the mind a false image, which produces the same effect with false reasoning. He ought to have recollected that this allegory might be employed against himself. When they see the law turned into a castle, is it not natural for ruined suitors to represent it as a castle inhabited by robbers?

A man's house, say the English, is his castle. This poetical expression is certainly no reason; for if a man's house be his castle by night, why not by day? If it is an inviolable asylum for the owner, why is it not so for every person whom he chooses to receive there? The course of justice is sometimes interrupted in England by this puerile notion of liberty. Criminals seem to be looked upon like foxes; they are suffered to have their burrows, in order to increase the sports of the chase.

A church in Catholic countries is the *House of God*. This metaphor has served to establish asylums for criminals. It would be a mark of disrespect for the Divinity to seize by force those who had taken refuge in his house.

The *balance of trade* has produced a multitude of reasonings founded upon metaphor. It has been imagined that in the course of mutual commerce nations rose and sank like the scales of a balance loaded with unequal weights; people have been terribly alarmed at what appeared to them a want of equilibrium; for it has been supposed that what one nation gained the other must lose, as if a weight had been transferred from one scale to the other.

The word *mother-country* has produced a great number of prejudices and false reasonings in all questions concerning colonies and the parent state. Duties have been imposed upon colonies, and they have been accused of offences, founded solely upon the metaphor of their filial dependence.

6. *A Fiction Is Not a Reason.* I understand by fiction an assumed fact notoriously false, upon which one reasons as if it were true. . . .

Blackstone, in the seventh chapter of his first book, in speaking of the royal authority, has given himself up to all the puerility of fiction. The king, he tells us, is everywhere present; he can do no wrong; he is immortal.

These ridiculous paradoxes, the fruits of servility, so far from furnishing just ideas of the prerogatives of royalty, only serve to dazzle, to mislead, and to give to reality itself an air of fable and of prodigy. . . .

But there are fictions more bold and more important, which have played a great part in politics, and which have produced celebrated works: these are *contracts*.

The *Leviathan* of Hobbes, a work now-a-days but little known, and detested through prejudice and at second-hand as a defence of despotism, is an attempt to base all political society upon a pretended contract between the people and the sovereign. The people by this contract have renounced their natural liberty, which produced nothing but evil; and have deposited all power in the hands of the prince. All opposing wills have been united in his, or rather annihilated by it. That which he *wills* is taken to be the will of all his subjects. . . .

Locke, whose name is as dear to the friends of liberty as that of Hobbes is odious, has also fixed the basis of government upon a contract. He agrees that there is a contract between the prince and the people; but according to him the prince takes an engagement to govern according to the laws, and for the public good; while the people, on their side, take an engagement of obedience so long as the prince remains faithful to the conditions in virtue of which he receives the crown.

Rousseau rejects with indignation the idea of this bilateral contract between the prince and the people. He has imagined a *social contract,* by which all are bound to all, and which is the only legitimate basis of government. Society exists only by virtue of this free convention of associates.

These three systems—so directly opposed—agree, however, in beginning the theory of politics with a fiction, for these three contracts are equally fictitious. They exist only in the imagination of their authors. Not only we find no trace of them in history, but everywhere we discover proofs to the contrary. . . .

It is not necessary to make the happiness of the human race dependent on a fiction. It is not necessary to erect the social pyramid upon a foundation of sand, or upon a clay which slips from beneath it. Let us leave such trifling to children; men ought to speak the language of truth and reason.

The true political tie is the immense interest which men have in maintaining a government. Without a government there can be no security, no domestic enjoyments, no property, no industry. It is in this fact that we ought to seek the basis and the reason of all governments, whatever may be their origin and their form; it is by comparing them with their object that we can reason with solidity upon their rights and their obligations, without having recourse to pretended contracts which can only serve to produce interminable disputes.

7. *Fancy Is Not a Reason.* Nothing is more common than to say, *reason decides, eternal reason orders, etc.* But what is this reason? If it is not a distinct view of good or evil, it is mere fancy; it is a despotism, which announces nothing but the interior persuasion of him who speaks. Let us see upon what foundation a distinguished jurist has sought to establish the paternal authority. A man of ordinary good sense would not see much difficulty in that question; but your learned men find a mystery everywhere.

"The right of a father over his children," says Cocceiji, "is founded in reason;—for, 1st, Children are born in a house, of which the father is the master; 2nd, They are born in a family of which he is the chief; 3rd, They are of his seed, and a part of his body." These are the reasons from which he concludes, among other things, that a man of forty ought not to marry without the consent of a father, who in the course of nature must by that time be in his dotage. What there is common to these three reasons is, that none of them has any relation to the interests of the parties. The author consults neither the welfare of father nor that of the children.

The right of a father is an improper phrase. The question is not of an unlimited, nor of an indivisible right. There are many kinds of rights which may be granted or refused to a father, each for particular reasons. . . .

And here we may remark an essential difference between false principles and the true one. The principle of utility, applying itself only to the interests of the parties, bends to circumstances, and accommodates itself to every case. False principles, being founded upon things which have nothing to do with individual interests, would be inflexible if they were consistent. Such is the character of this pretended right founded upon birth. The son naturally belongs to the father, because the matter of which the son is formed once circulated in the father's veins. No matter how unhappy he renders his son;—it is impossible to annihilate his right, because we cannot make his son cease to be his son. The corn of which your body is made formerly grew in my field; how is it that you are not my slave?

8. *Antipathy and Sympathy Are Not Reasons.* Reasoning by antipathy is most common upon subjects connected with penal law; for we have antipathies against actions reputed to be crimes; antipathies against individuals reputed to be criminals; antipathies against the ministers of justice; antipathies against such and such punishments. This false principle has reigned like a tyrant throughout this vast province of law. Beccaria first dared openly to attack it. His arms were of celestial temper; but if he did much towards destroying the usurper, he did very little towards the establishment of a new and more equitable rule.

It is the principle of antipathy which leads us to speak of offences as *deserving* punishment. It is the corresponding principle of sympathy which leads us to speak of certain actions as *meriting* reward. This word *merit* can only lead to passion and to error. It is *effects,* good or bad, which we ought alone to consider.

But when I say that *antipathies and sympathies are no reason,* I mean those of the legislator; for the antipathies and sympathies of the people may be reasons, and very powerful ones. However odd or pernicious a religion, a law, a custom may be, it is of no consequence, so long as the people are attached to it. To take away an enjoyment or a hope, chimerical though it may be, is to do the same injury as if we took away a real hope, a real enjoyment. In such a case the pain of a single individual becomes, by sympathy, the pain of all. . . .

But ought the legislator to be a slave to the fancies of those whom he governs? No. Between an imprudent opposition and a servile compliance there is a middle path, honourable and safe. It is to combat these fancies with the only arms that can conquer them—example and instruction. He must enlighten the people, he must address himself to the public reason; he must give time for error to be unmasked. Sound reasons, clearly set forth, are of necessity stronger than false ones. But the legislator ought not to show himself too openly in these instructions, for fear of compromising himself with the public ignorance. Indirect means will better answer his end.

It is to be observed, however, that too much deference for prejudices is a more common fault than the contrary excess. The best projects of laws are for ever stumbling against this common objection—"Prejudice is opposed to it; the people will be offended!" But how is that known? How has public opinion been consulted? What is its organ? Have the whole people but one uniform notion on the subject? Have all the individuals of the community the same sentiments, including perhaps nine out of ten, who never heard the subject spoken of? Besides, if the people are in error, are they compelled always to remain so? Will not an influx of light dissipate the darkness which produces error? Can we expect the people to possess sound knowledge, while it is yet unattained by their legislators, by those who are regarded as the wise men of the land? Have there not been examples of other nations who have come out of a similar ignorance, and where triumphs have been achieved over the same obstacles?

After all, popular prejudice serves oftener as a pretext than as a motive. It is a convenient cover for the weakness of statesmen. The ignorance of the people is the favourite argument of pusillanimity and of indolence; while the real motives are prejudices from which the legislators themselves have not been able to get free. The name of the people is falsely used to justify their leaders.

9. *Begging the Question Is Not a Reason.* The *petitio principii,* or begging the question, is one of the sophisms which is noted by Aristotle; but it is a Proteus which conceals itself artfully, and is reproduced under a thousand forms.

Begging the question, or rather assuming the question, consists in making use of the very proposition in dispute, as though it were already proved.

This false procedure insinuates itself into morals and legislation, under the disguise of *sentimental* or *impassioned* terms; that is, terms which, beside their principal sense, carry with them an accessory idea of praise or blame. *Neuter* terms are those which simply express the thing in question, without any attending presumption of good or evil; without introducing any foreign idea of blame or approbation.

Now it is to be observed that an impassioned term envelops a proposition not expressed, but understood, which always accompanies its employment, though in general unperceived by those who employ it. This concealed proposition implies either blame or praise; but the implication is always vague and undetermined.

Do I desire to connect an idea of utility with a term which commonly conveys an accessory idea of blame? I shall seem to advance a paradox, and to contradict myself. For example, should I say that such a piece of *luxury* is a good thing? The proposition astonishes those who are accustomed to attach to this word *luxury* a sentiment of disapprobation.

How shall I be able to examine this particular point without awakening a dangerous association? I must have recourse to a neuter word; I must say, for example, *such a manner of spending one's revenue* is good. This turn of expression runs counter to no prejudice, and permits an impartial examination of the object in question. When Helvetius advanced the idea that all actions have *interest* for their motive, the public cried out against his doctrine without stopping to understand it. Why? Because the word *interest* has an odious sense; a common acceptation, in which it seems to exclude every motive of pure attachment and of benevolence.

How many reasonings upon political subjects are founded upon nothing but impassioned terms! People suppose they are giving a reason for a law, when they say that it is conformable to the principles of monarchy or of democracy. But that means nothing. If there are persons in whose minds these words are associated with an idea of approbation, there are others who attach contrary ideas to them. Let these two parties begin to quarrel, the dispute will never come to an end, except through the weariness of the combatants. For, before beginning a true examination, we must renounce these impassioned terms, and calculate the effects of the proposed law in good and evil. . . .

If we attempt a theory upon the subject of *national representation,* in following out all that appears to be a natural consequence of that abstract idea, we come at last to the conclusion that *universal suffrage* ought to be established; and to the additional conclusion that the representatives ought to be re-chosen as frequently as possible, in order that the national representation may deserve to be esteemed such.

In deciding these same questions according to the principle of utility, it will not do to reason upon words; we must look only at effects. In the election of a legislative assembly, the right of suffrage should not be allowed except to those who are esteemed by the nation fit to exercise it; for a choice made by men who do not possess the national confidence will weaken the confidence of the nation in the assembly so chosen.

Men who would be thought fit to be electors, are those who cannot be presumed to possess political integrity, and a sufficient degree of knowledge. Now we cannot presume upon the political integrity of those whom want exposes to the temptation of selling themselves; nor of those who have no fixed abode; nor of those who have been found guilty in the courts of justice of certain offences forbidden by the law. We cannot presume a sufficient degree of knowledge in women, whom their domestic condition withdraws from the conduct of public affairs; in children and adults beneath a certain age; in those who are deprived by their poverty of the first elements of education, etc. etc.

It is according to these principles, and others like them, that we ought to fix the conditions necessary for becoming an elector; and it is in like manner, upon the advantages and disadvantages of frequent elections, without paying any attention to arguments drawn from abstract terms, that we ought to reason in establishing the duration of a legislative assembly. . . .

10. *An Imaginary Law Is Not a Reason. Natural law, natural rights* are two kinds of fictions or metaphors, which play so great a part in books of legislation that they deserve to be examined by themselves.

The primitive sense of the word *law,* and the ordinary meaning of the word, is—the will or command of a legislator. The *law of nature* is a figurative expression, in which nature is represented as a being; and such and such a disposition is attributed to her, which is figuratively called a law. In this sense, all the general inclinations of men, all those which appear to exist independently of human societies, and from which must proceed the establishment of political and civil law, are called *laws of nature.* This is the true sense of the phrase.

But this is not the way in which it is understood. Authors have taken it in a direct sense; as if there had been a real code of natural laws. They appeal to these laws; they cite them, and they oppose them, clause by clause, to the enactments of legislators. They do not see that these natural laws are laws of their own invention; that they are all at odds among themselves as to the contents of this pretended code; that they affirm without proof; that systems are as numerous as authors; and that, in reasoning in this manner, it is necessary to be always beginning anew, because every one can advance what he pleases touching laws which are only imaginary, and so keep on disputing for ever.

What is natural to man is sentiments of pleasure or pain, what are called inclinations. But to call these sentiments and these inclinations *laws,* is to introduce a false and dangerous idea. It is to set language in opposition to itself; for it is necessary to make *laws* precisely for the purpose of restraining these inclinations. Instead of regarding them as laws, they must be submitted to laws. It is against the strongest natural inclinations that it is necessary to have laws the most repressive. If there were a law of nature which directed all men towards their common good, laws would be useless; it would be employing a creeper to uphold an oak; it would be kindling a torch to add light to the sun. . . .

The word *rights,* the same as the word *law,* has two senses; the one a proper sense, the other a metaphorical sense. *Rights,* properly so called, are the creatures of *law* properly so called; real laws give birth to real rights. *Natural rights* are the creatures of natural law; they are a metaphor which derives its origin from another metaphor.

What there is natural in man is means,—faculties. But to call these means, these faculties, *natural rights,* is again to put language in opposition to itself. For *rights* are established to insure the exercise of means and faculties. The right is the *guarantee;* the faculty is the thing guaranteed. How can we understand each other with a language which confounds under the same term things so different? Where would be the nomenclature of the arts, if we gave to the *mechanic* who makes an article the same name as to the article itself?

Real rights are always spoken of in a legal sense; natural rights are often spoken of in a sense that may be called anti-legal. When it is said, for example, that *law cannot avail against natural rights,* the word rights is employed in a sense above the law; for, in this use of it, we acknowledge rights which attack the law; which overturn it, which annul it. In this anti-legal sense, the word *right* is the greatest enemy of reason, and the most terrible destroyer of governments.

There is no reasoning with fanatics, armed with *natural rights,* which each one understands as he pleases, and applies as he sees fit; of which nothing can be yielded, nor retrenched; which are inflexible, at the same time that they are unintelligible; which are consecrated as dogmas, from which it is a crime to vary. Instead of examining laws by their effects, instead of judging them as good or bad, they consider them in relation to these pretended natural rights; that is to say, they substitute for the reasoning of experience the chimeras of their own imaginations. . . .

Is not this arming every fanatic against all governments? In the immense variety of ideas respecting natural and Divine law, cannot some reason be found for resisting all human laws? Is there a single state which can maintain itself a day, if each individual holds himself bound in conscience to resist the laws, whenever they are not conformed to his particular ideas of natural or Divine law? What a cut-throat scene of it we should have between all the interpreters of the code of nature, and all the interpreters of the law of God!

"The pursuit of happiness is a natural right." The pursuit of happiness is certainly a natural inclination; but can it be declared to be a right? That depends on the way in which it is pursued. The assassin pursues his happiness, or what he esteems such, by committing an assassination. Has he a right to do so? If not, why declare that he has? What tendency is there in such a declaration to render men more happy or more wise? . . .

I propose a treaty of conciliation with the partisans of natural rights. If *nature* has made such or such a law, those who cite it with so much confidence, those who have modestly taken upon themselves to be its interpreters, must suppose that nature had some reasons for her law. Would it not be surer, shorter and more persuasive, to give us those reasons directly, instead of urging upon us the will of this unknown legislator, as itself an authority? . . .

All these false methods of reasoning can always be reduced to one or the other of the two false principles. This fundamental distinction is very useful in getting rid of words, and rendering ideas more clear. To refer such or such an argument to one or another of the false principles, is like tying weeds into bundles, to be thrown into the fire.

I conclude with a general observation. The language of error is always obscure and indefinite. An abundance of words serves to cover a paucity and a falsity of ideas. The oftener terms are changed, the easier it is to delude the reader. The language of truth is uniform and simple. The same ideas are always expressed by the same terms. Everything is referred to pleasures or to pains. Every expression is avoided which tends to disguise or intercept the familiar idea, that *from such and such actions result such and such pleasures and pains.* Trust not to me, but to experience, and especially your own. *Of two opposite methods of action, do you desire to know which should have the preference? Calculate their effects in good and evil, and prefer that which promises the greater sum of good.*

REACTION IN ENGLAND

WITH THE END of the Napoleonic wars in 1815, the British economy entered a period of depression marked by both falling prices for manufactured goods and consequent unemployment, and higher grain prices owing to poor crops and increased tariffs.

The disfranchised lower middle class and labor began to demand a reform of Parliament that would pave the way for legislation favorable to their interests. Radicals like William Cobbett led the fight against the ruling oligarchy, and an unsophisticated public turned to mass meetings to press for a political reform which they felt would in itself cure their economic ills. Some of the mass meetings produced riots, from the Spa Fields meeting at London in 1816, to the "Peterloo" massacre at Manchester in 1819, when local officials ordered soldiers to attack the crowd.

The government reacted with a series of measures, culminating in the Six Acts of 1819, that dealt a severe blow to such English liberties as habeas corpus, and the freedom of assembly and the press.

The following selections are taken from Hansard's *Parliamentary Debates*, Jan. 27–April 13, 1818, and Nov. 23, 1819–Feb. 28, 1820.

❦

REPORT OF THE SECRET COMMITTEE ON THE INTERNAL STATE OF THE COUNTRY

THE FIRST OBJECT of Your Committee, in examining the Papers which have been referred to their consideration, has been, to form a just estimate of the internal State of the Country, from the period when the Second Report of the Secret Committee, in the last Session of Parliament, was presented, to the present time.

The Insurrection, which broke out in the night between the 9th and 10th of June, on the borders of Derbyshire and Nottinghamshire, shortly before the close of the sitting of that Committee, was the last open attempt to carry into effect the Revolution, which had so long been the object of an extended Conspiracy. The arrest of some of the principal Promoters of these treasonable designs, in different parts of the Country, had deranged the plans, and distracted the councils, of the Disaffected; occasioned delays and hesitation in the appointment of the day for a simultaneous effort; and finally, left none, but the most infatuated, to hazard the experiment of Rebellion.

The suppression of this Insurrection (following the dispersion of the partial rising which had taken place the night before in the neighbourhood of Huddersfield,) the apprehension and committal of the leaders for trial in the regular course of law, under the charge of High Treason, and the detention of several others of the most active delegates and agitators, under the authority of the Act of the last Session, frustrated all further attempts at open violence. But the spirit of disaffection does not appear to have been subdued; disappointment was frequently expressed by the disaffected, at the failure of an enterprize, from the success of which a relief from all distress and grievances had been confidently predicted; and the projected Revolution was considered as not less certain, for being somewhat longer delayed.

In the course of the succeeding month, Bills of Indictment for High Treason were found against forty-six persons, at the Assizes at Derby; which must have tended still further to check the progress of Sedition, by apprizing the wavering of the danger to which they were exposed, and over-awing the remainder of the more determined leaders. On the Trials which took place in October, twenty-three were either convicted by the Verdict of the Jury, or pleaded guilty; against twelve, who were mostly young men, and related to some of the Prisoners already convicted, the Law Officers of the Crown declined offering any evidence. The remaining eleven had succeeded in absconding, and have not yet been apprehended. The result of these Trials, and the examples which followed, seem to have had the effect which might be expected, of striking a terror into the most violent of those engaged in the general conspiracy; whilst the lenity shown to the deluded, was gratefully felt by the individuals themselves, and restored quiet and subordination to the district, which had been the principal scene of disturbance.

In the course of the Autumn, a gradual reduction in the price of provisions, and still more an increased demand for labour, in consequence of a progressive improvement in the state of agriculture, as well as of trade and manufactures in some of their most important branches, afforded the means of subsistence and employment to numbers of those, who had been taught to ascribe all the privations to which they were unfortunately subjected, to defects in the existing Constitution.

Your Committee see fresh cause to be convinced of the truth of the opinion expressed by the first Secret Committee, which sat in the last year, of the general good disposition and loyalty of the great body of the People; and they advert with pleasure to the confirmation afforded by the late Trials at Derby, of the testimony borne in the Report of the last Committee, to the exemplary conduct of the mass of the population, in the Country through which the insurrection passed. They have no doubt, that the numbers of those who were either pledged, or prepared to engage in actual insurrection, has generally been much exaggerated by the leaders of the disaffected, from the obvious policy, both of giving importance to themselves, and of encouraging their followers. It is, however, impossible to calculate the extent to which any insurrection, not successfully opposed in its outset, might have grown in its progress through a population, in a state of reduced employment, of distress, and of agitation. In such a state of things, opportunity would, no doubt, have been afforded to active and plausible demagogues, for seducing into acts of violence and outrage, persons altogether unaware of the nature and consequences of the measures, to which they were called upon to lend their assistance; that these consequences would have involved the destruction of the lives and property of the loyal and well-affected, in the event of any decided, though temporary, success of the insurgents, is sufficiently evident, from the designs which have in some instances been proved.

It was therefore the duty of the Magistracy, and of the Government, not only to prepare the means of effectual resistance to open force; but, where they had the opportunity, to defeat the danger in its origin, by apprehending the leaders and instigators of conspiracy. Your Committee indulge the hope, that the hour of delusion, among those who have been misled into disaffection, may be passing away; and that some, even of the deluders themselves, may have seen, and repented of their error. But Your Committee would deceive the House, if they were not to state it as their opinion, that it will still require all the vigilance of Government, and of the Magistracy, to maintain the tranquillity, which has been restored. It will no less require a firm determination among the moral and reflecting members of the community, of whatever rank and station they may be, to lend the aid of their influence and example, to counteract the effect of those licentious and inflammatory publications, which are poured forth throughout the Country, with a profusion heretofore unexampled.

Your Committee have hitherto applied their observations to the lately disturbed districts in the Country. In adverting to the state of The Metropolis, during the same period, they have observed, with concern, that a small number of active and infatuated individuals have been unremittingly engaged, in arranging plans of insurrection, in endeavouring to foment disturbances that might lead to it, and in procuring the means of active operations, with the ultimate view of subverting all the existing establishments of the Country, and substituting some form of Revolutionary Government in their stead. Your Committee however, have the satisfaction to find, that, notwithstanding the desperation and confidence of the leaders, the proselytes that have been gained to their cause are not numerous. The sensible improvement in the comforts and employment of the labouring part of the community, has tended to diminish at once the motives of discontent, and the means of seduction. The mischief does not appear to have extended into any other rank of life, than that of the persons referred to in the First Report of the Secret Committee of last year, nor to have received countenance from any individuals of higher condition.

Eager as these agitators are, to avail themselves of any popular assemblage, still more, of any occasion that might happen to arise of popular discontent, and capable as they appear, from their own declarations, to be of any act of atrocity, Your Committee see no reason to apprehend that the vigilance of the Police, and the unrelaxed superintendence of Government, may not, under the present circumstances of the Country, be sufficient to prevent them from breaking out into any serious disturbance of the public peace.

The attention of Your Committee has next been directed to the Documents, which have been laid before them, relative to the apprehension of the several persons suspected of being engaged in treasonable practices, who have been detained under the authority of the Acts of the last Session. They have examined the charges upon which the several detentions have been founded, and find them, in all instances, substantiated by depositions on oath. Your Committee have no hesitation in declaring, that the discretion thus intrusted to His Majesty's Government, appears to them to have been temperately and judiciously exercised, and that the Government would, in their opinion, have failed in its duty, as Guardian of the Peace, and Tranquillity of the Realm, if it had not exercised, to the extent which it has done, the powers intrusted to it by the Legislature. Of the thirty-seven Persons, which is the whole number of those who were finally committed, one was discharged on the 4th of July, one on the 31st on account of illness, ten on the 12th of November, fourteen on the 3d of December, one on the 22d of December, six on the 29th of December, and three on the 20th of January, and one died in prison. From the circumstances of the Country, as laid before Your Committee, and as publickly notorious during the period in which those imprisonments took place, Your Committee see no reason to doubt that the detention of the several Prisoners, was governed by the same sound discretion, which, as Your Committee have already stated, appears to have been exercised in apprehending them. The whole of the arduous duties confided to the Executive Government, appears to Your Committee to have been discharged with as much moderation and lenity, as was compatible with the paramount object of general security.

27 *February,* 1818.

PAPERS RELATIVE TO THE INTERNAL STATE OF THE COUNTRY

Resolutions Passed at the Meeting Held on Hunslet Moor,
near Leeds, 19 July, 1819

RESOLVED, 1st. That there is no such thing as servitude in nature; and therefore all statutes and enactments that have tendency to injure one part of society for the benefit of the other, is a gross violation of the immutable law of God.

2d. That as our legislators have, in innumerable instances, manifested a cruel and criminal indifference to our truly distressed situation, and treated our petitions with contempt, we therefore make this solemn appeal to our oppressed fellow countrymen, praying them to join us in forming a National Union, the object of which is to obtain an overwhelming majority of the male population, to present such a petition as can scarcely fail to have the desired effect, and to adopt such other constitutional measures as may be deemed most expedient to procure for us the redress of our manifold grievances.

3d. That we are perfectly satisfied that our excellent Constitution, in its original purity, as it was bequeathed to us by our brave ancestors, is fully adequate to all the purposes of good government; we are therefore determined not to rest satisfied with any thing short of the Constitution—the whole Constitution—and nothing but the Constitution.

4th. That as we are perfectly satisfied that annual parliaments and universal suffrage constitute an essential part of our constitution, and are our rightful inheritance—we shall consider our grievances unredressed, and our indisputable rights withheld from us, until we are possessed of such annual parliament and universal suffrage.

5th. That this meeting cannot but view with regret the apathy of our should-be-leaders, that is our men of property, in not supporting our mutual rights, convinced that alienation of the rich from the poor, must, in the end, be the ruin of both; that whenever oppression or despotism militates, or is the ruin of one, it must, in the end, be the destruction of the other; we therefore entreat them, ere it be too late, to stand forward and espouse the constitutional rights of the people, by endeavouring to obtain a radical reform in the system of representation, which can alone save the trading and labouring classes from ruin.

6th. That we believe the distresses we now suffer have originated in boroughmongering system, aided by a depreciated paper currency, which has involved the nation in one hundred thousand millions of debt, and which has increased taxation to such an extent as has nearly destroyed our manufactures and commerce; and we are perfectly satisfied that nothing but a currency convertible into specie, a rigid economy, and an equal representation, can either put an end to our sufferings, or save our country from ruin.

7th. That the saving bank scheme, which was instituted under a pretence of benefiting the working classes, when nearly three-fourths of them were out of employ, is an insult to common sense and real understanding, and ought to be considered as what it really is,—an engine to work the last shilling out of the pockets of a few old servants and retired tradesmen, to enable the bank and boroughmongers to pay the fractional parts of the dividends, and to create a sort of lesser fund holders of those who know no better than to make a deposit of their hard earnings to fill the pockets of those who are draining them of their last shilling.

8th. That, as distress has become so general and extensive, we deem it highly necessary, that deputy meetings should be appointed, and out of these deputy meetings, district meetings, to meet at any place that may be thought proper; that these meetings shall extend throughout the three United Kingdoms, and that they do consist of men discreet and wise, and out of these shall be appointed men to form a National Meeting, that the whole may be brought to one focus, in order that they may devise the best plan of obtaining a Radical Reform, upon the principle of Annual Parliaments, Universal Suffrage, and Election by Ballot.

9th. That no redress can be obtained but from ourselves; that we amply possess the means; and if we fail to adopt them with vigour, and resolutely persevere therein, we shall merit every privation we may have to endure, and deserve the detestation of posterity, to whom we shall leave a greater legacy of tyranny and oppression than ever was bequeathed from one generation to another.

10th. That should the usurpers of our rights, in order to retain their power, proceed to acts of violence against the people, and even succeed in incarcerating individuals, we earnestly entreat our fellow-countrymen not to suffer their exertions to relax, but, on the contrary, persevere in the steady path of duty, looking to the end, even the salvation of our country; and our fellow-countrymen will endeavour to lighten the fetters, and enliven the dungeons of those men who are now suffering, or may hereafter suffer in the sacred cause of liberty.

11th. That we consider it to be the duty of every well-meaning subject, to stand with all his might against oppression and partial law; in doing which, an individual exposes himself to destruction, but if the whole community act as one man, success must be the result.

12th. That every well-wisher to mankind cannot but consider it to be his duty to endeavour, by every means in his power, to work a thorough reformation in the political and moral state of the country; and the surest mean is to lay aside every sordid maxim of avarice, and abandon the restraints of luxury and false ambition, which are at present so fatal to the nation.

13th. That a very small number of men who have guided the councils, and have plundered the people in order to complete their fraud, have hired the offscouring of society to print and publish newspapers, who have nearly succeeded in making thousands who might have been the leaders and friends of the people, believe the present system was for our good, when they were fattening on our property, and reducing all classes of society, till they have at last brought us to a strait from whence there are no issues but through a radical reform.

14th. That the passing of corn laws in opposition to the express will of the people—the combination act, in order to prevent work people from unitedly attempting to raise their wages in proportion to the advancement of provisions—and the imposing a duty on foreign wool, at a time when the woollen manufacture, and those employed therein, are in the most deplorable condition—appear to this meeting, proof positive, that until the Members of the Commons House are really appointed by the people at large, little improvement is to be expected in the circumstances of the people, or diminution of their distress.

15th. That as soon as an eligible person, who will accept the appointment, can be found to represent the unrepresented part of the inhabitants of Leeds, in the House of Commons, another meeting shall be called for the purpose of electing him to that situation.

My Lord,   Manchester, 16th August 1819,
                                                Quarter past Nine.

Mr. Norris being very much fatigued by the harassing duty of this day, it becomes mine now to inform your Lordship of the proceedings which have been had in consequence of the proposal put forward for a meeting. The Special Committee have been in constant attendance for the last three days, and contented themselves till they saw what the complexion of the meeting might be, or what circumstances might arise, with coming to this determination only, which they adopted in concurrence with some of the most intelligent gentlemen of the town, not to stop the numerous columns which were from various roads expected to pour in, but to allow them to reach the place of their destination.

The assistance of the military was of course required, and arrangements in consequence made with them, of such description as might be applicable to various circumstances.

About eleven o'clock the Magistrates, who were very numerous, repaired to a house, whence they might see the whole of the proceedings of the meeting. A body of special constables took their ground, about two hundred in number, close to the hustings; from them there was a line of communication to the house where we were. Mr. Trafford Trafford was so good as to take the situation of attending Colonel L'Estrange, the commanding officer.

From eleven till one o'clock, the various columns arrived, attended by flags, each by two or three flags; and there were four, if not more, caps of liberty. The ensigns were of the same description as those displayed on similar occasions, with this addition, that one had a bloody pike represented on it; another, "Equal representation or death." There was no appearance of arms or pikes, but great plenty of sticks and staves; and every column marched in regular files of three or four deep, attended with conductors, music, &c. The most powerful accession was in the last instance, when Hunt and his party came in. But, long before this, the Magistrates had felt a decided conviction that the whole bore the appearance of insurrection; that the array was such as to terrify all the King's subjects, and was such as no legitimate purpose could justify. In addition to their own sense of the meeting, they had very numerous depositions from the inhabitants, as to their fears for the public safety; and at length a man deposed as to the parties who were approaching, attended by the heaviest column. On a barouche-box was a woman in white, who, I believe, was a Mrs. Gant from Stockport, and who, it is believed, had a cap of liberty. In the barouche were Hunt, Johnson, Knight, and Moorhouse of Stockport: as soon as these four parties were ascertained, a warrant issued to apprehend them. The troops were mustered, and Nadin, preceding the Manchester Yeomanry Cavalry, executed it. While the Cavalry was forming, a most marked defiance of them was acted by the reforming part of the mob; however, they so far executed their purpose, as to apprehend Hunt and Johnson on the hustings: Knight and Moorhouse in the moment escaped. They also took on the hustings Saxton, and Sykes, who is the writer to the Manchester Observer, and which Saxton had before been addressing the mob. The parties thus apprehended, were brought to the house where the

Magistrates were. In the mean time the Riot Act was read, and the mob was completely dispersed, but not without very serious and lamentable effects. Hunt, &c. were brought down to the New Bailey; two Magistrates and myself, having promised them protection, preceded them; we were attended by special Constables and some Cavalry. The parties were lodged in the New Bailey; and since that have been added to them Knight and Moorhouse. On inquiry, it appeared that many had suffered from various instances; one of the Manchester Yeomanry, Mr. Holme, was, after the parties were taken, struck by a brick bat; he lost his power over his horse, and is supposed to have fractured his skull by a fall from his horse. I am afraid that he is since dead; if not, there are no hopes of his recovery. A special Constable of the name of Ashworth has been killed—cause unknown; and four women appear to have lost their lives by being pressed by the crowd; these, I believe, are the fatal effects of the meeting. A variety of instances of sabre wounds occurred, but I hope none mortal; several pistols were fired by the mob, but as to their effect, save in one instance deposed to before Colonel Fletcher, we have no account. We cannot but deeply regret all this serious attendant on this transaction; but we have the satisfaction of witnessing the very grateful and cheering countenances of the whole town; in fact, they consider themselves as saved by our exertions. All the shops were shut, and, for the most part, continued so all the evening. The capture of Hunt took place before two o'clock, and I forgot to mention, that all their colours, drums, &c. were taken or destroyed: since that I have been to the Infirmary, and found myself justified in making the report I have; but Mr. Norris now tells me, that one or two more than I have mentioned may have lost their lives. The parties apprehended will have their cases proceeded on to-morrow; but it appears that there may arise difficulties as to the nature of some of their crimes, on which it may be necessary to consult Government. The whole Committee of Magistrates will assemble to-morrow as usual. During the afternoon, and part of the evening, parts of the town have been in a very disturbed state, and numerous applications made for military. These have been supplied, but in some cases have, in the Irish part of the town, been obliged to fire, I trust without any bad effect as to life, in any instance. At present, every thing seems quiet; the reports agree with that, and I hope that we shall have a quiet night. I have omitted to mention, that the active part of the meeting may be said to have come in wholly from the country; and that it did not consist of less than 20,000 men, &c. The flag on which was "Equal representation or death," was a black one; and in addition, on the same side, had "No boroughmongering—unite, and be free;" at the bottom, "Saddleworth, Lees, and Morley Union;" on the reverse, "No

Corn Laws;—Taxation, without representation, is unjust and tyrannical." On the Middleton flag was, "Let us die like men, and not be sold like slaves;" reverse, "Liberty is the birthright of man."

I close my letter at a quarter before eleven; every thing remains quiet— many of the troops have returned to the barracks, with the consent of the Magistrates. I have to apologize to your Lordship for the haste in which this is written, but I trust that the haste will naturally be accounted for.

I have the honour to be, my Lord, with sincere respect,

Your Lordship's faithful and obedient humble servant,

To the Right Hon. Viscount Sidmouth, *W. R. Hay.*

One of His Majesty's Principal Secretaries of State, &c. &c. &c.

On my arrival in this county I found that the tone of feeling and proceedings of the vast population of this neighbourhood were of a description calculated to excite the utmost alarm in the well-affected, and that the public mind was considerably agitated by the insidious and too successful promulgation of seditious principles, as well as by the late more open audacious attempts to interrupt the public tranquillity.

In this populous manufacturing district, revolutionary principles have made alarming progress. For a considerable period the utmost pains have been taken to spread a spirit of disaffection in this country by an unexampled spirit of proselytism, to perpetuate the evil by instilling the most pernicious principles into the minds of youth, and to obliterate all religious feeling in this once religious district.

The statutes for repressing seditious clubs and societies have induced the disaffected to conduct all their proceedings by committees, which are appointed at smaller meetings to manage the preparations for the larger; and a system of rapid communication of political intelligence and orders is organized, in which, what are called "Unions," hold a conspicuous place. These "Unions," which are daily becoming more numerous, consist of classes or subdivisions of Reformers, who hire an apartment convenient for their local residence, where they procure newspapers and pamphlets of a seditious tendency. Notwithstanding the distresses of the times there are few operative manufacturers who do not find the means of reading such publications.

The assumed right of mustering from various quarters to the point of meeting, with banners, bearing seditious symbols and inscriptions, or with inscriptions, which, though unexceptionable in the abstract, are made to serve the same purpose, has swelled the ranks of the disaffected, in consequence of the temptations which are thus afforded to idle curiosity: and the impunity

with which this is done has added to the effect which the speeches delivered
on such occasions have on the minds of hearers already discontented, and pre-
disposed to listen with eagerness and credulity to the prospects of innovation
so confidently held out to them.

Three of these meetings have been held within the last three months in
the county of Renfrew. The second of these, held on the 11th of September, was
followed by disturbances which continued for three days before they were
effectually suppressed. At the last meeting, held on the 1st of November, at
a village some miles distant from Paisley, numerous flags were carried in
procession, bearing inscriptions calculated to convey alarm into the minds
of the well-affected, and inspire those of different dispositions with confidence
in an impending Revolution.—There were also at this last meeting, two important features which had not been witnessed in those by which it was preceded—the junction of bands of females as part of the exhibition, and the
display of arms. The ostensible arms were chiefly bludgeons, but it is well
known that many were prepared both with pistols and other weapons. Both
in proceeding to the place of meeting, and in returning from it, there was a
striking exhibition of movements executed in the streets of the town by several thousand persons, with military precision, silence and order. The pretence
alledged for arming was self defence, and this precautionary measure was said
to have reference to the late events at Manchester, and to the exertions of the
special constables and military in quelling the riots which commenced at
Paisley on the 11th of September.

While these public meetings, thus held with a display of banners and arms,
serve to inspire the disaffected with confidence in their numbers, they over-
awe and intimidate many who would otherwise have disclaimed seditious
principles, and have gladly arrayed themselves in aid of the Civil Authority.

Even the special constables who have been enrolled, and provided with
batons for the preservation of public tranquillity, feel reluctant to act with that
vigour which is necessary.

There is not, at present, in this county, any corps of Yeomanry Cavalry, nor
armed association of any description whatever, to counteract these menacing
preparations, nor any suitable accommodation for the reception of regular
troops, so that they can be kept united when called on by the civil Magistrate,
or saved from that contamination of principle, which is also an avowed object among the Reformers.

On the whole I think it my duty explicitly to state to your Lordship, that
while the Reformers of this district call out "Order" at their meetings, and
can systematically preserve it too when it suits their policy or humour, their
public harangues are of the most audacious and revolutionary description: the

expectation of a subversion of the Government is so deeply rooted in their minds, that whenever a leader shall arise, or a favourable moment occur, I fear a considerable portion of the population could not be depended on.

I have been induced to enter more fully into the situation of this county, as I believe the above will not be found an inaccurate representation of the management and proceedings of the Reformers in some other disturbed districts of the West of Scotland.

I have the honour to be,

With the greatest respect,

The Right Honourable My Lord, your Lordship's

Viscount Sidmouth, Most obedient and most humble Servant,

&c. &c.   *Glasgow.*

THE DUKE OF WELLINGTON ON THE
REFORM BILL

No MAN STANDS TRUER to type than Arthur Wellesley, duke of Wellington (1769–1852), the perfect British Tory. Soldier, statesman, landed gentleman, profoundly loyal to the Crown, the Iron Duke served his country for over fifty years with a rigid devotion and a stern sense of duty. He was no blind reactionary, incapable of accepting the least modification in things to which he was accustomed. His Toryism, which rose from his entire life and career, rested on a sense of Britain's achievements, and on his belief that these, in turn, rested on the institutions which had developed over centuries and taken form in the Glorious Revolution. Thus he was quick to accept the July Revolution in France, holding that the preservation of the peace of Europe far outweighed the maintenance of the structure which he had helped to build in 1815. He led some of his unwilling Tory followers, while losing others, into passage of the Catholic Emancipation Act of 1829, declaring that the only alternative was revolution and civil war.

But Wellington would not tolerate the actions of mobs or threats to the cautious balance of the British Constitution. On both these scores, and because his principles of government were at stake, he steadfastly opposed Parliamentary Reform by means of reapportionment and the extension of the suffrage. Reform petitions had been pouring into Parliament for a number of years; "Political Unions" were meeting throughout the country; the middle class were striving for their share of power; and the masses joined them in the hope that they would benefit from an extended suffrage, even though they were not included. Economic depression stimulated unrest, and Continental revolutions inspired British agitation. But the Tories, while admitting that there were irregularities and imperfections, held to Edmund Burke's belief that the nation was "virtually represented" by the traditional system. They maintained that the well-to-do would be guided by community interest to act for the good of all. The Duke of Wellington accordingly took an irretrievable stand against Reform in the debate on the Address in Answer to the King's Speech opening Parliament in the fall of 1830. When he resumed his seat he turned to Lord Aberdeen, the Foreign Secretary, and asked "I have not said too much, have I?" Aberdeen was acquainted with the temper of Commons and country, and later remarked that the Duke had ". . . said that we are going out." And shortly thereafter his government fell.

The Whigs, under Earl Grey, took office and introduced a reform measure. A dissolution of Parliament resulted, and the Whigs emerged strengthened from the election. A second bill was introduced, passed the Commons and was rejected by the Lords. A third time the measure was passed by the House of Commons. When the House of Lords rejected the bill once more, Grey called upon King William IV to name enough Whig peers to override the Tory majority in the upper house. The king refused, Grey resigned, and Wellington was summoned to resume the office of Prime Minister. He tried to form a Tory Cabinet, with the intention of passing a moderate Reform Bill and thereby drawing the sting from the reform movement. Wellington was not much concerned with parties. He was guided by his conception of his duties as the king's servant, not by party regularity. But the Tory party rejected the political inconsistency of voting for reform, and the country was severely disturbed by the impending return to power of the Tory Duke, whose motives were not generally understood. Wellington was forced to inform the king of his failure, and he advised him to recall Grey and the Whigs with the promise to create the necessary number of new peers. The House of Lords retreated before this final blow, Tory peers abstained from voting, and the Reform Bill was passed in 1832.

This law redistributed one hundred forty-three seats in the House of Commons, removing a few of the most glaring inequalities of representation and reducing property requirements for voting. It was the first of a series of measures, followed by those of 1867, 1884, 1885, 1918, and 1928, which brought England universal suffrage.

The following selections were taken from Hansard's *Parliamentary Debates*, 3d series, Vol. III.

DEBATE ON THE REFORM BILL

HOUSE OF LORDS, MARCH 28, 1831

THE DUKE OF WELLINGTON must say, in the outset, that up to the present moment he had heard nothing like an answer to the able address of his noble friend (Lord Wharncliffe) near him; and he had not, therefore, wished to address their Lordships until he heard the speech of the noble and learned Lord on the Woolsack.[1] That noble and learned Lord had only done him justice in supposing that his opinions had undergone no change since the declaration he had made to their Lordships at the opening of the Session. In his opinion, the state of the Representation ought not to be changed. In his opinion they could, on principle, no more deprive one of these boroughs of their franchise, without delinquency being proved, than they could deprive him of his seat in that House, or of his title, or the noble Lord on the Woolsack of his estate. The right in both cases was the same, and he contended that that argument had been held over and over again in that House, and would be held again, if the case of Liverpool should ever be brought forward. That House had always required proof of delinquency before it would consent to any act of disfranchisement. He admitted that there were circumstances of necessity, which would get rid of this strict letter of the law, as they

[1] [Lord Brougham, Whig Lord Chancellor, who presided by sitting on the "Woolsack."]

would get rid of the strict letter of the law in other cases; but he contended, that no circumstances of necessity, upon this subject, had, till this moment, been made out. Even the eloquent speech of the noble and learned Lord had done nothing to establish it. At the close of his speech, indeed, the noble and learned Lord had talked of the people who laboured by the sweat of their brow, and who shed their blood in our armies; but these were not the persons to whom this Bill gave the elective franchise—it was given to altogether another class of persons. On all this, the noble and learned Lord went upon the principle of expediency, as well as he did. But the noble and learned Lord, and his noble friend near him, had both left out of consideration, that it was the creation of a legislative assembly they were to look to, and not what the voters were to be—that they were to consider what a House of Commons ought to be, and not what the constituents ought to be. This, he contended, it was the duty of the Government to consider in framing a measure of this kind. But he had not yet done with the matter of principle. The noble and learned Lord had admitted that he would have preferred to keep some of the rotten boroughs in the place of other boroughs, but what then became of the noble and learned Lord's principle? The principle was at once given up here. Well, but he had said that they were to look more to the formation of a House of Commons, than to the formation of an elective body upon the principle of population. Now he thought that the present House of Commons was as complete a one as could be formed. He contended that the House of Commons, particularly since the peace, had shown itself to be the most efficient legislative body in the world, without any exception. It had rendered more services than any other House of Commons in this country during the same length of time. He contended that it had continued to render those services till the close of last Session; that it was prepared to continue them still in this Session; and that it was only interrupted by the introduction of the discussion of this subject of Reform. He would refer to the opinion of the noble Marquis (Lansdown) opposite, whom he always heard with great delight, whose opinions he believed did not much differ from his own, and who had said, that if he had to form a House of Commons, he would form one like the present, giving a large preponderance to property, and the most to landed property. . . . [It] was said that it became necessary for the Government to propose some plan of Reform in the representative system. Now, he must say here, that some observations which had fallen from the noble Lord, the Privy Seal, and from the noble and learned Lord, the Lord Chancellor of Ireland, were not quite correct as to facts; and upon those observations he felt himself called upon to make some remarks. It was quite true, that when the late Government brought forward the Catholic question, they were supported by many noble Lords who were generally in opposition to the Government. He had the misfortune on that occasion to lose the support and regard of a great number of friends, both there and in the other House of Parliament. That was a misfortune which he should never cease to lament; yet he had the consolation of knowing, that what he then did was no more than his public duty required of him. Believing, as he did, that civil war must be the consequence of continuing to refuse the settlement of that question, he thought that he should have been wanting in his duty, both as a man and as a minister, if he had hesitated to give up his former views with regard to that measure. Certainly the part he had taken on that occasion had lost him the confidence of many of his former friends, and the noble Lords who supported him in that measure were not willing to lend him the same support on the other measures which he thought necessary for the good of the country. Nevertheless, he thought he was bound to remain in the position he then occupied, as long as he enjoyed the confidence of his Sovereign, and the support of the House of Commons. He might, he believed, have continued in that position, but the late revolution in France had occurred at a critical period. Like former revolutions, such as those in Spain and Naples, it certainly did create a very great sensation in this country, and a strong desire was excited by speeches in various places, and by the spirit developed at the elections for Parliamentary Reform,— a desire more strong on the part of the people than had been displayed for many years with respect to any political object. But he did not then, nor did he now, think that desire irresistible—to be sure it would be irresistible if Parliament thought proper to make the alterations demanded in our representative system,—but if it should decide otherwise, he believed the country would in this, as in other instances, submit to the decision of Parliament. He admitted that there had been a growing wish for Parliamentary Reform in the country, but he thought that if the question were fairly discussed in Parliament, and if, after a fair hearing of the case, Parliament should decide against it, the country would submit without a murmur. The fashion resulting from the example of the French and Belgian revolutions had now subsided—people saw the consequences of revolution to be distress and ruin; and his belief was, if Parliament in its wisdom decided that Reform was not to be carried, that the country would submit to the decision. . . . He came now to the circumstance of the members of the present Government taking office, and he found the noble Earl [2] stating, on the first opportunity after having occupied office, the three principles of his Government; and these were,—Retrenchment, Peace and Reform. As for Retrenchment, and Peace, he maintained that there existed no difference between the noble Earl and himself. . . . Parliamentary Reform

[2] [Earl Grey, then Whig Prime Minister, who speaks later in the debate.]

was the remaining question,—for the introduction of that it appeared Ministers had obtained the consent of his Majesty, and certainly it appeared that his Majesty's name had been used upon the subject, and, he believed, frequently by persons who were by no means authorised to use it, and also upon occasions when it ought not to have been used. It was true Government had the sanction of his Majesty to bring forward the question of Reform—perhaps this measure of Reform; but to say his Majesty had taken a more active part in the matter than was implied in taking the advice of his Ministers, was not constitutional; and such being the case, he could not consider the assertion as being founded in fact. Let their Lordships look at what such a measure ought to be, and let them see what the measure was which had been brought forward by the Ministers. A measure of Parliamentary Reform brought forward by Government ought to be a measure which should enable Government to carry on the King's service in Parliament according to the Constitution as it was established at the Revolution, and as it had since proceeded. How had the public service been carried on since the Revolution? By persons of talent, property, and knowledge—scientific, political, commercial, and manufacturing,—men connected with or representing all the great interests of the country,—men noted for great abilities, who on all occasions had been a conservative party in the State, and who had supported the power and glory of the country in war, and had promoted her prosperity in peace during the last 140 years. If the country were to lose such a Parliament, Ministers were bound to see that their new system of election should be such as would secure the King's Government the support of this other Parliament when formed upon the new principle. Look at the new system. His noble friend, who had addressed the House earlier in the debate, stated with great clearness what would be the result of the Bill in certain respects. His noble friend stated, that throughout the towns of England and Wales many existing interests would be interfered with, and he also stated the effect of giving votes to £10 householders for counties. His noble friend's statements well deserved the attention of their Lordships. He himself had examined the Bill with reference to its effects on the county of Southampton. In that county were several towns—Winchester, Christchurch, Portsmouth, Southampton, and the borough of Lymington. Several boroughs in this county were struck out of the Representation by the Bill, and there were besides a number of considerable towns left unrepresented; but the voters of these places were to come into the county constituency. According to the old system, only the freeholders had votes for the county, but according to the new system the inhabitants of these unrepresented towns would have votes for the county. Now copyholders and £50 lease-holders were to vote for the county. In the towns those two classes were for the most part shopkeepers.

He was convinced that there were not less than 4,000 or 5,000 such inhabitants of towns in Hampshire, who would come to have votes for the county as well as for the freeholders. Now, of whom did this class of electors consist? As he had before stated, they were shopkeepers—respectable shopkeepers —in towns. He begged to ask, were they fit persons to be the only electors to return county Members to a Parliament which was to govern the affairs of this great nation, consisting of 100,000,000 of subjects, and so many various relations, foreign, domestic, colonial, commercial, and manufacturing? Men of the description he had mentioned, with their prejudices and peculiar interests, however respectable as a body, could not be fit to be the only electors of Members of the House of Commons. But he begged to say, that however respectable this or any other class of electors might be, there was a strong reason against any uniformity of system in the Representation of the country. He had heard already of the establishment in this town of a Committee formed for the purpose of recommending candidates for the Representation to the different towns throughout the country. Now, considering the means of combination, and the facilities of communication which existed, he thought such a body dangerous. Associations of a like kind had been found effectual in other countries to put down the Government. Was it fit to establish such a uniform system of election (he cared not in whose hands placed), that any Committee sitting in London could guide the determination of the entire country with respect to the Representation? He wanted to know what security there would be for their Lordships' seats in that House if such a Committee existed at the first general election of a Reformed Parliament? He was in France at the period when the law of elections was passed in 1817, at that period there were in each department 300 persons, who, paying the highest amount of taxes, were chosen to manage the Representation. The King and Government altered this, and gave the power of choosing representatives to persons paying taxes to the amount of 300 francs. Two years afterwards they were obliged to alter the law again, and form two classes of electors. Since then there had been two general elections, one more unfavourable than the other to the Government, and the matter ended in the formation of a Parliament, the spirit of which rendered it impossible for a Government to act. . . . He was not the apologist of Prince Polignac; but things had been brought to that state in France, that it was impossible there should not be a revolution. When he saw a similar mode of election recommended in this country— when he saw the adoption of a uniform system of election—when he saw the election placed in the hands of shopkeepers in towns and boroughs all over the country—he thought that we incurred considerable danger, and did put the country in that situation that no Minister could be certain that any one measure which he brought forward would succeed, or that he would be enabled to carry on the Government. The circumstances of France and England were in many particulars alike, and we ought to take warning by the dangers of the neighbouring country. He wished the House to advert to what the business of the King's Government in Parliament was. It was the duty of that Government to manage every thing. He had heard the noble and learned Lord on the Woolsack, in a speech of admirable eloquence and knowledge, propose a new judicial system at the commencement of the Session; but he maintained that it would be impossible for the Government ultimately to decide on that question, and he told the noble and learned Lord this—that if a Parliament were constructed on the new plan, it would be too strong for Government on that and many similar questions. So, also, in matters affecting commerce and manufactures, Government would depend entirely upon Parliament. He wanted to know how Government was to carry any measure on the appointment of a new Parliament. There was a great question now before the House of Commons on the subject of tithes. A Government might submit to the will of a majority opposed to its own views on other questions, but on the questions of Tithes and the Church, its duty was clearly pointed out, the King's Coronation Oath, and the acts of Union with Scotland and Ireland, guaranteeing the integrity of the Church establishment. But he wanted to know how Government was to maintain the safety of the Established Church, after placing Parliament on the footing proposed. He did not wish to carry this argument farther than it would safely go; but he inferred from every thing he could see, that the Government of the country could not be carried on as hitherto, if this plan were adopted. In such an event we must alter the Constitution. He did not say the Crown could not be preserved: the King's power might be limited and confined to the management of the Army, Navy, &c.; but that would not be the English Constitution,—the country could no longer go on as before—it would not be the same England. Assuming that the concession of the Catholic question, and that the Union with Ireland were great alterations, as the noble and learned Lord stated, in the Constitution, still they were both resorted to on the principle of expediency, which was clearly made out, and he could not admit that the expediency of the present measure had been demonstrated. On the contrary, all experience warranted him in saying, that the present Legislature had answered its purposes remarkably well, and that there must arise great danger, if not irremediable mischief, from altering its composition. The great difference, therefore, between those departures from the Constitution and the present measure was, that they were warranted by expediency, and it is not. He regretted being compelled to differ from many of his political friends with respect to Reform, but duty obliged him to do so. He had no desire for any thing, except to be useful for the service of the public in any way that might be required. He had no personal reasons for communicating his opinions; he spoke them broadly and openly, with a view to the country benefitting by their expression. He wished to God he could convince the noble Earl and his colleagues of the error into which they had fallen on the subject of Reform, being convinced that they would place the country in the greatest possible peril if they passed the Bill in its present shape. . . .

EARL GREY [3] found it impossible to remain silent after listening to the speech of the noble Duke opposite, though if he had consulted his own case, he certainly should not have addressed their Lordships at that late hour. He would begin by expressing the same wish towards the noble Duke, as the noble Duke had expressed with respect to him. He wished to God he could cure the noble Duke of the error into which he thought his Grace had fallen. The noble Duke thought him in error; he thought the noble Duke mistaken—which was right, time would show. He believed there was hardly one man in the House, and but a very small proportion of persons in the country, who concurred with the noble Duke in opinion, that there was nothing in the state of the Representation of the people in Parliament, or in the circumstances and character of the times, which required any alteration to be made in those laws by which the Representation of the people in Parliament was at present constituted. This opinion the noble Duke was pledged to,—that the system was perfect as it stood—that all those things which others called abuses, had contributed to the glory and welfare of the country,—that the abuses were an essential part of the system,—and that, if we attempted to correct them, we at once put an end to the glory, power, and prosperity of the empire. This was a bold doctrine, which few men could be brought to concur in; even the noble Duke himself did not say that one of those generally united with him in political principles agreed with him in this opinion. In all the discussions on the subject, he had hardly heard one person venture to say, that situated as this country was, and in the present state of public opinion, it was impossible to proceed safely without some attempt to restore the satisfaction and confidence of the people, by giving them a share in the right of Representation to which they considered themselves (and he thought justly considered themselves) entitled. The noble Duke had stated the circumstances under which he thought the question arose, and it was a satisfaction to him to hear, not only from his noble friend who opened the Debate, but also from the noble Duke, statements that relieved him from a charge under which he felt a good deal of uneasiness—namely, that to him and his colleagues was owing

[3] [Whig; Prime Minister.]

that state of excitement at present existing in the country, which alone seemed to make some change necessary. . . . He gathered from the noble Duke's own account of the matter, that there was existing in the country—the thing was manifested at the general election—a strong desire (whether augmented, as the noble Duke supposed, by the Belgian or French Revolution, or occasioned by some other cause), a strong desire among the people to procure parliamentary Reform. Nay, the noble Duke had gone farther; he acknowledged that this inclination was so far indulged in by the House of Commons itself, that if he had remained much longer in office, he apprehended the question might have been carried against him. The noble Duke had admitted then that there existed in the country, and in the House of Commons, at the time the present Government came into office, so strong a feeling in favour of Parliamentary Reform that it was impossible for the Government to avoid taking that subject into its earliest consideration. . . . A complaint had been made which, he thought, was reiterated by the noble Duke, of the use which had been made of the King's name on this occasion. The noble Duke admitted that the question could not have been introduced to Parliament by Ministers without the King's consent; but declared that nothing should have been said with respect to his Majesty for the purpose of influencing the votes of Members of Parliament. The noble Duke was quite correct in his position. The House, however, was frequently informed, by a Message from the Crown itself, that the Monarch was aware of particular measures recommended to him by his Ministers. This course was pursued with respect to the Catholic Question, when a noble Duke advised his Majesty to recommend to Parliament, in a Speech from the Throne to adopt measures on the subject. He could not but recollect the strong and emphatic manner in which the noble Duke, in introducing the Catholic Relief Bill into the House, stated that he had the cordial support of his late Majesty to that measure. He did not mean to instance one wrong act as an excuse for another, but when such complaints were made from such quarters, he might plead example by way of mitigation of censure. It had also been said, that he had resorted to threats. He had held out no threat, and he meant to hold out none—he was not authorised to hold out any, and he hoped that he knew his duty too well as a Minister of the Crown to say anything until he had received his Majesty's sanction. He would only repeat what he stated on a former occasion, that he thought the measure of Reform now recommended by the Ministers of the Crown was of the greatest importance to the well-being of the country; to that measure he was committed heart and soul, and he would not shrink from giving his advice to his Majesty to adopt every constitutional means to carry it into effect. The noble Duke said, that if the measure should become a law, it would be impossible that the business of the Government should be carried on. He did not understand how the noble Duke made out that proposition. The noble Duke said, rather curiously, that it should have been the object of Ministers to look rather to the constitution of the assembly than to the qualification of the voters. What Ministers had looked to, certainly, was the composition of the legislative assembly. It was an error to suppose that the consideration of the two things could be separated. The noble Duke said, the effect of the measure would be to add 5,000 voters to the constituent body in Hampshire. He could hardly believe it possible that the noble Duke was correctly informed upon this point, because the whole constituent body in Hampshire at the present moment was only 8,000 or 9,000. The noble Duke said, that after the Bill should pass, it would be impossible for Government to carry any questions relating to finance, colonial policy, and other intricate subjects. What was this but saying that the Government need no longer have the power of dictating what the decision of the House of Commons should be? The noble Duke shook his head, but that was really the result of his argument. He believed that the Government would continue to possess all the influence which it ought to have, and that, relying on the confidence of the people, there was no fear of the salutary measures which it might propose not being carried into effect. The noble Duke had endeavoured to excite alarm by dwelling on the subject of tithes. The people of England were attached to the national church establishment, and a free Representation of the people would, however they might correct the abuses, which were not the strength but the weakness of the Church, never countenance any attempt to invade the just rights of the establishment. There were several points to which he should have wished to call their Lordships' attention but for the lateness of the hour: but there was one point which he could not pass over. It was objected to the measure, that it was not a resting-place; that it would necessarily lead to ulterior consequences, which would be fatal to the peace and security of the empire. "Give," it was said, "to those who clamour for Reform, the measure you now propose, and they will force you to go forward to extremes which you would wish in vain to avoid." He believed that the result would be the very reverse. The prospect of the measure had given almost universal satisfaction, and he had no doubt that it would unite all those who were at present in a state of discontent in attachment to the Government. But supposing, which he did not, that such might be the consequences, how would it be remedied by not granting Reform? The noble Lord saw that Reform was irresistible; that, whatever Government was at the head of affairs, it could not exist, if it did not do something to satisfy the expectations of the people. No paltry, no half measure would do; there must be something, he admitted, substantial and effective.

Then what he (Earl Grey) wished, with his noble and learned friend on the Woolsack, was to bring those persons who held his opinion to state what was the measure they meant to propose. If he knew what that substantial and effective measure was, he should then be able to give an opinion. Short of this measure it must be less satisfactory to the people, and then would be more likely to lead to those extremes which his noble friend wished to avoid. The difference between his noble friend and himself was this—his noble friend was for an extension of the right of voting, and for the extinction of boroughs, for he admitted that not only was Reform necessary, but he admitted the principle of disfranchisement; he would go a certain length, but he would not go the whole length of this measure, and he would consequently leave discontent behind. The measure would be an imperfect measure, founded on admitted principles. It could not give satisfaction, and therefore all the consequences predicted from the present measure,—but which he did not expect,—would certainly flow from the partial Reform alluded to by his noble friend. With respect to the measure of Reform, he had considered himself pledged to it when out of office, and still more when in office, from a sense of public duty. He thought the state of the country required that the question should be looked at, and he asked himself what was to be done? Should he bring forward a short measure, that should "keep the word of promise to the ear and break it to the hope?" or should he bring forward a measure that would afford a reasonable hope of satisfying the people, and would put an end to the agitation by which the country was disturbed? He had been represented as if he had gone further than the intention he had at first held out. Undoubtedly he had said moderate Reform, but at the same time effective Reform, such as would produce the effect of satisfying the country. The first disposition of his mind undoubtedly was to limit the Reform within a much narrower compass; but after full consideration, and discussing the subject with his colleagues, he was convinced that nothing short of the present measure would tend to the desired result of satisfying the country, and give to the Government security and respect. Founded upon these principles the measure had been introduced, and had received the general approbation of the country. It had operated like oil on troubled water; agitation had subsided, and he had every expectation, that if the measure was suffered to pass into a law there would be a season of peace and tranquility, of improvement to the wealth and prosperity of the country, and an addition of strength to the Government, such as had not been witnessed for years past. Some persons had expressed a surprise that no opposition was made to it, but the current of opinion set too strong the other way. It would not do, at the present day, to talk of county meetings as farces, or to say they were not attended by a large proportion of the freeholders. Look at the meetings in Yorkshire, Derbyshire, Cheshire, counties which had hitherto been most adverse to Reform; look at the respectable names of the persons who attended those meetings, and then let their Lordships say if the question had not been favourably received by persons of all parties, and even by persons who were eminently Tories. There never had been a measure regarding which public opinion had so nearly approached to unanimity. He would refer to a criterion upon this head, sanctioned by an authority which even the noble Duke would think entitled to respect. In the discussion on the Catholic Question, a right hon. Gentleman had stated the proportion of counties and principal towns for and against that measure. He stated that there were nineteen counties for, and seventeen against the measure of Catholic Emancipation; of principal towns, twenty-six were for and nineteen against the measure. Assuming that as a practical and correct mode of estimating public opinion, let their Lordships see how that opinion was expressed upon this Question. Taking the same counties and towns, he found that twenty-seven counties were for, and nine against the measure; of principal towns, there were thirty-seven for, and eight against it. The noble Duke had said that if Parliament should reject the measure, he was satisfied the country would submit without a murmur. He would admit that, if the measure were rejected, there might be no opposition to the authority of the law or a throwing off attachment or allegiance to the Government and he trusted and hoped such would be the result; but that there would not be a murmur, let not the noble Duke "lay that flattering unction to his soul." That there would be a general attempt, by legal and constitutional means, to urge on Parliament the adoption of the measure, he had no doubt; there would be discontent and agitation throughout the country, which would be kept in alarm and irritation; and the consequence would be, a state of things similar to that which preceded Catholic Emancipation in Ireland. The very persons who now reject the measure would then find themselves obliged to agree to it. He had supported Catholic Emancipation for more than thirty years, through good report and evil report; he had been driven from office by an endeavour to make a slight step towards it; and it was a sacrifice he willingly made for that object. In all the discussions he had heard on that question, it had been contended that Catholic Emancipation must produce the subversion of the Constitution and the separation of the two countries. No man had argued more strongly against that measure than the noble Duke. He remembered the noble Duke saying that it was not Catholic Emancipation that Ireland wanted; adding—for the words sank deep into his ear—that Ireland had never been more than half conquered. These opinions had been uttered as confidently by the same persons who opposed Catholic Emancipation, as they now predicted similar results from Reform. But at the end of a few years these persons found the error they laboured under in resisting those claims, and the measure of Emancipation was proposed by those very men. Had the discovery been made sooner, the evils which now oppressed Ireland would perhaps have disappeared. The same would be the case in the event of the rejection of the proposition for Reform. Granted at the present moment, the people would consider it as an act of grace; refused, who could predict the consequences of the rejection? It was a rejection which might destroy the present Administration; but how would it operate on their successors? The people, disappointed of their just expectations, would be inflamed with resentment; and would eventually demand, with a voice of thunder, that which it would be found impossible longer to deny; but the granting of which would not only be unattended with the advantages that would now accompany its concession, but, in the strong excitement that would then exist, might be productive of evils which no man could foresee—evils that might throw the whole country into irremediable disorder. He was firmly convinced that the present measure would satisfy the people, and as firmly convinced that, without some large and liberal measure of Reform, the Government could not possibly be carried on advantageously for the country.

CHARTISM

AFTER THE COLLAPSE of the Owenite movement in 1834 the energies of radical reformers and of discontented British workingmen during the following two decades found political channels in "Chartism." In 1838 William Lovett (1800–1877) and Francis Place (1771–1854) drew up a bill to be presented to Parliament which was widely circulated in London and the provinces as *The People's Charter*. It embodied six demands: equality of representation, universal suffrage, vote by ballot, annual meetings of Parliament, no property qualifications for members of Parliament, and payment to members of Parliament. The *Charter* was presented to Parliament in 1839 where it was rejected, and its rejection led to a series of disorders. In 1842 and again, anticlimactically, in 1848 the *Charter* was vainly laid before the Parliament.

Chartism was a movement which arose among disaffected persons, some of whom hoped to find in a victory for political democracy a step toward a more generous social democracy. However, agreement on the principle of universal suffrage did not constitute an adequate basis for common action, and the movement was divided between those who would have put aside all other matters until the struggle for political democracy was won and those who saw in Chartism simply another way of registering fundamental economic discontents.

The selections included here give in a concise manner the gist of the demands included in *The People's Charter*. The first selection is the petition authorized at the "Crown and Anchor" meeting on February 28, 1837, and is described in the following words by Lovett: "In February, 1837, our Association [The London Working Men's Association] convened a public meeting at the Crown and Anchor in the Strand for the purpose of petitioning Parliament. . . . The prayer of that petition formed the nucleus of the far-famed *People's Charter*, which may be said to have had its origin at this meeting."

The second selection brings out the economic issues involved in the struggle of the Chartists. It was the first "National Petition" and was presented with the first *People's Charter* along with a list of 1,283,000 signatures. It was written by R. K. Douglas, editor of the *Birmingham Journal*, for the Birmingham Political Union, which was one of the sources of the stream of Chartist agitation.

PETITION AGREED TO AT THE "CROWN AND ANCHOR" MEETING, FEBRUARY 28TH, 1837

TO THE HONORABLE the Commons of Great Britain and Ireland. The Petition of the undersigned Members of the Working Men's Association and others sheweth—

That the only *rational use* of the institutions and laws of society is justly to protect, encourage, and support all that can be made to contribute *to the happiness of all the people.*

That, as the object to be obtained is mutual benefit, so ought the enactment of laws to be by mutual consent.

That obedience to laws can only be *justly enforced* on the certainty that those who are called on to obey them have had, either personally or by their representatives, the power to enact, amend, or repeal them.

That all those who are excluded from this share of political power are not justly included within the operation of the laws; to them the laws are only despotic enactments, and the legislative assembly from whom they emanate can only be considered parties to an unholy compact, devising plans and schemes for taxing and subjecting the many.

That the universal political right of every human being is superior and stands apart from all customs, forms, or ancient usage; a fundamental right not in the power of man to confer, or justly to deprive him of.

That to take away this sacred right from the *person* and to vest it in *property,* is a wilful perversion of justice and common sense, as the creation and security of property *are the consequences of society*—the great object of which is human happiness.

That any constitution or code of laws, formed in violation of men's political and social rights, are not rendered sacred by time nor sanctified by custom.

That the ignorance which originated, or permits their operation, forms no excuse for perpetuating the injustice; nor can aught but force or fraud sustain them, when any considerable number of people perceive and feel their degradation.

That the intent and object of your petitioners are to present such facts before your Honorable House as will serve to convince you and the country at large that you do not represent the people of these realms; and to appeal to your sense of right and justice as well as to every principle of honour, for directly making such legislative enactments as shall cause the mass of the people to be represented; with the view of securing *the greatest amount of happiness to all classes of society.*

Your Petitioners find, by returns ordered by your Honourable House, that the whole people of Great Britain and Ireland are about 24 millions, and that the males above 21 years of age are 6,023,752, who, in the opinion of your petitioners, are justly entitled to the elective right.

That according to S. Wortley's return (ordered by your Honourable House) the number of registered electors, who have the power to vote for members of Parliament, are only 839,519, and of this number only 8½ in 12 give their votes.

That on an analysis of the constituency of the United Kingdom, your petitioners find that 331 members (being a *majority* of your Honourable House) are returned by *one hundred and fifty-one thousand four hundred and ninety-two* registered electors!

That comparing the whole of the male population above the age of 21 with the 151,492 electors, it appears that 1–40 of them, or 1–160 of the entire population, have the power of passing all the laws in your Honourable House.

And your petitioners further find on investigation, that this majority of 331 members are composed of 163 Tories or Conservatives, 134 Whigs and Liberals, and only 34 who call themselves Radicals; and out of this limited number it is questionable whether 10 can be found who are truly the representatives of the wants and wishes of the producing classes.

Your petitioners also find that 15 members of your Honourable House are returned by electors under 200; 55 under 300; 90 under 400; 121 under 500; 150 under 600; 196 under 700; 214 under 800; 240 under 900; and 256 under 1,000; and that many of these constituencies are divided between two members.

They also find that your Honourable House, which is said to be exclusively the people's or the Commons House, contains *two hundred and five persons who are immediately or remotely related to the Peers of the Realm.*

Also that your Honourable House contains 1 marquess, 7 earls, 19 viscounts, 32 lords, 25 right honourables, 52 honourables, 63 baronets, 13 knights, 3 admirals, 7 lord-lieutenants, 42 deputy and vice-lieutenants, 1 general, 5 lieutenant-generals, 9 major-generals, 32 colonels, 33 lieutenant-colonels, 10 majors, 49 captains in army and navy, 10 lieutenants, 2 cornets, 58 barristers, 3 solicitors, 40 bankers, 33 East India proprietors, 13 West India proprietors, 52 place-men, 114 patrons of church livings having the patronage of 274 livings between them; the names of whom your petitioners can furnish at the request of your Honourable House.

Your petitioners therefore respectfully submit to your Honourable House that these facts afford abundant proofs that you do not represent the numbers or the interests of the millions; but that the persons composing it have interests for the most part foreign or directly opposed to the true interests of the great body of the people.

That perceiving the tremendous power you possess over the lives, liberty and labour of the unrepresented millions—perceiving the *military* and *civil forces* at your command—*the revenue* at your disposal—the *relief of the poor* in your hands—the *public press* in your power, by enactments expressly excluding the working classes alone—moreover, the power of delegating to others the whole control of the *monetary arrangements* of the Kingdom, by which the labouring classes may be silently plundered or suddenly suspended from employment—seeing all these elements of power wielded by your Honourable House as at present constituted, and fearing the consequences that may result if a thorough reform is not speedily had recourse to, your petitioners earnestly pray your Honourable House *to enact the following as the law of these realms,* with such other essential details as your Honourable House shall deem necessary:—

A LAW FOR EQUALLY REPRESENTING THE PEOPLE OF GREAT BRITAIN AND IRELAND

Equal Representation

That the United Kingdom be divided into 200 electoral districts; dividing, as nearly as possible, an equal number of inhabitants; and that each district do send a representative to Parliament.

Universal Suffrage

That every person producing proof of his being 21 years of age, to the clerk of the parish in which he has resided six months, shall be entitled to have his name registered as a voter. That the time for registering in each year be from the 1st of January to the 1st of March.

Annual Parliaments

That a general election do take place on the 24th of June in each year, and that each vacancy be filled up a fortnight after it occurs. That the hours for voting be from six o'clock in the morning till six o'clock in the evening.

No Property Qualifications

That there shall be no property qualification for members; but on a requisition, signed by 200 voters, in favour of any candidate being presented to the clerk of the parish in which they reside, such candidate shall be put in nomination. And the list of all the candidates nominated throughout the district shall be stuck on the church door in every parish, to enable voters to judge of their qualification.

Vote by Ballot

That each voter must vote in the parish in which he resides. That each parish provide as many balloting boxes as there are candidates proposed in the district; and that a temporary place be fitted up in each parish church for the purpose of *secret voting*. And, on the day of election, as each voter passes orderly on to the ballot, he shall have given to him, by the officer in attendance, a balloting ball, which he shall drop into the box of his favourite candidate. At the close of the day the votes shall be counted, by the proper officers, and the numbers stuck on the church doors. The following day the clerk of the district and two examiners shall collect the votes of all the parishes throughout the district, and cause the name of the successful candidate to be posted in every parish of the district.

Sittings and Payments to Members

That the members do take their seats in Parliament on the first Monday in October next after their election, and continue their sittings every day (Sundays excepted) till the business of the sitting is terminated, but not later than the 1st of September. They shall meet every day (during the Session) for business at 10 o'clock in the morning, and adjourn at 4. And every member shall be paid quarterly out of the public treasury £400 a year. That all electoral officers shall be elected by universal suffrage.

By passing the foregoing as the law of the land, you will confer a great blessing on the people of England; and your petitioners, as in duty bound, will ever pray.

NATIONAL PETITION

Unto the Honourable the Commons of the United Kingdom of Great Britain and Ireland in Parliament assembled, the Petition of the undersigned, their suffering countrymen,
Humbly Sheweth,

That we, your petitioners, dwell in a land whose merchants are noted for enterprise, whose manufacturers are very skilful, and whose workmen are proverbial for their industry.

The land itself is goodly, the soil rich, and the temperature wholesome; it is abundantly furnished with the materials of commerce and trade; it has numerous and convenient harbours; in facility of internal communication it exceeds all others.

For three-and-twenty years we have enjoyed a profound peace.

Yet, with all these elements of national prosperity, and with every disposition and capacity to take advantage of them, we find ourselves overwhelmed with public and private suffering.

We are bowed down under a load of taxes; which, notwithstanding, fall greatly short of the wants of our rulers; our traders are trembling on the verge of bankruptcy; our workmen are starving; capital brings no profit and labour no remuneration; the home of the artificer is desolate, and the warehouse of the pawnbroker is full; the workhouse is crowded, and the manufactory is deserted.

We have looked on every side, we have searched diligently in order to find out the causes of a distress so sore and so long continued.

We can discover none in nature, or in Providence.

Heaven has dealt graciously by the people; but the foolishness of our rulers has made the goodness of God of none effect.

The energies of a mighty kingdom have been wasted in building up the power of selfish and ignorant men, and its resources squandered for their aggrandisement.

The good of a party has been advanced to the sacrifice of the good of the nation; the few have governed for the interest of the few, while the interest of the many has been neglected, or insolently and tyrannously trampled upon.

It was the fond expectation of the people that a remedy for the greater part, if not for the whole, of their grievances, would be found in the Reform Act of 1832.

They were taught to regard that Act as a wise means to a worthy end; as the machinery of an improved legislation, when the will of the masses would be at length potential.

They have been bitterly and basely deceived.

The fruit which looked so fair to the eye has turned to dust and ashes when gathered.

The Reform Act has effected a transfer of power from one domineering faction to another, and left the people as helpless as before.

Our slavery has been exchanged for an apprenticeship to liberty, which has aggravated the painful feeling of our social degradation, by adding to it the sickening of still deferred hope.

We come before your Honourable House to tell you, with all humility, that this state of things must not be permitted to continue; that it cannot long continue without very seriously endangering the stability of the throne and the peace of the kingdom; and that if by God's help and all lawful and constitutional appliances, an end can be put to it, we are fully resolved that it shall speedily come to an end.

We tell your Honourable House that the capital of the master must no longer be deprived of its due reward; that the laws which make food dear, and those which by making money scarce, make labour cheap, must be abolished; that taxation must be made to fall on property, not on industry; that the good of the many, as it is the only legitimate end, so must it be the sole study of the Government.

As a preliminary essential to these and other requisite changes; as means by which alone the interests of the people can be effectually vindicated and secured, we demand that those interests be confided to the keeping of the people.

When the State calls for defenders, when it calls for money, no consideration of poverty or ignorance can be pleaded in refusal or delay of the call.

Required as we are, universally, to support and obey the laws, nature and reason entitle us to demand, that in the making of the laws, the universal voice shall be implicitly listened to.

We perform the duties of freemen; we must have the privileges of freemen. WE DEMAND UNIVERSAL SUFFRAGE.

The suffrage to be exempt from the corruption of the wealthy, and the violence of the powerful, must be secret.

The assertion of our right necessarily involves the power of its uncontrolled exercise.

WE DEMAND THE BALLOT.

The connection between the representatives and the people, to be beneficial must be intimate.

The legislative and constituent powers, for correction and for instruction, ought to be brought into frequent contact.

Errors, which are comparatively light when susceptible of a speedy popular remedy, may produce the most disastrous effects when permitted to grow inveterate through years of compulsory endurance.

To public safety as well as public confidence, frequent elections are essential. WE DEMAND ANNUAL PARLIAMENTS.

With power to choose, and freedom in choosing, the range of our choice must be unrestricted.

We are compelled, by the existing laws, to take for our representatives, men who are incapable of appreciating our difficulties, or who have little sympathy with them; merchants who have retired from trade, and no longer feel its harassings; proprietors of land who are alike ignorant of its evils and their cure; lawyers, by whom the honours of the senate are sought after only as means of obtaining notice in the courts.

The labours of a representative, who is sedulous in the discharge of his duty, are numerous and burdensome.

It is neither just, nor reasonable, nor safe, that they should continue to be gratuitously rendered.

We demand that in the future election of members of your Honourable House, the approbation of the constituency shall be the sole qualification; and that to every representative so chosen shall be assigned, out of the public taxes, a fair and adequate remuneration for the time which he is called upon to devote to the public service.

Finally, we would most earnestly impress on your Honourable House, that this petition has not been dictated by any idle love of change; that it springs out of no inconsiderate attachment to fanciful theories; but that it is the result of much and long deliberation, and of convictions, which the events of each succeeding year tend more and more to strengthen.

The management of this mighty kingdom has hitherto been a subject for contending factions to try their selfish experiments upon.

We have felt the consequences in our sorrowful experience—short glimmerings of uncertain enjoyment swallowed up by long and dark seasons of suffering.

If the self-government of the people should not remove their distresses, it will at least remove their repining.

Universal suffrage will, and it alone can, bring true and lasting peace to the nation; we firmly believe that it will also bring prosperity.

May it therefore please your Honourable House to take this our petition into your most serious consideration; and to use your utmost endeavours, by all constitutional means, to have a law passed, granting to every male of lawful age, sane mind, and unconvicted of crime, the right of voting for members of Parliament; and directing all future elections of members of Parliament to be in the way of secret ballot; and ordaining that the duration of Parliaments so chosen shall in no case exceed one year; and abolishing all property qualifications in the members; and providing for their due remuneration while in attendance on their Parliamentary duties.

And your petitioners, etc.

ALEXIS DE TOCQUEVILLE

ONE OF THE MOST thoughtful and perceptive observers of nineteenth-century political life, Alexis de Tocqueville (1805–59) achieved fame with the publication in 1835 of his profound and prophetic study, *Democracy in America*. During a visit to the United States in 1831–32 he investigated at first hand, and with a good deal of sympathy, the first vigorous manifestations of Jacksonian democracy. He returned to Europe, however, somewhat dismayed by his conclusion that "we are heading toward this unlimited democracy. What I see in this country [America] convinces me that it will work out badly in France; but we are pushed toward it by an irresistible force." His book, therefore, was intended "to diminish the ardor of those who thought democracy easy and brilliant, [and] to diminish the terror of those who thought it menacing and unworkable." The judicious tone of his book and the author's relative aloofness from partisan politics contributed to the almost universally enthusiastic reception of his book, which had a very large sale, and which one critic called "the greatest work of its kind since Montesquieu's *Esprit des lois.*"

Tocqueville's characteristic independence of mind made it difficult for him to play much part in politics under the July Monarchy. Although not fundamentally opposed to Louis-Philippe's government, he refused an easy opportunity to enter the Chamber in 1837 because he was unwilling to stand for election as an "official candidate." Two years later he managed to secure a deputy's mandate on his own terms, and maintained a position of critical neutrality between the government and the opposition until the Revolution of 1848, the outbreak of which he was almost alone in predicting.

During the revolutionary months of 1848 Tocqueville continued to plead for moderation and conciliation; he hoped that the new Republic could avoid the two great pitfalls in its path—the rule of the mob and eventual Caesarism. He approved of the drastic crushing of the June insurrection and as a member of the Constituent Assembly argued unsuccessfully for the adoption of a bicameral legislature and for the American system of indirect election of the President by an electoral college, because he correctly foresaw that the alternative (direct election by all adult males) would open the way to the dictatorship of a popular demagogue like Louis Napoleon Bonaparte. For several months he served as foreign minister of the Second Republic. He was imprisoned for two days after Bonaparte's coup d'état of December 2, 1851, against which he had publicly protested.

After the proclamation of the Second Empire had ended his political career, Tocqueville turned again to the study of political institutions. Convinced that the great French Revolution of 1789 had marked the decisive emergence of the new democratic order, he sought to see how the society of the Old Regime had given birth to the forces impelling the modern world in the direction of ever-greater mass participation in government. His last major work was *The Old Regime and the Revolution,* which was still unfinished at his death, though Part I had appeared in 1856. Tocqueville's general conclusion, that liberty and democracy (though often thought of as interchangeable terms) may well prove to be incompatible with one another under modern conditions, emerges as the central theme of his lifetime of observation and experience and represents one of his most influential contributions to modern political philosophy.

In his *Recollections* Tocqueville writes of events in which he was personally concerned with extraordinary detachment, and brings to bear on them the superlative analytical powers that distinguished his more theoretical writings. The manuscript was written at intervals during his retirement and was first published in French in 1893. It was translated in 1896 by Alexander Teixeira de Mattos. The Reeve translation of the following selections from *Democracy in America* appeared in 1835 and 1840. The selections from *The Recollections of Alexis de Tocqueville* were edited, with additions and an introduction, by J. P. Mayer (London: The Harvill Press, 1948).

DEMOCRACY IN AMERICA

AUTHOR'S INTRODUCTION

AMONG the novel objects that attracted my attention during my stay in the United States, nothing struck me more forcibly than the general equality of condition among the people. I readily discovered the prodigious influence that this primary fact exercises on the whole course of society; it gives a peculiar direction to public opinion and a peculiar tenor to the laws; it imparts new maxims to the governing authorities and peculiar habits to the governed.

I soon perceived that the influence of this fact extends far beyond the political character and the laws of the country, and that it has no less effect on civil society than on the government; it creates opinions, gives birth to new sentiments, founds novel customs, and modifies whatever it does not produce. The more I advanced in the study of American society, the more I perceived that this equality of condition is the fundamental fact from which all others seem to be derived and the central point at which all my observations constantly terminated.

I then turned my thoughts to our own hemisphere, and thought that I discerned there something analogous to the spectacle which the New World presented to me. I observed that equality of condition, though it has not there reached the extreme limit which it seems to have attained in the United

States, is constantly approaching it; and that the democracy which governs the American communities appears to be rapidly rising into power in Europe.

Hence I conceived the idea of the book that is now before the reader.

It is evident to all alike that a great democratic revolution is going on among us, but all do not look at it in the same light. To some it appears to be novel but accidental, and, as such, they hope it may still be checked; to others it seems irresistible, because it is the most uniform, the most ancient, and the most permanent tendency that is to be found in history.

I look back for a moment on the situation of France seven hundred years ago, when the territory was divided among a small number of families, who were the owners of the soil and the rulers of the inhabitants; the right of governing descended with the family inheritance from generation to generation; force was the only means by which man could act on man; and landed property was the sole source of power.

Soon, however, the political power of the clergy was founded and began to increase: the clergy opened their ranks to all classes, to the poor and the rich, the commoner and the noble; through the church, equality penetrated into the government, and he who as a serf must have vegetated in perpetual bondage took his place as a priest in the midst of nobles, and not infrequently above the heads of kings.

The different relations of men with one another became more complicated and numerous as society gradually became more stable and civilized. Hence the want of civil law was felt; and the ministers of law soon rose from the obscurity of the tribunals and their dusty chambers to appear at the court of the monarch, by the side of the feudal barons clothed in their ermine and their mail.

While the kings were ruining themselves by their great enterprises, and the nobles exhausting their resources by private wars, the lower orders were enriching themselves by commerce. The influence of money began to be perceptible in state affairs. The transactions of business opened a new road to power, and the financier rose to a station of political influence in which he was at once flattered and despised.

Gradually enlightenment spread, a reawakening of taste for literature and the arts became evident; intellect and will contributed to success; knowledge became an attribute of government, intelligence a social force; the educated man took part in affairs of state.

The value attached to high birth declined just as fast as new avenues to power were discovered. In the eleventh century, nobility was beyond all price; in the thirteenth, it might be purchased. Nobility was first conferred by gift in 1270, and equality was thus introduced into the government by the aristocracy itself.

In the course of these seven hundred years it sometimes happened that the nobles, in order to resist the authority of the crown or to diminish the power of their rivals, granted some political power to the common people. Or, more frequently, the king permitted the lower orders to have a share in the government, with the intention of limiting the power of the aristocracy.

In France the kings have always been the most active and the most constant of levelers. When they were strong and ambitious, they spared no pains to raise the people to the level of the nobles; when they were temperate and feeble, they allowed the people to rise above themselves. Some assisted democracy by their talents, others by their vices. Louis XI and Louis XIV reduced all ranks beneath the throne to the same degree of subjection; and finally Louis XV descended, himself and all his court, into the dust.

As soon as land began to be held on any other than a feudal tenure, and personal property could in its turn confer influence and power, every discovery in the arts, every improvement in commerce of manufactures, created so many new elements of equality among men. Henceforward every new invention, every new want which it occasioned, and every new desire which craved satisfaction were steps towards a general leveling. The taste for luxury, the love of war, the rule of fashion, and the most superficial as well as the deepest passions of the human heart seemed to co-operate to enrich the poor and to impoverish the rich.

From the time when the exercise of the intellect became a source of strength and of wealth, we see that every addition to science, every fresh truth, and every new idea became a germ of power placed within the reach of the people. Poetry, eloquence, and memory, the graces of the mind, the fire of imagination, depth of thought, and all the gifts which Heaven scatters at a venture turned to the advantage of democracy; and even when they were in the possession of its adversaries, they still served its cause by throwing into bold relief the natural greatness of man. Its conquests spread, therefore, with those of civilization and knowledge; and literature became an arsenal open to all, where the poor and the weak daily resorted for arms.

In running over the pages of our history, we shall scarcely find a single event of the last seven hundred years that has not promoted equality of condition.

The Crusades and the English wars decimated the nobles and divided their possessions: the municipal corporations introduced democratic liberty into the bosom of feudal monarchy; the invention of firearms equalized the vassal and the noble on the field of battle; the art of printing opened the same resources to the minds of all classes; the post brought knowledge alike to the door of the cottage and to the gate of the palace; and Protestantism proclaimed that all men are equally able to find the road to heaven. The discovery of America opened a thousand new paths to fortune and led obscure adventurers to wealth and power.

If, beginning with the eleventh century, we examine what has happened in France from one half-century to another, we shall not fail to perceive that at the end of each of these periods a two-fold revolution has taken place in the state of society. The noble has gone down the social ladder, and the commoner has gone up; the one descends as the other rises. Every half-century brings them nearer to each other, and they will soon meet.

Nor is this peculiar to France. Wherever we look, we perceive the same revolution going on throughout the Christian world.

The various occurrences of national existence have everywhere turned to the advantage of democracy: all men have aided it by their exertions, both those who have intentionally labored in its cause and those who have served it unwittingly; those who have fought for it and even those who have declared themselves its opponents have all been driven along in the same direction, have all labored to one end; some unknowingly and some despite themselves, all have been blind instruments in the hands of God.

The gradual development of the principle of equality is, therefore, a providential fact. It has all the chief characteristics of such a fact: it is universal, it is lasting, it constantly eludes all human interference, and all events as well as all men contribute to its progress.

Would it, then, be wise to imagine that a social movement the causes of which lie so far back can be checked by the efforts of one generation? Can it be believed that the democracy which has overthrown the feudal system and vanquished kings will retreat before tradesmen and capitalists? Will it stop now that it has grown so strong and its adversaries so weak?

Whither, then, are we tending? No one can say, for terms of comparison already fail us. There is greater equality of condition in Christian countries at the present day than there has been at any previous time, in any part of the world, so that the magnitude of what already has been done prevents us from foreseeing what is yet to be accomplished.

The whole book that is here offered to the public has been written under the influence of a kind of religious awe produced in the author's mind by the view of that irresistible revolution which has advanced for centuries in spite of every obstacle and which is still advancing in the midst of the ruins it has caused.

It is not necessary that God himself should speak in order that we may discover the unquestionable signs of his will. It is enough to ascertain what is the habitual course of nature and the constant tendency of events. I know, without special revelation, that the planets move in the orbits traced by the Creator's hand.

If the men of our time should be convinced, by attentive observation and sincere reflection, that the gradual and progressive development of social equality is at once the past and the future of their history, this discovery alone would confer upon the change the sacred character of a divine decree. To attempt to check democracy would be in that case to resist the will of God; and the nations would then be constrained to make the best of the social lot awarded them by Providence.

The Christian nations of our day seem to me to present a most alarming spectacle; the movement which impels them is already so strong that it cannot be stopped, but it is not yet so rapid that it cannot be guided. Their fate is still in their own hands; but very soon they may lose control.

The first of the duties that are at this time imposed upon those who direct our affairs is to educate democracy, to reawaken, if possible, its religious beliefs; to purify its morals; to mold its actions; to substitute a knowledge of statecraft for its blind instincts, to adapt its government to time and place, and to modify it according to men and to conditions. A new science of politics is needed for a new world.

This, however, is what we think of least; placed in the middle of a rapid stream, we obstinately fix our eyes on the ruins that may still be descried upon the shore we have left, while the current hurries us away and drags us backward towards the abyss.

In no country in Europe has the great social revolution that I have just described made such rapid progress as in France; but it has always advanced without guidance. The heads of the state have made no preparation for it, and it has advanced without their consent or without their knowledge. The most powerful, the most intelligent, and the most moral classes of the nation have never attempted to control it in order to guide it. Democracy has consequently been abandoned to its wild instincts, and it has grown up like those children who have no parental guidance, who receive their education in the public streets, and who are acquainted only with the vices and wretchedness of society. Its existence was seemingly unknown when suddenly it acquired supreme power. All then servilely submitted to its caprices; it was worshipped as the idol of strength; and when afterwards it was enfeebled by its own excesses, the legislator conceived the rash project of destroying it, instead of instructing it and correcting its vices. No attempt was made to fit it to govern, but all were bent on excluding it from the government.

The result has been that the democratic revolution has taken place in the body of society without that concomitant change in the laws, ideas, customs, and morals which was necessary to render such a revolution beneficial. Thus we have a democracy without anything to lessen its vices and bring out its natural advantages; and although we already perceive the evils it brings, we are ignorant of the benefits it may confer.

While the power of the crown, supported by the aristocracy, peaceably governed the nations of Europe, society, in the midst of its wretchedness, had several sources of happiness which can now scarcely be conceived or appreciated. The power of a few of his subjects was an insurmountable barrier to the tyranny of the prince; and the monarch, who felt the almost divine character which he enjoyed in the eyes of the multitude, derived a motive for the just use of his power from the respect which he inspired. The nobles, placed high as they were above the people, could take that calm and benevolent interest in their fate which the shepherd feels towards his flock; and without acknowledging the poor as their equals, they watched over the destiny of those whose welfare Providence had entrusted to their care. The people, never having conceived the idea of a social condition different from their own, and never expecting to become equal to their leaders, received benefits from them without discussing their rights. They became attached to them when they were clement and just and submitted to their exactions without resistance or servility, as to the inevitable visitations of the Deity. Custom and usage, moreover, had established certain limits to oppression and founded a sort of law in the very midst of violence.

As the noble never suspected that anyone would attempt to deprive him of the privileges which he believed to be legitimate, and as the serf looked upon his own inferiority as a consequence of the immutable order of nature, it is easy to imagine that some mutual exchange of goodwill took place between two classes so differently endowed by fate. Inequality and wretchedness were then to be found in society, but the souls of neither rank of men were degraded.

Men are not corrupted by the exercise of power or debased by the habit of obedience, but by the exercise of a power which they believe to be illegitimate, and by obedience to a rule which they consider to be usurped and oppressive.

On the one side were wealth, strength, and leisure, accompanied by the pursuit of luxury, the refinements of taste, the pleasures of wit, and the culti-vation of the arts; on the other were labor, clownishness, and ignorance. But in the midst of this coarse and ignorant multitude it was not uncommon to meet with energetic passions, generous sentiments, profound religious convic-tions, and wild virtues.

The social state thus organized might boast of its stability, its power, and above all, its glory.

But the scene is now changed. Gradually the distinctions of rank are done away with; the barriers that once severed mankind are falling; property is divided, power is shared by many, the light of intelligence spreads, and the capacities of all classes tend towards equality. Society becomes democratic, and the empire of democracy is slowly and peaceably introduced into institu-tions and customs.

I can conceive of a society in which all men would feel an equal love and respect for the laws of which they consider themselves the authors; in which the authority of the government would be respected as necessary, and not divine; and in which the loyalty of the subject to the chief magistrate would not be a passion, but a quiet and rational persuasion. With every individual in the possession of rights which he is sure to retain, a kind of manly confi-dence and reciprocal courtesy would arise between all classes, removed alike from pride and servility. The people, well acquainted with their own true interests, would understand that, in order to profit from the advantages of the state, it is necessary to satisfy its requirements. The voluntary association of the citizens might then take the place of the individual authority of the nobles, and the community would be protected from tyranny and license.

I admit that, in a democratic state thus constituted, society would not be stationary. But the impulses of the social body might there be regulated and made progressive. If there were less splendor than in an aristocracy, misery would also be less prevalent; the pleasures of enjoyment might be less exces-sive, but those of comfort would be more general; the sciences might be less perfectly cultivated, but ignorance would be less common; the ardor of the feelings would be constrained, and the habits of the nation softened; there would be more vices and fewer crimes.

In the absence of enthusiasm and ardent faith, great sacrifices may be ob-tained from the members of a commonwealth by an appeal to their under-standing and their experience; each individual will feel the same necessity of union with his fellows to protect his own weakness; and as he knows that he can obtain their help only on condition of helping them, he will readily per-ceive that his personal interest is identified with the interests of the whole com-munity. The nation, taken as a whole, will be less brilliant, less glorious, and perhaps less strong; but the majority of the people will enjoy a greater degree of prosperity, and the people will remain peaceable, not because they despair of a change for the better, but because they are conscious that they are well off already.

If all the consequences of this state of things were not good or useful, society would at least have appropriated all such as were useful and good; and having once and forever renounced the social advantages of aristocracy, mankind would enter into possession of all the benefits that democracy can offer.

But here it may be asked what we have adopted in the place of those institutions, those ideas, and those customs of our forefathers which we have abandoned.

The spell of royalty is broken, but it has not been succeeded by the majesty of the laws. The people have learned to despise all authority, but they still fear it; and fear now extorts more than was formerly paid from reverence and love.

I perceive that we have destroyed those individual powers which were able, single-handed, to cope with tyranny; but it is the government alone that has inherited all the privileges of which families, guilds, and individuals have been deprived; to the power of a small number of persons, which if it was sometimes oppressive was often conservative, has succeeded the weakness of the whole community.

The division of property has lessened the distance which separated the rich from the poor; but it would seem that, the nearer they draw to each other, the greater is their mutual hatred and the more vehement the envy and the dread with which they resist each other's claims to power; the idea of right does not exist for either party, and force affords to both the only argument for the present and the only guarantee for the future.

The poor man retains the prejudices of his forefathers without their faith, and their ignorance without their virtues; he has adopted the doctrine of self-interest as the rule of his actions without understanding the science that puts it to use; and his selfishness is no less blind than was formerly his devotion to others.

If society is tranquil, it is not because it is conscious of its strength and its well-being, but because it fears its weakness and its infirmities; a single effort may cost it its life. Everybody feels the evil, but no one has courage or energy enough to seek the cure. The desires, the repinings, the sorrows, and the joys of the present time lead to nothing visible or permanent, like the passions of old men, which terminate in impotence.

We have, then, abandoned whatever advantages the old state of things afforded, without receiving any compensation from our present condition; we have destroyed an aristocracy, and we seem inclined to survey its ruins with complacency and to accept them.

The phenomena which the intellectual world presents are not less deplorable. The democracy of France, hampered in its course or abandoned to its lawless passions, has overthrown whatever crossed its path and has shaken all that it has not destroyed. Its empire has not been gradually introduced or peaceably established, but it has constantly advanced in the midst of the disorders and the agitations of a conflict. In the heat of the struggle each partisan is hurried beyond the natural limits of his opinions by the doctrines and the excesses of his opponents, until he loses sight of the end of his exertions, and holds forth in a way which does not correspond to his real sentiments or secret instincts. Hence arises the strange confusion that we are compelled to witness.

I can recall nothing in history more worthy of sorrow and pity than the scenes which are passing before our eyes. It is as if the natural bond that unites the opinions of man to his tastes, and his actions to his principles, was now broken, the harmony that has always been observed between the feelings and the ideas of mankind appears to be dissolved and all the laws of moral analogy to be abolished.

Zealous Christians are still found among us, whose minds are nurtured on the thoughts that pertain to a future life, and who readily espouse the cause of human liberty as the source of all moral greatness. Christianity, which has declared that all men are equal in the sight of God, will not refuse to acknowledge that all citizens are equal in the eye of the law. But, by a strange coincidence of events, religion has been for a time entangled with those institutions which democracy destroys; and it is not infrequently brought to reject the equality which it loves, and to curse as a foe that cause of liberty whose efforts it might hallow by its alliance.

By the side of these religious men I discern others whose thoughts are turned to earth rather than to heaven. These are the partisans of liberty, not only as the source of the noblest virtues, but more especially as the root of all solid advantages; and they sincerely desire to secure its authority, and to impart its blessings to mankind. It is natural that they should hasten to invoke the assistance of religion, for they must know that liberty cannot be established without morality, nor morality without faith. But they have seen religion in the ranks of their adversaries, and they inquire no further; some of them attack it openly, and the rest are afraid to defend it.

In former ages slavery was advocated by the venal and slavish-minded, while the independent and the warm-hearted were struggling without hope to save the liberties of mankind. But men of high and generous character are now to be met with, whose opinions are directly at variance with their inclinations, and who praise that servility and meanness which they have themselves never known. Others, on the contrary, speak of liberty as if they were able to feel its sanctity and its majesty, and loudly claim for humanity those rights which they have always refused to acknowledge.

There are virtuous and peaceful individuals whose pure morality, quiet habits, opulence, and talents fit them to be the leaders of their fellow men. Their love of country is sincere, and they are ready to make the greatest sacrifices for its welfare. But civilization often finds them among its opponents; they confound its abuses with its benefits, and the idea of evil is inseparable in their minds from that of novelty.

Near these I find others whose object is to materialize mankind, to hit upon what is expedient without heeding what is just, to acquire knowledge without faith, and prosperity apart from virtue; claiming to be the champions of modern civilization, they place themselves arrogantly at its head, usurping a place which is abandoned to them, and of which they are wholly unworthy.

Where are we, then?

The religionists are the enemies of liberty, and the friends of liberty attack religion; the high-minded and the noble advocate bondage, and the meanest and most servile preach independence; honest and enlightened citizens are opposed to all progress, while men without patriotism and without principle put themselves forward as the apostles of civilization and intelligence.

Has such been the fate of the centuries which have preceded our own? and has man always inhabited a world like the present, where all things are not in their proper relationships, where virtue is without genius, and genius without honor; where the love of order is confused with a taste for oppression, and the holy cult of freedom with a contempt of law; where the light thrown by conscience on human actions is dim, and where nothing seems to be any longer forbidden or allowed, honorable or shameful, false or true?

I cannot believe that the Creator made man to leave him in an endless struggle with the intellectual wretchedness that surrounds us. God destines a calmer and a more certain future to the communities of Europe. I am ignorant of his designs, but I shall not cease to believe in them because I cannot fathom them, and I had rather mistrust my own capacity than his justice.

There is one country in the world where the great social revolution that I am speaking of seems to have nearly reached its natural limits. It has been effected with ease and simplicity; say rather that this country is reaping the fruits of the democratic revolution which we are undergoing, without having had the revolution itself.

The emigrants who colonized the shores of America in the beginning of the seventeenth century somehow separated the democratic principle from all the principles that it had to contend with in the old communities of Europe, and transplanted it alone to the New World. It has there been able to spread in perfect freedom and peaceably to determine the character of the laws by influencing the manners of the country.

It appears to me beyond a doubt that, sooner or later, we shall arrive, like the Americans, at an almost complete equality of condition. But I do not conclude from this that we shall ever be necessarily led to draw the same political consequences which the Americans have derived from a similar social organization. I am far from supposing that they have chosen the only form of government which a democracy may adopt; but as the generating cause of laws and manners in the two countries is the same, it is of immense interest for us to know what it has produced in each of them.

It is not, then, merely to satisfy a curiosity, however legitimate, that I have examined America; my wish has been to find there instruction by which we may ourselves profit. . . .

America, then, exhibits in her social state an extraordinary phenomenon. Men are there seen on a greater equality in point of fortune and intellect, or, in other words, more equal in strength, than in any other country of the world, or in any age of which history has preserved the remembrance.

The political consequences of such a social condition as this are easily deducible.

It is impossible to believe that equality will not eventually find its way into the political world, as it does everywhere else. To conceive of men remaining forever unequal upon a single point, yet equal on all others, is impossible; they must come in the end to be equal upon all.

Now, I know of only two methods of establishing equality in the political world; rights must be given to every citizen, or none at all to anyone. For nations which are arrived at the same stage of social existence as the Anglo-Americans, it is, therefore, very difficult to discover a medium between the sovereignty of all and the absolute power of one man: and it would be vain to deny that the social condition which I have been describing is just as liable to one of these consequences as to the other.

There is, in fact, a manly and lawful passion for equality that incites men to wish all to be powerful and honored. This passion tends to elevate the humble to the rank of the great; but there exists also in the human heart a depraved taste for equality, which impels the weak to attempt to lower the powerful to their own level and reduces men to prefer equality in slavery to inequality with freedom. Not that those nations whose social condition is democratic naturally despise liberty; on the contrary, they have an instinctive love of it. But liberty is not the chief and constant object of their desires; equality is their idol; they make rapid and sudden efforts to obtain liberty and, if they miss their aim, resign themselves to their disappointment; but nothing can satisfy them without equality, and they would rather perish than lose it.

On the other hand, in a state where the citizens are all practically equal, it becomes difficult for them to preserve their independence against the aggressions of power. No one among them being strong enough to engage in the struggle alone with advantage, nothing but a general combination can protect their liberty. Now, such a union is not always possible.

From the same social position, then, nations may derive one or the other of two great political results; these results are extremely different from each other, but they both proceed from the same cause.

The Anglo-Americans are the first nation who, having been exposed to this formidable alternative, have been happy enough to escape the dominion of absolute power. They have been allowed by their circumstances, their origin, their intelligence, and especially by their morals to establish and maintain the sovereignty of the people. . . .

IMPORTANCE OF WHAT PRECEDES WITH RESPECT TO
THE STATE OF EUROPE

. . . . If those nations whose social condition is democratic could remain free only while they inhabit uncultivated regions, we must despair of the future destiny of the human race; for democracy is rapidly acquiring a more extended sway, and the wilds are gradually peopled with men. If it were true that laws and customs are insufficient to maintain democratic institutions, what refuge would remain open to the nations, except the despotism of one man? I am aware that there are many worthy persons at the present time who are not alarmed at this alternative and who are so tired of liberty as to be glad of repose far from its storms. But these persons are ill acquainted with the haven towards which they are bound. Preoccupied by their remembrances, they judge of absolute power by what it has been and not by what it might become in our times.

If absolute power were re-established among the democratic nations of Europe, I am persuaded that it would assume a new form and appear under features unknown to our fathers. There was a time in Europe when the laws and the consent of the people had invested princes with almost unlimited authority, but they scarcely ever availed themselves of it. I do not speak of the prerogatives of the nobility, of the authority of high courts of justice, of corporations and their chartered rights, or of provincial privileges, which served to break the blows of sovereign authority and to keep up a spirit of resistance in the nation. Independently of these political institutions, which, however opposed they might be to personal liberty, served to keep alive the love of freedom in the mind and which may be esteemed useful in this respect, the manners and opinions of the nation confined the royal authority within barriers that were not less powerful because less conspicuous. Religion, the affections of the people, the benevolence of the prince, the sense of honor, family pride, provincial prejudices, custom, and public opinion limited the power of kings and restrained their authority within an invisible circle. The constitution of nations was despotic at that time, but their customs were free. Princes had the right, but they had neither the means nor the desire of doing whatever they pleased.

But what now remains of those barriers which formerly arrested tyranny? Since religion has lost its empire over the souls of men, the most prominent boundary that divided good from evil is overthrown; everything seems doubtful and indeterminate in the moral world; kings and nations are guided by chance, and none can say where are the natural limits of despotism and the bounds of license. Long revolutions have forever destroyed the respect which surrounded the rulers of the state; and since they have been relieved from the burden of public esteem, princes may henceforward surrender themselves without fear to the intoxication of arbitrary power.

When kings find that the hearts of their subjects are turned towards them, they are lenient, because they are conscious of their strength; and they are careful of the affection of their people because the affection of their people is the bulwark of the throne. A mutual interchange of goodwill then takes place between the prince and the people, which resembles the gracious intercourse of domestic life. The subjects may murmur at the sovereign's decree, but they are grieved to displease him; and the sovereign chastises his subjects with the light hand of parental affection.

But when once the spell of royalty is broken in the tumult of revolution, when successive monarchs have crossed the throne, so as alternately to display to the people the weakness of their right and the harshness of their power, the sovereign is no longer regarded by any as the father of the state, and he is feared by all as its master. If he is weak, he is despised; if he is strong, he is detested. He is himself full of animosity and alarm; he finds that he is a stranger in his own country, and he treats his subjects like conquered enemies.

When the provinces and the towns formed so many different nations in the midst of their common country, each of them had a will of its own, which was opposed to the general spirit of subjection; but now that all the parts of the same empire, after having lost their immunities, their customs, their prejudices, their traditions, and even their names, have become accustomed to obey the same laws, it is not more difficult to oppress them all together than it was formerly to oppress one of them separately.

While the nobles enjoyed their power, and indeed long after that power was lost, the honor of aristocracy conferred an extraordinary degree of force upon their personal opposition. Men could then be found who, notwithstanding their weakness, still entertained a high opinion of their personal value, and dared to cope single-handed with public authority. But at the present day, when all ranks are more and more undifferentiated, when the individual disappears in the throng and is easily lost in the midst of a common obscurity, when the honor of monarchy has almost lost its power, without being succeeded by virtue, and when nothing can enable man to rise above himself, who shall say at what point the exigencies of power and the servility of weakness will stop?

As long as family feeling was kept alive, the opponent of oppression was never alone; he looked about him and found his clients, his hereditary friends, and his kinsfolk. If this support was wanting, he felt himself sustained by his ancestors and animated by his posterity. But when patrimonial estates are divided, and when a few years suffice to confound the distinctions of race, where can family feeling be found? What force can there be in the customs of a country which has changed, and is still perpetually changing, its aspect, in which every act of tyranny already has a precedent and every crime an example, in which there is nothing so old that its antiquity can save it from destruction, and nothing so unparalleled that its novelty can prevent it from being done? What resistance can be offered by customs of so pliant a make that they have already often yielded? What strength can even public opinion have retained when no twenty persons are connected by a common tie, when not a man, nor a family, nor chartered corporation, nor class, nor free institution, has the power of representing or exerting that opinion, and when every citizen, being equally weak, equally poor, and equally isolated, has only his personal impotence to oppose to the organized force of the government?

The annals of France furnish nothing analogous to the condition in which that country might then be thrown. But it may more aptly be assimilated to the times of old, and to those hideous eras of Roman oppression when the manners of the people were corrupted, their traditions obliterated, their habits destroyed, their opinions shaken, and freedom, expelled from the laws, could find no refuge in the land; when nothing protected the citizens, and the citizens no longer protected themselves; when human nature was the sport of man, and princes wearied out the clemency of Heaven before they exhausted the patience of their subjects. Those who hope to revive the monarchy of Henry IV or of Louis XIV appear to me to be afflicted with mental blindness; and when I consider the present condition of several European nations, a condition to which all the others tend, I am led to believe that they will soon be left with no other alternative than democratic liberty or the tyranny of the Caesars.

Is not this deserving of consideration? If men must really come to this point, that they are to be entirely emancipated or entirely enslaved, all their rights to be made equal or all to be taken away from them; if the rulers of society were compelled either gradually to raise the crowd to their own level or to allow all the citizens to fall below that of humanity, would not the doubts of many be resolved, the consciences of many be confirmed, and the community prepared to make great sacrifices with little difficulty? In that case the gradual growth of democratic manners and institutions should be regarded, not as the best, but as the only means of preserving freedom; and, without caring for the democratic form of government, it might be adopted as the most applicable, and the fairest remedy for the present ills of society.

It is difficult to make the people participate in the government, but it is still more difficult to supply them with experience and to inspire them with the feelings which they need in order to govern well. I grant that the wishes of the democracy are capricious, its instruments rude, its laws imperfect. But if it were true that soon no just medium would exist between the rule of democracy and the dominion of a single man, should we not rather incline towards the former than submit voluntarily to the latter? And if complete equality be our fate, is it not better to be leveled by free institutions than by a despot?

Those who, after having read this book, should imagine that my intention in writing it was to propose the laws and customs of the Anglo-Americans for the imitation of all democratic communities would make a great mistake; they must have paid more attention to the form than to the substance of my thought. My aim has been to show, by the example of America, that laws, and especially customs, may allow a democratic people to remain free. But I am very far from thinking that we ought to follow the example of the

American democracy and copy the means that it has employed to attain this end; for I am well aware of the influence which the nature of a country and its political antecedents exercise upon its political constitution; and I should regard it as a great misfortune for mankind if liberty were to exist all over the world under the same features.

But I am of the opinion that if we do not succeed in gradually introducing democratic institutions into France, if we despair of imparting to all the citizens those ideas and sentiments which first prepare them for freedom and afterwards allow them to enjoy it, there will be no independence at all, either for the middle classes or for the nobility, for the poor or for the rich, but an equal tyranny over all; and I foresee that if the peaceable dominion of the majority is not founded among us in time, we shall sooner or later fall under the unlimited authority of a single man.

RECOLLECTIONS

ORIGIN AND CHARACTER OF THESE RECOLLECTIONS—GENERAL ASPECTS OF THE PERIOD PRECEDING THE REVOLUTION OF 1848—FIRST SYMPTOMS OF THE REVOLUTION

. . . OUR HISTORY from 1789 to 1830, viewed from a distance and as a whole, affords as it were the picture of a struggle to the death between the Ancien Régime, its traditions, memories, hopes, and men, as represented by the aristocracy, and the New France led by the Middle Class. The year 1830 closed the first period of our revolutions, or rather of our revolution: for there is but one, which has remained always the same in the face of varying fortunes, of which our fathers witnessed the beginning, and of which we, in all probability, shall not live to see the end. In 1830 the triumph of the middle class had been definite and so thorough that all political power, every franchise, every prerogative, and the whole government was confined and, as it were, heaped up within the narrow limits of this one class, to the statutory exclusion of all beneath them and the actual exclusion of all above. Not only did it thus rule society, but it may be said to have formed it. It entrenched itself in every vacant place, prodigiously augmented the number of places and accustomed itself to live almost as much upon the Treasury as upon its own industry.

No sooner had the Revolution of 1830 become an accomplished fact, than there ensued a great lull in political passion, a sort of general subsidence, accompanied by a rapid increase in public wealth. The particular spirit of the middle class became the general spirit of the government; it ruled the latter's foreign policy as well as affairs at home: an active, industrious spirit, often dishonourable, generally orderly, occasionally reckless through vanity or egoism, but timid by temperament, moderate in all things except in its love of ease and comfort, and last but not least mediocre. It was a spirit which, mingled with that of the people or of the aristocracy, can do wonders; but which, by itself, will never produce more than a government shorn of both virtue and greatness. Master of everything in a manner that no aristocracy has ever been or may ever hope to be, the middle class, when called upon to assume the government, took it up as an industrial enterprise; it entrenched itself behind its power, and before long, in their egoism, each of its members thought much more of his private business than of public affairs; of his personal enjoyment than of the greatness of the nation.

Posterity, which sees none but the more dazzling crimes, and which loses sight, in general, of mere vices, will never, perhaps, know to what extent the government of that day, towards its close, assumed the ways of an industrial enterprise, which conducts all its transactions with a view to the profits accruing to the shareholders. These vices were due to the natural instincts of the dominant class, to its absolute power, and also to the character of the time. King Louis-Philippe had contributed much to their growth. He was the accident which made the malady mortal. This prince was a singular medley of qualities, and one would have to have known him longer and more nearly than I did to be able to portray him in detail. But his main traits were easily seen even when one was far away or one was only passing by.

Though he came from one of the noblest families in Europe, he concealed all hereditary pride deeply in his soul; nevertheless he certainly believed that there was no other human being like him. All the same he had most of the qualities and defects which belong more particularly to the subaltern orders of society. He had regular habits and wanted those around him to have them too. He was orderly in his conduct, simple in his habits, his tastes were tempered; he was a born friend of the law, an enemy of all excesses, sober in his ways except in his desires. He was human without being sentimental, greedy and soft. He had no flaming passions, no ruinous weaknesses, no striking vices, and only one kingly virtue: courage. He was extremely polite, but without choice or greatness, a politeness of a merchant rather than of a Prince. He hardly appreciated literature or art, but he passionately loved industry. His memory was prodigious and capable of keeping the minutest detail. His conversation was prolix, diffuse, original and trivial, anecdotal, full of small facts, of salt and meaning; it gave all satisfaction which one may find in intellectual pleasures when delicacy and elevation are absent. His mind was distinguished, but withdrawn and embarrassed for his soul was neither high nor profound. He was enlightened, subtle, flexible; as he was only open to that which was useful, he was full of profound disdain for the truth, and he did so little believe in virtue that his sight was darkened. Thus he did not see the beauty which truth and decency show, he did not even understand any more their usefulness which they so often have. He had a profound knowledge of human beings, but he knew them only through their vices. He was unbeliever in religious matters as the eighteenth century and sceptical in politics as the 19th; having no belief himself, he did not believe in the belief of others. He was, as it were, naturally fond of power and of dishonest, mediocre, facile, and plain courtiers to be really born for the throne. His ambition only, limited by prudence, never satisfied, nor did it ever carry him away; it always kept him near to the ground.

There have been several princes who resemble this portrait, but the special case of Louis-Philippe was his analogy or rather kind of parentship and consanguinity which bound his faults to those of his time; this made him for his contemporaries and particularly for the class which held the power such an attractive, singularly dangerous and corruptive prince. Chief of the bourgeoisie,—he pushed them towards their natural bent which they had only too much inclination to follow. They married their vices, and this family union first made each of them strong, singly, then accomplished the demoralisation of the other, and finished by making them both perish. . . .

In this political world thus constituted and conducted, what was most wanting, particularly towards the end, was political life itself. It could neither come into being nor be maintained within the legal circle which the Constitution had traced for it: the old aristocracy was vanquished, the people excluded. As all business was discussed among members of one class, in the interest and in the spirit of that class, there was no battlefield for contending parties to meet upon. This singular homogeneity of position, of interests, and consequently of views, reigning in what M. Guizot had once called the legal country, deprived the parliamentary debates of all originality, of all reality, and therefore of all genuine passion. I have spent ten years of my life in the company of truly great minds, who were in a constant state of agitation without succeeding in heating themselves, and who spent all their perspicacity in vain endeavours to find subjects upon which they could seriously disagree.

On the other hand, the preponderating influence which King Louis-Philippe had acquired in public affairs, which never permitted the politicians to stray very far from that Prince's ideas, lest they should at the same time be removed from power, reduced the different colours of parties to the merest shades, and debates to the splitting of straws. I doubt whether any parliament (not except-ing the Constituent Assembly, I mean the true one, that of 1789) ever con-tained more varied and brilliant talents than did ours during the closing years of the Monarchy of July. Nevertheless, I am able to declare that these great orators were bored to death of listening to one another, and, what was worse the whole country was bored of listening to them. France grew unconsciously accustomed to look upon the debates in the Chambers as exercises of the intellect rather than as serious discussions, and upon all the differences be-tween the various parliamentary parties—the majority, the left centre, or the dynastic opposition—as domestic quarrels between children of one family trying to trick one another. A few glaring instances of corruption, discovered by accident, led the country to presuppose a number of hidden cases, and convinced it that the whole of the governing class was corrupt; whence it conceived for the latter a silent contempt, which was generally taken for confiding and contented submission.

The country was at that time divided into two unequal parts, or rather zones: in the upper, which alone was intended to contain the whole of the nation's political life, there reigned nothing but languor, impotence, stagna-tion, and boredom; in the lower, on the contrary, political life began to make itself manifest by means of feverish and irregular signs, of which the attentive observer was easily able to seize the meaning.

I was one of these observers; and although I was far from imagining that the catastrophe was so near at hand and fated to be so terrible, I felt a distrust springing up and insensibly growing in my mind, and the idea taking root more and more that we were making strides towards a fresh revolution. This denoted a great change in my thoughts; since the general appeasement and flatness that followed the Revolution of July had led me to believe for a long time that I was destined to spend my life amid an enervated and peaceful society. Indeed, anyone who had only examined the inside of the governmental fabric would have had the same conviction. Everything there seemed com-bined to produce with the machinery of liberty a preponderance of Royal power which verged upon despotism; and, in fact, this result was produced almost without effort by the regular and tranquil movement of the machine. King Louis-Philippe was persuaded that, so long as he did not himself lay hand upon that fine instrument, and allowed it to work according to rule, he was safe from all peril. His only occupation was to keep it in order, and to make it work according to his own views, forgetful of society, upon which this ingenious piece of mechanism rested; he resembled the man who refused to believe that his house was on fire, because he had the key to it in his pocket. I could neither have the same interests nor the same cares, and this permitted me to see through the mechanism of institutions and the agglomeration of petty every-day facts, and to observe the state of morals and opinions in the country. There I clearly saw the appearance of several of the portents that usually denote the approach of revolutions, and I began to believe that in 1830 I had taken for the end of the play what was nothing more than the end of an act.

A short unpublished document which I composed at the time, and a speech which I delivered early in 1848, will bear witness to these pre-occupations of my mind.

Several of my friends in Parliament met together in October 1847, to decide upon the policy to be adopted during the next session. It was agreed that we should issue a program in the form of a manifesto, and the task of drawing it up was deputed to me. Later, the idea of this publication was abandoned, but I had already written the document. I have discovered it among my papers, and I give the following extracts. After commenting on the symptoms of languor in Parliament, I continued:

. . . The time will come when the country will find itself once again divided between two great parties. The French Revolution which abolished all privileges and destroyed all exclusive rights, has allowed one to remain, that of property. Let not the proprietors deceive themselves as to the strength of their position, nor think that the rights of property form an insurmountable barrier because they have not as yet been surmounted; for our times are unlike any others. When the rights of property were merely the origin and commencement of a number of other rights, they were easily defended, or rather, they were never attacked; they then formed the surrounding wall of society, of which all other rights were the outposts; no blows reached them; no serious attempt was ever made to touch them. But to-day, when the rights of property are nothing more than the last remnants of an overthrown aristocratic world; when they alone are left intact, isolated privileges amid the universal levelling of society; when they are no longer protected behind a number of still more controversible and odious rights, the case is altered, and they alone are left daily to resist the direct and unceasing shock of democratic opinion.

. . . Before long, the political struggle will be restricted to those who have and those who have not; property will form the great field of battle; and the principal political questions will turn upon the more or less important modifications to be introduced into the right of property. We shall then have once more among us great public agitations and great political parties.

How is it that these premonitory symptoms escape the general view? Can anyone believe that it is by accident, through some passing whim of the human mind, that we see appearing on every side these curious doctrines, bearing different titles, but all characterized in their essence by their denial of the rights of property, and all tending, at least, to diminish and weaken the exercise of these rights? Who can fail here to recognise the final symptom of the old democratic disease of the time, whose crisis would seem to be at hand?

I was still more urgent and explicit in the speech which I delivered in the Chamber of Deputies on the 29th of January 1848, and which appeared in the *Moniteur* of the 30th.

The principal passages may be quoted here:

. . . I am told that there is no danger because there are no riots; I am told that, because there is no visible disorder on the surface of society, there is no revolution at hand.

Gentlemen, permit me to say that I believe you are mistaken. True, there is no actual disorder; but it has entered deeply into men's minds. See what is preparing itself amongst the working classes, who, I grant, are at present quiet. No doubt they are not disturbed by political passions, properly so-called, to the same extent that they have been; but can you not see that their passions, instead of political, have become social? Do you not see that they are gradually forming opinions and ideas which are destined not only to upset this or that law, ministry, or even form of government, but society itself, until it totters upon the foundations on which it rests to-day? Do you not listen to what they say to themselves each day? Do you not hear them repeating unceasingly that all that is above them is incapable and unworthy of governing them; that the distribution of goods prevalent until now throughout the world is unjust; that property rests on a foundation which is not an equitable one? And do you not realize that when such opinions take root, when they spread in an almost universal manner, when they sink deeply into the masses, they are bound to bring with them sooner or later, I know not when or how, a most formidable revolution?

This, gentlemen, is my profound conviction: I believe that we are at this moment sleeping on a volcano. I am profoundly convinced of it . . .

. . . I was saying just now that this evil would sooner or later, I know not how or whence it will come, bring with it a most serious revolution: be assured that that is so.

When I come to investigate what, at different times, in different periods, among different peoples, has been the effective cause that has brought about the downfall of the governing classes, I perceive this or that event, man, or accidental or superficial cause; but, believe me, the real reason, the effective reason which causes men to lose political power is, that they have become unworthy to retain it.

Think, gentlemen, of the old Monarchy: it was stronger than you are, stronger in its origin; it was able to lean more than you do upon ancient customs, ancient habits, ancient beliefs; it was stronger than you are, and yet it has fallen to dust. And why did it fall? Do you think it was by particular mischance? Do you think it was by the act of some man, by the deficit, the oath in the Tennis Court, La Fayette, Mirabeau? No, gentlemen; there was another reason: the class that was then the governing class had become, through its indifference, its selfishness and its vices, incapable and unworthy of governing the country.

That was the true reason.

Well, gentlemen, if it is right to have this patriotic prejudice at all times, how much more is it not right to have it in our own? Do you not feel, by some intuitive instinct which is not capable of analysis, but which is undeniable, that the earth is quaking once again in Europe? Do you not feel—what shall I say?—as it were a gale of revolution in the air? This gale, no one knows whence it springs, whence it blows, nor, believe me, whom it will carry with it; and it is in such times as these that you remain calm before the degradation of public morality—for the expression is not too strong. . . .

THE BANQUETS—SENSE OF SECURITY ENTERTAINED BY THE GOVERNMENT —ANXIETY OF THE LEADERS OF THE OPPOSITION—ARRAIGNMENT OF MINISTERS

I refused to take part in the affair of the banquets. I had both serious and petty reasons for abstaining. What I call petty reasons I am quite willing to describe as bad reasons, although they were consistent with honour, and would have been unexceptionable in a private matter. They were the irritation and disgust aroused in me by the character and the tactics of the leaders of this enterprise. Nevertheless, I confess that the private prejudice which we entertain with regard to individuals is a bad guide in politics. . . .

It will be remembered that, at the opening of the session of 1848, King Louis-Philippe, in his speech from the Throne, had described the authors of the banquets as men excited by blind or hostile passions. This was bringing Royalty into direct conflict with more than one hundred members of the Chamber. This insult, which added anger to all the ambitious passions which were already disturbing the hearts of the majority of these men, ended by making them lose their reason. A violent debate was expected, but did not take place at once. The earlier discussions on the Address were calm: the majority and the Opposition both restrained themselves at the beginning, like two men who feel that they have lost their tempers, and who fear lest while in their condition, they should perpetrate some folly in word or deed.

But the storm of passion broke out at last, and continued with unaccustomed violence. The extraordinary heat of these debates was already redolent of civil war for those who knew how to scent revolutions from afar. . . .

The debates on the Address were closed, if I remember rightly, on the 12th of February, and it is really from this moment that the revolutionary movement burst out. The Constitutional Opposition, which had for many months been constantly pushed on by the Radical party, was from this time forward led and directed not so much by the members of that party who occupied seats in the Chamber of Deputies (the greater number of these had become luke-warm and, as it were, enervated in the Parliamentary atmosphere), as by the younger, bolder, and more irresponsible men who wrote for the dema-gogic press. This change was especially apparent in two principal facts which had an overwhelming influence upon events—the program of the banquet and the arraignment of Ministers.

On the 20th of February, there appeared in almost all the Opposition news-papers, by way of program of the approaching banquet, what was really a proclamation, convoking the schools and inviting the National Guard itself to attend the ceremony as a body. It read like a decree emanating from the Provisional Government which was to be set up three days later. The Cabinet, which had already been blamed by many of its followers for tacitly authorising the banquet, considered that it was justified in retracing its steps. It officially announced that it forbade the banquet, and that it would prevent it by force.

It was this declaration of the Government which provided the field for the battle. I am in a position to state, although it sounds hardly credible, that the program which thus suddenly turned the banquet into an insurrection was resolved upon, drawn up and published without the participation or the knowledge of the members of Parliament who considered themselves to be still leading the movement which they had called into existence. The program was the hurried work of a nocturnal gathering of journalists and Radicals, and the leaders of the Dynastic Opposition heard of it at the same time as the public, by reading it in the papers in the morning.

And see by what counter-strokes human affairs are pushed on! M. Odilon Barrot, who disapproved of the program as much as anyone, dared not dis-claim it for fear of offending the men, who, till then, had seemed to be moving with him; and then, when the Government, alarmed by the publication of this document, prohibited the banquet, M. Barrot, finding himself brought face to face with civil war, drew back. He himself gave up this dangerous demon-stration; but at the same time that he was making this concession to the men of moderation, he granted to the extremists the impeachment of Ministers. He accused the latter of violating the Constitution by prohibiting the banquet, and thus furnished an excuse to those who were about to take up arms in the name of the violated Constitution.

Thus the principal leaders of the Radical Party, who thought that a revolu-tion would be premature, and who did not yet desire it, had considered them-selves obliged, in order to differentiate themselves from their allies in the Dynastic Opposition, to make very revolutionary speeches and fan the flame of insurrectionary passion. On the other hand, the Dynastic Opposition, which had had enough of the banquets, had been forced to persevere in this bad course so as not to present an appearance of retreating before the defiance of the Government. And finally the mass of the Conservatives, who believed in the necessity of great concessions and were ready to make them, were driven by the violence of their adversaries and the passions of some of their chiefs to deny even the right of meeting in private banquets and to refuse the country any hopes of reform.

One must have lived long amid political parties, and in the very whirlwind in which they move, to understand to what extent men mutually push each other away from their respective plans, and how the destinies of this world proceed as the result, but often as the contrary result, of the intentions that produce them, similarly to the kite which flies by the antagonistic action of the wind and the cord.

MY EXPLANATION OF THE 24TH OF FEBRUARY, AND MY THOUGHTS AS TO ITS EFFECTS UPON THE FUTURE

. . . The Revolution of February, in common with all other great events of this class, sprang from general causes, impregnated, if I am permitted the expression, by accidents; and it would be as superficial a judgment to ascribe it necessarily to the former or exclusively to the latter.

The industrial revolution which, during the past thirty years, had turned Paris into the principal manufacturing city of France and attracted within its walls an entire new population of workmen (to whom the works of the fortifications had added another population of labourers at present deprived of work), together with the excess in material pleasures fostered by the government itself, tended more and more to inflame this multitude. Add to this the democratic disease of envy, which was silently permeating it; the economical and political theories which were beginning to make their way and which strove to prove that human misery was the work of laws and not of Providence, and that poverty could be suppressed by changing the conditions of society; the contempt into which the governing class, and especially the men who led it, had fallen, a contempt so general and so profound that it paralyzed the resistance even of those who were most interested in maintaining the power that was being overthrown; the centralization which reduced the whole revolutionary movement to the overmastering of Paris and the seizing of the machinery of government; and lastly, the mobility of all this, institutions, ideas, men and customs, in a fluctuating state of society which had, in less than sixty years, undergone the shock of seven great revolutions, without numbering a multitude of smaller, secondary upheavals. These were the general causes without which the Revolution of February would have been impossible. The principal accidents which led to it were the passions of the dynastic Opposition, which brought about a riot in proposing a reform; the suppression of this riot, first over-violent and then abandoned; the sudden disappearance of the old Ministry, unexpectedly snapping the threads of power, which the new ministers, in their confusion, were unable either to seize upon or to reunite; the mistakes and disorder of mind of these ministers, so powerless to re-establish that which they had been strong enough to overthrow; the vacillation of the generals; the absence of the only princes who possessed either personal energy or popularity; and above all, the senile imbecility of King Louis-Philippe, his weakness, which no one could have foreseen, and which still remains almost incredible, after the event has proved it.

I have sometimes asked myself what could have produced this sudden and unprecedented depression in the King's mind. Louis-Philippe had spent his life in the midst of revolutions, and certainly lacked neither experience, courage, nor readiness of mind, although these qualities all failed him so completely on that day. In my opinion, his weakness was due to his excessive surprise; he was overwhelmed with consternation before he had grasped the meaning of things. The Revolution of February was *unforeseen* by all, but by him more than any other; he had been prepared for it by no warning from the outside, for since many years his mind had withdrawn into that sort of haughty solitude into which in the end the intellect almost always settles down of princes who have long lived happily, and who, mistaking luck for genius, refuse to listen to anything, because they think that there is nothing left for them to learn from anybody. Besides, Louis-Philippe had been deceived, as I have already said that his ministers were, by the misleading light cast by antecedent facts upon present times. One might draw a strange picture of all the errors which have thus been begotten, one by the other, without resembling each other. We see Charles I driven to tyranny and violence at the sight of the progress which the spirit of opposition had made in England during the gentle reign of his father; Louis XVI determined to suffer everything because Charles I had perished by refusing to endure anything; Charles X provoking the Revolution, because he had with his own eyes beheld the weakness of Louis XVI; and lastly, Louis-Philippe, who had more perspicacity than any of them, imagining that, in order to remain on the Throne, all he had to do was to observe the letter of the law while violating its spirit, and that, provided he himself kept within the bounds of the Charter, the nation would never exceed them. To warp the spirit of the Constitution without changing the letter; to set the vices of the country in opposition to each other; gently to drown revolutionary passion in the love of material enjoyment: such was the idea of his whole life. Little by little, it had become, not his leading, but his sole idea. He had wrapped himself in it, he had lived in it; and when he suddenly saw that it was a false idea, he became like a man who is awakened in the night by an earthquake, and who, feeling his house crumbling in the darkness, and the very ground seeming to yawn beneath his feet, remains distracted amid this unforeseen and universal ruin.

I am arguing very much at my ease to-day concerning the causes that brought about the events of the 24th of February; but on the afternoon of that day I had many other things in my head: I was thinking of the events themselves, and sought less for what had produced them than for what was to follow.

I returned slowly home. I explained in a few words to Madame de Tocqueville what I had seen, and sat down in a corner to think. I cannot remember ever feeling my soul so full of sadness. It was the second revolution I had seen accomplish itself, before my eyes, within seventeen years!

On the 30th of July, 1830, at daybreak, I had met the carriages of King Charles X on the outer boulevards of Versailles, with damaged escutcheons, proceeding at a foot pace, in Indian file, like a funeral, and I was unable to restrain my tears at the sight. This time my impressions were of another kind, but even keener. Both revolutions had afflicted me; but how much more bitter were the impressions caused by the last! I had until the end felt a remnant of hereditary affection for Charles X; but that King fell for having violated rights that were dear to me, and I had every hope that my country's freedom would be revived rather than extinguished by his fall. But now this freedom seemed dead; the Princes who were fleeing were nothing to me, but I felt that the cause I had at heart was lost.

I had spent the best days of my youth amid a society which seemed to increase in greatness and prosperity as it increased in liberty; I had conceived the idea of a balanced, regulated liberty, held in check by religion, custom and law; the attractions of this liberty had touched me; it had become the passion of my life; I felt that I could never be consoled for its loss, and that I must renounce all hope of its recovery.

I had gained too much experience of men to be able to content myself with empty words; I knew that, if one great revolution is able to establish liberty in a country, a number of succeeding revolutions make all regular liberty impossible for very many years.

I could not yet know what would issue from this last revolution, but I was already convinced that it could give birth to nothing that would satisfy me; and I foresaw that, whatever might be the lot reserved for our posterity, our own fate was to drag on our lives miserably amid alternate reactions of licence and oppression.

I began to pass in review the history of our last sixty years, and I smiled bitterly when I thought of the illusions formed at the conclusion of each period in this long revolution; the theories on which these illusions had been fed; the sapient dreams of our historians, and all the ingenious and deceptive systems by the aid of which it had been endeavoured to explain a present which was still incorrectly seen, and a future which was not seen at all.

The Constitutional Monarchy had succeeded the Ancien Régime; the Republic, the Monarchy; the Empire, the Republic; the Restoration, the Empire; and then came the Monarchy of July. After each of these successive changes it was said that the French Revolution, having accomplished what was presumptuously called its work, was finished; this had been said and it had been believed. Alas! I myself had hoped it under the Restoration, and again after the fall of the Government of the Restoration; and here is the French Revolution beginning over again, for it is still the same one. As we go on, its end seems farther off and shrouded in greater darkness. Shall we ever—as we are assured by other prophets, perhaps as delusive as their predecessors—shall we ever attain a more complete and more far-reaching social transformation than our fathers foresaw and desired, and than we ourselves are able to foresee; or are we not destined simply to end in a condition of intermittent anarchy, the well-known chronic and incurable complaint of old peoples? As for me, I am unable to say; I do not know when this long voyage will be ended; I am weary of seeing the shore in each successive mirage, and I often ask myself whether the *terra firma* we are seeking does really exist, and whether we are not doomed to rove upon the seas for ever! . .

PARIS ON THE MORROW OF THE 24TH OF FEBRUARY AND THE NEXT DAYS —THE SOCIALISTIC CHARACTER OF THE NEW REVOLUTION

. . . For a year past the dynastic Opposition and the republican Opposition had been living in fallacious intimacy, acting in the same way from different motives. The misunderstanding which had facilitated the revolution tended to mitigate its after effects. Now that the Monarchy had disappeared, the battle-field seemed empty; the people no longer clearly saw what enemies remained for them to pursue and strike down; the former objects of their anger, themselves, were no longer there; the clergy had never been completely reconciled to the new dynasty, and witnessed its ruin without regret; the old nobility were delighted at it, whatever the ultimate consequences might be: the first had suffered through the system of intolerance of the middle classes, the second through their pride: both either despised or feared their government.

For the first time in sixty years, the priests, the old aristocracy and the people met in a common sentiment—a feeling of revenge, it is true, and not of affection; but even that is a great thing in politics, where a community of hatred is almost always the foundation of friendships. The real, the only vanquished were the middle class; but even this had little to fear. Its reign had been exclusive rather than oppressive; corrupt, but not violent; it was despised rather than hated. Moreover, the middle class never forms a compact body in the heart of the nation, a part very distinct from the whole; it always participates a little with all the others, and in some places merges into them. This absence of homogeneity and of exact limits makes the government of the middle class weak and uncertain, but it also makes it intangible, and, as it were, invisible to those who desire to strike it when it is no longer governing.

From all these united causes proceeded that languor of the people which had struck me as much as its omnipotence, a languor which was the more discernible, in that it contrasted strangely with the turgid energy of the language used and the terrible recollections which it evoked. The truth is that never was a greater change in the government, and even in the very condition of a nation, brought about by citizens who were themselves so little moved. The *History of the Revolution* by M. Thiers, *The Girondins* by M. Lamartine, as well as other works, particularly plays, which are less well known, had rehabilitated the period of the Terror and brought it to some extent into fashion. The lukewarm passions of the time were made to speak in the bombastic periods of '93, and one heard cited at every moment the name and example of the illustrious ruffians whom no one possessed either the energy or even a sincere desire to resemble.

It was the Socialistic theories which I have already described as the philosophy of the Revolution of February that later kindled genuine passion, embittered jealousy, and ended by stirring up war between the classes. If the actions at the commencement were less disorderly than might have been feared, on the very morrow of the Revolution there was displayed an extraordinary agitation, an unequalled disorder, in the ideas of the people.

From the 25th of February onwards, a thousand strange systems came issuing pell-mell from the minds of innovators, and spread among the troubled minds of the crowd. Everything still remained standing except Royalty and Parliament; yet it seemed as though the shock of the Revolution had reduced society itself to dust, and as though a competition had been opened for the new form that was to be given to the edifice about to be erected in its place. Everyone came forward with a plan of his own: this one printed it in the papers, that other on the placards with which the walls were soon covered, a third proclaimed his loud-mouthed in the open air. One aimed at destroying inequality of fortune, another inequality of education, a third undertook to do away with the oldest of all inequalities, that between man and woman. Specifics were offered against poverty, and remedies for the disease of work which has tortured humanity since the first days of its existence.

These theories were of very varied natures, often opposed and sometimes hostile to one another; but all of them, aiming lower than the government and striving to reach society itself, on which government rests, adopted the common name of Socialism.

Socialism will always remain the essential characteristic and the most redoubtable remembrance of the Revolution of February. The Republic will only appear to the on-looker to have come upon the scene as a means, not as an end.

It does not come within the scope of these Recollections that I should seek for the causes which gave a socialistic character to the Revolution of February, and I will content myself with saying that the discovery of this new facet of the French Revolution was not of a nature to cause so great surprise as it did. Had it not been long perceived that the people had continually been improving and raising its condition, that its importance, its education, its desires, its power had been constantly increasing? Its prosperity had also grown greater, but less rapidly, and was approaching the limit which it hardly ever passes in old societies, where there are many men and but few places. How should the poor and humbler and yet powerful classes not have dreamt of issuing from their poverty and inferiority by means of their power, especially in an epoch when our view into another world has become dimmer, and the miseries of this world become more visible and seem more intolerable? They had been working to this end for the last sixty years. The people had first endeavoured to help itself by changing every political institution, but after each change it found that its lot was in no way improved, or was only improving with a slowness quite incompatible with the eagerness of its desire. Inevitably, it must sooner or later discover that that which held it fixed in its position was not the constitution of the government but the unalterable laws that constitute society itself; and it was natural that it should be brought to ask itself if it had not both the power and the right to alter those laws, as it had altered all the rest. And to speak more specially of property, which is, as it were, the foundation of our social order—all the privileges which covered it and which, so to speak, concealed the privilege of property having been destroyed, and the latter remaining the principal obstacle to equality among men, and appearing to be the only sign of inequality—was it not necessary, I will not say that it should be abolished in its turn, but at least that the thought of abolishing it should occur to the minds of those who did not enjoy it?

This natural restlessness in the minds of the people, this inevitable perturbation of its thoughts and its desires, these needs, these instincts of the crowd formed in a certain sense the fabric upon which the political innovators embroidered so many monstrous and grotesque figures. Their work may be regarded as ludicrous, but the material on which they worked is the most serious that it is possible for philosophers and statesmen to contemplate.

Will Socialism remain buried in the disdain with which the Socialists of 1848 are so justly covered? I put the question without making any reply. I do not doubt that the laws concerning the constitution of our modern society will in the long run undergo modification; they have already done so in many of their principal parts. But will they ever be destroyed and replaced by others? It seems to me to be impracticable. I say no more, because—the more I study the former condition of the world and see the world of our own day in greater detail, the more I consider the prodigious variety to be met with not only in laws, but in the principles of law, and the different forms even now taken and retained, whatever one may say, by the rights of property on this earth—the more I am tempted to believe that what we call necessary institutions are often no more than institutions to which we have grown accustomed, and that in matters of social constitution the field of possibilities is much more extensive than men living in their various societies are ready to imagine.

THE FIRST SITTING OF THE CONSTITUENT ASSEMBLY—THE APPEARANCE OF THIS ASSEMBLY

. . . There have certainly been more wicked revolutionaries than those of 1848, but I doubt if there were ever any more stupid; they neither knew how to make use of universal suffrage nor how to do without it. If they had held the elections immediately after the 24th of February, while the upper classes were still bewildered by the blow they had just received, and the people more amazed than discontented, they would perhaps have obtained an Assembly after their hearts; if, on the other hand, they had boldly seized the dictatorship, they might have been able for some time to retain it. But they trusted themselves to the nation, and at the same time did all that was most likely to set the latter against them; they threatened it while placing themselves in its power; they alarmed it by the recklessness of their proposals and the violence of their language, while inviting it to resistance by the feebleness of their actions; they pretended to lay down the law to it at the very time that they were placing themselves at its disposal. Instead of opening out their ranks after the victory, they jealously closed them up, and seemed, in one word, to be striving to solve this insoluble problem, namely, how to govern through the majority and yet against its inclination.

Following the examples of the past without understanding them, they foolishly imagined that to summon the crowd to take part in political life was sufficient to attach it to their cause; and that to popularise the Republic, it was enough to give the public rights without offering them any profits. They forgot that their predecessors, when they gave every peasant the vote, at the same time did away with tithes, abolished statute labour and the other seignorial privileges, and divided the property of the nobles among the peasants; whereas they were not in a position to do anything of the kind. In establishing universal suffrage they thought they were summoning the people to the assistance of the Revolution: they were only giving them arms against it. Nevertheless, I am far from believing that it was impossible to arouse revolutionary passions, even in the country districts. In France, every agriculturist owns some portion of the soil, and most of them are more or less involved in debt; it was not, therefore, the landlords that should have been attacked, but the creditors; not the abolition promised of the rights of property, but the abolition of debts. The demagogues of 1848 did not think of this scheme; they showed themselves much clumsier than their predecessors, but no less dishonest, for they were as violent and unjust in their desires as the others in their acts. Only, to commit violent and unjust acts, it is not enough for a government to have the will, or even the power; the habits, ideas, and passions of the time must lend themselves to the committal of them.

As the party which held the reins of government saw its candidates rejected one after the other, it displayed great vexation and rage, complaining now sadly and now rudely of the electors, whom it treated as ignorant, ungrateful blockheads, and enemies of their own good; it lost its temper with the whole nation; and, its impatience exhausted by the latter's coldness, it seemed ready to say with Molière's Arnolfe, when he addresses Agnès: *"Pourquoi ne m'aimer pas, madame l'impudente?"* [1]

One thing was not ridiculous, but really ominous and terrible; and that was the appearance of Paris on my return. I found in the capital a hundred thousand armed workmen formed into regiments, out of work, dying of hunger, but with their minds crammed with vain theories and visionary hopes. I saw society cut into two; those who possessed nothing, united in a common greed; those who possessed something, united in a common terror. There were no bonds, no sympathy between these two great sections; everywhere the idea of an inevitable and immediate struggle seemed at hand. Already the *bourgeois* and the *peuple* (for the old nicknames had been resumed) had come to blows, with varying fortunes, at Rouen, Limoges, Paris; not a day passed but the owners of property were attacked or menaced in either their capital or income: they were asked to employ labour without selling the produce; they were expected to remit the rents of their tenants when they themselves possessed no other means of living. They gave way as long as they could to this tyranny, and endeavoured at least to turn their weakness to account by publishing it. I remember reading in the papers of that time this advertisement, among others, which still strikes me as a model of vanity, poltroonery, and stupidity harmoniously mingled:

[1] [*"Why not love me, impudent lady?"*]

"Mr. Editor," it read, "I make use of your paper to inform my tenants that, desiring to put into practice in my relations with them the principles of fraternity that should guide all true democrats, I will hand to those of my tenants who apply for it a formal receipt for their next quarter's rent."

Meanwhile, a gloomy despair had overspread this bourgeoisie thus threatened and oppressed, and imperceptibly this despair was changing into courage. I had always believed that it was useless to hope to settle the movement of the Revolution of February peacefully and gradually, and that it could only be stopped suddenly, by a great battle fought in the streets of Paris. I had said this immediately after the 24th of February; and what I now saw persuaded me that this battle was not only inevitable but imminent, and that it would be well to seize the first opportunity to deliver it. . . .

The Revolution of 1792, when striking the upper classes, had cured them of their irreligiousness; it had taught them, if not the truth, at least the social usefulness of belief. This lesson was lost upon the middle class, which remained their political heir and their jealous rival; and the latter had even become more sceptical in proportion as the former seemed to become more religious. The Revolution of 1848 had just done on a small scale for our tradesmen what that of 1792 had done for the nobility: the same reverses, the same terrors, the same conversion; it was the same picture, only painted smaller and in less bright and, no doubt, less lasting colours. The clergy had facilitated this conversion by separating itself from all the old political parties, and entering into the old, true spirit of the Catholic clergy, which is that it should belong only to the Church. It readily, therefore, professed republican opinions, while at the same time it gave to long established interests the guarantee of its traditions, its custom and its hierarchy. It was accepted and made much of by all. The priests sent to the Assembly were treated with very great consideration, and they deserved it, through their good sense, their moderation and their modesty. Some of them endeavoured to speak from the tribune, but they were never able to learn the language of politics. They had forgotten it too long ago, and all their speeches turned imperceptibly into homilies.

For the rest, the universal franchise had shaken the country from top to bottom without bringing to light a single new man worthy of coming to the front. I have always held that, whatever method be followed in a general election, the great majority of the exceptional men whom the nation possesses definitively succeed in getting elected. The system of election adopted exercises a great influence only upon the class of ordinary individuals in the Assembly, who form the ground-work of every political body. These belong to very different orders and are of very diverse natures, according to the system upon which the election has been conducted. Nothing confirmed me in this belief more than did the sight of the Constituent Assembly. Almost all the men who played the first part in it were already known to me, but the bulk of the rest resembled nothing that I had seen before. They were imbued with a new spirit, and displayed a new character and new manners.

I will say that, in my opinion, and taken all round, this Assembly compared favourably with those which I had seen. One met in it more men who were sincere, disinterested, honest and, above all, courageous than in the Chambers of Deputies among which I had lived. . . .

MY RELATIONS WITH LAMARTINE—HIS SUBTERFUGES

Lamartine was now at the climax of his fame: to all those whom the Revolution had injured or alarmed, that is to say, to the great majority of the nation, he appeared in the light of a saviour. He had been elected to the Assembly by the city of Paris and no fewer than eleven departments; I do not believe that ever anybody inspired such keen enthusiasm as that to which he was then giving rise; one must have seen love thus stimulated by fear to know with what excess of idolatry men are capable of loving. The transcendental favour which was shown him at this time was not to be compared with anything except, perhaps, the excessive injustice which he shortly afterwards received. All the deputies who came to Paris with the desire to put down the excesses of the Revolution and to combat the demagogic party regarded him beforehand as their only possible leader, and looked to him unhesitatingly to place himself at their head to attack and overthrow the Socialists and demagogues. They soon discovered that they were deceived, and that Lamartine did not see the part he was called upon to play in so simple a light. It must be confessed that his was a very complex and difficult position. It was forgotten at the time, but he could not himself forget, that he had contributed more than any other to the success of the Revolution of February. Terror effaced this remembrance for the moment from the public mind; but a general feeling of security could not fail soon to restore it. It was easy to foresee that, so soon as the current which had brought affairs to their present pitch was arrested, a contrary current would set in, which would impel the nation in the opposite direction, and drive it faster and further than Lamartine could or would go. The success of the Montagnards would involve his immediate ruin; but their complete defeat would render him useless and must, sooner or later, remove the government from his hands. He saw, therefore, that for him there was almost as much danger and loss in triumph as in defeat.

As a matter of fact, I believe that, if Lamartine had resolutely, from the first, placed himself at the head of the immense party which desired to moderate and regulate the course of the Revolution, and had succeeded in leading it to victory, he would before long have been buried beneath his own triumph; he would not have been able to stop his army in time, and it would have left him behind and chosen other leaders.

I doubt whether, whatever line of conduct he had adopted, he could have retained his power for long. I believe his only remaining chance was to be gloriously defeated while saving his country. But Lamartine was the last man to sacrifice himself in this way. I do not know that I have ever, in this world of selfishness and ambition in which I lived, met a mind so void of any thought of the public welfare as his. I have seen a crowd of men disturbing the country in order to raise themselves: that is an everyday perversity; but he is the only one who seemed to me always ready to turn the world upside down in order to divert himself. Neither have I ever known a mind less sincere, nor one that had a more thorough contempt for the truth. When I say he despised it, I am wrong: he did not honour it enough to heed it in any way whatever. When speaking or writing, he spoke the truth or lied, without caring which he did, occupied only with the effect he wished to produce at the moment. . . .

THE COMMITTEE FOR THE CONSTITUTION

I now change my subject, and am glad to leave the scenes of the civil war and to return to the recollections of my parliamentary life. I wish to speak of what happened in the Committee for the Constitution, of which I was a member. . .

All were unanimous in the opinion that the Executive Power should be entrusted to one man alone. But what prerogatives and what agents should he be given, what responsibilities laid upon him? Clearly, none of these questions could be treated in an arbitrary fashion: each of them was necessarily in connection with all the others, and could, above all, be only decided by taking into special account the habits and customs of the country. These were old problems, no doubt; but they were made young again by the novelty of the circumstances.

. . . I first proposed to limit in various directions the sphere of the Executive Power; but I soon saw that it was useless to attempt anything serious on that side. I then fell back upon the method of election itself, and raised a discussion on that portion of Cormenin's clause which treated of it. The clause, as I said above, laid down that the President should be elected directly, by a relative majority, the minimum of this majority being fixed at two million votes. This method had several very serious drawbacks.

Since the President was to be elected directly by the citizens, the enthusiasm and infatuation of the people was very much to be feared; and moreover, the prestige and moral power which the newly elected would possess would be much greater. Since a relative majority was to be sufficient to make the election valid, it might be possible that the President should only represent the wishes of a minority of the nation. I asked that the President might not be elected directly by the citizens, but that this should be entrusted to delegates whom the people would elect.

In the second place, I proposed to substitute an actual for a relative majority; if an absolute majority was not obtained at the first vote, it would fall to the Assembly to make a choice. These ideas were, I think, sound, but they were not new; I had borrowed them from the American Constitution. I doubt whether anyone would have suspected this, had I not said so; so little was the Committee prepared to play its great part.

The first part of my amendment was rejected. I expected this: our great men were of opinion that this system was not sufficiently simple, and they considered it tainted with a touch of aristocracy. The second was accepted, and is part of the actual Constitution.

Beaumont proposed that the President should not be re-eligible; I supported him vigorously, and the proposal was carried. On this occasion we both fell into a great mistake which will, I fear, lead to very sad results. We had always been greatly struck with the dangers threatening liberty and public morality at the hands of a re-eligible president, who in order to secure his re-election would infallibly employ beforehand the immense resources of constraint and corruption which our laws and customs allow to the head of the Executive Power. Our minds were not supple or prompt enough to turn in time or to see that, so soon as it was decided that the citizens themselves should directly choose the President, the evil was irreparable, and that it would be only increasing it rashly to undertake to hinder the people in their choice. This vote, and the great influence I brought to bear upon it, is my most unpleasant memory of that period. . . .

ASPECT OF THE CABINET—ITS FIRST ACTS UNTIL AFTER THE INSURREC-
TIONARY ATTEMPTS OF THE 13TH OF JUNE

. . . I did not believe then, any more than I do now, that the republican form of government is the best suited to the needs of France. What I mean when I say the republican form of government, is the Executive Power. With a people among whom habit, tradition, custom have assured so great a place to the Executive Power, its instability will always be, in periods of excitement, a cause of revolution, and, in peaceful times, a cause of great uneasiness. Moreover, I have always considered the Republic an ill-balanced form of government, which always promised more, but gave less, liberty than the Constitutional Monarchy. And yet I sincerely wished to maintain the Republic; and although there were, so to speak, no Republicans in France, I did not look upon the maintenance of it as absolutely impossible.

I wished to maintain it because I saw nothing ready or fit to set in its place. The old Dynasty was profoundly antipathetic to the majority of the country. Amid this flagging of all political passion, which was the result of the fatigue of the revolutions and their vain promises, one genuine passion remained alive in France: hatred of the Ancien Régime and mistrust of the old privileged classes who represented it in the eyes of the people. This sentiment passes through revolutions without dissolving in them, like the water of those marvellous fountains which, according to the ancients, passed across the waves of the sea without mixing with or disappearing in them. As to the Orleans Dynasty, the experience the people had had of it did not particularly incline them to return to it so soon. It was bound once more to throw into Opposition all the upper classes and the clergy, and to separate itself from the people, as it had done before, leaving the cares and profits of government to those same middle classes whom I had already seen during eighteen years so inadequate for the good government of France. Moreover, nothing was ready for its triumph.

Louis Napoleon alone was ready to take the place of the Republic, because he already held the power in his hands. But what could come of his success, except a bastard Monarchy, despised by the enlightened classes, hostile to liberty, governed by intriguers, adventurers and valets? Not one of these results would justify a new revolution. . . .

Louis Napoleon plays so great a part in the rest of my narrative that he seems to me to deserve a special portrait amid the host of contemporaries of whom I have been content to sketch the features. Of all his ministers, and perhaps of all the men who refused to take part in his conspiracy against the Republic, I was the one who was most advanced in his good graces, who saw him closest, and who was best able to judge him.

He was vastly superior to what his preceding career and his mad enterprises might very properly have led one to believe of him. This was my first impression on conversing with him. In this respect he deceived his adversaries, and perhaps still more his friends, if this term can be applied to the politicians who patronised his candidature. The greater part of these, in fact, elected him, not because of his merits, but because of his presumed mediocrity. They expected to find him an instrument which they could handle as they pleased, and which it would always be lawful for them to break when they wished to. In this they were greatly deceived.

As a private individual, Louis Napoleon possessed certain attractive qualities: an easy and kindly humour, a mind which was gentle, and even tender, without being delicate, great confidence in his intercourse, perfect simplicity, a certain personal modesty amidst the immense pride derived from his origin. He was capable of showing affection, and able to inspire it in those who approached him. His conversation was brief and unsuggestive. He had not the art of drawing others out or of establishing intimate relations with them; nor any facility in expressing his views. He had the writer's habit, and a certain amount of the author's self-love. His dissimulation, which was the deep dissimulation of a man who has spent his life in plots, was assisted in a remarkable way by the immobility of his features and his want of expression: for his eyes were dull and opaque, like the thick glass used to light the cabins of ships, which admits the light but cannot be seen through. Careless of danger, he possessed a fine, cool courage in days of crisis; and at the same time—a common thing enough—he was very vacillating in his plans. He was often seen to change his direction, to advance, hesitate, draw back, to his great detriment: for the nation had chosen him in order to dare all things, and what it expected from him was audacity and not prudence. It was said that he had always been greatly addicted to pleasures, and not very delicate in his choice of them. This passion for vulgar enjoyment and this taste for luxury had increased still more with the facilities offered by his position. Each day he wore out his energy in indulgence, and deadened and degraded even his ambition. His intelligence was incoherent, confused, filled with great but ill-assorted thoughts, which he borrowed now from the examples of Napoleon, now from socialistic theories, sometimes from recollections of England, where he had lived: very different, and often very contrary, sources. These he had laboriously collected in his solitary meditations, far removed from the contact of men and facts, for he was naturally a dreamer and a visionary. But when he was forced to emerge from these vague, vast regions in order to confine his mind to the limits of a piece of business, it showed itself to be capable of justice, sometimes of subtlety and compass, and even of a certain depth, but never sure, and always prepared to place a grotesque idea by the side of a correct one.

Generally, it was difficult to come into long and very close contact with him without discovering a little vein of madness running through his better sense, the sight of which always recalled the escapades of his youth, and served to explain them.

It may be admitted, for that matter, that it was his madness rather than his reason which, thanks to circumstances, caused his success and his force: for the world is a strange theatre. There are moments in it when the worst plays are those which succeed best. If Louis Napoleon had been a wise man, or a man of genius, he would never have become President of the Republic.

He trusted in his star; he firmly believed himself to be the instrument of destiny and the necessary man. I have always believed that he was really convinced of his right, and I doubt whether Charles X was ever more infatuated with his legitimism than he with his. Moreover, he was quite as incapable of alleging a reason for his faith; for, although he had a sort of abstract adoration for the people, he had very little taste for liberty. The characteristic and fundamental feature of his mind in political matters was his hatred of and contempt for assemblies. The rule of the Constitutional Monarchy seemed to him even more insupportable than that of the Republic. His unlimited pride in the name he bore, which willingly bowed before the nations, revolted at the idea of yielding to the influence of a parliament.

Before attaining power he had had time to strengthen his natural taste for the footman class, which is always displayed by mediocre princes, by the habits of twenty years of conspiracy spent amid low-class adventurers, men of ruined fortunes or blemished reputations, and young debauchees, the only persons who, during all this time, could have consented to serve him as go-betweens or accomplices. He himself, in spite of his good manners, allowed a glimpse to pierce through of the adventurer and the prince of fortune. He continued to take pleasure in this inferior company after he was no longer obliged to live in it. I believe that his difficulty in expressing his thoughts otherwise than in writing attached him to people who had long been familiar with his current of thought and with his dreamings, and that his inferiority in conversation rendered him generally averse to contact with clever men. Moreover, he desired above all things to meet with devotion to his person and his cause, as though his person and his cause were such as to be able to arouse devotion: merit annoyed him when it displayed ever so little independence. He wanted believers in his star, and vulgar worshippers of his fortune. One could not approach him except through a group of special, intimate friends and servants, of whom General Changarnier told me that all could be described by these two words which go together: cheats and scoundrels. Nothing was more base than these intimates, except perhaps his family, which consisted, for the most part, of rogues and *femmes galantes*.

This was the man whom the need of a chief and the power of a memory had placed at the head of France, and with whom we would have to govern.

FOREIGN AFFAIRS

. . . It was especially in the conduct of foreign affairs that he [Louis Napoleon] showed how badly prepared he still was for the great part to which blind fortune had called him. I was not slow in perceiving that this man, whose pride aimed at leading everything, had not yet taken the smallest steps to inform himself of anything. I proposed to have an analysis drawn up every day of all the despatches and to submit it to his inspection. Before this, he knew what happened in the world only by hearsay, and only knew what the Minister for Foreign Affairs had thought fit to tell him. The solid basis of facts was always lacking to the operations of his mind, and this was easily seen in all the dreams with which the latter was filled.

I was sometimes frightened at perceiving how much there was in his plans that was vast, chimerical, unscrupulous, and confused; although it is true that, when explaining the real state of things to him, I easily made him recognize the difficulties which they presented, for discussion was not his strong point. He was silent, but never yielded.

One of his myths was an alliance with one of the two great powers of Germany, of which he proposed to make use to alter the map of Europe and erase the limits which the treaties of 1815 had traced for France. As he saw that I did not believe it possible to find either of these powers inclined for an alliance of this sort, and with such an object, he undertook himself to sound their ambassadors in Paris. One of them came to me one day in a state of great excitement to tell me that the President of the Republic had asked him if, in consideration of an equivalent, his Court would not consent to allow France to seize Savoy. On another occasion, he conceived the idea of sending a private agent, one of his own men, as he called them, to come to a direct understanding with the German Princes. He chose Persigny, and asked me to give him his credentials; and I consented, knowing well that nothing could come of a negotiation of this sort. I believe that Persigny had a two-fold mission: it was a question of facilitating the usurpation at home and an extension of territory abroad. He went first to Berlin and then to Vienna; as I expected, he was very well received, handsomely entertained, and politely bowed out.

But I have spoken enough of individuals; let us come to politics.

At the time when I took up office, Europe was, as it were, on fire, although the conflagration was already extinguished in certain countries.

Sicily was conquered and subdued; the Neapolitans had returned to their obedience and even to their servitude; the battle of Novara had been fought and lost; the victorious Austrians were negotiating with the son of Charles Albert, who had become King of Piedmont by his father's abdication; their armies, issuing from the confines of Lombardy, occupied Parma, a portion of the Papal States, Placentia, and Tuscany, which they had entered unasked, and in spite of the fact that the Grand Duke had been restored by his subjects, who have been but ill rewarded since for their zeal and fidelity.

But Venice still resisted, and Rome, after repelling our first attack, was calling all the demagogues of Italy to its assistance and exciting all Europe with its clamour. Never, perhaps, since February, had Germany seemed more divided or disturbed. Although the dream of German unity had been dispelled, the reality of the old Teutonic organization had not yet resumed its place. Reduced to a small number of members, the National Assembly, which had till then endeavoured to promote this unity, fled from Frankfort and hawked round the spectacle of its impotence and its ridiculous fury. But its fall did not restore order; on the contrary, it left a freer field for anarchy.

The moderate, one may say the innocent, revolutionaries, who had cherished the belief that they would be able, peacefully, and by means of arguments and decrees, to persuade the peoples and princes of Germany to submit to a single government, made way for the violent revolutionaries, who had always maintained that Germany could only be brought to a state of unity by the complete ruin of its old systems of government, and the entire abolition of the existing social order. Riots therefore followed in every land upon parliamentary discussion. Political rivalries turned into a war of classes; the natural hatred and jealousy entertained by the poor for the rich developed into socialistic theories in many quarters, but especially in the small states of Central Germany and in the great Rhine Valley. Wurtemberg was in a state of agitation; Saxony had just experienced a terrible insurrection, which had only been crushed with the assistance of Prussia; insurrections had also occurred in Westphalia; the Palatinate was in open revolt; and Baden had expelled its Grand Duke, and appointed a Provisional Government. And yet the final victory of the Princes, which I had foreseen when travelling through Germany, a month before, was no longer in doubt; the very violence of the insurrections hastened it. The larger monarchies had recaptured their capitals and their armies. Their heads had still difficulties to conquer, but no more dangers; and themselves masters, or on the point of becoming so, at home, they could not fail soon to triumph in the second-rate States. By thus violently disturbing public order, the insurgents gave them the wish, the opportunity and the right to intervene.

Prussia had already commenced to do so. The Prussians had just suppressed the Saxon insurrection by force of arms; they now entered the Rhine Palatinate, offered their intervention to Wurtemberg, and prepared to invade the Grand-Duchy of Baden, thus occupying almost the whole of Germany with their soldiers or their influence.

Austria had emerged from the terrible crisis which had threatened its existence, but it was still in great travail. Its armies, after conquering in Italy, were being defeated in Hungary.

Despairing of mastering its subjects unaided, it had called Russia to its assistance and the Tsar, in a manifesto dated 13 May, had announced to Europe that he was marching against the Hungarians. The Emperor Nicholas had till then remained at rest amid his uncontested might. He had viewed the agitation of the nations from afar in safety, but not with indifference. Thenceforward, he alone among the great powers of Europe represented the old state of society and the old traditional principle of authority. He was not only its representative: he considered himself its champion. His political theories, his religious belief, his ambition and his conscience, all urged him to adopt this part. He had, therefore, made for himself out of the cause of authority throughout the world a second empire yet vaster than the first. He encouraged with his letters and rewarded with his honours all those who, in whatever corner of Europe, gained victories over anarchy and even over liberty, as though they were his subjects and had contributed to strengthening his own power. He had thus sent, to the extreme South of Europe, one of his orders to Filangieri, the conqueror of the Sicilians, and had written that general an autograph letter to show to him that he was satisfied with his conduct. From the lofty position which he occupied, and whence he peacefully watched the various incidents of the struggle which shook Europe, the Emperor judged freely, and followed with a certain tranquil disdain, not only the follies of the revolutionaries whom he pursued, but also the vices and the faults of the parties and princes whom he assisted. . . .

In the midst of this Europe which I have depicted, the position of France was one of weakness and embarrassment. Nowhere had the Revolution succeeded in establishing a regular and stable system of liberty. On every side, the old powers were rising up again from amid the ruins which it had made —not, it is true, the same as when they fell, but very similar. We could not assist the latter in establishing themselves nor ensure their victory, for the system which they were setting up was antipathetic, I will say not only to the institutions created by the Revolution of February, but, at the root of our ideas, to all that was most permanent and unconquerable in our new habits. They, on their side, distrusted us, and rightly. The great part of restorers of the general order in Europe was therefore forbidden us. This part, moreover, was already played by another: it belonged by right to Russia, and only the second remained for us. As to placing France at the head of the innovators, this was to be still less thought of, for two reasons: first, that it would have been absolutely impossible to advise these latter or to hope to lead them, because of their extravagance and their detestable incapacity; secondly, that it was not possible to support them abroad without falling beneath their blows at home. The contact of their passions and doctrines would have put all

France in flame, revolutionary doctrines at that time dominating all others. Thus we were neither able to unite with the nations, who accused us of urging them on and then betraying them, nor with the princes, who reproached us with shaking thrones. We were reduced to accepting the sterile good-will of the English: it was the same isolation as before February, with the Continent more hostile to us and England more lukewarm. It was therefore necessary, as it had been then, to reduce ourselves to leading a small life, from day to day; but this was difficult. The French Nation, which had made and, in a certain way, still made so great a figure in the world, kicked against this necessity of the time: it had remained haughty while it ceased to be preponderant; it feared to act and tried to talk loudly; and it also expected its Government to be proud, without, however, permitting it to run the risks which such conduct entailed. . . .

. . . The struggles of the nations against the Governments were followed by quarrels of the princes among themselves. I followed this new phase of the Revolution with a very attentive gaze and a very perplexed mind.

The Revolution in Germany had not proceeded from a simple cause, as in the rest of Europe. It was produced at once by the general spirit of the time and by the unitarian ideas peculiar to the Germans. The democracy was now beaten, but the idea of German unity was not destroyed; the needs, the memories, the passions that had inspired it survived. The King of Prussia had undertaken to appropriate it and make use of it. This Prince, a man of intelligence but of very little sense, had been wavering for a year between his fear of the Revolution and his desire to turn it to account. He struggled as much as he could against the liberal and democratic spirit of the age; yet he favoured the German unitarian spirit, a blundering game in which, if he had dared to go to the length of his desires, he would have risked his Crown and his life. For, in order to overcome the resistance which existing institutions and the interests of the Princes were bound to oppose to the establishment of a central power, he would have had to summon the revolutionary passions of the peoples to his aid, and of these Frederic William could not have made use without soon being destroyed by them himself.

So long as the Frankfort Parliament retained its *prestige* and its power, the King of Prussia entreated it kindly and strove to get himself placed by it at the head of the new Empire. When the Parliament fell into discredit and powerlessness, the King changed his behaviour without changing his plans. He endeavoured to obtain the legacy of this Assembly and to combat the Revolution by realizing the chimera of German unity, of which the democrats had made use to shake every throne. With this intention, he invited all the German Princes to come to an understanding with him to form a new Confederation, which should be closer than that of 1815, and to give him the government of it. In return he undertook to establish and strengthen them in their States. These Princes, who detested Prussia, but who trembled before the Revolution, for the most part accepted the usurious bargain proposed to them. Austria, which the success of this proposal would have driven out of Germany, protested, being not yet in a position to do more. The two principal monarchies of the South, Bavaria and Wurtemberg, followed its example, but all North and Central Germany entered into this ephemeral Confederation, which was concluded on the 26th of May, 1849 and is known in history by the name of the Union of the Three Kings.

Prussia then suddenly became the dominating power in a vast stretch of country, reaching from Memel to Basle, and at one time saw twenty-six or twenty-seven million Germans marching under its orders. All this was completed shortly after my arrival in office.

I confess that, at the sight of this singular spectacle, my mind was crossed with strange ideas, and I was, for a moment tempted to believe that the President was not so mad in his foreign policy as I had at first thought him. That union of the great Courts of the North, which had so long weighed heavily upon us, was broken. Two of the great Continental monarchies, Prussia and Austria, were quarrelling and almost at war. Had not the moment come for us to contact one of those intimate and powerful alliances which we have been compelled to forego for sixty years, and perhaps in a measure to repair our losses of 1815? France, by platonically assisting Frederic William in his enterprises which England did not oppose, could divide Europe and bring on one of those great crises which entail a redistribution of territory. . . .

I quickly realized that Prussia was neither able nor willing to give us anything worth having in exchange for our good offices; that its power over the other German States was very precarious, and was likely to be ephemeral; that no reliance was to be placed in its King, who at the first obstacle would have failed us and failed himself; and, above all, that such extensive and ambitious designs were not suited to so ill-established a state of society and to such troubled and dangerous times as ours, nor to transient powers such as that which chance had placed in my hands.

I put a more serious question to myself, and it was this—I recall it here because it is bound constantly to crop up again: Is it to the interest of France that the bonds which hold together the German Confederation should be strengthened or relaxed? In other words, ought we to desire that Germany should in a certain sense become a single nation, or that it should remain an ill-joined conglomeration of disunited peoples and princes? There is an old tradition in our diplomacy that we should strive to keep Germany divided among a large number of independent powers; and this in fact, was self-evident at the time when there was nothing behind Germany except Poland and a semi-savage Russia; but is the case the same in our days? The reply to this question depends upon the reply to another: What is really the peril with which in our days Russia threatens the independence of Europe? For my part, believing as I do that our West is threatened sooner or later to fall under the yoke, or at least under the direct and irresistible influence of the Tsars, I think that our first object should be to favour the union of all the German races in order to oppose it to that influence. The conditions of the world are new; we must change our old maxims and not fear to strengthen our neigh-bours, so that they may one day be in a condition with us to repel the common enemy.

The Emperor of Russia, on his side, saw how great an obstacle an United Germany would prove in his way. [Ambassador] Lamoricière, in one of his private letters, informed me that the Emperor had said to him with his ordinary candour and arrogance:

"If the unity of Germany, which doubtless you wish for no more than I do, ever becomes a fact, there will be needed, in order to manage it, a man capable of what Napoleon himself was not able to do; and if this man were found, if that armed mass developed into a menace, it would then become your affair and mine."

But when I put these questions to myself, the time had not come to solve them nor even to discuss them, for Germany was of its own accord irresistibly returning to its old constitution and to the old anarchy of its powers. The Frankfort Parliament's attempt in favour of unity had fallen through. That made by the King of Prussia was destined to meet with the same fate.

It was the dread of the Revolution which alone had driven the German Princes into Frederic William's arms. In the measure that, thanks to the efforts of the Prussians, the Revolution was on all sides suppressed and ceased to make itself feared, the allies (one might almost say the new subjects) of Prussia, aimed at recovering their independence. The King of Prussia's enterprise was of that unfortunate kind in which success itself interferes with triumph, and to compare large things with smaller, I would say that his history was not unlike ours, and that, like ourselves, he was doomed to strike upon a rock so soon as, and for the reason that, he had re-established order. The princes who had adhered to what was known as the Prussian hegemony seized the first opportunity to renounce it. Austria supplied this opportunity, when, after defeating the Hungarians, she was able to re-appear upon the scene of Ger-man affairs with her material power and that of the memories which attached to her name. This is what happened in the course of September 1849. When the King of Prussia found himself face to face with that powerful rival, behind whom he caught sight of Russia, his courage suddenly failed him, as I expected, and he returned to his old part. The German Constitution of 1815 resumed its empire, the Diet its sittings; and soon, of all that great movement of 1848, there remained but two traces visible in Germany: a greater dependence of the small States upon the great monarchies, and an irreparable blow struck at all that remains of feudal institutions: their ruin, consummated by the nations, was sanctioned by the Princes. From one end of Germany to the other, the perpetuity of ground-rents, baronial tithes, forced labour, rights of mutation, of hunting, of justice, which constituted a great part of the riches of the nobility, remained abolished. The Kings were restored, but the aristocracies did not recover from the blow that had been struck them.[2]

[2] I had foreseen from the commencement that Austria and Prussia would soon return to their former sphere and fall back in each case within the influence of Russia. I find this provision set forth in the instructions which I gave to one of our ambassadors to Germany on the 24th of July, before the events which I have described had taken place. These instructions are drawn up in my own hand, as were all my more important despatches. I read as follows:

"I know that the malady which is ravaging all the old European society is incurable, that in changing its symptoms it does not change in character, and that all the old powers are, to a greater or lesser extent, threatened with modification or destruction. But I am inclined to believe that the next event will be the strengthening of authority throughout Europe. It would not be impossible that, under the pressure of a common instinct of defence or under the common influence of recent occurrences, Russia should be willing and able to bring about harmony between North and South Germany and to reconcile Austria and Prussia, and that all this great movement should merely resolve itself into a new alliance of principles between the three monarchies at the expense of the secondary governments and the liberty of the citizens. Consider the situation from this point of view, and give me an account of your observations."

GIUSEPPE MAZZINI

IUSEPPE MAZZINI (1805–72) towers above other spokesmen of liberal nationalism because he regarded Italy's struggle for independence and freedom as a step toward the organization of an international brotherhood of free and sovereign peoples. Mazzini's program stressed the need for popular equality and for unity as a means of achieving independence. "Young Italy," he said, "is republican and unitarian, republican because all the men of a nation are required by the laws of God and Humanity to be freemen, equals, and brothers, and the institution of the republic is the only one that can assure this result; unitarian because without unity there is no strength, and Italy, surrounded by powerful and jealous unitarian nations, must needs before all things be strong . . . Young Italy is the brotherhood of Italians believing in a law of Progress and Duty."

Young Italy was a secret association, founded by Mazzini in 1831 after he was exiled for his affiliation with the Carbonari (charcoal burners), an underground revolutionary movement composed mainly of officers and noblemen. Young Italy became the leading force behind the numerous unsuccessful local insurrections which broke out in the following years. It inspired the more popular and radical current in the great 1848–49 upheaval. Although King Charles Albert of Sardinia, Mazzini's unreconciled enemy, took the leadership of the moderate liberals he was forced to abdicate by the victorious Austrians. Mazzini was called to head the newly established Republic of Rome, from which the pope fled after a short period of half-hearted collaboration with the moderate liberals. French, Austrian, and Spanish troops at once attacked the Republic, which resisted gallantly from April 25 to July 4, 1849. The collapse of both Mazzini's and Charles Albert's attempts at liberating Italy "by her own efforts" indicated that a foreign ally was needed to oust Austria. In 1858 the diplomatic skill of Cavour secured for the Savoy monarchy that ally in the person of Napoleon III, who as president of the French republic had sent the troops which had destroyed Mazzini's Roman republic in 1849. Cavour's honesty won over not only the moderate liberals, but also many of Mazzini's own followers, including Garibaldi. Thus, in 1861, Italy was unified under Victor Emmanuel II, the son of Charles Albert.

Mazzini was willing to support the Savoy monarchs in any struggle for the unification of Italy, but he insisted that only a Constituent Assembly elected directly by the people could ultimately decide whether Italy should be a monarchy or a republic. Because of his opposition to the Crown's plans, Mazzini could return to his now unified fatherland only by taking shelter under an assumed name.

Mazzini, like Cobden and Bright in England, subscribed to the view that the nation is not an isolated end in itself, but that each nation has its own peculiar contribution to offer to the general wealth of all nations. Unlike them, however, he did not base this faith on free-trade economics but placed it on a broader cultural foundation. The nation, for Mazzini, existed only to make the cooperation of individuals possible. With Herder and Hegel he emphasized the peculiar value in the uniqueness of each national tradition. Mazzini still remains the symbol of this kind of internationalism.

The selection that follows is from Mazzini's best known and representative work, *The Duties of Man*. The first four chapters appeared in 1844 in the *Apostolato Popolare,* a journal published by Mazzini for Italians living in England. The remainder, containing the chapter on "Duties Towards Your Country," appeared in 1858 in the *Pensiero ed Azione*. The chapter that follows is a typical statement of the theory of liberal nationalism.

ॐ

DUTIES TOWARDS YOUR COUNTRY

YOUR FIRST DUTIES—first as regards importance—are . . . towards Humanity. You are *men* before you are either citizens or fathers. If you do not embrace the whole human family in your affection, if you do not bear witness to your belief in the Unity of that family—consequent upon the Unity of God;—and in that fraternity among the peoples which is destined to reduce that Unity to action; if, wheresoever a fellow-creature suffers, or the dignity of human nature is violated by falsehood or tyranny—you are not ready, if able, to aid the unhappy, and do not feel called upon to combat, if able, for the redemption of the betrayed or oppressed—you violate your Law of life, you comprehend not that Religion which will be the guide and blessing of the future.

But what can each of you, singly, *do* for the moral improvement and progress of Humanity? You can from time to time give sterile utterance to your belief; you may, on some rare occasions, perform some act of *charity* towards a brother man not belonging to your own land;—no more. But charity is not the watchword of the Faith of the future. The watchword of the Faith of the future is *association* and fraternal co-operation of all towards a common aim, and this is as far superior to all charity, as the edifice which all of you should unite to raise would be superior to the humble hut each one of you might build alone or with the mere assistance of lending and borrowing stone, mortar, and tools.

But, you tell me, you cannot attempt united action, distinct and divided as you are in language, customs, tendencies, and capacity. The individual is too insignificant, and Humanity too vast. The mariner of Brittany prays to God as he puts to sea: *Help me, my God! my boat is so small and Thy ocean so wide!* And this prayer is the true expression of the condition of each one of you, until you find the means of infinitely multiplying your forces and powers of action.

This means was provided for you by God when he gave you a country; when, even as a wise overseer of labour distributes the various branches of employment according to the different capacities of the workmen, he divided Humanity into distinct groups or nuclei upon the face of the earth, thus creating the germ of Nationalities. Evil governments have disfigured the Divine design. Nevertheless you may still trace it, distinctly marked out—at least as far as Europe is concerned—by the course of the great rivers, the direction of the higher mountains, and other geographical conditions. They have disfigured it by their conquests, their greed, and their jealousy even of the righteous power of others; disfigured it so far that, if we except England and France —there is not perhaps a single country whose present boundaries correspond to that Design.

These governments did not, and do not, recognise any country save their own families or dynasty, the egotism of caste. But the Divine design will infallibly be realised. Natural divisions, and the spontaneous innate tendencies of the peoples, will take the place of the arbitrary divisions sanctioned by evil governments. The map of Europe will be re-drawn. The countries of the Peoples, defined by the vote of free men, will arise upon the ruins of the countries of kings and privileged castes, and between these countries harmony and fraternity will exist. And the common work of Humanity, of great amelioration, and the gradual discovery and application of its law of life, being distributed according to local and general capacities, will be wrought out in peaceful and progressive development and advance.

Then may each one of you, fortified by the power and the affection of many millions, all speaking the same language, gifted with the same tendencies, and educated by the same historical tradition, hope even by your own single effort to be able to benefit all Humanity.

O my brothers, love your Country! Our country is our Home, the House that God has given us, placing therein a numerous family that loves us, and whom we love; a family with whom we sympathize more readily, and whom we understand more quickly, than we do others; and which, from its being centred round a given spot, and from the homogeneous nature of its elements, is adapted to a special branch of activity.

Our Country is our common workshop, whence the products of our activity are sent forth for the benefit of the whole world; wherein the tools and implements of labour we can most usefully employ are gathered together; nor may we reject them without disobeying the play of the Almighty, and diminishing our own strength.

In labouring for our own country on the right principle, we labour for Humanity. Our country is the fulcrum of the lever we have to wield for the common good. In abandoning that fulcrum, we run the risk of rendering ourselves useless not only to humanity but to our country itself.

Before men can *associate* with the nations of which humanity is composed, they must have a National existence. There is no true association except among equals. It is only through our country that we can have a recognized *collective* existence.

Humanity is a vast army advancing to the conquest of lands unknown, against enemies both powerful and astute. The peoples are the different corps, the divisions of that army. Each of them has its post assigned to it, and its special operation to execute; and the common victory depends upon the exactitude with which those distinct operations shall be fulfilled. Disturb not the order of battle. Forsake not the banner given to you by God. Wheresoever you may be, in the centre of whatsoever people circumstances may have placed you, be ever ready to combat for the liberty of that people should it be necessary, but combat in such wise that the blood you shed may reflect glory, not on yourselves alone, but on your country. Say not *I*, but *we*. Let each man among you strive to incarnate his country in himself. Let each man among you regard himself as a guarantee, responsible for his fellow-countrymen, and learn so to govern his actions as to cause his country to be loved and respected through him.

Your country is the sign of the mission God has given you to fulfil towards humanity. The faculties and forces of *all* her sons should be associated in the accomplishment of that mission.

The true country is a community of free men and equals, bound together in fraternal concord to labour towards a common aim. You are bound to make it and to maintain it such.

The country is not an *aggregation,* but an *association.*

There is therefore no true country without an uniform Right. There is no true country where the uniformity of that Right is violated by the existence of castes, privilege, and inequality.

Where the activity of a portion of the powers and faculties of the individual is either cancelled or dormant; where there is not a common Principle, recognised, accepted, and developed by all, there is no true Nation, no People; but only a multitude, a fortuitous agglomeration of men whom circumstances have called together, and whom circumstances may again divide.

In the name of the love you bear your country you must peacefully but untiringly combat the existence of privilege and inequality in the land that gave you life.

There is but one sole legitimate privilege, the privilege of Genius when it reveals itself united with virtue. But this is a privilege given by God, and when you acknowledge it and follow its inspiration, you do so freely, exercising your own reason and your own choice.

Every privilege which demands submission from you in virtue of power, inheritance, or any other right than the Right common to all, is an usurpation and a tyranny which you are bound to resist and destroy.

Be your country your Temple. God at the summit; a people of equals at the base.

Accept no other formula, no other moral law, if you would not dishonour alike your country and yourselves. Let all secondary laws be but the gradual regulation of your existence by the progressive application of this supreme law.

And in order that they may be such, it is necessary that *all* of you should aid in framing them. Laws framed only by a single fraction of the citizens, can never, in the very nature of things, be other than the mere expression of the thoughts, aspirations, and desires of that fraction; the representation, not of the Country, but of a third or fourth part, of a class or zone of the Country.

The laws should be the expression of the *universal* aspiration, and promote the universal good. They should be a pulsation of the heart of the Nation. The entire Nation should, either directly or indirectly, legislate.

By yielding up this mission into the hands of a few, you substitute the egotism of one class for the Country, which is the Union of all classes.

Country is not a mere zone of territory. The true Country is the Idea to which it gives birth; it is the Thought of love, the sense of communion which unites in one all the sons of that territory.

So long as a single one amongst your brothers has no vote to represent him in the development of the National life, so long as there is one left to vegetate in ignorance where others are educated, so long as a single man, able and willing to work, languishes in poverty through want of work to do, you have no Country in the sense in which Country ought to exist—the Country of all and for all.

Education, labour, and the franchise, are the three main pillars of the Nation. Rest not until you have built them strongly up with your own labour and exertions.

Never deny your sister Nations. Be it yours to evolve the life of your Country in loveliness and strength; free from all servile fears or sceptical doubts; maintaining as its basis the People; as its guide the consequences of the principles of its Religious Faith, logically and energetically applied; its strength, the united strength of all; its aim the fulfilment of the mission given to it by God.

And so long as you are ready to die for Humanity, the Life of your Country will be immortal.

THE FUNDAMENTAL RIGHTS OF
THE GERMAN PEOPLE

THE FUNDAMENTAL RIGHTS of the German People were proclaimed in December, 1848, by a national assembly at Frankfurt-am-Main, and in March of the following year these rights were included in the constitution proposed for a united liberal Germany. The members of the assembly had been elected by various systems of suffrage in the states formerly included in the dissolved German Confederation, but many conservatives had abstained from voting. The majority of the delegates were partisans of a federation of liberal monarchies. The large number of university professors and other intellectuals who participated in the Frankfurt Parliament accounts in part for the theoretical elaborateness of the document and for the special emphasis placed on educational problems.

Unlike the French Declaration of the Rights of Man and of the Citizen (1789), this German bill of rights was more frankly nationalistic. The loosely organized Confederation had been dissolved only in order to clear the ground for a more effective federal union. Sharp differences developed over the areas to be included in the new federation, but the delegates began their work with much idealistic optimism. "We are here," said the president, Heinrich von Gagern, "to create a Constitution for Germany, for the whole Reich. Our call to the work and the authority to proceed have their origin in the sovereignty of the People . . . Germany longs to be united and, with the co-operation of all her members, to be governed by the will of the People. It lies also in the province of this assembly to bring about this co-operation on the part of the State Governments."

The Frankfurt Assembly spent nearly a year in its deliberations, and by that time the liberals had lost influence with the governments of Austria and Prussia, as well as much of their popular support. The decision of the assembly to offer the crown to the king of Prussia, who at first seemed less hostile to the Frankfurt liberals than the Austrian emperor, meant the abandonment of the "Greater Germany" plan; Austria would never consent to take second place to Prussia. The king of Prussia then declined the offer of an imperial crown which came "from the gutter," as he said. It was an accurate representation of his personal aversion to the democratic parliament, but he had also a more practical reason for refusing: he knew full well that to accept would not have pleased his peers, the rulers of the kingdoms of Bavaria, Württemberg, Saxony, Hanover, and especially Austria. The Frankfurt Parliament then collapsed. In the following month (May, 1849), groups of liberal extremists tried to dethrone princes and set up republican governments in various parts of Germany. These "republics" were promptly suppressed. The Prussian king then invited all the German states, except Austria, to form a new union under his presidency.

So strong was the Austrian opposition to Frederick William of Prussia that the new German Union was dissolved, and the German Confederation under the presidency of Austria was revived. The restored Diet at Frankfurt formally repealed the

Fundamental Rights of the German People and directed a special commission to purge any state constitution of "revolutionary novelties."

The following selection embodies the whole of the Fundamental Rights in the form appearing as *Abschnitt* VI in *Die deutsche Verfassung vom 28. März 1849* (*Section VI, the German Constitution of 28th March 1849*).

THE FUNDAMENTAL RIGHTS OF THE GERMAN PEOPLE

THE FOLLOWING FUNDAMENTAL RIGHTS shall be guaranteed to the German people. They shall serve as a standard for the constitutions of the separate German states and no constitution or legislation of any German state may ever set aside or limit them.

Article I

1. The German people consists of the citizens of the states which make up the German Reich.

2. Every German has the rights of German citizenship. He may exercise these rights in every German state. The election laws of the Reich determine the right to vote in elections for the Reich's assembly.

3. Every German has the right to sojourn or establish his residence in any part of the territory of the Reich, to acquire real estate of any description and to control the same, to engage in any trade, to enjoy the rights of local citizenship.

The government of the Reich shall establish for the whole of Germany the conditions governing sojourn and residence by a law of residence, and those respecting trades by trade regulations.

4. No German state may make a distinction in matters of civil and criminal law and procedural rights between its citizens and other Germans which would place the latter in the category of aliens.

5. Punishment by deprivation of citizenship shall not take place, and where it has already been decreed it shall cease in its effects, in so far as this does not do injury to private rights acquired thereby.

6. The freedom to emigrate is not limited for reasons of state. Emigration fees may not be levied.

Matters pertaining to emigration come under the protection and care of the Reich.

Article II

7. No privilege of rank is valid before the law. Nobility is abolished as a rank.

All privileges of rank are abolished.

All Germans are equal before the law.

All titles, in so far as they do not pertain to an office, are abolished and may never again be introduced.

No member of the state may accept a decoration from a foreign state.

Every public office is open equally to all who are qualified.

Military duties are the same for all; the employment of substitutes is not permissible.

Article III

8. The freedom of the individual is inviolable.

The arrest of a person shall take place, except in case of his being apprehended in the deed, only on the authority of a court order stating the cause. This order must be presented to the arrested person at the time of his arrest or within the following twenty-four hours.

Everyone taken into custody by the police must either be set free in the course of the following day or be turned over to the judicial authorities.

Everyone accused shall be released on presentation of bail to be determined by the court, in so far as compelling evidence of serious criminal activity is not submitted against him. In case of an unlawfully imposed or prolonged imprisonment, the one who is responsible, even if it be the state, is obligated to give satisfaction and compensation to the person injured.

Modifications of this rule necessary for the army and the navy are reserved for special legislation.

9. The death penalty as well as the penalties of the pillory, branding, and corporal punishment are abolished, with the exception of cases in which they are prescribed by martial law or in which they are permissible according to maritime law in the event of mutiny.

10. The home is inviolable.

The searching of a domicile is permissible only:

(i) on authority of a judicial order stating reasons, which order must be presented to the parties concerned immediately or within the following twenty-four hours;

(ii) in case of pursuit of an offender caught in the act on the part of legally authorized officials;

(iii) in those cases and circumstances in which the law exceptionally permits designated officials to do so even without judicial order.

The searching of a domicile must take place, when feasible, with the assistance of the household.

The inviolability of a domicile is not to prevent the arrest of one who is legally pursued.

11. The confiscation of letters and papers may be undertaken only on authority of a judicial order stating reasons, except in case of arrest or of searching of a domicile. This order must be presented to the parties concerned immediately or within the following twenty-four hours.

12. The privacy of letters is guaranteed.

The restrictions necessitated by examinations of a criminal court or at time of war are to be determined by legislation.

Article IV

13. Every German has the right to express his opinion freely in speaking, writing, printing, or pictorial representation.

The freedom of the press may under no circumstances and in no way be limited, suspended, or annulled by means of preventive rules, namely censorship, concessions, safety provisions, state taxes, limitations on printing or the book trade, postal restrictions or other restrictions upon free intercourse.

Offenses of the press, which are officially prosecuted, will be tried before a jury.

Laws governing the press will be proclaimed by the Reich.

Article V

14. Every German has full freedom of belief and of conscience.

No one is obligated to reveal his religious convictions.

15. Every German is unrestricted in the common practice of his religion at home or in public.

The commission of a crime and infringement of law which are committed in the exercise of this freedom are to be punished according to law.

16. The enjoyment of civil and political rights is neither conditioned nor limited by religious belief. Religious belief is not an excuse for failure to perform one's obligations as a citizen of the state.

17. Every religious association directs and controls its own affairs independently, but remains subject to the common laws of the state.

No religious association shall enjoy special privileges from the state above any other association; furthermore there is no state church.

New religious associations may be formed; no recognition of their principles on the part of the state is required.

18. None may be coerced to participate in an ecclesiastical activity or ceremony.

19. In the future the form of the oath shall read: "So help me God."

20. The civil validity of marriage depends only upon the fulfilment of the civil ceremony; the religious ceremony may take place only after the completion of the civil ceremony.

Religious differences are not a civil obstacle to marriage.

21. Record books are kept by the civil authorities.

Article VI

22. Knowledge and the teaching of knowledge are free.

23. Instruction and the system of education are under the supervision of the state and are, with the exception of religious instruction, freed from supervision of the clergy as such.

24. Every German is free to establish, to lead, and to give instruction in institutions for instruction and education, if he has given evidence of his qualifications to do so to the proper authorities of the state.

Instruction at home is not restricted in any way.

25. Sufficient provision shall everywhere be made for the education of German youth through public schools.

Parents or their representatives may not permit their children or wards to be without the instruction which is prescribed for the lower public schools.

26. Public teachers have the rights of public officials.

The state appoints teachers of the public schools from the number of those who have been examined according to the legally established rules of the communities.

27. No tuition will be paid for instruction in the public schools and lower trade schools.

Those without means shall be granted free instruction in all public educational institutions.

28. Everyone is free to choose his occupation and to prepare himself for it, how and where he wishes.

Article VII

29. Every German has the right to apply in writing to the authorities, to the representatives, and to the Reichstag with requests and complaints.

This right may be exercised by individuals as well as by corporations and by a number jointly; but in the army and navy only in the manner prescribed by the regulations governing discipline.

30. Previous consent of the authorities is not necessary in order to prosecute public officials on account of their official activities.

Article VIII

31. Germans have the right to assemble peacefully and without arms; no special permission to do so is required.

Public assemblies in the open may be forbidden in times of urgent danger in the interest of public order and safety.

32. Germans have the right to form associations. This right shall not be limited by any preventive measure.

33. The provisions included in the last two paragraphs are applicable to army and navy in so far as they are not contrary to regulations for military discipline.

Article IX

34. Private property is inviolable.

Expropriation may take place only in the interest of the public welfare, only according to law and on the basis of just compensation.

Ecclesiastical property shall be protected by legislation.

35. Every owner of real estate may dispose of his property in whole or in part among the living or on account of death. The execution of the principle governing the divisibility of real estate by means of inheritance legislation is left to the separate states.

In the interest of the public welfare, it is permissible for the legislature to impose restrictions on the rights of deceased individuals to acquire and control real estate.

36. Every relationship of bondage or serfdom is ended forever.

37. The following are abolished without compensation:

i. the patrimonial jurisdiction and the police power of the lord of a manor, together with the authority, exemptions, and imposts emanating therefrom.

ii. the personal imposts and services which have their source in the manorial and feudal relationship.

With these rights the counter services and obligations also cease, which formerly had obligated those who had been entitled to the privileges revoked.

38. All imposts and services which have their basis in the soil, the tithe in particular, are revokable. The manner in which this is to be done, whether only on application of those on whom the burden falls or of those who are privileged, is left to the legislatures of the separate states.

Henceforth no piece of real estate may be burdened with an unredeemable impost or service.

39. The right to hunt on one's own property rests in the ownership of that property.

The right to hunt on the property of others, hunting services and fees, or other services for purposes of hunting are abolished without compensation.

Only revokable, however, is the right to hunt which demonstrably has been acquired by contract with the owner of the property thus encumbered. The manner and means of this revocation is to be determined by acts of the legislature.

The regulation of the exercise of the right to hunt for reasons of public safety and the general welfare is reserved to the legislature.

The right to hunt on the property of others may not in the future be determined again as a prerogative attaching to land.

40. The laws governing non-salable family real estate are to be annulled. The manner and conditions of this revocation are to be determined by the legislatures of the separate states.

Decisions regarding family entail of the ruling princely houses are reserved to the legislatures.

41. All feudal relations are to be annulled. Particulars regarding the manner and means of execution are to be ordered by the legislative acts of the separate states.

42. The punishment of confiscation of property shall not take place.

43. Taxation shall be so regulated that the privileged position of some occupations and property shall cease in the community and state.

Article X

44. All legal jurisdiction proceeds from the state. There shall be no patrimonial courts.

45. Judicial power will be exercised independently by the courts. Cabinet and ministerial jurisdiction is inadmissible.

None may be withdrawn from his legal court. Extraordinary courts shall never take place.

46. There shall be no privileged juridical position of persons or of property.

The military tribunal is limited to pass sentence on military crimes and offences as well as on military and disciplinary misdemeanors, with the exception of decrees for the state of war.

47. No judge may be removed from office, or reduced in rank or salary, except through sentence and law.

Suspension may not take place without a court decision.

No judge may against his will be removed to a different location or be retired, except through court decision in specified cases and ways determined by law.

48. Court proceedings shall be public and oral.

Exceptions from publicity are determined by law in the interest of morality.

49. Prosecution applies in criminal cases. Gross criminal cases and all political offences shall always be judged by trial by jury.

50. In matters pertaining to special practical or professional experience, the civil administration of justice shall be administered or assisted by specially qualified judges freely chosen by their colleagues.

51. The execution and administration of justice shall be separated and be independent of each other.

Cases of conflict of jurisdiction between administrative and judicial authorities in the individual states are decided by a court determined by law.

52. Judicial power on the part of administrative authorities ceases. All violations of law are determined by the courts.

The police authorities have no power to punish.

53. Legal decisions of German courts are equally valid and effective in all German states.

A law of the nation will determine details.

Article XI

54. The fundamental principles of the constitution of every community are: (i) the election of its head officer and representative; (ii) the independent administration of its community affairs including the local police, under the legally appointed supervision of the state; (iii) that all matters pertaining to public administration be open to the public; (iv) the rule that all negotiations will be public.

55. Every piece of property shall be under the jurisdiction of a community organization.

Limitations on account of forests or deserts remain reserved to the state legislature.

Article XII

56. Every German state shall have a constitution with representation of the people.

Ministers are responsible to the representatives of the people.

57. The representatives of the people have a decisive voice in legislation, in taxation, in the regulation of affairs of state. Also, in case there is a bicameral

legislature, each chamber has for itself the right of initiating legislation, presenting grievances, of petitioning, as well as of impeaching ministers.

The sessions of the representatives are as a rule public.

Article XIII

58. The non-German speaking races of Germany are guaranteed their racial development, namely the equal right of their languages in the regions which they occupy, their rights in church affairs, in instruction, in local government, and in administration of justice.

Article XIV

59. Every German citizen abroad is under the protection of the Reich.

C. A. L. HERMANN BAUMGARTEN

Carl August Ludwig Hermann Baumgarten was born in Hesse in 1825, the son of a Protestant clergyman. He received his primary education at the Gymnasium in Wolfenbüttel, and in 1842 entered the University of Jena to study theology. After studying philology at Halle and at Bonn, he received his degree from the University of Göttingen.

During the Revolution of 1848 Baumgarten was a correspondent for the *Deutschen Reichszeitung,* a liberal journal which favored the hereditary monarchy. Abandoning journalism for scholarship, Baumgarten in 1852 began his apprenticeship to G. G. Gervinus (1805–71), the German historian. When the latter became suspect for his political activities, Baumgarten came to his aid with an important pamphlet, *Gervinus and his Political Convictions* (1853). Before leaving Gervinus in 1855 to begin independent work, he played an important role in assembling the materials for Gervinus's massive *History of the Nineteenth Century.* Baumgarten now began work on a history of Spain which was completed after he accepted a position at the Technische Hochschule in Karlsruhe. Published in three volumes, the *History of Spain from the Outbreak of the French Revolution to the Present* (1865–71) earned for its author considerable scholarly repute in Germany, although it was not widely regarded elsewhere in Europe and is today largely discredited.

Baumgarten remained deeply concerned with German politics. He was at first opposed to Bismarck and mistrustful of his ambitions. After 1866, however, he became severely critical of the parochialism—*Kleinstaaterei*—of traditional German liberalism, and he attacked the Progressive party of Prussia for failing to come to terms with the larger political forces of the day. He attained national fame with his essay *German Liberalism: A Self-Criticism* (1867), in which he gave the fullest expression to these convictions. He urged the liberals to join forces in the effort to create a national state, and in effect sketched out the program followed by the National-Liberal party, newly formed after the split in the Progressive party in 1866. In 1870 Baumgarten published another important political work, *How We Have Become a People Once Again,* in which he accepted the Prussian state as the territorial basis for German unity. In 1872 he was called to a post at the University of Strasbourg, where he taught until 1890.

In many ways Baumgarten's political career was representative of German liberalism. Although he took the lead in demanding that liberals accept certain compromises for the sake of a unified Germany, he quickly became disillusioned with this "politics of unity." He viewed the development of the young empire with increasing skepticism, and complained bitterly in his letters of Bismarck's internal politics. His frank and unequivocal assault upon Treitschke's history of Germany exposed him to the wrath of important political and scholarly figures. His objection to Prussia's domination of the empire and his distaste for the anti-Semitism which came to mark German political life in the 1880s, under the influence of Adolph Stöcker, drove Baumgarten out of politics. From 1882 to 1892 he occupied himself with studies of Alsatian history; he died in 1893.

The following selection from *German Liberalism: A Self-Criticism* has been translated by Elinor Stoneman.

꧄

GERMAN LIBERALISM: A SELF-CRITICISM

MORE THAN three hundred years have passed since the German people, as one people, intervened with an action of great magnitude in human history. The Reformation was the last practical accomplishment of the entire German people; and this last work caused them to split apart, and ended their national existence. Luther's great and infinitely blessed deed rested upon the cooperation of the Franks, the Swabians, the Hessians, the Thüringians, and the Saxons; only the Bavarians had little share in it. But this deed, as it founded our spiritual life on the private conscience; as it taught us, according to the word of Christ and in the spirit of the oldest Christian communities, to despise this world and to contemplate Godhead; as it released the individual conscience, in accordance with the most fundamental characteristics of our German nature, from worldly considerations; precisely as it accomplished all this, Luther's deed broke the last weak bonds which still held together the Holy Roman Empire of the German nation. . . .

Even our Lutheran princes had some politics, indeed a kind of politics never before seen. Their politics were those that up until the present day have dominated the German destiny: the politics of moral meditation, of domestic conscientiousness, of diligence in small things and impotence in great; of eager industry within a limited sphere, and embarrassed inertia on the larger stage. These politics either caused or encouraged the formation of the solid bourgeoisie of our cities, the comfortable prosperity of our villages, the flowering of our schools and universities, the conscientious industry of our officials, the seriousness of our scholarship, the purity of our family life; these politics, in short, helped to form everything of which we can be proud, everything that tends toward our domestic, private, and economic happiness. These politics have also, however, created that miserable particularism which has a place only for the father of a family, but murders the man and the citizen. They have created that poverty-stricken Philistinism which hampers us at every turn; they have accustomed our minds to lay siege to heaven by the keenest fantasies, and yet to allow our arms to sink helplessly before the slightest difficulties of this world. These politics have sucked the manly marrow from the bones of the state and turned it into a kindergarten which protects us indeed from all the dangers, but also from all the greatness, of the evil world. . . .

The greatness of our actions of the intellect [in the period after the death of Frederick the Great] can never be admired enough: they will be for all time the highest ornament of our name. . . . It is nevertheless, I believe, unquestionably true that the essential tendency of our classical literature was to give exaggerated weight to the education of the intellect, to perception, to thought, and to feeling, and in neglecting the active part of our nature, to withdraw into an exclusively spiritual sphere, and to lose itself in an antique idealism inappropriate to modern, and particularly to German, life. Something of the misfortune of Renaissance humanism touched this literary epoch: no more than the clarity of the humanists could do away with the moral conditions which afflicted Europe at the beginning of the sixteenth century could the aesthetic and critical glory of Jena and Weimar hinder in the slightest degree the terrible catastrophe of 1806. Our country shone most brightly in poetry, in philosophy, and in scholarship precisely as the moment of its moral destruction approached. . . .

In fact, we were much in need of this chastisement, which reduced our trust in ideas, and taught the people that aesthetic creation and philosophical knowledge do not make up the sum of human affairs. The lamentable events of 1806 and 1807, and the hard struggles during the years following, could only issue in complete rebirth. Our rebirth was not limited to the restoration of political independence, but involved our most inward convictions. Our new convictions found a fertile place prepared for them by the great elector and the great king in the midst of the barren waste of the German realms. It was not with Weimar and Jena that we had then to do, not with the songs of the poets and the systems of the philosophers, but with the saving deeds of statesmen and soldiers, not with the fine circle of highly cultivated aesthetes, but with the hard fists of peasants accustomed all through a glorious history only to submission. The great minds which tarried with their elevated thoughts in the universal would perhaps have peacefully allowed the German way to perish; it was the mediocre talents, with their lower flight and narrower view, who felt the entire disgrace; and, indeed, it was not the powers of the creative imagination and of the abstract reason, until then almost alone esteemed, but force of character, until then almost wholly despised, which now provided the solution. We had the good fortune in these terrible circumstances, hitherto unknown to us, immediately to find among us a few worthy representatives of active patriotism in the grand style. The picture of those extraordinary times was honorably completed when, next to the heroes of poetry and of scientific inquiry, there arose the heroes of political and military action, and upon the hundreds of thousands who had listened enthusiastically to our poets followed other hundreds of thousands who understood how to act and to strike in the spirit of Stein, Scharnhorst, Gneisenau, and Blücher. . . .

From a human point of view, this was all very satisfactory and harmonious. After having won the highest honors in the ideal spheres of poetry, philosophy, and scholarship, we learned quickly, through severe trials, to occupy the neglected ground of the active life; after having sacrificed richly to antique humanism we served Christian Germanism; after having been the most enthusiastic cosmopolites and made secure forever the idea of world citizenship, we became equally enthusiastic patriots, in order to free the fatherland by glorious warfare as we had just freed the realm of ideas. But, from a political point of view, these accomplishments were not so satisfying. Support of the fight for freedom advanced rapidly from Prussia in all directions and inflamed tempers all the way to Swabia and Bavaria. This tendency was by no means exclusively Prussian; it was German. "As far as the German tongue is heard": that was the watchword. The glory of Germany was to rise up. But what was the situation of that Germany in actuality? Was Germany fighting for the German interest? Certainly not. The dismembered Prussia, and Brunswick, and Hanover, and Hesse, they rose to fight for freedom together with Russians and Britons, and the greater number of Germans fought under French banners, while Metternich's Austria sat waiting to see on which side she could win the greater advantage. . . . While Prussia with almost superhuman effort bore the burden of the war, not only the Confederation of the Rhine, but even Hanover, joined hands with Metternich to spoil the fruits of the war and to throw Germany back into the old miseries of petty dynastic egotism and lack of leadership. And not only did these enemies hasten to destroy the only advantages the moment offered, but Prussia herself, incomparable in war, proved herself politically unready and uncertain. . . . The characteristics of the Protestant state reappeared, that petty conscientiousness, that narrow private industry which was our political inheritance from the Reformation. And indeed not merely in the smaller states, but most eminently in Prussia herself. . . .

It would be of great value for us to know exactly the history of liberalism from 1815 to 1848. Today we know it only in its most general outlines, and I doubt that we shall ever have detailed, authentic information concerning it. For when shall we find ten or twelve historical specialists who would have the patience . . . to collect it . . . ? Where would we find the public for it

which would justify so much work on so little material? And what cannot
stimulate the historian to write cannot stimulate important men to act. If
we are to be honest, we must admit that while the activity of liberalism during
that period was of some service in the small states in improving conditions,
preventing worse, and, especially, in keeping the spirit of the nation alive and
giving it the first political schooling, nevertheless liberal politics remained
in general unfruitful and failed to provide the nation with what it required.
*If the man is to be effective in the state, he must have a state; all those single
German states, however, to which liberalism was confined by the resignation
of Prussia, were not states.* They did not possess the independence of action
which is essential to every state, nor did they have at their disposal the necessary intellectual and material resources. The narrowest limits were placed
upon all their activities. On the larger political scene they were either hemmed
in by the united pressure of Prussia and Austria or tossed back and forth involuntarily by the antagonism of those two great powers. In internal
politics they were embarrassed by the unavoidable influence of their numerous neighbors, and particularly by their lack of territory. . . . The best
intentions of the rulers were bound to be shattered against the limitations of
space and the insufficiency of available resources. This dwarf's politics, imposed by bitter necessity, distorted every expression of national life into a
caricature. . . .

Whoever takes stock fairly of all these circumstances will find natural the
ineffectiveness of the liberal strivings up to 1848. . . .

Finally it came to be understood that there was little to be gained from all
the freedom of the individual states, that a national state must be created.
Admittedly, the greatest disagreement arose on this point among those who
had hitherto been united. If all who until then had been liberals had perceived only the common enemy, without realizing how far apart their own
assumptions were, March 1848 soon revealed that the previous unhealthy
conditions had produced a full measure of the most fatal conflicts. Since
liberalism had until then formed the opposition exclusively, since its politics
had been limited to speech-making and writing, the most diverse theories
had been formulated as to the best method of organizing the government.
The negative elements, which had arisen out of the ineffectiveness of the
liberal efforts, had gained a dangerous strength in the forties, as the contradiction between the actual situation and the justified demands of the
nation became ever more obvious. The rash theories of the Young Hegelians
and the mad doctrines of French radicalism, encountering the romantic attempts at restoration by the Prussian king, had produced a frightful confusion in the minds of the young (and of some of maturer age). . . . The

sobriety of the people did not allow these extremes much scope for their destructive experiments; but, because the mass of educated men also lacked political experience, the saner party of moderates, which the majority of the nation followed, had its own attack of dreams which hindered them from working boldly and consistently toward an attainable goal. Prussia had now to pay dearly for having so long denied her people the opportunity of political action. Instead of being the stronghold of a reasonably creative reform policy, she became the arena for the wildest utopian schemes; and instead of assembling the German powers in her capital, she had to await moderating influences from Frankfurt. More than any other state she became the plaything of the destructive extremes, and after the Berlin National Assembly had been busy a while at the work of destroying the necessary foundations of monarchical order, there came to the fore that unholy restoration party whose chief aim seemed to be to place the Prussian nobility in unreconcilable opposition to all healthy political life and to the goals of Prussian policy itself.

While every kind of political corruption thus proceeded from Berlin, the attempt was made in Frankfurt radically to heal the German sickness, while preserving what could be preserved. How could such an undertaking not have encountered the most numerous difficulties? How could the Germans have been able safely to sail over the reefs on which nearly every constitution-making assembly has been wrecked? The men who in the Paulskirche [1] dared to make the attempt, although they tried in vain to maintain the rule of moderation in this time of the wildest political ferment, they at least succeeded in setting out a program for the new ordering of Germany which threw the first light on the main questions. Any just observer of the situation will give the center credit for the sober insight and political sophistication it exhibited, indeed to an extent which the previous course of our politics scarcely allowed us to hope. These men, suddenly lifted out of the restricted scene of provincial politics and placed on the greatest stage, removed from the discussion of often trivial enough theories and called to the solution of the most difficult world questions; almost without preparation for such a task, without any support from an organized governmental power, pressed on all sides by tumultuous demands, holding their sessions in a land where political conditions every month underwent the most vital changes; these men, for the most part summoned from the university or from other wholly unpolitical occupations, managed to maintain a firmness and prudence which, if it did not reach the desired end in its first attempt, nevertheless transformed the political thinking of the nation in the most gratifying fashion.

[1] [The Frankfurt Parliament met in a church in Frankfurt.]

This first attempt to solve the German question was bound to fail, if only because the true strength of the determining factors, the conflicting interests, were first revealed by the attempt itself. No one could have known in the summer of 1848 how Prussia and Austria and the various small states stood on the question, what the dynasties and the populace thought, in what way foreign powers would try to influence the results. Only as the majority of the group gathered in the Paulskirche brought their constitutional plans to maturity did the various conditions gradually come to light. The majority could not, therefore, draft their plan in accordance with these conditions, but were obliged to proceed on the basis of what they held in general to be desirable and possible according to their experience in German affairs, and on the basis of what seemed to correspond to the nature of the states to be united. In these circumstances it will surely be recognized that the assembly, aside from the unfortunate despotic and radical rights of man, understood how to draft a constitution which offered satisfaction to the needs of the nation in certain main points. . . .

The plan admittedly could not have been carried out. First, because the Prussia of 1849, the Prussia of Frederick William IV, was thoroughly unfit to carry out the task assigned to her by the Parliament. Also because the nation would have refused the necessary support to a better armed Prussia. And, finally, because the constitution, aside from other faults, was a theoretical work which did not rest upon a particular power. Instead of proceeding from the idea that the Prussian interest should be determining, it drew a certain ideal diagonal between the conflicting interests of Prussia and the smaller states; and in trying to be just to everyone, in fact satisfied no one. . . .

The German question slept, and German honor slept with it. We ourselves handed over the duchies of the Elbe to the brutal Danes, we ourselves laid hands on the German fleet. A lively people would never have borne the disgraces which the restored Bundestag heaped upon it. We were calm enough to accommodate ourselves to circumstances which seemed to us merely unpleasant. We crept back into our petty private existence, wrote and read once again innumerable books, and attended to our old business. Infinitely lamentable times for anyone who had any manly pride in him. . . .

At the moment when the danger of war with France came closer, the conviction had already hardened in Berlin that a reform of the military constitution of the Prussian state had become an unavoidable necessity. The mobilization of the summer of 1859 had made evident all the disadvantages attached to the old regime, and the experiences of the Italian war had revealed to those versed in the matter that the existing military arrangements were insufficient to allow Prussia to view calmly the prospect of a conflict with France. . . . The principle of universal conscription had become falsified in that the army, held within its old limits, now comprised only three-fifths of the available manpower, and allowed two-fifths to escape from duty. The principle of frugality which during the long period of peace had determined the activity of the state threatened to become the cause of terrible expenditure in a time which bore the seeds of war in its womb. Before the advent of Napoleonism, during the peace guaranteed by the alliance of the eastern powers, it was prudent for Prussia to organize her peaceful state with the utmost economy, even at the risk of having to send the flower of her people, the first ranks of the militia, into battle with little effect; for the danger of war had then been far away. But since the Russian and especially since the Italian war, this economizing in peacetime had begun to appear a highly risky procedure. . . .

For all these important reasons it was decided in the summer of 1859 to attempt a reform of the military organization. The Prince Regent pursued the matter personally; it seemed to him the most important task of his government. By the beginning of the winter the military had finished giving technical advice, and the matter came up for political consideration by the ministry. For them it was a question of deciding whether, and to what degree, the financial position of the state permitted the increase in forces. The ministers could not deceive themselves that the measure would be popular with the people. Liberal opinion was in all military questions subject to rather radical views. A peace of almost fifty years, dissatisfaction with a high and apparently superfluous appropriation for a standing army, the seductive example of Switzerland and the United States, the misleading memory of the great deeds of the militia in 1813-15, the opposition to the absolutist tendencies of the military aristocracy, the disinclination to all warlike disturbances whatsoever (this was only natural in a time of the greater and greater dominance of industrialism)—for all these reasons public opinion would be likely to oppose any increase in the military burden. It was obvious that precisely for these reasons only a liberal government had a chance of winning support for such a measure from the representatives; it was just as certain that even liberal ministers could hope to carry through the reform only if their liberalism were absolutely unquestionable. The liberals offered assurances to the people that the increase in the military establishment would be compensated for by the abolition of other disabilities under which they had labored for many years. Such an arrangement held the greatest opportunities for the liberal cause. Those persons and classes who had most to gain from the military reform could make the greatest difficulties for the liberalism of the ministry. The ministers, therefore, found themselves in an excellent bargaining position:

they could place the military and the general political question in the closest relationship, forward the one by means of the other, and make their cooperation on the military question contingent on the concessions they desired in the other. Herr von Manteuffel remarked, perfectly correctly, in January of 1860, that "if the Liberals were clever, they would use the military issue to take the rudder out of our hands forever."

But in their first great opportunity to assure Prussia of a firm and lasting liberal policy, the Liberals demonstrated a fateful incompetence. Even before the public learned any details of the projected reorganization, the sudden retirement of the popular war minister von Bonin was an evil omen for the further prosecution of the matter. Bonin was generally considered a liberal military man: it was naturally assumed that he had withdrawn because the reorganization of the army was to be carried out in a reactionary manner. In fact, the minister had quite other motives; in fact, he was not capable of undertaking the task. But his retirement, without the other ministers, indicated that they, not he, had failed to take the correct stand on a question which involved the very existence of the whole government. Nor did the other ministers seem to take such a stand as the question was further formulated. It was clearly not sufficient to demand from the Regent his approval of a series of drafts of reform legislation; it was necessary to demand guarantees that these proposals would actually be enacted, that they would not be defeated by the powers and influences of the old regime which still had tremendous strength in all the ministries, in the higher posts of the provincial government, in the House of Lords, and among the princes. . . .

I do not believe that the foregoing suggestions are the exaggerated demands of an ideal policy. . . . If someone wishes to point out that the ministers were confronted by great difficulties, I can only reply that great tasks inevitably involve great difficulties. And this was truly a great task. It was a matter of leading Prussia out of the byways of revolutionary and counterrevolutionary agitation onto the highroad of a healthy, progressive policy; it was a matter of giving Germany a happier future through a strong Prussia, of renewing the old order of Europe, now collapsing, through a Prussia supported by all of Germany, as the interests of Prussia, of Germany, and of civilization itself demanded. . . .

On the 12th of January, 1860, the Prince Regent opened the Landtag with a speech from the throne which emphasized the necessity of the military reorganization. . . . Everyone understood from his words, and from his tone, that his mind was set on the measure, that his attitude to the *Land* would be conditioned by the position it took on this issue. The speech did not neglect to give several assurances in advance, the importance of which cannot be denied. He spoke of the reform of the German constitution, which made plain the good will, at least, of the government. He made known his wish that "the activity of the German constitutional assembly be confined to practical suggestions for revising the constitutions of the individual states." He showed his sincerity by citing the Prussian guarantee, in the Hessian constitutional question, of a return to the constitution of 1831. He gave notice also of Prussia's attempt to create a constitution guaranteeing the recognized rights in the civil code to the duchies of the Elbe. In domestic affairs, he proposed to introduce bills on civil marriage, on the determination of the electoral districts, on the guarantee of freedom of the press, on revision of the land tax, and on a new local organization to satisfy the most pressing needs of the country. One cannot doubt that this speech developed a consistent system of domestic and foreign policy. If Prussia received what was promised by the speech, she would so certainly be on the right road to constitutional progress that she could afford a greater defense burden, and at the same time take up the position in Germany of which her internal reform would have made her worthy. In fact, the political situation was altered for the better by the speech. Everyone approached with fresh faith the work which seemed destined to consolidate the new era. But within a few weeks the parliamentary skies were overcast with the blackest clouds. On the tenth of February the ministers introduced a bill for military reform. Until that day the ministerial press had insisted that the increase in expenditure for the military would not exceed six million; the ministers themselves must have assured their friends in the House that this was so. For when Herr von Patow informed the House of an increase of nine million, the whole House was dumbfounded. They would not have been shocked by an appropriation double that amount, had they been prepared for it; but with one blow the good mood of the representatives, and of the entire liberal population, was destroyed. The representatives considered their party obligations to their former leaders in the ministry to have been dissolved; the evil prophecies of the radical doubters now found ready ears in many circles; and the worst was that few really examined the military situation itself with an unprejudiced eye. The procedure of the ministers seemed explicable only by their having had a bad conscience about the measure. The angry Liberals, readily aroused against anything which smacked of the military, immediately began to interpret the whole measure as a reactionary maneuver to supplant the militia and strengthen the influence of the Junker class over the army.

Immediately after the introduction of the military reform bill came the debate of the House of Lords on the marriage law. . . . The speech from the throne had expressed the "lively wish" that the law be passed. . . . The lords did not allow themselves to be swerved in the slightest degree from their appointed path; against the most weighty arguments of the minister of justice and of religion, they insisted upon adhering to the doctrines of extreme orthodoxy, supported, indeed, by the most ludicrous arguments. . . . If the government had entertained the illusion that the authority of the Regent would suffice to bend the House of Lords to its will, it could not after this experience doubt that the Lords would treat the equalization of the land tax as it had the marriage law, and thereby subvert the essential financial basis of the military reform. To hold to that reform, while all the other reforms failed, was impossible even for the most shameless liberalism. The speech from the throne had set forth a consistent political program; it could not be that one would allow all the reforms welcome to the liberals to be blocked by the House of Lords, and at the same time wish to pass the military reform which the Lords welcomed. . . . If, however, the state was against such a result, one had to take into account not only the power of the ministers, but also the will of the Regent. Did he perhaps, in spite of everything, share the views of the House of Lords?

I do not doubt that the ministers tried to win more votes in the House of Lords; but their attempts were unsuccessful. I cannot say why they failed. But the primary reason must have been that their relations with the Regent either were not of the best, or had undergone a fatal weakening through the difficulties of the last few months. I touch here upon a point which is of special significance for our liberal politics. Almost everywhere in Germany liberal ministers have the difficult task of dealing with princes who suspect them of wanting to deprive their masters of their princely rights. If the ministers' relations with the princes are in many respects the most delicate aspect of their mission, they are certain to be made the more thorny by this suspicion. The old opposition of the nobility makes itself felt too: if a prince really has decided, out of clear insight and honest intentions, to trust his liberal ministers, the atmosphere created by the nobles constantly acts to make him waver in his determination. . . . Probably the word of the prince would have been enough to bring the Lords into line. But when the ministers allowed the Lords to doubt whether the prince really wanted what he had so ceremoniously called for in his speech from the throne, when they allowed the Lords to hope that their insults to liberalism constituted support for the prince, then not even the creation of new peers would have sufficed to shake the House—apart from the fact that the ministers who failed to obtain from the throne the smaller favor, could scarcely have obtained the larger. So it went. The ministers were unsuccessful at the palace. Every day Herr von Auerswald drove in vain to the court. The Regent did not know what to make of his liberal advice; its influence was reduced by the growing power of the opposition. Thus the House of Lords remained as it was. It defeated the land tax bill as it had the marriage law. The ministerial strategy had failed completely.

Already in March, 1860, the situation was quite clear to the politically alert. The fall of the Auerswald ministry was feared. Did the fall signify the bankruptcy of liberalism in general?

A ministry is almost always a true expression of the party it represents. The faults and weaknesses which come to light in it are usually faults and weaknesses of the party itself. In our case this was certainly true. The party members who formed the government represented the best in the party. If the party knew, as it must have, that even the best would not be good enough, its duty was all the more to stand by its friends in the government, to support and strengthen them. It cannot be said that the party fulfilled this duty. And if we wish to point out the main reason for their negligence, we can only repeat what we said earlier of German liberalism in general: the Prussian liberals, like their comrades in the smaller states, carried on politics, with few exceptions, like dilettantes. . . .

The Liberal Party, as well as the Liberal ministry, broke down. If the liberal system nevertheless appeared to be in power for almost two more years, that seems to me only to prove once again that this system, otherwise handled, really had had a good chance of keeping the country and the Prince on the path which he had chosen at the beginning of his government. . . . But, after the session of 1860, one could no longer have any faith in the politics of the new era; the necessary relation between the government and public opinion, and between public opinion and the House of Representatives, had been too much shaken.

THE DECEMBRIST MOVEMENT

THE INSTITUTION of serfdom was established comparatively late in Russia. It attained its fullest development there in the eighteenth century, at the very time when in many other parts of Europe it was in process of rapid decline. By 1800, however, there were even in Russia unmistakable signs that serfdom must come to an end. The bloodily repressed mass uprisings led by peasant heroes like Pugachev, the bankruptcy of many landlords, the growth of industry and commerce, these were all signs that Russian serfdom was already in decay.

Then came the era of the French Revolution, with deeds and ideas that shook all Europe. The Revolution's main achievement was to sweep away the last vestiges of feudalism in France, and to establish a society based upon a new conception of man as a being endowed with human dignity and natural rights. Hence it captured the imagination of not a few of the Russian youth, and in particular of certain young army officers, members of the liberal nobility, who had fought through to Paris in 1814 and had had an opportunity to become personally acquainted with the land of the Revolution.

At the beginning of the nineteenth century, when Alexander I came to the throne, the atmosphere in Russia had been favorable to the discussion and dissemination of liberal ideas. The new Tsar himself had enjoyed the benefits of a liberal education, having been taught by the Swiss republican Frédéric Laharpe, and looked with a benevolent eye on the discussions and associations of the progressive nobility and intellectuals. Toward the close of his reign, however, the Tsar came increasingly under the influence of reactionary advisers at home and of conservative ministers like Metternich abroad. The last ten years of his reign were characterized by the imposition of a pedantically strict censorship and the establishment of barracks rule under the direction of the military sadist Arakchéev. Under these circumstances liberal thought was inevitably driven underground and compelled to take the form of secret societies somewhat analogous to masonic lodges.

Among the more prominent of these societies was one named "Association for Public Welfare." It grew up among a circle of young nobles and army officers in St. Petersburg in the period 1816–17 with the aim of establishing a limited monarchy. A southern branch of the society established at Tulchin had the more revolutionary aim of overthrowing the autocracy. This southern group also entered into relations with the United Slavs, a secret society of the Ukraine, and with the Polish Secret Patriotic Society, whose aim was to secure the national independence of Poland. The northern group carried on an active propaganda in the army, where it had many sympathizers.

The revolutionaries' great opportunity to do away with absolutism came in 1825. On November 19 of that year the death of the childless Alexander I inaugurated a period of confusion when it was not clear which of Alexander's two brothers, Constantine or Nicholas, would succeed to the throne. Plans were speedily made for an uprising, and Prince Trubetskoi, chief of the northern group, drafted a manifesto declaring the old régime to be at an end and a Provisional Government to be established. (This Manifesto is among the selections that follow.) On December 14 a mass of people—soldiers of the Guard, marines, members of the public and revolutionaries—gathered in the square of the Senate in St. Petersburg to protest the proclamation of Nicholas as Tsar.

The indecision, inexperience, and even panic of some of the revolutionary leaders doomed the movement to failure and turned the situation to Nicholas's advantage. Cannon were brought up and the rebellion was crushed with great loss of life. A similar fate befell a revolt organized by the societies of the south. The leaders were hanged, the rest sent to the living death of exile in Siberia. They are immortalized in Russian history as the *Dekabristi*, or men of December.

Tsar Nicholas, in his rage that nobles, army men and intellectuals should have dared revolt against the throne, spared no pains to lay bare all the circumstances of the rebellion, down to the most trifling details. He brought all the prisoners to St. Petersburg and conducted a very thorough examination. The material printed in the following selections is a part of the testimony extorted by him from the conspirators. These documents well reflect the conditions and the atmosphere in which the secret societies flourished, and the political, national and constitutional aims for which they worked.

The selections are from A. G. Mazour, *The First Russian Revolution, 1825* (Berkeley, University of California Press, 1937).

§

LETTER OF A. BESTUZHEV TO NICHOLAS I

Your Imperial Highness:

CONVINCED that You, Sovereign, love the truth, I dare to lay before You the historical development of free thinking in Russia and in general of many ideas which constitute the moral and political basis of the events of December 14. I shall speak in full frankness, without concealing evil, without even softening expressions, for the duty of a loyal subject is to tell his Monarch the truth without any embellishment. I commence.

The beginning of the reign of Emperor Alexander was marked with bright hopes for Russia's prosperity. The gentry had recuperated, the merchant class did not object to giving credit, the army served without making trouble, scholars studied what they wished, all spoke what they thought, and everyone expected better days. Unfortunately, circumstances prevented the realization of these hopes, which aged without their fulfillment. The unsuccessful, expensive war of 1807 and others disorganized our finances, though we had not yet realized it when preparing for the national war of 1812. Finally, Napoleon invaded Russia and then only, for the first time, did the Russian people become aware of their power; only then awakened in all our hearts a feeling of independence, at first political and finally national. That is the beginning of free thinking in Russia. The government itself spoke such words as "Liberty, Emancipation!" It had itself sown the idea of abuses resulting from the unlimited power of Napoleon, and the appeal of the Russian Monarch resounded on the banks of the Rhine and the Seine. The war was still on when the soldiers, upon their return home, for the first time disseminated grumbling among the masses. "We shed blood," they would say, "and then we are again forced to sweat under feudal obligations. We freed the Fatherland from the tyrant, and now we ourselves are tyrannized over by the ruling class." The army, from generals to privates, upon its return, did nothing but discuss how good it is in foreign lands. A comparison with their own country naturally brought up the question, "Why should it not be so in our own land?"

At first, as long as they talked without being hindered, it was lost in the air, for thinking is like gunpowder, only dangerous when pressed. Many cherished the hope that the Emperor would grant a constitution, as he himself had stated at the opening of the Legislative Assembly in Warsaw, and the attempt of some generals to free their serfs encouraged that sentiment. But after 1817 everything changed. Those who saw evil or who wished improvement, thanks to the mass of spies were forced to whisper about it, and this was the beginning of the secret societies. Oppression by the government of deserving officers irritated men's minds. Then the military men began to talk: "Did we free Europe in order to be ourselves placed in chains? Did we grant a constitution to France in order that we dare not talk about it, and did we buy at the price of blood priority among nations in order that we might be humiliated at home?" The destructive policy toward schools and the persecution of education forced us in utter despair to begin considering some important measures. And since the grumbling of the people, caused by exhaustion and the abuses of national and civil administrations, threatened bloody revolution, the Societies intended to prevent a greater evil by a lesser one and began their activities at the first opportunity. . . .

You, Sovereign, probably already know how we, inspired by such a situation in Russia and seeing the elements ready for change, decided to bring about a *coup d'état.* . . . Here are the plans we had for the future. We thought of creating a Senate of the oldest and wisest Russian men of the present administration, for we thought that power and ambition would always have their attraction. Then we thought of having a Chamber of Deputies composed of national representatives. . . . For enlightenment of the lower classes we wished everywhere to establish Lancasterian schools. And in order to bring about moral improvement we thought of raising the standard of the clergy by granting to them a means of livelihood. Elimination of nearly all duties, freedom from distillation and road improvement for the state, encouragement of agriculture and general protection of industry would result in satisfying the peasants. Assurance and stability would attract to Russia many resourceful foreigners. Factories would increase with the demand for commodities, while competition would stimulate improvement, which rises along with the prosperity of the people, for the need of commodities for life and luxury is constant. . . .

Most devoted servant of
Your Imperial Highness,
Alexander Bestuzhev. . . .

RELATIONS BETWEEN THE SOUTHERN AND POLISH SECRET SOCIETIES

(From the Testimony of M. Bestuzhev-Riumin)

AT THE Kiev fair in 1824 I learned from Chodkiewicz that there existed a Society, which, upon finding that we had a similar organization, wished to enter into negotiations. I reported this to the Directory, which gave me instructions to conclude an agreement. This agreement consisted:

On Our Part:

(1) Russia, preferring to have noble allies instead of secret enemies, upon completing her reforms would grant Poland independence.

(2) There would be a new delimitation, and for the sake of retaining friendly and beneficial relationships the provinces which have not been sufficiently Russified would be restored to Poland.

(3) At the same time the interests of those who would be compelled to remain on Russian soil on account of strategic demarcation would be respected.

(4) The Poles could, however, hope to receive back the Provinces of Grodna, part of Vilna, Minsk, and Volynsk.

(5) With the confirmation of the agreement, the Russian Society would give protection to Poles who happened to carry on their work in Russia, provided that that work was not in conflict with national interests.

(6) The Russian Society would use all means to eradicate the antagonism which exists between the two peoples, realizing that in the age of enlightenment in which we live the interests of all peoples are identical, and imbedded hatred is the attribute only of barbaric ages.

(7) For further relations each party appoints deputies who will be instructed:

(a) That they communicate to their respective directories everything designated for them or present information requested by the other party.

(b) Polish deputies will inform the Russian Society concerning developments in Western Europe.

(c) It is strictly forbidden to deputies to name or request them to name any members of either society.

(d) If a Russian deputy meets members of the Polish Society, or a Polish deputy meets members of the Russian Society, they must not reveal that the two organizations have entered into any relationships.

(e) All intercourse between the two directories is to be carried out through deputies only.

(f) The deputies cannot agree to nor promise anything without the consent of their respective directories.

On the Part of the Poles:

The Poles are obligated to:

(1) use all means, regardless of what kind, to prevent Grand Duke Constantine Pavlovich from returning to Russia;

(2) rebel simultaneously with us;

(3) attack the Lithuanian Corps, should it move against us;

(4) give us all possible assistance at their disposal;

(5) arrange relations between us and political societies which function in Western Europe;

(6) inform us about all important matters as soon as they know of them;

(7) act during the revolution according to the instructions of our Society, and recognize themselves as our subordinates;

(8) adopt a republican form of government.

THE OATH FOR MEMBERS WHO ENTER THE UNITED SLAVS

UPON JOINING the United Slavs for the liberation of myself from tyranny and for the restoration of freedom, which is so precious to the human race, I solemnly pledge on these arms brotherly love, which is to me divine and from which I expect the fulfillment of all my desires. I swear to be always virtuous, always loyal to our aim, and to observe the deepest secrecy. Hell itself with all its horrors will not be able to compel me to reveal to the tyrants my friends and their aims. I swear that only when a man proves undoubted desire to become a participant, will my tongue reveal the Society; I swear, to the last drop of my blood, to my last breath, to assist you, my friends, from this sacred moment. Special activity will be my first virtue, and mutual love and aid my sacred duty. I swear that nothing in the world will be able to move me. With sword in hand I shall attain the aim designated by us. I will pass through a thousand deaths, a thousand obstacles—I will pass through, and dedicate my last breath to freedom and the fraternal union of the noble Slavs. Should I violate this oath, then let remorse be the first vengeance for my hideous offense, let the point of this sword turn against my heart and fill it with hellish torment; let the moment of my life that is injurious to my friends, be the last one; let my existence be transformed into a chain of unheard misery from the fatal moment that I forget my pledge. May I see all that is dear to my heart perish by this weapon and in horrible suffering, and this weapon, reaching me, the criminal, cover my body with wounds and cast infamy upon me; and the accumulated burden of physical and moral evil shall impress on my forehead the sign of a monstrous son of Nature.

A MANIFESTO, DRAWN BY "DICTATOR" TRUBETSKOI ON THE EVE OF DECEMBER 14, 1825

The Manifesto of the Senate should proclaim:

(1) abolition of the former government;

(2) establishment of a Provisional Government until a permanent one is decided upon by representatives;

(3) freedom of the press, hence abolition of censorship;

(4) religious tolerance to all faiths;

(5) abolition of the right to own men;

(6) equality of all classes before the law and therefore abolition of military courts and all sorts of judicial commissions from which all cases proceed to civil courts;

(7) announcement of rights for every citizen to occupy himself with whatever he wishes and therefore—nobleman, merchant, middle-class man, peasant—all to have equal right to enter military, civil, or clerical service, trade wholesale or retail, paying established taxes for such trade; to acquire all kinds of property such as land, or houses in villages and cities; make all kinds of contracts among themselves, or summon each other for trial;

(8) cancellation of poll tax and arrears;

(9) abolition of monopolies on salt and alcohol; permission for free distillation and for the procuring of salt with payment of tax according to the respective amounts of salt and alcohol produced;

(10) abolition of recruiting and military colonies;

(11) reduction of the term of military service for privates to be followed by equalization of military service of all classes;

(12) retirement without exception of all privates who have served fifteen years;

(13) the creation of Community, County, Gubernia, and Regional administrations, which are to be substituted for all civil service men appointed formerly by the government;

(14) public trials;

(15) introduction of a jury system in criminal and civil courts. There shall be created an administration of two or three persons to which all the highest officers of the government shall be subordinated, such as the Ministry, the Council, the Ministerial Committee, the Army and Navy: in a word, the entire Supreme Executive government, but not the legislative nor judicial. For the latter there remains the Ministry subordinated to the Provisional Government, but for decision of cases not passed upon by the lower courts there will remain a department of the Senate which shall handle civil and criminal cases; its members shall remain in service until a permanent administration is established.

The Provisional Government is instructed to:

(1) equalize all classes;

(2) form all local, Community, County, Gubernia, and Regional administrations;

(3) form a National Guard;

(4) form a judicial branch with a jury;

(5) equalize recruiting obligations among all classes;

(6) abolish a permanent army;

(7) establish a form of election of representatives to the Lower Chamber which will have to ratify the future form of Government.

JOHN STUART MILL

JOHN STUART MILL (1806–73) was one of the most versatile British thinkers of the nineteenth century. He made important contributions to logic, ethics, economics, and politics. During the greater part of his life Mill was employed by the East India Company in a position which afforded him financial security and political experience as well as leisure. In 1865 he was elected to Parliament, and supported the Reform Bill of 1867. Until he failed to be reelected in 1868 he championed a number of the more liberal causes, such as Irish home rule and extension of the suffrage to the working classes and to women.

His father, James Mill, was a central figure among the utilitarians, and he designed an education for his son that was to develop in him a penetrating and logical mind. The education of John Stuart Mill, doctrinaire though it was, made him an incisive critic of liberalism as well as its greatest exponent. Although he waited until after his father's death in 1836 to give a forthright declaration of independence, he early showed signs of defection from the position of Jeremy Bentham, his father's friend.

Mill brought new qualities of imagination and temperament to the utilitarian position. His thought was influenced by the idealistic philosophy imported into England by such men as Coleridge, and he readily adopted for his own use Goethe's criterion of "many-sidedness." Although he remained the outstanding exponent of utilitarianism during the century, he subjected the philosophy of Bentham to penetrating criticism, holding against it its lack of historical perspective, its narrow view of human nature, and its tendency toward an unbridled individualism.

Mill's *Considerations on Representative Government* (1861) derives many of its insights from the earlier work of Alexis de Tocqueville. By 1861 Mill had retreated from his youthful limitless enthusiasm for democracy to the sober assessment of its strengths and weaknesses expressed in the selection printed below. As in his other later political works, Mill constantly oscillates between two poles—his habitual reluctance to admit government to too wide a power over individual activities and his readiness to espouse positive governmental reforms in order to bring about conditions more conducive to the general happiness.

Mill's essay *On Liberty,* published two years earlier than the *Considerations on Representative Government,* is the classic modern defense of civil liberties and cultural freedom. He wrote it with the cooperation of his wife and published it in 1859. Its argument departs from traditional liberal and utilitarian statements in a number of respects. Most important is its emphasis upon the principle of diversity and its consequent consideration of safeguards against the tyranny of the majority, in contrast with the more enthusiastic preoccupation of early "philosophic radicals" with majority rule. Mill's argument in *On Liberty* continues to appeal to the utilitarian "greatest happiness" motto by making freedom of inquiry and of discussion necessary ingredients of human happiness.

The selection reprinted below from Mill's *Considerations on Representative Government* is from the 1865 edition. The text of *On Liberty* is from the original edition of 1859.

భ

CONSIDERATIONS ON REPRESENTATIVE GOVERNMENT

CHAPTER II: THE CRITERION OF A GOOD GOVERNMENT

GOVERNMENT consist of acts done by human beings; and if the agents, or those who choose the agents, or those to whom the agents are responsible, or the lookers-on whose opinion ought to influence and check all these, are mere masses of ignorance, stupidity, and baleful prejudice, every operation of government will go wrong: while, in proportion as the men rise above this standard, so will the government improve in quality; up to the point of excellence, attainable but nowhere attained, where the officers of government, themselves persons of superior virtue and intellect, are surrounded by the atmosphere of a virtuous and enlightened public opinion.

The first element of good government, therefore, being the virtue and intelligence of the human beings composing the community, the most important point of excellence which any form of government can possess is to promote the virtue and intelligence of the people themselves. The first question in respect to any political institutions is, how far they tend to foster in the members of the community the various desirable qualities, moral and intellectual; or rather (following Bentham's more complete classification) moral, intellectual, and active. The government which does this the best, has every likelihood of being the best in all other respects, since it is on these qualities, so far as they exist in the people, that all possibility of goodness in the practical operations of the government depends.

We may consider, then, as one criterion of the goodness of a government, the degree in which it tends to increase the sum of good qualities in the governed, collectively and individually; since, besides that their well-being is the sole object of government, their good qualities supply the moving force which works the machinery. This leaves, as the other constituent element of the merit of a government, the quality of the machinery itself; that is, the degree in which it is adapted to take advantage of the amount of good qualities which may at any time exist, and make them instrumental to the right purposes. Let us again take the subject of judicature as an example and illustration. The judicial system being given, the goodness of the administration of justice is in the compound ratio of the worth of the men composing the tribunals, and the worth of the public opinion which influences or controls them. But all the difference between a good and a bad system of judicature lies in the contrivances adopted for bringing whatever moral and intellectual worth exists in the community to bear upon the administration of justice, and making it duly operative on the result. The arrangements for rendering the choice of the judges such as to obtain the highest average of virtue and intelligence; the salutary forms of procedure; the publicity which allows observation and criticism of whatever is amiss; the liberty of discussion and censure through the press; the mode of taking evidence, according as it is well or ill adapted to elicit truth; the facilities, whatever be their amount, for obtaining access to the tribunals; the arrangements for detecting crimes and apprehending offenders;—all these things are not the power, but the machinery for bringing the power into contact with the obstacle: and the machinery has no action of itself, but without it the power, let it be ever so ample, would be wasted and of no effect. A similar distinction exists in regard to the constitution of the executive departments of administration. Their machinery is good, when the proper tests are prescribed for the qualifications of officers, the proper rules for their promotion; when the business is conveniently distributed among those who are to transact it, a convenient and methodical order established for its transaction, a correct and intelligible record kept of it after being transacted; when each individual knows for what he is responsible, and is known to others as responsible for it; when the best-contrived checks are provided against negligence, favouritism, or jobbery, in any of the acts of the department. But political checks will not more act of themselves, than a bridle will direct a horse without a rider. If the checking functionaries are as corrupt or as negligent as those whom they ought to check and if the public, the mainspring of the whole checking machinery, are too ignorant, too passive, or too careless and inattentive, to do their part, little benefit will be derived from the best administrative apparatus. Yet a good apparatus is always preferable to a bad. It enables such insufficient moving or checking power as exists, to act at the greatest advantage; and without it, no amount of moving or checking power would be sufficient. Publicity, for instance, is no impediment to evil nor stimulus to good if the public will not look at what is done; but without publicity, how could they either check or encourage what they were not permitted to see? The ideally perfect constitution of a public office is that in which the interest of the functionary is entirely coincident with his duty. No mere system will make it so, but still less can it be made so without a system, aptly devised for the purpose. . . .

CHAPTER III: THAT THE REALLY BEST FORM OF GOVERNMENT IS REPRESENTATIVE GOVERNMENT

There is no difficulty in showing that the ideally best form of government is that in which the sovereignty, or supreme controlling power in the last resort, is vested in the entire aggregate of the community; every citizen not only having a voice in the exercise of that ultimate sovereignty, but being, at least occasionally, called on to take an actual part in the government, by the personal discharge of some public function, local or general.

To test this proposition, it has to be examined in reference to the two branches into which, as pointed out in the last chapter, the inquiry into the goodness of a government conveniently divides itself, namely, how far it promotes the good management of the affairs of society by means of the existing faculties, moral, intellectual, and active, of its various members, and what is its effect in improving or deteriorating those faculties.

The ideally best form of government, it is scarcely necessary to say, does not mean one which is practicable or eligible in all states of civilization, but the one which, in the circumstances in which it is practicable and eligible, is attended with the greatest amount of beneficial consequences, immediate and prospective. A completely popular government is the only polity which can make out any claim to this character. It is pre-eminent in both the departments between which the excellence of a political constitution is divided. It is both more favourable to present good government, and promotes a better and higher form of national character, than any other polity whatsoever.

Its superiority in reference to present well-being rests upon two principles, of as universal truth and applicability as any general propositions which can be laid down respecting human affairs. The first is, that the rights and interests of every or any person are only secure from being disregarded, when the person interested is himself able, and habitually disposed, to stand up for them. The second is, that the general prosperity attains a greater height, and is more widely diffused, in proportion to the amount and variety of the personal energies enlisted in promoting it. . . .

From these accumulated considerations it is evident, that the only government which can fully satisfy all the exigencies of the social state, is one in which the whole people participate; that any participation, even in the smallest public function, is useful; that the participation should everywhere be as great as the general degree of improvement of the community will allow; and that nothing less can be ultimately desirable, than the admission of all to a share in the sovereign power of the state. But since all cannot, in a community exceeding a single small town, participate personally in any but some very minor portions of the public business, it follows that the ideal type of a perfect government must be representative.

CHAPTER V: OF THE PROPER FUNCTIONS OF REPRESENTATIVE BODIES

Instead of the function of governing, for which it is radically unfit, the proper office of a representative assembly is to watch and control the government: to throw the light of publicity on its acts: to compel a full exposition and justification of all of them which any one considers questionable; to censure them if found condemnable, and, if the men who compose the government abuse their trust, or fulfil it in a manner which conflicts with the deliberate sense of the nation, to expel them from office, and either expressly or virtually appoint their successors. This is surely ample power, and security enough for the liberty of the nation. In addition to this, the Parliament has an office, not inferior even to this in importance; (to be at once the nation's Committee of Grievances, and its Congress of Opinions; an arena in which not only the general opinion of the nation, but that of every section of it, and as far as possible of every eminent individual whom it contains, can produce itself in full light and challenge discussion); where every person in the country may count upon finding somebody who speaks his mind, as well or better than he could speak it himself—not to friends and partisans exclusively, but in the face of opponents, to be tested by adverse controversy; where those whose opinion is overruled, feel satisfied that it is heard, and set aside not by a mere act of will, but for what are thought superior reasons, and commend themselves as such to the representatives of the majority of the nation; where every party or opinion in the country can muster its strength, and be cured of any illusion concerning the number or power of its adherents; where the opinion which prevails in the nation makes itself manifest as prevailing, and marshals its hosts in the presence of the government, which is thus enabled and compelled to give way to it on the mere manifestation, without the actual employment, of its strength; where statesmen can assure themselves, far more certainly than by any other signs, what elements of opinion and power are growing, and what declining, and are enabled to shape their measures with some regard not solely to present exigencies, but to tendencies in progress. Representative assemblies are often taunted by their enemies with being places of mere talk and *bavardage*. There has seldom been more misplaced derision. I know not how a representative assembly can more usefully employ itself than in talk, when the subject of talk is the great public interests of the country, and every sentence of it represents the opinion either of some important body of persons in the nation, or of an individual in whom some such body have reposed their confidence. A place where every interest and shade of opinion in the country can have its cause even passionately pleaded, in the face of the government and of all other interests and opinions, can compel them to listen, and either comply, or state clearly why they do not, is in itself, if it answered no other purpose, one of the most important political institutions that can exist anywhere, and one of the foremost benefits of free government. Such "talking" would never be looked upon with disparagement if it were not allowed to stop "doing"; which it never would, if assemblies knew and acknowledged that talking and discussion are their proper business, while *doing,* as the result of discussion, is the task not of a miscellaneous body, but of individuals specially trained to it; that the fit office of an assembly is to see that those individuals are honestly and intelligently chosen, and to interfere no further with them, except by unlimited latitude of suggestion and criticism, and by applying or withholding the final seal of national assent. It is for want of this judicious reserve, that popular assemblies attempt to do what they cannot do well—to govern and legislate—and provide no machinery but their own for much of it, when of course every hour spent in talk is an hour withdrawn from actual business. But the very fact which most unfits such bodies for a Council of Legislation, qualifies them the more for their other office—namely, that they are not a selection of the greatest political minds in the country, from whose opinions little could with certainty be inferred concerning those of the nation, but are, when properly constituted, a fair sample of every grade of intellect among the people which is at all entitled to a voice in public affairs. Their part is to indicate wants, to be an organ for popular demands, and a place of adverse discussion for all opinions relating to public matters, both great and small; and, along with this, to check by criticism, and eventually by withdrawing their support, those high public officers who really conduct the public business, or who appoint those by whom it is conducted. Nothing but the restriction of the function of representative bodies within these rational limits, will enable the benefits of popular control to be enjoyed in conjunction with the no less important requisites (growing ever more important as human affairs increase in scale and in complexity) of skilled legislation and administration. There are no means of combining these benefits, except by separating the functions which guarantee the one from those which essentially require the other; by disjoining the office of control and criticism from the actual conduct of affairs, and devolving the former on the representatives of the Many, while securing for the latter, under strict responsibility to the nation, the acquired knowledge and practised intelligence of a specially trained and experienced Few.

CHAPTER VI: OF THE INFIRMITIES AND DANGERS TO WHICH
REPRESENTATIVE GOVERNMENT IS LIABLE

The defects of any form of government may be either negative or positive. It is negatively defective if it does not concentrate in the hands of the authorities, power sufficient to fulfil the necessary offices of a government; or if it does not sufficiently develope by exercise the active capacities and social feelings of the individual citizens.

The *positive* evils and dangers of the representative, as of every other form of government, may be reduced to two heads: first, general ignorance and incapacity, or, to speak more moderately, insufficient mental qualifications, in the controlling body; secondly, the danger of its being under the influence of interests not identical with the general welfare of the community. . . .

One of the greatest dangers, therefore, of democracy, as of all other forms of government, lies in the sinister interest of the holders of power: it is the danger of class legislation; of government intended for (whether really effecting it or not) the immediate benefit of the dominant class, to the lasting detriment of the whole. And one of the most important questions demanding consideration, in determining the best constitution of a representative government, is how to provide efficacious securities against this evil.

If we consider as a class, politically speaking, any number of persons who have the same sinister interest,—that is, whose direct and apparent interest points towards the same description of bad measures; the desirable object would be that no class, and no combination of classes likely to combine, should be able to exercise a preponderant influence in the government. A modern community, not divided within itself by strong antipathies of race, language, or nationality, may be considered as in the main divisible into two sections, which, in spite of partial variations, correspond on the whole with two divergent directions of apparent interest. Let us call them (in brief general terms) labourers on the one hand, employers of labour on the other: including however along with employers of labour, not only retired capitalists, and the possessors of inherited wealth, but all that highly paid description of labourers (such as the professions) whose education and way of life assimilate them with the rich, and whose prospect and ambition it is to raise themselves into that class. With the labourers, on the other hand, may be ranked those smaller employers of labour, who by interests, habits, and educational impressions, are assimilated in wishes, tastes, and objects to the labouring classes; comprehending a large proportion of petty tradesmen. In a state of society thus composed, if the representative system could be made ideally perfect, and if it were possible to maintain it in that state, its organization must be such, that these two classes, manual labourers and their affinities on one side, employers of labour and their affinities on the other, should be, in the arrangement of the representative system, equally balanced, each influencing about an equal number of votes in Parliament: since, assuming that the majority of each class, in any difference between them, would be mainly governed by their class interests, there would be a minority of each in whom that consideration would be subordinate to reason, justice, and the good of the whole; and this minority of either, joining with the whole of the other, would turn the scale against any demands of their own majority which were not such as ought to prevail. The reason why, in any tolerably constituted society, justice and the general interest mostly in the end carry their point, is that the separate and selfish interests of mankind are almost always divided; some are interested in what is wrong, but some, also, have their private interest on the side of what is right: and those who are governed by higher considerations, though too few and weak to prevail against the whole of the others, usually after sufficient discussion and agitation become strong enough to turn the balance in favour of the body of private interests which is on the same side with them. The representative system ought to be so constituted as to maintain this state of things: it ought not to allow any of the various sectional interests to be so powerful as to be capable of prevailing against truth and justice and the other sectional interests combined. There ought always to be such a balance preserved among personal interests, as may render any one of them dependent for its successes, on carrying with it at least a large proportion of those who act on higher motives, and more comprehensive and distant views.

CHAPTER VII: OF TRUE AND FALSE DEMOCRACY; REPRESENTATION OF ALL, AND REPRESENTATION OF THE MAJORITY ONLY

It has been seen, that the dangers incident to a representative democracy are of two kinds: *danger of a low grade of intelligence in the representative body, and in the popular opinion which controls it; and danger of class legislation on the part of the numerical majority,* these being all composed of the same class. We have next to consider, how far it is possible so to organize the democracy, as, without interfering materially with the characteristic benefits of democratic government, to do away with these two great evils, or at least to abate them, in the utmost degree attainable by human contrivance.

The common mode of attempting this is by limiting the democratic character of the representation, through a more or less restricted suffrage. But there is a previous consideration which, duly kept in view, considerably modifies the circumstances which are supposed to render such a restriction necessary.

A completely equal democracy, in a nation in which a single class composes the numerical majority, cannot be divested of certain evils; but those evils are greatly aggravated by the fact, that the democracies which at present exist are not equal, but systematically unequal in favour of the predominant class. Two very different ideas are usually confounded under the name democracy. The pure idea of democracy, according to its definition, is the government of the whole people by the whole people, equally represented. Democracy as commonly conceived and hitherto practised, is the government of the whole people by a mere majority of the people, exclusively represented. The former is synonymous with the equality of all citizens; the latter, strangely confounded with it, is a government of privilege, in favor of the numerical majority, who alone possess practically any voice in the State. This is the inevitable consequence of the manner in which the votes are now taken, to the complete disfranchisement of minorities.

The confusion of ideas here is great, but it is so easily cleared up, that one would suppose the slightest indication would be sufficient to place the matter in its true light before any mind of average intelligence. It would be so, but for the power of habit; owing to which the simplest idea, if unfamiliar, has as great difficulty in making its way to the mind as a far more complicated one. That the minority must yield to the majority, the smaller number to the greater, is a familiar idea; and accordingly men think there is no necessity for using their minds any further, and it does not occur to them that there is any medium between allowing the smaller number to be equally powerful with the greater, and blotting out the smaller number altogether. In a representative body actually deliberating, the minority must of course be overruled; and in an equal democracy (since the opinions of the constituents, when they insist on them, determine those of the representative body) the majority of the people, through their representatives, will outvote and prevail over the minority and their representatives. But does it follow that the minority should have no representatives at all? Because the majority ought to prevail over the minority, must the majority have all the votes, the minority none? Is it necessary that the minority should not even be heard? Nothing but habit and old association can reconcile any reasonable being to the needless injustice. In a really equal democracy, every or any section would be represented, not disproportionately, but proportionately. A majority of the electors would always have a majority of the representatives; but a minority of the electors would always have a minority of the representatives. Man for man, they would be as fully represented as the majority. Unless they are, there is not equal government, but a government of inequality and privilege: one part of the people rule over the rest: there is a part whose fair and equal share of influence in the representation is withheld from them; contrary to all just government, but above all, contrary to the principle of democracy, which professes equality as its very root and foundation.

The injustice and violation of principle are not less flagrant because those who suffer by them are a minority; for there is not equal suffrage where every single individual does not count for as much as any other single individual in the community. But it is not only a minority who suffer. Democracy, thus constituted, does not even attain its ostensible object, that of giving the powers of government in all cases to the numerical majority. It does something very different: it gives them to a majority of the majority; who may be, and often are, but a minority of the whole. All principles are most effectually tested by extreme cases. Suppose then, that, in a country governed by equal and universal suffrage, there is a contested election in every constituency, and every election is carried by a small majority. The Parliament thus brought together represents little more than a bare majority of the people. This Parliament proceeds to legislate, and adopts important measures by a bare majority of itself. What guarantee is there that these measures accord with the wishes of a majority of the people? Nearly half the electors, having been outvoted at the hustings, have had no influence at all in the decision; and the whole of these may be, a majority of them probably are, hostile to the measures, having voted against those by whom they have been carried. Of the remaining electors, nearly half have chosen representatives who, by supposition, have voted against the measures. It is possible, therefore, and not at all improbable, that the opinion which has prevailed was agreeable only to a minority of the nation, though a majority of that portion of it, whom the institutions of the country have erected into a ruling class. If democracy means the certain ascendancy of the majority, there are no means of insuring that, but by allowing every individual figure to tell equally in the summing up. Any minority left out, either purposely or by the play of the machinery, gives the power not to the majority, but to a minority in some other part of the scale.

CHAPTER VIII: OF THE EXTENSION OF THE SUFFRAGE

No arrangement of the suffrage, therefore, can be permanently satisfactory, in which any person or class is peremptorily excluded; in which the electoral privilege is not open to all persons of full age who desire to obtain it.

There are, however, certain exclusions, required by positive reasons, which do not conflict with this principle, and which, though an evil in themselves, are only to be got rid of by the cessation of the state of things which requires them. I regard it as wholly inadmissible that any person should participate in the suffrage, without being able to read, write, and, I will add, perform the common operations of arithmetic. Justice demands, even when the suffrage does not depend on it, that the means of attaining these elementary acquirements should be within the reach of every person, either gratuitously, or at an expense not exceeding what the poorest, who earn their own living, can afford. If this were really the case, people would no more think of giving the suffrage to a man who could not read, than of giving it to a child who could not speak; and it would not be society that would exclude him, but his own laziness. When society has not performed its duty, by rendering this amount of instruction accessible to all, there is some hardship in the case, but it is a hardship that ought to be borne. If society has neglected to discharge two solemn obligations, the more important and more fundamental of the two must be fulfilled first: universal teaching must precede universal enfranchisement. No one but those in whom an *a priori* theory has silenced common sense, will maintain, that power over others, over the whole community, should be imparted to people who have not acquired the commonest and most essential requisites for taking care of themselves; for pursuing intelligently their own interests, and those of the persons most nearly allied to them. This argument, doubtless, might be pressed further, and made to prove much more. It would be eminently desirable that other things besides reading, writing, and arithmetic, could be made necessary to the suffrage; that some knowledge of the conformation of the earth, its natural and political divisions, the elements of general history, and of the history and institutions of their own country, could be required from all electors. But these kinds of knowledge, however indispensable to an intelligent use of the suffrage, are not, in this country, nor probably anywhere save in the Northern United States, accessible to the whole people; nor does there exist any trustworthy machinery for ascertaining whether they have been acquired or not. The attempt, at present, would lead to partiality, chicanery, and every kind of fraud. It is better that the suffrage should be conferred indiscriminately, or even withheld indiscriminately, than that it should be given to one and withheld from another at the discretion of a public officer. In regard, however, to reading, writing, and calculating, there need be no difficulty. It would be easy to require from every one who presented himself for registry, that he should, in the presence of the registrar, copy a sentence from an English book, and perform a sum in the rule of three; and to secure, by fixed rules and complete publicity, the honest application of so very simple a test. This condition, therefore, should in all cases accompany universal suffrage; and it would, after a few years, exclude none but those who cared so little for the privilege, that their vote, if given, would not in general be an indication of any real political opinion.

It is also important, that the assembly which votes the taxes, either general or local, should be elected exclusively by those who pay something towards the taxes imposed. Those who pay no taxes, disposing by their votes of other people's money, have every motive to be lavish, and none to economize. As far as money matters are concerned, any power of voting possessed by them is a violation of the fundamental principle of free government; a severance of the power of control, from the interest in its beneficial exercise. It amounts to allowing them to put their hands into other people's pockets, for any purpose which they think fit to call a public one; which in some of the great towns of the United States is known to have produced a scale of local taxation onerous beyond example, and wholly borne by the wealthier classes. That representation should be co-extensive with taxation, not stopping short of it, but also not going beyond it, is in accordance with the theory of British institutions. But to reconcile this, as a condition annexed to the representation, with universality, it is essential, as it is on many other accounts desirable, that taxation, in a visible shape, should descend to the poorest class. In this country, and in most others, there is probably no labouring family which does not contribute to the indirect taxes, by the purchase of tea, coffee, sugar, not to mention narcotics or stimulants. But this mode of defraying a share of the public expenses is hardly felt: the payer, unless a person of education and reflection, does not identify his interest with a low scale of public expenditure, as closely as when money for its support is demanded directly from himself; and even supposing him to do so, he would doubtless take care that, however lavish an expenditure he might, by his vote, assist in imposing upon the government, it should not be defrayed by any additional taxes on the articles which he himself consumes. It would be better that a direct tax, in the simple form of a capitation, should be levied on every grown person in the community; or that every such person should be admitted an elector, on allowing himself to be rated *extra ordinem* to the assessed taxes; or that a small annual payment, rising and falling with the gross expenditure of the country, should be required from every registered elector; that so every one might feel that the money which he assisted in voting was partly his own, and that he was interested in keeping down its amount.

However this may be, I regard it as required by first principles, that the receipt of parish relief should be a peremptory disqualification for the franchise. He who cannot by his labour suffice for his own support, has no claim to the privilege of helping himself to the money of others. By becoming dependent on the remaining members of the community for actual subsistence, he abdicates his claim to equal rights with them in other respects. Those to whom he is indebted for the continuance of his very existence, may justly claim the exclusive management of those common concerns, to which he now brings nothing, or less than he takes away. As a condition of the franchise, a term should be fixed, say five years previous to the registry, during which the applicant's name has not been on the parish books as a recipient of relief. To be an uncertified bankrupt, or to have taken the benefit of the Insolvent Act, should disqualify for the franchise until the person has paid his debts, or at least proved that he is not now, and has not for some long period been, dependent on eleemosynary support. Non-payment of taxes, when so long persisted in that it cannot have arisen from inadvertence, should disqualify while it lasts. These exclusions are not in their nature permanent. They exact such conditions only as all are able, or ought to be able, to fulfil if they choose. They leave the suffrage accessible to all who are in the normal condition of a human being: and if any one has to forego it, he either does not care sufficiently for it, to do for its sake what he is already bound to do, or he is in a general condition of depression and degradation in which this slight addition, necessary for the security of others, would be unfelt, and on emerging from which, this mark of inferiority would disappear with the rest.

In the long run, therefore (supposing no restrictions to exist but those of which we have now treated), we might expect that all, except that (it is to be hoped) progressively diminishing class, the recipients of parish relief, would be in possession of votes, so that the suffrage would be, with that slight abatement, universal. That it should be thus widely expanded, is, as we have seen, absolutely necessary to an enlarged and elevated conception of good government. Yet in this state of things, the great majority of voters, in most countries, and emphatically in this, would be manual labourers; and the twofold danger, that of too low a standard of political intelligence, and that of class legislation, would still exist, in a very perilous degree. It remains to be seen whether any means exist by which these evils can be obviated.

They are capable of being obviated, if men sincerely wish it; not by any artificial contrivance, but by carrying out the natural order of human life, which recommends itself to every one in things in which he has no interest or traditional opinion running counter to it. In all human affairs, every person directly interested, and not under positive tutelage, has an admitted claim to a voice, and when his exercise of it is not inconsistent with the safety of the whole, cannot justly be excluded from it. But though every one ought to have a voice—that every one should have an equal voice is a totally different proposition. When two persons who have a joint interest in any business, differ in opinion, does justice require that both opinions should be held of exactly equal value? If with equal virtue, one is superior to the other in knowledge and intelligence—or if with equal intelligence, one excels the other in virtue—the opinion, the judgment, of the higher moral or intellectual being, is worth more than that of the inferior: and if the institutions of the country virtually assert that they are of the same value, they assert a thing which is not. One of the two, as the wiser or better man, has a claim to superior weight: the difficulty is in ascertaining which of the two it is; a thing impossible as between individuals, but, taking men in bodies and in numbers, it can be done with a certain approach to accuracy. There would be no pretence for applying this doctrine to any case which could with reason be considered as one of individual and private right. In an affair which concerns only one of two persons, that one is entitled to follow his own opinion, however much wiser the other may be than himself. But we are speaking of things which equally concern them both; where, if the more ignorant does not yield his share of the matter to the guidance of the wiser man, the wiser man must resign his to that of the more ignorant. Which of these modes of getting over the difficulty is most for the interest of both, and most conformable to the general fitness of things? If it be deemed unjust that either should have to give way, which injustice is greatest? that the better judgment should give way to the worse, or the worse to the better?

Now, national affairs are exactly such a joint concern, with the difference, that no one needs ever be called upon for a complete sacrifice of his own opinion. It can always be taken into the calculation, and counted at a certain figure, a higher figure being assigned to the suffrages of those whose opinion is entitled to greater weight. There is not, in this arrangement, anything necessarily invidious to those to whom it assigns the lower degrees of influence. Entire exclusion from a voice in the common concerns, is one thing: the concession to others of a more potential voice, on the ground of greater capacity for the management of the joint interests, is another. The two things are not merely different, they are incommensurable. Every one has a right to feel insulted by being made a nobody, and stamped as of no account at all. No one but a fool, and only a fool of a peculiar description, feels offended by the acknowledgement that there are others whose opinion, and even whose wish, is entitled to a greater amount of consideration than his. To have no voice in what are partly his own concerns, is a thing which nobody willingly submits to; but when what is partly his concern is also partly another's, and he feels the other to understand the subject better than himself, that the other's opinion should be counted for more than his own, accords with his expectations, and with the course of things which in all other affairs of life he is accustomed to acquiesce in. It is only necessary that this superior influence should be assigned on grounds which he can comprehend, and of which he is able to perceive the justice.

I hasten to say, that I consider it entirely inadmissible, unless as a temporary makeshift, that the superiority of influence should be conferred in consideration of property. I do not deny that property is a kind of test; education in most countries, though anything but proportional to riches, is on the average better in the richer half of society than in the poorer. But the criterion is so imperfect; accident has so much more to do than merit with enabling men to rise in the world; and it is so impossible for any one, by acquiring any amount of instruction, to make sure of the corresponding rise in station, that this foundation of electoral privilege is always, and will continue to be, supremely odious. To connect plurality of votes with any pecuniary qualification would be not only objectionable in itself, but a sure mode of discrediting the principle, and making its permanent maintenance impracticable. The Democracy, at least of this country, are not at present jealous of personal superiority, but they are naturally and most justly so of that which is grounded on mere pecuniary circumstances. The only thing which can justify reckoning one person's opinion as equivalent to more than one, is individual mental superiority; and what is wanted is some approximate means of ascertaining that. If there existed such a thing as a really national education, or a trustworthy system of general examination, education might be tested directly. In the absence of these, the nature of a person's occupation is some test. An employer of labour is on the average more intelligent than a labourer; for he must labour with his head, and not solely with his hands. A foreman is generally more intelligent than an ordinary labourer, and a labourer in the skilled trades than in the unskilled. A banker, merchant, or manufacturer, is likely to be more intelligent than a tradesman, because he has larger and more complicated interests to manage. In all these cases it is not the having merely undertaken the superior function, but the successful performance of it, that tests the qualifications; for which reason, as well as to prevent persons from engaging nominally in an occupation for the sake of the vote, it would be proper to require that the occupation should have been persevered in for some length of time (say three years). Subject to some such condition, two or more votes might be allowed to every person who exercises any of these superior functions. The liberal professions, when really and not nominally practised, imply, of course, a still higher degree of instruction; and wherever a sufficient examination, or any serious conditions of education, are required before entering on a profession, its members could be admitted at once to a plurality of votes. The same rule might be applied to graduates of universities; and even to those who bring satisfactory certificates of having passed through the course of study required by any school at which the higher branches of knowledge are taught, under proper securities that the teaching is real, and not a mere pretence.

CHAPTER XIV: OF THE EXECUTIVE IN A REPRESENTATIVE GOVERNMENT

As a general rule, every executive function, whether superior or subordinate, should be the appointed duty of some given individual. It should be apparent to all the world, who did everything, and through whose default anything was left undone. Responsibility is null, when nobody knows who is responsible. Nor, even when real, can it be divided without being weakened. To maintain it at its highest, there must be one person who receives the whole praise of what is well done, the whole blame of what is ill. There are, however, two modes of sharing responsibility: by one it is only enfeebled, by the other, absolutely destroyed. It is enfeebled, when the concurrence of more than one functionary is required to the same act. Each one among them has still a real responsibility; if a wrong has been done, none of them can say he did not do it; he is as much a participant, as an accomplice is in an offence: if there has been legal criminality they may all be punished legally, and their punishment needs not be less severe than if there had been only one person concerned. But it is not so with the penalties, any more than with the rewards, of opinion: these are always diminished by being shared. Where there has been no definite legal offence, no corruption or malversation, only an error or an imprudence, or what may pass for such, every participator has an excuse to himself and to the world, in the fact that other persons are jointly involved with him. There is hardly anything, even to pecuniary dishonesty, for which men will not feel themselves almost absolved, if those whose duty it was to resist and remonstrate have failed to do it, still more if they have given a formal assent.

In this case, however, though responsibility is weakened, there still is responsibility: every one of those implicated has in his individual capacity assented to, and joined in, the act. Things are much worse when the act itself is only that of a majority—a Board, deliberating with closed doors, nobody knowing, or, except in some extreme case, being ever likely to know, whether an individual member voted for the act or against it. Responsibility in this case is a mere name. "Boards," it is happily said by Bentham, "are screens." What "the Board" does is the act of nobody; and nobody can be made to answer for it. The Board suffers, even in reputation, only in its collective character; and no individual member feels this, further than his disposition leads him to identify his own estimation with that of the body—a feeling often very strong when the body is a permanent one, and he is wedded to it for better, for worse; but the fluctuations of a modern official career give no time for the formation of such an *esprit de corps;* which, if it exists at all, exists only in the obscure ranks of the permanent subordinates. Boards, therefore, are not a fit instrument for executive business; and are only admissible in it, when, for other reasons, to give full discretionary power to a single minister would be worse.

On the other hand, it is also a maxim of experience, that in the multitude of counsellors there is wisdom; and that a man seldom judges right, even in his own concerns, still less in those of the public, when he makes habitual use of no knowledge but his own, or that of some single adviser. There is no necessary incompatibility between this principle and the other. It is easy to give the effective power, and the full responsibility, to one, providing him when necessary with advisers, each of whom is responsible only for the opinion he gives.

In general, the head of a department of the executive government is a mere politician. He may be a good politician, and a man of merit; and unless this is usually the case, the government is bad. But his general capacity, and the knowledge he ought to possess of the general interests of the country, will not, unless by occasional accident, be accompanied by adequate, and what may be called professional, knowledge of the department over which he is called to preside. Professional advisers must therefore be provided for him. Wherever mere experience and attainments are sufficient—wherever the qualities required in a professional adviser may possibly be united in a single well-selected individual (as in the case, for example, of a law officer), one such person for general purposes, and a staff of clerks to supply knowledge of details, meet the demands of the case. But, more frequently, it is not sufficient that the minister should consult some one competent person, and, when himself not conversant with the subject, act implicitly on that person's advice. It is often necessary that he should, not only occasionally but habitually, listen to a variety of opinions, and inform his judgment by the discussions among a body of advisers. This, for example, is emphatically necessary in military and naval affairs. The military and naval ministers, therefore, and probably several others, should be provided with a Council, composed, at least in those two departments, of able and experienced professional men. As a means of obtaining the best men for the purpose under every change of administration, they ought to be permanent: by which I mean, that they ought not, like the Lords of the Admiralty, to be expected to resign with the ministry by whom they were appointed: but it is a good rule that all who hold high appointments to which they have risen by selection, and not by the ordinary course of promotion, should retain their office only for a fixed term, unless reappointed; as is now the rule with Staff appointments in the British army. This rule renders appointments somewhat less likely to be jobbed, not being a provision for life, and at the same time affords a means, without affront to any one, of getting rid of those who are least worth keeping, and bringing in highly qualified persons of younger standing, for whom there might never be room if death vacancies, or voluntary resignations, were waited for.

The Councils should be consultative merely, in this sense, that the ultimate decision should rest undividedly with the minister himself: but neither ought they to be looked upon, or to look upon themselves, as ciphers, or as capable of being reduced to such at his pleasure. The advisers attached to a powerful and perhaps self-willed man, ought to be placed under conditions which make it impossible for them, without discredit, not to express an opinion, and impossible for him not to listen to and consider their recommendations, whether he adopts them or not. The relation which ought to exist between a chief and this description of advisers is very accurately hit by the constitution of the Council of the Governor-General and those of the different Presidencies in India. These Councils are composed of persons who have professional knowledge of Indian affairs, which the Governor-General and Governors usually lack, and which it would not be desirable to require of them. As a rule, every member of Council is expected to give an opinion, which is of course very often a simple acquiescence: but if there is a difference of sentiment, it is at the option of every member, and is the invariable practice, to record the reasons of his opinion: the Governor-General, or Governor, doing the same. In ordinary cases the decision is according to the sense of the majority; the Council, therefore, has a substantial part in the government: but if the Governor-General, or Governor, thinks fit, he may set aside even their unanimous opinion, recording his reasons. The result is, that the chief is individually and effectively responsible for every act of the Government. The members of Council have only the responsibility of advisers; but it is always known, from documents capable of being produced, and which if called for by Parliament or public opinion always are produced, what each has advised, and what reasons he gave for his advice: while, from their dignified position, and ostensible participation in all acts of government, they have nearly as strong motives to apply themselves to the public business, and to form and express a well-considered opinion on every part of it, as if the whole responsibility rested with themselves.

This mode of conducting the highest class of administrative business is one of the most successful instances of the adaptation of means to ends, which political history, not hitherto very prolific in works of skill and contrivance, has yet to show. It is one of the acquisitions with which the art of politics has been enriched by the experience of the East India Company's rule; and, like most of the other wise contrivances by which India has been preserved to this country, and an amount of good government produced which is truly wonderful considering the circumstances and the materials, it is probably destined to perish in the general holocaust which the traditions of Indian government seem fated to undergo, since they have been placed at the mercy of public ignorance, and the presumptuous vanity of political men. Already an outcry is raised for abolishing the Councils, as a superfluous and expensive clog on the wheels of government: while the clamour has long been urgent, and is daily obtaining more countenance in the highest quarters, for the abrogation of the professional civil service, which breeds the men that compose the Councils, and the existence of which is the sole guarantee for their being of any value.

A most important principle of good government in a popular constitution, is that no executive functionaries should be appointed by popular election: neither by the votes of the people themselves, nor by those of their representatives. The entire business of government is skilled employment; the qualifications for the discharge of it are of that special and professional kind, which cannot be properly judged of except by persons who have themselves some share of those qualifications, or some practical experience of them. The business of finding the fittest persons to fill public employments—not merely selecting the best who offer, but looking out for the absolutely best, and taking note of all fit persons who are met with, that they may be found when wanted—is very laborious, and requires a delicate as well as highly conscientious discernment; and as there is no public duty which is in general so badly performed, so there is none for which it is of greater importance to enforce the utmost practicable amount of personal responsibility, by imposing it as a special obligation on high functionaries in the several departments. All subordinate public officers who are not appointed by some mode of public competition, should be selected on the direct responsibility of the minister under whom they serve. The ministers, all but the chief, will naturally be selected by the chief; and the chief himself, though really designated by Parliament, should be, in a regal government, officially appointed by the Crown. The functionary who appoints should be the sole person empowered to remove any subordinate officer who is liable to removal; which the far greater number ought not to be, except for personal misconduct; since it would be vain to expect that the body of persons by whom the whole detail of the public business is transacted, and whose qualifications are generally of much more importance to the public than those of the minister himself, will devote themselves to their profession, and acquire the knowledge and skill on which the minister must often place entire dependence, if they are liable at any moment to be turned adrift for no fault, that the minister may gratify himself, or promote his political interest, by appointing somebody else.

To the principle which condemns the appointment of executive officers by popular suffrage, ought the chief of the executive, in a republican government, to be an exception? Is it a good rule, which, in the American constitution, provides for the election of the President once in every four years by the entire people? The question is not free from difficulty. There is unquestionably some advantage, in a country like America, where no apprehension needs be entertained of a *coup d'état,* in making the chief minister constitutionally independent of the legislative body, and rendering the two great branches of the government, while equally popular both in their origin and in their responsibility, an effective check on one another. The plan is in accordance with that sedulous avoidance of the concentration of great masses of power in the same hands, which is a marked characteristic of the American Federal Constitution. But the advantage, in this instance, is purchased at a price above all reasonable estimate of its value. It seems far better that the chief magistrate in a republic should be appointed avowedly, as the chief minister in a constitutional monarchy is virtually, by the representative body. In the first place, he is certain, when thus appointed, to be a more eminent man. The party which has the majority in Parliament would then, as a rule, appoint its own leader; who is always one of the foremost, and often the very foremost person in political life: while the President of the United States, since the last survivor of the founders of the republic disappeared from the scene, is almost always either an obscure man, or one who has gained any reputation he may possess in some other field than politics. And this, as I have before observed, is no accident, but the natural effect of the situation. The eminent men of a party, in an election extending to the whole country, are never its most available candidates. All eminent men have made personal enemies, or have done something, or at the lowest professed some opinion, obnoxious to some local or other considerable division of the community, and likely to tell with fatal effect upon the number of votes; whereas a man without antecedents, of whom nothing is known but that he professes the creed of the party, is readily voted for by its entire strength. Another important consideration is the great mischief of unintermitted electioneering. When the highest dignity in the State is to be conferred by popular election once in every few years, the whole intervening time is spent in what is virtually a canvass. President, ministers, chiefs of parties, and their followers, are all electioneerers: the whole community is kept intent on the mere personalities of politics, and every public question is discussed and decided with less reference to its merits than to its expected bearing on the presidential election. If a system had been devised to make party spirit the ruling principle of action in all public affairs, and create an inducement not only to make every question a party question, but to raise questions for the purpose of founding parties upon them, it would have been difficult to contrive any means better adapted to the purpose.

ON LIBERTY

CHAPTER I: INTRODUCTORY

... THE OBJECT of this Essay is to assert one very simple principle, as entitled to govern absolutely the dealings of society with the individual in the way of compulsion and control, whether the means used be physical force in the form of legal penalties, or the moral coercion of public opinion. That principle is, that the sole end for which mankind are warranted, individually or collectively, in interfering with the liberty of action of any of their number, is self-protection. That the only purpose for which power can be rightfully exercised over any member of a civilized community, against his will, is to prevent harm to others. His own good, either physical or moral, is not a sufficient warrant. He cannot rightfully be compelled to do or forbear because it will be better for him to do so, because it will make him happier, because, in the opinions of others, to do so would be wise, or even right. These are good reasons for remonstrating with him, or reasoning with him, or persuading him, or entreating him, but not for compelling him, or visiting him with any evil in case he do otherwise. To justify that, the conduct from which it is desired to deter him, must be calculated to produce evil to some one else. The only part of the conduct of any one, for which he is amenable to society, is that which concerns others. In the part which merely concerns himself, his independence is, of right, absolute. Over himself, over his own body and mind, the individual is sovereign.

... We may leave out of consideration those backward states of society in which the race itself may be considered as in its nonage. The early difficulties in the way of spontaneous progress are so great, that there is seldom any choice of means for overcoming them; and a ruler full of the spirit of improvement is warranted in the use of any expedients that will attain an end, perhaps otherwise unattainable. Despotism is a legitimate mode of government in dealing with barbarians, provided the end be their improvement, and the means justified by actually effecting that end. Liberty, as a principle, has no application to any state of things anterior to the time when mankind have become capable of being improved by free and equal discussion. Until then, there is nothing for them but implicit obedience to an Akbar or a Charlemagne, if they are so fortunate as to find one. But as soon as mankind have attained the capacity of being guided to their own improvement by conviction or persuasion ..., compulsion, either in the direct form or in that of pains and penalties for non-compliance, is no longer admissible as a means to their own good, and justifiable only for the security of others.

It is proper to state that I forgo any advantage which could be derived to my argument from the idea of abstract right, as a thing independent of utility. I regard utility as the ultimate appeal on all ethical questions; but it must be utility in the larger sense, grounded on the permanent interests of man as a progressive being. Those interests, I contend, authorize the subjection of individual spontaneity to external control, only in respect to those actions of each, which concern the interest of other people. If any one does an act hurtful to others, there is a prima facie case for punishing him, by law, or, where legal penalties are not safely applicable, by general disapprobation. There are also many positive acts for the benefit of others, which he may rightfully be compelled to perform; such as, to give evidence in a court of justice; to bear his fair share in the common defence, or in any other joint work necessary to the interest of the society of which he enjoys the protection; and to perform certain acts of individual beneficence, such as saving a fellow creature's life, or interposing to protect the defenceless against ill-usage, things which whenever it is obviously a man's duty to do, he may rightfully be made responsible to society for not doing. A person may cause evil to others not only by his actions but by his inaction, and in either case he is justly accountable to them for the injury. The latter case, it is true, requires a much more cautious exercise of compulsion than the former. To make any one answerable for doing evil to others, is the rule; to make him answerable for not preventing evil, is, comparatively speaking, the exception. Yet there are many cases clear enough and grave enough to justify that exception. In all things which regard the external relations of the individual, he is *de jure* amenable to those whose interests are concerned, and if need be, to society as their protector. There are often good reasons for not holding him to the responsibility; but these reasons must arise from the special expediencies of the case: either because it is a kind of case in which he is on the whole likely to act better, when left to his own discretion, than when controlled in any way in which society have it in their power to control him; or because the attempt to exercise control would produce other evils, greater than those which it would prevent. When such reasons as these preclude the enforcement of responsibility, the conscience of the agent himself should step into the vacant judgement-seat, and protect those interests of others which have no external protection; judging himself all the more rigidly, because the case does not admit of his being made accountable to the judgement of his fellow creatures.

But there is a sphere of action in which society, as distinguished from the individual, has, if any, only an indirect interest; comprehending all that portion of a person's life and conduct which affects only himself, or if it also affects others, only with their free, voluntary, and undeceived consent and participation. When I say only himself, I mean directly, and in the first instance: for whatever affects himself, may affect others through himself; and the objection which may be grounded on this contingency will receive consideration in the sequel. This, then, is the appropriate region of human liberty. It comprises, first, the inward domain of consciousness; demanding liberty of conscience, in the most comprehensive sense; liberty of thought and feeling; absolute freedom of opinion and sentiment on all subjects, practical or speculative, scientific, moral, or theological. The liberty of expressing and publishing opinions may seem to fall under a different principle, since it belongs to that part of the conduct of an individual which concerns other people; but, being almost of as much importance as the liberty of thought itself, and resting in great part on the same reasons, is practically inseparable from it. Secondly, the principle requires liberty of tastes and pursuits; of framing the plan of our life to suit our own character; of doing as we like, subject to such consequences as may follow: without impediment from our fellow creatures, so long as what we do does not harm them, even though they should think our conduct foolish, perverse, or wrong. Thirdly, from this liberty of each individual, follows the liberty, within the same limits, of combination among individuals; freedom to unite, for any purpose not involving harm to others: the persons combining being supposed to be of full age, and not forced or deceived.

No society in which these liberties are not, on the whole, respected, is free, whatever may be its form of government; and none is completely free in which they do not exist absolute and unqualified. The only freedom which deserves the name, is that of pursuing our own good in our own way, so long as we do not attempt to deprive others of theirs, or impede their efforts to obtain it. Each is the proper guardian of his own health, whether bodily, or mental and spiritual. Mankind are greater gainers by suffering each other to live as seems good to themselves, than by compelling each to live as seems good to the rest.

Though this doctrine is anything but new, and to some persons, may have the air of a truism, there is no doctrine which stands more directly opposed to the general tendency of existing opinion and practice. Society has expended fully as much effort in the attempt (according to its lights) to compel people to conform to its notions of personal, as of social excellence. The ancient commonwealths thought themselves entitled to practise, and the ancient philosophers countenanced, the regulation of every part of private conduct by public authority, on the ground that the State had a deep interest in the whole bodily and mental discipline of every one of its citizens; a mode of thinking which may have been admissible in small republics surrounded by powerful enemies, in constant peril of being subverted by foreign attack or internal commotion, and to which even a short interval of relaxed energy and self-command might so easily be fatal, that they could not afford to wait for the salutary permanent effects of freedom. In the modern world, the greater size of political communities, and, above all, the separation between spiritual and temporal authority (which placed the direction of men's consciences in other hands than those which controlled their worldly affairs), prevented so great an interference by law in the details of private life; but the engines of moral repression have been wielded more strenuously against divergence from the reigning opinion in self-regarding, than even in social matters; religion, the most powerful of the elements which have entered into the formation of moral feeling, having almost always been governed either by the ambition of a hierarchy, seeking control over every department of human conduct, or by the spirit of Puritanism. And some of those modern reformers who have placed themselves in strongest opposition to the religions of the past, have been no way behind either churches or sects in their assertion of the right of spiritual domination: M. Comte, in particular, whose social system, as unfolded in his *Système de Politique Positive,* aims at establishing (though by moral more than by legal appliances) a despotism of society over the individual, surpassing anything contemplated in the political ideal of the most rigid disciplinarian among the ancient philosophers. . . .

CHAPTER II: OF THE LIBERTY OF THOUGHT AND DISCUSSION

The time, it is to be hoped, is gone by, when any defence would be necessary of the "liberty of the press" as one of the securities against corrupt or tyrannical government. No argument, we may suppose, can now be needed, against permitting a legislature or an executive, not identified in interest with the people, to prescribe opinions to them, and determine what doctrines or what arguments they shall be allowed to hear. This aspect of the question, besides, has been so often and so triumphantly enforced by preceding writers, that it needs not be specially insisted on in this place. Though the law of England, on the subject of the press, is as servile to this day as it was in the time of the Tudors, there is little danger of its being actually put in force against political discussion, except during some temporary panic, when fear of insurrection drives ministers and judges from their propriety; and, speaking generally, it is not, in constitutional countries, to be apprehended, that the government, whether completely responsible to the people or not, will often attempt to control the expression of opinion, except when in doing so it makes itself the organ of the general intolerance of the public. Let us suppose, therefore, that the government is entirely at one with the people, and never thinks of exerting any power of coercion unless in agreement with what it conceives to be their voice. But I deny the right of the people to exercise such coercion, either by themselves or by their government. The power itself is illegitimate. The best government has no more title to it than the worst. It is as noxious, or more noxious, when exerted in accordance with public opinion, than when in opposition to it. If all mankind minus one, were of one opinion, and only one person were of the contrary opinion, mankind would be no more justified in silencing that one person, than he, if he had the power, would be justified in silencing mankind. Were an opinion a personal possession of no value except to the owner; if to be obstructed in the enjoyment of it were simply a private injury, it would make some difference whether the injury was inflicted only on a few persons or on many. But the peculiar evil of silencing the expression of an opinion is, that it is robbing the human race; posterity as well as the existing generation; those who dissent from the opinion, still more than those who hold it. If the opinion is right, they are deprived of the opportunity of exchanging error for truth: if wrong, they lose, what is almost as great a benefit, the clearer perception and livelier impression of truth, produced by its collision with error.

It is necessary to consider separately these two hypotheses, each of which has a distinct branch of the argument corresponding to it. We can never be sure that the opinion we are endeavouring to stifle is a false opinion; and if we were sure, stifling it would be an evil still . . .

We have . . . recognized the necessity to the mental well-being of mankind (on which all their other well-being depends) of freedom of opinion, and freedom of the expression of opinion, on four distinct grounds; which we will now briefly recapitulate.

First, if any opinion is compelled to silence, that opinion may, for aught we can certainly know, be true. To deny this is to assume our own infallibility.

Secondly, though the silenced opinion be an error, it may, and very commonly does, contain a portion of truth; and since the general or prevailing opinion on any subject is rarely or never the whole truth, it is only by the collision of adverse opinions that the remainder of the truth has any chance of being supplied.

Thirdly, even if the received opinion be not only true, but the whole truth; unless it is suffered to be, and actually is, vigorously and earnestly contested, it will, by most of those who receive it, be held in the manner of a prejudice, with little comprehension or feeling of its rational grounds. And not only this, but, fourthly, the meaning of the doctrine itself will be in danger of being lost, or enfeebled, and deprived of its vital effect on the character and conduct: the dogma becoming a mere formal profession, inefficacious for good, but cum-

bering the ground, and preventing the growth of any real and heartfelt conviction, from reason or personal experience.

Before quitting the subject of freedom of opinion, it is fit to take some notice
of those who say, that the free expression of all opinions should be permitted,
on condition that the manner be temperate, and do not pass the bounds of fair
discussion. Much might be said on the impossibility of fixing where these
supposed bounds are to be placed; for if the test be offence to those whose
opinion is attacked, I think experience testifies that this offence is given whenever the attack is telling and powerful, and that every opponent who pushes
them hard, and whom they find it difficult to answer, appears to them, if he
shows any strong feeling on the subject, an intemperate opponent. But this,
though an important consideration in a practical point of view, merges in a
more fundamental objection. Undoubtedly the manner of asserting an opinion, even though it be a true one, may be very objectionable, and may justly
incur severe censure. But the principal offences of the kind are such as it is
mostly impossible, unless by accidental self-betrayal, to bring home to conviction. The gravest of them is, to argue sophistically, to suppress facts or
arguments, to misstate the elements of the case, or misrepresent the opposite
opinion. But all this, even to the most aggravated degree, is so continually
done in perfect good faith, by persons who are not considered, and in many
other respects may not deserve to be considered, ignorant or incompetent, that
it is rarely possible on adequate grounds conscientiously to stamp the misrepresentation as morally culpable; and still less could law presume to interfere
with this kind of controversial misconduct. With regard to what is commonly
meant by intemperate discussion, namely invective, sarcasm, personality, and
the like, the denunciation of these weapons would deserve more sympathy if it
were ever proposed to interdict them equally to both sides; but it is only desired
to restrain the employment of them against the prevailing opinion: against
the unprevailing they may not only be used without general disapproval, but
will be likely to obtain for him who uses them the praise of honest zeal and
righteous indignation. Yet whatever mischief arises from their use, is greatest
when they are employed against the comparatively defenceless; and whatever
unfair advantage can be derived by any opinion from this mode of asserting
it, accrues almost exclusively to received opinions. The worst offence of this
kind which can be committed by a polemic, is to stigmatize those who hold
the contrary opinion as bad and immoral men. To calumny of this sort, those
who hold any unpopular opinion are peculiarly exposed, because they are in
general few and uninfluential, and nobody but themselves feels much interested in seeing justice done them; but this weapon is, from the nature of the

case, denied to those who attack a prevailing opinion: they can neither use it with safety to themselves, nor, if they could, would it do anything but recoil on their own cause. In general, opinions contrary to those commonly received can only obtain a hearing by studied moderation of language, and the most cautious avoidance of unnecessary offence, from which they hardly ever deviate even in a slight degree without losing ground: while unmeasured vituperation employed on the side of the prevailing opinion, really does deter people from professing contrary opinions, and from listening to those who profess them. For the interest, therefore, of truth and justice, it is far more important to restrain this employment of vituperative language than the other; and, for example, if it were necessary to choose, there would be much more need to discourage offensive attacks on infidelity, than on religion. It is, however, obvious that law and authority have no business with restraining either, while opinion ought, in every instance, to determine its verdict by the circumstances of the individual case; condemning every one, on whichever side of the argument he places himself, in whose mode of advocacy either want of candour, or malignity, bigotry, or intolerance of feeling manifest themselves; but not inferring these vices from the side which a person takes, though it be the contrary side of the question to our own: and giving merited honour to every one, whatever opinion he may hold, who has calmness to see and honesty to state what his opponents and their opinions really are, exaggerating nothing to their discredit, keeping nothing back which tells, or can be supposed to tell, in their favour. This is the real morality of public discussion: and if often violated, I am happy to think that there are many controversialists who to a great extent observe it, and a still greater number who conscientiously strive towards it.

CHAPTER III: OF INDIVIDUALITY, AS ONE OF THE ELEMENTS OF WELL-BEING

Such being the reasons which make it imperative that human beings should be free to form opinions, and to express their opinions without reserve; and such the baneful consequences to the intellectual, and through that to the moral nature of man, unless this liberty is either conceded, or asserted in spite of prohibition; let us next examine whether the same reasons do not require that men should be free to act upon their opinions—to carry these out in their lives, without hindrance, either physical or moral, from their fellow men, so long as it is at their own risk and peril. This last proviso is of course indispensable. No one pretends that actions should be as free as opinions. On the contrary, even opinions lose their immunity, when the circumstances in which they are expressed are such as to constitute their expression a positive instigation to some mischievous act. An opinion that corn-dealers are starvers of the poor, or that private property is robbery, ought to be unmolested when simply circulated through the press, but may justly incur punishment when delivered orally to an excited mob assembled before the house of a corn-dealer, or when handed about among the same mob in the form of a placard. Acts, of whatever kind, which, without justifiable cause, do harm to others, may be, and in the more important cases absolutely require to be, controlled by the unfavorable sentiments, and, when needful, by the active interference of mankind. The liberty of the individual must be thus far limited; he must not make himself a nuisance to other people. But if he refrains from molesting others in what concerns them, and merely acts according to his own inclination and judgement in things which concern himself, the same reasons which show that opinion should be free, prove also that he should be allowed, without molestation, to carry his opinions into practice at his own cost. That mankind are not infallible; that their truths, for the most part, are only half-truths; that unity of opinion, unless resulting from the fullest and freest comparison of opposite opinions, is not desirable, and diversity not an evil, but a good, until mankind are much more capable than at present of recognizing all sides of the truth, are principles applicable to men's modes of action, not less than to their opinions. As it is useful that while mankind are imperfect there should be different opinions, so is it that there should be different experiments of living; that free scope should be given to varieties of character, short of injury to others; and that the worth of different modes of life should be proved practically, when any one thinks fit to try them. It is desirable, in short, that in things which do not primarily concern others, individuality should assert itself. Where, not the person's own character, but the traditions or customs of other people are the rule of conduct, there is wanting one of the principal ingredients of human happiness, and quite the chief ingredient of individual and social progress.

In maintaining this principle, the greatest difficulty to be encountered does not lie in the appreciation of means towards an acknowledged end, but in the indifference of persons in general to the end itself. If it were felt that the free development of individuality is one of the leading essentials of well-being; that it is not only a co-ordinate element with all that is designated by the terms civilization, instruction, education, culture, but is itself a necessary part and condition of all those things; there would be no danger that liberty should be undervalued, and the adjustment of the boundaries between it and social control would present no extraordinary difficulty. But the evil is, that individual spontaneity is hardly recognized by the common modes of thinking, as having any intrinsic worth, or deserving any regard on its own account. The majority, being satisfied with the ways of mankind as they now are (for it is they who make them what they are), cannot comprehend why those ways should not be

good enough for everybody; and what is more, spontaneity forms no part
of the ideal of the majority of moral and social reformers, but is rather looked
on with jealousy, as a troublesome and perhaps rebellious obstruction to the
general acceptance of what these reformers, in their own judgement, think
would be best for mankind. Few persons, out of Germany, even comprehend
the meaning of the doctrine which Wilhelm von Humboldt, so eminent both
as a savant and as a politician, made the text of a treatise—that "the end of
man, or that which is prescribed by the eternal or immutable dictates of reason, and not suggested by vague and transient desires, is the highest and most
harmonious development of his powers to a complete and consistent whole";
that, therefore, the object "towards which every human being must ceaselessly
direct his efforts, and on which especially those who design to influence their
fellow men must ever keep their eyes, is the individuality of power and development"; that for this there are two requisites, "freedom, and variety of
situations"; and that from the union of these arise "individual vigour and manifold diversity," which combine themselves in "originality."

Little, however, as people are accustomed to a doctrine like that of Von
Humboldt, and surprising as it may be to them to find so high a value attached
to individuality, the question, one must nevertheless think, can only be one
of degree. No one's idea of excellence in conduct is that people should do
absolutely nothing but copy one another. No one would assert that people
ought not to put into their mode of life, and into the conduct of their concerns,
any impress whatever of their own judgement, or of their own individual
character. On the other hand, it would be absurd to pretend that people ought
to live as if nothing whatever had been known in the world before they came
into it; as if experience had as yet done nothing towards showing that one mode
of existence, or of conduct, is preferable to another. Nobody denies that people
should be so taught and trained in youth, as to know and benefit by the ascertained results of human experience. But it is the privilege and proper condition of a human being, arrived at the maturity of his faculties, to use and
interpret experience in his own way. It is for him to find out what part of
recorded experience is properly applicable to his own circumstances and character. The traditions and customs of other people are, to a certain extent, evidence of what their experience has taught *them;* presumptive evidence, and as
such, have a claim to his deference: but, in the first place, their experience may
be too narrow; or they may not have interpreted it rightly. Secondly, their
interpretation of experience may be correct, but unsuitable to him. Customs
are made for customary circumstances, and customary characters; and his circumstances or his character may be uncustomary. Thirdly, though the customs be both good as customs, and suitable to him, yet to conform to custom,

merely *as* custom, does not educate or develop in him any of the qualities which are the distinctive endowment of a human being. The human faculties of perception, judgement, discriminative feeling, mental activity, and even moral preference, are exercised only in making a choice. He who does anything because it is the custom, makes no choice. He gains no practice either in discerning or in desiring what is best. The mental and moral, like the muscular powers, are improved only by being used. The faculties are called into no exercise by doing a thing merely because others do it, no more than by believing a thing only because others believe it. If the grounds of an opinion are not conclusive to the person's own reason, his reason cannot be strengthened, but is likely to be weakened, by his adopting it: and if the inducements to an act are not such as are consentaneous to his own feelings and character (where affection, or the rights of others, are not concerned) it is so much done towards rendering his feelings and character inert and torpid, instead of active and energetic. . . .

It will probably be conceded that it is desirable people should exercise their understandings, and that an intelligent following of custom, or even occasionally an intelligent deviation from custom, is better than a blind and simply mechanical adhesion to it. To a certain extent it is admitted, that our understanding should be our own: but there is not the same willingness to admit that our desires and impulses should be our own likewise; or that to possess impulses of our own, and of any strength, is anything but a peril and a snare. Yet desires and impulses are as much a part of a perfect human being, as beliefs and restraints: and strong impulses are only perilous when not properly balanced; when one set of aims and inclinations is developed into strength, while others, which ought to co-exist with them, remain weak and inactive. It is not because men's desires are strong that they act ill; it is because their consciences are weak. There is no natural connexion between strong impulses and a weak conscience. The natural connexion is the other way. To say that one person's desires and feelings are stronger and more various than those of another, is merely to say that he has more of the raw material of human nature, and is therefore capable, perhaps of more evil, but certainly of more good. Strong impulses are but another name for energy. Energy may be turned to bad uses; but more good may always be made of an energetic nature, than of an indolent and impassive one. Those who have most natural feeling, are always those whose cultivated feelings may be made the strongest. The same strong susceptibilities which make the personal impulses vivid and powerful, are also the source from whence are generated the most passionate love of virtue, and the sternest self-control. It is through the cultivation of these, that society both does its duty and protects its interests: not by rejecting the stuff of which heroes are made, because it knows not how to make them. A person whose desires and impulses are his own—are the expression of his own nature, as it has been developed and modified by his own culture—is said to have a character. One whose desires and impulses are not his own, has no character, no more than a steam-engine has a character. If, in addition to being his own, his impulses are strong, and are under the government of a strong will, he has an energetic character. Whoever thinks that individuality of desires and impulses should not be encouraged to unfold itself, must maintain that society has no need of strong natures—is not the better for containing many persons who have much character—and that a high general average of energy is not desirable.

In some early states of society, these forces might be, and were, too much ahead of the power which society then possessed of disciplining and controlling them. There has been a time when the element of spontaneity and individuality was in excess, and the social principle had a hard struggle with it. The difficulty then was, to induce men of strong bodies or minds to pay obedience to any rules which required them to control their impulses. To overcome this difficulty, law and discipline, like the Popes struggling against the Emperors, asserted a power over the whole man, claiming to control all his life in order to control his character—which society had not found any other sufficient means of binding. But society has now fairly got the better of individuality; and the danger which threatens human nature is not the excess, but the deficiency, of personal impulses and preferences. Things are vastly changed, since the passions of those who were strong by station or by personal endowment were in a state of habitual rebellion against laws and ordinances, and required to be rigorously chained up to enable the persons within their reach to enjoy any particle of security. In our times, from the highest class of society down to the lowest, every one lives as under the eye of a hostile and dreaded censorship. Not only in what concerns others, but in what concerns only themselves, the individual or the family do not ask themselves—what do I prefer? or, what would suit my character and disposition? or, what would allow the best and highest in me to have fair play, and enable it to grow and thrive? They ask themselves, what is suitable to my position? what is usually done by persons of my station and pecuniary circumstances? or (worse still) what is usually done by persons of a station and circumstances superior to mine? I do not mean that they choose what is customary, in preference to what suits their own inclination. It does not occur to them to have any inclination, except for what is customary. Thus the mind itself is bowed to the yoke: even in what people do for pleasure, conformity is the first thing thought of; they like in crowds; they exercise choice only among things commonly done: peculiarity of taste, eccentricity of conduct, are shunned equally with crimes: until by dint of not following their own nature, they have no nature to follow: their human capacities are withered and starved: they become incapable of any strong wishes or native pleasures, and are generally without either opinions or feelings of home growth, or properly their own. Now is this, or is it not, the desirable condition of human nature?

It is so, on the Calvinistic theory. According to that, the one great offence of man is self-will. All the good of which humanity is capable, is comprised in obedience. You have no choice; thus you must do, and no otherwise: "whatever is not a duty, is a sin." Human nature being radically corrupt, there is no redemption for any one until human nature is killed within him. To one holding this theory of life, crushing out any of the human faculties, capacities, and susceptibilities, is no evil: man needs no capacity, but that of surrendering himself to the will of God: and if he uses any of his faculties for any other purpose but to do that supposed will more effectually, he is better without them. This is the theory of Calvinism; and it is held, in a mitigated form, by many who do not consider themselves Calvinists; the mitigation consisting in giving a less ascetic interpretation to the alleged will of God; asserting it to be his will that mankind should gratify some of their inclinations; of course not in the manner they themselves prefer, but in the way of obedience, that is, in a way prescribed to them by authority; and, therefore, by the necessary conditions of the case, the same for all.

In some such insidious form there is at present a strong tendency to this narrow theory of life, and to the pinched and hidebound type of human character which it patronizes. Many persons, no doubt, sincerely think that human beings thus cramped and dwarfed, are as their Maker designed them to be; just as many have thought that trees are a much finer thing when clipped into pollards, or cut out into figures of animals, than as nature made them. But if it be any part of religion to believe that man was made by a good Being, it is more consistent with that faith to believe, that this Being gave all human faculties that they might be cultivated and unfolded, not rooted out and consumed, and that he takes delight in every nearer approach made by his creatures to the ideal conception embodied in them, every increase in any of their capabilities of comprehension, of action, or of enjoyment. There is a different type of human excellence from the Calvinistic; a conception of humanity as having its nature bestowed on it for other purposes than merely to be abnegated. "Pagan self-assertion" is one of the elements of human worth, as well as "Christian self-denial." There is a Greek ideal of self-development, which the Platonic and Christian ideal of self-government blends with, but does not supersede. It may be better to be a John Knox than an Alcibiades, but it is better to be a Pericles than either; nor would a Pericles, if we had one in these days, be without anything good which belonged to John Knox.

It is not by wearing down into uniformity all that is individual in themselves, but by cultivating it and calling it forth, within the limits imposed by the rights and interests of others, that human beings become a noble and beautiful object of contemplation; and as the works partake the character of those who do them, by the same process human life also becomes rich, diversified, and animating, furnishing more abundant aliment to high thoughts and elevating feelings, and strengthening the tie which binds every individual to the race, by making the race infinitely better worth belonging to. In proportion to the development of his individuality, each person becomes more valuable to himself, and is therefore capable of being more valuable to others. There is a greater fullness of life about his own existence, and when there is more life in the units there is more in the mass which is composed of them. As much compression as is necessary to prevent the stronger specimens of human nature from encroaching on the rights of others, cannot be dispensed with; but for this there is ample compensation even in the point of view of human development. The means of development which the individual loses by being prevented from gratifying his inclinations to the injury of others, are chiefly obtained at the expense of the development of other people. And even to himself there is a full equivalent in the better development of the social part of his nature, rendered possible by the restraint put upon the selfish part. To be held to rigid rules of justice for the sake of others, develops the feelings and capacities which have the good of others for their object. But to be restrained in things not affecting their good, by their mere displeasure, develops nothing valuable, except such force of character as may unfold itself in resisting the restraint. If acquiesced in, it dulls and blunts the whole nature. To give any fair play to the nature of each, it is essential that different persons should be allowed to lead different lives. In proportion as this latitude has been exercised in any age, has that age been noteworthy to posterity. Even despotism does not produce its worst effects, so long as individuality exists under it; and whatever crushes individuality is despotism, by whatever name it may be called, and whether it professes to be enforcing the will of God or the injunctions of men. . . .

CHAPTER V: APPLICATIONS

The principles asserted in these pages must be more generally admitted as the basis for discussion of details, before a consistent application of them to all the various departments of government and morals can be attempted with any prospect of advantage. The few observations I propose to make on questions of detail, are designed to illustrate the principles, rather than to follow them out to their consequences. I offer, not so much applications, as specimens of application; which may serve to bring into greater clearness the meaning and limits of the two maxims which together form the entire doctrine of this Essay, and to assist the judgement in holding the balance between them, in the cases where it appears doubtful which of them is applicable to the case.

The maxims are, first, that the individual is not accountable to society for his actions, in so far as these concern the interests of no person but himself. Advice, instruction, persuasion, and avoidance by other people if thought necessary by them for their own good, are the only measures by which society can justifiably express its dislike or disapprobation of his conduct. Secondly, that for such actions as are prejudicial to the interests of others, the individual is accountable, and may be subjected either to social or to legal punishment, if society is of opinion that the one or the other is requisite for its protection.

In the first place, it must by no means be supposed, because damage, or probability of damage, to the interests of others, can alone justify the interference of society, that therefore it always does justify such interference. In many cases, an individual, in pursuing a legitimate object, necessarily and therefore legitimately causes pain or loss to others, or intercepts a good which they had a reasonable hope of obtaining. Such oppositions of interest between individuals often arise from bad social institutions, but are unavoidable while those institutions last; and some would be unavoidable under any institutions. Whoever succeeds in an over-crowded profession, or in a competitive examination; whoever is preferred to another in any contest for an object which both desire, reaps benefit from the loss of others, from their wasted exertion and their disappointment. But it is, by common admission, better for the general interest of mankind, that persons should pursue their objects undeterred by this sort of consequences. In other words, society admits no right, either legal or moral, in the disappointed competitors, to immunity from this kind of suffering; and feels called on to interfere, only when means of success have been employed which it is contrary to the general interest to permit—namely, fraud or treachery, and force.

Again, trade is a social act. Whoever undertakes to sell any description of goods to the public, does what affects the interest of other persons, and of society in general; and thus his conduct, in principle, comes within the jurisdiction of society: accordingly, it was once held to be the duty of governments, in all cases which were considered of importance, to fix prices, and regulate the processes of manufacture. But it is now recognized, though not till after a long struggle, that both the cheapness and the good quality of commodities are most effectually provided for by leaving the producers and sellers perfectly free, under the sole check of equal freedom to the buyers for supplying themselves elsewhere. This is the so-called doctrine of Free Trade, which rests on grounds different from, though equally solid with, the principle of individual liberty asserted in this Essay. Restrictions on trade, or on production for purposes of trade, are indeed restraints; and all restraint, *quâ* restraint, is an evil: but the restraints in question affect only that part of conduct which society is competent to restrain, and are wrong solely because they do not really produce the results which it is desired to produce by them. As the principle of individual liberty is not involved in the doctrine of Free Trade, so neither is it in most of the questions which arise respecting the limits of that doctrine; as for example, what amount of public control is admissible for the prevention of fraud by adulteration; how far sanitary precautions, or arrangements to protect workpeople employed in dangerous occupations, should be enforced on employers. Such questions involve considerations of liberty, only in so far as leaving people to themselves is always better, *caeteris paribus*,[1] than controlling them: but that they may be legitimately controlled for these ends, is in principle undeniable. On the other hand, there are questions relating to interference with trade, which are essentially questions of liberty; such as the Maine Law, already touched upon; the prohibition of the importation of opium into China; the restriction of the sale of poisons; all cases, in short, where the object of the interference is to make it impossible or difficult to obtain a particular commodity. These interferences are objectionable, not as infringements on the liberty of the producer or seller, but on that of the buyer.

One of these examples, that of the sale of poisons, opens a new question; the proper limits of what may be called the functions of police; how far liberty may legitimately be invaded for the prevention of crime, or of accident. It is one of the undisputed functions of government to take precautions against crime before it has been committed, as well as to detect and punish it afterwards. The preventive function of government, however, is far more liable to be abused, to the prejudice of liberty, than the punitory function; for there is hardly any part of the legitimate freedom of action of a human being which would not admit of being represented, and fairly too, as increasing the facilities for some form or other of delinquency. Nevertheless, if a public authority, or even a private person, sees any one evidently preparing to commit a crime, they are not bound to look on inactive until the crime is committed, but may interfere to prevent it. If poisons were never bought or used for any purpose except the commission of murder, it would be right to prohibit their manufacture and sale. They may, however, be wanted not only for innocent but for useful purposes, and restrictions cannot be imposed in the one case without operating in the other. Again, it is a proper office of public authority to guard

---

[1] [*Other things equal.*]

against accidents. If either a public officer or any one else saw a person attempting to cross a bridge which had been ascertained to be unsafe, and there were no time to warn him of his danger, they might seize him and turn him back, without any real infringement of his liberty; for liberty consists in doing what one desires, and he does not desire to fall into the river. Nevertheless, when there is not a certainty, but only a danger of mischief, no one but the person himself can judge of the sufficiency of the motive which may prompt him to incur the risk: in this case, therefore (unless he is a child, or delirious, or in some state of excitement or absorption incompatible with the full use of the reflecting faculty), he ought, I conceive, to be only warned of the danger; not forcibly prevented from exposing himself to it. Similar considerations, applied to such a question as the sale of poisons, may enable us to decide which among the possible modes of regulation are or are not contrary to principle. Such a precaution, for example, as that of labelling the drug with some word expressive of its dangerous character, may be enforced without violation of liberty: the buyer cannot wish not to know that the thing he possesses has poisonous qualities. But to require in all cases the certificate of a medical practitioner, would make it sometimes impossible, always expensive, to obtain the article for legitimate uses. The only mode apparent to me, in which difficulties may be thrown in the way of crime committed through this means, without any infringement, worth taking into account, upon the liberty of those who desire the poisonous substance for other purposes, consists in providing what, in the apt language of Bentham, is called "preappointed evidence." This provision is familiar to every one in the case of contracts. It is usual and right that the law, when a contract is entered into, should require as the condition of its enforcing performance, that certain formalities should be observed, such as signatures, attestation of witnesses, and the like, in order that in case of subsequent dispute, there may be evidence to prove that the contract was really entered into, and that there was nothing in the circumstances to render it legally invalid: the effect being, to throw great obstacles in the way of fictitious contracts, or contracts made in circumstances which, if known, would destroy their validity. Precautions of a similar nature might be enforced in the sale of articles adapted to be instruments of crime. The seller, for example, might be required to enter in a register the exact time of the transaction, the name and address of the buyer, the precise quality and quantity sold; to ask the purpose for which it was wanted, and record the answer he received. When there was no medical prescription, the presence of some third person might be required, to bring home the fact to the purchaser, in case there should afterwards be reason to believe that the article had been applied to criminal purposes. Such regulations would in general be no material impediment to obtaining the article, but a very considerable one to making an improper use of it without detection.

The right inherent in society, to ward off crimes against itself by antecedent precautions, suggests the obvious limitations to the maxim, that purely self-regarding misconduct cannot properly be meddled with in the way of prevention or punishment. Drunkenness, for example, in ordinary cases, is not a fit subject for legislative interference; but I should deem it perfectly legitimate that a person, who had once been convicted of any act of violence to others under the influence of drink, should be placed under a special legal restriction, personal to himself; that if he were afterwards found drunk, he should be liable to a penalty, and that if when in that state he committed another offence, the punishment to which he would be liable for that other offence should be increased in severity. The making himself drunk, in a person whom drunkenness excites to do harm to others, is a crime against others. So, again, idleness, except in a person receiving support from the public, or except when it constitutes a breach of contract, cannot without tyranny be made a subject of legal punishment; but if, either from idleness or from any other avoidable cause, a man fails to perform his legal duties to others, as for instance to support his children, it is no tyranny to force him to fulfil that obligation, by compulsory labour, if no other means are available.

Again, there are many acts which, being directly injurious only to the agents themselves, ought not to be legally interdicted, but which, if done publicly, are a violation of good manners, and coming thus within the category of offences against others, may rightfully be prohibited. Of this kind are offences against decency; on which it is unnecessary to dwell, the rather as they are only connected indirectly with our subject, the objection to publicity being equally strong in the case of many actions not in themselves condemnable, nor supposed to be so.

There is another question to which an answer must be found, consistent with the principles which have been laid down. In cases of personal conduct supposed to be blameable, but which respect for liberty precludes society from preventing or punishing, because the evil directly resulting falls wholly on the agent; what the agent is free to do, ought other persons to be equally free to counsel or instigate? This question is not free from difficulty. The case of a person who solicits another to do an act, is not strictly a case of self-regarding conduct. To give advice or offer inducements to any one, is a social act, and may, therefore, like actions in general which affect others, be supposed amenable to social control. But a little reflection corrects the first impression, by showing that if the case is not strictly within the definition of individual liberty, yet the reasons on which the principle of individual liberty is grounded, are applicable to it. If people must be allowed, in whatever concerns only themselves, to act as seems best to themselves at their own peril, they must equally be free to consult with one another about what is fit to be so done; to exchange opinions, and give and receive suggestions. Whatever it is permitted to do, it must be permitted to advise to do. The question is doubtful, only when the instigator derives a personal benefit from his advice; when he makes it his occupation, for subsistence or pecuniary gain, to promote what society and the State consider to be an evil. Then, indeed, a new element of complication is introduced; namely, the existence of classes of persons with an interest opposed to what is considered as the public weal, and whose mode of living is grounded on the counteraction of it. Ought this to be interfered with, or not? Fornication, for example, must be tolerated, and so must gambling; but should a person be free to be a pimp, or to keep a gambling-house? The case is one of those which lie on the exact boundary line between two principles, and it is not at once apparent to which of the two it properly belongs. There are arguments on both sides. On the side of toleration it may be said, that the fact of following anything as an occupation, and living or profiting by the practice of it, cannot make that criminal which would otherwise be admissible; that the act should either be consistently permitted or consistently prohibited; that if the principles which we have hitherto defended are true, society has no business, *as* society, to decide anything to be wrong which concerns only the individual; that it cannot go beyond dissuasion, and that one person should be as free to persuade, as another to dissuade. In opposition to this it may be contended, that although the public, or the State, are not warranted in authoritatively deciding, for purposes of repression or punishment, that such or such conduct affecting only the interests of the individual is good or bad, they are fully justified in assuming, if they regard it as bad, that its being so or not is at least a disputable question: That, this being supposed, they cannot be acting wrongly in endeavouring to exclude the influence of solicitations which are not disinterested, of instigators who cannot possibly be impartial—who have a direct personal interest on one side, and that side the one which the State believes to be wrong, and who confessedly promote it for personal objects only. There can surely, it may be urged, be nothing lost, no sacrifice of good, by so ordering matters that persons shall make their election, either wisely or foolishly, on their own prompting, as free as possible from the arts of persons who stimulate their inclinations for interested purposes of their own. Thus (it may be said) though the statutes respecting unlawful games are utterly indefensible —though all persons should be free to gamble in their own or each other's houses, or in any place of meeting established by their own subscriptions, and open only to the members and their visitors—yet public gambling-houses should not be permitted. It is true that the prohibition is never effectual, and that, whatever amount of tyrannical power may be given to the police, gambling-houses can always be maintained under other pretences; but they may be compelled to conduct their operations with a certain degree of secrecy and mystery, so that nobody knows anything about them but those who seek them; and more than this, society ought not to aim at. There is considerable force in these arguments. I will not venture to decide whether they are sufficient to justify the moral anomaly of punishing the accessary, when the principal is (and must be) allowed to go free; of fining or imprisoning the procurer, but not the fornicator, the gambling-house keeper, but not the gambler. Still less ought the common operations of buying and selling to be interfered with on analogous grounds. Almost every article which is bought and sold may be used in excess, and the sellers have a pecuniary interest in encouraging that excess; but no argument can be founded on this, in favour, for instance, of the Maine Law; because the class of dealers in strong drinks, though interested in their abuse, are indispensably required for the sake of their legitimate use. The interest, however, of these dealers in promoting intemperance is a real evil, and justifies the State in imposing restrictions and requiring guarantees which, but for that justification, would be infringements of legitimate liberty. . . .

It was pointed out in an early part of this Essay, that the liberty of the individual, in things wherein the individual is alone concerned, implies a corresponding liberty in any number of individuals to regulate by mutual agreement such things as regard them jointly, and regard no persons but themselves. This question presents no difficulty, so long as the will of all the persons implicated remains unaltered; but since that will may change, it is often necessary, even in things in which they alone are concerned, that they should enter into engagements with one another; and when they do, it is fit, as a general rule, that those engagements should be kept. Yet, in the laws, probably, of every country, this general rule has some exceptions. Not only persons are not held to engagements which violate the rights of third parties, but it is sometimes considered a sufficient reason for releasing them from an engagement, that it is injurious to themselves. In this and most other civilized countries, for example, an engagement by which a person should sell himself, or allow himself to be sold, as a slave, would be null and void; neither enforced by law nor by opinion. The ground for thus limiting his power of voluntarily disposing of his own lot in life, is apparent, and is very clearly seen in this extreme case. The reason for not interfering, unless for the sake of others, with a person's voluntary acts, is consideration for his liberty. His voluntary choice is evidence that what he so chooses is desirable, or at the least endurable, to him, and his good is on the whole best provided for by allowing him to take his own means of pursuing it. But by selling himself for a slave, he abdicates his liberty; he forgoes any future use of it beyond that single act. He therefore defeats, in his own case, the very purpose which is the justification of allowing him to dispose of himself. He is no longer free; but is thenceforth in a position which has no longer the presumption in its favour, that would be afforded by his voluntarily remaining in it. The principle of freedom cannot require that he should be free not to be free. It is not freedom, to be allowed to alienate his freedom. These reasons, the force of which is so conspicuous in this peculiar case, are evidently of far wider application; yet a limit is everywhere set to them by the necessities of life, which continually require, not indeed that we should resign our freedom, but that we should consent to this and the other limitation of it. The principle, however, which demands uncontrolled freedom of action in all that concerns only the agents themselves, requires that those who have become bound to one another, in things which concern no third party, should be able to release one another from the engagement: and even without such voluntary release, there are perhaps no contracts or engagements, except those that relate to money or money's worth, of which one can venture to say that there ought to be no liberty whatever of retractation. . . .

I have already observed that, owing to the absence of any recognized general principles, liberty is often granted where it should be withheld, as well as withheld where it should be granted; and one of the cases in which, in the modern European world, the sentiment of liberty is the strongest, is a case where, in my view, it is altogether misplaced. A person should be free to do as he likes in his own concerns; but he ought not to be free to do as he likes in acting for another, under the pretext that the affairs of the other are his own affairs. The State, while it respects the liberty of each in what specially regards himself, is bound to maintain a vigilant control over his exercise of any power which it allows him to possess over others. This obligation is almost entirely disregarded in the case of the family relations, a case, in its direct influence on human happiness, more important than all others taken together. The almost despotic power of husbands over wives needs not be enlarged upon here, because nothing more is needed for the complete removal of the evil, than that wives should have the same rights, and should receive the protection of law in the same manner, as all other persons; and because, on this subject, the defenders of established injustice do not avail themselves of the plea of liberty, but stand forth openly as the champions of power. It is in the case of children, that misapplied notions of liberty are a real obstacle to the fulfilment by the State of its duties. One would almost think that a man's children were supposed to be literally, and not metaphorically, a part of himself, so jealous is opinion of the smallest interference of law with his absolute and exclusive control over them; more jealous than of almost any interference with his own freedom of action:

so much less do the generality of mankind value liberty than power. Consider, for example, the case of education. Is it not almost a self-evident axiom, that the State should require and compel the education, up to a certain standard, of every human being who is born its citizen? Yet who is there that is not afraid to recognize and assert this truth? Hardly any one indeed will deny that it is one of the most sacred duties of the parents (or, as law and usage now stand, the father), after summoning a human being into the world, to give to that being an education fitting him to perform his part well in life towards others and towards himself. But while this is unanimously declared to be the father's duty, scarcely anybody, in this country, will bear to hear of obliging him to perform it. Instead of his being required to make any exertion or sacrifice for securing education to the child, it is left to his choice to accept it or not when it is provided gratis! It still remains unrecognized, that to bring a child into existence without a fair prospect of being able, not only to provide food for its body, but instruction and training for its mind, is a moral crime, both against the unfortunate offspring and against society; and that if the parent does not fulfil this obligation, the State ought to see it fulfilled, at the charge, as far as possible, of the parent.

Were the duty of enforcing universal education once admitted, there would be an end to the difficulties about what the State should teach, and how it should teach, which now convert the subject into a mere battle-field of sects and parties, causing the time and labour which should have been spent in educating, to be wasted in quarrelling about education. If the government would make up its mind to *require* for every child a good education, it might save itself the trouble of *providing* one. It might leave to parents to obtain the education where and how they pleased, and content itself with helping to pay the school fees of the poorer classes of children, and defraying the entire school expenses of those who have no one else to pay for them. The objections which are urged with reason against State education, do not apply to the enforcement of education by the State, but to the State's taking upon itself to direct that education: which is a totally different thing. That the whole or any large part of the education of the people should be in State hands, I go as far as any one in deprecating. All that has been said of the importance of individuality of character, and diversity in opinions and modes of conduct, involves, as of the same unspeakable importance, diversity of education. A general State education is a mere contrivance for moulding people to be exactly like one another: and as the mould in which it casts them is that which pleases the predominant power in the government, whether this be a monarch, a priesthood, an aristocracy, or the majority of the existing generation in proportion as it is efficient and successful, it establishes a despotism over the mind, leading by natural tendency to one over the body. An education established and controlled by the State should only exist, if it exist at all, as one among many competing experiments, carried on for the purpose of example and stimulus, to keep the others up to a certain standard of excellence. Unless, indeed, when society in general is in so backward a state that it could not or would not provide for itself any proper institutions of education, unless the government undertook the task: then, indeed, the government may, as the less of two great evils, take upon itself the business of schools and universities, as it may that of joint-stock companies, when private enterprise, in a shape fitted for undertaking great works of industry, does not exist in the country. But in general, if the country contains a sufficient number of persons qualified to provide education under government auspices, the same persons would be able and willing to give an equally good education on the voluntary principle, under the assurance of remuneration afforded by a law rendering education compulsory, combined with State aid to those unable to defray the expense.

The instrument for enforcing the law could be no other than public examinations, extending to all children, and beginning at an early age. An age might be fixed at which every child must be examined, to ascertain if he (or she) is able to read. If a child proves unable, the father, unless he has some sufficient ground of excuse, might be subjected to a moderate fine, to be worked out, if necessary, by his labour, and the child might be put to school at his expense. Once in every year the examination should be renewed, with a gradually extending range of subjects, so as to make the universal acquisition, and what is more, retention, of a certain minimum of general knowledge, virtually compulsory. Beyond that minimum, there should be voluntary examinations on all subjects, at which all who come up to a certain standard of proficiency might claim a certificate. To prevent the State from exercising, through these arrangements, an improper influence over opinion, the knowledge required for passing an examination (beyond the merely instrumental parts of knowledge, such as languages and their use) should, even in the higher classes of examinations, be confined to facts and positive science exclusively. The examinations on religion, politics, or other disputed topics, should not turn on the truth or falsehood of opinions, but on the matter of fact that such and such an opinion is held, on such grounds, by such authors, or schools, or churches. Under this system, the rising generation would be no worse off in regard to all disputed truths, than they are at present; they would be brought up either churchmen or dissenters as they now are, the State merely taking care that they should be instructed churchmen, or instructed dissenters. There would be nothing to hinder them from being taught religion, if their parents chose, at the same schools where they were taught other things. All attempts by the State to bias the conclusions of its citizens on disputed subjects, are evil; but it may very properly offer to ascertain and certify that a person possesses the knowledge, requisite to make his conclusions, on any given subject, worth attending to. . . .

It is not in the matter of education only, that misplaced notions of liberty prevent moral obligations on the part of parents from being recognized, and legal obligations from being imposed, where there are the strongest grounds for the former always, and in many cases for the latter also. The fact itself, of causing the existence of a human being, is one of the most responsible actions in the range of human life. To undertake this responsibility—to bestow a life which may be either a curse or a blessing—unless the being on whom it is to be bestowed will have at least the ordinary chances of a desirable existence, is a crime against that being. And in a country either over-peopled, or threatened with being so, to produce children, beyond a very small number, with the effect of reducing the reward of labour by their competition, is a serious offence against all who live by the remuneration of their labour. The laws which, in many countries on the Continent, forbid marriage unless the parties can show that they have the means of supporting a family, do not exceed the legitimate powers of the State: and whether such laws be expedient or not (a question mainly dependent on local circumstances and feelings), they are not objectionable as violations of liberty. Such laws are interferences of the State to prohibit a mischievous act—an act injurious to others, which ought to be a subject of reprobation, and social stigma, even when it is not deemed expedient to superadd legal punishment. Yet the current ideas of liberty, which bend so easily to real infringements of the freedom of the individual in things which concern only himself, would repel the attempt to put any restraint upon his inclinations when the consequence of their indulgence is a life or lives of wretchedness and depravity to the offspring, with manifold evils to those sufficiently within reach to be in any way affected by their actions. When we compare the strange respect of mankind for liberty, with their strange want of respect for it, we might imagine that a man had an indispensable right to do harm to others, and no right at all to please himself without giving pain to any one.

I have reserved for the last place a large class of questions respecting the limits of government interference, which, though closely connected with the subject of this Essay, do not, in strictness, belong to it. These are cases in which the reasons against interference do not turn upon the principle of liberty: the question is not about restraining the actions of individuals, but about helping them: it is asked whether the government should do, or cause to be done, something for their benefit, instead of leaving it to be done by themselves, individually, or in voluntary combination.

The objections to government interference, when it is not such as to involve infringement of liberty, may be of three kinds.

The first is, when the thing to be done is likely to be better done by individuals than by the government. Speaking generally, there is no one so fit to conduct any business, or to determine how or by whom it shall be conducted, as those who are personally interested in it. This principle condemns the interferences, once so common, of the legislature, or the officers of government, with the ordinary processes of industry. But this part of the subject has been sufficiently enlarged upon by political economists, and is not particularly related to the principles of this Essay.

The second objection is more nearly allied to our subject. In many cases, though individuals may not do the particular thing so well, on the average, as the officers of government, it is nevertheless desirable that it should be done by them, rather than by the government, as a means to their own mental education—a mode of strengthening their active faculties, exercising their judgement, and giving them a familiar knowledge of the subjects with which they are thus left to deal. This is a principal, though not the sole, recommendation of jury trial (in cases not political); of free and popular local and municipal institutions; of the conduct of industrial and philanthropic enterprises by voluntary associations. These are not questions of liberty, and are connected with that subject only by remote tendencies; but they are questions of development. It belongs to a different occasion from the present to dwell on these things as parts of national education; as being, in truth, the peculiar training of a citizen, the practical part of the political education of a free people, taking them out of the narrow circle of personal and family selfishness, and accustoming them to the comprehension of joint interests, the management of joint concerns—habituating them to act from public or semi-public motives, and guide their conduct by aims which unite instead of isolating them from one another. Without these habits and powers, a free constitution can neither be worked nor preserved; as is exemplified by the too-often transitory nature of political freedom in countries where it does not rest upon a sufficient basis of local liberties. The management of purely local business by the localities, and of the great enterprises of industry by the union of those who voluntarily supply the pecuniary means, is further recommended by all the advantages which have been set forth in this Essay as belonging to individuality of development, and diversity of modes of action. Government operations tend to be everywhere alike. With individuals and voluntary associations, on the contrary, there are varied experiments, and endless diversity of experience. What the State can usefully do, is to make itself a central depository, and active circulator and diffuser, of the experience resulting from many trials. Its business is to enable each experimentalist to benefit by the experiments of others; instead of tolerating no experiments but its own.

The third, and most cogent reason for restricting the interference of government, is the great evil of adding unnecessarily to its power. Every function superadded to those already exercised by the government, causes its influence over hopes and fears to be more widely diffused, and converts, more and more, the active and ambitious part of the public into hangers-on of the government, or of some party which aims at becoming the government. If the roads, the railways, the banks, the insurance offices, the great joint-stock companies, the universities, and the public charities, were all of them branches of the government; if, in addition, the municipal corporations and local boards, with all that now devolves on them, became departments of the central administration; if the employés of all these different enterprises were appointed and paid by the government, and looked to the government for every rise in life; not all the freedom of the press and popular constitution of the legislature would make this or any other country free otherwise than in name. And the evil would be greater, the more efficiently and scientifically the administrative machinery was constructed—the more skilful the arrangements for obtaining the best qualified hands and heads with which to work it. In England it has of late been proposed that all the members of the civil service of government should be selected by competitive examination, to obtain for those employments the most intelligent and instructed persons procurable; and much has been said and written for and against this proposal. One of the arguments most insisted on by its opponents, is that the occupation of a permanent official servant of the State does not hold out sufficient prospects of emolument and importance to attract the highest talents, which will always be able to find a more inviting career in the professions, or in the service of companies and other public bodies. One would not have been surprised if this argument had been used by the friends of the proposition, as an answer to its principal difficulty. Coming from the opponents it is strange enough. What is urged as an objection is the safety-valve of the proposed system. If indeed all the high talent of the country *could* be drawn into the service of the government, a proposal tending to bring about that result might well inspire uneasiness. If every part of the business of society which required organized concert, or large and comprehensive views, were in the hands of the government, and if government offices were universally filled by the ablest men, all the enlarged culture and practised intelligence in the country, except the purely speculative, would be concentrated in a numerous bureaucracy, to whom alone the rest of the community would look for all things: the multitude for direction and dictation in all they had to do; the able and aspiring for personal advancement. To be admitted into the ranks of this bureaucracy, and when admitted, to rise therein, would be the sole objects of ambition. Under this régime, not only is the outside public ill-qualified, for want of practical experience, to criticize or check the mode of operation of the bureaucracy, but even if the accidents of despotic or the natural working of popular institutions occasionally raise to the summit a ruler or rulers of reforming inclinations, no reform can be effected which is contrary to the interest of the bureaucracy. Such is the melancholy condition of the Russian empire, as shown in the accounts of those who have had sufficient opportunity of observation. The Czar himself is powerless against the bureaucratic body; he can send any one of them to Siberia, but he cannot govern without them, or against their will. On every decree of his they have a tacit veto, by merely refraining from carrying it into effect. In countries of more advanced civilization and of a more insurrectionary spirit, the public, accustomed to expect everything to be done for them by the State, or at least to do nothing for themselves without asking from the State not only leave to do it, but even how it is to be done, naturally hold the State responsible for all evil which befalls them, and when the evil exceeds their amount of patience, they rise against the government and make what is called a revolution; whereupon somebody else, with or without legitimate authority from the nation, vaults into the seat, issues his orders to the bureaucracy, and everything goes on much as it did before; the bureaucracy being unchanged, and nobody else being capable of taking their place.

A very different spectacle is exhibited among a people accustomed to transact their own business. In France, a large part of the people having been engaged in military service, many of whom have held at least the rank of non-commissioned officers, there are in every popular insurrection several persons competent to take the lead, and improvise some tolerable plan of action. What the French are in military affairs, the Americans are in every kind of civil business; let them be left without a government, every body of Americans is able to improvise one, and to carry on that or any other public business with a sufficient amount of intelligence, order, and decision. This is what every free people ought to be: and a people capable of this is certain to be free; it will never let itself be enslaved by any man or body of men because these are able to seize and pull the reins of the central administration. No bureaucracy can hope to make such a people as this do or undergo anything that they do not like. But where everything is done through the bureaucracy, nothing to which the bureaucracy is really adverse can be done at all. The constitution of such countries is an organization of the experience and practical ability of the nation, into a disciplined body for the purpose of governing the rest; and the more perfect that organization is in itself, the more successful in drawing to itself and educating for itself the persons of greatest capacity from all ranks of the community, the more complete is the bondage of all, the members of the bureaucracy included. For the governors are as much the slaves of their organization and discipline, as the governed are of the governors. A Chinese mandarin is as much the tool and creature of a despotism as the humblest cultivator. An individual Jesuit is to the utmost degree of abasement the slave of his order, though the order itself exists for the collective power and importance of its members. . . .

To determine the point at which evils, so formidable to human freedom and advancement, begin, or rather at which they begin to predominate over the benefits attending the collective application of the force of society, under its recognized chiefs, for the removal of the obstacles which stand in the way of its well-being; to secure as much of the advantages of centralized power and intelligence, as can be had without turning into governmental channels too great a proportion of the general activity—is one of the most difficult and complicated questions in the art of government. It is, in a great measure, a question of detail, in which many and various considerations must be kept in view, and no absolute rule can be laid down. But I believe that the practical principle in which safety resides, the ideal to be kept in view, the standard by which to test all arrangements intended for overcoming the difficulty, may be conveyed in these words: the greatest dissemination of power consistent with efficiency; but the greatest possible centralization of information, and diffusion of it from the centre. Thus, in municipal administration, there would be, as in the New England States, a very minute division among separate officers, chosen by the localities, of all business which is not better left to the persons directly interested; but besides this, there would be, in each department of local affairs, a central superintendence, forming a branch of the general government. The organ of this superintendence would concentrate, as in a focus, the variety of information and experience derived from the conduct of that branch of public business in all the localities, from everything analogous which is done in foreign countries, and from the general principles of political science. This central organ should have a right to know all that is done, and its special duty should be that of making the knowledge acquired in one place available for others. Emancipated from the petty prejudices and narrow views of a locality by its elevated position and comprehensive sphere of observation, its advice would naturally carry much authority, but its actual power, as a permanent institution, should, I conceive, be limited to compelling the local officers to obey the laws laid down for their guidance. In all things not provided for by general rules, those officers should be left to their own judgement, under responsibility to their constituents. For the violation of rules, they should be responsible to law, and the rules themselves should be laid down by the legislature; the central administrative authority only watching over their execution, and if they were not properly carried into effect, appealing, according to the nature of the case, to the tribunals to enforce the law, or to the constituencies to dismiss the functionaries who had not executed it according to its spirit. Such, in its general conception, is the central superintendence which the Poor Law Board is intended to exercise over the administrators of the Poor Rate throughout the country. Whatever powers the Board exercises beyond this limit, were right and necessary in that peculiar case, for the cure of rooted habits of maladministration in matters deeply affecting not the localities merely, but the whole community; since no locality has a moral right to make itself by mismanagement a nest of pauperism, necessity overflowing into other localities, and impairing the moral and physical condition of the whole labouring community. The powers of administrative coercion and subordinate legislation possessed by the Poor Law Board (but which, owing to the state of opinion on the subject, are very scantily exercised by them), though perfectly justifiable in a case of first-rate national interest, would be wholly out of place in the superintendence of interests purely local. But a central organ of information and instruction for all the localities, would be equally valuable in all departments of administration. A government cannot have too much of the kind of activity which does not impede, but aids and stimulates, individual exertion and development. The mischief begins when, instead of calling forth the activity and powers of individuals and bodies, it substitutes its own activity for theirs; when, instead of informing, advising, and, upon occasion, denouncing, it makes them work in fetters, or bids them stand aside and does their work instead of them. The worth of a State, in the long run, is the worth of the individuals composing it; and a State which postpones the interest of *their* mental expansion and elevation, to a little more of administrative skill, or of that semblance of it which practice gives, in the details of business; a State which dwarfs its men, in order that they may be more docile instruments in its hands even for beneficial purposes—will find that with small men no great thing can really be accomplished; and that the perfection of machinery to which it has sacrificed everything, will in the end avail it nothing, for want of the vital power which, in order that the machine might work more smoothly, it has preferred to banish.

MATTHEW ARNOLD

MATTHEW ARNOLD (1822–88) was the eldest son of Thomas Arnold, famous headmaster of Rugby and a leader of the liberals in the Church of England. From his father he inherited a high sense of duty, rigid intellectual honesty, and a deep interest in religious, ethical, and social problems. During his school years at Rugby, Arnold won a prize for his first published poem, and, in 1841, a scholarship to Balliol College, Oxford. Oxford was then the center of the Tractarian Movement, which sought to save the Church of England for orthodoxy from liberal Christians like Arnold's father. Even so, the movement interested him little. Though he admired the orthodox Newman's personal grace and charm, his intellectual influence on Arnold was slight. During these years Arnold made the first of many trips to France and formed the interest in French culture and national character that appears in much of his writing.

Between 1845 and 1857 Arnold was a Fellow of Oriel College, taught classics at Rugby, wrote poetry, and began his important work in education as an inspector of schools. In 1857 he became the first layman to be elected to the poetry chair at Oxford, where he broke all precedents by lecturing in English instead of Latin. From 1857 to 1869 Arnold published more poems, several articles in favor of the reform of English education, and his striking *Essays in Criticism*. In these essays he suggested a new critical method by treating criticism as a deliberate and disinterested art with ways and methods of its own, "a disinterested endeavor to learn and propagate the best that is known and thought in the world."

After 1867, Arnold wrote little poetry. He turned his energy to criticism, not just of literature, but also of religion and society. His standards for judging literature had, in fact, been ethical rather than strictly "aesthetic"; he considered poetry a "criticism of life." *Culture and Anarchy* (1869), in part an answer to Mill's *On Liberty,* was followed by *Literature and Dogma* (1873), *God and the Bible* (1875), and *Mixed Essays* (1879). A pension of £250 a year from Gladstone in 1883 gave Arnold a chance to tour America, where he had difficulty making audiences understand him, even after a few lessons in elocution. *Discourses in America,* a study of problems affecting national character, was the work by which he especially desired to be remembered. *Essays in Criticism, Second Series* appeared in 1888, the last year of his life.

Culture, for Arnold, was a way to self-realization. He sought to impress upon his generation humanistic ideals which would save society from "philistinism," by which he meant vulgarity, narrow-mindedness, and complacency. *Culture and Anarchy,* from which the following selection is taken, was the first book Arnold wrote to illustrate his broad conception of criticism as the vindication of an ideal humanity against corrupting influences. Because his special topic here is social conditions in England, the reader must remember that 1866 was the year of the Hyde Park riots; that the Second Reform Bill extended the suffrage in 1867, announcing to the consternation of conservatives that England was to be a democracy; and that imprisonment for debt was abolished in 1869, the year *Culture and Anarchy* was published.

CULTURE AND ANARCHY

CHAPTER II: DOING AS ONE LIKES

I HAVE BEEN TRYING to show that culture is, or ought to be, the study and pursuit of perfection; and that of perfection, as pursued by culture, beauty and intelligence, or, in other words, sweetness and light, are the main characters. But hitherto I have been insisting chiefly on beauty, or sweetness, as a character of perfection. To complete rightly my design, it evidently remains to speak also of intelligence, or light, as a character of perfection.

First, however, I ought perhaps to notice that, both here and on the other side of the Atlantic, all sorts of objections are raised against the "religion of culture," as the objectors mockingly call it, which I am supposed to be promulgating. It is said to be a religion proposing parmaceti, or some scented salve or other, as a cure for human miseries; a religion breathing a spirit of cultivated inaction, making its believer refuse to lend a hand at uprooting the definite evils on all sides of us, and filling him with antipathy against the reforms and reformers which try to extirpate them. In general, it is summed up as being not practical, or,—as some critics familiarly put it,—all moonshine. That Alcibiades, the editor of the *Morning Star,* taunts me, as its promulgator, with living out of the world and knowing nothing of life and men. That great austere toiler, the editor of the *Daily Telegraph,* upbraids me,—but kindly, and more in sorrow than in anger,—for trifling with aesthetics and poetical fancies, while he himself, in that arsenal of his in Fleet Street, is bearing the burden and heat of the day. An intelligent American newspaper, the *Nation,* says that it is very easy to sit in one's study and find fault with the course of modern society, but the thing is to propose practical improvements for it. While, finally, Mr. Frederic Harrison, in a very good tempered and witty satire, which makes me quite understand his having apparently achieved such a conquest of my young Prussian friend, Arminius, at last gets moved to an almost stern moral impatience, to behold, as he says, "Death, sin, cruelty stalk among us, filling their maws with innocence and youth," and me, in the midst of the general tribulation, handing out my poucet-box.

It is impossible that all these remonstrances and reproofs should not affect me, and I shall try my very best, in completing my design and speaking of light as one of the characters of perfection, and of culture as giving us light, to profit by the objections I have heard and read, and to drive at practice as much as I can, by showing the communications and passages into practical life from the doctrine which I am inculcating.

It is said that a man with my theories of sweetness and light is full of antipathy against the rougher or coarser movements going on around him, that he will not lend a hand to the humble operation of uprooting evil by their means, and that therefore the believers in action grow impatient with him. But what if rough and coarse action, ill-calculated action, action with insufficient insight is, and has for a long time been, our bane? What if our urgent want now is, not to act at any price, but rather to lay in a stock of light for our difficulties? In that case, to refuse to lend a hand to the rougher and coarser movements going on round us, to make the primary need, both for oneself and others, to consist in enlightening ourselves and qualifying ourselves to act less at random, is surely the best and in real truth the most practical line our endeavours can take. So that if I can show what my opponents call rough or coarse action, but what I would rather call random and ill-regulated action,—action with insufficient light, action pursued because we like to be doing something and doing it as we please, and do not like the trouble of thinking and the severe constraint of any kind of rule,—if I can show this to be, at the present moment, a practical mischief and dangerous to us, then I have found a practical use for light, in correcting this state of things, and have only to exemplify how, in cases which fall under everybody's observation, it may deal with it.

When I began to speak of culture, I insisted on our bondage to machinery, on our proneness to value machinery as an end in itself, without looking beyond it to the end for which alone, in truth, it is valuable. Freedom, I said, was one of those things which we thus worshipped in itself, without enough regarding the ends for which freedom is to be desired. In our common notions and talk about freedom, we eminently show our idolatry of machinery. Our prevalent notion is,—and I quoted a number of instances to prove it,—that it is a most happy and important thing for a man merely to be able to do as he likes. On what he is to do when he is thus free to do as he likes, we do not lay so much stress. Our familiar praise of the British Constitution under which we live, is that it is a system of checks—a system which stops and paralyses any power in interfering with the free action of individuals. To this effect Mr. Bright, who loves to walk in the old ways of the Constitution, said forcibly in one of his great speeches, what many other people are every day saying less forcibly, that the central idea of English life and politics is *the assertion of personal liberty*. Evidently this is so; but, evidently, also, as feudalism, which with its ideas and habits of subordination was for many centuries silently behind the British Constitution, dies out, and we are left with nothing but our system of checks, and our notion of its being the great right and happiness of an Englishman to do as far as possible what he likes, we are in danger of drifting towards anarchy. We have not the notion, so familiar on the Continent and to antiquity, *of the State,*—the nation in its collective and corporate character, entrusted with stringent powers for the general advantage, and controlling individual wills in the name of an interest wider than that of individuals. We say, what is very true, that this notion is often made instrumental to tyranny; we say that a State is in reality made up of the individuals who compose it, and that every individual is the best judge of his own interests. Our leading class is an aristocracy, and no aristocracy likes the notion of a State-authority greater than itself, with a stringent administrative machinery, superseding the decorative inutilities of lord-lieutenancy, deputy-lieutenancy, and the *posse comitatus,* which are all in its own hands. Our middle class, the great representative of trade and Dissent, with its maxims of every man for himself in business, every man for himself in religion, dreads a powerful administration which might somehow interfere with it; and besides, it has its own decorative inutilities of vestrymanship and guardianship, which are to this class what lord-lieutenancy and the country magistracy are to the aristocratic class, and a stringent administration might either take these functions out of its hands, or prevent its exercising them in its own comfortable, independent manner, as at present.

Then as to our working class. This class, pressed constantly by the hard daily compulsion of material wants, is naturally the very centre and stronghold of our national idea, that it is man's ideal right and felicity to do as he likes. I think I have somewhere related how M. Michelet said to me of the people of France, that it was "a nation of barbarians civilised by the conscription." He meant that through their military service the idea of public duty and discipline was brought to the mind of these masses, in other respects so raw and uncultivated. Our masses are quite as raw and uncultivated as the French; and so far from having the idea of public duty and of discipline, superior to the individual's self-will, brought to their mind by a universal obligation of military service, such as that of the conscription,—so far from their having this, the very idea of a conscription is so at variance with our English notion of the prime right and blessedness of doing as one likes, that I remember the manager of the Clay Cross works in Derbyshire told me during the Crimean war, when our want of soldiers was much felt and some people were talking of a conscription, that sooner than submit to a conscription the population of that district would flee to the mines, and lead a sort of Robin Hood life under ground.

For a long time, as I have said, the strong feudal habits of subordination and deference continue to tell upon the working class. The modern spirit has now almost entirely dissolved those habits, and the anarchical tendency of our worship of freedom in and for itself, of our superstitious faith, as I say, in machinery, because of our want of light to enable us to look beyond machinery to the end for which machinery is valuable, this and that man, and this and that body of men, all over the country, are beginning to assert and put in practice an Englishman's right to do what he likes; his right to march where he likes, meet where he likes, enter where he likes, hoot as he likes, threaten as he likes, smash as he likes. All this, I say, tends to anarchy; and though a number of excellent people, and particularly my friends of the Liberal or progressive party, as they call themselves, are kind enough to reassure us by saying that these are trifles, that a few transient outbreaks of rowdyism signify nothing, that our system of liberty is one which itself cures all the evils which it works, that the educated and intelligent classes stand in overwhelming strength and majestic repose, ready, like our military force in riots, to act at a moment's notice,—yet one finds that one's Liberal friends generally say this because they have such faith in themselves and their nostrums, when they shall return, as the public welfare requires, to place and power. But this faith of theirs one cannot exactly share, when one has so long had them and their nostrums at work, and sees that they have not prevented our coming to our present embarrassed condition. And one finds, also, that the outbreaks of rowdyism tend to become less and less of trifles, to become more frequent rather than less frequent; and that meanwhile our educated and intelligent classes remain in their majestic repose, and somehow or other, whatever happens, their overwhelming strength, like our military force in riots, never does act.

How, indeed, *should* their overwhelming strength act, when the man who gives an inflammatory lecture, or breaks down the park railings, or invades a Secretary of State's office, is only following an Englishman's impulse to do as he likes; and our own conscience tells us that we ourselves have always regarded this impulse as something primary and sacred? Mr. Murphy lectures at Birmingham, and showers on the Catholic population of that town "words" says the Home Secretary, "only fit to be addressed to thieves or murderers." What then? Mr. Murphy has his own reasons of several kinds. He suspects the Roman Catholic Church of designs upon Mrs. Murphy; and he says, if mayors and magistrates do not care for their wives and daughters, he does. But, above all, he is doing as he likes; or, in worthier language, asserting his personal liberty. "I will carry out my lectures if they walk over my body as a dead corpse; and I say to the Mayor of Birmingham that he is my servant while I am in Birmingham, and as my servant he must do his duty and protect me." Touching and beautiful words, which find a sympathetic chord in every British bosom! The moment it is plainly put before us that a man is asserting his personal liberty, we are half-disarmed; because we are believers in freedom, and not in some dream of a right reason to which the assertion of our freedom is to be subordinated. Accordingly, the Secretary of State had to say that although the lecturer's language was "only fit to be addressed to thieves or murderers," yet, "I do not think he is to be deprived, I do not think that anything I have said could justify the inference that he is to be deprived, of the right of protection in a place built by him for the purpose of these lectures; because the language was not language which afforded grounds for criminal prosecution." No, nor to be silenced by Mayor, or Home Secretary, or any administrative authority on earth, simply on their notion of what is discreet and reasonable! This is in perfect consonance with our public opinion, and with our national love for the assertion of personal liberty.

In quite another department of affairs, an experienced and distinguished Chancery Judge relates an incident which is just to the same effect as this of Mr. Murphy. A testator bequeathed £300 a year, to be for ever applied as a pension to some person who had been unsuccessful in literature, and whose duty should be to support and diffuse, by his writings, the testator's own views, as enforced in the testator's publications. The views were not worth a straw, and the bequest was appealed against in the Court of Chancery on the ground of its absurdity; but, being only absurd, it was upheld, and the so-called charity was established. Having, I say, at the bottom of our English hearts a very strong belief in freedom, and a very weak belief in right reason, we are soon silenced when a man pleads the prime right to do as he likes, because this is the prime right for ourselves too; and even if we attempt now and then to mumble something about reason, yet we have ourselves thought so little about this and so much about liberty, that we are in conscience forced, when our brother Philistine with whom we are meddling turns boldly round upon us and asks: *Have you any light?*—to shake our heads, ruefully, and to let him go his own way after all.

There are many things to be said on behalf of this exclusive attention of ours to liberty, and of the relaxed habits of government which it has engendered. It is very easy to mistake or to exaggerate the sort of anarchy from which we are in danger through them. We are not in danger from Fenianism, fierce and turbulent as it may show itself; for against this our conscience is free enough to let us act resolutely and put forth our overwhelming strength the moment there is any real need for it. In the first place, it never was any part of our creed that the great right and blessedness of an Irishman, or, indeed, of anybody on earth except an Englishman, is to do as he likes; and we can have no scruple at all about abridging, if necessary, a non-Englishman's assertion of personal liberty. The British Constitution, its checks, and its prime virtues, are for Englishmen. We may extend them to others out of love and kindness; but we find no real divine law written on our hearts constraining us to so extend them. And then the difference between an Irish Fenian and an English rough is so immense, and the case, in dealing with the Fenian, so much more clear! He is so evidently desperate and dangerous, a man of a conquered race, a Papist, with centuries of ill-usage to inflame him against us, with an alien religion established in his country by us at his expense, with no admiration of our institutions, no love of our virtues, no talents for our business, no turn for our comfort! Show him our symbolical Truss Manufactory on the finest site in Europe, and tell him that Bristish industrialism and individualism can bring a man to that, and he remains cold! Evidently, if we deal tenderly with a sentimentalist like this, it is out of pure philanthropy.

But with the Hyde Park rioter how different! He is our own flesh and blood; he is a Protestant; he is framed by nature to do as we do, hate what we hate, love what we love; he is capable of feeling the symbolical force of the Truss Manufactory; the question of questions, for him, is a wages question. That beautiful sentence Sir Daniel Gooch quoted to the Swindon workmen, and which I treasure as Mrs. Gooch's Golden Rule, or the Divine Injunction "Be ye Perfect" done into British—the sentence Sir Daniel Gooch's mother repeated to him every morning when he was a boy going to work: *"Ever remember, my dear Dan, that you should look forward to being some day manager of that concern!"*—this fruitful maxim is perfectly fitted to shine forth in the heart of the Hyde Park rough also, and to be his guiding-star through life. He has no visionary schemes of revolution and transformation, though of course he would like his class to rule, as the aristocratic class like their class to rule, and the middle class theirs. But meanwhile our social machine is a little out of order; there are a good many people in our paradisiacal centres of industrialism and individualism taking the bread out of one another's mouths. The rough has not yet quite found his groove and settled down to his work, and so he is just asserting his personal liberty a little, going where he likes, assembling where he likes, bawling as he likes, hustling as he likes. Just as the rest of us,—as the country squires in the aristocractic class, as the political Dissenters in the middle class,—he has no idea of a *State,* of the nation in its collective and corporate character controlling, as government, the free swing of this or that one of its members in the name of the higher reason of all of them, his own as well as that of others. He sees the rich, the aristocratic class, in occupation of the executive government, and so if he is stopped from making Hyde Park a bear-garden or the streets impassable, he says he is being butchered by the artistocracy.

His apparition is somewhat embarrassing, because too many cooks spoil the broth; because, while the aristocratic and middle classes have long been doing as they like with great vigour, he has been too undeveloped and submissive hitherto to join in the game; and now, when he does come, he comes in immense numbers, and is rather raw and rough. But he does not break many laws, or not many at one time: and, as our laws were made for very different circumstances from our present (but always with an eye to Englishmen doing as they like), and as the clear letter of the law must be against our Englishman who does as he likes and not only the spirit of the law and public policy, and as Government must neither have any discretionary power nor act resolutely on its own interpretation of the law if any one disputes it, it is evident our laws give our playful giant, in doing as he likes, considerable advantage. Besides, even if he can be clearly proved to commit an illegality in doing as he likes, there is always the resource of not putting the law in force, or of abolishing it. So he has his way, and if he has his way he is soon satisfied for the time. However, he falls into the habit of taking it oftener and oftener, and at last begins to create by his operations a confusion of which mischievous people can take advantage, and which at any rate, by troubling the common course of business throughout the country, tends to cause distress, and so to increase the sort of anarchy and social disintegration which had previously commenced. And thus that profound sense of settled order and security, without which a society like ours cannot live and grow at all, sometimes seems to be beginning to threaten us with taking its departure.

Now, if culture, which simply means trying to perfect oneself, and one's mind as part of oneself, brings us light, and if light shows us that there is nothing so very blessed in merely doing as one likes, that the worship of the mere freedom to do as one likes is worship of machinery, that the really blessed thing is to like what right reason ordains, and to follow her authority, then we have got a practical benefit out of culture. We have got a much wanted principle, a principle of authority, to counteract the tendency to anarchy which seems to be threatening us.

But how to organise this authority, or to what hands to entrust the wielding of it? How to get your *State,* summing up the right reason of the community, and giving effect to it, as circumstances may require, with vigour? And here I think I see my enemies waiting for me with a hungry joy in their eyes. But I shall elude them.

The *State,* the power most representing the right reason of the nation, and most worthy, therefore, of ruling,—of exercising, when circumsances require it, authority over us all,—is for Mr. Carlyle the aristocracy. For Mr. Lowe, it is the middle class with its incomparable Parliament. For the Reform League, it is the working class, the class with "the brightest powers of sympathy and readiest powers of action." Now culture, with its disinterested pursuit of perfection, culture, simply trying to see things as they are in order to seize on the best and to make it prevail, is surely well fitted to help us to judge rightly, by all the aids of observing, reading, and thinking, the qualifications and titles to our confidence of these three candidates for authority, and can thus render us a practical service of no mean value.

So when Mr. Carlyle, a man of genius to whom we have all at one time or other been indebted for refreshment and stimulus, says we should give rule to the aristocracy, mainly because of its dignity and politeness, surely culture is useful in reminding us, that in our idea of perfection the characters of beauty and intelligence are both of them present, and sweetness and light, the two noblest of things, are united. Allowing, therefore, with Mr. Carlyle, the aristocratic class to possess sweetness, culture insists on the necessity of light also, and shows us that aristocracies, being by the very nature of things inaccessible to ideas, unapt to see how the world is going, must be somewhat wanting in light, and must therefore be, at a moment when light is our great requisite, inadequate to our needs. Aristocracies, those children of the established fact, are for epochs of concentration. In epochs of expansion, epochs such as that in which we now live, epochs when always the warning voice is again heard: *Now is the judgment of this world,*—in such epochs aristocracies with their natural clinging to the established fact, their want of sense for the flux of things, for the inevitable transitoriness of all human institutions, are bewildered and helpless. Their serenity, their high spirit, their power of haughty resistance,—the great qualities of an aristocracy, and the secret of its distinguished manners and dignity,—these very qualities, in an epoch of expansion, turn against their possessors. Again and again I have said how the refinement of an aristocracy may be precious and educative to a raw nation as a kind of shadow of true refinement; how its serenity and dignified freedom from petty cares may serve as a useful foil to set off the vulgarity and hideousness of that type of life which a hard middle class tends to establish, and to help people to see this vulgarity and hideousness in their true colours. But the true grace and serenity is that of which Greece and Greek art suggest the admirable ideals of perfection,—a serenity which comes from having made order among ideas and harmonised them; whereas the serenity of aristocracies, at least the peculiar serenity of aristocracies of Teutonic origin, appears to come from their never having any ideas to trouble them. And so, in a time of expansion like the present, a time for ideas, one gets, perhaps, in regarding an aristocracy, even more than the idea of serenity, the idea of futility and sterility.

One has often wondered whether upon the whole earth there is anything so unintelligent, so unapt to perceive how the world is really going, as an ordinary young Englishman of our upper class. Ideas he has not, and neither has he that seriousness of our middle class which is, as I have often said, the great strength of this class, and may become its salvation. Why, a man may hear a young Dives of the aristocratic class, when the whim takes him to sing the praises of wealth and material comfort, sing them with a cynicism from which the conscience of the veriest Philistine of our industrial middle class would recoil in affright. And when, with the natural sympathy of aristocracies for firm dealing with the multitude, and his uneasiness at our feeble dealing with it at home, an unvarnished young Englishman of our aristocratic class applauds the absolute rulers on the Continent, he in general manages completely to miss the grounds of reason and intelligence which alone can give any colour of justification, any possibility of existence, to those rulers, and applauds them on grounds which it would make their own hair stand on end to listen to.

And all this time we are in an epoch of expansion; and the essence of an epoch of expansion is a movement of ideas, and the one salvation of an epoch of expansion is a harmony of ideas. The very principle of the authority which we are seeking as a defence against anarchy is right reason, ideas, light. The more, therefore, an aristocracy calls to its aid its innate forces,—its impenetrability, its high spirit, its power of haughty resistance,—to deal with an epoch of expansion, the graver is the danger, the greater the certainty of explosion, the surer the aristocracy's defeat; for it is trying to do violence to nature instead of working along with it. The best powers shown by the best men of an aristocracy at such an epoch are, it will be observed, non-aristocratical powers, powers of industry, powers of intelligence; and these powers thus exhibited, tend really not to strengthen the aristocracy, but to take their owners out of it, to expose them to the dissolving agencies of thought and change, to make them men of the modern spirit and of the future. If, as sometimes happens, they add to their non-aristocratical qualities also,—of pride, defiance, turn for resistance,—this truly aristocratical side of them, so far from adding any strength to them, really neutralises their force and makes them impracticable and ineffective.

Knowing myself to be indeed sadly to seek, as one of my many critics says, in "a philosophy with coherent, inter-dependent, subordinate and derivative principles," I continually have recourse to a plain man's expedient of trying to make what few simple notions I have, clearer and more intelligible to myself by means of example and illustration. And having been brought up at Oxford in the bad old times, when we were stuffed with Greek and Aristotle, and thought nothing of preparing ourselves by the study of modern languages,— as after Mr. Lowe's great speech at Edinburgh we shall do,—to fight the battle of life with the waiters in foreign hotels, my head is still full of a lumber of phrases we learnt at Oxford from Aristotle, about virtue being in a mean, and about excess and defect and so on. Once when I had had the advantage of listening to the Reform debates in the House of Commons, having heard a number of interesting speakers, and among them a well-known lord and a well-known baronet, I remember it struck me, applying Aristotle's machinery of the mean to my ideas about our aristocracy, that the lord was exactly the perfection, or happy mean, or virtue, of aristocracy, and the baronet the excess. And I fancied that by observing these two we might see both the inadequacy of aristocracy to supply the principle of authority needful for our present wants, and the danger of its trying to supply it when it was not really competent for the business. On the one hand, in the brilliant lord, showing plenty of high spirit, but remarkable, far above and beyond his gift of high spirit, for the fine tempering of his high spirit, for ease, serenity, politeness,— the great virtues, as Mr. Carlyle says, of aristocracy,—in this beautiful and virtuous mean, there seemed evidently some insufficiency of light; while, on the other hand, the worthy baronet, in whom the high spirit of aristocracy, its impenetrability, defiant courage, and pride of resistance, were developed even in excess, was manifestly capable, if he had his way given him, of causing us great danger, and, indeed, of throwing the whole commonwealth into confusion. Then I reverted to that old fundamental notion of mine about the grand merit of our race being really our honesty. And the very helplessness of our aristocratic or governing class in dealing with our perturbed social condition, their jealousy of entrusting too much power to the State as it now actually exists—that is to themselves—gave me a sort of pride and satisfaction; because I saw they were, as a whole, too honest to try and manage a business for which they did not feel themselves capable.

Surely, now, it is no inconsiderable boon which culture confers upon us, if in embarrassed times like the present it enables us to look at the ins and the outs of things in this way, without hatred and without partiality, and with a disposition to see the good in everybody all round. And I try to follow just the same course with our middle class as with our aristocracy. Mr. Lowe talks to us of this strong middle part of the nation, of the unrivaled deeds of our Liberal middle-class Parliament, of the noble, the heroic work it has performed in the last thirty years; and I begin to ask myself if we shall not, then, find in our middle class the principle of authority we want, and if we had not better take administration as well as legislation away from the weak extreme which now administers for us, and commit both to the strong middle part. I observe, too, that the heroes of middle-class liberalism, such as we have hitherto known it, speak with a kind of prophetic anticipation of the great destiny which awaits them, and as if the future was clearly theirs. The advanced party, the progressive party, the party in alliance with the future, are the names they like to give themselves. "The principles which will obtain recognition in the future," says Mr. Miall, a personage of deserved eminence among the political Dissenters, as they are called, who have been the backbone of middle-class liberalism —"the principles which will obtain recognition in the future are the principles for which I have long and zealously laboured. I qualified myself for joining in the work of harvest by doing to the best of my ability the duties of seed-time." These duties, if one is to gather them from the works of the great Liberal party in the last thirty years, are, as I have elsewhere summed them up, the advocacy of free trade, of Parliamentary reform, of abolition of church-rates, of voluntaryism in religion and education, of non-interference of the State between employers and employed, and of marriage with one's deceased wife's sister.

Now I know, when I object that all this is machinery, the great Liberal middle class has by this time grown cunning enough to answer that it always meant more by these things than meets the eye; that it has had that within which passes show, and that we are soon going to see, in a Free Church and all manner of good things, what it was. But I have learned from Bishop Wilson (if Mr. Frederic Harrison will forgive my again quoting that poor old hierophant of a decayed superstition) : "If we would really know our heart let us impartially view our actions"; and I cannot help thinking that if our Liberals had had so much sweetness and light in their inner minds as they allege, more of it must have come out in their sayings and doings.

An American friend of the English Liberals says, indeed, that their Dissidence of Dissent has been a mere instrument of the political Dissenters for making reason and the will of God prevail (and no doubt he would say the same of marriage with one's deceased wife's sister) ; and that the abolition of a State Church is merely the Dissenter's means to this end, just as culture is mine. Another American defender of theirs says just the same of their industrialism and free trade; indeed, this gentlemen, taking the bull by the horns, proposes that we should for the future call industrialism culture, and the industrialists the men of culture, and then of course there can be no longer any misapprehension about their true character; and besides the pleasure of being wealthy and comfortable, they will have authentic recognition as vessels of sweetness and light.

All this is undoubtedly specious; but I must remark that the culture of which I talked was an endeavour to come at reason and the will of God by means of reading, observing, and thinking; and that whoever calls anything else culture may, indeed, call it so if he likes, but then he talks of something quite different from what I talked of. And, again, as culture's way of working for reason and the will of God is by directly trying to know more about them, while the Dissidence of Dissent is evidently in itself no effort of this kind, nor is its Free Church, in fact, a church with worthier conceptions of God and the ordering of the whole than the State Church professes, but with mainly the same conceptions of these as the State Church has, only that every man is to comport himself as he likes in professing them,—this being so, I cannot at once accept the Nonconformity any more than the industrialism and the other great works of our Liberal middle class as proof positive that this class is in possession of light, and that here is the true seat of authority for which we are in search; but I must try a little further, and seek for other indications which may enable me to make up my mind.

Why should we not do with the middle class as we have done with the aristocratic class,—find in it some representative men who may stand for the virtuous mean of this class, for the perfection of its present qualities and mode of being, and also for the excess of them. Such men must clearly not be men of genius like Mr. Bright; for, as I have formerly said, so far as a man has genius, he tends to take himself out of the category of class altogether, and to become simply a man. Some more ordinary man would be more to the purpose,—would sum up better in himself, without disturbing influences, the general liberal force of the middle class, the force by which it has done its great works of free trade, Parliamentary reform, voluntaryism, and so on, and the spirit in which it has done them. Now it happens that a typical middle-class man, the member for one of our chief industrial cities, has given us a famous sentence which bears directly on the resolution of our present question: whether there is light enough in our middle class to make it the proper seat of the authority we wish to establish. When there was a talk some little while ago about the state of middle-class education, our friend, as the representative of that class, spoke some memorable words:—"There had been a cry that middle-class education ought to receive more attention. He confessed himself very much surprised by the clamour that was raised. He did not think that class need excited the sympathy either of the legislature or the public." Now this satisfaction of our middle-class member of Parliament with the mental state of the middle class was truly representative, and makes good his claim to stand as the beautiful and virtuous mean of that class. But it is obviously at variance with our definition of culture, or the pursuit of light and perfection, which made light and perfection consist, not in resting and being, but in growing and becoming, in a perpetual advance in beauty and wisdom. So the middle class is by its essence, as one may say, by its incomparable self-satisfaction decisively expressed through its beautiful and virtuous mean, self-excluded from wielding an authority of which light is to be the very soul.

Clear as this is, it will be made clearer still if we take some representative man as the excess of the middle class, and remember that the middle class, in general, is to be conceived as a body swaying between the qualities of its mean and of its excess, and on the whole, of course, as human nature is constituted, inclining rather towards the excess than the mean. Of its excess no better representative can possibly be imagined than a Dissenting minister from Walsall, who came before the public in connexion with the proceedings at Birmingham of Mr. Murphy, already mentioned. Speaking in the midst of an irritated population of Catholics, this Walsall gentleman exclaimed:—"I say, then, away with the Mass! It is from the bottomless pit; and in the bottomless pit shall all liars have their part, in the lake that burneth with fire and brimstone." And again: "When all the praties were black in Ireland, why didn't the priests say the hocus-pocus over them, and make them all good again?" He shared, too, Mr. Murphy's fear of some invasion of his domestic happiness: "What I wish to say to you as Protestant husbands, is, *Take care of your wives!*" And, finally, in the true vein of an Englishman doing as he likes, a vein of which I have at some length pointed out the present dangers, he recommended for imitation the example of some churchwardens at Dublin, among whom, said he, "there was a Luther and also a Melanchthon," who had made very short work of some ritualist or other, hauled him down from his pulpit, and kicked him out of church. Now it is manifest, as I said in the case of our aristocratical baronet, that if we let this excess of the sturdy English middle class, this conscientious Protestant Dissenter, so strong, so self-reliant, so fully persuaded in his own mind, have his way, he would be capable, with his want of light,—or, to use the language of the religious world, with his zeal without knowledge,—of stirring up strife which neither he nor anyone else could easily compose.

And then comes in, as it did also with the aristocracy, the honesty of our race, and by the voice of another middle-class man, Alderman of the City of London and Colonel of the City of London Militia, proclaims that it has

twinges of conscience, and that it will not attempt to cope with our social disorders, and to deal with a business which it feels to be too high for it. Every
one remembers how this virtuous Alderman-Colonel, or Colonel-Alderman,
led his militia through the London streets; how the bystanders gathered to
see him pass; how the London roughs, asserting an Englishman's best and
most blissful right of doing what he likes, robbed and beat the bystanders;
and how the blameless warrior-magistrate refused to let his troops interfere.
"The crowd," he touchingly said afterwards, "was mostly composed of fine
healthy strong men, bent on mischief; if he had allowed his soldiers to interfere they might have been overpowered, their rifles taken from them and used
against them by the mob; a riot in fact, might have ensued, and been attended
with bloodshed compared with which the assaults and loss of property that
actually occurred would have been as nothing." Honest and affecting testimony of the English middle class to its own inadequacy for the authoritative
part one's admiration would sometimes incline one to assign to it! "Who are
we," they say by the voice of their Alderman-Colonel, "that we should not be
overpowered if we attempt to cope with social anarchy, our rifles taken from
us and used against us by the mob, and we, perhaps, robbed and beaten ourselves? Or what light have we, beyond a free-born Englishman's impulse to
do as he likes, which could justify us in preventing, at the cost of bloodshed,
other free-born Englishman from doing as they like, and robbing and beating us as much as they please?"

This distrust of themselves as an adequate centre of authority does not mark
the working class, as was shown by their readiness the other day in Hyde Park
to take upon themselves all the functions of government. But this comes from
the working class being, as I have often said, still an embryo, of which no one
can foresee the final development; and from its not having the same experience and self-knowledge as the aristocratic and middle classes. Honesty it no
doubt has, just like the other classes of Englishmen, but honesty is an inchoate and untrained state; and meanwhile its powers of action, which are,
as Mr. Frederic Harrison says, exceedingly ready, easily run away with it.
That it cannot at present have a sufficiency of light which comes by culture,—
that is, by reading, observing, and thinking,—is clear from the very nature
of its condition; and, indeed, we saw that Mr. Frederic Harrison, in seeking
to make a free stage for its bright powers of sympathy and ready powers of
action, had to begin by throwing overboard culture, and flouting it as only fit
for a professor of *belles lettres*. Still, to make it perfectly manifest that no more
in the working class than in the aristocratic and middle classes can one find
an adequate centre of authority,—that is, as culture teaches us to conceive

our required authority, of light,—let us again follow, with this class, the method we have followed with the aristocratic and middle classes, and try to bring before our minds representative men, who may figure to us its virtue and its excess.

We must not take, of course, men like the chiefs of the Hyde Park demonstration, Colonel Dickson or Mr. Beales; because Colonel Dickson, by his martial profession and dashing exterior, seems to belong properly, like Julius Caesar and Mirabeau and other great popular leaders, to the aristocratic class, and to be carried into the popular ranks only by his ambition or his genius; while Mr. Beales belongs to our solid middle class, and, perhaps, if he had not been a great popular leader, would have been a Philistine. But Mr. Odger, whose speeches we have all read, and of whom his friends relate, besides, much that is favourable, may very well stand for the beautiful and virtuous mean of our present working class; and I think everybody will admit that in Mr. Odger there is manifestly, with all his good points, some insufficiency of light. The excess of the working class, in its present state of development, is perhaps best shown in Mr. Bradlaugh, the iconoclast, who seems to be almost for baptizing us all in blood and fire into his new social dispensation, and to whose reflexions, now that I have once been set going on Bishop Wilson's track, I cannot forbear commending this maxim of the good old man: "Intemperance in talk makes a dreadful havoc in the heart." Mr. Bradlaugh, like our types of excess in the aristocratic and middle classes, is evidently capable, if he had his head given him, of running us all into great dangers and confusion. I conclude, therefore,—what, indeed, few of those who do me the honour to read this disquisition are likely to dispute,—that we can as little find in the working class as in the aristocratic or in the middle class our much-wanted source of authority, as culture suggests it to us.

Well, then, what if we tried to rise above the idea of class to the idea of the whole community, *the State,* and to find our centre of light and authority there? Every one of us has the idea of country, as a sentiment; hardly any one of us has the idea of *the State,* as a working power. And why? Because we habitually live in our ordinary selves, which do not carry us beyond the ideas and wishes of the class to which we happen to belong. And we are all afraid of giving to the State too much power, because we only conceive of the State as something equivalent to the class in occupation of the executive government, and are afraid of that class abusing power to its own purposes. If we strengthen the State with the aristocratic class in occupation of the executive government, we imagine we are delivering ourselves up captive to the ideas and wishes of our fierce aristocratical baronet; if with the middle class in occupation of the executive government, to those of our truculent middle-class Dissenting minister; if with the working class, to those of its notorious tribune, Mr. Bradlaugh. And with justice; owing to the exaggerated notion which we English, as I have said, entertain of the right and blessedness of the mere doing as one likes, of the affirming oneself, and oneself just as it is. People of the aristocratic class want to affirm their ordinary selves, their likings and dislikings; people of the middle class the same, people of the working class the same. By our every-day selves, however, we are separate, personal, at war; we are only safe from one another's tyranny when no one has any power; and this safety, in its turn, cannot save us from anarchy. And when, therefore, anarchy presents itself as a danger to us, we know not where to turn.

But by our *best self* we are united, impersonal, at harmony. We are in no peril from giving authority to this, because it is the truest friend we all of us can have; and when anarchy is a danger to us, to this authority we may turn with sure trust. Well, and this is the very self which culture, or the study of perfection, seeks to develop in us; at the expense of our old untransformed self, taking pleasure only in doing what it likes or is used to do, and exposing us to the risk of clashing with every one else who is doing the same! So that our poor culture, which is flouted as so unpractical, leads us to the very ideas capable of meeting the great want of our present embarrassed times! We want an authority, and we find nothing but jealous classes, checks, and a deadlock; culture suggests the idea of *the State*. We find no basis for a firm State-power in our ordinary selves; culture suggests one to us in our *best self*.

It cannot but acutely try a tender conscience to be accused, in a practical country like ours, of keeping aloof from the work and hope of a multitude of earnest-hearted men, and of merely toying with poetry and aesthetics. So it is with no little sense of relief that I find myself thus in the position of one who makes a contribution in aid of the practical necessities of our times. The great thing, it will be observed, is to find our *best* self, and to seek to affirm nothing but that; not,—as we English with our over-value for merely being free and busy have been so accustomed to do,—resting satisfied with a self which comes uppermost long before our best self, and affirming that with blind energy. In short,—to go back yet once more to Bishop Wilson,—of these two excellent rules of Bishop Wilson's for a man's guidance: "Firstly, never go against the best light you have; secondly, take care that your light be not darkness," we English have followed with praiseworthy zeal the first rule, but we have not given so much heed to the second. We have gone manfully according to the best light we have; but we have not taken enough care that this should be really the best light possible for us, that it should not be dark-ness. And, our honesty being very great, conscience has whispered to us that the light we were following, our ordinary self, was, indeed, perhaps, only an inferior self, only darkness, and that it would not do to impose this seriously on all the world.

But our best self inspires faith, and is capable of affording a serious principle of authority. For example. We are on our way to what the late Duke of Wellington, with his strong sagacity, foresaw and admirably described as "a revolution by due course of law." This is undoubtedly,—if we are still to live and grow, and this famous nation is not to stagnate and dwindle away on the one hand, or, on the other, to perish miserably in mere anarchy and confusion,—what we are on the way to. Great changes there must be, for a revolution cannot accomplish itself by due course of law. So whatever brings risk of tumult and disorder, multitudinous processions in the streets of our crowded towns, multitudinous meetings in their public places and parks,— demonstrations perfectly unnecessary in the present course of our affairs,—our best self, or right reason, plainly enjoins us to set our faces against. It enjoins us to encourage and uphold the occupants of the executive power, whoever they may be, in firmly prohibiting them. But it does this clearly and resolutely, and is thus a real principle of authority, because it does it with a free conscience; because in thus provisionally strengthening the executive power, it knows that it is not doing this merely to enable our aristocratical baronet to affirm himself as against our working men's tribune, or our middle-class Dissenter to affirm himself as against both. It knows that it is establishing *the State*, or organ of our collective best self, of our national right reason. And it has the testimony of conscience that it is stablishing the State on behalf of whatever great changes are needed, just as much as on behalf of order; stablishing it to deal just as stringently, when the time comes, with our baronet's aristocratical prejudices, or with the fanaticism of our middle-class Dissenter, as it deals with Mr. Bradlaugh's street-processions.

POPE PIUS IX

W HEN Giovanni Maria Mastai-Ferret was elected to the papacy on June 16, 1846, he began the longest pontificate in the history of the Roman Catholic Church. He adopted the name Pius in memory of his friend and mentor, Pius VII (1800–23), who had been, like himself, Bishop of Imola. Pius IX was widely regarded as a "liberal" and an Italian patriot in the early years of his administration.

The revolutions of 1848 in Italy and Austria convinced Pius of the incompatibility of political liberalism with ecclesiastical authority. Italian rebels forced him to flee from Rome in 1849, and his policy became one of utter hostility toward Italian nationalism. Papal relations with Piedmont became steadily worse as Italy moved closer to unification. After the Romans voted to join the Kingdom of Italy in 1870 the papacy was awarded a financial settlement by the new government and guarantees of sovereignty for the Vatican, but Pius chose to regard himself as a prisoner in Vatican City for the rest of his life and refused any dealings with the Italian government.

Pius IX was convinced that the chief danger to the Church lay in modern secular ideas which liberal Catholics were trying to incorporate into its doctrines. In the encyclical *Iamdudum cernimus* (March 18, 1861) he denounced "Piedmontese aggression" and those secular political doctrines which sought to undermine the authority of the Church. Two years later the Pope expressed his opposition to the sentiments espoused by Montalembert, the French leader of liberal Catholics.

On December 8, 1864, Pius issued the encyclical *Quanta cura*. Attached to it was the *Syllabus of Errors* listing eighty of the principle "errors of our times" which had previously been condemned in allocutions, encyclicals, and other apostolic letters. The *Syllabus* thus represented a reformulation and underlining of positions Pius had already taken during his pontificate; it was not a new pronouncement, except in so far as it made general what had previously been specific denunciations concerned with particular events. Representing a wholesale attack on the liberal Catholic position, the *Syllabus* immediately became the source of great controversy among clerics as well as lay members of the Church. The government of Napoleon III forbade its publication in France. Theologians like Newman questioned its binding power, concluding that it did not have the force of dogma and that each proposition was subject to theological comment and interpretation. The proclamation of the doctrine of papal infallibility at the Vatican Council in July, 1870, confirmed papal strength and represented final defeat for the liberal Catholic party.

Pius IX died on February 5, 1878. His long pontificate had been confronted with some of the most serious challenges in the history of the Church, the last of them being Bismarck's *Kulturkampf;* in his response to these challenges, Pius had a determining influence on the development of the modern papacy.

The text of the *Syllabus of Errors* comes from the *Dogmatic Canons and Decrees*, published by Devin-Adair in 1912.

꧁꧂

THE SYLLABUS OF PIUS IX

SYLLABUS *of the principal errors of our time, which are censured in the consistorial Allocutions, Encyclical and other Apostolic Letters of our Most Holy Lord, Pope Pius IX.*

I. PANTHEISM, NATURALISM AND ABSOLUTE RATIONALISM

1. There exists no Supreme, all-wise, all-provident Divine Being, distinct from the universe, and God is identical with the nature of things, and is, therefore, subject to changes. In effect, God is produced in man and in the world, and all things are God and have the very substance of God, and God is one and the same thing with the world, and, therefore, spirit with matter, necessity with liberty, good with evil, justice with injustice.—*Allocution "Maxima quidem," June 9, 1862.*

2. All action of God upon man and the world is to be denied.—*Ibid.*

3. Human reason, without any reference whatsoever to God, is the sole arbiter of truth and falsehood, and of good and evil; it is law to itself, and suffices, by its natural force, to secure the welfare of men and of nations.—*Ibid.*

4. All the truths of religion proceed from the innate strength of human reason; hence reason is the ultimate standard by which men can and ought to arrive at the knowledge of all truths of every kind.—*Ibid.* and *Encyclical "Qui pluribus," Nov. 9, 1846, etc.*

5. Divine revelation is imperfect, and therefore subject to a continual and indefinite progress, corresponding with the advancement of human reason.—*Ibid.*

6. The faith of Christ is in opposition to human reason, and divine revelation not only is not useful, but is even hurtful to the perfection of man.—*Ibid.*

7. The prophecies and miracles set forth and recorded in the Sacred Scriptures are the fiction of poets, and the mysteries of the Christian faith the result of philosophical investigations. In the books of the Old and the New Testament there are contained mythical inventions, and Jesus Christ is Himself a myth.—*Ibid.*

II. MODERATE RATIONALISM

8. As human reason is placed on a level with religion itself, so theological must be treated in the same manner as philosophical sciences.—*Allocution "Singulari quadam," Dec. 9, 1854.*

9. All the dogmas of the Christian religion are indiscriminately the object of natural science or philosophy; and human reason, enlightened solely in an historical way, is able, by its own natural strength and principles, to attain to the true science of even the most abstruse dogmas; provided only that such dogmas be proposed to reason itself as its object.—*Letters to the Archbishop of Munich, "Gravissimas inter," Dec. 11, 1862, and "Tuas libenter," Dec. 21, 1863.*

10. As the philosopher is one thing, and philosophy another, so it is the right and duty of the philosopher to subject himself to the authority which he shall have proved to be true; but philosophy neither can nor ought to submit to any such authority.—*Ibid., Dec. 11, 1862.*

11. The Church not only ought never to pass judgment on philosophy, but ought to tolerate the errors of philosophy, leaving it to correct itself.—*Ibid., Dec. 21, 1863.*

12. The decrees of the Apostolic See and of the Roman congregations impede the true progress of science.—*Ibid.*

13. The method and principles by which the old scholastic doctors cultivated theology are no longer suitable to the demands of our times and to the progress of the sciences.—*Ibid.*

14. Philosophy is to be treated without taking any account of supernatural revelation.—*Ibid.*

N.B. To the rationalistic system belong in great part the errors of Anthony Günther, condemned in the letter to the Cardinal Archbishop of Cologne, "Eximiam tumam," June 15, 1857, and in that to the Bishop of Breslau, "Dolore haud mediocri," April 30, 1860.

III. INDIFFERENTISM, LATITUDINARIANISM

15. Every man is free to embrace and profess that religion which, guided by the light of reason, he shall consider true.—*Allocution "Maxima quidem," June 9, 1862; Damnatio "Multiplices inter," June 10, 1851.*

16. Man may, in the observance of any religion whatever, find the way of eternal salvation, and arrive at eternal salvation.—*Encyclical "Qui pluribus," Nov. 9, 1846.*

17. Good hope at least is to be entertained of the eternal salvation of all

those who are not at all in the true Church of Christ.—*Encyclical "Quanto conficiamur," Aug. 10, 1863,* etc.

18. Protestantism is nothing more than another form of the same true Christian religion, in which form it is given to please God equally as in the Catholic Church.—*Encyclical "Noscitis," Dec. 8, 1849.*

IV. SOCIALISM, COMMUNISM, SECRET SOCIETIES, BIBLICAL SOCIETIES, CLERICO-LIBERAL SOCIETIES

Pests of this kind are frequently reprobated in the severest terms in the Encyclical "Qui pluribus," Nov. 9, 1846, Allocution "Quibus quantisque," April 20, 1849, Encyclical "Noscitis et nobiscum," Dec. 8, 1849, Allocution "Singulari quadam," Dec. 9, 1854, Encyclical "Quanto conficiamur," Aug. 10, 1863.

V. ERRORS CONCERNING THE CHURCH AND HER RIGHTS

19. The Church is not a true and perfect society, entirely free; nor is she endowed with proper and perpetual rights of her own, conferred upon her by her Divine Founder; but it appertains to the civil power to define what are the rights of the Church, and the limits within which she may exercise those rights.—*Allocution "Singulari quadam," Dec. 9, 1854,* etc.

20. The ecclesiastical power ought not to exercise its authority without the permission and assent of the civil government.—*Allocution "Meminit unusquisque," Sept. 30, 1861.*

21. The Church has not the power of defining dogmatically that the religion of the Catholic Church is the only true religion.—*Damnatio "Multiplices inter," June 10, 1851.*

22. The obligation by which Catholic teachers and authors are strictly bound is confined to those things only which are proposed to universal belief as dogmas of faith by the infallible judgment of the Church.—*Letter to the Archbishop of Munich, "Tuas libenter," Dec. 21, 1863.*

23. Roman pontiffs and ecumenical councils have wandered outside the limits of their powers, have usurped the rights of princes, and have even erred in defining matters of faith and morals.—*Damnatio "Multiplices inter," June 10, 1851.*

24. The Church has not the power of using force, nor has she any temporal power, direct or indirect.—*Apostolic Letter "Ad Apostolicae," Aug. 22, 1851.*

25. Besides the power inherent in the episcopate, other temporal power has been attributed to it by the civil authority, granted either explicitly or tacitly, which on that account is revocable by the civil authority whenever it thinks fit.—*Ibid.*

26. The Church has no innate and legitimate right of acquiring and possessing property.—*Allocution "Nunquam fore," Dec. 15, 1856; Encyclical "Incredibili," Sept. 7, 1863.*

27. The sacred ministers of the Church and the Roman pontiff are to be absolutely excluded from every charge and dominion over temporal affairs.—*Allocution "Maxima quidem," June 9, 1862.*

28. It is not lawful for bishops to publish even letters Apostolic without the permission of Government.—*Allocution "Nunquam fore," Dec. 15, 1856.*

29. Favours granted by the Roman pontiff ought to be considered null, unless they have been sought for through the civil government.—*Ibid.*

30. The immunity of the Church and of ecclesiastical persons derived its origin from civil law.—*Damnatio "Multiplices inter." June 10, 1851.*

31. The ecclesiastical forum or tribunal for the temporal causes, whether civil or criminal, of clerics, ought by all means to be abolished, even without consulting and against the protest of the Holy See.—*Allocution "Nunquam fore," Dec. 15, 1856; Allocution "Acerbissimum," Sept. 27, 1852.*

32. The personal immunity by which clerics are exonerated from military conscription and service in the army may be abolished without violation either of natural right or equity. Its abolition is called for by civil progress, especially in a society framed on the model of a liberal government.—*Letter to the Bishop of Monreale "Singularis nobisque," Sept. 29, 1864.*

33. It does not appertain exclusively to the power of ecclesiastical jurisdiction by right, proper and innate, to direct the teaching of theological questions.—*Letter to the Archbishop of Munich, "Tuas libenter," Dec. 21, 1863.*

34. The teaching of those who compare the Sovereign Pontiff to a prince, free and acting in the universal Church, is a doctrine which prevailed in the Middle Ages.—*Apostolic Letter "Ad Apostolicae," Aug. 22, 1851.*

35. There is nothing to prevent the decree of a general council, or the act of all peoples, from transferring the supreme pontificate from the bishop and city of Rome to another bishop and another city.—*Ibid.*

36. The definition of a national council does not admit of any subsequent discussion, and the civil authority can assume this principle as the basis of its acts.—*Ibid.*

37. National churches, withdrawn from the authority of the Roman pontiff and altogether separated, can be established.—*Allocution "Multis gravibusque," Dec. 17, 1860.*

38. The Roman pontiffs have, by their too arbitrary conduct, contributed to the division of the Church into Eastern and Western.—*Apostolic Letter "Ad Apostolicae," Aug. 22, 1851.*

VI. ERRORS ABOUT CIVIL SOCIETY, CONSIDERED BOTH IN ITSELF AND IN ITS RELATION TO THE CHURCH

39. The State, as being the origin and source of all rights, is endowed with a certain right not circumscribed by any limits.—*Allocution "Maxima quidem," June 9, 1862.*

40. The teaching of the Catholic Church is hostile to the well-being and interests of society.—*Encyclical "Qui pluribus," Nov. 9, 1846; Allocution "Quibus quantisque," April 20, 1849.*

41. The civil government, even when in the hands of an infidel sovereign, has a right to an indirect negative power over religious affairs. It therefore possesses not only the right called that of *exsequatur,* but also that of appeal, called *appellatio ab abusu.*—*Apostolic Letter "Ad Apostolicae," Aug. 22, 1851.*

42. In the case of conflicting laws enacted by the two powers, the civil law prevails.—*Ibid.*

43. The secular power has authority to rescind, declare and render null, solemn conventions, commonly called concordats, entered into with the Apostolic See, regarding the use of rights appertaining to ecclesiastical immunity, without the consent of the Apostolic See, and even in spite of its protest.— *Allocution "Multis gravibusque," Dec. 17, 1860; Allocution "In consistoriali," Nov. 1, 1850.*

44. The civil authority may interfere in matters relating to religion, morality and spiritual government: hence, it can pass judgment on the instructions issued for the guidance of consciences, conformably with their mission, by the pastors of the Church. Furthermore, it has the right to make enactments regarding the administration of the divine sacraments, and the dispositions necessary for receiving them.—*Allocutions "In consistoriali," Nov. 1, 1850, and "Maxima quidem," June 9, 1862.*

45. The entire government of public schools in which the youth of a Christian state is educated, except (to a certain extent) in the case of episcopal seminaries, may and ought to appertain to the civil power, and belong to it so far that no other authority whatsoever shall be recognized as having any right to interfere in the discipline of the schools, the arrangement of the studies, the conferring of degrees, in the choice or approval of the teachers.—*Allocutions "Quibus luctuosissimis," Sept. 5, 1851, and "In consistoriali," Nov. 1, 1850.*

46. Moreover, even in ecclesiastical seminaries, the method of studies to be adopted is subject to the civil authority.—*Allocution "Nunquam fore," Dec. 15, 1856.*

47. The best theory of civil society requires that popular schools open to children of every class of the people, and, generally, all public institutes in-

tended for instruction in letters and philosophical sciences and for carrying on the education of youth, should be freed from all ecclesiastical authority, control and interference, and should be fully subjected to the civil and political power at the pleasure of the rulers, and according to the standard of the prevalent opinions of the age.—*Epistle to the Archbishop of Freiburg,* "Cum non sine," *July 14, 1864.*

48. Catholics may approve of the system of educating youth unconnected with Catholic faith and the power of the Church, and which regards the knowledge of merely natural things, and only, or at least primarily, the ends of earthly social life.—*Ibid.*

49. The civil power may prevent the prelates of the Church and the faithful from communicating freely and mutually with the Roman pontiff.—*Allocution* "Maxima quidem," *June 9, 1862.*

50. Lay authority possesses of itself the right of presenting bishops, and may require of them to undertake the administration of the diocese before they receive canonical institution, and the Letters Apostolic from the Holy See.—*Allocution* "Nunquam fore," *Dec. 15, 1856.*

51. And, further, the lay government has the right of deposing bishops from their pastoral functions, and is not bound to obey the Roman pontiff in those things which relate to the institution of bishoprics and the appointment of bishops.—*Allocution* "Acerbissimum," *Sept. 27, 1852; Damnatio* "Multiplices inter," *June 10, 1851.*

52. Government can, by its own right, alter the age prescribed by the Church for the religious profession of women and men; and may require of all religious orders to admit no person to take solemn vows without its permission.—*Allocution* "Nunquam fore," *Dec. 15, 1856.*

53. The laws enacted for the protection of religious orders and regarding their rights and duties ought to be abolished; nay, more, civil Government may lend its assistance to all who desire to renounce the obligation which they have undertaken of a religious life, and to break their vows. Government may also suppress the said religious orders, as likewise collegiate churches and simple benefices, even those of advowson, and subject their property and revenues to the administration and pleasure of the civil power.—*Allocutions* "Acerbissimum," *Sept. 27, 1852;* "Probe memineritis," *Jan. 22, 1855;* "Cum saepe," *July 26, 1855.*

54. Kings and princes are not only exempt from the jurisdiction of the Church, but are superior to the Church in deciding questions of jurisdiction. —*Damnatio* "Multiplices inter," *June 10, 1851.*

55. The Church ought to be separated from the State, and the State from the Church.—*Allocution* "Acerbissimum," *Sept. 27, 1852.*

VII. ERRORS CONCERNING NATURAL AND CHRISTIAN ETHICS

56. Moral laws do not stand in need of the divine sanction, and it is not at all necessary that human laws should be made conformable to the laws of nature, and receive their power of binding from God.—*Allocution "Maxima quidem," June 9, 1862.*

57. The science of philosophical things and morals and also civil laws may and ought to keep aloof from divine and ecclesiastical authority.—*Ibid.*

58. No other forces are to be recognized except those which reside in matter, and all the rectitude and excellence of morality ought to be placed in the accumulation and increase of riches by every possible means, and the gratification of pleasure.—*Ibid.; Encyclical "Quanto conficiamur," Aug. 10, 1863.*

59. Right consists in the material fact. All human duties are an empty word, and all human facts have the force of right.—*Allocution "Maxima quidem," June 9, 1862.*

60. Authority is nothing else but numbers and the sum total of material forces.—*Ibid.*

61. The injustice of an act when successful inflicts no injury on the sanctity of right.—*Allocution "Jamdudum cernimus," March 18, 1861.*

62. The principle of non-intervention, as it is called, ought to be proclaimed and observed.—*Allocution "Novos et ante," Sept. 28, 1860.*

63. It is lawful to refuse obedience to legitimate princes, and even to rebel against them.—*Encyclical "Qui pluribus," Nov. 9, 1864; Allocution "Quibusque vestrum," Oct. 4, 1847; "Noscitis et Nobiscum," Dec. 8, 1849; Letter Apostolic "Cum Catholica."*

64. The violation of any solemn oath, as well as any wicked and flagitious action repugnant to the eternal law, is not only not blamable but is altogether lawful and worthy of the highest praise when done through love of country. —*Allocution "Quibus quantisque," April 20, 1849.*

VIII. ERRORS CONCERNING CHRISTIAN MARRIAGE

65. The doctrine that Christ has raised marriage to the dignity of a sacrament cannot be at all tolerated.—*Apostolic Letter "Ad Apostolicae," Aug. 22, 1851.*

66. The Sacrament of Marriage is only a something accessory to the contract and separate from it, and the sacrament itself consists in the nuptial benediction alone.—*Ibid.*

67. By the law of nature, the marriage tie is not indissoluble, and in many cases divorce properly so called may be decreed by the civil authority.—*Ibid.; Allocution "Acerbissimum," Sept. 27, 1852.*

68. The Church has not the power of establishing diriment impediments of marriage, but such a power belongs to the civil authority by which existing impediments are to be removed.—*Damnatio "Multiplices inter," June 10, 1851.*

69. In the dark ages the Church began to establish diriment impediments, not by her own right, but by using a power borrowed from the State.—*Apostolic Letter "Ad Apostolicae," Aug. 22, 1851.*

70. The canons of the Council of Trent, which anathematized those who dare to deny to the Church the right of establishing diriment impediments, either are not dogmatic, or must be understood as referring to such borrowed power.—*Ibid.*

71. The form of solemnizing marriage prescribed by the Council of Trent, under pain of nullity, does not bind in cases where the civil law lays down another form, and declares that when this new form is used the marriage will be valid.—*Ibid.*

72. Boniface VIII was the first who declared that the vow of chastity taken at ordination renders marriage void.—*Ibid.*

73. In force of a merely civil contract there may exist between Christians a real marriage, and it is false to say either that the marriage contract between Christians is always a sacrament, or that there is no contract if the sacrament be excluded.—*Ibid.; Letter to the King of Sardinia, Sept. 9, 1852; Allocutions "Acerbissimum," Sept. 27, 1852; "Multis gravibusque," Dec. 17, 1860.*

74. Matrimonial causes and espousals belong by their nature to civil tribunals.—*Encyclical "Qui pluribus," Nov. 9, 1846; Damnatio "Multiplices inter," June 10, 1851; "Ad Apostolicae," Aug. 22, 1851; Allocution "Acerbissimum," Sept. 27, 1852.*

N.B. To the preceding questions may be referred two other errors regarding the celibacy of priests and the preference due to the state of marriage over that of virginity. These have been stigmatized: the first in the Encyclical "Qui pluribus," Nov. 9, 1846; the second, in the Letter Apostolic "Multiplices inter," June 10, 1851.

IX. ERRORS REGARDING THE CIVIL POWER OF THE SOVEREIGN PONTIFF

75. The children of the Christian and Catholic Church are divided amongst themselves about the compatibility of the temporal with the spiritual power.—*"Ad Apostolicae," Aug. 22, 1851.*

76. The abolition of the temporal power of which the Apostolic See is possessed would contribute in the greatest degree to the liberty and prosperity of the Church.—*Allocutions "Quibus quantisque," April 20, 1849; "Si semper antea," May 20, 1850.*

N.B. Besides these errors, explicitly censured, very many others are implicitly condemned by the doctrine propounded and established, which all Catholics are bound most firmly to hold touching the temporal sovereignty of the Roman pontiff. This doctrine is clearly stated in the Allocutions "Quibus quantisque," April 20, 1849; and "Si semper antea," May 20, 1850; Letter Apostolic "Cum Catholica ecclesia," March 26, 1860; Allocutions, "Noves et antea," Sept. 28, 1860; "Jamdudum cernimus," March 18, 1861; "Maxima quidem," June 9, 1862.

X. ERRORS HAVING REFERENCE TO MODERN LIBERALISM

77. In the present day it is no longer expedient that the Catholic religion should be held as the only religion of the State, to the exclusion of all other forms of worship.—*Allocution "Nemo vestrum," July 26, 1855.*

78. Hence it has been wisely decided by law, in some Catholic countries, that persons coming to reside therein shall enjoy the public exercise of their own peculiar worship.—*Allocution "Acerbissimum," Sept. 27, 1852.*

79. Moreover, it is false that the civil liberty of every form of worship, and the full power, given to all, of overtly and publicly manifesting any opinions whatsoever and thoughts, conduce more easily to corrupt the morals and minds of the people, and to propagate the pest of indifferentism.—*Allocution "Nunquam fore," Dec. 15, 1856.*

80. The Roman Pontiff can, and ought to, reconcile himself and come to terms with progress, liberalism and modern civilization.—*Allocution "Jamdudum cernimus," March 18, 1861.*

LORD ACTON

John Emerich Edward Dalberg Acton was born in Naples on January 10, 1834. He was educated at Oscott until 1848, then at Edinburgh and Munich, where he studied under the Catholic historian, Döllinger. Himself a Catholic, Acton could not study at Cambridge, the university of his choice, because it was then closed to Catholics.

Acton was a Liberal in politics, and he served in Parliament as representative for Carlow from 1859 to 1865. He traveled to the intellectual centers of Europe and America and was friendly with many of the great literary figures of his time. In 1859, Acton assumed the editorship of a Roman Catholic monthly, *The Rambler,* which was merged in 1862 with the *Home and Foreign Review.* Although a sincere Catholic, Acton soon came into conflict with ultramontanism, and in August, 1852, Cardinal Wiseman (under whom Acton had studied at Oscott) publicly censured his *Review.*

Acton was married in 1865 to the daughter of a Bavarian count. In 1869 he was made a peer—Baron Acton—by Gladstone, his lifelong admirer.

The promulgation of the doctrine of Papal Infallibility by Pius IX in 1870 involved Acton once again in religious controversy. He had been in agreement with the opposition, which was led by his old teacher, Döllinger, but after the doctrine was sanctioned by the Vatican Council, he deferred to Rome, while Döllinger was excommunicated. The following essay, which first appeared in 1864, explains Acton's dilemma and the principles on which he later decided to submit to papal authority.

In 1895, Acton was appointed Regius Professor of Modern History at Cambridge. His powerful personal influence on others was as important to later historians as were his writings. Two courses of lectures that he delivered at Cambridge—on the French Revolution and on modern history—were published in his lifetime, as was his inaugural lecture, published as *The Study of History* (1895). It was under his direction that the great *Cambridge Modern History* was conceived and planned, although it was not completed until long after his death on June 19, 1902.

The essay "Conflicts with Rome" first appeared in *The Rambler, New Series,* IV (January, 1864).

CONFLICTS WITH ROME

Among the causes which have brought dishonour on the Church in recent years, none have had a more fatal operation than those conflicts with science and literature which have led men to dispute the competence, or the justice, or the wisdom, of her authorities. Rare as such conflicts have been, they have awakened a special hostility which the defenders of Catholicism have not succeeded in allaying. They have induced a suspicion that the Church, in her zeal for the prevention of error, represses that intellectual freedom which is essential to the progress of truth; that she allows an administrative interference with convictions to which she cannot attach the stigma of falsehood; and that she claims a right to restrain the growth of knowledge, to justify an acquiescence in ignorance, to promote error, and even to alter at her arbitrary will the dogmas that are proposed to faith. There are few faults or errors imputed to Catholicism which individual Catholics have not committed or held, and the instances on which these particular accusations are founded have sometimes been supplied by the acts of authority itself. Dishonest controversy loves to confound the personal with the spiritual element in the Church—to ignore the distinction between the sinful agents and the divine institution. And this confusion makes it easy to deny, what otherwise would be too evident to question, that knowledge has a freedom in the Catholic Church which it can find in no other religion; though there, as elsewhere, freedom degenerates unless it has to struggle in its own defence.

. . . The Church is interested, not in the triumph of a principle or cause which may be dated as that of 1789, or of 1815, or of 1830, but in the triumph of justice and the just cause, whether it be that of the people or of the Crown, of a Catholic party or of its opponents. She admits the tests of public law and political science. When these proclaim the existence of the conditions which justify an insurrection or a war, she cannot condemn that insurrection or that war. She is guided in her judgment on these causes by criteria which are not her own, but are borrowed from departments over which she has no supreme control. This is as true of science as it is of law and politics. Other truths are as certain as those which natural or positive law embraces, and other obligations as imperative as those which regulate the relations of subjects and authorities. The principle which places right above expedience in the political action of the Church has an equal application in history or in astronomy. The Church can no more identify her cause with scientific error than with political wrong. Her interests may be impaired by some measure of political justice, or by the admission of some fact or document. But in neither case can she guard her interests at the cost of denying the truth.

This is the principle which has so much difficulty in obtaining recognition in an age when science is more or less irreligious, and when Catholics more or less neglect its study. Political and intellectual liberty have the same claims and the same conditions in the eyes of the Church. The Catholic judges the measures of governments and the discoveries of science in exactly the same manner. Public law may make it imperative to overthrow a Catholic monarch, like James II, or to uphold a Protestant monarch, like the King of Prussia. The demonstrations of science may oblige us to believe that the earth revolves around the sun, or that the *Donation of Constantine* is spurious. The apparent interests of religion have much to say against all this; but religion itself prevents those considerations from prevailing. This has not been seen by those writers who have done most in defence of the principle. They have usually considered it from the standing ground of their own practical aims, and have therefore failed to attain that general view which might have been suggested to them by the pursuit of truth as a whole. French writers have done much for political liberty, and Germans for intellectual liberty; but the defenders of the one cause have generally had so little sympathy with the other, that they have neglected to defend their own on the grounds common to both. There is hardly a Catholic writer who has penetrated to the common source from which they spring. And this is the greatest defect in Catholic literature, even to the present day. . . .

On the other hand, it appeared that a blow which struck the Catholic scholars of Germany would assure to the victorious congregation of Roman divines an easy supremacy over the writers of all other countries. The case of Dr. Frohschammer might be made to test what degree of control it would be possible to exercise over his countrymen, the only body of writers at whom alarm was felt, and who insisted, more than others, on their freedom. But the suspicion of such a possibility was likely only to confirm him in the idea that he was chosen to be the experimental body on which an important principle was to be decided, and that it was his duty, till his dogmatic error was proved, to resist a questionable encroachment of authority upon the rights of freedom. He therefore refused to make the preliminary submission which was required of him, and allowed the decree to go forth against him in the usual way. Hereupon it was intimated to him —though not by Rome—that he had incurred excommunication. This was the measure which raised the momentous question of the liberties of Catholic science, and gave the impulse to that new theory on the limits of authority with which his name has become associated.

In the civil affairs of mankind it is necessary to assume that the knowledge of the moral code and the traditions of law cannot perish in a Christian nation. Particular authorities may fall into error; decisions may be appealed against; laws may be repealed, but the political conscience of the whole people cannot be irrecoverably lost. The Church possesses the same privilege, but in a much higher degree, for she exists expressly for the purpose of preserving a definite body of truths, the knowledge of which she can never lose. Whatever authority, therefore, expresses that knowledge of which she is the keeper must be obeyed. But there is no institution from which this knowledge can be obtained with immediate certainty. A council is not *a priori* oecumenical; the Holy See is not separately infallible. The one has to await a sanction, the other has repeatedly erred. Every decree, therefore, requires a preliminary examination.

A writer who is censured may, in the first place, yield an external submission, either for the sake of discipline, or because his conviction is too weak to support him against the weight of authority. But if the question at issue is more important than the preservation of peace, and if his conviction is strong, he inquires whether the authority which condemns him utters the voice of the Church. If he finds that it does, he yields to it, or ceases to profess the faith of Catholics. If he finds that it does not, but is only the voice of authority, he owes it to his conscience, and to the supreme claims of truth, to remain constant to that which he believes, in spite of opposition. No authority has power to impose error, and, if it resists the truth, the truth must be upheld until it is admitted. . . .

On the 21st of December 1863, the Pope addressed a Brief to the Archbishop of Munich, which was published on the 5th of March. . . .

Besides the censure of the doctrines of Frohschammer, and the approbation given to the acts of the Munich Congress, the Brief contains passages of deeper and more general import, not directly touching the action of the German divines, but having an important bearing on the position of this *Review*. The substance of these passages is as follows: In the present condition of society the supreme authority in the Church is more than ever necessary, and must not surrender in the smallest degree the exclusive direction of ecclesiastical knowledge. An entire obedience to the decrees of the Holy See and the Roman congregations cannot be inconsistent with the freedom and progress of science. The disposition to find fault with the scholastic theology, and to dispute the conclusions and the method of its teachers, threatens the authority of the Church, because the Church has not only allowed theology to remain for centuries faithful to their system, but has urgently recommended it as the safest bulwark of the faith, and an efficient weapon against her enemies. Catholic writers are not bound only by those decisions of the infallible Church which regard articles of faith. They must also submit to the theological decisions of the Roman congregations, and to the opinions which are commonly received in the schools. And it is wrong, though not heretical, to reject those decisions or opinions.

In a word, therefore, the Brief affirms that the common opinions and explanations of Catholic divines ought not to yield to the progress of secular science, and that the course of theological knowledge ought to be controlled by the decrees of the Index.

There is no doubt that the letter of this document might be interpreted in a sense consistent with the habitual language of the *Home and Foreign Review*. On the one hand, the censure is evidently aimed at that exaggerated claim of independence which would deny to the Pope and the Episcopate any right of interfering in literature, and would transfer the whole weight heretofore belonging to the traditions of the schools of theology to the incomplete, and therefore uncertain, conclusions of modern science. On the other hand, the *Review* has always maintained, in common with all Catholics, that if the one Church has an organ it is through that organ that she must speak; that her authority is not limited to the precise sphere of her infallibility; and that opinions which she has long tolerated or approved, and has for centuries found compatible with the secular as well as religious knowledge of the age, cannot be lightly supplanted by new hypotheses of scientific men, which have not yet had time to prove their consistency with dogmatic truth. But such a plausible accommodation, even if it were honest or dignified, would only disguise and obscure those ideas which it has been the chief object of the *Review* to proclaim. It is, therefore, not only more respectful to the Holy See, but more serviceable to the principles of the *Review* itself, and more in accordance with the spirit in which it has been conducted, to interpret the words of the Pope as they were really meant, than to elude their consequences by subtle distinctions, and to profess a formal adoption of maxims which no man who holds the principles of the *Review* can accept in their intended signification.

One of these maxims is that theological and other opinions long held and allowed in the Church gather truth from time, and an authority in some sort binding from the implied sanction of the Holy See, so that they cannot be rejected without rashness; and that the decrees of the congregation of the Index possess an authority quite independent of the acquirements of the men composing it. This is no new opinion; it is only expressed on the present occasion with unusual solemnity and distinctness. But one of the essential principles of this *Review* consists in a clear recognition, first, of the infinite gulf which in theology separates what is of faith from what is not of faith,—revealed dogmas from opinions unconnected with them by logical necessity, and therefore, incapable of anything higher than a natural certainty—and next, of the practical difference which exists in ecclesiastical discipline between the acts of infallible authority and those which possess no higher sanction than that of canonical legality. That which is not decided with dogmatic infallibility is for the time susceptible only of a scientific determination, which advances with the progress of science, and becomes absolute only where science has attained its final results. On the one hand, this scientific progress is beneficial, and even necessary, to the Church; on the other, it must inevitably be opposed by the guardians of traditional opinion, to whom, as such, no share in it belongs, and who, by their own acts and those of their predecessors, are committed to views which it menaces or destroys. The same principle which, in certain conjunctures, imposes the duty of surrendering received opinions imposes in equal extent, and under like conditions, the duty of disregarding the fallible authorities that uphold them.

It is the design of the Holy See not, of course, to deny the distinction between dogma and opinion, upon which this duty is founded, but to reduce the practical recognition of it among Catholics to the smallest possible limits. A grave question therefore arises as to the position of a *Review* founded in great part for the purpose of exemplifying this distinction. In considering the solution of this question two circumstances must be borne in mind; first, that the antagonism now so forcibly expressed has always been known and acknowledged; and secondly, that no part of the Brief applies directly to the *Review*. The *Review* was as distinctly opposed to the Roman sentiment before the Brief as since, and it is still as free from censure as before. It was at no time in virtual sympathy with authority on the points in question, and it is not now in formal conflict with authority.

But the definiteness with which the Holy See has pronounced its will, and the fact that it has taken the initiative, seem positively to invite adhesion, and to convey a special warning to all who have expressed opinions contrary to the maxims of the Brief. A periodical which not only has done so, but exists in a measure for the purpose of doing so, cannot with propriety refuse to survey the new position in which it is placed by this important act. For the conduct of a *Review* involves more delicate relations with the government of the Church than the authorship of an isolated book. When opinions which the author defends are rejected at Rome, he either makes his submission, or, if his mind remains unaltered, silently leaves his book to take its chance, and to influence men according to its merits. But such passivity, however right and seemly in the author of a book, is inapplicable to the case of a *Review*. The periodical iteration of rejected propositions would amount to insult and defiance, and would probably provoke more definite measures; and thus the result would be to commit authority yet more irrevocably to an opinion which otherwise might take no deep root, and might yield ultimately to the influence of time. For it is hard to surrender a cause on behalf of which a struggle has been sustained, and spiritual evils have been inflicted. In an isolated book, the author need discuss no more topics than he likes, and any want of agreement with ecclesiastical authority may receive so little prominence as to excite no attention. But a continuous *Review,* which adopted this kind of reserve, would give a negative prominence to the topics it persistently avoided, and by thus keeping before the world the position it occupied would hold out a perpetual invitation to its readers to judge between the Church and itself. Whatever it gained of approbation and assent would be so much lost to the authority and dignity of the Holy See. It could only hope to succeed by trading on the scandal it caused.

But in reality its success could no longer advance the cause of truth. For what is the Holy See in its relation to the masses of Catholics, and where does its strength lie? It is the organ, the mouth, the head of the Church. Its strength consists in its agreement with the general conviction of the faithful. When it expresses the common knowledge and sense of the age, or of a large majority of Catholics, its position is impregnable. The force it derives from this general support makes direct opposition hopeless, and therefore disedifying, tending only to division and promoting reaction rather than reform. The influence by which it is to be moved must be directed first on that which gives it strength, and must pervade the members in order that it may reach the head. While the general sentiment of Catholics is unaltered, the course of the Holy See remains unaltered too. As soon as that sentiment is modified, Rome sympathises with the change. The ecclesiastical government, based upon the public opinion of the Church, and acting through it, cannot separate itself from the mass of the faithful, and keep pace with the progress of the instructed minority. It follows slowly and warily, and sometimes begins by resisting and denouncing what in the end it thoroughly adopts. Hence a direct controversy with Rome holds out the prospect of great evils, and at best a barren and unprofitable victory. The victory that is fruitful springs from that gradual change in the knowledge, the ideas, and the convictions of the Catholic body, which, in due time, overcomes the natural reluctance to forsake a beaten path, and by insensible degrees constrains the mouthpiece of tradition to conform itself to the new atmosphere with which it is surrounded. The slow, silent, indirect action of public opinion bears the Holy See along, without any demoralising conflict or dishonourable capitulation. This action belongs essentially to the graver scientific literature to direct; and the inquiry what form that literature should assume at any given moment involves no question which affects its substance, though it may often involve questions of moral fitness sufficiently decisive for a particular occasion.

It was never pretended that the *Home and Foreign Review* represented the opinions of the majority of Catholics. The Holy See has had their support in maintaining a view of the obligations of Catholic literature very different from the one which has been upheld in these pages; nor could it explicitly abandon that view without taking up a new position in the Church. All that could be hoped for on the other side was silence and forbearance, and for a time they have been conceded. But this is the case no longer. The toleration has now been pointedly withdrawn; and the adversaries of the Roman theory have been challenged with the summons to submit.

If the opinions for which submission is claimed were new, or if the opposition now signalised were one of which there had hitherto been any doubt, a question might have arisen as to the limits of the authority of the Holy See over the conscience, and the necessity or possibility of accepting the view which it propounds. But no problem of this kind has in fact presented itself for consideration. The differences which are now proclaimed have all along been acknowledged to exist; and the conductors of this *Review* are unable to yield their assent to the opinions put forward in the Brief.

In these circumstances there are two courses which it is impossible to take. It would be wrong to abandon principles which have been well considered and are sincerely held, and it would also be wrong to assail the authority which contradicts them. The principles have not ceased to be true, nor the authority to be legitimate, because the two are in contradiction. To submit the intellect and conscience without examining the reasonableness and justice of this decree, or to reject the authority on the ground of its having been abused, would equally be a sin, on one side against morals, on the other against faith. The conscience cannot be relieved by casting on the administrators of ecclesiastical discipline the whole responsibility of preserving religious truth; nor can it be emancipated by a virtual apostasy. For the Church is neither a despotism in which the convictions of the faithful possess no power of expressing themselves and no means of exercising legitimate control, nor is it an organised anarchy where the judicial and administrative powers are destitute of that authority which is conceded to them in civil society—the authority which commands submission even where it cannot impose a conviction of the righteousness of its acts.

No Catholic can contemplate without alarm the evil that would be caused by a Catholic journal persistently labouring to thwart the published will of the Holy See, and continuously defying its authority. The conductors of this *Review* refuse to take upon themselves the responsibility of such a position. And if it were accepted, the *Review* would represent no section of Catholics. But the representative character is as essential to it as the opinions it professes, or the literary resources it commands. There is no lack of periodical publications representing science apart from religion, or religion apart from science. The distinctive feature of the *Home and Foreign Review* has been that it has attempted to exhibit the two in union; and the interest which has been attached to its views proceeded from the fact that they were put forward as essentially Catholic in proportion to their scientific truth, and as expressing more faithfully than even the voice of authority the genuine spirit of the Church in relation to intellect. Its object has been to elucidate the harmony which exists between religion and the established conclusions of secular knowledge, and to exhibit the real amity and sympathy between the methods of science and the methods employed by the Church. That amity and sympathy the enemies of the Church refuse to admit, and her friends have not learned to understand. Long disowned by a large part of our Episcopate, they are now rejected by the Holy See; and the issue is vital to a *Review* which, in ceasing to uphold them, would surrender the whole reason of its existence.

Warned, therefore, by the language of the Brief, I will not provoke ecclesiastical authority to a more explicit repudiation of doctrines which are necessary to secure its influence upon the advance of modern science. I will not challenge a conflict which would only deceive the world into a belief that religion cannot be harmonised with all that is right and true in the progress of the present age. But I will sacrifice the existence of the *Review* to the defence of its principles, in order that I may combine the obedience which is due to legitimate ecclesiastical authority, with an equally conscientious maintenance of the rightful and necessary liberty of thought. A conjuncture like the present does not perplex the conscience of a Catholic; for his obligation to refrain from wounding the peace of the Church is neither more nor less real than that of professing nothing beside or against his convictions. If these duties have not been always understood, at least the *Home and Foreign Review* will not betray them; and the cause it has imperfectly expounded can be more efficiently served in future by means which will neither weaken the position of authority nor depend for their influence on its approval.

If, as I have heard, but now am scarcely anxious to believe, there are those, both in the communion of the Church and out of it, who have found comfort in the existence of this *Review,* and have watched its straight short course with hopeful interest, trusting it as a sign that the knowledge deposited in their minds by study, and transformed by conscience into inviolable convictions, was not only tolerated among Catholics, but might be reasonably held to be of the very essence of their system; who were willing to accept its principles as a possible solution of the difficulties they saw in Catholicism, and were even prepared to make its fate the touchstone of the real spirit of our hierarchy; or who deemed that while it lasted it promised them some immunity from the overwhelming pressure of uniformity, some safeguard against resistance to the growth of knowledge and of freedom, and some protection for themselves, since, however weak its influence as an auxiliary, it would, by its position, encounter the first shock, and so divert from others the censures which they apprehended; who have found a welcome encouragement in its confidence, a satisfaction in its sincerity when they shrank from revealing their own thoughts, or a salutary restraint when its moderation failed to satisfy their ardour; whom, not being Catholics, it has induced to think less hardly of the Church, or, being Catholics, has bound more strongly to her;—to all these I would say that the principles it has upheld will not die with it, but will find their destined advocates, and triumph in their appointed time. From the beginning of the Church it has been a law of her nature, that the truths which eventually proved themselves the legitimate products of her doctrine, have had to make their slow way upwards through a phalanx of hostile habits and traditions, and to be rescued, not only from open enemies, but also from friendly hands that were not worthy to defend them. It is right that in every arduous enterprise someone who stakes no influence on the issue should make the first essay, whilst the true champions, like the Triarii of the Roman legions, are behind, and wait, without wavering, until the crisis calls them forward.

And already it seems to have arrived. All that is being done for ecclesiastical learning by the priesthood of the Continent bears testimony to the truths which are now called in question; and every work of real science written by a Catholic adds to their force. The example of great writers aids their cause more powerfully than many theoretical discussions. Indeed, when the principles of the antagonism which divides Catholics have been brought clearly out, the part of theory is accomplished, and most of the work of a *Review* is done. It remains that the principles which have been made intelligible should be translated into practice, and should pass from the arena of discussion into the ethical code of literature. In that shape their efficacy will be acknowledged, and they will cease to be the object of alarm. Those who have been indignant at hearing that their methods are obsolete and their labours vain, will be taught by experience to recognise in the works of another school services to religion more momentous than those which they themselves have aspired to perform; practice will compel the assent which is denied to theory; and men will learn to value in the fruit what the germ did not reveal to them. Therefore it is to the prospect of that development of Catholic learning which is too powerful to be arrested or repressed that I would direct the thoughts of those who are tempted to yield either to a malignant joy or an unjust despondency at the language of the Holy See. If the spirit of the *Home and Foreign Review* really animates those whose sympathy it enjoyed, neither their principles, nor their confidence, nor their hopes will be shaken by its extinction. It was but a partial and temporary embodiment of an imperishable idea— the faint reflection of a light which still lives and burns in the hearts of the silent thinkers of the Church.

V THE GROWTH OF SOCIALISM

ROBERT OWEN

UNTIL 1815 ROBERT OWEN (1771–1858) was known as "Mr. Owen the Philanthropist," the benevolently disposed manager of a factory in New Lanarck, Scotland, who had been unexpectedly successful in making philanthropy pay. He had published in 1813 a book entitled *A New View of Society; or, Essays on the Formation of Character*. Like many other manufacturers, Owen was aware of the responsibility involved in organizing industrial communities for an uprooted rural population; and he seemed more than ordinarily sensitive to the dislocations implicit in the mushroom growth of towns organized around the factory. The critical years following 1815, however, brought Owen into widespread public notice as the advocate of a "plan of amelioration and reform without revolution." Owen proposed that a capital sum be set aside by the government for the founding of so-called "Villages of Co-operation"—his own New Lanarck became a model—organized around scientific agriculture and based on the principles of "co-operation" and "united labor."

Owen's most thoughtful and comprehensive work, the *Report to the County of Lanarck* (1821), part of which is given as the first selection which follows, marks his transition from a reformer to an advocate of a system of communities founded upon socialist principles. Between 1824 and 1829 he attempted to put his plan of a largely self-sufficient community of cooperating producers into practice in the village of New Harmony, which he set up in the United States, in Indiana. Internal dissension wrecked the scheme, and he returned to England convinced that "the habits of the individual system were so powerful" that a communal effort for the general good was impracticable without previous moral training.

The Reform Bill of 1832 disillusioned many workingmen who had put their faith in political action, and Owen, who had never shared this faith, became the acknowledged leader of a movement against the English aristocracy and the relatively younger manufacturing interest. In 1833 he formed the Grand National Consolidated Trades Union, a producers' association which sought to bring about revolutionary changes in the industrial system by threatening a general strike. By 1834, however, the movement had collapsed under the direct attack of the newly entrenched industrial interests.

Owen did not believe that political measures were adequate to a crisis which was fundamentally economic and cultural. He emphasized that not even thoroughgoing economic change is stable unless it is founded upon a previous revolution in moral character. His educational proposals were not attempts to cut all men to a single pattern, but to impart to a community a common desire for moral cooperation on the basis of which individual qualities might be fostered.

Owen's disinclination for political agitation removed him from the mainstream of the workers' movement. After the collapse of his Trades Union his former associates became supporters of such political movements as Chartism. In addition, his antidemocratic propensities and his attacks on established religion alienated many who might otherwise have followed his lead. William Lovett, the Chartist leader, reports a remark by Owen to the effect that his followers "must consent to be ruled by despots till they have acquired sufficient knowledge to govern themselves."

Despite this practical failure, Owen made a number of significant contributions. He was active in the rise of British trade unionism as an independent force. His education reforms are still influential. He is also credited with being the first writer to use the word "socialism."

The second selection which follows is from a prospectus to *The Economist, a* weekly paper devoted to the propagation of Owen's views. The paper first appeared on January 27, 1821, and was discontinued in January, 1822. It was written and edited by George Mudie, a confirmed and passionate Owenite, and was dedicated "to the development of principles calculated assuredly to banish poverty from society, and to the discussion of all questions connected with the amelioration of the condition of mankind."

Mudie's views, as projected in *The Economist,* inspired the printers of London to establish a plan for a cooperative community, under the name of the "Economical and Cooperative Society." Lack of sufficient funds compelled the Society to abandon its efforts.

❧

REPORT TO THE COUNTY OF LANARCK

THE EVIL for which your Reporter has been required to provide a remedy, is the general want of employment, at wages sufficient to support the family of a working man beneficially for the community. After the most earnest consideration of the subject, he has been compelled to conclude, that such employment cannot be procured through the medium of trade, commerce, or manufactures, or even of agriculture, until the Government and the Legislature, cordially supported by the country, shall previously adopt measures to remove obstacles, which, without their interference, will now permanently keep the working classes in poverty and discontent, and gradually deteriorate all the resources of the empire. . . .

Your Reporter has been impressed with the truth of this conclusion, by the following considerations:—

1st, That manual labour, properly directed, is the source of all wealth, and of national prosperity.

2nd, That, when properly directed, labour is of far more value to the community than the expense necessary to maintain the labourer in considerable comfort.

3d, That manual labour, properly directed, may be made to continue of this value in all parts of the world, under any supposable increase of its population, for many centuries to come.

4th, That, under a proper direction of manual labour, Great Britain and its dependencies may be made to support an incalculable increase of population, most advantageously for all its inhabitants.

5th, That, when manual labour shall be so directed, it will be found that population cannot for many years, be stimulated to advance, as rapidly as society might be benefited by its increase.

These considerations, deduced from the first and most obvious principles of the science of political economy, convinced your Reporter, that some formidable artificial obstacle intervened to obstruct the natural improvement and progress of society. . . .

It is admitted that, under the present system, no more hands can be employed advantageously in agriculture or manufactures; and that both interests are on the eve of bankruptcy. It is also admitted, that the prosperity of the country, or rather that which ought to create prosperity, the improvement in mechanical and chemical science, has enabled the population to produce more than the present system permits to be consumed. In consequence, new arrangements become necessary, by which *consumption* may be made to keep pace with *production;* and the following are recommended:

1st, To cultivate the soil with the spade instead of the plough.

2nd, To make such changes as the spade cultivation requires, to render it easy and profitable to individuals, and beneficial to the country.

3d, To adopt a standard of value, by means of which, the exchange of the products of labour may proceed without check or limit, until wealth shall become so abundant, that any further increase to it will be considered useless, and will not be desired.

We proceed to give the reasons for recommending these arrangements in preference to all others. And first, those for preferring the spade to the plough for the universal cultivation of the soil. . . .

The action of the plough upon the soil is the reverse of that of the spade, in these important particulars:

Instead of *loosening* the subsoil, it *hardens* it; the heavy smooth surface of the plough, and the frequent trampling of the horses' feet, tend to form a surface on the subsoil, well calculated to prevent the water from penetrating below it; and in many soils, after a few years ploughing, it is there retained to drown the seed or plant in rainy seasons, and to be speedily evaporated when it would be the most desirable to retain it. Thus the crop is injured, and often destroyed, in dry weather, for the want of that moisture, which, under a different system, might have been retained in the subsoil.

It is evident, therefore, that the plough conceals from the eye its own imperfections, and deceives its employers, being in truth, a *mere surface implement,* and extremely defective in principle; that the spade, on the contrary, makes a good subsoil, as well as a superior surface, and the longer it is used on the same soil, the more easily will it be worked; and by occasional trenching, where there is sufficient depth of soil, new earth will be brought into action, and the benefits to be derived from a well prepared subsoil will be increased.

These facts being incontrovertible, few perhaps will hesitate to admit them. But it may be said, that admitting the statement to be true to the full extent, yet the plough, with a pair of horses and one man, performs so much work in a given time, that, with all its imperfections, it may be a more economical instrument for the purpose required. Such has been the almost universal impression for ages past, and, in consequence, the plough has superseded the spade, and is considered to be an improved machine for ordinary cultivation.

All this is plausible, and is sanctioned by the old prejudices of the world; but your Reporter maintains, that it is not true that the plough is, or has ever been, in any stage of society, the most economical instrument for the cultivation of the soil. It has been so in appearance only, not in reality. . . .

Agriculture, instead of being, as heretofore, the occupation of the mere peasant and farmer, with minds as defective in their cultivation as their soils, will then become the delightful employment of a race of men, trained in the best habits and dispositions; familiar with the most useful practice in the arts and sciences; and with minds fraught with the most valuable information, and extensive general knowledge,—capable of forming and conducting combined arrangements in agriculture, trade, commerce, and manufactures, far superior to those which have yet existed in any of these departments, as they have been hitherto disjoined, and separately conducted. It will be readily perceived, that this is an advance in civilization and general improvement, that is to be effected solely *through the science of the influence of circumstances over human nature, and the knowledge of the means by which those circumstances may be easily controlled.*

Closet theorists, and inexperienced persons, suppose, that to exchange the plough for the spade, would be to turn back in the road of improvement,—to give up a superior for an inferior implement of cultivation. Little do they imagine, that the introduction of the spade, with the scientific arrangements which it requires, will produce far greater improvements in agriculture, than the steam engine has effected in manufactures. Still less do they imagine, that the change from the plough to the spade, will prove to be a far more extensive and beneficial innovation, than that which the invention of the spinning machine has occasioned, by the introduction of which, instead of the single wheel in a corner of a farm house, we now see thousands of spindles, revolving with the noise of a water-fall, in buildings palace-like for their cost, magnitude, and appearance.

Yet this extraordinary change is at hand. It will immediately take place; for the interest and well-being of all classes require it. Society cannot longer proceed another step in advance without it, and until it is adopted, civilization must retrograde, and the working classes starve for want of employment.

The introduction of the steam engine, and the spinning machine, added, in an extraordinary manner, to the powers of human nature. In their consequences they have, in half a century, multiplied the productive power, or the means of creating wealth, among the population of these islands, more than 12 fold, besides giving a great increase to the means of creating wealth in other countries.

The steam engine and spinning machines, with the endless mechanical inventions to which they have given rise, have, however, inflicted evils on society, which now greatly overbalance the benefits which are derived from them. They have created an aggregate of wealth, and placed it in the hands of a few, who, by its aid, continue to absorb the wealth produced by the industry of the many. Thus the mass of the population are become mere slaves to the ignorance and caprice of these monopolists, and are far more truly helpless and wretched than they were before the names of WATT and ARKWRIGHT were known. Yet these celebrated and ingenious men have been the instruments of preparing society for the important beneficial changes which are about to occur.

All now know and feel, that the good which these inventions are calculated to impart to the community, has not yet been realized. The condition of society, instead of being improved, has been deteriorated, under the new circumstances to which they have given birth; and is now experiencing a retrograde movement.

"Something," therefore, "must be done," as the general voice exclaims, to give to our suffering population, and to society at large, the means of deriving from these inventions the advantages which all men of science expect from them.

In recommending the change from the plough to the spade cultivation, your Reporter has in view such scientific arrangements, as, he is persuaded, will, upon due examination, convince every intelligent mind, that they offer the only means by which Great Britain can be enabled to maintain in future her rank among nations. They are the only effectual remedy for the evils which the steam engine and the spinning machine have, by their misdirection, created, and are alone capable of giving a real and substantial value to these and other late scientific inventions. Of all our splendid improvements in art and science, the effect has hitherto been, to demoralize society, through the misapplication of the new wealth created. The arrangements to which your Reporter now calls the attention of the Public, present the certain means of renovating the moral character, and of improving, to an unlimited extent, the general condition of the population, and while they lead to a far more rapid multiplication of wealth than the present system permits to take place, they will effectually preclude all the evils with which wealth is now accompanied.

It is estimated, that, in Great Britain and Ireland, there are now under cultivation upwards of 60 millions of acres; and of these, 20 millions are arable, and 40 millions in pasture;—that, under the present system of cultivation by the plough, and of pasturing, about 2 millions at most of *actual labourers* are employed on the soil, giving immediate support to about three times that number, and supplying food for a population of about 18 millions. Sixty millions of acres, under a judicious arrangement of spade cultivation, with manufactures as an appendage, might be made to give healthy advantageous employment to 60 millions of labourers at the least, and support, in high comfort, a population greatly exceeding 100 millions. But, in the present low state of population in these islands, not more than 5 or 6 millions of acres could be properly cultivated by the spade, although all the operative manufacturers were to be chiefly in this mode of agriculture. Imperfect, therefore, as the plough is for the cultivation of the soil, it is probable, that, in this country, for want of an adequate population, many centuries will elapse before it can be entirely superseded by the spade; yet, under the plough system, Great Britain and Ireland are even now supposed to be greatly overpeopled.

It follows from this statement, that we possess the means of supplying the labouring poor, however numerous they may be, with permanent beneficial employment for many centuries to come. . . .

Having given the outline of the considerations, which show the superiority in principle of the spade over the plough, as a scientific and economical instrument of cultivation; having also described, briefly, the objects to be attended to in forming economical arrangements for the change proposed;—it now remains that the principle should be generally explained by which an advantageous interchange and exchange may be made of the greatly increased products of labour, which will be created by the spade cultivation, aided by the improved arrangements now contemplated.

These incalculably increased products will render gold, the old artificial standard of value, far more unfit for the task which is to be performed than it was in 1797, when it ceased to be the British legal standard of value, or than it is now, when wealth has so much increased.

Your Reporter is of opinion, that the natural standard of human labour, fixed to represent its natural worth, or power of creating new wealth, will alone be found adequate to the purposes required.

To a mind coming first to this subject, innumerable and apparently insurmountable difficulties will occur; but by the steady application of that fixed and persevering attention, which is alone calculated successfully to contend against and overcome difficulties, every obstacle will vanish, and the practice will prove simple and easy.

That which can create new wealth, is of course worth the wealth which it creates. Human labour, whenever common justice shall be done to human beings, can now be applied to produce, advantageously for all ranks in society, many times the amount of wealth that is necessary to support the individual in considerable comfort. Of this new wealth so created, the labourer who produces it is justly entitled to his fair proportion; and the best interests of every community require that the producer should have a fair and fixed proportion of all the wealth which he creates. This can be assigned to him on no other principle, than by forming arrangements by which the *natural* standard of value shall become the *practical* standard of value. To make labour the standard of value, it is necessary to ascertain the amount of it in all articles to be bought and sold. This is, in fact, already accomplished, and is denoted, by what in commerce is technically termed, "the prime cost," or the net value of the whole labour contained in any article of value,—the material contained in, or consumed by, the manufacture of the article, forming a part of the whole labour.

The great object of society is, to obtain wealth, and to enjoy it.

The genuine principle of barter was, to exchange the supposed prime cost of, or value of labour, in one article, against the prime cost of, or amount of labour contained in any other article. This is the only equitable principle of exchange; but, as inventions increased, and human desires multiplied, it was found to be inconvenient in practice. Barter was succeeded by commerce, the principle of which is, to produce or procure every article at the lowest, and to obtain for it in exchange, the *highest* amount of labour. To effect this, an artificial standard of value was necessary; and the metals were, by common consent among nations, permitted to perform the office. This principle, in the progress of its operation, has been productive of important advantages, and of very great evils; but, like barter, it has been suited to a certain stage of society. It has stimulated invention; it has given industry and talent to the human character, and secured the future exertion of those energies which otherwise might have remained dormant and unknown. But it has made man ignorantly, individually selfish; placed him in opposition to his fellows; engendered fraud and deceit; blindly urged him forward to create, but deprived him of the wisdom to enjoy. In striving to take advantage of others, he has overreached himself. The strong hand of necessity will now force him into the path which conducts to that wisdom in which he has been so long deficient. He will discover the advantages to be derived from uniting in practice the best parts of the principles of barter and commerce, and dismissing those which experience has proved to be inconvenient and injurious. This substantial improvement in the progress of society, may be easily effected by exchanging all articles with each other at their prime cost, or with reference to the amount of labour in each, which can be equitably ascertained, and by permitting the exchange to be made through a convenient medium, to represent this value, and which will thus represent a real and unchanging value, and be issued only as substantial wealth increases. The profit of production will arise, in all cases, from the value of the labour contained in the article produced, and it will be for the interest of society that this profit should be most ample. Its exact amount will depend upon what, by strict examination, shall be proved to be the present real value of a day's labour; calculated with reference to the amount of wealth, in the necessaries and comforts of life, which an average labourer may, by temperate exertions, be now made to produce. . . .

It has been, and still is, a received opinion among theorists in political economy, that man can provide better for himself, and more advantageously for the public, when left to his own individual exertions, opposed to, and in competition with his fellows, than when aided by any social arrangement, which shall unite his interests individually and generally with society. This principle of individual interest, opposed, as it is perpetually, to the public good, is considered, by the most celebrated political economists, to be the corner stone of the social system, and without which, society could not subsist. Yet when they shall know themselves, and discover the wonderful effects, which combination and unity can produce, they will acknowledge that the present arrangement of society is the most antisocial, impolitic, and irrational, that can be devised; that under its influence, all the superior and valuable qualities of human nature are repressed from infancy, and that the most unnatural means are used to bring out the most injurious propensities;

in short, that the utmost pains are taken to make that which by nature is the most delightful compound for producing excellence and happiness, absurd, imbecile, and wretched. Such is the conduct now pursued by those who are called the best and wisest of the present generation, although there is not one rational object to be gained by it. From this principle of individual interest have arisen all the divisions of mankind, the endless errors and mischiefs of class, sect, party, and of national antipathies, creating the angry and malevolent passions, and all the crimes and misery with which the human race has been hitherto afflicted. In short, if there be one closet doctrine more contrary to truth than another, it is the notion that individual interest, as the term is now understood, is a more advantageous principle on which to found the social system, for the benefit of all, or of any, than the principle of union and mutual cooperation. The former acts like an immense weight to repress the most valuable faculties and dispositions, and to give a wrong direction to all the human powers. It is one of those magnificent errors (if the expression may be allowed) that when enforced in practice, brings ten thousand evils in its train. The principle on which these economists proceed, instead of adding to the wealth of nations or of individuals, is itself the sole cause of poverty; and but for its operation, wealth would long ago have ceased to be a subject of contention in any part of the world. If, it may be asked, experience has proved that union, combination, and extensive arrangement among mankind, are a thousand times more powerful to *destroy,* than the efforts of an unconnected multitude, where each acts individually for himself,—would not a similar increased effect be produced by union, combination, and extensive arrangement, to *create and conserve?* Why should not the result be the same in the one case as in the other? But it is well known that a combination of men and of interests, can effect that which it would be futile to attempt, and impossible to accomplish, by individual exertions and separate interests. Then why, it may be inquired, have men so long acted individually, and in opposition to each other?

This is an important question, and merits the most serious attention.

Men have not yet been trained in principles that will permit them *to act in unison,* except to defend themselves or to destroy others. For self-preservation, they were early compelled to unite for these purposes in war. A necessity, however, equally powerful will now compel men to be trained to act together, to *create and conserve,* that in like manner they may preserve life in peace. Fortunately for mankind, the system of individual opposing interests, has now reached the extreme point of error and inconsistency;—in the midst of the most ample means to create wealth, all are in poverty, or in imminent danger, from the effects of poverty upon others.

The reflecting part of mankind, have admitted in theory, that the characters of men are formed chiefly by the circumstances in which they are placed; yet the science of the influence of circumstances, which is the most important of all the sciences, remains unknown for the great practical business of life. When it shall be fully developed, it will be discovered, that to unite the mental faculties of men, for the attainment of pacific and civil objects, will be a far more easy task than it has been to combine their physical powers to carry on extensive warlike operations.

The discovery of the distance and movements of the heavenly bodies; of the time-pieces; of a vessel to navigate the most distant parts of the ocean; of the steam engine, which performs, under the easy control of one man, the labour of many thousands; and of the press, by which knowledge and improvements may be speedily given to the most ignorant, in all parts of the earth;—these have, indeed, been discoveries of high import to mankind; but important as these and others have been in their effects, on the condition of human society, their combined benefits in practice, will fall far short of those which will be speedily attained by the new intellectual power, which men will acquire through the knowledge of "the science of the influence of circumstances over the whole conduct, character, and proceedings of the human race." By this latter discovery, more shall be accomplished in one year, for the well-being of human nature, including, without any exceptions, all ranks and descriptions of men, than has ever yet been effected in one or in many centuries. Strange as this language may seem to those whose minds have not yet had a glimpse of the real state in which society now is, it will prove to be not more strange than true.

Are not the mental energies of the world at this moment in a state of high effervescence. Is not society at a stand, incompetent to proceed in its present course, and do not all men cry out that "something must be done?" That "something," to produce the effect desired, must be a complete renovation of the whole social compact; one not forced on prematurely, by confusion and violence; not one to be brought about by the futile measures of the Radicals, Whigs, or Tories, of Britain,—the Liberals or Royalists of France. —the Illuminati of Germany, or the mere party proceedings of any little local portion of human beings, trained as they have hitherto been, in almost every kind of error, and without any true knowledge of themselves. No! The change sought for, must be preceded by the clear development of a great and universal principle which shall unite in one, all the petty jarring interests, by which, till now, nature has been made a most inveterate enemy to itself. No! extensive, nay, rather, universal as the re-arrangement of society must be, to relieve it from the difficulties with which it is now over-whelmed, it will be effected in peace and quietness, with the good will and hearty concurrence of all parties, and of every people. It will necessarily com mence by common consent, on account of its advantages, almost simultane-ously among all civilized nations; and, once begun, will daily advance with an accelerating ratio, unopposed, and bearing down before it the existing systems of the world. The only astonishment then will be that such systems could so long have existed. . . .

Under the present system, there is the most minute division of mental power and manual labour in the individuals of the working classes; private interests are placed perpetually at variance with the public good, and, in every nation, men are purposely trained from infancy to suppose, that their well-being is incompatible with the progress and prosperity of other nations. Such are the means by which old society seeks to obtain the desired effects of life. The details now to be submitted, have been devised upon principles which will lead to an opposite practice; to the combination of extensive mental and manual powers in the individuals of the working classes; to a complete identity of private and public interest, and to the training of na-tions to comprehend that their power and happiness cannot attain their full and natural development, but through an equal increase of the power and happiness of all other states. These, therefore, are the real points at variance between that which *is,* and that which *ought to be.*

It is upon these principles that arrangements are now proposed for the new agricultural villages, by which the food of the inhabitants may be pre-pared in one establishment, where they will eat together as one family. Various objects have been urged against this practice, but they have come from those only, who, whatever may be their pretensions in other respects, are mere children in the knowledge of the principle and economy of social life. By such arrangements, the members of these new associations may be supplied with food at far less expense, and with much more comfort, than by any individual or family arrangements; and when the parties have been once trained and accustomed, as they easily may be, to the former mode, they will never afterwards feel any inclination to return to the latter. If a saving in the quantity of food,—the obtaining of a superior quality of pre-pared provisions from the same materials,—and the operation of preparing them being effected in much less time, with far less fuel, and with greater ease, comfort, and health, to all the parties employed,—be advantages, these will be obtained in a remarkable manner by the new arrangements pro-posed. And if, to partake of viands so prepared, served up with every regard to comfort, in clean, spacious, well-lighted, and pleasantly-ventilated apartments, and in the society of well-dressed, well-trained, well-educated, and well-informed associates, possessing the most benevolent dispositions, and desirable habits, can give zest and proper enjoyment to meals, then will the inhabitants of the proposed villages experience all this in an eminent degree. When the new arrangements shall become familiar to the parties, this superior mode of living may be enjoyed at far less expense, and with much less trouble, than are necessary to procure such meals as the poor are now compelled to eat, surrounded by every object of discomfort and disgust, in the cellars and garrets of the most unhealthy courts, alleys and lanes, in London, Dublin, and Edinburgh, or Glasgow, Manchester, Leeds, and Birmingham. Striking, however, as the contrast is in description, and although the actual practice will far exceed what words can convey, yet there are many closet theorists, and inexperienced persons, probably, who will contend for individual arrangements and interests, in preference to that which they cannot comprehend. These individuals must be left to be convinced by the facts themselves.

We now proceed to describe the interior accommodations of the private lodging-houses which will occupy three sides of the parallelogram. As it is of essential importance that there should be abundance of space within the line of the private dwelling, the parallelogram, in all cases, whether the association is intended to be near the maximum or minimum in numbers, should be of large dimensions; and to accommodate a greater or less population, the private dwelling should be of one, two, three, or four storeys, and the interior arrangements formed accordingly. This will be very simple; no kitchen will be necessary, as the public arrangements for cooking will supersede the necessity for any. The apartments will be always well ventilated, and, when necessary, heated or cooled on the improved principles lately introduced in the Derby Infirmary. The expense and trouble, to say nothing of the superior health and comforts which these improvements will give, will be very greatly less than attach to the present practice. To heat, cool, and ventilate their apartments, the parties will have no further trouble than to open or shut two slides, or valves, in each room, the atmosphere of which, by this simple contrivance, may be always kept temperate and pure. One stove of proper dimensions, judiciously placed, will supply the apartments of several dwellings with little trouble, and at a very light expense, when the buildings are originally adapted for this arrangement. Thus will all the inconveniences and expense of separate fires and fireplaces, and their appendages, be avoided, as well as the trouble and disagreeable effects of mending fires and removing ashes, &c. &c. Good sleeping apartments looking over the gardens into the country, and sitting-rooms of proper dimensions, fronting the square, will afford as much lodging-accommodation, as, with the other public arrangements, can be useful to, or desired by, these associated cultivators. . . .

A paper representative of the value of labour, manufactured on the principle of the new notes of the Bank of England, will serve for every purpose of their domestic commerce or exchanges, and will be issued only for intrinsic value received and in store. It has been mentioned already, that all motives to deception will be effectually removed from the minds of the inhabitants of these new villages, and of course, forgeries, though not guarded against by this new improvement, would not have any existence among them; and as this representative would be of no use in the old society, no injury could come from that quarter.

But these associations must contribute their fair quota to the exigencies of the state. This consideration leads your Reporter to the next general head, or, The connection of the new establishments with the government of the country, and with old society.

Under this head are to be noticed, the amount and collection of the revenue, and the public or legal duties of the association in peace and war.

Your Reporter concludes, that whatever taxes are paid from land, capital, and labour, under the existing arrangements of society, the same amount for the same proportion of each may be collected with far more ease under those now proposed. The government would of course require its revenue to be paid in the legal circulating medium, to obtain which, the associations would have to dispose of as much of their surplus produce to common society for the legal coin or paper of the realm, as would discharge the demands of government. In time of peace, these associations would give no trouble to government, their internal regulations being founded on principle of prevention, not only with reference to public crimes, but to the private evils and errors which so fatally abound in common society. Courts of law, prisons, and punishments, would not be required. These are requisite only where human nature is greatly misunderstood; where society rests on the demoralizing system of individual rewards and punishments;—they are necessary only in a stage of existence previous to the discovery of the science of the certain and overwhelming influence of circumstances, over the whole character and conduct of mankind. Whatever courts of law, prisons, and punishments, have yet effected for society, the influence of other circumstances which may now be easily introduced, will accomplish infinitely more, for they will effectually prevent the growth of those evils, of which our present Institutions do not take cognizance, till they are already full formed, and in baneful activity.

In time of peace, therefore, these associations will save much charge and trouble to government. In reference to war also, they will be equally beneficial. Bodily exercises, adapted to improve the dispositions, and increase the health and strength of the individual, will form part of the training and education of the children. In these exercises they may be instructed to acquire facility in the execution of combined movements, a habit which is calculated to produce regularity and order in time of peace, as well as to aid defensive and offensive operations in war. The children therefore, at an early age, will acquire *through their amusements* those habits which will render them capable of becoming, in a short time, at any future period of life, the best defenders of their country, if necessity should again arise to defend it, since they would in all probability be far more to be depended upon than those whose physical, intellectual, and moral training, had been less carefully conducted. In furnishing their quotas for the militia or common army, they would probably adopt the pecuniary alternative; by which means they would form a reserve, that, in proportion to their numbers, would be a great security for the nation's safety. They would prefer this alternative, to avoid the demoralizing effects of recruiting.

But the knowledge of the science of the influence of circumstances over mankind, will speedily enable all nations to discover, not only the evils of war, but the folly of it. Of all modes of conduct adopted by mankind to obtain advantages in the present stage of society, this is the most certain to defeat its object. It is, in truth, a system of demoralization and of destruction, while it is the highest interest of all individuals, and of all countries, to *remoralize and conserve*. Men surely cannot with truth be termed rational beings, until they shall discover and put in practice the principles which shall enable them to conduct their affairs without war. The arrangement we are considering, would speedily show how easily these principles and practices may be introduced into general society. . . .

Possessing, in human nature, a soil capable of yielding abundantly the product which man most desires, we have in our ignorance, planted the thorn instead of the vine. The evil principle, which has been instilled into all minds from infancy, "that the character is formed *by* the individual," has produced, and so long as it shall continue to be cherished, will ever produce, the unwelcome harvest of evil passions,—hatred, revenge, and all uncharitableness, and the innumerable crimes and miseries to which they have given birth; for these are the certain and necessary effects of the institutions which have arisen among mankind, in consequence of the universally received, and long coerced belief in this erroneous principle.

"That the character is formed *for* and not *by* the individual," is a truth to which every fact connected with man's history bears testimony, and of which the evidence of our senses affords us daily and hourly proof. It is also a truth which, when its practical application shall be fully understood, will be of inestimable value to mankind. Let us not, therefore, continue to act as if the reverse of this proposition were true. Let us cease to do violence to human nature; and having at length discovered the vine, or the good principle, let us henceforward substitute it for the thorn. The knowledge of this principle will necessarily lead to the gradual and peaceful introduction of other institutions and improved arrangements, which will preclude all the existing evils, and permanently secure the well-being and happiness of mankind.

THE ECONOMIST

THE COLLECTIVE AFFAIRS OF MEN have hitherto been very grossly mismanaged.

The true Principles of Society have been very little, if at all, understood.

The real causes of the vice, poverty, and wretchedness, which have scourged the great mass of every people, and have finally consigned the mightiest empires to destruction, have, till very lately, been overlooked, or entirely unknown.

The powers acquired by mankind, for the production and distribution of wealth, the diffusion of knowledge, the growth of virtue, the reduction of human labour, the enjoyment of comfort, and the establishment of security, have been rendered, with relation to the great majority of every people, nearly useless, but the influence of counteracting principles, inherent in, and nearly coeval with, the frame of society itself.

The ECONOMIST undertakes to PROVE these assertions, by a few self-evident, intelligible, common-sense statements, as plain, as simple, and as palpable, as they are true.

He will take England as the portion of the globe on which his proofs are to be exhibited: England, with all her means, with all her power, all her glory, all her wealth, all her learning, all her beneficence,—England (strange, and hitherto unaccountable anomaly) with all her wretchedness, all her vice, all her poverty, all her ignorance, all her dissensions and degradation.

England possesses the means and the power of creating more Manufactured Goods than the world can consume; and her soil is capable of furnishing several times the number of her present population with food.

Notwithstanding this power, and this inalienable source of superabundant subsistence, millions of her own people are but imperfectly supplied with some, and are entirely destitute of most, of the necessaries and comforts of life, and of the numberless articles of convenience or of elegance which inventive skill has contrived for the accommodation or embellishment of society.

Here, then, is a source of wealth which is not sufficiently opened, and a power of production which is not exerted;—and, here, on the other hand, are unsatisfied wants, which the inert power, if we remove the causes that now restrain its activity, is much more than adequate to supply.

The sphere of wretchedness (to state the case again) enlarges; the wants of the people increase; yet the power, which is able almost immediately to satisfy these wants, and in a short time to pour a superabundance upon the whole nation, becomes more and more inert.

The manufacturer, the merchant, and all who have not yet looked to the bottom of this long-perplexing subject, are in the habit of remarking, or rather complaining, that there is *no demand for goods;* that the *market is overstocked;* and that *the times are bad;* because, say they, *more goods are produced than can be consumed.*

The ECONOMIST utterly denies the truth of these allegations. He hesitates not to declare, That the parties advancing them are mistaken; nor to pronounce that they have deceived themselves, and are guilty, however unintentionally, of deceiving the public, on a question of the highest importance: a question involving our very *existence,* as individuals and as a nation.

For what description of goods is there *no demand?* With what commodities is the world *over-stocked?* Of what articles, the product of land or of industry, does there exist a *greater quantity* than can be *consumed.*

Is it of *bread,* or any other necessary of life, the product of the soil?

I will show the landholder, even in this rich and flourishing land, hundreds of thousands of half-starved wretches, whose cry of distress, whose clamorous *demand* for *bread,* has at length penetrated the palaces and the breasts of their astonished and alarmed superiors.

Does the complaint come from the clothier, the hatter, the hosier, the tanner, the cutler, the potter, the joiner, the upholsterer, the founder, the builder, or even the scholar, the teacher, and the moralist?

I will take the first four through the streets of London; and I will show them, in London alone, a multitude in abject poverty and squalid attire, the supply of whom, with comfortable apparel, would empty their full warehouses, and for a season exhaust their stores.

I will carry the cutler, the potter, the joiner, the upholsterer, the bedding-maker, the founder, &c. into the miserable abodes of millions of Britons; and I will exhibit to them an almost endless succession of bare and dreary dwellings, the equipment of which with the necessaries and comforts, to say nothing of the elegancies of life, would, for a time, engross all their means and employ all their industry.

I will expose to the builder multitudes of human beings, crowded together in filthy, incommodious, and unhealthful hovels, languishing in garrets, and expiring in damp and dismal cellars, in workhouses, in hospitals, in jails. I will even show him thousands of houseless and unsheltered wretches, inhaling their mortal malady with the distillations of the night, or perhaps breathing their last sigh on the inhospitable threshold, which is closed upon the pleading eloquence of Nature and Humanity, and repels the heartbreaking *demand* of silent Misery; and I will ask him, If he does not think there is ample scope for the extended consumption of our inexhaustible materials for building, and for the increased employment of him and all his labourers. . . .

That, though Vice and Crime (the progeny of Political Errors) are rapidly decomposing the elements of society, and preparing the volcanic mass of conflicting principles for an explosion that shall level the proud institutions and distinctions of civilization with the ground, and bury in their ruins all the graces, the charities, the intelligence, which ages of assiduous culture have brought to their present growth,—we, nevertheless, possess the certain means of averting the catastrophe which threatens us, and of almost instantly allaying those portentous grumblings, which too plainly indicate the approach of a terrible convulsion, that would hurl mankind back into barbarism:

That, though hundreds of thousands of English families are inadequately supplied with food, and though this country even depends upon Foreign Nations for a portion of the first necessaries of life; yet, that our own soil, and our vast unemployed powers of production are capable of immediately furnishing a superabundance of produce for the satisfaction of the first urgent and indispensable demand of nature:

That, though we have an immense population, not only ill-instructed, and ill-fed, but inadequately lodged, uncomfortably clothed, and wholly unfurnished with innocent pleasures, with healthful and agreeable recreations, with all the articles and arrangements of convenience or of comfort which engage the minds, cheer the spirits, adorn the persons, and embellish the abodes of mankind,—yet we have materials,—we have the command of means,—we have hands,—above all, we have science and mechanism, capable of surrounding each individual with more of all these goods than his utmost wishes can desire. . . .

The measures which are calculated to effect this great change, may be commenced almost without an effort.

All the persons who at present have employment, may instantly begin to climb the ascent without soliciting a helping hand from those who stand above them.

The utterly destitute will require less aid to render them and their descendants happy and independent, than that which must, under the present system, be afforded them for the prolongation of a miserable existence, from public and private charity.

The poor will be relieved from their wretchedness, and the rich will be benefited by the process.

The ignorant will be instructed, while the learned will derive vast accessions to the sum of human knowledge and wisdom.

The vicious will be reclaimed, while the virtuous will, in great measure, be withdrawn from temptation.

The humble will be placed in a situation of safety, and of gradual elevation, while the great will gain in security.

Land and labour will become of greatly increased value, and will always command their true worth.

Of the latter (labour) there will for a long time be too little for the demand, though there is at present so great a scarcity of employment.

The present *money* wealth of the country will become many times more valuable, active, and useful, than it now is;—so truly and obviously so, indeed, that the effect will be the same as if foreign nations were suddenly to pay us a tribute, equal to several times the amount of our present money wealth; and as if that vast accession of wealth were equally divided among the population.

Plenty will overspread the land!—Knowledge will increase!—Virtue will flourish!—Happiness will be recognized, secured, and enjoyed. . . .

[The ECONOMIST] has already shown that there are almost boundless wants, and that we possess equally boundless powers of production, for the creation of all the goods by which those wants are to be satisfied. He hopes we shall at least hear no more, therefore, of their being *no market* for our produce,—of there being *no demand* for our commodities,—of the necessity of looking into every corner of the globe for customers, while we have so many millions of ill-supplied consumers at home. He trusts that mankind, at length convinced of this great truth, will set about emancipating themselves from the thraldom of ignorance, which has hitherto rendered all their energies nearly nugatory;—that they will now complain, not of the want of goods, of means, or of power, but of the errors which prevent the exercise of their power, the command of their means, and the distribution of their goods;—that, having at length discovered that their multifarious evils arise, not from the absence of markets,—not from the limited extent of the demand,—not from the paucity of consumers,—but from the prevalence of erroneous principles, which continually interpose between the consumers and the producers, and which tend perpetually to close the channels of circulation;—they will set themselves seriously to remove the real causes of all their calamities,—to break down the barriers which have shut out man from man,—and so to open, renovate, and enlarge the channels through which alone their boundless treasures can be circulated, as to afford an easy passage to the full-swelling tide of their wealth, knowledge, and happiness.

THE COMMUNIST MANIFESTO

KARL MARX (1818–83) came from a well-to-do Rhineland Jewish family. Planning an academic career, Marx studied first at Bonn and then at Berlin, where he was influenced by the so-called "left Hegelians." Because he anticipated political difficulties as a teacher, he went into journalism. In 1843 he had to flee to Paris because of his revolutionary activities.

The next year he met Friedrich Engels (1820–95) who had been sent to England by his father, a wealthy Rhineland industrialist, to supervise a branch factory near Manchester. Engels was revolted by working-class conditions, wrote an exposé of them, and took part in the Chartist agitation. After meeting Marx in 1844 he remained his constant co-worker and financial supporter. During 1843 and 1844 in Paris Marx met and quarreled with the socialists Louis Blanc and Proudhon, and with the Saint-Simonians. In 1845 he moved to Brussels, his basic theories already shaped. In 1847 he and Engels joined a secret workingmen's society, the Communist League. The jointly written *Communist Manifesto* of 1848 was a program for this group, but it became the core of all later Communist doctrine.

The *Manifesto* was entitled "Communist" to differentiate it from programs of mere reform, especially the paternalistic socialism of Owen and Fourier, and to attach it to working-class movements. Part III of the *Manifesto,* a criticism of other types of socialism, is omitted here. The translation from the German is the authorized English version done by Samuel F. Moore under the supervision of Engels. The notes are those supplied by Engels in 1888.

MANIFESTO OF
THE COMMUNIST PARTY

A SPECTRE is haunting Europe—the spectre of Communism. All the powers of old Europe have entered into a holy alliance to exorcise this spectre; Pope and Czar, Metternich and Guizot, French Radicals and German police-spies.

Where is the party in opposition that has not been decried as communistic by its opponents in power? Where the Opposition that has not hurled back the branding reproach of Communism, against the more advanced opposition parties, as well as against its reactionary adversaries?

Two things result from this fact.

I. Communism is already acknowledged by all European Powers to be itself a Power.

II. It is high time that Communists should openly, in the face of the whole world, publish their views, their aims, their tendencies, and meet this nursery tale of the Spectre of Communism with a Manifesto of the party itself.

To this end, Communists of various nationalities have assembled in London, and sketched the following manifesto, to be published in the English, French, German, Italian, Flemish and Danish languages.

I. BOURGEOIS AND PROLETARIANS [1]

The history of all hitherto existing society [2] is the history of class struggles.

Freeman and slave, patrician and plebeian, lord and serf, guild-master [3] and journeyman, in a word, oppressor and oppressed, stood in constant opposition to one another, carried on an uninterrupted, now hidden, now open fight, a fight that each time ended, either in a revolutionary re-constitution of society at large, or in the common ruin of the contending classes.

In the earlier epochs of history, we find almost everywhere a complicated arrangement of society into various orders, a manifold graduation of social rank. In ancient Rome we have patricians, knights, plebeians, slaves; in the middle ages, feudal lords, vassals, guildmasters, journeymen, apprentices, serfs; in almost all of these classes, again, subordinate gradations.

The modern bourgeois society that has sprouted from the ruins of feudal society, has not done away with class antagonisms. It has but established new classes, new conditions of oppression, new forms of struggle in place of the old ones.

Our epoch, the epoch of the bourgeoisie, possesses, however, this distinctive feature; it has simplified the class antagonisms. Society as a whole

[1] By bourgeoisie is meant the class of modern Capitalists, owners of the means of social production and employers of wage-labor. By proletariat, the class of modern wage-laborers who, having no means of production of their own, are reduced to selling their labor-power in order to live.

[2] That is, all written history. In 1847, the pre-history of society, the social organization existing previous to recorded history, was all but unknown. Since then, Haxthausen discovered common ownership of land in Russia, Maurer proved it to be the social foundation from which all Teutonic races started in history, and by and by village communities were found to be, or to have been, the primitive form of society everywhere from India to Ireland. The inner organization of this primitive Communistic society was laid bare, in its typical form, by Morgan's crowning discovery of the true nature of the gens and its relation to the tribe. With the dissolution of these primeval communities society begins to be differentiated into separate and finally antagonistic classes. I have attempted to retrace this process of dissolution in "The Origin of the Family, Private Property and the State."

[3] Guildmaster, that is, a full member of a guild, a master within, not a head of, a guild.

tinctive feature; it has simplified the class antagonisms. Society as a whole is more and more splitting up into two great hostile camps, into two great classes directly facing each other: Bourgeoisie and Proletariat.

From the serfs of the middle ages sprang the chartered burghers of the earliest towns. From these burgesses the first elements of the bourgeoisie were developed.

The discovery of America, the rounding of the Cape, opened up fresh ground for the rising bourgeoisie. The East-Indian and Chinese markets, the colonization of America, trade with the colonies, the increase in the means of exchange and in commodities generally, gave to commerce, to navigation, to industry, an impulse never before known, and thereby, to the revolutionary element in the tottering feudal society, a rapid development.

The feudal system of industry, under which industrial production was monopolized by close guilds, now no longer sufficed for the growing wants of the new markets. The manufacturing system took its place. The guild-masters were pushed on one side by the manufacturing middle-class; division of labor between the different corporate guilds vanished in the face of division of labor in each single workshop.

Meantime the markets kept ever growing, the demand, ever rising. Even manufacture no longer sufficed. Thereupon, steam and machinery revolutionized industrial production. The place of manufacture was taken by the giant, Modern Industry, the place of the industrial middle-class, by industrial millionaires, the leaders of whole industrial armies, the modern bourgeois.

Modern industry has established the world-market, for which the discovery of America paved the way. This market has given an immense development to commerce, to navigation, to communication by land. This development has, in its turn, reacted on the extension of industry; and in proportion as industry, commerce, navigation, railways extended, in the same proportion the bourgeoisie developed, increased its capital, and pushed into the background every class handed down from the Middle Ages.

We see, therefore, how the modern bourgeoisie is itself the product of a long course of development, of a series of revolutions in the modes of production and of exchange.

Each step in the development of the bourgeoisie was accompanied by a corresponding political advance of that class. An oppressed class under the sway of the feudal nobility, an armed and self-governing association in the mediaeval commune,[4] here independent urban republic (as in Italy and Germany), there taxable "third estate" of the monarchy (as in France), after-

---

[4] "Commune" was the name taken, in France, by the nascent towns even before they had conquered from their feudal lords and masters, local self-government and political rights as "the Third Estate." Generally speaking, for the economical development of the bourgeoisie, England is here taken as the typical country, for its political development, France.

wards, in the period of manufacture proper, serving either the semi-feudal or the absolute monarchy as a counterpoise against the nobility, and, in fact. corner stone of the great monarchies in general, the bourgeoisie has at last. since the establishment of Modern Industry and of the world-market, con quered for itself, in the modern representative State, exclusive political sway. The executive of the modern State is but a committee for managing the common affairs of the whole bourgeoisie.

The bourgeoisie, historically, has played a most revolutionary part.

The bourgeoisie, wherever it has got the upper hand, has put an end to all feudal, patriarchal, idyllic relations. It has pitilessly torn asunder the motley feudal ties that bound man to his "natural superiors," and has left remaining no other nexus between man and man than naked self-interest, than callous "cash payment." It has drowned the most heavenly ecstasies of religious fervor, of chivalrous enthusiasm, of philistine sentimentalism, in the icy water of egotistical calculation. It has resolved personal worth into exchange value, and in place of the numberless indefeasible chartered free-doms, has set up that single, unconscionable freedom—Free Trade. In one word, for exploitation, veiled by religious and political illusions, it has sub-stituted naked, shameless, direct, brutal exploitation.

The bourgeoisie has stripped of its halo every occupation hitherto hon ored and looked up to with reverent awe. It has converted the physician, the lawyer, the priest, the poet, the man of science, into its paid wage-laborers.

The bourgeoisie has torn away from the family its sentimental veil, and has reduced the family relation to a mere money relation.

The bourgeoisie has disclosed how it came to pass that the brutal display of vigor in the Middle Ages, which Reactionists so much admire, found its fitting complement in the most slothful indolence. It has been the first to show what man's activity can bring about. It has accomplished wonders far surpassing Egyptian pyramids, Roman aqueducts, and Gothic cathedrals; it has conducted expeditions that put in the shade all former Exoduses of nations and crusades.

The bourgeoisie cannot exist without constantly revolutionizing the in-struments of production, and thereby the relations of production, and with them the whole relations of society. Conservation of the old modes of pro-duction in unaltered form, was, on the contrary, the first condition of exist-ence for all earlier industrial classes. Constant revolutionizing of production, uninterrupted disturbance of all social conditions, everlasting uncertainty and agitation distinguish the bourgeois epoch from all earlier ones. All fixed, fast-frozen relations, with their train of ancient and venerable prejudices and opinions, are swept away, all new-formed ones become antiquated before they can ossify. All that is solid melts into air, all that is holy is profaned, and man is at last compelled to face with sober senses, his real conditions of life, and his relations with his kind.

The need of a constantly expanding market for its products chases the bourgeoisie over the whole surface of the globe. It must nestle everywhere, settle everywhere, establish connections everywhere.

The bourgeoisie has through its exploitation of the world-market given a cosmopolitan character to production and consumption in every country. To the great chagrin of Reactionists, it has drawn from under the feet of industry the national ground on which it stood. All old-established national industries have been destroyed or are daily being destroyed. They are dislodged by new industries, whose introduction becomes a life and death question for all civilized nations, by industries that no longer work up indigenous raw material, but raw material drawn from the remotest zones; industries whose products are consumed, not only at home, but in every quarter of the globe. In place of the old wants, satisfied by the productions of the country, we find new wants, requiring for their satisfaction the products of distant lands and climes. In place of the old local and national seclusion and self-sufficiency, we have intercourse in every direction, universal inter-dependence of nations. And as in material, so also in intellectual production. The intellectual creations of individual nations become common property. National one-sidedness and narrow-mindedness become more and more impossible, and from the numerous national and local literatures there arises a world-literature.

The bourgeoisie, by the rapid improvement of all instruments of production, by the immensely facilitated means of communication, draws all, even the most barbarian, nations into civilization. The cheap prices of its commodities are the heavy artillery with which it batters down all Chinese walls, with which it forces the barbarians' intensely obstinate hatred of foreigners to capitulate. It compels all nations, on pain of extinction, to adopt the bourgeois mode of production; it compels them to introduce what it calls civilization into their midst, i. e., to become bourgeois themselves. In a word, it creates a world after its own image.

The bourgeoisie has subjected the country to the rule of the towns. It has created enormous cities, has greatly increased the urban population as compared with the rural, and has thus rescued a considerable part of the population from the idiocy of rural life. Just as it has made the country dependent on the towns, so it has made barbarian and semi-barbarian countries dependent on the civilized ones, nations of peasants on nations of bourgeois, the East on the West.

The bourgeoisie keeps more and more doing away with the scattered state of the population, of the means of production, and of property. It has agglomerated population, centralized means of production, and has concentrated property in a few hands. The necessary consequence of this was political centralization. Independent, or but loosely connected provinces, with separate interests, laws, governments and systems of taxation, became lumped together in one nation, with one government, one code of laws, one national class-interest, one frontier and one customs-tariff.

The bourgeoisie, during its rule of scarce one hundred years, has created more massive and more colossal productive forces than have all preceding generations together. Subjection of Nature's forces to man, machinery, application of chemistry to industry and agriculture, steam-navigation, railways, electric telegraphs, clearing of whole continents for cultivation, canalization of rivers, whole populations conjured out of the ground—what earlier century had even a presentiment that such productive forces slumbered in the lap of social labor?

We see then: the means of production and of exchange on whose foundation the bourgeoisie built itself up, were generated in feudal society. At a certain stage in the development of these means of production and of exchange, the conditions under which feudal society produced and exchanged, the feudal organization of agriculture and manufacturing industry, in one word, the feudal relations of property became no longer compatible with the already developed productive forces; they became so many fetters. They had to burst asunder; they were burst asunder.

Into their places stepped free competition, accompanied by a social and political constitution adapted to it, and by the economical and political sway of the bourgeois class.

A similar movement is going on before our own eyes. Modern bourgeois society with its relations of production, of exchange and of property, a society that has conjured up such gigantic means of production and of exchange, is like the sorcerer, who is no longer able to control the powers of the nether world whom he has called up by his spells. For many a decade past the history of industry and commerce is but the history of the revolt of modern productive forces against modern conditions of production, against the property relations that are the conditions for the existence of the bourgeoisie and of its rule. It is enough to mention the commercial crises that by their periodical return put on its trial, each time more threateningly, the existence of the entire bourgeois society. In these crises a great part not only of the existing products, but also of the previously created productive forces, are periodically destroyed. In these crises there breaks out an epi-

demic that, in all earlier epochs, would have seemed an absurdity—the epidemic of over-production. Society suddenly finds itself put back into a state
of momentary barbarism; it appears as if a famine, a universal war of devastation had cut off the supply of every means of subsistence; industry and
commerce seem to be destroyed; and why? Because there is too much
civilization, too much means of subsistence, too much industry, too much
commerce. The productive forces at the disposal of society no longer tend
to further the development of the conditions of bourgeois property; on the
contrary, they have become too powerful for these conditions, by which they
are fettered, and so soon as they overcome these fetters, they bring disorder
into the whole of bourgeois society, endanger the existence of bourgeois
property. The conditions of bourgeois society are too narrow to comprise
the wealth created by them. And how does the bourgeoisie get over these
crises? On the one hand by enforced destruction of a mass of productive
forces; on the other, by the conquest of new markets, and by the more
thorough exploitation of the old ones. That is to say, by paving the way for
more extensive and more destructive crises, and by diminishing the means
whereby crises are prevented.

The weapons with which the bourgeoisie felled feudalism to the ground
are now turned against the bourgeoisie itself.

But not only has the bourgeoisie forged the weapons that bring death to
itself; it has also called into existence the men who are to wield those weapons—the modern working-class—the proletarians.

In proportion as the bourgeoisie, i. e., capital, is developed, in the same
proportion is the proletariat, the modern working-class, developed, a class
of laborers, who live only so long as they find work, and who find work
only so long as their labor increases capital. These laborers, who must sell
themselves piecemeal, are a commodity, like every other article of commerce, and are consequently exposed to all the vicissitudes of competition,
to all the fluctuations of the market.

Owing to the extensive use of machinery and to division of labor, the
work of the proletarians has lost all individual character, and, consequently,
all charm for the workman. He becomes an appendage of the machine, and
it is only the most simple, most monotonous, and most easily acquired knack
that is required of him. Hence, the cost of production of a workman is restricted, almost entirely, to the means of subsistence that he requires for his
maintenance, and for the propagation of his race. But the price of a commodity, and also of labor, is equal to its cost of production. In proportion,
therefore, as the repulsiveness of the work increases, the wage decreases.
Nay more, in proportion as the use of machinery and division of labor in-

creases, in the same proportion the burden of toil also increases, whether by prolongation of the working hours, by increase of the work enacted in a given time, or by increased speed of the machinery, etc.

Modern industry has converted the little workshop of the patriarchal master into the great factory of the industrial capitalist. Masses of laborers, crowded into the factory, are organized like soldiers. As privates of the industrial army they are placed under the command of a perfect hierarchy of officers and sergeants. Not only are they the slaves of the bourgeois class, and of the bourgeois State, they are daily and hourly enslaved by the machine, by the over-looker, and, above all, by the individual bourgeois manufacturer himself. The more openly this despotism proclaims gain to be its end and aim, the more petty, the more hateful and the more embittering it is.

The less the skill and exertion or strength implied in manual labor, in other words, the more modern industry becomes developed, the more is the labor of men superseded by that of women. Differences of age and sex have no longer any distinctive social validity for the working class. All are instruments of labor, more or less expensive to use, according to their age and sex.

No sooner is the exploitation of the laborer by the manufacturer, so far at an end, that he receives his wages in cash, than he is set upon by the other portions of the bourgeoisie, the landlord, the shopkeeper, the pawnbroker, etc.

The lower strata of the middle class—the small tradespeople, shopkeepers, and retired tradesmen generally, the handicraftsmen and peasants—all these sink gradually into the proletariat, partly because their diminutive capital does not suffice for the scale on which Modern Industry is carried on, and is swamped in the competition with the large capitalists, partly because their specialized skill is rendered worthless by new methods of production. Thus the proletariat is recruited from all classes of the population.

The proletariat goes through various stages of development. With its birth begins its struggle with the bourgeoisie. At first the contest is carried on by individual laborers, then by the workpeople of a factory, then by the operatives of one trade, in one locality, against the individual bourgeois who directly exploits them. They direct their attacks not against the bourgeois conditions of production, but against the instruments of production themselves; they destroy imported wares that compete with their labor, they smash to pieces machinery, they set factories ablaze, they seek to restore by force the vanished status of the workman of the Middle Ages.

At this stage the laborers still form an incoherent mass scattered over the whole country, and broken up by their mutual competition. If anywhere they unite to form more compact bodies, this is not yet the consequence of their own active union, but of the union of the bourgeoisie, which class, in order to attain its own political ends, is compelled to set the whole proletariat in motion, and is moreover yet, for a time, able to do so. At this stage, therefore, the proletarians do not fight their enemies, but the enemies of their enemies, the remnants of absolute monarchy, the landowners, the non-industrial bourgeois, the petty bourgeoisie. Thus the whole historical movement is concentrated in the hands of the bourgeoisie; every victory so obtained is a victory for the bourgeoisie.

But with the development of industry the proletariat not only increases in number, it becomes concentrated in greater masses, its strength grows, and it feels that strength more. The various interests and conditions of life within the ranks of the proletariat are more and more equalized, in proportion as machinery obliterates all distinctions of labor, and nearly everywhere reduces wages to the same low level. The growing competition among the bourgeois, and the resulting commercial crises, make the wages of the workers ever more fluctuating. The unceasing improvement of machinery, ever more rapidly developing, makes their livelihood more and more precarious; the collisions between individual workmen and individual bourgeois take more and more the character of collisions between two classes. Thereupon the workers begin to form combinations (Trades' Unions) against the bourgeois; they club together in order to keep up the rate of wages; they found permanent associations in order to make provision beforehand for these occasional revolts. Here and there the contest breaks out into riots.

Now and then the workers are victorious, but only for a time. The real fruit of their battles lies, not in the immediate result, but in the ever expanding union of the workers. This union is helped on by the improved means of communication that are created by modern industry, and that place the workers of different localities in contact with one another. It was just this contact that was needed to centralize the numerous local struggles, all of the same character, into one national struggle between classes. But every class struggle is a political struggle. And that union, to attain which the burghers of the Middle Ages, with their miserable highways, required centuries, the modern proletarians, thanks to railways, achieve in a few years.

This organization of the proletarians into a class, and consequently into a political party, is continually being upset again by the competition between the workers themselves. But it ever rises up again, stronger, firmer, mightier.

It compels legislative recognition of particular interests of the workers, by taking advantage of the divisions among the bourgeoisie itself. Thus the ten-hour bill in England was carried.

Altogether collisions between the classes of the old society further, in many ways, the course of development of the proletariat. The bourgeoisie finds itself involved in a constant battle. At first with the aristocracy; later on, with those portions of the bourgeoisie itself, whose interests have become antagonistic to the progress of industry; at all times, with the bourgeoisie of foreign countries. In all these battles it sees itself compelled to appeal to the proletariat, to ask for its help, and thus, to drag it into the political arena. The bourgeoisie itself, therefore, supplies the proletariat with its own elements of political and general education, in other words, it furnishes the proletariat with weapons for fighting the bourgeoisie.

Further, as we have already seen, entire sections of the ruling classes are, by the advance of industry, precipitated into the proletariat, or are at least threatened in their conditions of existence. These also supply the proletariat with fresh elements of enlightenment and progress.

Finally, in times when the class-struggle nears the decisive hour, the process of dissolution going on within the ruling class, in fact, within the whole range of old society, assumes such a violent, glaring character, that a small section of the ruling class cuts itself adrift, and joins the revolutionary class, the class that holds the future in its hands. Just as, therefore, at an earlier period, a section of the nobility went over to the bourgeoisie, so now a portion of the bourgeoisie goes over to the proletariat, and in particular, a portion of the bourgeois ideologists, who have raised themselves to the level of comprehending theoretically the historical movements as a whole.

Of all the classes that stand face to face with the bourgeoisie today, the proletariat alone is a really revolutionary class. The other classes decay and finally disappear in the face of modern industry; the proletariat is its special and essential product.

The lower middle class, the small manufacturer, the shopkeeper, the artisan, the peasant, all these fight against the bourgeoisie, to save from extinction their existence as fractions of the middle class. They are, therefore, not revolutionary, but conservative. Nay more, they are reactionary, for they try to roll back the wheel of history. If by chance they are revolutionary, they are so, only in view of their impending transfer into the proletariat, they thus defend not their present, but their future interests, they desert their own standpoint to place themselves at that of the proletariat.

The "dangerous class," the social scum, that passively rotting mass thrown off by the lowest layers of old society, may, here and there, be swept into the movement by a proletarian revolution; its conditions of life, however, prepare it far more for the part of a bribed tool of reactionary intrigue.

In the conditions of the proletariat, those of old society at large are already virtually swamped. The proletarian is without property; his relation to his wife and children has no longer anything in common with the bourgeois family-relations; modern industrial labor, modern subjection to capital, the same in England as in France, in America as in Germany, has stripped him of every trace of national character. Law, morality, religion, are to him so many bourgeois prejudices, behind which lurk in ambush just as many bourgeois interests.

All the preceding classes that got the upper hand, sought to fortify their already acquired status by subjecting society at large to their conditions of appropriation. The proletarians cannot become masters of the productive forces of society, except by abolishing their own previous mode of appropriation, and thereby also every other previous mode of appropriation. They have nothing of their own to secure and to fortify; their mission is to destroy all previous securities for, and insurances of, individual property.

All previous historical movements were movements of minorities, or in the interest of minorities. The proletarian movement is the self-conscious, independent movement of the immense majority, in the interest of the immense majority. The proletariat, the lowest stratum of our present society, cannot stir, cannot raise itself up, without the whole superincumbent strata of official society being sprung into the air.

Though not in substance, yet in form, the struggle of the proletariat with the bourgeoisie is at first a national struggle. The proletariat of each country must, of course, first of all settle matters with its own bourgeoisie.

In depicting the most general phases of the development of the proletariat, we traced the more or less veiled civil war, raging within existing society, up to the point where that war breaks out into open revolution, and where the violent overthrow of the bourgeoisie lays the foundation for the sway of the proletariat.

Hitherto, every form of society has been based, as we have already seen, on the antagonism of oppressing and oppressed classes. But in order to oppress a class, certain conditions must be assured to it under which it can, at least, continue its slavish existence. The serf, in the period of serfdom, raised himself to membership in the commune, just as the petty bourgeois, under the yoke of feudal absolutism, managed to develop into a bourgeois. The modern laborer, on the contrary, instead of rising with the progress of industry, sinks deeper and deeper below the conditions of existence of his own class. He becomes a pauper, and pauperism develops more rapidly than population and wealth. And here it becomes evident, that the bourgeoisie is unfit any longer to be the ruling class in society, and to impose its conditions of existence upon society as an over-riding law. It is unfit to rule, because it is incompetent to assure an existence to its slave within his slavery, because it cannot help letting him sink into such a state that it has to feed him, instead of being fed by him. Society can no longer live under this bourgeoisie, in other words, its existence is no longer compatible with society.

The essential condition for the existence, and for the sway of the bourgeois class, is the formation and augmentation of capital; the condition for capital is wage-labor. Wage-labor rests exclusively on competition between the laborers. The advance of industry, whose involuntary promoter is the bourgeoisie, replaces the isolation of the laborers, due to competition, by their revolutionary combination, due to association. The development of Modern Industry, therefore, cuts from under its feet the very foundation on which the bourgeoisie produces and appropriates products. What the bourgeoisie therefore produces, above all, are its own grave-diggers. Its fall and the victory of the proletariat are equally inevitable.

II. PROLETARIANS AND COMMUNISTS

In what relation do the Communists stand to the proletarians as a whole?

The Communists do not form a separate party opposed to other working-class parties.

They have no interests separate and apart from those of the proletariat as a whole.

They do not set up any sectarian principles of their own, by which to shape and mould the proletarian movement.

The Communists are distinguished from the other working class parties by this only: 1. In the national struggles of the proletarians of the different countries, they point out and bring to the front the common interests of the entire proletariat independently of all nationality. 2. In the various stages of development which the struggle of the working class against the bourgeoisie has to pass through, they always and everywhere represent the interests of the movement as a whole.

The Communists, therefore, are on the one hand, practically, the most advanced and resolute section of the working class parties of every country, that section which pushes forward all others; on the other hand, theoretically, they have over the great mass of the proletariat the advantage of clearly understanding the line of march, the conditions, and the ultimate general results of the proletarian movement.

The immediate aim of the Communists is the same as that of all the other proletarian parties; formation of the proletariat into a class, overthrow of the bourgeois supremacy, conquest of political power by the proletariat.

The theoretical conclusions of the Communists are in no way based on ideas or principles that have been invented, or discovered, by this or that would-be universal reformer.

They merely express, in general terms, actual relations springing from an existing class struggle, from a historical movement going on under our very eyes. The abolition of existing property relations is not at all a distinctive feature of Communism.

All property relations in the past have continually been subject to historical change consequent upon the change in historical conditions.

The French Revolution, for example, abolished feudal property in favor of bourgeois property.

The distinguishing feature of Communism is not the abolition of property generally, but the abolition of bourgeois property. But modern bourgeois private property is the final and most complete expression of the system of producing and appropriating products, that is based on class antagonism, on the exploitation of the many by the few.

In this sense, the theory of the Communists may be summed up in the single sentence: Abolition of private property.

We Communists have been reproached with the desire of abolishing the right of personally acquiring property as the fruit of a man's own labor, which property is alleged to be the ground work of all personal freedom, activity and independence.

Hard-won, self-acquired, self-earned property! Do you mean the property of the petty artisan and of the small peasant, a form of property that preceded the bourgeois form? There is no need to abolish that; the development of industry has to a great extent already destroyed it, and is still destroying it daily.

Or do you mean modern bourgeois private property?

But does wage-labor create any property for the laborer? Not a bit. It creates capital, i. e., that kind of property which exploits wage-labor, and which cannot increase except upon condition of getting a new supply of wage-labor for fresh exploitation. Property, in its present form, is based on the antagonism of capital and wage-labor. Let us examine both sides of this antagonism.

To be a capitalist, is to have not only a purely personal, but a social status in production. Capital is a collective product, and only by the united action of many members, nay, in the last resort, only by the united action of all members of society, can it be set in motion.

Capital is therefore not a personal, it is a social power.

When, therefore, capital is converted into common property, into the property of all members of society, personal property is not thereby transformed into social property. It is only the social character of the property that is changed. It loses its class-character.

Let us now take wage-labor.

The average price of wage-labor is the minimum wage, i. e., that quantum of the means of subsistence, which is absolutely requisite to keep the laborer in bare existence as a laborer. What, therefore, the wage-laborer appropriates by means of his labor, merely suffices to prolong and reproduce a bare existence. We by no means intend to abolish this personal appropriation of the products of labor, an appropriation that is made for the maintenance and reproduction of human life, and that leaves no surplus wherewith to command the labor of others. All that we want to do away with is the miserable character of this appropriation, under which the laborer lives merely to increase capital, and is allowed to live only in so far as the interest of the ruling class requires it.

In bourgeois society, living labor is but a means to increase accumulated labor. In communist society, accumulated labor is but a means to widen, to enrich, to promote the existence of the laborer.

In bourgeois society, therefore, the past dominates the present; in communist society, the present dominates the past. In bourgeois society capital is independent and has individuality, while the living person is dependent and has no individuality.

And the abolition of this state of things is called by the bourgeois, abolition of individuality and freedom! And rightly so. The abolition of bourgeois individuality, bourgeois independence, and bourgeois freedom is undoubtedly aimed at.

By freedom is meant, under the present bourgeois conditions of production, free trade, free selling and buying.

But if selling and buying disappears, free selling and buying disappears also. This talk about free selling and buying, and all the other "brave words" of our bourgeoisie about freedom in general, have a meaning, if any, only in contrast with restricted selling and buying, with the fettered traders of the Middle Ages, but have no meaning when opposed to the Communistic abolition of buying and selling, of the bourgeois conditions of production, and of the bourgeoisie itself.

You are horrified at our intending to do away with private property. But in your existing society, private property is already done away with for nine-tenths of the population; its existence for the few is solely due to its non-existence in the hands of those nine-tenths. You reproach us, therefore, with intending to do away with a form of property, the necessary condition for whose existence is, the non-existence of any property for the immense majority of society.

In one word, you reproach us with intending to do away with your property. Precisely so; that is just what we intend.

From the moment when labor can no longer be converted into capital, money, or rent, into a social power capable of being monopolized, i. e., from the moment when individual property can no longer be transformed into bourgeois property, into capital, from that moment, you say, individuality vanishes.

You must, therefore, confess that by "individual" you mean no other person than the bourgeois, than the middle-class owner of property. This person must, indeed, be swept out of the way, and made impossible.

Communism deprives no man of the power to appropriate the products of society: all that it does is to deprive him of the power to subjugate the labor of others by means of such appropriation.

It has been objected, that upon the abolition of private property all work will cease, and universal laziness will overtake us.

According to this, bourgeois society ought long ago to have gone to the dogs through sheer idleness; for those of its members who work, acquire nothing, and those who acquire anything, do not work. The whole of this objection is but another expression of the tautology: that there can no longer be any wage-labor when there is no longer any capital.

All objections urged against the Communistic mode of producing and appropriating material products, have, in the same way, been urged against the Communistic modes of producing and appropriating intellectual products. Just as, to the bourgeois, the disappearance of class property is the disappearance of production itself, so the disappearance of class culture is to him identical with the disappearance of all culture.

That culture, the loss of which he laments, is, for the enormous majority, a mere training to act as a machine.

But don't wrangle with us so long as you apply, to our intended abolition of bourgeois property, the standard of your bourgeois notions of freedom, culture, law, etc. Your very ideas are but the outgrowth of the conditions of your bourgeois production and bourgeois property, just as your jurisprudence is but the will of your class made into a law for all, a will, whose essential character and direction are determined by the economic conditions of existence of your class.

The selfish misconception that induces you to transform into eternal laws of nature and of reason, the social forms springing from your present mode of production and form of property—historical relations that rise and disappear in the progress of production—this misconception you share with every ruling class that has preceded you. What you see clearly in the case of ancient property, what you admit in the case of feudal property, you are of course forbidden to admit in the case of your own bourgeois form of property.

Abolition of the family! Even the most radical flare up at this infamous proposal of the Communists.

On what foundation is the present family, the bourgeois family, based? On capital, on private gain. In its completely developed form this family exists only among the bourgeoisie. But this state of things finds its complement in the practical absence of the family among the proletarians, and in public prostitution.

The bourgeois family will vanish as a matter of course when its complement vanishes, and both will vanish with the vanishing of capital.

Do you charge us with wanting to stop the exploitation of children by their parents? To this crime we plead guilty.

But, you will say, we destroy the most hallowed of relations, when we replace home education by social.

And your education! Is not that also social, and determined by the social conditions under which you educate, by the intervention, direct or indirect, of society by means of schools, etc.? The Communists have not invented the intervention of society in education; they do but seek to alter the character of that intervention, and to rescue education from the influence of the ruling class.

The bourgeois clap-trap about the family and education, about the hallowed co-relation of parent and child, becomes all the more disgusting, the more, by the action of Modern Industry, all family ties among the proletarians are torn asunder, and their children transformed into simple articles of commerce and instruments of labor.

But you Communists would introduce community of women, screams the whole bourgeoisie in chorus.

The bourgeois sees in his wife a mere instrument of production. He hears that the instruments of production are to be exploited in common, and, naturally, can come to no other conclusion, than that the lot of being common to all will likewise fall to the women.

He has not even a suspicion that the real point aimed at is to do away with the status of women as mere instruments of production.

For the rest, nothing is more ridiculous than the virtuous indignation of our bourgeois at the community of women which, they pretend, is to be openly and officially established by the Communists. The Communists have no need to introduce community of women; it has existed almost from time immemorial.

Our bourgeois, not content with having the wives and daughters of their proletarians at their disposal, not to speak of common prostitutes, take the greatest pleasure in seducing each other's wives.

Bourgeois marriage is in reality a system of wives in common and thus, at the most, what the Communists might possibly be reproached with, is that they desire to introduce, in substitution for a hypocritically concealed, an openly legalized community of women. For the rest, it is self-evident, that the abolition of the present system of production must bring with it the abolition of the community of women springing from that system, i. e., of prostitution both public and private.

The Communists are further reproached with desiring to abolish countries and nationalities.

The working men have no country. We cannot take from them what they have not got. Since the proletariat must first of all acquire political supremacy, must rise to be the leading class of the nation, must constitute itself the nation, it is, so far, itself national, though not in the bourgeois sense of the word.

National differences, and antagonisms between peoples, are daily more and more vanishing, owing to the development of the bourgeoisie, to freedom of commerce, to the world-market, to uniformity in the mode of production and in the conditions of life corresponding thereto.

The supremacy of the proletariat will cause them to vanish still faster. United action, of the leading civilized countries at least, is one of the first conditions for the emancipation of the proletariat.

In proportion as the exploitation of one individual by another is put an end to, the exploitation of one nation by another will also be put an end to. In proportion as the antagonism between classes within the nation vanishes, the hostility of one nation to another will come to an end.

The charges against Communism made from a religious, a philosophical, and generally, from an ideological standpoint, are not deserving of serious examination.

Does it require deep intuition to comprehend that man's ideas, views, and conceptions, in one word, man's consciousness, changes with every change in the conditions of his material existence, in his social relations and in his social life?

What else does the history of ideas prove, than that intellectual production changes in character in proportion as material production is changed? The ruling ideas of each age have ever been the ideas of its ruling class.

When people speak of ideas that revolutionize society, they do but express the fact, that within the old society, the elements of a new one have been created, and that the dissolution of the old ideas keeps even pace with the dissolution of the old conditions of existence.

When the ancient world was in its last throes, the ancient religions were overcome by Christianity. When Christian ideas succumbed in the 18th century to rationalist ideas, feudal society fought its death-battle with the then revolutionary bourgeoisie. The ideas of religious liberty and freedom of conscience, merely gave expression to the sway of free competition within the domain of knowledge.

"Undoubtedly," it will be said, "religious, moral, philosophical and juridical ideas have been modified in the course of historical development. But religion, morality, philosophy, political science, and law, constantly survived this change.

"There are, besides, eternal truths, such as Freedom, Justice, etc., that are common to all states of society. But Communism abolishes eternal truths, it abolishes all religion, and all morality, instead of constituting them on a new basis; it therefore acts in contradiction to all past historical experience."

What does this accusation reduce itself to? The history of all past society has consisted in the development of class antagonisms, antagonisms that assumed different forms at different epochs.

But whatever form they may have taken, one fact is common to all past ages, viz., the exploitation of one part of society by the other. No wonder, then, that the social consciousness of past ages, despite all the multiplicity and variety it displays, moves within certain common forms, or general ideas, which cannot completely vanish except with the total disappearance of class antagonisms.

The Communist revolution is the most radical rupture with traditional property-relations; no wonder that its development involves the most radical rupture with traditional ideas.

But let us have done with the bourgeois objections to Communism.

We have seen above, that the first step in the revolution by the working class, is to raise the proletariat to the position of ruling class, to win the battle of democracy.

The proletariat will use its political supremacy, to wrest, by degrees, all capital from the bourgeoisie, to centralize all instruments of production in the hands of the State, i. e., of the proletariat organized as the ruling class; and to increase the total of productive forces as rapidly as possible.

Of course, in the beginning, this cannot be effected except by means of despotic inroads on the rights of property, and on the conditions of bourgeois production; by means of measures, therefore, which appear economically insufficient and untenable, but which, in the course of the movement, outstrip themselves, necessitate further inroads upon the old social order, and are unavoidable as a means of entirely revolutionizing the mode of production.

These measures will of course be different in different countries.

Nevertheless in the most advanced countries the following will be pretty generally applicable:

1. Abolition of property in land and application of all rents of land to public purposes.

2. A heavy progressive or graduated income tax.

3. Abolition of all right of inheritance.

4. Confiscation of the property of all emigrants and rebels.

5. Centralization of credit in the hands of the state, by means of a national bank with State capital and an exclusive monopoly.

6. Centralization of the means of communication and transport in the hands of the State.

7. Extension of factories and instruments of production owned by the State; the bringing into cultivation of waste lands, and the improvement of the soil generally in accordance with a common plan.

8. Equal liability of all to labor. Establishment of industrial armies, especially for agriculture.

9. Combination of agriculture with manufacturing industries; gradual abolition of the distinction between town and country, by a more equable distribution of population over the country.

10. Free education for all children in public schools. Abolition of children's factory labor in its present form. Combination of education with industrial production, etc., etc.

When, in the course of development, class distinctions have disappeared, and all production has been concentrated in the hands of a vast association of the whole nation, the public power will lose its political character. Political power, properly so called, is merely the organized power of one class for oppressing another. If the proletariat during its contest with the bourgeoisie is compelled, by the force of circumstances, to organize itself as a class, if, by means of a revolution, it makes itself the ruling class, and, as such, sweeps away by force the old conditions of production, then it will, along with these conditions, have swept away the conditions for the existence of class antagonisms, and of classes generally, and will thereby have abolished its own supremacy as a class.

In place of the old bourgeois society, with its classes and class antagonisms, we shall have an association, in which the free development of each is the condition for the free development of all.

IV. POSITION OF THE COMMUNISTS IN RELATION TO THE VARIOUS EXISTING OPPOSITION PARTIES

Section II has made clear the relations of the Communists to the existing working class parties, such as the Chartists in England and the Agrarian Reformers in America.

The Communists fight for the attainment of the immediate aims, for the enforcement of the momentary interests of the working class; but in the movement of the present, they also represent and take care of the future of that movement. In France the Communists ally themselves with the Social-Democrats,[5] against the conservative and radical bourgeoisie, reserving, however, the right to take up a critical position in regard to phrases and illusions traditionally handed down from the great Revolution.

In Switzerland they support the Radicals, without losing sight of the fact that this party consists of antagonistic elements, partly of Democratic Socialists, in the French sense, partly of radical bourgeois.

In Poland they support the party that insists on an agrarian revolution, as the prime condition of national emancipation, that party which fomented the insurrection of Cracow in 1846.

In Germany they fight with the bourgeoisie whenever it acts in a revolutionary way, against the absolute monarchy, the feudal squirearchy, and the petty bourgeoisie.

But they never cease, for a single instant, to instill into the working class the clearest possible recognition of the hostile antagonism between bourgeoisie and proletariat, in order that the German workers may straightway use, as so many weapons against the bourgeoisie, the social and political conditions that the bourgeoisie must necessarily introduce along with its supremacy, and in order that, after the fall of the reactionary classes in Germany, the fight against the bourgeoisie itself may immediately begin.

The Communists turn their attention chiefly to Germany, because that

---

[5] The party then represented in parliament by Ledru-Rollin, in literature by Louis Blanc, in the daily press by the Reforme. The name of Social Democracy signified, with these its inventors, a section of the Democratic or Republican party more or less tinged with Socialism.

country is on the eve of a bourgeois revolution, that is bound to be carried out under more advanced conditions of European civilization, and with a more developed proletariat, than that of England was in the seventeenth, and of France in the eighteenth century, and because the bourgeois revolution in Germany will be but the prelude to an immediately following proletarian revolution.

In short, the Communists everywhere support every revolutionary movement against the existing social and political order of things.

In all these movements they bring to the front, as the leading question in each, the property question, no matter what its degree of development at the time.

Finally, they labor everywhere for the union and agreement of the democratic parties of all countries.

The Communists disdain to conceal their views and aims. They openly declare that their ends can be attained only by the forcible overthrow of all existing social conditions. Let the ruling classes tremble at a Communistic revolution. The proletarians have nothing to lose but their chains. They have a world to win.

Working men of all countries, unite!

FRIEDRICH ENGELS

THE PUBLICATION of his early work, *The Condition of the Working Class in England,* in 1845, secured for Friedrich Engels, a reputation throughout Europe. For the next five years he traveled widely in France, Germany, and Belgium, and organized revolutionary groups. During this time he was also involved with Karl Marx in the collaboration which resulted in the *Communist Manifesto* of 1848. When he returned to business in England in 1850, he devoted much of his time and money to the support of Marx. He retired from business in 1864 and gave his efforts to revolutionary activity.

Following Marx's death in 1883, Engels became the leading figure in European Marxian socialism: he edited the second and third volumes of *Capital* from rough drafts and notes; he played a key role in the formation of Socialist thought by his own writing of articles and letters; and he became chief adviser to the German Socialist Party, founded by Marx and Ferdinand Lassalle in 1875. Engels died on August 5, 1895, having entrusted Eduard Bernstein and August Bebel with the joint responsibility for administering his literary remains.

Among Engels's most important works is *Eugen Dühring's Revolution in Science* (the *Anti-Dühring*), 1878, from which the following selection is taken. In this and other works he elaborated the theoretical implications of dialectical materialism and applied the dialectic to the earliest stages in human history. In 1880 Engels prepared three chapters of the *Anti-Dühring* for translation into French, and these have since been known under the title *Socialism: Utopian and Scientific.* The present selection is from the translation by Edward Aveling (New York: International Publishers, 1935).

SOCIALISM: UTOPIAN AND SCIENTIFIC

II

WHEN WE CONSIDER and reflect upon nature at large, or the history of mankind, or our own intellectual activity, at first we see the picture of an endless entanglement of relations and reactions, permutations and combinations, in which nothing remains what, where, and as it was, but everything moves, changes, comes into being and passes away. We see, therefore, at first the picture as a whole, with its individual parts still more or less kept in the background; we observe the movements, transitions, connections, rather than the things that move, combine, and are connected. This primitive, naïve, but intrinsically correct conception of the world is that of ancient Greek philosophy, and was first clearly formulated by Heraclitus: everything is and is not, for everything is fluid, is constantly changing, constantly coming into being and passing away.

But this conception, correctly as it expresses the general character of the picture of appearances as a whole, does not suffice to explain the details of which this picture is made up, and so long as we do not understand these, we have not a clear idea of the whole picture. In order to understand these details we must detach them from their natural or historical connection and examine each one separately, its nature, special causes, effects, etc. This is, primarily, the task of natural science and historical research; branches of science which the Greeks of classical times, on very good grounds, relegated to a subordinate position, because they had first of all to collect materials for these sciences to work upon. A certain amount of natural and historical material must be collected before there can be any critical analysis, comparison and arrangement in classes, orders and species. The foundations of the exact natural sciences were, therefore, first worked out by the Greeks of the Alexandrian period, and later, in the Middle Ages, by the Arabs. Real natural science dates from the second half of the fifteenth century, and thence onward it has advanced with constantly increasing rapidity. The analysis of nature into its individual parts, the grouping of the different natural processes and objects in definite classes, the study of the internal anatomy of organised bodies in their manifold forms—these were the fundamental conditions of the gigantic strides in our knowledge of nature that have been made during the last four hundred years. But this method of work has also left us as legacy the habit of observing natural objects and processes in isolation, apart from their connection with the vast whole; of observing them in repose, not in motion; as constants, not as essentially variables; in their death, not in their life. And when this way of looking at things was transferred by Bacon and Locke from natural science to philosophy, it begot the narrow, metaphysical mode of thought peculiar to the last century.

To the metaphysician, things and their mental reflexes, ideas, are isolated, are to be considered one after the other and apart from each other, are objects of investigation fixed, rigid, given once for all. He thinks in absolutely irreconcilable antitheses. "His communication is 'yea, yea; nay, nay'; for whatsoever is more than these cometh of evil." For him a thing either exists or does not exist; a thing cannot at the same time be itself and something else. Positive and negative absolutely exclude one another; cause and effect stand in a rigid antithesis one to the other.

At first sight this mode of thinking seems to us very luminous, because it is that of so-called sound common sense. Only sound common sense, respectable fellow that he is, in the homely realm of his own four walls, has very wonderful adventures directly he ventures out into the wide world of research. And the metaphysical mode of thought, justifiable and necessary as it is in a number of domains whose extent varies according to the nature of the particular object of investigation, sooner or later reaches a limit, beyond which it becomes one-sided, restricted, abstract, lost in insoluble contradictions. In the contemplation of individual things, it forgets the connection between them; in the contemplation of their existence, it forgets the beginning and end of that existence; of their repose, it forgets their motion. It cannot see the wood for the trees.

For everyday purposes we know and can say, *e.g.,* whether an animal is alive or not. But, upon closer inquiry, we find that this is, in many cases, a very complex question, as the jurists know very well. They have cudgelled their brains in vain to discover a rational limit beyond which the killing of the child in its mother's womb is murder. It is just as impossible to determine absolutely the moment of death, for physiology proves that death is not an instantaneous, momentary phenomenon, but a very protracted process.

In like manner, every organised being is every moment the same and not the same; every moment it assimilates matter supplied from without, and gets rid of other matter; every moment some cells of its body die and others build themselves anew; in a longer or shorter time the matter of its body is completely renewed, and is replaced by other molecules of matter, so that every organised being is always itself, and yet something other than itself.

Further, we find upon closer investigation that the two poles of an antithesis, positive and negative, *e.g.,* are as inseparable as they are opposed, and that despite all their opposition, they mutually interpenetrate. And we find, in like manner, that cause and effect are conceptions which only hold good in their application to individual cases; but as soon as we consider the individual cases in their general connection with the universe as a whole, they run into each other, and they become confounded when we contemplate that universal action and reaction in which causes and effects are eternally changing places, so that what is effect here and now will be cause there and then, and *vice versa.*

None of these processes and modes of thought enters into the framework of metaphysical reasoning. Dialectics, on the other hand, comprehends things and their representations, ideas, in the essential connection, concatenation, motion, origin and ending. Such processes as those mentioned above are, therefore, so many corroborations of its own method of procedure.

Nature is the proof of dialectics, and it must be said for modern science that it has furnished this proof with very rich materials increasing daily, and thus has shown that, in the last resort, nature works dialectically and not metaphysically; that she does not move in the eternal oneness of a perpetually recurring circle, but goes through a real historical evolution. In this connection Darwin must be named before all others. He dealt the metaphysical conception of nature the heaviest blow by his proof that all organic beings, plants, animals and man himself, are the products of a process of evolution going on through millions of years. But the naturalists who have learned to think dialectically are few and far between, and this conflict of the results of discovery with preconceived modes of thinking explains the endless confusion now reigning in theoretical natural science, the despair of teachers as well as learners, of authors and readers alike.

An exact representation of the universe, of its evolution, of the development of mankind, and of the reflection of this evolution in the minds of men, can therefore only be obtained by the methods of dialectics, with its constant regard to the innumerable actions and reactions of life and death, of progressive or retrogressive changes. And in this spirit the new German philosophy has worked. Kant began his career by resolving the stable solar system of Newton and its eternal duration, after the famous initial impulse had once been given, into the result of a historic process, the formation of the sun and all the planets out of a rotating nebulous mass. From this he at the same time drew the conclusion that, given this origin of the solar system, its future death followed of necessity. His theory half a century later was established mathematically by Laplace, and half a century after that the spectroscope proved the existence in space of such incandescent masses of gas in various stages of condensation.

This new German philosophy culminated in the Hegelian system. In this system—and herein is its great merit—for the first time the whole world, natural, historical, intellectual, is represented as a process, *i.e.,* as in constant motion, change, transformation, development; and the attempt is made to trace out the internal connection that makes a continuous whole of all this movement and development. From this point of view the history of mankind no longer appeared as a wild whirl of senseless deeds of violence, all equally condemnable at the judgment seat of mature philosophic reason, and which are best forgotten as quickly as possible, but as the process of evolution of man himself. It was now the task of the intellect to follow the gradual march of this process through all its devious ways, and to trace out the inner law running through all its apparently accidental phenomena.

That the Hegelian system did not solve the problem it propounded is here immaterial. Its epoch-making merit was that it propounded the problem. This problem is one that no single individual will ever be able to solve. Although Hegel was—with Saint-Simon—the most encyclopaedic mind of his time, yet he was limited, first, by the necessarily limited extent of his own knowledge, and, second, by the limited extent and depth of the knowledge and conceptions of his age. To these limits a third must be added. Hegel was an idealist. To him the thoughts within his brain were not the more or less abstract pictures of actual things and processes, but, conversely, things and their evolution were only the realised pictures of the "Idea," existing somewhere from eternity before the world was. This way of thinking turned everything upside down, and completely reversed the actual connection of things in the world. Correctly and ingeniously as many individual groups of facts were grasped by Hegel, yet, for the reasons just given, there is much that is botched, artificial, laboured, in a word, wrong in point of detail. The Hegelian system, in itself, was a colossal miscarriage— but it was also the last of its kind. It was suffering, in fact, from an internal and incurable contradiction. Upon the one hand, its essential proposition was the conception that human history is a process of evolution, which, by its very nature, cannot find its intellectual final term in the discovery of any so-called absolute truth. But, on the other hand, it laid claim to being the very essence of this absolute truth. A system of natural and historical knowledge embracing everything, and final for all time, is a contradiction to the fundamental law of dialectic reasoning. This law, indeed, by no means excludes, but, on the contrary, includes the idea that the systematic knowledge of the external universe can make giant strides from age to age.

The perception of the fundamental contradiction in German idealism led necessarily back to materialism, but *nota bene,* not to the simply metaphysical, exclusively mechanical materialism of the eighteenth century. Old materialism looked upon all previous history as a crude heap of irrationality and violence; modern materialism sees in it the process of evolution of humanity, and aims at discovering the laws thereof. With the French of the eighteenth century, and even with Hegel, the conception obtained of nature as a whole, moving in narrow circles, and forever immutable, with its eternal celestial bodies, as Newton, and unalterable organic species, as Linnaeus, taught. Modern materialism embraces the more recent discoveries of natural science according to which nature also has its history in time, the celestial bodies, like the organic species that, under favourable conditions, people them, being born and perishing. And even if nature, as a whole, must still be said to move in recurrent cycles, these cycles assume infinitely larger dimensions. In both aspects, modern materialism is essentially dialectic, and no longer requires the assistance of that sort of philosophy which, queen-like, pretended to rule the remaining mob of sciences. As soon as each special science is bound to make clear its position in the great totality of things and of our knowledge of things, a special science dealing with this totality is superfluous or unnecessary. That which still survives of all earlier philosophy is the science of thought and its laws—formal logic and dialectics. Everything else is subsumed in the positive science of nature and history.

Whilst, however, the revolution in the conception of nature could only be made in proportion to the corresponding positive materials furnished by research, already much earlier certain historical facts had occurred which led to a decisive change in the conception of history. In 1831, the first working class rising took place in Lyons; between 1838 and 1842, the first national working class movement, that of the English Chartists, reached its height. The class struggle between proletariat and bourgeoisie came to the front in the history of the most advanced countries in Europe, in proportion to the development, upon the one hand, of modern industry, upon the other, of the newly-acquired political supremacy of the bourgeoisie. Facts more and more strenuously gave the lie to the teachings of bourgeois economy as to the identity of the interests of capital and labour, as to the universal harmony and universal prosperity that would be the consequence of unbridled competition. All these things could no longer be ignored, any more than the French and English socialism, which was their theoretical, though very imperfect, expression. But the old idealist conception of history, which was not yet dislodged, knew nothing of class struggles based upon economic interests, knew nothing of economic interests; production and all economic relations appeared in it only as incidental, subordinate elements in the "history of civilisation."

The new facts made imperative a new examination of all past history. Then it was seen that *all* past history, with the exception of its primitive stages, was the history of class struggles; that these warring classes of society are always the products of the modes of production and of exchange —in a word, of the *economic* conditions of their time; that the economic structure of society always furnishes the real basis, starting from which we can alone work out the ultimate explanation of the whole superstructure of juridical and political institutions as well as of the religious, philosophical and other ideas of a given historical period. Hegel had freed history from metaphysics—he had made it dialectic; but his conception of history was essentially idealistic. But now idealism was driven from its last refuge, the philosophy of history; now a materialistic treatment of history was propounded, and a method found of explaining man's "knowing" by his "being," instead of, as heretofore, his "being" by his "knowing."

From that time forward socialism was no longer an accidental discovery of this or that ingenious brain, but the necessary outcome of the struggle between two historically developed classes—the proletariat and the bourgeoisie. Its task was no longer to manufacture a system of society as perfect as possible, but to examine the historico-economic succession of events from which these classes and their antagonisms had of necessity sprung, and to discover in the economic conditions thus created the means of ending the conflict. But the socialism of earlier days was as incompatible with this materialistic conception as the conception of nature of the French materialists was with dialectics and modern natural science. The socialism of earlier days certainly criticised the existing capitalistic mode of production and its consequences. But it could not explain them, and, therefore, could not get the mastery of them. It could only simply reject them as bad. The more strongly this earlier socialism denounced the exploitation of the working class, inevitable under capitalism, the less able was it clearly to show in what this exploitation consisted and how it arose. But for this it was necessary— 1) to present the capitalistic method of production in its historical connection and its inevitableness during a particular historical period, and therefore, also, to present its inevitable downfall; and 2) to lay bare its essential character, which was still a secret. This was done by the discovery of *surplus value*. It was shown that the appropriation of unpaid labour is the basis of the capitalist mode of production and of the exploitation of the worker that occurs under it; that even if the capitalist buys the labour power of his labourer at its full value as a commodity on the market, he yet extracts more value from it than he paid for; and that in the ultimate analysis this surplus value forms those sums of value from which are heaped up the constantly increasing masses of capital in the hands of the possessing classes. The genesis of capitalist production and the production of capital were both explained.

These two great discoveries, the materialistic conception of history and the revelation of the secret of capitalistic production through surplus value, we owe to Marx. With these discoveries socialism became a science. The next thing was to work out all its details and relations.

III

The materialist conception of history starts from the proposition that the production of the means to support human life and, next to production, the exchange of things produced, is the basis of all social structure; that in every society that has appeared in history, the manner in which wealth is distributed and society divided into classes or orders is dependent upon what is produced, how it is produced, and how the products are exchanged. From this point of view the final causes of all social changes and political revolutions are to be sought, not in men's brains, not in man's better insight into eternal truth and justice, but in changes in the modes of production and exchange. They are to be sought, not in the *philosophy,* but in the *economics* of each particular epoch. The growing perception that existing social institutions are unreasonable and unjust, that reason has become unreason, and right wrong, is only proof that in the modes of production and exchange changes have silently taken place, with which the social order, adapted to earlier economic conditions, is no longer in keeping. From this it also follows that the means of getting rid of the incongruities that have been brought to light must also be present, in a more or less developed condition, within the changed modes of production themselves. These means are not to be invented by deduction from fundamental principles, but are to be discovered in the stubborn facts of the existing system of production.

What is, then, the position of modern socialism in this connection?

The present structure of society—this is now pretty generally conceded —is the creation of the ruling class of today, of the bourgeoisie. The mode of production peculiar to the bourgeoisie, known, since Marx, as the capitalist mode of production, was incompatible with the feudal system, with the privileges it conferred upon individuals, entire social ranks and local corporations, as well as with the hereditary ties of subordination which constituted the framework of its social organization. The bourgeoisie broke up the feudal system and built upon its ruins the capitalist order of society, the kingdom of free competition, of personal liberty, of equality before the law of all commodity owners, and of all the rest of the capitalist blessings. Thenceforward the capitalist mode of production could develop in freedom. Since steam, machinery and the making of machines by machinery transformed the older manufacture into modern industry, the productive forces evolved under the guidance of the bourgeoisie developed with a rapidity and in a degree unheard of before. But just as the older manufacture, in its time, and handicraft, becoming more developed under its influence, had come into collision with the feudal trammels of the guilds, so now modern industry, in its more complete development, comes into collision with the bounds within which the capitalistic mode of production holds it confined. The new productive forces have already outgrown the capitalistic mode of using them. And this conflict between productive forces and modes of production is not a conflict engendered in the mind of man, like that between original sin and divine justice. It exists, in fact, objectively, outside us, independently of the will and actions even of the men that have brought it on. Modern socialism is nothing but the reflex, in thought, of this conflict in fact; its ideal reflection in the minds, first, of the class directly suffering under it, the working class.

Now, in what does this conflict consist?

Before capitalistic production, *i.e.,* in the Middle Ages, the system of petty industry obtained generally, based upon the private property of the labourers in their means of production; in the country, the agriculture of the small peasant, freeman or serf; in the towns, the handicrafts organised in guilds. The instruments of labour—land, agricultural implements, the workshop, the tool—were the instruments of labour of single individuals, adapted for the use of one worker, and, therefore, of necessity, small, dwarfish, circumscribed. But for this very reason they belonged, as a rule, to the producer himself. To concentrate these scattered, limited means of production, to enlarge them, to turn them into the powerful levers of production of the present day—this was precisely the historic role of capitalist production and of its upholder, the bourgeoisie. In Part IV of *Capital* Marx has explained in detail, how since the fifteenth century this has been historically worked out through the three phases of simple co-operation, manufacture and modern industry. But the bourgeoisie, as is also shown there, could not transform these puny means of production into mighty productive forces, without transforming them, at the same time, from means of production of the individual into *social* means of production only workable by a collectivity of men. The spinning-wheel, the hand-loom, the blacksmith's hammer were replaced by the spinning machine, the power-loom, the steam-hammer; the individual workshop, by the factory, implying the co-operation of hundreds and thousands of workmen. In like manner, production itself changed from a series of individual into a series of social acts, and the products from individual to social products. The yarn, the cloth, the metal articles that now came out of the factory were the joint product of many workers, through whose hands they had successively to pass before they were ready. No one person could say of them: "I made that; this is *my* product."

But where, in a given society, the fundamental form of production is that spontaneous division of labour which creeps in gradually and not upon any preconceived plan, there the products take on the form of *commodities,* whose mutual exchange, buying and selling, enable the individual producers to satisfy their manifold wants. And this was the case in the Middle Ages. The peasant, *e.g.,* sold to the artisan agricultural products and bought from him the products of handicraft. Into this society of individual producers, of commodity producers, the new mode of production thrust itself. In the midst of the old division of labour, grown up spontaneously and upon *no definite plan,* which had governed the whole of society, now arose division of labour upon *a definite plan,* as organised in the factory; side by side with *individual* production appeared *social* production. The products of both were sold in the same market, and, therefore, at prices at least approximately equal. But organisation upon a definite plan was stronger than spontaneous division of labour. The factories working with the combined social forces of a collectivity of individuals produced their commodities far more cheaply than the individual small producers. Individual production succumbed in one department after another. Socialised production revolutionised all the old methods of production. But its revolutionary character was, at the same time, so little recognised, that it was, on the contrary, introduced as a means of increasing and developing the production of commodities. When it arose, it found ready-made, and made liberal use of, certain machinery for the production and exchange of commodities; merchants' capital, handicraft, wage labour. Socialised production thus introducing itself as a new form of the production of commodities, it was a matter of course that under it the old forms of appropriation remained in full swing, and were applied to its products as well.

In the mediaeval stage of evolution of the production of commodities, the question as to the owner of the product of labour could not arise. The individual producer, as a rule, had, from raw material belonging to himself, and generally his own handiwork, produced it with his own tools, by the labour of his own hands or of his family. There was no need for him to appropriate the new product. It belonged wholly to him, as a matter of course. His property in the product was, therefore, based *upon his own labour.* Even where external help was used, this was, as a rule, of little importance, and very generally was compensated by something other than wages. The apprentices and journeymen of the guilds worked less for board and wages than for education, in order that they might become master craftsmen themselves.

Then came the concentration of the means of production and of the producers in large workshops and manufactories, their transformation into actual socialised means of production and socialised producers. But the socialised producers and means of production and their products were still treated, after this change, just as they had been before, *i.e.,* as the means of production and the products of individuals. Hitherto, the owner of the instruments of labour had himself appropriated the product, because as a rule it was his own product and the assistance of others was the exception. Now the owner of the instruments of labour always appropriated to himself the product, although it was no longer *his* product but exclusively the product of the *labour of others*. Thus, the products now produced socially were not appropriated by those who had actually set in motion the means of production and actually produced the commodities, but by the *capitalists*. The means of production, and production itself, had become in essence socialised. But they were subjected to a form of appropriation which presupposes the private production of individuals, under which, therefore, every one owns his own product and brings it to market. The mode of production is subjected to this form of appropriation, although it abolished the conditions upon which the latter rests.

This contradiction, which gives to the new mode of production its capitalistic character, *contains the germ of the whole of the social antagonisms of today*. The greater the mastery obtained by the new mode of production over all important fields of production and in all manufacturing countries, the more it reduced individual production to an insignificant residuum, *the more clearly was brought out the incompatibility of socialised production with capitalistic appropriation*.

The first capitalists found, as we have said, alongside of other forms of labour, wage labour ready-made for them on the market. But it was exceptional, complementary, necessary, transitory wage labour. The agricultural labourer, though, upon occasion, he hired himself out by the day, had a few acres of his own land on which he could at all events live at a pinch. The guilds were so organised that the journeyman of today became the master of tomorrow. But all this changed, as soon as the means of production became socialised and concentrated in the hands of capitalists. The means of production, as well as the product of the individual producer became more and more worthless; there was nothing left for him but to turn wage worker under the capitalist. Wage labour, aforetime the exception and accessory, now became the rule and basis of all production; aforetime complementary, it now became the sole remaining function of the worker. The wage worker for a time became the wage worker for life. The number of these permanent wage workers was further enormously increased by the breaking up of the feudal system that occurred at the same time, by the disbanding of the retainers of the feudal lords, the eviction of the peasants from their homesteads, etc. The separation was made complete between the means of production concentrated in the hands of the capitalists on the one side, and the producers, possessing nothing but their labour power, on the other. *The contradiction between socialised production and capitalistic appropriation manifested itself as the antagonism of proletariat and bourgeoisie.*

We have seen that the capitalistic mode of production thrust its way into a society of commodity producers, of individual producers, whose social bond was the exchange of their products. But every society, based upon the production of commodities, has this peculiarity: that the producers have lost control over their own social inter-relations. Each man produces for himself with such means of production as he may happen to have, and for such exchange as he may require to satisfy his remaining wants. No one knows how much of his particular article is coming on the market, nor how much of it will be wanted. No one knows whether his individual product will meet an actual demand, whether he will be able to make good his cost of production or even to sell his commodity at all. Anarchy reigns in socialised production.

But the production of commodities, like every other form of production, has its peculiar inherent laws inseparable from it; and these laws work, despite anarchy, in and through anarchy. They reveal themselves in the only persistent form of social inter-relations, *i.e.,* in exchange, and here they affect the individual producers as compulsory laws of competition. They are, at first, unknown to these producers themselves, and have to be discovered by them gradually and as the result of experience. They work themselves out, therefore, independently of the producers, and in antagonism to them, as inexorable natural laws of their particular form of production. The product governs the producers.

In mediaeval society, especially in the earlier centuries, production was essentially directed towards satisfying the wants of the individual. It satisfied, in the main, only the wants of the producer and his family. Where relations of personal dependence existed, as in the country, it also helped to satisfy the wants of the feudal lord. In all this there was, therefore, no exchange; the products, consequently, did not assume the character of commodities. The family of the peasant produced almost everything they wanted: clothes and furniture, as well as means of subsistence. Only when it began to produce more than was sufficient to supply its own wants and the payments in kind to the feudal lord, only then did it also produce commodities. This surplus, thrown into socialised exchange and offered for sale, became commodities.

The artisans of the towns, it is true, had from the first to produce for exchange. But they, also, themselves supplied the greatest part of their own individual wants. They had gardens and plots of land. They turned their cattle out into the communal forest, which, also, yielded them timber and firing. The women spun flax, wool, and so forth. Production for the purpose of exchange, production of commodities was only in its infancy. Hence, exchange was restricted, the market narrow, the methods of production stable; there was local exclusiveness without, local unity within; the mark in the country, in the town, the guild.

But with the extension of the production of commodities, and especially with the introduction of the capitalist mode of production, the laws of commodity production, hitherto latent, came into action more openly and with greater force. The old bonds were loosened, the old exclusive limits broken through, the producers were more and more turned into independent, isolated producers of commodities. It became apparent that the production of society at large was ruled by absence of plan, by accident, by anarchy; and this anarchy grew to greater and greater height. But the chief means by aid of which the capitalist mode of production intensified this anarchy of socialised production was the exact opposite of anarchy. It was the increasing organisation of production, upon a social basis, in every individual productive establishment. By this, the old, peaceful, stable condition of things was ended. Wherever this organisation of production was introduced into a branch of industry, it brooked no other method of production by its side. The field of labour became a battle ground. The great geographical discoveries, and the colonisation following upon them, multiplied markets and quickened the transformation of handicraft into manufacture. The war did not simply break out between the individual producers of particular localities. The local struggles begat in their turn national conflicts, the commercial wars of the seventeenth and the eighteenth centuries.

Finally, modern industry and the opening of the world market made the struggle universal, and at the same time gave it an unheard-of virulence. Advantages in natural or artificial conditions of production now decide the existence or non-existence of individual capitalists, as well as of whole industries and countries. He that falls is remorselessly cast aside. It is the Darwinian struggle of the individual for existence transferred from nature to society with intensified violence. The conditions of existence natural to the animal appear as the final term of human development. The contradiction between socialised production and capitalistic appropriation now presents itself as *an antagonism between the organisation of production in the individual workshop and the anarchy of production in society generally.*

The capitalistic mode of production moves in these two forms of the antagonism immanent to it from its very origin. It is never able to get out of that "vicious circle," which Fourier had already discovered. What Fourier could not, indeed, see in his time is: that this circle is gradually narrowing; that the movement becomes more and more a spiral, and must come to an end, like the movement of the planets, by collision with the centre. It is the compelling force of anarchy in the production of society at large that more and more completely turns the great majority of men into proletarians; and it is the masses of the proletariat again who will finally put an end to anarchy in production. It is the compelling force of anarchy in social production that turns the limitless perfectibility of machinery under modern industry into a compulsory law by which every individual industrial capitalist must perfect his machinery more and more, under penalty of ruin.

But the perfecting of machinery is making human labour superfluous. If the introduction and increase of machinery means the displacement of millions of manual, by a few machine workers, improvement in machinery means the displacement of more and more of the machine workers themselves. It means, in the last instance, the production of a number of available wage workers in excess of the average needs of capital, the formation of a complete industrial reserve army, as I called it in 1845,[1] available at the times when industry is working at high pressure, to be cast out upon the street when the inevitable crash comes, a constant dead weight upon the limbs of the working class in its struggle for existence with capital, a regulator for the keeping of wages down to the low level that suits the interests of capital. Thus it comes about, to quote Marx, that machinery becomes the most powerful weapon in the war of capital against the working class; that the instruments of labour constantly tear the means of subsistence out of the hands of the labourer; that the very product of the worker is turned into an instrument for his subjugation. Thus it comes about that the economising of the instruments of labour becomes at the same time, from the outset, the most reckless waste of labour power, and robbery based upon the normal conditions under which labour functions; that machinery, "the most powerful instrument for shortening labour time, becomes the most unfailing means for placing every moment of the labourer's time and that of his family at the disposal of the capitalist for the purpose of expanding the value of his capital." Thus it comes about that overwork of some becomes the preliminary condition for the idleness of others, and that modern industry, which hunts after new consumers over the whole world, forces the consumption of the masses at home down to a starvation minimum, and in doing thus destroys its own home market. "The law that always equilibrates the relative sur-

[1] *The Condition of the Working Class in England,* Sonnenschein and Co., p. 84.

plus population, or industrial reserve army, to the extent and energy of accumulation, this law rivets the labourer to capital more firmly than the wedges of Vulcan did Prometheus to the rock. It establishes an accumulation of misery, corresponding with accumulation of capital. Accumulation of wealth at one pole is, therefore, at the same time, accumulation of misery, agony of toil, slavery, ignorance, brutality, mental degradation, at the opposite pole, *i.e.,* on the side of the class that produces *its own product in the form of capital."* And to expect any other division of the products from the capitalistic mode of production is the same as expecting the electrodes of a battery not to decompose acidulated water, not to liberate oxygen at the positive, hydrogen at the negative pole, so long as they are connected with the battery.

We have seen that the ever-increasing perfectibility of modern machinery is, by the anarchy of social production, turned into a compulsory law that forces the individual industrial capitalist always to improve his machinery, always to increase its productive force. The bare possibility of extending the field of production is transformed for him into a similar compulsory law. The enormous expansive force of modern industry, compared with which that of gases is mere child's play, appears to us now as a *necessity* for expansion, both qualitative and quantitative, that laughs at all resistance. Such resistance is offered by consumption, by sales, by the markets for the products of modern industry. But the capacity for extension, extensive and intensive, of the markets is primarily governed by quite different laws, that work much less energetically. The extension of the markets cannot keep pace with the extension of production. The collision becomes inevitable, and as this cannot produce any real solution so long as it does not break in pieces the capitalist mode of production, the collisions become periodic. Capitalist production has begotten another "vicious circle."

As a matter of fact, since 1825, when the first general crisis broke out, the whole industrial and commercial world, production and exchange among all civilised peoples and their more or less barbaric hangers-on, are thrown out of joint about once every ten years. Commerce is at a standstill, the markets are glutted, products accumulate, as multitudinous as they are unsaleable, hard cash disappears, credit vanishes, factories are closed, the mass of the workers are in want of the means of subsistence, because they have produced too much of the means of subsistence; bankruptcy follows upon bankruptcy, execution upon execution. The stagnation lasts for years; productive forces and products are wasted and destroyed wholesale, until the accumulated mass of commodities finally filter off, more or less depreciated in value, until production and exchange gradually begin to move again. Little by little the pace quickens. It becomes a trot. The industrial trot breaks into a canter, the canter in turn grows into the headlong gallop of a perfect steeplechase of industry, commercial credit and speculation, which finally, after breakneck leaps, ends where it began—in the ditch of a crisis. And so over and over again. We have now, since the year 1825, gone through this five times, and at the present moment (1877) we are going through it for the sixth time. And the character of these crises is so clearly defined that Fourier hit all of them off when he described the first as *"crise pléthorique,"* a crisis from plethora.

In these crises, the contradiction between socialised production and capitalist appropriation ends in a violent explosion. The circulation of commodities is, for the time being, stopped. Money, the means of circulation, becomes a hindrance to circulation. All the laws of production and circulation of commodities are turned upside down. The economic collision has reached its apogee. *The mode of production is in rebellion against the mode of exchange.*

The fact that the socialised organisation of production within the factory has developed so far that it has become incompatible with the anarchy of production in society, which exists side by side with and dominates it, is brought home to the capitalists themselves by the violent concentration of capital that occurs during crises, through the ruin of many large, and a still greater number of small, capitalists. The whole mechanism of the capitalist mode of production breaks down under the pressure of the productive forces, its own creations. It is no longer able to turn all this mass of means of production into capital. They lie fallow, and for that very reason the industrial reserve army must also lie fallow. Means of production, means of subsistence, available labourers, all the elements of production and of general wealth, are present in abundance. But "abundance becomes the source of distress and want." (Fourier), because it is the very thing that prevents the transformation of the means of production and subsistence into capital. For in capitalistic society the means of production can only function when they have undergone a preliminary transformation into capital, into the means of exploiting human labour power. The necessity of this transformation into capital of the means of production and subsistence stands like a ghost between these and the workers. It alone prevents the coming together of the material and personal levers of production; it alone forbids the means of production to function, the workers to work and live. On the one hand, therefore, the capitalistic mode of production stands convicted of its own incapacity to further direct these productive forces. On the other, these productive forces themselves, with increasing energy, press forward to the removal of the existing contradiction, to the abolition of their quality as capital, to the *practical recognition of their character as social productive forces.*

This rebellion of the productive forces, as they grow more and more power-ful, against their quality as capital, this stronger and stronger command that their social character shall be recognised, forces the capitalist class itself to treat them more and more as social productive forces, so far as this is possible under capitalist conditions. The period of industrial high pressure, with its unbounded inflation of credit, not less than the crash itself, by the collapse of great capitalist establishments, tends to bring about that form of the socialisation of great masses of means of production, which we meet with in the different kinds of joint-stock companies. Many of these means of pro-duction and of distribution are, from the outset, so colossal, that, like the railroads, they exclude all other forms of capitalistic exploitation. At a further stage of evolution this form also becomes insufficient. The producers on a large scale in a particular branch of industry in a particular country unite in a "trust," a union for the purpose of regulating production. They determine the total amount to be produced, parcel it out among themselves, and thus enforce the selling price fixed beforehand. But trusts of this kind, as soon as business becomes bad, are generally liable to break up, and, on this very account, compel a yet greater concentration of association. The whole of the particular industry is turned into one gigantic joint-stock company; internal competition gives place to the internal monopoly of this one com-pany. This has happened in 1890 with the English *alkali* production, which is now, after the fusion of 48 large works, in the hands of one company, con-ducted upon a single plan, and with a capital of £6,000,000.

In the trusts, freedom of competition changes into its very opposite—into monopoly; and the production without any definite plan of capitalistic society capitulates to the production upon a definite plan of the invading socialistic society. Certainly this is so far still to the benefit and advantage of the capi-talists. But in this case the exploitation is so palpable that it must break down. No nation will put up with production conducted by trusts, with so barefaced an exploitation of the community by a small band of dividend mongers.

In any case, with trusts or without, the official representative of capitalist society—the state—will ultimately have to undertake the direction of pro-duction. This necessity of conversion into state property is felt first in the great institutions for intercourse and communication—the post-office, the telegraphs, the railways.

If the crises demonstrate the incapacity of the bourgeoisie for managing any longer modern productive forces, the transformation of the great estab-lishments for production and distribution into joint-stock companies, trusts and state property, show how unnecessary the bourgeoisie are for that purpose. All the social functions of the capitalist are now performed by salaried employees. The capitalist has no further social function than that of pocketing dividends, tearing off coupons, and gambling on the Stock Exchange, where the different capitalists despoil one another of their capital. At first the capitalistic mode of production forces out the workers. Now it forces out the capitalists, and reduces them, just as it reduced the workers, to the ranks of the surplus population, although not immediately into those of the industrial reserve army.

But the transformation, either into joint-stock companies and trusts, or into state ownership, does not do away with the capitalistic nature of the productive forces. In the joint-stock companies and trusts this is obvious. And the modern state, again, is only the organisation that bourgeois society takes on in order to support the external conditions of the capitalist mode of production against the encroachments, as well of the workers as of individual capitalists. The modern state, no matter what its form, is essentially a capitalist machine, the state of the capitalists, the ideal personification of the total national capital. The more it proceeds to the taking over of productive forces, the more does it actually become the national capitalist, the more citizens does it exploit. The workers remain wage workers—proletarians. The capitalist relation is not done away with. It is rather brought to a head. But, brought to a head, it topples over. State ownership of the productive forces is not the solution of the conflict, but concealed within it are the technical conditions that form the elements of that solution.

This solution can only consist in the practical recognition of the social nature of the modern forces of production, and therefore in the harmonising of the modes of production, appropriation and exchange with the socialised character of the means of production. And this can only come about by society openly and directly taking possession of the productive forces which have outgrown all control except that of society as a whole. The social character of the means of production and of the products today reacts against the producers, periodically disrupts all production and exchange, acts only like a law of nature working blindly, forcibly, destructively. But with the taking over by society of the productive forces, the social character of the means of production and of the products will be utilised by the producers with a perfect understanding of its nature, and instead of being a source of disturbance and periodical collapse, will become the most powerful lever of production itself.

Active social forces work exactly like natural forces; blindly, forcibly, destructively, so long as we do not understand and reckon with them. But when once we understand them, when once we grasp their action, their direction, their effects, it depends only upon ourselves to subject them more and more to our own will, and by means of them to reach our own ends. And this holds quite especially of the mighty productive forces of today. As long as we obstinately refuse to understand the nature and the character of these social means of action—and this understanding goes against the grain of the capitalist mode of production and its defenders—so long these forces are at work in spite of us, in opposition to us, so long they master us, as we have shown above in detail.

But when once their nature is understood, they can, in the hands of the producers working together, be transformed from master demons into willing servants. The difference is as that between the destructive force of electricity in the lightning of the storm, and electricity under command in the telegraph and the voltaic arc; the difference between a conflagration, and fire working in the service of man. With this recognition at last of the real nature of the productive forces of today, the social anarchy of production gives place to a social regulation of production upon a definite plan, according to the needs of the community and of each individual. Then the capitalist mode of appropriation of the products that is based upon the nature of the modern means of production; upon the one hand, direct social appropriation, as means to the maintenance and extension of production—on the other, direct individual appropriation, as means of subsistence and of enjoyment.

Whilst the capitalist mode of production more and more completely transforms the great majority of the population into proletarians, it creates the power which, under penalty of its own destruction, is forced to accomplish this revolution. Whilst it forces on more and more the transformation of the vast means of production, already socialised, into state property, it shows itself the way to accomplishing this revolution. *The proletariat seizes political power and turns the means of production into state property.*

But, in doing this, it abolishes itself as proletariat, abolishes all class distinctions and class antagonisms, abolishes also the state as state. Society thus far, based upon class antagonisms, had need of the state. That is, of an organisation of the particular class which was *pro tempore* the exploiting class, an organisation for the purpose of preventing any interference from without with the existing conditions of production, and therefore, especially, for the purpose of forcibly keeping the exploited classes in the condition of oppression corresponding with the given mode of production (slavery, serfdom, wage labour). The state was the official representative of society as a whole; the gathering of it together into a visible embodiment. But it was this only in so far as it was the state of that class which itself represented, for the time being, society as a whole; in ancient times, the state of slave-owning citizens; in the Middle Ages, the feudal lords; in our own time, the bourgeoisie. When at last it becomes the real representative of the whole of society, it renders itself unnecessary. As soon as there is no longer any social class to be held in subjection; as soon as class rule and the individual struggle for existence based upon our present anarchy in production, with the collisions and excesses arising from these, are removed, nothing more remains to be repressed, and a special repressive force, a state, is no longer necessary. The first act by virtue of which the state really constitutes itself the representative of the whole of society—the taking possession of the means of production in the name of society—this is, at the same time, its last independent act as a state. State interference in social relations becomes, in one domain after another, superfluous, and then dies out of itself; the government of persons is replaced by the administration of things, and by the conduct of processes of production. The state is not "abolished." *It dies out.* This gives the measure of the value of the phrase "a free state," both as to its justifiable use at times by agitators, and as to its ultimate scientific insufficiency; and also of the demands of the so-called anarchists for the abolition of the state out of hand.

Since the historical appearance of the capitalist mode of production, the appropriation by society of all the means of production has often been dreamed of, more or less vaguely, by individuals, as well as by sects, as the ideal of the future. But it could become possible, could become a historical necessity, only when the actual conditions for its realisation were there. Like every other social advance, it becomes practicable, not by men understanding that the existence of classes is in contradiction to justice, equality, etc., not by the mere willingness to abolish these classes, but by virtue of certain new economic conditions. The separation of society into an exploiting and an exploited class, a ruling and an oppressed class, was the necessary consequence of the deficient and restricted development of production in former times. So long as the total social labour only yields a produce which but slightly exceeds that barely necessary for the existence of all; so long, therefore, as labour engages all or almost all the time of the great majority of the members of society—so long, of necessity, this society is divided into classes. Side by side with the great majority, exclusively bond slaves to labour, arises a class freed from directly productive labour, which looks after the general affairs of society, the direction of labour, state business, law, science, art, etc. It is, therefore, the law of division of labour that lies at the basis of the division into classes. But this does not prevent this division into classes from being carried out by means of violence and robbery, trickery and fraud. It does not prevent the ruling class, once having the upper hand, from consolidating its power at the expense of the working class, from turning their social leadership into an intensified exploitation of the masses.

But if, upon this showing, division into classes has a certain historical justification, it has this only for a given period, only under given social conditions. It was based upon the insufficiency of production. It will be swept away by the complete development of modern productive forces. And, in fact, the abolition of classes in society presupposes a degree of historical evolution, at which the existence, not simply of this or that particular ruling class, but of any ruling class at all, and, therefore, the existence of class distinction itself has become an obsolete anachronism. It presupposes, therefore, the development of production carried out to a degree at which appropriation of the means of production and of the products, and, with this, of political domination, of the monopoly of culture, and of intellectual leadership by a particular class of society, has become not only superfluous, but economically, politically, intellectually a hindrance to development.

This point is now reached. Their political and intellectual bankruptcy is scarcely any longer a secret to the bourgeoisie themselves. Their economic bankruptcy recurs regularly every ten years. In every crisis, society is suffocated beneath the weight of its own productive forces and products, which it cannot use, and stands helpless, face to face with the absurd contradiction that the producers have nothing to consume, because consumers are wanting. The expansive force of the means of production bursts the bonds that the capitalist mode of production had imposed upon them. Their deliverance from these bonds is the one precondition for an unbroken, constantly accelerated development of the productive forces, and therewith for a practically unlimited increase of production itself. Nor is this all. The socialised appropriation of the means of production does away not only with the present artificial restrictions upon production, but also with the positive waste and devastation of productive forces and products that are at the present time the inevitable concomitants of production, and that reach their height in the crises. Further, it sets free for the community at large a mass of means of production and of products, by doing away with the senseless extravagance of the ruling classes of today, and their political representatives. The possibility of securing for every member of society, by means of socialised production, an existence not only fully sufficient materially, and becoming day by day more full, but an existence guaranteeing to all the free development and exercise of their physical and mental faculties—this possibility is now for the first time here, but *it is here*.

With the seizing of the means of production by society, production of commodities is done away with, and, simultaneously, the mastery of the product over the producer. Anarchy in social production is replaced by systematic definite organisation. The struggle for individual existence disappears. Then for the first time, man, in a certain sense, is finally marked off from the rest of the animal kingdom, and emerges from mere animal conditions of existence into really human ones. The whole sphere of the conditions of life which environ man, and which have hitherto ruled man, now comes under the dominion and control of man, who for the first time becomes the real, conscious lord of nature, because he has now become master of his own social organisation. The laws of his own social action, hitherto standing face to face with man as laws of nature foreign to and dominating him, will then be used with full understanding, and so mastered by him. Man's own social organisation, hitherto confronting him as a necessity imposed by nature and history, now becomes the result of his own free action. The extraneous objective forces that have hitherto governed history pass under the control of man himself. Only from that time will man himself, more and more consciously, make his own history—only from that time will the social causes set in movement by him have, in the main and in a constantly growing measure, the results intended by him. It is the ascent of man from the kingdom of necessity to the kingdom of freedom.

Let us briefly sum up our sketch of historical evolution.

I. *Mediaeval Society*—Individual production on a small scale. Means of production adapted for individual use; hence primitive, ungainly, petty, dwarfed in action. Production for immediate consumption, either of the producer himself or of his feudal lords. Only where an excess of production over this consumption occurs is such excess offered for sale, enters into exchange. Production of commodities, therefore, is only in its infancy. But already it contains within itself, in embryo, *anarchy in the production of society at large*.

II. *Capitalist Revolution*—Transformation of industry, at first by means of simple co-operation and manufacture. Concentration of the means of production, hitherto scattered, into great workshops. As a consequence, their transformation from individual to social means of production—a transformation which does not, on the whole, affect the form of exchange. The old forms of appropriation remain in force. The capitalist appears. In his capacity as owner of the means of production, he also appropriates the products and turns them into commodities. Production has become a *social* act. Exchange and appropriation continue to be *individual* acts, the acts of individuals. *The social product is appropriated by the individual capitalist*. Fundamental contradiction, whence arise all the contradictions in which our present day society moves, and which modern industry brings to light.

A. Severance of the producer from the means of production. Condemnation of the worker to wage labour for life. *Antagonism between the proletariat and the bourgeoisie.*

B. Growing predominance and increasing effectiveness of the laws governing the production of commodities. Unbridled competition. *Contradiction between socialised organisation in the individual factory and social anarchy in production as a whole.*

C. On the one hand, perfecting of machinery, made by competition compulsory for each individual manufacturer, and complemented by a constantly growing displacement of labourers. *Industrial reserve army.* On the other hand, unlimited extension of production, also compulsory under competition, for every manufacturer. On both sides, unheard of development of productive forces, excess of supply over demand, overproduction, glutting of the markets, crises every ten years, the vicious circle: excess here, of means of production and products—excess there, of labourers, without employment and without means of existence. But these two levers of production and of social well-being are unable to work together because the capitalist form of production prevents the productive forces from working and the products from circulating, unless they are first turned into capital—which their very superabundance prevents. The contradiction has grown into an absurdity. *The mode of production rises in rebellion against the form of exchange.* The bourgeoisie are convicted of incapacity further to manage their own social productive forces.

D. Partial recognition of the social character of the productive forces forced upon the capitalists themselves. Taking over of the great institutions for production and communication, first by joint-stock companies, later on by trusts, then by the state. The bourgeoisie demonstrated to be a superfluous class. All its social functions are now performed by salaried employees.

III. *Proletarian Revolution*—Solution of the contradictions. The proletariat seizes the public power, and by means of this transforms the socialised means of production, slipping from the hands of the bourgeoisie, into public property. By this act, the proletariat frees the means of production from the character of capital they have thus far borne, and gives their socialised character complete freedom to work itself out. Socialised production upon a predetermined plan becomes henceforth possible. The development of production makes the existence of different classes of society thenceforth an anachronism. In proportion as anarchy in social production vanishes, the political authority of the state dies out. Man, at last the master of his own form of social organisation, becomes at the same time the lord over nature, his own master—free.

To accomplish this act of universal emancipation is the historical mission of the modern proletariat. To thoroughly comprehend the historical conditions and thus the very nature of this act, to impart to the now oppressed proletarian class a full knowledge of the conditions and of the meaning of the momentous act it is called upon to accomplish, this is the task of the theoretical expression of the proletarian movement, scientific socialism.

KARL MARX

A T THE OUTBREAK of the revolutions of 1848, Marx left Paris for Cologne, where he assumed the editorship of the *Neue Rheinische Zeitung*. He was tried by Prussia for high treason and acquitted, but was forced to leave the country. Expelled from France, he settled in London, and spent the rest of his life there. He published another newspaper, and contributed an important series of articles analyzing the French Revolution of 1848. These articles were later published as a book by Engels under the title *The Class Struggle in France after 1848*. In 1859 he published *Towards a Critique of Political Economy* which formed the basis for his magnum opus, *Capital,* the first volume of which appeared in 1867. (It was subsequently revised by Marx in 1873 and 1875; the second and third volumes were edited and published by Engels from Marx's manuscripts and notes.)

In 1864, he founded the International Workingmen's Association in London. He wrote all the addresses and proclamations of the First International, and explained them in lectures to his colleagues on the General Council. It was at such a lecture that Marx outlined in simplified form the views on *Value, Price and Profit* (edited by Eleanor Marx Aveling, New York: International Publishers, 1935) which he was developing in his *Capital*. Selections from that edition appear below, as do extracts from *The Class Struggle in France after 1848* (New York: International Publishers, 1934) and *The Eighteenth Brumaire of Louis Bonaparte* (New York: International Publishers, 1951).

The First International was dissolved in 1876 after many years of strife, chiefly between Marx and Michael Bakunin, the Russian anarchist. Marx died seven years later, and was buried in Highgate Cemetery, London.

VALUE, PRICE AND PROFIT

VI. VALUE AND LABOUR

CITIZENS, I have now arrived at a point where I must enter upon the real development of the question. I cannot promise to do this in a very satisfactory way, because to do so I should be obliged to go over the whole field of political economy. I can, as the French would say, but *effleurer la question,* touch upon the main points.

The first question we have to put is: What is the *value* of a commodity? How is it determined?

At first sight it would seem that the value of a commodity is a thing quite *relative,* and not to be settled without considering one commodity in its relation to all other commodities. In fact, in speaking of the value, the value in exchange of a commodity, we mean the proportional quantities in which it exchanges with all other commodities. But then arises the question: How are the proportions in which commodities exchange with each other regulated?

We know from experience that these proportions vary infinitely. Taking one single commodity, wheat, for instance, we shall find that a quarter of wheat exchanges in almost countless variations of proportion with different commodities. Yet, *its value remaining always the same,* whether expressed in silk, gold, or any other commodity, it must be something distinct from, and independent of, these *different rates of exchange* with different articles. It must be possible to express, in a very different form, these various equations with various commodities.

Besides, if I say a quarter of wheat exchanges with iron in a certain proportion, or the value of a quarter of wheat is expressed in a certain amount of iron, I say that the value of wheat and its equivalent in iron are equal *to some third thing,* which is neither wheat nor iron, because I suppose them to express the same magnitude in two different shapes. Either of them, the wheat or the iron, must, therefore, independently of the other, be reducible to this third thing which is their common measure.

To elucidate this point I shall recur to a very simple geometrical illustration. In comparing the areas of triangles of all possible forms and magnitudes, or comparing triangles with rectangles, or any other rectilinear figure, how do we proceed? We reduce the area of any triangle whatever to an expression quite different from its visible form. Having found from the nature of the triangle that its area is equal to half the product of its base by its height, we can then compare the different values of all sorts of triangles, and of all rectilinear figures whatever, because all of them may be resolved into a certain number of triangles.

The same mode of procedure must obtain with the values of commodities. We must be able to reduce all of them to an expression common to all, and distinguishing them only by the proportions in which they contain that same and identical measure.

As the *exchangeable values* of commodities are only *social functions* of those things, and have nothing at all to do with the *natural* qualities, we must first ask: What is the common *social substance* of all commodities? It is *labour.* To produce a commodity a certain amount of labour must be bestowed upon it, or worked up in it. And I say not only *labour,* but *social labour.* A man who produces an article for his own immediate use, to consume it himself, creates a *product*, but not a *commodity*. As a self-sustaining producer he has nothing to do with society. But to produce a *commodity*, a man must not only produce an article satisfying some *social* want, but his labour itself must form part and parcel of the total sum of labour expended by society. It must be subordinate to the *division of labour within society*. It is nothing without the other division of labour, and on its part is required to *integrate* them.

If we consider *commodities as values*, we consider them exclusively under the single aspect of *realised, fixed*, or, if you like, *crystallised social labour*. In this respect they can *differ* only by representing greater or smaller quantities of labour, as, for example, a greater amount of labour may be worked up in a silken handkerchief than in a brick. But how does one measure *quantities of labour?* By the *time the labour lasts*, in measuring the labour by the hour, the day, etc. Of course, to apply this measure, all sorts of labour are reduced to average or simple labour as their unit.

We arrive, therefore, at this conclusion. A commodity has a *value*, because it is a *crystallisation of social labour*. The *greatness* of its value, or its *relative* value, depends upon the greater or less amount of that social substance contained in it; that is to say, on the relative mass of labour necessary for its production. The *relative values of commodities* are, therefore, determined by the *respective quantities or amounts of labour, worked up, realised, fixed in them*. The *correlative* quantities of commodities which can be produced in the *same time of labour* are *equal*. Or the value of one commodity is to the value of another commodity as the quantity of labour fixed in the one is to the quantity of labour fixed in the other.

I suspect that many of you will ask: Does then, indeed, there exist such a vast, or any difference whatever, between determining the values of commodities by *wages*, and determining them by the *relative quantities of labour* necessary for their production? You must, however, be aware that the *reward* for labour, and *quantity* of labour, are quite disparate things. Suppose, for example, *equal quantities of labour* to be fixed in one quarter of wheat and one ounce of gold. I resort to the example because it was used by Benjamin Franklin in his first essay published in 1721, and entitled: *A Modest Enquiry into the Nature and Necessity of a Paper Currency*, where he, one of the first, hit upon the true nature of value. Well. We suppose, then, that one quarter of wheat and one ounce of gold are *equal values* or *equivalents*, because they are *crystallisations of equal amounts of average labour*, of so many days' or so many weeks' labour respectively fixed in them. In thus determining the relative values of gold and corn, do we refer in any way whatever to the *wages* of the agricultural labourer and the miner? Not a bit. We leave it quite *inde-*

terminate how their day's or week's labour was paid, or even whether wages labour was employed at all. If it was, wages may have been very unequal. The labourer whose labour is realised in the quarter of wheat may receive two bushels only, and the labourer employed in mining may receive one half of the ounce of gold. Or, supposing their wages to be equal, they may deviate in all possible proportions from the values of the commodities produced by them. They may amount to one half, one third, one fourth, one fifth, or any other proportional part of the one quarter of corn or the one ounce of gold. Their *wages* can, of course, not *exceed,* nor be more than the values of the commodities they produced, but they can be *less* in every possible degree. Their *wages* will be *limited* by the *values* of the products, but the *values of their products* will not be limited by the wages. And above all, the values, the relative values of corn and gold, for example, will have been settled without any regard whatever to the value of the labour employed, that is to say, to *wages.* To determine the values of commodities by the *relative quantities of labour fixed in them,* is therefore, a thing quite different from the tautological method of determining the values of commodities by the value of labour, or by wages. This point, however, will be further elucidated in the progress of our inquiry.

In calculating the exchangeable value of a commodity we must add to the quantity of labour *last* employed the quantity of labour *previously* worked up in the raw material of the commodity, and the labour bestowed on the implements, tools, machinery, and buildings, with which such labour is assisted. For example, the value of a certain amount of cotton yarn is the crystallisation of the quantity of labour added to the cotton during the spinning process, the quantity of labour previously realised in the cotton, itself, the quantity of labour realised in the coal, oil, and other auxiliary matter used, the quantity of labour fixed in the steam-engine, the spindles, the factory building, and so forth. Instruments of production properly so-called, such as tools, machinery, buildings, serve again and again for a longer or shorter period during repeated processes of production. If they were used up at once, like the raw material, their whole value would at once be transferred to the commodities they assist in producing. But as a spindle, for example, is but gradually used up, and average calculation is made, based upon the average time it lasts, and its average waste or wear and tear during a certain period, say a day. In this way we calculate how much of the value of the spindle is transferred to the yarn daily spun, and how much, therefore, of the total amount of labour realised in a pound of yarn, for example, is due to the quantity of labour previously realised in the spindle. For our present purpose it is not necessary to dwell any longer upon this point.

It might seem that if the value of a commodity is determined by the *quan-*

tity of labour bestowed upon its production, the lazier a man, or the clumsier a man, the more valuable his commodity, because the greater the time of labour required for finishing the commodity. This, however, would be a sad mistake. You will recollect that I used the word *"social* labour," and many points are involved in this qualification of *"social."* In saying that the value of a commodity is determined by the *quantity of labour* worked up or crystallised in it, we mean the *quantity of labour necessary* for its production in a given state of society, under certain social average conditions of production, with a given social average intensity, and average skill of the labour employed. When, in England, the power-loom came to compete with the hand-loom, only one-half the former time of labour was wanted to convert a given amount of yarn into a yard of cotton or cloth. The poor hand-loom weaver now worked seventeen and eighteen hours daily, instead of the nine or ten hours he had worked before. Still the product of twenty hours of his labour represented now only ten social hours of labour, or ten hours of labour socially necessary for the conversion of a certain amount of yarn into textile stuffs. His product of twenty hours had, therefore, no more value than his former product of ten hours.

If then the quantity of socially necessary labour realised in commodities regulates their exchangeable values, every increase in the quantity of labour wanted for the production of a commodity must augment its value, as every diminution must lower it.

If the respective quantities of labour necessary for the production of the respective commodities remained constant, their relative values also would be constant. But such is not the case. The quantity of labour necessary for the production of a commodity changes continuously with the changes in the productive powers of the labour employed. The greater the productive powers of labour, the more produce is finished in a given time of labour; and the smaller the productive powers of labour, the less produce is finished in the same time. If, for example, in the progress of population it should become necessary to cultivate less fertile soils, the same amount of produce would be only attainable by a greater amount of labour spent, and the value of agricultural produce would consequently rise. On the other hand, if with the modern methods of production, a single spinner converts into yarn, during one working day, many thousand times the amount of cotton which he could have spun during the same time with the spinning wheel, it is evident that every single pound of cotton will absorb many thousand times less of spinning labour than it did before, and, consequently, the value added by spinning to every single pound of cotton will be a thousand times less than before. The value of yarn will sink accordingly.

Apart from the different natural energies and acquired working abilities of different peoples, the productive powers of labour must principally depend:

Firstly. Upon the *natural* conditions of labour, such as fertility of soil, mines, and so forth.

Secondly. Upon the progressive improvement of the *social powers of labour,* such as are derived from production on a grand scale, concentration of capital and combination of labour, subdivision of labour, machinery, improved methods, appliance of chemical and other natural agencies, shortening of time and space by means of communication and transport, and every other contrivance by which science presses natural agencies into the service of labour, and by which the social or co-operative character of labour is developed. The greater the productive powers of labour, the less labour is bestowed upon a given amount of produce; hence the smaller the value of this produce. The smaller the productive powers of labour, the more labour is bestowed upon the same amount of produce; hence the greater its value. As a general law, we may, therefore, set it down that:

The values of commodities are directly as the times of labour employed in their production, and are inversely as the productive powers of the labour employed.

Having till now only spoken of *value,* I shall add a few words about *price,* which is a peculiar form assumed by value.

Price, taken by itself, is nothing but the *monetary expression of value.* The values of all commodities of this country, for example, are expressed in gold prices, while on the Continent they are mainly expressed in silver prices. The value of gold or silver, like that of all other commodities, is regulated by the quantity of labour necessary for getting them. You exchange a certain amount of your national products, in which a certain amount of your national labour is crystallised, for the produce of the gold and silver producing countries, in which a certain quantity of *their* labour is crystallised. It is in this way, in fact by barter, that you learn to express in gold and silver the values of all commodities, that is the respective quantities of labour bestowed on them. Looking somewhat closer into *the monetary expression of value,* or what comes to the same, the *conversion of value into price,* you will find that it is a process by which you give to the *values* of all commodities an *independent* and *homogeneous form,* or by which you express them as quantities of *equal* social labour. So far as it is but the monetary expression of value, price has been called *natural price* by Adam Smith, *prix nécessaire* by the French physiocrats.

What then is the relation between *value* and *market prices,* or between *natural prices* and *market prices?* You all know that the *market price* is the *same* for all commodities of the same kind, however the conditions of production may differ for the individual producers. The market price expresses only the *average amount of social labour* necessary, under the average conditions of production to supply the market with a certain mass of a certain article. It is calculated upon the whole lot of a commodity of a certain description.

So far the *market price* of a commodity coincides with its *value*. On the other hand, the oscillations of market prices, rising now over, sinking now under the value or natural price, depend on the fluctuations of supply and demand. The deviations of market prices from values are continual, but as Adam Smith says: "The natural price is the central price to which the prices of commodities are continually gravitating. Different accidents may sometimes keep them suspended a good deal above it, and sometimes force them down even somewhat below it. But whatever may be the obstacles which hinder them from settling in this centre of repose and continuance, they are constantly tending towards it."

I cannot now sift this matter. It suffices to say that *if* supply and demand equilibrate each other, the market prices of commodities will correspond with their natural prices, that is to say with their values, as determined by the respective quantities of labour required for their production. But supply and demand *must* constantly tend to equilibrate each other, although they do so only by compensating one fluctuation by another, a rise by a fall, and *vice versa*. If instead of considering only the daily fluctuations you analyse the movement of market prices for longer periods, as Mr. Tooke, for example, has done in his *History of Prices,* you will find that the fluctuations of market prices, their deviations from values, their ups and downs, paralyse and compensate each other; so that apart from the effect of monopolies and some other modifications I must now pass by, all descriptions of commodities are, on the average, sold at their respective *values* or natural prices. The average periods during which the fluctuations of market prices compensate each other are different for different kinds of commodities, because with one kind it is easier to adapt supply to demand than with the other.

If then, speaking broadly, and embracing somewhat longer periods, all descriptions of commodities sell at their respective values, it is nonsense to suppose that profit, not in individual cases, but that the constant and usual profits of different trades spring from surcharging the prices of commodities, or selling them at a price over and above their *value*. The absurdity of this notion becomes evident if it is generalised. What a man would constantly win as a seller he would as constantly lose as a purchaser. It would not do to say that there are men who are buyers without being sellers, or consumers without being producers. What these people pay to the producers, they must first get from them for nothing. If a man first takes your money and afterwards returns that money in buying your commodities, you will never enrich yourselves by selling your commodities too dear to that same man. This sort of transaction might diminish a loss, but would never help in realising a profit.

To explain, therefore, the *general nature of profits,* you must start from the theorem that, on an average, commodities are *sold at their real values,* and that *profits are derived from selling them at their values,* that is, in proportion to the quantity of labour realised in them. If you cannot explain profit upon this supposition, you cannot explain it at all. This seems paradox and contrary to everyday observation. It is also paradox that the earth moves round the sun, and that water consists of two highly inflammable gases. Scientific truth is always paradox, if judged by everyday experience, which catches only the delusive appearance of things.

VII. LABOURING POWER

Having now, as far as it could be done in such a cursory manner, analysed the nature of *Value,* of the *Value of any commodity whatever,* we must turn our attention to the specific *Value of Labour.* And here, again, I must startle you by a seeming paradox. All of you feel sure that what they daily sell is their Labour; that, therefore, Labour has a Price, and that, the price of a commodity being only the monetary expression of its value, there must certainly exist such a thing as the *Value of Labour.* However, there exists no such thing as the *Value of Labour* in the common acceptance of the word. We have seen that the amount of necessary labour crystallised in a commodity constitutes its value. Now, applying this notion of value, how could we define, say, the value of a ten hours' working day? How much labour is contained in that day? Ten hours' labour. To say that the value of a ten hours' working day is equal to ten hours' labour, or the quantity of labour contained in it, would be a tautological and, moreover, a nonsensical expression. Of course, having once found out the true but hidden sense of the expression "*Value of Labour,*" we shall be able to interpret this irrational, and seemingly impossible application of value, in the same way that, having once made sure of the real movement of the celestial bodies, we shall be able to explain their apparent or merely phenomenal movements.

What the working man sells is not directly his *Labour,* but his *Labouring Power,* the temporary disposal of which he makes over to the capitalist. This is so much the case that I do not know whether by the English laws, but certainly by some Continental laws, the *maximum time* is fixed for which a man is allowed to sell his labouring power. If allowed to do so for any indefinite period whatever, slavery would be immediately restored. Such a sale, if it comprised his lifetime, for example, would make him at once the lifelong slave of his employer.

One of the oldest economists and most original philosophers of England—Thomas Hobbes—has already, in his *Leviathan,* instinctively hit upon this point overlooked by all his successors. He says: "The *value or worth of a man* is, as in all other things, his *price:* that is so much as would be given for the *Use of his Power."*

Proceeding from this basis, we shall be able to determine the *Value of Labour* as that of all other commodities.

But before doing so, we might ask, how does this strange phenomenon arise, that we find on the market a set of buyers, possessed of land, machinery, raw material, and the means of life, all of them, save land in its crude state, the *products of labour,* and on the other hand, a set of sellers who have nothing to sell except their labouring power, their working arms and brains? That the one set buys continually in order to make a profit and enrich themselves, while the other set continually sells in order to earn their livelihood? The inquiry into this question would be an inquiry into what the economists call *"Previous, or Original Accumulation,"* but which ought to be called *Original Expropriation.* We should find that this so-called *Original Accumulation* means nothing but a series of historical processes, resulting in a *Decomposition of the Original Union* existing between the Labouring Man and his Means of Labour. Such an inquiry, however, lies beyond the pale of my present subject. The *Separation* between the Man of Labour and the Means of Labour once established, such a state of things will maintain itself and reproduce itself upon a constantly increasing scale, until a new and fundamental revolution in the mode of production should again overturn it, and restore the original union in a new historical form.

What, then, is the *Value of Labouring Power?*

Like that of every other commodity, its value is determined by the quantity of labour necessary to produce it. The labouring power of a man exists only in his living individuality. A certain mass of necessaries must be consumed by a man to grow up and maintain his life. But the man, like the machine, will wear out, and must be replaced by another man. Beside the mass of necessaries required for his *own* maintenance, he wants another amount of necessaries to bring up a certain quota of children that are to replace him on the labour market and to perpetuate the race of labourers. Moreover, to develop his labouring power, and acquire a given skill, another amount of values must be spent. For our purpose it suffices to consider only average labour, the costs of whose education and development are vanishing magnitudes. Still I must seize upon this occasion to state that, as the costs of producing labouring powers of different quality do differ, so must differ the values of the labouring powers employed in different trades. To cry for an *equality of wages* rests, therefore, upon a mistake, is an inane wish never to be fulfilled. It is an offspring of that false and superficial radicalism that accepts premises and tries to evade conclusions. Upon the basis of the wages system the value of labouring power is settled like that of every other commodity; and as different kinds of labouring power have different values, or require different quantities of labour for their production, they *must* fetch different prices in the labour market. To clamour for *equal or even equitable retribution* on the basis of the wages system is the same as to clamour for *freedom* on the basis of the slavery system. What you think just or equitable is out of the question. The question is: What is necessary and unavoidable with a given system of production?

After what has been said, the *value of labouring power* is determined by the *value of the necessaries* required to produce, develop, maintain, and perpetuate the labouring power.

VIII. PRODUCTION OF SURPLUS VALUE

Now suppose that the average amount of the daily necessaries of a labouring man require *six hours of average labour* for their production. Suppose moreover, six hours of average labour to be also realised in a quantity of gold equal to 3*s*. Then 3*s*. would be the *Price,* or the monetary expression of the *Daily Value* of that man's *Labouring Power.* If he worked daily six hours he would daily produce a value sufficient to buy the average amount of his daily necessaries, or to maintain himself as a labouring man.

But our man is a wages labourer. He must, therefore, sell his labouring power to a capitalist. If he sells it at 3*s*. daily, or 18*s*. weekly, he sells it at its value. Suppose him to be a spinner. If he works six hours daily he will add to the cotton a value of 3*s*. daily. This value, daily added by him, would be an exact equivalent for the wages, or the price of his labouring power, received daily. But in that case no *surplus value* or *surplus produce* whatever would go to the capitalist. Here, then, we come to the rub.

In buying the labouring power of the workman, and paying its value, the capitalist, like every other purchaser, has acquired the right to consume or use the commodity bought. You consume or use the labouring power of a man by making him work, as you consume or use a machine by making it run. By paying the daily or weekly value of the labouring power of the workman, the capitalist has, therefore, acquired the right to use or make that labouring power work during the *whole day or week*. The working day or the working week has, of course, certain limits, but those we shall afterwards look more closely at.

For the present I want to turn your attention to one decisive point.

The *value* of the labouring power is determined by the quantity of labour necessary to maintain or reproduce it, but the *use* of that labouring power is only limited by the active energies and physical strength of the labourer. The daily or weekly *value* of the labouring power is quite distinct from the daily or weekly exercise of that power, the same as the food a horse wants and the time it can carry the horseman are quite distinct. The quantity of labour by which the *value* of the workman's labouring power is limited forms by no means a limit to the quantity of labour which his labouring power is apt to perform. Take the example of our spinner. We have seen that, to daily reproduce his labouring power, he must daily reproduce a value of three shillings, which he will do by working six hours daily. But this does not disable him from working ten or twelve or more hours a day. But by paying the daily or weekly *value* of the spinner's labouring power the capitalist has acquired the right of using that labouring power during *the whole day or week*. He will, therefore, make him work daily, say, *twelve* hours. *Over and above* the six hours required to replace his wages, or the value of his labouring power, he will, therefore, have to work *six other hours,* which I shall call hours of *surplus labour,* which surplus labour will realise itself in a *surplus value* and a *surplus produce*. If our spinner, for example, by his daily labour of six hours, added three shillings' value to the cotton, a value forming an exact equivalent to his wages, he will, in twelve hours, add six shillings' worth to the cotton, and produce a *proportional surplus of yarn*. As he has sold his labouring power to the capitalist, the whole value or produce created by him belongs to the capitalist, the owner *pro tem*. of his labouring power. By advancing three shillings, the capitalist will, therefore, realise a value of six shillings, because, advancing a value in which six hours of labour are crystallised, he will receive in return a value in which twelve hours of labour are crystallised. By repeating this same process daily, the capitalist will daily advance three shillings and daily pocket six shillings, one half of which will go to pay wages anew, and the other half of which will form the *surplus value,* for which the capitalist pays no equivalent. It is this sort of *exchange between capital and labour* upon which capitalistic production, or the wages system, is founded, and which must constantly result in reproducing the working man as a working man, and the capitalist as a capitalist.

The *rate of surplus value,* all other circumstances remaining the same, will depend on the proportion between that part of the working day necessary to reproduce the value of the labouring power and the *surplus time* or *surplus labour* performed for the capitalist. It will, therefore, depend on the *ratio in which the working day is prolonged over and above that extent,* by working which the working man would only reproduce the value of his labouring power, or replace his wages.

IX. VALUE OF LABOUR

We must now return to the expression, *"Value, or Price of Labour."*

We have seen that, in fact, it is only the value of the labouring power, measured by the values of commodities necessary for its maintenance. But since the workman receives his wages *after* his labour is performed, and knows, moreover, that what he actually gives to the capitalist is his labour, the value or price of his labouring power necessarily appears to him as the *price* or *value of his labour itself.* If the price of his labouring power is three shillings, in which six hours of labour are realised, and if he works twelve hours, he necessarily considers these three shillings as the value or price of twelve hours of labour, although these twelve hours of labour realise themselves in a value of six shillings. A double consequence flows from this.

Firstly. The *value or price of the labouring power* takes the semblance of the *price or value of labour itself,* although, strictly speaking, value and price of labour are senseless terms.

Secondly. Although one part only of the workman's daily labour is *paid,* while the other part is *unpaid,* and while that unpaid or surplus labour constitutes exactly the fund out of which *surplus value* or *profit* is formed, it seems as if the aggregate labour was paid labour.

This false appearance distinguishes *wages labour* from other *historical* forms of labour. On the basis of the wages system even the *unpaid* labour seems to be *paid* labour. With the *slave,* on the contrary, even that part of his labour which is paid appears to be unpaid. Of course, in order to work the slave must live, and one part of his working day goes to replace the value of his own maintenance. But since no bargain is struck between him and his master, and no acts of selling and buying are going on between the two parties, all his labour seems to be given away for nothing.

Take, on the other hand, the peasant serf, such as he, I might say, until yesterday existed in the whole east of Europe. This peasant worked, for example, three days for himself on his own field or the field allotted to him, and the three subsequent days he performed compulsory and gratuitous labour on the estate of his lord. Here, then, the paid and unpaid parts of labour were visibly separated, separated in time and space; and our Liberals overflowed with moral indignation at the preposterous notion of making a man work for nothing.

In point of fact, however, whether a man works three days of the week for himself on his own field and three days for nothing on the estate of his lord, or whether he works in the factory or the workshop six hours daily for himself and six for his employer, comes to the same, although in the latter case the paid and unpaid portions of his labour are inseparably mixed up with each other, and the nature of the whole transaction is completely masked by the *intervention of a contract* and the *pay* received at the end of the week. The gratuitous labour appears to be voluntarily given in the one instance, and to be compulsory in the other. That makes all the difference.

In using the word *"value of labour,"* I shall only use it as a popular slang term for *"value of labouring power."*

X. PROFIT IS MADE BY SELLING A COMMODITY AT ITS VALUE

Suppose an average hour of labour to be realised in a value equal to six-pence, or twelve average hours of labour to be realised in six shillings. Suppose, further, the value of labour to be three shillings or the produce of six hours' labour. If, then, in the raw material, machinery, and so forth, used up in a commodity, twenty-four average hours of labour were realised, its value would amount to twelve shillings. If, moreover, the workman employed by the capitalist added twelve hours of labour to those means of production, these twelve hours would be realised in an additional value of six shillings. The *total value of the product* would, therefore, amount to thirty-six hours of realised labour, and be equal to eighteen shillings. But as the value of labour, or the wages paid to the workman, would be three shillings only, no equivalent would have been paid by the capitalist for the six hours of surplus labour worked by the workman, and realised in the value of the commodity. By selling this commodity at its value for eighteen shillings, the capitalist would, therefore, realise a value of three shillings, for which he had paid no equivalent. These three shillings would constitute the surplus value or profit pocketed by him. The capitalist would consequently realise the profit of three shillings, not by selling his commodity at a price *over and above* its value, but by selling it *at its real value.*

The value of a commodity is determined by the *total quantity of labour* contained in it. But part of that quantity of labour is realised in a value, for which an equivalent has been paid in the form of wages; part of it is realised in a value for which no equivalent has been paid. Part of the labour contained in the commodity is *paid* labour; part is *unpaid* labour. By selling, therefore, the commodity *at its value,* that is, as the crystallisation of the *total quantity of labour* bestowed upon it, the capitalist must necessarily sell it at a profit. He sells not only what has cost him an equivalent, but he sells also what has cost him nothing, although it has cost the labour of his workman. The cost of the commodity to the capitalist and its real cost are different things, I repeat, therefore, that normal and average profits are made by selling commodities not *above,* but *at their real values.*

XI. THE DIFFERENT PARTS INTO WHICH SURPLUS VALUE IS DECOMPOSED

The *surplus value,* or that part of the total value of the commodity in which the *surplus labour* or *unpaid labour* of the working man is realised, I call *Profit.* The whole of that profit is not pocketed by the employing capitalist. The monopoly of land enables the landlord to take one part of that *surplus value,* under the name of *rent,* whether the land is used for agriculture or buildings or railways, or for any other productive purpose. On the other hand, the very fact that the possession of the *means of labour* enables the employing capitalist to produce a *surplus value,* or what comes to the same, *to appropriate to himself a certain amount of unpaid labour,* enables the owner of the means of labour, which he lends wholly or partly to the employing capitalist—enables, in one word, the *money-lending capitalist* to claim for himself under the name of *interest* another part of that surplus value, so that there remains to the employing capitalist *as such* only what is called *industrial* or *commercial profit.*

By what laws this division of the total amount of surplus value amongst the three categories of people is regulated is a question quite foreign to our subject. This much, however, results from what has been stated.

Rent, Interest, and Industrial Profit are only *different names for different parts* of the *surplus value* of the commodity, or the *unpaid labour realised in it,* and they are *equally derived from this source, and from this source alone.* They are not derived from *land* as such nor from *capital* as such, but land and capital enable their owners to get their respective shares out of the surplus value extracted by the employing capitalist from the labourer. For the labourer himself it is a matter of subordinate importance whether that surplus value, the result of his surplus labour, or unpaid labour, is altogether pocketed by the employing capitalist, or whether the latter is obliged to pay portions of it, under the names of rent and interest, away to third parties. Suppose the employing capitalist to use only his own capital and to be his own landlord, then the whole surplus value would go into his pocket.

It is the employing capitalist who immediately extracts from the labourer this surplus value, whatever part of it he may ultimately be able to keep for himself. Upon this relation, therefore, between the employing capitalist and the wages labourer the whole wages system and the whole present system of production hinge. Some of the citizens who took part in our debate were, therefore, wrong in trying to mince matters, and to treat this fundamental relation between the employing capitalist and the working man as a secondary question, although they were right in stating that, under given circumstances, a rise of prices might affect in very unequal degrees the employing capitalist, the landlord, the moneyed capitalist, and, if you please, the tax-gatherer.

Another consequence follows from what has been stated.

That part of the value of the commodity which represents only the value of the raw materials, the machinery, in one word, the value of the means of production used up, forms *no revenue* at all, but replaces *only capital*. But apart from this, it is false that the other part of the value of the commodity *which forms revenue,* or may be spent in the form of wages, profits, rent, interest, is *constituted* by the value of wages, the value of rent, the value of profit, and so forth. We shall, in the first instance, discard wages, and only treat industrial profits, interest, and rent. We have just seen that the *surplus value* contained in the commodity, or that part of its value in which *unpaid labour* is realised, resolves itself into different fractions, bearing three different names. But it would be quite the reverse of the truth to say that its value is *composed* of, or *formed* by, the *addition* of the *independent values of these three constituents.*

If one hour of labour realises itself in a value of sixpence, if the working day of the labourer comprises twelve hours, if half of this time is unpaid labour, that surplus labour will add to the commodity a *surplus value* of three shillings, that is value for which no equivalent has been paid. This surplus value of three shillings constitutes the *whole fund* which the employing capitalist may divide, in whatever proportions, with the landlord and the money-lender. The value of these three shillings constitutes the limit of the value they have to divide amongst them. But it is not the employing capitalist who adds to the value of the commodity an arbitrary value for his profit, to which another value is added for the landlord, and so forth, so that the addition of these arbitrarily fixed values would constitute the total value. You see, therefore, the fallacy of the popular notion, which confounds the *decomposition* of a *given value* into three parts, with the *formation* of that value by the addition of three *independent* values, thus converting the aggregate value, from which rent, profit, and interest are derived, into an arbitrary magnitude.

If the total profit realised by a capitalist be equal to £100, we call this sum, considered as absolute magnitude, the *amount of profit*. But if we calculate the ratio which those £100 bear to the capital advanced, we call this *relative* magnitude, *the rate of profit*. It is evident that this rate of profit may be expressed in a double way.

Suppose £100 to be the capital *advanced in wages*. If the surplus value created is also £100—and this would show us that half of the working day of the labourer consists of *unpaid* labour—and if we measured this profit by the value of the capital advanced in wages, we should say that the *rate of profit* amounted to one hundred per cent, because the value advanced would be one hundred and the value realised would be two hundred.

If, on the other hand, we should not only consider the *capital advanced in wages,* but the *total capital* advanced, say, for example, £500, of which £400 represented the value of raw materials, machinery, and so forth, we should say that the *rate of profit* amounted only to twenty per cent, because the profit of one hundred would be but the fifth part of the *total* capital advanced.

The first mode of expressing the rate of profit is the only one which shows you the real ratio between paid and unpaid labour, the real degree of *exploitation* (you must allow me this French word) *of labour.* The other mode of expression is that in common use, and is, indeed, appropriate for certain purposes. At all events, it is very useful for concealing the degree in which the capitalist extracts gratuitous labour from the workman.

In the remarks I have still to make, I shall use the word *Profit* for the whole amount of the surplus value extracted by the capitalist without any regard to the division of that surplus value between different parties, and in using the words *Rate of Profit,* I shall always measure profits by the value of the capital advanced in wages. . . .

THE CLASS STRUGGLES IN FRANCE

AFTER the July revolution (of 1830), when the liberal banker Laffitte led his godfather, the Duke of Orleans, in triumph to the Hôtel de Ville, he let fall the words: *"From now on the bankers will rule."* Laffitte had betrayed the secret of the revolution.

It was not the French bourgeoisie that ruled under Louis Philippe, but *one section* of it: bankers, stock-exchange kings, railway kings, owners of coal and iron mines and forests, a part of the landed proprietors that rallied round them—the so-called *finance aristocracy.* It sat on the throne, it dictated laws in the Chambers, it distributed public offices, from cabinet portfolios to tobacco bureau posts.

The *industrial bourgeoisie,* properly so called, formed part of the official opposition, i.e., it was represented only as a minority in the Chambers. Its opposition was expressed all the more resolutely, the more unalloyed the autocracy of the finance aristocracy became, and the more it itself imagined that its domination over the working class was ensured after the mutinies of 1832, 1834, and 1839, which had been drowned in blood. *Grandin,* Rouen manufacturer and the most fanatical instrument of bourgeois reaction in the Constituent as well as in the Legislative National Assembly, was the most violent opponent of Guizot in the Chamber of Deputies. *Léon Faucher,* later known for his impotent efforts to climb into prominence as the Guizot of the French counterrevolution, in the last days of Louis Philippe waged a war of the pen for industry against speculation and its trainbearer, the government. *Bastiat* agitated in the name of Bordeaux and the whole of wine-producing France against the ruling system.

The *petty bourgeoisie* of all gradations and the *peasantry* also, were completely excluded from political power. Finally, in the official opposition or entirely outside the *pays légal,* there were the *ideological* representatives and spokesmen of the above classes, their savants, lawyers, doctors, etc.—in a word, their so-called *men of talent.*

Owing to its financial straits, the July monarchy was dependent from the beginning on the big bourgeoisie, and its dependence on the big bourgeoisie was the inexhaustible source of increasing financial straits. It was impossible to subordinate the administration of the state to the interests of national production without balancing the budget, without establishing a balance beween state expenditures and revenues. And how was this balance to be established without limiting state extravagance, i.e., without encroaching on interests which were so many props of the ruling system, and without redistributing taxes, i. e., without shifting a considerable share of the burden of taxation onto the shoulders of the big bourgeoisie itself?

Moreover, the faction of the bourgeoisie that ruled and legislated through the Chambers had a *direct interest in the indebtedness of the state.* The *state deficit* was really the main object of its speculation and the chief source of its enrichment. At the end of each year, a new deficit. After expiry of four of five years, a new loan. And every new loan offered new opportunities to the finance aristocracy for defrauding the state, which was kept artificially on the verge of bankruptcy—it had to negotiate with the bankers under the most unfavorable conditions. Each new loan gave a further opportunity, that of plundering the public, which invested its capital in state bonds by means of stock-exchange manipulations, into the secrets of which the government and the majority in the Chambers were initiated. In general, the fluctuations in state credits and the possession of state secrets gave the bankers and their associates in the Chambers and on the throne the possibility of evoking sudden, extraordinary fluctuations in the quotations of state bonds, the result of which was always bound to be the ruin of a mass of smaller capitalists and the fabulously rapid enrichment of the big gamblers. As the state deficit was in the direct interest of the ruling section of the bourgeoisie, it is clear why the *extraordinary* state expenditure in the last years of Louis Philippe's reign was far more than double the extraordinary state expenditure under Napoleon, indeed reached a yearly sum of nearly four hundred million francs, whereas the whole average annual export of France seldom attained a volume amounting to seven hundred and fifty million francs. The enormous sums which, in this way, flowed through the hands of the state facilitated, moreover, swindling contracts for deliveries, bribery, defalcations, and all kinds of roguery. The defrauding of the state, practiced wholesale in connection with loans, was repeated retail in public works. What occurred in the relations between Chamber and government became multiplied in the relations between individual departments and individual *entrepreneurs*.

The ruling class exploited the *building of railways* in the same way as it exploited state expenditures in general and state loans. The Chambers piled the main burdens on the state, and secured the golden fruits to the speculating finance aristocracy. One recalls the scandals in the Chamber of Deputies, when by chance it leaked out that all the members of the majority, including a number of ministers, had been interested as shareholders in the very railroad construction which as legislators they caused to be carried out afterwards at the cost of the state.

On the other hand, the smallest financial reform was wrecked due to the influence of the bankers. For example, the *postal reform*. Rothschild protested. Was it permissible for the state to curtail sources of revenue out of which interest was to be paid on its ever increasing debt?

The July monarchy was nothing other than a joint-stock company for the exploitation of France's national wealth, the dividends on which were divided among ministers, Chambers, two hundred and forty thousand voters and their adherents. Louis Philippe was the director of this company—Robert Macaire on the throne. Trade, industry, agriculture, shipping, the interests of the industrial bourgeoisie, were bound to be continually endangered and prejudiced under this system. *Gouvernement à bon marché,* cheap government, was what it had inscribed in the July days on its banner.

Since the finance aristocracy made the laws, was at the head of the administration of the state, had command of all the organized public authorities, dominated public opinion through the actual state of affairs and through the press, the same prostitution, the same shameless cheating, the same mania

to get rich were repeated in every sphere, from the court to the Café Borgne
—to get rich not by production, but by pocketing the already available wealth
of others. Clashing every moment with the bourgeois laws themselves, an
unbridled assertion of unhealthy and dissolute appetites manifested itself,
particularly at the top of bourgeois society—lusts wherein wealth derived
from gambling naturally seeks its satisfaction, where pleasure becomes debauched, where money, filth, and blood commingle. The finance aristocracy,
in its mode of acquisition as well as in its pleasures, is nothing but the
resurrection of the lumpenproletariat *transported to the heights of bourgeois
society.* . . .

The eruption of the general discontent was finally accelerated and the mood
for revolt ripened by *two economic world events.*

The potato blight and the crop failures of 1845 and 1846 increased the general ferment among the people. The dearth of 1847 called forth bloody conflicts in France as well as on the rest of the Continent. As against the shameless orgies of the finance aristocracy, the struggle of the people for the prime
necessities of life! At Buzançais hunger rioters executed; in Paris oversatiated
swindlers snatched from the courts by the royal family!

The second great economic event which hastened the outbreak of the revolution was a *general commercial and industrial* crisis in England. Already
heralded in the autumn of 1845 by the wholesale reverses of the speculators in
railway shares, staved off during 1846 by a number of incidents such as the
impending abolition of the corn duties, the crisis finally burst in the autumn
of 1847 with the bankruptcy of the London wholesale grocers, on the heels
of which followed the insolvencies of the land banks and the closing of the
factories in the English industrial districts. The aftereffect of this crisis on
the Continent had not yet spent itself when the February revolution broke
out.

The devastation of trade and industry caused by the economic epidemic
made the autocracy of the finance aristocracy still more unbearable. Throughout the whole of France the bourgeois opposition *agitated at banquets* for an
electoral reform which should win for it the majority in the Chambers and
overthrow the Ministry of the Bourse. In Paris the industrial crisis had,
moreover, the particular result of throwing a number of manufacturers and
big traders, who under the existing circumstances could no longer do any
business in the foreign market, onto the home market. They set up large
establishments, the competition of which ruined the small grocers and shopkeepers *en masse*. Hence the innumerable bankruptcies among this section
of the Paris bourgeoisie, and hence their revolutionary action in February.
It is well known how Guizot and the Chambers answered the reform pro-

posals with an unambiguous challenge, how Louis Philippe too late resolved on a ministry led by Barrot, how things went as far as hand-to-hand fighting between people and the army, how the army was disarmed by the passive conduct of the National Guard, how the July monarchy had to give way to a provisional government.

The provisional government which emerged from the February barricades necessarily mirrored in its composition the different parties which shared in the victory. It could not be anything but a *compromise between the different classes* which together had overturned the July throne, but whose interests were mutually antagonistic. The *great majority* of its members consisted of representatives of the bourgeoisie. The republican petty bourgeoisie was represented by Ledru-Rollin and Flacon, the republican bourgeoisie by the people from the *National,* the dynastic opposition by Cremieux, Dupont de l'Eure, etc. The working class had only two representatives, Louis Blanc and Albert. Finally, Lamartine in the provisional government; this was actually no real interest, no definite class; this was the February revolution itself, the common uprising with its illusions, its poetry, its visionary content, and its phrases. For the rest, the spokesman of the February revolution, by his position and his views, belonged to the *bourgeoisie.*

If Paris, as a result of political centralization, rules France, the workers, in moments of revolutionary earthquakes, rule Paris. The first act in the life of the provisional government was an attempt to escape from this over-powering influence by an appeal from intoxicated Paris to sober France. Lamartine disputed the right of the barricade fighters to proclaim a republic on the ground that only the majority of Frenchmen had that right; they must await their votes, the Parisian proletariat must not besmirch its victory by a usurpation. The bourgeoisie allows the proletariat only one usurpation—that of fighting.

Up to noon of February 25 the republic had not yet been proclaimed; on the other hand, all the ministries had already been divided among the bourgeois elements of the provisional government and among the generals, bankers, and lawyers of the *National*. But the workers were determined this time not to put up with any bamboozlement like that of July 1830. They were ready to take up the fight anew, and to get a republic by force of arms. With this message, *Raspail* betook himself to the Hôtel de Ville. In the name of the Parisian proletariat he commanded the provisional government to proclaim a republic; if this order of the people was not fulfilled within two hours, he would return at the head of two hundred thousand men. The bodies of the fallen were scarcely cold, the barricades were not yet cleared away, the workers not yet disarmed, and the only force which could be opposed to them was the National Guard. Under these circumstances the doubts born

of considerations of state policy and the juristic scruples of conscience entertained by the provisional government suddenly vanished. The time limit
of two hours had not yet expired when all the walls of Paris were resplendent
with the gigantesque historical words:

République française! Liberté, Egalité, Fraternité!

Even the memory of the limited aims and motives which drove the
bourgeoisie into the February revolution was extinguished by the proclamation of the republic on the basis of universal suffrage. Instead of only a few
sections of the bourgeoisie all classes of French society were suddenly hurled
into the orbit of political power, forced to leave the boxes, the stalls, and the
gallery and to act in person upon the revolutionary stage! With the constitutional monarchy also vanished the semblance of a state power independently confronting bourgeois society as well as the whole series of subordinate struggles which this semblance of power called forth!

By dictating the republic to the provisional government, and through the
provisional government to the whole of France, the proletariat stepped into
the foreground forthwith as an independent party, but at the same time
challenged the whole of bourgeois France to enter the lists against it. What
it won was the terrain for the fight for its revolutionary emancipation, but
by no means this emancipation itself.

The first thing that the February republic had to do was rather to *complete
the rule of the bourgeoisie* by allowing, besides the finance aristocracy, *all
the propertied classes* to enter the orbit of political power. The majority of
the great landowners, the Legitimists, were emancipated from the political
nullity to which they had been condemned by the July monarchy. Not for
nothing had the *Gazette de France* agitated in common with the opposition
papers; not for nothing had Larochejaquelin taken the side of the revolution
in the session of the Chamber of Deputies on February 24. The nominal
proprietors, who form the great majority of the French people, the *peasants,*
were put by universal suffrage in the position of arbiters of the fate of
France. The February republic finally brought the rule of the bourgeoisie
clearly into view, since it struck off the crown behind which capital kept
itself concealed.

Just as the workers in the July days had fought for and won the *bourgeois
monarchy,* so in the February days they fought for and won the *bourgeois
republic.* Just as the July monarchy had to proclaim itself a *monarchy surrounded by republican institutions,* so the February republic was forced to
proclaim itself a *republic surrounded by social institutions.* The Paris proletariat *compelled* this concession, too.

Marche, a worker, dictated the decree by which the newly formed provisional government pledged itself to guarantee the workers a livelihood by means of work, to provide work for all citizens, etc. And when, a few days later, it forgot its promises and seemed to have lost sight of the proletariat, a mass of twenty thousand workers marched on the Hôtel de Ville with the cry: *"We want the organization of work! We want our own Ministry of Labor!"* Reluctantly, and after long debate, the provisional government nominated a permanent special commission charged with *finding* means of improving the lot of the working classes! This commission consisted of delegates from the corporations of Paris artisans, and was presided over by Louis Blanc and Albert. The Luxembourg Palace was assigned to it as its meeting place. In this way the representatives of the working class were exiled from the seat of the provisional government, the bourgeois section of which retained the real state power and the reins of administration exclusively in its hands; and *side by side* with the Ministries of Finance, Trade, and Public Works, *side by side* with the Banks and the Bourse, there arose a *socialist synagogue* whose high priests, Louis Blanc and Albert, had the task of discovering the promised land, of preaching the new gospel, and of providing work for the Paris proletariat. Unlike any profane state power, they had no budget, no executive authority at their disposal. They were supposed to use their heads to break the pillars of bourgeois society. While at the Palais de Luxembourg they sought the philosopher's stone, in the Hôtel de Ville they minted the current coinage.

And yet the claims of the Paris proletariat, so far as they went beyond the bourgeois republic, could win no other existence than the nebulous one of the Luxembourg Commission.

In common with the bourgeoisie the workers had made the February revolution, and *alongside* the bourgeoisie they sought to put through their interests, just as they had installed a worker in the provisional government itself alongside the bourgeois majority. *Organization of work!* But the existing, the bourgeois organization of work is wage labor. Without it there is no capital, no bourgeoisie, no bourgeois society. *Their own Ministry of Labor!* But the Ministries of Finance, of Trade, of Public Works—are not these the bourgeois Ministries of Labor? And *alongside* these a *proletarian* Ministry of Labor had to be a ministry of impotence, a ministry of pious wishes, a Luxembourg Commission. Just as the workers thought they would be able to emancipate themselves side by side with the bourgeoisie, so they thought they would be able to consummate a proletarian revolution within the national walls of France, side by side with the remaining bourgeois nations. But French production relations are conditioned by the foreign trade of

France, by her position on the world market and the laws thereof; how was France to break them without a European revolutionary war; which would strike back at the despot of the world market, England?

As soon as it has risen up, a class in which the revolutionary interests of society are concentrated finds the content and the material for its revolutionary activity directly in its own situation: foes to be laid low, measures dictated by the needs of the struggle to be taken; the consequences of its own deeds drive it on. It makes no theoretical inquiries into its own task. The French working class had not attained this level; it was still incapable of accomplishing its own revolution.

The development of the industrial proletariat is, in general, conditioned by the development of the industrial bourgeoisie. Only under its rule does the proletariat gain that extensive national existence which can raise its revolution to a national one and does it itself create the modern means of production, which become just so many means of its revolutionary emancipation. Only its rule tears up the material roots of feudal society and levels the ground on which alone a proletarian revolution is possible. In France industry is more developed and the bourgeoisie more revolutionary than elsewhere on the Continent. But was not the February revolution leveled directly against the finance aristocracy? This fact proved that the industrial bourgeoisie did not rule France. The industrial bourgeoisie can rule only where modern industry shapes all property relations to suit itself, and industry can win this power only when it has conquered the world market, for national bounds are not wide enough for its development. But French industry, to a great extent, maintains its command even of the national market only through a more or less modified system of prohibitive duties. While, therefore, the French proletariat, at the moment of a revolution, possesses in Paris actual power and influence which spur it on to a drive beyond its means, in the rest of France it is crowded into separate, scattered industrial centers, being almost lost in the superior numbers of peasants and petty bourgeois. The struggle against capital in its developed, modern form, in its culminating phase, the struggle of the industrial wage workers against the industrial bourgeois, is in France a partial phenomenon, which after the February days could so much the less supply the national content of the revolution, since the struggle against capital's secondary modes of exploitation, that of the peasants against the usury in mortgages or of the petty bourgeois against the wholesale dealer, banker, and manufacturer, in a word against bankruptcy, was still hidden in the general uprising against the finance aristocracy. Nothing is more understandable, then, than that the Paris proletariat sought to put through its own interests *side by side* with those of the bourgeoisie instead of enforcing them as the revolutionary interests of society itself, and that it let the *red* flag be lowered to the *tricolor*. The French workers could not take a step forward, could not touch a hair of the bourgeois order, until the course of the revolution had aroused the mass of the nation, peasants and petty bourgeois, standing between the proletariat and the bourgeoisie, against this order, against the rule of capital, and had forced it to attach itself to the proletariat as its protagonist. The workers could buy this victory only through the tremendous defeat of June. . . .

On May 4 the *National Assembly,* the result of the direct *general elections,* convened. Universal suffrage did not possess the magic power which republicans of the old school had ascribed to it. They saw in the whole of France, at least in the majority of Frenchmen, *citoyens* with the same interests, the same understanding, etc. This was their *cult of the people.* Instead of their *imaginary* people the elections brought the *real* people to the light of day, i. e., representatives of the different classes into which it falls. We have seen why peasants and petty bourgeois had to vote under the leadership of a bourgeoisie spoiling for a fight and of big landowners frantic for restoration. But if universal suffrage was not the miracle-working magic wand for which the republican worthies had taken it, it possessed the incomparably higher merit of unchaining the class struggle, of letting the various middle sections of bourgeois society rapidly get over their illusions and disappointments, of tossing all the sections of the exploiting class at one throw to the apex of the state, and thus tearing from them their treacherous mask, whereas the monarchy with its property qualifications let only certain sections of the bourgeoisie compromise themselves, allowing the others to lie hidden behind the scenes and surrounding them with the halo of a common opposition.

In the Constituent National Assembly, which met on May 4, the *bourgeois republicans,* the republicans of the *National,* had the upper hand. Even Legitimists and Orleanists at first dared to show themselves only under the mask of bourgeois republicanism. The fight against the proletariat could be undertaken only in the name of the republic.

The republic dates from May 4, not from February 25, i. e., the republic recognized by the French people; it is not the republic which the Paris proletariat thrust upon the provisional government, not the republic with social institutions, not the vision which hovered before the fighters on the barricades. The republic proclaimed by the National Assembly, the sole legitimate republic, is a republic which is no revolutionary weapon against the bourgeois order, but rather its political reconstitution, the political reconsolidation of bourgeois society, in a word, *a bourgeois republic.* This contention resounded from the tribune of the National Assembly, and in the entire republican and antirepublican bourgeois press it found its echo.

And we have seen how the February republic in reality was not and could not be other than a *bourgeois* republic; how the provisional government, nevertheless, was forced by the immediate pressure of the proletariat to announce it as a *republic with social institutions;* how the Paris proletariat was still incapable of going beyond the bourgeois republic otherwise than in its *fancy,* in *imagination;* how everywhere it acted in its service when it really came to action; how the promises made to it became an unbearable danger for the new republic; how the whole life process of the provisional government was comprised in a continuous fight against the demands of the proletariat.

In the National Assembly all France sat in judgment upon the Paris proletariat. The Assembly broke immediately with the social illusions of the February revolution; it roundly proclaimed the *bourgeois republic,* nothing but the bourgeois republic. It at once excluded the representatives of the proletariat, Louis Blanc and Albert, from the Executive Commission appointed by it; it threw out the proposal of a special Labor Ministry, and received with wild applause the statement of the Minister Trélat: "The question now is merely one of *bringing labor back to its old conditions.*"

But all this was not enough. The February republic was won by the workers with the passive support of the bourgeoisie. The proletarians rightly regarded themselves as the victors of February, and they made the arrogant claims of victors. They had to be vanquished in the streets, they had to be shown that they were worsted as soon as they did not fight *with* the bourgeoisie, but *against* the bourgeoisie. Just as the February republic, with its socialist concessions, required a battle of the proletariat, united with the bourgeoisie, against monarchy, so a second battle was necessary in order to sever the republic from the socialist concessions, in order to officially work out the *bourgeois republic* as dominant. Arms in hand, the bourgeoisie had to refute the demands of the proletariat. And the real birthplace of the bourgeois republic is not the *February victory;* it is the *June defeat.*

The proletariat hastened the decision when, on the fifteenth of May, it pushed its way into the National Assembly, sought in vain to recapture its revolutionary influence, and only delivered its energetic leaders to the jailers of the bourgeoisie. *"Il faut en finir* (This situation must end)!" With this cry the National Assembly gave vent to its determination to force the proletariat into a decisive struggle. The Executive Commission issued a series of provocative decrees, such as that prohibiting congregations of people, etc. The workers were directly provoked, insulted, and derided from the tribune of the Constituent National Assembly. But the real point of the attack was, as we have seen, the national workshops. The Constituent Assembly imperiously pointed these out to the Executive Commission, which only waited to hear its own plan proclaimed the command of the National Assembly.

The Executive Commission began by making admission to the national workshops more difficult, by turning the day wage into a piece wage, by banishing workers not born in Paris to Sologne, ostensibly for the construction of earthworks. These earthworks were only a rhetorical formula with which to gloss over their exile, as the workers, returning disillusioned, announced to their comrades. Finally, on June 21, a decree appeared in the *Moniteur* which ordered the forcible expulsion of all unmarried workers from the national workshops, or their enrollment in the army.

The workers were left no choice; they had to starve or start to fight. They answered on June 22 with the tremendous insurrection in which the first great battle was fought between the two classes that split modern society. It was a fight for the preservation or annihilation of the *bourgeois* order. The veil that shrouded the republic was torn asunder.

It is well known how the workers, with unexampled bravery and ingenuity, without leaders, without a common plan, without means, and, for the most part, lacking weapons, held in check for five days the army, the Mobile Guard, the Paris National Guard, and the National Guard that streamed in from the provinces. It is well known how the bourgeoisie compensated itself for the mortal anguish it suffered by unheard-of brutality, massacring over three thousand prisoners.

The official representatives of French democracy were steeped in republican ideology to such an extent that it was only some weeks later that they began to have an inkling of the significance of the June fight. They were stupefied by the gunpowder smoke in which their fantastic republic had dissolved.

The immediate impression which the news of the June defeat made on us, the reader will allow us to describe in the words of the *Neue Rheinische Zeitung:*

The last official remnant of the February revolution, the Executive Commission, has melted away, like an apparition, before the seriousness of events. The fireworks of Lamartine have turned into the war rockets of Cavaignac. *Fraternité,* the fraternity of antagonistic classes, of which one exploits the other, this *fraternité,* proclaimed in February, written in capital letters on the brow of Paris, on every prison, on every barracks—its true, unadulterated, its prosaic expression is *civil war,* civil war in its most frightful form, the war of labor and capital. This fraternity flamed in front of all the windows of Paris on the evening of June 25, when the Paris of the bourgeoisie was illuminated, while the Paris of the proletariat burned, bled, moaned. Fraternity endured just as long as the interests of the bourgeoisie were in fraternity with the interests of the proletariat. Pedants of the old revolutionary traditions of 1793; socialist doctrinaires who begged at the doors of the bourgeoisie on behalf of the people and were allowed to preach long sermons and to compromise themselves as long as the proletarian lion had to be lulled to sleep; republicans who demanded the old bourgeois order in its entirety, with the exception of the crowned head; adherents of the dynasty among the opposition upon whom accident foisted the overthrow of the dynasty instead of a change of ministers; Legitimists who did not want to cast aside the livery but to change its cut—these were the allies with whom the people made its February.

The February revolution was the *beautiful* revolution, the revolution of universal sympathy, because the antagonisms which had flared up in it against the monarchy slumbered peacefully side by side, still *undeveloped,* because the social struggle which formed its background had won only an airy existence, an existence of phrases, of words. The *June revolution* is the *ugly* revolution, the repulsive revolution, because deeds have taken the place of phrases, because the republic uncovered the head of the monster itself by striking off the crown that shielded and concealed it.

"Order!" was the battle cry of Guizot. *"Order!"* cried Sebastiani, the follower of Guizot, when Warsaw became Russian. *"Order!"* shouted Cavaignac, the brutal echo of the French National Assembly and of the republican bourgeoisie. *"Order!"* thundered his grapeshot as it ripped up the body of the proletariat. None of the numerous revolutions of the French bourgeoisie since 1789 was an attack on *order,* for they allowed the rule of the class, they allowed the slavery of the workers, they allowed the *bourgeois* order to endure, no matter how often the political form of this rule and of this slavery changed. June has violated this order. Woe to June!

"Woe to June!" re-echoes Europe.

The Paris proletariat was *forced* into the June insurrection by the bourgeoisie. In this lay its doom. Its immediate, avowed needs did not drive it to engage in a fight for the forcible overthrow of the bourgeoisie, nor was it equal to this task. The *Moniteur* had to inform it officially that the time was past when the republic saw any occasion to bow and scrape to its illusions, and only its defeat convinced it of the truth that the slightest improvement in its position remains a *utopia within* the bourgeois republic, a utopia that becomes a crime as soon as it wants to realize it. In place of its demands, exuberant in form, but petty and even bourgeois still in content, the concession of which it wanted to wring from the February republic, there appeared the bold slogan of revolutionary struggle: *Overthrow of the bourgeoisie! Dictatorship of the working class!*

By making its burial place the birthplace of the *bourgeois republic* the proletariat compelled the latter to come out forthwith in its pure form as the state whose admitted object it is to perpetuate the rule of capital, the slavery of labor. Having constantly before its eyes the scarred, irreconcilable, invincible enemy—invincible because his existence is the condition of the bourgeoisie's own life—bourgeois rule, freed from all fetters, was bound to turn immediately into *bourgeois terrorism*. With the proletariat removed for the time being from the stage and bourgeois dictatorship recognized officially, the middle sections of bourgeois society, the petty bourgeoisie and the peasant class, had to adhere more and more closely to the proletariat as their position became more and more unbearable and their antagonism to the bourgeoisie more acute. Just as earlier they had to find the cause of their misery in its upsurge, so now in its defeat.

The June insurrection raised the self-assurance of the bourgeoisie all over the Continent, and caused it to league itself openly with the feudal monarchy against the people; but who was the first victim of this alliance? The Continental bourgeoisie itself. The June defeat prevented it from consolidating its rule, and from bringing the people, half satisfied and half out of humor, to a standstill at the lowest stage of the bourgeois revolution.

Finally, the defeat of June divulged to the despotic powers of Europe the secret that France must under all conditions maintain peace abroad in order to be able to wage civil war at home. Thus the peoples who had begun the fight for their national independence were abandoned to the superior power of Russia, Austria, and Prussia, but, at the same time, the fate of these national revolutions was subordinated to the fate of the proletarian revolutions, and they were robbed of their apparent independence, their independence of the great social revolution. The Hungarian shall not be free, nor the Pole, nor the Italian, as long as the worker remains a slave!

Finally, with the victories of the Holy Alliance, Europe has taken on a form that makes every fresh proletarian upheaval in France directly coincide with a *world war*. The new French revolution is forced to leave its national soil forthwith and *conquer the European terrain,* on which alone the social revolution of the nineteenth century can be accomplished.

Thus only the June defeat has created all the conditions under which France can seize the *initiative* of the European revolution. Only after baptism in the blood of the *June insurgents* did the tricolor become the flag of the European revolution—the *red flag*.

And we exclaim: *"The revolution is dead! Long live the revolution!"*

THE EIGHTEENTH BRUMAIRE
OF LOUIS BONAPARTE

HEGEL remarks somewhere that all facts and personages of great importance in world history occur, as it were, twice. He forgot to add: the first time as tragedy, the second as farce. Caussidière for Danton, Louis Blanc for Robespierre, the *Montagne* of 1848 to 1851 for the *Montagne* of 1793 to 1795, the nephew for the uncle. And the same caricature occurs in the circumstances attending the second edition of the eighteenth Brumaire!

Men make their own history, but they do not make it just as they please; they do not make it under circumstances chosen by themselves, but under circumstances directly encountered, given, and transmitted from the past. The tradition of all the dead generations weighs like a nightmare on the brain of the living. And just when they seem engaged in revolutionizing themselves and things, in creating something that has never yet existed, precisely in such periods of revolutionary crisis they anxiously conjure up the spirits of the past to their service and borrow from them names, battle cries, and costumes in order to present the new scene of world history in this time-honored disguise and this borrowed language. Thus Luther donned the mask of the apostle Paul, the Revolution of 1789 to 1814 draped itself alternately as the Roman Republic and the Roman Empire, and the Revolution of 1848 knew nothing better to do than to parody, now 1789, now the revolutionary tradition of 1793 to 1795. In like manner a beginner who has learned a new language always translates it back into his mother tongue, but he has assimilated the spirit of the new language and can freely express himself in it only when he finds his way in it without recalling the old and forgets his native tongue in the use of the new.

Consideration of this conjuring up of the dead of world history reveals at once a salient difference. Camille Desmoulins, Danton, Robespierre, St. Just, Napoleon, the heroes as well as the parties and the masses of the old French Revolution performed the task of their time in Roman costume and with Roman phrases, the task of unchaining and setting up modern *bourgeois* society. The first ones knocked the feudal basis to pieces and mowed off the feudal heads which had grown on it. The other created inside France the conditions under which alone free competition could be developed, parceled landed property exploited, and the unchained industrial productive power of the nation employed; and beyond the French borders he everywhere swept the feudal institutions away, so far as was necessary to furnish bourgeois society in France with a suitable up-to-date environment on the European continent. The new social formation once established, the antediluvian colossi disappeared and with them resurrected Romanity—the Brutuses, Gracchi, Publicolas, the tribunes, the senators, and Caesar himself. Bourgeois society in its sober reality had begotten its true interpreters and mouthpieces in the Says, Cousins, Royer-Collards, Benjamin Constants, and Guizots; its real military leaders sat behind the office desks, and the hogsheaded Louis XVIII was its political chief. Wholly absorbed in the production of wealth and in peaceful competitive struggle, it no longer comprehended that ghosts from the days of Rome had watched over its cradle. But unheroic as bourgeois society is, it nevertheless took heroism, sacrifice, terror, civil war, and battles of peoples to bring it into being. And in the classically austere traditions of the Roman Republic its gladiators found the ideals and the art forms, the self-deceptions that they needed in order to conceal from themselves the bourgeois limitations of the content of their struggles and to keep their enthusiasm on the high plane of the great historical tragedy. Similarly, at another stage of development, a century earlier, Cromwell and the English people had borrowed speech, passions, and illusions from the Old Testament for their bourgeois revolution. When the real aim had been achieved, when the bourgeois transformation of English society had been accomplished, Locke supplanted Habakkuk.

Thus the awakening of the dead of those revolutions served the purpose of glorifying the new struggles, not of parodying the old; of magnifying the given task in imagination, not of fleeing from its solution in reality; of finding once more the spirit of revolution, not of making its ghost walk about again.

From 1848 to 1851 only the ghost of the old revolution walked about, from Marrast, the *républicain en gants jaunes,* who disguised himself as the old Bailly, down to the adventurer, who hides his commonplace repulsive features under the iron death mask of Napoleon. An entire people, which had imagined that by means of a revolution it had imparted to itself an accelerated power of motion, suddenly finds itself set back into a defunct epoch and, in order that no doubt as to the relapse may be possible, the old dates arise again, the old chronology, the old names, the old edicts, which had long become a subject of antiquarian erudition, and the old minions of the law, who had seemed long decayed. The nation feels like that mad Englishman in Bedlam who fancies that he lives in the times of the ancient Pharaohs and daily bemoans the hard labor that he must perform in the Ethiopian mines as a gold digger, immured in this subterranean prison, a dimly burning lamp fastened to his head, the overseer of the slaves behind him with a long whip, and at the exits a confused welter of barbarian mercenaries, who understand neither the forced laborers in the mines nor one another, since they speak no common language. "And all this is expected of me," sighs the mad Englishman, "of me, a freeborn Briton, in order to make gold for the old Pharaohs." "In order to pay the debts of the Bonaparte family," sighs the French nation. The Englishman, so long as he was in his right mind, could not get rid of the fixed idea of making gold. The French, so long as they were engaged in revolution, could not get rid of the memory of Napoleon, as the election of December 10 proved. They hankered to return from the perils of revolution to the fleshpots of Egypt, and December 2, 1851, was the answer. They have not only a caricature of the old Napoleon, they have the old Napoleon himself, caricatured as he must appear in the middle of the nineteenth century. . . .

And yet the state power is not suspended in mid-air. Bonaparte represents a class, and the most numerous class of French society at that, the *small-holding (Parzellen) peasants*.

Just as the Bourbons were the dynasty of big landed property and just as the Orleans' were the dynasty of money, so the Bonapartes are the dynasty of the peasants, who submitted to the bourgeois parliament, but the Bonaparte who dispersed the bourgeois parliament is the chosen of the peasantry. For three years the towns had succeeded in falsifying the meaning of the election of December 10 and in cheating the peasants out of the restoration of the empire. The election of December 10, 1848, has been consummated only by the *coup d'état* of December 2, 1851.

The small-holding peasants form a vast mass, the members of which live in similar conditions but without entering into manifold relations with one another. Their mode of production isolates them from one another instead of bringing them into mutual intercourse. The isolation is increased by France's bad means of communication and by the poverty of the peasants. Their field of production, the small holding, admits of no division of labor in its cultivation, no application of science, and, therefore, no diversity of development, no variety of talent, no wealth of social relationships. Each individual peasant family is almost self-sufficient; it itself directly produces the major part of its consumption, and thus acquires its means of life more through exchange with nature than in intercourse with society. A small holding, a peasant and his family; alongside them another small holding, another peasant and another family. A few score of these make up a village, and a few score of villages make up a Department. In this way the great mass of the French nation is formed by simple addition of homologous magnitudes, much as potatoes in a sack form a sack of potatoes. In so far as millions of families live under economic conditions of existence that separate their mode of life, their interests, and their culture from those of the other classes and put them in hostile opposition to the latter, they form a class. In so far as there is merely a local interconnection among these small-holding peasants and the identity of their interests begets no community, no national bond, and no political organization among them, they do not form a class. They are consequently incapable of enforcing their class interest in their own name, whether through a parliament or through a convention. They cannot represent themselves, they must be represented. Their representative must at the same time appear as their master, as an authority over them, as an unlimited government power that protects them against the other classes and sends them rain and sunshine from above. The political influence of the small-holding peasants, therefore, finds its final expression in the executive power subordinating society itself.

Historical tradition gave rise to the belief of the French peasants in the miracle that a man named Napoleon would bring all the glory back to them. And an individual turns up who gives himself out as the man because he bears the name of Napoleon, in consequence of the Code Napoléon, which lays down that *la recherche de la paternité est interdite*. (Research into paternity is forbidden.) After a vagabondage of twenty years and after a series of grotesque adventures the legend finds fulfillment and the man becomes Emperor of the French. The fixed idea of the nephew was realized because it coincided with the fixed idea of the most numerous class of the French people.

But, it may be objected, what about the peasant risings in half of France, the raids on the peasants by the army, the mass incarceration and transportation of peasants?

Since Louis XIV, France has experienced no similar persecution of the peasants "on account of demagogic practices."

But let there be no misunderstanding. The Bonaparte dynasty represents not the revolutionary, but the conservative peasant; not the peasant that strikes out beyond the condition of his social existence, the small holding, but rather the peasant who wants to consolidate this holding, not the country folk who, linked up with the towns, want to overthrow the old order through their own energies, but on the contrary, those who, in stupefied seclusion within this old order, want to see themselves and their small holdings saved and favored by the ghost of the empire. It represents not the enlightenment, but the superstition of the peasant; not his judgment, but his prejudice; not his future, but his past; not his modern Cevennes, but his modern Vendée.

The three-year rigorous rule of the parliamentary republic had freed a part of the French peasants from the Napoleonic illusion and had revolutionized them, even if only superficially; but the bourgeoisie violently repressed them as often as they set themselves in motion. Under the parliamentary republic the modern and the traditional consciousness of the French peasant contended for mastery. This progress took the form of an incessant struggle between the schoolmasters and the priests. The bourgeoisie struck down the schoolmasters. For the first time the peasants made efforts to behave independently in the face of the activity of the government. This was shown in the continual conflict between the *maires* and the prefects. The bourgeoisie deposed the *maires*. Finally, during the period of the parliamentary republic, the peasants of different localities rose against their own offspring, the army. The bourgeoisie punished them with states of siege and punitive expeditions. And this same bourgeoisie now cries out about the stupidity of the masses, the vile multitude, that has betrayed it to Bonaparte. It has itself forcibly strengthened the empire sentiments (*Imperialismus*) of the peasant class, it conserved the conditions that form the birthplace of this peasant religion. The bourgeoisie, to be sure, is bound to fear the stupidity of the masses as long as they remain conservative and the insight of the masses as soon as they become revolutionary.

In the risings after the *coup d'état* a part of the French peasants protested, arms in hand, against their own vote of December 10, 1848. The school they had gone through since 1848 had sharpened their wits. But they had made themselves over to the underworld of history; history held them to their word, and the majority was still so prejudiced that in precisely the reddest Departments the peasant population voted openly for Bonaparte. In its view, the National Assembly had hindered his progress. He had now merely broken the fetters that the towns had imposed on the will of the countryside. In some parts the peasants even entertained the grotesque notion of a convention side by side with Napoleon.

After the first revolution had transformed the peasants from semi-villeins into freeholders, Napoleon confirmed and regulated the conditions on which they could exploit undisturbed the soil of France which had only just fallen to their lot and slake their youthful passion for property. But what is now causing the ruin of the French peasant is his small holding itself, the division of the land, the form of property which Napoleon consolidated in France. It is precisely the material conditions which made the feudal peasant a small-holding peasant and Napoleon an emperor. Two generations have sufficed to produce the inevitable result: progressive deterioration of agriculture, progressive indebtedness of the agriculturist. The "Napoleonic" form of property, which at the beginning of the nineteenth century was the condition for the liberation and enrichment of the French country folk, has developed in the course of this century into the law of their enslavement and pauperization. And precisely this law is the first of the *"idées napoléoniennes"* which the second Bonaparte has to uphold. If he still shares with the peasants the illusion that the cause of their ruin is to be sought not in this small-holding property itself but outside it, in the influence of secondary circumstances, his experiments will burst like soap bubbles when they come in contact with the relations of production.

The economic development of small-holding property has radically changed the relation of the peasants to the other classes of society. Under Napoleon the fragmentation of the land in the countryside supplemented free competition and the beginning of big industry in the towns. The peasant class was the ubiquitous protest against the landed aristocracy, which had just been overthrown. The roots that small-holding property struck in French soil deprived feudalism of all nutriment. Its landmarks formed the natural fortifications of the bourgeoisie against any surprise attack on the part of its old overlords. But in the course of the nineteenth century the feudal lords were replaced by urban usurers; the feudal obligation that went with the land was replaced by the mortgage; aristocratic landed property was replaced by bourgeois capital. The small holding of the peasant is now only the pretext that allows the capitalist to draw profits, interest, and rent from the soil, while leaving it to the tiller of the soil himself to see how he can extract his wages. The mortgage debt burdening the soil of France imposes on the French peasantry payment of an amount of interest equal to the annual interest on the entire British national debt. Small-holding property, in this enslavement by capital to which its development inevitably pushes forward, has transformed the mass of the French nation into troglodytes. Sixteen million peasants (including women and children) dwell in hovels, a large number of which have but one opening, others only two, and the most favored only three. And windows are to a house what the five senses are to the head. The bourgeois order, which at the beginning of the century set the state to stand guard over the newly arisen small holding and manured it with laurels, has become a vampire that sucks out its blood and brains and throws them into the alchemistic cauldron of capital. The Code Napoléon is now nothing but a *codex* of distraints, forced sales, and compulsory auctions. To the four million (including children, etc.) officially recognized paupers, vagabonds, criminals, and prostitutes in France must be added five million who hover on the margin of existence and either have their haunts in the countryside itself, or, with their rags and their children, continually desert the countryside for the towns and the towns for the countryside. The interests of the peasants, therefore, are no longer, as under Napoleon, in accord with, but in opposition to the interest of the bourgeoisie, to capital. Hence the peasants find their natural ally and leader in the *urban proletariat,* whose task is the overthrow of the bourgeois order. But *strong and unlimited government*—and this is the second *"idée napoléonienne"* which the second Napoleon has to carry out —is called upon to defend this "material" order by force. This *"ordre matériel"* also serves as the catchword in all of Bonaparte's proclamations against the rebellious peasants.

Besides the mortgage which capital imposes on it, the small holding is burdened by *taxes*. Taxes are the source of life for the bureaucracy, the army, the priests, and the court, in short, for the whole apparatus of the executive power. Strong government and heavy taxes are identical. By its very nature small-holding property forms a suitable basis for an all-powerful and innumerable bureaucracy. It creates a uniform level of relationships and persons over the whole surface of the land. Hence it also permits of uniform action from a supreme center on all points of this uniform mass. It annihilates the aristocratic intermediate grades between the mass of the people and the state power. On all sides, therefore, it calls forth the direct interference of this state power and the interposition of its immediate organs. Finally, it produces an unemployed surplus population for which there is no place either on the land or in the towns, and which accordingly reaches out for state offices as a sort of respectable alms and provokes the creation of state posts. By the new markets which he opened at the point of the bayonet, by the plundering of the Continent, Napoleon repaid the compulsory taxes with interest. These taxes were a spur to the industry of the peasant, whereas now they rob his industry of its last resources and complete his inability to resist pauperism. And an enormous bureaucracy, well gallooned and well fed, is the *"idée napoléonienne"* which is most congenial of all to the second Bonaparte. How could it be otherwise, seeing that alongside the actual classes of society he is forced to create an artificial caste, for which the maintenance of his regime becomes a bread-and-butter question? Accordingly, one of his first financial operations was the raising of officials' salaries to their old level and the creation of new sinecures.

Another *"idée napoléonienne"* is the domination of the *priests* as an instrument of government. But while in its accord with society, in its dependence on natural forces and its submission to the authority which protected it from above the small holding that had newly come into being was naturally religious, the small holding that is ruined by debts, at odds with society and authority, and driven beyond its own limitations naturally becomes irreligious. Heaven was quite a pleasing accession to the narrow strip of land just won, more particularly as it makes the weather; it becomes an insult as soon as it is thrust forward as substitute for the small holding. The priest then appears as only the anointed bloodhound of the earthly police— another *"idée napoléonienne."* On the next occasion, the expedition against Rome will take place in France itself, but in a sense opposite to that of M. de Montalembert.

Lastly, the culminating point of the *"idées napoléoniennes"* is the preponderance of the *army*. The army was the *point d'honneur* of the small-holding peasants; it was they themselves transformed into heroes, defending their new possessions against the outer world, glorifying their recently won nationhood, plundering and revolutionizing the world. The uniform was their own state dress; war was their poetry; the small holding, extended and rounded off in imagination, was their fatherland, and patriotism the ideal form of the sense of property. But the enemies against whom the French peasant has now to defend his property are not the Cossacks; they are the *huissiers* and the tax collectors. The small holding lies no longer in the so-called fatherland, but in the register of mortgages. The army itself is no longer the flower of the peasant youth; it is the swamp flower of the peasant *lumpenproletariat.* It consists in large measure of *remplaçants,* of substitutes, just as the second Bonaparte is himself only a *remplaçant,* the substitute for Napoleon. It now performs its deeds of valor by hounding the peasants in masses like chamois, by doing *gendarme* duty, and if the internal contradictions of his system chase the chief of the Society of December 10 over the French border, his army, after some acts of brigandage, will reap not laurels, but thrashings.

One see all *"idées napoléoniennes" are ideas of the undeveloped small holding in the freshness of its youth;* for the small holding that has outlived its day, they are an absurdity. They are only the hallucinations of its death struggle, words that are transformed into phrases, spirits transformed into ghosts. But the parody of the empire (*das Imperialismus*) was necessary to free the mass of the French nation from the weight of tradition and to work out in pure form the opposition between the state power and society. With the progressive undermining of small-holding property, the state structure erected upon it collapses. The centralization of the state that modern society requires arises only on the ruins of the military bureaucratic government machinery which was forged in opposition to feudalism.

The condition of the French peasants provides us with the answer to the riddle of the *general elections of December 20 and 21,* which bore the second Bonaparte up Mount Sinai not to receive laws, but to give them.

Manifestly the bourgeoisie had now no choice but to elect Bonaparte. When the puritans at the Council of Constance complained of the dissolute lives of the popes and wailed about the necessity of moral reform, Cardinal Pierre d'Ailly thundered at them: "Only the devil in person can still save the Catholic Church, and you ask for angels." In like manner, after the *coup d'état,* the French bourgeoisie cried: "Only the chief of the Society of December 10 can still save bourgeois society! Only theft can still save property; only perjury, religion, bastardy, the family; disorder, order!"

As the executive authority which has made itself an independent power, Bonaparte feels it to be his mission to safeguard "bourgeois order." But the strength of this bourgeois order lies in the middle class. He looks on himself, therefore, as the representative of the middle class, and issues decrees in this sense. Nevertheless, he is somebody solely due to the fact that he has broken the political power of this middle class and daily breaks it anew. Consequently he looks on himself as the adversary of the political and literary power of the middle class. But by protecting its material power he generates its political power anew. The cause must accordingly be kept alive, but the effect, where it manifests itself, must be done away with. But this cannot pass off without slight confusions of cause and effect, since in their interaction both lose their distinguishing features. New decrees that obliterate the border line. As against the bourgeoisie, Bonaparte looks on himself, at the same time, as the representative of the peasants and of the people in general, who wants to make the lower classes of the people happy within the frame of bourgeois society. New decrees that cheat the "true socialists" of their statecraft in advance. But, above all, Bonaparte looks on himself as the chief of the Society of December 10, as the representative of the *lumpenproletariat,* to which he himself, his *entourage,* his government, and his army belong, and whose prime consideration is to benefit itself and draw California lottery prizes from the state treasury. And he vindicates his position as chief of the Society of December 10 with decrees, and despite decrees.

This contradictory task of the man explains the contradictions of his government, the confused groping about which seeks now to win, now to humiliate first one class and then another and arrays all of them uniformly against him, whose practical uncertainty forms a highly comical contrast to the imperious, categorical style of the government decrees, a style which is faithfully copied from the uncle.

Industry and trade, hence the business affairs of the middle class, are to prosper in hothouse fashion under the strong government. The grant of innumerable railway concessions. But the Bonapartist *lumpenproletariat* is to enrich itself. The initiated play *tripotage* on the Bourse with the railway concessions. But no capital is forthcoming for the railways. Obligation of the Bank to make advances on railway shares. But, at the same time, the Bank is to be exploited for personal ends and therefore must be cajoled. Release of the Bank from the obligation to publish its report weekly. Leonine agreement of the Bank with the government. The people are to be given employment. Initiation of public works. But the public works increase the obligations of the people in respect of taxes. Hence reduction of the taxes by an onslaught on the *rentiers,* by conversion of the 5 per cent bonds to 4½ per cents. But, once more, the middle class must receive a *douceur.* Therefore doubling of the wine tax for the people, who buy it *en détail,* and halving of the wine tax for the middle class, who drink it *en gros*. Dissolution of the actual workers' associations, but promises of miracles of association in the future. The peasants are to be helped. Mortgage banks that expedite their getting into debt and accelerate the concentration of property. But these banks are to be used to make money out of the confiscated estates of the house of Orleans. No capitalist wants to agree to this condition, which is not in the decree, and the mortgage bank remains a mere decree, etc.

Bonaparte would like to appear as the patriarchal benefactor of all classes. But he cannot give to one class without taking from another. Just as at the time of the Fronde it was said of the Duke of Guise that he was the most *obligeant* man in France because he had turned all his estates into his partisans' obligations to him, so Bonaparte would fain be the most *obligeant* man in France and turn all the property, all the labor of France into a personal obligation to himself. He would like to steal the whole of France in order to be able to make a present of her to France or, rather, in order to be able to buy France anew with French money, for as the chief of the Society of December 10 he must needs buy what ought to belong to him. And all the state institutions, the Senate, the Council of State, the legislative body, the Legion of Honor, the Soldiers' medals, the washhouses, the public works, the railways, the *état major* of the National Guard to the exclusion of privates, and the confiscated estates of the house of Orleans—all become parts of the institution of purchase. Every place in the army and in the government machine becomes a means of purchase. But the most important feature of this process, whereby France is taken in order to give to her, is the percentages that find their way into the pockets of the head and the members of the Society of December 10 during the turnover. The witticism with which Countess L., the mistress of M. de Morny, characterized the confiscation of the Orleans' estates: *"C'est le premier vol de l'aigle,"* is applicable to every flight of this *eagle*, which is more like a *raven*. He himself and his adherents call out to one another daily like that Italian Carthusian admonishing the miser, who, with boastful display, counted up the goods on which he could yet live for years to come: *"Tu fai conto sopra i beni, bisogna prima far il conto sopra gli anni* (Thou countest thy goods, thou shouldst first count thy years)."* Lest they make a mistake in the years, they count the minutes. A bunch of blokes push their way forward to the court, into the ministries, to the head of the administration and the army, a crowd of the best of whom it must be said that no one knows whence he comes, a noisy, disreputable, rapacious *bohème* that crawls into gallooned coats with the same grotesque dignity as the high dignitaries of Soulouque. One can visualize clearly this upper stratum of the Society of December 10 if one reflects that *Véron-Crevel* is its preacher of morals and *Granier de Cassagnac* its thinker. When Guizot, at the time of his ministry, utilized this Granier on a hole-and-corner newspaper against the dynastic opposition, he used to boast of him with the quip: "*C'est le roi des drôles* (He is the king of buffoons)." One would do wrong to recall the regency of Louis XV in connection with Louis Bonaparte's court and clique. For "often already, France has experienced a government of mistresses, but never before a government of *hommes entretenus* (kept men)."

Driven by the contradictory demands of his situation and being at the same time, like a conjurer, under the necessity of keeping the public gaze fixed on himself, as Napoleon's substitute, by springing constant surprises, that is to say, under the necessity of executing a *coup d'état en miniature* every day, Bonaparte throws the entire bourgeois economy into confusion, violates everything that seemed inviolable to the Revolution of 1848, makes some tolerant of revolution, others desirous of revolution, and produces actual anarchy in the name of order, while at the same time stripping its halo from the entire state machine, profanes it and makes it at once loathsome and ridiculous. The cult of the Holy Tunic of Treves he duplicates at Paris in the cult of the Napoleonic imperial mantle. But when the imperial mantle finally falls on the shoulders of Louis Bonaparte, the bronze statue of Napoleon will crash from the top of the Vendôme Column.

VI RELIGION AND ETHICS IN THE AGE OF DARWIN

AUGUSTE COMTE

Auguste Comte (1798–1857), born at Montpellier of Catholic royalist parents, developed into intellectual maturity during the period of reaction to the predominantly individualistic social philosophy of the Enlightenment. The writings of Joseph de Maistre and others had made him sensitive to the historical and "organic" nature of society; and he soon became impatient with attempts, such as that of the Jacobins of the French Revolution, to create new systems of society without taking into account the laws of historical development. "Society does not and cannot progress in this way," he wrote in 1822; "the pretension of constructing offhand in a few months or even years a social system, in its complete and definite shape, is an extravagant chimera absolutely incompatible with the weakness of the human intellect." His lifework had a twofold objective: (1) the generalization of scientific conceptions so that they could be applied to the study of society; and (2) the systematization of the art of social life so that intellect could be subordinated to social feeling. Consonant with his conviction that a new moral faith must be developed to replace the spiritual loyalties destroyed by the French Revolution, the culmination of his system was a new "religion of humanity," whose aim was to foster universal altruism and whose motto was "Order and progress—live for others."

Comte's importance as a thinker derives from his systematic use of the method of comparative historical analysis in social studies and his ambitious attempt to trace the main course of social development. He borrowed heavily not only from Maistre and Saint–Simon but also from Plato, Hume, Montesquieu, Turgot, Kant, and Condorcet. In the first of his two major works, the *System of Positive Philosophy* (published in six volumes between 1830 and 1842), he tried to show by a detailed analysis of science and history that sociology (a word he coined) could and inevitably must become a full-fledged science. He argued that every science must pass through three stages of development and that all sciences except sociology have gone through the full cycle of evolution.

Comte believed that sociology, which he regarded as being still in a metaphysical stage of growth, was about to enter the positivistic period of its development. The full details of Comte's conception of society were provided in the *System of Positive Polity* (published in four volumes between 1851 and 1854), where he argued that a natural need for a central coordinating agency in a positivistic society would have to be performed by the priests of a new "Religion of Humanity" who would be specialists in sociology rather than theology.

The first of the following selections is taken from *The Positive Philosophy,* as "freely translated and condensed" by Harriet Martineau (3d ed., 1856). The second selection is from the second edition of the *General View of Positivism* (1851), which first appeared in 1848. It was translated from the French by J. H. Bridges.

THE POSITIVE PHILOSOPHY

IN ORDER TO UNDERSTAND the true value and character of the Positive Philosophy, we must take a brief general view of the progressive course of the human mind, regarded as a whole; for no conception can be understood otherwise than through its history.

From the study of the development of human intelligence, in all directions, and through all times, the discovery arises of a great fundamental law, to which it is necessarily subject, and which has a solid foundation of proof, both in the facts of our organization and in our historical experience. The law is this:—that each of our leading conceptions—each branch of our knowledge —passes successively through three different theoretical conditions: the Theological, or fictitious; the Metaphysical, or abstract; and the Scientific, or positive. In other words, the human mind, by its nature, employs in its progress three methods of philosophizing, the character of which is essentially different, and even radically opposed: viz., the theological method, the metaphysical, and the positive. Hence arise three philosophies, or general systems of conceptions on the aggregate of phenomena, each of which excludes the others. The first is the necessary point of departure of the human understanding; and the third is its fixed and definite state. The second is merely a state of transition.

In the theological state, the human mind, seeking the essential nature of beings, the first and final causes (the origin and purpose) of all effects—in short, Absolute knowledge—supposes all phenomena to be produced by the immediate action of supernatural beings.

In the metaphysical state, which is only a modification of the first, the mind supposes, instead of supernatural beings, abstract forces, veritable entities (that is, personified abstractions) inherent in all beings, and capable of producing all phenomena. What is called the explanation of phenomena is, in this stage, a mere reference of each to its proper entity.

In the final, the positive state, the mind has given over the vain search after Absolute notions, the origin and destination of the universe, and the causes of phenomena, and applies itself to the study of their laws—that is, their invariable relations of succession and resemblance. Reasoning and observation, duly combined, are the means of this knowledge. What is now understood when we speak of an explanation of facts is simply the establishment of a connection between single phenomena and some general facts, the number of which continually diminishes with the progress of science.

The Theological system arrived at the highest perfection of which it is capable when it substituted the providential action of a single Being for the varied operations of the numerous divinities which had been before imagined. In the same way, in the last stage of the Metaphysical system, men substitute one great entity (Nature) as the cause of all phenomena, instead of the multitude of entities at first supposed. In the same way, again, the ultimate perfection of the Positive system would be (if such perfection could be hoped for) to represent all phenomena as particular aspects of a single general fact—such as Gravitation, for instance.

The importance of the working of this general law will be established hereafter. At present, it must suffice to point out some of the grounds of it.

There is no science which, having attained the positive stage, does not bear the marks of having passed through the others. Some time since it was (whatever it might be) composed, as we can now perceive, of metaphysical abstractions; and, further back in the course of time, it took its form from theological conceptions. We shall have only too much occasion to see, as we proceed, that our most advanced sciences still bear very evident marks of the two earlier periods through which they have passed.

The progress of the individual mind is not only an illustration, but an indirect evidence of that of the general mind. The point of departure of the individual and of the race being the same, the phases of the mind of a man correspond to the epochs of the mind of the race. Now, each of us is aware, if he looks back upon his own history, that he was a theologian in his childhood, a metaphysician in his youth, and a natural philosopher in his manhood. All men who are up to their age can verify this for themselves.

Besides the observation of facts, we have theoretical reasons in support of this law.

The most important of these reasons arises from the necessity that always exists for some theory to which to refer our facts, combined with the clear impossibility that, at the outset of human knowledge, men could have formed theories out of the observation of facts. All good intellects have repeated, since Bacon's time, that there can be no real knowledge but that which is based on observed facts. This is incontestable, in our present advanced stage; but, if we look back to the primitive stage of human knowledge, we shall see that it must have been otherwise then. If it is true that every theory must be based upon observed facts, it is equally true that facts can not be observed without the guidance of some theory. Without such guidance, our facts would be desultory and fruitless; we could not retain them: for the most part we could not even perceive them.

Thus, between the necessity of observing facts in order to form a theory, and having a theory in order to observe facts, the human mind would have been entangled in a vicious circle, but for the natural opening afforded by Theological conceptions. This is the fundamental reason for the theological character of the primitive philosophy. This necessity is confirmed by the perfect suitability of the theological philosophy to the earliest researches of the human mind. It is remarkable that the most inaccessible questions—those of the nature of beings, and the origin and purpose of phenomena—should be the first to occur in a primitive state, while those which are really within our reach are regarded as almost unworthy of serious study. The reason is evident enough:—that experience alone can teach us the measure of our powers; and if men had not begun by an exaggerated estimate of what they can do, they would never have done all that they are capable of. Our organization requires this. At such a period there could have been no reception of a positive philosophy, whose function is to discover the laws of phenomena, and whose leading characteristic it is to regard as interdicted to human reason those sublime mysteries which theology explains, even to their minutest details, with the most attractive facility. It is just so under a practical view of the nature of the researches with which men first occupied themselves. Such inquiries offered the powerful charm of unlimited empire over the external world—a world destined wholly for our use, and involved in every way with our existence. The theological philosophy, presenting this view, administered exactly the stimulus necessary to incite the human mind to the irksome labor without which it could make no progress. We can now scarcely conceive of such a state of things, our reason having become sufficiently mature to enter upon laborious scientific researches, without needing any such stimulus as wrought upon the imaginations of astrologers and alchemists. We have motive enough in the hope of discovering the laws of phenomena, with a view to the confirmation or rejection of a theory. But it could not be so in the earliest days; and it is to the chimeras of astrology and alchemy that we owe the long series of observations and experiments on which our positive science is based. Kepler felt this on behalf of astronomy, and Berthollet on behalf of chemistry. Thus was a spontaneous philosophy, the theological, the only possible beginning, method, and provisional system, out of which the Positive philosophy could grow. It is easy, after this, to perceive how Metaphysical methods and doctrines must have afforded the means of transition from the one to the other.

The human understanding, slow in its advance, could not step at once from the theological into the positive philosophy. The two are so radically opposed, that an intermediate system of conceptions has been necessary to render the transition possible. It is only in doing this, that metaphysical conceptions have any utility whatever. In contemplating phenomena, men substitute for supernatural direction a corresponding entity. This entity may have been supposed to be derived from the supernatural action: but it is more easily lost sight of, leaving attention free from the facts themselves, till, at length, metaphysical agents have ceased to be anything more than the abstract names of phenomena. It is not easy to say by what other process than this our minds could have passed from supernatural considerations to natural; from the theological system to the positive. . . .

Though involved with the physiological, Social phenomena demand a distinct classification, both on account of their importance and of their difficulty. They are the most individual, the most complicated, the most dependent on all others; and therefore they must be the latest,—even if they had no special obstacle to encounter. This branch of science has not hitherto entered into the domain of Positive philosophy. Theological and metaphysical methods, exploded in other departments, are as yet exclusively applied, both in the way of inquiry and discussion, in all treatment of Social subjects, though the best minds are heartily weary of eternal disputes about divine right and the sovereignty of the people. This is the great, while it is evidently the only gap which has to be filled, to constitute, solid and entire, the Positive Philosophy. Now that the human mind has grasped celestial and terrestrial physics,—mechanical and chemical; organic physics, both vegetable and animal,—there remains one science, to fill up the series of sciences of observation,—Social physics. . . .

The philosophical principle of the science being that social phenomena are subject to natural laws, admitting of rational prevision, we have to ascertain what is the precise subject, and what the peculiar character of those laws. The distinction between the Statical and Dynamical conditions of the subject must be extended to social science. . . .

The statical study of sociology consists in the investigation of the laws of action and reaction of the different parts of the social system—apart, for the occasion, from the fundamental movement which is always gradually modifying them. In this view, sociological prevision, founded upon the exact general knowledge of those relations, acts by judging by each other the various statical indications of each mode of social existence, in conformity with direct observation—just as is done daily in the case of anatomy. This view condemns the existing philosophical practice of contemplating social elements separately, as if they had an independent existence; and it leads us to regard them as in mutual relation, and forming a whole which compels us to treat them in combination. By this method, not only are we furnished with the only possible basis for the study of social movement, but we are put in possession of an important aid to direct observation; since many social elements which can not be investigated by immediate observation, may be estimated by their scientific relation to others already known. . . .

It follows from this attribute that there can be no scientific study of society, either in its conditions or its movements, if it is separated into portions, and its divisions are studied apart. . . . Materials may be furnished by the observation of different departments; and such observation may be necessary for that object; but it can not be called science. The methodical division of studies which takes place in the simple inorganic sciences is thoroughly irrational in the recent and complex science of society, and can produce no results. The day may come when some sort of subdivision may be practicable and desirable; but it is impossible for us now to anticipate what the principle of distribution may be; for the principle itself must arise from the development of the science; and that development can take place not otherwise than by our formation of the science as a whole. The complete body will indicate for itself, at the right season, the particular points which need investigation; and then will be the time for such special study as may be required. By any other method of proceeding, we shall only find ourselves encumbered with special discussions, badly instituted, worse pursued, and accomplishing no other purpose than that of impeding the formation of real science. It is no easy matter to study social phenomena in the only right way,—viewing each element in the light of the whole system. It is no easy matter to exercise such vigilance as that no one of the number of contemporary aspects shall be lost sight of. But it is the right and the only way; and we may perceive in it a clear suggestion that this lofty study should be reserved for the highest order of scientific minds, better prepared than others, by wise educational discipline, for sustained speculative efforts, aided by an habitual subordination of the passions to the reason. . . .

Though the statical view of society is the basis of sociology, the dynamical view is not only the more interesting of the two, but the more marked in its philosophical character from its being more distinguished from biology by the master-thought of continuous progress, or rather, of the gradual development of humanity. If I were writing a methodical treatise on political philosophy, it would be necessary to offer a preliminary analysis of the individual impulsions which make up the progressive force of the human race, by referring them to that instinct which results from the concurrence of all our natural tendencies, and which urges man to develop the whole of his life, physical, moral, and intellectual, as far as his circumstances allow. But this view is admitted by all enlightened philosophers; so that I may proceed at once to consider the continuous succession of human development, regarded in the whole race, as if humanity were one. For clearness, we may take advantage of Condorcet's device of supposing a single nation to which we may refer all the consecutive social modifications actually witnessed among distinct peoples. This rational fiction is nearer the reality than we are accustomed to suppose; for, in a political view, the true successors of such or such a people are certainly those who, taking up and carrying out their primitive endeavors, have prolonged their social progress, whatever may be the soil which they inhabit, or even the race from which they spring. In brief, it is political continuity which regulates sociological succession, though the having a common country must usually affect this continuity in a high degree. As a scientific artifice merely, however, I shall employ this hypothesis, and on the ground of its manifest utility.

The true general spirit of social dynamics then consists in conceiving of each of these consecutive social states as the necessary result of the preceding, and the indispensable move of the following, according to the axiom of Leibnitz—*the present is big with the future*. In this view, the object of science is to discover the laws which govern this continuity, and the aggregate of which determines the course of human development. In short, social dynamics studies the laws of succession, while social statics inquires into those of co-existence; so that the use of the first is to furnish the true theory of progress to political practice, while the second performs the same service in regard to order; and this suitability to the needs of modern society is a strong confirmation of the philosophical character of such a combination.

If the existence of sociological laws has been established in the more difficult and uncertain case of the statical condition, we may assume that they will not be questioned in the dynamical province. In all times and places, the ordinary course of even our brief individual life has disclosed certain remarkable modifications which have occurred, in various ways, in the social state; and all the most ancient representations of human life bear unconscious and most interesting testimony to this, apart from all systematic estimate of the fact. Now it is the slow, continuous accumulation of these successive changes which gradually constitutes the social movement, whose steps are ordinarily marked by generations, as the most appreciable elementary variations are wrought by the constant renewal of adults. At a time when the average rapidity of this progression seems to all eyes to be remarkably accelerated, the reality of the movement can not be disputed, even by those who most abhor it. The only question is about the constant subjection of these great dynamical phenomena to invariable natural laws, a proposition about which there is no question to any one who takes his stand on positive philosophy. It is easy however to establish, from any point of view, that the successive modifications of society have always taken place in a determinate order, the rational explanation of which is already possible in so many cases that we may confidently hope to recognise it ultimately in all the rest. So remarkable is the steadiness of this order, moreover, that it exhibits an exact parallelism of development among distinct and independent populations, as we shall see when we come to the historical portion of this volume. Since, then, the existence of the social movement is unquestionable, on the one hand, and, on the other, the succession of social states is never arbitrary, we can not but regard this continuous phenomenon as subject to natural laws as positive as those which govern all other phenomena, though more complex. There is in fact no intellectual alternative; and thus it is evident that it is on the ground of social science that the great conflict must soon terminate which has gone on for three centuries between the positive and the theologico-metaphysical spirit. Banished for ever from all other classes of speculation, in principle at least, the old philosophies now prevail in social science alone; and it is from this domain that they have to be excluded, by the conception of the social movement being subject to invariable natural laws, instead of to any will whatever. . . .

. . . Whatever may be the importance of the ideas communicated by the inorganic sciences to sociology, the scientific office must especially belong to biology, which, from the nature of the subjects concerned, must always furnish the fundamental ideas that must guide sociological research; and often even rectify or improve the results. Moreover, it is biology which presents to us the domestic state, intermediate between individual and social existence, which is more or less common to all the superior animals, and which is, in our species, the true primitive basis of the more vast collective organism. However, the first elaboration of this new science could not but be essentially dynamical; so that the laws of harmony have nearly throughout been implicitly considered among the laws of succession, in which alone social physics can at present consist. The scientific link between biology and sociology is the connection of their two series, by which the second may be regarded as the prolongation of the first, though the terms of the one may be successive, and of the other, coexisting. With this difference, we find that the essential character of the human evolution results from the growing power of the superior attributes which place Man at the head of the animal hierarchy, where they also enable us to assign the chief degrees of animality. Thus we see the vast organic system really connecting the humblest vegetative existence with the noblest social life through a long succession, which, if necessarily discontinuous, is not the less essentially homogeneous. And, in as far as the principle of such a connection consists in the decreasing generality of the chief phenomena, this double organic series is connected with the rudimentary inorganic, the interior succession of which is determined by the same principle. The necessary direction of the human movement being thus ascertained, the only remaining task, in constituting sociology, was to mark out its general course. This was done by my ascertaining the law of evolution, which in connection with the hierarchical law, establishes a true philosophical system, the two chief elements of which are absolutely interconnected. In this dynamical conception, sociology is radically connected with biology, since the original state of humanity essentially coincides with that in which the superior animals are detained by their organic imperfection,—their speculative ability never transcending the primitive fetichism from which man could not have issued but for the strong impulsion of the collective development. The resemblance is yet stronger in the practical aspect. The sociological theory being thus constituted, nothing remained but to put it to the proof by an historical application of it to the intellectual and social progression of the most advanced portion of the human race through forty centuries. This test has discredited all the historical conceptions proposed before, and has shown the reality of the theory by explaining and estimating each phase as it passed in review, so as to enable us to do honor to the services of the most opposite influences,—as in the case of the polytheistic and monotheistic states. A political and philosophical preparation like this was necessary to emancipate the mind of the inquirer from the old philosophy and critical prejudices, and to substitute for them the scientific condition of mind which is indispensable for the humblest speculations, but far more necessary, and at the same time more difficult, in the case of the most transcendent and the most impassioned researches that the human mind can undertake.

A GENERAL VIEW OF POSITIVISM

POSITIVISM CONSISTS essentially of a Philosophy and a Polity. These can never be dissevered; the former being the basis, and the latter the end of one comprehensive system, in which our intellectual faculties and our social sympathies are brought into close correlation with each other. For, in the first place, the science of Society, besides being more important than any other, supplies the only logical and scientific link by which all our varied observations of phenomena can be brought into one consistent whole. Of this science it is even more true than of any of the preceding sciences, that its real character cannot be understood without explaining its exact relation in all general features with the art corresponding to it. Now here we find a coincidence which is assuredly not fortuitous. At the very time when the theory of society is being laid down, an immense sphere is opened for the application of that theory; the direction, namely, of the social regeneration of Western Europe. For, if we take another point of view, and look at the great crisis of modern history, as its character is displayed in the natural course of events, it becomes every day more evident how hopeless is the task of reconstructing political institutions without the previous remodelling of opinion and of life. To form then a satisfactory synthesis of all human conceptions is the most urgent of our social wants: and it is needed equally for the sake of Order and of Progress. During the gradual accomplishment of this great philosophical work, a new moral power will arise spontaneously throughout the West, which, as its influence increases, will lay down a definite basis for the reorganization of society. It will offer a general system of education for the adoption of all civilized nations, and by this means will supply in every department of public and private life fixed principles of judgment and of conduct. Thus the intellectual movement and the social crisis will be brought continually into close connection with each other. Both will combine to prepare the advanced portion of humanity for the acceptance of a true spiritual power, a power more coherent, as well as more progressive, than the noble but premature attempt of mediaeval Catholicism.

The primary object, then, of Positivism is twofold: to generalize our scientific conceptions, and to systematize the art of social life. These are but two aspects of one and the same problem. They will form the subjects of the two first chapters of this work. I shall first explain the general spirit of the new philosophy. I shall then show its necessary connection with the whole course of that vast revolution which is now about to terminate under its guidance in social reconstruction.

This will lead us naturally to another question. The regenerating doctrine cannot do its work without adherents; in what quarter should we hope to find them? Now, with individual exceptions of great value, we cannot expect the adhesion of any of the upper classes in society. They are all more or less under the influence of baseless metaphysical theories, and of aristocratic self-seeking. They are absorbed in blind political agitation, and in disputes for the possession of the useless remnants of the old theological and military system. Their action only tends to prolong the revolutionary state indefinitely, and can never result in true social renovation.

Whether we regard its intellectual character or its social objects, it is certain that Positivism must look elsewhere for support. It will find a welcome in those classes only whose good sense has been left unimpaired by our vicious system of education, and whose generous sympathies are allowed to develop themselves freely. It is among Women, therefore, and among the Working classes that the heartiest supporters of the new doctrines will be found. It is intended, indeed, ultimately for all classes of society. But it will never gain much real influence over the higher ranks till it is forced upon their notice by these powerful patrons. When the work of spiritual reorganization is completed, it is on them that its maintenance will principally depend; and so too, their combined aid is necessary for its commencement. Having but little influence in political government, they are the more likely to appreciate the need of a moral government the special object of which it will be to protect them against the oppressive action of the temporal power. . . .

Thus it is that a philosophy originating in speculations of the most abstract character, is found applicable not merely to every department of practical life, but also to the sphere of our moral nature. But to complete the proof of its universality I have still to speak of another very essential feature. I shall show, in spite of prejudices which exist very naturally on this point, that Positivism is eminently calculated to call the Imaginative faculties into exercise. It is by these faculties that the unity of human nature is most distinctly represented: they are themselves intellectual, but their field lies principally in our moral nature, and the result of their operation is to influence the active powers. The subject of women treated in the fourth chapter, will lead me by a natural transition to speak in the fifth of the Esthetic aspects of Positivism. I shall attempt to show that the new doctrine by the very fact of embracing the whole range of human relations in the spirit of reality, discloses the true theory of Art, which has hitherto been so great a deficiency in our speculative conceptions. The principle of the theory is that, in co-ordinating the primary functions of Humanity, Positivism places the Idealities of the poet midway between the Ideas of the philosopher and the Realities of the statesman. We see from this theory how it is that the poetical power of Positivism cannot be manifested at present. We must wait until moral and mental regeneration has advanced far enough to awaken the sympathies which naturally belong to it, and on which Art in its renewed state must depend for the future. The first mental and social shock once passed, Poetry will at last take her proper rank. She will lead Humanity onward towards a future which is now no longer vague and visionary while at the same time she enables us to pay due honour to all phases of the past. The great object which Positivism sets before us individually and socially, is the endeavour to become more perfect. The highest importance is attached therefore to the imaginative faculties, because in every sphere with which they deal they stimulate the sense of perfection. Limited as my explanations in this work must be, I shall be able to show that Positivism, while opening out a new and wide field for art, supplies in the same spontaneous way new means of expression. . . .

As summed up in the Positivist motto, *Love, Order, Progress* they lead us to the conception of Humanity, which implicitly involves and gives new force of each of them. Rightly interpreting this conception, we view Positivism at last as a complete and consistent whole. The subject will naturally lead us to speak in general terms of the future progress of social regeneration, as far as the history of the past enables us to foresee it. The movement originates in France, and is limited at first to the great family of Western nations. I shall show that it will afterwards extend, in accordance with definite laws, to the rest of the white race, and finally to the other two great races of man. . .

It will now not be difficult to show that all the characteristics of Positivism are summed up in its motto, *Order and Progress,* a motto which has a philosophical as well as political bearing, and which I shall always feel glad to have put forward.

Positivism is the only school which has given a definite significance to these two conceptions, whether regarded from their scientific or their social aspect. With regard to Progress, the assertion will hardly be disputed, no definition of it but the Positive ever having yet been given. In the case of Order, it is less apparent; but as I have shown in the first chapter, it is no less profoundly true. All previous philosophies had regarded Order as stationary, a conception which rendered it wholly inapplicable to modern politics. But Positivism, by rejecting the absolute, and yet not introducing the arbitrary, represents Order in a totally new light, and adapts it to our progressive civilization. It places it on the firmest possible foundation, that is, on the doctrine of the invariability of the laws of nature, which defends it against all danger from subjective chimeras. The Positivist regards artificial Order in Social phenomena, as in all others, as resting necessarily upon the Order of nature, in other words, upon the whole series of natural laws.

But Order has to be reconciled with Progress: and here Positivism is still more obviously without a rival. Necessary as the reconciliation is, no other system has even attempted it. But the facility with which we are now enabled, by the encyclopaedic scale, to pass from the simplest mathematical phenomena to the most complicated phenomena of political life, leads at once to a solution of the problem. Viewed scientifically, it is an instance of that necessary correlation of existence and movement, which we find indicated in the inorganic world, and which becomes still more distinct in Biology. Finding it in all the lower sciences, we are prepared for its appearance in a still more definite shape in Sociology. Here its practical importance becomes more obvious, though it had been implicitly involved before. In Sociology the correlation assumes this form: Order is the condition of all Progress; Progress is always the object of Order. Or, to penetrate the question still more deeply, Progress may be regarded simply as the development of Order; for the order of nature necessarily contains within itself the germ of all possible progress. The rational view of human affairs is to look on all their changes, not as new Creations, but as new Evolutions. And we find this principle fully borne out in history. Every social innovation has its roots in the past; and the rudest phases of savage life show the primitive trace of all subsequent improvement. Progress then is in its essence identical with Order, and may be looked upon as Order made manifest.

Therefore, in explaining this double conception on which the Science and Art of society depend, we may at present limit ourselves to the analysis of Progress. Thus simplified it is more easy to grasp, especially now that the novelty and importance of the question of Progress are attracting so much attention. For the public is becoming instinctively alive to its real significance, as the basis on which all sound moral and political teaching must henceforth rest.

Taking, then, this point of view, we may say that the one great object of life, personal and social, is to become more perfect in every way; in our external condition first, but also, and more especially, in our own nature. The first kind of Progress we share in common with the higher animals; all of which make some efforts to improve their material position. It is of course the least elevated stage of progress; but being the easiest, it is the point from which we start towards the higher stages. A nation that has made no efforts to improve itself materially, will take but little interest in moral or mental improvement. This is the only ground on which enlightened men can feel much pleasure in the material progress of our own times. It stirs up influences that tend to the nobler kinds of Progress; influences which would meet with even greater opposition than they do, were not the temptations presented to the coarser natures by material prosperity so irresistible. Owing to the mental and moral anarchy in which we live, systematic efforts to gain the higher degrees of Progress are as yet impossible; and this explains, though it does not justify, the exaggerated importance attributed nowadays to material improvements. But the only kinds of improvement really characteristic of Humanity are those which concern our own nature; and even here we are not quite alone; for several of the higher animals show some slight tendencies to improve themselves physically.

Progress in the higher sense includes improvements of three sorts; that is to say, it may be Physical, Intellectual, or Moral progress; the difficulty of each class being in proportion to its value and the extent of its sphere. Physical progress, which again might be divided on the same principle, seems under some of its aspects almost the same thing as material. But regarded as a whole it is far more important and far more difficult: its influence on the well-being of Man is also much greater. We gain more, for instance, by the smallest addition to length of life, or by any increased security for health, than by the most elaborate improvements in our modes of travelling by land or water, in which birds will probably always have a great advantage over us. However, as I said before, physical progress is not exclusively confined to Man. Some of the animals, for instance, advance as far as cleanliness, which is the first step in the progressive scale.

Intellectual and Moral progress, then, is the only kind really distinctive of our race. Individual animals sometimes show it, but never a whole species, except as a consequence of prolonged intervention on the part of Man. Between these two highest grades, as between the two lower, we shall find a difference of value, extent, and difficulty; always supposing the standard to be the manner in which they affect Man's well-being collectively or individually. To strengthen the intellectual powers, whether for art or for science, whether it be the powers of observation or those of induction and deduction, is, when circumstances allow of their being made available for social purposes, of greater and more extensive importance, than all physical and a fortiori than all material improvements. But we know from the fundamental principle laid down in the first chapter of this work that moral progress has even more to do with our well-being than intellectual progress. The moral faculties are more modifiable, although the effort required to modify them is greater. If the benevolence or courage of the human race were increased, it would bring more real happiness than any addition to our intellectual powers. Therefore, to the question, What is the true object of human life, whether looked at collectively or individually? the simplest and most precise answer would be, the perfection of our moral nature; since it has a more immediate and certain influence on our well-being than perfection of any other kind. All the other kinds are necessary, if for no other reason than to prepare the way for this; but from the very fact of this connection, it may be regarded as their representative; since it involves them all implicitly and stimulates them to increased activity. Keeping then to the question of moral perfection, we find two qualities standing above the rest in practical importance, namely, Sympathy and Energy. Both these qualities are included in the word *Heart,* which in all European languages has a different meaning for the two sexes. Both will be developed by Positivism, more directly, more continuously, and with greater result, than under any former system. The whole tendency of Positivism is to encourage sympathy; since it subordinates every thought, desire, and action to social feeling. Energy is also presupposed, and at the same time fostered by the system. For it removes a heavy weight of superstition, it reveals the true dignity of man, and it supplies an unceasing motive for individual and collective action. The very acceptance of Positivism demands some vigour of character, it implies the braving of spiritual terrors, which were once enough to intimidate the firmest minds.

Progress, then, may be regarded under four successive aspects: Material, Physical, Intellectual, and Moral. Each of these might again be divided on the same principle, and we should then discover several intermediate phases. These cannot be investigated here; and I have only to note that the philosophical principle of this analysis is precisely the same as that on which I have based the Classification of the Sciences. In both cases the order followed is that of increasing generality and complexity in the phenomena. The only difference is in the mode in which the two arrangements are developed. For scientific purposes the lower portion of the scale has to be expanded into greater detail; while from the social point of view attention is concentrated on the higher parts. But whether it be the scale of the True or that of the Good, the conclusion is the same in both. Both alike indicate the supremacy of social considerations; both point to universal Love as the highest ideal.

I have now explained the principal purpose of Positive Philosophy, namely spiritual reorganization; and I have shown how that purpose is involved in the Positivist motto, Order and Progress. Positivism, then, realizes the highest aspirations of mediaeval Catholicism, and at the same time fulfils the conditions, the absence of which caused the failure of the Convention. It combines the opposite merits of the Catholic and the Revolutionary spirit, and by so doing supersedes them both. Theology and Metaphysics may now disappear without danger, because the service which each of them rendered is now harmonised with that of the other, and will be performed more perfectly. The principle on which this result depends is the separation of spiritual from temporal power. This, it will be remembered, had always been the chief subject of contention between the two antagonistic parties. . . .

The peculiar reality of Positivism, and its invariable tendency to concentrate our intellectual powers upon social questions, are attributes, both of which involve its adoption of the essential principle of Communism; that principle being, that Property is in its nature social, and that it needs control.

Property has been erroneously represented by most modern jurists as conferring an absolute right upon the possessor, irrespectively of the good or bad use made of it. This view is instinctively felt by the working classes to be un-sound, and all true philosophers will agree with them. It is an anti-social theory, due historically to exaggerated reaction against previous legislation of a peculiarly oppressive kind, but it has no real foundation either in justice or in fact. Property can neither be created, nor even transmitted by the sole agency of its possessor. The co-operation of the public is always necessary, whether in the assertion of the general principle or in the application of it to each special case. Therefore the tenure of property is not to be regarded as a purely individual right. In every age and in every country the state has intervened, to a greater or less degree, making property subservient to social requirements. Taxation evidently gives the public an interest in the private fortune of each individual; an interest which, instead of diminishing with the progress of civilization, has been always on the increase, especially in modern times, now that the connection of each member of society with the whole is becoming more apparent. The practice of confiscation which also is in uni-versal use, shows that in certain extreme cases the community considers itself authorised to assume entire possession of private property. Confiscation has, it is true, been abolished for a time in France. But this isolated exception is due only to the abuses which recently accompanied the exercise of what was in itself an undoubted right; and it will hardly survive when the causes which led to it are forgotten, and the power which introduced it has passed away. In their abstract views of property, then, Communists are perfectly able to main-tain their ground against the jurists.

They are right, again, in dissenting as deeply as they do from the Econo-mists, who lay it down as an absolute principle that the application of wealth should be entirely unrestricted by society. This error, like the one just spoken of, is attributable to instances of unjustifiable interference. But it is utterly opposed to all sound philosophical teaching, although it has a certain appear-ance of truth, in so far as it recognizes the subordination of social phenomena to natural laws. But the Economists seem to have adopted this important principle only to show how incapable they are of comprehending it. Before they applied the conception of Law to the higher phenomena of nature, they ought to have made themselves well acquainted with its meaning, as applied to the lower and more simple phenomena. Not having done so, they have been utterly blind to the fact that the Order of nature becomes more and more modifiable as it grows more complicated. This conception lies at the very root of our whole practical life; therefore nothing can excuse the metaphysical school of Economists for systematically resisting the intervention of human wisdom in the various departments of social action. That the movement of society is subject to natural laws is certain; but this truth, instead of inducing us to abandon all efforts to modify society, should rather lead to a wiser application of such efforts, since they are at once more efficacious, and more necessary in social phenomena than in any other.

So far, therefore, the fundamental principle of Communism is one which the Positivist school must obviously adopt. Positivism not only confirms this principle, but widens its scope, by showing its application to other departments of human life; by insisting that, not wealth only, but that all our powers shall be devoted in the true republican spirit to the continuous service of the community. The long period of revolution which has elapsed since the Middle Ages has encouraged individualism in the moral world, as in the intellectual it has fostered the specialising tendency. But both are equally inconsistent with the final order of modern society. In all healthy conditions of Humanity, the citizen, whatever his position, has been regarded as a public functionary, whose duties and claims were determined more or less distinctly by his faculties. The case of property is certainly no exception to this general principle. Proprietorship is regarded by the Positivist as an important social function; the function, namely, of creating and administering that capital by means of which each generation lays the foundation for the operation of its successor. This is the only tenable view of property; and wisely interpreted, it is one which, while ennobling to its possessor, does not exclude a due measure of freedom. It will in fact place his position on a firmer basis than ever.

But the agreement here pointed out between sociological science and the spontaneous inspirations of popular judgment goes no farther. Positivists accept, and indeed enlarge, the programme of Communism; but we reject its practical solution on the ground that it is at once inadequate and subversive. The chief difference between our own solution and theirs is that we substitute moral agencies for political. Thus we come again to our leading principle of separating spiritual from temporal power; a principle which, disregarded, as it has hitherto been in the system of modern renovators, will be found in every one of the important problems of our time to be the sole possible issue. In the present case, while throwing such light on the fallacy of Communism, it should lead us to excuse the fallacy, by reminding us that politicians of every accredited school are equally guilty of it. At a time when there are so very few, even of cultivated minds, who have a clear conception of this the primary principle of modern politics, it would be harsh to blame the people for still accepting a result of revolutionary empiricism, which is so universally adopted by other classes. . . .

The ignorance of the true laws of social life under which Communists labour is evident in their dangerous tendency to suppress individuality. Not only do they ignore the inherent preponderance in our nature of the personal instincts; but they forget that, in the collective Organism, the separation of functions is a feature no less essential than the co-operation of functions. Suppose for a moment that the connection between men could be made such that they were physically inseparable, as has been actually the case with twins in certain cases of monstrosity; society would obviously be impossible. Extravagant as this supposition is, it may illustrate the fact that in social life individuality cannot be dispensed with. It is necessary in order to admit of that variety of simultaneous efforts which constitutes the immense superiority of the Social Organism over every individual life. The great problem for man is to harmonize, as far as possible, the freedom resulting from isolation, with the equally urgent necessity for convergence. To dwell exclusively upon the necessity of convergence would tend to undermine not merely our practical energy, but our true dignity; since it would do away with the sense of personal responsibility. In exceptional cases where life is spent in forced subjection to domestic authority, the comforts of home are often not enough to prevent existence from becoming an intolerable burden, simply from the want of sufficient independence. What would it be, then, if everybody stood in a similar position of dependence towards a community that was indifferent to his happiness? Yet no less a danger than this would be the result of adopting any of these utopian schemes which sacrifice true liberty to uncontrolled equality, or even to an exaggerated sense of fraternity. Wide as the divergence between Positivism and the Economic schools is, Positivists adopt substantially the strictures which they have passed upon Communism; especially those of Dunoyer, their most advanced writer.

There is another point in which Communism is equally inconsistent with the laws of Sociology. Acting under false views of the constitution of our modern industrial system, it proposes to remove its directors, who form so essential a part of it. An army can no more exist without officers than without soldiers; and this elementary truth holds good of Industry as well as of War. The organization of modern industry has not been found practicable as yet; but the germ of such organization lies unquestionably in the division which has arisen spontaneously between Capitalist and Workman. No great works could be undertaken if each worker were also to be a director, or if the management, instead of being fixed, were entrusted to a passive and irresponsible body. It is evident that under the present system of industry there is a tendency to a constant enlargement of undertakings: each fresh step leads at once to still further extension. Now this tendency, so far from being opposed to the interests of the working classes, is a condition which will most seriously facilitate the real organization of our material existence, as soon as we have a moral authority competent to control it. For it is only the larger employers that the spiritual power can hope to penetrate with a strong and habitual sense of duty to their subordinates. Without a sufficient concentration of material power, the means of satisfying the claims of morality would be found wanting, except at such exorbitant sacrifices as would be incompatible with all industrial progress. This is the weak point of every plan of reform which limits itself to the mode of acquiring power, whether public power or private, instead of aiming at controlling its use in whose ever hands it may be placed. It leads to a waste of those forces which, when rightly used, form our principal resource in dealing with grave social difficulties.

The motives, therefore, from which modern Communism has arisen, however estimable, lead at present, in the want of proper scientific teaching, to a very wrong view both of the nature of the disease and of its remedy. A heavier reproach against it is, that in one point it shows a manifest insufficiency of social instinct. Communists boast of their spirit of social union; but they limit it to the union of the present generation, stopping short of historical continuity, which yet is the principal characteristic of Humanity. When they have matured their moral growth, and have followed out in Time that connection which at present they only recognise in Space, they will at once see the necessity of these general conditions which at present they would reject. They will understand the importance of inheritance, as the natural means by which each generation transmits to its successor the result of its own labours and the means of improving them. The necessity of inheritance, as far as the community is concerned, is evident, and its extension to the individual is an obvious consequence. But whatever reproaches Communists may deserve in this respect are equally applicable to all the other progressive sects. They are all pervaded by an anti-historic spirit, which leads them to conceive of Society as though it had no ancestors; and this, although their own ideas for the most part can have no bearing except upon posterity. . . .

Love, then, is our principle; Order our basis; and Progress our end. Such is the essential character of the system of life which Positivism offers for the definite acceptance of society; a system which regulates the whole course of our private and public existence, by bringing Feeling, Reason, and Activity into permanent harmony. In this final synthesis, all essential conditions are far more perfectly fulfilled than in any other. Each special element of our nature is more fully developed, and at the same time the general working of the whole is more coherent. Greater distinctness is given to the truth that the affective element predominates in our nature. Life in all its actions and thoughts is brought under the control and inspiring charm of Social Sympathy.

By the supremacy of the Heart, the Intellect, so far from being crushed, is elevated; for all its powers are consecrated to the service of the social instincts, with the purpose of strengthening their influence and directing their employment. By accepting its subordination to Feeling, Reason adds to its own authority. To it we look for the revelation of the laws of nature, of the established Order which dictates the inevitable conditions of human life. The objective basis thus discovered for human effort reacts most beneficially on our moral nature. Forced as we are to accept it, it controls the fickleness to which our affections are liable, and acts as a direct stimulus to social sympathy. Concentrated on so high an office, the intellect will be preserved from useless digression; and will yet find a boundless field for its operations in the study of all the natural laws by which human destinies are affected, and especially those which relate to the constitution of man or of society. The fact that every subject is to be regarded from the sociological point of view, so far from discouraging even the most abstract order of speculations, adds to their logical coherence as well as to their moral value by introducing the central principle round which alone they can be co-ordinated into a whole.

And whilst Reason is admitted to its due share of influence on human life, Imagination is also strengthened and called into constant exercise. Henceforth it will assume its proper function, the idealization of truth. For the objective basis of our conceptions scientific investigation is necessary. But this basis once obtained, the constitution of our mind is far better adapted to esthetic than to scientific study, provided always that imagination never disregard the truths of science, and degenerate into extravagance. Subject to this condition, Positivism gives every encouragement to esthetic studies, being as they are so closely related to its guiding principle and to its practical aim, to Love namely, and to Progress. Art will enter largely into the social life of the Future, and will be regarded as the most pleasurable and most salutary exercise of our intellectual powers, because it leads them in the most direct manner to the culture and improvement of our moral nature.

Originating in the first instance from practical life, Positivism will return thither with increased force, now that its long period of scientific preparation is accomplished, and that it has occupied the field of moral truth, which henceforth will be its principal domain. Its principle of sympathy, so far from relaxing our efforts, will stimulate all our faculties to universal activity by urging them onwards towards perfection of every kind. Scientific study of the natural Order is inculcated solely with the view of directing all the forces of Man and of Society to its improvement by artificial effort. Hitherto this aim has hardly been recognized, even with regard to the material world, and but a very small proportion of our energies has been spent upon it. Yet the aim is high, provided always that the view taken of human progress extend beyond its lower and more material stages. Our theoretical powers once con-

centrated on the moral problems which form their principal field, our practical
energies will not fail to take the same direction, devoting themselves to that
portion of the natural Order which is most imperfect, and at the same time
most modifiable. With these larger and more systematic views of human life,
its best efforts will be given to the improvement of the mind, and still more to
the improvement of the character, and to the increase of affection and courage.
Public and private life are now brought into close relation by the identity
of their principal aim, which, being kept constantly in sight, ennobles every
action in both. Practical questions must ever continue to preponderate, as
before, over questions of theory; but this condition, so far from being adverse
to speculative power, concentrates it upon the most difficult of all problems,
the discovery of moral and social laws, our knowledge of which will never
be fully adequate to our practical requirements. Mental and practical activity
of this kind can never result in hardness of feeling. On the contrary, it impresses us more strongly with the conviction that Sympathy is not merely our
highest happiness, but the most effectual of all our means of improvement;
and that without it, all other means can be of little avail.

Thus it is that in the Positive system, the Heart, the Intellect, and the
Character mutually strengthen and develop one another, because each is
systematically directed to the mode of action for which it is by nature adapted.
Public and private life are brought into a far more harmonious relation than
in any former time, because the purpose to which both are consecrated is
identical; the difference being merely in the range of their activities. The
aim in both is to secure to the utmost possible extent, the victory of Social
feeling over Self-love; and to this aim all our powers, whether of affection,
thought, or action, are in both unceasingly directed.

This, then, is the shape in which the great human problem comes definitely
before us. Its solution demands all the appliances of Social Art. The primary
principle on which the solution rests, is the separation of the two elementary
powers of society; the moral power of counsel, and the political power of
command. The necessary preponderance of the latter, which rests upon material force, corresponds to the fact that in our imperfect nature, where the
coarser wants are the most pressing and the most continuously felt; the selfish
instincts are naturally stronger than the unselfish. In the absence of all compulsory authority, our action even as individuals would be feeble and purposeless, and social life still more certainly would lose its character and its energy.
Moral force, therefore, by which is meant the force of conviction and persuasion, is to be regarded simply as a modifying influence, not as a means of
authoritative direction.

Moral force originates in Feeling and in Reason. It represents the social side of our nature, and to this its direct influence is limited. Indeed by the very fact that it is the expression of our highest attributes, it is precluded from that practical ascendancy which is possessed by faculties of a lower but more energetic kind. Inferior to material force in power, though superior to it in dignity, it contrasts and opposes its own classification of men according to the standard of moral and intellectual worth, to the classification by wealth and worldly position which actually prevails. True, the higher standard will never be adopted practically, but the effort to uphold it will react beneficially on the natural order of society. It will inspire those larger views, and reanimate that sense of duty, which are so apt to become obliterated in the ordinary current of life. . . .

The highest progress of man and of society consists in gradual increase of our mastery over all our defects, especially the defects of our moral nature. Among the nations of antiquity the progress in this direction was but small; all that they could do was to prepare the way for it by certain necessary phases of intellectual and social development. The whole tendency of Greek and Roman society was such as made it impossible to form a distinct conception of the great problem of our moral nature. In fact, Morals were with them invariably subordinate to Politics. Nevertheless, it is moral progress which alone can satisfy our nature; and in the Middle Ages it was recognised as the highest aim of human effort, notwithstanding that its intellectual and social conditions were as yet very imperfectly realised. The creeds of the Middle Ages were too unreal and imperfect, the character of society was too military and aristocratic, to allow Morals and Politics to assume permanently their right relation. The attempt was made, however; and, inadequate as it was, it was enough to allow the people of the West to appreciate the fundamental principle involved in it, a principle destined to survive the opinions and the habits of life from which it arose. Its full weight could never be felt until the Positive spirit had extended beyond the elementary subjects to which it had been so long subjected, to the sphere of social truth; and had thus reached the position at which a complete synthesis became possible. Equally essential was it that in those countries which had been incorporated into the Western Empire, and had passed from it into Catholic Feudalism, war should be definitely superseded by industrial activity. In the long period of transition which has elapsed since the Middle Ages, both these conditions have been fulfilled, while at the same time the old system had been gradually decomposed. Finally the great crisis of the Revolution has stimulated all advanced minds to reconsider, with better intellectual and social principles, the same problem that Christianity and Chivalry had attempted. The radical solution of it was then begun, and it is now completed and enunciated in a systematic form by Positivism.

All essential phases in the evolution of society answer to corresponding phases in the growth of the individual, whether it has proceeded spontaneously or under systematic guidance, supposing always that this development be complete. But it is not enough to prove the close connection which exists between all modes and degrees of human regeneration. We have yet to find a central point round which all will naturally meet. In this point consists the unity of Positivism as a system of life. Unless it can be thus condensed, round one single principle, it will never wholly supersede the synthesis of Theology, notwithstanding its superiority in the reality and stability of its component parts, and in their homogeneity and coherence as a whole. There should be a central point in the system, towards which Feeling, Reason, and Activity alike converge. The proof that Positivism possesses such a central point will remove the last obstacle to its complete acceptance as the guide of private or of public life.

Such a centre we find in the great conception of Humanity, towards which every aspect of Positivism naturally converges. By it the conception of God will be entirely superseded, and a synthesis be formed, more complete and permanent than that provisionally established by the old religions. Through it the new doctrine becomes at once accessible to men's hearts in its full extent and application. From their hearts it will penetrate their minds, and thus the immediate necessity of beginning with a long and difficult course of study is avoided, though this must of course be always indispensable to its systematic teachers.

This central point of Positivism is even more moral than intellectual in character; it represents the principle of Love upon which the whole system rests. It is the peculiar characteristic of the Great Being who is here set forth, to be compounded of separable elements. Its existence depends therefore entirely upon mutual Love knitting together its various parts. The calculations of self-interest can never be substituted as a combining influence for the sympathetic instincts.

Yet the belief in Humanity, while stimulating Sympathy, at the same time enlarges the scope and vigour of the Intellect. For it requires high powers of generalization to conceive clearly of this vast organism, as the result of spontaneous co-operation, abstraction made of all partial antagonisms. Reason, then, has its part in this central dogma as well as Love. It enlarges and completes our conception of the Supreme Being, by revealing to us the external and internal conditions of its existence.

Lastly, our active powers are stimulated by it no less than our feelings and our reason. For since Humanity is so far more complex than any other organism, it will react more strongly and more continuously on its environment, submitting to its influence and so modifying it. Hence results Progress which is simply the development of Order, under the influence of Love.

Thus, in the conception of Humanity, the three essential aspects of Positivism, its subjective principle, its objective dogma, and its practical object are united. Towards Humanity, who is for us the only true Great Being, we, the conscious elements of whom she is composed, shall henceforth direct every aspect of our life, individual or collective. Our thoughts will be devoted to the knowledge of Humanity, our affections to her love, our actions to her service.

Positivists then may, more truly than theological believers of whatever creed, regard life as a continuous and earnest act of worship; worship which will elevate and purify our feelings, enlarge and enlighten our thoughts, ennoble and invigorate our actions. It supplies a direct solution, so far as a solution is possible, of the great problem of the Middle Ages, the subordination of Politics to Morals. For this follows at once from the consecration now given to the principle that social sympathy should preponderate over self-love.

Thus Positivism becomes, in the true sense of the word, a Religion; the only religion which is real and complete; destined therefore to replace all imperfect and provisional systems resting on the primitive basis of theology. . . .

By entirely renouncing wealth and worldly position, and that not as individuals merely, but as a body, the priests of Humanity will occupy a position of unparalleled dignity. For with their moral influence they will combine what since the downfall of the old theocracies has always been separated from it, the influence of superiority in art and science. Reason, Imagination, and Feeling will be brought into unison: and so united, will react strongly on the imperious conditions of practical life; bringing it into closer accordance with the laws of universal morality, from which it is so prone to deviate. And the influence of this new modifying power will be the greater that the synthesis on which it rests will have preceded and prepared the way for the social system of the future; whereas theology could not arrive at its central principle, until the time of its decline was approaching. All functions, then, that co-operate in the elevation of man will be regenerated by the Positive priesthood. Science, Poetry, Morality, will be devoted to the study, the praise, and the love of Humanity, in order that under their combined influence, our political action may be more unremittingly given to her service.

With such a mission, Science acquires a position of unparalleled importance, as the sole means through which we come to know the nature and conditions of this great Being, the worship of whom should be the distinctive feature of our whole life. For this all-important knowledge, the study of Sociology would seem to suffice: but Sociology itself depends upon preliminary study, first of the outer world, in which the actions of Humanity take place; and secondly, of Man, the individual agent.

The object of Positivist worship is not like that of theological believers, an absolute, isolated, incomprehensible Being, whose existence admits of no demonstration, or comparison with anything real. The evidence of the Being here set forward is spontaneous, and is shrouded in no mystery. Before we can praise love, and serve Humanity as we ought, we must know something of the laws which govern her existence, an existence more complicated than any other of which we are cognizant.

ESSAYS AND REVIEWS

IN MARCH, 1860, on the eve of the Darwinian controversy, a small book called *Essays and Reviews* was published. Its authors were six parsons and one layman, among whom were Benjamin Jowett (1817–93), afterwards master of Balliol College, and Frederick Temple (1821–1902), headmaster of Rugby, later Archbishop of Canterbury. The seven writers intended to prove to Christians that discoveries in natural science and biblical scholarship or the "Higher Criticism," as it was called, did not threaten but actually strengthened the foundations of their faith. One writer went so far as to claim that Darwin's *Origin of Species* illustrated "the grand principle of the self-evolving powers of Nature." The response to *Essays and Reviews* was heated. One declaration of belief in the infallibility of the Bible aimed against the work obtained over eleven thousand clerical signatures; the authors were denounced as "Septem Contra Christum," and "the seven extinguishers of the seven lamps of the Apocalypse"; two of them were persecuted and condemned in the ecclesiastical court. Both sentences were later reversed on appeal to the Privy Council.

The intention of the authors to "reconcile intellectual persons to Christianity" grew out of the belief that science and Christianity were being fallaciously but increasingly represented as antagonistic. The authors argued that the discoveries in science and biblical scholarship could be accepted as proofs of God's work and that the discovery of scientific laws was the growing recognition of God's laws as manifested in nature. Jowett, for example, held that if Christianity could not comprehend the new discoveries, it was itself at fault; "The Christian religion is in a false position when all the tendencies of knowledge are opposed to it"; Christianity must be reconciled with its criticism; the "eternal import" of Christianity could not be threatened by any new discovery, and could only be made stronger by the removal of "incrustations."

This liberal Christianity received attacks from both sides at once, from orthodox Christians like Bishop Wilberforce and from positivists like Frederic Harrison. Temple's idea that Christianity might have powers of growth and change like a living organism did not suit Harrison's notion that it was merely "a crumbling edifice." Such ideas, according to Harrison, could only debase the whole religious structure, and the seven authors had better either remain firm in the "religious belief of the mass of the Christian public" or declare themselves positivists.

Bishop Wilberforce, for the opposite reasons, agreed with Harrison that there was no middle way: "They believe too much not to believe more, and they disbelieve too much not to disbelieve everything." Wilberforce took the book as "infidelity, if not atheism," and as a dangerous effort to defend Christianity by surrendering all that had always been thought its substance. Temple's notion of a gradual education of the human race seemed to him to deny the fall of man by making history the record of a gradual improvement. It did not occur to Wilberforce that the liberals might be trying to repair damage already done by at least a century of intellectual challenge rather than surrender the faith.

The following selection is from a sermon, "The Present Relations of Science to Religion," included as an appendix to *Essays and Reviews* and preached by Frederick Temple on July 1, 1860, four months after the publication of the controversial volume. Though his contribution to the book was perhaps the least objectionable to conservative Christians, a storm of protest arose when Temple was offered the see of Exeter a few years later. As Bishop of Exeter he continued to lecture on "the relation between science and religion," but when he became Bishop of London, in 1869, the clergy who had opposed him before almost unanimously signed a memorial of regret at his departure. Temple became Archbishop of Canterbury, primate of the Church of England, in 1897.

This selection is taken from the second American edition of *Essays and Reviews*, 1861 (published as *Recent Inquiries in Theology*).

THE PRESENT RELATIONS OF SCIENCE
TO RELIGION

ECCLESIASTES 1.17: *"I gave my heart to know wisdom, and to know madness and folly: I perceive that this also is vexation of spirit."*

The writer of the Book of Ecclesiastes tells us that he made it his business to inquire into all that went out upon the earth, in the hope that he might find "what was that good for the sons of men which they should do under the heaven all the days of their life." His inquiry led him, in every instance, to the same conclusion, that all was vanity. The word "vanity" here, however, plainly does not mean an absolute, but only a relative, condemnation. The preacher does not mean to say that human pursuits contain nothing in them that is good, nor does he wish to exhort his hearers to quit altogether what he has condemned. On the contrary, the book abounds with the fullest acknowledgments of the excellence of each human occupation and enjoyment in its turn. There is much in the praise of pleasure: "There is nothing better for a man than that he should eat and drink, and that he should make his soul enjoy good in his labor." There is much in praise of labor: "Whatsoever thy hand findeth to do, do it with thy might." There is much in praise of wisdom: "Wisdom is better than strength;" "Wisdom is as good as an inheritance;" "Wisdom is profitable to direct." There is much in praise of upright conduct: "God giveth to a man that is good in his sight wisdom and knowledge and joy, but to the sinner he giveth travail." There is much in praise of the happy heart of youth: "Let thy heart cheer thee in the days of thy youth, and walk in the ways of thine heart and in the sight of thine eyes." And all these praises, and the exhortations that go along with them to enjoy the good that God hath given, are not ironical, but seriously meant. But, notwithstanding, one after another, all human pursuits, all human gifts, all human enjoyments, are branded with the same mark of deficiency; all, even the most excellent, are still vanity and vexation of spirit. Not wisdom only, and labor, and youth, and pleasure, but even the upright walk and the keeping of the ordinances of religion, even they too are in the same sense vanity. "There is one event to the righteous and to the wicked, to the clean and to the unclean, to him that sacrificeth and to him that sacrificeth not; as is the good so is the sinner, and he that sweareth as he that feareth an oath."

It is plain that the sense in which all these things are vanity is, that they cannot satisfy. They are all, without exception, shadows and not substance. They all, without exception, promise what they cannot perform. Each in its turn promises to fill the whole man and give him all that he wants. There are excellent enjoyments which, some for a shorter, some for a longer time, seem to be all that the soul desires. There are occupations and labors which aim at so worthy an end, and are rewarded by so noble an appreciation, that for a time the soul believes them equal to all its needs. The fire of youthful happiness burns so brightly, and so warmly, and so purely, that we are tempted to declare it the one best gift of God. There is a path of life so honored by men, so approved by conscience, namely, the path of duty, that in it surely might well seem to be comprised all that man can possibly require. And yet each one of these will be found wanting: good as far as it goes, but not the whole; promising to satisfy, and never fulfilling its promise; in fact, only then fulfilling its function when it proclaims its own vanity, and bids the seeker seek further still. The very excellence of the most excellent of all these will the more emphatically condemn it, for that excellence is the false light which allures men to believe in its perfection, and to fancy that all that is wanted shall here be found.

So we are led to the conclusion of the whole matter. "Fear God and keep his commandments, for this is the whole of man." Not in pleasure, however pure and however heavenly; not in wisdom, however searching; not in labor, however successful; not in worldly duty, however self-denying; but in God shall we find the true substance of all that is done under the sun, the reality of which all else is the image, the brightness of which all else is the reflection.

This conclusion has been in the minds of the vast majority of thinkers ever since. It is possible to forget God altogether in the whirl of pleasure, in the absorbing interests of business or of ambition. But the student cannot well forget the question which underlies all other questions: "What is it that gives any unity or consistency to all these studies? What is the relation between our knowledge and the source of all knowledge? What can human science tell me of divine nature?" And those who have been more than students, who have been Christians in heart as well as searchers after truth, have sought for an answer to this question, not as the solution of an intellectual puzzle, but as the true end of all their studies. The desire to find God in all his works is certainly not rare, the desire to clear up the relation between faith and science is almost universal in those who devote themselves to scientific investigation. Hence no sooner is any physical theory or hypothesis proposed which in the remotest way can affect the belief of Christians, than its bearing on every article of the Christian faith, and even on every detail of the commonly received religious opinions, are discussed at the fullest length, and not unfrequently with an eager anxiety to identify faith and science which overshoots the mark, by attempting to decide before there is evidence enough for a decision.

On the present occasion it seems to be not unfitting to examine some of the leading relations between religion and science, especially with a view to point out some of the changes which the progress of science is producing in them.

Science has been called the handmaid of theology, and theology has often had recourse to science for arguments to prove or confirm her fundamental propositions. But it is remarkable that theology has almost always for this purpose dwelt chiefly, not on the scientific, but on the unscientific statements of science. Arguments have been commonly extracted, not from the revelations of science, but from her confessions; and theology has begun where science has ended. It has been common to trace the power of God, not in that which is universal, but in that which is individual; not in the laws of nature, but in any apparent interference with those laws; not in the maintenance, but in the creation of the universe. And sometimes such stress has been laid upon these arguments, that to deny them was held to be a denial of their own conclusions; and men were thought impious who attempted to represent the present order of the solar system or the existence of animal life as the work of natural causes, and not the direct handiwork of God himself. And yet spontaneous generation was long believed in by the most religious men, and there seems no more reason why the solar system should not have been brought into its present form by the slow working of natural causes than the surface of the earth, about whose gradual formation most students are now agreed. The fact is, that one idea is now emerging into supremacy in science, a supremacy which it never possessed before, and for which it still has to fight a battle; and that is the idea of law. Different orders of natural phenomena have in time past been held to be exempt from that idea, either tacitly or avowedly. The weather, the thunder and lightning, the crops of the earth, the progress of disease, whether over a country or in an individual, these have been considered as regulated by some special interference, even when it was already known that the recurrence of the seasons, the motions of the planets, the periodic winds, and other phenomena of the same kind, were subject to invariable laws. But the steady march of science has now reached the point when men are tempted, or rather compelled, to jump at once to a universal conclusion: all analogy points one way, and none another. And the student of science is learning to look upon fixed laws as universal, and many of the old arguments which science once supplied to religion are in consequence rapidly disappearing. How strikingly altered is our view from that of a few centuries ago is shown by the fact that the miracles recorded in the Bible, which once were looked on as the bulwarks of the faith, are now felt by very many to be difficulties in their way; and commentators endeavor to represent them, not as mere interferences with the laws of nature, but as the natural action of still higher laws belonging to a world whose phenomena are only half revealed to us.

It is evident that this change in science necessitates a change in its relation to faith. If law be either almost or altogether universal, we must look for the finger of God in that law: we must expect to find him manifesting his love, his wisdom, his infinity, not in individual acts of will, but in a perfection of legislation rendering all individual action needless; we must find his providence in that perfect adaptation of all the parts of the machine to one another which shall have the effect of tender care, though it proceed by an invariable action. The vast consequences which flow from a few simple properties of matter, the profusion of combinations, the beauty, the order, the happiness which abound in the creation in consequence of these, such must be now the teachers of the man of science to make him feel that God is with him in all his studies.

It may be, indeed, that the scientific student is every day less and less driven to confession of the narrowness of his knowledge: he has less occasion for the humility which once allowed vast realms of nature to lie out of the domain of science, and was wont to say, when baffled, "Here human powers can go no further; this knowledge God has reserved for himself." On the contrary, he is now inclined to think that, if only time enough be given, there seems to be no kind of phenomenon under the sun which patient study will not bring within the range of science. But this only amounts to saying that he must learn humility in another way. God will not stop human science in order to teach man humility. He will not have man ignorant in order to be humble. He will have him study and learn, and be humble notwithstanding. And already we can see that, as the bar is removed which once seemed to stop man's progress in knowledge, so all the clearer is the bar made manifest which limits his powers of action. You have studied the laws of God's creation; can you alter one of them in the very slightest degree? You have weighed the matter of the earth; can you create or can you (as would have been thought not long ago) annihilate one grain of its dust? The creation of matter and the creation of the laws of matter is absolutely beyond all your power and all your wisdom; and the longer you study and the wider appears to your eye the possible range of your science, the more clear and certain is this conclusion. There we find the hand of God; there we shall never find the hand of man.

The natural objection to find God in laws rather than in acts is that it tends to a kind of pantheism which robs us of our belief in God's personality. There is not perhaps much, though there is some, tendency to that gross material pantheism which identifies the universe with God, and making all created matter to be as it were his body, destroys our conception of his nature. But there is considerable tendency to the subtler pantheism, which forgets him in the idea of a universal law or system of laws, with a rigid mechanical action; without tenderness, without consciousness, without any answer to affection. It is clear, however, that this tendency to pantheism is not in the conception of law, but in our own minds; and the proper corrective is to lift our minds up to the level which science demands of us. For we form our idea of God, and indeed we must do so, by analogy from ourselves. In the infancy of knowledge the spiritual faculty in man appears to be his will. The ideal of manhood is that of a will working at every moment by pure and high instincts, by the instincts of love, and tenderness, and unselfish generosity, and noble self-respect. But as knowledge grows, even in the short course of our own life, the reason and not the will, the principles and not the in-stincts, become the supreme characteristic of man, and that which most dis-tinguishes him from all lower creatures. Then the ideal of manhood is that of a will subordinate to an enlightened reason or conscience, acting by laws the ground of which is understood, with a forethought of consequences, with a deliberateness of purpose, not swayed hither and thither by even the highest impulses, but joining to the tenderest feelings the power of harmonizing them with a consistent, unvarying rule of action. So, too, we may think of God as love, but as love already acquainted with all that will happen or that can happen, and therefore able to harmonize that love with a fixed system of laws, and not driven, as human love is often driven, to shift its course by the occurrence or the discovery of circumstances previously unknown. We can think of his tenderness as shown, not in stopping the machinery of the world to adapt our circumstances to our short-sighted wishes, but in supplying our souls with a spiritual power which will enable us to rise above all circumstances whatever.

This, however, is not all that we get from the idea of law. The laws of conscience, quite as much as the laws of nature, are capable of being represented to our minds in their highest forms as absolutely fixed. Not only are they capable of being so represented, but it is the shape which they naturally wear. We naturally think, as soon as we conceive the idea of law at all, of the laws of morals as being in their supreme manifestation eternal and immutable. And while science demands our recognition of the universal dominion of physical laws, and treats all exceptions as so rare that we may safely disregard them in our estimate, so conscience perpetually proclaims the existence and loftier dominion of her moral law, and requires us to believe, under pain of her displeasure, and as we value the dignity of our own manhood, that all laws are subordinate to hers, and that, whatever appearances there may be to the contrary, holiness and goodness and justice are the final arbiters of all that is, or hath been, or shall be, in the universe. Thus, above and beyond all the physical laws that we know, rises another of a different kind, proclaiming a different authority, demanding a completer obedience. Long induction compels our unhesitating belief in the properties of matter, or, in other words, in the laws of nature. No one doubts that fire will burn, that ice will chill, that poison will destroy; and the proof of the faith is given by the obedience rendered. Precisely the same unhesitating faith will conscience require for the moral law; we are to believe with the same unhesitating certainty that justice and goodness and holiness rule the universe, and we are to act on that belief.

And further, this moral law is not capable, like the physical law, of being conceived as impersonal, but carries in it the conviction of its own personality. For a moral law differs from a physical law in this, that a physical law is satisfied by mere verification: it is enough for a physical law if the facts invariably accord with the predictions of the law. Not so with a moral law. It is not justice if by some mere external accident it so happens that I get my deserts; a murderer is not really punished for a murder because he is accidentally hung by those who know nothing of his crime; a servant would not consider himself to have receive his wages because he found an equal amount by a lucky accident. The intention is essential to the morality; it would not satisfy the demands of justice that by some accident it should turn out that justice was always done; it must not only be done, it must be intended. And if there is intention, there is will; and if there is will, there is personality. And thus the moral law, whose sovereign authority is incessantly proclaimed within us, becomes the embodiment of the God of holiness, and in obeying it we are worshipping Him.

It is true that we rise to the belief in the universal dominion of the moral law by an act of faith, and not by demonstration; but the moral spring is not greater in this case than the intellectual spring in the other. No man can say that it is yet demonstrated in detail that all nature is subject to fixed laws; in fact, many who are not themselves students of science, and are therefore only bound to accept the conclusions of science so far as they are demonstrated, will still maintain that the health of the body and the changes of the weather are under some special government, and not under absolutely fixed laws at all. Yet such is the power of the perpetually operating analogy of science, that no student of nature seriously doubts the universality, or, at any rate, the generality, of the principle. Exceptions may still be possible, for our ignorance is, after all, greater than our knowledge, but assuredly they are so extremely rare that they need not be counted. And why do we thus leap to this conclusion? Because without it all science becomes incomplete and unaccountable; because we have tried it over and over again, and it has never yet failed us; because it perpetually opens new paths of knowledge, and no other principle ever has. Now for precisely the same reasons do we leap to the parallel conclusion in religion. We have not evidence enough to show that the moral law rules the world; there is, indeed, much that obeys it, but there is also much that seems to disobey it; but never for a moment does conscience relax her demand upon our assent: for without it all our morality becomes incomplete and unaccountable; the belief in it has always promised to raise us in the scale of moral being, and, whenever we have tried it, it has never failed to do so; it perpetually lifts us above ourselves to all we find noblest and purest and best, and no other principle ever did or will.

Thus, while the fixed laws of science can supply natural religion with numberless illustrations of the wisdom, the beneficence, the order, the beauty that characterize the workmanship of God; while they illustrate his infinity by the marvellous complexity of natural combinations, by the variety and order of his creatures, by the exquisite finish alike bestowed on the very greatest and on the very least of his works, as if size were absolutely nothing in his sight; so, too, they supply the analogy by which we can rise above themselves to that still higher law in which we find the very presence of the person of the Godhead.

Similar to this relation between science and natural religion is the relation between science and revelation. There was a time when the spheres of these two were distinct; or, if there was ever an appearance of collision, science was required to give place. That time ceased with Galileo, and can never return. The student of science now feels himself bound by the interests of truth, and can admit no other obligation. And if he be a religious man, he believes that both books, the book of Nature and the book of Revelation, come alike from God, and that he has no more right to refuse to accept what he finds in the one than in the other. The two books are indeed on totally different subjects; the one may be called a treatise on theology and morals. But they are both by the same Author; and the difference in their importance is derived from the difference in their matter, and not from any difference in their authority. Whenever, therefore, there is a collision between them, the dispute becomes simply a question of evidence. Here, you have in nature God's handiwork; there, you have in the Bible the message which he commissioned certain servants of his to give you. They do not appear to agree. Now, on the one side, are you quite certain in your interpretation of his handiwork? on the other, are you quite certain that you are not mixing up with his message some extraneous matter which belongs not to the message, but to the messenger? In the case of Galileo the question has been answered; the astronomer was right, the theologians were wrong. The apparent statement that the sun went round the earth is now acknowledged to belong to the messenger, not to the message; to the language, not to the substance. The present state of science indicates that there will be more answers in the same direction. Geology, for instance, has already altered our conception of a great part of the book of Genesis. Researches into ancient records seem likely to affect the details of the history of the early races of mankind. How each one of the many questions thus started will be ultimately answered it is impossible to say. The probability is that both the agreements and the discrepancies between science and the Biblical narrative will be very different from what we now suppose: but, at any rate, it is tolerably plain that the Bible is not to look to science for that confirmation of minute details which not very long ago was confidently expected, and in many cases apparently produced.

Is there, then, no harmony between the Bible and science? Are they, if not foes, yet so distinct as to have no point of meeting? Not so. But this harmony is to be looked for in a different direction; not in petty details of facts are we to find it, but in the deep identity of tone, character, and spirit which pervade both the books. Where, for instance, in all literature is the wonderful patience of God's operations more clearly exhibited than in the Bible? Again and again are we, as it were, reminded that to him a thousand years are as one day, and one day as a thousand years. To him, an absolutely infinite being, what difference can there be between long and short? why should he not spend ages as willingly as seconds? So he chooses out a people two thousand years before it is wanted, and drills it and disciplines it from the call of Abraham to the coming of our Lord; all, as it seems, to make a fit scene for that four years of our Lord's ministry, and a fit instrument for conveying his message to the world. Is not this like the same Hand that lavishes in unmeasured profusion thousands of years to make a continent, to stock it with mountains and rivers, with mines and stone-quarries, all, as it seems, to be a scene for the history of one of our passing nations? Or again, look at the enormous waste that seems to meet us in the very conception of choosing a people at all. The Jews were God's chosen, but what were all the rest? Some few races, we can see, were trained up for similar, though inferior, purposes; but how vast a number seem no more than a mere store of material useless for the present. And is there not a similar waste in the creation of nature, stores of fossils buried where they can be of no value, plants growing where none can enjoy them, seeds and eggs by millions that never come to life at all? Or again, look at the marvellous adaptation to human feeling which marks every precept of the Bible and compare it with the wonderful beauty and beneficence of nature. Or again, look at the awful sternness with which the Bible threatens all disobedience, and compare it with the merciless severity of the physical laws when they are disobeyed. Or again, look at the mystery of repentance, the restoration to favor so often accompanied by no remission of the penalty, and see if nature does not often repair a fault in such a way as to leave the punishment for life. Or again, look at the strange instances of curses turned to blessings, and men apparently raised in some sense to a higher state by having fallen, and compare it with those strange caprices, as we call them, by which nature sometimes changes mischief into downright improvement. Whatever may be the case as regards the details of the narrative, assuredly there can be no mistake regarding the spirit of the author. The more the Bible is studied, and the more nature is studied, the deeper will be found the harmony between them in character, the more assured the certainty that whoever inspired the one also made the other. And most assured will that certainty be in the mind of him who studies the Bible as it was meant to be studied, not as an interesting historical record, but as the guide of life, the revelation of spiritual truth, the awakener and the kindler of religious inspiration.

But when we have reached this point, when we have made science help us into religion, have we indeed reached, according to the Preacher, the conclusion of the whole matter? No, indeed. Religious speculations, though the highest of all speculations, are yet but speculations; and if we rest in them we shall certainly be compelled to pronounce them also vanity and vexation of spirit. When we fight the battle with besetting sins; when we have to resist some terrible attack from sensuality, from ambition, from vanity, from pride; in the great crises of our life, when we stand where several ways meet, and our better nature is at war with our lower, and we seem to say, What shall I do to inherit eternal life? and a still small voice seems to answer, Sell what thou hast and give unto the poor, and come, follow Me; on the bed of sickness and of death, when this world seems to fade out of sight; in the day of sharp trouble, of anxiety, of wounded affection, of hopeless misery,—then we need something more than religious speculations, even of the loftiest kind; then we are not contented to hear of the moral law or of the nature of God: we want God himself, and without the living God we feel that we cannot stand. Then it is that the student of science knows that the most unlettered peasant can penetrate to the true reality of all things as surely as the wisest philosopher; then science is called vanity, and theology is forgotten; then pain is God's scourge to chastise, and his judgments are warnings, and the cry of our hearts is the echo of the groanings of his spirit, and the Bible is a letter written in his own hand, and we are his children, and he is our Father. Then all else fails us, and we cannot be content except we are clasped to his bosom and feel the Shepherd's arms around us. If our science is incompatible with this; if it stifles the voice of nature, and prevents us from knowing that God is our Father and that we are his children, and that all his anger even against our sins is still the anger of a Father who never ceases to love us; if its mechanical accuracy chills our feelings and blunts the keen edge of our desire to be like him, to be with him, to belong to him,—then certainly is such science vanity, and worse than vanity; if it is truth to others, it is a deadly lie to ourselves. But the reverent study of the works of God assuredly need not ever lead in this direction. Rather in such study, as men behold the marvellous balance whereby the Father ever restores all things to their true rest, can they learn, if they will, the quiet calmness, the trust in the Almighty's power and goodness, which best befits a Christian soul. The reverent study of His works can and will bring us nearer in temper to their Divine Author. For of Him, and through Him, and to Him, are all things; to whom be glory forever. Amen.

JOHN HENRY NEWMAN

JOHN HENRY NEWMAN (1801–90) was born in London, eldest son of John Newman, a banker. A quiet and serious boy, sometime in 1816 he had a religious "conversion" in which he experienced a vivid conviction of the reality of God and his own soul which lasted the rest of his life. In December of 1816 he entered Oxford. Although he failed to gain high honors, he nevertheless was elected to a fellowship at Oriel College in 1822.

Newman took Holy Orders in the Anglican Church in 1824, became Vicar of St. Mary's, Oxford, four years later, and select preacher to the University in 1831. He developed close friendships with Hurrell Froude, John Keble, and Edward Pusey, who shared his antipathy to rationalistic and liberal tendencies in the Church of England.

When in July, 1833, Newman returned from a Mediterranean tour, he found England in a turmoil of political and religious reform. The Whigs had abolished ten bishoprics in Ireland, and some of them wanted to disestablish the Church of England, which they regarded as little more than a department of state. When Keble delivered a sermon on the "National Apostasy" on July 14, Newman greeted it as the beginning of a new movement. The Tractarian, or Oxford, movement attempted to retrieve the tradition of piety, spirituality, and authority founded on the early church fathers; to find a firmer foundation for the Catholic tradition latent in Anglicanism; to combat liberals and rationalists who, according to Newman, led one to "prefer intellectual excellence to moral," and to assert the spiritual independence of the Church from the state. The *Tracts for the Times,* which Newman began in September, 1833, set forth these aims in an attempt to save the Church of England from liberal theology and subordination to the state. Newman and his Oriel colleagues wanted a definite and more Catholic basis for doctrine and discipline.

Between 1833 and 1841 Newman moved closer to a Roman Catholic position. The famous *Tract XC* met with great indignation in Oxford and elsewhere. The bishop of Oxford requested him to discontinue the *Tracts.* He complied, considering himself no longer an Anglican. In 1843 he published anonymously a retraction of all he had said against the Roman Catholic Church, which he joined in 1845. Newman was ordained a priest in Rome the following year.

The last half of Newman's life was less public. He continued to write and lecture. In 1864 he wrote his *Apologia pro Vita Sua,* a history of his religious opinions, as a reply to an attack on his motives by Charles Kingsley. This religious autobiography restored Newman to a high place in British public opinion. He was created a cardinal in 1879 and lived in quiet retirement until his death in 1890.

The following selection is from the appendix on "Liberalism" in the *Apologia.* A study of Newman's definition of liberalism, not just in its religious meaning but in its broad political and ethical implications, will reveal some of the conflicts of faith which characterized the period of the Oxford Movement in particular and the Victorian era in general. Elsewhere in the *Apologia* Newman said, "There are but two alternatives, the way to Rome, and the way to Atheism: Anglicanism is the halfway house on the one side, and Liberalism is the halfway house on the other."

Newman's *Apologia* appeared in book form in 1865.

LIBERALISM

I HAVE BEEN ASKED to explain more fully what it is I mean by "Liberalism," because merely to call it the Anti-dogmatic Principle is to tell very little about it. An explanation is the more necessary, because such good Catholics and distinguished writers as Count Montalembert and Father Lacordaire use the word in a favourable sense, and claim to be Liberals themselves. "The only singularity," says the former of the two in describing his friend, "was his Liberalism. By a phenomenon, at that time unheard of, this convert, this seminarist, this confessor of nuns, was just as stubborn a liberal, as in the days when he was a student and a barrister."

I do not believe that it is possible for me to differ in any important matter from two men whom I so highly admire. In their general line of thought and conduct I enthusiastically concur, and consider them to be before their age. And it would be strange indeed if I did not read with a special interest, in M. de Montalembert's beautiful volume, of the unselfish aims, the thwarted projects, the unrequited toils, the grand and tender resignation of Lacordaire. If I hesitate to adopt their language about Liberalism, I impute the necessity of such hesitation to some differences between us in the use of words or in the circumstances of country; and thus I reconcile myself to remaining faithful to my own conception of it, though I cannot have their voices to give force to mine. Speaking then in my own way, I proceed to explain what I meant as a Protestant by Liberalism, and to do so in connexion with the circumstances under which that system of opinion came before me at Oxford.

If I might presume to contrast Lacordaire and myself, I should say, that we had been both of us inconsistent;—he, a Catholic, in calling himself a Liberal; I, a Protestant, in being an anti-liberal; and moreover, that the cause of this inconsistency had been in both cases one and the same. This is, we were both of us such good conservatives, as to take up with what we happened to find established in our respective countries, at the time when we came into active life. Toryism was the creed of Oxford; he inherited, and made the best of, the French Revolution.

When, in the beginning of the present century, not very long before my own time, after many years of moral and intellectual declension, the University of Oxford woke up to a sense of its duties, and began to reform itself, the first instruments of this change, to whose zeal and courage we all owe so much, were naturally thrown together for mutual support, against the numerous obstacles which lay in their path, and soon stood out in relief from the body of residents, who, though many of them men of talent themselves, cared little for the object which the others had at heart. These Reformers, as they may be called, were for some years members of scarcely more than three or four Colleges and their own Colleges, as being under their direct influence, of course had the benefit of those stricter views of discipline and teaching, which they themselves were urging on the University. They had, in no long time, enough of real progress in their several spheres of exertion, and enough of reputation out of doors, to warrant them in considering themselves the *élite* of the place; and it is not wonderful if they were in consequence led to look down upon the majority of Colleges, which had not kept pace with the reform, or which had been hostile to it. And, when those rivalries of one man with another arose, whether personal or collegiate, which befall literary and scientific societies, such disturbances did but tend to raise in their eyes the value which they had already set upon academical distinction, and increase their zeal in pursuing it. Thus was formed an intellectual circle or class in the University,—men who felt they had a career before them, as soon as the pupils, whom they were forming, came into public life; men, whom non-residents, whether country parsons or preachers of the Low Church, on coming up from time to time to the old place, would look at, partly with admiration, partly with suspicion, as being an honour indeed to Oxford, but withal exposed to the temptation of ambitious views, and to the spiritual evils signified in what is called the "pride of reason."

Nor was this imputation altogether unjust; for, as they were following out the proper idea of a University, of course they suffered more or less from the moral malady incident to such a pursuit. The very object of such great institutions lies in the cultivation of the mind and the spread of knowledge: if this object, as all human objects, has its dangers at all times, much more would these exist in the case of men, who were engaged in a work of reformation, and had the opportunity of measuring themselves, not only with those who were their equals in intellect, but with the many who were below them. In this select circle or class of men, in various Colleges, the direct instruments and the choice of real University Reform, we see the rudiments of the Liberal party.

Whenever men are able to act at all, there is the chance of extreme and intemperate action; and therefore, when there is exercise of mind, there is the chance of wayward or mistaken exercise. Liberty of thought is in itself a good; but it gives an opening to false liberty. Now by Liberalism I mean false liberty of thought or the exercise of thought upon matters, in which, from the constitution of the human mind, thought cannot be brought to any successful issue, and therefore is out of place. Among such matters are first principles of whatever kind; and of these the most sacred and momentous are especially to be reckoned the truths of Revelation. Liberalism then is the mistake of subjecting to human judgment those revealed doctrines which are in their nature beyond and independent of it, and of claiming to determine on intrinsic grounds the truth and value of propositions which rest for their reception simply on the external authority of the Divine Word.

Now certainly the party of whom I have been speaking, taken as a whole, were of a character of mind out of which Liberalism might easily grow up, as in fact it did; certainly they breathed around an influence which made men of religious seriousness shrink into themselves. But, while I say as much as this, I have no intention whatever of implying that the talent of the University in the years before and after 1820, was liberal in its theology, in the sense in which the bulk of the educated classes through the country are liberal now. I would not for the world be supposed to detract from the Christian earnestness, and the activity in religious works, above the average of men, of many of the persons in question. They would have protested against their being supposed to place reason before faith, or knowledge before devotion; yet I do consider that they unconsciously encouraged and successfully introduced into Oxford a licence of opinion which went far beyond them. In their day they did little more than take credit of sentiment, without drawing the line between what was just and what was inadmissible in speculation, and without seeing the tendency of their own principles; and engrossing, as they did, the mental energy of the University, they met for a time with no effectual hindrance to the spread of their influence, except (what indeed at the moment was most effectual, but not of an intellectual character) the thorough-going Toryism and traditionary Church-of-Englandism of the great body of the Colleges and Convocation.

Now and then a man of note appeared in the Pulpit or Lecture Rooms of the University, who was a worthy representative of the more religious and devout Anglicans. These belonged chiefly to the High-Church party; for the party called Evangelical never has been able to breathe freely in the atmosphere of Oxford, and at no time has been conspicuous, as a party, for talent or learning. But of the old High Churchmen several exerted some sort of Anti-liberal influence in the place, at least from time to time, and that influence of an intellectual nature. Among these especially may be mentioned Mr. John Miller, of Worcester College, who preached the Bampton Lecture in the year 1817. But, as far as I know, he who turned the tide, and brought the talent of the University round to the side of the old theology, and against what was familiarly called "march-of-mind," was Mr. Keble. In and from Keble the mental activity of Oxford took that contrary direction which issued in what was called Tractarianism.

Keble was young in years when he became a University celebrity, and younger in mind. He had the purity and simplicity of a child. He had few sympathies with the intellectual party, who sincerely welcomed him as a brilliant specimen of young Oxford. He instinctively shut up before literary display, and pomp and donnishness of manner, faults which always will beset academical notabilities. He did not respond to their advances. His collision with them (if it may be so called) was thus described by Hurrell Froude in his own way. "Poor Keble," he used gravely to say, "he was asked to join the aristocracy of talent, but he soon found his level." He went into the country, but his instance serves to prove that men need not, in the event, lose that influence which is rightly theirs, because they happen to be thwarted in the use of the channels natural and proper to its exercise. He did not lose his place in the minds of men because he was out of their sight.

Keble was a man who guided himself and formed his judgments, not by processes of reason, by inquiry or by argument, but, to use the word in a broad sense, by authority. Conscience is an authority; the Bible is an authority; such is the Church; such is Antiquity; such are the words of the wise; such are hereditary lessons; such are ethical truths; such are historical memories; such are legal saws and state maxims; such are proverbs; such are sentiments, presages, and prepossessions. It seemed to me as if he ever felt happier, when he could speak or act under some such primary or external sanction; and could use argument mainly as means of recommending or explaining what had claims on his reception prior to proof. He even felt a tenderness, I think, in spite of Bacon for the Idols of the Tribe and the Den, of the Market and the Theatre. What he hated instinctively was heresy, insubordination, resistance to things established, claims of independence, disloyalty, innovation, a critical, censorious spirit. And such was the main principle of the school which in the course of years was formed around him; nor is it easy to set limits to its influence in its day; for multitudes of men, who did not profess its teaching or accept its peculiar doctrines, were willing nevertheless, or found it to their purpose, to act in company with it.

Indeed for a time it was practically the champion and advocate of the political doctrines of the great clerical interest through the country, who found in Mr. Keble and his friends an intellectual, as well as moral support to their cause, which they looked for in vain elsewhere. His weak point, in their eyes, was his consistency; for he carried his love of authority and old times so far, as to be more than gentle towards the Catholic Religion, with which the Toryism of Oxford and of the Church of England had no sympathy. Accordingly, if my memory be correct, he never could get himself to throw his heart into the opposition made to Catholic Emancipation, strongly as he revolted from the politics and the instruments by means of which that Emancipation was won. I fancy he would have had no difficulty in accepting Dr. Johnson's saying about "the first Whig"; and it grieved and offended him that the "Via prima salutis" should be opened to the Catholic body from the Whig quarter. In spite of his reverence for the Old Religion, I conceive that on the whole he would rather have kept its professors beyond the pale of the Constitution with the Tories, than admit them on the principles of the Whigs. Moreover, if the Revolution of 1688 was too lax in principle for him and his friends, much less, as is very plain, could they endure to subscribe to the revolutionary doctrines of 1776 and 1789, which they felt to be absolutely and entirely out of keeping with theological truth.

The old Tory or Conservative party in Oxford had in it no principle or power of development, and that from its very nature and constitution: it was otherwise with the Liberals. They represented a new idea, which was but gradually learning to recognize itself, to ascertain its characteristics and external relations, and to exert an influence upon the University. The party grew, all the time that I was in Oxford, even in numbers, certainly in breadth and definiteness of doctrine, and in power. And, what was a far higher consideration, by the accession of Dr. Arnold's pupils, it was invested with an elevation of character which claimed the respect even of its opponents. On the other hand, in proportion as it became more earnest and less self-applauding, it became more free-spoken; and members of it might be found who, from the mere circumstance of remaining firm to their original professions, would in the judgment of the world, as to their public acts, seem to have left it for the Conservative camp. Thus, neither in its component parts nor in its policy, was it the same in 1832, 1836, and 1841, as it was in 1845.

These last remarks will serve to throw light upon a matter personal to myself, which I have introduced into my Narrative, and to which my attention has been pointedly called, now that my Volume is coming to a second edition.

It has been strongly urged upon me to reconsider the following passages which occur in it: "The men who had driven me from Oxford were distinctly the Liberals, it was they who had opened the attack upon Tract 90," and "I found no fault with the Liberals; they had beaten me in a fair field."

I am very unwilling to seem ungracious, or to cause pain in any quarter; still I am sorry to say I cannot modify these statements. It is surely a matter of historical fact that I left Oxford upon the University proceedings of 1841; and in those proceedings, whether we look to the Heads of Houses or the resident Masters, the leaders, if intellect and influence make men such, were members of the Liberal party. Those who did not lead, concurred or acquiesced in them,—I may say, felt a satisfaction. I do not recollect any Liberal who was on my side on that occasion. Excepting the Liberal, no other party, as a party, acted against me. I am not complaining of them; I deserved nothing else at their hands. They could not undo in 1845, even had they wished it, (and there is no proof they did,) what they had done in 1841. In 1845, when I had already given up the contest for four years, and my part in it had passed into the hands of others, then some of those who were prominent against me in 1841, feeling (what they had not felt in 1841) the danger of driving a number of my followers to Rome, and joined by younger friends who had come into University importance since 1841 and felt kindly towards me, adopted a course more consistent with their principles, and proceeded to shield from the zeal of the Hebdomadal Board, not me, but, professedly, all parties through the country—Tractarians, Evangelicals, Liberals in general,— who had to subscribe to the Anglican formularies, on the ground that those formularies, rigidly taken, were, on some point or other, a difficulty to all parties alike.

However, besides the historical fact, I can bear witness to my own feeling at the time, and my feeling was this: that those who in 1841 had considered it to be a duty to act against me, had then done their worst. What was it to me what they were now doing in opposition to the New Test proposed by the Hebdomadal Board? I owed them no thanks for their trouble. I took no interest at all, in February 1845, in the proceedings of the Heads of Houses and of the Convocation. I felt myself dead as regarded my relations to the Anglican Church. My leaving it was all but a matter of time. I believe I did not even thank my real friends, the two Proctors, who in Convocation stopped by their Veto the condemnation of Tract 90; nor did I make any acknowledgment to Mr. Rogers nor to Mr. James Mozley, nor, as I think, to Mr.

Hussey, for their pamphlets on my behalf. My frame of mind is best described by the sentiment of the passage in Horace, which at the time I was fond of quoting, as expressing my view of the relation that existed between the Vice-Chancellor and myself.

"Pentheu
Rector Thebarum quid me perferre patique
Indignum cogas?" 'Adimam bona.' "Nempe pecus, rem,
Lectos, argentum; tollas licet." 'In manicis et
Compedibus, saevi, te sub custode tenebo.' (viz. the 39 Articles)
"Ipse Deus, simul atque volam, me solvet." Opinor
Hoc sentit; Moriar. Mors ultima linea rerum est.[1]

I conclude this notice of Liberalism in Oxford, and the party which was antagonistic to it, with some propositions in detail, which, as a member of the latter, and together with the High Church, I earnestly denounced and abjured.

1. No religious tenet is important, unless reason shows it to be so.
Therefore, e.g. the doctrine of the Athanasian Creed is not to be insisted on, unless it tends to convert the soul; and the doctrine of the Atonement is to be insisted on, if it does convert the soul.

2. No one can believe what he does not understand.
Therefore, e.g. there are no mysteries in true religion.

3. No theological doctrine is any thing more than an opinion which happens to be held by bodies of men.
Therefore, e.g. no creed, as such, is necessary for salvation.

4. It is dishonest in a man to make an act of faith in what he has not had brought home to him by actual proof.
Therefore, e.g. the mass of men ought not absolutely to believe in the divine authority of the Bible.

5. It is immoral in a man to believe more than he can spontaneously receive as being congenial to his moral and mental nature.
Therefore, e.g. a given individual is not bound to believe in eternal punishment.

6. No revealed doctrines or precepts may reasonably stand in the way of scientific conclusions.
Therefore, e.g. Political Economy may reverse our Lord's declarations about

[1] [*"Pentheus, king of Thebes, what indignities will you compel me to suffer and endure?" 'I will take away your goods.' "My cattle, I suppose, my land, my moveables and money: you may take them." 'I will confine you with handcuffs and fetters under a merciless jailer.' (viz. the 39 Articles) "The deity himself will discharge me, whenever I please." In my opinion, this is his meaning; I will die. Death is the ultimate boundary of human matters.*—Horace, *Epistles*, Bk. i, No. xvi]

poverty and riches, or a system of Ethics may teach that the highest condition of body is ordinarily essential to the highest state of mind.

7. Christianity is necessarily modified by the growth of civilization and the exigencies of times.

Therefore, e.g. the Catholic Priesthood, though necessary in the Middle Ages, may be superseded now.

8. There is a system of religion more simply true than Christianity as it has ever been received.

Therefore, e.g. we may advance that Christianity is the "corn of wheat" which has been dead for 1800 years, but at length will bear fruit; and that Mahometanism is the manly religion, and existing Christianity the womanish.

9. There is a right of Private Judgment: that is, there is no existing authority on earth competent to interfere with the liberty of individuals in reasoning and judging for themselves about the Bible and its contents, as they severally please.

Therefore, e. g. religious establishments requiring subscriptions are Antichristian.

10. There are rights of conscience such, that every one may lawfully advance a claim to profess and teach what is false and wrong in matters, religion, social, and moral, provided that to his private conscience it seems absolutely true and right.

Therefore, e.g. individuals have a right to preach and practise fornication and polygamy.

11. There is no such thing as a national or state conscience.

Therefore, e.g. no judgments can fall upon a sinful or infidel nation.

12. The civil power has no positive duty, in a normal state of things, to maintain religious truth.

Therefore, e.g. blasphemy and sabbath-breaking are not rightly punishable by law.

13. Utility and expedience are the measure of political duty.

Therefore, e.g. no punishment may be enacted, on the ground that God commands it, e.g. on the text, "Whoso sheddeth man's blood, by man shall his blood be shed."

14. The Civil Power may dispose of Church property without sacrilege.

Therefore, e.g. Henry VIII committed no sin in his spoliations.

15. The Civil Power has the right of ecclesiastical jurisdiction and administration.

Therefore, e.g. Parliament may impose articles of faith on the Church or suppress Dioceses.

16. It is lawful to rise in arms against legitimate princes.

Therefore, e.g. the Puritans in the 17th century, and the French in the 18th, were justifiable in their Rebellion and Revolution respectively.

17. The people are the legitimate source of power.

Therefore, e.g. Universal Suffrage is among the natural rights of man.

18. Virtue is the child of knowledge, and vice of ignorance.

Therefore, e.g. education, periodical literature, railroad travelling, ventilation, drainage, and the arts of life, when fully carried out, serve to make a population moral and happy.

All of these propositions, and many others too, were familiar to me thirty years ago, as in the number of the tenets of Liberalism, and, while I gave into none of them except No. 12, and perhaps No. 11 and partly No. 1, before I began to publish, so afterwards I wrote against most of them in some part or other of my Anglican works.

If it is necessary to refer to a work, not simply my own, but of the Tractarian school which contains a similar protest, I should name the *Lyra Apostolica.* This volume, which by accident has been left unnoticed, except incidentally, in my Narrative, was collected together from the pages of the *British Magazine,* in which its contents originally appeared, and published in a separate form, immediately after Hurrell Froude's death in 1836. Its signatures a, β, γ, δ, ϵ, ζ, denote respectively as authors, Mr. Bowden, Mr. Hurrell Froude, Mr. Keble, Mr. Newman, Mr. Robert Wilberforce, and Mr. Isaac Williams.

There is one poem on "Liberalism," beginning "Ye cannot halve the Gospel of God's grace:" which bears out the account of Liberalism as above given; and another upon "the Age to come," defining from its own point of view the position and prospects of Liberalism.

I need hardly say that the above Note is mainly historical. How far the Liberal party of 1830-40 really held the above eighteen Theses, which I attributed to them, and how far and in what sense I should oppose those Theses now, could scarcely be explained without a separate Dissertation.

CHARLES DARWIN

CHARLES DARWIN (1809–82) was descended from a line of physicians; his grandfather, Erasmus Darwin, had been a pioneer evolutionist. After studying medicine, and preparing at Cambridge for theology, Darwin became naturalist for the surveying expedition of the *Beagle*. During its five-year voyage to remote corners of the globe he collected the basic evidence and obtained the initial inspiration for his theory of evolution. On his return he served as secretary of the Geological Society, in close association with Charles Lyell. Lyell's revolutionary *Principles of Geology* (1830–33) had accustomed men to the immensity of geological time and to the principle of the "uniformity" of nature—the idea that all changes must be understood as caused by the operation of essentially similar natural processes. In accordance with this principle, Darwin looked to "artificial selection" (the way the breeder of new varieties of animals and plants selects those he will preserve) as the observable process that bears the closest analogy to the "natural selection" by which species might have been modified. But what automatic mechanism takes the place of the breeder? In 1838 Darwin found the answer in Malthus's *Essay on Population*. In the competition for survival in human society, Darwin saw the analogue of the struggle for existence he had long observed among living things. "Under these circumstances, favourable variations would tend to be preserved and unfavourable ones to be destroyed. The result of this would be the formation of new species. Here, then, I had a theory by which to work."

Illness forced Darwin to retire to a country seat at Down, where he patiently experimented with plants and collected further evidence. He worked carefully and slowly, and he had a book about half completed when Alfred Russel Wallace sent him from the Moluccas a paper which read like an abstract of his own theory of natural selection. On the advice of his friends Lyell and Hooker he sent Wallace's paper, together with an abstract of his own, to the Linnaean Society, where both were read on July 1, 1858. The next year he issued his completed treatise, the *Origin of Species*. In 1871 the *Descent of Man* crowned his theory by including man in the evolutionary process.

The *Origin of Species* brought together a mass of cumulative evidence drawn from geographical distribution, paleontology, embryology, comparative anatomy, and experimental breeding—sufficient to convince biologists that, whatever its explanation, the evolution of species was a fact. The idea of organic evolution had long been familiar and had found able exponents for almost a century, as the "Historical Sketch" Darwin prefixed to the second edition makes clear. The opening passage of the following selections emphasizes, for example, the work of Lamarck and Geoffroy Saint-Hilaire. But most naturalists had rejected "transformism," partly because of the limited time then allowed for the history of the earth, partly because not even Lamarck had been able to suggest a credible and verifiable theory of the way in which the process could have taken place.

Besides collecting evidence for the fact of evolution, the *Origin of Species* emphasizes the novel idea of "natural selection" through the survival and perpetuation of the fittest variations in the struggle for existence. This was Darwin's theory of the factors involved in the evolutionary process. As the first plausible account of the method of evolution, the "natural selection" of chance variations played a large part in winning general acceptance of the fact of evolution. Ironically enough, it is Darwin's causal theory that has had to be most drastically supplemented and reconstructed in the light of closer analysis and of detailed knowledge of the mechanisms of heredity. In the Conclusion of the *Origin* Darwin rejects "great and abrupt modifications." Since the work of Hugo DeVries, most biologists have accepted the view that only large and sudden variations can be inherited—the complete jumps or mutations. In the words of T. H. Morgan, "The causes of the mutations that give rise to new characters we do not know, although we have no reason for supposing that they are due to other than natural processes."

The repercussions of the central ideas of the *Origin of Species* form a large part of the intellectual history of the later nineteenth century. At first, after an initial struggle to win popular acceptance, Darwin was taken as supplying solid scientific evidence for various conflicting social programs of "progress." Evolution was broadened to a single inevitable cosmic process, and became an up-to-date version of God's providence—or a substitute for it. Only slowly did men come to understand that the idea of organic evolution, taken seriously, did not give "answers" but transformed the problems to which philosophies of progress and social reform programs seemed answers. By the turn of the century men began to comprehend that the real significance of biological evolution lay in the new attitudes and novel ideas to which it pointed: the abolition of the last fixity in nature, the breakdown of sharp lines of demarcation between species, the emphasis on the detailed causal analysis of specific processes of change, a general pluralism and relativism stressing the functional role of ideas involved in the observable temporal "process," and the abandonment of the earlier exclusively mechanistic approach to nature.

THE ORIGIN OF SPECIES

HISTORICAL SKETCH

Until recently the great majority of naturalists believed that species were immutable productions, and had been separately created. This view has been ably maintained by many authors. Some few naturalists, on the other hand, have believed that species undergo modification, and that the existing forms of life are the descendants by true generation of pre-existing forms. Passing over allusions to the subject in the classical writers,[1] the first author who in modern times has treated it in a scientific spirit was Buffon. But as his opinions fluctuated greatly at different periods, and as he does not enter on the causes or means of the transformation of species, I need not here enter on details.

Lamarck was the first man whose conclusions on the subject excited much attention. This justly-celebrated naturalist first published his views in 1801; he much enlarged them in 1809 in his "Philosophie Zoologique," and subsequently, in 1815, in the Introduction to his "Hist. Nat. des Animaux sans Vertébres." In these works he upholds the doctrine that all species, including man, are descended from other species. He first did the eminent service of arousing attention to the probability of all change in the organic, as well as in the inorganic world, being the result of law, and not of miraculous interposition. [Lamarck seems to have been chiefly led to his conclusion on the gradual change of species, by the difficulty of distinguishing species and varieties, by the almost perfect gradation of forms in certain groups, and by the analogy of domestic productions. With respect to the means of modification, he attributed something to the direct action of the physical conditions of life, something to the crossing of already existing forms, and much to use and disuse, that is, to (the effects of habit.) To this latter agency he seems to attribute all the beautiful adaptations in nature;—such as the long neck of the giraffe for browsing on the branches of trees. But he likewise believed in a law of progressive development; and as all the forms of life thus tend to progress, in order to account for the existence at the present day of simple productions, he maintains that such forms are now spontaneously generated.[2] . . .]

[1] Aristotle, in his "Physicae Auscultationes" (lib. 2, cap. 8, s. 2), after remarking that rain does not fall in order to make the corn grow, any more than it falls to spoil the farmer's corn when threshed out of doors, applies the same argument to organisation; and adds (as translated by Mr. Clair Grece, who first pointed out the passage to me), "So what hinders the different parts [of the body] from having this merely accidental relation in nature? as the teeth, for example, grow by necessity, the front ones sharp, adapted for dividing, and the grinders flat, and serviceable for masticating the food; since they were not made for the sake of this, but it was the result of accident. And in like manner as to the other parts in which there appears to exist an adaptation to an end. Wheresoever, therefore, all things together (that is all the parts of one whole) happened like as if they were made for the sake of something, these were preserved, having been appropriately constituted by an internal spontaneity; and whatsoever things were not thus constituted, perished, and still perish." We here see the principle of natural selection shadowed forth, but how little Aristotle fully comprehended the principle, is shown by his remarks on the formation of the teeth.

[2] I have taken the date of the first publication of Lamarck from Isid. Geoffroy Saint-Hilaire's ("Hist. Natl. Générale," tom. ii., p. 405, 1859) excellent history of opinion on this subject. In this work a full account is given on Buffon's conclusions on the same subject. It is curious how largely my grandfather, Dr. Erasmus Darwin, anticipated the views and erroneous grounds of opinion

INTRODUCTION

When on Board H.M.S. "Beagle," as naturalist, I was much struck with certain facts in the distribution of the organic beings inhabiting South America, and in the geological relations of the present to the past inhabitants of that continent. These facts, as will be seen in the latter chapters of this volume, seemed to throw some light on the origin of species—that mystery of mysteries, as it has been called by one of our greatest philosophers. . . .

This Abstract, which I now publish, must necessarily be imperfect. I cannot here give references and authorities for my several statements; and I must trust to the reader reposing some confidence in my accuracy. No doubt errors will have crept in, though I hope I have always been cautious in trusting to good authorities alone. I can here give only the general conclusions at which I have arrived, with a few facts in illustration, but which, I hope, in most cases will suffice. No one can feel more sensible than I do of the necessity of hereafter publishing in detail all the facts, with references, on which my conclusions have been grounded; and I hope in a future work to do this. For I am well aware that scarcely a single point is discussed in this volume on which facts cannot be adduced, often apparently leading to conclusions directly opposite to those at which I have arrived. A fair result can be obtained only by fully stating and balancing the facts and arguments on both sides of each question; and this is here impossible. . . .

In considering the origin of species, it is quite conceivable that a naturalist, reflecting on the mutual affinities of organic beings, on their embryological relations, their geographical distribution, geological succession, and other such facts, might come to the conclusion that species had not been independently created, but had descended, like varieties, from other species. Nevertheless, such a conclusion, even if well founded, would be unsatisfactory, until it could be shown how the innumerable species inhabiting this world have been modified, so as to acquire that perfection of structure and coadaptation which justly excites our admiration. Naturalists continually refer to external conditions, such as climate, food, &c., as the only possible cause of variation. In one limited sense, as we shall hereafter see, this may be true; but it is preposterous to at-

---

of Lamarck in his "Zoonomia" (vol. i., pp. 500–510), published in 1794. According to Isid. Geoffroy there is no doubt that Goethe was an extreme partisan of similar views, as shown in the Introduction to a work written in 1794 and 1795, but not published till long afterwards: he has pointedly remarked ("Goethe als Naturforscher," von Dr. Karl Meding, s. 34) that the future question for naturalists will be how, for instance, cattle got their horns, and not for what they are used. It is rather a singular instance of the manner in which similar views arise at about the same time, that Goethe in Germany, Dr. Darwin in England, and Geoffroy Saint-Hilaire (as we shall immediately see) in France, came to the same conclusion on the origin of species, in the years 1794–5.

tribute to mere external condition, the structure, for instance, of the wood-pecker, with its feet, tail, beak and tongue, so admirably adapted to catch insects under the bark of trees. In the case of the mistletoe, which draws its nourishment from certain trees, which has seeds that must be transported by certain birds, and which has flowers with separate sexes absolutely requiring the agency of certain insects to bring pollen from one flower to the other, it is equally preposterous to account for the structure of this parasite, with its relations to several distinct organic beings, by the effects of external conditions, or of habit, or of the volition of the plant itself.

It is, therefore, of the highest importance to gain a clear insight into the means of modification and co-adaptation. At the commencement of my obser-vations it seemed to me probable that a careful study of domesticated animals and of cultivated plants would offer the best chance of making out this obscure problem. Nor have I been disappointed; in this and in all other perplexing cases I have invariably found that our knowledge, imperfect though it be, of variation under domestication, afforded the best and safest clue. I may venture to express my conviction of the high value of such studies, although they have been very commonly neglected by naturalists.

From these considerations, I shall devote the first chapter of this Abstract to Variation under Domestication. We shall thus see that a large amount of hereditary modification is at least possible; and, what is equally or more im-portant, we shall see how great is the power of man in accumulating by his Selection successive slight variations. I will then pass on to the variability of species in a state of nature; but I shall, unfortunately, be compelled to treat this subject far too briefly, as it can be treated properly only by giving long catalogues of facts. We shall, however, be enabled to discuss what circum-stances are most favourable to variation. In the next chapter the Struggle for Existence amongst all organic beings throughout the world, which inevitably follows from the higher geometrical ratio of their increase, will be considered. This is the doctrine of Malthus, applied to the whole animal and vegetable kingdoms. As many more individuals of each species are born than can pos-sibly survive; and as, consequently, there is a frequently recurring struggle for existence, it follows that any being, if it vary however slightly in any man-ner profitable to itself, under the complex and sometimes varying conditions of life, will have a better chance of surviving, and thus be *naturally selected*. From the strong principle of inheritance, any selected variety will tend to propagate its new and modified form.

This fundamental subject of Natural Selection will be treated at some length in the fourth chapter; and we shall then see how Natural Selection al-most inevitably causes much Extinction of the less improved forms of life, and leads to what I have called Divergence of Character. In the next chapter I shall discuss the complex and little known laws of variation. In the five succeeding chapters, the most apparent and gravest difficulties in accepting the theory will be given: namely, first, the difficulties of transitions, or how a simple being or a simple organ can be changed and perfected into a highly developed being or into an elaborately constructed organ; secondly, the subject of Instinct, or the mental powers of animals; thirdly, Hybridism, or the infertility of species and the fertility of varieties when intercrossed; and fourthly, the imperfection of the Geological Record. In the next chapter I shall consider the geological succession of organic beings throughout time; in the twelfth and thirteenth, their geographical distribution throughout space; in the fourteenth, their classification or mutual affinities, both when mature and in an embryonic condition. In the last chapter I shall give a brief recapitulation of the whole work, and a few concluding remarks.

No one ought to feel surprise at much remaining as yet unexplained in regard to the origin of species and varieties, if he make due allowance for our profound ignorance in regard to the mutual relations of the many beings which live around us. Who can explain why one species ranges widely and is very numerous, and why another allied species has a narrow range and is rare? Yet these relations are of the highest importance, for they determine the present welfare and, as I believe, the future success and modification of every inhabitant of this world. Still less do we know of the mutual relations of the innumerable inhabitants of the world during the many past geological epochs in its history. Although much remains obscure, and will long remain obscure, I can entertain no doubt, after the most deliberate study and dispassionate judgment of which I am capable, that the view which most naturalists until recently entertained, and which I formerly entertained—namely, that each species has been independently created—is erroneous. I am fully convinced that species are not immutable; but that those belonging to what are called the same genera are lineal descendants of some other and generally extinct species, in the same manner as the acknowledged varieties of any one species are the descendants of that species. Furthermore, I am convinced that Natural Selection has been the most important, but not the exclusive, means of modification.

CHAPTER IV: NATURAL SELECTION; OR THE SURVIVAL OF THE FITTEST

. . . If under changing conditions of life organic beings present individual differences in almost every part of their structure, and this cannot be disputed; if there be, owing to their geometrical rate of increase, a severe struggle for life at some age, season, or year, and this certainly cannot be disputed; then, considering the infinite complexity of the relations of all organic beings to each other and to their conditions of life, causing an infinite diversity in structure, constitution, and habits, to be advantageous to them, it would be a most extraordinary fact if no variations had ever occurred useful to each being's own welfare, in the same manner as so many variations have occurred useful to man. But if variations useful to any organic being ever do occur, assuredly individuals thus characterised will have the best chance of being preserved in the struggle for life; and from the strong principle of inheritance, these will tend to produce offspring similarly characterised. This principle of preservation, or the survival of the fittest, I have called Natural Selection. It leads to the improvement of each creature in relation to its organic and inorganic conditions of life; and consequently, in most cases, to what must be regarded as an advance in organisation. Nevertheless, low and simple forms will long endure if well fitted for their simple conditions of life.

Natural selection, on the principle of qualities being inherited at corresponding ages, can modify the egg, seed, or young, as easily as the adult. Amongst many animals, sexual selection will have given its aid to ordinary selection, by assuring to the most vigorous and best adapted males the greatest number of offspring. Sexual selection will also give characters useful to the males alone, in their struggles or rivalry with other males; and these characters will be transmitted to one sex or to both sexes, according to the form of inheritance which prevails. . . .

. . . It is the common, the widely-diffused and widely-ranging species, belonging to the larger genera within each class, which vary most; and these tend to transmit to their modified offspring that superiority which now makes them dominant in their own countries. Natural selection, as has just been remarked, leads to divergence of character and to much extinction of the less improved and intermediate forms of life. On these principles, the nature of the affinities, and the generally well-defined distinctions between the innumerable organic beings in each class throughout the world, may be explained. It is a truly wonderful fact—the wonder of which we are apt to overlook from familiarity—that all animals and all plants throughout all time and space should be related to each other in groups, subordinate to groups, in the manner which we everywhere behold—namely, varieties of the same species most closely related, species of the same genus less closely and unequally related, forming sections and sub-genera, species of distinct genera much less closely related, and genera related in different degrees, forming sub-families, families, orders, sub-classes and classes. The several subordinate groups in any class cannot be ranked in a single file, but seem clustered round points, and these round other points, and so on in almost endless cycles. If species had been independently created, no explanation would have been possible of this kind of classification; but it is explained through inheritance and the complex action of natural selection, entailing extinction and divergence of character. . . .

The affinities of all the beings of the same class have sometimes been represented by a great tree. I believe this simile largely speaks the truth. The green and budding twigs may represent existing species; and those produced during former years may represent the long succession of extinct species. At each period of growth all the growing twigs have tried to branch out on all sides, and to overtop and kill the surrounding twigs and branches, in the same manner as species and groups of species have at all times overmastered other species in the great battle for life. The limbs divided into great branches, and these into lesser and lesser branches, were themselves once, when the tree was young, budding twigs; and this connection of the former and present buds by ramifying branches may well represent the classification of all extinct and living species in groups subordinate to groups. Of the many twigs which flourished when the tree was a mere bush, only two or three, now grown into great branches, yet survive and bear the other branches; so with the species which lived during long-past geological periods, very few have left living and modified descendants. From the first growth of the tree, many a limb and branch has decayed and dropped off; and these fallen branches of various sizes may represent those whole orders, families, and genera which have now no living representatives, and which are known to us only in a fossil state. As we here and there see a thin straggling branch springing from a fork low down in a tree, and which by some chance has been favoured and is still alive on its summit, so we occasionally see an animal like the Ornithorhynchus or Lepidosiren, which in some small degree connects by its affinities two large branches of life, and which has apparently been saved from fatal competition by having inhabited a protected station. As buds give rise by growth to fresh buds, and these, if vigorous, branch out and overtop on all sides many a feebler branch, so by generation I believe it has been with the great Tree of Life, which fills with its dead and broken branches the crust of the earth, and covers the surface with its ever-branching and beautiful ramifications.

CHAPTER XV: RECAPITULATION AND CONCLUSION

. . . Under domestication we see much variability, caused, or at least excited, by changed conditions of life; but often in so obscure a manner, that we are tempted to consider the variations as spontaneous. Variability is governed by many complex laws,—by correlated growth, compensation, the increased use and disuse of parts, and the definite action of the surrounding conditions. There is much difficulty in ascertaining how largely our domestic productions have been modified; but we may safely infer that the amount has been large, and that modifications can be inherited for long periods. . . .

There is no reason why the principles which have acted so efficiently under domestication should not have acted under nature. In the survival of favoured individuals and races, during the constantly-recurrent Struggle for Existence, we see a powerful and ever-acting form of Selection. The struggle for existence inevitably follows from the high geometrical ratio of increase which is common to all organic beings. This high rate of increase is proved by calculation, —by the rapid increase of many animals and plants during a succession of peculiar seasons, and when naturalised in new countries. More individuals are born than can possibly survive. A grain in the balance may determine which individual shall live and which shall die,—which variety or species shall increase in number, and which shall decrease, or finally become extinct. As the individuals of the same species come in all respects into the closest competition with each other, the struggle will generally be most severe between them; it will be almost equally severe between the varieties of the same species, and next in severity between the species of the same genus. On the other hand the struggle will often be severe between beings remote in the scale of nature. The slightest advantage in certain individuals, at any age or during any season, over those with which they come into competition, or better adaptation in however slight a degree to the surrounding physical conditions, will, in the long run, turn the balance.

With animals having separated sexes, there will be in most cases a struggle between the males for the possession of the females. The most vigorous males, or those which have most successfully struggled with their conditions of life, will generally leave most progeny. But success will often depend on the males having special weapons, or means of defence, or charms; and a slight advantage will lead to victory.

As geology plainly proclaims that each land has undergone great physical changes, we might have expected to find that organic beings have varied under nature, in the same way as they have varied under domestication. And if there has been any variability under nature, it would be an unaccountable fact if natural selection had not come into play. It has often been asserted, but the assertion is incapable of proof, that the amount of variation under nature is a strictly limited quantity. Man, though acting on external characters alone and often capriciously, can produce within a short period a great result by adding up mere individual differences in his domestic productions; and every one admits that species present individual differences. But, besides such differences, all naturalists admit that natural varieties exist, which are considered sufficiently distinct to be worthy of record in systematic works. No one has drawn any clear distinction between individual differences and slight varieties; or between more plainly marked varieties and sub-species, and species. On separate continents, and on different parts of the same continent when divided by barriers of any kind, and on outlying islands, what a multitude of forms exist, which some experienced naturalists rank as varieties, others as geographical races or sub-species, and others as distinct, though closely allied species!

[If then, animals and plants do vary, let it be ever so slightly or slowly, why should not variations or individual differences, which are in any way beneficial, be preserved and accumulated through natural selection, or the survival of the fittest?] If man can by patience select variations useful to him, why, under changing and complex conditions of life, should not variations useful to nature's living products often arise, and be preserved or selected? What limit can be put to this power, acting during long ages and rigidly scrutinising the whole constitution, structure, and habits of each creature,—favouring the good and rejecting the bad? I can see no limit to this power, in slowly and beautifully adapting each form to the most complex relations of life. The theory of natural selection, even if we look no farther than this, seems to be in the highest degree probable. . . .

On the view that species are only strongly marked and permanent varieties, and that each species first existed as a variety, we can see why it is that no line of demarcation can be drawn between species, commonly supposed to have been produced by special acts of creation, and varieties which are acknowledged to have been produced by secondary laws. On this same view we can understand how it is that in a region where many species of a genus have been produced, and where they now flourish, these same species should present many varieties; for where the manufactory of species has been active, we might expect, as a general rule, to find it still in action; and this is the case if varieties be incipient species. Moreover, the species of the larger genera, which afford the greater number of varieties or incipient species, retain to a certain degree the character of varieties; for they differ from each other by a less amount of difference than do the species of smaller genera. The closely allied species also of the larger genera apparently have restricted ranges, and in their affinities they are clustered in little groups round other species—in both respects resembling varieties. These are strange relations on the view that each species was independently created, but are intelligible if each existed first as a variety.

As each species tends by its geometrical rate of reproduction to increase inordinately in number; and as the modified descendants of each species will be enabled to increase by as much as they become more diversified in habits and structure, so as to be able to seize on many and widely different places in the economy of nature, there will be a constant tendency in natural selection to preserve the most divergent offspring of any one species. Hence, during a long continued course of modification, the slight differences characteristic of varieties of the same species, tend to be augmented into the greater differences characteristic of the species of the same genus. New and improved varieties will inevitably supplant and exterminate the older, less improved, and intermediate varieties; and thus species are rendered to a large extent defined and distinct objects. Dominant species belonging to the larger groups within each class tend to give birth to new and dominant forms; so that each large group tends to become still larger, and at the same time more divergent in character. But as all groups cannot thus go on increasing in size, for the world would not hold them, the more dominant groups beat the less dominant. This tendency in the large groups to go on increasing in size and diverging in character, together with the inevitable contingency of much extinction, explains the arrangement of all the forms of life in groups subordinate to groups, all within a few great classes, which has prevailed throughout all time. This grand fact of the grouping of all organic beings under what is called the Natural System, is utterly inexplicable on the theory of creation.

As natural selection acts solely by accumulating slight, successive, favourable variations, it can produce no great or sudden modifications; it can act only by short and slow steps. Hence, the canon of "Natura non facit saltum," which every fresh addition to our knowledge tends to confirm, is on this theory intelligible. We can see why throughout nature the same general end is gained by an almost infinite diversity of means, for every peculiarity when once acquired is long inherited, and structures already modified in many different ways have to be adapted for the same general purpose. We can, in short, see why nature is prodigal in variety, though niggard in innovation. But why this should be a law of nature if each species has been independently created no man can explain.

Many other facts are, as it seems to me, explicable on this theory. How strange it is that a bird, under the form of a woodpecker, should prey on insects on the ground; that upland geese which rarely or never swim, should possess webbed feet; that a thrush-like bird should dive and feed on sub-aquatic insects; and that a petrel should have the habits and structure fitting it for the life of an auk! and so in endless other cases. But on the view of each species constantly trying to increase in number, with natural selection always ready to adapt the slowly varying descendants of each to any unoccupied or ill-occupied place in nature, these facts cease to be strange, or might even have been anticipated.

We can to a certain extent understand how it is that there is so much beauty throughout nature; for this may be largely attributed to the agency of selection. That beauty, according to our sense of it, is not universal, must be admitted by every one who will look at some venomous snakes, at some fishes, and at certain hideous bats with a distorted resemblance to the human face. Sexual selection has given the most brilliant colours, elegant patterns, and other ornaments to the males, and sometimes to both sexes of many birds, butterflies, and other animals. With birds it has often rendered the voice of the male musical to the female, as well as to our ears. Flowers and fruit have been rendered conspicuous by brilliant colours in contrast with the green foliage, in order that the flowers may be readily seen, visited and fertilized by insects, and the seeds disseminated by birds. How it comes that certain colours, sounds, and forms should give pleasure to man and the lower animals,—that is, how the sense of beauty in its simplest form was first acquired,—we do not know any more than how certain odours and flavours were first rendered agreeable.

As natural selection acts by competition, it adapts and improves the inhabitants of each country only in relation to their co-inhabitants; so that we need feel no surprise at the species of any one country, although on the ordinary view supposed to have been created and specially adapted for that country, being beaten and supplanted by the naturalised productions from another land. Nor ought we to marvel if all the contrivances in nature be not, as far as we can judge, absolutely perfect, as in the case even of the human eye; or if some of them be abhorrent to our ideas of fitness. We need not marvel at the sting of the bee, when used against an enemy, causing the bee's own death; at drones being produced in such great numbers for one single act, and being then slaughtered by their sterile sisters; at the astonishing waste of pollen by our fir-trees; at the instinctive hatred of the queen-bee for her own fertile daughters; and the ichneumonidae feeding within the living bodies of caterpillars; or at other such cases. The wonder indeed is, on the theory of natural selection, that more cases of the want of absolute perfection have not been detected.

The complex and little known laws governing the production of varieties are the same, as far as we can judge, with the laws which have governed the production of distinct species. In both cases physical conditions seem to have produced some direct and definite effect, but how much we cannot say. Thus, when varieties enter any new station, they occasionally assume some of the characters proper to the species of that station. With both varieties and species, use and disuse seem to have produced a considerable effect; for it is impossible to resist this conclusion when we look, for instance, at the logger headed duck, which has wings incapable of flight, in nearly the same condition as in the domestic duck; or when we look at the burrowing tucu-tucu, which is occasionally blind, and then at certain moles, which are habitually blind and have their eyes covered with skin; or when we look at the blind animals inhabiting the dark caves of America and Europe. With varieties and species, correlated variation seems to have played an important part, so that when one part has been modified other parts have been necessarily modified. With both varieties and species, reversions to long-lost characters occasionally occur. How inexplicable on the theory of creation is the occasional appearance of stripes on the shoulders and legs of the several species of the horse-genus and of their hybrids! How simply is this fact explained if we believe that these species are all descended from a striped progenitor, in the same manner as the several domestic breeds of the pigeon are descended from the blue and barred rock-pigeon.

On the ordinary view of each species having been independently created, why should specific characters, or those by which the species of the same genus differ from each other, be more variable than generic characters in which they all agree? Why, for instance, should the colour of a flower be more likely to vary in any one species of a genus, if the other species possess differently coloured flowers, than if all possessed the same coloured flowers? If species are only well-marked varieties, of which the characters have become in a high degree permanent, we can understand this fact; for they have already varied since they branched off from a common progenitor in certain characters, by which they have come to be specifically distinct from each other; therefore these same characters would be more likely again to vary than the generic characters which have been inherited without change for an immense period. It is inexplicable on the theory of creation why a part developed in a very unusual manner in one species alone of a genus, and therefore, as we may naturally infer, of great importance to that species, should be eminently liable to variation; but, on our view, this part has undergone, since the several species branched off from a common progenitor, an unusual amount of variability and modification, and therefore we might expect the part generally to be still variable. But a part may be developed in the most unusual manner, like the wing of a bat, and yet not be more variable than any other structure, if the part be common to many subordinate forms, that is, if it has been inherited for a very long period; for in this case it will have been rendered constant by long-continued natural selection. . . .

The similar framework of bones in the hand of a man, wing of a bat, fin of the porpoise, and leg of the horse,—the same number of vertebrae forming the neck of the giraffe and of the elephant,—and innumerable other such facts, at once explain themselves on the theory of descent with slow and slight successive modifications. The similarity of pattern in the wing and in the leg of a bat, though used for such different purpose,—in the jaws and legs of a crab,—in the petals, stamens, and pistils of a flower, is likewise, to a large extent, intelligible on the view of the gradual modification of parts or organs, which were aboriginally alike in an early progenitor in each of these classes. On the principle of successive variations not always supervening at an early age, and being inherited at a corresponding not early period of life, we clearly see why the embryos of mammals, birds, reptiles, and fishes should be so closely similar, and so unlike the adult forms. We may cease marvelling at the embryo of an air breathing mammal or bird having branchial slits and arteries running in loops, like those of a fish which has to breathe the air dissolved in water by the aid of well-developed branchiae.

Disuse, aided sometimes by natural selection, will often have reduced organs when rendered useless under changed habits or conditions of life; and we can understand on this view the meaning of rudimentary organs. But disuse and selection will generally act on each creature, when it has come to maturity and has to play its full part in the struggle for existence, and will thus have little power on an organ during early life; hence the organ will not be reduced or rendered rudimentary at this early age. The calf, for instance, has inherited teeth, which never cut through the gums of the upper jaw, from an early progenitor having well-developed teeth; and we may believe, that the teeth in the mature animal were formerly reduced by disuse, owing to the tongue and palate, or lips, having become excellently fitted through natural selection to browse without their aid; whereas in the calf, the teeth have been left unaffected, and on the principle of inheritance at corresponding ages have been inherited from a remote period to the present day. On the view of each organism with all its separate parts having been specially created, how utterly inexplicable is it that organs bearing the plain stamp of inutility, such as the teeth in the embryonic calf or the shrivelled wings under the soldered wing-covers of many beetles, should so frequently occur. Nature may be said to have taken pains to reveal her scheme of modification, by means of rudimentary organs, of embryological and homologous structures, but we are too blind to understand her meaning.

I have now recapitulated the facts and considerations which have thoroughly convinced me that species have been modified, during a long course of descent. This has been effected chiefly through the natural selection of numerous successive, slight, favourable variations; aided in an important manner by the inherited effects of the use and disuse of parts; and in an unimportant manner, that is in relation to adaptive structures, whether past or present, by the direct action of external conditions, and by variations which seem to us in our ignorance to arise spontaneously. It appears that I formerly underrated the frequency and value of these latter forms of variation, as leading to permanent modifications of structure independently of natural selection. But as my conclusions have lately been much misrepresented, and it has been stated that I attribute the modification of species exclusively to natural selection, I may be permitted to remark that in the first edition of this work, and subsequently, I placed in a most conspicuous position—namely, at the close of the Introduction—the following words: "I am convinced that natural selection has been the main but not the exclusive means of modification." This has been of no avail. Great is the power of steady misrepresentation; but the history of science shows that fortunately this power does not long endure.

It can hardly be supposed that a false theory would explain, in so satisfactory a manner as does the theory of natural selection, the several large classes of facts above specified. It has recently been objected that this is an unsafe method of arguing; but it is a method used in judging of the common events of life, and has often been used by the greatest natural philosophers. The undulatory theory of light has thus been arrived at; and the belief in the revolution of the earth on its own axis was until lately supported by hardly any direct evidence. It is no valid objection that science as yet throws no light on the far higher problem of the essence or origin of life. Who can explain what is the essence of the attraction of gravity? No one now objects to following out the results consequent on this unknown element of attraction; notwithstanding that Leibnitz formerly accused Newton of introducing "occult qualities and miracles into philosophy."

I see no good reason why the views given in this volume should shock the religious feelings of any one. It is satisfactory, as showing how transient such impressions are, to remember that the greatest discovery ever made by man, namely the law of the attraction of gravity, was also attacked by Leibnitz, "as subversive of natural, and inferentially of revealed, religion." A celebrated author and divine has written to me that "he has gradually learnt to see that it is just as noble a conception of the Deity to believe that He created a few original forms capable of self-development into other and needful forms, as to believe that He required a fresh act of creation to supply the voids caused by the action of His laws."

Why, it may be asked, until recently did nearly all the most eminent living naturalists and geologists disbelieve in the mutability of species. It cannot be asserted that organic beings in a state of nature are subject to no variation; it cannot be proved that the amount of variation in the course of long ages is a limited quantity; no clear distinction has been, or can be, drawn between species and well-marked varieties. It cannot be maintained that species when intercrossed are invariably sterile, and varieties invariably fertile; or that sterility is a special endowment and sign of creation. The belief that species were immutable productions was almost unavoidable as long as the history of the world was thought to be of short duration; and now that we have acquired some idea of the lapse of time, we are too apt to assume, without proof, that the geological record is so perfect that it would have afforded us plain evidence of the mutation of species, if they had undergone mutation.

But the chief cause of our natural unwillingness to admit that one species has given birth to clear and distinct species, is that we are always slow in admitting great changes of which we do not see the steps. The difficulty is the same as that felt by so many geologists, when Lyell first insisted that long lines of inland cliffs had been formed, and great valleys excavated, by the agencies which we see still at work. The mind cannot possibly grasp the full meaning of the term of even a million years; it cannot add up and perceive the full effects of many slight variations, accumulated during an almost infinite number of generations.

Although I am fully convinced of the truth of the views given in this volume under the form of an abstract, I by no means expect to convince experienced naturalists whose minds are stocked with a multitude of facts all viewed, during a long course of years, from a point of view directly opposite to mine. It is so easy to hide our ignorance under such expressions as the "plan of creation," "unity of design," &c., and to think that we give an explanation when we only re-state a fact. Any one whose disposition leads him to attach more weight to unexplained difficulties than to the explanation of a certain number of facts will certainly reject the theory. A few naturalists, endowed with much flexibility of mind, and who have already begun to doubt the immutability of species, may be influenced by this volume; but I look with confidence to the future,—to young and rising naturalists, who will be able to view both sides of the question with impartiality. Whoever is led to believe that species are mutable will do good service by conscientiously expressing his conviction; for thus only can the load of prejudice by which this subject is overwhelmed be removed.

Several eminent naturalists have of late published their belief that a multitude of reputed species in each genus are not real species; but that other species are real, that is, have been independently created. This seems to me a strange conclusion to arrive at. They admit that a multitude of forms, which till lately they themselves thought were special creations, and which are still thus looked at by the majority of naturalists, and which consequently have all the external characteristic features of true species,—they admit that these have been produced by variation, but they refuse to extend the same view to other and slightly different forms. Nevertheless they do not pretend that they can define, or even conjecture, which are the created forms of life, and which are those produced by secondary laws. They admit variation as a *vera causa* [3] in one case, they arbitrarily reject it in another, without assigning any distinction in the two cases. The day will come when this will be given as a curious illustration of the blindness of preconceived opinion. These authors seem no more startled at a miraculous act of creation than at an ordinary birth. But do they really believe that at innumerable periods in the earth's history certain elemental atoms have been commanded suddenly to flash into living tissues? Do they believe that at each supposed act of creation one individual or many were produced? Were all the infinitely numerous kinds of animals and plants created as eggs or seed, or as full grown? and in the case of mammals, were they created bearing the false marks of nourishment from the mother's womb? Undoubtedly some of these same questions cannot be answered by those who believe in the appearance or creation of only a few forms of life, or of some one form alone. It has been maintained by several authors that it is as easy to believe in the creation of a million beings as of one; but Maupertuis' philosophical axiom "of least action" leads the mind more willingly to admit the smaller number; and certainly we ought not to believe that innumerable beings within each great class have been created with plain, but deceptive, marks of descent from a single parent.

As a record of a former state of things, I have retained in the foregoing paragraphs, and elsewhere, several sentences which imply that naturalists believe in the separate creation of each species; and I have been much censured for having thus expressed myself. But undoubtedly this was the general belief when the first edition of the present work appeared. I formerly spoke to very many naturalists on the subject of evolution, and never once met with any sympathetic agreement. It is probable that some did then believe in evolution, but they were either silent, or expressed themselves so ambiguously that it was not easy to understand their meaning. Now things are wholly changed, and almost every naturalist admits the great principle of evolution. There are, however, some who still think that species have suddenly given birth, through quite unexplained means, to new and totally different forms: but, as I have attempted to show, weighty evidence can be opposed to the admission of great and abrupt modifications. Under a scientific point of view, and as leading to further investigation, but little advantage is gained by believing that new forms are suddenly developed in an inexplicable manner from old and widely different forms, over the old belief in the creation of species from the dust of the earth.

[3] [*True cause.*]

It may be asked how far I extend the doctrine of the modification of species. The question is difficult to answer, because the more distinct the forms are which we consider, by so much the arguments in favour of community of descent become fewer in number and less in force. But some arguments of the greatest weight extend very far. All the members of whole classes are connected together by a chain of affinities, and all can be classed on the same principle, in groups subordinate to groups. Fossil remains sometimes tend to fill up very wide intervals between existing orders.

Organs in a rudimentary condition plainly show that an early progenitor had the organ in a fully developed condition; and this in some cases implies an enormous amount of modification in the descendants. Throughout whole classes various structures are formed on the same pattern, and at a very early age the embryos closely resemble each other. Therefore I cannot doubt that the theory of descent with modification embraces all the members of the same great class or kingdom. I believe that animals are descended from at most only four or five progenitors, and plants from an equal or lesser number.

Analogy would lead me one step farther, namely, to the belief that all animals and plants are descended from some one prototype. But analogy may be a deceitful guide. Nevertheless all living things have much in common, in their chemical composition, their cellular structure, their laws of growth, and their liability to injurious influences. We see this even in so trifling a fact as that the same poison often similarly affects plants and animals; or that the poison secreted by the gall-fly produces monstrous growths on the wild rose or oak-tree. With all organic beings, excepting perhaps some of the very lowest, sexual production seems to be essentially similar. With all, as far as is at present known, the germinal vesicle is the same; so that all organisms start from a common origin. If we look even to the two main divisions—namely, to the animal and vegetable kingdoms—certain low forms are so far intermediate in character that naturalists have disputed to which kingdom they should be referred. As Professor Asa Gray has remarked, "the spores and other reproductive bodies of many of the lower algae may claim to have first a characteristically animal, and then an unequivocally vegetable existence." Therefore, on the principle of natural selection with divergence of character, it does not seem incredible that, from some such low and intermediate form, both animals and plants may have been developed; and, if we admit this, we must likewise admit that all the organic beings which have ever lived on this earth may be descended from some one primordial form. But this inference is chiefly grounded on analogy, and it is immaterial whether or not it be accepted. . . .

Authors of the highest eminence seem to be fully satisfied with the view that each species has been independently created. To my mind it accords better with what we know of the laws impressed on matter by the Creator, that the production and extinction of the past and present inhabitants of the world should have been due to secondary causes, like those determining the birth and death of the individual. When I view all beings not as special creations, but as the lineal descendants of some few beings which lived long before the first bed of the Cambrian system was deposited, they seem to me to become ennobled. Judging from the past, we may safely infer that not one living species will transmit its unaltered likeness to a distant futurity. And of the species now living very few will transmit progeny of any kind to a far distant futurity; for the manner in which all organic beings are grouped, shows that the greater number of species in each genus, and all the species in many genera, have left no descendants, but have become utterly extinct. We can so far take a prophetic glance into futurity as to foretell that it will be the common and widely-spread species, belonging to the larger and dominant groups within each class, which will ultimately prevail and procreate new and dominant species. As all the living forms of life are the lineal descendants of those which lived long before the Cambrian epoch, we may feel certain that the ordinary succession by generation has never once been broken, and that no cataclysm has desolated the whole world. Hence we may look with some confidence to a secure future of great length. And as natural selection works solely by and for the good of each being, all corporeal and mental endowments will tend to progress towards perfection.

It is interesting to contemplate a tangled bank, clothed with many plants of many kinds, with birds singing on the bushes, with various insects flitting about, and with worms crawling through the damp earth, and to reflect that these elaborately constructed forms, so different from each other, and dependent upon each other in so complex a manner, have all been produced by laws acting around us. These laws, taken in the largest sense, being Growth with Reproduction; Inheritance which is almost implied by reproduction; Variability from the indirect and direct action of the conditions of life, and from use and disuse: a Ratio of Increase so high as to lead to a Struggle for Life, and as a consequence to Natural Selection, entailing Divergence of Character and the Extinction of less-improved forms. Thus, from the war of nature, from famine and death, the most exalted object which we are capable of conceiving, namely, the production of the higher animals, directly follows. There is grandeur in this view of life, with its several powers, having been originally breathed by the Creator into a few forms or into one; and that, whilst this planet has gone cycling on according to the fixed law of gravity,

from so simple a beginning endless forms most beautiful and most wonderful
have been, and are being evolved.

THE DESCENT OF MAN

CHAPTER XXI: GENERAL SUMMARY AND CONCLUSION

The main conclusion here arrived at, and now held by many naturalists,
who are well competent to form a sound judgment, is that man is descended
from some less highly organized form. The grounds upon which this conclusion rests will never be shaken, for the close similarity between man and
the lower animals in embryonic development, as well as in innumerable
points of structure and constitution, both of high and of the most trifling
importance—the rudiments which he retains, and the abnormal reversions to
which he is occasionally liable—are facts which cannot be disputed. They
have long been known, but, until recently, they told us nothing with respect
to the origin of man. Now, when viewed by the light of our knowledge of
the whole organic world, their meaning is unmistakable. The great principle
of evolution stands up clear and firm when these groups of facts are considered in connection with others, such as the mutual affinities of the members of the same group, their geographical distribution in past and present
times, and their geological succession. It is incredible that all these facts should
speak falsely. He who is not content to look, like a savage, at the phenomena
of nature as disconnected, cannot any longer believe that man is the work
of a separate act of creation. He will be forced to admit that the close resemblance of the embryo of man to that, for instance, of a dog—the construction of his skull, limbs, and whole frame on the same plan with that of
other mammals, independently of the uses to which the parts may be put—
the occasional reappearance of various structures, for instance of several muscles, which man does not normally possess, but which are common to the
Quadrumana—and a crowd of analogous facts—all point in the plainest manner to the conclusion that man is the co-descendant with other mammals of
a common progenitor. . . .

[This] conclusion . . . will, I regret to think, be highly distasteful to many.
But there can hardly be a doubt that we are descended from barbarians. The
astonishment which I felt on first seeing a party of Fuegians on a wild and
broken shore will never be forgotten by me, for the reflections at once rushed
into my mind—such were our ancestors. These men were absolutely naked
and bedaubed with paint, their long hair was tangled, their mouths frothed
with excitement, and their expression was wild, startled and distrustful. They

possessed hardly any arts, and like wild animals lived on what they could catch; they had no government, and were merciless to every one not of their own small tribe. He who has seen a savage in his native land will not feel much shame, if forced to acknowledge that the blood of some more humble creature flows in his veins. For my own part I would as soon be descended from that heroic little monkey who braved his dreaded enemy in order to save the life of his keeper, or from that old baboon, who, descending from the mountains, carried away in triumph his young comrade from a crowd of astonished dogs—as from a savage who delights to torture his enemies, offers up bloody sacrifices, practices infanticide without remorse, treats his wives like slaves, knows no decency, and is haunted by the grossest superstitions.

Man may be excused for feeling some pride at having risen, though not through his own exertions, to the very summit of the organic scale; and the fact of his having thus risen, instead of having been aboriginally placed there, may give him hope for a still higher destiny in the distant future. But we are not here concerned with hopes or fears, only with the truth as far as our reason permits us to discover it; and I have given the evidence to the best of my ability. We must, however, acknowledge, as it seems to me, that man, with all his noble qualities, with sympathy which feels for the most debased, with benevolence which extends not only to other men but to the humblest living creature, with his godlike intellect which has penetrated into the movements and constitution of the solar system—with all these exalted powers—man still bears in his bodily frame the indelible stamp of his lowly origin.

HERBERT SPENCER

ERBERT SPENCER (1820–1903) was born in Derby, England, of parents
who were religious Nonconformists. An uncle took a prominent part
in the agitation for universal suffrage and for the abolition of the Corn
Laws, and Philosophic Radicalism was the dominant intellectual temper of
Spencer's early environment. His career as a social philosopher began in 1850 with
the publication of his first book, the important and highly influential *Social
Statics;* writing did not end until his death in 1903. He lived on the income from
the sale of his books and on the stipend provided by American admirers.

Spencer adopted the scientific positivism of Auguste Comte and reinterpreted
its essential conclusions in his own evolutionary cosmology. His philosophy en-
visaged a universal pattern of evolution and supplied a cosmic foundation for
optimism concerning human progress; it applied the categories of physical and
biological evolution to the study of human psychology and history; and it provided what seemed like a definitive justification for England's policy of free
trade and the doctrine of *laissez faire.* Spencer's *Synthetic Philosophy* (published
in ten volumes between 1860 and 1896) and his numerous other books and essays surveyed the entire scope of man's knowledge from physics to ethics in terms
of one comprehensive law of evolution; his writings influenced not only the
method and direction of inquiry in the social sciences, but also the formulation
of issues in practical matters of politics, law, and reform.

The bearing of Spencer's conception of social evolution upon practical issues
was made evident in his *Social Statics and Man versus the State* (published with
this title in 1884), and other writings. The ideal society is one which provides
the maximum opportunity for the elimination of the unfit and for the realization
of individual potentialities; in such a society each individual will enjoy as perfect
a degree of freedom as is compatible with similar privileges of other individuals.
The state is formed for the mutual protection of its members; and it must refrain from any acts which do not contribute to this aim. It must not interfere with
the operation of natural selection and thus must do nothing other than enforce
contracts and provide safety against physical assault and foreign aggression.
Spencer undoubtedly convinced many of his contemporaries that individualistic
liberalism was part of the inherent pattern of the universe.

He attacked the socialistic tendencies of his day with great vigor, declaring
that those supporting "paternalistic" legislation were shortsighted sentimentalists
who were preparing the ground for a new slavery. Even when admitting that his
conception of the true limits of state activity would not be adopted for generations to come, he was supremely confident that the future was on his side. However that may be, there is no doubt that Spencer's writings did much to fortify
and to popularize the notion of individual liberty; and he was not without influence even within the ranks of philosophical anarchists and evolutionary socialists.

The following selections, taken from an essay of 1857 reprinted in *Illustrations of Universal Progress,* and from *Social Statics and Man versus the State,* are intended to convey the essential concepts in Spencer's scheme of progress and the main burden of his application of the evolutionary theory to social problems in support of liberalism.

ಌ

ILLUSTRATIONS OF
UNIVERSAL PROGRESS

PROGRESS: ITS LAW AND CAUSE

THE CURRENT CONCEPTION of Progress is somewhat shifting and indefinite. Sometimes it comprehends little more than simple growth—as of a nation in the number of its members and the extent of territory over which it has spread. Sometimes it has reference to quantity of material products—as when the advance of agriculture and manufactures is the topic. Sometimes the superior quality of these products is contemplated: and sometimes the new or improved appliances by which they are produced. When, again, we speak of moral or intellectual progress, we refer to the state of the individual or people exhibiting it; while, when the progress of Knowledge, of Science, of Art, is commented upon, we have in view certain abstract results of human thought and action. Not only, however, is the current conception of Progress more or less vague, but it is in great measure erroneous. It takes in not so much the reality of Progress as its accompaniments—not so much the substance as the shadow. That progress in intelligence seen during the growth of the child into the man, or the savage into the philosopher, is commonly regarded as consisting in the greater number of facts known and laws understood: whereas the actual progress consists in those internal modifications of which this increased knowledge is the expression. Social progress is supposed to consist in the produce of a greater quantity and variety of the articles required for satisfying men's wants; in the increasing security of person and property; in widening freedom of action: whereas, rightly understood, social progress consists in those changes of structure in the social organism which have entailed these consequences. The current conception is a teleological one. The phenomena are contemplated solely as bearing on human happiness. Only those changes are held to constitute progress which directly or indirectly tend to heighten human happiness. And they are thought to constitute progress simply *because* they tend to heighten human happiness. But rightly to understand progress, we must inquire what is the nature of these changes, considered apart from our interests.⏋Ceasing, for example, to regard the successive geological modifications that have taken place in the Earth, as modifications that have gradually fitted it for the habitation of Man, and as *therefore* a geological progress, we must seek to determine the character common to these modifications—the law to which they all conform. And similarly in every other case. Leaving out of sight concomitants and beneficial consequences, let us ask what Progress is in itself.

In respect to that progress which individual organisms display in the course of their evolution, this question has been answered by the Germans. The investigations of Wolff, Goethe, and Von Baer, have established the truth that the series of changes gone through during the development of a seed into a tree, or an ovum into an animal, constitute an advance from homogeneity of structure to heterogeneity of structure. In its primary stage, every germ consists of a substance that is uniform throughout, both in texture and chemical composition. The first step is the appearance of a difference between two parts of this substance; or, as the phenomenon is called in physiological language, a differentiation. Each of these differentiated divisions presently begins itself to exhibit some contrast of parts; and by and by these secondary differentiations become as definite as the original one. This process is continuously repeated—is simultaneously going on in all parts of the growing embryo; and by endless such differentiations there is finally produced that complex combination of tissues and organs constituting the adult animal or plant. This is the history of all organisms whatever. It is settled beyond dispute that organic progress consists in a change from the homogeneous to the heterogeneous.

Now, we propose in the first place to show, that this law of organic progress is the law of all progress. Whether it be in the development of the Earth, in the development of Life upon its surface, in the development of Society, of Government, of Manufactures, of Commerce, of Language, Literature, Science, Art, this same evolution of the simple into the complex, through successive differentiations, holds throughout. From the earliest traceable cosmical changes down to the latest results of civilization, we shall find that the transformation of the homogeneous into the heterogeneous, is that in which Progress essentially consists. . . .

It is clearly enough displayed in the progress of the latest and most heterogeneous creature—Man. It is alike true that, during the period in which the Earth has been peopled, the human organism has grown more heterogeneous among the civilized divisions of the species; and that the species, as a whole, has been growing more heterogeneous in virtue of the multiplication of races and the differentiation of these races from each other.

In proof of the first of these positions, we may cite the fact that, in the relative development of the limbs, the civilized man departs more widely from the general type of the placental mammalia than do the lower human races. While often possessing well-developed body and arms, the Papuan has extremely small legs: thus reminding us of the quadrumana, in which there is no great contrast in size between the hind and fore limbs. But in the European, the greater length and massiveness of the legs has become very marked —the fore and hind limbs are relatively more heterogeneous. Again, the greater ratio which the cranial bones bear to the facial bones illustrates the same truth. Among the vertebrata in general, progress is marked by an increasing heterogeneity in the vertebral column, and more especially in the vertebræ constituting the skull: the higher forms being distinguished by the relatively larger size of the bones which cover the brain, and the relatively smaller size of those which form the jaw, &c. Now, this characteristic, which is stronger in Man than in any other creature, is stronger in the European than in the savage. Moreover, judging from the greater extent and variety of faculty he exhibits, we may infer that the civilized man has also a more complex or heterogeneous nervous system than the uncivilized man: and indeed the fact is in part visible in the increased ratio which his cerebrum bears to the subjacent ganglia.

If further elucidation be needed, we may find it in every nursery. The infant European has sundry marked points of resemblance to the lower human races; as in the flatness of the alæ of the nose, the depression of its bridge, the divergence and forward opening of the nostrils, the form of the lips, the absence of a frontal sinus, the width between the eyes, the smallness of the legs. Now, as the developmental process by which these traits are turned into those of the adult European, is a continuation of that change from the homogeneous to the heterogeneous displayed during the previous evolution of the embryo, which every physiologist will admit; it follows that the parallel developmental process by which the like traits of the barbarous races have been turned into those of the civilized races, has also been a continuation of the change from the homogeneous to the heterogeneous. The truth of the second position—that Mankind, as a whole, have become more heterogeneous—is so obvious as scarcely to need illustration. Every work on Ethnology, by its divisions and subdivisions of races, bears testimony to it. Even were we to admit the hypothesis that Mankind originated from several separate stocks, it would still remain true, that as, from each of these stocks, there have sprung many now widely different tribes, which are proved by philological evidence to have had a common origin, the race as a whole is far less homogeneous than it once was. Add to which, that we have, in the Anglo-Americans, an example of a new variety arising within these few generations; and that, if we may trust to the description of observers, we are likely soon to have another such example in Australia.

On passing from Humanity under its individual form, to Humanity as socially embodied, we find the general law still more variously exemplified. The change from the homogeneous to the heterogeneous is displayed equally in the progress of civilization as a whole, and in the progress of every tribe or nation; and is still going on with increasing rapidity. As we see in existing barbarous tribes, society in its first and lowest form is a homogeneous aggregation of individuals having like powers and like functions: the only marked difference of function being that which accompanies difference of sex. Every man is warrior, hunter, fisherman, tool-maker, builder; every woman performs the same drudgeries; every family is self-sufficing, and save for purposes of aggression and defence, might as well live apart from the rest. Very early, however, in the process of social evolution, we find an incipient differentiation between the governing and the governed. Some kind of chieftainship seems coeval with the first advance from the state of separate wandering families to that of a nomadic tribe. The authority of the strongest makes itself felt among a body of savages as in a herd of animals, or a posse of schoolboys. At first, however, it is indefinite, uncertain; is shared by others of scarcely inferior power; and is unaccompanied by any difference in occupation or style of living: the first ruler kills his own game, makes his own weapons, builds his own hut, and economically considered, does not differ from others of his tribe. Gradually, as the tribe progresses, the contrast between the governing and the governed grows more decided. Supreme power becomes hereditary in one family; the head of that family, ceasing to provide for his own wants, is served by others; and he begins to assume the sole office of ruling.

At the same time there has been arising a co-ordinate species of government—that of Religion. As all ancient records and traditions prove, the earliest rulers are regarded as divine personages. The maxims and commands they uttered during their lives are held sacred after their deaths, and are enforced by their divinely-descended successors; who in their turns are promoted to the pantheon of the race, there to be worshipped and propitiated along with their predecessors: the most ancient of whom is the supreme god, and the rest subordinate gods. For a long time these connate forms of government—civil and religious—continue closely associated. For many generations the king continues to be the chief priest, and the priesthood to be members of the royal race. For many ages religious law continues to contain more or less of civil regulation, and civil law to possess more or less of religious sanction; and even among the most advanced nations these two controlling agencies are by no means completely differentiated from each other.

Having a common root with these, and gradually diverging from them, we find yet another controlling agency—that of Manners or ceremonial usages. All titles of honour are originally the names of the god-king; afterwards of God and the king; still later of persons of high rank; and finally come, some of them, to be used between man and man. All forms of complimentary address were at first the expressions of submission from prisoners to their conqueror, or from subjects to their ruler, either human or divine—expressions that were afterwards used to propitiate subordinate authorities, and slowly descended into ordinary intercourse. All modes of salutation were once obeisances made before the monarch and used in worship of him after his death. Presently others of the god-descended race were similarly saluted; and by degrees some of the salutations have become the due of all. Thus, no sooner does the originally homogeneous social mass differentiate into the governed and the governing parts, than this last exhibits an incipient differentiation into religious and secular—Church and State; while at the same time there begins to be differentiated from both, that less definite species of government which rules our daily intercourse—a species of government which, as we may see in heralds' colleges, in books of the peerage, in masters of ceremonies, is not without a certain embodiment of its own. Each of these is itself subject to successive differentiations. In the course of ages, there arises, as among ourselves, a highly complex political organization of monarch, ministers, lords and commons, with their subordinate administrative departments, courts of justice, revenue offices, &c., supplemented in the provinces by municipal governments, county governments, parish or union governments—all of them more or less elaborated. By its side there grows up a highly complex religious organization, with its various grades of officials, from archbishops down to sextons, its colleges, convocations, ecclesiastical courts, &c.; to all which must be added the ever multiplying independent sects, each with its general and local authorities. And at the same time there is developed a highly complex aggregation of customs, manners, and temporary fashions, enforced by society at large, and serving to control those minor transactions between man and man which are not regulated by civil and religious law. Moreover it is to be observed that this ever increasing heterogeneity in the governmental appliances of each nation, has been accompanied by an increasing heterogeneity in the governmental appliances of different nations; all of which are more or less unlike in their political systems and legislation, in their creeds and religious institutions, in their customs and ceremonial usages.

Simultaneously there has been going on a second differentiation of a more familiar kind; that, namely, by which the mass of the community has been segregated into distinct classes and orders of workers. . . .

Long after considerable progress has been made in the division of labour among different classes of workers, there is still little or no division of labour among the widely separated parts of the community; the nation continues comparatively homogeneous in the respect that in each district the same occupations are pursued. But when roads and other means of transit become numerous and good, the different districts begin to assume different functions, and to become mutually dependent. The calico manufacture locates itself in this county, the woollen-cloth manufacture in that; silks are produced here, lace there; stockings in one place, shoes in another; pottery, hardware, cutlery, come to have their special towns; and ultimately every locality becomes more or less distinguished from the rest by the leading occupation carried on in it. Nay, more, this subdivision of functions shows itself not only among the different parts of the same nation, but among different nations. That exchange of commodities which free-trade promises so greatly to increase, will ultimately have the effect of specializing, in a greater or less degree, the industry of each people. *exchange*

Not only is the law thus clearly exemplified in the evolution of the social organism, but it is exemplified with equal clearness in the evolution of all products of human thought and action, whether concrete or abstract, real or ideal. . . .

And now, from this uniformity of procedure, may we not infer some fundamental necessity whence it results? May we not rationally seek for some all-pervading principle which determines this all-pervading process of things? Does not the universality of the *law* imply a universal *cause*? . . .

Just as it was possible to interpret Kepler's laws as necessary consequences of the law of gravitation; so it may be possible to interpret this law of Progress, in its multiform manifestations, as the necessary consequence of some similarly universal principle. As gravitation was assignable as the *cause* of each of the groups of phenomena which Kepler formulated; so may some equally simple attribute of things be assignable as the cause of each of the groups of phenomena formulated in the foregoing pages. We may be able to affiliate all these varied and complex evolutions of the homogeneous into the heterogeneous, upon certain simple facts of immediate experience, which, in virtue of endless repetition, we regard as necessary.

The probability of a common cause, and the possibility of formulating it, being granted, it will be well, before going further, to consider what must be the general characteristics of such cause, and in what direction we ought to look for it. We can with certainty predict that it has a high degree of generality; seeing that it is common to such infinitely varied phenomena: just in proportion to the universality of its application must be the abstractness of its character. We need not expect to see in it an obvious solution of this or that form of Progress; because it equally refers to forms of Progress bearing little apparent resemblance to them: its association with multiform orders of facts, involves its dissociation from any particular order of facts. Being that which determines Progress of every kind—astronomic, geologic, organic, ethnologic, social, economic, artistic, &c.—it must be concerned with some fundamental attribute possessed in common by these; and must be expressible in terms of this fundamental attribute. The only obvious respect in which all kinds of Progress are alike, is, that they are modes of *change;* and hence, in some characteristic of changes in general, the desired solution will probably be found. We may suspect *à priori* that in some law of change lies the explanation of this universal transformation of the homogeneous into the heterogeneous.

Thus much premised, we pass at once to the statement of the law, which is this:—*Every active force produces more than one change—every cause produces more than one effect.*

Before this law can be duly comprehended, a few examples must be looked at. When one body is struck against another, that which we usually regard as the effect, is a change of position or motion in one or both bodies. But a moment's thought shows us that this is a careless and very incomplete view of the matter. Besides the visible mechanical result, sound is produced; or, to speak accurately, a vibration in one or both bodies, and in the surrounding air: and under some circumstances we call this the effect. Moreover, the air has not only been made to vibrate, but has had sundry currents caused in it by the transit of the bodies, further, there is a disarrangement of the particles of the two bodies in the neighbourhood of their point of collision; amounting in some cases to a visible condensation. Yet more, this condensation is accompanied by the disengagement of heat. In some cases a spark—that is, light—results, from the incandescence of a portion struck off; and sometimes this incandescence is associated with chemical combination.

Thus, by the original mechanical force expended in the collision, at least five, and often more, different kinds of changes have been produced. Take, again, the lighting of a candle. Primarily this is a chemical change consequent on a rise of temperature. The process of combination having once been set going by extraneous heat, there is a continued formation of carbonic acid, water, &c.—in itself a result more complex than the extraneous heat that first caused it. But accompanying this process of combination there is a production of heat; there is a production of light; there is an ascending column of hot gases generated; there are currents established in the surrounding air. Moreover, the decomposition of one force into many forces does not end here: each of the several changes produced becomes the parent of further changes. The carbonic acid given off will by and by combine with some base; or under the influence of sunshine give up its carbon to the leaf of a plant. The water will modify the hygrometric state of the air around; or, if the current of hot gases containing it come against a cold body, will be condensed: altering the temperature, and perhaps the chemical state, of the surface it covers. The heat given out melts the subjacent tallow, and expands whatever it warms. The light, falling on various substances, calls forth from them reactions by which it is modified; and so divers colours are produced. Similarly even with these secondary actions, which may be traced out into ever-multiplying ramifications, until they become too minute to be appreciated. And thus it is with all changes whatever. No case can be named in which an active force does not evolve forces of several kinds, and each of these, other groups of forces. Universally the effect is more complex than the cause. . . .

However, to avoid committing ourselves to more than is yet proved, we must be content with saying that such are the law and the cause of all progress that is known to us. Should the Nebular Hypothesis ever be established, then it will become manifest that the Universe at large, like every organism, was once homogeneous; that as a whole, and in every detail, it has unceasingly advanced towards greater heterogeneity; and that its heterogeneity is still increasing. It will be seen that as in each event of to-day, so from the beginning, the decomposition of every expended force into several forces has been perpetually producing a higher complication; that the increase of heterogeneity so brought about is still going on, and must continue to go on; and that thus Progress is not an accident, not a thing within human control, but a beneficent necessity.

SOCIAL STATICS AND MAN VERSUS THE STATE

THE EVANESCENCE OF EVIL

ALL EVIL results from the non-adaptation of constitution to conditions. Does a shrub dwindle in poor soil, or become sickly when deprived of light, or die outright if removed to a cold climate? it is because the harmony between its organization and its circumstances has been destroyed. Those experiences of the farm-yard and the menagerie which show that pain, disease, and death, are entailed upon animals by certain kinds of treatment, may be similarly generalized. Every suffering incident to the human body, from a headache up to a fatal illness, from a burn or a sprain up to accidental loss of life, is similarly traceable to the having placed that body in a situation for which its powers did not fit it. Nor is the expression confined in its application to physical evil. Is the bachelor unhappy because his means will not permit him to marry? does the mother mourn over her lost child? does the emigrant lament leaving his father-land? The explanation is still the same. No matter what the special nature of the evil, it is invariably referable to the one generic cause—want of congruity between the faculties and their spheres of action.

Equally true is it that evil perpetually tends to disappear. In virtue of an essential principle of life, this non-adaptation of an organism to its conditions is ever being rectified; and modification of one or both, continues until the adaptation is complete. Whatever possesses vitality, from the elementary cell up to man himself, inclusive, obeys this law. . . .

We must adopt one of three propositions. We must either affirm that the human being is unaltered by the influences brought to bear on him—his circumstances; or that he tends to become *un*fitted to those circumstances; or that he tends to become fitted to them. If the first be true, then all schemes of education, of government, of social reform are useless. If the second be true, then the way to make a man virtuous is to accustom him to vicious practices, and *vice versa*. Both of which propositions being absurd, we are impelled to admit the remaining one. . . .

But why is not man adapted to the social state?

Simply because he yet partially retains the characteristics appropriate to an antecedent state. The respects in which he is not fitted to society, are the respects in which he is fitted for his original predatory life. His primitive circumstances required that he should sacrifice the welfare of other beings to his own; his present circumstances require that he shall not do so; and in so far as his old attribute still clings to him, he is unfit for the social state. All sins of men against one another, from the cannibalism of the Fijian to the crimes and venalities we see around us, the felonies which fill our prisons, the trickeries of trade, the quarrellings of class with class and of nation with nation, have their causes comprehended under this generalization.

Man needed one moral constitution to fit him for his original state; he needs another to fit him for his present state; and he has been, is, and will long continue to be, in process of adaptation. And the belief in human perfectibility merely amounts to the belief that, in virtue of this process, man will eventually become completely suited to his mode of life.

Progress, therefore, is not an accident, but a necessity. Instead of civilization being artificial it is a part of nature; all of a piece with the development of an embryo or the unfolding of a flower. The modifications mankind have undergone, and are still undergoing, result from a law underlying the whole organic creation; and provided the human race continues, and the constitution of things remains the same, those modifications must end in completeness. As surely as the tree becomes bulky when it stands alone, and slender if one of a group; as surely as a blacksmith's arm grows large, and the skin of a laborer's hand thick; as surely as the eye tends to become long-sighted in the sailor, and short-sighted in the student; as surely as a clerk acquires rapidity in writing and calculation; as surely as the musician learns to detect an error of a semitone amidst what seems to others a very babel of sound; as surely as a passion grows by indulgence and diminishes when restrained; as surely as a disregarded conscience becomes inert, and one that is obeyed active; as surely as there is any meaning in such terms as habit, custom, practice;—so surely must the human faculties be moulded into complete fitness for the social state; so surely must evil and immorality disappear; so surely must man become perfect.[1]

POOR LAWS

. . . Pervading all Nature we may see at work a stern discipline which is a little cruel that it may be very kind. That state of universal warfare maintained throughout the lower creation, to the great perplexity of many worthy people, is at bottom the most merciful provision which the circumstances admit of. It is much better that the ruminant animal, when deprived by age of the vigour which made its existence a pleasure, should be killed by some beast of prey, than that it should linger out a life made painful by infirmities, and eventually die of starvation. By the destruction of all such, not only is existence ended before it becomes burdensome, but room is made for a younger generation capable of the fullest enjoyment; and, moreover, out of the very act of substitution happiness is derived for a tribe of predatory creatures. Note, further, that their carnivorous enemies not only remove from herbivorous herds individuals past their prime, but also weed out the sickly, the malformed, and the least

[1] [This note appears in the 1892 edition of *Social Statics:* "With the exception of small verbal improvements, I have let this chapter stand unaltered, though it is now clear to me that the conclusions drawn in it should be largely qualified. 1. Various races of mankind, inhabiting bad habitats, and obliged to lead miserable lives, cannot by any amount of adaptation be moulded into satisfactory types. 2. Astronomical and geological changes must continue hereafter to cause such changes of surface and climate as must entail migrations from habitats rendered unfit to fitter habitats; and such migrations must entail modified modes of life, with consequent re-adaptations. 3. The rate of progress towards any adapted form must diminish with the approach to complete adaptation, since the force producing it must diminish; so that, other causes apart, perfect adaptation can be reached only in infinite time."]

fleet or powerful. By the aid of which purifying process, as well as by the fighting so universal in the pairing season, all vitiation of the race through the multiplication of its inferior samples is prevented; and the maintenance of a constitution completely adapted to surrounding conditions, and therefore most productive of happiness, is ensured.

The development of the higher creation is a progress towards a form of being, capable of a happiness undiminished by these drawbacks. It is in the human race that the consummation is to be accomplished. Civilization is the last stage of its accomplishment. And the ideal man is the man in whom all the conditions to that accomplishment are fulfilled. Meanwhile, the well-being of existing humanity and the unfolding of it into this ultimate perfection, are both secured by that same beneficial though severe discipline, to which the animate creation at large is subject. It seems hard that an unskilfulness which with all his efforts he cannot overcome, should entail hunger upon the artizan. It seems hard that a labourer incapacitated by sickness from competing with his stronger fellows, should have to bear the resulting privations. It seems hard that widows and orphans should be left to struggle for life or death. Nevertheless, when regarded not separately but in connexion with the interests of universal humanity, these harsh fatalities are seen to be full of beneficence—the same beneficence which brings to early graves the children of diseased parents, and singles out the intemperate and the debilitated as the victims of an epidemic.

There are many very amiable people who have not the nerve to look this matter fairly in the face. Disabled as they are by their sympathies with present suffering, from duly regarding ultimate consequences, they pursue a course which is injudicious, and in the end even cruel. We do not consider it true kindness in a mother to gratify her child with sweetmeats that are likely to make it ill. We should think it a very foolish sort of benevolence which led a surgeon to let his patient's disease progress to a fatal issue, rather than inflict pain by an operation. Similarly, we must call those spurious philanthropists who, to prevent present misery, would entail greater misery on future generations. That rigorous necessity which, when allowed to operate, becomes so sharp a spur to the lazy and so strong a bridle to the random, these paupers' friends would repeal, because of the wailings it here and there produces. Blind to the fact that under the natural order of things society is constantly excreting its unhealthy, imbecile, slow, vacillating, faithless members, these unthinking, though well-meaning, men advocate an interference which not only stops the purifying process, but even increases the vitiation—absolutely encourages the multiplication of the reckless and incompetent by offering them an unfailing provision, and *dis*courages the multiplication of the competent and provident by heightening the difficulty of maintaining a family. And thus, in their eagerness to prevent the salutary sufferings that surround us, these sigh-wise and groan-foolish people bequeath to posterity a continually increasing curse.

Returning again to the highest point of view, we find that there is a second and still more injurious mode in which law-enforced charity checks the process of adaptation. To become fit for the social state, man has not only to lose his savageness but he has to acquire the capacities needful for civilized life. Power of application must be developed; such modification of the intellect as shall qualify it for its new tasks must take place; and, above all, there must be gained the ability to sacrifice a small immediate gratification for a future great one. The state of transition will of course be an unhappy state. Misery inevitably results from incongruity between constitution and conditions. Humanity is being pressed against the inexorable necessities of its new position—is being moulded into harmony with them, and has to bear the resulting happiness as best it can. The process *must* be undergone and the sufferings *must* be endured. No power on Earth, no cunningly-devised laws of statesmen, no world-rectifying schemes of the humane, no communist panaceas, no reforms that men ever did broach or ever will broach, can diminish them one jot. Intensified they may be, and are; and in preventing their intensification the philanthropic will find ample scope for exertion. But there is bound up with the change a *normal* amount of suffering, which cannot be lessened without altering the very laws of life. Every attempt at mitigation of this eventuates in exacerbation of it. All that a poor-law or any kindred institution can do, is to partially suspend the transition—to take off for a time, from certain members of society, the painful pressure which is effecting their transformation. At best this is merely to postpone what must ultimately be borne. But it is more than this: it is to undo what has already been done. For the circumstances to which adaptation is taking place cannot be superseded without causing a retrogression; and as the whole process must some time or other be passed through, the lost ground must be gone over again, and the attendant pain borne afresh.

At first sight these considerations seem conclusive against *all* relief to the poor—voluntary as well as compulsory; and it is no doubt true that they imply a condemnation of whatever private charity enables the recipients to elude the necessities of our social existence. With this condemnation, however, no rational man will quarrel. That careless squandering of pence which has fostered into perfection a system of organized begging—which has made skilful mendicancy more profitable than ordinary manual labour—which induces the simulation of diseases and deformities—which has called into existence warehouses for the sale and hire of impostor's dresses—which has given to pity-inspiring babes a market value of 9*d.* per day—the unthinking benevolence which has generated all this, cannot but be disapproved by every one. Now it is only against this injudicious charity that the foregoing argument tells. To that charity which may be described as helping men to help themselves, it makes no objection—countenances it rather. And in helping men to help themselves, there remains abundant scope for the exercise of a people's sympathies. Accidents will still supply victims on whom generosity may be legitimately expended. Men thrown off the track by unforeseen events, men who have failed for want of knowledge inaccessible to them, men ruined by the dishonesty of others, and men in whom hope long delayed has made the heart sick, may, with advantage to all parties, be assisted. Even the prodigal, after severe hardships has branded his memory with the unbending conditions of social life to which he must submit, may properly have another trial afforded him. And, although by these ameliorations the process of adaptation must be remotely interfered with, yet, in the majority of cases, it will not be so much retarded in one direction as it will be advanced in another.

Objectionable as we find a poor-law to be, even under the supposition that it does what it is intended to do—diminish present suffering—how shall we regard it on finding that in reality it does no such thing—cannot do any such thing? Yet, paradoxical as the assertion looks, this is absolutely the fact. Let but the observer cease to contemplate so fixedly one side of the phenomenon—pauperism and its relief, and begin to examine the other side—rates and the *ultimate* contributors of them, and he will discover that to suppose the sum-total of distress diminishable by act-of-parliament bounty is a delusion.

Here, at any specified period, is a given quantity of food and things exchangeable for food, in the hands or at the command of the middle and upper classes. A certain portion of this food is needed by these classes themselves, and is consumed by them at the same rate, or very near it, be there scarcity or abundance. Whatever variation occurs in the sum-total of food and its equivalents, must therefore affect the remaining portion, not used by these classes for personal sustenance. This remaining portion is paid by them to the people in return for their labour, which is partly expended in the production of a further supply of necessaries, and partly in the production of luxuries. Hence, by how much this portion is deficient, by so much must the people come short. A re-distribution by legislative or other agency cannot make that sufficient for them which was previously insufficient. It can do nothing but change the parties by whom the insufficiency is felt. If it gives enough to some who else would not have enough, it must inevitably reduce certain others to the condition of not having enough. . . .

THE COMING SLAVERY

The kinship of pity to love is shown among other ways in this, that it idealizes its object. Sympathy with one in suffering suppresses, for the time being, remembrance of his transgressions. The feeling which vents itself in "poor fellow!" on seeing one in agony, excludes the thought of "bad fellow," which might at another time arise. Naturally, then, if the wretched are unknown or but vaguely known, all the demerits they may have are ignored; and thus it happens that when the miseries of the poor are dilated upon, they are thought of as the miseries of the deserving poor, instead of being thought of as the miseries of the undeserving poor, which in large measure they should be. Those whose hardships are set forth in pamphlets and proclaimed in sermons and speeches which echo throughout society, are assumed to be all worthy souls, grievously wronged; and none of them are thought of as bearing the penalties of their misdeeds.

On hailing a cab in a London street, it is surprising how frequently the door is officiously opened by one who expects to get something for his trouble. The surprise lessens after counting the many loungers about tavern-doors, or after observing the quickness with which a street-performance, or procession, draws from neighbouring slums and stable-yards a group of idlers. Seeing how numerous they are in every small area, it becomes manifest that tens of thousands of such swarm through London. "They have no work," you say. Say rather that they either refuse work or quickly turn themselves out of it. They are simply good-for-nothings, who in one way or other live on the good-for-somethings—vagrants and sots, criminals and those on the way to crime, youths who are burdens on hard-worked parents, men who appropriate the wages of their wives, fellows who share the gains of prostitutes; and then, less visible and less numerous, there is a corresponding class of women.

Is it natural that happiness should be the lot of such? or is it natural that they should bring unhappiness on themselves and those connected with them? Is it not manifest that there must exist in our midst an immense amount of misery which is a normal result of misconduct, and ought not to be dissociated from it? There is a notion, always more or less prevalent and just now vociferously expressed, that all social suffering is removable, and that it is the duty of somebody or other to remove it. Both these beliefs are false. To separate pain from ill-doing is to fight against the constitution of things, and will be followed by far more pain. Saving men from the natural penalties of dissolute living, eventually necessitates the infliction of artificial penalties in solitary cells, on tread-wheels, and by the lash. I suppose a dictum on which the current creed and the creed of science are at one, may be considered to have as high an authority as can be found. Well, the command "if any would not work neither should he eat," is simply a Christian enunciation of that universal law of Nature under which life has reached its present height—the law that a creature not energetic enough to maintain itself must die: the sole difference being that the law which in the one case is to be artificially enforced, is, in the other case, a natural necessity. And yet this particular tenet of their religion which science so manifestly justifies, is the one which Christians seem least inclined to accept. The current assumption is that there should be no suffering, and that society is to blame for that which exists. . . .

. . . Influences of various kinds conspire to increase corporate action and decrease individual action. And the change is being on all sides aided by schemers, each of whom thinks only of his pet plan and not at all of the general reorganization which his plan, joined with others such, are working out. It is said that the French Revolution devoured its own children. Here, an analogous catastrophe seems not unlikely. The numerous socialistic changes made by Act of Parliament, joined with the numerous others presently to be made, will by-and-by be all merged in State-socialism—swallowed in the vast wave which they have little by little raised.

"But why is this change described as 'the coming slavery'?" is a question which many will still ask. The reply is simple. All socialism involves slavery. What is essential to the idea of a slave? We primarily think of him as one who is owned by another. To be more than nominal, however, the ownership must be shown by control of the slave's actions—a control which is habitually for the benefit of the controller. That which fundamentally distinguishes the slave is that he labours under coercion to satisfy another's desires. The relation admits of sundry gradations. Remembering that originally the slave is a prisoner whose life is at the mercy of his captor, it suffices here to note that there is a harsh form of slavery in which, treated as an animal, he has to expend his entire effort for his owner's advantage. Under a system less harsh, though occupied chiefly in working for his owner, he is allowed a short time in which to work for himself, and some ground on which to grow extra food. A further amelioration gives him power to sell the produce of his plot and keep the proceeds. Then we come to the still more moderated form which commonly arises where, having been a free man working on his own land, conquest turns him into what we distinguish as a serf; and he has to give to his owner each year a fixed amount of labour or produce, or both: retaining the rest himself. Finally, in some cases, as in Russia before serfdom was abolished, he is allowed to leave his owner's estate and work or trade for himself elsewhere, under the condition that he shall pay an annual sum. What is it which, in these cases, leads us to qualify our conception of the slavery as more or less severe? Evidently the greater or smaller extent to which effort is compulsorily expended for the benefit of another instead of for self-benefit. If all the slave's labour is for his owner the slavery is heavy, and if but little it is light. Take now a further step. Suppose an owner dies, and his estate with its slaves comes into the hands of trustees; or suppose the estate and everything on it to be bought by a company; is the condition of the slave any the better if the amount of his compulsory labour remains the same? Suppose that for a company we substitute the community; does it make any difference to the slave if the time he has to work for others is as great, and the time left for himself is as small, as before? The essential question is—How much is he compelled to labour for other benefit than his own, and how much can he labour for his own benefit? The degree of his slavery varies according to the ratio between that which he is forced to yield up and that which he is allowed to retain; and it matters not whether his master is a single person or a society. If, without option, he has to labour for the society, and receives from the general stock such portion as the society awards him, he becomes a slave to the society. Socialistic arrangements necessitate an enslavement of this kind; and towards such an enslavement many recent measures, and still more the measures advocated, are carrying us. . . .

Evidently then, the changes made, the changes in progress, and the changes urged, will carry us not only towards State-ownership of land and dwellings and means of communication, all to be administered and worked by State-agents, but towards State-usurpation of all industries: the private forms of which, disadvantaged more and more in competition with the State, which can arrange everything for its own convenience, will more and more die away; just as many voluntary schools have, in presence of Board-schools. And so will be brought about the desired ideal of the socialists.

And now when there has been compassed this desired ideal, which "practical" politicians are helping socialists to reach, and which is so tempting on that bright side which socialists contemplate, what must be the accompanying shady side which they do not contemplate? It is a matter of common remark, often made when a marriage is impending, that those possessed by strong hopes habitually dwell on the promised pleasures and think nothing of the accompanying pains. A further exemplification of this truth is supplied by these political enthusiasts and fanatical revolutionists. Impressed with the miseries existing under our present social arrangements, and not regarding these miseries as caused by the ill-working of a human nature but partially adapted to the social state, they imagine them to be forthwith curable by this or that rearrangement. Yet, even did their plans succeed it could only be by substituting one kind of evil for another. A little deliberate thought would show that under their proposed arrangements, their liberties must be surrendered in proportion as their material welfares were cared for.

For no form of co-operation, small or great, can be carried on without regulation, and an implied submission to the regulating agencies. Even one of their own organizations for effecting social changes yields them proof. It is compelled to have its councils, its local and general officers, its authoritative leaders, who must be obeyed under penalty of confusion and failure. And the experience of those who are loudest in their advocacy of a new social order under the paternal control of a Government, shows that even in private voluntarily-formed societies, the power of the regulative organization becomes great, if not irresistible: often, indeed, causing grumbling and restiveness among those controlled. Trades-unions which carry on a kind of industrial war in defence of workers' interests *versus* employers' interests, find that subordination almost military in its strictness is needful to secure efficient action; for divided councils prove fatal to success. And even in bodies of co-operators, formed for carrying on manufacturing or distributing businesses, and not needing that obedience to leaders which is required where the aims are offensive or defensive, it is still found that the administrative agency gains such supremacy that there arise complaints about "the tyranny of organization." Judge then what must happen when, instead of relatively small combinations, to which men may belong or not as they please, we have a national combination in which each citizen finds himself incorporated, and from which he cannot separate himself without leaving the country. Judge what must under such conditions become the despotism of a graduated and centralized officialism, holding in its hands the resources of the community, and having behind it whatever amount of force it finds requisite to carry out its decrees and maintain what it calls order. Well may Prince Bismarck display leanings towards State-socialism.

And then after recognizing, as they must if they think out their scheme, the power possessed by the regulative agency in the new social system so temptingly pictured, let its advocates ask themselves to what end this power must be used. Not dwelling exclusively, as they habitually do, on the material well-being and the mental gratifications to be provided for them by a beneficent administration, let them dwell a little on the price to be paid. The officials cannot create the needful supplies: they can but distribute among individuals that which the individuals have joined to produce. If the public agency is required to provide for them, it must reciprocally require them to furnish the means. There cannot be, as under our existing system, agreement between employer and employed—this the scheme excludes. There must in place of it be command by local authorities over workers, and acceptance by the workers of that which the authorities assign to them. And this, indeed, is the arrangement distinctly, but as it would seem inadvertently, pointed to by the members of the Democratic Federation. For they propose that production should be carried on by "agricultural and industrial *armies* under State-control": apparently not remembering that armies pre-suppose grades of officers, by whom obedience would have to be insisted upon; since otherwise neither order nor efficient work could be ensured. So that each would stand toward the governing agency in the relation of slave to master.

"But the governing agency would be a master which he and others made and kept constantly in check; and one which therefore would not control him or others more than was needful for the benefit of each and all."

To which reply the first rejoinder is that, even if so, each member of the community as an individual would be a slave to the community as a whole. Such a relation has habitually existed in militant communities, even under quasi-popular forms of government. In ancient Greece the accepted principle was that the citizen belonged neither to himself nor to his family, but belonged to his city—the city being with the Greek equivalent to the community. And this doctrine, proper to a state of constant warfare, is a doctrine which socialism unawares re-introduces into a state intended to be purely industrial. The services of each will belong to the aggregate of all; and for these services, such returns will be given as the authorities think proper. So that even if the administration is of the beneficent kind intended to be secured, slavery, however mild, must be the outcome of the arrangement.

A second rejoinder is that the administration will presently become not of the intended kind, and that the slavery will not be mild. The socialist speculation is vitiated by an assumption like that which vitiates the speculations of the "practical" politician. It is assumed that officialism will work as it is intended to work, which it never does. The machinery of Communism, like existing social machinery, has to be framed out of existing human nature; and the defects of existing human nature will generate in the one the same evils as in the other. The love of power, the selfishness, the injustice, the untruthfulness, which often in comparatively short times bring private organizations to disaster, will inevitably, where their effects accumulate from generation to generation, work evils far greater and less remediable; since, vast and complex and possessed of all the resources, the administrative organization once developed and consolidated, must become irresistible. And if there needs proof that the periodic exercise of electoral power would fail to prevent this, it suffices to instance the French Government, which, purely popular in origin, and subject at short intervals to popular judgment, nevertheless tramples on the freedom of citizens to an extent which the English delegates to the late Trades Unions Congress say "is a disgrace to, and an anomaly in, a Republican nation."

The final result would be a revival of despotism. A disciplined army of civil officials, like an army of military officials, gives supreme power to its head—a power which has often led to usurpation, as in mediæval Europe and still more in Japan—nay, has thus so led among our neighbours, within our own times. The recent confessions of M. de Maupas have shown how readily a constitutional head, elected and trusted by the whole people, may, with the aid of a few unscrupulous confederates, paralyze the representative body and make himself autocrat. That those who rose to power in a socialistic organization would not scruple to carry out their aims at all costs, we have good reason for concluding. When we find that shareholders who, sometimes gaining but often losing, have made that railway-system by which national prosperity has been so greatly increased, are spoken of by the council of the Democratic Federation as having "laid hands" on the means of communication, we may infer that those who directed a socialistic administration might interpret with extreme perversity the claims of individuals and classes under their control. And when, further, we find members of this same council urging that the State should take possession of the railways, "with or without compensation," we may suspect that the heads of the ideal society desired, would be but little deterred by considerations of equity from pursuing whatever policy they thought needful: a policy which would always be one identified with their own supremacy. It would need but a war with an adjacent society, or some internal discontent demanding forcible suppression, to at once transform a socialistic administration into a grinding tyranny like that of ancient Peru; under which the mass of the people, controlled by grades of officials, and leading lives that were inspected out-of-doors and in-doors, laboured for the support of the organization which regulated them, and were left with but a bare subsistence for themselves. And then would be completely revived, under a different form, that *régime* of status—that system of compulsory co-operation, the decaying tradition of which is represented by the old Toryism, and towards which the new Toryism is carrying us back.

"But we shall be on our guard against all that—we shall take precautions to ward off such disasters," will doubtless say the enthusiasts. Be they "practical" politicians with their new regulative measures, or communists with their schemes for re-organizing labour their reply is ever the same;—"It is true that plans of kindred nature have, from unforeseen causes or adverse accidents, or the misdeeds of those concerned, been brought to failure; but this time we shall profit by past experiences and succeed." There seems no getting people to accept the truth, which nevertheless is conspicuous enough, that the welfare of a society and the justice of its arrangements are at bottom dependent on the characters of its members; and that improvement in neither can take place without that improvement in character which results from carrying on peaceful industry under the restraints imposed by an orderly social life. The belief, not only of the socialists but also of those so-called Liberals who are diligently preparing the way for them, is that by due skill an ill-working humanity may be framed into well-working institutions. It is a delusion. The defective natures of citizens will show themselves in the bad acting of whatever social structure they are arranged into. There is no political alchemy by which you can get golden conduct out of leaden instincts.

THOMAS HENRY HUXLEY

THE MAN who more than anyone else made "Darwinism" a household word for his contemporaries, synonymous with a "new reformation" in thought, was Thomas Henry Huxley (1825-95). While still in his teens he chanced upon the writings of Sir William Hamilton, the philosopher, and Thomas Carlyle. Both men left a permanent mark upon his outlook: the former's insistence on the "relativity of all knowledge" bore fruit in Huxley's subsequent agnosticism, while from the latter he acquired a passionate resolve "to make things clear and get rid of cant and shams of all sorts." In 1839, under the guidance of two brothers-in-law who were physicians, he began to study medicine privately, and in 1846 he entered into practice.

The publication of Darwin's *Origin of Species* in 1859 converted Huxley to evolution and embarked him on his career as "Darwin's Bulldog." After a first reading of the book he wrote to Darwin expressing his adherence to the central evolutionary doctrine contained in it, though making some reservations as to details; and he added: "I trust you will not allow yourself to be in any way disgusted or annoyed by the considerable abuse and misrepresentation which, unless I greatly mistake, is in store for you. . . . I am sharpening up my claws and beak in readiness." Huxley's first opportunity to test his claws came in 1860, during a famous session of the British Association for the Advancement of Science. In the course of an attack on the theory of evolution as both factually invalid and inimical to religion, Samuel Wilberforce, the Bishop of Oxford, addressed himself at one point to Huxley to ask with apparent solicitude whether the latter was descended from the apes on the side of his grandfather or grandmother. Huxley rose to the occasion, and after controverting the Bishop's facts (on which the latter had been coached by Richard Owen), he declared: "A man has no reason to be ashamed of having an ape for his grandfather. If there were an ancestor whom I should feel shame in recalling it would rather be a *man*—a man of restless and versatile intellect—who, not content with an equivocal success in his own sphere of activity, plunges into scientific questions with which he has no real acquaintance, only to obscure by an aimless rhetoric, and distract the attention of his hearers from the real point at issue by eloquent digressions and skilled appeals to religious prejudice." This retort made Huxley immediately notorious; and perhaps inevitably evolution was turned into a public question—to be fought over as much for its anti-religious implications as for its validity. For almost two-score years thereafter, at meetings of scientific societies, on the public platform, as well as in books and articles, Huxley went about fulfilling an early vow "to smite all humbugs, however big"—expounding and defending Darwin's ideas, though without accepting them slavishly.

It was Huxley rather than Darwin who established by experimental analyses the anatomical kinship of man to the apes. In 1875 he was invited to attend the opening of the Johns Hopkins University in Baltimore; and on a visit to

Nashville, Tennessee (years later the scene of a renewed struggle over the teaching of evolution), he was hailed publicly for his scientific achievements. Because of failing health he retired from regular teaching in 1885.

Huxley dismissed as so much ungrounded speculation the philosophic systems which tried to discover the reality lying behind the opaque curtain of "consciousness." He therefore called himself an "agnostic" because, as he once wrote to Charles Kingsley, "I don't know whether Matter is anything distinct from Force. I don't know that the atoms are anything but pure myths . . . I am quite as ready to admit your doctrine that souls secrete bodies as I am the opposite that bodies secrete souls—simply because I deny the possibility of obtaining any evidence as to the truth and falsehood of either hypothesis. My fundamental axiom of speculative philosophy is that materialism and spiritualism are opposite poles of the same absurdity—the absurdity of imagining that we know anything about either spirit or matter."

Huxley's acceptance of Darwin's theories was always qualified by doubts concerning the adequacy of the doctrine of natural selection to explain all the facts regarding the transmutation of species. Nevertheless, he subscribed to evolution as a reasonable hypothesis on the available data, and he admitted that natural selection is a factor—even if not the exclusive one—in the evolutionary process. On the other hand, he was dismayed by attempts to use Darwinism as the basis for the theory of morals; and he was impatient with those who tried to derive political theory from *a priori* assumptions concerning natural rights. The present selection is from *Evolution and Ethics,* the Romanes Lecture for 1893, one of the essays in which he opposed such attempts.

Huxley was also very determined in his criticisms of social theores based on *a priori* and other unfounded assumptions concerning the "natural" state of mankind. He was particularly effective in destroying the foundations upon which the conception of the state as a mere policeman was built—although, because Spencer was a close friend, Huxley's explicit criticisms of him were sparing. Nevertheless, in the two essays *Administrative Nihilism* (1870) and *Government: Anarchy or Regimentation* (1890) he made short work of Spencer's "anarchic individualism" and showed that the latter's advocacy of governmental abstention from all regulative activity was without rational foundation.

EVOLUTION AND ETHICS

FROM VERY LOW FORMS up to the highest—in the animal no less than in the vegetable kingdom—the process of life presents the same appearance of cyclical evolution. Nay, we have but to cast our eyes over the rest of the world and cyclical change presents itself on all sides. It meets us in the water that flows to the sea and returns to the springs; in the heavenly bodies that wax and wane, go and return to their places; in the inexorable sequence of the ages of man's life; in that successive rise, apogee, and fall of dynasties and of states which is the most prominent topic of civil history.

As no man fording a swift stream can dip his foot twice into the same water, so no man can, with exactness, affirm of anything in the sensible world that it is. As he utters the words, nay, as he thinks them, the predicate ceases to be applicable; the present has become the past; the "is" should be "was." And the more we learn of the nature of things, the more evident is it that what we call rest is only unperceived activity; that seeming peace is silent but strenuous battle. In every part, at every moment, the state of the cosmos is the expression of a transitory adjustment of contending forces; a scene of strife, in which all the combatants fall in turn. What is true of each part, is true of the whole. Natural knowledge tends more and more to the conclusion that "all the choir of heaven and furniture of the earth" are the transitory forms of parcels of cosmic substance wending along the road of evolution, from nebulous potentiality, through endless growths of sun and planet and satellite; through all varieties of matter; through infinite diversities of life and thought; possibly, through modes of being of which we neither have a conception, nor are competent to form any, back to the indefinable latency from which they arose. Thus the most obvious attribute of the cosmos is its impermanence. It assumes the aspect not so much of a permanent entity as of a changeful process in which naught endures save the flow of energy and the rational order which pervades it. . . .

But there is another aspect of the cosmic process, so perfect as a mechanism, so beautiful as a work of art. Where the cosmopoietic energy works through sentient beings, there arises, among its other manifestations, that which we call pain or suffering. This baleful product of evolution increases in quantity and in intensity, with advancing grades of animal organization, until it attains its highest level in man. Further, the consummation is not reached in man, the mere animal; nor in man, the whole or half savage; but only in man, the member of an organized polity. And it is a necessary consequence of his attempt to live in this way; that is, under those conditions which are essential to the full development of his noblest powers.

Man, the animal, in fact, has worked his way to the headship of the sentient world, and has become the superb animal which he is, in virtue of his success in the struggle for existence. The conditions having been of a certain order, man's organization has adjusted itself to them better than that of his competitors in the cosmic strife. In the case of mankind, the self-assertion, the unscrupulous seizing upon all that can be grasped, the tenacious holding of all that can be kept, which constitute the essence of the struggle for existence, have answered. For his successful progress, throughout the savage state, man has been largely indebted to those qualities which he shares with the ape and the tiger; his exceptional physical organization; his cunning, his sociability, his curiosity, and his imitativeness; his ruthless and ferocious destructiveness when his anger is roused by opposition.

But, in proportion as men have passed from anarchy to social organization, and in proportion as civilization has grown in worth, these deeply ingrained serviceable qualities have become defects. After the manner of successful persons, civilized man would gladly kick down the ladder by which he has climbed. He would be only too pleased to see "the ape and tiger die." But they decline to suit his convenience; and the unwelcome intrusion of these boon companions of his hot youth into the ranged existence of civil life adds pains and griefs, innumerable and immeasurably great, to those which the cosmic process necessarily brings on the mere animal. In fact, civilized man brands all these ape and tiger promptings with the name of sins; he punishes many of the acts which flow from them as crimes; and, in extreme cases, he does his best to put an end to the survival of the fittest of former days by axe and rope.

I have said that civilized man has reached this point; the assertion is perhaps too broad and general; I had better put it that ethical man has attained thereto. The science of ethics professes to furnish us with a reasoned rule of life; to tell us what is right action and why it is so. Whatever differences of opinion may exist among experts there is a general consensus that the ape and tiger methods of the struggle for existence are not reconcilable with sound ethical principles. . . .

Theories of the universe, in which the conception of evolution plays a leading part, were extant at least six centuries before our era. Certain knowledge of them, in the fifth century, reaches us from localities as distant as the valley of the Ganges and the Asiatic coasts of the Ægean. To the early philosophers of Hindostan, no less than to those of Ionia, the salient and characteristic feature of the phenomenal world was its changefulness; the unresting flow of all things, through birth to visible being and thence to not being, in which they could discern no sign of a beginning and for which they saw no prospect of an ending. It was no less plain to some of these antique forerunners of modern philosophy that suffering is the badge of all the tribe of sentient things; that it is no accidental accompaniment, but an essential constituent of the cosmic process. The energetic Greek might find fierce joys in a world in which "strife is father and king"; but the old Aryan spirit was subdued to quietism in the Indian sage; the mist of suffering which spread over humanity hid everything else from his view; to him life was one with suffering and suffering with life.

In Hindostan, as in Ionia, a period of relatively high and tolerably stable civilization had succeeded long ages of semi-barbarism and struggle. Out of wealth and security had come leisure and refinement, and, close at their heels, had followed the malady of thought. To the struggle for bare existence, which never ends, though it may be alleviated and partially disguised for a fortunate few, succeeded the struggle to make existence intelligible and to bring the order of things into harmony with the moral sense of man, which also never ends, but, for the thinking few, becomes keener with every increase of knowledge and with every step towards the realization of a worthy ideal of life.

Two thousand five hundred years ago, the value of civilization was as apparent as it is now; then, as now, it was obvious that only in the garden of an orderly polity can the finest fruits humanity is capable of bearing be produced. But it had also become evident that the blessings of culture were not unmixed. The garden was apt to turn into a hothouse. The stimulation of the senses, the pampering of the emotions, endlessly multiplied the sources of pleasure. The constant widening of the intellectual field indefinitely extended the range of that especially human faculty of looking before and after, which adds to the fleeting present those old and new worlds of the past and the future, wherein men dwell the more the higher their culture. But that very sharpening of the sense and that subtle refinement of emotion, which brought such a wealth of pleasures, were fatally attended by a proportional enlargement of the capacity for suffering; and the divine faculty of imagination, while it created new heavens and new earths, provided them with the corresponding hells of futile regret for the past and morbid anxiety for the future. Finally, the inevitable penalty of over-stimulation, exhaustion, opened the gates of civilization to its great enemy, ennui; the stale and flat weariness when man delights not, nor woman neither; when all things are vanity and vexation; and life seems not worth living except to escape the bore of dying.

Even purely intellectual progress brings about its revenges. Problems settled in a rough and ready way by rude men, absorbed in action, demand renewed attention and show themselves to be still unread riddles when men have time to think. The beneficent demon, doubt, whose name is Legion and who dwells amongst the tombs of old faiths, enters into mankind and thenceforth refuses to be cast out. Sacred customs, venerable dooms of ancestral wisdom, hallowed by tradition and professing to hold good for all time, are put to the question. Cultured reflection asks for their credentials; judges them by its own standards; finally, gathers those of which it approves into ethical systems, in which the reasoning is rarely much more than a decent pretext for the adoption of foregone conclusions.

One of the oldest and most important elements in such systems is the conception of justice. Society is impossible unless those who are associated agree to observe certain rules of conduct towards one another; its stability depends on the steadiness with which they abide by that agreement; and, so far as they waver, that mutual trust which is the bond of society is weakened or destroyed. Wolves could not hunt in packs except for the real, though unexpressed, understanding that they should not attack one another during the chase. The most rudimentary polity is a pack of men living under the like tacit, or expressed, understanding; and having made the very important advance upon wolf society, that they agree to use the force of the whole body against individuals who violate it and in favour of those who observe it. This observance of a common understanding, with the consequent distribution of punishments and rewards according to accepted rules, received the name of justice, while the contrary was called injustice. Early ethics did not take much note of the animus of the violator of the rules. But civilization could not advance far, without the establishment of a capital distinction between the case of involuntary and that of wilful misdeed; between a merely wrong action and a guilty one. And, with increasing refinement of moral appreciation, the problem of desert, which arises out of this distinction, acquired more and more theoretical and practical importance. If life must be given for life, yet it was recognized that the unintentional slayer did not altogether deserve death; and, by a sort of compromise between the public and the private conception of justice, a sanctuary was provided in which he might take refuge from the avenger of blood.

The idea of justice thus underwent a gradual sublimation from punishment and reward according to acts, to punishment and reward according to desert; or, in other words, according to motive. Righteousness, that is, action from right motive, not only became synonymous with justice, but the positive constituent of innocence and the very heart of goodness.

Now when the ancient sage, whether Indian or Greek, who had attained to this conception of goodness, looked the world, and especially human life, in the face, he found it as hard as we do to bring the course of evolution into harmony with even the elementary requirements of the ethical ideal of the just and the good.

If there is one thing plainer than another, it is that neither the pleasures nor the pains of life, in the merely animal world, are distributed according to desert; for it is admittedly impossible for the lower orders of sentient beings to deserve either the one or the other. If there is a generalization from the facts of human life which has the assent of thoughtful men in every age and country, it is that the violator of ethical rules constantly escapes the punishment which he deserves; that the wicked flourishes like a green bay tree, while the righteous begs his bread; that the sins of the fathers are visited upon the children; that, in the realm of nature, ignorance is punished just as severely as wilful wrong; and that thousands upon thousands of innocent beings suffer for the crime, or the unintentional trespass of one.

Greek and Semite and Indian are agreed upon this subject. The book of Job is at one with the "Works and Days" and the Buddhist Sutras; the Psalmist and the Preacher of Israel, with the Tragic Poets of Greece. What is a more common motive of the ancient tragedy in fact, than the unfathomable injustice of the nature of things; what is more deeply felt to be true than its presentation of the destruction of the blameless by the work of his own hands, or by the fatal operation of the sins of others? Surely Œdipus was pure of heart; it was the natural sequence of events—the cosmic process—which drove him, in all innocence, to slay his father and become the husband of his mother, to the desolation of his people and his own headlong ruin. Or to step, for a moment, beyond the chronological limits I have set myself, what constitutes the sempiternal attraction of Hamlet but the appeal to deepest experience of that history of a no less blameless dreamer, dragged, in spite of himself, into a world out of joint; involved in a tangle of crime and misery, created by one of the prime agents of the cosmic process as it works in and through man?

Thus, brought before the tribunal of ethics, the cosmos might well seem to stand condemned. The conscience of man revolted against the moral indifference of nature, and the microcosmic atom should have found the illimitable macrocosm guilty. But few, or none, ventured to record that verdict. . . .

We are more than sufficiently familiar with modern pessimism, at least as a speculation; for I cannot call to mind that any of its present votaries have sealed their faith by assuming the rags and the bowl of the mendicant

Bhikku, or the cloak and the wallet of the Cynic. The obstacles placed in the way of sturdy vagrancy by an unphilosophical police have, perhaps, proved too formidable for philosophical consistency. We also know modern speculative optimism, with its perfectibility of the species, reign of peace, and lion and lamb transformation scenes; but one does not hear so much of it as one did forty years ago; indeed, I imagine it is to be met with more commonly at the tables of the healthy and wealthy, than in the congregations of the wise. The majority of us, I apprehend, profess neither pessimism nor optimism. We hold that the world is neither so good, nor so bad, as it conceivably might be; and, as most of us have reason, now and again, to discover that it can be. Those who have failed to experience the joys that make life worth living are, probably, in as small a minority as those who have never known the griefs that rob existence of its savour and turn its richest fruits into mere dust and ashes.

Further, I think I do not err in assuming that, however diverse their views on philosophical and religious matters, most men are agreed that the proportion of good and evil in life may be very sensibly affected by human action. I never heard anybody doubt that the evil may be thus increased, or diminished; and it would seem to follow that good must be similarly susceptible of addition or subtraction. Finally, to my knowledge, nobody professes to doubt that, so far forth as we possess a power of bettering things, it is our paramount duty to use it and to train all our intellect and energy to this supreme service of our kind.

Hence the pressing interest of the question, to what extent modern progress in natural knowledge, and, more especially, the general outcome of that progress in the doctrine of evolution, is competent to help us in the great work of helping one another?

The propounders of what are called the "ethics of evolution," when the "evolution of ethics" would usually better express the object of their speculations, adduce a number of more or less interesting facts and more or less sound arguments in favour of the origin of the moral sentiments, in the same way as other natural phenomena, by a process of evolution. I have little doubt, for my own part, that they are on the right track; but as the immoral sentiments have no less been evolved, there is, so far, as much natural sanction for the one as the other. The thief and the murderer follow nature just as much as the philanthropist. Cosmic evolution may teach us how the good and the evil tendencies of man may have come about; but, in itself, it is incompetent to furnish any better reason why what we call good is preferable to what we call evil than we had before. Some day, I doubt not, we shall arrive at an understanding of the evolution of the æsthetic faculty; but all the understanding in the world will neither increase nor diminish the force of the intuition that this is beautiful and that is ugly.

There is another fallacy which appears to me to pervade the so-called "ethics of evolution." It is the notion that because, on the whole, animals and plants have advanced in perfection of organization by means of the struggle for existence and the consequent "survival of the fittest"; therefore men in society, men as ethical beings, must look to the same process to help them towards perfection. I suspect that this fallacy has arisen out of the unfortunate ambiguity of the phrase "survival of the fittest." "Fittest" has a connotation of "best"; and about "best" there hangs a moral flavour. In cosmic nature, however, what is "fittest" depends upon the conditions. Long since, I ventured to point out that if our hemisphere were to cool again, the survival of the fittest might bring about, in the vegetable kingdom, a population of more and more stunted and humbler and humbler organisms, until the "fittest" that survived might be nothing but lichens, diatoms, and such microscopic organisms as those which give red snow its colour; while, if it became hotter, the pleasant valleys of the Thames and Isis might be uninhabitable by any animated beings save those that flourish in a tropical jungle. They, as the fittest, the best adapted to the changed conditions, would survive.

Men in society are undoubtedly subject to the cosmic process. As among other animals, multiplication goes on without cessation, and involves severe competition for the means of support. The struggle for existence tends to eliminate those less fitted to adapt themselves to the circumstances of their existence. The strongest, the most self-assertive, tend to tread down the weaker. But the influence of the cosmic process on the evolution of society is the greater the more rudimentary its civilization. Social progress means a checking of the cosmic process at every step and the substitution for it of another, which may be called the ethical process; the end of which is not the survival of those who may happen to be the fittest, in respect of the whole of the conditions which obtain, but of those who are ethically the best.

As I have already urged, the practice of that which is ethically best—what we call goodness or virtue—involves a course of conduct which, in all respects, is opposed to that which leads to success in the cosmic struggle for existence. In place of ruthless self-assertion it demands self-restraint; in place of thrusting aside, or treading down, all competitors, it requires that the individual shall not merely respect, but shall help his fellows; its influence is directed, not so much to the survival of the fittest, as to the fitting of as many as possible to survive. It repudiates the gladiatorial theory of existence. It demands that each man who enters into the enjoyment of the advantages of a polity shall be mindful of his debt to those who have laboriously constructed it; and shall take heed that no act of his weakens the fabric in which he has been permitted to live. Laws and moral precepts are directed to the end of curbing the cosmic process and reminding the individual of his duty to the community, to the protection and influence of which he owes, if not existence itself, at least the life of something better than a brutal savage.

It is from neglect of these plain considerations that the fanatical individualism of our time attempts to apply the analogy of cosmic nature to society. Once more we have a misapplication of the stoical injunction to follow nature; the duties of the individual to the state are forgotten, and his tendencies to self-assertion are dignified by the name of rights. It is seriously debated whether the members of a community are justified in using their combined strength to constrain one of their number to contribute his share to the maintenance of it; or even to prevent him from doing his best to destroy it. The struggle for existence which has done such admirable work in cosmic nature, must, it appears, be equally beneficent in the ethical sphere. Yet if that which I have insisted upon is true; if the cosmic process has no sort of relation to moral ends; if the imitation of it by man is inconsistent with the first principles of ethics; what becomes of this surprising theory?

Let us understand, once for all, that the ethical progress of society depends, not on imitating the cosmic process, still less in running away from it, but in combating it. It may seem an audacious proposal thus to pit the microcosm against the macrocosm and to set man to subdue nature to his higher ends; but I venture to think that the great intellectual difference between the ancient times with which we have been occupied and our day, lies in the solid foundation we have acquired for the hope that such an enterprise may meet with a certain measure of success.

The history of civilization details the steps by which men have succeeded in building up an artificial world within the cosmos. Fragile reed as he may be, man, as Pascal says, is a thinking reed: there lies within him a fund of energy operating intelligently and so far akin to that which pervades the universe, that it is competent to influence and modify the cosmic process. In virtue of his intelligence, the dwarf bends the Titan to his will. In every family, in every polity that has been established, the cosmic process in man has been restrained and otherwise modified by law and custom; in surrounding nature, it has been similarly influenced by the art of the shepherd, the agriculturist, the artisan. As civilization has advanced, so has the extent of this interference increased; until the organized and highly developed sciences and arts of the present day have endowed man with a command over the course of non-human nature greater than that once attributed to the magicians. The most impressive, I might say startling, of these changes have been brought about in the course of the last two centuries; while a right comprehension of the process of life and of the means of influencing its manifestations is only just dawning upon us. We do not yet see our way beyond generalities; and we are befogged by the obtrusion of false analogies and crude anticipations. But Astronomy, Physics, Chemistry, have all had to pass through similar phases, before they reached the stage at which their influence became an important factor in human affairs. Physiology, Psychology, Ethics, Political Science, must submit to the same ordeal. Yet it seems to me irrational to doubt that, at no distant period, they will work as great a revolution in the sphere of practice.

The theory of evolution encourages no millennial anticipations. If, for millions of years, our globe has taken the upward road, yet, some time, the summit will be reached and the downward route will be commenced. The most daring imagination will hardly venture upon the suggestion that the power and the intelligence of man can ever arrest the procession of the great year.

Moreover, the cosmic nature born with us and, to a large extent, necessary for our maintenance, is the outcome of millions of years of severe training, and it would be folly to imagine that a few centuries will suffice to subdue its masterfulness to purely ethical ends. Ethical nature may count upon having to reckon with a tenacious and powerful enemy as long as the world lasts. But, on the other hand, I see no limit to the extent to which intelligence and will, guided by sound principles of investigation, and organized in common effort, may modify the conditions of existence, for a period longer than that now covered by history. And much may be done to change the nature of man himself. The intelligence which has converted the brother of the wolf into the faithful guardian of the flock ought to be able to do something towards curbing the instincts of savagery in civilized men.

But if we may permit ourselves a larger hope of abatement of the essential evil of the world than was possible to those who, in the infancy of exact knowledge, faced the problem of existence more than a score of centuries ago, I deem it an essential condition of the realization of that hope that we should cast aside the notion that the escape from pain and sorrow is the proper object of life.

We have long since emerged from the heroic childhood of our race, when good and evil could be met with the same "frolic welcome"; the attempts to escape from evil, whether Indian or Greek, have ended in flight from the battle-field; it remains to us to throw aside the youthful over-confidence and the no less youthful discouragement of nonage. We are grown men, and must play the man

> strong in will
> To strive, to seek, to find, and not to yield,

cherishing the good that falls in our way, and bearing the evil, in and around us, with stout hearts set on diminishing it. So far, we all may strive in one faith towards one hope:

> It may be that the gulfs will wash us down,
> It may be we shall touch the Happy Isles,
>
> . . . . but something ere the end,
> Some work of noble note may yet be done.[1]

[1] [These lines are from Tennyson's *Ulysses*.]

VII

BIG BUSINESS
AND ITS CRITICS

BIG BUSINESS

THE CLASSICAL ECONOMISTS trusted to competition to prevent the plundering of the consumer and to secure some relationship between prices and costs. For competition to be effective in keeping prices down there must be many enterprises each seeking to sell its goods in a free market. Such conditions were realized in most phases of agriculture, at least, down to the 1930s.

But in other types of business the story was different. Even in Adam Smith's day, as he remarked, it was normal for people in the same kind of trade to get together in a more or less covert conspiracy to raise prices. None the less, until the latter part of the nineteenth century trusts and combines were not yet a serious problem, though there were always some elements of monopoly in public utilities, like railways, and in patented or copyrighted articles. About 1880 a new trend became apparent. The size of business enterprises was growing. The larger ones were tending to swallow up the smaller ones. As the number in a given line of activity was reduced to a few hundred, or a few score, it became possible for the various firms to get together to fix prices, or even for most of them to coalesce into one giant combine. In some cases, the objectives were the economies of large-scale production, the avoidance of duplication of sales forces or advertising, and the allocation of markets to avoid cross-hauls in transportation. But frequently the main purpose was to increase profits by restricting the supply and raising prices.

In each country the movement in business to eliminate competition took a somewhat different form. In America gigantic trusts, like the Standard Oil Company, or the American Tobacco Company, perfected horizontal combinations, and once they had achieved a monopoly or a near monopoly exploited the consumer by charging high prices. At a later date, the trusts were replaced by informal or gentlemen's agreements, like Judge Gary's famous dinners which influenced steel prices. Still later, holding companies and trade associations were used to obviate "the evils of cut-throat competition."

In Germany the cartel or *Kartell* was the usual device for getting rid of competition. A cartel is an association of semi-independent concerns for a specified purpose or purposes—selling, buying, dividing the market, "stabilizing prices," and so on. Sometimes the cartel amounted to little more than an annual meeting to discuss and decide common problems. More often the members carried on important joint activities. They might, for example, sell through a single sales organization. Before the First World War the cartel had penetrated nearly every line of business in Germany. There were mighty cartels in coal and potash, chemicals and electrical goods, and minor ones, like that of the hotelkeepers of the Black Forest. The cartel grew important in the international economy also. In aluminum, electrical goods, chemicals, oils, and other lines, the combines formed on a national basis got together more or less formally to divide the world's markets and agree on price policies. This trend was evident from about 1900 on and continued in the two decades after the First World War.

In England, the union of competing firms usually took one of two forms—the amalgamation in which one company absorbed others, and the combine in which two or more companies got together to form a new concern. Such deals were much facilitated by the intricacies of the corporate form of organization. They could often be effected merely by the purchase or exchange of stock. Great combines and amalgamations in England after 1880 came to dominate such diverse fields as salt, sewing thread, chemicals, tires, and tobacco.

In the following selection Lord Furness is urging the stockholders of an engine-building company to accept a scheme for an amalgamation. His speech was delivered on December 29, 1908, before the Eighth Ordinary General Meeting of the Shareholders of Richardsons, Westgarth and Company, Ltd.

❧

LORD FURNESS'S SPEECH ON AMALGAMATION

THE USUAL ROUTINE with regard to our annual meeting has this year been interfered with on account of a proposal which has been made to your directors for the amalgamation of our business with those of several other engine building firms on this coast. I may at once say that I was in no way responsible for the proposal, and am neither directly nor indirectly interested in the scheme except as your chairman and as a shareholder in your company, but the commercial possibilities of such an amalgamation are in the opinion of your directors so important, that we feel it our duty, even at the sacrifice of very considerable time, to investigate the position thoroughly and to take part in what are proving to be very prolonged negotiations.

You will, I know, agree with me that the past year has been one of the most disastrous in the annals of the North-East Coast, involving as it did the practical stoppage of the engineering industry for no less than seven months by the engineers' strike, this in our own case being preceded by partial stoppage and complete disorganisation owing to sectional strikes in the shipyards. We have lost, in fact, an entire year, and the immense efforts we have made in laboriously building up additional branches to our business by the creation of new departments for the manufacture of steam turbines, pumping machinery, steel works' equipment and electric installations, have been ruthlessly upset by one of the most ill-advised and calamitous strikes on record. The general public have grown so accustomed to the continuous succession of strikes that nothing short of the stoppage of the nation's railway system or coal supply creates more than ordinary interest, but the alarming fact remains that British industries are being jeopardised and British capital destroyed to an extent unparalleled in British industrial history. Take our own case as an example. We have three works, in Hartlepool, Middlesbrough, and Sunderland, with staffs of highly trained technical experts for the conduct and development of our various manufactures, each department having an organisation of designers and draughtsmen complete in itself. To supervise the actual manufacture there is a further organisation of works managers, departmental foremen and assistants, and in addition the usual commercial and clerical staffs, numbering in all some 250 men, whose services cannot, of course, be dispensed with the moment the general body of employés decide to go out on strike. At the commencement of the strike it also happened that we had an unusual number of important contracts in process of erection in various parts of the kingdom, and at a stroke everything was brought to a complete stoppage, this being followed by the virtual paralysis of our entire business for seven weary months, each successive month bringing possibilities of settlement by various proposals, including the intervention of the Board of Trade, whose good offices were so flouted by the men as to result in the resignation of Mr. Barnes, the General Secretary of the Amalgamated Engineers' Society. For ourselves, we were compelled to see our profits turned into losses, grass actually growing in our yards, our customers disappointed and disgusted, and our prospective business brought to a dead standstill by reason of our inability to accept orders. In the town, as you know, men were brought to beggary, women and children to the verge of starvation, and tradesmen's savings reduced almost to vanishing point. This, then, is the sorry picture of a strike for which there was no justification whatever and which was blindly persisted in notwithstanding many friendly efforts, including those of a Cabinet Minister and the men's leaders.

We are still among the wreckage, but let us hope that this epidemic of strikes is over, for otherwise it will be quite impossible to maintain the prosperity which has hitherto been associated with the engineering industry on this coast. Indeed, even with a mutual desire to recover lost ground, it is problematical whether we can do so unless we adopt methods by which the cost of production can be reduced by the elimination of wastage. The position we have to face is one of intense competition, and what that competition means is well illustrated by the fact that our once highly-remunerative forge department, together with many others in the district, is now practically closed, as we can obtain forgings at considerably lower prices than we can either produce them ourselves or buy them in this country. This competition will surely spread to other departments unless we adopt wise measures, and the points we must always keep prominently in view are—that there must be no strikes, that greater individual interest must be taken in the day's work, that contract dates must be kept and the confidence of buyers restored, and that the cost of production must be reduced.

If commercial success is to be achieved by any scheme of amalgamation, however, it is obvious that it can only result from increasing the excellence of our manufactures and decreasing the cost of their production. Any attempt at artificially creating a range of selling prices higher than the market standard prevailing at any given time is foredoomed to failure, as we should deservedly lose our trade by sacrificing the goodwill of our friends and customers. The one objective must, therefore, be to beneficially influence the shipbuilding industry by supplying machinery at prices which will compare favourably with those of other competing centres, and at the same time secure, if possible, a fair manufacturing profit. It is unquestionable that marine engine building presents an ideal proposition for the application of such a scheme, and if it becomes an accomplished fact and is carried out with an enthusiastic determination to make it a great success, then, in my opinion, it cannot fail to have a favourable and permanent influence on the shipbuilding industry on this coast.

Experience has shown that the highest success in any manufacture can only be obtained by specialised production in large quantities under expert management. The production of marine machinery, and the mass of detail in particular connection therewith, involves so many trades each requiring a separate department, that specialised production in bulk under highly concentrated management becomes practically impossible for the average engine builder; but under an adequate scheme of amalgamation the entire proposition is simplified and is feasibly desirable. For example, the firms considering this scheme have, during the past seven years, supplied complete engine equipment to 1206 steam-ships, having an aggregate horse-power of 2,150,000. The detail alone in connection with the yearly output of 172 sets of machinery is enormous, and were it standardised and manufactured under modern conditions, profits would be obtained which, under the present conditions, are quite impossible.

In view of the highly progressive nature, not only of the manufacture of marine and other machinery but also of its design, every single builder is now constantly face to face with heavy expenditures for plant in order to keep pace with the times. Take another example: since this Company was formed, seven years ago, we have spent £133,000 in new machinery and buildings, besides another £140,000 or thereabouts in maintaining our three works in a high state of efficiency, this expenditure being entirely apart from the cost of our turbine works, which are practically independent and constitute what is to us an entirely new business, and which have involved an outlay of fully £50,000. We are, of course, not alone in this expenditure, as all firms recognise that it is necessary for their very existence, and, heavy as it is now, it will undoubtedly become more so in the future by reason of the ever-increasing severity of competition throughout the industrial world. By amalgamating several of these big businesses, however, and localising, as far as practically possible, the manufacture of standard details, this enormous aggregate expenditure could either be very greatly reduced or, if spent as freely as at present, would inevitably result in far greater profit-earning capacity. This is to my mind the most important requirement of the present-day engineering manufacture. Experience has proved beyond question that in order to exist at all every engine manufacturer must, no matter how well his works may be equipped at present, continue to spend money very freely, and the essence of the contemplated scheme of amalgamation is to spend that money in such a manner as will enable a united body of manufacturers to meet competition with far greater success than is possible as independent units, each repeating the others' work in a fashion which, in years to come, will be regarded as tantamount to commercial suicide. The suggested amalgamation is therefore a commercial proposition of the first order, its anticipated effect being to conserve and ultimately to considerably enhance the value of the capital embarked in the industry, an effect which will apply equally to all the capital invested in engineering works on this coast. This is possible because an amalgamation offers facilities for the high development of an organisation on commercial, technical, and practical lines quite beyond those afforded by independent competitive units. Of course, any scheme of amalgamation decreases internal competition and automatic benefit would accrue under that head, but it would be a mere bye-product in comparison with the central aim and object, viz.: decreased cost of production. It would, of course, require time and immense energy on the part of everyone concerned to organise the new departure, but there would be compensation in the fact that the energy would be centred in the useful channel of progressive construction rather than in competitive destruction, and, therefore, it would beget that enthusiasm which is invariably associated with success.

It is a pertinent fact that all the firms on the coast buy many details in this country cheaper than they themselves can produce them, and yet the manufacturers of these details make very substantial profits. They do so, of course, by specialised production and concentrated management. Again, we all make details which cost us just as much as we could buy them for, and we content ourselves with the thought that they contribute their quota to our working expenses. To obtain the profits we now lose, however, is only possible if the scheme of amalgamation is sufficiently large, so that unless all the firms at present interested in the matter are in agreement it cannot be carried through.

Under the present system engines and boilers are built by each of the firms to the requirements of the several classifications, and whilst the average result of each firm's productions closely approximates that obtained by the others, yet each builder has some points of excellence, either in design, method of manufacture, arrangement of parts, quality of material or of workmanship, which in combination would yield greater excellence, and being reflected in the higher general efficiency of the entire machinery, would tend to place British construction on a higher plane in the markets of the world. Again, each firm has an expensive staff, producing designs practically identical with those of its competitors, as well as pattern-shops producing equally identical patterns. The useless expenditure under these two heads alone may be estimated from the fact that the designs and patterns for a cargo boat's engines cost about £500 to produce, and for passenger steamers a correspondingly higher figure.

It is impossible for me to enumerate within the limits of a speech all the sources of economy that are open to such an amalgamation, but its possibilities are sufficiently indicated if you consider the matter on its broad lines. The adoption of a single scheme of buying under the control of the commercial directors would alone tend to a considerable diminution in first cost.

With regard to the works, one system of organisation would be established, all antiquated tools would be replaced, and the latest methods of manufacture adopted. Overtime, which is at all times highly expensive, would be abolished as far as manufacturing conditions permitted, and night shift at high rates of pay only resorted to when it was warranted by the conditions of trade and obtainable prices—the productive capacity of the whole of the works acting in union would in all ordinary circumstances dispel the conditions which lead the individual to resort to overtime. Broadly, the leading principle would be to limit the working hours to the standard length of the working week and to divide the work amongst the various shops to that end—an arrangement, one would suppose, that would be as satisfactory to the workmen as it would undoubtedly be to the employers.

An important advantage to the shipbuilders would result from contract deliveries being strictly maintained, as in the event of local pressure relief could always be given by one or other of the amalgamated works. There would also be no reason why ships should not always be engined in the port in which they are built, as the same standard of workmanship would prevail in each of the amalgamated works. Last year the expenses incurred in this connection alone amounted approximately to £18,000 for insurance, towage, etc., all of which represents unnecessary cost, apart altogether from the loss involved by the delay in completion consequent on the ship's absence in a distant port for approximately a fortnight.

It is intended to retain the identity of the several firms as at present, and each firm would therefore trade under the name upon which its business has been built up, and by which its productions are known and celebrated the world over. Moreover, the local boards of management would continue and the executive staffs would be retained, as only by their united efforts could the new scheme of organisation be developed with dispatch and success.

I would again emphasise the fact that I am simply putting before you the proposition which has been put before your Directors, and before all the firms interested in this matter, and it is only by force of circumstances and not by intention that it falls to my lot to give public expression to the views which prompted any of us to give the scheme our consideration. I am convinced, however, that if we are to advance our industries and protect the capital invested in them we must recognise facts and modernise our methods, and in dealing with this scheme we must also endeavour to sink personal considerations of every kind. We cannot but realise that the industrial world is advancing at a pace unparalleled in its history. To have been told ten years ago, or even five years ago, that Japan would be building, and building with the greatest success, her "Dreadnoughts," her fast torpedo boat destroyers, and her 23-knot passenger liners, would have been regarded as a dream, yet they are accomplished facts. Continental competition is also, as you know, increasing by leaps and bounds, but in spite of all I am convinced that we can hold our own, nay more than hold our own, if we will but shake off the incubus of our stereotyped industrial methods. In Germany, which is in the forefront of industrial progress, there are some hundreds of amalgamations of one kind and another, so there it has been amply demonstrated that the secret of commercial success lies in a policy of combined effort. At this stage I cannot say whether the scheme will mature or not; if it does it will involve an adjustment of our capital to a basis which, it has been decided, shall be the standard basis for every firm, although on that point I am unable, and it is altogether unnecessary that I should say more on the present occasion. Your Board propose to you that this meeting shall stand adjourned until a convenient date, and that in the meantime you will patiently await the maturing of the negotiations that are now afoot, relying upon the ability and zeal of your directors to safeguard and protect your interests in every possible way, and as soon as the negotiations are sufficiently advanced we will lose no time in putting the matter fully before you for your final decision.

THE DOCKERS' STRIKE

THE GREAT DOCK STRIKE of 1889 marked a turning point in the British labor movement. Up to that time the English unions had been in the main composed of skilled workers. They did not include unskilled low-paid workers such as dockers (stevedores and longshoremen who loaded and unloaded ships).

The dockers of London were overworked, underpaid, and exploited mercilessly through unfavorable conditions of hiring and employment. In 1889, a small strike broke out at the West India Dock and quickly spread to other piers. Led by Ben Tillett and his lieutenants, Tom Mann and John Burns (who were trade unionists and engineers), the dockers were quickly organized into a union. Despite lack of funds and trade-union experience, the dockers held firm during the strike, which lasted for more than a month. Meanwhile their cause had awakened much sympathy not only among labor, both organized and unorganized, but also among the middle class. Young liberals, radicals, Fabian socialists, and humanitarians rallied to their cause, took up collections, passed out soup to the strikers, wrote articles, and made speeches. The employers could not find scabs (called blacklegs in England) to replace the strikers because of the general sympathy for the strikers. Nearly £50,000 was raised to help the dockers, by public subscription.

Finally, through the mediation of Cardinal Manning, the leading Catholic churchman of England, and Sydney Buxton, the strike was ended. The dockers won all their main demands: sixpence an hour as a minimum wage, extra pay for overtime, four hours as the minimum period of employment, abolition of piecework, and improved conditions of hiring.

In the ensuing years the organization of unskilled workers progressed rapidly in England and there was an increased solidarity among the ranks of labor. Many regard the dock strike as the beginning of this trend.

The passage below is Tom Mann's own story of the strike, one of many which he helped to organize and lead in his long career in the forefront of the English labor movement. It is taken from *Tom Mann's Memoirs* (London, Labour Publishing Company, 1923).

TOM MANN'S MEMOIRS

THE LONDON DOCK STRIKE of 1889 involved a much wider issue than that of a large number of port workers fighting for better conditions. There had long been no more than a dogged acquiescence in the conditions insisted upon by the employers, more particularly on the part of those classed as unskilled labourers. Skilled and unskilled alike were dominated over by their employers; and at the same time the unskilled, not being yet organised, were in many instances subject to further dictation and domination by the organised skilled men. The industrial system was (as it still is, with some modification) creating an army of surplus workers, who, never having been decently paid for their work, had never been decently fed; every occupation had its proportion of this surplus. Irregularity of work, coupled with liability to arduous and dangerous toil when employed, characterised the dock workers in an exceptional degree; and although dock labour was classed as unskilled, in grim reality it often required a considerable amount of skill; moreover, accidents were frequent. Nevertheless, in the struggle against death by starvation, a larger percentage of worn-out men (cast-offs from other occupations) made their way to compete for casual labour at the docks and wharves of London, than to any other place or to any similar occupation.

This does not mean that all the dock workers were weaklings! Far from it. Some of the finest built men in the country would always be found amongst the dockers; but the above generalisation was true. Again, whilst dockers were in a very large number of cases badly paid per hour, and could only get a few hours' work per week, in the work of a large port there is always a number who get regular work, and some, of course, who get relatively good wages.

Many circumstances seem to have conspired to make the upheaval of 1889 the assertion of the rights of a large class in the community—the rights of those who had never before been recognised as possessing the rights and the title to respect of civilised humans. It was nothing less than a challenge to all hostile forces, and an assertion of the claim for proper treatment. The challenge was successful; the claim was enforced.

I was at the office of the "Labour Elector" in Paternoster Row, on August 14th in that year, when, about midday, I received a wire from Ben Tillett asking me to make my way to the South West India Dock. I went at once. There was no difficulty in finding the men, for Ben was with them, and they were about to hold a meeting. I was soon put in possession of the main facts.

The men had been discharging a sailing ship named "The Lady Armstrong." They were working for fivepence an hour and "plus," this meaning that, in a vague fashion, very ill defined, there was a recognised time for discharging certain goods, and if the men did the work in less time they received a surplus of a halfpenny or penny per hour. The men argued they had kept correct tally, but the dock superintendent refused to admit the claim. The dockers were told that their demand for more pay would have to be dealt with by the chief authority, The London and India Docks Joint Committee. The men refused to return to work.

Serious discussion must have taken place prior to the "Lady Armstrong" difficulty, because almost immediately it was proposed that now they were out, they should insist in the future upon an established minimum of sixpence per hour for ordinary time and eightpence per hour for overtime. When I arrived, they had already decided to claim at least as much as this, and to call upon their fellow dockers to help them. No need here to go into detail beyond that of giving a correct idea of the definiteness of aim, and the effect of the achievement. For myself, I kept at that strike until it was over; and for long after I remained in touch with the dockers, and with the movement of which they were a part.

Burns, as all know, was, like Tillett, in the thick of the struggle, being active in every phase of it, except when absolutely compelled to take rest. The Strike Committee at the start made its headquarters at Wroots' Coffee House, Poplar, and the first day that relief tickets were given out I had a very difficult duty. There was a crowd of several thousand men to deal with, and each had to be given one ticket, and only one. As yet there had been no time to organise the distribution systematically. The men were in urgent need; they had been told a few hours before that tickets would be issued that day. Now they had assembled, and the committee had just received the tickets from the printer. Wroots' Coffee House door opened out on to a main thoroughfare. If only we could admit the men at a quiet walking pace they could go out at a side door; but naturally they were eager; they were fearful there might not be enough tickets to go round; they would hardly listen to instructions that order must be preserved. I, therefore, stood on the doorstep and briefly addressed the crowd, telling them that every one would get a ticket, but that we must keep control of the position, and I asked them to pass me quietly. To their great credit, they entirely agreed. Almost immediately a thousand men were right close to me, but endeavouring to be perfectly orderly. I put my back against one of the doorposts, and stretched out my leg with my foot on the opposite post, jamming myself in. I talked pleasantly to the men, and passed each man in under my leg, by this means steadying the rush. The fact that they did not make it impossible for me to remain at the task was exceedingly creditable, for, to prevent a stampede, many had to keep their mates back, and it was all done in good humour. At the close I was so stiff and bruised, I could scarcely walk for a while. I pulled my shirt off and wrung it out. It was soaked with perspiration, and my back had a good deal of skin off; but the job was completed satisfactorily.

The stevedores, the men who load the long-distance boats, and therefore stow the cargo, had organised in 1872, and had established a rate of eightpence an hour ordinary time and one shilling an hour overtime, thus giving evidence of the disciplinary effects of organisation. Their meeting place was at the Wades' Arms, Jeremiah Street, Poplar; and as the accommodation was more suitable there than at Wroots', the Strike Committee moved to the stevedores' headquarters. Tom McCarthy (dead now this twenty-two years) was a prominent and active member. Another stevedore, James Twomey, was chairman of the Strike Committee—for these and all other waterside workers were out in sympathy, if not directly affected.

The Strike Committee sat every day and evening, usually till midnight. The questions to be dealt with were multitudinous; occasionally there would be warmth of temper shown, but generally speaking the proceedings were conducted in a most orderly fashion. I was told off to give special attention to picketing, and to the organisation of forces on the south side of the river. This left others available for public speaking, attempts at negotiations, etc. I usually turned up at committee about 11 P.M., unless special questions demanded consideration.

What stress and strain and responsibility! What opportunities for demonstrating capacity, a knowledge of what was necessary, a readiness to do it! And, speaking generally, wonderfully good work was done. Apart from public speaking, picketing, and negotiating, a thousand things every day required attention, and as a rule they were well attended to. Besides the thirty thousand dock and wharf workers, there were sailors and firemen, carmen, lightermen, and dry-dock workers, making another thirty thousand. These, with their dependents, all had to be provided for. Four hundred and forty thousand food tickets were distributed during the five weeks the dispute lasted, and many thousands of meals were organised and provided by friendly agencies. Public sympathy was entirely with the men, and practically the whole press was kindly disposed. Large sums were collected, but in spite of this help the time came when finances were at a very low ebb and the prospects of a settlement seemed remote. Next day, however, came a cable from Australia sending two thousand pounds, with promise of more; a few days later, the Australians cabled fifteen hundred pounds more. All told they sent no less than thirty thousand pounds. What a godsend! How it delighted the men; how it encouraged the leaders; and how it must have told the other way on the dock directors!

The dockers' fight in London fired the imagination of all classes in Australia; and employers, as readily and as heartily as workers, contributed to the London Dockers' Fund. I have had opportunities of thanking the people of Australia by addressing them in person at public meetings in nearly every city and township. What of it, that many Australians who subscribed to the London Dockers' Fund in 1889, fought determinedly against the transport workers in Australasia in 1890? These are the vagaries of human nature. As Yorkshire people say: "Ther's nowt so queer as folk."

John Burns and Ben Tillett were two very different men in temperament and style, but each of them possessed exactly the right qualities to fire audiences and keep up the struggle to a successful finish. John Burns—with his assertiveness, his businesslike readiness to deal with emergencies, his power and disposition to keep at arm's length those who would have foisted themselves on the movement to its disadvantage, his cheery jocularity and homely remarks to the men on the march or on Tower Hill, his scathing criticism of hostile comments in the press or on the part of the dock directors—vitally contributed to the continuous encouragement of the mass of the strikers.

Ben Tillett, who had a close relationship to the men as general secretary of the Tea Operatives' and General Labourers' Union, would pour forth invectives upon all opponents, would reach the heart's core of the dockers by his description of the way in which they had to beg for work and the paltry pittance they received, and by his homely illustrations of their life as it was and as it ought to be. He was short in stature, but tough; pallid, but dauntless; affected with a stammer at this time, but the real orator of the group. Ben was a force to be reckoned with all through the fight.

H. H. Champion, cooler than a cucumber, would make statements of a revolutionary character, would deal with the weak points in the men's position, and would encourage them to rectify the same. Occasionally R. B. Cunninghame Graham would appear, as neat as a West End dude, with an eye keener than a hawk's and a voice and manner that riveted attention as he drove home his satirical points, but always leaving a nice impression.

Tom McCarthy was a keen-witted, eloquent, versatile Irishman, full of personal knowledge of the actual life and work of a waterside man. Harry Orbell was a simple-spoken, frank, honest fellow, familiar with all the difficulties of the unskilled labourer, but was himself a highly-skilled man in the furnishing business. He had been squeezed out of this employment by the exigencies of trade depression. On the south side, Harry Quelch took a keen interest in the organisation of the men, and built up the Labour Protection League.

When at length the dock directors agreed to the demands, with certain reservations as to the date when they should become operative, the position became critical. At the Mansion House many conferences had been held. The Lord Mayor, the dock directors, the men's representatives, and with general acquiescence a few prominent persons not identified directly with the business side of life, including the Bishop of London and Cardinal Manning, participated.

I had never seen the Cardinal before, and it was a matter of no small interest to me to find myself closely identified with such a man for a colleague.

A large percentage of the men at the docks were (and are) Roman Catholics. Now that a stage had been reached when the men's representatives were of opinion that the offers of the company merited serious consideration, the Cardinal, on the suggestion of the Strike Committee chairman, agreed to go to Poplar and put the case to the men, who held him in the greatest respect and reverence.

The meeting was held in the Kirby Street Catholic School at Poplar. The Cardinal was a very slender man; his face was most arresting, so thin, so refined, so kindly. In the whole of my life I have never seen another like unto it. He spoke to the dockers in such a quiet, firm, and advising fatherly manner, that minute by minute as he was speaking one could feel the mental atmosphere changing. The result was an agreement that the conditions should be accepted, to become operative in November.

The chief gains were: a minimum of sixpence an hour instead of five-pence (only fourpence formerly at Tilbury); eightpence an hour for over-time; none to be paid off with less than two shillings, or four hours' work. This seems a trifling gain now, but it was an important matter then, to have regular taking-on times instead of taking-on at any hour of the day, and to have gangs properly made up. The last point was not included in the original settlement, but it became a current practice at the docks and wharves, to the great advantage of the men. The change for the better was very real; and although subsequently difficulties arose, when many of the men became careless, and when petty bosses sought to score over the dockers, still, all who knew and know the facts will admit that the struggle of 1889 was a real landmark.

Ben Tillett, who had been general secretary all the time, writing of what happened in 1889 and its effects, when reviewing the position twenty-one years later, in *A Brief History of the Dockers' Union*, wrote:

We had established a new spirit; the bully and the thief, for a time at least, were squelched; no more would the old man be driven and cursed to death by the younger man, threatened and egged on to murder by an overmastering bully. The whole tone and conduct of work, of management of the men, was altered, and for the best.

The goad of the sack was not so fearful; the filthiness and foulness of language was altered for an attempt at courtesy, which, if not refined, was at least a recognition of the manhood of our brothers.

From a condition of the foulest blackguardism in directing the work, the men found a greater respect shown them; they, too, grew in self-respect, and the men we saw after the strike were comparable to the most self-respecting of the other grades of labour.

The "calls" worked out satisfactorily; organisation took the place of the haphazard; the bosses who lazed and loafed on their subordinates were perforce obliged to earn instead of thieving their money; the work was better done; the men's lives were more regular as the work was—the docker had, in fact, become a man!

The man became greater in the happiness of a better supplied larder and home; and the women folk, with the children, shared the sense of security and peace the victory at the docks had wrought.

I must give myself the satisfaction here of putting on record the great kindness and forebearance shown to the Strike Committee, and to the stream of deputations they had to deal with, by Mrs. Hickey of the Wades' Arms. The hostess, her son, and her daughters had, indeed, a heavy task. We practically took possession of the house, not for an hour or two, but for all day and every day during the five weeks the strike lasted. But Mrs. Hickey treated these fellows—ourselves of the Committee included—as though she had been mother to the lot. She literally kept a shillelah handy, with which she frequently, in a half-serious way, would threaten any young fellow who was too noisy; but it was fine that these rough chaps respected her so thoroughly, and that she had the splendid tact to make it easy for them to keep good order all through the trying time.

I was generally one of the last members of the committee to get away. Often enough I left the premises nearer one o'clock than midnight—not to go home, for there was little chance of doing that, but to get to the house of Brother Jem Twomey, the chairman of the Strike Committee, with whom I used to stay.

I can honestly say, for my own part, that I cared nothing at all for the public meetings, whether on Tower Hill or elsewhere, or for what was thought of the fight by the public. I concentrated on the work of organisation, and was indifferent to outside opinion. I had been at it about three weeks, and was now dealing specially with the south side of the Thames.

One day I realised that my boots had become so worn out, and that I must get others, or go barefoot (we always had long marches, and I invariably marched with the crowd). I slipped away from the marching column as soon as I noticed a boot shop. Hastily buying a pair of boots, I put them on and hurried to catch up with the crowd. When we reached Sayes Court, Deptford, I spoke as usual upon the general situation. A few days later, we were marching again along the thoroughfare where I had bought the boots. My eye lighted on the shop window, and to my amazement I noticed my name on a card. I approached the window, and to my still greater astonishment I saw that the card bearing my name was on the pair of old boots I had shed a few days before. The writing on the card ran: "The boots worn by Tom Mann during the long marches in the Dock Strike." I was positively flabbergasted, to think that importance of any kind could attach to such articles, or to me.

I had become so inextricably involved in the dispute, and felt so completely a part of everything that was taking place, that I had left work, home, and all else, and paid no regard to anything other than the fight I was in. I scarcely noticed the papers, and had it not been for the subscriptions from Australia, I doubt if I should have known that the activities in which I was swallowed up had arrested attention outside this country. But, as events proved, the dock strike started a wave which spread over a great part of the world, and the working conditions of many millions were affected by it.

ANDREW CARNEGIE

BORN IN SCOTLAND, the son of a hand-loom weaver forced to flee to America, when hand work was displaced by the advance of machine industry, Andrew Carnegie (1835–1919) found in the New World the realized dream of equality of opportunity. He began work at the age of thirteen and at eighteen found his opportunity when he took a position with the Pennsylvania Railroad as a telegraph clerk. Carnegie exploited his personal contacts, and in six years he was superintendent of the western division of the Pennsylvania. By dint of scrupulous saving and sagacious investments Carnegie built up his fortune, and by 1863, in the midst of the Civil War, the young capitalist reckoned his income at $47,860.67. In 1865 he left his job with the railroad (which was anything but the essential source of his income, since he had never earned more than $2,400 a year through his work as superintendent) and entered the iron business. In 1873 he turned his energies to the organization of steel companies—the industry in connection with which he is best remembered. Carnegie's opening ventures in steel were capitalized at a total sum of $700,000: it was characteristic of his career that by 1892 he and his associates had acquired $40,000,000 on this original investment.

In his own way Carnegie personified the spirit of the industrial capitalism in which he flourished. His business methods were always individualistic, his companies were organized around him, and his successes were usually the fruits of his personal connections. Thus, he remained scrupulously away from the banks and the investment market; he kept his partners within the firm, and always kept a controlling interest; he was his own sales manager and his own public-relations man; he was sometimes on favorable terms with labor unions, sometimes at odds with them—but whatever his relations with labor, and whatever his relations with his competitors, they were always on his own terms. It was he more than any other who was responsible for the tremendous expansion of America's steel industry in the last quarter of the nineteenth century. His retirement in 1901 was symbolic of the passing of an era: for he sold out (at his own price) to the newly formed United States Steel Corporation, controlled by Morgan, who was primarily a financier.

Carnegie, the rugged individualist, was not unaware of his debt to the New World, nor did his conception of the gospel of wealth omit the sense of social obligation. In a series of essays he set forth his belief that wealth was a public trust. Always the individualist, however, he refused to accept the government as the seat of that trust, but insisted that the philanthropic individual must be the source of social services. His beliefs did not end in theory. Carnegie gave away a total of $288,000,000 within the United States and $62,000,000 in Great Britain. The primary interest of this social program arose out of Carnegie's antagonism to the imperialism associated with finance capital. Perhaps closest to his heart was the movement for world peace; to advance it, he established the Carnegie Foundation for International Peace.

The following selections are from three of Carnegie's essays, "The Gospel of Wealth," "Popular Illusions about Trusts," and "An Employer's View of the Labor Question," which appeared together in book form under the title *The Gospel of Wealth* (New York, The Century Company, 1900).

℘

THE GOSPEL OF WEALTH

The Gospel of Wealth

THE PROBLEM OF THE ADMINISTRATION OF WEALTH

THE PROBLEM of our age is the proper administration of wealth, that the ties of brotherhood may still bind together the rich and poor in harmonious relationship. The conditions of human life have not only been changed, but revolutionized, within the past few hundred years. In former days there was little difference between the dwelling, dress, food, and environment of the chief and those of his retainers. The Indians are to-day where civilized man then was. When visiting the Sioux, I was led to the wigwam of the chief. It was like the others in external appearance, and even within the difference was trifling between it and those of the poorest of his braves. The contrast between the palace of the millionaire and the cottage of the laborer with us to-day measures the change which has come with civilization. This change, however, is not to be deplored, but welcomed as highly beneficial. It is well, nay, essential, for the progress of the race that the houses of some should be homes for all that is highest and best in literature and the arts, and for all the refinements of civilization, rather than that none should be so. Much better this great irregularity than universal squalor. Without wealth there can be no Mæcenas. The "good old times" were not good old times. Neither master nor servant was as well situated then as to-day. A relapse to old conditions would be disastrous to both—not the least so to him who serves—and would sweep away civilization with it. But whether the change be for good or ill, it is upon us, beyond our power to alter, and, therefore, to be accepted and made the best of. It is a waste of time to criticize the inevitable.

It is easy to see how the change has come. One illustration will serve for almost every phase of the cause. In the manufacture of products we have the whole story. It applies to all combinations of human industry, as stimulated and enlarged by the inventions of this scientific age. Formerly, articles were manufactured at the domestic hearth, or in small shops which formed part of the household. The master and his apprentices worked side by side, the latter living with the master, and therefore subject to the same conditions. When these apprentices rose to be masters, there was little or no change in their mode of life, and they, in turn, educated succeeding apprentices in the same routine. There was, substantially, social equality, and even political equality, for those engaged in industrial pursuits had then little or no voice in the State.

The inevitable result of such a mode of manufacture was crude articles at high prices. To-day the world obtains commodities of excellent quality at prices which even the preceding generation would have deemed incredible. In the commercial world similar causes have produced similar results, and the race is benefited thereby. The poor enjoy what the rich could not before afford. What were the luxuries have become the necessaries of life. The laborer has now more comforts than the farmer had a few generations ago. The farmer has more luxuries than the landlord had, and is more richly clad and better housed. The landlord has books and pictures rarer and appointments more artistic than the king could then obtain.

The price we pay for this salutary change is, no doubt, great. We assemble thousands of operatives in the factory, and in the mine, of whom the employer can know little or nothing, and to whom he is little better than a myth. All intercourse between them is at an end. Rigid castes are formed, and, as usual, mutual ignorance breeds mutual distrust. Each caste is without sympathy with the other, and ready to credit anything disparaging in regard to it. Under the law of competition, the employer of thousands is forced into the strictest economies, among which the rates paid to labor figure prominently, and often there is friction between the employer and employed, between capital and labor, between rich and poor. Human society loses homogeneity.

The price which society pays for the law of competition, like the price it pays for cheap comforts and luxuries, is also great; but the advantages of this law are also greater still than its cost—for it is to this law that we owe our wonderful material development, which brings improved conditions in its train. But, whether the law be benign or not, we must say of it, as we say of the change in the conditions of men to which we have referred: It is here; we cannot evade it; no substitutes for it have been found; and while the law may be sometimes hard for the individual, it is best for the race, because it insures the survival of the fittest in every department. We accept and welcome, therefore, as conditions to which we must accommodate ourselves, great inequality of environment; the concentration of business, industrial and commercial, in the hands of a few; and the law of competition between these, as being not only beneficial, but essential to the future progress of the race. Having accepted these, it follows that there must be great scope for the exercise of special ability in the merchant and in the manufacturer who has to conduct affairs upon a great scale. That this talent for organization and management is rare among men is proved by the fact that it invariably secures enormous rewards for its possessor, no matter where or under what laws or conditions. The experienced in affairs always rate the MAN whose services can be obtained as a partner as not only the first consideration, but such as renders the question of his capital scarcely worth considering: for able men soon create capital; in the hands of those without the special talent required, capital soon takes wings. Such men become interested in firms or corporations using millions; and, estimating only simple interest to be made upon the capital invested, it is inevitable that their income must exceed their expenditure and that they must, therefore, accumulate wealth. Nor is there any middle ground which such men can occupy, because the great manufacturing or commercial concern which does not earn at least interest upon its capital soon becomes bankrupt. It must either go forward or fall behind; to stand still is impossible. It is a condition essential to its successful operation that it should be thus far profitable, and even that, in addition to interest on capital, it should make profit. It is a law, as certain as any of the others named, that men possessed of this peculiar talent for affairs, under the free play of economic forces must, of necessity, soon be in receipt of more revenue than can be judiciously expended upon themselves; and this law is as beneficial for the race as the others.

Objections to the foundations upon which society is based are not in order, because the condition of the race is better with these than it has been with any other which has been tried. Of the effect of any new substitutes proposed we cannot be sure. The Socialist or Anarchist who seeks to overturn present conditions is to be regarded as attacking the foundation upon which civilization itself rests, for civilization took its start from the day when the capable, industrious workman said to his incompetent and lazy fellow, "If thou dost not sow, thou shalt not reap," and thus ended primitive Communism by separating the drones from the bees. One who studies this subject will soon be brought face to face with the conclusion that upon the sacredness of property civilization itself depends—the right of the laborer to his hundred dollars in the savings-bank, and equally the legal right of the millionaire to his millions. Every man must be allowed "to sit under his own vine and fig-tree, with none to make afraid," if human society is to advance, or even to remain so far advanced as it is. To those who propose to substitute Communism for this intense Individualism, the answer therefore is: The race has tried that. All progress from that barbarous day to the present time has resulted from its displacement. Not evil, but good, has come to the race from the accumulation of wealth by those who have had the ability and energy to produce it. But even if we admit for a moment that it might be better for the race to discard its present foundation, Individualism,—that it is a nobler ideal that man should labor, not for himself alone, but in and for a brotherhood of his fellows, and share with them all in common, realizing Swedenborg's idea of heaven, where, as he says, the angels derive their happiness, not from laboring for self, but for each other,—even admit all this, and a sufficient answer is, This is not evolution, but revolution. It necessitates the changing of human nature itself—a work of eons, even if it were good to change it, which we cannot know.

It is not practicable in our day or in our age. Even if desirable theoretically, it belongs to another and long-succeeding sociological stratum. Our duty is with what is practicable now—with the next step possible in our day and generation. It is criminal to waste our energies in endeavoring to uproot, when all we can profitably accomplish is to bend the universal tree of humanity a little in the direction most favorable to the production of good fruit under existing circumstances. We might as well urge the destruction of the highest existing type of man because he failed to reach our ideal as to favor the destruction of Individualism, Private Property, the Law of Accumulation of Wealth, and the Law of Competition; for these are the highest result of human experience, the soil in which society, so far, has produced the best fruit. Unequally or unjustly, perhaps, as these laws sometimes operate, and imperfect as they appear to the Idealist, they are, nevertheless, like the highest type of man, the best and most valuable of all that humanity has yet accomplished.

We start, then, with a condition of affairs under which the best interests of the race are promoted, but which inevitably gives wealth to the few. Thus far, accepting conditions as they exist, the situation can be surveyed and pronounced good. The question then arises,—and if the foregoing be correct, it is the only question with which we have to deal,—What is the proper mode of administering wealth after the laws upon which civilization is founded have thrown it into the hands of the few? And it is of this great question that I believe I offer the true solution. It will be understood that fortunes are here spoken of, not moderate sums saved by many years of effort, the returns from which are required for the comfortable maintenance and education of families. This is not wealth, but only competence, which it should be the aim of all to acquire, and which it is for the best interests of society should be acquired.

There are but three modes in which surplus wealth can be disposed of. It can be left to the families of the decedents; or it can be bequeathed for public purposes; or, finally, it can be administered by its possessors during their lives.

Under the first and second modes most of the wealth of the world that has reached the few has hitherto been applied. Let us in turn consider each of these modes. The first is the most injudicious. In monarchical countries, the estates and the greatest portion of the wealth are left to the first son, that the vanity of the parent may be gratified by the thought that his name and title are to descend unimpaired to succeeding generations. The condition of this class in Europe to-day teaches the failure of such hopes or ambitions. The successors have become impoverished through their follies, or from the fall in the value of land. Even in Great Britain the strict law of entail has been found inadequate to maintain an hereditary class. Its soil is rapidly passing into the hands of the stranger. Under republican institutions the division of property among the children is much fairer; but the question which forces itself upon thoughtful men in all lands is, Why should men leave great fortunes to their children? If this is done from affection, is it not misguided affection? Observation teaches that, generally speaking, it is not well for the children that they should be so burdened. Neither is it well for the State. Beyond providing for the wife and daughters moderate sources of income, and very moderate allowances indeed, if any, for the sons, men may well hesitate; for it is no longer questionable that great sums bequeathed often work more for the injury than for the good of the recipients. Wise men will soon conclude that, for the best interests of the members of their families, and of the State, such bequests are an improper use of their means.

It is not suggested that men who have failed to educate their sons to earn a livelihood shall cast them adrift in poverty. If any man has seen fit to rear his sons with a view to their living idle lives, or, what is highly commendable, has instilled in them the sentiment that they are in a position to labor for public ends without reference to pecuniary considerations, then, of course, the duty of the parent is to see that such are provided for in moderation. There are instances of millionaires' sons unspoiled by wealth, who, being rich, still perform great services to the community. Such are the very salt of the earth, as valuable as, unfortunately, they are rare. It is not the exception, however, but the rule, that men must regard; and, looking at the usual result of enormous sums conferred upon legatees, the thoughtful man must shortly say, "I would as soon leave to my son a curse as the almighty dollar," and admit to himself that it is not the welfare of the children, but family pride, which inspires these legacies.

As to the second mode, that of leaving wealth at death for public uses . . . the cases are not few in which the real object sought by the testator is not attained, nor are they few in which his real wishes are thwarted. In many cases the bequests are so used as to become only monuments of his folly.

It is well to remember that it requires the exercise of not less ability than that which acquires it, to use wealth so as to be really beneficial to the community. Besides this, it may fairly be said that no man is to be extolled for doing what he cannot help doing, nor is he to be thanked by the community to which he only leaves wealth at death. Men who leave a vast sum in this way may fairly be thought men who would not have left it at all had they been able to take it with them. The memories of such cannot be held in grateful remembrance, for there is no grace in their gifts. It is not to be wondered at that such bequests seem so generally to lack the blessing. . . .

There remains, then, only one mode of using great fortunes; but in this we have the true antidote for the temporary unequal distribution of wealth, the reconciliation of the rich and the poor—a reign of harmony, another ideal, differing, indeed, from that of the Communist in requiring only the further evolution of existing conditions, not the total overthrow of our civilization. It is founded upon the present most intense Individualism, and the race is prepared to put it in practice by degrees whenever it pleases. Under its sway we shall have an ideal State, in which the surplus wealth of the few will become, in the best sense, the property of the many, because administered for the common good: and this wealth, passing through the hands of the few, can be made a much more potent force for the elevation of our race than if distributed in small sums to the people themselves. Even the poorest can be made to see this, and to agree that great sums gathered by some of their fellow-citizens and spent for public purposes, from which the masses reap the principal benefit, are more valuable to them than if scattered among themselves in trifling amounts through the course of many years. . . .

The best uses to which surplus wealth can be put have already been indicated. Those who would administer wisely must, indeed, be wise; for one of the serious obstacles to the improvement of our race is indiscriminate charity. It were better for mankind that the millions of the rich were thrown into the sea than so spent as to encourage the slothful, the drunken, the unworthy. Of every thousand dollars spent in so-called charity to-day, it is probable that nine hundred and fifty dollars is unwisely spent—so spent, indeed, as to produce the very evils which it hopes to mitigate or cure. A well-known writer of philosophic books admitted the other day that he had given a quarter of a dollar to a man who approached him as he was coming to visit the house of his friend. He knew nothing of the habits of this beggar, knew not the use that would be made of this money, although he had every reason to suspect that it would be spent improperly. This man professed to be a disciple of Herbert Spencer; yet the quarter-dollar given that night will probably work more injury than all the money will do good which its thoughtless donor will ever be able to give in true charity. He only gratified his own feelings, saved himself from annoyance—and this was probably one of the most selfish and very worst actions of his life, for in all respects he is most worthy.

In bestowing charity, the main consideration should be to help those who will help themselves; to provide part of the means by which those who desire to improve may do so; to give those who desire to rise the aids by which they may rise; to assist, but rarely or never to do all. Neither the individual nor the race is improved by almsgiving. Those worthy of assistance, except in rare cases, seldom require assistance. The really valuable men of the race never do, except in case of accident or sudden change. Every one has, of course, cases of individuals brought to his own knowledge where temporary assistance can do genuine good, and these he will not overlook. But the amount which can be wisely given by the individual for individuals is necessarily limited by his lack of knowledge of the circumstances connected with each. He is the only true reformer who is as careful and as anxious not to aid the unworthy as he is to aid the worthy, and, perhaps, even more so, for in almsgiving more injury is probably done by rewarding vice than by relieving virtue.

The rich man is thus almost restricted to following the examples of Peter Cooper, Enoch Pratt of Baltimore, Mr. Pratt of Brooklyn, Senator Stanford, and others, who know that the best means of benefiting the community is to place within its reach the ladders upon which the aspiring can rise—free libraries, parks, and means of recreation, by which men are helped in body and mind; works of art, certain to give pleasure and improve the public taste; and public institutions of various kinds, which will improve the general condition of the people; in this manner returning their surplus wealth to the mass of their fellows in the forms best calculated to do them lasting good.

Thus is the problem of rich and poor to be solved. The laws of accumulation will be left free, the laws of distribution free. Individualism will continue, but the millionaire will be but a trustee for the poor, intrusted for a season with a great part of the increased wealth of the community, but administering it for the community far better than it could or would have done for itself. The best minds will thus have reached a stage in the development of the race in which it is clearly seen that there is no mode of disposing of surplus wealth creditable to thoughtful and earnest men into whose hands it flows, save by using it year by year for the general good. This day already dawns. Men may die without incurring the pity of their fellows, still sharers in great business enterprises from which their capital cannot be or has not been withdrawn, and which is left chiefly at death for public uses; yet the day is not far distant when the man who dies leaving behind him millions of available wealth, which was free for him to administer during life, will pass away "unwept, unhonored, and unsung," no matter to what uses he leaves the dross which he cannot take with him. Of such as these the public verdict will then be: "The man who dies thus rich dies disgraced."

Such, in my opinion, is the true gospel concerning wealth, obedience to which is destined some day to solve the problem of the rich and the poor, and to bring "Peace on earth, among men good will."

Popular Illusions About Trusts

. . . The day of small concerns within the means of many able men seems to be over, never to return. The rise to partnership in vast concerns must come chiefly through such means as these permitted by the laws of limited partnership.

To-day we hear little of the joint-stock corporation, which has settled into its proper sphere and escapes notice. It was succeeded by the "syndicate," a combination of corporations which pulled together for a time, and expected to destroy destructive competition. The word has already almost passed out of use, and now the syndicate has given place to the trust.

We see in all these efforts of men the desire to furnish opportunities to mass capital, to concentrate the small savings of the many and to direct them to one end. The conditions of human society create for this an imperious demand; the concentration of capital is a necessity for meeting the demands of our day, and as such should not be looked at askance, but be encouraged. There is nothing detrimental to human society in it, but much that is, or is bound soon to become, beneficial. It is an evolution from the heterogeneous to the homogeneous [sic], and is clearly another step in the upward path of development.

Abreast of this necessity for massing the wealth of the many in even larger and larger sums for huge enterprises, another law is seen in operation in the invariable tendency from the beginning till now to lower the cost of all articles produced by man. Through the operation of this law the home of the laboring man of our day boasts luxuries which even in the palaces of monarchs as recent as Queen Elizabeth were unknown. It is a trite saying that the comforts of to-day were the luxuries of yesterday, and conveys only a faint impression of the contrast, until one walks through the castles and palaces of older countries, and learns that two or three centuries ago these had for carpets only rushes, small open spaces for windows, glass being little known, and were without gas or water-supply, or any of what we consider to-day the conveniences of life. As for those chief treasures of life, books, there is scarcely a workingman's family which has not at its command, without money and without price, access to libraries to which the palace was recently a stranger.

If there be in human history one truth clearer and more indisputable than another, it is that the cheapening of articles, whether of luxury or of necessity or of those classed as artistic, insures their more general distribution, and is one of the most potent factors in refining and lifting a people, and in adding to its happiness. In no period of human activity has this great agency been so potent or so wide-spread as in our own. Now, the cheapening of all these good things, whether it be in the metals, in textiles, or in food, or especially in books and prints, is rendered possible only through the operation of the law, which may be stated thus: cheapness is in proportion to the scale of production. To make ten tons of steel a day would cost many times as much per ton as to make one hundred tons; to make one hundred tons would cost double as much per ton as a thousand; and to make one thousand tons per day would cost greatly more than to make ten thousand tons. Thus, the larger the scale of operation the cheaper the product. The huge steamship of twenty thousand tons burden carries its ton of freight at less cost, it is stated, than the first steamships carried a pound. It is, fortunately, impossible for man to impede, much less to change, this great and beneficent law, from which flow most of his comforts and luxuries, and also most of the best and most improving forces in his life.

In an age noted for its inventions, we see the same law running through these. Inventions facilitate big operations, and in most instances require to be worked upon a great scale. Indeed, as a rule, the great invention which is beneficent in its operation would be useless unless operated to supply a thousand people where ten were supplied before. Every agency in our day labors to scatter the good things of life, both for mind and body, among the toiling millions. Everywhere we look we see the inexorable law ever producing bigger and bigger things. One of the most notable illustrations of this is seen in the railway freight-car. When the writer entered the service of the Pennsylvania Railroad from seven to eight tons were carried upon eight wheels; to-day they carry fifty tons. The locomotive has quadrupled in power. The steamship to-day is ten times bigger, the blast-furnace has seven times more capacity, and the tendency everywhere is still to increase. The contrast between the hand printing-press of old and the elaborate newspaper printing-machine of to-day is even more marked.

We conclude that this overpowering, irresistible tendency toward aggregation of capital and increase of size in every branch of product cannot be arrested or even greatly impeded, and that, instead of attempting to restrict either, we should hail every increase as something gained, not for the few rich, but for the millions of poor, seeing that the law is salutary, working for good and not for evil. Every enlargement is an improvement, step by step, upon what has preceded. It makes for higher civilization, for the enrichment of human life, not for one, but for all classes of men. It tends to bring to the laborer's cottage the luxuries hitherto enjoyed only by the rich, to remove from the most squalid homes much of their squalor, and to foster the growth of human happiness relatively more in the workman's home than in the millionaire's palace. It does not tend to make the rich poorer, but it does tend to make the poor richer in the possession of better things, and greatly lessens the wide and deplorable gulf between the rich and the poor. Superficial politicians may, for a time, deceive the uninformed, but more and more will all this be clearly seen by those who are now led to regard aggregations as injurious.

In all great movements, even of the highest value, there is cause for criticism, and new dangers arising from new conditions, which must be guarded against. There is no nugget free from more or less impurity, and no good cause without its fringe of scoria. The sun itself has spots, but, as has been wisely said, these are rendered visible only by the light it itself sends forth. . . .

An Employer's View of the Labor Question

. . . A strike or lockout is, in itself, a ridiculous affair. Whether a failure or a success, it gives no direct proof of its justice or injustice. In this it resembles war between two nations. It is simply a question of strength and endurance between the contestants. The gage of battle, or the duel, is not more senseless, as a means of establishing what is just and fair, than an industrial strike or lockout. It would be folly to conclude that we have reached any permanent adjustment between capital and labor until strikes and lockouts are as much things of the past as the gage of battle or the duel have become in the most advanced communities.

Taking for granted, then, that some further modifications must be made between capital and labor, I propose to consider the various plans that have been suggested by which labor can advance another stage in its development in relation to capital. And, as a preliminary, let it be noted that it is only labor and capital in their greatest masses which it is necessary to consider. It is only in large establishments that the industrial unrest of which I have spoken ominously manifests itself. The farmer who hires a man to assist him, or the gentleman who engages a groom or a butler, is not affected by strikes. The innumerable cases in which a few men only are directly concerned, which comprise in the aggregate the most of labor, present upon the whole a tolerably satisfactory condition of affairs. This clears the ground of much, and leaves us to deal only with the immense mining and manufacturing concerns of recent growth, in which capital and labor often array themselves in alarming antagonism.

Among the expedients suggested for their better reconciliation, the first place must be assigned to the idea of coöperation, or the plan by which the workers are to become part-owners in enterprises, and share their fortunes. There is no doubt that if this could be effected it would have the same beneficial effect upon the workman which the ownership of land has upon the man who has hitherto tilled the land for another. The sense of ownership would make of him more of a man as regards himself, and hence more of a citizen as regards the commonwealth. But we are here met by a difficulty which I confess I have not yet been able to overcome, and which renders me less sanguine than I should like to be in regard to coöperation. The difficulty is this, and it seems to me to be inherent in all gigantic manufacturing, mining, and commercial operations. Two men or two combinations of men will erect blast-furnaces, iron-mills, cotton-mills, or piano manufactories adjoining each other, or engage in shipping or commercial business. They will start with equal capital and credit; and to those only superficially acquainted with the personnel of these concerns, success will seem as likely to attend the one as the other. Nevertheless, one will fail after dragging along a lifeless existence, and pass into the hands of its creditors; while the neighboring mill or business will make a fortune for its owners. Now, the successful manufacturer, dividing every month or every year a proportion of his profits among his workmen, either as a bonus or as dividends upon shares owned by them, will not only have a happy and contented body of operatives, but he will inevitably attract from his rival the very best workmen in every department. His rival, having no profits to divide among his workmen, and paying them only a small assured minimum to enable them to live, finds himself despoiled of foremen and of workmen necessary to carry on his business successfully. His workmen are discontented and, in their own opinion, defrauded of the proper fruits of their skill, through incapacity or inattention of their employers. Thus, unequal business capacity in the management produces unequal results.

It will be precisely the same if one of these manufactories belongs to the workmen themselves; but in this case, in the present stage of development of the workmen, the chances of failure will be enormously increased. It is, indeed, greatly to be doubted whether any body of working-men in the world could to-day organize and successfully carry on a mining or manufacturing or commercial business in competition with concerns owned by men trained to affairs. If any such coöperative organization succeeds, it may be taken for granted that it is principally owing to the exceptional business ability of one of the managers, and only in a very small degree to the efforts of the mass of workmen-owners. This business ability is excessively rare, as is proved by the incredibly large proportion of those who enter upon the stormy sea of business only to fail. I should say that twenty coöperative concerns would fail to every one that would succeed. There are, of course, a few successful establishments, notably two in France and one in England, which are organized upon the coöperative plan, in which the workmen participate directly in the profits. But these were all created by the present owners, who now generously share the profits with their workmen, and are making the success of their manufactories upon the coöperative plan the proud work of their lives. What these concerns will become when the genius for affairs is no longer with them to guide, is a matter of grave doubt and, to me, of foreboding. I can, of course, picture in my mind a state of civilization in which the most talented business men shall find their most cherished work in carrying on immense concerns, not primarily for their own personal aggrandizement, but for the good of the masses of workers engaged therein, and their families; but this is only a foreshadowing of a dim and distant future. When a class of such men has evolved, the problem of capital and labor will be permanently solved to the entire satisfaction of both. But as this manifestly belongs to a future generation, I cannot consider coöperation, or common ownership, as the next immediate step in advance which it is possible for labor to make in its upward path.

The next suggestion is that peaceful settlement of differences should be reached through arbitration. Here we are upon firmer ground. I would lay it down as a maxim that there is no excuse for a strike or a lockout until arbitration of differences has been offered by one party and refused by the other. No doubt serious trouble attends even arbitration at present, from the difficulty of procuring suitable men to judge intelligently between the disputants. There is a natural disinclination among business men to expose their business to men in whom they have not entire confidence. We lack, so far, in America a retired class of men of affairs. Our vile practice is to keep on accumulating more dollars until we die. If it were the custom here, as it is in England, for men to withdraw from active business after acquiring a fortune, this class would furnish the proper arbitrators. . . .

The influence of trades-unions upon the relations between the employer and employed has been much discussed. Some establishments in America have refused to recognize the right of the men to form themselves into these unions, although I am not aware that any concern in England would dare to take this position. This policy, however, may be regarded as only a temporary phase of the situation. The right of the working-men to combine and to form trades-unions is no less sacred than the right of the manufacturer to enter into associations and conferences with his fellows, and it must sooner or later be conceded. Indeed, it gives one but a poor opinion of the American workman if he permits himself to be deprived of a right which his fellow in England long since conquered for himself. My experience has been that trades-unions, upon the whole, are beneficial both to labor and capital. They certainly educate the working-men, and give them a truer conception of the relations of capital and labor than they could otherwise form. The ablest and best workmen eventually come to the front in these organizations; and it may be laid down as a rule that the more intelligent the workman the fewer the contests with employers. It is not the intelligent workman, who knows that labor without his brother capital is helpless, but the blatant ignorant man, who regards capital as the natural enemy of labor, who does so much to embitter the relations between employer and employed; and the power of this ignorant demagogue arises chiefly from the lack of proper organization among the men through which their real voice can be expressed. This voice will always be found in favor of the judicious and intelligent representative. Of course, as men become intelligent more deference must be paid to them personally and to their rights, and even to their opinions and prejudices; and, upon the whole, a greater share of profits must be paid in the day of prosperity to the intelligent than to the ignorant workman. He cannot be imposed upon so readily. On the other hand, he will be found much readier to accept reduced compensation when business is depressed; and it is better in the long run for capital to be served by the highest intelligence, and to be made well aware of the fact that it is dealing with men who know what is due to them, both as to treatment and compensation.

One great source of the trouble between employers and employed arises from the fact that the immense establishments of to-day, in which alone we find serious conflicts between capital and labor, are not managed by their owners, but by salaried officers, who cannot possibly have any permanent interest in the welfare of the working-men. These officials are chiefly anxious to present a satisfactory balance-sheet at the end of the year, that their hundreds of shareholders may receive the usual dividends, and that they may therefore be secure in their positions, and be allowed to manage the business without unpleasant interference either by directors or shareholders. It is notable that bitter strikes seldom occur in small establishments where the owner comes into direct contact with his men, and knows their qualities, their struggles, and their aspirations. It is the chairman, situated hundreds of miles away from his men, who only pays a flying visit to the works and perhaps finds time to walk through the mill or mine once or twice a year, that is chiefly responsible for the disputes which break out at intervals. I have noticed that the manager who confers oftenest with a committee of his leading men has the least trouble with his workmen. Although it may be impracticable for the presidents of these large corporations to know the working-men personally, the manager at the mills, having a committee of his best men to present their suggestions and wishes from time to time, can do much to maintain and strengthen amicable relations, if not interfered with from headquarters. I, therefore, recognize in trades-unions, or, better still, in organizations of the men of each establishment, who select representatives to speak for them, a means, not of further embittering the relations between employer and employed, but of improving them. . . .

Whatever the future may have in store for labor, the evolutionist, who sees nothing but certain and steady progress for the race, will never attempt to set bounds to its triumphs, even to its final form of complete and universal industrial coöperation, which I hope is some day to be reached. But I am persuaded that the next step forward is to be in the direction I have here ventured to point out; and as one who is now most anxious to contribute his part toward helping forward the day of amicable relations between the two forces of capital and labor, which are not enemies, but are really auxiliaries who stand or fall together, I ask at the hands of both capital and labor a careful consideration of these views.

THORSTEIN VEBLEN

THORSTEIN VEBLEN (1857–1929) was born in Wisconsin. He spent his early years in a pioneer farming community in Minnesota, and attended Carleton College. He studied there under John Bates Clark (1847–1938), who encouraged him to pursue a career of teaching and scholarship. After his graduation in 1880, he went on to Johns Hopkins and Yale and received his Ph. D. from the latter institution in 1884. He taught at Cornell from 1890 to 1892, the University of Chicago from 1892 to 1906, Stanford from 1906 to 1910, and Missouri from 1911 to 1918. He spent the next nine years in New York as lecturer at the New School for Social Research, and served as managing editor of the *Journal of Political Economy*.

In 1899 Veblen published *The Theory of the Leisure Class;* it was followed in 1904 by *The Theory of Business Enterprise.* These works presented a radically new approach to the study of economics. In his analysis and critique of American capitalism at the turn of the century Veblen made use of psychological insights and anthropological lore. For him, the classical economists' "mechanical" explanation of the operation of the market was insufficient to account for the nature of an economic system. The sanction of custom, the force of social proprieties, the different types of human personalities and attitudes—all were needed to explain the American economy, and all, for Veblen, had historical rather than *a priori* foundations.

Veblen's highly unorthodox teachings gained him few disciples among traditional economists. For historians, philosophers, sociologists, and social critics, however, he became a source of information and inspiration. Among his most important works, other than those already mentioned, are *The Instinct of Workmanship and the State of the Industrial Revolution* (1915), *The Higher Learning in America* (1919), and *The Place of Science in Modern Civilization* (1919). In later works, such as *The Engineers and the Price System* (1921), Veblen advocated a "technocratic" system directed by industrialists and engineers as the only permanent way of resolving the antagonism between money and craftsmanship in Western society.

This selection comes from the original edition of *The Theory of Business Enterprise* (New York, 1904).

THE THEORY OF BUSINESS ENTERPRISE

CHAPTER II: THE MACHINE PROCESS

WHEREVER manual dexterity, the rule of thumb, and the fortuitous conjunctures of the seasons have been supplanted by a reasoned procedure on the basis of a systematic knowledge of the forces employed, there the mechanical industry is to be found, even in the absence of intricate mechanical contrivances. It is a question of the character of the process rather than a question of the complexity of the contrivances employed. Chemical, agricultural, and animal industries, as carried on by the characteristically modern methods and in due touch with the market, are to be included in the modern complex of mechanical industry.

No one of the mechanical processes carried on by the use of a given outfit of appliances is independent of other processes going on elsewhere. Each draws upon and presupposes the proper working of many other processes of a similarly mechanical character. None of the processes in the mechanical industries is self-sufficing. Each follows some and precedes other processes in an endless sequence, into which each fits and to the requirements of which each must adapt its own working. The whole concert of industrial operations is to be taken as a machine process, made up of interlocking detail processes, rather than as a multiplicity of mechanical appliances each doing its particular work in severalty. This comprehensive industrial process draws into its scope and turns to account all branches of knowledge that have to do with the material sciences, and the whole makes a more or less delicately balanced complex of sub-processes.

Looked at in this way the industrial process shows two well-marked general characteristics: (*a*) the running maintenance of interstitial adjustments between the several sub-processes or branches of industry, wherever in their working they touch one another in the sequence of industrial elaboration; and (*b*) an unremitting requirement of quantitative precision, accuracy in point of time and sequence, in the proper inclusion and exclusion of forces affecting the outcome, in the magnitude of the various physical characteristics (weight, size, density, hardness, tensile strength, elasticity, temperature, chemical reaction, actinic sensitiveness, etc.) of the materials handled as well as of the appliances employed. This requirement of mechanical accuracy and nice adaptation to specific uses has led to a gradual pervading enforcement of uniformity, to a reduction to staple grades and staple character in the materials handled, and to a thorough standardizing of tools and units of measurement. Standard physical measurements are of the essence of the machine's régime. . . . The adjustment and adaptation of part to part and of process to process has passed out of the category of craftsmanlike skill into the category of mechanical standardization. Hence, perhaps, the greatest, most wide-reaching gain in productive celerity and efficiency through modern methods, and hence the largest saving of labor in modern history.

Tools, mechanical appliances and movements, and structural materials are scheduled by certain conventional scales and gauges; and modern industry has little use for, and can make little use of, what does not conform to the standard. What is not competently standardized calls for too much of craftsmanlike skill, reflection, and individual elaboration, and is therefore not available for economical use in the processes. Irregularity, departure from standard measurements in any of the measurable facts, is of itself a fault in any item that is to find a use in the industrial process, for it brings delay, it detracts from its ready usability in the nicely adjusted process into which it is to go; and a delay at any point means a more or less far-reaching and intolerable retardation of the comprehensive industrial process at large. Irregularity in products intended for industrial use carries a penalty to the nonconforming producer which urges him to fall into line and submit to the required standardization.

The materials and moving forces of industry are undergoing a like reduction to staple kinds, styles, grades, and gauge. Even such forces as would seem at first sight not to lend themselves to standardization, either in their production or their use, are subjected to uniform scales of measurement; as, e.g., water-power, steam, electricity, and human labor. The latter is perhaps the least amenable to standardization, but for all that, it is bargained for, delivered, and turned to account on schedules of time, speed, and intensity which are continually sought to be reduced to a more precise measurement and a more sweeping uniformity.

The like is true of the finished products. Modern consumers in great part supply their wants with commodities that conform to certain staple specifications of size, weight, and grade. The consumer (that is to say the vulgar consumer) furnishes his house, his table, and his person with supplies of standard weight and measure, and he can to an appreciable degree specify his needs and his consumption in the notation of the standard gauge. As regards the mass of civilized mankind, the idiosyncrasies of the individual consumers are required to conform to the uniform gradations imposed upon consumable goods by the comprehensive mechanical processes of industry. "Local color," it is said, is falling into abeyance in modern life, and where it is still found it tends to assert itself in units of the standard gauge. . . .

Machine production leads to a standardization of services as well as of goods. So, for instance, the modern means of communication and the system into which these means are organized are also of the nature of a mechanical process, and in this mechanical process of service and intercourse the life of all civilized men is more or less intimately involved. To make effective use of the modern system of communication in any or all of its ramifications (streets, railways, steamship lines, telephone, telegraph, postal service, etc.), men are required to adapt their needs and their motions to the exigencies of the process whereby this civilized method of intercourse is carried into effect. The service is standardized, and therefore the use of it is standardized also. Schedules of time, place, and circumstance rule throughout. The scheme of everyday life must be arranged with a strict regard to the exigencies of the process whereby this range of human needs is served, if full advantage is to be taken of this system of intercourse, which means that, in so far, one's plans and projects must be conceived and worked out in terms of those standard units which the system imposes.

For the population of the towns and cities, at least, much the same rule holds true of the distribution of consumable goods. So, also, amusements and diversions, much of the current amenities of life, are organized into a more or less sweeping process to which those who would benefit by the advantages offered must adapt their schedule of wants and the disposition of their time and effort. The frequency, duration, intensity, grade, and sequence are not, in the main, matters for the free discretion of the individuals who participate. Throughout the scheme of life of that portion of mankind that clusters about the centres of modern culture the industrial process makes itself felt and enforces a degree of conformity to the canon of accurate quantitative measurement. There comes to prevail a degree of standardization and precise mechanical adjustment of the details of everyday life, which presumes a facile and unbroken working of all those processes that minister to these standardized human wants.

As a result of this superinduced mechanical regularity of life, the livelihood of individuals is, over large areas, affected in an approximately uniform manner by any incident which at all seriously affects the industrial process at any point.

As was noted above, each industrial unit, represented by a given industrial "plant," stands in close relations of interdependence with other industrial processes going forward elsewhere, near or far away, from which it receives supplies—materials, apparatus, and the like—and to which it turns over its output of products and waste, or on which it depends for auxiliary work, such as transportation. The resulting concatenation of industries has been noticed by most modern writers. It is commonly discussed under the head of the division of labor. Evidently the prevalent standardization of industrial means, methods, and products greatly increases the reach of this concatenation of industries, at the same time that it enforces a close conformity in point of time, volume, and character of the product, whether the product is goods or services.

By virtue of this concatenation of processes the modern industrial system at large bears the character of a comprehensive, balanced mechanical process. In order for an efficient working of this industrial process at large, the various constituent sub-processes must work in due coördination throughout the whole. Any degree of maladjustment in the interstitial coördinations of this industrial process at large in some degree hinders its working. Similarly, any given detail process or any industrial plant will do its work to full advantage only when due adjustment is had between its work and the work done by the rest. The higher the degree of development reached by a given industrial community, the more comprehensive and urgent becomes this requirement of interstitial adjustment. And the more fully a given industry has taken on the character of a mechanical process, and the more extensively and closely it is correlated in its work with other industries that precede or follow it in the sequence of elaboration, the more urgent, other things equal, is the need of maintaining the proper working relations with these other industries, the greater is the industrial detriment suffered from any derangement of the accustomed working relations, and the greater is the industrial gain to be derived from a closer adaptation and a more facile method of readjustment in the event of a disturbance,—the greater is also the chance for an effectual disturbance of industry at the particular point. This mechanical concatenation of industrial processes makes for solidarity in the administration of any group of related industries, and more remotely it makes for solidarity in the management of the entire industrial traffic of the community. . . .

CHAPTER III: BUSINESS ENTERPRISE

The motive of business is pecuniary gain, the method is essentially purchase and sale. The aim and usual outcome is an accumulation of wealth. Men whose aim is not increase of possessions do not go into business, particularly not on an independent footing. . . .

In early modern times, before the régime of the machine industry set in, business enterprise on any appreciable scale commonly took the form of commercial business—some form of merchandising or banking. Shipping was the only considerable line of business which involved an investment in or management of extensive mechanical appliances and processes, comparable with the facts of the modern mechanical industry. And shipping was commonly combined with merchandising. But even the shipping trade of earlier times had much of a fortuitous character, in this respect resembling agriculture or any other industry in which wind and weather greatly affect the outcome. The fortunes of men in shipping were on a more precarious footing than to-day, and the successful outcome of their ventures was less a matter of shrewd foresight and daily pecuniary strategy than are the affairs of the modern large business concerns in transportation or the foreign trade. Under these circumstances the work of the business man was rather to take advantage of the conjunctures offered by the course of the seasons and the fluctuations of demand and supply than to adapt the course of affairs to his own ends. The large business man was more of a speculative buyer and seller and less of a financiering strategist than he has since become.

Since the advent of the machine age the situation has changed. The methods of business have, of course, not changed fundamentally, whatever may be true of the methods of industry; for they are, as they had been, conditioned by the facts of ownership. But instead of investing in the goods as they pass between producer and consumer, as the merchant does, the business man now invests in the processes of industry; and instead of staking his values on the dimly foreseen conjunctures of the seasons and the act of God, he turns to the conjunctures arising from the interplay of the industrial processes, which are in great measure under the control of business men.

So long as the machine processes were but slightly developed, scattered, relatively isolated, and independent of one another industrially, and so long as they were carried on on a small scale for a relatively narrow market, so long the management of them was conditioned by circumstances in many respects similar to those which conditioned the English domestic industry of the eighteenth century. It was under the conditions of this inchoate phase of the machine age that the earlier generation of economists worked out their theory of the business man's part in industry. It was then still true, in great measure, that the undertaker was the owner of the industrial equipment, and that he kept an immediate oversight of the mechanical processes as well as of the pecuniary transactions in which his enterprise was engaged; and it was also true, with relatively infrequent exceptions, that an unsophisticated productive efficiency was the prime element of business success. A further feature of the precapitalistic business situation is that business, whether handicraft or trade, was customarily managed with a view to earning a livelihood rather than with a view to profits on investment.

In proportion as the machine industry gained ground, and as the modern concatenation of industrial processes and of markets developed, the conjunctures of business grew more varied and of larger scope at the same time that they became more amenable to shrewd manipulation. The pecuniary side of the enterprise came to require more unremitting attention, as the chances for gain or loss through business relations simply, aside from mere industrial efficiency, grew greater in number and magnitude. The same circumstances also provoked a spirit of business enterprise, and brought on a systematic investment for gain. With a fuller development of the modern close-knit and comprehensive industrial system, the point of chief attention for the business man has shifted from the old-fashioned surveillance and regulation of a given industrial process, with which his livelihood was once bound up, to an alert redistribution of investments from less to more gainful ventures, and to a strategic control of the conjunctures of business through shrewd investments and coalitions with other business men.

As shown above, the modern industrial system is a concatenation of processes which has much of the character of a single, comprehensive, balanced mechanical process. A disturbance of the balance at any point means a differential advantage (or disadvantage) to one or more of the owners of the sub-processes between which the disturbance falls; and it may also frequently mean gain or loss to many remoter members in the concatenation of processes, for the balance throughout the sequence is a delicate one, and the transmission of a disturbance often goes far. It may even take on a cumulative character, and may thereby seriously cripple or accelerate branches of industry that are out of direct touch with those members of the concatenation upon which the initial disturbance falls. Such is the case, for instance, in an industrial crisis, when an apparently slight initial disturbance may become the occasion of a widespread derangement. And such, on the other hand, is also the case when some favorable condition abruptly supervenes in a given industry; as, *e.g.,* when a sudden demand for war stores starts a wave of prosperity by force of a large and lucrative demand for the products of certain industries, and these in turn draw on their neighbors in the sequence, and so transmit a wave of business activity.

The keeping of the industrial balance, therefore, and adjusting the several industrial processes to one another's work and needs, is a matter of grave and far-reaching consequence in any modern community, as has already been shown. Now, the means by which this balance is kept is business transactions, and the men in whose keeping it lies are the business men. The channel by which disturbances are transmitted from member to member of the comprehensive industrial system is the business relations between the several members of the system; and, under the modern conditions of ownership, disturbances, favorable or unfavorable, in the field of industry are transmitted by nothing but these business relations. Hard times or prosperity spread through the system by means of business relations, and are in their primary expression phenomena of the business situation simply. It is only secondarily that the disturbances in question show themselves as alterations in the character or magnitude of the mechanical processes involved. Industry is carried on for the sake of business, and not conversely; and the progress and activity of industry are conditioned by the outlook of the market, which means the presumptive chance of business profits.

All this is a matter of course which it may seem simply tedious to recite. But its consequences for the theory of business make it necessary to keep the nature of this connection between business and industry in mind. The adjustments of industry take place through the mediation of pecuniary transactions, and these transactions take place at the hands of the business men and are carried on by them for business ends, not for industrial ends in the narrower meaning of the phrase.

The economic welfare of the community at large is best served by a facile and uninterrupted interplay of the various processes which make up the industrial system at large; but the pecuniary interests of the business men in whose hands lies the discretion in the matter are not necessarily best served by an unbroken maintenance of the industrial balance. Especially is this true as regards those greater business men whose interests are very extensive. The pecuniary operations of these latter are of large scope, and their fortunes commonly are not permanently bound up with the smooth working of a given subprocess in the industrial system. Their fortunes are rather related to the larger conjunctures of the industrial system as a whole, the interstitial adjustments, or to conjunctures affecting large ramifications of the system. Nor is it at all uniformly to their interest to enhance the smooth working of the industrial system at large in so far as they are given disturbance of the system whether the disturbance makes for heightened facility or for widespread hardship, very much as a speculator in grain futures may be either a bull or a bear. To the business man who aims at a differential gain arising out of interstitial adjustments or disturbances of the industrial system, it is not a material question whether his operations have an immediate furthering or hindering effect upon the system at large. The end is pecuniary gain, the means is disturbance of the industrial system,—except so far as the gain is sought by the old-fashioned method of permanent investment in some one industrial or commercial plant, a case which is for the present left on one side as not bearing on the point immediately in hand. The point immediately in question is the part which the business man plays in what are here called the interstitial adjustments of the industrial system; and so far as touches his transactions in this field it is, by and large, a matter of indifference to him whether his traffic affects the system advantageously or disastrously. His gains (or losses) are related to the magnitude of the disturbances that take place, rather than to their bearing upon the welfare of the community.

The outcome of this management of industrial affairs through pecuniary transactions, therefore, has been to dissociate the interests of those men who exercise the discretion from the interests of the community. This is true in a peculiar degree and increasingly since the fuller development of the machine industry has brought about a close-knit and wide-reaching articulation of industrial processes, and has at the same time given rise to a class of pecuniary experts whose business is the strategic management of the interstitial relations of the system. Broadly, this class of business men, in so far as they have no ulterior strategic ends to serve, have an interest in making the disturbances of the system large and frequent, since it is in the conjunctures of change that their gain emerges. Qualifications of this proposition may be needed, and it will be necessary to return to this point presently.

It is, as a business proposition, a matter of indifference to the man of large affairs whether the disturbances which his transactions set up in the industrial system help or hinder the system at large, except in so far as he has ulterior strategic ends to serve. But most of the modern captains of industry have such ulterior ends, and of the greater ones among them this is peculiarly true. Indeed, it is this work of far-reaching business strategy that gives them full title to the designation, "Captains of Industry." This large business strategy is the most admirable trait of the great business men who with force and insight swing the fortunes of civilized mankind. And due qualification is accordingly to be entered in the broad statement made above. The captain's strategy is commonly directed to gaining control of some large portion of the industrial system. When such control has been achieved, it may be to his interest to make and maintain business conditions which shall facilitate the smooth and efficient working of what has come under his control, in case he continues to hold a large interest in it as an investor; for, other things equal, the gains from what has come under his hands permanently in the way of industrial plant are greater the higher and more uninterrupted its industrial efficiency.

An appreciable portion of the larger transactions in railway and "industrial" properties, e.g., are carried out with a view to the permanent ownership of the properties by the business men into whose hands they pass. But also in a large proportion of these transactions the business men's endeavors are directed to a temporary control of the properties in order to close out at an advance or to gain some indirect advantage; that is to say, the transactions have a strategic purpose. The business man aims to gain control of a given block of industrial equipment—as, e.g., given railway lines or iron mills that are strategically important—as a basis for further transactions out of which gain is expected. In such a case his efforts are directed, not to maintaining the permanent efficiency of the industrial equipment, but to influencing the tone of the market for the time being, the apprehensions of other large operators, or the transient faith of investors. His interest in the particular block of industrial equipment is, then, altogether transient, and while it lasts it is of a factitious character.

The exigencies of this business of interstitial disturbance decide that in the common run of cases the proximate aim of the business man is to upset or block the industrial process at some one or more points. His strategy is commonly directed against other business interests and his ends are commonly accomplished by the help of some form of pecuniary coercion. This is not uniformly true, but it seems to be true in appreciably more than half of the transactions in question. In general, transactions which aim to bring a coalition of industrial plants or processes under the control of a given business man are directed to making it difficult for the plants or processes in question to be carried on in severalty by their previous owners or managers. It is commonly a struggle between rival business men, and more often than not the outcome of the struggle depends on which side can inflict or endure the greater pecuniary damage. And pecuniary damage in such a case not uncommonly involves a set-back to the industrial plants concerned and a derangement, more or less extensive, of the industrial system at large. . . .

Taking the industrial process as a whole, it is safe to say that at no time is it free from derangements of this character in any of the main branches of modern industry. This chronic state of perturbation is incident to the management of industry by business methods and is unavoidable under existing conditions. So soon as the machine industry had developed to large proportions, it became unavoidable, in the nature of the case, that the business men in whose hands lies the conduct of affairs should play at cross-purposes and endeavor to derange industry. But chronic perturbation is so much a matter of course and prevails with so rare interruptions, that, being the normal state of affairs, it does not attract particular notice.

In current discussion of business, indeed ever since the relation of business men to the industrial system has seriously engaged the attention of economists, the point to which attention has chiefly been directed is the business man's work as an organizer of comprehensive industrial processes. During the later decades of the nineteenth century, particularly, has much interest centred, as there has been much provocation for its doing, on the formation of large industrial consolidations; and the evident good effects of this work in the way of heightened serviceability and economies of production are pointed to as the chief and characteristic end of this work of reorganization. So obvious are these good results and so well and widely has the matter been expounded, theoretically, that it is not only permissible, but it is a point of conscience, to shorten this tale by passing over these good effects as a matter of common notoriety. But there are other features of the case, less obtrusive and less attractive to the theoreticians, which need more detailed attention than they have commonly received.

The circumstances which condition the work of consolidation in industry and which decide whether a given move in the direction of a closer and wider organization of industrial processes will be practicable and will result in economies of production,—these circumstances are of a mechanical nature. They are facts of the comprehensive machine process. The conditions favorable to industrial consolidation on these grounds are not created by the business men. They are matters of "the state of the industrial arts," and are the outcome of the work of those men who are engaged in the industrial employments rather than of those who are occupied with business affairs. The inventors, engineers, experts, or whatever name be applied to the comprehensive class that does the intellectual work involved in the modern machine industry, must prepare the way for the man of pecuniary affairs by making possible and putting in evidence the economies and other advantages that will follow from a prospective consolidation.

But it is not enough that the business man should see a chance to effect economies of production and to heighten the efficiency of industry by a new combination. Conditions favorable to consolidation on these grounds must be visible to him before he can make the decisive business arrangements; but these conditions, taken by themselves, do not move him. The motives of the business man are pecuniary motives, inducements in the way of pecuniary gain to him or to the business enterprise with which he is identified. The end of his endeavors is, not simply to effect an industrially advantageous consolidation, but to effect it under such circumstances of ownership as will give him control of large business forces or bring him the largest possible gain. The ulterior end sought is an increase of ownership, not industrial serviceability. His aim is to contrive a consolidation in which he will be at an advantage, and to effect it on the terms most favorable to his own interest.

But it is not commonly evident at the outset what are the most favorable terms that he can get in his dealings with other business men whose interests are touched by the proposed consolidation, or who are ambitious to effect some similar consolidation of the same or of competing industrial elements for their own profit. It rarely happens that the interests of the business men whom the prospective consolidation touches all converge to a coalition on the same basis and under the same management. The consequence is negotiation and delay. It commonly also happens that some of the business men affected see their advantage in staving off the coalition until a time more propitious to their own interest, or until those who have the work of consolidation in hand can be brought to compound with them for the withdrawal of whatever obstruction they are able to offer. Such a coalition involves a loss of independent standing, or even a loss of occupation, to many of the business men interested in the deal. If a prospective industrial consolidation is of such scope as to require the concurrence or consent of many business interests, among which no one is very decidedly preponderant in pecuniary strength or in strategic position, a long time will be consumed in the negotiations and strategy necessary to define the terms on which the several business interests will consent to come in and the degree of solidarity and central control to which they will submit.

It is notorious, beyond the need of specific citation, that the great business coalitions and industrial combinations which have characterized the situation of the last few years have commonly been the outcome of a long-drawn struggle, in which the industrial ends, as contrasted with business ends, have not been seriously considered, and in which great shrewdness and tenacity have commonly been shown in the staving off of a settlement for years in the hope of more advantageous terms. The like is true as regards further coalitions, further consolidations of industrial processes which have not been effected, but which are known to be feasible and desirable so far as regards the mechanical circumstances of the case. The difficulties in the way are difficulties of ownership, of business interest, not of mechanical feasibility.

These negotiations and much of the strategy that leads up to a business consolidation are of the nature of derangements of industry, after the manner spoken of above. So that business interests and manoeuvres commonly delay consolidations, combinations, correlations of the several plants and processes, for some appreciable time after such measures have become patently advisable on industrial grounds. In the meantime the negotiators are working at cross-purposes and endeavoring to put their rivals in as disadvantageous a light as may be, with the result that there is chronic derangement, duplication, and misdirected growth of the industrial equipment while the strategy is going forward, and expensive maladjustment to be overcome when the negotiations are brought to a close.

Serviceability, industrial advisability, is not the decisive point. The decisive point is business expediency and business pressure. In the normal course of business touching this matter of industrial consolidation, therefore, the captain of industry works against, as well as for, a new and more efficient organization. He inhibits as well as furthers the higher organization of industry. Broadly, it may be said that industrial consolidations and the working arrangements made for the more economical utilization of resources and mechanical contrivances are allowed to go into effect only after they are long overdue.

In current economic theory the business man is spoken of under the name of "Entrepreneur" or "undertaker," and his function is held to be the co-ordinating of industrial processes with a view to economies of production and heightened serviceability. The soundness of this view need not be questioned. It has a great sentimental value and is useful in many ways. There is also a modicum of truth in it as an account of facts. In common with other men, the business man is moved by ideals of serviceability and an aspiration to make the way of life easier for his fellows. Like other men, he has something of the instinct of workmanship. No doubt such aspirations move the great business man less urgently than many others, who are, on that account, less successful in business affairs. Motives of this kind detract from business efficiency, and an undue yielding to them on the part of business men is to be deprecated as an infirmity. Still, throughout men's dealings with one another and with the interests of the community there runs a sense of equity, fair dealing, and workmanlike integrity; and in an uncertain degree this bent discountenances gain that is got at an undue cost to others, or without rendering some colorable equivalent. Business men are also, in a measure, guided by the ambition to effect a creditable improvement in the industrial processes which their business traffic touches. These sentimental factors in business exercise something of a constraint, varying greatly from one person to another, but not measurable in its aggregate results. The careers of most of the illustrious business men show the presence of some salutary constraint of this kind. Not infrequently an excessive sensitiveness of this kind leads to a withdrawal from business, or from certain forms of business which may appeal to a vivid fancy as peculiarly dishonest or peculiarly detrimental to the community. Such grounds of action, and perhaps others equally genial and equally unbusinesslike, would probably be discovered by a detailed scrutiny of any large business deal. Probably in many cases the business strategist, infected with this human infirmity, reaches an agreement with his rivals and his neighbors in the industrial system without exacting the last concession that a ruthless business strategy might entitle him to. The result is, probably, a speedier conclusion and a smoother working of the large coalitions than would follow from the unmitigated sway of business principles.

But the sentiment which in this way acts in constraint of business traffic proceeds on such grounds of equity and fair dealing as are afforded by current business ethics; it acts within the range of business principles, not in contravention of them; it acts as a conventional restraint upon pecuniary advantage, not in abrogation of it. This code of business ethics consists, after all, of mitigations of the maxim, *Caveat emptor*. It touches primarily the dealings of man with man, and only less directly and less searchingly inculcates temperance and circumspection as regards the ulterior interests of the community at large. Where this moral need of a balance between the services rendered the community and the gain derived from a given business transaction asserts itself at all, the balance is commonly sought to be maintained in some sort of pecuniary terms; but pecuniary terms afford only a very inadequate measure of serviceability to the community.

Great and many are the items of service to be set down to the business man's account in connection with the organization of the industrial system, but when all is said, it is still to be kept in mind that his work in the correlation of industrial processes is chiefly of a permissive kind. His furtherance of industry is at the second remove, and is chiefly of a negative character. In his capacity as business man he does not go creatively into the work of perfecting mechanical processes and turning the means at hand to new or larger uses. That is the work of the men who have in hand the devising and oversight of mechanical processes. The men in industry must first create the mechanical possibility of such new and more efficient methods and correlations, before the business man sees the chance, makes the necessary business arrangements, and gives general directions that the contemplated industrial advance shall go into effect. The period between the time of earliest practicability and the effectual completion of a given consolidation in industry marks the interval by which the business man retards the advance of industry. Against this are to be offset the cases, comparatively slight and infrequent, where the business men in control push the advance of industry into new fields and prompt the men concerned with the mechanics of the case to experiment and exploration in new fields of mechanical process.

When the recital is made, therefore, of how the large consolidations take place at the initiative of the business men who are in control, it should be added that the fact of their being in control precludes industrial correlations from taking place except by their advice and consent. The industrial system is organized on business principles and for pecuniary ends. The business man is at the centre; he holds the discretion and he exercises it freely, and his choice falls out now on one side, now on the other. The retardation as well as the advance is to be set down to his account.

As regards the economies in cost of production effected by these consolidations, there is a further characteristic feature to be noted, a feature of some significance for any theory of modern business. In great measure the saving effected is a saving of the costs of business management and of the competitive costs of marketing products and services, rather than a saving in the prime costs of production. The heightened facility and efficiency of the new and larger business combinations primarily affect the expenses of office work and sales, and it is in great part only indirectly that this curtailment and consolidation of business management has an effect upon the methods and aims of industry proper. It touches the pecuniary processes immediately, and the mechanical processes indirectly and in an uncertain degree. It is of the nature of a partial neutralization of the wastes due to the presence of pecuniary motives and business management,—for the business management involves waste wherever a greater number of men or transactions are involved than are necessary to the effective direction of the mechanical processes employed. The amount of "business" that has to be transacted per unit of product is much greater where the various related industrial processes are managed in severalty than where several of them are brought under one business management. A pecuniary discretion has to be exercised at every point of contact or transition, where the process or its product touches or passes the boundary between different spheres of ownership. Business transactions have to do with ownership and changes of ownership. The greater the parcelment in point of ownership, the greater the amount of business work that has to be done in connection with a given output of goods or services, and the slower, less facile, and less accurate, on the whole, is the work. This applies both to the work of bargain and contract, wherein pecuniary initiative and discretion are chiefly exercised, and to the routine work of accounting, and of gathering and applying information and misinformation.

The standardization of industrial processes, products, services, and consumers, spoken of in an earlier chapter, very materially facilitates the business man's work in reorganizing business enterprises on a larger scale; particularly does this standardization serve his ends by permitting a uniform routine in accounting, invoices, contracts, etc., and so admitting a large central accounting system, with homogeneous ramifications, such as will give a competent conspectus of the pecuniary situation of the enterprise at any given time.

The great, at the present stage of development perhaps the greatest, opportunity for saving by consolidation, in the common run of cases, is afforded by the ubiquitous and in a sense excessive presence of business enterprise in the economic system. It is in doing away with unnecessary business transactions and industrially futile manoeuvring on the part of independent firms that the promoter of combinations finds his most telling opportunity. So that it is scarcely an overstatement to say that probably the largest, assuredly the securest and most unquestionable, service rendered by the great modern captains of industry is this curtailment of the business to be done,—this sweeping retirement of business men as a class from the service and the definitive cancelment of opportunities for private enterprise.

So long as related industrial units are under different business managements, they are, by the nature of the case, at cross-purposes, and business consolidation remedies this untoward feature of the industrial system by eliminating the pecuniary element from the interstices of the system as far as may be. The interstitial adjustments of the industrial system at large are in this way withdrawn from the discretion of rival business men, and the work of pecuniary management previously involved is in large part dispensed with, with the result that there is a saving of work and an avoidance of that systematic mutual hindrance that characterizes the competitive management of industry. To the community at large the work of pecuniary management, it appears, is less serviceable the more there is of it. The heroic rôle of the captain of industry is that of a deliverer from an excess of business management. It is a casting out of business men by the chief of business men.

The theory of business enterprise sketched above applies to such business as is occupied with the interstitial adjustments of the system of industries. This work of keeping and of disturbing the interstitial adjustments does not look immediately to the output of goods as its source of gain, but to the alterations of values involved in disturbances of the balance, and to the achievement of a more favorable business situation for some of the enterprises engaged. This work lies in the middle, between commercial enterprise proper, on the one hand, and industrial enterprise in the stricter sense, on the other hand. It is directed to the acquisition of gain through taking advantage of those conjunctures of business that arise out of the concatenation of processes in the industrial system.

In a similar manner commercial business may be said to be occupied with conjunctures that arise out of the circumstances of the industrial system at large, but not originating in the mechanical exigencies of the industrial processes. The conjunctures of commercial business proper are in the main fortuitous, in so far that they are commonly not initiated by the business men engaged in these commercial pursuits. Commercial business, simply as such, does not aim to guide the course of industry.

On the other hand, the large business enterprise spoken of above initiates changes in industrial organization and seeks its gain in large part through such alterations of value levels as take place on its own initiative. These alterations of the value levels, of course, have their effect upon the output of goods and upon the material welfare of the community; but the effect which they have in this way is only incidental to the quest of profits.

But apart from this remoter and larger guidance of the course of industry, the business men also, and more persistently and pervasively, exercise a guidance over the course of industry in detail. The production of goods and services is carried on for gain, and the output of goods is controlled by business men with a view to gain. Commonly, in ordinary routine business, the gains come from this output of goods and services. By the sale of the output the business man in industry "realizes" his gains. To "realize" means to convert salable goods into money values. The sale is the last step in the process and the end of the business man's endeavor. When he has disposed of the output, and so has converted his holdings of consumable articles into money values, his gains are as nearly secure and definitive as the circumstances of modern life admit. It is in terms of price that he keeps his accounts, and in the same terms he computes his output, its convertibility into money values, not its serviceability for the needs of mankind. A modicum of serviceability, for some purpose or other, the output must have if it is to be salable. But it does not follow that the highest serviceability gives the largest gains to the business man in terms of money, nor does it follow that the output need in all cases have other than a factitious serviceability. There is, on the one hand, such a possibility as over-stocking the market with any given line of goods, to the detriment of the business man concerned, but not necessarily to the immediate disadvantage of the body of consumers. And there are, on the other hand, certain lines of industry, such as many advertising enterprises, the output of which may be highly effective for its purpose but of quite equivocal use to the community. Many well-known and prosperous enterprises which advertise and sell patent medicines and other proprietary articles might be cited in proof.

In the older days, when handicraft was the rule of the industrial system, the personal contact between the producer and his customer was somewhat close and lasting. Under these circumstances the factor of personal esteem and disesteem had a considerable play in controlling the purveyors of goods and services. This factor of personal contact counted in two divergent ways: (1) producers were careful of their reputation for workmanship, even apart from the gains which such a reputation might bring; and (2) a degree of irritation and ill-will would arise in many cases, leading to petty trade quarrels and discriminations on other grounds than the gains to be got, at the same time that the detail character of dealings between producer and consumer admitted a degree of petty knavery and huckstering that is no longer practicable in the current large-scale business dealings. Of these two divergent effects resulting from close personal relations between producer and consumer the former seems on the whole to have been of preponderant consequence. Under the system of handicraft and neighborhood industry, the adage that "Honesty is the best policy" seems on the whole to have been accepted and to have been true. The adage has come down from the days before the machine's régime and before modern business enterprise.

Under modern circumstances, where industry is carried on on a large scale, the discretionary head of an industrial enterprise is commonly removed from all personal contact with the body of customers for whom the industrial process under his control purveys goods or services. The mitigating effect which personal contact may have in dealings between man and man is therefore in great measure eliminated. The whole takes on something of an impersonal character. One can with an easier conscience and with less of a sense of meanness take advantage of the necessities of people whom one knows of only as an indiscriminate aggregate of consumers. Particularly is this true when, as frequently happens in the modern situation, this body of consumers belongs in the main to another, inferior class, so that personal contact and cognizance of them is not only not contemplated, but is in a sense impossible. Equity, in excess of the formal modicum specified by law, does not so readily assert its claims where the relations between the parties are remote and impersonal as where one is dealing with one's necessitous neighbors who live on the same social plane. Under these circumstances the adage cited above loses much of its axiomatic force. Business management has a chance to proceed on a temperate and sagacious calculation of profit and loss, untroubled by sentimental considerations of human kindness or irritation or of honesty.

The broad principle which guides producers and merchants, large and small, in fixing the prices at which they offer their wares and services is what is known in the language of the railroads as "charging what the traffic will bear." Where a given enterprise has a strict monopoly of the supply of a given article or of a given class of services this principle applies in the un-qualified form in which it has been understood among those who discuss railway charges. But where the monopoly is less strict, where there are competitors, there the competition that has to be met is one of the factors to be taken account of in determining what the traffic will bear; competition may even become the most serious factor in the case if the enterprise in question has little or none of the character of a monopoly. But it is very doubtful if there are any successful business ventures within the range of the modern industries from which the monopoly element is wholly absent. They are, at any rate, few and not of great magnitude. And the endeavor of all such enterprises that look to a permanent continuance of their business is to establish as much of a monopoly as may be. Such a monopoly position may be a legally established one, or one due to location or the control of natural resources, or it may be a monopoly of a less definite character resting on custom and prestige (good-will). This latter class of monopolies are not commonly classed as such; although in character and degree the advantage which they give is very much the same as that due to a differential advantage in location or in the command of resources. The end sought by the systematic advertising of the larger business concerns is such a monopoly of custom and prestige. This form of monopoly is sometimes of great value, and is frequently sold under the name of good-will, trademarks, brands, etc. Instances are known where such monopolies of custom, prestige, prejudice, have been sold at prices running up into the millions.

The great end of consistent advertising is to establish such differential monopolies resting on popular conviction. And the advertiser is successful in this endeavor to establish a profitable popular conviction, somewhat in proportion as he correctly apprehends the manner in which a popular conviction on any given topic is built up. The cost as well as the pecuniary value and the magnitude, of this organized fabrication of popular convictions is indicated by such statements as that the proprietors of a certain well-known household remedy, reputed among medical authorities to be of entirely dubious value, have for a series of years found their profits in spending several million dollars annually in advertisements. The case is by no means unique.

It has been said, no doubt in good faith and certainly with some reason, that advertising as currently carried on gives the body of consumers valuable information and guidance as to the ways and means whereby their wants can be satisfied and their purchasing power can best be utilized. To the extent to which this holds true, advertising is a service to the community. But there is a large reservation to be made on this head. Advertising is competitive; the greater part of it aims to divert purchases, etc., from one channel to another channel of the same general class. And to the extent to which the efforts of advertising in all its branches are spent on this competitive disturbance of trade, they are, on the whole, of slight if any immediate service to the community. Such advertising, however, is indispensable to most branches of modern industry; but the necessity of most of the advertising is not due to its serving the needs of the community nor to any aggregate advantage accruing to the concerns which advertise, but to the fact that a business concern which falls short in advertising fails to get its share of trade. Each concern must advertise, chiefly because the others do. The aggregate expenditure that could advantageously be put into advertising in the absence of competition would undoubtedly be but an inconsiderable fraction of what is actually incurred, and necessarily incurred under existing circumstances.

Not all advertising is wholly competitive, or at least it is not always obviously so. In proportion as an enterprise has secured a monopoly position, its advertising loses the air of competitive selling and takes on the character of information designed to increase the use of its output independently. But such an increase implies a redistribution of consumption on the part of the customers. So that the element of competitive selling is after all not absent in these cases, but takes the form of competition between different classes of wares instead of competitive selling of different brands of the same class of wares.

Attention is here called to this matter of advertising and the necessity of it in modern competitive business for the light which it throws on "cost of production" in the modern system, where the process of production is under the control of business men and is carried on for business ends. Competitive advertising is an unavoidable item in the aggregate costs of industry. It does not add to the serviceability of the output, except it be incidentally and unintentionally. What it aims at is the sale of the output, and it is for this purpose that it is useful. It gives vendibility, which is useful to the seller, but has no utility to the last buyer. Its ubiquitous presence in the costs of any business enterprise that has to do with the production of goods for the market enforces the statement that the "cost of production" of commodities under the modern business system is cost incurred with a view to vendibility, not with a view to serviceability of the goods for human use.

There is, of course, much else that goes into the cost of competitive selling, besides the expense of advertising, although advertising may be the largest and most unequivocal item to be set down to that account. A great part of the work done by merchants and their staff of employees, both wholesale and retail, as well as by sales-agents not exclusively connected with any one mercantile house, belongs under the same head. Just how large a share of the costs of the distribution of goods fairly belongs under the rubric of competitive selling can of course not be made out. It is largest, on the whole, in the case of consumable goods marketed in finished form for the consumer, but there is more or less of it throughout. The goods turned out on a large scale by the modern industrial processes, on the whole, carry a larger portion of such competitive costs than the goods still produced by the old-fashioned detail methods, this distinction does not hold hard and fast. In some extreme cases the cost of competitive selling may amount to more than ninety per cent of the total cost of the goods when they reach the consumer. In other lines of business, commonly occupied with the production of staple goods, this constituent of cost may perhaps fall below ten per cent of the total. Where the average, for the price of finished goods delivered to the consumers, may lie would be a hazardous guess.

It is evident that the gains which accrue from this business of competitive selling and buying bear no determinable relation to the services which the work in question may render the community. If a comparison may be hazarded between two unknown and indeterminate quantities, it may perhaps be said that the gains from competitive selling bear something more of a stable relation to the service rendered than do the gains derived from speculative transactions or from the financiering operations of the great captains of industry. It seems at least safe to say that the converse will not hold true. Gains and services seem more widely out of touch in the case of the large-scale financiering work. Not that the work of the large business men in reorganizing and consolidating the industrial process is of slight consequence; but as a general proposition, the amount of the business man's gains from any given transaction of this latter class bear no traceable relation to any benefit which the community may derive from the transaction.

As to the wages paid to the men engaged in the routine of competitive selling, as salesmen, buyers, accountants, and the like,—much the same holds true of them as of the income of the business men who carry on the business on their own initiative. Their employers pay the wages of these persons, not because their work is productive of benefit to the community, but because it brings a gain to the employers. The point to which the work is directed is profitable sales, and the wages are in some proportion to the efficiency of this work as counted in terms of heightened vendibility.

The like holds true for the work and pay of the force of workmen engaged in the industrial processes under business management. It holds, in a measure, of all modern industry that produces for the market, but it holds true, in an eminent degree, of those lines of industry that are more fully under the guidance of modern business methods. These are most closely in touch with the market and are most consistently guided by considerations of vendibility. They are also, on the whole, more commonly carried on by hired labor, and the wages paid are competitively adjusted on grounds of the vendibility of the product. The brute serviceability of the output of these industries may be a large factor in its vendibility, perhaps the largest factor; but the fact remains that the end sought by the business men in control is a profitable sale, and the wages are paid as a means to that end, not to the end that the way of life may be smoother for the ultimate consumer of the goods produced.

The outcome of this recital, then, is that wherever and in so far as business ends and methods dominate modern industry the relation between the usefulness of the work (for other purposes than pecuniary gain) and the remuneration of it is remote and uncertain to such a degree that no attempt at formulating such a relation is worth while. This is eminently and obviously true of the work and gains of business men, in whatever lines of business they are engaged. This follows as a necessary consequence of the nature of business management.

Work that is, on the whole, useless or detrimental to the community at large may be as gainful to the business man and to the workmen whom he employs as work that contributes substantially to the aggregate livelihood. This seems to be peculiarly true of the bolder flights of business enterprise. In so far as its results are not detrimental to human life at large, such unproductive work directed to securing an income may seem to be an idle matter in which the rest of the community has no substantial interests. Such is not the case. In so far as the gains of these unproductive occupations are of a substantial character, they come out of the aggregate product of the other occupations in which the various classes of the community engage. The aggregate profits of the business, whatever its character, are drawn from the aggregate output of goods and services, and whatever goes to the maintenance of the profits of those who contribute nothing substantial to the output is, of course, deducted from the income of the others, whose work tells substantially.

There are, therefore, limits to the growth of the industrially parasitic lines of business just spoken of. A disproportionate growth of parasitic industries, such as most advertising and much of the other efforts that go into competitive selling, as well as warlike expenditure and other industries directed to turning out goods for conspicuously wasteful consumption, would lower the effective vitality of the community to such a degree as to jeopardize its chances of advance or even its life. The limits which the circumstances of life impose in this respect are of a selective character, in the last resort. A persistent excess of parasitic and wasteful efforts over productive industry must bring on a decline. But owing to the very high productive efficiency of the modern mechanical industry, the margin available for wasteful occupations and wasteful expenditures is very great. The requirements of the aggregate livelihood are so far short of the possible output of goods by modern methods as to leave a very wide margin for waste and parasitic income. So that instances of such a decline, due to industrial exhaustion, drawn from the history of any earlier phase of economic life, carry no well-defined lesson as to what a modern industrial community may allow itself in this respect.

While it is in the nature of things unavoidable that the management of industry by modern business methods should involve a large misdirection of effort and a very large waste of goods and services, it is also true that the aims and ideals to which this manner of economic life gives effect act forcibly to offset all this incidental futility. These pecuniary aims and ideals have a very great effect, for instance, in making men work hard and unremittingly, so that on this ground alone the business system probably compensates for any wastes involved in working. There seems, therefore, to be no tenable ground for thinking that the working of the modern business system involves a curtailment of the community's livelihood. It makes up for its wastefulness by the added strain which it throws upon those engaged in the productive work.

CHAPTER VII: THE THEORY OF MODERN WELFARE

Wasteful expenditure on a scale adequate to offset the surplus productivity of modern industry is nearly out of the question. Private initiative cannot carry the waste of goods and services to nearly the point required by the business situation. Private waste is no doubt large, but business principles, leading to saving and shrewd investment, are too ingrained in the habits of modern men to admit an effective retardation of the rate of saving. Something more to the point can be done, and indeed is being done, by the civilized governments in the way of effectual waste. Armaments, public edifices, courtly and diplomatic establishments, and the like, are almost altogether wasteful, so far as bears on the present question. They have the additional advantage that the public securities which represent this waste serve as attractive investment securities for private savings, at the same time that, taken in the aggregate, the savings so invested are purely fictitious savings and therefore do not act to lower profits or prices. Expenditures met by taxation are less expedient for this purpose; although indirect taxes have the peculiar advantage of keeping up the prices of the goods on which they are imposed, and thereby act directly toward the desired end. The waste of time and effort that goes into military service, as well as the employment of the courtly, diplomatic, and ecclesiastical personnel, counts effectually in the same direction. But however extraordinary this public waste of substance latterly has been, it is apparently altogether inadequate to offset the surplus productivity of the machine industry, particularly when this productivity is seconded by the great facility which the modern business organization affords for the accumulation of savings in relatively few hands. There is also the drawback that the waste of time involved in military service reduces the purchasing power of the classes that are drawn into the service, and so reduces the amount of wasteful consumption which these classes might otherwise accomplish.

So long as industry remains at its present level of efficiency, and especially so long as incomes continue to be distributed somewhat after the present scheme, waste cannot be expected to overtake production, and can therefore not check the untoward tendency to depression. But if the balance cannot be maintained by accelerating wasteful consumption, it may be maintained by curtailing and regulating the output of goods.

"Cutthroat" competition, that is to say, free competitive selling, can be done away by "pooling the interests" of the competitors, so soon as all or an effective majority of the business concerns which are rivals in the market combine and place their business management under one directive head. When this is done, by whatever method, selling of goods or services at competitively varying prices is replaced by collective selling ("collective bargaining") at prices fixed on the basis of "what the traffic will bear." That is to say, prices are fixed by consideration of what scale of prices will bring the largest aggregate net earnings, due regard being had to the effect of a lower price in increasing sales as well as to the reduction of cost through the increase of output. The outcome, as regards the scale of prices, may easily be a reduction of the price to consumers; but it may also, and equally readily, be an increase of the average price. But the prices of the output which is in this way brought to a monopoly basis are nearly certain to run more even than prices of the like output while sold competitively by rival concerns.

What has been said in the last paragraph supposes that the combination of business enterprises is so comprehensive as to place the resulting coalition in a position of practical monopoly. Such a result is not always attained, however, especially not in the earlier attempts at coalition in any particular branch of industry; although the endeavor is commonly repeated until at last a virtual monopoly is achieved. But even where no effective monopoly is achieved, a coalition of this kind has a salutary effect, at least temporarily. In almost all cases a consolidation of this kind is able to effect considerable economies in the cost of production, as pointed out in an earlier chapter, and such economies bring relief through enabling the combined industrial ventures to earn a reasonable profit at a lower price for their product than before. They are therefore able to go on on a scale of prices which was not remunerative while they stood on their old footing of severalty. But the relief which comes of such measures, so long as competitive selling goes on in rivalry with concerns standing outside the coalition, is only transient. The declining cost of production, and the consequent competitive investment and extension in the industry, presently catches up with the gain in economy; the margin of advantage in the competition is lost, and depression again overtakes the consolidated enterprises on their new footing. The remedy again is a wider coalition, making possible farther economies, and making some approach to a position of secure monopoly.

It is only on a footing of monopoly that this grinding depression can be definitively set aside. But the monopoly need not be absolute in order to afford a somewhat enduring relief. What is necessary is that the monopoly should comprehend all but a negligible fraction of the business concerns and the equipment engaged in the field within which competition has kept profits below a reasonable level. What is a negligible quantity in such a case is not to be determined on general considerations, since it depends in each case on circumstances affecting the particular industry. But, in a general way, the more nearly complete the monopoly, the more effectually is it likely to serve its purpose.

Such business coalitions have the effect of bringing profits to a reasonable level, not only by making it possible to regulate output and prices, but also by the economies which are made practicable on this footing. Coalitions of a less comprehensive character, as spoken of above, also effect economies in the cost of production. But the larger coalitions which bring the business to a monopoly basis have not only the advantage which comes of the large-scale organization of the industrial process, but they also enjoy peculiar advantages in the matter of cost, due to their monopoly position. These added advantages are more particularly advantages in buying or bargaining for all goods, materials, and services required, as well as in selling the output. So long as the coalitions are not comprehensive enough effectually to eliminate competition, they are constrained to both buy and sell in competition with others. But when the coalition comes effectually to cover its special field of operation, it is able, not only to fix the prices which it will accept (on the basis of what the traffic will bear), but also in a considerable measure to fix the prices or rates which it will pay for materials, labor, and other services (such as transportation) on a similar basis,—unless it should necessarily have to do with another coalition that is in a similar position of monopoly.

The rule which governs the fixing of rates on this side of the business dealings of a monopolistic coalition is similar to that which guides its transactions in the matter of sales. Prices and rates, as, *e.g.,* for materials and labor, are not depressed to the lowest possible point, but to the lowest practicable point,—to the point compatible with the largest net profits. This may or may not be a point below the rates necessary under a régime of competitive buying. It may be added that only in rare cases does a coalition attain so strong a position in respect of its purchases (of materials or services) as to lift this side of its business entirely above the reach of competition.

Wherever this expedient of coalition has been found practicable, the chronic depression of recent times and the confusion and uncertainty which goes with a depressed competitive business situation have been obviated. The great coalitions do not suffer acutely from the ills of depression, except in cases where their industrial processes are to a peculiar degree in the position of intermediaries within the range of the competitive industries, as is the case, *e.g.,* with most railroads. But even in such a case the coalition which has a monopoly is more fortunate as regards the stability of its balance sheet than the same traffic would be without the advantage of monopoly.

Barring providential intervention, then, the only refuge from chronic depression, according to the view here set forth, is thoroughgoing coalition in those lines of business in which coalition is practicable. But since this would include the greater part of those lines of industry which are dominated by the machine process, it seems reasonable to expect that the remedy should be efficacious. The higher development of the machine process makes competitive business impracticable, but it carries a remedy for its own evils in that it makes coalition practicable. The ulterior effects of thoroughgoing monopoly, as regards the efficiency of industry, the constancy of employment, the rates of wages, the prices of goods to consumers, and the like, are, of course, largely matter of surmise, and cannot be taken up in this inquiry, the present purpose being merely to give in outline an economic theory of current business enterprise.

A further consideration bearing on the later phases of the business situation may be added. The great coalitions and the business manoeuvres connected with them have the effect of adding to the large fortunes of the greater business men; which adds to the large incomes that cannot be spent in consumptive expenditures; which accelerates the increase of investments; which brings competition if there is a chance for it; which tends to bring on depression, in the manner already indicated. The great coalitions, therefore, seem to carry the seed of this malady of competition, and this evil consequence can accordingly be avoided only on the basis of so comprehensive and rigorous a coalition of business concerns as shall wholly exclude competition, even in the face of any conceivable amount of new capital seeking investment.

What has made chronic depression the normal course of things in modern industrial business is the higher development of the machine process,—given, of course, the traits of human nature as it manifests itself in business traffic. The machine process works this effect by virtue, chiefly if not altogether, of these two characteristics: (1) a relatively rapid rate of increasing efficiency; and (2) the close interdependence of the several lines of industrial activity in a comprehensive system, which is growing more comprehensive and close-knit as improvement and specialization of industrial processes go on. The last-named factor counts for more in proportion as the interdependence grows closer and more comprehensive. Disturbances are progressively transmitted with greater facility and effect throughout the system, and each line of industrial business comes to stand in relatively intimate relations to an ever increasing range of other lines with which it carries on a traffic of purchase or sale. A consequence of this state of things is that any business coalition, in order effectually to serve its purpose of maintaining earnings and capitalization, is required to be of larger scope and closer texture. As the exigencies which enforce the resort to coalition uninterruptedly gain in scope and urgency, the "trust" must take the same course of growth to meet these exigencies; until, with some slight further advance along the accustomed lines, the trust which shall serve the modern business situation must comprehend in one close business coalition virtually the whole field of industry within which the machine process is the dominant industrial factor.

To this there is a broad exception, given by the circumstances of the industrial organization. This organization rests on the distinction between business management and ownership. The workmen do not and cannot own or direct the industrial equipment and processes, so long as ownership prevails and industry is to be managed on business principles. The labor supply, or the working population, can therefore not be included in the ideally complete business coalition suggested above, however consummate the machine system and the business organization built upon it may become. So that when the last step in business coalition has been taken, there remains the competitive friction between the combined business capital and the combined workmen.

From the considerations recited above it appears that the competitive management of industry becomes incompatible with continued prosperity so soon as the machine process has been developed to its fuller efficiency. Further technological advance must act to heighten the impracticability of competitive business. As it is sometimes expressed, the tendency to consolidation is irresistible. Modern circumstances do not permit the competitive management of property invested in industrial enterprise, much less its management in detail by the individual owners. In short, the exercise of free contract, and the other powers inhering in the natural right of ownership, are incompatible with the modern machine technology. Business discretion necessarily centres in other hands than those of the general body of owners. In the ideal case, so far as the machine technology and its business concomitants are consistently carried through, the general body of owners are necessarily reduced to the practical status of pensioners dependent on the discretion of the great holders of immaterial wealth; the general body of business men are similarly, in the ideal outcome, disfranchised in point of business initiative and reduced to a bureaucratic hierarchy under the same guidance; and the rest, the populace, is very difficult to bring into the schedule except as raw material of industry. What may take place to accentuate or mitigate this tendency is a question of the drift of sentiment on the matter of property rights, business obligations, and economic policy. So far as the economic factors at play in the modern situation shape this drift of sentiment they do so in large part indirectly, through the disciplinary effect of new and untried circumstances of politics and legal relation to which their working gives rise.

WALTER RATHENAU

I**N THE OPENING** years of the twentieth century, Walter Rathenau (1867–1922) made, among his other creative achievements, a notable contribution, both practical and theoretical, to the development of cartel organization in German industry. His father had founded Germany's greatest electrical combine, the Allgemeine Elecktrizitäts Gesellschaft (AEG), and after taking his doctorate in theoretical physics, Rathenau became a "captain of industry," first as his father's chief assistant, then his successor as head of AEG. His mind was an unusually complex one, and it ranged over a vast panorama of topics, of which economics was only one. Although he was engaged in a multitude of far-flung business enterprises, he found time to employ his versatile gifts and his incredibly prolific pen in the service of science, philosophy, aesthetics, religion and mysticism, metaphysics, ethics, literature, history, politics, psychology, and autobiography—altogether Rathenau's collected works in these fields comprise five brilliantly written volumes.

When the German war effort threatened to collapse in the fall and winter of 1914 for lack of imported raw materials, Rathenau volunteered his services to the War Ministry and organized a thoroughgoing system of planned economy whose primary purpose was to ensure the allocation of scarce supplies to factories producing munitions. A "war cartel," in which the government had the deciding vote, was established for each main branch of German industry, and every firm was obliged to be a member for the duration of the war. Thus, the first comprehensive attempt to plan a modern nation's entire economic activity came into existence. The first achievement of Rathenau's organization was to avert a critical shortage of nitrates (without which explosives could not be made) by moving quickly to collect manure before it could be spread on the fields by farmers, extracting from it the needed saltpeter, and thus enabling the German guns to go on firing until synthetic nitrates became available thanks to the development of the Haber fixation process.

Despite his vital contribution to the war effort—or rather because the anti-Semitic military bureaucracy found it humiliating to have been rescued from their own short-sighted blunders by a Jewish civilian—Rathenau was forced out of the War Office in 1915. He occupied his leisure during the next few years in writing a series of widely read books that attempted to chart a path for Germany in the postwar world. The war cartels, he argued, had represented "a decisive step in the direction of state socialism," but they had simultaneously aimed at "self-government in industry to the highest possible degree." He looked forward to a "New Economy" based on universal cartelization of industry, with the public interest safeguarded by the participation of workers and consumers in the making of all important decisions. *Laissez-faire* and competition for markets would thus be entirely superseded by a totally planned, but decentralized and nonbureaucratic, economy operating to secure maximum efficiency. In politics a parliament chosen to represent economic interests would supplement or take the place of the Reichstag based on geographic constituencies. Thus a "German Collective Economy" (*Gemeinwirt-*

schaft) would arise as a logical development out of large-scale industry, and Germany's closely knit structure of cartels would evolve into a nonauthoritarian corporative state.

Though his ideas found many followers, and were widely regarded as Germany's most acceptable alternative to Bolshevism on the one hand and to the "anarchy of private economy" on the other, the only institutional change directly inspired by the "New Economy" was the National Economic Council provided for in Article 165 of the Weimar Constitution, which had little practical significance during the republican period. Rathenau's ideas did have a powerful effect in shaping the "rationalization movement"—the drive for greater technical efficiency and for a higher integration of plants—in German industry, which was carried out on a large scale with the aid of large American loans in the latter nineteen-twenties. Some of his phrases also were taken over by Nazi economic planners, though his basically democratic ideals were, of course, thoroughly perverted.

Rathenau became a martyr to his liberal and internationalist convictions when he was assassinated in 1922, while serving as Foreign Minister of the Weimar Republic, by nationalist fanatics who were enraged at his policy of reconciliation and of loyal fulfillment of the Treaty of Versailles. After 1933 his name was *verboten* in Germany.

The following selection is taken from *In Days to Come,* which first appeared in 1918, was translated from the German by Eden and Cedar Paul (London, George Allen & Unwin Ltd., 1921), and is here reprinted by permission of The Macmillan Company, New York.

§

IN DAYS TO COME

IF WE CONTEMPLATE the extant functioning of large-scale private property, looking at the matter in a purely mechanical way, and leaving the ethico-social implications of the problem unconsidered, we see that such property performs a duty which, however uncongenial it appears in its essential nature, is nevertheless of great importance from the economic outlook. Private property shoulders the risk of the world economy.

All the enterprises of the capitalist system share common characteristics; they all require large means, and they are all risky. The revenue department of any properly organised community can supply the requisite means. Much more difficult, however, is it for a municipality or a state to engage in bold virtues. These corporations lack the passionate stimulus of private enterprise; the sense of responsibility renders them timid; they are devoid of that autocratic and instinctive judgment which makes the prospects of success outweigh the possibilities of danger. Onlookers are apt to imagine that specialised skill can provide a substitute for the aforesaid incisive powers of judgment, but the desiderated substitute will not prove effective when the risks of great enterprises are under consideration; the experts will differ among themselves, and by the time they have settled their differences, the favourable opportunity will have been lost.

Private capital secures ample funds by the joint-stock method; it encounters the risks of enterprise by indefatigable endeavours towards success and profit; it overcomes the uncertainties of the future by exercising the greatest possible care in the choice of its agents, and by the number and variety of its enterprises.

Hitherto this demand could be met only by means of the surplus capital which, accumulating in the hands of the well-to-do after these had consumed all they considered requisite for daily life, clamoured for reinvestment and increase. The smaller savings were satisfied with increased security and less risk. . . .

Almost without exception these enterprises assume the impersonal form of the joint-stock company. No one is a permanent owner. The composition of the thousandfold complex which functions as lord of the undertaking, is in a state of perpetual flux. The original arrangement, in accordance with which a number of well-to-do merchants combined for the joint conduct of some business which was too extensive for any one of them to undertake single-handed, has become a matter of purely historical interest. Almost fortuitously, one person or another acquires one or several shares in an enterprise; he may hold on for a dividend or for a rise in values; in many cases he has bought merely to sell again as soon as possible. The fact that he has become a shareholder in a limited company hardly enters into his consciousness. In a great many instances, all that he has done is to bet upon the prosperity of some branch of business enterprise, and the scrip which he holds is merely the symbol of this bet.

The investor, however, is likewise the possessor of other stock and scrip, perhaps in a great many different enterprises; he is the point of intersection of various rights of ownership, and in each case the ownership is a fluctuating complex. In many cases he knows nothing more of these enterprises than the name; he may have been personally advised to invest in them; he may have been attracted by a newspaper article; he may have followed a popular craze in favour of some particular investment.

The relationship we have been describing signifies that ownership has been de-individualised. The primitive personal relationship between a man and a tangible, accurately known affair, has given place to an impersonal claim upon a theoretical yield.

The de-individualisation of ownership simultaneously implies the objectification of the thing owned. The claims to ownership are subdivided in such a fashion, and are so mobile, that the enterprise assumes an independent life, as if it belonged to no one; it takes on an objective existence, such as in earlier days was embodied only in state and church, in a municipal corporation, in the life of a guild or a religious order.

In the vital activity of the undertaking, this relationship manifests itself as a shifting of the centre of gravity. The executive instruments of an official hierarchy become the new centre. The community of owners still retains the sovereign right of decision, but this right grows increasingly theoretical, inasmuch as a multiplicity of other collective organisms (especially banks) are entrusted by the shareholders with the maintenance of their rights, and inasmuch as these fiduciaries in their turn work hand in hand with the directors of the enterprise.

To-day, already, the paradox is conceivable that the enterprise might come to own itself inasmuch as with the profits it could buy out the individual shareholders. German law imposes restrictions upon such a process, insisting that the original shareholders must retain their voting rights. Nevertheless, there is no organic contradiction to the complete detachment of ownership from the owner.

The de-individualisation of ownership, the objectification of enterprise, the detachment of property from the possessor, leads to a point where the enterprise becomes transformed as it were into a trusteeship, or perhaps it would be better to say into an institution resembling the state. This condition, which I shall denote by the term "autonomy," can be reached by many routes. One of these, the repayment of capital, has previously been mentioned. A second method, the distribution of ownership among the employees and officials of the undertaking, has been followed somewhat closely by one of our German manufacturers. The right of ownership can be vested in official positions, universities, town councils, governments; this has happened in the case of one of the oldest mining corporations in Germany. Nothing more is requisite than that there should be adequate and practical stipulations, which provide that the enterprise shall be permanently conducted by the best discoverable instruments.

If its constitution be wisely drafted, the enterprise will be able to provide for all future requirements of capital, however extensive these may become. Its first resource will be to lay hands upon the revenues which hitherto from year to year it has distributed to the shareholders. Next, transiently or permanently, it can issue debentures. In case of need, it can retreat a step, and can issue new shares. Above all, if under the protection of a state whose wealth is inexhaustible, and if subjected to the control of this state, it has a right to expect that in case of need the state will provide it with funds in return for sufficient guarantees. Nay more, the state itself will wish and demand that autonomous enterprises shall be willing at any time, under proper supervision, to take over and to invest surpluses from the state treasury.

The counterpart of the objective tendency towards autonomy is the subjective psychological evolution of the enterprise and its organs.

In so far as wealthy private entrepreneurs still exist, they have long been accustomed to regard their businesses as independent entities, incorporated objectively as companies. Such an entity has its own personal responsibility; it works, grows, makes contracts and alliances on its own account; it is nourished by its own profits; it lives for its own purposes. The fact that it nourishes the proprietor may be purely accessory, and in most cases is not the main point. A good man of business will incline to restrict unduly his own and his family's consumption, in order to provide more abundant means for the strengthening and extension of the firm. The growth and the power of this organism is a delight to the owner, a far greater delight than lucre. The desire for gain is overshadowed by ambition and by the joys of creation.

Such an outlook is accentuated among the chiefs of great corporate undertakings. Here we already encounter an official idealism identical with that which prevails in the state service. The executive instruments labour for the benefit of times when, in all human probability, they will long have ceased to be associated with the enterprise. Almost without exception, they do their utmost to reserve for the undertaking the larger moiety of its profits, and to distribute no more than the lesser moiety in the form of dividends, although to the detriment of their individual incomes. They try to preserve for their successors the yield of the period during which they have been the administrators. A leading official in such an enterprise, if offered the choice between having his salary doubled and becoming one of the directors, will prefer responsibility to wealth. The power, the archetypal reality, of the institution has become an end in itself. Covetousness, as the motive force, has been completely superseded by the sense of responsibility.

Thus the psyche of the enterprise works towards the same end as the evolution of the possessional relationships. Both culminate in the production of autonomy.

In ultimate analysis, the economic meaning of the whole movement grows clear. It is no longer the wealthy capitalist's desire for gain which shapes the enterprise. The undertaking itself, now grown into an objective personality, maintains itself, creates its own means just as much as it creates its own tasks. It is ready to provide these means out of its own profits, by the temporary issue of debentures, out of state loans, out of foundations, out of the savings of its staff and its workmen—or in any way that may be possible.

Thus, between the domain of state organisations and the domain of private businesses, there arises a domain of intermediate structures. In this we find autonomous enterprises, arising out of and conducted by private initiative, subjected to state supervision, and leading an independent life. Essentially, they are transitional varieties between private economy and state economy. Presumably, in future centuries, this objective and de-individualised ownership will become the leading mode of existence for all permanent property. In contrast therewith, property in articles of consumption will remain private, whilst property in goods of communal utility will continue to be vested in the state. Industrial monopolies will be conducted under the form of mixed-economic enterprises.

The laws of property must take into account the characteristics of autonomous undertakings, no less than the characteristics of foundations, which will likewise prove of increasing importance in days to come. Both kinds of institution should be authorised to accept legacies, in so far at least as their aims meet with public approval. Thus the creator of an economic organism will be empowered to give expression to his ideal will, to the will permanently incorporated in his work, without transmitting property rights and revenues to idle generations. The economic will thus secures enduring existence in so far as it works productively, whereas it is mortal in so far as it strives for the accumulation of material goods. The foundation, grown objective, and detached from the individual life, becomes the true monument of an outwardly-working existence. It acquires an analogy with the ideal creation of a work of art, an analogy which is manifest in respect of absolute existence if not in respect of spiritual content. . . .

If we now survey the economic life of a country which we assume to have realised the principles of the new order, we shall discern the following series of effects.

The aspect of production has changed. All the energies of the land have become active; none but invalids and the elderly are idle. The import and manufacture of needless, ugly, and noxious products has been reduced to a minimum. Thereby a third of the national labour power has been saved, so that the production of necessary goods has been notably cheapened and increased.

The concentration of manufacturing energy upon necessary and useful products increases the effectiveness of human labour in relation to the goods produced. The factor of attainability grows. The average share of products available for consumption rises, so that for an equal amount of labour a higher standard of life becomes possible.

Whilst the general wellbeing of the country is doubled or trebled by the setting of idle hands to work and by the rationalisation of production, the accumulation of private wealth is checked. Consequently the growth of property must advantage the community. These benefits accrue in two different ways.

First of all, the state grows rich beyond imagination.

All the tasks it has hitherto performed, can now be performed much better. The state can abolish poverty and unemployment; it can fulfil to an unprecedented degree all obligations of a generally useful character, without having recourse to increased taxation. Sources of revenue which to-day are utilised by methods that exploit economic life and thus work immense harm, can in the new order be dealt with apart from fiscal considerations. Considering in this connection one problem alone, that of traffic and transport, it is obvious that the abandonment of profit-making considerations by the state would result in a great multiplication of productive capacity and in an almost incredible cheapening of manufacture. For, practically speaking, the whole transport system in the hands of the state would be made free. The effect would be the same as if all the sources of raw material and all the means of production throughout the country had been concentrated into a single area. The same considerations apply to the generation and distribution of mechanical energy.

The state becomes the guardian and administrator of enormous means for investment. On the most moderate terms, it places these means at the disposal of all productive occupations, while making it a condition that those to whom such means are ceded shall pay the normal rate of wages. A new middle class comes into existence through the national financing of such medium-scale enterprises as it is expedient to maintain side by side with the large-scale industries. The influx of nationalised capital lowers the rate of interest in industrial undertakings throughout the country and facilitates the establishment of enterprises of moderate proportions.

At the same time, the state is enabled to liberate intellectual labour from the mechanism of material industry, and to ensure to brainworkers that adequate return which to-day depends upon the chances of an unspiritual success. The artist, the thinker, and the man of learning, grow independent of the decrees of a market which will not reward the genuine unless it is lucky enough to be confounded with the spurious.

As the state becomes more prosperous, so concomitantly does the wellbeing of the people increase, not indeed through an increase in great private fortunes, but through the general diffusion of civic comfort. Class contrasts have disappeared; the path towards independence and responsibility has been thrown open to all; the means of culture are accessible to every person of talent. No longer has the man of ability to struggle against the closed phalanx of the privileged; we see a continuous intermingling, an enduring ascent and descent, in the ranks of the active and in the ranks of the leaders. In proportion as, on the one hand, the accumulation of savings facilitates the securing of economic credits, and, on the other hand, the recommencement of existences becomes a daily occurrence through withdrawal into the battalions of the less highly skilled workers—wage struggles grow less bitter, all the more so since moral and intellectual qualities are increasingly influential in deciding choice of occupation. Above all we shall find that the conditions of the supply of labour have changed. Whereas to-day hands are at times idle, while machines and the means of production are in excessive demand, in the new order, machines and capital will wait for the hands to set them at work, and consequently willing workers will secure an enhanced share of the values produced by labour.

The stratum of new structures, the stratum of autonomous enterprises which has been intercalated between the private economy and the state economy, contributes to promote these results. The autonomous economic instrument has its activities predominantly determined by other considerations than those of high profit. It aims at the accumulation of surpluses only in so far as is requisite for renovation and extension. The conflict with the interests of the wage-earners is mitigated. Nay more, some of these new organisms will as a matter of principle admit the workers to a share in the profits; others will seek to secure the advantages of an economic form which is no longer subordinated to the monetary interests of shareholders and capitalists, by improving the status of their workers through high wages, and thus securing work of better quality and a greater degree of intensity. The existence and the competition of these autonomous enterprises will have a stimulating reaction upon the labour market.

When economic life assumes such characters, it becomes possible to ensure equality in education and the careful selection of all available talent, these measures decisively contributing to strengthen the whole life of the nation; whereas to-day the best attempts towards an unprejudiced popular education are shipwrecked through the diversities in the domestic circumstances of the pupils, and through the variations in their bodily and mental qualities. A nation can only come to full maturity, can only develop its spiritual and moral powers to the maximum, when no grain of corn falls on barren ground, and when every shoot secures the care which comports with the worth and the divine calling of the human spirit. Lest any fallacy should creep in to invalidate the understanding of what might seem to be a utopian picture, the contrast between the existing system and that which is destined to replace it may be briefly summarised:

1. Production and wellbeing must be increased throughout the country, for:

    extravagance will be put a stop to;

    superfluous production will be replaced by useful production;

    idleness will be abolished, and all available forces will be harnessed to the work of spiritual and material production;

    free competition and the spirit of private enterprise will be preserved;

    responsibility will be placed in the hands of those who are most capable both morally and intellectually.

2. The accumulation of immoderate and dead wealth will be checked.

3. Caste barriers will be broken down; in place of permanently burdened and permanently burdening members, there will be a system characterised by organic movement and by organic ascent and descent.

4. Therewith will increase:

    the power of the state, its material strength, and its equalising energy;

    and simultaneously there will arise an equable condition of average wellbeing, which will permeate all classes, will do away with class contrasts, and will promote throughout the land the highest conceivable development of intellectual and economic energies.

PHILIP WICKSTEED

PHILIP HENRY WICKSTEED was born on October 25, 1844, in Leeds, the son of an eminent Unitarian minister. The boy received a sound grammar school education and distinguished himself in classics and mathematics. He then studied at the University of London. Wicksteed received his M.A. with a gold medal in classics from Manchester New College in 1867, and accepted a position as Unitarian minister in a small, poor town in Somersetshire. There Wicksteed preached from the same pulpit Coleridge had once occupied, and was widely hailed as an orator of eloquence and conviction. In a subsequent post in London, his congregation included many prominent literary and intellectual figures. From 1887 to 1918, he served as University Extension Lecturer in London.

Wicksteed was a scholar of the most catholic interests, and a man of letters in the finest tradition of that term. He translated a number of important Dutch biblical studies into English, and was responsible for the popularizing of much of the "modern" continental biblical scholarship in England. He lectured widely on Ibsen, Wordsworth, and Dante, and translated most of Dante's works into English. In 1911 Wicksteed delivered the Jowett lecture at Oxford on *Dante and Aquinas* (published 1913). Always keenly interested in mathematics, he kept abreast of the latest scholarship and was intrigued with attempts to apply the mathematical method to economics. It was this interest as well as his concern with social problems that led him to study economics, which resulted in his *Alphabet of Economic Science* (1888), and *The Common Sense of Political Economy* (1910). The latter work represents the most elaborate statement of his views on economic questions, as well as a non-mathematical exposition of the technicalities of the new system of "marginal analysis."

Although marginal analysis is still an official economic doctrine, its original formulation goes back to Wicksteed's time. In the 1870s Carl Menger in Germany, Stanley Jevons in England, and Léon Walras in France almost simultaneously wrote treaties which contained explanations of price in the new marginal utility terms. It took another two decades before a new group of economists, the marginal productivity theorists, extended marginal analysis from consumer behavior to business behavior. The leaders among this second generation of marginalists include John Bates Clark, an American; Knut Wicksell, a Swede; and Alfred Marshall, like Wicksteed, English. By the opening years of the 20th century the marginal revolution was complete: marginal utility explained consumer behavior and marginal productivity explained business behavior.

For consumers, marginal choices imply the balancing of satisfactions to be derived from one purchase against those to be derived from alternative uses of income. For businessmen, marginal choices imply choosing one factor of production rather than another according to the varying productive worths of the factors. The theory assumes rational behavior, limited incomes, and a wish to maximize utility on the part of consumers and profits on the part of businessmen. As a theory it replaces the earlier cost explanations of price determination,

Wicksteed was awarded the honorary degree of Doctor of Letters by the University of Leeds in 1915, and by the University of Manchester in 1919. He died on March 18, 1927.

The popular exposition of marginalism below comes from an article published in the magazine *To-Day* in October, 1884.

THE MARXIAN THEORY OF VALUE

Das Kapital: A Criticism

I HAVE LONG wished to lay before the disciples of Karl Marx certain theoretical objections to the more abstract portions of *Das Kapital* which suggested themselves to me on my reading of that great work, and which a patient and repeated study of it have failed to remove.

The editors of *To-Day*, with equal candour and courtesy, have given me the opportunity I sought; and my first duty is to thank them for opening the pages of their review to a critical analysis of the teaching of the great Socialist thinker. The sense of obligation will be more than doubted if any student of Marx should think my criticisms deserving of a reply; for while making no illusions to myself as to the probability of serious and mature convictions being shaken, on either side, by such a controversy, I am none the less persuaded that in studying so profound and abstruse a work as *Das Kapital*, neither disciples nor opponents can afford to neglect the sidelights that may be thrown upon the subject by any earnest and intelligent attempt to analyse and discuss it from a point of view differing from their own.

As a challenge, then, to a renewed study of the theoretical basis of *Das Kapital*, the following remarks may perhaps be regarded as not altogether out of place in *To-Day*, even by those Socialists who are most convinced that a vigorous propaganda, rather than a discussion of first principles, is the specific work to which the Socialist press is now called.

It has been held by Economists of the most widely divergent schools that the wages of manual labour normally tend, under existing conditions, to sink to a point at which they barely suffice to support existence and allow of reproduction; and that the only means (always under existing conditions) by which wages could be permanently raised would be a collective refusal on the part of the working-classes to live and propagate on the terms at present granted—i.e. a raising of the standard of minimum comfort. This position—

which I do not stay to examine—is accepted by Marx (*Das Kapital,* pp. 155–163 [73–5]).[1]

But if his results coincide, in this respect, with those of the old school of Economics, the grounds on which he rests them are, of course, entirely different.

In the Malthusian philosophy the reason why wages steadily tend to the minimum allowed by the "standard of comfort" (*aliter dictum*—to starvation point) is sufficiently obvious. It is a law not of society but of nature. The point of "diminishing returns" has been reached and passed, and every additional labourer whom the increase of population throws upon the field reduces the average productiveness of labour, so that there really is less wealth per head to be consumed, and each labourer, of course, gets less for himself. This is supposed to go on until the labourers refuse to add to their numbers (standard of comfort check) or are unable to do so because their children cannot live (starvation check).

On the monstrous assumptions of Malthusianism all this is obvious enough; but it need hardly be said that Marx does not grant these assumptions, and must, therefore, find some other explanation of the phenomenon they are called on to account for. It is not in the material environment of humanity, but in the social and industrial organisation of capitalistic societies that we must look, according to Marx, for the reasons that force men to accept starvation wages.

What is it, then, in the conditions of modern industralism that compels the producers of all wealth to make such hard terms with the non-producers? What is it that constantly fills the markets with men willing and anxious to sell their "labour force" for the wages of bare subsistence?

As far as I can see, Karl Marx gives two distinct and disconnected answers to this question. In the later portion of *Das Kapital* (I speak, of course, of the single volume published), he shows how the alternate expansions and contractions of the several branches of industry, aggravated by the disturbances caused by the introduction of "labour-saving" machinery, and so forth, tend constantly to throw upon the market a number of unemployed labourers, who will offer their "labour-force" to the purchaser at prices barely adequate to support existence. All this seems to me worthy of the most earnest attention; but it is not my present purpose to dwell upon it further; for according to Marx there is a deeper cause of the phenomenon we are examining, immanent in the very fact of the purchase of "labour-force" in the market at all, and essentially independent of any such influences as I have just referred to which may

---

[1] I cite from the second German edition (1872) which is probably the one in the hands of most of my readers. References to the French translation are added in square brackets.

depress or disturb that market when once established. It is to this alleged inherent necessity of "capitalistic" production that I wish to direct attention.

I must ask leave to restate the main positions which lead up to Marx's conclusions in the order which will be most convenient for subsequent analysis. According to Marx, then, the (exchange) value of wares is determined by the amount of labour necessary on the average to produce them, and in the last resort their average selling price depends upon their value (pp. 52, 81, 151 note 37, etc. [30a, 42b, 70b note, etc.]), so that in dealing with normal relations we must always assume that whatever is sold or purchased, is sold or purchased at its full value and no more.

The manufacturer, then, must be supposed to sell his product at its value, which is as good as to say that he receives a sum of money for it representing the number of days of labour required to produce it. But he must also be supposed to have purchased all the machines, raw material, labour-force, etc., necessary to production at their value, i.e. he must have given as much money for them as represents the number of days of labour needed to produce them. Now if we take any one of these necessities of production, such as the coal needed to work the engines, and inquire into the relation in which it stands to the value of the product, the problem seems to be a very simple one. Inasmuch as a certain amount of coal must be burned before so much cotton cloth can be produced, the labour expended in getting the coal is in reality a part of the labour expended in producing the cotton cloth, and in estimating the value of the cotton cloth, we must reckon in so many days' labour expended in getting coal. The cloth, then, is more valuable than it would have been had the coal been unnecessary to its production by the precise amount of labour needed to produce the coal: but by hypothesis this is exactly represented by the money paid for the coal, so that the price of the coal (if purchased at its value) will reappear in the price of the cloth (if sold at its value)—so much *and no more*. The same reasoning will apply to the machinery, raw cotton, and so forth. The labour needed to produce each of these is labour needed to produce the cotton, and the fact that they are all necessary to the production of cotton enhances the value of cotton by precisely the amount of their own value—so much *and no more*. But when we come to labour-force, the case is different. Labour-force, like every other ware, has its value determined by the amount of labour needed to produce it. Now the amount of labour needed to produce, say, a day's labour-force, is the amount of labour needed to produce food, clothing, etc., adequate to maintaining the labourer in working condition for one day, allowance being made for the support of a number of children adequate to keeping up the supply of labourers, and so forth. Our capitalist then goes into the market and purchases labour-force *at its value*. We may suppose, for the sake of argument, that this value represents six hours' work, i.e. that it would need so much work to provide the labourer with all things needful to keep him in working condition for one day. The capitalist, then, by expending a sum of money representing six hours' work, has purchased at its value, and becomes the possessor of, a day's labour-force. It is now at his complete disposal, and on the supposition that a man can work eight or ten hours a day without any undue strain upon his system (so that the labour-force, the value of which the capitalist has paid, is labour-force capable of being applied over eight or ten hours), it is obvious that the capitalist will realize a gain of two or four hours' work. He (virtually) puts into the labourer (in the shape of food, clothing, etc.) a value representing six hours' work, and in virtue of this transaction, he causes the labourer to put eight or ten hours' work into the cotton. Hence the result that, though he buys all the things needful to the production of the cotton (including labour-force) *at their value,* and sells his cotton *at its value,* yet *more value comes out than goes in.* This "more" is the "surplus value" to secure which is the capitalist's aim, and from which interest, rent and profit are ultimately cut out as so many slices.

The production and appropriation of this surplus value is, according to Marx, the immanent law of capitalistic production, and no mere incidental development of it. If the extraction of surplus value from the application of labour-force were rendered impossible, the capitalist would lose his sole motive for engaging in his peculiar form of production at all.

I believe this is a fair summary of Marx's argument, and if so, its essential positions are as follows:—

First. The (exchange) value of a ware is determined by the amount of labour needed on the average to produce it.

Second. There is such a degree of correspondence between the value of a ware and its average selling price, that for theoretical purposes we must assume that nominally wares are bought and sold at their values.

Third. Labour-force is (in our industrial societies) a ware subject to the same laws and conditions of value and exchange as other wares.

Whether Marx's conclusions can be logically deduced from these positions or not is a question which I will not attempt to answer now, for I am concerned with the positions themselves. Against the second (when a correct definition of value has been reached)—I have nothing to urge. It is the first and third that I wish to test.

With reference to the theory of value, it will be convenient to follow Marx in his fundamental analysis of the process of exchange.

He begins by pointing out that the fact of two wares being exchangeable (no matter in what proportion) implies of necessity both *Verschiedenheit* and

Gleichheit; i.e. that they are *not identical* (else the exchange would leave things exactly where it found them), and that they are different manifestations or forms of a *common something* (else they could not be equated against each other). In other words, things which are exchangeable must be *dissimilar in quality,* but yet they must have some common measure, by reduction to which the equivalent portions of each will be seen to be *identical in quantity.*

Now with regard to the qualitative dissimilarity, I do not see that there is any room for difference of opinion. It consists in the divergent nature of the services rendered by the respective wares. Cast-iron nails and new-laid eggs differ in respect to their "value in use." They serve different purposes. Even a red and blue ribbon, though they both serve purposes of adornment, are capable each of rendering some particular services of adornment under circumstances which would make the other a mere disfigurement. I agree with Marx, then, that the *Verschiedenheit* of the wares is to be found in the respective *Gebrauchswerth* of each, or, as I should express it, *commodities differ one from another in their specific utilities.*

But in what does the *Gleichheit* consist? What is the *common something* of which each ware is a more or less? Marx replies that to get at this something, whatever it is, we must obviously set on one side all geometrical, physical, chemical and other natural properties of the several wares, for it is precisely in these that they differ from one another, and we are seeking that in which they are all identical. Now in setting aside all these natural properties, we are setting aside all that gives the wares a value in use, and there is nothing left them but the single property of being *products of labour.* But the wares, as they stand, are the products of many *different kinds* of labour, each of which was engaged in conferring upon them the special physical properties in virtue of which they possess specific utilities. Now to get at that in which all wares are identical we have been obliged to strip off all these physical properties in which they differ, so that if we still regard them as products of labour, it must be labour that has no specific character or direction, mere "abstract and indifferent human labour," the expenditure of so much human brain and muscle, etc. The *Gleichheit,* then, of the several wares consists in the fact that they are all products of abstract human labour, and the equation x of ware A = y of ware B, holds in virtue of the fact that it requires the same amount of abstract human labour to produce x of ware A or y of ware B (pp. 12, 13, cf. 19, 23, sq. [14b, 15a, cf. 17a, 19 sq.]).

Now the leap by which this reasoning lands us in labour as the sole constituent element of value appears to me so surprising that I am prepared to learn that the yet unpublished portions of *Das Kapital* contain supplementary or elucidatory matter which may set it in a new light. Meanwhile the analysis appears to be given as complete and adequate, so far as it goes, and I can, therefore, only take it as I find it and try to test its validity. But instead of directly confronting it with what seems to be the true analysis of the phenomenon of exchange, I will follow it out a little further, and we shall see that Marx himself introduces a modification into his result (or develops a half-latent implication in it), in such a way as to vitiate the very analysis on which that result is founded, and to lead us, if we work it out, to what I regard as the true solution of the problem.

A few pages, then, after we have been told that wares regarded as "valuables" must be stripped of all their physical attributes, *i.e.* of everything that gives them their value in use, and reduced to one identical spectral objectivity, as mere jellies of undistinguishable abstract human labour, and that it is this abstract human labour which constitutes them valuables, we find the important statement that the *labour does not count unless it is useful* (pp. 15, 16, 64 [16a, 35a]). Simple and obvious as this seems, it in reality surrenders the whole of the previous analysis, for if it is only useful labour that counts, then in stripping the wares of all the specific properties conferred upon them by specific kinds of useful work, we must not be supposed to have stripped them of the abstract utility, conferred upon them by abstractly useful work. If only useful labour counts, then when the wares are reduced to mere indifferent products of such labour in the abstract, they are still *useful* in the abstract, and therefore it is not true that "nothing remains to them but the one attribute of being products of labour" (p. 12 [14b]), for the attribute of being useful also remains to them. In this all wares are alike.

Armed with this result, let us return to the fundamental analysis of the phenomenon of exchange.

The exchange of two wares implies a heterogeneity (*Verschiedenheit*) and a homogeneity (*Gleichheit*). *This is implied in the fact that they are exchangeable.* And here I must challenge the attention of students of *Das Kapital* to the fact that the analysis by which "labour" is reached as the ultimate constituent element of (exchange) value, starts from the naked fact of exchangeability and is said to be involved in that fact. It is true that in the instances given by Marx the articles exchanged are wares (*i.e.* commodities which have been produced for the express purpose of exchange), and moreover wares which can practically be produced in almost unlimited quantities. It is true also that Marx elsewhere virtually *defines* value so as to make it essentially dependent upon human labour (p. 81 [43a]). But for all that his analysis is based on the bare fact of exchangeability. This fact alone establishes *Verschiedenheit* and *Gleichheit,* heterogeneity and homogeneity. Any two things which normally exchange for each other, whether products of labour or not, whether they have, or have not, what we choose to *call* value, must have that "common something" in virtue of which things exchange and can be equated with each other; and all legitimate inferences as to wares which are drawn from the bare fact of exchange must be equally legitimate when applied to other exchangeable things.

Now the "common something" which all exchangeable things contain, is neither more nor less than abstract *utility, i.e.* power of satisfying human desires. The exchanged articles differ from each other in the *specific desires* which they satisfy, they resemble each other in the *degree of satisfaction* which they confer. The *Verschiedenheit* is qualitative, the *Gleichheit* is quantitative.

It cannot be urged that there is no common measure to which we can reduce the satisfaction derived from such different articles as Bibles and brandy, for instance (to take an illustration suggested by Marx), for as a matter of fact we are all of us making such reductions every day. If I am willing to give the same sum of money for a family Bible and for a dozen of brandy, it is because I have reduced the respective satisfactions their possession will afford me to a common measure, and have found them equivalent. In economic phrase, the two things have equal abstract utility for me. In popular (and highly significant) phrase, each of the two things is *worth* as much to me as the other.

Marx is, therefore, wrong in saying that when we pass from that in which the exchangeable wares differ (value in use) to that in which they are identical (value in exchange) we must put their utility out of consideration, leaving only jellies of abstract labour. What we really have to do is to put out of consideration the concrete and specific qualitative utilities in which they differ, leaving only the abstract and general quantitative utility in which they are identical.

This formula applies to all exchangeable commodities, whether producible in indefinite quantities, like family Bibles and brandy, or strictly limited in quantity, like the "Raphaels," one of which has just been purchased for the nation. The equation which always holds in the case of a normal exchange is an equation not of labour, but of abstract utility, significantly called *worth*. The precise nature of this equation we shall presently examine; but let it be observed, meanwhile, that "labour" is indeed one of the sources (not the only one) alike of value in use (specific utility) and value in exchange (abstract utility), but in no case is it a constituent *element* of the latter any more than of the former. A coat is *made* specifically useful by the tailor's work, but it *is* specifically useful (has a value in use) because it protects us. In the same way, it is *made* valuable by abstractly useful work, but it *is* valuable because it has abstract utility. Labour, in its two-fold capacity of specifically useful work (tailoring, joinery, etc.) and abstractly useful work, *confers* upon suitable substances both *Gebrauchswerth* (value in use) and *Tauschwerth* (value in exchange), but it is not an element of either.

I venture to think that if any student of Marx will candidly re-peruse the opening portion of *Das Kapital,* and especially the remarkable section on "the two-fold character of the labour represented in wares" (pp. 16–21 [16–18]), he will be compelled to admit that the great logician has at any rate fallen into formal (if not, as I believe to be the case, into substantial) error, has passed unwarrantably and without warning, from one category into another, when he makes the great leap from specific utilities into objectivised abstract labour (p. 12 [14b]), and has given us an argument which can only become formally correct when so modified and supplemented as to accept *abstract utility* as the measure of value.

But to many of my readers this will appear to be an absurd and contradictory conclusion. "When all is said and done," they will think, "we know that as a matter of fact the exchange value of all ordinary articles *is* fixed by the amount of labour required to produce them. It may be true that *I am willing to give* equal sums for A and B because they will gratify equally intense or imperious desires, but, for all that, the reason why *I have to give* equal sums for them, and why *I can get them* for equal sums, is that it took equal amounts of labour to produce them; and the proof is that if owing to some new invention A could be made henceforth with half the labour that it requires to make B it would still perform the same service for me as it did before, and would therefore be equally useful *but its exchange value would be less."*

It is the complete and definitive solution of the problem thus presented that will immortalise the name of Stanley Jevons, and all that I have attempted or shall attempt in this article is to bring the potent instrument of investigation which he has placed in our hands to bear upon the problems under discussion. Under his guidance we shall be able to account for the *coincidence,* in the case of ordinary manufactured articles, between "exchange value" and "amount of labour contained," while clearly perceiving that exchange value itself is always immediately dependent not upon "amount of labour," but upon abstract utility.

The clue to the investigation we are now to enter on is furnished by the combined effects of "the law of indifference" and "the law of the variation of utility" (see Jevons's *Theory of Political Economy,* pp. 49 and 98). By the former of these laws "when a commodity is perfectly uniform or homogeneous in quality, any portion may be indifferently used in place of an equal portion; hence, in the same market, and at the same moment, all portions must be exchanged at the same ratio," and by the latter, each successive increment of any given commodity (at any rate after a certain point has been reached) satisfies a less urgent desire or need, and has, therefore, a less utility than the previous increment had. For example, one coat possessed by each member of a community would satisfy the urgent needs of protection and decency; whereas a second coat possessed by each member would serve chiefly to satisfy the less urgent needs of convenience, taste, luxury, etc. Now in a community every member of which possessed two coats already, a further increment of coats would (*ceteris paribus*) satisfy a less urgent need, possess a less utility, and therefore have a lower exchange value than would be the case in a community each member of which possessed only one coat; and, by the "law of indifference," all coats (of identical quality) would exchange with other goods at this lower ratio. Thus the abstract utility of the last available increment of any commodity determines the ratio of exchange of the whole of it. The importance of these facts in their bearing on our problem, I must endeavour briefly to indicate, while referring to Jevons for their full elaboration.

Exchange value is a phenomenal manifestation (conditioned by our present social and industrial organisation) of *equivalence of utility,* which equivalence of utility would, and does, exist even under industrial conditions which render its manifestation, in the particular form of exchange value impossible. Let us, then, try to track it down on ground where it is less surrounded by complications and prejudices than it is at home. "All the mystery," says Marx, "of the world of wares, all the false lights and magic which play about the creations of labour when produced as wares, disappear at once when we have recourse to other forms of production. And since Political Economy delights in Robinsoniads, let us begin with Robinson on his island" (p. 53 [30]). I accept this invitation, and proceed to make my own observations on what I see.

Robinson, then, has to perform various kinds of useful work, such as making tools or furniture, taming goats, fishing, hunting, etc.; and although he does not ever exchange things against each other, having no one with whom to exchange, yet he is perfectly conscious of the equivalence of utility existing between certain products of his labour, and as he is at liberty to distribute that labour as he likes, he will always apply it where it can produce the greatest utility in a given time. The need of food being the most urgent of all his needs, his first hours (if we suppose him to start with nothing) will be devoted to procuring food, but when he has got some little food, a further increment of it, however acceptable it would be, is not so necessary as the first instalment was, and will, therefore, not be so useful. By devoting a few hours to the search for or construction of, some rude shelter he will now be producing a greater utility than he could produce in the same time by obtaining food; and thus he continues always producing so much of what he wants most that the next increment would have a less utility than some other thing which it would take the same time to secure. He has arrived at a state of equilibrium, so to speak, when his stock of each product is such that his desire for a further increment of it is proportional to the time it would take to produce it, for when this state of things is realised, equal expenditures of labour, wherever applied, would result in equal utilities.

Let us now take the case of an industrial community the labour of which is directed to the immediate supply of the wants of its own members, without the intervention of any system of exchange, and let us suppose, for instance, that it takes a working member of such a community four days to make a coat and half a day to make a hat. We will put all other branches of industry out of consideration, we will suppose that at a given moment the members of the community are, owing to some special cause, equally ill-provided with coats and hats, and that under the climatic and other conditions to which they are subject, it would cause them equal discomfort to go without coats or without hats. A hat is therefore, at the present moment, as useful as a coat, and it only takes one-eight of the time to make it. Labour will, therefore, be directed to hat-making rather than to coat-making; for why should I spend four days in producing a certain utility when I could produce another utility exactly equivalent to it in half a day? But when a certain number of hats have been made the inconvenience caused by the insufficient supply becomes less acute, whereas the want of coats is as great as ever. Additional hats, therefore, would no longer be as useful as the same number of additional coats, but would be, say, half as useful. But since a man can produce eight hats in the time it would take him to make one coat, and since each hat is worth half as much (*i.e.* is half as useful) as a coat, he can still produce four times the utility by making hats which he could produce in the same time by making coats. He therefore goes on making hats. But the need of hats is now rapidly diminishing, and the time soon arrives when additional hats would be only *one-eighth* as useful as the same number of additional coats. A man can now produce equal utilities in a given time whether he works at coats or hats, for though it will take him eight times as long to make a coat as to make a hat, it will be *worth* eight hats to the community. Equilibrium will now be established, because the stock of coats and hats is such that the utility of more coats would be to the utility of more hats as the time it takes to make a coat to the time it takes to make a hat. But observe a coat is not worth eight times as much as a hat to this community, because it takes eight times as long to make it (that it always did, even when *one* hat was worth as much to the community as a coat)—but the community is willing to devote eight times as long to the making of a coat, because when made it will be worth eight times as much to it.

The transition to the industrial conditions under which we actually live is easy. Indeed it is already contained in the word "worth." The popular instinct has appropriated this word to the "common something" which all exchangeable commodities embody, irrespective of the industrial conditions of their production and of the commercial conditions of their circulation and consumption. From my own individual standpoint I may say that A is worth as much to me as B, *i.e.* that there is to me an *equivalence of utility* between A and B, though their specific utilities may be wholly unlike. From the standpoint of communistic or patriarchal economics, I might use the same language with the same meaning. A is worth as much to the community as B, *i.e.* there is an equivalence of utility to the community between A and B. Lastly, from the point of view of a commercially organised society in which no man's wants are reckoned unless he can give something for their gratification (the ordinary point of view) we may say "A and B are *worth* the same," = "there is an equivalence of utility to 'the purchaser' between A and B," = "there are persons who want more A and persons who want more B; and the desire for more A on the part of the former (as measured against their desire for other commodities), is equivalent to the desire for more B on the part of the latter, measured in the same way" = "the (exchange) values of A and B are equal."

One point remains to be cleared up. In the case of manufactured articles, such as hats and coats, for instance, there is always a certain stream of supply flowing, and when we speak of the "desire for more hats," we must be understood to mean, not the desire on behalf of purchasers for more hats *than they have,* but their desire for more hats *than are being supplied, i.e.* the pressure (or rather suction) which seeks to widen supply. By the "law of indifference" it is the force of demand *at the margin* of supply which determines the exchange value of the whole. For example, a watch of a certain quality is worth £15 to me, *i.e.* it would have as great a utility to me as anything else which I have not got, and which I could obtain for £15. But watches of the quality in question are now being supplied to the commercial society of which I am a member at the rate of fifty *per diem,* and the ranks of the men to whom such watches are worth £15, are only recruited at the rate of ten *per diem.* The ranks of those to whom they are worth at least £10 are, however, recruited at the rate of fifty *per diem, i.e.* the worth or utility of watches of such and such a quality, supplied at the rate of fifty *per diem* is, at the margin of supply, £10, and, therefore, by the "law of indifference" all the watches exchange at that same rate. A desire for *all* the watches that are available (theoretically identical with the desire for an infinitesimal increment of watches *beyond* what are available) is felt by persons to whom each watch has a utility represented by at least £10. A desire for *some* of the watches (but not all) is felt by persons to whom each watch would have a utility represented by some larger amount, in some cases perhaps £15 or even more, but this high utility of watches to *some* people does not affect their utility at the margin of supply, and therefore does not affect their exchange value. Thus, while value in exchange is rigidly determined by value in use, yet it may happen that any number of persons short of the whole body of purchasers, may obtain for £10 each, watches which have a utility *for them* represented by something more than £10. It is needless to add that the "margin of supply" may be fixed by the holding back from the market of a certain part of the commodities in question by the traders, or by the deliberate limitation of the production by the manufacturers, or by the physical limits imposed on the manufacture, or perhaps by other causes. This does not affect the matter.

Let us now take up the problem from the other side. Watches are being produced at the rate of fifty *per diem,* and they are worth £10 each when produced. It requires, say, twelve days' labour to produce a watch, and (due allowance being made for the quality of the labour (cf. *Das Kapital,* p. 19 [17a]) we will suppose there is no other direction which could be given to this labour by which in the same time it would produce anything worth more than £10, *i.e.* having a greater utility at the margin of supply than the watch has.

Now suppose an improvement in the manufacture of watches to be made which saves twenty-five per cent of the labour. This does not, in itself, affect the utility of watches, and therefore, nine days' labour applied to watch-making will now produce as great a utility as twelve days applied to any other industry. Anyone who has the free disposal of labour will, of course, now apply it to watch-making, but the watches he makes *will no longer be as useful* as watches have been hitherto, and for the following reason. There are more watches available now than there were formerly. If they are all to be bought (or indeed used) they must, some of them, be bought (or used) by persons to whom (in comparison with other things) they are *less useful* than the watches formerly sold were to their purchasers. All the persons to whom a watch was as useful as 200 lbs. of beef (supposing beef to be a shilling a pound), or anything else they would get for £10, are already supplied (or are being coninuously supplied as they continuously appear), and if more watches are sold it must be to persons to whom they are only as useful as, say, 180 lbs. of beef would be. A man to whom *one* watch was as useful as 200 lbs. of beef, but to whom a second watch in the family (though a great convenience) was not so imperiously required as the first, will now determine to buy a second watch which *will be less useful* than the first, but still as useful as 180 lbs. of beef. Others to whom even a single watch would not have been as useful as the greater amount of food, purchase one now because it is as useful as the smaller amount. The usefulness of a watch at the margin of supply is now represented by £9. The value of watches has fallen, *not because they contain less labour,* but because the recent increments have been *less useful,* and by the "law of indifference" the utility of the last increment determines the value of the whole.

Still, however, there is an advantage in making watches. Nine days' labour applied in any other direction would only produce a utility represented by £7:10s., whereas if applied to watch-making it will produce a utility represented by £9. Labour free to take any direction will still be directed to watch-making, and by increasing still further the number of watches available, will again lower their *usefulness* (measured by its ratio to the usefulness of other things) at the margin of supply, till at last there are so many watches already in the possession of those to whom they are useful, or in the normal stream of supply, that any further increment of watches would not be more useful to anyone than 150 lbs. of beef or a dress suit, or a new sofa, or new clothes for the children, or something else which he wants, which he has not got, and which he can get for £7:10s. When this point is reached equilibrium is restored. Nine days' labour produces a utility represented by £7:10s., whether devoted to watch-making or anything else. The value of the watch now coincides with the amount of labour it contains, yet it is not worth £7:10s., neither more nor less, because it contains nine days of a certain quality of labour, but men are willing to put nine days and no more of such labour into it, because when made it will be worth £7:10s., and it will be worth that sum in virtue of its utility at the margin of supply, which, by the "law of indifference," determines its exchange value.

The correctness of this theory of value may be tested in another way. Utility arises from the power possessed by certain things of gratifying human desires. We have seen that as these things are multiplied, the desires to which each successive increment ministers, become relatively less intense, by which their utility at the margin of supply (called by Jevons their "final utility") is lowered. We have seen that this "law of variation of utility" fully accounts for all the phenomena of supply and demand and for the coincidence, in the case of articles that can be indefinitely multiplied, between the relative amounts of labour they contain and their relative values. But if utility is the real constituent element of value, there must be another aspect of the question. Utility rising out of a relation between human desires and certain *things* (whether material or immaterial), must be affected by any modification either in the things or in the desires. We have seen that in many cases labour can indefinitely modify the number of the things, and by so doing can modify their (final) utility, and so affect their value. But there are other things which are normally exchanged (and which we must, therefore, regard as containing that "common something" which is implied in every equation of exchange, and to which it is the height of arbitrariness to refuse the name of "value"), the number and quality of which labour is powerless to affect; and yet they, too, rise and fall in value. Such are specimens of old china, pictures by deceased masters, and to a greater or less degree, the yield of all natural or artificial monopolies. The value of these things changes because their utility changes. And their utility changes, not because of any change in their own number or quality, but because of a change in the desires to which they minister. I cannot see how any analysis of the act of exchange, which reduces the "common something" implied in that act to *labour* can possibly be applied to this class of phenomena.

We have now a theory of value which is equally applicable to things that can, and things that can not, be multiplied by labour, which is equally applicable to market and to normal values, which moves with perfect ease amongst the "bourgeois categories" that have been prominent in the latter part of our argument, and fits all the complicated phenomena of our commercial societies like a glove, and yet all the while shows that these phenomena are but the specially conditioned manifestations of the ultimate and universal facts of industry, and find their analogues in the economy of a self-supplying patriarchal community or of Robinson Crusoe's island.

It only remains to apply our results to Marx's theory of surplus value. The keystone of the argument by which that theory is supported is, as we have seen, the proposition that the value of the labour-force is fixed by the amount of labour needed to produce it, whereas in its expenditure that same labour-force liquefies into a greater amount of labour than it took to produce it, so that if a man purchases labour-force at its value, he will be able to draw out at one end of his bargain more labour (and therefore more value) than he puts in at the other.

We have now learned, however, that value does not depend upon "amount of labour contained," and does not always coincide with it. Under what conditions does it so coincide? And does labour-force comply with those conditions? Whenever labour can be freely directed to the production of A or B optionally, so that x days of labour can be converted at will into y units of A, or z units of B, then, but then only, will labour be directed to the production of one or the other until the relative abundance or scarcity of A and B is such that y units of A are as useful at the margin of supply as z units of B. Equilibrium will then be reached.

But if there is any commodity C, to the production of which a man who has labour at this disposal can *not* direct that labour at his will, then there is no reason whatever to suppose that the value of C will stand in any relation to the amount of labour which it contains, for its value is determined by its utility at the margin of supply, and by hypothesis it is out of the power of labour to raise or lower that margin.

Now this is the case with labour-force in every country in which the labourer is not personally a slave. If I have obtained by purchase or otherwise the right to apply a certain amount of labour to any purpose I choose, I can-not direct it at my option to the production of hats (for instance) *or to the production of labour-force,* unless I live in a country where slave-breeding is possible; and, therefore, there is no economic law the action of which will bring the value of labour-force, and the value of other commodities, into the ratio of the amounts of labour respectively embodied in them.

It appears to me, therefore, that Marx has failed to indicate any immanent law of capitalistic production by which a man who purchases labour-force at its value will extract from its consumption a surplus value. We are simply thrown back upon the fact that a man can purchase (not produce) as much labour-force as he likes at the price of bare subsistence. But this fact is the problem we are to investigate, not the solution of the problem.

The object of this paper is purely critical, and my task is, therefore, for the present completed. Only let me repeat that in the latter portion of the published volume of *Das Kapital* Marx appears to me to have made contribu-tions of extreme importance to the solution of the great problem, though I cannot see that they stand in any logical connection with the abstract reason-ing of his early chapters.

SIDNEY WEBB

Sidney James Webb was born in London on July 13, 1859, to lower middle-class parents. He was educated in Switzerland and Mecklenburg-Schwerin, at the Birkbeck Institute and at the City of London College. After entering the civil service by open examination in 1878, he began to study law and received his LL.B. from the University of London in 1886.

In 1879 Webb met George Bernard Shaw, who later introduced him into the Fabian Society. Webb joined in 1885 and became, along with Sidney (later Lord) Olivier and Graham Wallas, one of the dominating figures of the group. He wrote, as Fabian tracts, *Facts for Socialists* (1887) and *Facts for Londoners* (1889), while making an important contribution to the *Fabian Essays in Socialism* (1889).

In 1892 Webb married Beatrice Potter, the daughter of a railway and industrial magnate. She was herself much interested in social problems—having published articles on "The Dock Life of East London," and "Sweated Labor"—and it was in the course of her work on the cooperative movement, work which culminated in the publication of *The Co-operative Movement in Great Britain* (1891), that she met Webb. Within the wedding rings they exchanged was inscribed the motto *pro bono publico* (for the public weal).

From this time, most of their work was done in common. In 1894 they published *The History of Trade Unionism,* a pioneering work in the scholarly study of trade unionism, and three years later their two-volume study of *Industrial Democracy* appeared. In 1895 the Webbs conceived the idea which resulted in the founding of the London School of Economics and Political Science, to which they both devoted unwearying service. From 1906 to 1929 they were occupied in publishing the nine volumes of their comprehensive *English Local Government,* a monument of historical scholarship.

In 1909 the failure of their vigorous campaign against the Poor Laws disillusioned the Webbs with the possibility of turning the older parties in the direction of massive social reform. For this reason they abandoned their old antagonism to the Labour Party and entered into cooperation with its secretary, Arthur Henderson. In 1915 Sidney Webb became a member of the party executive, and in 1918 he drafted *Labour and the New Social Order,* the statement of policy which was to become the official program of the Labour Party after the First World War. In 1922 he was elected to Parliament for the coal constituency of Durham, and in 1924 he was made president of the Board of Trade in the first Labour government. Under the 1929 Labour government Webb was made Baron Passfield, and he served as Secretary of State for Dominion Affairs from 1929 to 1930, and as Secretary of State for the Colonies from 1930 to 1931.

In 1932 the Webbs made a trip to Russia. They returned profoundly impressed with what they had seen, and published *Soviet Communism: A New Civilization* in 1935. A later edition, however, was more skeptical.

Beatrice Webb died at Passfield Corner in 1943. Her husband died in the same place in 1947. Their ashes were buried in Westminster Abbey. The following early essay on the relation of the growth of the state to the development of capitalism was Sidney Webb's contribution to *Fabian Essays in Socialism* (1889).

THE BASIS OF SOCIALISM

THE DEVELOPMENT OF THE DEMOCRATIC IDEAL

In discussing the historic groundwork of Socialism, it is worth remembering that no special claim is made for Socialism in the assertion that it possesses a basis in history. Just as every human being has an ancestry, unknown to him though it may be; so every idea, every incident, every movement has in the past its own long chain of causes, without which it could not have been. Formerly we were glad to let the dead bury their dead: nowadays we turn lovingly to the records, whether of persons or things; and we busy ouselves willingly among origins, even without conscious utilitarian end. We are no longer proud of having ancestors, since everyone has them; but we are more than ever interested in our ancestors, now that we find in them the fragments which compose our very selves. The historic ancestry of the English social organization during the present century stands witness to the irresistible momentum of the ideas which Socialism denotes. The record of the century in English social history begins with the trial and hopeless failure of an almost complete industrial individualism, in which, however, unrestrained private ownership of land and capital was accompanied by subjection to a political oligarchy. So little element of permanence was there in this individualistic order that, with the progress of political emancipation, private ownership of the means of production has been, in one direction or another, successively regulated, limited and superseded, until it may now fairly be claimed that the Socialist philosophy of to-day is but the conscious and explicit assertion of principles of social organization which have been already in great part unconsciously adopted. The economic history of the century is an almost continuous record of the progress of Socialism.

Socialism too, has in the record of its internal development a history of its own. Down to the present generation, the aspirant after social regeneration naturally vindicated the practicability of his ideas by offering an elaborate plan with specifications of a new social order from which all contemporary evils were eliminated. Just as Plato had his Republic and Sir Thomas More his Utopia, so Baboeuf had his Charter of Equality, Cabet his Icaria, St.

Simon his Industrial System, and Fourier his ideal Phalanstery. Robert Owen spent a fortune in pressing upon an unbelieving generation his New Moral World; and even Auguste Comte, superior as he was to many of the weaknesses of his time, must needs add a detailed Polity to his Philosophy of Positivism.

The leading feature of all these proposals was what may be called their statical character. The ideal society was represented as in perfectly balanced equilibrium, without need or possibility of future organic alteration. Since their day we have learned that social reconstruction must not be gone at in this fashion. Owing mainly to the efforts of Comte, Darwin, and Herbert Spencer, we can no longer think of the ideal society as an unchanging State. The social ideal from being static has become dynamic. The necessity of the constant growth and development of the social organism has become axiomatic. No philosopher now looks for anything but the gradual evolution of the new order from the old, without breach of continuity or abrupt change of the entire social tissue at any point during the process. The new becomes itself old, often before it is consciously recognized as new; and history shews us no example of the sudden substitutions of Utopian and revolutionary romance.

Though Socialists have learnt this lesson better than most of their opponents, the common criticism of Socialism has not yet noted the change, and still deals mainly with the obsolete Utopias of the pre-evolutionary age. Parodies of the domestic details of an imaginary Phalanstery, and homilies on the failure of Brook Farm or Icaria, may be passed over as belated and irrelevant now that Socialists are only advocating the conscious adoption of a principle of social organization which the world has already found to be the inevitable outcome of Democracy and the Industrial Revolution. For Socialism is by this time a wave surging throughout all Europe; and for want of a grasp of the series of apparently unconnected events by which and with which it has been for two generations rapidly coming upon us—for want, in short, of knowledge of its intellectual history, we in England to-day see our political leaders in a general attitude of astonishment at the changing face of current politics; both great parties drifting vaguely before a nameless undercurrent which they fail utterly to recognize or understand. With some dim impression that Socialism is one of the Utopian dreams they remember to have heard comfortably disposed of in their academic youth as the impossible ideal of Humanity-intoxicated Frenchmen, they go their ways through the nineteenth century as a countryman blunders through Cheapside. One or two are history fanciers, learned in curious details of the past:

the present eludes these no less than the others. They are so near to the individual events that they are blind to the onward sweep of the column. They cannot see the forest for the trees. . . .

The main stream which has borne European society towards Socialism during the past 100 years is the irresistible progress of Democracy. De Tocqueville drove and hammered this truth into the reluctant ears of the Old World two generations ago; and we have all pretended to carry it about as part of our mental furniture ever since. But like most epigrammatic commonplaces, it is not generally realized; and De Tocqueville's book has, in due course, become a classic which everyone quotes and nobody reads. The progress of Democracy is, in fact, often imagined, as by Sir Henry Maine to be merely the substitution of one kind of political machinery for another; and there are many political Democrats to-day who cannot understand why social or economic matters should be mixed up with politics at all. It was not for this that they broke the power of the aristocracy: they were touched not so much with love of the many as with hatred of the few; and, as has been acutely said—though usually by foolish persons—they are Radicals merely because they are not themselves lords. But it will not long be possible for any man to persist in believing that the political organization of society can be completely altered without corresponding changes in economic and social relations. De Tocqueville expressly pointed out that the progress of Democracy meant nothing less than a complete dissolution of the nexus by which society was held together under the old *régime*. This dissolution is followed by a period of anarchic spiritual isolation of the individual from his fellows, and to that extent by a general denial of the very idea of society. But man is a social animal; and after more or less interval there necessarily comes into existence a new nexus, differing so entirely from the old-fashioned organization that the historic fossil goes about denying that it is a nexus at all, or that any new nexus is possible or desirable. To him, mostly through lack of economics, the progress of Democracy is nothing more than the destruction of old political privileges; and, naturally enough, few can see any beauty in mere dissolution and destruction. Those few are the purely political Radicals abhorred of Comte and Carlyle: they are in social matters the empiricist survivals from a pre-scientific age.

The mere Utopians, on the other hand, who wove the baseless fabric of their visions of reconstructed society on their own private looms, equally failed, as a rule, to comprehend the problem of the age. They were, in imagination, resuscitated Joseph the Seconds, benevolent despots who would have poured the old world, had it only been fluid, into their new moulds. Against their crude plans the Statesman, the Radical, and the Political Economist were united; for they took no account of the blind social forces which they could not control, and which went on inexorably working out social salvation in ways unsuspected by the Utopian.

In the present Socialist movement these two streams are united: advocates of social reconstruction have learnt the lesson of Democracy, and know that it is through the slow and gradual turning of the popular mind to new principles that social reorganization bit by bit comes. All students of society who are abreast of their times, Socialists as well as Individualists, realize that important organic changes can only be (1) democratic, and thus acceptable to a majority of the people, and prepared for in the minds of all; (2) gradual, and thus causing no dislocation, however rapid may be the rate of progress; (3) not regarded as immoral by the mass of the people, and thus not subjectively demoralizing to them; and (4) in this country at any rate, constitutional and peaceful. Socialists may therefore be quite at one with Radicals in their political methods. Radicals, on the other hand, are perforce realizing that mere political levelling is insufficient to save a State from anarchy and despair. Both sections have been driven to recognize that the root of the difficulty is economic; and there is every day a wider consensus that the inevitable outcome of Democracy is the control by the people themselves, not only of their own political organization, but, through that, also of the main instruments of wealth production; the gradual substitution of organized cooperation for the anarchy of the competitive struggle; and the consequent recovery, in the only possible way, of what John Stuart Mill calls "the enormous share which the possessors of the instruments of industry are able to take from the produce." The economic side of the democratic ideal is, in fact, Socialism itself.

THE DISINTEGRATION OF THE OLD SYNTHESIS

At the middle of the last century Western Europe was still organized on a system of which the basis was virtually a surviving feudalism. The nexus between man and man was essentially a relation of superiority and inferiority. Social power still rested either with the monarch, or with the owners of large landed estates. Some inroads had already been made in the perfect symmetry of the organization, notably by the growth of towns, and the rise of the still comparatively small trading class; but the bulk of the population was arranged in an hierarchical series of classes, linked to one another by the bond of Power. . . .

Even in England the whole political administration was divided between the king and the great families; and not one person in 500 possessed so much as a vote. As lately as 1831 one hundred and fifty persons returned a majority of the House of Commons (Molesworth, "History of the Reform Bill," p. 347). The Church, once a universal democratic organization of international fraternity, had become a mere *appanage* of the landed gentry. The administration of justice and of the executive government was entirely in their hands, while Parliament was filled with their leaders or nominees. No avenue of advancement existed for even exceptionally gifted sons of the people; and the masses found themselves born into a position of lifelong dependence upon a class of superior birth.

The economic organization was of similar character. Two-thirds of the population tilled the soil, and dwelt in lonely hamlets scattered about the still sparsely inhabited country. Though possessing the remnants of ancient communal rights, they were practically dependent on the farmers of the parish, who fixed their wages by a constant tacit conspiracy. The farmers themselves were the obedient serfs of the large proprietors, to whom they paid a customary rent. Though nominally free to move, both farmers and laborers were practically fettered to the manor by their ignorance and their poverty; and though the lord had lost the criminal jurisdiction of his manorial courts, his powers as Justice of the Peace formed a full equivalent. His unrestrained ownership of the land enabled him to take for himself as rent the whole advantage of all but the very worst of the soils in use; and the lingering manorial rights gave him toll even from that worst. Throughout the countryside his word was law and his power irresistible. It was a world whose nexus was might, economic and political, tempered only by custom and lack of stimulus to change. The poor were not necessarily worse off in material matters than they are now: the agricultural laborer, indeed, was apparently better off in 1750 than at any other time between 1450 and 1850. But it was a world still mainly mediaeval in political, in economic, and in social relations: a world of status and of permanent social inequalities not differing essentially from the feudalism of the past.

The system had, however, already begun to decay. The rise of the towns by the growth of trade gradually created new centres of independence and new classes who broke the bonds of innate status. The intrusion of the moneyed city classes and the Indian "Nabobs" into the rural districts tended to destroy the feudal idea. The growth of new sects in religion made fresh points of individual resistance, degenerating often into spiritual anarchy or unsocial quietism. The spread of learning built up a small but active disintegrating force of those who had detected the shams around them. But the real Perseus who was to free the people from their political bondage was Newcomen or Watt, Hargreaves or Crompton, Kay or Arkwright, whichever may be considered to have contributed the main stroke towards the

Industrial Revolution of the last century. From the inventions of these men came the machine industry with its innumerable secondary results—the Factory System and the upspringing of the Northern and Midland industrial towns,[1] and the evangelization of the waste places of the earth by the sale of grey shirtings. Throughout one-third of England the manor gave way to the mill or the mine; and the feudal lord had to slacken his hold of political and social power in order to give full play to the change which enriched him with boundless rents and mining royalties. And so it happened in England that the final collapse of Mediaevalism came, not by the Great Rebellion nor by the Whig Treason of 1688, nor yet by the rule of the Great Commoner, but by the Industrial Revolution of the eighteenth century, which created the England of to-day. Within a couple of generations the squire faded away before the mill-owner; and feudalism lingered thenceforth only in the rapidly diminishing rural districts, and in the empty remnants of ceremonial organization. The mediaeval arrangement, in fact, could not survive the fall of the cottage industry; and it is, fundamentally, the use of new motors which has been for a generation destroying the individualist conception of property. The landlord and the capitalist are both finding that the steam-engine is a Frankenstein which they had better not have raised; for with it comes inevitably urban Democracy, the study of Political Economy, and Socialism.

The event which brought to a head the influences making for political change was the French Revolution. The fall of the Bastille was hailed by all who had been touched by the new ideas. "How much the greatest event it is that ever happened in the world; and how much the best!" wrote Charles James Fox. It shewed, or seemed to shew, to men that a genuine social reconstruction was not only desirable but possible. The National Assembly, respectable old oligarchy as it was, pointed the way to legislative fields not even yet completely worked out.

When the rulers of England perceived that in France at least Humpty Dumpty was actually down, the effect at first was to tighten the existing organization. The mildest agitation was put down with a cruelly strong hand. The Whig party in the House of Commons sank to half-a-dozen members. Prices were kept up and wages down, while the heaviest possible load of taxation was imposed on the suffering people. Then came the Peace, and Castlereagh's "White Terror," culminating in the "massacre of Peterloo" (1819) and Lord Sidmouth's infamous "Six Acts." But the old order was doomed. The suicide of Castlereagh was not only the end of the man but

[1] Between 1801–1845 the population of Manchester grew 109 per cent., Glasgow 108 per cent., Liverpool 100 per cent., and Leeds 99 per cent. (Report of Commissioners on State of Health of Larger Towns, 1843–5.)

also the sign of the collapse of the system. With a series of political wrenches there came the Repeal of the Test and Corporation Acts (1828), Catholic Emancipation (1829), the beginnings of legal and administrative reform, and finally the great Reform Bill of 1832, by which the reign of the middle class superseded aristocratic rule. But the people were no more enfranchised than they had been before. The Factory had beaten the Manor for the benefit, not of the factory hand, but of the mill-owner. Democracy was at the gates; but it was still on the wrong side of them. Its entry, however, was only a matter of time. Since 1832 English political history is the record of the reluctant en-franchisement of one class after another, by mere force of the tendencies of the age. None of these enfranchised classes has ever sincerely desired to ad-mit new voters to share the privileges and submerge the power which it had won; but each political party in turn has been driven to "shoot Niagara" in order to compete with its opponents. The Whig Bill of 1832 enfranchised the middle-class for Parliament: the Municipal Corporations Act of 1835 gave them control of the provincial towns. After a generation of agitation, it was ultimately the Tory party which gave the townspeople in 1867 Household Suffrage. Eleven years later a Conservative majority passed Sir Charles Dilke's Act enfranchising the tenement occupier (1878). In 1885 the Liberals, intending permanently to ruin their opponents, gave the vote to the agricul-tural laborer; and last year (1888) it was the Tories, not to be outdone, who gave him the control of the local administration of the counties, and placed the government of London in the hands of a popularly elected council. Neither party can claim much credit for its reform bills, extorted as they have been, not by belief in Democracy, but by fear of the opposing faction. Even now the citizen is tricked out of his vote by every possible legal and administrative technicality; so that more than one-third of our adult men are unenfranchised, together with the whole of the other sex. Neither the Con-servative party nor the self-styled "Party of the Masses" gives proof of any real desire to give the vote to this not inconsiderable remnant; but both sides pay lip-homage to Democracy; and everyone knows that it is merely a wait-ing race between them as to which shall be driven to take the next step. The virtual completion of the political revolution is already in sight; and no more striking testimony can be given of the momentum of the new ideas which the Fall of the Bastille effectually spread over the world than this democratic triumph in England, within less than a century, over the political mediaeval-ism of ten centuries growth.

The full significance of this triumph is as yet unsuspected by the ordinary politician. The industrial evolution has left the laborer a landless stranger in his own country. The political evolution is rapidly making him its ruler. Samson is feeling for his grip on the pillars.

THE PERIOD OF ANARCHY

The result of the industrial revolution, with its dissolution of mediaevalism amid an impetuous reaction against the bureaucratic tyranny of the past, was to leave all the new elements of society in a state of unrestrained license. Individual liberty, in the sense of freedom to privately appropriate the means of production, reached its maximum at the commencement of the century. No sentimental regulations hindered the free employment of land and capital to the greatest possible pecuniary gain of the proprietors, however many lives of men, women and children were used up in the process. Ignorant or unreflecting capitalists still speak of that terrible time with exultation. "It was not five per cent or ten per cent," says one, "but thousands per cent that made the fortunes of Lancashire."

Mr. Herbert Spencer and those who agree in his worship of Individualism, apparently desire to bring back the legal position which made possible the "white slavery" of which the "sins of legislators" have deprived us; but no serious attempt has ever been made to get repealed any one of the Factory Acts. Women working half naked in the coal mines; young children dragging trucks all day in the foul atmosphere of the underground galleries; infants bound to the loom for fifteen hours in the heated air of the cotton mill, and kept awake only by the overlooker's lash; hours of labor for all, young and old, limited only by the utmost capabilities of physical endurance; complete absence of the sanitary provisions necessary to a rapidly growing population: these and other nameless iniquities will be found recorded as the results of freedom of contract and complete *laisser faire* in the impartial pages of successive blue-book reports. But the Liberal mill-owners of the day, aided by some of the political economists, stubbornly resisted every attempt to interfere with their freedom to use "their" capital and "their" hands as they found most profitable, and (like their successors to-day) predicted of each restriction as it arrived that it must inevitably destroy the export trade and deprive them of all profit whatsoever.

But this "acute outbreak of individualism, unchecked by the old restraints, and invested with almost a religious sanction by a certain soulless school of writers," [2] was inevitable, after the economic blundering of governments in the eighteenth century. Prior to the scientific investigation of economic

[2] Professor H. S. Foxwell (University College, London), p. 249 of Essay in "The Claims of Labor" (Edinburgh: Co-operative Printing Company, 1886).

laws, men had naturally interfered in social arrangements with very unsatisfactory results. A specially extravagant or a specially thrifty king debased the currency, and then was surprised to find that in spite of stringent prohibitions prices went up and all good money fled the country. Wise statesmen, to keep up wages, encouraged the woollen manufactures of England by ruining those of Ireland, and were then astonished to find English wages cut by Irish pauper immigration. Benevolent parliaments attempted to raise the worker's income by poor law allowances, and then found that they had lowered it. Christian kings eliminated half the skilled artisans from their kingdoms, and then found that they had ruined the rest by disabling industry. Government inspectors ordered how the cloth should be woven, what patterns should be made, and how broad the piece should be, until the manufacturers in despair cried out merely to be let alone.

When the early economists realized how radically wrong had been even the well-meant attempts to regulate economic relations by legislation, and how generally these attempts multiplied private monopolies, they leaned in their deductions heavily towards complete individual liberty. The administration of a populous state is such a very difficult matter, and when done on false principles is so certain to be badly done, that it was natural to advocate rather no administration at all than the interference of ignorant and interested bunglers. Nature, glorified by the worship of a famous school of French philosophers and English poets, and as yet unsuspected of the countless crimes of "the struggle for existence," appeared at least more trustworthy than Castlereagh. Real democratic administration seemed, in the time of the "White Terror," and even under the milder Whig hypocrisy which succeeded it, hopelessly remote. The best thing to work and fight for was, apparently, the reduction to impotence and neutrality of all the "Powers that Be." Their influence being for the moment hostile to the people, it behoved the people to destroy their influence altogether. And so grew up the doctrine of what Professor Huxley has since called "Administrative Nihilism." It was the apotheosis of *Laisser Faire, Laisser Aller*.

Though the economists have since had to bear all the blame for what nearly everyone now perceives to have been an economic and social mistake, neither Hume nor Adam Smith caught the *laisser faire* fever to as great an extent as their French contemporaries and imitators. The English industrial position was not the same as that of France. The "mercantile system" by which, as by "Fair Trade" to-day, foreign trade was to be regulated and encouraged according as it tended to cause the stock of goods, especially coin and bullion, to increase in the country, was the same on both sides of the Channel. But our political revolution had already been partly accomplished; and the more obvious shackles of feudalism had been long since struck off. No Englishman was compelled to grind his corn at the mill of the lord of the manor; to give up unpaid days to plough the lord's field and cart the lord's hay; or to spend his nights in beating the waters of the lord's marsh so that the croaking of the frogs might not disturb the lord's repose. Our labor dues had long before been commuted for money payments; and these had become light owing to the change in currency values. Our apprenticeship laws and guild regulations were becoming rapidly inoperative. No vexatious excise or gabelle hampered our manufactures.

Tyranny there was, enough and to spare, and economic spoliation; but they did not take the form of personal interferences and indignities. The non-noble Frenchman was bond, and he knew it; the middle-class Englishman to a great extent thought himself free; his economic servitude, though it galled him, was not clearly distinguishable from the niggardliness of nature. The landlord in France was an obvious tyrant: here he certainly caused (by the abstraction of the economic rent) an artificial barrenness of the workers' labor; but the barrenness was so old and had been so constant that it was not seen to be artificial, and was not resented as such. No peasant rebels against the blight. Accordingly, we have, since 1381, never had in England a burning of the *châteaux;* and accordingly, too, Adam Smith is no complete champion of *laisser faire,* though his great work was effective mainly in sweeping away foreign trade restrictions and regulations, and in giving viability to labor by establishing the laborer's geographical freedom to move and to enter into the wage contract when and where best he could. The English economists, stopping illogically short of the complete freedom preached by Rousseau and Godwin and the scientific Anarchists of to-day, advocated just as much freedom as sufficed to make the fortunes of Lancashire capitalists and to create the modern proletariat. The Utilitarians are appropriately coupled with the Political Economists in connexion with this phase of thought. Although Adam Smith did not belong to their school, almost the whole work of developing and popularizing the new science was done by them. It was not until after the Peace—when Bentham and James Mill were in full vigor, and soon to be reinforced by Austin, Villiers, John Stuart Mill, Roebuck, Grote, Ricardo, and others—that Political Economy became a force in England. The motive and enthusiasm for the new science undoubtedly came from the Utilitarian ethics. If the sole masters of man were pleasure and pain, the knowledge of the natural laws expressing the course of social action, and thus regulating pleasure and pain, became of vital importance. If it is God's will, as Paley and Austin asserted, that men should seek for happiness, then the study of how to obtain economic comfort becomes a sacred duty, and has even been so regarded by such rational divines as Malthus, Chalmers, Maurice, Kingsley, and the young High Church party of to-day. Christianity and the course of modern thought began to join hands; and we may see in Bishop Berkeley and Paley the forerunners of such a development as the Guild of St. Matthew.

The Utilitarian philosophy, besides aiding in the popularization of economic science, strongly influenced its early character. The tendency to *Laisser Faire* inherited from the country and century of upheaval and revolt against authority, was fostered by Bentham's destructive criticism of all the venerable relics of the past. What is the use of it, he asked, of every shred of social institution then existing. What is the net result of its being upon individual happiness? Free of the laws and customs—little, indeed, of the social organization of that time could stand this test. England was covered with rotten survivals from bygone circumstances; the whole administration was an instrument for class domination and parasite nurture; the progress of the industrial revolution was rapidly making obsolete all laws, customs, proverbs, maxims, and nursery tales; and the sudden increase of population was baffling all expectations and disconcerting all arrangements. At last it came to be carelessly accepted as the teaching of both philosophy and of experience that every man must fight for himself; and "devil take the hindmost" became the accepted social creed of what was still believed to be a Christian nation. Utilitarianism became the Protestantism of Sociology, and "how to make for self and family the best of both worlds" was assumed to be the duty, as it certainly was the aim, of every practical Englishman.

THE INTELLECTUAL AND MORAL REVOLT, AND ITS POLITICAL OUTCOME

The new creed of "Philosophic Radicalism" did not have matters all its own way. Its doctrines might suit millowners and merchant princes, and all who were able to enjoy the delight of their own strength in the battle of life. But it was essentially a creed of Murdstones and Gradgrinds; and the first revolt came from the artistic side. The "nest of singing birds" at the Lakes would have none of it, though De Quincey worked out its abstract economics in a manner still unsurpassed. Coleridge did his best to drown it in German Transcendentalism. Robert Owen and his following of enthusiastic communistic co-operators steadfastly held up a loftier ideal. The great mass of the wage earners never bowed the knee to the principles upon which the current "White Slavery" was maintained. But the first man who really made a dint on the individualist shield was Carlyle, who knew how to compel men to listen to him. Oftener wrong than right in his particular proposals, he managed to keep alive the faith in nobler ends than making a fortune in this world and saving one's soul in the next. Then came Maurice, Kingsley, Ruskin, and others who dared to impeach the current middle class cult; until finally, through Comte and John Stuart Mill, Darwin and Herbert Spencer, the conception of the Social Organism has at last penetrated to the minds, though not yet to the books, even of our professors of Political Economy.

Meanwhile, caring for none of these things, the practical man had been irresistibly driven in the same direction. In the teeth of the current Political Economy, and in spite of all the efforts of the millowning Liberals, England was compelled to put forth her hand to succor and protect her weaker members. Any number of Local Improvement Acts, Drainage Acts, Mines Regulation Acts, Factory Acts, Public Health Acts, Adulteration Acts, were passed into law. The liberty of the property owner to oppress the propertyless by the levy of the economic tribute of rent and interest began to be circumscribed, pared away, obstructed and forbidden in various directions. Slice after slice has gradually been cut from the profits of capital, and therefore from its selling value, by socially beneficial restrictions on its user's liberty to do as he liked with it. Slice after slice has been cut off the incomes from rent and interest by the gradual shifting of taxation from consumers to persons enjoying incomes above the average of the kingdom. Step by step the political power and political organization of the country have been used for industrial ends, until to-day the largest employer of labor is one of the ministers of the Crown (the Postmaster-General); and almost every conceivable trade is, somewhere or other, carried on by a parish, municipality, or the National Government itself without the intervention of any middleman or capitalist. The theorists who denounce the taking by the community into its own hands of the organization of its own labor as a thing economically unclean, repugnant to the sturdy individual independence of Englishmen, and as yet outside the sphere of practical politics, seldom have the least suspicion of the extent to which it has already been carried. Besides our international relations and the army, navy, police and the courts of justice, the community now carries on for itself, in some part or another of these islands, the post office, telegraphs, carriage of small commodities, coinage, surveys, the regulation of the currency and note issue, the provision of weights and measures, the making, sweeping, lighting, and repairing of streets, roads, and bridges, life insurance, the grant of annuities, shipbuilding, stockbroking, banking, farming, and money-lending. It provides for many thousands of us from birth to burial—midwifery, nursery, education, board and lodging, vaccination, medical attendance, medicine, public worship, amusements, and interment. It furnishes and maintains its own museums, parks, art galleries, libraries, concert-halls, roads, streets, bridges, markets, slaughter-houses, fire-engines, lighthouses, pilots, ferries, surfboats, steamtugs, life-boats, cemeteries, public baths, washhouses, pounds, harbours, piers, wharves, hospitals, dispensaries, gasworks, waterworks, tramways, telegraph cables, allotments, cow meadows, artisans' dwellings, schools, churches, and reading-rooms. It carries on and publishes its own researches in geology, meteorology, statistics, zoology, geography, and even theology. In our Colonies the English Government further allows and encourages the communities to provide for themselves railways, canals, pawnbroking, theatres, forestry, cinchona farms, irrigation, leper villages, casinos, bathing establishments, and immigration, and to deal in ballast, guano, quinine, opium, salt, and what not. Every one of these functions, with those of the army, navy, police, and courts of justice, were at one time left to private enterprise, and were a source of legitimate individual investment of capital. Step by step the community has absorbed them, wholly or partially; and the area of private exploitation has been lessened. Parallel with this progressive nationalization or municipalization of industry, there has gone on the elimination of the purely personal element in business management. The older economists doubted whether anything but banking and insurance could be carried on by joint stock enterprise: now every conceivable industry, down to baking and milk-selling, is successfully managed by the salaried officers of large corporations of idle shareholders. More than one-third of the whole business of England, measured by the capital employed, is now done by joint stock companies, whose shareholders could be expropriated by the community with no more dislocation of the industries carried on by them than is caused by the daily purchase of shares on the Stock Exchange.

Besides its direct supersession of private enterprise, the State now registers, inspects, and controls nearly all the industrial functions which it has not yet absorbed. In addition to births, marriages, deaths, and electors, the State registers all solicitors, barristers, notaries, patent agents, brokers, newspaper proprietors, playing-card makers, brewers, bankers, seamen, captains, mates, doctors, cabmen, hawkers, pawnbrokers, tobacconists, distillers, plate dealers, game dealers; all insurance companies, friendly societies, endowed schools and charities, limited companies, lands, houses, deeds, bills of sale, compositions, ships, arms, dogs, cabs, omnibuses, books, plays, pamphlets, newspapers, raw cotton movements, trademarks, and patents; lodging-houses, public-houses, refreshment-houses, theatres, music-halls, places of worship, elementary schools, and dancing rooms.

Nor is the registration a mere form. Most of the foregoing are also inspected and criticised, as are all railways, tramways, ships, mines, factories, canal-boats, public conveyances, fisheries, slaughter-houses, dairies, milk-shops, bakeries, babyfarms, gasmeters, schools of anatomy, vivisection labora-tories, explosive works, Scotch herrings, and common lodging-houses.

The inspection is often detailed and rigidly enforced. The State in most of the larger industrial operations prescribes the age of the worker, the hours of work, the amount of air, light, cubic space, heat, lavatory accommodation, holidays, and mealtimes; where, when, and how wages shall be paid; how machinery staircases, lift holes, mines, and quarries are to be fenced and guarded; how and when the plant shall be cleaned, repaired, and worked. Even the kind of package in which some articles shall be sold is duly pre-scribed, so that the individual capitalist shall take no advantage of his posi-tion. On every side he is being registered, inspected, controlled, and even-tually superseded by the community; and in the meantime he is compelled to cede for public purposes an ever-increasing share of his rent and interest.

Even in the fields still abandoned to private enterprise, its operations are thus every day more closely limited, in order that the anarchic competition of private greed, which at the beginning of the century was set up as the only infallibly beneficent principle of social action, may not utterly destroy the State. All this has been done by "practical" men, ignorant, that is to say, of any scientific sociology believing Socialism to be the most foolish of dreams, and absolutely ignoring, as they thought, all grandiloquent claims for social reconstruction. Such is the irresistible sweep of social tendencies, that in their every act they worked to bring about the very Socialism they despised; and to destroy the Individualist faith which they still professed. They builded better than they knew.

It must by no means be supposed that these beginnings of social reorganiza-tion have been effected, or the proposals for their extension brought to the front, without the conscious efforts of individual reformers. The "Zeitgeist" is potent; but it does not pass Acts of Parliament without legislators, or erect municipal libraries without town councillors. Though our decisions are moulded by the circumstances of the time, and the environment at least roughhews our ends, shape them as we will; yet each generation decides for itself. It still rests with the individual to resist or promote the social evolu-tion, consciously or unconsciously, according to his character and informa-tion. The importance of complete consciousness of the social tendencies of the age lies in the fact that its existence and comprehensiveness often deter-mine the expediency of our particular action: we move with less resistance with the stream than against it.

The general failure to realize the extent to which our unconscious Social-ism has already proceeded—a failure which causes much time and labor to

be wasted in uttering and elaborating on paper the most ludicrously unpractical anti-socialist demonstrations of the impossibility of matters of daily
occurrence—is due to the fact that few know anything of local administration outside their own town. It is the municipalities which have done most
to "socialize" our industrial life; and the municipal history of the century
is yet unwritten. . . .

Nor is there any apparent prospect of a slackening of the pace of this unconscious abandonment of individualism. No member of Parliament has so
much as introduced a Bill to give effect to the anarchist principles of Mr.
Herbert Spencer's "Man *versus* the State." The not disinterested efforts of
the Liberty and Property Defence League fail to hinder even Conservative
Parliaments from further Socialist legislation. Mr. Gladstone remarked to
a friend in 1886 that the Home Rule question would turn the Liberal party
into a Radical party. He might have said that it would make both parties
Socialist. Free elementary and public technical education is now practically
accepted on both sides of the House, provided that the so-called "voluntary
schools," themselves half maintained from public funds, are not extinguished.
Mr. Chamberlain and the younger Conservatives openly advocate far reaching projects of social reform through State and municipal agency, as a means
of obtaining popular support. The National Liberal Federation adopts the
special taxation of urban ground values as the main feature in its domestic
programme, notwithstanding that this proposal is characterized by old-
fashioned Liberals as sheer confiscation of so much of the landlords' property. The London Liberal and Radical Union, which has Mr. John Morley
for its president, even proposes that the County Council shall have power to
rebuild the London slums at the sole charge of the ground landlord. It is,
therefore, not surprising that the Trades Union Congress should now twice
have declared in favor of "Land Nationalization" by large majorities, or
that the bulk of the London County Council should be returned on an essentially Socialist platform. The whole of the immediately practicable demands of the most exacting Socialist are, indeed, now often embodied in the
current Radical programme; and the following exposition of it, from the
pages of the *Star* newspaper, 8th August, 1888, may serve as a statement of
the current Socialist demands for further legislation.

REVISION OF TAXATION

Object.—Complete shifting of burden from the workers, of whatever grade,
to the recipients of rent and interest, with a view to the ultimate and gradual
extinction of the latter class.

Means.—1. Abolition of all customs and excise duties, except those on spirits. 2. Increase of income tax, differentiating in favor of earned as against unearned incomes, and graduating cumulatively by system of successive levels of abatement. 3. Equalization and increase of death duties and the use of the proceeds as capital, not income. 4. Shifting of local rates and house duty from occupier to owner, any contract to the contrary notwithstanding. 5. Compulsory redemption of existing land tax and reimposition on all ground rents and increased values. 6. Abolition of fees on licenses for employment. 7. Abolition of police-court fees.

EXTENSION OF FACTORY ACTS

Object.—To raise, universally, the standard of comfort by obtaining the general recognition of a minimum wage and a maximum working day.

Means.—1. Extension of the general provisions of the Factory and Workshops Acts (or the Mines Regulation Acts, as the case may be) to all employers of labor. 2. Compulsory registration of all employers of more than three (?) workers. 3. Largely increased number of inspectors, and these to include women, and to be mainly chosen from the wage-earning class. 4. Immediate reduction of maximum hours to eight per day in all Government and municipal employment, in all mines, and in all licensed monopolies, such as railways, tramways, gasworks, waterworks, docks, harbors, etc.; and in any trade in which a majority of the workers desire it. 5. The compulsory insertion of clauses in all contracts for Government or municipal supplies, providing that (a) there shall be no sub-contracting, (b) that no worker shall be employed more than eight hours per day, and (c) that no wages less than a prescribed minimum shall be paid.

EDUCATIONAL REFORM

Object—To enable, all, even the poorest, children to obtain not merely some, but the best education they are capable of.

Means—1. The immediate abolition of all fees in public elementary schools, Board or voluntary, with a corresponding increase in the Government grant. 2. Creation of a Minister for Education, with control over the whole educational system, from the elementary school to the University, and over all educational endowments. 3. Provision of public technical and secondary schools wherever needed, and creation of abundant public secondary scholarships. 4. Continuation, in all cases, of elementary education at evening schools. 5. Registration and inspection of all private educational establishments.

RE-ORGANIZATION OF POOR LAW ADMINISTRATION

Object—To provide generously, and without stigma, for the aged, the sick, and those destitute through temporary want of employment, without relaxing the "tests" against the endowment of able-bodied idleness.

Means—1. The separation of the relief of the aged and the sick from the workhouse system, by a universal system of aged pensions, and public infirmaries. 2. The industrial organization and technical education of all able-bodied paupers. 3. The provision of temporary relief works for the unemployed. 4. The supersession of the Board of Guardians by the local municipal authorities.

EXTENSION OF MUNICIPAL ACTIVITY

Object—The gradual public organization of labor for all public purposes, and the elimination of the private capitalist and middleman.

Means—1. The provision of increased facilities for the acquisition of land, the destruction without compensation of all dwellings found unfit for habitation, and the provision of artisan dwellings by the municipality. 2. The facilitation of every extension of municipal administration, in London and all other towns, of gas, water, markets, tramways, hospitals, cemeteries, parks, museums, art galleries, libraries, reading-rooms, schools, docks, harbors, rivers, etc. 3. The provision of abundant facilities for the acquisition of land by local rural authorities, for allotments, common pastures, public halls, reading rooms, etc.

AMENDMENT OF POLITICAL MACHINERY

Object—To obtain the most accurate representation and expression of the desires of the majority of the people at every moment.

Means—1. Reform of registration so as to give a vote, both Parliamentary and municipal, to every adult. 2. Abolition of any period of residence as a qualification for registration. 3. Bi-annual registration by special public officer. 4. Annual Parliaments. 5. Payment of election expenses, including postage of election addresses and polling cards. 6. Payment of all public representatives, parliamentary, county, or municipal. 7. Second ballot. 8. Abolition or painless extinction of the House of Lords.

This is the programme to which a century of industrial revolution has brought the Radical working man. Like John Stuart Mill, though less explicitly, he has turned from mere political Democracy to a complete, though unconscious, Socialism.

EDUARD BERNSTEIN

AFTER the repeal of the antisocialist law in 1890 the German Social-Democratic party emerged into the open and took an active part in government. In addition, economic prosperity was breaking down fixed class barriers and making it possible for many individual workers to rise to new stations, thus apparently refuting, or at least blurring the edges of, the Marxist prophecy. The task of closing the gap between the revolutionary formulas embodied in the *Communist Manifesto* and the new situation of social fluidity of classes and active class collaboration was taken up by the formulation of "revisionist" socialism by Eduard Bernstein (1850–1932).

The main burden of Bernstein's argument rests upon his criticism of Marx's analysis of the historical tendency of capitalist accumulation, a theory which Bernstein believed could continue to be supported in his own day only on the basis of falsification of the facts. In place of this theory that "progress depends on the deterioration of social conditions," Bernstein offered the notion that the prospects of working-class amelioration depended upon "the growth of social wealth and of the social productive forces, in conjunction with general social progress, and, particularly, in conjunction with the intellectual and moral advance of the working classes themselves."

Such an interpretation meant for Bernstein a reformulation of socialist tactics and policies. He rejected the tactics of unremitting class conflict and suggested that it be replaced by a policy of collaboration with all "progressive" forces, whether or not such forces were rooted in the proletariat. His "evolutionary" or "gradualist" version of socialism deviated from the orthodox Marxist dependence on the ability of a revolutionized state to take over large-scale industry; Bernstein put his trust rather in the gradual movement towards a cooperative scheme of production. While he does not reject a theoretical allegiance to the ultimate aim of socialism, he emphasized that it need hardly be an ever-present factor in the day-to-day experience of socialist practice, and that, indeed, such an inflexible principle (the inheritance from the Utopian elements in Marx) may become dangerous when it leads to the neglect of or contempt for the facts.

Bernstein's program was rejected by the majority of the German Social-Democratic party, led by Karl Kautsky. Bernstein was one of the leaders of the minority of the Social Democrats who early in 1916 refused to approve further military expenditure. In the last analysis, the struggle in German socialism did not stem from the disagreements of Kautsky and Bernstein, but from the division of opinion between the Social Democrats who supported the war, the "Independent Socialists," who opposed it, and the "Spartacists," led by Karl Liebknecht and Rosa Luxemburg, who advocated the Leninist policy of turning the imperialist war into a civil war.

The following selection is from a letter Bernstein wrote to the Stuttgart Congress of the Social-Democratic party in 1898. It was reprinted in the preface to *Evolu-*

tionary Socialism (New York, 1911), a translation by Edith C. Harvey of *Die Voraussetzungen des Sozialismus und die Aufgaben der Sozialdemokratie* [1] (1899).

❧

EVOLUTIONARY SOCIALISM

. . . IT HAS been maintained in a certain quarter that the practical deductions from my treatises would be the abandonment of the conquest of political power by the proletariat organized politically and economically. That is quite an arbitrary deduction, the accuracy of which I altogether deny.

I set myself against the notion that we have to expect shortly a collapse of the bourgeois economy, and that social democracy should be induced by the prospect of such an imminent, great, social catastrophe to adapt its tactics to that assumption. That I maintain most emphatically.

The adherents of this theory of a catastrophe base it especially on the conclusions of the *Communist Manifesto*. This is a mistake in every respect.

The theory which the *Communist Manifesto* sets forth of the evolution of modern society was correct as far as it characterized the general tendencies of that evolution. But it was mistaken in several special deductions, above all in the estimate of the *time* the evolution would take. The last has been unreservedly acknowledged by Friedrich Engels, the joint author with Marx of the *Manifesto,* in his preface to the *Class War in France*. But it is evident that if social evolution takes a much greater period of time than was assumed, it must also take upon itself *forms* and lead to forms that were not foreseen and could not be foreseen then.

Social conditions have not developed to such an acute opposition of things and classes as is depicted in the *Manifesto*. It is not only useless, it is the greatest folly to attempt to conceal this from ourselves. The number of members of the possessing classes is to-day not smaller but larger. The enormous increase of social wealth is not accompanied by a decreasing number of large capitalists but by an increasing number of capitalists of all degrees. The middle classes change their character but they do not disappear from the social scale.

The concentration in productive industry is not being accomplished even to-day in all its departments with equal thoroughness and at an equal rate. In a great many branches of production it certainly justifies the forecasts of the socialist critic of society; but in other branches it lags even to-day behind them. The process of concentration in agriculture proceeds still more slowly. Trade statistics show an extraordinarily elaborated graduation of enterprises

[1] *The Assumptions of Socialism and the Tasks of Social Democracy.*

in regard to size. No rung of the ladder is disappearing from it. The significant changes in the inner structure of these enterprises and their interrelationship cannot do away with this fact.

In all advanced countries we see the privileges of the capitalist bourgeoisie yielding step by step to democratic organizations. Under the influence of this, and driven by the movement of the working classes which is daily becoming stronger, a social reaction has set in against the exploiting tendencies of capital, a counteraction which, although it still proceeds timidly and feebly, yet does exist, and is always drawing more departments of economic life under its influence. Factory legislation, the democratization of local government, and the extension of its area of work, the freeing of trade unions and systems of cooperative trade from legal restrictions, the consideration of standard conditions of labour in the work undertaken by public authorities—all these characterize this phase of the evolution.

But the more the political organizations of the modern nations are democratized the more the needs and opportunities of great political catastrophes are diminished. He who holds firmly to the catastrophic theory of evolution must, with all his power, withstand and hinder the evolution described above, which, indeed, the logical defenders of that theory formerly did. But is the conquest of political power by the proletariat simply to be by a political catastrophe? Is it to be the appropriation and utilization of the power of the State by the proletariat exclusively against the whole nonproletarian world?

He who replies in the affirmative must be reminded of two things. In 1872 Marx and Engels announced in the preface to the new edition of the *Communist Manifesto* that the Paris Commune had exhibited a proof that "the working classes cannot simply take possession of the ready-made State machine and set it in motion for their own aims." And in 1895 Friedrich Engels stated in detail in the preface to *War of the Classes* that the time of political surprises, of the "revolutions of small conscious minorities at the head of unconscious masses" was to-day at an end, that a collision on a large scale with the military would be the means of checking the steady growth of social democracy and of even throwing it back for a time—in short, that social democracy would flourish far better by lawful than by unlawful means and by violent revolution. And he points out in conformity with this opinion that the next task of the party should be "to work for an uninterrupted increase of its vote" or to carry on a slow *propaganda of parliamentary activity*.

Thus Engels, who, nevertheless, as his numerical examples show, still somewhat overestimated the rate of process of the evolution! Shall we be told that he abandoned the conquest of political power by the working classes, because he wished to avoid the steady growth of social democracy secured by lawful means being interrupted by a political revolution?

If not, and if one subscribes to his conclusions, one cannot reasonably take any offense if it is declared that for a long time yet the task of social democracy is, instead of speculating on a great economic crash, "to organize the working classes politically and develop them as a democracy and to fight for all reforms in the State which are adapted to raise the working classes and transform the state in the direction of democracy."

That is what I have said in my impugned article and what I still maintain in its full import. As far as concerns the question propounded above it is equivalent to Engel's dictum, for democracy is, at any given time, as much government by the working classes as these are capable of practising according to their intellectual ripeness and the degree of social development they have attained. Engels, indeed, refers at the place just mentioned to the fact that the *Communist Manifesto* has "proclaimed the conquest of the democracy as one of the first and important tasks of the fighting proletariat."

In short, Engels is so thoroughly convinced that the tactics based on the presumption of a catastrophe have had their day, that he even considers a revision of them necessary in the Latin countries where tradition is much more favourable to them than in Germany. "If the conditions of war between nations have altered," he writes, "no less have those for the war between classes." Has this already been forgotten?

No one has questioned the necessity for the working classes to gain the control of government. The point at issue is between the theory of social cataclysm and the question whether with the given social development in Germany and the present advanced state of its working classes in the towns and the country, a sudden catastrophe would be desirable in the interest of the social democracy. I have denied it and deny it again, because in my judgment a greater security for lasting success lies in a steady advance than in the possibilities offered by a catastrophic crash.

And as I am firmly convinced that important periods in the development of nations cannot be leapt over I lay the greatest value on the next tasks of social democracy, on the struggle for the political rights of the working man, on the political activity of working men in town and country for the interests of their class, as well as on the work of the industrial organization of the workers.

In this sense I wrote the sentence that the movement means everything for me and that what is *usually* called "the final aim of socialism" is nothing; and in this sense I write it down again to-day. Even if the word "usually" had not shown that the proposition was only to be understood conditionally, it was obvious that it *could* not express indifference concerning the final carrying out of socialist principles, but only indifference—or, as it would be better expressed, carelessness—as to the form of the final arrangement of things. I have at no time had an excessive interest in the future, beyond general principles; I have not been able to read to the end of any picture of the future. My thought and efforts are concerned with the duties of the present and the nearest future, and I only busy myself with the perspectives beyond so far as they give me a line of conduct for suitable action now.

The conquest of political power by the working classes, the expropriation of capitalists, are no ends in themselves but only means for the accomplishment of certain aims and endeavours. As such they are demands in the programme of social democracy and are not attacked by me. Nothing can be said beforehand as to the circumstances of their accomplishments; we can only fight for their realization. But the conquest of political power necessitates the possession of political *rights;* and the most important problem of tactics which German social democracy has at the present time to solve, appears to me to be to devise the best ways for the extension of the political and economic rights of the German working classes. . . .

VLADIMIR ILICH LENIN

VLADIMIR ILICH ULYANOV (1870–1924), was born in Simbirsk, Russia, the son of an inspector of schools. When Vladimir was seven, his eldest brother was hanged for his part in an abortive conspiracy against Alexander III. Vladimir was educated at the universities of Kazan and St. Petersburg and received a law degree from the latter institution. Although called to the bar in St. Petersburg, he practiced for only a short while, resolving at the age of twenty-three to devote his whole life to revolutionary activity.

In 1895 Lenin (the revolutionary pseudonym adopted by Ulyanov) was imprisoned and exiled to Siberia until 1900 for his involvement in radical movements. It was during this period that he acquired his extraordinary knowledge of Marxist theory, and in 1899 he published the *Development of Capitalism in Russia*. In 1900 he was sent abroad by the Russian Social Democratic Party for propaganda and organizational activity and—except for a brief period in 1905—he did not return to Russia until 1917, when he organized the successful *coup d'état* against the democratic Kerensky regime.

In Lenin there emerges Communism's characteristic emphasis upon the decisive role of a centralized party with a tightly knit ideology. In the pamphlet *What Is to Be Done?* (1902) Lenin distinguished between ordinary trade-union psychology, produced in the everyday struggle of workers for immediate reforms, and socialist ideology. In Lenin's view, without the Communist Party the proletarian revolution against imperialist monopoly capitalism is unthinkable. This idea constituted a significant addition to Marxism, for Marx had never regarded the spread of socialist ideology as uniquely dependent on a political party, but had regarded it as a natural articulation of the experience of workers in the class struggle. The role of the Communist Party, "the vanguard of the proletariat," is thus to take advantage of the inherent breakdown of capitalism by the creation and direction under its own control of a revolutionary sentiment, through the propagation to all classes of the ideology of revolt.

At the London Conference of the Russian Social Democratic Party in 1903, Lenin won over a temporary majority to his view, but was almost immediately defeated by the advocates of mass party action through the legal and parliamentary framework. At that point Lenin became the acknowledged leader of the left-wing revolutionaries, the Bolsheviks. The failure of the Revolution of 1905 in Russia confirmed Lenin in his commitment to disciplined and coordinated revolutionary activity, and he continued his organizational and propaganda work as a political exile.

The following selections are from *What Is to Be Done?* (New York: International Publishers, 1929).

WHAT IS TO BE DONE?

. . . The case of the Russian Social-Democrats strikingly illustrates the fact observed in the whole of Europe (and long ago observed in German Marxism) that the notorious freedom of criticism implies, not the substitution of one theory by another, but freedom from every complete and thought-out theory; it implies eclecticism and absence of principle. Those who are in the least acquainted with the actual state of our movement cannot but see that the spread of Marxism was accompanied by a certain deterioration of theoretical standards. Quite a number of people, with very little, and even totally lacking in, theoretical training, joined the movement for the sake of its practical significance and its practical successes. We can judge, therefore, how tactless *Rabocheye Dyelo* is when, with an air of invincibility, it quotes the statement of Marx that: "A single step of the real movement is worth a dozen programmes." To repeat these words in the epoch of theoretical chaos is sheer mockery. Moreover, these words of Marx are taken from his letter on the Gotha Programme, in which he *sharply condemns* eclecticism in the formulation of principles: "If you must combine," Marx wrote to the party leaders, "then enter into agreements to satisfy the practical aims of the movement, but do not haggle over principles, do not make 'concessions' in theory." This was Marx's idea, and yet there are people among us who strive—in his name! —to belittle the significance of theory.

Without a revolutionary theory there can be no revolutionary movement. This cannot be insisted upon too strongly at a time when the fashionable preaching of opportunism is combined with absorption in the narrowest forms of practical activity. . . .

We shall quote what Engels said in 1874 concerning the significance of theory in the Social-Democratic movement. Engels recognizes *not two* forms of the great struggle Social-Democracy is conducting (political and economic), as is the fashion among us, *but three, adding to the first two also the theoretical struggle.* His recommendations to the German labour movement, which has now become practically and politically strong, are so instructive from the point of view of present-day controversies, that we hope the reader will forgive us for quoting a long passage from his Introduction to the *Peasant War in Germany,* which long ago became a literary rarity.

The German workers have two important advantages compared with the rest of Europe. First, they belong to the most theoretical people of Europe; second, they have retained that sense of theory which the so-called "educated" people of

Germany have totally lost. Without German philosophy, particularly that of Hegel, German scientific Socialism (the only scientific Socialism extant) would never have come into existence. Without a sense for theory, scientific Socialism would have never become blood and tissue of the workers. What an enormous advantage this is, may be seen on the one hand, from the indifference of the English labour movement towards all theory, which is one of the reasons why it moves so slowly, in spite of the splendid organisation of the individual unions; on the other hand, from the mischief and confusion created by Proudhonism in its original form among the Frenchmen and Belgians, and in its caricature form as presented by Bakunin, among the Spaniards and Italians.

The second advantage is that, chronologically speaking, the Germans were the last to appear in the labour movement. In the same manner as German theoretical Socialism will never forget that it rests on the shoulders of Saint Simon, Fourier and Owen, the three who, in spite of their fantastic notions and Utopianism, belonged to the most significant heads of all time, and whose genius anticipated the correctness of what can now be proved in a scientific way, so the practical German labour movement must never forget that it has developed on the shoulders of the English and French movements, that it had utilised their experience, acquired at a heavy price, and that for this reason it was in a position to avoid their mistakes which in their time were unavoidable. Without the English trade unions and the French political workers' struggles preceding the German labour movement, without the mighty impulse given by the Paris Commune, where would we now be?

It must be said to the credit of the German workers that they utilised the advantages of their situation with rare understanding. For the first time in the history of the labour movement, the struggle is being so conducted that its three sides, the theoretical, the political, and the practical economic (resistance to the capitalists), form one harmonious and well-planned entity. In this concentric attack, as it were, lies the strength and invincibility of the German movement.

It is due to this advantageous situation on the one hand, to the insular peculiarities of the British, and to the cruel oppression of the French movements on the other, that for the present moment the German workers form the vanguard of the proletarian struggle. How long events will allow them to occupy this post of honour cannot be foreseen. But as long as they are placed in it, let us hope that they will discharge their duties in the proper manner. To this end it will be necessary to double our energies in all the spheres of struggle and agitation. It is the specified duty of the leaders to gain an ever-clearer understanding of the theoretical problems, to free themselves more and more from the influence of traditional phrases inherited from the old conception of the world, and constantly to keep in mind that Socialism, having become a science, demands the same treatment as every other science—it must be studied. The task of the leaders will be to bring understanding, thus acquired and clarified, to the working masses, to spread it with increased enthusiasm, to close the ranks of the party organisations and of the labour unions with ever-greater energy. . . .

If the German workers proceed in this way they may not march exactly at the head of the movement—it is not in the interest of the movement that the workers of one country should march at the head of all—but they will occupy an honourable place on the battle line, and they will stand armed for battle when other unexpected grave trials or momentous events will demand heightened courage, heightened determination, and the will to act.

Engels' words proved prophetic. Within a few years, the German workers were subjected to severe trials in the form of the anti-Socialist laws; but they were fully armed to meet the situation, and succeeded in emerging from it victoriously.

The Russian workers will have to undergo trials immeasurably more severe; they will have to take up the fight against a monster, compared with which anti-Socialist laws in a constitutional country are but pigmies. History has now confronted us with an immediate task which is *more revolutionary than all the immediate tasks* that confront the proletariat of any other country. The fulfilment of this task, the destruction of the most powerful bulwark, not only of European, but also (it may now be said) of Asiatic reaction, places the Russian proletariat in the vanguard of the international revolutionary proletariat. We shall have the right to count upon acquiring the honourable title already earned by our predecessors, the revolutionists of the seventies, if we succeed in inspiring our movement—which is a thousand times wider and deeper—with the same devoted determination and vigor. . . .

We said that *there could not yet be* Social-Democratic consciousness among the workers. This consciousness could only be brought to them from without. The history of all countries shows that the working class, exclusively by its own effort, is able to develop only trade-union consciousness, *i.e.,* it may itself realise the necessity for combining in unions, to fight against the employers and to strive to compel the government to pass necessary labour legislation, etc.

The theory of Socialism, however, grew out of the philosophic, historical and economic theories that were elaborated by the educated representatives of the propertied classes, the intellectuals. The founders of modern scientific Socialism, Marx and Engels, themselves belonged to the bourgeois intelligentsia. Similarly in Russia, the theoretical doctrine of Social-Democracy arose quite independently of the spontaneous growth of the labour movement; it arose as a natural and inevitable outcome of the development of ideas among the revolutionary Socialist intelligentsia. At the time of which we are speaking, *i.e.,* the middle of the nineties, this doctrine not only represented the completely formulated programme of the Emancipation of Labour group but had already won the adhesion of the majority of the revolutionary youth in Russia. . . .

. . . Subservience to the spontaneity of the labour movement, the belittling of the rôle of "the conscious element," of the rôle of Social-Democracy, *means, whether one likes it or not, growth of influence of bourgeois ideology among the workers.* All those who talk about "exaggerating the importance of ideology," about exaggerating the rôle of the conscious elements, etc., imagine that the pure and simple labour movement can work out an independent ideology for itself, if only the workers "take their fate out of the hands of the leaders." But in this they are profoundly mistaken. To supplement what has been said above, we shall quote the following profoundly true and important utterances by Karl Kautsky on the new programme of the Austrian Social-Democratic Party:

Many of our revisionist critics believe that Marx asserted that economic development and the class struggle create, not only the conditions for Socialist production, but also, and directly, the *consciousness* (K.K.'s italics) of its necessity. And these critics advance the argument that the most highly capitalistically developed country, England, is more remote than any other from this consciousness. Judging from the draft, one must come to the conclusion that the committee which drafted the Austrian Programme shared this alleged orthodox-Marxian view which is thus refuted. In the draft programme it is stated: "The more capitalist development increases the numbers of the proletariat, the more the proletariat is compelled, and obtains the opportunity to fight against capitalism." The proletariat becomes "conscious" of the possibility and necessity for Socialism. In this connection Socialist consciousness is represented as a necessary and direct result of the proletarian class struggle. But this is absolutely untrue. Of course, Socialism, as a theory, has its roots in a modern economic relationship in the same way as the class struggle of the proletariat has, and in the same way as the latter emerges from the struggle against the capitalist-created poverty and misery of the masses. But Socialism and the class struggle arise side by side and not one out of the other; each arises out of different premises. Modern Socialist consciousness can arise only on the basis of profound scientific knowledge. Indeed, modern economic science is as much a condition for Socialist production, as say, modern technology, and the proletariat can create neither the one nor the other, no matter how much it may desire to do so; both arise out of the modern social process. The vehicles of science are not the proletariat, but the *bourgeois intelligentsia* (K.K.'s italics): It was out of the heads of members of this stratum that modern Socialism originated, and it was they who communicated it to the more intellectually developed proletarians who, in their turn, introduced it into the proletarian class struggle where conditions allow that to be done. Thus, Socialist consciousness is something introduced into the proletarian class struggle from without (*von Aussen Hineingetragenes*), and not something that arose within it spontaneously (*urwüchsig*). Accordingly, the old Hainfeld programme quite rightly stated that the task of Social-Democracy is to imbue the proletariat with the *consciousness* of its position and the consciousness of its tasks. There would be no need for this if consciousness emerged from the class struggle. The new draft copied this postulate from the old programme, and attached it to the postulate mentioned above. But this completely broke the line of thought. . . .

Since there can be no talk of an independent ideology being developed by the masses of the workers in the process of their movement then *the only choice is:* Either bourgeois, or Socialist ideology. There is no middle course (for humanity has not created a "third" ideology, and, moreover, in a society torn by class antagonisms there can never be a non-class or above-class ideology). Hence, to belittle Socialist ideology *in any way,* to *deviate from it in the slightest degree* means strengthening bourgeois ideology. There is a lot of talk about spontaneity, but the *spontaneous* development of the labour movement leads to its becoming subordinated to bourgeois ideology . . . for the spontaneous labour movement is pure and simple trade unionism, is *Nur-Gewerkschaftlerei,* and trade unionism means the ideological subordination of the workers to the bourgeoisie. Hence, our task, the task of Social-Democracy, is to *combat spontaneity,* to *divert* the labour movement, with its spontaneous trade-unionist striving, from under the wing of the bourgeoisie, and bring it under the wing of revolutionary Social-Democracy. . . .

It is only natural that a Social-Democrat who conceives the political struggle as being identical with the "economic struggle against the employers and the government," should conceive "organisation of revolutionists" as being more or less identical with "organisation of workers." And this, in fact, is what actually happens; so that when we talk about organisation, we literally talk in different tongues. I recall a conversation I once had with a fairly consistent Economist, with whom I had not been previously acquainted. We were discussing the brochure *Who Will Make the Political Revolution?* and we were very soon agreed that the principal defect in that brochure was that it ignored the question of organisation. We were beginning to think that we were in complete agreement with each other—but as the conversation proceeded, it became clear that we were talking of different things. My interlocutor accused the author of the brochure just mentioned of ignoring strike funds, mutual-aid societies, etc.; whereas I had in mind an organisation of revolutionists, as an essential factor in "making" the political revolution. After that became clear, I hardly remember a single question of importance upon which I was in agreement with that Economist!

What was the source of our disagreement? It is the fact that on questions of organisation and politics the Economists are forever lapsing from Social-Democracy into trade unionism. The political struggle carried on by the Social-Democrats is far more extensive and complex than the economic struggle the workers carry on against the employers and the government. Similarly (and indeed for that reason), the organisation of revolutionary Social-Democrats must inevitably *differ* from the organisations of the workers designed for the latter struggle. The workers' organisations must in the first place be trade organisations; secondly, they must be as wide as possible; and thirdly, they must be as public as conditions will allow (here, of course, I have only autocratic Russia in mind). On the other hand, the organisations of revolutionists must be comprised first and foremost of people whose profession is that of revolutionists (that is why I speak of organisations of *revolutionists,* meaning revolutionary Social-Democrats). As this is the common feature of the members of such an organisation, *all distinctions as between workers and intellectuals,* and certainly distinctions of trade and profession, must be dropped. Such an organisation must of necessity be not too extensive and as secret as possible. Let us examine this three-fold distinction.

In countries where political liberty exists the distinction between a labour union and a political organisation is clear, as is the distinction between trade unions and Social-Democracy. . . . In Russia, however, the yoke of autocracy appears at first glance to obliterate all distinctions between a Social-Democratic organisation and trade unions, because *all* trade unions and *all* circles are prohibited, and because the principal manifestation and weapon of the workers' economic struggle—the strike—is regarded as a crime (and sometimes even as a political crime!). Conditions in our country, therefore, strongly "impel" the workers who are conducting the economic struggle to concern themselves with political questions. . . .

"A committee of students is no good, it is not stable." Quite true. But the conclusion that should be drawn from this is that we must have a committee of professional *revolutionists* and it does not matter whether a student or a worker is capable of qualifying himself as a professional revolutionist. The conclusion you draw, however, is that the working-class movement must not be pushed on from outside! In your political innocence you fail to observe that you are playing into the hands of our Economists and furthering our primitiveness. I would like to ask, what is meant by the students "pushing on" the workers? *All* it means is that the students bring to the worker the fragments of political knowledge they possess, the crumbs of Socialist ideas they have managed to acquire (for the principal intellectual diet of the present-day student, legal Marxism, can furnish only the A.B.C., only the crumbs of knowledge). *Such* "pushing on from outside" can never be too excessive; on the contrary, so far there has been too little, all too little of it in our movement; we have been stewing in our own juice far too long; we have bowed far too slavishly before the spontaneous "economic struggle of the workers against the employers and the government." We professional revolutionists must continue, and will continue, *this kind* of "pushing," and a hundred times more forcibly than we have done hitherto. . . .

As I have already said, by "wise men," in connection with organisation, I mean *professional revolutionists,* irrespective of whether they are students or working men. I assert: 1. That no movement can be durable without a stable organisation of leaders to maintain continuity; 2. that the more widely the masses are drawn into the struggle and form the basis of the movement, the more necessary is it to have such an organisation and the more stable must it be (for it is much easier then for demagogues to side-track the more backward sections of the masses); 3. that the organisation must consist chiefly of persons engaged in revolution as a profession; 4. that in a country with a despotic government, the more we *restrict* the membership of this organisation to persons who are engaged in revolution as a profession and who have been professionally trained in the art of combating the political police, the more difficult will it be to catch the organisation; and 5. the *wider* will be the circle of men and women of the working class or of other classes of society able to join the movement and perform active work in it. . . .

But to concentrate all secret functions in the hands of as small a number of professional revolutionists as possible, does not mean that the latter will "do the thinking for all" and that the crowd will not take an active part in the movement. On the contrary, the crowd will advance from its ranks increasing numbers of professional revolutionists, for it will know that it is not enough for a few students and workingmen waging economic war to gather together and form a "committee," but that professional revolutionists must be trained for years. . . .

. . . A "dozen" experienced revolutionists, no less professionally trained than the police, will concentrate all the secret side of the work in their hands —prepare leaflets, work out approximate plans and appoint bodies of leaders for each town district, for each factory district, and for each educational institution (I know that exception will be taken to my "undemocratic" views, but I shall reply to this altogether unintelligent objection later on). The centralisation of the more secret functions in an organisation of revolutionists will not diminish, but rather increase the extent and the quality of the activity of a large number of other organisations intended for wide membership and which, therefore, can be as loose and as public as possible, for example, trade unions, workers' circles for self-education, and the reading of illegal literature, and Socialist, and also democratic, circles for *all other sections of the population,* etc., etc. . . .

The most grievous sin we have committed in regard to organisation is that *by our primitiveness we have lowered the prestige of revolutionists in Russia.* A man who is weak and vacillating on theoretical questions, who has a narrow outlook, who makes excuses for his own slackness on the ground that the masses are awakening spontaneously, who resembles a trade-union secretary more than a people's tribune, who is unable to conceive a broad and bold plan, who is incapable of inspiring even his enemies with respect for himself, and who is inexperienced and clumsy in his own professional art—the art of combating the political police—such a man is not a revolutionist but a hopeless amateur!

Let no active worker take offense at these frank remarks, for as far as insufficient training is concerned, I apply them first and foremost to myself. I used to work in a circle that set itself a great and all-embracing task: and every member of that circle suffered to the point of torture from the realisation that we were proving ourselves to be amateurs at a moment in history when we might have been able to say—paraphrasing a well-known epigram: "Give us an organisation of revolutionists, and we shall over-turn the whole of Russia!" And the more I recall the burning sense of shame I then experienced, the more bitter are my feelings towards those pseudo-Social-Democrats whose teachings bring disgrace on the calling of a revolutionist, who fail to understand that our task is not to degrade the revolutionist to the level of an amateur, but to exalt the amateur to the level of a revolutionist. . . .

. . . The *form* a strong revolutionary organisation . . . may take in an autocratic country may be described as a "conspirative" organisation, because the French word *"conspiration"* means in Russian *"conspiracy,"* and we must have the utmost conspiracy for an organisation like that. Secrecy is such a necessary condition for such an organisation that all the other conditions (number and selection of members, functions, etc.) must all be subordinated to it. . . .

It is further argued against us that the views on organisation here expounded contradict the "principles of democracy." Now while the first mentioned accusation was of purely Russian origin, this one is of *purely foreign* origin. And only an organisation abroad (the League of Russian Social-Democrats) would be capable of giving its editorial board instructions like the following:

Principles of Organisation. In order to secure the successful development and unification of Social-Democracy, broad democratic principles of party organisation must be emphasised, developed and fought for; and this is particularly necessary in view of the anti-democratic tendencies that have become revealed in the ranks of our party. (*Two Congresses,* p. 18.)

We shall see how *Rabocheye Dyelo* fights against *Iskra's* "anti-democratic tendencies" in the next chapter. Here we shall examine more closely the "principle" that the Economists advance. Every one will probably agree that "broad principles of democracy" presupposes the two following conditions:

first, full publicity and second, election to all functions. It would be absurd to speak about democracy without publicity, that is a publicity that extends beyond the circle of the membership of the organisation. We call the German Socialist Party a democratic organisation because all it does is done publicly; even its party congresses are held in public. But no one would call an organisation that is hidden from every one but its members by a veil of secrecy, a democratic organisation. What is the use of advancing *"broad* principles of democracy" when the fundamental condition for this principle *cannot be fulfilled* by a secret organisation. "Broad principles" turns out to be a resonant, but hollow phrase. More than that, this phrase proves that the urgent tasks in regard to organisation are totally misunderstood. Every one knows how great is the lack of secrecy among the "broad" masses of revolutionists. We have heard the bitter complaints of B—v on this score, and his absolutely just demand for a "strict selection of members." And yet people who boast about their "sensitiveness to life" come forward in a situation like this and *urge* that strict secrecy and a strict (and therefore more restricted) selection of members is unnecessary, and that what is necessary are—*"broad* principles of democracy"! This is what we call being absolutely wide of the mark.

Nor is the situation with regard to the second attribute of democracy, namely, the principle of election, any better. In politically free countries, this condition is taken for granted. "Membership of the party is open to those who accept the principles of the party programme, and render all the support they can to the party"—says paragraph 1 of the rules of the German Social-Democratic Party. And as the political arena is as open to the public view as is the stage in a theatre, this acceptance or non-acceptance, support or opposition is announced to all in the press and at public meetings. Every one knows that a certain political worker commenced in a certain way, passed through a certain evolution, behaved in difficult periods in a certain way; every one knows all his qualities, and consequently, knowing all the facts of the case, *every party member can decide for himself whether or not to elect this person for a certain party office.* The general control (in the literal sense of the term) that the party exercises over every act this person commits on the political field brings into being an automatically operating mechanism which brings about what in biology is called "survival of the fittest." "Natural selection," full publicity, the principle of election and general control provide the guarantee that, in the last analysis, every political worker will be "in his proper place," will do the work for which he is best fitted, will feel the effects of his mistakes on himself, and prove before all the world his ability to recognise mistakes and to avoid them.

Try to put this picture in the frame of our autocracy! Is it possible in Russia for all those "who accept the principles of the party programme and render it all the support they can," to control every action of the revolutionist working in secret? Is it possible for all the revolutionists to elect one of their number to any particular office when, in the very interests of the work, he *must conceal his identity* from nine out of ten of these "all"? Ponder a little over the real meaning of the high-sounding phrases that *Rabocheye Dyelo* gives utterance to, and you will realise that "broad democracy" in party organisation, amidst the gloom of autocracy and the domination of the gendarmes, is nothing more than a *useless and harmful toy*. It is a useless toy, because as a matter of fact, no revolutionary organisation has ever practiced *broad* democracy, nor could it, however much it desired to do so. It is a harmful toy, because any attempt to practice the "broad principles of democracy" will simply facilitate the work of the police in making big raids, it will perpetuate the prevailing primitiveness, divert the thoughts of the practical workers from the serious and imperative task of training themselves to become professional revolutionists to that of drawing up detailed "paper" rules for election systems. Only abroad, where very often people who have no opportunity of doing real live work gather together, can the "game of democracy" be played here and there, especially in small groups.

VIII

POLITICS IN THE UNIFIED NATION STATE

HEINRICH VON TREITSCHKE

PROBABLY the most eloquent defender of Prussian militarism was a non Prussian civilian who as a boy had been disappointed by the liberal failure of 1848–49. Heinrich von Treitschke (1834–96) was a university professor and writer of history and political science. His development is an early example of the conversion of a German intellectual from the liberal idealism of the Frankfurt Assembly to the hard-boiled Bismarckian realism. The delegates to the Frankfurt Assembly expressed the feelings of most political-minded Germans only insofar as they advocated national unification and moral leadership. Their liberalism had little popular appeal and it failed to shake the ingrained convictions of the real leading class in Prussia and elsewhere—the aristocracy of great landowners, officers, and bureaucrats. These men clung to the feudal tradition of associating the virtues of courage, honor, and nobility with the practice of war, and had little sympathy for the abstract ideologies of the unarmed "professors." Events seemed to prove that they were right. The 1848–49 liberal revolution collapsed and Frederick William IV, Prussia's conservative king, had to bow in 1850 to the apparently overwhelming might of Austria, supported by Russia, and was forced to restore the loose Confederation of 1815.

It was at this time that Treitschke, the son of a Saxon army officer whose forebears were Slavic, concluded that Austria's opposition and the local interests of the petty German states precluded unification except by methods which Bismarck adopted later—blood and iron. First as a student, then as a teacher at the universities of Freiburg and Heidelberg he advocated unity under Prussian military leadership. Somewhat later most of Germany rallied around Bismarck when he successively defeated Denmark, Austria, and France with an army he had built up by unconstitutional means and against the opposition of Prussian liberals. The renunciation was made easier for the liberals by the fact that Bismarck then adopted for the whole of Germany an ostensibly liberal constitution with a Lower House elected by universal suffrage. Most of the "liberals" became "national liberals" and supported the successful Iron Chancellor; most of the German professors turned away from philosophical idealism. Nevertheless, they continued to regard themselves, like Treitschke, as liberals and idealists in matters where national interests were not threatened. With his characteristic blend of professed liberalism, of state worship, and of frank, brutal acceptance of "reality," Treitschke struck many responsive chords.

Treitschke never published his lectures on politics which were delivered at the University of Berlin, where he lectured from 1874–96. After his death they were compiled from his rough notes and the careful stenographic records of some of his students. They were printed in 1897. The following selections have been taken from a translation from the German by Blanche Dugdale and Torben de Bille, (London: Constable and Company, 1916).

POLITICS

THE STATE IDEA

THE STATE is the people, legally united as an independent entity. By the word "people" we understand briefly a number of families permanently living side by side. This definition implies that the State is primordial and necessary, that it is as enduring as history, and no less essential to mankind than speech. . . .

The human race was once for all created with certain innate qualities amongst which speech and political genius must undoubtedly be counted. . . .

If, then, political capacity is innate in man, and is to be further developed, it is quite inaccurate to call the State a necessary evil. We have to deal with it as a lofty necessity of Nature. Even as the possibility of building up a civilization is dependent upon the limitation of our powers combined with the gift of reason, so also the State depends upon our inability to live alone. This Aristotle has already demonstrated. The State, says he, arose in order to make life possible; it endured to make good life possible.

This natural necessity of a constituted order is further displayed by the fact that the political institutions of a people, broadly speaking, appear to be the external forms which are the inevitable outcome of its inner life. Just as its language is not the product of caprice but the immediate expression of its most deep-rooted attitude towards the world, so also its political institutions regarded as a whole, and the whole spirit of its jurisprudence, are the symbols of its political genius and of the outside destinies which have helped to shape the gifts which Nature bestowed. . . .

We may say with certainty that the evolution of the State is, broadly speaking, nothing but the necessary outward form which the inner life of a people bestows upon itself, and that peoples attain to that form of government which their moral capacity enables them to reach. Nothing can be more inverted than the opinion that constitutional laws were artificially evolved in opposition to the conception of a Natural Law. Ultramontanes and Jacobins both start with the assumption that the legislation of a modern State is the work of sinful man. They thus display their total lack of reverence for the objectively revealed Will of God, as unfolded in the life of the State.

When we assert the evolution of the State to be something inherently necessary, we do not thereby deny the power of genius or of creative Will in history. For it is of the essence of political genius to be national. There has never been an example of the contrary. The summit of historical fame was never attained by Wallenstein because he was never a national hero, but a Czech who played the German for the sake of expediency. He was, like Napoleon, a splendid Adventurer of history. The truly great maker of history always stands upon a national basis. This applies equally to men of letters. He only is a great writer who so writes that all his countrymen respond, "Thus it must be. Thus we all feel,"—who is in fact a microcosm of his nation.

If we have grasped that the State is the people legally constituted we thereby imply that it aims at establishing a permanent tradition throughout the Ages. A people does not only comprise the individuals living side by side, but also the successive generations of the same stock. This is one of the truths which Materialists dismiss as a mystical doctrine, and yet it is an obvious truth. Only the continuity of human history makes man a ζῶον πολιτικόν.[1] He alone stands upon the achievements of his forebears, and deliberately continues their work in order to transmit it more perfect to his children and children's children. Only a creature like man, needing aid and endowed with reason, can have a history; and it is one of the ineptitudes of the Materialists to speak of animal States. It is just a play upon words to talk of a bee State. Beasts merely reproduce unconsciously what has been from all time, and none but human beings can possess a form of government which is calculated to endure. There never was a form of Constitution without a law of inheritance. The rational basis for this is obvious, for by far the largest part of a nation's wealth was not created by the contemporary generation. The continuous legalized intention of the past, exemplified in the law of inheritance, must remain a factor in the distribution of property amongst posterity. In a nation's continuity with bygone generations lies the specific dignity of the State. It is consequently a contradiction to say that a distribution of property should be regulated by the deserts of the existing generation. Who would respect the banners of a State if the power of memory had fled? There are cases when the shadows of the past are invoked against the perverted will of the present, and prove more potent. Today in Alsace we appeal from the distorted opinions of the Francophobes to Geiler von Kaisersberg and expect to see his spirit revive again. No one who does not recognize the continued action of the past upon the present can ever understand the nature and necessity of War. Gibbon calls Patriotism "the living sense of my own interest in society"; but if we simply look upon the State as intended to secure life and property to the individual, how comes it that the individual will also sacrifice life and property to the State? It is a false conclusion that wars are waged for the sake of material advantage. Modern wars are not fought for the sake of booty. Here the high moral ideal of national honour is a factor

[1] [*Political animal.*]

handed down from one generation to another, enshrining something positively sacred, and compelling the individual to sacrifice himself to it. This ideal is above all price and cannot be reduced to pounds, shillings, and pence. Kant says, "Where a price can be paid, an equivalent can be substituted. It is he which is above price and which consequently admits of no equivalent, that possesses real value." Genuine patriotism is the consciousness of cooperating with the body-politic, of being rooted in ancestral achievements and of transmitting them to descendants. Fichte has finely said, "Individual man sees in his country the realisation of his earthly immortality."

This involves that the State has a personality, primarily in the juridical, and secondly in the politico-moral sense. Every man who is able to exercise his will in law has a legal personality. Now it is quite clear that the State possesses this deliberate will; nay more, that it has the juridical personality in the most complete sense. In State treaties it is the will of the State which is expressed, not the personal desires of the individuals who conclude them, and the treaty is binding as long as the contracting State exists. When a State is incapable of enforcing its will, or of maintaining law and order at home and prestige abroad, it becomes an anomaly and falls a prey either to anarchy or a foreign enemy. The State therefore must have the most emphatic will that can be imagined. . . .

Treat the State as a person, and the necessary and rational multiplicity of States follows. Just as in individual life the ego implies the existence of the non-ego, so it does in the State. The state is power, precisely in order to assert itself as against other equally independent powers. War and the administration of justice are the chief tasks of even the most barbaric States. But these tasks are only conceivable where a plurality of States are found existing side by side. Thus the idea of one universal empire is odious—the ideal of a State coextensive with humanity is no ideal at all. In a single State the whole range of culture could never be fully spanned; no single people could unite the virtues of aristocracy and democracy. All nations, like all individuals, have their limitations, but it is exactly in the abundance of these limited qualities that the genius of humanity is exhibited. The rays of the Divine light are manifested, broken by countless facets among the separate peoples, each one exhibiting another picture and another idea of the whole. Every people has a right to believe that certain attributes of the Divine reason are exhibited in it to their fullest perfection. No people ever attains to national consciousness without overrating itself. The Germans are always in danger of enervating their nationality through possessing too little of this rugged pride. The average German has very little political pride; but even our Philistines generally revel in the intellectual boast of the freedom and universality of the German spirit, and this is well, for such a sentiment is necessary if a people is to maintain and assert itself.

Since in so many nations the race becomes exhausted, and since various types of national culture exist side by side, single peoples can refresh themselves from the sources of other countries' intellectual vigour after a barren period of their own, as the Germans did from the French and English after the Thirty Years' War. The daily life of nations is founded upon mutual give and take, and since Christianity has brought this fact to universal recognition we may lay down that modern civilizations will not perish in the same sense as those of the ancient world, which lacked this knowledge. But it is no mere kindly interchange which takes place; the supreme need is to preserve what has been won. Historical greatness depends less on the first discovery or invention than on forming and keeping. The terrible saying, *Sic vos non vobis*,[2] is once more vindicated. How tragic is the fate of Spain, which discovered the New World and to-day can show no trophy of that mighty civilizing achievement. Her one remaining advantage is that Spanish is still the language of millions beyond the seas. Other nations advanced and snatched from the Iberian races the fruits of their labour, first the Dutch and then the English. The features of history are virile, unsuited to sentimental or feminine natures. Brave peoples alone have an existence, an evolution or a future; the weak and cowardly perish, and perish justly. The grandeur of history lies in the perpetual conflict of nations, and it is simply foolish to desire the suppression of their rivalry. Mankind has ever found it to be so. . . .

Further, if we examine our definition of the State as "the people legally united as an independent entity," we find that it can be more briefly put thus: "The State is the public force for Offence and Defence." It is, above all, Power which makes its will to prevail, it is not the totality of the people as Hegel assumes in his deification of it. The nation is not entirely comprised in the State, but the State protects and embraces the people's life, regulating its external aspects on every side. It does not ask primarily for opinion, but demands obedience, and its laws must be obeyed, whether willingly or no.

A step forward has been taken when the mute obedience of the citizens is transformed into a rational inward assent, but it cannot be said that this is absolutely necessary. Powerful, highly-developed Empires have stood for centuries without its aid. Submission is what the State primarily requires; it insists upon acquiescence; its very essence is the accomplishment of its will. . . . A State which can no longer carry out its purpose collapses in anarchy. . . .

The State is not an Academy of Arts. If it neglects its strength in order to promote the idealistic aspirations of man, it repudiates its own nature and

2 [Roughly, *What you do is not done for yourself.*]

perishes. This is in truth for the State equivalent to the sin against the Holy Ghost, for it is indeed a mortal error in the State to subordinate itself for sentimental reasons to a foreign Power, as we Germans have often done to England. . . .

We have described the State as an independent force. This pregnant theory of independence implies firstly so absolute a moral supremacy that the State cannot legitimately tolerate any power above its own, and secondly a temporal freedom entailing a variety of material resources adequate to its protection against hostile influences. Legal sovereignty, the State's complete independence of any other earthly power, is so rooted in its nature that it may be said to be its very standard and criterion. . . .

Human communities do exist which in their own fashion pursue aims no less lofty than those of the State, but which must be legally subject to it in their outward relations with the world. It is obvious that contradictions must arise, and that two such authorities, morally but not legally equal, must sometimes collide with each other. Nor is it to be wished that the conflicts between Church and State should wholly cease, for if they did one party or the other would be soulless and dead, like the Russian Church for example. Sovereignty, however, which is the peculiar attribute of the State, is of necessity supreme, and it is a ridiculous inconsistency to speak of a superior and inferior authority within it. The truth remains that the essence of the State consists in its incompatibility with any power over it. How proudly and truly statesmanlike is Gustavus Adolphus' exclamation, "I recognize no power over me but God and the conqueror's sword." This is so unconditionally true that we see at once that it cannot be the destiny of mankind to form a single State, but that the ideal towards which we strive is a harmonious comity of nations, who, concluding treaties of their own free will, admit restrictions upon their sovereignty without abrogating it.

For the notion of sovereignty must not be rigid, but flexible and relative, like all political conceptions. Every State, in treaty making, will limit its power in certain directions for its own sake. States which conclude treaties with each other thereby curtail their absolute authority to some extent. But the rule still stands, for every treaty is a voluntary curb upon the power of each, and all international agreements are prefaced by the clause "Rebus sic stantibus." No State can pledge its future to another. It knows no arbiter, and draws up all its treaties with this implied reservation. This is supported by the axiom that so long as international law exists all treaties lose their force at the very moment when war is declared between the contracting parties; moreover, every sovereign State has the undoubted right to declare war at its pleasure, and is consequently entitled to repudiate its treaties. Upon this constantly recurring alteration of treaties the progress of history depends; every State must take care that its treaties do not survive their effective value, lest another Power should denounce them by a declaration of war; for antiquated treaties must necessarily be denounced and replaced by others more consonant with circumstances.

It is clear that the international agreements which limit the power of a State are not absolute, but voluntary self-restrictions. Hence, it follows that the establishment of a permanent international Arbitration Court is incompatible with the nature of the State, which could at all events only accept the decision of such a tribunal in cases of second- or third-rate importance. When a nation's existence is at stake there is no outside Power whose impartiality can be trusted. Were we to commit the folly of treating the Alsace-Lorraine problem as an open question, by submitting it to arbitration, who would seriously believe that the award could be impartial? It is, moreover, a point of honour for a State to solve such difficulties for itself. International treaties may indeed become more frequent, but a finally decisive tribunal of the nations is an impossibility. The appeal to arms will be valid until the end of history, and therein lies the sacredness of war.

However flexible the conception of Sovereignty may be we are not to infer from that any self-contradiction, but rather a necessity to establish in what its pith and kernel consists. Legally it lies in the competence to define the limits of its own authority, and politically in the appeal to arms. An unarmed State, incapable of drawing the sword when it sees fit, is subject to one which wields the power of declaring war. To speak of a military suzerainty in time of peace obviously implies a *contradictio in adjecto*.[3] A defenceless State may still be termed a Kingdom for conventional or courtly reasons, but science, whose first duty is accuracy, must boldly declare that in point of fact such a country no longer takes rank as a State.

This, then, is the only real criterion. The right of arms distinguishes the State from all other forms of corporate life, and those who cannot take up arms for themselves may not be regarded as States, but only as members of a federated constellation of States. The difference between the Prussian Monarchy and the other German States is here apparent, namely, that the King of Prussia himself wields the supreme command, and therefore Prussia, unlike the others, has not lost its sovereignty.

The other test of sovereignty is the right to determine independently the limits of its power, and herein lies the difference between a federation of States and a Federal State. In the latter the central power is sovereign and can extend its competence according to its judgment, whereas in the former, every individual State is sovereign. The various subordinate countries of Germany

[3] [*Contradiction in terms.*]

are not genuine States; they must at any moment be prepared to see a right, which they possess at present, withdrawn by virtue of Imperial authority. Since Prussia alone has enough votes on the Federal Council to be in a position to prevent an alteration of the Constitution by its veto, it becomes evident that she cannot be outvoted on such decisive questions. She is therefore, in this second respect also, the only truly sovereign State which remains.

In such matters one must not be guided by historians, but by statesmen. When Bismarck once pointed out to the Emperor William I. that the consent of the Empire would not be forthcoming for a certain political step, the latter exclaimed irritably, "Rubbish! The Empire is after all only an extension of Prussia." This was certainly a crudely military point of view, but it was correct. As history knows of no case in which the conqueror has not strengthened his own organization, so it has come to pass by means of treaties that the might of Prussia has been indirectly extended over the whole Empire; and under these conditions we have prospered, for even the Kings of Bavaria, Wurtemberg, and Saxony have not lost but rather increased their effective influence through the creation of the German Empire. They have had to abandon a military power which only existed upon paper, and which 1866 had proved to be illusory, but they have gained a channel, through the formation of the Federal Council, by which they can exercise an influence on the collective will of the Empire at large. This influence is so considerable that the actual power of these rulers is at present greater than formerly, since it depends on realities rather than on titles.

Over and above these two essential factors of the State's sovereignty there belongs to the nature of its independence what Aristotle called "αὐτάρκεια," *i.e.* the capacity to be self-sufficing. This involves firstly that it should consist of a large enough number of families to secure the continuance of the race, and secondly, a certain geographical area. A ship an inch long, as Aristotle truly observes, is not a ship at all, because it is impossible to row it. Again, the State must possess such material resources as put it in a position to vindicate its theoretic independence by force of arms. Here everything depends upon the form of the community to which the State in question belongs. One cannot reckon its quality by its mileage, it must be judged by its proportionate strength compared with other States. The City State of Athens was not a petty State, but stood in the first rank in the hierarchy of nations of antiquity; the same is true of Sparta, and of Florence and Milan in the Middle Ages. But any political community not in a position to assert its native strength as against any given group of neighbours will always be on the verge of losing its characteristics as a State. This has always been the case. Great changes in the art of war have destroyed numberless States. It is because an army of 20,000 men can only be reckoned to-day as a weak army corps that the small States of Central Europe cannot maintain themselves in the long run.

There are, indeed, States which do not assert themselves positively by virtue of their own strength, but negatively through the exigencies of the balance of power in Europe. Switzerland, Holland, and Belgium are cases in point. They are sustained by the international situation, a foundation which is, however, extremely solid, and so long as the present grouping of the Powers continues Switzerland may look forward to prolonged existence.

If we apply the test of αὐτάρκεια we perceive that, as Europe is now constituted, the larger States are constantly gaining influence in proportion as our international system assumes a more and more aristocratic complexion. The time is not yet very distant when the adhesion or withdrawal of such States as Piedmont and Savoy could actually decide the fate of a coalition. To-day such a thing would be impossible. Since the Seven Years' War the domination of the five great Powers has been necessarily evolved. The big European questions are decided within this circle. Italy is on the verge of being admitted into it, but neither Belgium, Sweden, nor Switzerland have a voice unless their interests are directly concerned.

The entire development of European polity tends unmistakably to drive the second-rate Powers into the background, and this raises issues of immeasurable gravity for the German nation, in the world outside Europe. Up to the present Germany has always had too small a share of the spoils in the partition of non-European territories among the Powers of Europe, and yet our existence as a State of the first rank is vitally affected by the question whether we can become a power beyond the seas. If not, there remains the appalling prospect of England and Russia dividing the world between them, and in such a case it is hard to say whether the Russian knout or the English money bags would be the worst alternative.

On close examination then, it becomes clear that if the State is power, only that State which has power realizes its own idea, and this accounts for the undeniably ridiculous element which we discern in the existence of a small State. Weakness is not itself ridiculous, except when masquerading as strength. In small States that puling spirit is hatched, which judges the State by the taxes it levies, and does not perceive that if the State may not enclose and repress like an egg-shell, neither can it protect. Such thinkers fail to understand that the moral benefits for which we are indebted to the State are above all price. It is by generating this form of materialism that small States have so deleterious an effect upon their citizens.

Moreover, they are totally lacking in that capacity for justice which characterises their greater neighbours. Any person who has plenty of relations and is not a perfect fool is soon provided for in a small country, while in a large one, although justice tends to become stereotyped, it is not possible to be so much influenced by personal and local circumstances as in the narrower sphere. French centralization is an alarming example. The incurable nuisance of our examinations is unluckily of Prussian origin, for a country with hundreds of *Gymnasien* [4] cannot give a free hand to the teachers, and with our uncontrolled freedom of domicile and frequent change of employees it will be hard to find a better method of selection for the mass of Government posts which have to be filled than that afforded by the routine of examinations, which have verily become the curse of Germany. Red tape is an inevitable evil in the administration of big States, but it may be sensibly diminished by the increased autonomy of Provinces and Communes.

Everything considered, therefore, we reach the conclusion that the large State is the nobler type. This is more especially true of its fundamental functions such as wielding the sword in defence of the hearth and of justice. Both are better protected by a large State than a small one. The latter cannot wage war with any prospect of success. There is, however, nothing mechanical in the administration of justice, it must be constantly modified by the daily practice of the Courts, which is nourished by experience of life as well as by the science of law, and it is only when the practical experience of numberless Law Courts is continuously accumulating that the administration of Justice can be really effective. There neither is nor ever can be a Swiss jurisprudence; French, German, Italian law exists in Switzerland, but a national code can never be evolved; Swiss jurists continue to develop our German law.

The economic superiority of big countries is patent. A splendid security springs from the mere largeness of their scale. They can overcome economic crises far more easily. Famine, for instance, can hardly attack every part of them at once, and only in them can that truly national pride arise which is a sign of the moral stamina of a people. Their citizens' outlook upon the world will be freer and greater. The command of the sea more especially promotes it. The poet's saying is true indeed that "wide horizons liberate the mind." The time may come when no State will be counted great unless it can boast of territories beyond the seas.

Another essential for the State is a capital city to form a pivot for its culture. No great nation can endure for long without a centre in which its political, intellectual, and material life is concentrated, and its people can feel themselves united. London, Paris, Rome, Madrid, Stockholm, Copenhagen are the towns where the political life of the respective countries has culminated. Such capitals are necessary, their sins and their crimes notwithstanding, but it was not until the nineteenth century that we Germans possessed such a city.

4 [Roughly, *high school*.]

Examining closely, we find that culture in general, and in the widest sense of the word, matures more happily in the broader conditions of powerful countries than within the narrow limits of a little State. . . .

We come now to consider the last point which arises out of our definition of the State as the people legally united as an independent entity. . . .

It is a fundamental rule of human nature that the largest portion of the energy of the human race must be consumed in supplying the primary necessities of existence. The chief aim of a savage's life is to make that life secure, and mankind is by nature so frail and needy that the immense majority of men, even on the higher levels of culture, must always and everywhere devote themselves to bread-winning and the material cares of life. To put it simply: the masses must for ever remain the masses. There would be no culture without kitchenmaids.

Obviously education could never thrive if there was nobody to do the rough work. Millions must plough and forge and dig in order that a few thousands may write and paint and study.

It sounds harsh, but it is true for all time, and whining and complaining can never alter it. . . .

It is precisely in the differentiation of classes that the moral wealth of mankind is exhibited. The virtues of wealth stand side by side with those of poverty, with which we neither could nor should dispense, and which by their vigour and sincerity put to shame the jaded victim of over-culture. There is a hearty joy in living which can only flourish under simple conditions of life. Herein we find a remarkable equalization of the apparently cruel classifications of society. Want is a relative conception. It is the task of government to reduce and mitigate distress, but its abolition is neither possible nor desirable. The economy of Nature has here set definite limits upon human endeavour, and on the other hand man's pleasure in life is so overwhelming that a healthy race will increase and spread wherever there is space for them. . . .

From all this a result emerges which closer examination will verify: that there is in fact no actual entity corresponding to the abstract conception of civil society which exists in the brain of the student. Where do we find its concrete embodiment? Nowhere. Any one can see for himself that society, unlike the State, is intangible. We know the State is a unit, and not as a mythical personality. Society, however, has no single will, and we have no duties to fulfil towards it. In all my life I have never once thought of my moral obligations towards society, but I think constantly of my countrymen, whom I seek to honour as much as I can. Therefore, when a savant like Jhering talks of the ethical aim which society is supposed to have set itself, he falls into a logical error. Society is composed of all manner of warring interests, which if left to themselves would soon lead to a *bellum omnium contra omnes*,[5] for its natural tendency is towards conflict, and no suggestion of any aspiration after unity is to be found in it. . . .

When we draw our conclusions from all the foregoing we shall not follow Hegel in pronouncing the State to be absolutely the people's life.

In the State he saw the moral idea realized, which is able to accomplish whatever it may desire. Now the State, as we have seen, is not the whole of a nation's life, for its function is only to surround the whole, regulating and protecting it. When the Hegelian Philosophy was at its zenith, a number of gifted men tried to make out that the State, like the Leviathan, should swallow up everything. The modern man will not find this idea easy to accept. No Christian could live for the State alone, because he must cling fast to his destiny in eternity. Out of this arises a youthful error of Richard Rothe's, when, in his work on the history of the Christian Church, he develops the idea that if the State would in the future take over the Church's civilizing duties, the two might amalgamate. This can never be, nor can any one seriously wish it. The State can only work by an outward compulsion: it is only the people as a force; but in saying this we express an endlessly wide and great ideal, for the State is not only the arena for the great primitive forces of human nature, it is also the framework of all national life. In short, a people which is not in a position to create and maintain under the wing of the State an external organization of its own intellectual existence deserves to perish. The Jewish race affords the most tragic example of a richly gifted nation, who were incapable of defending their State, and are now scattered to the ends of the earth. Their life is crippled, for no man can belong to two nations at once. The State, therefore, is not only a high moral good in itself, but is also the assurance for the people's endurance. Only through it can their moral development be perfected, for the living sense of citizenship inspires the community in the same way as a sense of duty inspires the individual. . . .

THE AIM OF THE STATE

Theoretically, therefore, no limit can be set to the functions of a State. It will attempt to dominate the outer life of its members as far as it is able to do so. A more fruitful subject for speculation will be to fix the theoretic minimum for its activity, and decide what functions it must at the least fulfil before it can be given the name of State. When we have set this minimum we shall come to the further question of how far beyond it the State may reasonably extend its action. We then see at once that since its first duty, as we have already said, is the double one of maintaining power without, and law within, its primary obligations must be the care of its Army and its Jurisprudence, in order to

5 [*War of all against all.*]

protect and to restrain the community of its citizens. The fulfilment of these two functions is attained by certain material means; therefore some form of fiscal system must exist, even in the most primitive of States, in order to provide these means.

No State can endure which can no longer fulfil these elementary duties. It is only in abnormal circumstances that we find any exception to this rule, as when an artificial balance of power protects the smaller States which can no longer protect themselves.

The functions of the State in maintaining its own internal administration of justice are manifold. It must firstly, in civil law, place the prescribed limit upon the individual will. It will nevertheless proportionately restrict its own activity in this sphere, since no individual is compelled to exercise his own legal rights. Here the State will issue no direct commands, but merely act as mediator, leaving the carrying out of its decrees to the free will of the contracting parties. . . .

The next essential function of the State is the conduct of war. The long oblivion into which this principle had fallen is a proof of how effeminate the science of government had become in civilian hands. In our century this sentimentality was dissipated by Clausewitz, but a one-sided materialism arose in its place, after the fashion of the Manchester school, seeing in man a biped creature, whose destiny lies in buying cheap and selling dear. It is obvious that this idea is not compatible with war, and it is only since the last war that a sounder theory arose of the State and its military power.

Without war no State could be. All those we know of arose through war, and the protection of their members by armed force remains their primary and essential task. War, therefore, will endure to the end of history, as long as there is multiplicity of States. The laws of human thought and of human nature forbid any alternative, neither is one to be wished for. The blind worshipper of an eternal peace falls into the error of isolating the State, or dreams of one which is universal, which we have already seen to be at variance with reason.

Even as it is impossible to conceive of a tribunal above the State, which we have recognized as sovereign in its very essence, so it is likewise impossible to banish the idea of war from the world. It is a favourite fashion of our time to instance England as particularly ready for peace. But England is perpetually at war; there is hardly an instant in her recent history in which she has not been obliged to be fighting somewhere. The great strides which civilization makes against barbarism and unreason are only made actual by the sword. Between civilized nations also war is the form of litigation by which States make their claims valid. The arguments brought forward in these terrible law suits of the nations compel as no argument in civil suits can ever do. Often as we have tried by theory to convince the small States that Prussia alone can be the leader in Germany, we had to produce the final proof upon the battlefields of Bohemia and the Main.

Moreover, war is a uniting as well as a dividing element among nations; it does not draw them together in enmity only, for through its means they learn to know and to respect each other's peculiar qualities.

It is important not to look upon war always as a judgment from God. Its consequences are evanescent; but the life of a nation is reckoned by centuries, and the final verdict can only be pronounced after the survey of whole epochs.

Such a State as Prussia might indeed be brought near to destruction by a passing phase of degeneracy; but being by the character of its people more reasonable and more free than the French, it retained the power to call up the moral force within itself, and so to regain its ascendancy. Most undoubtedly war is the one remedy for an ailing nation. Social selfishness and party hatreds must be dumb before the call of the State when its existence is at stake. Forgetting himself, the individual must only remember that he is a part of the whole, and realize the unimportance of his own life compared with the common weal.

The grandeur of war lies in the utter annihilation of puny man in the great conception of the State, and it brings out the full magnificence of the sacrifice of fellow-countrymen for one another. In war the chaff is winnowed from the wheat. Those who have lived through 1870 cannot fail to understand Niebuhr's description of his feelings in 1813, when he speaks of how no one who has entered into the joy of being bound by a common tie to all his compatriots, gentle and simple alike, can ever forget how he was uplifted by the love, the friendliness, and the strength of that mutual sentiment.

It is war which fosters the political idealism which the materialist rejects. What a disaster for civilization it would be if mankind blotted its heroes from memory. The heroes of a nation are the figures which rejoice and inspire the spirit of its youth, and the writers whose words ring like trumpet blasts become the idols of our boyhood and our early manhood. He who feels no answering thrill is unworthy to bear arms for his country. To appeal from this judgment to Christianity would be sheer perversity, for does not the Bible distinctly say that the ruler shall rule by the sword, and again that greater love hath no man than to lay down his life for his friend? To Aryan races, who are before all things courageous, the foolish preaching of everlasting peace has always been vain. They have always been men enough to maintain with the sword what they have attained through the spirit.

Goethe once said that the North Germans were always more civilized than the South Germans. No doubt they were, and a glance at the history of the Princes of Lower Saxony shows that they were for ever either attacking or defending themselves. One-sided as Goethe's verdict is, it contains a core of truth. Our ancient Empire was great under the Saxons; under the Swabian and the Salic Emperors it declined. Heroism, bodily strength, and chivalrous spirit is essential to the character of a noble people.

Such matters must not be examined only by the light of the student's lamp. The historian who moves in the world of the real Will sees at once that the demand for eternal peace is purely reactionary. He sees that all movement and all growth would disappear with war, and that only the exhausted, spiritless, degenerate periods of history have toyed with the idea.

There are then no two opinions about the duty of the State to maintain its own laws and protect its own people. For this purpose every State must have an Exchequer. The machinery of the law, the upkeep of the army, and some system of finance are their first duties. Up to this point no argument need be entertained, for it is of no importance to science whether a truth be accepted quietly, or with wailing and gnashing of teeth. The dispute concerning the aims and business of the State only begins over the question of its ability and vocation to assume other duties towards the human race. No such question was admitted into the political conceptions of classical antiquity, for where the citizen is nothing but a member of the State the idea of its undue interference with his concerns does not arise. It never occurred to Aristotle to inquire whether the State was exceeding its prerogative when it appointed an official to superintend feminine morality. It acted within its rights, and he did not consider whether in so doing it did damage to family life. In the same way it did not strike the Ancients as possible that the State could legislate too much. The words of Tacitus, *in pessima republica plurimæ leges,*[6] which are so often and so willingly quoted in this context, simply mean that when the morals of a State are bad it may seek in vain to remedy the evil by a multitude of laws.

The modern theory of individualism, decked with its various titles, stands as the poles asunder from these conceptions of antiquity. From it the doctrine emanates that the State should content itself with protection of life and property, and with wings thus clipped be pompously dubbed a Constitutional State.

This teaching is the legitimate child of the old doctrine of Natural Law. According to it the State can only exist as a means for the individual's ends. The more ideal the view adopted of human life, the more certain does it seem that the State should content itself with the purely exterior protective functions. . . . But when we probe this theory which has cast its spell over so many distinguished men, we find that it has totally overlooked the continuity of history, and the bond which unites the succeeding generations. The State, as

[6] [*The worst state has the most laws.*]

we have seen, is enduring; humanly speaking, it is eternal. Its work therefore is to prepare the foundations for the future. If it existed only to protect the life and goods of its citizens it would not dare to go to war, for wars are waged for the sake of honour, and not for protection of property. They cannot therefore be explained by the empty theory which makes the State no more than an Insurance Society. Honour is a moral postulate, not a juridical conception.

OTTO VON BISMARCK

O TTO EDUARD LEOPOLD VON BISMARCK was born at Schönhausen in 1815, to an old Prussian family, and was educated at Berlin and Göttingen. He entered the diplomatic corps and opposed any concessions to the liberals during the Revolution of 1848. As Prussian minister from 1851 to 1859 to the Federal Diet at Frankfort he distinguished himself by his vigorous denunciation of democratic doctrines and his consistent protest against Prussia's subordinate position in the German Confederation. With the accession of the "liberal" William as Prince Regent, Bismarck was sent in 1859 as ambassador to Russia, "in cold storage" as he put it, and from there to Paris.

In 1862 William (now King William I) was confronted with a political crisis. The Prussian Chambers refused to authorize increased military expenditures without the guarantee of a strengthened citizen militia and the reduction of the period of service from three years to two. Bismarck was appointed Premier, and delivered his famous "blood and iron" speech to the Chambers, imposing an unconstitutional regime on the weak legislature. Bismarck referred to his actions as "exploiting the gap in the constitution." For the next twenty-eight years he directed the internal policies and foreign affairs of Prussia and (after 1871) of Germany.

In a series of wars—against Denmark in 1864, against Austria in 1866, and against France in 1870—Bismarck succeeded in uniting the German states around Prussia. The German Empire which was proclaimed in the Hall of Mirrors at Versailles on January 18, 1871, was as much the product of his resourcefulness in dealing with the lesser German princes as of his shrewd manipulation of foreign policy. In March, 1871, Bismarck was made a Prince of the Empire and was appointed Imperial Chancellor.

In domestic politics Bismarck was an opportunist. He tolerated a moderate parliamentarianism in the new empire, granting an electoral system based on universal suffrage. Nevertheless, he saw to it that the chancellor was responsible solely to the emperor (not to the Chambers, as in the parliamentary democracies of France and Britain), and gave Prussia a dominant voice in the upper house of the Chambers. He took his political allies where he could find them, working first with the Conservatives, then with the National Liberals, then again with the Conservatives. During the 1870s Bismarck held a real parliamentary majority, and he used it to provide a uniform code of commercial and civil law for Germany, as well as a unified currency and a central bank. His bitter campaign against the Catholic Center Party from 1870 to 1879, the *Kulturkampf,* and his struggle with the socialists after 1880 ended by strengthening his control over the government, although he did not succeed in quelling political opposition. Bismarck provided protection for agricultural and industrial interests, built canals and nationalized the railroads. He also organized a comprehensive system of state insurance for workers, providing old age, sickness, and accident benefits.

In foreign affairs, Bismarck regarded himself as the keeper of the "Concert of

Europe," a role which he fulfilled most skillfully at the Congress of Berlin in 1878. Although he disclaimed any imperialist ambitions, between 1884 and 1886 he acquired for Germany extensive holdings in Africa.

With the accession of the young William in 1888, Bismarck's control of German policy came to an end. In 1890 he was forced by the emperor to resign and he spent his last years as a bitter critic of the young ruler's policies. He died in 1898.

The selections dealing with social legislation have been translated partly from Bismarck's *Gesammelte Werke* (Vol. XII, Berlin, 1929), and partly taken from W. H. Dawson, *Bismarck and State Socialism* (London: Swan Sonnenschein, 1891). "The Triple Alliance" is from Bismarck's *Autobiography*, Vol. II, translated under the supervision of A. J. Butler, 1899.

SPEECH OPENING THE REICHSTAG, FEBRUARY 15, 1881

AT THE OPENING of the Reichstag in February, 1879, the Emperor, in reference to the [Anti-Socialist] law of October 21st, 1878, gave expression to the hope that this House would not refuse its cooperation in the remedying of social ills by means of legislation. A remedy cannot alone be sought in the repression of Socialistic excesses; there must be simultaneously the positive advancement of the welfare of the working classes. And here the care of those workpeople who are incapable of earning their livelihood is of the first importance. In the interest of these the Emperor has caused a bill for the insurance of workpeople against the consequences of accident to be sent to the Bundesrath—a bill which, it is hoped, will meet a need felt both by workpeople and employers. His Majesty hopes that the measure will in principle receive the assent of the Federal Governments, and that it will be welcomed by the Reichstag as a complement of the legislation affording protection against Social-Democratic movements. Past institutions intended to insure working people against the danger of falling into a condition of helplessness owing to the incapacity resulting from accident or age have proved inadequate, and their insufficiency has to no small extent contributed to cause the working classes to seek help by participating in Social-Democratic movements.

OFFICIAL JUSTIFICATION OF THE FIRST ACCIDENT INSURANCE BILL OF MARCH 8, 1881

THAT THE STATE should interest itself to a greater degree than hitherto in those of its members who need assistance, is not only a duty of humanity and Christianity—by which State institutions should be permeated—but a duty of State-preserving policy, whose aim should be to cultivate the conception —and that, too, amongst the non-propertied classes, which form at once the most numerous and the least instructed part of the population—that the State is not merely a necessary but a beneficent institution. These classes must, by the evident and direct advantages which are secured to them by legislative measures, be led to regard the State not as an institution contrived for the protection of the better classes of society, but as one serving their own needs and interests. The apprehension that a Socialist element might be introduced into legislation if this end were followed should not check us. So far as that may be the case it will not be an innovation but the further development of the modern State idea, the result of Christian ethics, according to which the State should discharge, besides the defensive duty of protecting existing rights, the positive duty of promoting the welfare of all its members, and especially those who are weak and in need of help, by means of judicious institutions and the employment of those resources of the community which are at its disposal. In this sense the legal regulation of poor relief which the modern State, in opposition to that of antiquity and of the Middle Ages, recognises as a duty incumbent upon it, contains a Socialistic element, and in truth the measures which may be adopted for improving the condition of the non-propertied classes are only a development of the idea which lies at the basis of poor relief. Nor should the fear that legislation of this kind will not attain important results unless the resources of the Empire and of the individual States be largely employed be a reason for holding back, for the value of measures affecting the future existence of society and the State should not be estimated according to the sacrifice of money which may be entailed. With a single measure, such as is at present proposed, it is of course impossible to remove entirely, or even to a considerable extent, the difficulties which are contained in the social question. This is, in fact, but the first step in a direction in which a difficult work, that will last for years, will have to be overcome gradually and cautiously, and the discharge of one task will only produce new ones.

MESSAGE OF WILLIAM I TO THE REICHSTAG, NOVEMBER 17, 1881

WE HOLD IT as our imperial duty to urge upon the Reichstag anew the promotion of the welfare of the worker, and we should have so much the greater satisfaction in the achievement, with which God has certainly blessed our reign, to look back, if it should be attained in the future, with the consciousness that we had left the Fatherland new and growing assurance of its inner peace and greater certainty and productiveness of assistance to those needing help, to which they are entitled. In our carefully considered plan we are certain of the assent of all cooperating governments and rely upon the aid of the Reichstag without distinction of party alignment. Pursuant thereto the draft of a law concerning the insurance of the worker against industrial accidents has been prepared first. Supplementary to it a proposal accompanies it which puts forward the task of uniform organization of the industrial sickness fund affairs. But also those of the working population who become incapable of work because of age or invalidity, on the other hand, have an established claim upon a higher measure of state care, when it can be had for them. To find the right means and method for this care is a difficult, but also one of the highest, tasks of every community, which stands upon the common basis of Christian public life.

SPEECH OF BISMARCK IN SUPPORT OF THE NEW ACCIDENT INSURANCE BILL, MARCH 15, 1884

I SHOULD LIKE us and the German Reichstag to have the merit of having made at least a beginning in this domain of legislation, and thus of having preceded the other European States. The limitation of the measure is dictated by the consideration that the wider and more comprehensive it is the more numerous are the interests touched, and therefore the greater the opposition on the part of the representatives of these interests, which will be aroused and will find expression here, so that the passing of the measure would be all the more difficult. The extent of the limitation should in my opinion be determined by the extent of the Employers' Liability Act of 1871, for I regarded it as our first duty to remove the deficiencies of the first attempt made in this domain by that law.

According to Frederick the Great, it is the duty of government to serve the people . . . The opposite would be to rule the people. We desire to serve the people . . . Only if you have decided not to improve the conditions of the workers do I understand why you reject the Anti-Socialist Law. For it is unjust to prevent a numerous class of compatriots from taking the necessary steps for their self defence and not to offer them a hand in removing the cause of their discontent. I can well understand that the leaders of the Social Democratic Party are not in favor of this law. What they need are precisely dissatisfied workers. They want to lead and to rule and in order to achieve this goal they need numerous dissatisfied classes. They must oppose each attempt of the government . . . to remove the causes of dissatisfaction since they do not want to lose their hold over the masses which they had led astray.

As soon as the State takes this matter [of insurance] in hand—and I believe it is its duty to take it in hand—it must seek the cheapest form of insurance, and, not aiming at profit for itself, must keep primarily in view the benefit of the poor and needy. Otherwise we might leave the fulfilment of certain State duties—such as poor relief, in the widest sense of the words, is amongst others—like education and national defence with more right to share-companies, only asking ourselves, Who will do it most cheaply? who will do it most effectively? If provision for the necessitous in a greater degree than is possible with the present poor relief legislation is a State duty, the State must take the matter in hand; it cannot rest content with the thought that a share-company will undertake it.

The whole matter centres in the question, Is it the duty of the State, or is it not, to provide for its helpless citizens? I maintain that it is its duty, that it is the duty not only of the "*Christian* State," as I ventured once to call it when speaking of "practical Christianity," but of every State. It would be foolish for a corporation to undertake matters which the individual can attend to alone; and similarly the purposes which the parish can fulfil with justice and with advantage are left to the parish. But there are purposes which only the State as a whole can fulfil. To these belong national defence, the general system of communications, and, indeed, everything spoken of in Article 4 of the constitution. To these, too, belong the help of the necessitous and the removal of those just complaints which provide Social Democracy with really effective material for agitation. This is a duty of the State, a duty which the State cannot permanently disregard.

I am not impressed if some people consider this law as socialistic. The question is rather how far one is to go in applying the principles of state socialism. Without the latter our economic life would become impossible. Every poor law is socialism. Indeed there are nations which do not want to have anything to do with socialism and which consequently have no poor laws at all. I need only mention the case of France. These conditions in France are reflected in the ideas of the eminent political economist Leon Say . . . whose views are based upon the conception that every French citizen has the right to starve and that the government is not obliged to prevent him from exercising this right. . . .

THE TRIPLE ALLIANCE

THE TRIPLE ALLIANCE which I originally sought to conclude after the peace of Frankfort, and about which I had already sounded Vienna and St. Petersburg, from Meaux, in September 1870, was an alliance of the three Emperors with the further idea of bringing into it monarchical Italy. It was designed for the struggle which, as I feared, was before us; between the two European tendencies which Napoleon called Republican and Cossack, and which I, according to our present ideas, should designate on the one side as the system of order on a monarchical basis, and on the other as the social republic to the level of which the antimonarchical development is wont to sink, either slowly or by leaps and bounds, until the conditions thus created become intolerable, and the disappointed populace are ready for a violent return to monarchical institutions in a Caesarean form. I consider that the task of escaping from this *circulus vitiosus,* or, if possible, of sparing the present generation and their children an entrance into it, ought to be more closely incumbent on the strong existing monarchies, those monarchies which still have a vigorous life, than any rivalry over the fragments of nations which people the Balkan peninsula. If the monarchical governments have no understanding of the necessity for holding together in the interests of political and social order, but make themselves subservient to the chauvinistic impulses of their subjects, I fear that the international revolutionary and social struggles which will have to be fought out will be all the more dangerous, and take such a form that the victory on the part of monarchical order will be more difficult. Since 1871 I have sought for the most certain assurance against those struggles in the alliance of the three Emperors, and also in the effort to impart to the monarchical principle in Italy a firm support in that alliance. I was not without hope of a lasting success when the meeting of the three Emperors took place in Berlin in September 1872, and this was followed by the visits of my Emperor to St. Petersburg in May, of the King of Italy to Berlin in September, and of the German Emperor to Vienna in October of the next year. The first clouding over of that hope was caused in 1875 by the provocations of Prince Gortchakoff, who spread the lie that we intended to fall upon France before she had recovered from her wounds.

At the time of the Luxemburg question (1867) I was on principle an adversary of preventive wars, that is, of offensive wars to be waged because we thought that later on we should have to wage them against an enemy who would be better prepared. According to the views of our military men it was probable that in 1875 we should have conquered France; but it was not so probable that the other Powers would have remained neutral. Even during the last months of the negotiations at Versailles the danger of European intervention had been daily a cause of anxiety to me, and the apparent hatefulness of an attack undertaken merely in order not to give France time to recover her breath would have offered a welcome pretext first for English phrases about humanity, but afterwards also to Russia for making a transition from the policy of the personal friendship of the two Emperors, to that of the cool consideration of Russian interests which had held the balance at the delimitation of French territory in 1814 and 1815. That for the Russian policy there is a limit beyond which the importance of France in Europe must not be decreased is explicable. That limit was reached, as I believe, at the peace of Frankfort—a fact which in 1870 and 1871 was not so completely realised at St. Petersburg as five years later. I hardly think that during our war the Russian cabinet clearly foresaw that, when it was over, Russia would have as neighbour so strong and consolidated a Germany. In 1875 I had the impression that some doubt prevailed on the Neva as to whether it had been prudent to let things go so far without interfering in their development. The sincere esteem and friendship of Alexander II for his uncle concealed the uneasiness already felt in official circles. If we had wished to renew the war at that time, so as not to give invalided France time to recover, after some unsuccessful conferences for preventing the war, our military operations in France would undoubtedly have come into the situation which I had feared at Versailles during the dragging on of the siege. The termination of the war would not have been brought about by a peace concluded tête-à-tête, but, as in 1814, in a congress to which the defeated France would have been admitted, and perhaps, considering the enmity to which we were exposed, just as in those days, at the dictation of a new Talleyrand. . . .

Count Shuvaloff was perfectly right when he said that the idea of coalitions gave me nightmares. We had waged victorious wars against two of the European Great Powers; everything depended on inducing at least one of the two mighty foes whom we had beaten in the field to renounce the anticipated design of uniting with the other in a war of revenge. To all who knew history and the character of the Gallic race, it was obvious that that Power could not be France, and if a secret treaty of Reichstadt was possible without our consent, without our knowledge, so also was a renewal of the old coalition—Kaunitz's handiwork—of France, Austria, and Russia, whenever the elements which it represented, and which beneath the surface were still present in Austria, should gain the ascendency there. They might find points of connexion which might serve to infuse new life into the ancient rivalry, the ancient struggle for the hegemony of Germany, making it once more a factor in Austrian policy, whether by an alliance with France, which in the time of Count Beust and the Salzburg meeting with Louis Napoleon, August 1867, was in the air, or by a closer accord with Russia, the existence of which was attested by the secret convention of Reichstadt. The question of what support Germany had in such a case to expect from England I will not answer without more in the way of historical retrospect of the Seven Years' War and the Congress of Vienna. I merely take note of the probability that, but for the victories of Frederick the Great, the cause of the King of Prussia would have been abandoned by England even earlier than it actually was.

The situation demanded an effort to limit the range of the possible anti-German coalition by means of treaty arrangements placing our relations with at least one of the Great Powers upon a firm footing. The choice could only lie between Austria and Russia, for the English constitution does not admit of alliances of assured permanence, and a union with Italy alone did not promise an adequate counterpoise to a coalition of the other three Great Powers, even supposing her future attitude and formation to be considered independently not only of French but also of Austrian influence. The area available for the formation of the coalition would therefore be narrowed till only the alternative remained which I have indicated.

In point of material force I held a union with Russia to have the advantage. I had also been used to regard it as safer, because I placed more reliance on traditional dynastic friendship, on community of conservative monarchical instincts, on the absence of indigenous political divisions, than on the fits and starts of public opinion among the Hungarian, Slav, and Catholic population of the monarchy of the Habsburgs. Complete reliance could be placed upon the durability of neither union, whether one estimated the strength of the dynastic bond with Russia, or of the German sympathies of the Hungarian populace. If the balance of opinion in Hungary were always determined by sober political calculation, this brave and independent people, isolated in the broad ocean of Slav populations, and comparatively insignificant in numbers, would still remain constant to the conviction that its position can only be secured by the support of the German elements that remained loyal to the Empire, with other symptoms showed that among Hungarian hussars and lawyers self-confidence is apt in critical moments to get the better of political calculation and self-control. Even in quiet times many a Magyar will get the gypsies to play to him the song, "Der Deutsche ist ein Hundsfott" ("The German is a blackguard").

In the forecast of the future relations of Austria and Germany an essential element was the imperfect appreciation of political possibilities displayed by the German element in Austria, which has caused it to lose touch with the dynasty and forfeit the guidance which it had inherited from its historical development. Misgivings as to the future of an Austro-German confederation were also suggested by the religious question, by the remembered influence of the father confessors of the imperial family, by the anticipated possibility of renewed relations with France, on the basis of a *rapprochement* by that country to the Catholic Church, whenever such a change should have taken place in the character and principles of French statesmanship. How remote or near such a change may be in France is quite beyond the scope of calculation.

Last of all came the Austrian policy in regard to Poland. We cannot demand of Austria that she should forgo the weapon which she possesses as against Russia in her fostering care of the Polish spirit in Galicia. The policy which in 1846 resulted in a price being set by Austrian officials on the heads of insurgent Polish patriots was possible because, by a conformable attitude in Polish and Eastern affairs, Austria paid (as by a contribution to a common insurance fund) for the advantages which she derived from the holy alliance, the league of the three Eastern Powers. So long as the triple alliance of the Eastern Powers held good, Austria could place her relations with the Ruthenes in the foreground of her policy; as soon as it was dissolved, it was more advisable to have the Polish nobility at her disposal in case of a war with Russia. Galicia is altogether more loosely connected with the Austrian monarchy than Poland and West Prussia with the Prussian monarchy. The Austrian trans-Carpathian eastern province lies open without natural boundary on that side, and Austria would be by no means weakened by its abandonment provided she could find compensation in the basin of the Danube for its five or six million Poles and Ruthenes. Plans of the sort, but taking the shape of the transference of Roumanian and Southern-Slav populations to Austria in exchange for Galicia, and the resuscitation of Poland under the sway of an archduke, were considered officially and unofficially during the Crimean war and in 1863. The Old-Prussian provinces are, however, separated from Posen and West Prussia by no natural boundary, and their abandonment by Prussia would be impossible. Hence among the pre-conditions of an offensive alliance between Germany and Austria the settlement of the future of Poland presents a problem of unusual difficulty. . . .

An alliance with Russia was popular with nearly all parties, with the Conservatives from an historical tradition, the entire consonance of which, with the point of view of a modern Conservative group, is perhaps doubtful. The fact, however, is that the majority of Prussian Conservatives regard alliance with Austria as congruous with their tendencies, and did so none the less when there existed a sort of temporary rivalry in Liberalism between the two governments. The Conservative halo of the Austrian name outweighed with most of the members of this group the advances, partly out of date, partly recent, made in the region of Liberalism, and the occasional leaning to *rapprochements* with the Western Powers, and especially with France. The considerations of expediency which commended to Catholics an alliance with the preponderant Catholic Great Power came nearer home. In a league, having the form and force of a treaty, between the new German Empire and Austria the National-Liberal party discerned a way of approximating to the quadrature of the political circle of 1848, by evading the difficulties which stood in the way of the complete unification, not only of Austria and Prussia-Germany, but also of the several constituents of the Austro-Hungarian Empire. Thus, outside of the social democratic party, whose approval was not to be had for any policy whatever which the government might adopt, there was in parliamentary quarters no opposition to the alliance with Austria, and much partiality for it.

Moreover, the traditions of international law from the time of the Holy Roman Empire, German by nation, and of the German confederation tended to the theory that between Germany as a whole and the Habsburg monarchy there existed a legal tie binding these central European territories together for purposes of mutual support. Practical effect had indeed rarely been given to this *consortium* in former ages; but it was possible to vindicate in Europe, and especially in Russia, the position that a permanent confederation of Austria and the modern German Empire was, from the point of view of international law, no new thing. These questions, whether the alliance would be popular in Germany, how far it could be justified by international law, were to me matters of subordinate importance, merely subsidiary to its eventual completion. In the foreground stood the question whether the execution of the design should be begun at once or deferred for a time, and with what degree of decision it would be advisable to combat the opposition which might be anticipated on the part of Emperor William—an opposition sure to be determined rather by his idiosyncrasy than by policy. So cogent seemed to me the considerations which in the political situation pointed us to an alliance with Austria that I would have striven to conclude one even in the face of a hostile public opinion. . . .

If the united Austro-German power had by the closeness of its cohesion and the unity of its counsels as assured a position as either the Russian or the French power regarded *per se,* I should not consider a simultaneous attack by our two great neighbour empires, even though Italy were not the third in the alliance, as a matter of life and death. But if in Austria anti-German proclivities, whether national or religious, were to gain strength; if Russian tentatives and overtures in the sphere of eastern policy, such as were made in the days of Catherine and Joseph II, were to be thrown into the scale, if Italian ambitions were to threaten Austria's possession on the Adriatic sea, and require the exertion of her strength to the same degree as in Radetzky's time—then the struggle, the possibility of which I anticipate, would be unequal. And if we suppose the French monarchy restored, and France and Austria in league with the Roman Curia and our enemies for the purpose of making a clean sweep of the results of 1866, no words are needed to show how greatly aggravated would then be the peril of Germany. This idea, pessimistic, but by no means chimerical, nor without justification in the past, induced me to raise the question whether it might not be advisable to establish between the German Empire and Austria-Hungary an organic connexion which should be incorporated in the legislation of both Empires, and require for its dissolution a new legislative Act on the part of one of them.

Such a guarantee has a tranquillising effect on the mind; but whether it would stand the actual strain of events may reasonably be doubted, when it is remembered that the constitution of the Holy Roman Empire, which in theory had much more effective sanctions, yet failed to assure the cohesion of the German nation, and that we should never be able to embody our relation with Austria in any more binding treaty-form than the earlier confederation treaties, which in theory excluded the possibility of the battle of Königgrätz. All contracts between great states cease to be unconditionally binding as soon as they are tested by "the struggle for existence." No great nation will ever be induced to sacrifice its existence on the altar of fidelity to contract when it is compelled to choose between the two. The maximum "ultra posse nemo obligatur" holds good in spite of all treaty formulas whatsoever, nor can any treaty guarantee the degree of zeal and the amount of force that will be devoted to the discharge of obligations when the private interest of those who lie under them no longer reinforces the text and its earliest interpretation. If, then, changes were to occur in the political situation of Europe of such a kind as to make an anti-German policy appear *salus publica* for Austria-Hungary, public faith could no more be expected to induce her to make an act of self-sacrifice than we saw gratitude do during the Crimean war, though the obligation was perhaps stronger than any can be established by the wax and parchment of a treaty.

An alliance under legislative sanction would have realised the constitutional project which hovered before the minds of the most moderate members of the assembly of the Paulskirche, both those who stood for the narrower Imperial-German and those who represented the wider Austro-German confederation; but the very reduction of such a scheme to contractual form would militate against the durability of its mutual obligations. The example of Austria between 1850 and 1866 was a warning to me that the political changes which such arrangements essay to control outrun the credits which independent states can assure to one another in the course of their political transactions. I think, therefore, that to ensure the durability of a written treaty it is indispensable that the various elements of political interest, and the perils involved therein, should not be left out of account. The German alliance is the best calculated to secure for Austria a peaceful and conservative policy.

The dangers to which our union with Austria are exposed by tentatives toward a Russo-Austrian understanding, such as was made in the days of Joseph II and Catherine, or by the secret convention of the Reichstadt, may, so far as possible, be minimized by keeping the strictest possible faith with Austria, and at the same time taking care that the road from Berlin to St. Petersburg is not closed. Our principal concern is to keep the peace between our two imperial neighbours. We shall be able to assure the future of the fourth great dynasty in Italy in proportion as we succeed in maintaining the unity of the three empire states, and in either bridling the ambition of our two neighbours on the east or satisfying it by an *entente cordiale* with both. Both are for us indispensable elements in the European political equilibrium; the lack of either would be our peril—but the maintenance of monarchical government in Vienna and St. Petersburg, and in Rome as dependent upon Vienna and St. Petersburg, is for us in Germany a problem which coincides with the maintenance of our own state régime. . . .

Anyhow, in the future not only military equipment but also a correct political eye will be required to guide the German ship of state through the currents of coalitions to which we are exposed in consequence of our geographical position and our previous history. We shall not avoid the dangers which lie in the bosom of the future by amiability and commercial *pourboires* to friendly Powers. We should only increase the greed of our former friends and teach them to reckon on our anxieties and necessities. What I fear is, that by following the road in which we have started our future will be sacrificed to small and temporary feelings of the present. Former rulers looked more to the capacity than the obedience of their advisers; if obedience alone is the criterion, then demands will be made on the general ability of the monarch, which Frederick the Great himself would not satisfy, although in his time politics, both in war and peace, were less difficult than they are to-day.

Our reputation and our security will develop all the more permanently, the more, in all conflicts which do not immediately touch us, we hold ourselves in reserve and do not show ourselves sensitive to every attempt to stir up and utilise our *vanity*. Attempts of this kind were made during the Crimean war by the English press and the English Court, and the men who tried to push themselves forward at our own Court by depending on England; we were then so successfully threatened with the loss of the title of a Great Power, that Herr von Manteuffel at Paris exposed us to great humiliations in order that we might be admitted to take part in signing a treaty, which it would have been useful to us not to be bound by. Now also Germany would be guilty of a great folly if in Eastern struggles which did not affect her interests she were to take a side sooner than the other Powers who were more directly concerned. Even during the Crimean war there were moments in which Prussia, weaker though she then was, by resolutely arming to support Austrian demands, and even going beyond them, could command peace and further an understanding with Austria on German questions; and just in the same way in future Eastern negotiations Germany, by holding back, will be able to turn to its advantage the fact that it is the Power which has least interest in Oriental questions, and will gain the more the longer it holds up its stake, even if the advantage were to consist in nothing more than a longer enjoyment of peace. Austria, England, Italy will always have to take up a position with regard to a Russian move forward upon Constantinople sooner than the French, for the Oriental interests of France are less imperative, and must be considered more in connexion with the question of the German frontier. In Russo-Oriental crises France would not be able to entangle herself either in a new policy for gaining power in the West, or in threats against England based upon friendship with Russia, unless she had previously come to an understanding or a breach with Germany.

If Germany has the advantage that her policy is free from direct interests in the East, on the other side is the disadvantage of the central and exposed position of the German Empire, with its extended frontier which has to be defended on every side, and the ease with which anti-German coalitions are made. At the same time Germany is perhaps the single Great Power in Europe which is not tempted by any objects which can be only attained by a successful war. It is our interest to maintain peace, while without exception our continental neighbours have wishes, either secret or officially avowed, which cannot be fulfilled except by war. We must direct our policy in accordance with these facts—that is, we must do our best to prevent war or limit it. We must reserve our hand, and not allow ourselves before the proper time to be pushed out of a waiting into an active attitude by any impatience, by the desire to oblige others at the expense of the country, by vanity or other provocation of this kind; otherwise *plectuntur Achivi.*

Our non-interference cannot reasonably be directed to sparing our forces so as, after the others have weakened themselves, to fall upon any of our neighbours or a possible opponent. On the contrary, we ought to do all we can to weaken the bad feeling which has been called through our growth to the position of a real Great Power, by honourable and peaceful use of our influence, and so convince the world that a German hegemony in Europe is more useful and less partisan and also less harmful for the freedom of others than that of France, Russia, or England. That respect for the rights of other states in which France especially has always been so wanting at the time of her supremacy, and which in England lasts only so long as English interests are not touched, is made easy for the German Empire and its policy, on one side owing to the practicality of the German character, on the other by the fact (which has nothing to do with our deserts) that we do not require an increase of our immediate territory, and also that we could not attain it without strengthening the centrifugal elements in our own territory. It has always been my ideal aim, after we had established our unity within the possible limits, to win the confidence not only of the smaller European states, but also of the Great Powers, and to convince them that German policy will be just and peaceful, now that it has repaired the *injuria temporum,* the disintegration of the nation. In order to produce this confidence it is above everything necessary that we should be honourable, open, and easily reconciled in case of friction or *untoward events.* I have followed this recipe not without some personal reluctance in cases like that of Schnäbele (April 1887), Boulanger, Kauffmann (September 1887); as towards Spain in the question of the Caroline Islands, towards the United States in that of Samoa, and I imagine that in the future also opportunities will not be wanting of showing that we are appeased and peaceful. During the time that I was in office I advised three wars, the Danish, the Bohemian, and the French; but every time I first made myself clear whether the war, if it were successful, would bring a prize of victory worth the sacrifices which every war requires, and which are so much greater than in the last century. Had I had to say to myself that after one of these wars we should find some difficulty in discovering conditions of peace which were desirable, I should scarcely have convinced myself of the necessity for these sacrifices as long as we were not actually attacked. I have never looked at international quarrels which can only be settled by a national war, from the point of view of the Göttingen student code of honour which governs a private duel, but I have always considered simply their reaction on the claim of the German people, in equality with the other great states and Powers of Europe, to lead an autonomous political life, so far as is possible on the basis of our peculiar national capacity.

CHURCH AND STATE IN GERMANY

BARON WILHELM EMMANUEL VON KETTELER (1811–77) was admitted to the priesthood in 1844. He became a leading organizer of the Catholic Center party in Germany. Von Ketteler's zeal for his Church never flagged, and after the formation of the German Empire he served in the Reichstag until he thought it best to resign because of the violent controversies of the day. He remained a leading figure in opposition to Bismarck's *Kulturkampf* (Fight for Civilization). The first of the following selections has been translated from *The Catholics in the German Empire,* which he wrote toward the end of the Franco-Prussian War of 1870–71 and which influenced the Center party in Germany for many years.

The second selection is a translation of an address by Bismarck (1815–98) before the Prussian House of Lords on March 10, 1873. In a straightforward manner and with little oratorical flourish, the Imperial Chancellor and Minister of Foreign Affairs makes his point of view clear regarding the conflict of church and state.

The specific problem before the House was the government's proposal to modify Articles 15 and 18 of the Constitution of 1850 of the Prussian State. Bismarck's point of view was supported on April 4, 1873. Religious institutions would continue to enjoy their property and management of their affairs, with the proviso that they "remain subject to the laws of the state and the legally provided supervision of the state." The following provision was added elsewhere: "However, the law authorizes the state to regulate the education, appointment, and dismissal of clergymen and ecclesiastical officials and determines the limits of ecclesiastical disciplinary authority."

The effect of these amendments, which became law on April 5, 1873, was clearly to place all religious institutions under the supervision and control of the state. In the following month came the May laws which were the center of the *Kulturkampf.* Two years later, on June 18, 1875, the above mentioned articles, together with Article 16, of the Prussian Constitution were completely annulled.

WILHELM VON KETTELER: THE CATHOLICS IN THE GERMAN EMPIRE

PROGRAM

I. Unreserved acceptance of the German government's authority within the limits of its present jurisdiction.

II. Firm national union with Austria, the German *Ostmark*.[1]

III. Just recognition of the independence of the separate lands belonging to the German Empire, as far as the necessary unity of the Empire permits and according to the laws of the Empire.

IV. The Christian religion is the foundation in the Empire as well as in the separate states on all matters pertaining to the practice of religion insofar as such practice is not detrimental to religious freedom.

V. The recognized Christian denominations order and control their affairs independently and remain in possession and enjoyment of their institutions and capital (endowments) founded for purposes of denominational, educational, and welfare activities.

VI. The German Empire demands, above all, German law and German freedom in the sense of an assured jurisdiction of justice for individual and social freedom and in contrast to the lying freedom of absolutism and liberalism which destroy the freedom of the individual and of association.

VII. Connected therewith is freedom of higher, secondary, and primary education, under legally controlled state supervision, and organization of the state school not at the option of state authorities, but in accordance with the genuine, religious, spiritual, and moral circumstances of the people.

VIII. The German Empire demands German constitutional forms in all spheres, not only a constitution for the Empire and country, but also a complete social constitution of the people for all their needs; corporate organization in contrast to the mechanistic constitutional forms of liberalism; self-administration in contrast to mere bureaucracy.

IX. In particular, a constitution expressing integrally these principles for the nation, the community, and the district.

X. The development of the constitution of the Empire:

(1) through an upper chamber;

(2) through a supreme court of the Empire as an inviolable bulwark of the entire German legal system, as bulwark of public law, and as juridical control for the administration of the Empire and country.

XI. Regulation of the national debt, reduction of obligations imposed by the state, equalization of taxes. As means thereto:

(1) introduction of a stock exchange tax;

(2) introduction of an income tax for commercial enterprises and corporations;

(3) operation of railroads at state expense;

(4) reduction of military burdens;

(5) abolition of taxes on the most essential necessities of life.

XII. Corporate reorganization of laboring and artisan classes.

[1] [*Eastern border-country.*]

Legal protection of children and women of the working classes against the exploitation of capitalists.

Protection of workers through laws governing hours of labor and Sabbath rest.

Legal protection of health and morals of workers with reference to working places.

Establishment of inspectors to supervise the laws enacted for the protection of the working class.

XIII. Legal prohibition of all secret societies, in particular the order of Freemasons as a secret society.

IV. RELATION OF THE GERMAN EMPIRE TO THE CHRISTIAN RELIGION

The constitution of the North German Confederation has hitherto been regarded as the model for the constitution of the German Empire and has been transferred with few modifications to the new Empire. It may have suited previous circumstances. However, this point of view cannot be maintained for the future. Such an Empire would not have the right to bear the name of the old German Empire. The German Empire, in contrast to the German Confederation, must serve not only material but also spiritual interests and must respond to the spirit of the German people. The institutions and laws of the Empire must therefore be permeated with respect for religion and morality. They must respect the honorable for its own sake, and protect the moral fibre through which the states are inwardly strengthened; they must renounce the materialistic conception of the state which has made many European countries sick unto death.

This ideal and moral content, however, is thoroughly lacking in the provisional constitution of the Empire. Convincing evidence for this is found in Article IV of the constitution of the North German Confederation, which enumerates the concerns underlying the Confederation and its legislation. Tariffs and taxes, trade, banking, and railroad matters constitute, in addition to military affairs, almost its only content. Important though these are, they give an insufficient content for the lofty concept of the German Empire. A North German paper recently made a significant comment on the July monarchy: "The political trading company which in 1830 took possession of the government in the name of the bourgeoisie, needed a name for the firm and found the same in Louis Philippe of Orleans." This king, it continued, "with his woolen umbrella and high finance" remained an "unintelligible interlude" to the people. The more this is confirmed to be true, the more must the German Empire guard itself against the appearance that it, too, was set up by a trading company which was only seeking an establishment for itself. The German title of Emperor demands something higher than the management of business interests, and even the lustre of the German armed forces is not able here to take the place of the higher spiritual blessings.

From this point of view, first of all, two propositions follow for our program.

The foundation of the whole historical development of the German people, its culture and its moral being, is the Christian religion. To it the German people owe their higher spiritual blessings. It would be a disgraceful disavowal of the entire past if the constitution of the German Empire should not mention in a single word the Christian religion, that spring from which Germany has derived its spiritual and moral life. In recognition of the fact that the Christian religion is the historical foundation of the religious life in Germany and is the religion of the entire German people with the exception of the Jewish subjects of the state, no attempt was made after the storms of the year 1848 to remove from the Prussian constitution of January 31, 1850, the statement that "the Christian religion will be made the foundation of those arrangements of the state which are related to the practice of religion, safeguarded by the guaranteed freedom of religion." This same statement, in recognition of the same fact, was also included in the German fundamental principles of the Union parliament in its decision of April 27, 1850, and a series of German constitutional charters followed this example.

We demand, therefore, in the first place, the inclusion of the same statement in the constitution of the Empire also. This demand satisfies the most sacred right of the great majority of the Christian population in Germany. Indeed it would be intolerable to belie the fact that the great mass of the German people is Christian. It would be intolerable to withhold from the Christian consciousness of the German people the very thing that was conscientiously guaranteed them even in the year 1848. A refusal to include this or a similar statement in the constitution of the Empire would come pretty close to an open declaration that the German Empire dissociates itself from the Christian religion. Such a declaration, however, would not injure the Christian religion so much as it would the very foundations of the Empire.

OTTO VON BISMARCK: THE ANCIENT STRUGGLE FOR POWER BETWEEN MONARCHY AND PRIESTHOOD

THE QUESTION before us, is in my opinion, misrepresented and is viewed in a false light, if it is considered as a denominational, ecclesiastical question. It is really a political issue. Our Catholic fellow citizens are being told that it is concerned with a struggle between a Protestant dynasty and the Catholic Church.

It is not a conflict between belief and unbelief. It is the ancient struggle for power, which is as old as the human race; the conflict between monarchy and priesthood, which is much older than the advent of our Saviour in this world. It is the conflict in which Agamemnon found himself with his seers, in which he lost his daughter, and which prevented the Greeks from putting to sea. It is the conflict which under the name of the struggles between the popes and the German emperors filled the history of the Middle Ages. . . . It is the conflict which found its end in the death of the last representative of the illustrious Swabian imperial family who died on the scaffold under the ax of a French conqueror. And this French conqueror was at that time in alliance with the Pope. We have been very near to an analogous solution of the situation, translated of course into the customs of our time. If the French war of conquest, whose outbreak coincided with the publication of the Vatican decrees, had been successful, I do not know what would have been said in German ecclesiastical circles of the *gesta Dei per Francos*.[2] Similar designs were proposed before the last war with Austria, similar designs were proposed at Olmütz,[3] where a similar alliance stood opposed to the monarchy as it exists in our land on a basis which is not recognized by Rome. It is, in my opinion, a falsification of politics and of history in general to regard His Holiness the Pope exclusively as the high priest of a denomination or the Catholic Church as the representative of ecclesiasticism. The papacy has always been a political power which has intervened in the affairs of the world with the greatest determination and the greatest results. It strives after these encroachments on the state and makes them its program. The programs are known. The goal which continually hovers before the papal power, as the Rhine boundary does before the French, the program, which at the time of the medieval emperors was near realization, is the subjection of the temporal to the spiritual power, an eminently political project. But it is a striving which is as old as humanity, for ever since there have been clever men, real priests, they have maintained that the will of God is more clearly known to them than to their fellow men and that on that basis they had the right to rule their fellow creatures. It is known that this tenet is the basis of papal pretensions to sovereign authority. I need not remind you here of the official papal documents which have been mentioned and criticized a hundred times. . . . The struggle between priesthood and monarchy, the struggle in this case between the Pope and the German Emperor, as we have already seen it in the Middle Ages, is to be judged

[2] [*Works of God through the French.*]

[3] [To avert war, the Prussian King, Frederick William IV, signed a treaty with Austria at Olmütz in November 1850, providing for the dissolution of the German Union under the leadership of Prussia and for the restoration of the German Confederation under the presidency of Austria.]

as every other contest. It has its alliances, its treaties of peace, its temporary lulls, its truces. . . .

This contest for power, then, is subject to the same conditions as every other political struggle, and it is a perversion of the problem, calculated to impress people of no judgment, to present it as if it were a matter of persecuting the Church. It is a question of protecting the state; it is a question of fixing the boundary between rule by priesthood and rule by monarchy, and the boundary line must be so established that the state on its part can maintain its existence. For in the realm of this world, it has the power and precedence.

We in Prussia have not always been parties to this struggle through any choice of ours. On the part of the Roman curia we were for a long time not regarded as the main adversary. Frederick the Great lived completely at peace with the Roman Church, while his contemporary, the emperor of the predominantly Catholic Austrian state was engaged in a violent contest with the Catholic Church. I wish only to point out that the problem is thus quite independent of denominationalism. In this same way I can cite the fact that it was really the thoroughly Protestant King, Frederick William III, whose faith was, one may almost say, anti-Catholic, who at the Congress of Vienna urged and accomplished the restoration of the temporal sovereignty of the Pope. Nevertheless he departed from this world while in conflict with the Catholic Church. We have found then, in the constitutional provisions which concern us here a *modus vivendi,* an armistice, which was concluded at a time when the state felt itself to be helpless and believed that it could find support at the hands of the Catholic Church, at least a partial support. This was probably due to the recollection that in the National Assembly of 1848 all the districts with overwhelming Catholic populations elected, I will not say, royalists, but at least friends of order, which was not the case in Protestant districts. In consideration of this, the compromise in the struggle for power between the secular and spiritual forces was concluded but, as was shortly revealed, quite mistakenly so far as the practical consequences were concerned. For it was not the support of the electors for whom those who wanted order had voted, but rather it was the Ministry of Brandenburg and the army of the King who restored order. The state indeed finally had to help itself; the protection which could be granted to it on the part of the various churches had not extricated it. At that time, however, arose the *modus vivendi* under which we lived for a number of years in a peaceful relationship. To be sure, this peace was purchased only by means of continual yielding on the part of the state. The state entrusted its rights with reference to the Catholic Church quite unreservedly to the hands of authorities whose function supposedly was to look after the interests of the Prussian King and state over against the Catholic Church. Actually, however, these authorities came into the service of the Pope to look after the rights of the Church as opposed to the Prussian state. . . . Meanwhile, because of my aversion to any internal conflict and quarrel of this kind, I preferred this peace with all its disadvantages and on my part have refused to engage in the conflict, although I have often been urged by others to do so. Perhaps there has never been a time, without regard to other issues when the government was more inclined to come to an understanding with the papacy, if it had not been attacked, than at the conclusion of the French War. . . . It is known to everyone who was with us in France that our otherwise naturally good relations with Italy succumbed to a discord, I will not say a gloom, during the entire war and lasted to the conclusion of peace. In our opinion, Italy's entire attitude was that her love for the French was greater than her own interests; otherwise Italy would have had to defend her independence along with us against France. It was a very striking phenomenon for us, and doubts arose as to which of the various interests would be decisive for the Italian government. It was a fact that Italian military forces were hostile to us under Garibaldi, whose departure from Italy, could as we believed, have been prevented if more energy had been used. Fortunately this discord between Italian and German politics has now been overcome. It is thus far from true that a partiality for Italy influenced our political affairs at that time.

While we were still at Versailles, it surprised me somewhat to learn that an appeal was issued to Catholic members of legislative bodies asking them to declare whether they were in favor of joining a denominational fraction, such as we know today as the Center Party; and whether in the politics of the Empire they would agree to work for and vote for the propositions which we are considering today in order that they might be incorporated in the constitution of the Empire. At that time this program did not alarm me so very much—I was peace-loving to that degree—I knew from whom it originated; in part from a highly ranking prince of the Church, Bishop von Ketteler of Mainz, who has the assignment to do whatever he can for papal politics; and partly from an outstanding member of the Center Party, von Savigny, the former Prussian representative of the federal diet. This movement had an advantage in being begun by them. I had not believed of the latter that he would use his influence in a direction hostile to the government. Therein I was completely mistaken. I only add the reasons for not attaching true significance to these matters at that time, for I would not have returned to Germany if I had not been convinced that we could get along with this party and its endeavors. However, when I returned here, I saw for the first time how strong the organization of the party had become, the party of the Church which is in conflict with the state. I saw the progress which the activities of the Catholic group in the ministry of ecclesiastical affairs and public instruction had made in its attack on the German language in the Polish territories. In Silesia, where this had never happened before, there emerged a Polish party under substantial priestly encouragement and actual protection of ecclesiastical policy. But even that would not in itself have been decisive. What first called my attention to the danger was the power which this newly formed faction had acquired. Representatives who had resided and been respected in their districts and for long had always been elected were set aside by orders from Berlin, and the election ordered of new representatives who were not even known by name in their election districts. That happened not in one but in several election districts. They had such a rigid organization and had won such power over the people to bring about the program of the previously mentioned prince of the Church, the Bishop of Mainz, as revealed in his published writings. To what does this program lead? Read them. These writings are ingeniously written and pleasant to read, and in everyone's hands. Their purpose is to create a political dualism in Prussia, a state within the state; that all Catholics be brought to the point where they receive the direction of their attitude in politics as in private life exclusively from this Center Party. We would thereby come to a dualism of the worst kind. The Austro-Hungarian Empire shows us that a state in propitious circumstances can govern with a dualistic constitution. But there is no denominational dualism there. Here we are concerned with the creation of two denominational states which would have to stand in a dualistic conflict with one another. The highest sovereign of the one is a foreign ecclesiastical prince who has his seat in Rome, a prince of the Church who through the newest changes in the constitution of the Catholic Church has become stronger than he was before. We would thus have, were this program realized, in place of the hitherto united Prussian state, in place of the realizable German Empire, two parallel bodies politic, running side by side. The one would have its general staff in the Center faction; the other would have its general staff in the principle of temporal power and in the government and person of His Majesty the Emperor. This situation was completely unacceptable to the government; it was a duty to protect the state against this danger. The government would have failed to recognize and would have neglected its duty if it had waited quietly while this amazing progress was being revealed by closer examination of the matter. Formerly there had been no occasion to make this examination. This progress was made by infringing upon the state's proper domain, and if the government on its side had quietly folded its hands in its lap, that same infringement would have continued. But the government found it necessary to terminate the armistice which had been provided for by terms of the constitution of 1848 and to establish a new *modus vivendi* between the secular and the priestly powers. The state cannot permit the situation to endure without being driven to internal conflicts which would deeply affect its stability. The entire question lies in this: are these provisions in the sense in which His Majesty's government bears witness, dangerous to the state or are they not? If they are, you fulfill a conservative duty if you vote against their maintenance. If you regard them to be completely harmless, that would be a conviction which His Majesty's government does not share and it cannot with these constitutional provisions continue to carry on its affairs and meet its responsibilities. The government must then leave it to those who regard these provisions as not dangerous. In its struggle to protect the state, the government turns to the House of Lords with the appeal for support and aid in fortifying the state and for defense against attacks that undermine it and endanger its peace and future. We have confidence that the majority of the House of Lords will not fail us in this support.

(The Count von Landsberg-Velen protested against the expression: "The Center faction with its sovereign in Rome." This resulted in the following remarks by the minister.)

As a matter of fact, I wished to remark that as far as pertains to constitutional circumstances, there is of course no doubt that legally the Center faction also recognizes its sovereign in His Majesty the Emperor, but I wished to say by means of the expression (to which exception is taken) that actually the party follows another power and other influences. I can also recollect in this connection literature and data which issued from the different leaders of the party. Also I would like to remind you that in the suggestions of the program of the party which first came to Versailles—and I could name witnesses who partly accepted and partly declined this program—, there was mention of representing the Pope and of the interests of the Pope as sovereign in his church and in his country. However, I believe that this question will not lead us any further. We all know what the Center Party is. I believe that it would never place itself in a strong opposition to Rome, not even the new Protestant members who have joined it, although they never shrink from strong opposition to their legal and public sovereign. This indicates the conflicts which lie before us. The purpose of my address was really not to go so far into the past as I had to, in order to document my conviction that this problem concerns itself not with ecclesiastical but with political struggles, which under ecclesiastical cloaking have been made to appear in a false light. If one attributes an ecclesiastical character to these conflicts, it is done for the impression this creates in the nation. The same was said, too, in the case of the school supervision law but experience has proved otherwise, and in the future you will continue to fail to produce evidence that the church was endangered by means of a higher degree of education for its officials.[4]

[4] [This refers to the Falk laws which put under state control the education of the Catholic clergy.]

JULES FERRY

IN 1877 LÉON GAMBETTA (1838–82), leader of the republican group in favor of the newly formed Third Republic, coined what was to become a famous phrase, "Clericalism, there is the enemy," and thereby pointed to the conviction that the most pressing problem facing the Third Republic was that of its relations with the clergy. For most partisans of the Republic the terms "clerical" and "monarchist" were to become practically synonymous during the ensuing years.

From the time of Condorcet the hope of establishing the secular goods of liberty and equality and especially of fraternity was founded largely upon a faith in education. And education was therefore conceived largely in terms of cultivating not only the reason but also a secular community fused by the allegiance to common principles. The first and perhaps most fundamental source of friction between clerical and anticlerical revolved around proposals for educational reform, and the man who bore the brunt of the conflict was Jules Ferry (1832–93). Lawyer and journalist, Ferry incurred the enmity of the Right with his "laic laws," and the enmity of the Radical Socialist Left with his imperialism. Guided by the principles worked out by Condorcet in connection with his own experience with the administration of a secular system of education, and believing in the principles of the positivists, Ferry proposed through the "laic laws," which have since become known under his name, to establish the compulsory school attendance of all children. The choice between a church school and one maintained by the state was to be left to the discretion of the individual family, but only the non-religious school was to be supported by state funds. At these schools only laymen were to be allowed to teach and no religious instruction was to be allowed. In addition, members of unauthorized religious orders were forbidden to teach even in private schools and all such orders were dissolved.

From 1879 to 1882, Ferry was several times premier of France. In addition, he was minister of public instruction and from 1883 to 1885 he took over the ministry of foreign affairs, working in a single-minded fashion on behalf of French colonial expansion. The exaggerated report of reverses to his policy in China led to his overthrow by Clemenceau and the Radical Socialists in 1885.

Ferry was anything but a popular public official. Nevertheless, he laid the foundations for the modern French Empire. And in addition, his attempt to establish the "moral unity" of France through a program of "neutral" education was the basis for the centralized system of French education which persisted through the entire history of the Third Republic.

The following selections are taken from Ferry's speeches in the Chamber of Deputies. The first was delivered in 1870 at the beginning of the Republic and the second in 1879.

[ON EDUCATION]

THE RETARDING of the progress of natural inequalities is, as I see it, the very basis and justification of society. Humanity has made this conquest; the advantage of physical force is already annulled, or almost so. But at the same time, isn't it true that modern society, which has done away with that kind of inequality, has preserved another and perhaps more formidable one, which results from wealth? It is true, gentlemen. Nevertheless, consider how in the present this inequality, which results from wealth, is attenuated, enfeebled, and moderated by the progress of time. For a long time here in France wealth has conferred no special rights. The possession of land, in the last century, was still a source of social power, of public right. . . .

That state of things has disappeared; the Revolution has come to grips with these outrages to human conscience; but, a little after the Revolution—and several of those here can remember—the possession of land, the enjoyment of a certain amount of capital still brought a privilege: the right to vote, the right to contribute to the formation of public powers; twenty years ago they still existed; happily these times are gone.

Even the right to work, the most essential of all rights, was eighty years ago, in a sense, a privilege of birth; craftsmen were organized in guilds; guilds recruited under certain conditions; the sons of masters had a right of priority, of preference over those who had the misfortune to be born outside the bounds of the guild; the Revolution came and swept away this inequality, this privilege of birth, just as it had caused other privileges and inequalities to disappear.

In sum, these are the two great victories of this century: the freedom of labor and universal suffrage; henceforth, neither the right to work nor the right to vote, that is to say of contributing to the formation of public powers, are attached to the accident of birth: they are the inheritance of all men coming into the world.

That being so, our century can say to itself that it is a great century. I often hear talk of the decadence of the present time; I confess to you, gentlemen, I am tired of these lamentations, and, moreover, I have noticed for a long time that this complaint comes from those people who resist, without explaining why, the current of modern civilization, and who cannot make up their minds to take their part in the democratic era we are now entering. No! we are not a society in decay, because we are a democratic society, we have done these two great things: we have freed the right to vote and the right to work. . . .

But we are a great century only under certain conditions: we are a great century if we know well what the work, the mission, and the duty of our century are. The last century and the beginning of this one have abolished the privileges of property, the privileges and distinction of class; assuredly the work of our time is not more difficult. Surely, it will necessitate fewer storms, it will exact less grievous sacrifices; it is a peaceful work, it is a generous work, and I define it thus: to get rid of the last, the most formidable of the inequalities founded on birth, the inequality of education. It is the problem of the century and we ought to apply ourselves to it. And as for me, when the supreme honor of representing a portion of the Paris population in the Chamber of Deputies fell to me, I took an oath: among all the necessities of the present time, among all the problems, I would choose one to which I would consecrate all that I have of intelligence, all that I have of soul, of heart, of physical and moral power—the problem of the education of the people.

From the social point of view, inequality of education is, in effect, one of the most glaring and most grievous consequences of the accident of birth. With the inequality of education, I defy you ever to have the equality of rights, not theoretical equality but real equality, and the equality of rights is the very basis and essence of democracy.

Let us construct an hypothesis and take the situation in its extreme terms: let us suppose that he who is born poor is by the same token necessarily and fatally ignorant; I know well that this is an hypothesis, and that the humanitarian instinct and social institutions, even those of the past, have always prevented such an extremity from developing; there have always been in all times—it must be said to the honor of humanity—there have always been means of instruction, more or less organized, accessible to those who were born poor, without resources, without capital. But, since we are concerned with the philosophy of the question, we can suppose a state of things where predestined ignorance is added necessarily to predestined poverty, and such would be, in effect, the logical consequence inevitable to a situation in which knowledge would be the exclusive privilege of wealth. Well, gentlemen, what is the name of that extreme situation in the history of humanity? It is the caste system. The caste system makes knowledge the exclusive prerogative of certain classes. And if modern society does not see to the separation of education and science from wealth, that is to say from the accident of birth, it simply returns to the caste system.

From another point of view, the inequality of education is the greatest obstacle in the way of the creation of truly democratic customs. This creation goes on under our eyes; it is already the work of today, it will be above all the work of tomorrow; it consists essentially in replacing the relations of inferior to superior by which the world has lived for so many centuries, by relations of equality. Here I ask for the attention of all in this kind of audience while I give an explanation. I do not come to preach any absolute equalizing of social conditions which would suppress the social relations of command and obedience. No, I do not suppress them, I modify them. Ancient societies admitted that humanity was divided into two classes: those who command and those who obey. The notion of command and obedience in a democratic society like ours, is this: there are always, without doubt, men who command, and others who obey, but commanding and obeying are alternatives, and it is for everyone in his turn to command and to obey.

That is the great distinction between democratic societies and those which are not democratic. What I call democratic command does not consist then in the distinction between inferior and superior; there is no longer either inferior or superior; there are two equal men who contract together; in the master and in the servant you do not see anything more than two contracting parties each with his own precise rights, limited and known in advance; each with his duties and, as a consequence, each with his dignity.

That is what modern society one day must be; but—and it is thus that I come back to my subject—what is the primary condition for the establishment of these equal customs (whose birth we are witnessing), for the spreading of democratic reform throughout the world? This condition is that a certain education must be given to him who at another time one called an *inferior,* to him who one still calls a *worker,* in such a way as to inspire him or to give him a sense of his dignity; and, since a contract regulates the two positions, it is necessary at least that it comprise two parties.

Finally, in a society which has as its task to establish liberty, it is very necessary to suppress the distinctions of classes. I ask you, in good faith, all of you who are here and who have received varying degrees of education, whether there are not still distinctions of classes? I say that they still exist; there is one that is fundamental and, moreover, difficult to erase, and that is between those who have received an education and those who have received none at all. Then, gentlemen, I defy you ever to make a nation of equals out of these two classes, a nation animated by that spirit of harmony and by that fraternity of ideas which are the strength of true democracies, if between the two classes there has not been that first drawing together, that first fusion which results from the mixing of the rich and the poor on the benches of some school.

Antiquity understood it, and the ancient republics stated it as a principle that, for both the children of the poor and the children of the rich, there must be only one kind of education. Ancient society, excessive in all things and easily oppressive because it was confined in general within the walls of one narrow city, was not afraid to separate the child from his family and deliver him wholly, body and soul, to the republic.

When Christianity came to replace ancient civilization, a similar conception was found among the superior men who were during many centuries the leaders of Christian society. I am, gentlemen, one of those who have a very great and sincere historical admiration for Christianity: I find that a work has been achieved during the past eighteen centuries, a work of men and of men's brains which is beyond praise when it is studied from the vantage point of today and analyzed in its entirety. Ah! there we had men with powerful minds; they were not simply priests, they were statesmen, these organizers of Christian and Catholic societies who founded so many of the things which we are having so much trouble in transforming. Well then, we find among them the very principle of which we speak; in Catholic society, in the society of the Middle Ages, one recognizes easily, one can put one's finger upon, the principle of the equality of education.

In the same way as the ancient republics separated children from their families and said the child belongs to the republic; so Christianity, coming in a different time to establish a sort of Christian republic over political divisions and differences of nationality, said: the child belongs to the Church, and then it established for the child, not only for the rich child—I say this to its honor—but just as much for the poor child, a kind of education of which the principle characteristic was rigorous equality. In the first grade, they studied the catechism; in the second grade they studied the sacred language, Latin, and having learned these two things, everything that it is important to know in Christian society was known; one is an accomplished Christian, a savant, a scholar, one has all Christian science. . . .

In effect, there is in America, in all cities which have five hundred families, a school in which one learns, in the first place, all the positive sciences which are the object of our three grades of French education; where one learns, in the second place, all of Latin and Greek that it is important to know; one does not learn to make Latin verses, but one learns to read Latin authors who are not too difficult. That is what is taught free to *seven million children* while in France we have only 500,000 children who go to primary school. America has 2,000 free and public schools. The budget for public instruction in America is not the budget of the American republic, but is the budget of the various states, and, above all, the budget of the townships. Do you know what its total is? It is tremendous: free America spends annually 450 millions for public schools; and by means of these 450 millions they generously open the great sources of learning to seven million children, and they give to these children of all classes instruction which is received only by a small number of children of the bourgeoisie of France.

And that is not all, gentlemen: there is not only free instruction, common and public; there are enough great colleges, academies, universities, special foundations, to make us hide in humiliation. . . .

In America the rich pay for the instruction of the poor. And I am prepared to find this just.

Gentlemen, in this world there are two ways of understanding the right of wealth; there is the wealthy man, content with himself, who shows off his comforts and casts aspersions on the poor, in saying, as the Pharisee of the Gospel said: "Thank God that I did not have to be born among these miserable people!" He is a satisfied man; he considers that he is within his right and that he owes nothing to anyone; let him bloom in his tranquility; but, without raising any question of social principle, let us say that finer souls have another idea of the duty of wealth. He who has never been struck by the unheard of and shocking aspects of the division of wealth in this world is very much a stranger to the finer qualities of the human soul. . . .

So I declare explicitly that it is just and necessary that the rich should pay for the education of the poor; for in this way their property is justified, and that the degree of moral advancement and civilization is marked by the gradual substitution for the right of the stronger or the richer *the duty of the stronger!* . . .

The equality of educations restores unity within the family. There is today a barrier between woman and man, between wife and husband, which makes many marriages, harmonious in appearance, hide the most profound differences of opinion, of tastes, of sentiments; this is not true marriage, for true marriage, gentlemen, is the marriage of souls. Well, then, tell me, is this marriage of souls frequent? Tell me if there are very many couples united by ideas, sentiments, and opinions? There are many households where the two mates are in accord on all external things, where there is absolute agreement concerning common interests; but as for the intimate thoughts and sentiments which are the whole of the human being, they are as strange to each other as if they were mere acquaintances.

So much for the well-to-do households. But in poor households, what resources are found when the wife brings to the marriage intelligence and wisdom! In place of a deserted house, there is a bright home, animated by conversation, embellished by reading, lit by a sun which puts sad and painful reality into a different light. Condorcet understood this well, and he said that the equality of education makes the wife of the worker both the guardian of the home and the guardian of the common wisdom.

In any case, it is necessary to realize and to understand that this problem of the education of the woman is connected with the problem of the very existence of actual society.

Today there is going on a hidden but persistent battle between the society of former times, the old régime with its structure of regrets, of beliefs and institutions which do not accept modern democracy, and the society which descends from the French Revolution; there is an old régime among us that is always persistent, active, and when this fight, which is at the bottom of modern anarchy, when this internal fight is over, the political battle will end at the same time. In this struggle woman cannot be neutral; optimists, who do not wish to see to the bottom of things, can imagine that the role of woman is nothing, that she does not take part in the battle, but they do not perceive the secret and persistent help which she brings to that society which is on the way out and which we wish to get rid of forever. . . .

THE FREEDOM OF HIGHER EDUCATION

. . . WHEN WE speak of an act of the State in education, operating to maintain unity, we attribute to the state the only role that it can have in regard to instruction and education.

The State is certainly not at all an instructor in mathematics, an instructor in physiology or in chemistry. If it suits it in the public interest to pay the chemists and the physiologists, if it suits it to pay the professors, it is not in order to create scientific truths; this is not its concern in fostering education; its concern is to maintain a certain state morale, certain state doctrines which are important for its conservation.

What will the most ardent among our adversaries say, and will they not consider this single question as an offense if I say to them: "Is it in the name of the right of the father and family that you tolerate instruction which tends to the negation and discredit of our country?" You have replied, No; haven't you? Well then, I ask this Chamber, I ask this republican majority which listens to me, I ask whether the fatherland is only a piece of land which events can extend or reduce, and whether, along with this native land there is not a moral native land, a set of ideas and aspirations which the government ought to defend as the inheritance of the souls of which it has charge?

I ask them whether there is not in this French society a certain number of ideas nourished on the most pure and generous blood; for twenty-five years, soldiers, writers, philosophers, orators, political men, have continuously striven for these ideas, have poured out their blood for them; I ask whether there is not a heritage of which you are the guardians, a heritage which you ought to transmit to your children just as your fathers left it to you. . . .

We have, then, to ask ourselves whether the restoration to the State of the right to bestow academic degrees and to reëstablish the laws governing unauthorized religious congregations, whether these two enactments (both of which restore to the public domain some of the prerogatives it had yielded to the private domain and which together comprehend in its entirety the law that is submitted to you), exceed the rights of the State—especially in the light of the definition of these rights that has just been given, and in view of the responsibility of the state for conserving unity. . . .

Where is the danger, gentlemen? I answer without hesitating: It is in the Jesuits . . . , it is in their growth, it is in their progress, it is in their incontestable and uncontested power. . . .

In 1861 they had 46 residences, distributed in 33 departments and in Algeria. In 1877, there were 1,509 members, distributed in 74 residences spread over 51 departments, in Algeria and in Reunion island.

How many of these establishments were devoted to secondary education? In 1865, the Jesuits possessed 14 establishments for secondary education, with 5,074 pupils. In 1876 they possessed, according to the statistics of the ministry, 27—I believe that the true figure is 31—27 with 9,131 pupils. Do you know how many pupils there are besides these, belonging to authorized and instructed congregations . . . ? There are . . . 7,854. . . .

In the face of this instruction, the sad picture of which I unfolded yesterday, . . . [it is said in some quarters] that there is only one thing for the government and the Chamber to do: give freedom to individuals and draw up a law of associations.

In making such an eloquent appeal (which surely finds sensitive chords in a French assembly) to the courage of the conviction of those who are in the majority here, to the generous sentiments which are those of the republican party, he says to you: "You are afraid of the Society of Jesus; but these terrors, justifiable a hundred years ago, are part of the government of the ancient régime; but you, have you forgotten? you are a free government! You have these two great forces: liberty and universal suffrage. Liberty you possess completely; power you have without reserve; universal suffrage backs you up; and it is in this situation of predominant and expanding control that you come to ask us for repressive measures against the Society of Jesus!" . . .

Do you not perceive that lay and civil society before 1789, represented by the parlements, had, in the face of the ultramontane and clerical danger, some powers which you do not have? It had absolute power, the power of an ancient historic dynasty; it had the courts, that is to say all the bourgeoisie; it had more than half, perhaps two-thirds of the French clergy; it was supported at the same time by royal authority, sometimes called episcopacy outside the Church, and by the power of the parlements; . . . it had a great theological and religious current behind it; thus endowed with all material and moral forces, it still felt that it ought to rely for its defense on measures identical with those we have just advised you to adopt.

What remains to us of all this arsenal? Not the absolute power, certainly, but in place of absolute power, governments by opinion, that is fleeting, essentially weak governments; a sovereign and uncontested power, which nothing resists, but which we do not know how to raise to the level of permanent, invariable, and indisputable forces. . . .

Well, I ask you as statesmen who feel the weight of your responsibility, at this hour when it depends on you to abolish the existing laws by your vote or to maintain them solemnly for the future and in the interest of the future, I ask you whether the situation and the moment are well chosen for the republican government to disinterest itself in the education of the younger generation; if the moment appears to have come to give young minds up to the anarchy of opinions, and to make a Republic which abandons to chance the intellectual development of the nation, which lets everything alone, and which is content to remain the scrupulous manager of the material interests of the country, to be a great builder of railroads and an honest collector of taxes.

If you think that this moment has come, it behooves you to recognize all the consequences of the course which you are going to take. . . .

I say that we wish to attack them [Jesuits], and we feel capable of attacking them, because they are the promoters of that attempt at religious revolution which is not yet ended . . . of that attempt so dangerous to civil power and modern society; because it dominates the Church; because it has a large part of the clergy in slavery; because the clergy of France is its captive . . . because these serve as models for all ecclesiastical establishments; because it is from them that these establishments ask for books, and modern histories, and travesties on the history of France! . . .

Finally, we attack the Jesuits because the Jesuits and their adherents are the soul of that new kind of lay army which we have fought for seven years; which has been the master in the national Assembly; which, by means of the Catholic committees extends over the whole of France and covers it like a net; which has a political personnel; which is a party—I am mistaken—which is a faction.

As for warring against Catholicism, truly I am surprised, grievously surprised, at finding this accusation on the lips of M. Lamy, who knows us, who knows very well that there is in the thought of no one of us, in the thought of no member of the government from which this project emanates, any desire, not the smallest desire, as remote as can be, of attempting, I will not say a persecution, but even an attack against Catholicism.

To attack Catholicism, to go to war with the belief held by the great number of our fellow citizens, why that would be the last and the most criminal of follies! . . .

You have duties, gentlemen, to the generation which have preceded you, and it is not, I think, so that young France might be left to the instruction of the Jesuits that they effected in this country two great revolutions, that of 1789 and that of 1830, both directed against the old régime!

As for your mandate, do you have any doubts as to its character? Did the people of the republic of France send you here simply to fold your arms? Was not a mandate given to you, not only to affirm the Republic and to carry it on here, but also to put it on a solid foundation? Is it in keeping with your mandate, after having chased your eternal adversaries from the political fortresses which they occupied, to permit them to fortify themselves in education?

MAURICE BARRÈS

Born of the disastrous war of 1870, the Third French Republic led a troubled existence in its early years, and it was not till the last decade of the nineteenth century that it seemed beyond the danger of destruction from within. Lingering royalism, anticlericalism and traditional Catholicism, radicalism, and conservatism rose in conflict each time some untoward incident occurred. And there were many such incidents: the *Seize mai*—the attempt of President MacMahon to dissolve the Chamber in 1877; the Wilson affair—when President Grévy's son-in-law was implicated in the selling of awards of the Legion of Honor; the Boulanger episode—the very abortive attempt at dictatorship by General Boulanger in 1889; the Panama scandal—which involved many republican deputies and officials; and, most serious of all, the Dreyfus case—which tore France asunder. And in the background there were the eternal shame of the loss of Alsace-Lorraine and the burning desire for revenge. These crises and this shame often prevented the French bourgeoisie from deriving full satisfaction from the otherwise bright picture of a nation rapidly growing in economic prosperity and in democratic stability. Though the Third Republic was much nearer to the ideal of an orderly government for the people and by the people than had been the "bourgeois" monarchy of Louis Philippe, it also drew considerable criticism both from the extreme Left and the extreme Right.

It was in this political atmosphere that Maurice Barrès (1862–1923) entered public life, and rose to be one of the great literary figures of modern France. His writings were shot through with the sadism, exoticism, and sensualized religiosity characteristic of post-Romantic "Decadence." The early work—three novels forming the trilogy of *Le Culte du moi*—was born of dissatisfaction with the skepticism which was the main fruit of his formal education and was devoted to the development of the individual. But Barrès was a native of Lorraine, the lost territory, and he soon began to ground his individualism, and cultivation of the self, in collective entities: the nation, the soil, the ancestors. Between 1892 and 1902 appeared his second trilogy, *L'Energie nationale*. Barrès turned to traditional elements for strength—the army, Catholic faith, monarchy. Thus he took part in the debates over the Dreyfus case and, with Paul Déroulède, whom he later succeeded as head of the League of Patriots, he was one of those who cried loudest in defense of what the army and the anti-Dreyfusards called "the honor of the army," while it was only a deliberate attempt at convicting Captain Alfred Dreyfus of "treason" which had been committed by another man. Another great figure in French literature, Emile Zola, put his reputation and his life itself at stake to defend the Jewish officer and to denounce those who had not hesitated to forge documents to strengthen the case against Dreyfus. But Zola was a realistic novelist and a radical republican. Barrès like his Italian contemporary, Gabriele D'Annunzio, and like Thomas Carlyle, belonged to that group whose deference to truth was sometimes beclouded by a mystical worship of beautiful "heroism."

Barrès arrived at a definition of nationalism, "integral nationalism," as the identification of the individual spirit with the national past and of individual life with that of the nation. This doctrine easily could and, with many did, unite with social Catholic concepts of corporatism within the state. It represented the extreme development of French nationalism, beyond which passed only the lunatic fringe and far short of which the vast majority of the French people stopped. It is worth noting that Barrès rejected for France the racist doctrines in his fellow countryman, Count de Gobineau, while the German Richard Wagner took them to heart and joined the newly founded *Gobineau Vereinigung*. But Barrès went far enough in the direction of exclusiveness. His French nationalism could appeal to Frenchmen only and therefore contradicted the more liberal nationalism of republican France—the nationalism of 1789, 1848, and even that of men like Charles Péguy which appealed to ideals of significance to the world at large as well as to France.

The following selection was translated from Barrès' *Scènes et doctrines du nationalisme* (1902).

FRENCH NATIONALISM

I WAS ASKED to deliver the third lecture of the League of the French Nation. I undertook to define nationalism, that is to say, to seek its basic principles and implications.

We must begin, I said, by understanding the causes of our weakness.

The Dreyfus Affair is only the tragic symptom of a general malady. When a wound fails to heal the physician thinks of diabetes. Beneath the accident let us seek out the underlying condition.

Our deeply ingrained disease is that we are divided, disturbed by a thousand individual wills, by a thousand individual imaginations. We have fallen apart, we have no common awareness of our aim, of our resources, of our core.

Happy are those nations where movements are linked together, where efforts harmonize as if a plan had been developed by a superior mind!

There are many ways in which a country can have this moral unity. Loyalism may rally a nation about its sovereign. In the absence of a dynasty, traditional institutions can provide a center. But a century ago, our France suddenly cursed and destroyed its dynasty and its institutions. Lastly, some races succeed in becoming aware of themselves organically. Such is the case with the Anglo-Saxon and Teutonic groups which are developing more and more into races. Alas! there is no French race, but a French people, a French nation, that is to say, an entity consisting of a political grouping. Yes, unfortunately, as compared with rival, and, in the struggle for existence, necessarily enemy groups, ours has not achieved a conscious awareness of itself. We implicitly admit this in the way in which our publicists, writers, and artists call us sometimes Latins, sometimes Gauls, sometimes "the soldier of the Church" and then again the great nation, "the emancipator of peoples," depending on the needs of the moment.

In the absence of a moral unity, of a common understanding of what France is, we have contradictory words, varied banners beneath which men eager to exercise leadership can gather their following. Each of these groups understands in its own way the internal law of the development of this country.

Nationalism means the resolution of all questions by reference to France. But how are we to do this when we have no common understanding and idea of France?

Should an incident occur, it is interpreted by each party according to the particular meaning the party gives to the concept of France. Hence we can understand the real importance of this Dreyfus Affair: instead of being handled, in a common spirit, by Frenchmen who had the same idea of their country and of what is good for it, it has been considered by doctrinaires who are guided by the precepts of their own taste.

Given this lack of moral unity in a country which has neither dynasty nor traditional institutions, and which is not a race, it is quite natural that dangerous metaphysicians should gain authority over our imaginations, provided that they are eloquent, persuasive, *kindly*. By offering us an ideal, they undertake to give us moral unity. But far from delivering us from confusion, they only increase it by their contradictory assertions.

This is what must be remedied. Only a lazy heart and a mind thoroughly corrupted by anarchy could be content in this France torn and leaderless in thought.

But how can this lacking national consciousness be developed?

First let us repudiate philosophic systems and the political parties to which they give rise. Let us all join our efforts, not behind a vision of our own mind, but behind realities.

We are men of good will: whatever be the opinions which our family, education, environment and many little personal events have given us, we are decided to take as our starting point that which is, and not our own intellectual ideal. One among us may find that the Revolution has turned us from the most prosperous and happy paths, another may regret that the First Consul, by the Concordat, returned France to the influence of Rome; a third is convinced that the destinies of our country are closely linked to those of Catholicism. Each rewrites the history of France. Let us cast aside these fictions. Why mire ourselves in these hypothetical roads which France might have followed? We shall derive a more certain profit from delving into all the moments of

French history, living in our thoughts with all her dead, with every one of her experiences. What moral problems we shall face if our own preference must choose among all these seemingly contradictory revolutions which have occurred in France over a century! After all, the France of the Consulate, the France of the Restoration, the France of 1830, the France of 1848, the France of the authoritarian Empire, all these Frances which go to contradictory extremes with such astonishing agility, all come from the same root, and tend toward the same end; they are the fruits of different seasons from the same seed on the same tree. . . .

If the League of the French Nation could succeed in giving its followers this sense of the real and the relative, if it could convince those honest and devoted professors (who at times have done us so much harm) to judge things as historians rather than as metaphysicians, it would transform the abominable political spirit of our nation, it would restore our moral unity, it would indeed create what we have lacked: a national consciousness.

To have this national, realistic view of the Fatherland accepted, we must develop sentiments which already exist naturally in the country. Union cannot be built on ideas, so long as they are only processes of reason; they must be bulwarked with emotional strength. At the root of all things is feeling. One would try in vain to establish truth by reason alone, for intelligence can always find a new motive for reopening the question.

To create a national consciousness we must combine with this dominant intellectualism whose methods the historians teach, a less conscious, less deliberate element.

Misled by a university training that spoke only of Man and Humanity, I feel that like so many others I should have embroiled myself in anarchical agitation had not certain feelings of veneration warned me and strengthened my heart. . . . [*There follows a description of his emotions on a visit to the military cemetery at Metz.*]

Nothing is more valuable in forming a people's soul than this voice of our ancestors, than this lesson of the soil which Metz teaches so well. Our soil gives us a discipline, for we are the continuation of our dead. That is the reality on which we should build. . . .

The dead! What would a man mean to himself if he stood only by himself? When each of us looks backward he sees an endless train of mysteries, whose recent embodiment is called France. We are the product of a collective being which speaks in us. Let the influence of the ancestors be enduring and the sons will be vigorous and upright, and the nation one. . . . In vain does the foreigner, on naturalization, swear that he will think and live as a Frenchman; in vain has he bound his interests with ours, blood persists in following the order of nature against all vows, against all laws. He is our guest, this son from beyond the Rhine, or English Channel, and we offer him safety and our generous friendship, but we do not owe him a share in the government of the country. Let him first feel our pulse, and, from roots that will grow, nourish himself from our soil and our dead. His grandchildren, indeed, will be French, genuinely, and not merely through a legal fiction.

CHARLES PÉGUY

CHARLES PÉGUY was born in Orléans in 1873. His father died when he was ten months old, and he was raised by his mother and grandmother. The family, of peasant stock themselves, lived on the outskirts of the city where Péguy gained the intimate familiarity with, and abiding respect for, peasant life which permeated much of his later writing. He was a scholarship student at the Lycée at Orléans, and continued his studies at the École Normale in Paris, where he heard Henri Bergson lecture on philosophy, and Romain Rolland on the history of art.

During his school days Péguy regarded himself as a socialist and an atheist. On May Day of 1898 he opened a socialist bookshop in Paris which was subsequently taken over by the future Premier of France, Léon Blum and some of his colleagues. In 1900 Péguy founded a periodical entitled *Cahiers de la quinzaine* (Fortnightly Notebooks). It became an organ for leftists of varying positions, and earned a considerable reputation by printing the early writings of Romain Rolland, Anatole France, and Jean Jaurès. Both the bookshop and the offices of the magazine became rallying places for the supporters of Dreyfus, and Péguy and his associates were not slow in "going into the streets" with their case for the condemned Captain.

The *Cahiers* served an important purpose in the development of Péguy's own thought. Many of his writings during this period reveal that humane patriotism which characterizes his later work. In 1905 he published *Notre Patrie,* and in 1908 he confessed to his friends that he had undergone a spiritual conversion and considered himself a Catholic. His Catholicism was as eclectic as his socialism had been, however, and assumed an individual character which was mystical and personal rather than dogmatic and antirepublican. In 1910 he published *Notre Jeunesse,* from which the following excerpt on the betrayal of republican ideals is taken.

Péguy had always been fascinated by the story of Joan of Arc; a Catholic mystic of the greatest intensity, and at the same time a French nationalist of the greatest dedication, she had achieved her most glorious triumph in his own birthplace, Orléans. For years, while studying at Paris, Péguy worked on a dramatic poem which he finally published in 1897, *Jeanne d'Arc.* It was revised in 1910 and published as *La Charité de Jeanne d'Arc,* followed by *Le Porche du-Mystère de la Deuxième Vertu* (1911), and *Le Mystère des Saints Innocents* (1912). One of his most important poems, *Eve,* was published in 1913.

With the outbreak of the First World War Péguy immediately enlisted in the army and refused a commission in order to be able to march along with his men to the front. He was killed in action during the first day of the Battle of the Marne, September 5, at Villeroy. He ended his life in defense of the French republic that he had sought to save from the fanaticism and opportunism of the Catholic and royalist right and from the dishonesty of his comrades on the republican and socialist left.

This selection is from Alexander Dru's translation of *Notre Jeunesse* in the volume *Temporal and Eternal* (New York: Harper and Bros., 1958).

OUR YOUTH

. . . . HISTORY will always tell us about the big chiefs, the leaders of history, more or less well, less rather than more, that's its *métier;* and if history does not, then historians will, and if historians do not then the professors (of history) will. What we want to know, and what we cannot invent, what we want to know more about, are not the principal roles, the leading stars, the grand drama, the stage, the spectacle; what we want to know is what went on behind, below, beneath the surface, what the people of France were like; in fact, what we want to know is the *tissue* of the people in that heroic age, the texture of the republican party. What we want to know is the texture, the very tissue of the bourgeoisie, of the Republic, of the people, when the bourgeoisie was great, when the people was great, when the republicans were heroic, and the Republic had clean hands. And to leave nothing unsaid, when the Republicans were republicans, and the Republic was the republic. What we want is not a Sunday version of history, but the history of every day of the week, a people in the ordinary texture of its daily life; working and earning, working for its daily bread, *panem quotidianum;* a race in its reality, displayed in all its depth.

. . . . The Republic was founded, preserved and saved and is still sustained by a small number of loyal families. Do they still preserve it in the same way? As they did for a century or more, in a sense almost since the second half of the eighteenth century? I am ready to agree, that a small number of families, of dynastic, hereditary loyalties, preserved the tradition, the *mystique* and what Halévy very rightly calls "republican conservation." But where I should not, perhaps, follow him, is that I think that we are literally the last representatives, and, unless our children take on the task, almost the last, posthumous survivals.

In any case, the last *witnesses.*

I mean precisely this: we do not yet know whether our children will reunite the threads of tradition, of the republican *mystique.* It has become completely foreign to the intermediary generation—and that makes twenty years.

We are the rearguard; not only a rearguard, but a somewhat isolated rearguard, sometimes almost abandoned. A company left in the lurch. We are almost specimens. We are going to be, we ourselves will be, archives, tablets, fossils, witnesses and survivors from those historic times. Tablets to be consulted.

We are extremely badly placed. Chronologically. In the succession of generations. We are the rearguard, in very poor touch, out of touch with the main body, the generations of the past. We are the last generation with a republican *mystique*. And our Dreyfus Affair will have been the last operation of the republican *mystique*.

We are the last. Almost the ones after the last. Immediately after us begins the world we call, which we have called, which we shall not cease calling, the modern world. The world that tries to be clever. The world of the intelligent, of the advanced, of those who know, who don't have to be shown a thing twice, who have nothing more to learn. The world of those who are not had on by fools. Like us. *That is to say:* the world of those who believe in nothing, not even in atheism, who devote themselves, who sacrifice themselves to nothing. *More precisely:* the world of those without a *mystique*. And who boast of it. Let no one make a mistake, and no one, consequently, rejoice over it, on either side. The *de-republicanisation* of France is essentially the same movement as the *de-christianisation* of France. Both together are one and the same movement, a profound *de-mystification*. It is one and the same movement which makes people no longer believe in the Republic and no longer believe in God, no longer want to lead a republican life, and no longer want to lead a Christian life, they have had enough of it, and one might almost say that they no longer believe in idols, and that they no longer want to believe in idols, and that they no longer want to believe in the true God. The *same* incredulity, *one single* incredulity, strikes at the idols and at God, strikes at the false gods and the true God, the old God and the new gods, the ancient gods and the God of the Christians. One and the same sterility withers the city and Christendom. The political city and the Christian city. The city of man and the City of God. That is the specific sterility of modern times. Let no one, therefore, rejoice on seeing the misfortune that befalls his enemy, his adversary, his neighbour. For the *same* misfortune, the same sterility, falls upon him . . . The argument is not really between the Republic and the Monarchy, between republicanism and royalism, particularly if one considers them as political forms, as two political forms; the modern world is not only opposed to the old *régime* and the new *régime* in France, it is opposed and contrary to all old cultures, to all old *régimes*, to all old cities, to everything which is culture, to everything which is the city. In fact, it is the first time in the history of the world that a whole world lives and prospers, *appears* to prosper, *in opposition to all culture.*

But let me not be misunderstood. I don't say this will last for ever. Our race has seen as bad times. But, anyway, that is how things stand.

And there we are.

We even have very deep reasons for hoping that it will not be for long.

We are extremely badly placed. We are in fact situated at a critical point, a distinguishing point, a dividing line. We are placed between the generations which had the republican *mystique* and those which have not got it, between those who still have it and those who no longer have it. So no one believes us. On either side. *Neutri,* neither the ones nor the others. The old republicans do not want to believe that there are no more young republicans. The young do not want to believe that there were old republicans.

We are between the two. No one, therefore, will believe us. To both we seem wrong. When we say to the old republicans: be careful, there's no one to come after us, they shrug their shoulders. They think there always will be someone. And when we say to the young: be careful, don't talk so airily about the Republic, it was not always a pack of politicians, behind it there is a *mystique,* it has its *mystique,* behind it lies a glorious past, an honourable past, and what is perhaps more important still, nearer the essence, there is a whole race behind it, heroism and perhaps sanctity; when we say that to the young, they stare at us with mild contempt and start treating us as old fogies.

Ready to regard us as fanatics.

But I repeat, I do not say it is for ever. On the contrary, the deepest reasons, the most serious indications all make us believe, and oblige us to think that the next generation which comes immediately after us, and which will soon be our children's generation, is going to be a mystical generation. Our race has too much blood in its veins to remain for more than a generation in the ashes and mildew of criticism. It is too vital not to reintegrate itself, organically, at the end of a generation.

Everything leads one to think that the two *mystiques,* the republican and the Christian, will flower again at the same time. As part of the same movement. In a single movement, just as they disappeared together (momentarily), and as they were obliterated together. However, what I say goes for the present, for the whole present. And after all much may happen in the course of a generation.

Misfortunes may befall us.

Such is our meagre position. We are meagre. As thin as a blade. We are squeezed in and flattened between the antecedent generations on the one hand, and on the other hand an already thick layer of succeeding generations. Such is the principal reason for our meagreness, our thinness, the wretchedness of our situation. We have the ungrateful task, the meagre office, the meagre duty of keeping the communications between them open, of enlightening the ones about the others, of informing them about one another. We shall, therefore, as a rule, be spewed out by the one and the other. That is commonly the fate of anyone who tries to tell a little (of the) truth. . . .

I am horrified when I see, when I discover, that the older men among us do not want to see what is self-evident, and which only has to be seen to be believed: the extent to which the young have become estranged from everything related to republican thought and its *mystique*. This is seen, above all, naturally, in the fact that thoughts, which were thoughts to us, have become, for them, ideas, in the fact that what was to us an instinct, a race, thoughts, have become for them *propositions,* from the fact that what was to us organic, has become for them a matter of logic.

Thoughts, instinct, races, habits which were nature itself to us, which we took for granted, on which we lived, and which were the forms of life, and which consequently no one thought about, which were more than legitimate, more than unquestioned: unreasoned, have become what is worst of all: theses, historical theses, hypotheses, I mean all that is least solid, most inexistent. The basis of a thesis. When a *régime,* from being organic has become logical, and from being alive has become historical, that *régime* is done for.

To-day we prove and demonstrate the Republic. When it was alive no one proved it.

One lived it. When a *régime* is demonstrated, easily, comfortably, victoriously, that means it is hollow, done for.

The Republic to-day is a thesis, accepted by the young. Accepted, rejected; it doesn't matter which. Proved, refuted. What is important, what is serious, what signifies, is not that it is held up, bolstered up, more or less indifferently, but that it should be a thesis.

That means that it must be supported or held together.

When a *régime* is a thesis among others (among so many others) it is down and out. A *régime* which is standing, which is alive, is not a thesis. . . .

The republicans and the monarchists, the governing republicans and the royalist theoreticians, reason in the same way, because they are intellectuals both together and separately, together and contrary to one another; they are politicians, and believe in a certain sense in politics, speak a political language, move and are situated on a political plane. So they speak the same language and move on the same plane. They believe in *régimes,* and that it is the *régime* which makes peace and war, provides the strength and virtue, the health and sickness, the steadiness, the duration and the tranquility of a people. The strength of a race. It is as though one believed that the Châteaux of the Loire caused or did not cause earthquakes.

We believe on the contrary (in opposition to both sides) that there are infinitely deeper forces and realities, and that it is the people on the contrary who are the strength or the weakness of *régimes;* and much less *régimes* of the people.

We believe that neither side sees nor wants to see those forces, those infinitely deeper realities.

If the republic and the neighbouring monarchies enjoy the same tranquility, it is because they are bathed in the same period, walking together along the same corridor. It is because they lead the same life fundamentally, are following the same diet. On those matters the republicans and the monarchists reason conjointly, though in opposition. We, on the other hand, place ourselves on an entirely different plane, descending on to a different level; trying to descend to quite other depths, we think, we believe, on the contrary, that it is the people who make the *régimes,* peace and war, strength and weakness, sickness and health.

We therefore turn towards the young, we turn to another side, and we can only say: "Take care. You treat us as old fogies. That's quite all right. But take care. When you talk airily, when you treat the Republic lightly, you do not only risk being unjust (which is not perhaps very important, at least so you say, in your system, but risk what in your system *is* serious), you risk something much worse, you risk being stupid. You forget, you fail to recognise that there is a republican *mystique;* but ignoring it and failing to recognise it will not prevent its having existed. Men have died for liberty as men have died for the Faith. The elections, nowadays, seem to you a grotesque formality, uniformly false and bogus in every respect. You have the right to say so. But men have lived, men without number, heroes, martyrs and I would even say saints—and when I say *saints* perhaps I know what I am saying— men have lived, numberless men, heroically, like saints, and have suffered and died, a whole people lived in order that the last of fools to-day should have the right to accomplish that bogus formality. It was a laborious and fearful birth. It was not always grotesquely funny. And all around us other peoples, whole races, are labouring in the same agonising birth, working and struggling for that contemptible formality. The elections nowadays are ridiculous. But there was a time, a heroic times, when the sick and the dying had themselves carried on their chairs in order *to deposit their ballot in the urn.* To deposit one's ballot in the urn; to you, to-day, the expression is pure comedy. It was prepared by a century of heroism. Not by literary heroism, that costs nothing. But by a century of incontestable heroism, of the most authentic quality. And, I should add, typically French. The elections are ridiculous. But there was an election. The great divide in the world, the great election of the modern world, between the *ancien régime* and the Revolution.

"The elections are ridiculous. But the heroism and the holiness with which one obtains contemptible results, temporally contemptible, are the greatest and most sacred things in the world. The most beautiful. You reproach us with the temporal degradation of the results. Look at yourselves. Look at your own results. You are always talking about republican degradation. But isn't the degradation of a *mystique* into a *politique* the common law? You talk of the decay of the republic, that is to say of the collapse of the republican *mystique* into the republican *politique*. Have there not been, are there not other degradations? Everything begins as a *mystique* and ends as a *politique*. Everything begins with *la mystique*, in mysticism, with its own *mystique*, and everything ends in politics, in *la politique*, in a policy. The important point is not that such and such a *politique* should triumph over another such, and that one should succeed. The whole point (what matters), the essential thing, is that *in each order, in each system*, THE MYSTIQUE SHOULD NOT BE DEVOURED BY THE POLITIQUE TO WHICH IT GAVE BIRTH.

"The essential thing, the thing that matters, is not that such and such a policy should triumph, but that in each order, in each system, in each *mystique*, the *mystique* should not be devoured by the policy that issues from it.

"In other words, it possibly matters, it obviously does matter, that the republicans should carry the day against the royalists, or that the royalists should carry the day against the republicans, but that is of infinitely little importance compared with the importance of the republicans remaining republicans.

"And I would add, not merely for the sake of symmetry, I should add as complementary: that the royalists should be and remain royalists. Which is, perhaps, what they are not doing at the present moment, just when they think they are doing so. You are always talking to us of the degradation of republicanism. But has there not been, by virtue of the same movement, has there not been a parallel degradation of monarchism, a similar royalist degradation? This is to say, properly speaking, a degradation of the royalist *mystique* into a certain policy issuing from it and corresponding to it, into a royalist policy. Have we not seen the effects of that *politique* for centuries, do we not see them daily? Have we not for centuries watched the royalist *mystique* being devoured by the royalist *politique*? And even to-day, although the royalist party is not in power, do we not read daily in its two principle newspapers, do we not see the miserable effects of that policy daily; and I should even go so far as to say that for those who know how to read, a constant struggle, a continual tension, an almost painful struggle, really painful, between a *mystique* and a *politique* between their *mystique* and their *politique*, the *mystique* belonging of course to the *Action Française*, using a rationalist terminology which deceives none but themselves; the *politique* being that of the *Gaulois* using a worldly terminology. What would they be like if they were in power? (Like us, alas.)"

People are always talking of the degradation of republicanism. When one sees what the clerical *politique* has made of the Christian *mystique*, why be astonished at what the radical policy has made of the republican *mystique*? When one sees what the clerks have, in general, made of the saints, why be surprised at what our parliamentarians have made of heroes? When one sees what the reactionaries have, by and large, made of sanctity, why be astonished at what the revolutionaries have made of heroism?

And then, all the same, one must be fair. If one wants to compare one order with another, one system with another, one must compare them on the same plane. One must compare the *mystiques* with one another and the *politiques* with one another. One must not compare a *mystique* with a *politique;* nor a *politique* with a *mystique*. In all the primary schools of the Republic, and in some of the secondary schools, and in many of the high schools they never tire of comparing the royalist *politique* and the republican *mystique*. In the *Action Française* everything comes down to comparing the republican *politique* with the royalist *mystique*. There is no end to it.

No one will ever agree. But that is perhaps what the parties want.

Perhaps it is the party game.

Our masters in the primary schools once used to hide the *mystique* of the *ancien régime* from us, the *mystique* of the old France, and concealed ten centuries of France from us. To-day our adversaries want to conceal *the mystique of the old France which was the republican mystique.*

And in particular the revolutionary mystique.

For the quarrel is not, as is said, between the old *régime* and the Revolution. The old *régime* was a *régime* belonging to the old France. The Revolution is eminently the work, the operation of the old France. The dividing date is not the first of January 1789 between midnight and one minute after midnight. The dividing line is somewhere about 1881.

Here again the republicans and the royalists, the republican government and the royalist theoreticians, reason in the same way, give two complementary arguments, twin arguments. Our good masters at the primary school told us, in effect, that, up to the first of January 1789 (Paris time), our poor old

France was an abyss of darkness and ignorance, of horrifying miseries, of crude barbarity (in fact, they did their job, taught their lesson), and so well you could hardly believe it: on the first of January 1789, electric light was installed everywhere. Our good adversaries in the School opposite told us, roughly speaking, that up to the first of January 1789, nature's sun was shining; since the first of January 1789, we have only got electric light. Both the ones and the others exaggerate.

The argument is not between an *ancien régime,* an old France, that supposedly ended in 1789, and a new France supposedly beginning in 1789. The fight goes much deeper. It is between the whole of the old France, pagan France (the Renaissance, the humanities, culture, ancient and modern letters, Greek and Latin and French), Christian France, traditional and revolutionary, monarchist, royalist and republican—and on the other hand, on the other side, in opposition, the dominion of a certain form of elementary, primary thought, which became established about 1881, which is not the Republic though calling itself the Republic, which is a parasite on the Republic and is properly speaking the domination of the intellectual party.

The contest is not between heroes and saints; the fight is against the intellectuals, against those who despise heroes and saints equally.

The argument is not between two orders of greatness. The fight is between those who hate greatness itself, who hate the one and the other equally, who have made themselves the official upholders of all that is base, small-minded and vile. . . .

The French Revolution founded a tradition that had already been prepared for a number of years, it founded a new order, a new conservatism. And a number of intelligent men have been led to think, nowadays, that the new order is not worth the old. But it certainly founded a new order, and not a disorder, as the reactionaries maintain. That order degenerated and became disorder, followed by disorders which became serious under the Directoire. . . .

The Revolution, on the contrary, the great Revolution, had been an inauguration. A more or less fortunate inauguration, but, in any case, an inauguration.

An inauguration; that is to say, that every subsequent restoration was nothing more than a repetition, a pale image, an attempted renewal of that inauguration. . . .

One must be very careful not to judge by names and indeed appearance, and one must mistrust them so much that just as the Second Empire, historically and really, is not the *continuation* of the First Empire, so the Third Republic, really and historically, does not *continue* itself. The continuation of the Third Republic does not *continue* the beginning of the Third Republic. Without there having been any great event, I mean any inscribably historical event in 1881, the Republic then began to reveal its discontinuity. From having been a republic it became Caesarism.

Not only can one say: everything is explained, I would say, everything is illuminated by that distinction. The incredible difficulties of public and private action are suddenly illuminated by the full light of day, flooded in light, if only one gives heed, gives audience so to say, to that distinction, to the discrimination we have just recognised. The source of all the sophism, of all the paralogisms of action, of all the *parapragmatisms*—or, at any rate, of all the worth-while ones, the only ones into which *we* can fall, the only ones we could commit, the only innocent ones—for all their culpability—lies in the fact that in politics we unduly prolong a line of action duly begun as a *mystique*. A line of action had emerged and sprung out of a *mystique,* with its source and spring in a *mystique*. That action was well and truly aligned. It was not only natural, legitimate, but due. Life follows its course. Action follows action in its train. One looks through the door. There is an engine-driver in control. Why bother about the driving? Life carries on. Action continues. And because it continues and the people, the mechanism, the institutions and surroundings, the apparatus, furniture and habits, all remain the same, one fails to notice that one has passed over the points where the line branches off. History itself has moved forward; events themselves march on. The points have been crossed. And by the mere succession of events, the continuation of the game, the baseness of man and his sinfulness, the *mystique* has become political action, or rather politics have usurped the place of the *mystique,* have devoured the *mystique*. That is the unchanging story that recurs again and again, only to begin all over again. The very same action which was legitimate becomes illegitimate. And that is how one becomes a criminal in all innocence.

The action that was decent becomes dirty, becomes another action, a dirty one. That is how one becomes an innocent criminal, the most dangerous of all, perhaps.

An action begun as a *mystique* continues in politics, and we do not notice that we are crossing the dividing line. Politics devour the *mystique,* and we fail to jump out when we are passing over the points, the point of discrimination.

If a man with his heart in the right place discerns the dividing point, stops at that point, and refuses to move in order to remain faithful to a *mystique,* refuses to adopt the abuses of the political game, which is itself an abuse, and refuses to enter into the derivative, parasitical, devouring *politique,* then politicians call him by a little word much used nowadays: they are quick to call us traitors.

Moreover, they call us traitors without conviction and for the sake of the electors. One must, after all, put something into electoral manifestos and pamphlets.

Everyone may as well know it, that is the sort of traitor we have always been and always will be. That is what we were, especially, pre-eminently, in the Dreyfus Affair, and the matter of Dreyfusism. The real traitor, in the full sense of the word, in the strong sense of the word, is the man who sells his faith, who sells his soul and gives himself up, loses his soul, betrays his principles, his ideal, his very being, who betrays his *mystique* and enters into its corresponding *politique,* the policy issuing from it and complacently passes over the dividing point.

. . . . If our first rule of conduct is not to continue (across the dividing point) an action begun as *mystique* and which ends in politics, similarly, our first rule of knowledge, of judgment, will be not to continue blindly (past the dividing point), the judgment, the knowledge, the knowing, concerned with an action begun as a *mystique* and ending in politics. Above all, one must be suspicious of one's judgment, of one's *knowing,* one's knowledge.

Above all, one must be careful of continuing. Continuing, persevering, in that sense, is all that is most dangerous to justice and to intelligence itself. To take one's ticket on departure in a party, in a faction, and never to bother where the train is rolling to, and above all, what it is rolling on, is to put one-self resolutely in the very best situation for becoming a criminal.

A great deal of light would be shed on all the rubbish, on the chatter and the nonsense and the apparent contradictions, on the difficulties and incomprehensibilities, the impossibilities, and the tiresome and tiring repetitions of the same incoherent views, on the good and bad faith of opponents—if only people would attend to what they are saying, if they made sure of talking about a *mystique* or about a *politique*. If only they would talk of the *mystique* or, more generally, of the *politique* of any particular action or order of things. That explains why, in so many polemics, and debates, the adversaries, the enemies, both seem to be in the right, and equally wrong. One of the main causes is that the one is talking about the *mystique,* and the other about the *politique* issued from it. Not only justice, in the moral order, requires that one should compare two actions on the same plane, and not on different planes, the *mystique* to a *mystique* and the *politique* to a *politique;* justice in the intellectual order requires as much.

The first consequence of the distinction, a first application of that principle, is that *mystiques* are far less inimical to each other than *politiques,* and in quite a different way. *Mystiques* should not, therefore, be blamed for the faults, the wars, the dissensions, the political enmities of the *politiques. Mystiques* are much less antagonistic to one another than are *politiques.* Because unlike *politiques,* they do not invariably have to divide the temporal world, temporal matters, limited temporal power, between themselves. And when they are enemies, it is in quite a different way, at a much deeper, more essential level, and with an infinitely nobler profundity. For example, the civic *mystique,* the *mystique* of antiquity, of the city, of the suppliants, was never opposed to, never could have opposed the *mystique* of salvation in the same way that the pagan *politique* opposed the Christian *politique;* so crudely, so basely, so temporally, so morally, as the pagan Emperors opposed the Christian Emperors and vice versa. And the *mystique* of salvation can never oppose the *mystique* of liberty in the same way as the clerical *politique* opposes, for example, the Radical *politique.* It is simple enough to be a good Christian and a good citizen as long as one does not go in for politics.

When politicians exchange their *mystique* for a *politique,* they accuse you of changing if you do not follow them. Let us put it more simply, and less harshly to the great men. Their *politique* has become a merry-go-round. "Monsieur," they say, "you have changed, you are no longer at the same place. The proof is that you are no longer opposite the same horse." *"Pardon, Monsieur le Député,* it is the horses that have moved."

We have had an eminent example of this in the Dreyfus Affair, continued in the affair of Dreyfusism. One could say that where there are already so many natural difficulties, the politicians have introduced supplementary, supererogatory, artificial difficulties. They always want those who serve the *mystique* to become the agents of their *politique,* from political motives, or, more usually, from natural incomprehension. They introduce further gratuitous breaches, as though the mystical ones were not enough.

And so we have in the Dreyfus Affair a unique example, a model almost, of what is meant by the degradation of a human action; but not only that, a précis of the degradation of a *mystique* into a *politique.*

There was a singular virtue in the Affair, perhaps an eternal virtue. I mean a singular power. And we can see this clearly to-day now that it is all over. It was not an illusion of our youth. First of all, it should be noted that it possessed a very singular virtue. In two senses. A singular power of virtue, as long as it remained a *mystique.* A singular power of malice as soon as it entered the field of politics. One of the greatest mysteries of history and of reality, and naturally therefore one that is most easily overlooked, is the sort of absolute difference (irrevocable, irreversible,) which there is in the *price* of events. The fact that certain events have a certain price, their own price; and that other events, of the same order, and of the same material or similar material, with the same form and the same value, should nevertheless have a price and value infinitely different; that every event should have its own price, its own mysterious power and value; that there should be wars and treaties of peace with their own value, heroisms and sanctities with their own value, is assuredly one of the great mysteries; that there should not only be men (and gods) who count for more than others, but peoples; entire peoples marked out in history, for the whole of temporal history, and perhaps, no doubt, for the other history too; and that the rest, the immense majority of people, almost all of them, on the contrary, should be marked out for silence, destined to silence, only rising to fall—that is a mystery we hardly see, like all great mysteries we do not observe, because we are bathed in it, as in all great mysteries; certainly it is one of the most poignant mysteries of history. The great problem of creation.

One should therefore say, with all due solemnity, that the Dreyfus Affair is one of the "chosen" events of history. It was a crisis in three histories, each of them outstanding. It was a crisis in the history of Israel. A crisis, obviously, in the history of France. And above all, it was a supreme crisis, as appears more and more distinctly, in the history of Christianity. And perhaps in several others. And thus, by a unique election, it was a triple crisis. Of triple eminence. A culmination. As for me, if I am able to continue the studies which we have begun on the situation accorded to history and to sociology in the general philosophy of the modern world, following the methods we always observe, of never writing anything except what we have experienced ourselves, we shall certainly take that great crisis as an example of what a crisis is, an event with its own, eminent, price.

As for me, if I finish an infinitely more serious work and reach the age of *confessions,* which as everyone knows is at fifty years old and at nine o'clock in the morning, that is what I should most certainly propose to describe. Taking up again and concluding my old study of "the decomposition of Dreyfusism in France," I should try to give, not so much an idea, as a picture of that immortal Affair and of what it was like in reality. It was like all self-respecting affairs, essentially mystical. It lived by its *mystique.* It died of its *politique.* Such is the rule; such is the law. Such is the level of life. All parties live by their *mystique* and die by their *politique.* That is what I should try to depict. I admit I am beginning to think that it would not be entirely useless. I suspect that there are any number of misunderstandings about the Affair.

. . . . What I mean is that if one only considers the Dreyfusists who are to the fore, in the public eye, the journalists, publicists, lecturers, candidates, parliamentarians and politicians, all those who talk and chatter and scribble and publish, the immense majority who appear on the scene, almost the whole lot hurried to take part in the Dreyfusist demagogy, and by that I mean the political demagogy that issued from the Dreyfusist *mystique*. But what I contest is that those who *appear* in history (and whom history seizes upon, in return, with such avidity) have a great importance in the depths of reality. At that depth, where the only important realities are found, I maintain that *all* the mystical Dreyfusists remained Dreyfusists, that they remained mystics, and kept their hands clean. What does it matter whether appearances, *phenomena*, whether all the officials, all those out for profit, should have abandoned, denied, betrayed and ridiculed the *mystique* in favour of the *politique*, and of the policies which issued from it, and of political demagogy? What does it matter if they sneer at us? We alone represent something, and they do not. What does it matter if they turn us to ridicule? They themselves live through us, and only exist by virtue of our existence. Their very vanity would not exist but for us.

. . . . What I maintain is that the whole mystical body of Dreyfusism remained intact. Who cares whether the politicians betrayed the *mystique*? It is their office to do so.

"Then," you will say, "neither the General Staff nor the various Committees, nor the Leagues, belonged to the *mystique*." Of course not. You surely did not expect them to. What does the League of the Rights of Man, and even of the Citizen, matter, what does it stand for by comparison with a conscience, a *mystique*? What does a policy, or a hundred policies matter by comparison with a *mystique*? *Mystiques* are always the creditors of policies.

You will add that the victim himself did not belong to the *mystique*. To his own *mystique*. That has become clear. We would have died for Dreyfus. Dreyfus did not die for Dreyfus. It is quite a good rule that the victim should not belong to the *mystique* of his own affair.

There you have the triumph of human weakness, the crown of our vanity, the supreme proof; the great masterpiece and demonstration of our infirmity.

It had to be so, in order that the masterpiece of our misery should be complete, in order that the bitterness should be drunk to the dregs, and ingratitude crowned.

So that it should be complete. In order that the disillusionment should be complete.

. . . . Our Socialism, our original socialism need I say, was not in the least anti-French, not in the least anti-patriotic, not in the least *anti*-national. It was rigorously, precisely, *inter*national. Theoretically it was not in the least anti-national. It was quite definitely international. Far from reducing or weakening the race, it exalted it, strengthened it. On the contrary, our thesis was, and still is, that, on the contrary, it is the bourgeoisie, bourgeois capitalism, capitalist sabotage, bourgeois and capitalist sabotage, which wiped out nation and people. It should be realised that there was nothing in common between the socialism of those days and the thing we know under that name to-day. Here again politics have done their work, and nowhere have politics undone and altered the nature of the *mystique* so completely as in this instance. The politics, I say, of the professional politicians, of the parliamentary politicians. But it has done still more, without a doubt, through the invention, the intervention, interpolation of sabotage, which is a political invention, in the same sense as the vote, *more political still than the vote,* worse, by which I mean more political; more even, without a doubt, than the professional anti-politicians, the syndicalists, the anti-parliamentarians. We thought then and we still think, though fifteen years ago everyone thought as we did, or affected to do so, that there was not a shadow of doubt, nor a suggestion of disagreement on that point, that principle. It is quite obvious that it was the bourgeois and the capitalist who began it. I mean to say, the bourgeois and the capitalist ceased to perform their office, their social task, before the working man, long before the working man stopped doing his. There can be no doubt about it: sabotage antedates sabotage from below; the bourgeois and the capitalist stopped loving bourgeois and capitalist work long before the working men stopped loving their work. It is in that order, beginning with the bourgeois capitalist world, that the general turning away from work occurred; the deepest stain, the central stain on the modern world, this aversion from work. Such is the general situation in the modern world; there was no question, as our syndicalist politicians like to pretend, of inventing, *adding* the disorder of the working-class to the disorder of the bourgeoisie, working-class sabotage to bourgeois and capitalist disorder. *On the contrary,* our socialism was essentially, and officially moreover, a theory, a general theory, a doctrine and method, a philosophy of organisation and of the re-organisation of work, the *restoration* of work. Our socialism was essentially, and moreover officially, a restoration, a general and even universal restoration. Nobody at the time contested the fact. But the politicians have been on the move for fifteen years. Two kinds of politicians, the politicians strictly speaking, and the anti-politicians. The politicians have passed on. What was at stake was a general restoration, beginning with the working-class world. A total restoration founded on the previous restoration of the world of the worker. It was a matter, and no one contested it at the time, on the contrary they all taught it, it was very definitely a matter of making the world of the worker in general healthy, of restoring the whole city to health, organically and atomically, beginning with the individual. That was the method and the ethics and the general philosophy of M. Sorel, himself a moralist and philosopher, which found its highest expression in his work. I add that it could be nothing else.

There can be no question of its being anything else. Let us say it without mincing our words. To the philosopher, and to any man philosophising, our socialism was a religion of temporal salvation, and nothing less. In seeking to restore health to the world of the worker, by restoring health to work and the world of work, by giving work back its dignity, and restoring the whole economic and industrial world, we were seeking nothing short of the temporal salvation of humanity. That is what we call the industrial world as opposed to the intellectual and political world, the world of learning, the parliamentary world; that is what we call *economics;* the morale of the producer; industrial morale; the world of producers; the economic world, the world of the working man; the (organic and molecular) structure, economic and industrial; that is what we call industry, the industrial régime, industrial production. The intellectual and political world, on the contrary, and the learned and parliamentary world belong together. By restoring health to the factory we hoped for no less, we aimed at no less than the temporal salvation of humanity. A joke only to those who do not want to see that Christianity, the religion of eternal salvation, is bogged down in the mud of rotten economic and industrial morals; and that it cannot extricate itself, will not get free, except at the price of an economic and industrial revolution; for in fact there is nowhere, no place better conceived, no source of perdition better organised and fitted out, so to say, no instrument better adapted to perdition than a modern factory. . . .

One must not conceal the fact that while the Church has ceased to act as the official religion of the State, it has not ceased to act as the official religion of the bourgeoisie in the State. Politically, she has cast off the burdens involved by her official position, but socially she has not cast them off. That is why there is no reason to claim a victory. That is why the factory is still closed to the Church, and the Church to the factory. She acts as, and is, the official formal religion of the rich. That is what the people, obscurely or explicitly, very certainly feel quite well. That is what they see. She is therefore nothing; that is why she is nothing. And above all, she is unlike what she was, having become all that is most contrary to herself, to her institution. And she will not reopen the factory doors, she will not reopen the way to the people except by *bearing the cost* of a revolution, an economic, social, industrial revolution, and, to call a spade a spade, a *temporal* revolution for *eternal* salvation. Such is, eternally, temporally (eternally temporally, and temporally eternally), the mysterious subjection of the eternal itself to the temporal. Such, properly speaking, is the inscription of the eternal itself on the temporal. The economic, social and industrial price must be paid, the temporal price. Nothing can evade it, not even the eternal, not even the spiritual, not even the inward life. That is why our socialism was not so stupid after all, and why it was profoundly Christian.

The clerical bourgeois affect to believe that it is the arguments, that it is cerebral modernism which is important, simply in order not to have to pay for an industrial revolution, an economic revolution.

Such being our socialism, and it being no secret, it is clear that it did not and could not endanger the legitimate rights of nations, but being and involving a general purification and restoration to health, could but serve the most essential interests of the nation and the legitimate rights of the people, within that process of restoration. The most sacred rights and interests. And it alone did so. It did not violate or obliterate nations and peoples; it did not force or falsify them, or twist them; on the contrary it worked to bring about a substitution, to replace the anarchic competition of nations with a growing forest of prosperous people, a whole world of flourishing peoples. It was not a denial of nations and of peoples. On the contrary it implied founding them, bringing them to birth and making them grow. It meant *making* them. From that moment we knew, we were certain that the world suffered infinitely more from bourgeois capitalist sabotage than from the sabotage of the working class. Contrary to what is generally believed, to what the intellectual and the bourgeois believe, to what publicists and sociologists believe, sabotage in the working man's world did not originate in this working man's world. It did not come from below, rising up from the mud, from the depths of the working man's world. It comes from above. Socialism is the only thing that can avoid it, avoid that contamination. It is bourgeois sabotage that, little by little, has extended down through all levels, down into the world of the working man. It is not his own peculiar vices which are gradually poisoning his world. It is his world which is gradually becoming bourgeois. Contrary to what is thought, sabotage is not innate, is not native to the worker. It is learnt. Taught dogmatically, intellectually, like a foreign language. It is a bourgeois invention. It meets with a resistance which is never met with in the bourgeois world. It has not won the battle. The city is not taken. And it remains, all things considered, artificial. It comes up against the most unforeseen resistance, resistance that goes incredibly deep, to that perennial love of work which enriches the hard-working heart. The capitalist and bourgeois world is almost entirely, almost completely, given up to pleasure. One can still find a large number of working men, and not only among the old, who *love* work.

Such being our socialism, it is clear that it implied, that it meant the restoration of health to the nation and the people, a strengthening hitherto unknown, prosperity, flowering, fertility. . . . Need I say, need I note, for the sake of order, need I recall how truly that socialism of ours was in the pure French tradition? The French vocation, destination, the French office, has always been to enlighten and give health to the world. To give health to what is sick, to enlighten what is troubled, to give order to what is disordered, to organise what is inchoate. Is it necessary to note the extent to which our socialism was based on generosity, how clear that generosity was, how full and pure and in the French tradition? In the sap and in the race itself. In the sap and in the blood of the race. A generosity at once abundant and sober, generous and well balanced, full, pure, fertile, clear, delicate, exuberant yet not giddy, well balanced but not sterile. In fact, a heroism at once sober, gay and prudent, a French heroism.

We were heroes. One must say it quite simply, for I really do not think any-one will say it for us. And here, very exactly, is how and why we were heroes. In the world in which we moved, where we were completing our years of apprenticeship, in all the circles in which we moved and worked, the ques-tion which was asked, during those two or three years of the rising curve, was never whether Dreyfus was in reality innocent (or guilty). The question was whether one could have the courage to recognise and to declare his innocence. To proclaim his innocence. Whether one had the double courage. First of all the first courage, the outward, crude courage, difficult enough in itself, the social courage to proclaim him innocent publicly, to testify publicly to him. To bet on it, to risk everything, to *put* everything one had on him, all one's miserable gains, the little man's money, the money of the poor; to put time, life and career on him; health, the heart-break of family feuds, the quarrels with one's nearest friends, the averted gaze, the silent or violent reprobation; the isolation, the quarantine; friendships of twenty years' standing broken, which meant, for us, friendships that had always been. The whole of social life. One's whole life in fact, everything. Secondly, the second courage, more difficult still, the inward courage, the secret courage, to admit to oneself in oneself that he was innocent. To give up one's peace of mind for the sake of that man.

Not only the peace of the city, the peace of one's home. The peace of one's family and household. But the peace of one's heart.

To the supreme good, the only good.

The courage to enter the kingdom of an incurable unrest for the sake of this man.

And of a bitterness that would never be cured. . . .

In reality the true position of those opposed to us was not of saying or thinking Dreyfus guilty, but of thinking and saying that whether he was innocent or guilty, one did not disturb, overthrow, or compromise, that one did not risk, for one man's sake, the life and salvation of a whole people. Meaning of course: the *temporal* salvation, *salut temporel*. Now our Christian *mystique* was merged so perfectly, so exactly with our patriotic *mystique,* that what must be recognised, and what I shall say, what I shall put into my confessions, is that *the point of view we adopted was none other than The Eternal Salvation of France.* What, in fact, did we say? Everything was against us, wisdom and law, human wisdom that is, and human law. What we did was in the order of madness and the order of sanctity, which have so many things in common, so many secret understandings, with human wisdom and the human eye. We went against wisdom, against the law. That is what I mean. What did we say in effect? The others said: "A people, a whole people is a great assemblage of interests, of the most legitimate rights. The most sacred rights. Thousands, millions of lives depend upon them, in the present, in the past, in the future, hundreds of millions of lives. Rights that are legitimate, sacred and incalculable.

"And the first duty of a people is not to risk the whole thing, not to endanger itself for the sake of one man, whoever he may be, however legitimate his interests and his rights. One does not sacrifice a city, a city is not lost, for one citizen. That was the language of reason. From that point of view it was clear that Dreyfus had to devote himself to France: not only for the peace of France, but for the safety and salvation of France, which we endangered. And if he would not sacrifice himself it would, if need be, be done for him." And we, what did we say? We said that a single injustice, a single crime, a single illegality, particularly if it were officially confirmed, particularly if it were universally, legally, nationally condoned, a single crime is enough to make a breach in the social compact, in the social contract, a single forfeit, a single dishonour is enough to dishonour a people. It becomes a source of infection, a poison that corrupts the whole body. What we defend is not only our honour, not only the honour of a whole people, in the present, but the historical honour of our whole race, the honour of our forefathers and children. And the more past we have the more memory (the more, as you say, responsibility we have), then the more we have to defend. The more past there is behind us, the more we must defend it. *"Je rendrai mon rang pur comme je l'ai recu."* That was the Cornelian impulse, the old Cornelian rule of honour. And the rule and the honour and the impulse of Christianity. A single stain stains a whole family. And a whole people. A people cannot rest on an injury suffered, on a crime as solemnly and definitely accepted. The honour of a people is all of a piece.

What does all this mean, unless one doesn't know a word of French, except that our adversaries were speaking the language of the *raison d'état,* which is not only the language of political and parliamentary reason, of contemptible political and parliamentary interests, but the very respectable language of continuity, of the temporal continuity of the race, *of the temporal salvation of the people and the race?* They aimed at nothing less. And we, by a profoundly Christian movement, a profoundly revolutionary and traditionally Christian impulse and effort, following one of the deepest Christian traditions, one of the most vital and central, and in line with the axis of Christianity, at its very heart, we aimed at no less than raising ourselves, I do not say to the conception, but to the passion, to the care of the eternal salvation, *le salut éternel,* of this people; we achieved an existence full of care and preoccupation, full of mortal anguish and anxiety for the eternal salvation of our race. Deep down within us, we were the men of eternal salvation, and our adversaries were the men of temporal salvation. That was the real division of the Dreyfus Affair. Deep down within us we were determined that France should not fall into a state of mortal sin. Christian doctrine, alone in the whole world, in the modern world, in any world, deliberately counts death at nought, at zero, in terms of the price of eternal death, and the risk of temporal death as nothing compared with the price of sin, mortal sin, eternal death.

Political, parliamentary parties cannot speak except in political, parliamentary language, they cannot undertake or support any action except on the political plane. And above all, naturally, they want us to do the same. For us to be constantly with them, among them. Everything we do, everything that goes to make the life and the strength of a people or actions and achievements, our transactions and conduct, our very souls and lives—all these they automatically and continuously, almost innocently, translate into political language; they diminish, reduce and project it on to the political plane. As a result they understand nothing, and prevent others from understanding anything. They deform and alter the nature of the thing, both in their own minds and in the imaginations of those who follow them. They translate everything we say and do, translate and betray. *Traducunt. Tradunt.* One never knows whether they do one more harm as opponents, or as supporters; for when they oppose one, they fight in political language on the political plane, and when they support one it is almost worse, for they support one and adopt one in political language on the political plane. As they pull one this way and that, they are equally wrong in opposite ways, equally inadequate. In each case they alter the very nature of the thing. They can only conceive and offer a diminished life, robbed of its essential nature. A phantom, a skeleton, a plan, a projection of life.

When they are for you and think you are for them, they take possession of you and are sure to do you fatal harm. They want to take you up and be taken up by you. To protect you. When they oppose you, then they oppose their *politique* to your *mystique,* their base politics to your *mystique.* And they translate your *mystique* into politics, into their ignominious politics. And having interpreted what we have done for our *mystique* in terms of their politics, the corresponding politics—issued from the *mystique*—they base themselves upon it and argue from it to bind us to their policy, and to forbid us other *mystiques.* In that way they arbitrarily transfer oppositions and contradictions, which only exist and only occur and function on the political plane, into the world of *mystique.*

That is how the parties reward you for what you have done for them at moments when they were in danger; I mean for what you have done for the *mystique* from which they issue, for the *mystique* on which they live, on which they are parasites. That is precisely how they "try to get a grip on you," and in that way hope to bind you to their policies, and forbid you other *mystiques.*

And because we have fought against the current of power and tyranny and demagogy of our (political) friends since the degradation of the Dreyfusist *mystique,* because we risked and sustained fifteen years of hardship for the defence of private liberties, of profound Christian liberties and Christian consciences, the reactionary politicians want to prevent us from calling ourselves republicans. And because we have put, not weeks and months, but fifteen years of hardship at the service of the Republic, the republican politicians would like nothing better than to prevent us from calling ourselves Christians. So the Republic is the *régime* of liberty of conscience for all, excepting for us, just in order to reward us for having defended it for fifteen years, and for still defending it. We shall have to forgo their permission. We do not live or move on the same plane as they do. Their disputes are not ours. The painful disputes which we sometimes sustain have nothing in common with their facile, superficial polemics.

The Republic, one might suppose, was a *régime* of liberty of conscience for everyone, excepting republicans.

. . . . You will observe, you will catch the tone of these *mémoires.* It is the very tone of the times. I should not be surprised if some idiot, with no sense of history, were to find the tone slightly ridiculous. It is already past. The men to whom that tone belonged did great things. And we?

To-day civic virtue too, seems ridiculous. Civic is an adjective which it is difficult to wear becomingly. Like all adjectives in *ic*.

The one value, the only strength of royalism, the only strength of a traditional monarchy lies in the fact that the King should be, more or less, loved. The only strength of a republic is that the republic should be, more or less, loved. The only strength, the only dignity that exists, is to be loved. That so many men should have lived and suffered so much for the Republic, should have believed so strongly in it, that so many should have died for it and should often have borne so many and such great trials for it, that is what counts, that is what interests me, that is what exists. That is what founds a *régime;* that is what makes it legitimate. When I find contempt and sarcasm and insults filling the pages of the *Action Française,* I am pained, for there we have men whose aim is to restore the oldest dignities of our race, and one does not found, one does not reform any culture upon derision, for derision and sarcasm and insults are barbarities. Puns will not restore a culture. When I find in the *Action Française,* the implacable, impeccable, invincible reasoning and logic of M. Maurras, showing that Monarchy is better than a Republic, and royalism better than republicanism, I confess that if I were to speak crudely I should say it just didn't take. Everyone will know what I mean. It doesn't bite. Our whole education, our whole intellectual formation, our university training has taught us how to make and give explanations, till we are saturated with them. If need be we could make theirs for them. We can see them coming, and that spoils their point for us. We know how it's done. But when, in an article, M. Maurras lets his pen run along, no doubt without thinking about it, and writes, not in the form of argument, but almost as though unconsciously, when I come across this phrase: "We should be prepared to die for the King, for the re-establishment of our King"; well, then you are saying something, you are beginning to talk. Knowing as I do that what he says is true, then I begin to listen, to understand; I pause and am struck. And the other day, after we had talked endlessly and committed the sin of explaining everything, all of a sudden Michel Arnauld, who was nearing the end of his tether, interrupted and said almost brusquely: *"That is all very fine, because the dangers are only vague and theoretical. But the day they become a real menace people will see that we are still capable of doing something for the Republic."* Then everyone understood that at last something had been said.

JEAN JAURÈS

THE THIRD REPUBLIC lost one of its greatest statesmen and the French socialist movement its greatest leader when Jean Jaurès (born at Castres in the *département* of Tarn in 1859) was shot in the back of the head by an unbalanced youth on July 31, 1914. Two days later, on August 2, general mobilization was proclaimed in France, and Europe was swept into the holocaust which Jaurès had desperately sought to avert. His assassin had been incited by the chauvinistic right-wing press, which for the past month had been openly advocating the murder of "Herr" Jaurès.

Trained in philosophy at the École Normale, Jaurès had resigned his professorship at the University of Toulouse when, at the age of twenty-six, he was elected to the Chamber of Deputies in 1885 as an independent republican. By 1893 his theoretical interest in Marxism and his deep practical concern for the welfare of the underprivileged had led him to call himself a socialist. During the next five years he emerged as a parliamentary orator and tactician of the first rank. By 1898, when the Dreyfus Affair broke over France, he had achieved a personal ascendency in the French socialist movement and had done much to bring about greater unity among its various factions. Jaurès threw himself heart and soul into the struggle to secure justice for Captain Dreyfus, refusing to accept defeat even when his party refused to follow him (on the ground that socialists were under no obligation to defend a bourgeois army officer). He lost his seat in Parliament as a result of his defense of the "traitor" Dreyfus, though he regained it again in 1902 after Dreyfus' vindication and retained it to the end of his life. His part in the "Affair" was second only to that of Zola, and the triumph of the Dreyfusard cause made Jaurès a national figure, the idol of young intellectuals and the hero of all republicans and liberals. His prestige redounded to the benefit of his party, which notably increased its strength in the Chamber as a result of Jaurès' demonstration that a socialist could be a sincere and effective defender of the democratic cause.

A prodigious worker all his life, Jaurès had managed during the most hectic months of the crisis, to plan a twenty-volume *Histoire socialiste de la France* which began to appear in 1900, and to complete five volumes of the work himself between 1898 and 1902. This history—praised for its accurate and original scholarship by no less an authority than Aulard—was intended to prepare the workers of France for their future political responsibilities in much the same way that the *Encyclopédie* of the eighteenth century had educated the bourgeoisie for its revolutionary role in the generation before 1789. Jaurès also became a pioneer in adult education with his organization of "popular universities" where workers could attend evening lectures given *gratis* by qualified professors and other intellectuals who had volunteered to bring general culture to the masses.

Jaurès was never belligerently anticlerical, and he was more a pantheist than a materialist. He greatly admired Marx, but he also retained strong loyalties to Hegel, Kant, Renan, and Michelet. He agreed, however, with the bourgeois republicans that French democracy would never be safe until Church and State were made completely separate, and that clerical influence in education must consequently be ended once and for all. Hence he played a leading part in the achievement of these purposes through the laws depriving religious congregations of their right to teach and through the abrogation (in 1905) of the Concordat with the Papacy which had been in effect since 1801. In 1904 Jaurès founded *L'Humanité* as a daily newspaper speaking officially for French socialism, and he remained its editor until his death. At the International Socialist Congress of Amsterdam in 1905 he came into conflict with the leadership of the powerful German wing of the Second International, and the influence of the latter was strong enough to defeat his motion to approve of socialist participation in bourgeois governments which were committed to the defense of democratic institutions. Jaurès loyally carried out the resolution even though it meant a considerable sacrifice of strength for the French party and the loss of some of its ablest leaders.

Beginning with the Moroccan crisis of 1905 Jaurès grew more and more alarmed by the upsurge of competitive militarism, chauvinistic nationalism, and insatiable imperialism on all sides. Though he never ceased to express his deeply patriotic devotion to France, he was convinced that the working class had no vital interests at stake in the sordid rivalries that were coming, as he thought, to divide the capitalists of Europe into two hostile camps. He hoped that the socialist movement, expressing the international solidarity of the workers, might stand as an effective barrier blocking the path to war. By insisting in each country that the government submit its case to arbitration, and by refusing to answer the call to the colors until such an offer had been made by their own country and refused by the enemy, Jaurès believed that the workers could hold in check the warlike propensities of munitions makers and recklessly ambitious militarists. An integral part of this ten-year struggle to preserve the peace was his carefully worked out proposal to substitute a democratic but highly trained militia for the existing bureaucratic and rigidly disciplined army dominated by a reactionary General Staff whose consuming ambition was to secure *revanche* (revenge) for the French defeat in 1870. He urged this reform from 1910 onward, advocating its adoption as much in the interests of flexible strategy and effective military defense as in the interests of peace.

The following selections, which include Jaurès' proposed Army Reorganization Bill and some of his commentary concerning it, are taken from *Democracy and Military Service,* edited by G. G. Coulton (London, Simpkin, 1916), which is an abbreviated translation from the French of Jaurès' *L'Armée nouvelle* (1910).

ARMY REORGANIZATION BILL

1. All able-bodied citizens from 20 to 45 are bound to help in national defense. From 20 to 34 they are in the first line, thence until 40, in the reserve; thence until 45, in the Territorial army.

2. The citizens of the Active army will be organized in divisions corre-

sponding to the regions of recruitment. Each division will include infantry, cavalry, artillery and engineers.

3. The recruiting is done by districts; the citizens are drafted into units corresponding with their districts of domicile: these limits may only be slightly extended for cavalry, artillery and engineers.

4. The education of the army will be in three steps: (*a*) preparatory (boys and youths), (*b*) recruit school, and (*c*) periodical after-trainings.

5. *Preparatory,* for boys from 10 to 20. This education will be more than a mere anticipation of military drill and maneuvers. It will be, above all, an education in health and activity, by gymnastics, marchings, rhythmical drill, games of skill and swiftness, and musketry-drill.

This physical education will be directed and controlled (1) by the officers (commissioned and non-commissioned) of the units to which the boys will be drafted, (2) by masters of public and private schools, (3) by local doctors and (4) by a Council of Promotion. This Council, of 30 members, shall be elected in the regimental district by universal suffrage and shall comprise representatives of all four arms. . . .

The families of the boys and youths under exercises shall be warned that notes will be taken of the pupils' punctuality and zeal. Habitual negligence will be punished by different penalties on a cumulative scale, notably by being debarred (at least for a time) from all public functions and by being kept longer than the rest in the Recruit School. Prizes, on the other hand, will be offered for the best pupils.

6. *Recruit School.* Youths of 20 will be called for six months to the nearest garrison-town to learn company, squadron, or battery maneuvers. This work may be done in two instalments, but always within the limits of one year. The times shall be so chosen as to permit open-air drill and maneuvers on all sorts of ground.

7. *After-training.* In the 13 years of active service which they have yet to render, these soldiers shall be called out eight times for exercises and maneuvers. These will be alternately (*a*) minor maneuvers, lasting 10 days and covering a fairly narrow radius; (*b*) grand maneuvers, lasting 21 days, covering a wider radius and including instruction-camps.

Besides these compulsory maneuvers, the Officers and Councils will try to arrange as much voluntary marching and rifle-practice as possible.

Each soldier keeps his uniform and kit at home, and is personally responsible for them. Armories will be kept up, under guard of the civil and military authorities, in the towns or chief villages of the district.

In the Departments near the Eastern frontier, every soldier shall have his arms at home. Depots of artillery and cavalry shall be distributed about these districts, and a close network of communications of every kind—railways, steam-trams, motor-cars—shall be instituted, in order that all the citizens of that region, by an immediate mobilization, may serve as a covering force for the general concentration. Aviation centers will also be created; and recruits from the whole of France, after a preliminary instruction of three months, may be called to do their remaining three months in the instruction-camps of these Eastern districts.

8. *Promotion.* The officers, commissioned and non-commissioned, will be divided into two classes—professional and civil. There will be no professional non-commissioned officers except the recruit-school instructors.

After three months of recruit-school, the smartest and best-educated recruits will be prepared to become non-coms. This choice will be made by the instructors, assisted by delegates of a Regimental Council. This Council will be composed of (*a*) the corps-commander, (*b*) representative officers of different ranks, and (*c*) members of the Council of Promotion (which is elected by universal suffrage). These candidates, if they are still approved after the first three months' preparation at the recruit-school, will be sent for another three months to a non-commissioned officers' school, and employed as corporals or sergeants either in their own or in a neighboring unit.

No recruit may decline such an appointment; if there are not enough voluntary candidates, the authorities may select recruits to fill the gaps.

Those who are in training at this non-com. school will receive daily pay equivalent to their loss of time. When promoted to non-com. rank, they shall be sufficiently indemnified for the time that they spend at their duties. In every public employment their rank shall give them a certain seniority. Private employers (who will be formed into Divisionary Associations) will be bound to give them employment suitable to their aptitudes. At the age of fifty, they will be entitled to a pension. Moreover, promotion will be so arranged that non-coms. may obtain seniority, and that a considerable proportion may rise to sub-lieutenant or lieutenant.

9. One-third of the commissioned officers shall be professional soldiers.

Labor organizations of all kinds—trades unions, benefit and cooperative societies—are authorized to contribute toward the expenses of such sons of their own members as have passed the necessary examinations and can study for promotion to the rank of officer.

Students who have passed the Bachelor examination shall be admitted by competition to sections of military studies created in the six most important universities, so that each main region of France shall have a section of its own. Such candidates must first have gone through their six months' recruit-school.

These studies shall last four years and shall be specialized for different branches of the army. These military students shall be taught as far as possible in conjunction with the other university students, in history, philosophy, political economy and science. They will use the neighboring recruit-schools to learn the habit of command. They shall receive a daily allowance from the State, until the end of their course.

If their families are poor, these also shall receive an allowance. After these four years, they shall be gazetted sub-lieutenants. Their university years shall be counted for seniority, in order to hasten their promotion to captain. Before each fresh promotion, they must again follow a special preparatory course of at least twenty days at the university which shall prescribe the subjects of study.

The duty of these professional officers shall be to assist the teachers and the delegates of the Council of Promotion in the aforesaid preparatory training of boys and youths; also, to help in the training of civilian officers.

The officers shall be admitted by competition to a higher military school in which they will secure advantages for further promotion, and which will prepare them for the General Staff. This higher military school, one of whose duties will be to coordinate the teaching in the universities, will give successive courses of instruction in each of the universities which has a military department.

10. Two-thirds of the officers will be civilians, chosen from among the civilian sergeants and attached to their Territorial unit, or to a neighboring unit.

A certificate of military studies, securing seniority for promotion to higher rank, will be given to any citizen who has followed special courses of study, either at the university or at the capital of his department. No man may receive a diploma as doctor, lawyer, engineer or teacher if he has not obtained this certificate of military study.

The civilian officers will receive pay. They will also enjoy a right of seniority in the different public departments in which they work. At fifty they may claim a pension. No non-commissioned officer may refuse a commission. If the number or the quality of voluntary candidates is insufficient, the authorities will have power to fill the vacancies. . . .

15. The Minister of War will aim at utilizing the whole Active army as a first-line army and will keep this object in view in all arrangements for districts of mobilization, for means of transport and for commissariat.

16. The Army thus constituted has one single object—to protect the independence and the soil of France against all aggression. All war is criminal if it is not manifestly defensive; and it can be manifestly and certainly de-

fensive only if our Government proposes to the foreign Government with which we are in dispute to settle that dispute by arbitration.

17. Any Government which plunges into war without having publicly and loyally proposed arrangement by arbitration shall be held to have committed treason against France and humanity and to be a public enemy of our country and of the human race. Any Parliament which has consented to this act shall be guilty of felony and legally dissolved. The constitutional and national duty of all citizens will then be to overthrow this Government and replace it by a Government acting in good faith, which, while perfectly safeguarding national independence, shall offer the foreign power either to forestall or to stop hostilities by a sentence of arbitration.

18. The French Government is herewith invited to complete treaties of arbitration with all countries represented at the Court of the Hague and to regulate procedure for arbitration in agreement with those countries.

THE NEW ARMY

IT IS FROM the point of view of National Defense and International Peace that I propose to begin explaining the plan for the organization of the State upon a socialistic basis, which I shall submit to Parliament in a succession of Bills.

It is imperative, both for Socialism and for the Nation, to define what the military institutions and the external policy of Republican France should be. In order to hasten and to accomplish its evolution towards entire social justice, to inaugurate, or even to prepare, a new order in which labor shall be organized and supreme, France needs above all things peace and security. We must not allow her to be tempted into the sinister diversion of foreign adventures; on the other hand, we must protect her from the threat of foreign violence.

The first problem, therefore, with which a great party of Social Reform has to deal is this:

How can we best secure the chances of peace for France and for the uncertain world which surrounds her? And if, in spite of her efforts and her wish for peace, she is attacked, how can we best secure the chances of safety, the means of Victory?

It would be childish and futile to propose a great program, a great sustained and systematic project of reform to a Country which is not its own master, which is ever at the mercy of adventurers within who are anxious to fish in troubled waters, or exposed to aggressors from without, and hence always under the threat, and on the brink, of War.

To ensure peace by a plain policy of wisdom, moderation and rectitude, by the definitive repudiation of all aggressive enterprises, by the loyal acceptance and practice of the new methods of international law which are capable of solving conflicts without violence; on the other hand, to ensure peace, courageously, by the establishment of a defensive organization so formidable that every thought of aggression is put out of the mind of even the most insolent and rapacious: these are the highest aims of the Socialist Party. Indeed, I ought rather to say that they are the very condition of its action and of its life. It is not enough that we should aim equally and simultaneously at international peace and national independence; we must persuade the whole country, the whole democracy, of the sincerity and the strength of our aims. For how can we invite and persuade the Nation to a bold policy of social reform if it has reason to think that its very existence is menaced by our doctrines? In order to perform the task of higher justice at which Socialism aims France needs the whole of her life, that is, the whole of her liberty: and how shall the sap rise to the fruit of the tree if the roots are injured? Above all, how can the Socialist Party speak with authority in proposing that form of national defense which seems to us most efficacious, if there is a doubt in the mind of one single individual as to whether we have a real interest in national defense itself? . . .

[Socialism] must not content itself with vague formulas in favor of a Militia System, but must show precisely the strong system of organization at which it aims. Socialism must prove this by the conduct of its advocates and by their propaganda among the working-classes, by their assiduity and their zeal in the living work of military education, in the gymnastic societies and the Rifle Clubs, in those field exercises which are so much more valuable than the sterile mechanism of the barrack square. *They must show, in fine, by their joyous activity that, while they fight Militarism and War, it is not from timid egotism or a cowardly servility and indolence, and that they are as resolved and ready to secure the full working of a thoroughly popular and defensive military system as they are to beat down the breeders of strife. If they act in this manner they may defy all slander, and they will carry with them, not only the strength which their historic country has garnered through the ages, but the ideal strength of a new country, the Motherland of Labor and of Justice. . . .*

There is only one social rôle which France can fill in the world to-day, which can give universal value to her actions and inspire the souls of Frenchmen with a higher emotion in which the life of France shall vibrate in accord with the life of humanity. That rôle is to help the workers of France to achieve the rights of property with the whole strength of the Republican Democracy. It is to help the World to the attainment of peace by an emphatic repudiation of all aggressive thought, and by an ardent propaganda in favor of arbitration and equity. The People, defending itself against aggression and acting as the champion of this ideal, would feel inspired with the nobility of a great national tradition and the grandeur of a human hope, and this great concentration of moral power would radiate Victory.

At the same time there is no need that officers should swallow any particular scheme of Social Organization. The point is that they should understand and appreciate the wealth of moral driving power which is to be found in the Socialism of the Working Classes, who aim both at national liberty and the solidarity of mankind. For without the driving power derived from such a faith and from such ideals it will be impossible for the officers adequately to fulfil their own mission, which is to protect the Mother country from every threat of attack from without.

In order to appreciate the advantages of the military system which Socialism puts forward, and which aims at identifying the Army with the Nation, the officer class must understand that the strength of the Army as an instrument of defense lies in its close union with the people, which represents productive labor and is inspired by the energy of its ideals. Thus they will understand the value of that diplomacy of peace which the working class desires to found on certain clearly defined lines.

In fact, the organization of national defense and the organization of international peace are but two different aspects of the same great task. For whatever adds to the defensive strength of France increases the hope of peace, and whatever success France attains in organizing peace on the basis of law and founding it upon arbitration and right will add to its own defensive strength. This is the reason why I put forward my projects for the organization of defense and the organization of peace as parts of the same scheme. I am not working simply for the propagation of ideas and the creation of mental tendencies. I am not devoting myself merely to the task of preaching a doctrine; my object is not merely to sweep away misunderstandings which tend to injure both the noble Country which I love and the great Party which I serve. I aim at a practical result, which is enormously important both for the present and for the future. . . .

If General Foch, and the officers whose teacher he is, will think the matter over, they will see that we have come to a critical moment for their conscience and their intellect. It is absurd and retrograde to attribute a thoroughly and essentially national character to wars kindled by the greed of rival capitalist groups. Our officers themselves must take a definite side in this great social and moral drama which the age is unrolling. They must not only realize in their minds but also proclaim in public that a policy which sets two nations by the ears for the sake of Colonial competition or stock-exchange speculations is an infamous and fatal policy. They must proclaim publicly, as officers, that troops cannot be expected to fight with the necessary dash when they are dragged to butchery for such an ignoble traffic as this. There are only two possibilities of truly national war nowadays. If a nation which wants peace and which proves its wish for peace—a nation which has no thought of aggression or robbery—is assailed by predatory and adventurous governments in quest of some colossal plunder or some startling diversion from their domestic difficulties, then we get a truly national war. Or, again, if a people were to carry out at home, without armed proselytism, some great social reform which should provoke the fears of neighboring oligarchies and should impel them to attempt to quench this revolution in blood. Then, but in no other cases, can we call a war really national. . . .

The best way of protecting every region of France is to protect France herself. Our army, in order to secure full liberty for decisive maneuvers and for the victory which shall at last free us, may be obliged to abandon some part of our territory for a time. Yet this would be better, in the long run, even for the districts thus abandoned, than to cling so closely to the frontier as to lose all chance of a great victory. In a truly democratic and popular France, in which army affairs were understood by the general public, it would be possible to appeal to the highest intelligence of the nation. How are we to break the shock of the enemy's onset? We must have two millions of French citizens in the very first line; and this enormous mass must have free play to combine for attack when the time comes. As soon as our General Staff, animated by a thoroughly republican, popular and national spirit, has understood this, then they will persuade all their fellow-citizens to let France have full liberty of maneuver. The enemy would then have to move slowly and cautiously; for the country would have made full preparations against invasion; and he would therefore meet the resistance which would most embarrass him. He would then have to reckon neither with a limited resistance nor, on the other hand, with a compact and motionless resistance of our whole forces. He would find us resisting, not only in full force, but also with a suppleness of movement which would add to his difficulties as much as our vast numbers would add to them.

We must have a new system with more elasticity and freedom and life than the present: only thus can we command the real interest of the people. We must have a system which develops all citizens better, both physically and morally; it must give us firmer certainty and a fresh pledge of the people's will for peace. Remember that governments will be far less ready to dream of adventurous foreign policies if the mobilization of the army is the mobilization of the nation itself. France must adopt this policy and thus take a step forward beyond all other nations, seeing that she can do so without risk; for such a system would rather strengthen than weaken her defensive force. Then the other nations will have to follow suit. Germany in especial—whatever may be her political and social reasons for putting nearly all her force and hope into her first-line army—will be compelled, in her turn, to organize and to wield masses of soldiers no less vast than the masses maneuvered by democratic France. She may begin by laughing at us; but, sooner or later, she will have to take us seriously; and then (as her own General Falkenhaus puts it) she will be obliged to deepen the sources of her army and to depend more seriously upon the older men. Then, Germany, in turn, will gain greater defensive power against invasion and less power of aggressive militarism. This will bring to Europe a new era; it will bring hopes of justice and peace which will help the French proletariat to understand the sense, the interest and the necessity of our proposals. Meanwhile we labor with passion but with perseverance to realize this scheme, since it forms part of the vast plan of social reform which in these days must be in the thoughts of all good citizens, of all good Frenchmen.

IX IMPERIALISM AFTER 1870

IMPERIALISM AFTER 1870

IX

VLADIMIR ILICH LENIN

AMONG LENIN's most important theoretical contributions was his attempt to apply the teachings of Marx and Engels to imperialistic expansion. In Lenin's view between 1871 (with the fall of the Paris commune) and 1914 (with the opening of an imperialist war) capitalism had entered a period which he characterized as "the substitution of capitalist monopolies for capitalist free competition." Imperialism, according to Lenin, marked the end of capitalism as a genuinely progressive force moving toward the constant expansion of production; it marked also a period of relative stagnation in which the bourgeoisie took on the distinguishing features of a static rentier class and in which imperialism itself was pressed toward ever more reactionary measures for maintaining its monopoly of economic resources. Historically speaking, modern imperialism is thus "capitalism in transition, or, more precisely. . . . dying capitalism." All the "inherent contradictions" of capitalism were sharpened during this period.

The following selections are from *Imperialism: The Highest Stage of Capitalism*, written in Zurich in 1916 and published in English by International Publishers (New York, 1939).

IMPERIALISM THE HIGHEST STAGE
OF CAPITALISM

THE ENORMOUS GROWTH of industry and the remarkably rapid process of concentration of production in ever-larger enterprises represent one of the most characteristic features of capitalism. Modern censuses of production give very complete and exact data on this process.

In Germany, for example, for every 1,000 industrial enterprises, large enterprises, *i.e.,* those employing more than 50 workers, numbered three in 1882, six in 1895 and nine in 1907; and out of every 100 workers employed, this group of enterprises employed 22, 30 and 37 respectively. Concentration of production, however, is much more intense than the concentration of workers, since labour in the large enterprises is much more productive. This is shown by the figures available on steam engines and electric motors. If we take what in Germany is called industry in the broad sense of the term, that is, including commerce, transport, etc., we get the following picture: Large-scale enterprises: 30,588 out of a total of 3,265,623, that is to say, 0.9 per cent. These large-scale enterprises employ 5,700,000 workers out of a total of 14,400,000, that is,

39.4 per cent; they use 6,660,000 steam horse power out of a total of 8,800,000, that is, 75.3 per cent and 1,200,000 kilowatts of electricity out of a total of 1,500,000, that is, 77.2 per cent.

Less than one-hundredth of the total enterprises utilise *more than three-fourths* of the steam and electric power! Two million nine hundred and seventy thousand small enterprises (employing up to five workers), representing 91 per cent of the total, utilise only 7 per cent of the steam and electric power. Tens of thousands of large-scale enterprises are everything; millions of small ones are nothing.

In 1907, there were in Germany 586 establishments employing one thousand and more workers. They employed nearly *one-tenth* (1,380,000) of the total number of workers employed in industry and utilised *almost one-third* (32 per cent) of the total steam and electric power employed. As we shall see, money capital and the banks make this superiority of a handful of the largest enterprises still more overwhelming, in the most literal sense of the word, since millions of small, medium, and even some big "masters" are in fact in complete subjection to some hundreds of millionaire financiers.

In another advanced country of modern capitalism, the United States, the growth of the concentration of production is still greater. Here statistics single out industry in the narrow sense of the word and group enterprises according to the value of their annual output. In 1904 large-scale enterprises with an annual output of one million dollars and over numbered 1,900 (out of 216,180, *i.e.,* 0.9 per cent). These employed 1,400,000 workers (out of 5,500,000, *i.e.,* 25.6 per cent) and their combined annual output was valued at $5,600,000,000 (out of $14,800,000,000, *i.e.,* 38 per cent). Five years later, in 1909, the corresponding figures were: large-scale enterprises: 3,060 out of 268,491, *i.e.,* 1.1 per cent; employing: 2,000,000 workers out of 6,600,000, *i.e.,* 30.5 per cent; output: $9,000,000,000 out of $20,700,000,000, *i.e.,* 43.8 per cent.

Almost half the total production of all the enterprises of the country was carried on by a *hundredth part* of those enterprises! These 3,000 giant enterprises embrace 268 branches of industry. From this it can be seen that, at a certain stage of its development, concentration itself, as it were, leads right to monopoly; for a score or so of giant enterprises can easily arrive at an agreement, while on the other hand, the difficulty of competition and the tendency towards monopoly arise from the very dimensions of the enterprises. This transformation of competition into monopoly is one of the most important —if not the most important—phenomena of modern capitalist economy. . . .

Fifty years ago, when Marx was writing *Capital,* free competition appeared to most economists to be a "natural law." Official science tried, by a conspiracy of silence, to kill the works of Marx, which by a theoretical and historical analysis of capitalism showed that free competition gives rise to the concentration of production, which, in turn, at a certain stage of development, leads to monopoly. Today, monopoly has become a fact. The economists are writing mountains of books in which they describe the diverse manifestations of monopoly, and continue to declare in chorus that "Marxism is refuted." But facts are stubborn things, as the English proverb says, and they have to be reckoned with, whether we like it or not. The facts show that differences between capitalist countries, *e.g.,* in the matter of protection or free trade, only give rise to insignificant variations in the form of monopolies or in the moment of their appearance; and that the rise of monopolies, as the result of the concentration of production, is a general and fundamental law of the present stage of development of capitalism.

For Europe, the time when the new capitalism *definitely* superseded the old can be established with fair precision: it was the beginning of the twentieth century. . . .

This is no longer the old type of free competition between manufacturers, scattered and out of touch with one another, and producing for an unknown market. Concentration has reached the point at which it is possible to make an approximate estimate of all sources of raw materials (for example, the iron ore deposits) of a country and even, as we shall see, of several countries, or of the whole world. Not only are such estimates made, but these sources are captured by gigantic monopolist combines. An approximate estimate of the capacity of markets is also made, and the combines divide them up amongst themselves by agreement. Skilled labour is monopolised, the best engineers are engaged; the means of transport are captured: railways in America, shipping companies in Europe and America. Capitalism in its imperialist stage arrives at the threshold of the most complete socialisation of production. In spite of themselves, the capitalists are dragged, as it were, into a new social order, a transitional social order from complete free competition to complete socialisation.

Production becomes social, but appropriation remains private. The social means of production remain the private property of a few. The general framework of formally recognised free competition remains, but the yoke of a few monopolists on the rest of the population becomes a hundred times heavier, more burdensome and intolerable. . . .

Translated into ordinary human language this means that the development of capitalism has arrived at a stage when, although commodity production still "reigns" and continues to be regarded as the basis of economic life, it has in reality been undermined and the big profits go to the "geniuses" of financial manipulation. At the basis of these swindles and manipulations lies socialised production; but the immense progress of humanity, which achieved this socialisation, goes to benefit the speculators. We shall see later how "on these grounds" reactionary, petty-bourgeois critics of capitalist imperialism dream of going back to "free," "peaceful" and "honest" competition. . . . the concentration of capital and the growth of their turnover is radically changing the significance of the banks. Scattered capitalists are transformed into a single collective capitalist. When carrying the current accounts of a few capitalists, the banks, as it were, transact a purely technical and exclusively auxiliary operation. When, however, these operations grow to enormous dimensions we find that a handful of monopolists control all the operations, both commercial and industrial, of the whole of capitalist society. They can, by means of their banking connections, by running current accounts and transacting other financial operations, first *ascertain exactly* the position of the various capitalists, then *control* them, influence them by restricting or enlarging, facilitating or hindering their credits, and finally they can *entirely determine* their fate, determine their income, deprive them of capital, or, on the other hand, permit them to increase their capital rapidly and to enormous dimensions, etc. . . .

The banking system, Marx wrote half a century ago in *Capital,* "presents indeed the form of common bookkeeping and distribution of means of production on a social scale, but only the form." The figures we have quoted on the growth of bank capital, on the increase in the number of the branches and offices of the biggest banks, the increase in the number of their accounts, etc., present a concrete picture of this "common bookkeeping" of the *whole* capitalist class; and not only of the capitalists, for the banks collect, even though temporarily, all kinds of financial revenues of small business men, office clerks, and of a small upper stratum of the working class. It is "common distribution of means of production" that, from the formal point of view, grows out of the development of modern banks, the most important of which, numbering from three to six in France, and from six to eight in Germany, control billions and billions. In point of fact, however, the distribution of means of production is by no means "common," but private, *i.e.,* it conforms to the interests of big capital, and primarily, of very big monopoly capital, which operates in conditions in which the masses of the population live in want, in which the whole development of agriculture hopelessly lags behind the development of industry, and within industry itself the "heavy industries" exact tribute from all other branches of industry. . . .

The concentration of production; the monopoly arising therefrom; the merging or coalescence of banking with industry—this is the history of the rise of finance capital and what gives the term "finance capital" its content.

We now have to describe how, under the general conditions of commodity production and private property, the "domination" of capitalist monopolies inevitably becomes the domination of a financial oligarchy. . . .

It is characteristic of capitalism in general that the ownership of capital is separated from the application of capital to production, that money capital is separated from industrial or productive capital, and that the rentier, who lives entirely on income obtained from money capital, is separated from the entrepreneur and from all who are directly concerned in the management of capital. Imperialism, or the domination of finance capital, is that highest stage of capitalism in which this separation reaches vast proportions. The supremacy of finance capital over all other forms of capital means the predominance of the rentier and of the financial oligarchy; it means the crystallisation of a small number of financially "powerful" states from among all the rest. The extent to which this process is going on may be judged from the statistics on emissions, *i.e.,* the issue of all kinds of securities. . . .

Under the old capitalism, when free competition prevailed, the export of *goods* was the most typical feature. Under modern capitalism, when monopolies prevail, the export of *capital* has become the typical feature.

Capitalism is commodity production at the highest stage of development, when labour power itself becomes a commodity. The growth of internal exchange, and particularly of international exchange, is the characteristic distinguishing feature of capitalism. The uneven and spasmodic character of the development of individual enterprises, of individual branches of industry and individual countries, is inevitable under the capitalist system. England became a capitalist country before any other, and in the middle of the nineteenth century, having adopted free trade, claimed to be the "workshop of the world," the great purveyor of manufactured goods to all countries, which in exchange were to keep her supplied with raw materials. But in the last quarter of the nineteenth century, *this* monopoly was already undermined. Other countries, protecting themselves by tariff walls, had developed into independent capitalist states. On the threshold of the twentieth century, we see a new type of monopoly coming into existence. Firstly, there are monopolist capitalist combines in all advanced capitalist countries; secondly, a few rich countries, in which the accumulation of capital reaches gigantic proportions, occupy a monopolist position. An enormous "superabundance of capital" has accumulated in the advanced countries.

It goes without saying that if capitalism could develop agriculture, which today lags far behind industry everywhere, if it could raise the standard of living of the masses, who are everywhere still poverty-stricken and underfed, in spite of the amazing advance in technical knowledge, there could be no talk of a superabundance of capital. This "argument" the petty-bourgeois critics of capitalism advance on every occasion. But if capitalism did these things it would not be capitalism; for uneven development and wretched conditions of the masses are fundamental and inevitable conditions and premises of this mode of production. As long as capitalism remains what it is, surplus capital will never be utilised for the purpose of raising the standard of living of the masses in a given country, for this would mean a decline in profits for the capitalists; it will be used for the purpose of increasing those profits by exporting capital abroad to the backward countries. In these backward countries profits are usually high, for capital is scarce, the price of land is relatively low, wages are low, raw materials are cheap. The possibility of exporting capital is created by the fact that numerous backward countries have been drawn into international capitalist intercourse; main railways have either been built or are being built there; the elementary conditions for industrial development have been created, etc. The necessity for exporting capital arises from the fact that in a few countries capitalism has become "over-ripe" and (owing to the backward state of agriculture and the impoverished state of the masses) capital cannot find "profitable" investment. . . .

In his book, *The Territorial Development of the European Colonies*, A. Supan, the geographer, gives the following brief summary of this development at the end of the nineteenth century:

PERCENTAGE OF TERRITORIES BELONGING TO THE
EUROPEAN COLONIAL POWERS

(Including United States)

	1876	1900	Increase or Decrease
Africa	10.8	90.4	+79.6
Polynesia	56.8	98.9	+42.1
Asia	51.5	56.6	+ 5.1
Australia	100.0	100.0	—
America	27.5	27.2	— 0.3

"The characteristic feature of this period," he concludes, "is therefore, the division of Africa and Polynesia."

As there are no unoccupied territories—that is, territories that do not belong to any state—in Asia and America, Mr. Supan's conclusion must be carried further, and we must say that the characteristic feature of this period is the final partition of the globe—not in the sense that a *new* partition is impossible —on the contrary, new partitions are possible and inevitable—but in the sense that the colonial policy of the capitalist countries has *completed* the seizure of the unoccupied territories on our planet. For the first time the world is completely divided up, so that in the future *only* redivision is possible; territories can only pass from one "owner" to another, instead of passing as unowned territory to an "owner."

Hence, we are passing through a peculiar period of world colonial policy, which is closely associated with the "latest stage in the development of capitalism," with finance capital. . . .

We must now try to sum up and put together what has been said above on the subject of imperialism. Imperialism emerged as the development and direct continuation of the fundamental attributes of capitalism in general. But capitalism only became capitalist imperialism at a definite and very high stage of its development, when certain of its fundamental attributes began to be transformed into their opposites, when the features of a period of transition from capitalism to a higher social and economic system began to take shape and reveal themselves all along the line. Economically, the main thing in this process is the substitution of capitalist monopolies for capitalist free competition. Free competition is the fundamental attribute of capitalism, and of commodity production generally. Monopoly is exactly the opposite of free competition; but we have seen the latter being transformed into monopoly before our very eyes, creating large-scale industry and eliminating small industry, replacing large-scale industry by still larger-scale industry, finally leading to such a concentration of production and capital that monopoly has been and is the result: cartels, syndicates and trusts, and merging with them, the capital of a dozen or so banks manipulating thousands of millions. At the same time monopoly, which has grown out of free competition, does not abolish the latter, but exists over it and alongside of it, and thereby gives rise to a number of very acute, intense antagonisms, friction and conflicts. Monopoly is the transition from capitalism to a higher system.

If it were necessary to give the briefest possible definition of imperialism we should have to say that imperialism is the monopoly stage of capitalism. Such a definition would include what is most important, for, on the one hand, finance capital is the bank capital of a few big monopolist banks, merged with the capital of the monopolist combines of manufacturers; and, on the other hand, the division of the world is the transition from a colonial policy which has extended without hindrance to territories unoccupied by any capitalist power, to a colonial policy of monopolistic possession of the territory of the world which has been completely divided up. . . .

We have seen that the economic quintessence of imperialism is monopoly capitalism. This very fact determines its place in history, for monopoly that grew up on the basis of free competition, and precisely out of free competition, is the transition from the capitalist system to a higher social-economic order. We must take special note of the four principal forms of monopoly, or the four principal manifestations of monopoly capitalism, which are characteristic of the epoch under review.

Firstly, monopoly arose out of the concentration of production at a very advanced stage of development. This refers to the monopolist capitalist combines, cartels, syndicates and trusts. We have seen the important part that these play in modern economic life. At the beginning of the twentieth century, monopolies acquired complete supremacy in the advanced countries. And although the first steps towards the formation of the cartels were first taken by countries enjoying the protection of high tariffs (Germany, America), Great Britain, with her system of free trade, was not far behind in revealing the same basic phenomenon, namely, the birth of monopoly out of the concentration of production.

Secondly, monopolies have accelerated the capture of the most important sources of raw materials, especially for the coal and iron industries, which are the basic and most highly cartelised industries in capitalist society. The monopoly of the most important sources of raw materials has enormously increased the power of big capital, and has sharpened the antagonism between cartelised and non-cartelised industry.

Thirdly, monopoly has sprung from the banks. The banks have developed from modest intermediary enterprises into the monopolists of finance capital. Some three or five of the biggest banks in each of the foremost capitalist countries have achieved the "personal union" of industrial and bank capital, and have concentrated in their hands the disposal of thousands upon thousands of millions which form the greater part of the capital and income of entire countries. A financial oligarchy, which throws a close net of relations of dependence over all the economic and political institutions of contemporary bourgeois society without exception—such is the most striking manifestation of this monopoly.

Fourthly, monopoly has grown out of colonial policy. To the numerous "old" motives of colonial policy, finance capital has added the struggle for the sources of raw materials, for the export of capital, for "spheres of influence," *i.e.,* for spheres for profitable deals, concessions, monopolist profits and so on; in fine, for economic territory in general. When the colonies of the European powers in Africa, for instance, comprised only one-tenth of that territory (as was the case in 1876), colonial policy was able to develop by methods other than those of monopoly—by the "free grabbing" of territories, so to speak. But when nine-tenths of Africa had been seized (approximately by 1900), when the whole world had been divided up, there was inevitably ushered in a period of colonial monopoly and, consequently, a period of particularly intense struggle for the division and the redivision of the world.

The extent to which monopolist capital has intensified all the contradictions of capitalism is generally known. It is sufficient to mention the high cost of living and the oppression of the cartels. This intensification of contradictions constitutes the most powerful driving force of the transitional period of history, which began from the time of the definite victory of world finance capital.

Monopolies, oligarchy, the striving for domination instead of the striving for liberty, the exploitation of an increasing number of small or weak nations by an extremely small group of the richest or most powerful nations—all these have given birth to those distinctive characteristics of imperialism which compel us to define it as parasitic or decaying capitalism. More and more prominently there emerges, as one of the tendencies of imperialism, the creation of the "bondholding" (rentier) state, the usurer state, in which the bourgeoisie lives on the proceeds of capital exports and by "clipping coupons." It would be a mistake to believe that this tendency to decay precludes the possibility of the rapid growth of capitalism. It does not. In the epoch of imperialism, certain branches of industry, certain strata of the bourgeoisie and certain countries betray, to a more or less degree, one or other of these tendencies. On the whole, capitalism is growing far more rapidly than before. But this growth is not only becoming more and more uneven in general; its unevenness also manifests itself, in particular, in the decay of the countries which are richest in capital (such as England). . . .

From all that has been said in this book on the economic nature of imperialism, it follows that we must define it as capitalism in transition, or, more precisely, as moribund capitalism. It is very instructive in this respect to note that the bourgeois economists, in describing modern capitalism, frequently employ terms like "interlocking," "absence of isolation," etc.; "in conformity with their functions and course of development," banks are "not purely private business enterprises; they are more and more outgrowing the sphere of purely private business regulation." And this very Riesser, who uttered the words just quoted, declares with all seriousness that the "prophecy" of the Marxists concerning "socialisation" has "not come true"!

What then does this word "interlocking" express? It merely expresses the most striking feature of the process going on before our eyes. It shows that the observer counts the separate trees, but cannot see the wood. It slavishly copies the superficial, the fortuitous, the chaotic. It reveals the observer as one who is overwhelmed by the mass of raw material and is utterly incapable of appreciating its meaning and importance. Ownership of shares and relations between owners of private property "interlock in a haphazard way." But the underlying factor of this interlocking, its very base, is the changing social relations of production. When a big enterprise assumes gigantic proportions, and, on the basis of exact computation of mass data, organises according to plan the supply of primary raw materials to the extent of two-thirds, or three-fourths of all that is necessary for tens of millions of people; when the raw materials are transported to the most suitable place of production, sometimes hundreds or thousands of miles away, in a systematic and organised manner; when a single centre directs all the successive stages of work right up to the manufacture of numerous varieties of finished articles; when these products are distributed according to a single plan among tens and hundreds of millions of consumers (as in the case of the distribution of oil in America and Germany by the American "oil trust")—then it becomes evident that we have socialisation of production, and not mere "interlocking"; that private economic relations and private property relations constitute a shell which is no longer suitable for its contents, a shell which must inevitably begin to decay if its destruction be delayed by artificial means; a shell which may continue in a state of decay for a fairly long period (particularly if the cure of the opportunist abscess is protracted), but which will inevitably be removed.

JOSEPH SCHUMPETER

JOSEPH ALOIS SCHUMPETER was born in Moravia (now Czechoslovakia), on February 8, 1883. After his father died and his mother remarried the family moved to Vienna, where Schumpeter was educated at a Mittelschule. He was graduated from secondary school with honors in Latin and Greek. In 1901 he entered the University of Vienna from which he received his Doctor of Laws degree. His fellow students there included Ludwig von Mises, the economist; Otto Bauer, future leader of the Austrian socialists; and Rudolph Hilferding, minister of finance under the Weimar Republic.

Schumpeter practiced law in Egypt from 1907 to 1908, and in 1909 returned to Austria as a professor of political economy in the University of Czernowitz. In 1911 he was appointed to a professorship at the University of Graz, and during 1913 and 1914 he was an Austrian exchange professor at Columbia University where he was awarded an honorary D. Litt. in March, 1914.

Schumpeter established his reputation as a brilliant scholar at the age of twenty-five, with the publication of his *Wesen und Hauptinhalt der theoretischen Nationalökonomie* (1908), followed four years later by *The Theory of Economic Development.* During the war Schumpeter was a pacifist, and frequently expressed his antagonism to German policy and his admiration for the Allies, especially Britain. His *Soziologie des Imperialismus,* from which the following excerpt is taken, was written in 1919 but had to await an English translation for a period well past a generation. After the war Schumpeter was a member of the German Socialization Commission, set up to study the prospects for the nationalization of industry; he joined his old classmates Lederer and Hilferding—but not as a socialist. When asked by one of his pupils about the inconsistency of his membership with his own principles of private enterprise, he replied: "If somebody wants to commit suicide, it is a good thing if a doctor is present." For seven months in 1919 he served as Minister of Finance of the Austrian Republic, but he was forced to resign by the socialists, who objected to many of his economic policies.

From 1927 to 1932, Schumpeter taught at Bonn and Harvard, and lectured in Japan. In 1932 he left Germany, never to return, and took up permanent residence at Harvard. In ensuing years he increased his world-wide reputation as an economist who brought to technical work an immense humanistic learning and the insights of history, sociology, and psychology. He was one of the founders of the Econometric Society, and served as its president from 1937 to 1941. In 1948 Schumpeter was elected president of the American Economic Association, and while plans were being formed for an International Economic Association (1949), there was unanimous agreement that he would be its first president.

Among Schumpeter's later works are *Business Cycles* (1939), and *Capitalism, Socialism, and Democracy* (1942). The latter work met with great popular success, and was translated into many languages. Schumpeter died on January 7, 1950, a week after delivering a paper to the American Economic Association.

"The Sociology of Imperialism" was translated by Heinz Norden in the volume entitled *Imperialism and Social Classes* (New York: Augustus M. Kelley, Inc., 1951).

ତୁ

THE SOCIOLOGY OF IMPERIALISM

CHAPTER V: IMPERIALISM AND CAPITALISM

OUR ANALYSIS of the historical evidence has shown, first, the unquestionable fact that "objectless" tendencies toward forcible expansion, without definite, utilitarian limits—that is, non-rational and irrational, purely instinctual in- clinations toward war and conquest—play a very large role in the history of mankind. It may sound paradoxical, but numberless wars—perhaps the major- ity of all wars—have been waged without adequate "reason"—not so much from the moral viewpoint as from that of reasoned and reasonable interest. The most herculean efforts of the nations, in other words, have faded into the empty air. Our analysis, in the second place, provides an explanation for this drive to action, this will to war—a theory by no means exhausted by mere references to an "urge" or an "instinct." The explanation lies, instead, in the vital needs of situations that molded peoples and classes into warriors—if they wanted to avoid extinction—and in the fact that psychological dispositions and social structures acquired in the dim past in such situations, once firmly established, tend to maintain themselves and to continue in effect long after they have lost their meaning and their life-preserving function. Our analysis, in the third place, has shown the existence of subsidiary factors that facilitate the survival of such dispositions and structures—factors that may be divided into two groups. The orientation toward war is mainly fostered by the do- mestic interests of ruling classes, but also by the influence of all those who stand to gain individually from a war policy, whether economically or socially. Both groups of factors are generally overgrown by elements of an altogether differ- ent character not only in terms of political phraseology, but also of psychologi- cal motivation. Imperialisms differ greatly in detail, but they all have at least these traits in common, turning them into a single phenomenon in the field of sociology, as we noted in the introduction.

Imperialism thus is atavistic in character. It falls into that large group of surviving features from earlier ages that play such an important part in every concrete social situation. In other words, it is an element that stems from the living conditions, not of the present, but of the past—or, put in terms of the economic interpretation of history, from past rather than present relations of production. It is an atavism in the social structure, in individual, psychological habits of emotional reaction. Since the vital needs that created it have passed away for good, it too must gradually disappear, even though every warlike involvement, no matter how non-imperialist in character, tends to revive it. It tends to disappear as a structural element because the structure that brought it to the fore goes into a decline giving way, in the course of social development, to other structures that have no room for it and eliminate the power factors that supported it. It tends to disappear as an element of habitual emotional reaction, because of the progressive rationalization of life and mind, a process in which old functional needs are absorbed by new tasks, in which heretofore military energies are functionally modified. If our theory is correct, cases of imperialism should decline in intensity the later they occur in the history of a people and of a culture. Our most recent examples of unmistakable, clear-cut imperialism are the absolute monarchies of the eighteenth century. They are unmistakably "more civilized" than their predecessors.

It is from absolute autocracy that the present age has taken over what imperialist tendencies it displays. And the imperialism of absolute autocracy flourished before the Industrial Revolution, that created the modern world, or rather, before the consequences of that revolution began to be felt in all their aspects. These two statements are primarily meant in a historical sense, and as such they are no more than self-evident. We shall nevertheless try, within the framework of our theory, to define the significance of capitalism for our phenomenon. . . .

The "instinct" that is *only* "instinct" that has lost its purpose, languishes relatively in the capitalist world, just as does an inefficient economic practice. We see this process of rationalization at work even in the case of the strongest impulses. We observe it, for example, in the facts of procreation. We must therefore anticipate finding it in the case of the imperialist impulse as well; we must expect to see this impulse, which rests on the primitive contingencies of physical combat, gradually disappear, washed away by new exigencies of daily life. There is another factor too. The competitive system absorbs the full energies of most of the people at all economic levels. Constant application, attention, and concentration of energy are the conditions of survival within it, primarily in the specifically economic professions, but also in other activities organized on their model. There is much less excess energy to be vented in war and conquest than in any precapitalist society. What excess energy there is flows largely into industry itself, accounts for its shining figures—the type of the captain of industry—and for the rest is applied to art, science, and the social struggle. In a purely capitalist world, what was once energy for war becomes simply energy for labor of every kind. Wars of conquest and adventurism in foreign policy in general are bound to be regarded as troublesome distractions, destructive of life's meaning, a diversion from the accustomed and therefore "true" task.

A purely capitalist world therefore can offer no fertile soil to imperialist impulses. That does not mean that it cannot still maintain an interest in imperialist expansion. We shall discuss this immediately. The point is that its people are likely to be essentially of an unwarlike disposition. Hence we must expect that anti-imperialist tendencies will show themselves wherever capitalism penetrates the economy and, through the economy, the mind of modern nations—most strongly, of course, where capitalism itself is strongest, where it has advanced furthest, encountered the least resistance, and pre-eminently where its types and hence democracy—in the "bourgeois" sense—come closest to political dominion. We must further expect that the types formed by capitalism will actually be the carriers of these tendencies. Is such the case? . . .

We cannot readily derive from it [capitalism] such imperialist tendencies as actually exist, but must evidently see them only as alien elements, carried into the world of capitalism from the outside, supported by non-capitalist factors in modern life. The survival of interest in a policy of forcible expansion does not, by itself, alter these facts—not even, it must be steadily emphasized, from the viewpoint of the economic interpretation of history. For objective interests become effective—and, what is important, become powerful political factors—only when they correspond to attitudes of the people or of sufficiently powerful strata. Otherwise they remain without effect, are not even conceived of as interests. The economic interest in the forcible conquest of India had to await free-booter personalities, in order to be followed up. In ancient Rome the domestic class interest in an expansive policy had to be seized upon by a vigorous, idle aristocracy, otherwise it would have been ruled out on internal political grounds. Even the purely commercial imperialism of Venice—assuming that we can speak of such a thing, and not merely of a policy of securing trade routes in a limitary sense, which was then necessary—even such a policy needed to have examples of a policy of conquest at hand on every side, needed mercenary groups and bellicose adventurers among the *nobili* in order to become true imperialism. The capitalist world, however, suppresses rather than creates such attitudes. Certainly, all expansive interests within it are likely to ally themselves with imperialist tendencies following from noncapitalist sources, to use them, to make them serve as pretexts, to rationalize them, to point the way toward action on account of them.

And from this union the picture of modern imperialism is put together; but for that very reason it is not a matter of capitalist factors alone. Before we go into this at length, we must understand the nature and strengh of the economic stake which capitalist society has in a policy of imperialism—especially the question of whether this interest is or is not inherent in the nature of capitalism —either capitalism generally, or a special phase of capitalism.

It is in the nature of a capitalist economy—and of an exchange economy generally—that many people stand to gain economically in any war. Here the situation is fundamentally much as it is with the familiar subject of luxury. War means increased demand at panic prices, hence high profits and also high wages in many parts of the national economy. This is primarily a matter of money incomes, but as a rule (though to a lesser extent) real incomes are also affected. There are, for example, the special war interests, such as the arms industry. If the war lasts long enough, the circle of money profiteers naturally expands more and more—quite apart from a possible paper-money economy. It may extend to every economic field, but just as naturally the commodity content of money profits drops more and more, indeed, quite rapidly to the point where actual losses are incurred. The national economy as a whole, of course, is impoverished by the tremendous excess in consumption brought on by war. It is, to be sure, conceivable that either the capitalists or the workers might make certain gains as a class, namely, if the volume either of capital or of labor should decline in such a way that the remainder receives a greater share in the social product and that, even from the absolute viewpoint the total sum of interest or wages becomes greater than it was before. But these advantages cannot be considerable. They are probably, for the most part, more than outweighed by the burdens imposed by war and by losses sustained abroad. Thus the gain of the capitalists as a class cannot be a motive for war— and it is this gain that counts, for any advantage to the working class would be contingent on a large number of workers falling in action or otherwise perishing. There remain the entrepreneurs in the war industries, in the broader sense, possibly also the large landowner—a small but powerful minority. Their war profits are always sure to be an important supporting element. But few will go so far as to assert that this element alone is sufficient to orient the people of the capitalist world along imperialist lines. At most, an interest in expansion may make the capitalists allies of those who stand for imperialist trends.

It may be stated as being beyond controversy that where free trade prevails no class has an interest in forcible expansion as such. For in such a case the citizens and goods of every nation can move in foreign countries as freely as though those countries were politically their own—free trade implying far more than mere freedom from tariffs. In a genuine state of free trade, foreign raw materials and foodstuffs are as accessible to each nation as though they were within its own territory. Where the cultural backwardness of a region makes normal economic intercourse dependent on colonization, it does not matter, assuming free trade, which of the "civilized" nations undertakes the task of colonization. Dominion of the seas, in such a case, means little more than a maritime traffic police. Similarly, it is a matter of indifference to a nation whether a railway concession in a foreign country is acquired by one of its own citizens or not—just so long as the railway is built and put into efficient operation. For citizens of any country may use the railway, just like the fellow countrymen of its builder—while in the event of war it will serve whoever controls it in the military sense, regardless of who built it. It is true, of course, that profits and wages flowing from its construction and operation will accrue, for the greater part, to the nation that built it. But capital and labor that go into the railway have to be taken from somewhere, and normally the other nations fill the gap. It is a fact that in a regime of free trade the essential advantages of international intercourse are clearly evident. The gain lies in the enlargement of the commodity supply by means of the division of labor among nations, rather than in the profits and wages of the export industry and the carrying trade. For these profits and wages would be reaped even if there were no export, in which case import, the necessary complement, would also vanish. Not even monopoly interests—if they existed—would be disposed toward imperialism in such a case. For under free trade only international cartels would be possible. Under a system of free trade there would be conflicts in economic interests neither among different nations nor among the corresponding classes of different nations. And since protectionism is not an essential characteristic of the capitalist economy—otherwise the English national economy would scarcely be capitalist—it is apparent that any economic interest in forcible expansion on the part of a people or a class is not necessarily a product of capitalism.

Protective tariffs alone—and harassment of the alien and of foreign commodities—do not basically change this situation as it affects interests. True, such barriers move the nations economically farther apart, making it easier for imperialist tendencies to win the upper hand; they line up the entrepreneurs of the different countries in battle formation against one another, impeding the rise of peaceful interests; they also hinder the flow of raw materials and foodstuffs and thus the export of manufactures, or conversely, the import of manufactures and the export of raw materials and foodstuffs, possibly creating an interest in—sometimes forcible—expansion of the customs area; they place entrepreneurs in a position of dependence on regulations of governments that may be serving imperialist interests, giving these governments occasion to pervert economic relations for purposes of sharpening economic conflicts for adulterating the competitive struggle with diplomatic methods outside the field of economics, and, finally, for imposing on peoples the heavy sacrifices exacted by a policy of autarchy, thus accustoming them to the thought of war by constant preparation for war. Nevertheless, in this case the basic alignment of interests remains essentially what it was under free trade. We might reiterate our example of railway construction, though in the case of mining concessions, for example, the situation is somewhat different. Colonial possessions acquire more meaning in this case, but the exclusion from the colonies of aliens and foreign capital is not altogether good business since it slows down the development of the colonies. The same is true of the struggle for third markets. When, for example, France obtains more favorable tariff treatment from the Chinese government than England enjoys, this will avail only those French exporters who are in a position to export the same goods as their English confreres; the others are only harmed. It is true, of course, that protectionism adds another form of international capital movement to the kind that prevails under free trade—or rather, a modification of it—namely, the movement of capital for the founding of enterprises inside the tariff wall, in order to save customs duties. But this capital movement too has no aggressive element; on the contrary, it tends toward the creation of peaceful interests. Thus an aggressive economic policy on the part of a country with a unified tariff—with preparedness for war always in the background—serves the economy only seemingly rather than really. Actually, one might assert that the economy becomes a weapon in the political struggle, a means for unifying the nation, for severing it from the fabric of international interests, for placing it at the disposal of the state power.

This becomes especially clear when we consider which strata of the capitalist world are actually economically benefited by protective tariffs. They do harm to both workers and capitalists—in contrast to entrepreneurs—not only in their role as consumers, but also as producers. The damage to consumers is universal, that to producers almost so. As for entrepreneurs, they are benefited only by the tariff that happens to be levied on their own product. But this advantage is substantially reduced by the countermeasures adopted by other countries—universally, except in the case of England—and by the effect of the tariff on the prices of other articles, especially those which they require for their own productive process. Why then, are entrepreneurs so strongly in favor of protective tariffs? The answer is simple. Each industry hopes to score *special* gains in the struggle of political intrigue, thus enabling it to realize a net gain. Moreover, every decline in freight rates, every advance in production abroad, is likely to affect the economic balance, making it necessary for domestic enterprises to adapt themselves, indeed often to turn to other lines of endeavor. This is a difficult task to which not everyone is equal. Within the industrial organism of every nation, there survive antiquated methods of doing business that would cause enterprises to succumb to foreign competition —because of poor management rather than lack of capital, for before 1914 the banks were almost forcing capital on the entrepreneurs. If, still, in most countries virtually *all* entrepreneurs are protectionists, this is owing to a reason which we shall presently discuss. Without that reason, their attitude would be different. The fact that all industries today demand tariff protection must not blind us to the fact that even the entrepreneur interest is not unequivocally protectionist. For this demand is only the consequence of a protectionism already in existence, of a protectionist spirit springing from the economic interests of relatively small entrepreneur groups and from noncapitalist elements—a spirit that ultimately carried along all groups, occasionally even the representatives of working-class interests. Today the protective tariff confers its full and immediate benefits—or comes close to conferring them—only on the large landowners.

A protectionist policy, however, does facilitate the formation of cartels and trusts. And it is true that this circumstance thoroughly alters the alignment of interests. It was neo-Marxist doctrine that first tellingly described this causal connection (Bauer) and fully recognized the significance of the "functional change in protectionism" (Hilferding). Union in a cartel or trust confers various benefits on the entrepreneur—a saving in costs, a stronger position as against the workers—but none of these compares with this one advantage: a monopolistic price policy, possible to any considerable degree *only* behind an adequate protective tariff. Now the price that brings the maximum monopoly profit is generally far above the price that would be fixed by fluctuating competitive costs, and the volume that can be marketed at that maximum price is generally far below the output that would be technically and economically feasible. Under free competition that output *would* be produced and offered, but a trust cannot offer it, for it could be sold only at a competitive price. Yet the trust *must* produce it—or approximately as much—otherwise the advantages of large-scale enterprise remain unexploited and unit costs are likely to be uneconomically high. The trust thus faces a dilemma. Either it renounces the monopolistic policies that motivated its founding: or it fails to exploit and expand its plant, with resultant high costs. It extricates itself from this dilemma by producing the full output that is economically feasible, thus securing low costs, and offering in the protected domestic market only the quantity corresponding to the monopoly price—insofar as the tariff permits: while the

rest is sold, or "dumped" abroad at a lower price, sometimes (but not necessarily) *below* cost.

What happens when the entrepreneurs successfully pursue such a policy is
something that did not occur in the cases discussed so far—a conflict of interests between nations that becomes so sharp that it cannot be overcome by the
existing basic community of interests. Each of the two groups of entrepreneurs
and each of the two states seeks to do something that is rendered illusory by
a similar policy on the part of the other. In the case of protective tariffs *without*
monopoly formation, an understanding is sometimes possible, for only a few
would be destroyed, while many would stand to gain; but when monopoly
rules it is very difficult to reach an agreement for it would require self-
negation on the part of the new rulers. All that is left to do is to pursue the
course once taken, to beat down the foreign industry wherever possible, forcing it to conclude a favorable "peace." This requires sacrifices. The excess
product is dumped on the world market at steadily lower prices. Counter-
attacks that grow more and more desperate must be repulsed on the domestic
scene. The atmosphere grows more and more heated. Workers and consumers
grow more and more troublesome. Where this situation prevails, capital export, like commodity export, becomes aggressive, belying its ordinary character.
A mass of capitalists competing with one another has no means of counteracting the decline in the interest rate. Of course they always seek out the places
where the interest rate is highest, and in this quest they are quite willing
to export their capital. But they are unable to adopt a policy of forced capital
exports; and where there is freedom of capital movement they also lack the
motive. For any gaps which might be opened up at home would be filled by
foreign capital flowing in from abroad, thus preventing a rise of the domestic
interest rate. But *organized* capital may very well make the discovery that the
interest rate can be maintained above the level of free competition, if the resulting surplus can be sent abroad and if any foreign capital that flows in can be
intercepted and—whether in the form of loans or in the form of machinery and
the like—can likewise be channeled into foreign investment outlets. Now it is
true that capital is nowhere cartelized. But it is every where subject to the
guidance of the big banks which, even without a capital cartel, have attained
a position similar to that of the cartel magnates in industry, and which are in a
position to put into effect similar policies. It is necessary to keep two factors
in mind. In the first place, everywhere except, significantly, in England, there
has come into being a close alliance between high finance and the cartel
magnates, often going as far as personal identity. Although the relation between capitalists and entrepreneurs is one of the typical and fundamental *conflicts* of the capitalist economy, monopoly capitalism has virtually fused the big

banks and cartels into one. Leading bankers are often leaders of the national economy. Here capitalism has found a central organ that supplants its automatism by conscious decisions. In the second place, the interests of the big banks coincide with those of their depositors even less than do the interests of cartel leaders with those of the firms belonging to the cartel. The policies of high finance are based on control of a large proportion of the national capital, but they are in the actual interest of only a small proportion and, indeed, with respect to the alliance with big business, sometimes not even in the interest of capital as such at all. The ordinary "small" capitalist foots the bills for a policy of forced exports, rather than enjoying its profits. He is a tool; his interests do not really matter. This possibility of laying all the sacrifices connected with a monopoly policy on one part of capital while removing them from another, makes capital exports far more lucrative for the favored part than they would otherwise be. Even capital that is independent of the banks is thus forced abroad—forced into the role of shock troop for the real leaders, because cartels successfully impede the founding of new enterprises. Thus the customs area of a trustified country generally pours a huge wave of capital into new countries. There it meets other, similar waves of capital, and a bitter, costly struggle begins but never ends.

In such a struggle among "dumped" products and capitals, it is no longer a matter of indifference who builds a given railroad, who owns a mine or a colony. Now that the law of costs is no longer operative, it becomes necessary to fight over such properties with desperate effort and with every available means, including those that are not economic in character, such as diplomacy. The concrete objects in question often become entirely subsidiary considerations; the anticipated profit may be trifling, because of the competitive struggle—a struggle that has very little to do with normal competition. What matters is to gain a foothold of some kind and then to exploit this foothold as a base for the conquest of new markets. This costs all the participants dear —often more than can be reasonably recovered, immediately or in the future. Fury lays hold of everyone concerned—and everyone sees to it that his fellow countrymen share his wrath. Each is constrained to resort to methods that he would regard as evidence of unprecedented moral depravity in the other.

It is not true that the capitalist system as such must collapse from immanent necessity, that it necessarily makes its continued existence impossible by its own growth and development. Marx's line of reasoning on this point shows serious defects, and when these are corrected the proof vanishes. It is to the great credit of Hilferding that he abandoned this thesis of Marxist theory. Nevertheless, the situation that has just been described is really untenable both politically and economically. Economically, it amounts to a *reductio ad absurdum*. Politically, it unleashes storms of indignation among the exploited consumers at home and the threatened producers abroad. Thus the idea of military force readily suggests itself. Force may serve to break down foreign customs barriers and thus afford relief from the vicious circle of economic aggression. If that is not feasible, military conquest may at least secure control over markets in which heretofore one had to compete with the enemy. In this context, the conquest of colonies takes on an altogether different significance. Nonmonopolist countries, especially those adhering to free trade, reap little profit from such a policy. But it is a different matter with countries that function in a monopolist role *vis-à-vis* their colonies. There being no competition, they can use cheap native labor without its ceasing to be cheap; they can market their products, even in the colonies, at monopoly prices; they can, finally, invest capital that would only depress the profit rate at home and that could be placed in other civilized countries only at very low interest rates. And they can do all these things even though the consequence may be much slower colonial development. It would seem as though there could be no such interest in expansion at the expense of other advanced capitalist countries—in Europe, for example—because their industry would merely offer competition to the domestic cartels. But it is sufficient for the industry of the conquering state to be superior to that of the one to be subjugated—superior in capital power, organization, intelligence, and self-assertion—to make it possible to treat the subjugated state, perhaps not quite, but very much like a colony, even though it may become necessary to make a deal with individual groups of interests that are particularly powerful. A much more important fact is that the conqueror can face the subjugated nation with the bearing of the victor. He has countless means at his disposal for expropriating raw material resources and the like and placing them in the service of his cartels. He can seize them outright, nationalize them, impose a forced sale, or draft the proprietors into industrial groups of the victor nation under conditions that insure control by the domestic captains of industry. He can exploit them by a system of quotas or allotments. He can administer the conquered means of communication in the interests of his own cartels. Under the pretext of military and political security, he can deprive the foreign workers of the right to organize, thus not only making cheap labor in the annexed territory available to his cartels, but also holding a threat over the head of domestic labor.

Thus we have here, within a social group that carries great political weight, a strong, undeniable, economic interest in such things as protective tariffs, cartels, monopoly prices, forced exports (dumping), an aggressive economic policy, an aggressive foreign policy generally, and war, including wars of expansion with a typically imperialist character. Once this alignment of interests exists, an even stronger interest in a somewhat differently motivated expansion must be added, namely, an interest in the conquest of lands producing raw materials and foodstuffs, with a view to facilitating self-sufficient warfare. Still another interest is that in rising wartime consumption. A mass of unorganized capitalists competing with one another may at best reap a trifling profit from such an eventuality, but organized capital is sure to profit hugely. Finally there is the political interest in war and international hatred which flows from the insecure position of the leading circles. They are small in numbers and highly unpopular. The essential nature of their policy is quite generally known, and most of the people find it unnatural and contemptible. An attack on all forms of property has revolutionary implications, but an attack on the privileged position of the cartel magnates may be politically rewarding, implying comparatively little risk and no threat to the existing order. Under certain circumstances it may serve to unite all the political parties. The existence of such a danger calls for diversionary tactics.

Yet the final word in any presentation of this aspect of modern economic life must be one of warning against over-estimating it. The conflicts that have been described, born of an export-dependent monopoly capitalism, may serve to submerge the real community of interests among nations; the monopolist press may drive it underground; but underneath the surface it never completely disappears. Deep down, the normal sense of business and trade usually prevails. Even cartels cannot do without the custom of their foreign economic kin. Even national economies characterized by export monopoly are dependent on one another in many respects. And their interests do not always conflict in the matter of producing for third markets. Even when the conflicting interests are emphasized parallel interests are not altogether lacking. Furthermore, if a policy of export monopolism is to be driven to the extremes of forcible expansion, it is necessary to win over all segments of the population—at least to the point where they are halfway prepared to support the war; but the real interest in export monopolism as such is limited to the entrepreneurs and their ally, high finance. Even the most skillful agitation cannot prevent the independent traders, the small producers who are not covered by cartels, the "mere" capitalists, and the workers from occasionally realizing that they are the victims of such a policy. In the case of the traders and small producers this is quite clear. It is not so clear in the case of the capitalists, because of the possibility of "dumping" capital in order to raise the domestic interest rate. Against this, however, stands the high cost of such a policy and the curtailment of the competition of entrepreneurs for domestic capital. It is of the greatest importance, finally, to understand that export monopolism injures the workers far more unequivocally than the capitalists. There can be no dumping of labor power, and employment abroad or in the colonies is not even a quantitative substitute. Curiously enough, this injury to the working class is a matter of controversy. Even neo-Marxist doctrine— and not merely those writers properly characterized as "vulgar marxists," who in every respect resemble their ilk of other persuasions—is inclined to admit that the workers derive temporary benefits from export monopolism, limiting the polemic against it to proof that the ultimate effects—economic and especially political—are doubtful, and that even the temporary benefits are purchased by an injury to foreign workers which conflicts with the spirit of socialism. There is an error here. Apparently it is assumed that production for export—and, to the extent that it fosters such production, monopoly capitalist expansion as well—increases the demand for labor and thus raises wages. Suppose we accept as correct the premises implied in this argument, that the increase in demand will outweigh any decrease flowing from monopolistic labor-saving production methods, and also that it will outweigh the disadvantage flowing from the fact that the workers are now confronted, rather than by many entrepreneurs in a single industry, by a single party of the second part who, on the local labor market at least, can engage in monopolistic policies with respect to them, both as workers and as consumers. Even if we accept these premises—which seem doubtful to me—the balance is not even temporarily in favor of the workers. We have already pointed out that the interest of workers in export, even when free trade prevails, is essentially a consumer interest; that is, it is based on the fact that exports make imports possible. But as a producer the worker will usually fare no worse without exports, since the lack of exports must also eliminate imports. The workers, moreover, have no interest whatever in exports that may result from a policy of export monopolism—in other words, that would not otherwise be exported at all. For if it were impossible to dump these quantities they would by no means remain unproduced. On the contrary, most, if not all, would be offered at home, in general affording the same employment opportunities to the workers and in addition cheapening consumption. If that is not possible—that is to say, if the profit from the increased supply at home, together with the profit from the reduced supply abroad, fails to cover total costs including interest—then the industry in question is expanded beyond economically justifiable limits, and it is in the interest of all the productive factors concerned, excepting only the cartel magnates, for capital and labor to move into other industries, something that is necessary and always possible. This constellation of interests is not altered by the circumstance that export monopolism is often able and willing to do things for its workers in the social welfare sphere, thus allowing them to share in its profits. For what makes this possible is, after all, nothing but exploitation of the consumer. If we may speak of the impoverishment of the workers anywhere within the world of capitalism, then a tendency to such impoverishment is apparent here, at least in a relative sense—though actually that tendency has slowed up since the turn of the century. If it is ever true that there is not a trace of parallelism of economic interests between entrepreneurs and workers, but instead only a sharp economic conflict—and usually there is much exaggeration in such statements—then this is true here. Chamberlain had every reason to appeal to national sentiment, to mock the petty calculation of immediate advantage, and to call out to the workers: "Learn to think imperially!" For the English worker knew what he was about, despite the banner headlines on the front pages of the yellow press: "Tariff Reform Means Work For All," and so on.

The fact that the balance sheet of export monopolism is anything but a brilliant success, even for the entrepreneurs, has been glossed over only by an upswing that stemmed from sources other than export monopolism itself. The hope of a future of dominion, to follow the struggles of the present, is but poor solace for the losses in that struggle. Should such a policy become general, the losses—admitted or not—of each individual nation would be even greater, the winnings even smaller. . . . Thus we can understand the fact that even in entrepreneurial circles dissatisfaction with such a policy arose, and while one group entertained the thought of forcible expansion as a last resort, another was led into an attitude of opposition. In all the protectionist countries, therefore, we have had, for the past twenty years, anti-dumping legislation, primarily as an instrument of tariff policy. This legislation, it is true, is directed against foreign dumping rather than against dumping by domestic enterprise, and hence it becomes a new weapon in the hands of the monopoly interests. But it is also true that its political basis lies partly in circles and attitudes opposed on principle to export aggression and for this reason anxious to make such a policy impossible for domestic enterprise. It must be admitted that such opposition often suffers from inappropriate techniques and from the influence of lay catch-words. But given peaceful development, it may be assumed that the opposition would gradually turn directly against dumping by domestic cartels.

This countermovement against export monopolism, within capitalism rather than opposed to it, would mean little if it were merely the political death struggle of a moribund economic order which is giving way to a new phase of development. If the cartel with its policy of export aggression stood face to face with non-cartelized factory industry, as that industry once faced handicraft industry, then even the most vigorous opposition could scarcely change the ultimate outcome or the fundamental significance of the process. But it cannot be emphasized sharply enough that such is not the case. Export monopolism does *not* grow from the inherent laws of capitalist development. The character of capitalism leads to large-scale production, but with few exceptions large-scale production does *not* lead to the kind of unlimited concentration that would leave but one or only a few firms in each industry. On the contrary, any plant runs up against limits to its growth in a given location; and the growth of combinations which would make sense under a system of free trade encounters limits of organizational efficiency. Beyond these limits there is no tendency toward combination inherent in the competitive system. In particular, the rise of trusts and cartels—a phenomenon quite different from the trend to large-scale production with which it is often confused—can never be explained by the automatism of the competitive system. This follows from the very fact that trusts and cartels can attain their primary purpose—to pursue a monopoly policy—only behind protective tariffs, without which they would lose their essential significance. But protective tariffs do not automatically grow from the competitive system. They are the fruit of political action—*a type of action that by no means reflects the objective interests of all those concerned* but that, on the contrary, becomes impossible as soon as the majority of those whose consent is necessary realize their true interests. To some extent it is obvious, and for the rest it will be presently shown, that the interests of the minority, quite appropriately expressed in support of a protective tariff, do not stem from capitalism as such. It follows that *it is a basic fallacy to describe imperialism as a necessary phase of capitalism, or even to speak of the development of capitalism into imperialism.* We have seen before that the mode of life of the capitalist world does not favor imperialist attitudes. We now see that the alignment of interests in a capitalist economy—even the interests of its upper strata— by no means points unequivocally in the direction of imperialism. We now come to the final step in our line of reasoning.

Since we cannot derive even export monopolism from any tendencies of the competitive system toward big enterprise, we must find some other explanation. A glance at the original purpose of tariffs provides what we need. Tariffs sprang from the financial interests of the monarchy. They were a method of exploiting the trader which differed from the method of the robber baron in the same way that the royal chase differed from the method of the poacher. They were in line with the royal prerogatives of safe conduct, of protection for the Jews, of the granting of market rights, and so forth. From the thirteenth century onward this method was progressively refined in the autocratic state, less and less emphasis being placed on the direct monetary yield of customs revenues and more and more on their indirect effect in creating productive taxable objects. In other words, while the protective value of a tariff counted, it counted only from the viewpoint of the ultimate monetary advantage of the sovereign. It does not matter, for our purposes, that occasionally this policy, under the influence of lay notions of economics, blundered badly in the choice of its methods. (From the viewpoint of autocratic interest, incidentally, such measures were not nearly so self-defeating as they were from the viewpoint of the national economy.) Every customs house, every privilege conferring the right to produce, market, or store, thus created a new economic situation which deflected trade and industry into "unnatural" channels. All tariffs, rights, and the like became the seed bed for economic growth that could have neither sprung up nor maintained itself without them. Further, all such economic institutions dictated by autocratic interest were surrounded by manifold interests of people who were dependent on them and now began to demand their continuance—a wholly paradoxical though at the same time quite understandable situation. The trading and manufacturing bourgeoisie was all the more aware of its dependence on the sovereign, since it needed his protection against the remaining feudal powers; and the uncertainties of the times, together with the lack of great consuming centers, impeded the rise of free economic competition. Insofar as commerce and manufacturing came into being at all, therefore, they arose under the sign of monopolistic interest. Thus the bourgeoisie willingly allowed itself to be molded into one of the power instruments of the monarchy, both in a territorial and in a national sense. It is even true that the bourgeoisie, because of the character of its interests and the kind of economic outlook that corresponded to those interests, made an essential contribution to the emergence of modern nationalism. Another factor that worked in the same direction was the financial relation between the great merchant houses and the sovereign. This theory of the nature of the relationship between the autocratic state and the bourgeoisie is not refuted by pointing out that it was precisely the mercantile republics of the Middle Ages and the early modern period that initially pursued a policy of mercantilism. They were no more than enclaves in a world pervaded by the struggle among feudal powers. The Hanseatic League and Venice, for example, could maintain themselves only as military powers, could pursue their business only by means of fortified bases, warehousing privileges, protective treaties. This forced the people to stand shoulder to shoulder, made the exploitation of political gains more important than domestic competition, infused them with a corporate and monopolistic spirit.

Wherever autocratic power vanished at an early date—as in the Netherlands and later in England—and the protective interest receded into the background, they swiftly discovered that trade must be free—"free to the nethermost recesses of hell."

Trade and industry of the early capitalist period thus remained strongly pervaded with precapitalist methods, bore the stamp of autocracy, and served its interests, either willingly or by force. With its traditional habits of feeling, thinking and acting molded along such lines, the bourgeoisie entered the Industrial Revolution. It was shaped, in other words, by the needs and interests of an environment that was essentially noncapitalist, or at least precapitalist—needs stemming not from the nature of the capitalist economy as such but from the fact of the coexistence of early capitalism with another and at first overwhelmingly powerful mode of life and business. Established habits of thought and action tend to persist, and hence the spirit of guild and monopoly at first maintained itself, and was only slowly undermined, even where capitalism was in sole possession of the field. Actually, capitalism did not fully prevail *anywhere* on the Continent. Existing economic interests, "artificially" shaped by the autocratic state, remained dependent on the "protection" of the state. The industrial organism, such as it was, would not have been able to withstand free competition. Even where the old barriers crumbled in the autocratic state, the people did not all at once flock to the clear track. They were creatures of mercantilism and even earlier periods, and many of them huddled together and protested against the affront of being forced to depend on their own ability. They cried for paternalism, for protection, for forcible restraint of strangers, and above all for tariffs. They met with partial success, particularly because capitalism failed to take radical action in the agrarian field. Capitalism did bring about many changes on the land, springing in part from its automatic mechanisms, in part from the political trends it engendered—abolition of serfdom, freeing the soil from feudal entanglements, and so on—but initially it did not alter the basic outlines of the social structure of the countryside. Even less did it affect the spirit of the people, and least of all their political goals. This explains why the features and trends of autocracy—including imperialism—proved so resistant, why they exerted such a powerful influence on capitalist development, why the old export monopolism could live on and merge into the new. . . .

The bourgeoisie did not simply supplant the sovereign, nor did it make him its leader, as did the nobility. It merely wrested a portion of his power from him and for the rest submitted to him. It did not take over from the sovereign the state as an abstract form of organization. The state remained a special social power, confronting the bourgeoisie. In some countries it has continued to play that role to the present day. It is in the state that the bourgeoisie with its interests seeks refuge, protection against external and even domestic enemies. The bourgeoisie seeks to win over the state for itself, and in return serves the state and state interests that are different from its own. Imbued with the spirit of the old autocracy, trained by it, the bourgeoisie often takes over its ideology, even where, as in France, the sovereign is eliminated and the official power of the nobility has been broken. Because the sovereign needed soldiers, the modern bourgeois—at least in his slogans—is an even more vehement advocate of an increasing population. Because the sovereign was in a position to exploit conquests, needed them to be a victorious warlord, the bourgeoisie thirsts for national glory—even in France, worshipping a headless body, as it were. Because the sovereign found a large gold hoard useful, the bourgeoisie even today cannot be swerved from its bullionist prejudices. Because the autocratic state paid attention to the trader and manufacturer chiefly as the most important sources of taxes and credits, today even the intellectual who has not a shred of property looks on international commerce, not from the viewpoint of the consumer, but from that of the trader and exporter. Because pugnacious sovereigns stood in constant fear of attack by their equally pugnacious neighbors, the modern bourgeois attributes aggressive designs to neighboring peoples. All such modes of thought are essentially noncapitalist. . . .

This significant dichotomy in the bourgeois mind—which in part explains its wretched weakness in politics, culture, and life generally, earns it the understandable contempt of the Left and the Right: and proves the accuracy of our diagnosis—is best exemplified by two phenomena that are very close to our subject: present-day nationalism and militarism. Nationalism is affirmative awareness of national character, together with an aggressive sense of superiority. It arose from the autocratic state. In conservatives, nationalism in general is understandable as an inherited orientation, as a mutation of the battle instincts of the medieval knights, and finally as a political stalking horse on the domestic scene; and conservatives are fond of reproaching the bourgeois with a lack of nationalism, which, from their point of view, is evaluated in a positive sense. Socialists, on the other hand, equally understandably exclude nationalism from their general ideology, because of the essential interests of the proletariat, and by virtue of their domestic opposition to the conservative stalking horse; they, in turn, not only reproach the bourgeoisie with an excess of nationalism (which they, of course, evaluate in a negative sense) but actually identify nationalism and even the very idea of the nation with bourgeois ideology. The curious thing is that both of these groups are right in their criticism of the bourgeoisie. For, as we have seen, the mode of life that flows logically from the nature of capitalism necessarily implies an antinationalist orientation in politics and culture. This orientation actually prevails. We find a great many antinationalist members of the middle class, and even more who merely parrot the catchwords of nationalism. In the capitalist world it is actually not big business and industry at all that are the carriers of nationalist trends, but the intellectual, and the content of *his* ideology is explained not so much from definite class interests as from chance emotion and individual interest. But the submission of the bourgeoisie to the powers of autocracy, its alliance with them, its economic and psychological patterning by them—all these tend to push the bourgeois in a nationalist direction; and this too we find prevalent, especially among the chief exponents of export monopolism. The relationship between the bourgeoisie and militarism is quite similar. Militarism is not necessarily a foregone conclusion when a nation maintains a large army, but only when high military circles become a political power. The criterion is whether leading generals as such wield political influence and whether the responsible statesmen can act only with their consent. That is possible only when the officer corps is linked to a definite social class, as in Japan, and can assimilate to its position individuals who do not belong to it by birth. Militarism too is rooted in the autocratic state. And again the same reproaches are made against the bourgeois from both sides—quite properly too. According to the "pure" capitalist mode of life, the bourgeois is unwarlike. The alignment of capitalist interests should make him utterly reject military methods, put him in opposition to the professional soldier. Significantly, we see this in the example of England where, first the struggle against a standing army generally and, next, opposition to its elaboration, furnished bourgeois politicians with their most popular slogan: "retrenchment." Even naval appropriations have encountered resistance. We find similar trends in other countries, though they are less strongly developed. The continental bourgeois, however, was used to the sight of troops. He regarded an army almost as a necessary component of the social order, ever since it had been his terrible taskmaster in the Thirty Years' war. He had no power at all to abolish the army. He might have done so if he had had the power; but not having it, he considered the fact that the army might be useful to him. In his "artificial" economic situation and because of his submission to the sovereign, he thus grew disposed toward militarism, especially where export monopolism flourished. The intellectuals, many of whom still maintained special relationships with feudal elements, were so disposed to an even greater degree.

Just as we once found a dichotomy in the social pyramid, so now we find everywhere, in every aspect of the bourgeois portion of the modern world, a dichotomy of attitudes and interests. Our examples also show in what way the two components work together. Nationalism and militarism, while not creatures of capitalism, become "capitalized" and in the end draw their best energies from capitalism. Capitalism involves them in its workings and thereby keeps them alive, politically as well as economically. And they, in turn, affect capitalism, cause it to deviate from the course it might have followed alone, support many of its interests.

Here we find that we have penetrated to the historical as well as the socio-logical sources of modern imperialism. It does not *coincide* with nationalism and militarism, though it *fuses* with them by supporting them as it is sup-ported by them. It too is—not only historically, but also sociologically—a heritage of the autocratic state, of its structural elements, organizational forms, interest alignments, and human attitudes, the outcome of precapitalist forces which the autocratic state has reorganized, in part by the methods of early capitalism. It would never have been evolved by the "inner logic" of capital-ism itself. This is true even of mere export monopolism. It too has its sources in absolutist policy and the action habits of an essentially precapitalist environ-ment. That it was able to develop to its present dimensions is owing to the momentum of a situation once created, which continued to engender ever new "artificial" economic structures, that is, those which maintain themselves by political power alone. In most of the countries addicted to export monopo-lism it is also owing to the fact that the old autocratic state and the old atti-tude of the bourgeoisie toward it were so vigorously maintained. But export monopolism, to go a step further, is not yet imperialism. And even if it had been able to arise without protective tariffs, it would never have developed into imperialism in the hands of an unwarlike bourgeoisie. If this did happen, it was only because the heritage included the war machine, together with its socio-psychological aura and aggressive bent, and because a class oriented toward war maintained itself in a ruling position. This class clung to its domestic interest in war, and the pro-military interests among the bourgeoisie were able to ally themselves with it. This alliance kept alive war instincts and ideas of overlordship, male supremacy, and triumphant glory—ideas that would have otherwise long since died. It led to social conditions that, while they ultimately stem from the conditions of production, cannot be explained from capitalist production methods alone. And it often impresses its mark on present-day politics, threatening Europe with the constant danger of war.

This diagnosis also bears the prognosis of imperialism. The precapitalist ele-ments in our social life may still have great vitality; special circumstances in national life may revive them from time to time; but in the end the climate of the modern world must destroy them. This is all the more certain since their props in the modern capitalist world are not of the most durable material. Whatever opinion is held concerning the vitality of capitalism itself, whatever the life span predicted for it, it is bound to withstand the onslaughts of its enemies and its own irrationality much longer than essentially untenable export monopolism—untenable even from the capitalist point of view. Export monopolism may perish in revolution, or it may be peacefully relinquished; this may happen soon, or it may take some time and require desperate struggle; but one thing is certain—it *will* happen. This will immediately dispose of neither warlike instincts nor structural elements and organizational forms oriented toward war—and it is to their dispositions and domestic interests that, in my opinion, much more weight must be given in every concrete case of imperialism than to export monopolist interests, which furnish the financial "outpost skirmishes"—a most appropriate term—in many wars. But such factors will be politically overcome in time, no matter what they do to maintain among the people a sense of constant danger of war, with the war machine forever primed for action. And with them, imperialisms will wither and die.

BENJAMIN DISRAELI

BENJAMIN DISRAELI was born in London in 1804. His father, the son of a prominent Jewish merchant and financier, severed his own relationship with Judaism in 1813, and permitted Benjamin to be baptized in 1817. The boy studied at private academies in London, and at the age of seventeen was apprenticed to a solicitors' firm. Disraeli did not take to business, and after a number of failures decided to give it up. He captured public attention with a novel, *Vivian Grey,* published in 1826, the first of a number of literary successes.

In 1832, Disraeli returned from a trip to the East to offer himself as a candidate for Parliament. After losing twice as a radical, he ran for a county borough as a Tory. Although defeated again, he laid the basis for his political future with a pamphlet entitled *What Is He?* (1833), in which he explained his apparent inconsistency by insisting that it was possible to be an honest democrat and an honest Tory. Between 1835 and 1837 he published a series of pamphlets in which he developed a consistent philosophy of conservatism, emphasizing his organic view of society, along with his ideas about the nature of social change and the determining influence of national character. He accused the Whigs of being a party of oligarchy and faction.

With the accession of Queen Victoria in 1837, Disraeli finally gained a seat as Tory member for Maidstone. His first speech in the House of Commons was a failure: he was laughed down as much for his exotic attire as for his extravagant similes. Disraeli soon gained the respect of the House, however, and after he was refused a place in the ministry of 1841 by Peel assumed the leadership of the "Young England" group, which harassed Peel with criticism and sarcasm in the House, and through the medium of Disraeli's novels—*Coningsby, or the Younger Generation* (1844), and *Sybil or the Two Nations* (1845)—secured popularity for their cause. Young Englanders believed that only the influence of the landed aristocracy and the good offices of a revivified Church could protect the laboring class and rescue them from degradation. Disraeli led the attack on Peel's Corn Law Repeal in 1846, and gained recognition as the most distinguished orator in the House. Although repeal was passed on June 25, 1846, Peel was turned out on the same day; the Tories were split and condemned to the position of an opposition party for the next twenty years. It was during this period that Disraeli took the lead in healing the breach among the Tories.

It was not until 1867 that the Conservatives became powerful enough to bring forward an important measure in Parliament: the Reform Bill of 1867. It was Disraeli who introduced the Bill, providing for a household franchise in boroughs, and a reduction in the qualification for county suffrage—in effect enfranchising great numbers of the urban working class. Disraeli was forced into opposition again in 1868, and it was during this period that his views on the Empire began to gain prominence, as he criticized the Liberals mercilessly for their "cosmopolitan" indifference to England's colonial empire.

Disraeli was returned to power in 1874. When in 1875 the Khedive of Egypt was forced to sell 177,000 shares in the French-built Suez Canal, Disraeli borrowed £4 million from the Rothschilds in the name of the cabinet, bought the shares, and demanded that parliament sanction his action. The next year, he secured for the Queen a new title with the passage of the "Empress of India Act," symbolizing the importance of the Empire in British life. When trouble threatened in the Near East, Disraeli secured a satisfactory settlement for Britain, and returned from the Congress of Berlin in 1878, announcing "peace with honour."

Disraeli was made Earl of Beaconsfield in 1876. The Conservatives were defeated at the polls in 1880, and Disraeli died in retirement on April 19, 1881. The first of the following selections is Disraeli's speech of 1872 at the Crystal Palace, London. It is said to mark the introduction of imperialism as a plank in the Conservative party program. The second is extracted from his speech to the House of Commons after his return from Berlin in 1878.

Both addresses are taken from *Selected Speeches of the Late Right Honorable the Earl of Beaconsfield*, ed. by T. E. Kebbel (12 vols.; London, 1882).

CONSERVATIVE AND LIBERAL PRINCIPLES

Speech at Crystal Palace, June 24, 1872

MY LORD DUKE AND GENTLEMEN:—I am very sensible of the honour which you have done me in requesting that I should be your guest to-day, and still more for your having associated my name with the important toast which has been proposed by the Lord Mayor. In the few observations that I shall presume to make on this occasion I will confine myself to some suggestions as to the present state of the Constitutional cause and the prospects which you, as a great Constitutional party, have before you. Gentlemen, some years ago—now, indeed, not an inconsiderable period, but within the memory of many who are present—the Tory party experienced a great overthrow. I am here to admit that in my opinion it was deserved. A long course of power and prosperity had induced it to sink into a state of apathy and indifference, and it had deviated from the great principles of that political association which had so long regulated the affairs and been identified with the glory of England. Instead of the principles professed by Mr. Pitt and Lord Grenville, and which those great men inherited from Tory statesmen who had preceded them not less illustrious, the Tory system had degenerated into a policy which found an adequate basis on the principles of exclusiveness and restriction. Gentlemen, the Tory party, unless it is a national party, is nothing. It is not a confederacy of nobles, it is not a democratic multitude; it is a party formed from all the numerous classes in the realm—classes alike and equal before the law, but whose different conditions and different aims give vigour and variety to our national life.

Gentlemen, a body of public men distinguished by their capacity took advantage of these circumstances. They seized the helm of affairs in a manner the honour of which I do not for a moment question, but they introduced a new system into our political life. Influenced in a great degree by the philosophy and the politics of the Continent, they endeavoured to substitute cosmopolitan for national principles; and they baptized the new scheme of politics with the plausible name of "Liberalism." Far be it from me for a moment to intimate that a country like England should not profit by the political experience of Continental nations of not inferior civilisation; far be it from me for a moment to maintain that the party which then obtained power and which has since generally possessed it did not make many suggestions for our public life that were of great value, and bring forward many measures which, though changes, were nevertheless improvements. But the tone and tendency of Liberalism cannot be long concealed. It is to attack the institutions of the country under the name of Reform, and to make war on the manners and customs of the people of this country under the pretext of Progress. During the forty years that have elapsed since the commencement of this new system—although the superficial have seen upon its surface only the contentions of political parties—the real state of affairs has been this: the attempt of one party to establish in this country cosmopolitan ideas, and the efforts of another—unconscious efforts, sometimes, but always continued—to recur to and resume those national principles to which they attribute the greatness and glory of the country.

The Liberal party cannot complain that they have not had fair play. Never had a political party such advantages, never such opportunities. They are still in power; they have been for a long period in power. And yet what is the result? I speak not I am sure the language of exaggeration when I say that they are viewed by the community with distrust and, I might even say, with repugnance. And, now, what is the present prospect of the national party? I have ventured to say that in my opinion Liberalism, from its essential elements, notwithstanding all the energy and ability with which its tenets have been advocated by its friends—notwithstanding the advantage which has accrued to them, as I will confess, from all the mistakes of their opponents, is viewed by the country with distrust. Now in what light is the party of which we are members viewed by the country, and what relation does public opinion bear to our opinions and our policy? That appears to me to be an instructive query; and on an occasion like the present it is as well that we should enter into its investigation as pay mutual compliments to each other, which may in the end, perhaps prove fallacious.

Now, I have always been of opinion that the Tory party has three great objects. The first is to maintain the institutions of the country—not from any sentiment of political superstition, but because we believe that they embody the principles upon which a community like England can alone safely rest. The principles of liberty, of order, of law, and of religion ought not to be entrusted to individual opinion or to the caprice and passion of multitudes, but should be embodied in a form of permanence and power. We associate with the Monarchy the ideas which it represents—the majesty of law, the administration of justice, the fountain of mercy and of honour. We know that in the Estates of the Realm and the privileges they enjoy, is the best security for public liberty and good government. We believe that a national profession of faith can only be maintained by an Established Church, and that no society is safe unless there is a public recognition of the Providential man. Well, it is a curious circumstance that during all these same forty years of triumphant Liberalism, every one of these institutions has been attacked and assailed—I say, continuously attacked and assailed. And what, gentlemen, has been the result? For the last forty years the most depreciating comparisons have been instituted between the Sovereignty of England and the Sovereignty of a great Republic. We have been called upon in every way, in Parliament, in the Press, by articles in newspapers, by pamphlets, by every means which can influence opinion, to contrast the simplicity and economy of the Sovereignty of the United States with the cumbrous cost of the Sovereignty of England.

Gentlemen, I need not in this company enter into any vindication of the Sovereignty of England on that head. I have recently enjoyed the opportunity, before a great assemblage of my countrymen, of speaking upon that subject. I have made statements with respect to it which have not been answered either on this side of the Atlantic or the other. Only six months ago the advanced guard of Liberalism, acting in entire unison with that spirit of assault upon the Monarchy which the literature and the political confederacies of Liberalism have for forty years encouraged, flatly announced itself as Republican, and appealed to the people of England on that distinct issue. Gentlemen, what was the answer? I need not dwell upon it. It is fresh in your memories and hearts. The people of England have expressed, in a manner which cannot be mistaken, that they will uphold the ancient Monarchy of England, the Constitutional Monarchy of England, limited by the co-ordinate authority of the Estates of the Realm, but limited by nothing else. Now, if you consider the state of public opinion with regard to those Estates of the Realm, what do you find? Take the case of the House of Lords. The House of Lords has been assailed during the Reign of Liberalism in every manner and unceasingly. Its constitution has been denounced as anomalous, its influence declared pernicious; but what has been the result of this assault and criticism of forty years? Why, the people of England, in my opinion, have discovered that the existence of a second Chamber is necessary to Constitutional Government; and, while necessary to Constitutional Government, is, at the same time, of all political inventions the most difficult. Therefore, the people of this country have congratulated themselves that, by the aid of an ancient and famous history, there has been developed in this country an Assembly which possesses all the virtues which a Senate should possess—independence, great local influence, eloquence, all the accomplishments of political life, and a public training which no theory could supply.

The assault of Liberalism upon the House of Lords has been mainly occasioned by the prejudice of Liberalism against the land laws of this country. But in my opinion, and in the opinion of wiser men than myself, and of men in other countries beside this, the liberty of England depends much upon the landed tenure of England—upon the fact that there is a class which can alike defy despots and mobs, around which the people may always rally, and which must be patriotic from its intimate connection with the soil. Well, gentlemen, so far as these institutions of the country—the Monarchy and the Lords Spiritual and Temporal—are concerned, I think we may fairly say, without exaggeration, that public opinion is in favour of those institutions, the maintenance of which is one of the principal tenets of the Tory party, and the existence of which has been unceasingly criticised for forty years by the Liberal party. Now, let me say a word about the other Estate of the Realm, which was first attacked by Liberalism.

One of the most distinguishing features of the great change effected in 1832 was that those who brought it about at once abolished all the franchises of the working classes. They were franchises as ancient as those of the Baronage of England; and, while they abolished them, they proposed no substitute. The discontent upon the subject of the representation which has from that time more or less pervaded our society dates from that period, and that discontent, all will admit, has now ceased. It was terminated by the Act of Parliamentary Reform of 1867–8. The Act was founded on a confidence that the great body of the people of this country were "Conservative." When I say "Conservative," I use the word in its purest and loftiest sense. I mean that the people of England, and especially the working classes of England, are proud of belonging to a great country, and wish to maintain its greatness—that they are proud of belonging to an Imperial country, and are resolved to maintain, if they can, their empire—that they believe, on the whole, that the greatness and the empire of England are to be attributed to the ancient institutions of the land.

Gentlemen, I venture to express my opinion, long entertained, and which has never for a moment faltered, that this is the disposition of the great mass of the people; and I am not misled for a moment by wild expressions and eccentric conduct which may occur in the metropolis of this country. There are people who may be, or who at least affect to be, working men, and who, no doubt, have a certain influence with a certain portion of the metropolitan working classes, who talk Jacobinism. But, gentlemen, that is no novelty. That is not the consequence of recent legislation or of any political legislation that has occurred in this century. There always has been a Jacobinical section in the City of London. I don't particularly refer to that most distinguished and affluent portion of the metropolis which is ruled by my right honourable friend the Lord Mayor. Mr. Pitt complained of and suffered by it. There has always been a certain portion of the working class in London who have sympathised—perverse as we may deem the taste—with the Jacobin feelings of Paris. Well, gentlemen, we all know now, after eighty years' experience, in what the Jacobinism of Paris has ended, and I hope I am not too sanguine when I express my conviction that the Jacobinism of London will find a very different result.

I say with confidence that the great body of the working class of England utterly repudiate such sentiments. They have no sympathy with them. They are English to the core. They repudiate cosmopolitan principles. They adhere to national principles. They are for maintaining the greatness of the kingdom and the empire, and they are proud of being subjects of our Sovereign and members of such an Empire. Well, then, as regards the political institutions of this country, the maintenance of which is one of the chief tenets of the Tory party, so far as I can read public opinion, the feeling of the nation is in accordance with the Tory party. It was not always so. There was a time when the institutions of this country were decried. They have passed through a scathing criticism of forty years; they have passed through that criticism when their political upholders have, generally speaking, been always in opposition. They have been upheld by us when we were unable to exercise any of the lures of power to attract force to us, and the people of this country have arrived at these conclusions from their own thought and their own experience.

Let me say one word upon another institution, the position of which is most interesting at this time. No institution of England, since the advent of Liberalism, has been so systematically, so continuously assailed as the Established Church. Gentlemen, we were first told that the Church was asleep, and it is very possible, as everybody, civil and spiritual, was asleep forty years ago, that

that might have been the case. Now we are told that the Church is too active, and that it will be destroyed by its internal restlessness and energy. I see in all these efforts of the Church to represent every mood of the spiritual mind of man, no evidence that it will fall, no proof that any fatal disruption is at hand. I see in the Church, as I believe I see in England, an immense effort to rise to national feelings and recur to national principles. The Church of England, like all our institutions, feels it must be national, and it knows that, to be national, it must be comprehensive. Gentlemen, I have referred to what I look upon as the first object of the Tory party—namely, to maintain the institutions of the country, and reviewing what has occurred, and referring to the present temper of the times upon these subjects, I think that the Tory party, or, as I will venture to call it, the National party, has everything to encourage it. I think that the nation, tested by many and severe trials, has arrived at the conclusion which we have always maintained, that it is the first duty of England to maintain its institutions, because to them we principally ascribe the power and prosperity of the country.

Gentlemen, there is another and second great object of the Tory party. If the first is to maintain the institutions of the country, the second is, in my opinion, to uphold the Empire of England. If you look to the history of this country since the advent of Liberalism—forty years ago—you will find that there has been no effort so continuous, so subtle, supported by so much energy, and carried on with so much ability and acumen, as the attempts of Liberalism to effect the disintegration of the Empire of England.

And, gentlemen, of all its efforts, this is the one which has been the nearest to success. Statesmen of the highest character, writers of the most distinguished ability, the most organised and efficient means have been employed in this endeavour. It has been proved to all of us that we have lost money by our colonies. It has been shown with precise, with mathematical demonstration, that there never was a jewel in the Crown of England that was so truly costly as the possession of India. How often has it been suggested that we should at once emancipate ourselves from this incubus. Well, that result was nearly accomplished. When those subtle views were adopted by the country under the plausible plea of granting self-government to the Colonies, I confess that I myself thought that the tie was broken. Not that I for one object to self-government. I cannot conceive how our distant colonies can have their affairs administered except by self-government. But self-government, in my opinion, when it was conceded, ought to have been conceded as part of a great policy of Imperial consolidation. It ought to have been accompanied by an Imperial tariff, by securities for the people of England for the enjoyment of the unappropriated lands which belonged to the Sovereign as their trustee, and by a military code which should have precisely defined the means and the responsibilities by which the colonies should be defended, and by which, if necessary, this country should call for aid from the colonies themselves. It ought, further, to have been accompanied by the institution of some representative council in the metropolis, which would have brought the Colonies into constant and continuous relations with the Home Government. All this, however, was omitted because those who advised that policy—and I believe their convictions were sincere—looked upon the Colonies of England, looked even upon our connection with India, as a burden upon this country, viewing everything in a financial aspect, and totally passing by those moral and political considerations which make nations great, and by the influence of which alone men are distinguished from animals.

Well, what has been the result of this attempt during the reign of Liberalism for the disintegration of the Empire? It has entirely failed. But how has it failed? Through the sympathy of the Colonies with the Mother Country. They have decided that the Empire shall not be destroyed, and in my opinion no minister in this country will do his duty who neglects any opportunity of reconstructing as much as possible our Colonial Empire, and of responding to those distant sympathies which may become the source of incalculable strength and happiness to this land. Therefore, gentlemen, with respect to the second great object of the Tory party also—the maintenance of the Empire—public opinion appears to be in favour of our principles—that public opinion which, I am bound to say, thirty years ago, was not favourable to our principles, and which, during a long interval of controversy, in the interval had been doubtful.

Gentlemen, another great object of the Tory party, and one not inferior to the maintenance of the Empire, or the upholding of our institutions, is the elevation of the condition of the people. Let us see in this great struggle between Toryism and Liberalism that has prevailed in this country during the last forty years what are the salient features. It must be obvious to all who consider the condition of the multitude with a desire to improve and elevate it, that no important step can be gained unless you can effect some reduction of their hours of labour and humanise their toil. The great problem is to be able to achieve such results without violating those principles of economic truth upon which the prosperity of all States depends. You recollect well that many years ago the Tory party believed that these two results might be obtained—that you might elevate the condition of the people by the reduction of their toil and the mitigation of their labour, and at the same time inflict no injury on the wealth of the nation. You know how that effort was encountered—how these views and principles were met by the triumphant statesmen of Liberalism. They told you that the inevitable consequence of your policy was to diminish capital, that this, again, would lead to the lowering of wages, to a great diminution of the employment of the people, and ultimately to the impoverishment of the kingdom.

These were not merely the opinions of Ministers of State, but those of the most blatant and loud-mouthed leaders of the Liberal party. And what has been the result? Those measures were carried, but carried, as I can bear witness, with great difficulty and after much labour and a long struggle. Yet they were carried; and what do we now find? That capital was never accumulated so quickly, that wages were never higher, that the employment of the people was never greater, and the country never wealthier. I ventured to say a short time ago, speaking in one of the great cities of this country, that the health of the people was the most important question for a statesman. It is, gentlemen, a large subject. It has many branches. It involves the state of the dwellings of the people, the moral consequences of which are not less considerable than the physical. It involves their enjoyment of some of the chief elements of nature—air, light, and water. It involves the regulation of their industry, the inspection of their toil. It involves the purity of their provisions, and it touches upon all the means by which you may wean them from habits of excess and of brutality. Now, what is the feeling upon these subjects of the Liberal party—that Liberal party, who opposed the Tory party when, even in their weakness, they advocated a diminution of the toil of the people, and introduced and supported those Factory Laws, the principles of which they extended, in the brief period when they possessed power, to every other trade in the country? What is the opinion of the great Liberal party—the party that seeks to substitute cosmopolitan for national principles in the government of this country—on this subject? Why, the views which I expressed in the great capital of the county of Lancaster have been held up to derision by the Liberal Press. A leading member—a very rising member, at least, among the new Liberal members—denounced them the other day as the "policy of sewage."

Well, it may be the "policy of sewage" to a Liberal member of Parliament. But to one of the labouring multitude of England, who has found fever always to be one of the inmates of his household—who has, year after year, seen stricken down the children of his loins, on whose sympathy and material support he has looked with hope and confidence, it is not a "policy of sewage," but a question of life and death. And I can tell you this, gentlemen, from personal conversation with some of the most intelligent of the labouring class—and I think there are many of them in this room who can bear witness to what I say—that the policy of the Tory party—the hereditary, the traditionary policy of the Tory party, that would improve the condition of the people—is more appreciated by the people than the ineffable mysteries and all the pains and penalties of the Ballot Bill. Gentlemen, is that wonderful? Consider the condition of the great body of the working classes of this country. They are in possession of personal privileges—of personal rights and liberties—which are not enjoyed by the aristocracies of other countries. Recently they have obtained—and wisely obtained—a great extension of political rights; and when the people of England see that under the constitution of this country, by means of the constitutional cause which my right honourable friend the Lord Mayor has proposed, they possess every personal right of freedom, and, according to the conviction of the whole country, also an adequate concession of political rights, is it at all wonderful that they should wish to elevate and improve their condition, and is it unreasonable that they should ask the Legislature to assist them in that behest as far as it is consistent with the general welfare of the realm?

Why, the people of England would be greater idiots than the Jacobinical leaders of London even suppose, if, with their experience and acuteness, they should not long have seen that the time had arrived when social, and not political improvement is the object which they ought to pursue. I have touched, gentlemen, on the three great objects of the Tory party. I told you I would try to ascertain what was the position of the Tory party with reference to the country now. I have told you also with frankness what I believe the position of the Liberal party to be. Notwithstanding their proud position, I believe they are viewed by the country with mistrust and repugnance. But on all the three great objects which are sought by Toryism—the maintenance of our institutions, the preservation of our Empire, and the improvement of the condition of the people—I find a rising opinion in the country sympathising with our tenets, and prepared, I believe, if the opportunity offers, to uphold them until they prevail.

Before sitting down, I would make one remark particularly applicable to those whom I am now addressing. This is a numerous assembly; this is an assembly individually influential; but it is not on account of its numbers, it is not on account of its individual influence, that I find it to me deeply interesting. It is because I know that I am addressing a representative assembly. It is because I know that there are men here who come from all districts and all quarters of England, who represent classes and powerful societies, and who meet here not merely for the pleasure of a festival, but because they believe that our assembling together may lead to national advantage. Yes, I tell all who are here present that there is a responsibility which you have incurred to-day, and which you must meet like men. When you return to your homes, when you return to your counties and to your cities, you must tell to all those whom you can influence that the time is at hand, that, at least, it cannot be far distant, when England will have to decide between national and cosmopolitan principles. The issue is not a mean one. It is whether you will be content to be a comfortable England, modelled and moulded upon Continental principles and meeting in due course an inevitable fate, or whether you will be a great country,—an Imperial country—a country where your sons, when they rise, rise to paramount positions, and obtain not merely the esteem of their countrymen, but command the respect of the world.

Upon you depends the issue. Whatever may be the general feeling, you must remember that in fighting against Liberalism or the Continental system you are fighting against those who have the advantage of power—against those who have been in high places for nearly half a century. You have nothing to trust to but your own energy and the sublime instinct of an ancient people. You must act as if everything depended on your individual efforts. The secret of success is constancy of purpose. Go to your homes, and teach there these truths, which will soon be imprinted on the conscience of the land. Make each man feel how much rests on his own exertions. The highest, like my noble friend the chairman, may lend us his great aid. But rest assured that the assistance of the humblest is not less efficient. Act in this spirit, and you will succeed. You will maintain your country in its present position. But you will do more than that—you will deliver to your posterity a land of liberty, of prosperity, of power, and of glory.

THE BERLIN TREATY

My LORDS, in laying on the table of your lordships' House, as I am about to do, the protocols of the Congress of Berlin, I have thought I should be only doing my duty to your lordships' House, to Parliament generally, and to the country, if I made some remarks on the policy which was supported by the representatives of Her Majesty at the Congress, and which is embodied in the Treaty of Berlin and in the convention which was placed on your lordships' table during my absence.

My lords, you are aware that the treaty of San Stefano was looked on with much distrust and alarm by Her Majesty's Government—that they believed it was calculated to bring about a state of affairs dangerous to European independence and injurious to the interests of the British Empire. Our impeachment of that policy is before your lordships and the country, and is contained in the circular of my noble friend the Secretary of State for Foreign Affairs in April last. Our present contention is, that we can show that, by the changes and modifications which have been made in the treaty of San Stefano by the Congress of Berlin and the Convention of Constantinople, the menace to European independence has been removed, and the threatened injury to the British Empire has been averted. Your lordships will recollect that by the treaty of San Stefano about one half of Turkey in Europe was formed into a State called Bulgaria—a State consisting of upwards of 50,000 geographical square miles, and containing a population of 4,000,000, with harbours on either sea—both on the shores of the Euxine and of the Archipelago. That disposition of territory severed Constantinople and the limited district which was still spared to the possessors of that city—severed it from the provinces of Macedonia and Thrace by Bulgaria descending to the very shores of the Ægean; and, altogether, a State was formed, which, both from its natural resources and its peculiarly favourable geographical position, must necessarily have exercised a predominant influence over the political and commercial interests of that part of the world. The remaining portion of Turkey in Europe was reduced also to a considerable degree by affording what was called compensation to previous rebellious tributary principalities, which have now become independent States—so that the general result of the treaty of San Stefano was, that while it spared the authority of the Sultan so far as his capital and its immediate vicinity, it reduced him to a state of subjection to the great Power which had defeated his armies, and which was present at the gates of his capital. Accordingly, though it might be said that he still seemed to be invested with one of the highest functions of public duty—the protection and custody of the Straits—it was apparent that his authority in that respect could be exercised by him in deference only to the superior Power which had vanquished him, and to whom the proposed arrangements would have kept him in subjection.

My lords, in these matters, the Congress of Berlin have made great changes. They have restored to the Sultan two-thirds of the territory which was to have formed the great Bulgarian State. They have restored to him upwards of 30,000 geographical square miles, and 2,500,000 of population—that territory being the richest in the Balkans, where most of the land is rich, and the population one of the wealthiest, most ingenious, and most loyal of his subjects. The frontiers of his State have been pushed forward from the mere environs of Salonica and Adrianople to the lines of the Balkans and Trajan's pass; the new principality, which was to exercise such an influence, and produce a revolution in the disposition of the territory and policy of that part of the globe, is now merely a State in the Valley of the Danube, and both in its extent and its population is reduced to one-third of what was contemplated by the treaty of San Stefano. . . .

My lords, in consequence of that arrangement cries have been raised against our "partition of Turkey." My lords, our object has been directly the reverse, our object has been to prevent partition. The question of partition is one upon which, it appears to me, very erroneous ideas are in circulation. Some two years ago—before, I think, the war had commenced, but when the disquietude and dangers of the situation were very generally felt—there was a school of statesmen who were highly in favour of what they believed to be the only remedy, what they called the partition of Turkey. Those who did not agree with them were those who thought we should, on the whole, attempt the restoration of Turkey. Her Majesty's Government at all times have resisted the partition of Turkey. They have done so because, exclusive of the high moral considerations that are mixed up with the subject, they believed an attempt, on a great scale, to accomplish the partition of Turkey, would inevitably lead to a long, a sanguinary, and often recurring struggle, and that Europe and Asia would both be involved in a series of troubles and sources of disaster and danger of which no adequate idea could be formed.

These professors of partition—quite secure, no doubt, in their own views—have freely spoken to us on this subject. We have been taken up to a high mountain and shown all the kingdoms of the earth, and they have said, "All these shall be yours if you will worship Partition." But we have declined to do so for the reasons I have shortly given. And it is a remarkable circumstance that after the great war, and after the prolonged diplomatic negotiations, which lasted during nearly a period of three years, on this matter, the whole Powers of Europe, including Russia, have strictly, and as completely as ever, come to the unanimous conclusion that the best chance for the tranquility and order of the world is to retain the Sultan as part of the acknowledged political system of Europe. My lords, unquestionably after a great war—and I call the late war a great war, because the greatness of a war now must not be calculated by its duration, but by the amount of the forces brought into the field, and where a million of men have struggled for supremacy, as has been the case recently, I call that a great war—but, I say, after a great war like this, it is utterly impossible that you can have a settlement of any permanent character without a redistribution of territory and considerable changes. But that is not partition. My lords, a country may have lost provinces, but that is not partition. We know that not very long ago a great country—one of the foremost countries of the world—lost provinces; yet is not France one of the great Powers of the world, and with a future—a commanding future?

Austria herself has lost provinces—more provinces even than Turkey, perhaps; even England has lost provinces—the most precious possessions—the loss of which every Englishman must deplore to this moment. We lost them from bad government. Had the principles which now obtain between the metropolis and her dependencies prevailed then, we should not, perhaps, have lost those provinces, and the power of this Empire would have been proportionally increased. It is perfectly true that the Sultan of Turkey has lost provinces; it is true that his armies have been defeated; it is true that his enemy is even now at his gates; but all that has happened to other Powers. But a sovereign who has not yet forfeited his capital, whose capital has not yet been occupied by his enemy—and that capital one of the strongest in the world— who has armies and fleets at his disposal, and who still rules over 20,000,000 of inhabitants, cannot be described as a Power whose dominions have been partitioned. My lords, it has been said that no limit has been fixed to the occupation of Bosnia by Austria. Well, I think that was a very wise step. The moment you limit an occupation you deprive it of half its virtue. All those opposed to the principles which occupation was devised to foster and strengthen, feel that they have only to hold their breath and wait a certain time, and the opportunity for their interference would again present itself. Therefore, I cannot agree with the objection which is made to the arrangement with regard to the occupation of Bosnia by Austria on the question of its duration. . . .

Now, my lords, I have touched upon most of the points connected with Turkey in Europe. My summary is that at this moment—of course, no longer counting Servia or Roumania, once tributary principalities, as part of Turkey; not counting even the New Bulgaria, though it is a tributary principality, as part of Turkey; and that I may not be taunted with taking an element which I am hardly entitled to place in the calculation, omitting even Bosnia—European Turkey still remains a dominion of 60,000 geographical square miles, with a population of 6,000,000, and that population in a very great degree concentrated and condensed in the provinces contiguous to the capital. My lords, it was said, when the line of the Balkans was carried—and it was not carried until after long and agitating discussions—it was said by that illustrious statesman who presided over our labours, that "Turkey in Europe once more exists." My lords, I do not think that, so far as European Turkey is concerned, this country has any right to complain of the decisions of the Congress, or, I would hope, of the labours of the plenipotentiaries. You cannot look at the map of Turkey as it had been left by the treaty of San Stefano, and as it has been rearranged by the Treaty of Berlin, without seeing that great results have accrued. If these results had been the consequences of a long war—if they had been the results of a struggle like that we underwent in the Crimea—I do not think they would have been even then unsubstantial or unsatisfactory. My lords, I hope that you and the country will not forget that these results have been obtained without shedding the blood of a single Englishman; and if there has been some expenditure, it has been an expenditure which, at least, has shown the resources and determination of this country. Had you entered into that war—for which you were prepared—and well prepared—probably in a month you would have exceeded the whole expenditure you have now incurred.

My lords, I now ask you for a short time to quit Europe and to visit Asia, and consider the labours of the Congress in another quarter of the world. My lords, you well know that the Russian arms met with great success in Asia, and that in the treaty of San Stefano considerable territories were yielded by Turkey to Russia. . . . The Congress have so far approved the treaty of San Stefano that they have sanctioned the retention by Russia of Kars and Batoum. . . . Now is that a question for which England would be justified in going to war with Russia? My lords, we have, therefore, thought it advisable not to grudge Russia those conquests which have been made—especially after obtaining the restoration of the town of Bayazid and its important district. . . .

But I must make this observation to your lordships. We have a substantial interest in the East; it is a commanding interest, and its behest must be obeyed. But the interest of France in Egypt, and her interest in Syria, are, as she acknowledges, sentimental and traditionary interests; and, although I respect them, and although I wish to see in the Lebanon and Egypt the influence of France fairly and justly maintained, and although her officers and ours in that part of the world—and especially in Egypt—are acting together with confidence and trust, we must remember that our connection with the East is not merely an affair of sentiment and tradition, but that we have urgent and substantial and enormous interests which we must guard and keep. Therefore, when we find that the progress of Russia is a progress which, whatever may be the intentions of Russia, necessarily in that part of the world produces such a state of disorganisation and want of confidence in the Porte, it comes to this—that if we do not interfere in vindication of our own interests, that part of Asia must become the victim of anarchy, and ultimately become part of the possessions of Russia.

Now, my lords, I have ventured to review the chief points connected with the subject on which I wished to address you—namely, what was the policy pursued by us, both at the Congress of Berlin and in the Convention of Constantinople? I am told, indeed, that we have incurred an awful responsibility by the Convention into which we have entered. My lords, a prudent minister certainly would not recklessly enter into any responsibility; but a minister who is afraid to enter into any responsibility is, to my mind, not a prudent minister. We do not, my lords, wish to enter into any unnecessary responsibility; but there is one responsibility from which we certainly shrink; we shrink from the responsibility of handing to our successors a weakened or a diminished Empire. Our opinion is, that the course we have taken will arrest the great evils which are destroying Asia Minor and the equally rich countries beyond. We see in the present state of affairs the Porte losing its influence over its subjects; we see a certainty, in our opinion, of increasing anarchy, of the dissolution of all those ties which, though feeble, yet still exist and which have kept society together in those countries. We see the inevitable result of such a state of things, and we cannot blame Russia for availing herself of it. But, yielding to Russia what she has obtained, we say to her—"Thus far, and no farther." Asia is large enough for both of us. There is no reason for these constant wars, or fears of wars, between Russia and England. Before the circumstances which led to the recent disastrous war, when none of those events which we have seen agitating the world had occurred, and when we were speaking in "another place" of the conduct of Russia in Central Asia, I vindicated that conduct, which I thought was unjustly attacked, and I said then —what I repeat now—there is room enough for Russia and England in Asia.

But the room that we require we must secure. We have, therefore, entered into an alliance—a defensive alliance—with Turkey, to guard her against any further attack from Russia. We believe that the result of this Convention will be order and tranquility. And then it will be for Europe—for we ask no exclusive privileges or commercial advantages—it will then be for Europe to assist England in availing ourselves of the wealth which has been so long neglected and undeveloped in regions once so fertile and so favoured. We are told, as I have said before, that we are undertaking great responsibilities. From those responsibilities we do not shrink. We think that, with prudence and discretion, we shall bring about a state of affairs as advantageous for Europe as for ourselves; and in that conviction we cannot bring ourselves to believe that the act which we have recommended is one that leads to trouble and to warfare. No, my lords, I am sure there will be no jealousy between England and France upon this subject. In taking Cyprus the movement is not Mediterranean, it is Indian. We have taken a step there which we think necessary for the maintenance of our Empire and for its preservation in peace. . . .

My lords, I have now laid before you the general outline of the policy we have pursued, both in the Congress of Berlin and at Constantinople. They are intimately connected with each other, and they must be considered together. I only hope that the House will not misunderstand—and I think the country will not misunderstand—our motives in occupying Cyprus, and in encouraging those intimate relations between ourselves and the Government and the population of Turkey. They are not movements of war; they are operations of

peace and civilisation. We have no reason to fear war. Her Majesty has fleets
and armies which are second to none. England must have seen with pride
the Mediterranean covered with her ships; she must have seen with pride the
discipline and devotion which have been shown to her and her Government
by all her troops, drawn from every part of her Empire. I leave it to the illustrious duke, in whose presence I speak, to bear witness to the spirit of imperial
patriotism which has been exhibited by the troops from India, which he recently reviewed at Malta. But it is not on our fleets and armies, however necessary they may be for the maintenance of our imperial strength, that I alone
or mainly depend in that enterprise on which this country is about to enter.
It is on what I most highly value—the consciousness that in the Eastern nations there is confidence in this country, and that, while they know we can
enforce our policy, at the same time they know that our Empire is an Empire
of liberty, of truth, and of justice.

THEODORE ROOSEVELT

THEODORE ROOSEVELT was born in New York City on October 27, 1858, the scion of an old and respected New York commercial family. He was a sickly and feeble youth and received his early education from private tutors. After graduating from Harvard in 1880, he studied law at Columbia.

In 1881 Roosevelt shocked his staid and respectable friends by joining a local political club. Thus began his remarkable ascent through the ranks of the Republican party, and in national political life. He served three terms as a member of the New York Assembly and in 1886 waged an unsuccessful campaign for the mayoralty of New York. From 1889 to 1895 he was a member of the Federal Civil Service Commission, then he returned to New York and served as president of the police board (1895-97). The outbreak of the Spanish-American War in 1898 found Roosevelt serving as the jingoist Assistant Secretary of the Navy. He resigned his post to organize the "Rough Riders," whose charge up San Juan Hill, with Roosevelt at their head, became a part of the Roosevelt legend. He was elected governor of New York in November of that year, and two years later was elected Vice-President of the United States. President William McKinley was assassinated on September 6, 1901, and eight days later Theodore Roosevelt became our twenty-sixth president.

Despite his conservative background, Roosevelt made it clear early in his political career that he was not a tool of the business interests. As governor of New York he had matched wits with "Boss" Platt and succeeded in passing important economic and conservation legislation, including the corporation franchise tax. As President he followed a policy of increased but mild government supervision of large corporate and banking groups. Antitrust suits were filed against powerful commercial interests: the Northern Securities Company, Standard Oil, United States Steel, and others. The Interstate Commerce Commission was strengthened while a Pure Food Act was passed to guarantee the consumer against adulterated food and drugs.

Roosevelt was much influenced by the writings of Admiral Mahan (1840-1914), American naval expert and expansionist. Roosevelt publicly expressed his own expansionism as early as 1894 when he demanded the annexation of Hawaii; he also advocated the acquisition of the Philippines. He was animated less by commercial ambition than by a desire to see the United States play a major role in world affairs. His support for the Panama Canal project, agitation for a large navy, announcement of the "Roosevelt Corollary" to the Monroe doctrine, and sending of the American fleet around the world were all expressions of this commitment. But Roosevelt was alive to the dangers which militarism posed to the United States' interests in other parts of the world, and in 1905 he brought the Russo-Japanese War to a conclusion by his mediation, for which he was awarded the Nobel Peace Prize.

After serving a second term, Roosevelt supported William Howard Taft for the Republican nomination in 1908. In 1912, however, believing that Taft had betrayed the reform principles to which he had been pledged, Roosevelt was the Progressive party nominee and outran Taft in the presidential election, although he himself was defeated by Woodrow Wilson. Roosevelt's last years were spent in foreign travel and speechmaking. After the outbreak of the First World War, he became one of the most impassioned advocates of preparedness and eventually of American intervention.

Roosevelt died a national hero on January 6, 1919. "The Strenuous Life," which expresses Roosevelt's belief in the imperial virtues, was delivered as an address to the Hamilton Club in Chicago in 1899 and was reprinted in *The Strenuous Life, Essays and Addresses* (New York: The Century Co., 1900).

THE STRENUOUS LIFE

IN SPEAKING to you, men of the greatest city of the West, men of the State which gave to the country Lincoln and Grant, men who preëminently and distinctly embody all that is most American in the American character, I wish to preach, not the doctrine of ignoble ease, but the doctrine of the strenuous life, the life of toil and effort, of labor and strife; to preach that highest form of success which comes, not to the man who desires mere easy peace, but to the man who does not shrink from danger, from hardship, or from bitter toil, and who out of these wins the splendid ultimate triumph.

A life of slothful ease, a life of that peace which springs merely from lack either of desire or of power to strive after great things, is as little worthy of a nation as of an individual. I ask only that what every self-respecting American demands from himself and from his sons shall be demanded of the American nation as a whole. Who among you would teach your boys that ease, that peace, is to be the first consideration in their eyes—to be the ultimate goal after which they strive? You men of Chicago have made this city great, you men of Illinois have done your share, and more than your share, in making America great, because you neither preach nor practise such a doctrine. You work yourselves, and you bring up your sons to work. If you are rich and are worth your salt, you will teach your sons that though they may have leisure, it is not to be spent in idleness; for wisely used leisure merely means that those who possess it, being free from the necessity of working for their livelihood, are all the more bound to carry on some kind of non-remunerative work in science, in letters, in art, in exploration, in historical research—work of the type we most need in this country, the successful carrying out of which reflects most honor upon the nation. We do not admire the man of timid peace. We admire the man who embodies victorious effort;

the man who never wrongs his neighbor, who is prompt to help a friend, but who has those virile qualities necessary to win in the stern strife of actual life. It is hard to fail, but it is worse never to have tried to succeed. In this life we get nothing save by effort. Freedom from effort in the present merely means that there has been stored up effort in the past. A man can be freed from the necessity of work only by the fact that he or his fathers before him have worked to good purpose. If the freedom thus purchased is used aright, and the man still does actual work, though of a different kind, whether as a writer or a general, whether in the field of politics or in the field of exploration and adventure, he shows he deserves his good fortune. But if he treats this period of freedom from the need of actual labor as a period, not of preparation, but of mere enjoyment, even though perhaps not of vicious enjoyment, he shows that he is simply a cumberer of the earth's surface, and he surely unfits himself to hold his own with his fellows if the need to do so should again arise. A mere life of ease is not in the end a very satisfactory life, and, above all, it is a life which ultimately unfits those who follow it for serious work in the world.

In the last analysis a healthy state can exist only when the men and women who make it up lead clean, vigorous, healthy lives; when the children are so trained that they shall endeavor, not to shirk difficulties, but to overcome them; not to seek ease, but to know how to wrest triumph from toil and risk. The man must be glad to do a man's work, to dare and endure and to labor; to keep himself, and to keep those dependent upon him. The woman must be the housewife, the helpmeet of the homemaker, the wise and fearless mother of many healthy children. In one of Daudet's powerful and melancholy books he speaks of "the fear of maternity, the haunting terror of the young wife of the present day." When such words can be truthfully written of a nation, that nation is rotten to the heart's core. When men fear work or fear righteous war, when women fear motherhood, they tremble on the brink of doom; and well it is that they should vanish from the earth, where they are fit subjects for the scorn of all men and women who are themselves strong and brave and high-minded.

As it is with the individual, so it is with the nation. It is a base untruth to say that happy is the nation that has no history. Thrice happy is the nation that has a glorious history. Far better it is to dare mighty things, to win glorious triumphs, even though checkered by failure, than to take rank with those poor spirits who neither enjoy much nor suffer much, because they live in the gray twilight that knows not victory nor defeat. If in 1861 the men who loved the Union had believed that peace was the end of all things, and war and strife the worst of all things, and had acted up to their belief, we would have saved hundreds of thousands of lives, we would have saved hundreds of millions of dollars. Moreover, besides saving all the blood and treasure we then lavished, we would have prevented the heartbreak of many women, the dissolution of many homes, and we would have spared the country those months of gloom and shame when it seemed as if our armies marched only to defeat. We could have avoided all this suffering simply by shrinking from strife. And if we had thus avoided it, we would have shown that we were weaklings, and that we were unfit to stand among the great nations of the earth. Thank God for the iron in the blood of our fathers, the men who upheld the wisdom of Lincoln, and bore sword or rifle in the armies of Grant! Let us, the children of the men who proved themselves equal to the mighty days, let us, the children of the men who carried the great Civil War to a triumphant conclusion, praise the God of our fathers that the ignoble counsels of peace were rejected; that the suffering and loss, the blackness of sorrow and despair, were unflinchingly faced, and the years of strife endured; for in the end the slave was freed, the Union restored, and the mighty American republic placed once more as a helmeted queen among nations.

We of this generation do not have to face a task such as that our fathers faced, but we have our tasks, and woe to us if we fail to perform them! We cannot, if we would, play the part of China, and be content to rot by inches in ignoble ease within our borders, taking no interest in what goes on beyond them, sunk in scrambling commercialism; heedless of the higher life, the life of aspiration, of toil and risk, busying ourselves only with the wants of our bodies for the day, until suddenly we should find, beyond a shadow of question, what China has already found, that in this world the nation that has trained itself to a career of unwarlike and isolated ease is bound, in the end, to go down before other nations which have not lost the manly and adventurous qualities. If we are to be a really great people, we must strive in good faith to play a great part in the world. We cannot avoid meeting great issues. All that we can determine for ourselves is whether we shall meet them well or ill. In 1898 we could not help being brought face to face with the problem of war with Spain. All we could decide was whether we should shrink like cowards from the contest, or enter into it as beseemed a brave and high-spirited people; and, once in, whether failure or success should crown our banners. So it is now. We cannot avoid the responsibilities that confront us in Hawaii, Cuba, Porto Rico, and the Philippines. All we can decide is whether we shall meet them in a way that will redound to the national credit, or whether we shall make of our dealings with these new problems a dark and shameful page in our history. To refuse to deal with them at all merely amounts to dealing with them badly. We have a given problem to solve. If we undertake the solution, there is, of course, always danger that we may not solve it aright; but to refuse to undertake the solution simply renders it certain that we cannot possibly solve it aright. The timid man, the lazy man, the man who distrusts his country, the over-civilized man, who has lost the great fighting, masterful virtues, the ignorant man, and the man of dull mind, whose soul is incapable of feeling the mighty lift that thrills "stern men with empires in their brains"—all these, of course, shrink from seeing the nation undertake its new duties; shrink from seeing us build a navy and an army adequate to our needs; shrink from seeing us do our share of the world's work, by bringing order out of chaos in the great, fair tropic islands from which the valor of our soldiers and sailors has driven the Spanish flag. These are the men who fear the strenuous life, who fear the only national life which is really worth leading. They believe in that cloistered life which saps the hardy virtues in a nation, as it saps them in the individual; or else they are wedded to that base spirit of gain and greed which recognizes in commercialism the be-all and end-all of national life, instead of realizing that, though an indispensable element, it is, after all, but one of the many elements that go to make up true national greatness. No country can long endure if its foundations are not laid deep in the material prosperity which comes from thrift, from business energy and enterprise, from hard, unsparing effort in the fields of industrial activity; but neither was any nation ever yet truly great if it relied upon material prosperity alone. All honor must be paid to the architects of our material prosperity, to the great captains of industry who have built our factories and our railroads, to the strong men who toil for wealth with brain or hand; for great is the debt of the nation to these and their kind. But our debt is yet greater to the men whose highest type is to be found in a statesman like Lincoln, a soldier like Grant. They showed by their lives that they recognized the law of work, the law of strife; they toiled to win a competence for themselves and those dependent upon them; but they recognized that there were yet other and even loftier duties—duties to the nation and duties to the race.

We cannot sit huddled within our own borders and avow ourselves merely an assemblage of well-to-do hucksters who care nothing for what happens beyond. Such a policy would defeat even its own end; for as the nations grow to have ever wider and wider interests, and are brought into closer and closer contact, if we are to hold our own in the struggle for naval and commercial supremacy, we must build up our power without our own borders. We must build the isthmian canal, and we must grasp the points of vantage which will enable us to have our say in deciding the destiny of the oceans of the East and the West.

So much for the commercial side. From the standpoint of international honor the argument is even stronger. The guns that thundered off Manila and Santiago left us echoes of glory, but they also left us a legacy of duty. If we drove out a medieval tyranny only to make room for savage anarchy, we had better not have begun the task at all. It is worse than idle to say that we have no duty to perform, and can leave to their fates the islands we have conquered. Such a course would be the course of infamy. It would be followed at once by utter chaos in the wretched islands themselves. Some stronger, manlier power would have to step in and do the work, and we would have shown ourselves weaklings, unable to carry to successful completion the labors that great and high-spirited nations are eager to undertake.

The work must be done; we cannot escape our responsibility; and if we are worth our salt, we shall be glad of the chance to do the work—glad of the chance to show ourselves equal to one of the great tasks set modern civilization. But let us not deceive ourselves as to the importance of the task. Let us not be misled by vainglory into underestimating the strain it will put on our powers. Above all, let us, as we value our own self-respect, face the responsibilities with proper seriousness, courage, and high resolve. We must demand the highest order of integrity and ability in our public men who are to grapple with these new problems. We must hold to a rigid accountability those public servants who show unfaithfulness to the interest of the nation or inability to rise to the high level of the new demands upon our strength and our resources.

Of course we must remember not to judge any public servant by any one act, and especially should we beware of attacking the men who are merely the occasions and not the causes of disaster. Let me illustrate what I mean by the army and the navy. If twenty years ago we had gone to war, we should have found the navy as absolutely unprepared as the army. At that time our ships could not have encountered with success the fleets of Spain any more than nowadays we can put untrained soldiers, no matter how brave, who are armed with archaic black-powder weapons, against well-drilled regulars armed with the highest type of modern repeating rifle. But in the early eighties the attention of the nation became directed to our naval needs. Congress most wisely made a series of appropriations to build up a new navy, and under a succession of able and patriotic secretaries, of both political parties, the navy was gradually built up, until its material became equal to its splendid personnel, with the result that in the summer of 1898 it leaped to its proper place as one of the most brilliant and formidable fighting navies in the entire world. We rightly pay all honor to the men controlling the navy at the time it won these great deeds, honor to Secretary Long and Admiral Dewey, to the captains who handled the ships in action, to the daring lieutenants who braved death in the smaller craft, and to the heads of bureaus at Washington who saw that the ships were so commanded, so armed, so equipped, so well engined, as to insure the best results. But let us also keep ever in mind that all of this would not have availed if it had not been for the wisdom of the men who during the preceding fifteen years had built up the navy. Keep in mind the secretaries of the navy during those years; keep in mind the senators and congressmen who by their votes gave the money necessary to build and to armor the ships, to construct the great guns, and to train the crews; remember also those who actually did build the ships, the armor, and the guns; and remember the admirals and captains who handled battle-ship, cruiser, and torpedo-boat on the high seas, alone and in squadrons, developing the seamanship, the gunnery, and the power of acting together, which their successors utilized so gloriously at Manila and off Santiago. And, gentlemen, remember the converse, too. Remember that justice has two sides. Be just to those who built up the navy, and, for the sake of the future of the country, keep in mind those who opposed its building up. Read the "Congressional Record." Find out the senators and congressmen who opposed the grants for building the new ships; who opposed the purchase of armor, without which the ships were worthless; who opposed any adequate maintenance for the Navy Department, and strove to cut down the number of men necessary to man our fleets. The men who did these things were one and all working to bring disaster on the country. They have no share in the glory of Manila, in the honor of Santiago. They have no cause to feel proud of the valor of our sea-captains, of the renown of our flag. Their motives may or may not have been good, but their acts were heavily fraught with evil. They did ill for the national honor, and we won in spite of their sinister opposition.

Now, apply all this to our public men of to-day. Our army has never been built up as it should be built up. I shall not discuss with an audience like this the puerile suggestion that a nation of seventy millions of freemen is in danger of losing its liberties from the existence of an army of one hundred thousand men, three fourths of whom will be employed in certain foreign islands, in certain coast fortresses, and on Indian reservations. No man of good sense and stout heart can take such a proposition seriously. If we are such weaklings as the proposition implies, then we are unworthy of freedom in any event. To no body of men in the United States is the country so much indebted as to the splendid officers and enlisted men of the regular army and navy. There is no body from which the country has less to fear, and none of which it should be prouder, none which it should be more anxious to upbuild.

Our army needs complete reorganization,—not merely enlarging,—and the reorganization can only come as the result of legislation. A proper general staff should be established, and the positions of ordnance, commissary, and quartermaster officers should be filled by detail from the line. Above all, the army must be given the chance to exercise in large bodies. Never again should we see, as we saw in the Spanish war, major-generals in command of divisions who had never before commanded three companies together in the field. Yet, incredible to relate, Congress has shown a queer inability to learn some of the lessons of the war. There were large bodies of men in both branches who opposed the declaration of war, who opposed the ratification of peace, who opposed the upbuilding of the army, and who even opposed the purchase of armor at a reasonable price for the battle-ships and cruisers, thereby putting an absolute stop to the building of any new fighting-ships for the navy. If, during the years to come, any disaster should befall our arms, afloat or ashore, and thereby any shame come to the United States, remember that the blame will lie upon the men whose names appear upon the roll-calls of Congress on the wrong side of these great questions. On them will lie the burden of any loss of our soldiers and sailors, of any dishonor to the flag; and upon you and the people of this country will lie the blame if you do not repudiate, in no unmistakable way, what these men have done. The blame will not rest upon the untrained commander of untried troops, upon the civil officers of a department the organization of which has been left utterly inadequate, or upon the admiral with an insufficient number of ships; but upon the public men who have so lamentably failed in forethought as to refuse to remedy these evils long in advance, and upon the nation that stands behind those public men.

So, at the present hour, no small share of the responsibility for the blood shed in the Philippines, the blood of our brothers, and the blood of their wild and ignorant foes, lies at the thresholds of those who so long delayed the adoption of the treaty of peace, and of those who by their worse than foolish words deliberately invited a savage people to plunge into a war fraught with sure disaster for them—a war, too, in which our own brave men who follow the flag must pay with their blood for the silly, mock humanitarianism of the prattlers who sit at home in peace.

The army and the navy are the sword and the shield which this nation must carry if she is to do her duty among the nations of the earth—if she is not to stand merely as the China of the western hemisphere. Our proper conduct toward the tropic islands we have wrested from Spain is merely the form which our duty has taken at the moment. Of course we are bound to handle the affairs of our own household well. We must see that there is civic honesty, civic cleanliness, civic good sense in our home administration of city, State, and nation. We must strive for honesty in office, for honesty toward the creditors of the nation and of the individual; for the widest freedom of individual initiative where possible, and for the wisest control of individual initiative where it is hostile to the welfare of the many. But because we set our own household in order we are not thereby excused from playing our part in the great affairs of the world. A man's first duty is to his own home, but he is not thereby excused from doing his duty to the State; for if he fails in this second duty it is under the penalty of ceasing to be a freeman. In the same way, while a nation's first duty is within its own borders, it is not thereby absolved from facing its duties in the world as a whole; and if it refuses to do so, it merely forfeits its right to struggle for a place among the peoples that shape the destiny of mankind.

In the West Indies and the Philippines alike we are confronted by most difficult problems. It is cowardly to shrink from solving them in the proper way; for solved they must be, if not by us, then by some stronger and more manful race. If we are too weak, too selfish, or too foolish to solve them, some bolder and abler people must undertake the solution. Personally, I am far too firm a believer in the greatness of my country and the power of my country-men to admit for one moment that we shall ever be driven to the ignoble alternative.

The problems are different for the different islands. Porto Rico is not large enough to stand alone. We must govern it wisely and well, primarily in the interest of its own people. Cuba is, in my judgment, entitled ultimately to settle for itself whether it shall be an independent state or an integral portion of the mightiest of republics. But until order and stable liberty are secured, we must remain in the island to insure them, and infinite tact, judgment, moderation, and courage must be shown by our military and civil representatives in keeping the island pacified, in relentlessly stamping out brigandage, in protecting all alike, and yet in showing proper recognition to the men who have fought for Cuban liberty. The Philippines offer a yet graver problem. Their population includes half-caste and native Christians, warlike Moslems, and wild pagans. Many of their people are utterly unfit for self-government, and show no signs of becoming fit. Others may in time become fit but at present can only take part in self-government under wise supervision, at once firm and beneficent. We have driven Spanish tyranny from the islands. If we now let it be replaced by savage anarchy, our work has been for harm and not for good. I have scant patience with those who fear to undertake the task of governing the Philippines, and who openly avow that they do fear to undertake it, or that they shrink from it because of the expense and trouble; but I have even scanter patience with those who make a pretense of humanitarianism to hide and cover their timidity, and who cant about "liberty" and the "consent of the governed," in order to excuse themselves for their unwillingness to play the part of men. Their doctrines, if carried out, would make it incumbent upon us to leave the Apaches of Arizona to work out their own salvation, and to decline to interfere in a single Indian reservation. Their doctrines condemn your forefathers and mine for ever having settled in these United States.

England's rule in India and Egypt has been of great benefit to England, for it has trained up generations of men accustomed to look at the larger and loftier side of public life. It has been of even greater benefit to India and Egypt. And finally, and most of all, it has advanced the cause of civilization. So, if we do our duty aright in the Philippines, we will add to that national renown which is the highest and finest part of national life, will greatly benefit the people of the Philippine Islands, and, above all, we will play our part well in the great work of uplifting mankind. But to do this work, keep ever in mind that we must show in a very high degree the qualities of courage, of honesty, and of good judgment. Resistance must be stamped out. The first and all-important work to be done is to establish the supremacy of our flag. We must put down armed resistance before we can accomplish anything else, and there should be no parleying, no faltering, in dealing with our foe. As for those in our own country who encourage the foe, we can afford contemptuously to disregard them; but it must be remembered that their utterances are not saved from being treasonable merely by the fact that they are despicable.

When once we have put down armed resistance, when once our rule is acknowledged, then an even more difficult task will begin, for then we must see to it that the islands are administered with absolute honesty and with good judgment. If we let the public service of the islands be turned into the prey of the spoils politician, we shall have begun to tread the path which Spain trod to her own destruction. We must send out there only good and able men, chosen for their fitness, and not because of their partizan service, and these men must not only administer impartial justice to the natives and serve their own government with honesty and fidelity, but must show the utmost tact and firmness, remembering that, with such people as those with whom we are to deal, weakness is the greatest of crimes, and that next to weakness comes lack of consideration for their principles and prejudices.

I preach to you, then, my countrymen, that our country calls not for the life of ease but for the life of strenuous endeavor. The twentieth century looms before us big with the fate of many nations. If we stand idly by, if we seek merely swollen, slothful ease and ignoble peace, if we shrink from the hard contests where men must win at hazard of their lives and at the risk of all they hold dear, then the bolder and stronger peoples will pass us by, and will win for themselves the domination of the world. Let us therefore boldly face the life of strife, resolute to do our duty well and manfully; resolute to uphold righteousness by deed and by word; resolute to be both honest and brave, to serve high ideals, yet to use practical methods. Above all, let us shrink from no strife, moral or physical, within or without the nation, provided we are certain that the strife, is justified, for it is only through strife, through hard and dangerous endeavor, that we shall ultimately win the goal of true national greatness.

JOHN CECIL RHODES

FACTORS IN European imperialism of the late nineteenth century are sometimes catalogued under such headings as: the search for markets, raw materials, and investment opportunities; population pressure; humanitarian and missionary enterprise; national patriotism and the search for prestige and naval bases. The British seizure of Rhodesia is an example of enterprise in which the economic motive, combined with patriotism, played a major role.

By the year 1888, the "dark continent" of Africa had been opened to the light of Western civilization by traders, explorers, patriots, and missionaries, and much of the interior was already claimed by European powers. There remained, however, a broad corridor from south to north through the heart of Africa over which native chieftains still exercised control. One of these areas lay between the Limpopo and Zambezi rivers, directly west of Portuguese Mozambique. Far to the northeast were lands claimed by the German East Africa Association. To the south and southwest were the Boer Republic of Transvaal and the newly acquired British Protectorate of Bechuanaland.

The recognized ruler of this territory, comprising more than 100,000 square miles, was a wily native chieftain named Lo Bengula, King of Matabeleland and Mashonaland of the Amandebele and related tribes. This chieftain had been able to cope with the few white traders, exporters, and missionaries who entered his domain, and he refused to sign away his independence to any company or country, as others had done.

In 1886, however, the discovery of gold in Transvaal brought to Lo Bengula's territory a parade of quarrelsome prospectors and concessions seekers whose demands became so insistent and whose rivalry so intense that Lo Bengula was hard put to it to maintain order, peace, and his own independence. His people were herders and farmers, with no interest in the subsoil, and they wished only to be let alone—vain hope! The importunate white men infested the Royal Kraal with the persistence of rats.

The rivalry was not international, except as the Boers were involved. The Germans remained far to the north and west, although they might not always remain so. The Portuguese, who talked of expansion, were so embarrassed financially and so weak militarily that no serious competition was expected from them. The concessions hunters were mostly English and a few Boers. In the end, the successful men were the agents of John Cecil Rhodes (1853–1902), trust builder, financier, mine operator, railway builder, and Cape Colony politician. Rhodes was also a British patriot, imperialist, and dreamer, and his most persistent vision was of a broad band of British pink stretching from the Cape to Cairo through the heart of Africa.

In the hope of finding new sources of income, new mines, new paths for his railways, and new land for the British Empire, Rhodes sent agents to join the others seeking concessions in Matabeleland. They represented interests which were vast and financially reliable, and they apparently persuaded Lo Bengula that, since he could not keep white men from his lands, he might as well put everything into the hands of men who could pay well, meet their financial obligations, and who could help him maintain order. Lo Bengula signed.

Shortly thereafter the disappointed concessions seekers banded together and persuaded Lo Bengula that he had given too much for too little, and the chieftain tried to undo what he had done. But it was too late. Rhodes had already enlisted some distinguished British lords and financiers in a new company to exploit the territory and persuaded the British government to give the enterprise its blessing. Lo Bengula had to submit.

The sequel is interesting too. Rhodes sent pioneers into the country, not to mine but to farm. Lo Bengula and the natives were not cooperative and, in order to protect the English settlers, Rhodes followed up with troops who conquered the king and his army and took his cattle. Lo Bengula's sons became Rhodes scholars, but Matabeleland became Rhodesia.

The following selections from the official British documents, it is hoped, will tell the story. A note about names in the text may be helpful. Charles Rudd was one of Rhodes' earliest partners. George Cawston was his attorney in London. Umsheti and Babaan were natives, members of Lo Bengula's council of *Indunas*, or nobles.

❦

THE TRAGEDY OF LO BENGULA

The Treaty of Peace and Amity

THE CHIEF Lo Bengula, Ruler of the tribe known as the Amandebele, together with the Mashuma and Makakalaka, tributaries of the same, hereby agrees to the following articles and conditions:

That peace and amity shall continue for ever between Her Britannic Majesty, Her subjects, and the Amandebele people; and the contracting chief Lo Bengula engages to use his utmost endeavours to prevent any rupture of the same, to cause the strict observance of this treaty, and so to carry out the spirit of the treaty of friendship which was entered into between his late father, the Chief Umsiligaas, with the then Governor of the Cape of Good Hope in the year of our Lord 1836.

It is hereby further agreed by Lo Bengula, Chief in and over the Amandebele country with its dependencies as aforesaid, on behalf of himself and people, that he will refrain from entering into any correspondence or treaty with any Foreign State or Power to sell, alienate, or cede, or permit or countenance any sale, alienation, or cession of the whole or any part of the said Amandebele country under his chieftainship, or upon any other subject, without the previous knowledge and sanction of Her Majesty's High Commissioner for South Africa.

In faith of which I, Lo Bengula, on my part have hereunto set my hand at Gubulawayo, Amandebeleland, this eleventh day of February, and of Her Majesty's reign the fifty-first.

(Signed)   Lo BENGULA, his X mark.
Witnesses (Signed)   W. GRAHAM.
                                                       G. B. VAN WYK
Before me,
(Signed)   J. S. MOFFAT,
                                                       Assistant Commissioner.
February 11, 1888.

G. Cawston, Esq., to Colonial Office

Hatton Court, Threadneedle Street, London, E.C.
My Lord,

I have the honour to request you to permit me to draw your attention to the Treaty of Peace and Amity which has been signed between the High Commissioner of the British Government in South Africa and Lo Bengula, Chief of the Matebeles.

It is the intention of myself, in conjunction with others, to send a representative to Matebeleland to negotiate with Lo Bengula a treaty for trading, mining, and general purposes.

Before doing so we are desirous of ascertaining whether we shall have the support of the British Government. For, of course, capital will not be expended in the development of the country unless encouraged, as we trust it will be.

In the event of such encouragement being obtained would the High Commissioner at the Cape be requested to render such assistance as will be compatible with the wishes of Lo Bengula, and with the best interests of his country.

I have, etc.
(Signed) GEO. CAWSTON
To the Right Hon. Lord Knutsford, G.C.M.G.,
Her Majesty's Principal Secretary of State for the Colonies
May 4, 1888

The Mining Concession

Know all men by these presents that whereas Charles Dunell Rudd of Kimberley, Rochfort Maguire of London, and Francis Robert Thompson of Kemberley, herein-after called the grantees, have covenanted and agreed and do hereby covenant and agree to pay to me my heirs and successors the sum of one hundred pounds sterling British currency on the first day of every lunar month, and further to deliver at my Royal Kraal one thousand Martini-Henry breech-loading rifles, together with one hundred thousand rounds of suitable ball cartridge, five hundred of the said rifles and fifty thousand of the said cartridges to be ordered from England forthwith and delivered with reasonable despatch, and the remainder of the said rifles and cartridges to be delivered as soon as the said grantees shall have commenced to work mining machinery within my territory, and further to deliver on the Zambesi River a steamboat with guns suitable for defensive purposes on the said river, or in lieu of the said steamboat, should I so elect, to pay me the sum of five hundred pounds sterling British currency on the execution of these presents, I, Lo Bengula, King of Matabeleland, Mashonaland, and other adjoining territories, in the exercise of my sovereign powers, and in the presence and with the consent of my Council of Indunas, do hereby grant and assign unto the said grantees, their heirs, representatives, and assigns, jointly and severally, the complete and exclusive charge over all metals and minerals situated and contained in my kingdoms, principalities, and dominions, together with full power to do all things that they may deem necessary to win and procure the same, and to hold, collect, and enjoy the profits and revenues, if any, derivable from the said metals and minerals subject to the aforesaid payment, and whereas I have been much molested of late by divers persons seeking and desiring to obtain grants and concessions of land and mining rights in my territories, I do hereby authorise the said grantees, their heirs, representatives, and assigns, to take all necessary and lawful steps to exclude from my kingdoms, principalities, and dominions all persons seeking land, metals, minerals, or mining rights therein, and I do hereby undertake to render them such needful assistance as they may from time to time require for the exclusion of such persons and to grant no concessions of land or mining rights from and after this date without their consent and concurrence, provided that if at any time the said monthly payment of one hundred pounds shall be in arrear for a period of three months then this grant shall cease and determine from the date of the last made payment, and further provided that nothing contained in these presents shall extend to or affect a grant made by me of certain mining rights in a portion of my territory south of the Ramakoban River, which grant is commonly known as the Tati Concession.

This given under my hand this thirtieth day of October in the year of our Lord eighteen hundred and eighty-eight at my Royal Kraal.

(Signed) Lo BENGULA

his X mark

C. D. RUDD

ROCHFORT MAGUIRE

F. R. THOMPSON

Witnesses

(Signed) CHAS. D. HELM

J. G. DREYER

I hereby certify that the accompanying document has been fully interpreted and explained by me to the Chief Lo Bengula and his full Council of Indunas, and that all the constitutional usages of the Matabele nation had been complied with prior to his executing the same.

Dated at Umgusa River this thirtieth day of October 1888.

(Signed) CHAS. D. HELM

Message of Lo Bengula to Queen Victoria

Lo Bengula desires to know that there is a Queen. Some of the people who come into his land tell him there is a Queen, some of them tell him there is not.

Lo Bengula can only find out the truth by sending eyes to see whether there is a Queen.

The Indunas are his eyes.

Lo Bengula desires, if there is a Queen, to ask her to advise and help him, as he is much troubled by white men who come into his country and ask to dig gold.

There is no one with him upon whom he can trust, and he asks that the Queen will send someone from herself.

March 2, 1889

Message of the Queen to Lo Bengula

The Queen has heard the words of Lo Bengula. She is glad to receive the messengers from Lo Bengula, and to learn the message which he has sent.

The Queen will send words in reply through her Secretary of State, for the messengers to take to Lo Bengula.

A reply to the letter of Lo Bengula will be sent through the High Commissioner. Lo Bengula may trust in the advice and words of that officer, as he is specially appointed by the Queen to receive the words of all friendly Chiefs in South Africa, and to send to them any reply which the Queen may be pleased to give.

March 2, 1889

Lord Knutsford to Lo Bengula

(ENTRUSTED TO UMSHETI AND BABAAN)

I, Lord Knutsford, one of Her Majesty's Principal Secretaries of State, am commanded by the Queen to give the following reply to the message delivered by Umsheti and Babaan.

The Queen has heard the words of Lo Bengula. She was glad to receive these messengers and to learn the message which they have brought.

They say that Lo Bengula is much troubled by white men, who come into his country and ask to dig gold, and that he begs for advice and help.

Lo Bengula is the ruler of his country, and the Queen does not interfere in the government of that country, but as Lo Bengula desires her advice, Her Majesty is ready to give it, and having therefore consulted Her Principal Secretary of State holding the Seals of the Colonial Department, now replies as follows:

In the first place, the Queen wishes Lo Bengula to understand distinctly that Englishmen who have gone out to Matabeleland to ask leave to dig for stones, have not gone with the Queen's authority, and that he should not believe any statements made by them or any of them to that effect.

The Queen advises Lo Bengula not to grant hastily concessions of land, or leave to dig, but to consider all applications very carefully.

It is not wise to put too much power into the hands of the men who come first, and to exclude other deserving men. A King gives a stranger an ox, not his whole herd of cattle, otherwise what would other strangers arriving have to eat?

Umsheti and Babaan say that Lo Bengula asks that the Queen will send him some one from herself. To this request the Queen is advised that Her Majesty may be pleased to accede. But they cannot say whether Lo Bengula wishes to have an Imperial officer to reside with him permanently, or only to have an officer sent out on a temporary mission, nor do Umsheti and Babaan state what provision Lo Bengula would be prepared to make for the expenses and maintenance of such an officer.

Upon this and any other matters Lo Bengula should write, and should send his letters to the High Commissioner at the Cape, who will send them direct to the Queen. The High Commissioner is the Queen's officer, and she places full trust in him, and Lo Bengula should also trust him. Those who advise Lo Bengula otherwise deceive him.

The Queen sends Lo Bengula a picture of herself to remind him of this message, and that he may be assured that the Queen wishes him peace and order in his country.

The Queen thanks Lo Bengula for the kindness which, following the example of his father, he has shown to many Englishmen visiting and living in Matabeleland.

This message has been interpreted to Umsheti and Babaan in my presence, and I have signed it in their presence, and affixed the seal of the Colonial Office.

(Signed) KNUTSFORD

Colonial Office,
March 26, 1889 [Seal]

To Her Majesty Queen Victoria from Lo Bengula, King of the Amandebele

King's Kraal, Ungusa River

Greeting:

Some time ago a party of men came into my country, the principal one appearing to be a man named Rudd. They asked me for a place to dig for gold, and said they would give me certain things for the right to do so. I told them to bring what they would give and I would then show them what I would give.

A document was written and presented to me for signature. I asked what it contained and was told that in it were my words and the words of those men.

I put my hand to it.

About three months afterwards I heard from other sources that I had given by that document the right to all the minerals in my country.

I called a meeting of my Indunas and also of the white men, and demanded a copy of the document. It was proved to me that I *had* signed away the mineral rights of my whole country to Rudd and his friends.

I have since had a meeting of my Indunas, and they will not recognise the paper as it contains neither my words nor the words of those who got it.

After the meeting I demanded that the original document be returned to me. It has not come yet, although it is two months since, and they promised to bring it back soon.

The men of the party who were in my country at the time were told to remain until the document was brought back. One of them, Maguire, has now left without my knowledge and against my orders.

I write to you that you may know the truth about this thing and may not be deceived.

With renewed and cordial greetings.

I am your friend,

As Witnesses:	(Signed) Lo BENGULA
G. A. PHILLIPS	his X mark
Moss COHEN	
JAMES FAIRBAIRN	[Elephant seal of Lo Bengula]

W. F. USHER, Interpreter

April 23, 1889

Creation of the British South Africa Company

VICTORIA BY THE GRACE OF GOD, OF THE UNITED KINGDOM OF GREAT BRITAIN AND IRELAND QUEEN, DEFENDER OF THE FAITH

To all to whom these presents shall come, Greeting:

Whereas a Humble Petition has been presented to Us in Our Council by the Most Noble James Duke of Abercorn, Companion of the Most Honourable Order of the Bath; the Most Noble Alexander William George Duke of Fife, Knight of the Most Ancient and Most Noble Order of the Thistle, Privy Councillor; the Right Honourable Edric Frederick Lord Gifford, V.C.; Cecil John Rhodes, of Kimberley, in the Cape Colony, Member of the Executive Council and of the House of Assembly of the Colony of the Cape of Good Hope; Alfred Beit, of 29, Holborn Viaduct, London, Merchant; Albert Henry George Grey, of Howick, Northumberland, Esquire; and George Cawston, of 18, Lennox Gardens, London, Esquire, Barrister-at-law.

And whereas the said Petition states amongst other things:

That the Petitioners and others are associated, for the purpose of forming a Company or Association, to be incorporated, if to Us should seem fit, for the objects in the said Petition set forth under the corporate name of The British South Africa Company.

That the existence of a powerful British Company, controlled by those of Our subjects in whom We have confidence, and having its principal field of operations in that region of South Africa lying to the north of Bechuanaland and to the west of Portuguese East Africa, would be advantageous to the commercial and other interests of Our subjects in the United Kingdom and in Our Colonies.

That the Petitioners desire to carry into effect divers concessions and agreements which have been made by certain of the chiefs and tribes inhabiting the said region, and such other concessions agreements grants and treaties as the Petitioners may hereafter obtain within the said region or elsewhere in Africa with the view of promoting trade commerce civilisation and good government (including the regulation of liquor traffic with the Natives) in the territories which are or may be comprised or referred to in such concessions agreements grants and treaties as aforesaid.

That the Petitioners believe that if the said concessions agreements grants and treaties can be carried into effect, the condition of the Natives inhabiting the said territories will be materially improved and their civilisation advanced and an organisation established which will tend to the suppression of the slave trade in the said territories, and to the opening up of the said territories, to the immigration of Europeans, and to the lawful trade and commerce of Our subjects and of other nations.

That the success of the enterprise in which the Petitioners are engaged would be greatly advanced if it should seem fit to Us to grant them Our Royal Charter of incorporation as a British Company under the said name or title, or such other name or title, with such powers, as to Us may seem fit for the purpose of more effectually carrying into effect the objects aforesaid.

That large sums of money have been subscribed for the purposes of the intended Company by the Petitioners and others, who are prepared also to subscribe or to procure such further sums as may hereafter be found requisite for the development of the said enterprise, in the event of Our being pleased to grant to them Our Royal Charter of incorporation as aforesaid.

Now, therefore, We having taken the said Petition into Our Royal consideration in Our Council, and being satisfied that the intentions of the petitioners are praiseworthy and deserve encouragement, and that the enterprise in the petition described may be productive of the benefits set forth therein, by Our Prerogative Royal and of Our especial grace, certain knowledge and mere motion, have constituted, erected, and incorporated, and by this Our Charter for Us and Our heirs and Royal successors do constitute, erect, and incorporate into one body politic and corporate by the name of the British South Africa Company the said James Duke of Abercorn, Alexander William George Duke of Fife, Edric Frederick Lord Gifford, Cecil John Rhodes, Alfred Beit, Albert Henry George Grey and George Cawston, and such other persons and such bodies as from time to time become and are members of the body politic and corporate by these presents constituted, erected and incorporated, with perpetual succession and a common seal, with power to break, alter, or renew the same at discretion, and with the further authorities, powers, and privileges conferred, and subject to the conditions imposed by this Our Charter: And We do hereby accordingly will ordain give grant constitute appoint and declare as follows (that is to say)—

1. The principal field of the operations of The British South Africa Company (in this our Charter referred to as "the Company") shall be the region of South Africa lying immediately to the north of British Bechuanaland, and to the north and west of the South African Republic, and to the west of the Portuguese Dominions.

2. The Company is hereby authorised and empowered to hold, use, and retain for the purposes of the Company and on the terms of this Our Charter the full benefit of the concessions and agreements made as aforesaid, so far as they are valid, or any of them, and all interests, authorities and powers comprised or referred to in the said concessions and agreements. Provided always that nothing herein contained shall prejudice or affect any other valid and subsisting concessions or agreements which may have been made by any of the chiefs or tribes aforesaid, and in particular nothing herein contained shall prejudice or affect certain concessions granted in and subsequent to the year 1880 relating to the territory usually known as the district of the Tati; nor shall anything herein contained be construed as giving any jurisdiction, administrative or otherwise within the said district of the Tati. . . .

3. The Company is hereby further authorized and empowered, subject to the approval of one of Our Principal Secretaries of State . . . , from time to time, to acquire by any concession agreement grant or treaty, all or any rights, interests, authorities, jurisdictions, and powers of any kind of nature whatever, including powers necessary for the purposes of government, and the preservation of public order in or for the protection of territories, lands, or property, comprised or referred to in the concessions and ageements made as aforesaid, or affecting other territories, lands, or property in Africa, or the inhabitants thereof, and to hold, use, and exercise such territories, lands, property, rights, interests, authorities, jurisdictions, and powers respectively for the purposes of the Company, and on the terms of this Our Charter. . . .

Witness Ourself at Westminster, the (29th) day of (October) in the fifty (third) year of Our reign.

By warrant under the Queen's Sign Manual.

Message to Lo Bengula

I, Lord Knutsford, one of the Queen's Principal Secretaries of State, am commanded by Her Majesty to send this further message to Lo Bengula. The Queen has kept in her mind the letter sent by Lo Bengula, and the message brought by Umsheti and Babaan in the beginning of this year, and she has now desired Mr. Moffat, whom she trusts, and whom Lo Bengula knows to be his true friend, to tell him what she has done for him and what she advises him to do.

2. Since the visit of Lo Bengula's Envoys, the Queen has made the fullest inquiries into the particular circumstances of Matabeleland, and understands the trouble caused to Lo Bengula by different parties of white men coming to his country to look for gold; but wherever gold is, or wherever it is reported to be, there it is impossible for him to exclude white men, and, therefore, the wisest and safest course for him to adopt, and that which will give least trouble to himself and his tribe, is to agree, not with one or two white men separately, but with one approved body of white men, who will consult Lo Bengula's wishes and arrange where white people are to dig, and who will be responsible to the Chief for any annoyance or trouble caused to himself or his people. If he does not agree with one set of people there will be endless disputes among the white men, and he will have all this time taken up in deciding their quarrels.

3. The Queen, therefore, approves of the concession made by Lo Bengula to some white men, who were represented in his country by Messrs. Rudd, Maguire, and Thompson. The Queen has caused inquiry to be made respecting these persons, and is satisfied that they are men who will fulfil their undertakings, and who may be trusted to carry out the working for gold in the Chief's country without molesting his people, or in any way interfering with their kraals, gardens, or cattle. And, as some of the Queen's highest and most trusted subjects have joined themselves with those to whom Lo Bengula gave his concessions, the Queen now thinks Lo Bengula is acting wisely in carrying out his agreement with these persons, and hopes that he will allow them to conduct their mining operations without interference or molestation from his subjects.

4. The Queen understands that Lo Bengula does not like deciding disputes among white men or assuming jurisdiction over them. This is very wise, as these disputes would take up much time, and Lo Bengula cannot understand the laws and customs of white people; but it is not well to have people in his country who are subject to no law, therefore the Queen thinks Lo Bengula would be wise to entrust to that body of white men, of whom Mr. Jamieson is now the principal representative in Matabeleland, the duty of deciding disputes and keeping the peace among white persons in his country.

5. In order to enable them to act lawfully and with full authority, the Queen has, by her Royal Charter, given to that body of men leave to undertake this duty, and will hold them responsible for their proper performance of such duty. Of course this must be as Lo Bengula likes, as he is King of the country,

and no one can exercise jurisdiction in it without his permission; but it is believed that this will be very convenient for the Chief, and the Queen is informed that he has already made such an arrangement in the Tati district, by which he is there saved all trouble.

6. The Queen understands that Lo Bengula wishes to have some one from her residing with him. The Queen, therefore, has directed her trusted servant, Mr. Moffat, to stay with the Chief as long as he wishes. Mr. Moffat is, as Lo Bengula knows, a true friend to himself and the Matabele tribe, while he is also in the confidence of the Queen and will from time to time convey the Queen's words to the Chief, and the Chief should always listen to and believe Mr. Moffat's words.

(Signed) KNUTSFORD
Her Majesty's Secretary of State for the Colonies

Downing Street
November 15 1889

E. M. FORSTER

Novelist, essayist, and critic, Edward Morgan Forster was born in 1879 and received his education at the Tonbridge School and King's College, Cambridge. He gained some early reputation as a short story writer, and after moving to Italy he published his first novel, *Where Angels Fear to Tread* (1905). He returned to England in 1907 and published his second novel in 1908, *A Room with a View. Howard's End* (1910), his most mature work of this period, attracted a wide audience and marked Forster as a young writer of distinction.

In 1911 Forster traveled to India. During the First World War he did civilian war work in Alexandria. After the war he returned to England to assume the literary editorship of the Labour *Daily Herald* and to write reviews for the *New Statesman* and *Spectator*. Forster returned to India in 1921, and three years later published his most famous work, *A Passage to India. Abinger Harvest,* a collection of essays and reviews, was published in 1926.

In 1927 at King's College he delivered the Clark Lectures, published later that year as *Aspects of the Novel.* During the 1930s he was outspoken in his condemnation of totalitarianism and in his criticism of hindrances to freedom of expression which existed in his native country. He openly opposed the British government's attitude toward the works of James Joyce and D. H. Lawrence.

After the Second World War, Forster visited India again. In 1947 he traveled through the United States on a lecture tour. He began a series of lectures for the B.B.C., and in 1953 published the book from which the following selection has been taken, *The Hill of Devi,* an account of his own experiences as secretary in India to the Maharajah of Dewas Senior. Another volume of his criticism, *Two Cheers for Democracy,* appeared in 1951. In January, 1953, Forster was awarded membership in the Order of Companions of Honour by Queen Elizabeth II.

THE HILL OF DEVI

Delhi
March 6th, 1913

The Rajah has just been talking to me, cross-legged and barefoot on a little cane chair. We had a long talk about religion, during which I often thought of you. Indians are so easy and communicative on this subject, whereas English people are mostly offended when it is introduced, or else shocked if there is a difference of opinion. His attitude was very difficult for a Westerner.

He believes that we—men, birds, everything—are part of God, and that men
have developed more than birds because they have come nearer to realising
this.

That isn't so difficult; but when I asked why we had any of us ever been
severed from God, he explained it by God becoming unconscious that we
were parts of him, owing to his energy at some time being concentrated elsewhere. "So," he said, "a man who is thinking of something else may become
unconscious of the existence of his own hand for a time, and feel nothing
when it is touched." Salvation, then, is the thrill which we feel when God
again becomes conscious of us, and all our life we must train our perceptions
so that we many be capable of feeling when the time comes.

I think I see what lies at the back of this—if you believe that the universe
was God's conscious creation, you are faced with the fact that he has consciously created suffering and sin, and this the Indian refuses to believe. "We
were either put here intentionally or unintentionally," said the Rajah, "and it
raises fewer difficulties if we suppose it was unintentionally."

April 6th [*1921*]

Today Malarao Sahib took me to his village. Deolekr Sahib drove the car,
and with us came Malarao's cousin, a Sirdar whom I take to a great deal,
but who is unfortunately out of favour at court. It was he who lent me Indian
clothes on my first visit. He is now a grey-haired young man. The four of
us had a pleasant morning and the car did not break down until we were
returning. We walked first, along the banks of the Sipra, a deep green river,
haunted by sweet skipping birds. There we had an exciting and typical adventure. Our train of villagers stopped and pointed to the opposite bank with
cries of a snake. At last I saw it—a black thing reared up to the height of
three feet and motionless. I said, "It looks a small dead tree," and was told
"Oh no," and exact species and habits of snakes were indicated—not a cobra,
but very fierce and revengeful, and if we shot it would pursue us several
days later all the way to Dewas. We then took stones and threw them across
the Sipra (half the width of the Thames at Weybridge) in order to make
snake crawl away. Still he didn't move and when a stone hit his base still
didn't move. He was a small dead tree. All the villagers shrieked with
laughter. The young Sirdar told them that I was much disappointed and
displeased about the snake, and that they must find a real one. So they dispersed anxiously for a few moments over the country, after which all was
forgotten.

I call the adventure "typical" because it is even more difficult here than in
England to get at the rights of a matter. Everything that happens is said to

be one thing and proves to be another, and as it is further said in an unknown tongue I live in a haze. After our walk we returned to the village (150 inhabitants) and I was asked by Malarao and his cousin to select a place to sit down. I avoided a manure heap which had attracted them and we squatted on a mattress beneath a great tree or sat on bedsteads. Cool breeze and all very nice.

We ate enormous cucumbers and drank tea while the villagers sang and tried out of politeness to cover our clothes with red powder. They were an ill-favoured crew, but cheerful. Meanwhile, out of a gap in the village mud-wall, the ladies issued with a strange cry. They, like the red powder, were part of the Hindu festivity of Holi, and squatting at a little distance, they made a bright spot in the dust.

The men continued their songs—one about the coming of Europeans to India, the other about the coming of Man to the Earth. Then my companions made me give the company some rupees (which they afterwards replaced stealthily in my pocket). I chose a site for a house, and we passed into the village by the seated ladies who abused us violently—so violently that even the young Sirdar could not understand what was said. This abuse is of course traditional and has nothing personal in it: 3,000 years ago in Greece the women did just the same thing at certain festivals.

We departed via the temple, where Malarao did a rapid worship for the party generally, then to the car which broke down as aforesaid, and we crawled home, depositing the Sirdar at his house. We had picked him up at it in the morning—of course no one had told him we were coming—and he was stripped for his prayers.

"Come up, Sahib!" he called, leaning from an upper window in this condition. "I was about to pray, but now will not, for it takes a half-hour."

People talk about Oriental seclusion: what strikes me is Oriental publicity. Here I am among Maratha nobles, a conservative and lofty race, yet I eat with them, sit in their bedrooms and visit their womenfolk. . . .

The Dewas Literary Society arose out of Macaulay's essay on Frederick the Great. I had been reading to H. H., Macaulay's account of the adventures of Voltaire at the tyrant's court, and we were both struck by the piquant parallel. Here was I a literary man at his court, and presumably in his power. A resident Voltaire, ought I not to do something?

So I drew up a manifesto, which still survives. Its tone is intentionally formal. I informed my Maratha peers that there are two reasons for the pursuit of literature: it introduces the reader to the noble writings of the past and the present, and it introduces him to other readers, similarly employed.

Our proceedings were to be in English, but works in other languages would also be discussed. No subscription would be necessary, only sympathy and practical support. The first meeting would be held on April 20th at 7:30 in the front room, ground floor, north wing, Shri Anand Bhuvan Palace. "Will the undermentioned gentlemen (most of whom I have the pleasure and privilege of knowing personally) be so kind as to signify whether they will support the scheme, and attend the meetings when their other engagements permit?" The names of about two dozen nobles followed. All signified their support, most of them proved to have other engagements. Still a few meetings were held before we petered out.

I remember a paper of my own where I quoted that story out of Dostoevsky about the wicked woman and the onion. She had been so wicked that in all her life she had only done one good deed—given an onion to a beggar. So she went to hell. As she lay in torment she saw the onion, lowered down from Heaven by an angel. She caught hold of it. He began to pull her up. The other damned saw what was happening and caught hold of it too. She was indignant and cried, "Let go—it's my onion," and as soon as she said "my onion" the stalk broke and she fell back into the flames.

I had always thought this story touching, but I had no idea of the effect it would produce on the Dewas Literary Society. Hitherto they had been polite, bored, straining to follow. Now their faces softened, and they murmured, "Ah that is good, good. That is *bhakti*." They had encountered something that they loved and understood. I have often thought of that moment since—that flash of comprehension in the midst of India. Of the many English writers I had quoted, not one had touched them. Their hearts were unlocked by a Russian. . . .

It is strange that the Political Department, which has to deal with princes, should specialise in bad manners. It was just the same ten years ago, though it is less painful now, as the princes are more uppish. I don't see, nor am I likely to see, anything of present movements in India, except indirectly. I mean that the Government, frightened of Bolshevism and Ghandi, is polite to the princes, and the princes, equally frightened, do all that they can to stop the spread of new ideas. There are said to be new ideas, even in Dewas, but they are not perceptible to a Western eye. Politically—though not socially—we are still living in the fourteenth century. Masood was scared at our backwardness and had a conversation (very polite) with H. H. on the point. A new constitution is to be drafted, so that the people may be educated gradually, but a new constitution was being drafted when I was here ten years ago, and if the people ever get educated it will be from outside. They look happy, work in moderation, and block the roads with bullock carts, which deploy in fan formation as soon as they hear a motor approaching. This palace, with its warped pianos and broken telephones, is really only an excrescence on the ancient countryside, and I love driving away from it in the evening to a garden about two miles off, where everything is peaceful and I can sit on the edge of a cistern under huge trees. . . .

May 9th

The birth of a little baby has turned everything upside down, so far as it wasn't already in that position. The rites—they are more than customs—are extraordinary, and seem designed to cause the greatest possible discomfort to mother and child. The unfortunate pair have to listen to music outside their door for nearly fifteen days. It began with fireworks and a discharge of rifles from the entire army in batches: then drums, trumpets, stringed instruments and singing. For five days the husband is supposed not to see his wife, but during the whole fifteen he must sleep in the compound where her house stands and his friends and attendants stay with him and listen to the continual music. So here I am. I come down from the Palace after dinner and squat amid discordant sounds till I fall asleep. My bed is next to H.H.'s, Malarao's on the other side. The courtyard is tidier than it was, but the first night we lay with bullocks all around.

Yesterday being the fifth day the music did go on all night. Nautch girls and boys dressed as girls howled, there were farces, dialogues, dances, the military band moaned Western melodies. I went to bed at midnight, but at 3 A.M. something unusual aroused me—the music became beautiful; so I fitted on my turban and rejoined the company. H.H. was asleep on his bed, the townsfolk had gone off to their homes, and only a few experts survived. Why save your best singers until 3 A.M.? "Ask India another" is the only answer to such a question. I am as far as ever from understanding Indian singing, but have no doubt that I was listening to great art, it was so complicated and yet so passionate. The singer (man) and the drummer were of almost equal importance and wove round the chord of C major elaborate patterns that came to an end at the same moment—at least that's as near as I can explain it: it was like Western music reflected in trembling water, and it continued in a single burst for half an hour. The words were unimportant, mere excuses for the voice to function.

But what fun the lady and the little baby get out of the above I don't know. H.H. quite agrees that it is monstrous—he has all the right feelings—but says tradition is too strong to be changed! At one time the band was actually in the bedroom. The courtiers haven't even the feelings. One of them, when I suggested that a fortnight's row is not the best of starts, replied, "Why so? It will prevent the mother from sadness. It is not as if she was ill"!! If it had been a boy baby the noises would have been doubled and the bill for festivities have reached £2,000, instead of the modest £1,000 that is anticipated at present. We need the money elsewhere and the work of the state is being postponed. . . .

Today—King-Emperor's Birthday—there was a formal Durbar. I wore a long dressing gown of palish purple spattered with gold flowers and beneath it a green waistcoat, also begolded, and on my head a fantastic headdress of red and gold; also white trousers; and the dressing gown and waistcoat were trimmed with red that was supposed to match the turban but did not. I thought I looked a perfect ass (was much admired) but you will see for yourself, for these clothes really are my own, being flung together desperately for the occasion. I have quite an Indian wardrobe now. It was a chair-durbar —no squatting. The telegram to the King-Emperor was read by the Dewan, "God Save the King" was excruciatingly rendered, attar and pan were handed round, and there followed a pleasant tea party.

The day before I spent in a more Western way, paying bills. I got hold of 1,500 rupees (i.e. £100; I don't know where it came from—I am rather good at getting hold of money) and banged it all away, settling small accounts—I cannot tackle the large ones. I cannot grasp the finances of the state. I am told they are admirable. They may be, but they do not look it. The treasury, as far as I have observed, pays nobody and nothing. But a loud lamentation, in which I am now expert, often raises a bag of silver coins, or even two or three bags, which Baldeo carries to my bedroom and inters in various boxes. Sometimes there is not even a bag, but the coins lie in a heap in the courtyard, a crowd around them. Then Baldeo brings linen boot-bags and we load them up.

Simla sounds imminent. I trust there will be some hitch, for I dread stirring out of this bearable, and sometimes delightful, climate, and frying in a train. Masood writes, as always affectionately, wanting me to come and stop. It will be curious to see something of the India that is changing. There is no perceptible change here, indeed the atmosphere is in some ways less Western than it was nine years ago. No one, except myself, wears European clothes, for instance—nine years ago H.H. often did. The place is altogether exceptional, and generalisations from it, which I am sure to make, are sure to be wrong. There is no anti-English feeling. It is Gandhi whom they dread and hate. . . .

This month is to be devoted, not to say abandoned, to religion, and we move down to the Old Palace in the heart of the town, to be stung by mosquitoes and bitten by bugs. I have already helped to choose the "Lord of the Universe" some new clothes. He is fortunately only six inches high, but he had to have eight suits, and he has several companions who must also be dressed, and the bill for this alone will be not far short of £30.

Well, what's it all about? It's called Gokul Ashtami—i.e., the eight days feast in honour of Krishna who was born at Gokul near Muttra, and I cannot yet discover how much of it is traditional and how much due to H.H. What troubles me is that every detail, almost without exception, is fatuous and in bad taste. The altar is a mess of little objects, stifled with rose leaves, the walls are hung with deplorable oleographs, the chandeliers, draperies—everything bad. Only one thing is beautiful—the expression on the faces of the people as they bow to the shrine, and he himself is, as always, successful in his odd role. I have never seen religious ecstasy before and don't take to it more than I expected I should, but he manages not to be absurd. Whereas the other groups of singers stand quiet, he is dancing all the time, like David before the ark, jigging up and down with a happy expression on his face, and twanging a stringed instrument that hangs by a scarf round his neck. At the end of his two hours he gets wound up and begins composing poetry which is copied down by a clerk, and yesterday he flung himself flat on his face on the carpet. Ten minutes afterwards I saw him as usual, in ordinary life. He complained of indigestion but seemed normal and discussed arrangements connected with the motor cars. . . .

Things began to warm up at 11:30 P.M. on the 26th when, dressed in our best, we sat cross-legged in the temple aisles, awaiting the Birth. The altar was as usual smothered in mess and the gold and silver and rich silks that make up its equipment were so disposed as to produce no effect. Choked somewhere in rose leaves, lay chief Dolly, but I could not locate him. Why, since he had been listening to hymns for eight days, he was now to be born was a puzzle to me; but no one else asked the question, and of course the festival is no more illogical than Christmas, though it seemed so, owing to its realism. My memory is so bad and the muddle so great, that I forget the details of the Birth already, but the Maharajah announced it from his end of the carpet and then went to the altar and buried his face in the rose leaves, much moved. Next, a miniature cradle was set up in the aisle, and a piece of crimson silk, folded so that it looked like an old woman over whom a traction engine has passed, was laid in it and rocked by him, Bhau Sahib, the Dewan, the Finance Member, and other leading officials of the state. Noise, I need hardly add, never stopped—the great horn brayed, the cymbals clashed, the harmonium and drums did their best, while in the outer courtyard the three elephants were set to bellow and the band played "Nights of Gladness" as loudly as possible.

Under these circumstances the child was named "Krishna" by H.H. . . .

I must get on to the final day—the most queer and also the most enjoyable day of the series. There was a sermon in the morning, but after it we began to play games before the altar in a ceremonial fashion; there were games of this sort in the Christian Middle Ages and they still survive in the Cathedral of Seville at Easter. With a long stick in his hand H.H. churned imaginary milk and threshed imaginary wheat and hit (I suppose) imaginary enemies and then each took a pair of little sticks, painted to match the turban, and whacked them together. (You must never forget that cymbals never cease, nor does a harmonium.) Real butter came next and was stuck on the forehead of a noble in a big lump and when he tried to lick it off another noble snatched it from behind. (Very deep meaning in all this, says H.H., though few know it.) I had a little butter too. Then we went under a large black vessel, rather handsome, that was hung up in the aisle, and we banged it with our painted sticks, and the vessel broke and a mass of grain soaked in milk fell down on our heads. We fed each other with it. This was the last of the games, and the mess was now awful and swarms of flies came.

Still holding our painted sticks we went into the court and began to form the procession. . . .

The procession started with an elephant—no one on its back, to indicate humility—then all of the army that possess uniforms or musical instruments, then the twelve bands of singers who had been at it all week, but they showed no signs of feebleness, H.H. leading the last band, just in front of the palanquin, which another elephant followed. The view, looking back, after we had passed through the outer palace gateway, was really fine. The eighteenth-century architecture, though not splendid, is better than anything Dewas has produced since—blue birds over the arch and elephants tussling on the cornice—and the rich round banners that accompanied the palanquin (shaped like magnifying-glasses) and the pennons, and the fans of peacock's feather —all under a pink evening sky. . . .

By ten we reached the Tank and the queer impressive ceremony of drowning the Town of Gokul was performed. The town—about a yard square— was stripped of its flagstaffs and after prayers and meals, was handed to a man whose hereditary duty it is to drown the Town of Gokul. He was half naked and waded into the water and the darkness, pushing the city before him on a floating tray. When he was far out he upset it, all the dolls fell into the water and were seen no more, and the town, being of mud, dissolved immediately. The tray was brought back and worshipped slightly, while elephants trumpeted and cannon were fired.

I limped to a victoria which I had waiting and drove straight to the Guest House at the other side of the Tank, there to wash my face, drink sherry, eat sardines, sausages and stewed fruit, and reel to my bed. The others had two more hours of it, getting back to the Old Palace at midnight.

As to the explanation of this, as apart from what one was told by the pious, I know too little to conjecture, but was reminded of the Adonis festival, where the God is born, dies, and is carried to the water, all in a short time. H.H. says the Town of Gokul is meant to represent Krishna who cannot of course be drowned. His end came next morning, but my own end was too near for me to go down to the Old Palace to witness it. At mid-day the purple and green curtain was drawn before the altar and all the prominent officials burst into tears.

. . . But what did he (Bapu Sahib) feel when he danced like King David before the altar? What were his religious opinions?

The first question is easier to answer than the second. He felt as King David and other mystics have felt when they are in the mystic state. He presented well-known characteristics. He was convinced that he was in touch with the reality he called Krishna. And he was unconscious of the world around him. "You can come in during my observances tomorrow and see me if you like, but I shall not know that you are there," he once told Malcolm. And he didn't know. He was in an abnormal but recognisable state; psychologists have studied it.

More interesting, and more elusive, are his religious opinions. The unseen was always close to him, even when he was joking or intriguing. Red paint on a stone could evoke it. Like most people, he implied beliefs and formulated rules for behavior, and since he had a lively mind, he was often inconsistent. It was difficult to be sure what he did believe (outside the great mystic moments) or what he thought right or wrong. Indians are even more puzzling than Westerners here. Mr. Shastri, a spiritual and subtle Brahmin, once uttered a puzzler: "If the Gods do a thing, it is a reason for men not to do it." No doubt he was in a particular religious mood. In another mood he would have urged us to imitate the Gods. And the Maharajah was all moods. They played over his face, they agitated his delicate feet and hands. To get any pronouncement from so mercurial a creature on the subject, say, of asceticism, was impossible. As a boy, he had thought of retiring from the world, and it was an ideal he cherished throughout his life, and which, at the end, he would have done well to practise. Yet he would condemn asceticism, declare that salvation could not be reached through it, that it might be

Vedantic but it was not Bedic, and matter and spirit must both be given their due. Nothing too much! In such moods he seemed Greek.

He believed in the heart, and here we reach firmer ground. "I stand for the heart. To the dogs with the head," cries Herman Melville, and he would have agreed. Affection, or the possibility of it, quivered through everything, from Gokul Ashtami down to daily human relationships. When I returned to England and he heard that I was worried because the post-war world of the '20's would not add up into sense, he sent me a message. "Tell him," it ran, "tell him from me to follow his heart, and his mind will see everything clear." The message as phrased is too facile: doors open into silliness at once. But to remember and respect and prefer the heart, to have the instinct which follows it wherever possible—what surer help than that could one have through life? What better hope of clarification? Melville goes on: "The reason that the mass of men fear God and at bottom dislike Him, is because they rather distrust His heart." With that too he would have agreed. . . .

It is India and 3 P.M. but so dark that I can scarcely see to write and not at all to find your letter. I go off on the royal progress tomorrow.

I tap about over this place and wonder whether I grow deaf or whether there really is no echo. Except in the direction of religion, where I allow them much, these people don't seem to move towards anything important; there is no art, the literature is racial and I suspect its value; there is no intellectual interest, although His Highness at least has an excellent intellect. The music —some singers are good but most that I have heard are not, and all become bawdy at the least encouragement. It is a great misfortune for art to be associated with prostitution, not for moral reasons but because every flight of beauty or fancy is apt to be cut short. H.H. leads a "good" life as it is called, and our singing parties at the Palace are only a debauch to the superficial observer. But there is much verbal and histrionic indecency which amused me at first, not now, because I see that it takes the place of so much that I value. I am afraid that Indian singing is doomed for this reason, because all the reformers and Westernisers will have none of it. And it is, or has been, a great art.

Night has fallen, and our excellent electric light has enabled me to find your letter. . . .

About the Prince of Wales' visit I might also write much. It is disliked and dreaded by nearly everyone. The chief exceptions are the motor firms and caterers, who will make fortunes, and the non-cooperators and extremists, who will have an opportunity for protest which they would otherwise have lacked. Masood is an exception too, because he believes that the Prince will make some important announcement, perhaps in regard to Turkey; if he doesn't do something dramatic and fundamental, his visit will be worse than useless, Masood agrees. The National Congress meets in December at Ahmedabad, and it will certainly carry through its resolution in favour of Civil Disobedience, and if there is general response, this expensive royal expedition will look rather foolish.

I have been with pro-Government and pro-English Indians all this time, so cannot realise the feeling of the other party: and am only sure of this— that we were paying for the insolence of Englishmen and Englishwomen out here in the past. I don't mean that good manners can avert a political upheaval. But they can minimise it, and come nearer to averting it in the East than elsewhere. English manners out here have improved wonderfully in the last eight years. Some people are frightened, others seem really to have undergone a change of heart.

But it's too late. Indians don't long for social intercourse with Englishmen any longer. They have made a life of their own.

ANDRÉ GIDE

T HE RIGHTS and wrongs of modern colonialism have been discussed at great length and with much moral fervor by writers on both sides of the question, but perhaps no critic has brought greater psychological discernment or more searching objectivity to his task than did André Gide (1869–1951). In his two books (*Voyage au Congo*, 1927, and *Le Retour du Tchad*, 1928) he used no second-hand evidence but presented only a calm description of what he had seen on a vacation trip through French Equatorial Africa in 1925. His indictment of the colonial administration was all the more telling in that his account was presented dispassionately and without exaggeration. His personal influence—as one of France's leading men of letters—and the pressure of public opinion which his books aroused, compelled the Chamber of Deputies to launch an official investigation of the abuses he had exposed. Some corrective measures were eventually taken, but most of these were subsequently nullified by the influence of the great rubber companies operating in the Congo.

Gide's criticism did not stem from any doctrinaire political or economic philosophy—indeed at the time his *Travels in the Congo* appeared he was known primarily as a convinced protagonist of "pure literature" and of "art for art's sake." He was equally famous as the apostle of an individualism so extreme that it demanded liberation not only from the shackles of family, church, and social convention, but even from the individual's own moral scruples. He had previously concerned himself but little with social questions, and—far from having any preconceived opinions about capitalism or colonialism—he had believed that the human condition could be improved only by changing men's own natures. He had been content to leave such matters as colonial policy to the constituted authorities and their expert advisers. In the Congo, however, ". . . it was not the same thing. There I could not doubt that, as far as the wronged were concerned, nobody would be there to hear them."

The following passages are reprinted from *Travels in the Congo*, which includes both *To the Congo* and *Back from Chad*. The book was translated from the French by Dorothy Bussy and published in 1929 by Alfred A. Knopf, Inc.; this selection is used by permission of the publisher.

ॐ

TRAVELS IN THE CONGO

Bangui, 27 October

W E WENT to bed early and were both fast asleep under our mosquito-nets in the post hut when, at about two o'clock in the morning, a noise of steps and voices woke us up. Someone wanted to come in. We called out in Sango: *"Zo niè?* (Who is there?)" It was a native chief of some importance, who had called before that same evening while we were at dinner, but, being afraid of disturbing us, he had put off the interview he wished to have until the next morning; in the mean time, a messenger, sent after him by Pacha, the administrator of Boda, had just arrived with orders that he should return at once to his village. He was obliged to obey. But in despair at seeing his last chance of speaking to us vanish, he had made so bold as to wake us up at this impossible hour. He talked with extreme volubility in a language of which we understood not a single word. We begged him to let us sleep. He could come back later when we should have an interpreter. We promised to take the responsibility of the delay on ourselves and to shield him from the terrible Pacha. Why should this latter be so anxious to prevent the chief Samba N'Goto from giving us his message? We easily understood the reason when next morning, with Mobaye acting as interpreter, we learnt the following circumstances from Samba N'Goto.

On October 21 last (six days ago, that is) Sergeant Yemba was sent by the administrator of Boda to Bodembéré in order to execute reprisals on the inhabitants of this village (between Boda and N'Goto), who had refused to obey the order to move their settlement on to the Carnot road. They pleaded that they were anxious not to abandon their plantations and urged besides that the people established on the Carnot road are Bayas, while they are Bofis.

Sergeant Yemba therefore left Boda with three guards (whose names we carefully noted). This small detachment was accompanied by the capita Baoué, and two men under his command. On the road, Sergeant Yemba requisitioned two or three men from each of the villages they passed through, and after having put them in chains, took them along with the party. When they arrived at Bodempéré, the reprisals began; twelve men were seized and tied up to trees, while the chief of the village, a man called Cobelé, took flight. Sergeant Yemba and the guard Bonjo then shot and killed the twelve men who had been tied up. Then followed a great massacre of women, whom Yemba struck down with a matchet; after which he seized five young children, shut them up in a hut, and set fire to it. In all, said Samba N'Goto, there were thirty-two victims.

We must add to this number the capita of M'Biri, who had fled from his village (Boubakara, near N'Goto) and whom Yemba came upon at Bossué, the first village north of N'Goto.

We also learnt that Samba N'Goto was returning to Boda, where he lives and had nearly reached it when on the road he met Governor Lamblin's car, which was taking us to N'Goto. At this he turned back, thinking that it contained the Governor himself and anxious to appeal to him in person. He must have walked very quickly, as he arrived at N'Goto a very short time after us.

He was determined not to let this unhoped-for chance of appealing to the white chief escape him.[1]

28 October

Samba N'Goto's deposition lasted more than two hours. It was raining. This was no passing tornado shower. The sky was thickly covered; the rain had set in for long. We started nevertheless at ten o'clock. I sat beside Mobaye; Marc and Zézé settled themselves inside the lorry as comfortably as they could on the sleeping-bags, though they found it very stifling under the tarpaulin. The road was sodden and the car's progress was despairingly slow. At the slightest hill and also in the parts where the road was too sandy, we had to get out in the rain and push, to prevent the lorry from sticking in the mud.

We were so much upset by Samba N'Goto's deposition and by Garron's tales that when, in the forest, we came across a group of women who were mending the road, we had no heart even to smile at them. These poor creatures, more like cattle than human beings, were in the streaming rain, a number of them with babies at the breast. Every twenty yards or so there were huge pits by the side of the road, generally about ten feet deep; it was out of these that the poor wretches had dug the sandy earth with which to bank the road, and this *without proper tools*. It has happened more than once that the loose earth has given way and buried the women and children who were working at the bottom of the pit. We were told this by several persons.[2] As they usually work too far from the village to return at night, the poor women have built themselves temporary huts in the forest, wretched shelters of branches and reeds, useless against the rain. We heard that the native soldier who is their overseer had made them work all night in order to repair the damage done by a recent storm and to enable us to pass. . . .

29 October

This morning I went to see one of the native chiefs who came to meet us yesterday. This evening he returned my visit. We had a long conversation. Adoum, sitting on the ground between the chief and me, acted as interpreter.

[1] Needless to say, Samba N'Goto was flung into prison as soon as he returned to Boda. A letter to Pacha which I had given him in order to excuse his delay and protect him if possible was of no avail. He was flung into prison with several members of his family whom Pacha was easily able to lay his hands on. In the mean time, Pacha absented himself on tour, accompanied by that very Yemba, whose exploits had by no means brought him into disgrace. I hasten to add that this impunity did not last long, nor the incarceration of Samba N'Goto either. On the receipt of my letter the Governor ordered an official inquiry. It was entrusted to M. Marchessou, inspector of Ubangui-Shari, who confirmed everything stated above. This led to the prosecution of Pacha.

[2] It is to be noted that this murderous road, which was particularly difficult to lay, owing to the nature of the soil, serves exclusively for the car which once a month takes the Forestière's representative, Mr. M., accompanied by the administrator Pacha to the market at Bambio.

The information of the Bambio chief confirms everything that I heard from Samba N'Goto. In particular, he gave me an account of "the ball" last market day at Boda. I here transcribe the story as I copied it from Garron's private diary.

At Bambio, on September 8, ten rubber-gatherers (twenty, according to later information [3]) belonging to the Goundi gang, who work for the Compagnie Forestière—because they had not brought in any rubber the month before (but this month they brought in double, from 40 to 50 kilogrammes)—were condemned to go round and round the factory under a fierce sun, carrying very heavy wooden beams. If they fell down, they were forced up by guards flogging them with whips.

The "ball" began at eight o'clock and lasted the whole day, with Messrs. Pacha and Maudurier, the company's agent, looking on. At about eleven o'clock a man from Bagouma, called Malongué, fell to get up no more. When M. Pacha was informed of this, he merely replied: *"Je m'en f——"* and ordered the "ball" to go on. All this took place in the presence of the assembled inhabitants of Bambio and of all the chiefs who had come from the neighbouring villages to attend the market.

The chief spoke to us also of the conditions reigning in the Boda prison; of the wretched plight of the natives and of how they are fleeing to some less accursed country. My indignation against Pacha is naturally great, but the Compagnie Forestière plays a part in all this, which seems to be very much graver, though more secret. For, after all, it—its representatives, I mean— knew everything that was going on. It (or its agents) profited by this state of things. Its agents approved Pacha, encouraged him, were his partners. It was at their request that Pacha arbitrarily threw into prison the natives who did not furnish enough stuff; etc. . . .

As I am anxious to make a good job of my letter to the Governor, I have decided to put off leaving here till the day after tomorrow. The short time I have passed in French Equatorial Africa has already put me on my guard against "authentic accounts," exaggerations and deformations of the smallest facts. I am terribly afraid, however, that this scene of the "ball" was nothing exceptional, if the stories of several eyewitnesses, whom I questioned one after the other, are to be believed. The terror Pacha inspires makes them implore me not to name them. No doubt they will withdraw everything later on and deny that they ever saw anything. When a Governor goes on tour, his subordinates usually present reports containing the facts they think most likely to please him. Those that I have to place before him are of a kind, I fear, that may never come to his notice, and the voices that might inform him of them will be carefully stifled. A simple tourist like myself may, I feel sure,

---

[3] They were all fined a sum equal to the price of their work. Consequently they worked for two months for nothing. One of them, who tried "to argue," was besides condemned to a month's imprisonment.

often hear and see things which never reach a person in his high position.

When I accepted this mission, I failed to grasp at first what it was I was undertaking, what part I could play, how I could be useful. I understand it now and I am beginning to think that my coming will not have been in vain.

During my stay in the colony I have come to realize how terribly the problems which I have to solve are interwoven one with the other. Far be it from me to raise my voice on points which are not within my competence and which necessitate a prolonged study. But this is a matter of certain definite facts, completely independent of questions of a general order. Perhaps the *chef de circonscription* has been already informed of them. From what the natives tell me, he seems to be ignorant of them. The circumscription is too vast; a single man who is without the means of rapid transport is unable to keep his eye on the whole of it. One is here, as everywhere else in French Equatorial Africa, brought up against those two terrible impediments: want of sufficient staff; want of sufficient money.

We held a grand view of our porters this evening by moonlight on the vast open space behind the shelter house. Marc told them off, arranged them in groups of ten, showed them how to count themselves. The ones who could understand shouted with laughter at those who could not. We distributed a spoonful of salt to each man, which caused an outburst of lyrical gratitude and enthusiastic protestations of devotion.

30 October

Impossible to sleep. The Bambio "ball" haunted my night. I cannot content myself with saying, as so many do, that the natives were still more wretched before the French occupation. We have shouldered responsibilities regarding them which we have no right to evade. The immense pity of what I have seen has taken possession of me; I know things to which I cannot reconcile myself. What demon drove me to Africa, What did I come out to find in this country, I was at peace. I know now. I must speak.

But how can I get people to listen, Hitherto I have always spoken without the least care whether I was heard or not; always written for tomorrow, with the single desire of lasting. Now I envy the journalist, whose voice carries at once, even if it perishes immediately after. Have I been walking hitherto between high walls of falsehood? I must get behind them, out on to the other side, and learn what it is they are put to hide, even if the truth is horrible. The horrible truth that I suspect is what I must see.

Spent the whole day composing my letter. . . .

31 October

. . . Long conversation with the two chiefs of the Bakongo village. But the one who was at first talking to us alone, stopped as soon as the other came up. He would not say another word; and nothing could be more harrowing than his silence and his fear of compromising himself when we questioned him about the Boda prison, where he has himself been confined. When he was again alone with us later on, he told us that he had seen ten men die in it in a single day, as a result of ill treatment. He himself bears the marks of flogging and showed us his scars. He confirmed what we had already heard,[4] that the prisoners receive as sole food, once a day, a ball of manioc as big as—he showed us his fist.

He spoke of the fines that the Compagnie Forestière are in the habit of inflicting on the natives who fail to bring in sufficient quantities of rubber—fines of forty francs—that is to say, the whole of one month's pay. He added that when the wretched man has not enough to pay the fine, he can only escape being thrown into prison by borrowing from someone better off than himself; if he can find such a person—and then he is sometimes thrown into prison "into the bargain." Terror reigns and the surrounding villages are deserted. We talked to other chiefs. When they are asked: "How many men in your village," they count them by putting down a finger for each one. There are rarely more than ten. Adoum acts as interpreter.

Adoum is intelligent, but he does not know French very well. When we halt in the forest, he says it is because we have found a "palace" (for a *"place"*). He says *"un nomme"* (instead of *"un homme"*), and when we tell him to ask a chief: "How many men have run away from your village, or have been put in prison?" Adoum answers: "Here ten *nommes;* there six *nommes;* and eight *nommes* farther on."

A great many natives come to see us. So-and-so asks for a paper to certify that he is sorcerer-in-chief to a great many villages; so-and-so wants a paper to authorize him to go away and "make a little village all by himself." When I inquire how many prisoners there are in the Boda jail, the only answer I get, whoever it may be who gives it, is: "Many; many; me can't count." There seem to be numbers of women and children as well among the prisoners. . . .

9 November

. . . I should like to preserve here some record of yesterday evening's fantastic party. We were dining at Dr. B.'s with A., the young agent of the Société Wial (only twenty-two years old), and L., the river steamship captain, who has just arrived from Brazzaville. We very soon noticed that the doctor

[4] Confirmed in turn by the official inquiry.

was not in a perfectly normal state; it was not only his excited remarks, but I saw that when he offered me wine, I had the greatest difficulty in keeping my glass under the bottle—he kept trying to pour it out *on the other side*. And on several occasions he put the piece of meat on his fork down on the tablecloth, instead of putting it into his mouth. He got more and more excited, without, however, drinking too much; but perhaps he had already drunk a good deal, in honour of the steamer's arrival. But it was not so much drink that I suspected as . . . The day before, I had shown him my letter to Governor Alfassa, containing the serious charges against Pacha; he had seemed indignant; then, that evening, when I imprudently spoke of sending my letter to the minister, seized with fear, no doubt, or from a sort of feeling of solidarity, he burst out into protests that there were numbers of officials and administrators who were honest, devoted, conscientious, excellent workers. I, in my turn, protested that I had never doubted it, and that I knew a great many such; but that it was all the more important that a few unfortunate exceptions (and I added that of the quantities of officials of all ranks I had seen, I had never met but one) should not bring discredit upon the others.

"But," he cried, "you won't be able to prevent attention's being called especially to that exception, and public opinion will be formed on it. It is deplorable."

There was a good deal of truth in what he said, and I was aware of it. He seemed to be afraid that he had gone too far in approving my letter the day before, and to be making a protest against that very approbation. For immediately afterwards he started approving a policy of brutality towards the blacks, affirming that one could get nothing out of them except by blows, and by making examples, even bloody ones. He went so far as to say that he himself had one day killed a Negro; then he added hastily that it was in defence, not of himself, but of a friend, who would otherwise have certainly been done in. Then he said that the only way to be respected by the Negroes was to make oneself feared, and he spoke of a confrere, Dr. X., the doctor who had preceded him at Nola, who, as he was peacefully going through the village of Katakouo (or Katapo), which we had gone through the day before, was seized, bound, stripped, daubed with paint from head to foot, and forced to dance to the sound of the tamtam for two days on end. He was only delivered by a squadron that was sent from Nola. . . . All this was said more and more queerly, more and more incoherently and excitedly. We were all silent; no one else spoke a word. And if we had not finally broken up the party, because we had our packing to attend to for the next morning's start, he would certainly have said more. He almost went so far as to approve Pacha; at any rate, everything he said was with the unavowed object of excusing him and of repudiating me. He said besides (and, if true, this is very important) that the recognized chiefs of the villages are more often than not men who are held in no consideration among the natives they are supposed to rule; that they are former slaves, mere figure-heads, chosen to shoulder responsibilities and suffer any punishments that may be inflicted; and that all the inhabitants of the villages were delighted when they were flung into jail. The real chief is a secret chief, whom the French government hardly ever get to know of.

I can only repeat his remarks more or less roughly; I cannot give any idea of the fantastic, uncanny atmosphere of the scene. One could only manage this with a great deal of art and I am writing as it comes. It should be noted that the doctor began the subject abruptly, by a direct attack, evidently premeditated; the soup had not been cleared away before he suddenly asked me whether I had been to see the Nola cemetery. And when I said no, "Well! there are sixteen white men's graves there," etc. . . .

10 November

. . . The obligingness and attentiveness and zeal of our boys is beyond words; as for our cook, his cooking is the best we have tasted in this country. I continue to think, and think more and more, that most of the faults people complain of in the servants here come more than anything from the way in which they are treated and spoken to. We can only be congratulated on ours —to whom we have never spoken an unkind word, to whom we trust all our possessions, and who, so far, have shown themselves scrupulously honest. More than that: we leave all our small objects lying about in view of our porters, and in view of the inhabitants of the villages we pass through—objects that are exceedingly tempting to them and the theft of which it would be exceedingly difficult to discover—a thing we should never dare do in France—and so far nothing has disappeared. A mutual confidence and cordiality have sprung up between our servants and us, and all, without a single exception, are as nice to us as we make a point of being to them.[5]

---

[5] This judgment, which might seem premature, was only more and more confirmed as time went on. And I confess I cannot understand why all Europeans, almost without exception, officials as well as traders, women as well as men, think it necessary to treat their servants roughly —in speech, at any rate—even when they show them real kindness. I know a lady, who is otherwise charming and gentle, who never calls her boy anything but *"tête de brute"* ("blockhead" is a mild translation of this), though she never raises her hand against him. Such is the custom. "You will end by it too. Wait and see." We waited ten months without changing our servants and we did not end by it. Were we particularly lucky? Perhaps. . . . But I am inclined to think that every master has the servants he deserves, and what I say does not apply only to the Congo. What servant in our country would care to remain honest if he heard his master deny him the possession of a single virtue? If I had been Mr. X.'s boy, I should have robbed him the very same night I heard him declare that all Negroes were cheats, liars, and thieves.

I am going on with Adoum's reading-lessons. His application is touching; he is getting on steadily, and every day I am becoming more attached to him. When the white man gets angry with the blacks' stupidity, he is usually showing up his own foolishness! Not that I think them capable of any but the slightest mental development; their brains as a rule are dull and stagnant— but how often the white man seems to make it his business to thrust them back into their darkness.

"Doesn't your boy understand French?" I asked with some uneasiness.

"He speaks it admirably. . . . Why?"

"Aren't you afraid that what you have just said . . . ?"

"It'll teach him that I'm not taken in by him."

At the same dinner I heard a guest declare that all women (and he wasn't talking of Negresses this time) care for nothing but pleasure as long as they are worthy of our attentions, and that no woman is ever really pious before the age of forty.

These gentlemen have the same knowledge of Negroes that they have of women. Experience rarely teaches us anything. A man uses everything he comes across to strengthen him in his own opinion and sweeps everything into his net to prove his convictions. . . . No prejudice so absurd but finds its confirmation in experience.

Negroes, who are prodigiously malleable, oftener than not become what people think, or want, or fear them to be. I would not swear that our boys too might not have been turned into rascals. One has only to set about it in the right way; and colonials are extraordinarily ingenious in this matter. One teaches his parrot to say: "Get out, dirty nigger!" Another is angry because his boy brings vermouth and bitters after dinner instead of liqueurs. "Double-dyed idiot! Don't you know yet what an *apéritif* is? . . ." Another time a poor boy who, thinking he was doing right, had warmed a porcelain tea-pot with boiling water is railed at before the whole company and again called a fool. Hadn't he been taught that hot water broke glasses?

X REAPPRAISING THE NINETEENTH CENTURY

WILLIAM JAMES

WILLIAM JAMES was born in New York in 1842. His father, Henry, a man of strong character and mystical tendencies (he was a Swedenborgian), had a powerful influence on William and his younger brother Henry, the future novelist. William was educated in France, Switzerland, and the United States, and just before his twentieth birthday he entered Harvard to study science. In 1865 he interrupted his studies to travel with Louis Agassiz, the famed naturalist, on an expedition to the Amazon. William returned in ill health, and after another term at Harvard journeyed to Germany, where he studied medicine. Throughout this period he suffered from chronic physical illness and severe depression. He received his medical degree but felt himself unable to practice, and spent the years 1869 to 1872 as a semi-invalid in his father's home. There, James wrote occasional reviews and read widely in psychology and philosophy. He devoted much time to the writings of Renouvier.

James taught anatomy and physiology at Harvard for three years, and in 1875 he was appointed to teach psychology and philosophy. It was while occupying this position that he effected a revolution in the study of psychology by removing it from the domain of philosophy and making it into a laboratory science. He established the first experimental laboratory in psychology in the United States. In 1891 he published his two-volume study, *The Principles of Psychology*, at once acclaimed as a pioneering yet definitive work.

After this triumph, James turned from psychology to problems of a more general philosophical nature. Here too he gained recognition as an innovator. Emphasizing individuality, spontaneity, and initiative, in opposition to fatalistic philosophies like Herbert Spencer's, James insisted that the true criterion for the evaluation of ideas and actions lay in their success or failure, not in some supposed intrinsic qualities. Like his friend Justice Oliver Wendell Holmes, he regarded all life as an experiment with no guarantees of permanence for any idea in a ceaseless evolutionary process.

James developed these ideas as they applied to religion in two important works, *The Will to Believe* (1897) and *The Varieties of Religious Experience* (1902). He elaborated his pragmatic philosophy in the Lowell Lectures of 1906, later published as *Pragmatism: A New Name for Old Ways of Thinking*. The pragmatic philosophy, and James himself, soon became the center of a storm of controversy: while Americans eventually championed the new school, European and English intellectuals—with a few exceptions—were in fierce opposition. At his final lecture at Harvard in 1907, James was presented by his students with a loving cup, while his lectures on "Pragmatism" at Columbia in the spring of that year were little short of triumphs. He was called to deliver the Hibbert lectures at Oxford in 1909, later published as *A Pluralistic Universe*.

William James died in New Hampshire on August 26, 1910. Some of his most important essays were collected and published posthumously as *Essays in Radical Empiricism* (1912). The following selection was a speech delivered before the

Harvard Natural History Society and published in the *Atlantic Monthly* of October, 1880.

❧

GREAT MEN AND THEIR ENVIRONMENT

A REMARKABLE PARALLEL, which I think has never been noticed, obtains between the facts of social evolution on the one hand, and of zoölogical evolution as expounded by Mr. Darwin on the other.

It will be best to prepare the ground for my thesis by a few very general remarks on the method of getting at scientific truth. It is a common platitude that a complete acquaintance with any one thing, however small, would require a knowledge of the entire universe. Not a sparrow falls to the ground but some of the remote conditions of his fall are to be found in the milky way, in our federal constitution, or in the early history of Europe. That is to say, alter the milky way, alter the federal constitution, alter the facts of our barbarian ancestry, and the universe would so far be a different universe from what it now is. One fact involved in the difference might be that the particular little street-boy who threw the stone which brought down the sparrow might not find himself opposite the sparrow at that particular moment; or, finding himself there, he might not be in that particular serene and disengaged mood of mind which expressed itself in throwing the stone. But, true as all this is, it would be very foolish for any one who was inquiring the cause of the sparrow's fall to overlook the boy as too personal, proximate, and so to speak anthropomorphic an agent, and to say that the true cause is the federal constitution, the westward migration of the Celtic race, or the structure of the milky way. If we proceeded on that method, we might say with perfect legitimacy that a friend of ours, who had slipped on the ice upon his door-step and cracked his skull, some months after dining with thirteen at the table, died because of that ominous feast. I know, in fact, one such instance; and I might, if I chose, contend with perfect logical propriety that the slip on the ice was no real accident. "There are no accidents," I might say, "for science. The whole history of the world converged to produce that slip. If anything had been left out, the slip would not have occurred just there and then. To say it would is to deny the relations of cause and effect throughout the universe. The real cause of the death was not the slip, *but the conditions which engendered the slip,*—and among them his having sat at a table, six months previous, one among thirteen. *That* is truly the reason why he died within the year."

It will soon be seen whose arguments I am, in form, reproducing here. I would fain lay down the truth without polemics or recrimination. But unfortunately we never fully grasp the import of any true statement until we have a clear notion of what the opposite untrue statement would be. The error is needed to set off the truth, much as a dark background is required for exhibiting the brightness of a picture. And the error which I am going to use as a foil to set off what seems to me the truth of my own statements is contained in the philosophy of Mr. Herbert Spencer and his disciples. Our problem is, What are the causes that make communities change from generation to generation,—what makes the England of Queen Anne so different from the England of Elizabeth, the Harvard College of to-day so different from that of thirty years ago?

I shall reply to this problem. The difference is due to the accumulated influences of individuals, of their examples, their initiatives, and their decisions. The Spencerian school replies, The changes are irrespective of persons, and independent of individual control. They are due to the environment, to the circumstances, the physical geography, the ancestral conditions, the increasing experience of outer relations; to everything, in fact, except the Grants and the Bismarcks, the Joneses and the Smiths.

Now I say that these theorizers are guilty of precisely the same fallacy as he who should ascribe the death of his friend to the dinner with thirteen, or the fall of the sparrow to the milky way. Like the dog in the fable, who drops his real bone to snatch at others, which from no possible human point of view are avaliable or attainable. Their fallacy is a practical one. Let us see where it lies. Although I believe in free-will myself, I will waive that belief in this discussion, and assume with the Spencerians the predestination of all human actions. On that assumption I gladly allow that were the intelligence investigating the man's or the sparrow's death omniscient and omnipresent, able to take in the whole of time and space at a single glance, there would not be the slightest objection to the milky way or the fatal feast being invoked among the sought-for causes. Such a divine intelligence would see instantaneously all the infinite lines of convergence towards a given result, and it would, moreover, see impartially: it would see the fatal feast to be as much a condition of the sparrow's death as of the man's; it would see the boy with the stone to be as much a condition of the man's fall as of the sparrow's.

The human mind, however, is constituted on an entirely different plan. It has no such power of universal intuition. Its finiteness obliges it to see but two or three things at a time. If it wishes to take wider sweeps it has to use "general ideas," as they are called, and in so doing to drop all concrete truths. Thus, in the present case, if we as men wish to feel the connection between the milky way and the boy . . . we can do so only by falling back on the enormous emptiness of what is called an abstract proposition. We must say, All things in the world are fatally pre-determined, and hang together in the adamantine fixity of a system of natural law. But in the vagueness of this vast proposition we have lost all the concrete facts and links; and in all practical matters the concrete links are the only things of importance. The human mind is essentially partial. It can be efficient at all only by *picking out* what to attend to, and ignoring everything else,—by narrowing its point of view. . . .

It is, then, a necessity laid upon us as human beings to limit our view. . . . An astronomer, in dealing with the tidal movements of the ocean, takes no account of the waves made by the wind, or by the pressure of all the steamers which day and night are moving their thousands of tons upon its surface. Just so the marksman, in sighting his rifle, allows for the motion of the wind, but not for the equally real motion of the earth and solar system. Just so a business man's punctuality may overlook an error of five minutes, while a physicist, measuring the velocity of light, must count each thousandth of a second.

There are, in short, *different cycles of operation* in nature; different departments, so to speak, relatively independent of one another, so that what goes on at any moment in one may be compatible with almost any condition of things at the same time in the next. The mould on the biscuit in the store-room of a man-of-war vegetates in absolute indifference to the nationality of the flag, the direction of the voyage, the weather, and the human dramas that may go on on board; and a mycologist may study it in complete abstraction from all these larger details. Only by so studying it, in fact, is there any chance of the mental concentration by which alone he may hope to learn something of its nature. On the other hand, the captain, who in manoeuvring the vessel through a naval fight should think it necessary to bring the mouldy biscuit into his calculations would very likely lose the battle by reason of the excessive "thoroughness" of his mind.

The causes which operate in these incommensurable cycles are connected with one another only *if we take the whole universe into account*. For all lesser points of view it is lawful—nay, more, it is for human wisdom necessary —to regard them as disconnected and irrelevant to one another.

And this brings us nearer to our special topic. If we look at an animal or a human being, distinguished from the rest of his kind by the possession of some extraordinary peculiarity, good or bad, we shall be able to discriminate between the causes which originally *produced* the peculiarity in him and the causes that *maintain* it after it is produced; and we shall see, if the peculiarity be one that he was born with, that these two sets of causes belong to two such irrelevant cycles. It was the triumphant originality of Darwin to see this, and to act accordingly. Separating the causes of production under the title of "tendencies to spontaneous variation," and relegating them to a physiological cycle which he forthwith agreed to ignore altogether, he confined his attention to the causes of preservation, and under the names of natural selection and sexual selection studied them exclusively as functions of the cycle of the environment.

Pre-Darwinian philosophers had also tried to establish the doctrine of descent with modification; but they all committed the blunder of clumping the two cycles of causation into one. What preserves an animal with his peculiarity, if it be a useful one, they saw to be the nature of the environment to which the peculiarity was adjusted. The giraffe with his peculiar neck is preserved by the fact that there are in his environment tall trees whose leaves he can digest. But these philosophers went further, and said that the presence of the trees not only maintained an animal with a long neck to browse upon their branches, but also produced him. They *made* his neck long by the constant striving they aroused in him to reach up to them. The environment, in short, was supposed by these writers to mould the animal by a kind of direct pressure, very much as a seal presses the wax into harmony with itself. Numerous instances were given of the way in which this goes on under our eyes. The exercise of the forge makes the right arm strong, the palm grows callous to the oar, the mountain air distends the chest, the chased fox grows cunning and the chased bird shy, the arctic cold stimulates the animal combustion, and so forth. Now these changes, of which many more examples might be adduced, are at present distinguished by the special names of *adapative* changes. Their peculiarity is that that very feature in the environment to which the animal's nature grows adjusted, itself produces the adjustment. The "inner relation," to use Mr. Spencer's phrase, "corresponds" with its own efficient cause.

Darwin's first achievement was to show the utter insignificance in amount of these changes produced by direct adaptation, the immensely greater mass of changes being produced by internal molecular accidents, of which we know nothing. His next achievement was to define the true problem with which we have to deal when we study the effects of the visible environment on the animal. That problem is simply this: Is the environment more likely to *preserve or to destroy him*, on account of this or that peculiarity with which he may be born? In giving the name of "accidental variations" to those pecularities with which an animal is born, Darwin does not for a moment mean to suggest that they are not the fixed outcome of natural law. If the total system of the universe be taken into account, the causes of these variations and the visible en-vironment which preserves or destroys them, undoubtedly do, in some remote and roundabout way, hang together. What Darwin means is, that since that environment is a perfectly known thing, and its relations to the organism in the way of destruction or preservation are tangible and distinct, it would ut-terly confuse our finite understandings and frustrate our hopes of science to mix in with it facts from such a disparate and incommensurable cycle as that in which the variations are produced. This last cycle is that of occurrences before the animal is born. It is the cycle of influences upon ova and embryos; in which lie the causes that tip them and tilt them towards masculinity or femininity, towards strength or weakness, towards health or disease, and towards divergence from the parent type. What are the causes there?

In the first place, they are molecular and invisible,—inaccessible, therefore, to direct observation of any kind. Secondly, their operations are compatible with any social, political, and physical conditions of environment. The same parents, living in the same environing conditions, may at one birth produce a genius, at the next an idiot or a monster. The visible external conditions are therefore not direct determinants of this cycle; and the more we consider the matter, the more we are forced to believe that two children of the same parents are made to differ from each other by causes as disproportionate to their ulti-mate effects as is the famous pebble on the Rocky Mountain crest, which separates two rain-drops, to the Gulf of St. Lawrence and the Pacific Ocean toward which it makes them severally flow.

The great mechanical distinction between transitive forces and discharging forces is nowhere illustrated on such a scale as in physiology. Almost all causes there are forces of *detent,* which operate by simply unlocking energy already stored up. They are upsetters of unstable equlibria, and the resultant effect depends infinitely more on the nature of the materials upset than on that of the particular stimulus which joggles them down. Galvanic work, equal to unity, done on a frog's nerve will discharge from the muscle to which the nerve belongs mechanical work equal to seventy thousand; and exactly the same muscular effect will emerge if other irritants than galvanism are em-ployed. The irritant has merely started or provoked something which then went on of itself,—as a match may start a fire which consumes a whole town. And qualitatively as well as quantitatively the effect may be absolutely incom-mensurable with the cause. We find this condition of things in all organic matter. Chemists are distracted by the difficulties which the instability of albuminoid compounds opposes to their study. Two specimens, treated in what outwardly seem scrupulously identical conditions, behave in quite different ways. You know about the invisible factors of fermentation, and how the fate of a jar of milk—whether it turn into a sour clot or a mass of koumiss —depends on whether the lactic acid ferment or the alcoholic is introduced first, and gets ahead of the other in starting the process. Now, when the result is the tendency of an ovum, itself invisible to the naked eye, to tip towards this direction or that in its further evolution,—to bring forth a genius or a dunce, even as the rain-drop passes east or west of the pebble,—is it not obvious that the deflecting cause must lie in a region so recondite and minute, must be such a ferment of a ferment, an infinitesimal of so high an order, that surmise itself may never succeed even in attempting to frame an image of it?

Such being the case, was not Darwin right to turn his back upon that region altogether, and to keep his own problem carefully free from all entanglement with matters such as these? The success of his work is a sufficiently affirmative reply.

And this brings us at last to the heart of our subject. The causes of production of great men lie in a sphere wholly inaccessible to the social philosopher. He must simply accept geniuses as data, just as Darwin accepts his spontaneous variations. For him, as for Darwin, the only problem is, these data being given, How does the environment affect them, and how do they affect the environment? Now, I affirm that the relation of the visible environment to the great man is in the main exactly what it is to the "variation" in the Darwinian philosophy. It chiefly adopts or rejects, preserves or destroys, in short *selects* him. And whenever it adopts and preserves the great man, it becomes modified by his influence in an entirely original and peculiar way. He acts as a ferment, and changes its constitution, just as the advent of a new zoölogical species changes the faunal and floral equilibrium of the region in which it appears. We all recollect Mr. Darwin's famous statement of the influence of cats on the growth of clover in their neighborhood. We have all read of the effects of the European rabbit in New Zealand, and we have many of us taken part in the controversy about the English sparrow here,—whether he kills most canker-worms, or drives away most native birds. Just so the great man, whether he be an importation from without like Clive in India or Agassiz here, or whether he spring from soil like Mahomet or Franklin, brings about a rearrangement, on a large or a small scale, of the pre-existing social relations.

The mutations of societies, then, from generation to generation, are in the main due directly or indirectly to the acts or the example of individuals whose genius was so adapted to the receptivities of the moment, or whose accidental position of authority was so critical that they became ferments, initiators of movement, setters of precedent or fashion, centres of corruption, or destroyers of other persons, whose gifts, had they had free play, would have led society in another direction.

We see this power of individual initiative exemplified on a small scale all about us, and on a large scale in the case of the leaders of history. It is only following the common-sense method of a Lyell, a Darwin, and a Whitney to interpret the unknown by the known, and reckon up cumulatively the only causes of social change we can directly observe. Societies of men are just like individuals, in that both at any given moment offer ambiguous potentialities of development. Whether a young man enters business or the ministry may depend on a decision which has to be taken before a certain day. He takes the place offered in the counting-house, and is *committed*. Little by little, the habits, the knowledges, of the other career, which once lay so near, cease to be reckoned even among his possibilities. At first, he may sometimes doubt whether the self he murdered in that decisive hour might not have been the better of the two; but with the years such questions themselves expire, and the old alternative *ego,* once so vivid, fades into something less substantial than a dream. It is no otherwise with nations. They may be committed by kings and ministers to peace or war, by generals to victory or defeat, by prophets to this religion or to that, by various geniuses to fame in art, science, or industry. A war is a true point of bifurcation of future possibilities. Whether it fail or succeed, its declaration must be the starting-point of new policies. Just so does a revolution, or any great civic precedent, become a deflecting influence, whose operations widen with the course of time. Communities obey their ideals; and an accidental success fixes an ideal, as an accidental failure blights it. . . .

The fermentative influence of geniuses must be admitted as, at any rate, one factor in the changes that constitute social evolution. The community *may* evolve in many ways. The accidental presence of this or that ferment decides in which way it *shall* evolve. Why, the very birds of the forest, the parrot, the mino, have the power of human speech, but never develop it of themselves, some one must be there to teach them. So with us individuals. Rembrandt must teach us to enjoy the struggle of light with darkness, Wagner to enjoy peculiar musical effects; Dickens give a twist to our sentimentality, Artemus Ward to our humor; Emerson kindles a new moral light within us. But it is like Columbus's egg. "All can raise the flowers now, for all have got the seed." But if this be true of the individuals in the community, how can it be false of the community as a whole? If shown a certain way, a community may take it; if not, it will never find it. And the ways are to a large extent indeterminate in advance. A nation may obey either of many alternative impulses given by different men of genius, and still live and be prosperous, just as a man may enter either of many businesses. Only, the prosperities may differ in their type.

But the indeterminism is not absolute. Not every "man" fits every "hour." Some incompatibilities there are. A given genius may come either too early or too late. Peter the Hermit would now be sent to a lunatic asylum. John Mill in the tenth century would have lived and died unknown. Cromwell and Napoleon need their revolutions, Grant his civil war. An Ajax gets no fame in the day of telescopic-sighted rifles; and to express differently an instance which Spencer uses, what could a Watt have effected in a tribe which no precursive genius had taught to smelt iron or to turn a lathe?

Now, the important thing to notice is that what makes a certain genius now incompatible with his surroundings is usually the fact that some previous genius of a different strain has warped the community away from the sphere of his possible effectiveness. After Voltaire, no Peter the Hermit; after Charles IX. and Louis XIV., no general protestantization of France; after a Manchester school, a Beaconsfield's success is transient; after a Philip II., a Castelar makes little headway; and so on. Each bifurcation cuts off certain sides of the field altogether, and limits the future possible angles of deflection. A community is a living thing, and in words which I can do no better than quote from Professor Clifford,[1]

it is the peculiarity of living things not merely that they change under the influence of surrounding circumstances, but that any change which takes place in them is not lost but retained, and as it were built into the organism to serve as the foundation for future actions. If you cause any distortion in the growth of a tree and make it crooked, whatever you may do afterwards to make the tree straight the mark of your distortion is there; it is absolutely indelible; it has become part of the tree's nature. . . . Suppose, however, that you take a lump of gold, melt it, and let it cool. . . . No one can tell by examining a piece of gold how often it has been melted and cooled in geologic ages, or even in the last year by the hand of man. Any one who cuts down an oak can tell by the rings in its trunk how many times winter has frozen it into widowhood, and how many times summer has warmed it into life. A living being must always contain within itself the history, not merely of its own existence, but of all its ancestors.

Every painter can tell us how each added line deflects his picture in a certain sense. Whatever lines follow must be built on those first laid down. Every author who starts to rewrite a piece of work knows how impossible it becomes to use any of the first-written pages again. The new beginning has already excluded the possibility of those earlier phrases and transitions, while it has at the same time created the possibility of an indefinite set of new ones,

[1] *Lectures and Essays*, i. 82.

no one of which, however, is completely determined in advance. Just so the social surroundings of the past and present hour exclude the possibility of accepting certain contributions from individuals; but they do not positively define what contributions shall be accepted, for in themselves they are powerless to fix what the nature of the individual offerings shall be.

Thus social evolution is a resultant of the interaction of two wholly distinct factors,—the individual, deriving his peculiar gifts from the play of physiological and infra-social forces, but bearing all the power of initiative and origination in his hands; and, second, the social environment, with its power of adopting or rejecting both him and his gifts. Both factors are essential to change. The community stagnates without the impulse of the individual. The impulse dies away without the sympathy of the community.

All this seems nothing more than common-sense. . . . But there are never wanting minds to whom such views seem personal and contracted, and allied to an anthropomorphism long exploded in other fields of knowledge. "The individual withers, and the world is more and more," to these writers; and in a Buckle, a Draper, and a Taine we all know how much the "world" has come to be almost synonymous with the *climate*. We all know, too, how the controversy has been kept up between the partisans of a "science of history" and those who deny the existence of anything like necessary "laws" where human societies are concerned. Mr. Spencer, at the opening of his *Study of Sociology,* makes an onslaught on the "great-man theory" of history, from which a few passages may be quoted:—

The genesis of societies by the action of great men may be comfortably believed so long as, resting in general notions, you do not ask for particulars. But now, if dissatisfied with vagueness, we demand that our ideas shall be brought into focus and exactly defined, we discover the hypothesis to be utterly incoherent. If, not stopping at the explanation of social progress as due to the great man, we go back a step, and ask, Whence comes the great man? we find that the theory breaks down completely. The question has two conceivable answers: his origin is supernatural, or it is natural. Is his origin supernatural? Then he is a deputy god, and we have theocracy once removed,—or rather, not removed at all. . . . Is this an unacceptable solution? Then the origin of the great man is natural; and immediately this is recognized, he must be classed with all other phenomena in the society that gave him birth as a product of its antecedents. Along with the whole generation of which he forms a minute part, along with its institutions, language, knowledge, manners, and its multitudinous arts and appliances, he is a *resultant.* . . . You must admit that the genesis of the great man depends on the long series of complex influences which has produced the race in which he appears, and the social state into which that race has slowly grown. . . . Before he can remake his society, his society must make him. All those changes of which he is the proximate initiator have their chief causes in the generations he descended from. If there is to be anything like a real explanation of those changes, it must be sought in that aggregate of conditions out of which both he and they have arisen.[2]

Now, it seems to me that there is something which one might almost call impudent in the attempt which Mr. Spencer makes, in the first sentence of this extract, to pin the reproach of vagueness upon those who believe in the power of initiative of the great man.

Suppose I say that the singular moderation which now distinguishes social, political, and religious discussion in England, and contrasts so strongly with the bigotry and dogmatism of sixty years ago, is largely due to J. S. Mill's example. I may possibly be wrong about the facts; but I am, at any rate "asking for particulars," and not "resting in general notions." And if Mr. Spencer should tell me it started from no personal influence whatever, but from the "aggregate of conditions," the "generations," Mill and all his contemporaries "descended from," the whole past order of nature in short, surely he, not I, would be the person "satisfied with vagueness."

The fact is that Mr. Spencer's sociological method is identical with that of one who would invoke the zodiac to account for the fall of the sparrow, and the thirteen at table to explain the gentlemen's death. It is of little more scientific value than the Oriental method of reply to whatever question arises by the unimpeachable truism, "God is great." *Not* to fall back on the gods, where a proximate principle may be found, has with us Westerners long since become the sign of an efficient as distinguished from an inefficient intellect.

To believe that the cause of everything is to be found in its antecedents is the starting-point, the initial postulate, not the goal and consummation, of science. If she is simply to lead us out of the labyrinth by the same hole we went in by three or four thousand years ago, it seems hardly worth while to have followed her through the darkness at all. If anything is humanly certain it is that the great man's society, properly so called, does *not* make him before he can remake it. Physiological forces, with which the social, political, geographical, and to a great extent anthropological conditions have just as much and just as little to do as the condition of the crater of Vesuvius has to do with the flickering of this gas by which I write, are what makes him. Can it be that Mr. Spencer holds the convergence of sociological pressures to have so impinged on Stratford-upon-Avon about the 26th of April, 1564, that a W. Shakespeare, with all his mental peculiarities, had to be born there,—as the pressure of water outside a certain boat will cause a stream of a certain form to ooze into a particular leak? And does he mean to say that if the aforesaid W. Shakespeare had died of cholera infantum, another mother at Stratford-upon-Avon would

[2] *Study of Sociology,* pages 33–35.

needs have engendered a duplicate copy of him, to restore the sociologic equilibrium,—just as the same stream of water will reappear, no matter how often you pass a sponge over the leak, so long as the outside level remains unchanged? Or might the substitute arise at "Stratford-atte-Bowe"? Here, as elsewhere, it is very hard to tell what he does mean at all.

We have, however, in his disciple, Mr. Grant Allen, one who leaves us in no doubt whatever of his precise meaning. This widely informed, suggestive, and brilliant writer published last year a couple of articles in the Gentleman's Magazine, in which he maintained that individuals have no initiative in determining social change. . . .

Mr. Allen, writing of the Greek culture, says:—

It was absolutely and unreservedly the product of the geographical Hellas, acting upon the given factor of the undifferentiated Aryan brain. . . . To me it seems a self-evident proposition that nothing whatsoever can differentiate one body of men from another, except the physical conditions in which they are set,—including, of course, under the term *physical conditions* the relations of place and time in which they stand with regard to other bodies of men. To suppose otherwise is to deny the primordial law of causation. To imagine that the mind can differentiate itself is to imagine that it can be differentiated without a cause.

This outcry about the law of universal causation being undone, the moment we refuse to invest in the kind of causation which is peddled round by a particular school, makes one impatient. These writers have no imagination of alternatives. With them there is no *tertium quid* between outward environment and miracle. *Aut Caesar, aut nullus! Aut* Spencerism, *aut* catechism!

If by "physical conditions" Mr. Allen means what he does mean, the outward cycle of visible nature and man, his assertion is simply physiologically false. For a national mind differentiates "itself" whenever a genius is born in its midst by causes acting in the invisible and molecular cycle. But if Mr. Allen means by "physical conditions" the whole of nature, his assertion, though true, forms but the vague Asiatic profession of belief in an all-enveloping fate, which certainly need not plume itself on any specially advanced or scientific character.

And how can a thinker so clever as Mr. Allen fail to have distinguished in these matters between *necessary* conditions and *sufficient* conditions of a given result? The French say that to have an omelet we must break our eggs; that is, the breaking of eggs is a necessary condition of the omelet. But is it a sufficient condition? Does an omelet appear whenever three eggs are broken? So of the Greek mind. To get such versatile intelligence it may be that such commercial dealings with the world as the geographical Hellas afforded are a necessary condition. But if they are a sufficient condition, why did not the Phoenicians outstrip the Greeks in intelligence? No geographical environment can produce a given type of mind. It can only foster and further certain types fortuitously produced, and thwart and frustrate others. Once again, its function is simply selective, and determines what shall actually be only by destroying what is positively incompatible. An Arctic environment is incompatible with improvident habits in its denizens; but whether the inhabitants of such a region shall unite with their thrift the peacefulness of the Eskimo or the pugnacity of the Norseman is, so far as climate is concerned, an accident. Evolutionists should not forget that we all have five fingers not because four or six would not do just as well, but merely because the first vertebrate above the fishes *happened* to have that number. He owed his prodigious success in founding a line of descent to some entirely other quality,—we know not which,—but the inessential five fingers were taken in tow and preserved to the present day. So of most social peculiarities. Which of them shall be taken in tow by the few qualities which the environment necessarily exacts is a matter of what physiological accidents shall happen among individuals. Mr. Allen promises to prove his thesis in detail by the examples of China, India, England, Rome, etc. I have not the smallest hesitation in predicting that he will do no more with these examples than he has done with Hellas. He will appear upon the scene after the fact, and show that the quality developed by each race was, naturally enough, not incompatible with its habitat. But he will utterly fail to show that the particular form of compatibility fallen into in each case was the one necessary and only possible form. . . .

Sporadic great men come everywhere. But for a community to get vibrating through and through with intense active life, many geniuses coming together and in rapid succession are required. This is why great epochs are so rare,—why the sudden bloom of a Greece, an early Rome, a Renaissance, is such a mystery. Blow must follow blow so fast that no cooling can occur in the intervals. Then the mass of the nation grows incandescent, and may continue to glow by pure inertia long after the originators of its internal movement have passed away. We often hear surprise expressed that in these high tides of human affairs not only the people should be filled with stronger life, but that individual geniuses should seem so exceptionally abundant. This mystery is just about as deep as the time-honored conundrum as to why great rivers flow by great towns. It is true that great public fermentations awaken and adopt many geniuses, who in more torpid times would have had no chance to work. But over and above this there must be an exceptional concourse of genius about a time, to make the fermentation begin at all. The unlikeliness of the concourse is far greater than the unlikeliness of any particular genius; hence the rarity of these periods and the exceptional aspect which they always wear.

It is folly, then, to speak of the "laws of history" as of something inevitable, which science has only to discover, and whose consequences any one can then foretell but do nothing to alter or avert. Why, the very laws of physics are conditional, and deal with *ifs*. The physicist does not say, "The water will boil anyhow"; he only says it will boil if a fire be kindled beneath it. And so the utmost the student of sociology can ever predict is that *if* a genius of a certain sort show the way, society will be sure to follow. It might long ago have been predicted with great confidence that both Italy and Germany would reach a stable unity if some one could but succeed in starting the process. It could not have been predicted, however, that the *modus operandi* in each case would be subordination to a paramount state rather than federation, because no historian could have calculated the freaks of birth and fortune which gave at the same moment such positions of authority to three such peculiar individuals as Napoleon III., Bismarck, and Cavour. So of our own politics. It is certain now that the movement of the independents, reformers, or whatever one please to call them, will triumph. But whether it do so by converting the Republican party to its ends, or by rearing a new party on the ruins of both our present factions, the historian cannot say. There can be no doubt that the reform movement would make more progress in one year with an adequate personal leader than as now in ten without one. Were there a great citizen, splendid with every civic gift, to be its candidate, who can doubt that he would lead us to victory? But, at present, we, his environment, who sigh for him and would so gladly preserve and adopt him if he came, can neither move without him, nor yet do anything to bring him forth.

To conclude: The evolutionary view of history, when it denies the vital importance of individual initiative, is, then, an utterly vague and unscientific conception, a lapse from modern scientific determinism into the most ancient oriental fatalism. The lesson of the analysis that we have made (even on the completely deterministic hypothesis with which we started) forms an appeal of the most stimulating sort to the energy of the individual. Even the dogged resistance of the reactionary conservative to changes which he cannot hope entirely to defeat is justified and shown to be effective. He retards the movement; deflects it a little by the concessions he extracts; gives it a resultant momentum, compounded of his inertia and his adversaries' speed; and keeps up, in short, a constant lateral pressure, which, to be sure, never heads it round about, but brings it up at last at a goal far to the right or left of that to which it would have drifted had he allowed it to drift alone.

I now pass to the last division of my subject, the function of the environment in *mental* evolution. After what I have already said, I may be quite concise. Here, if anywhere, it would seem at first sight as if that school must be right which makes the mind passively plastic, and the environment actively productive of the form and order of its conceptions; which, in a word, thinks that all mental progress must result from a series of adaptive changes, in the sense already defined of that word. We know what a vast part of our mental furniture consists of purely remembered, not reasoned, experience. The entire field of our habits and associations by contiguity belongs here. The entire field of those abstract conceptions which were taught us with the language into which we were born belongs here also. And, more than this, there is reason to think that the order of "outer relations" experienced by the individual may itself determine the order in which the general characters imbedded therein shall be noticed and extracted by his mind. The pleasures and benefits, moreover, which certain parts of the environment yield, and the pains and hurts which other parts inflict, determine the direction of our interest and our attention, and so decide at which points the accumulation of mental experiences shall begin. It might, accordingly, seem as if there were no room for any other agency than this; as if the distinction we have found so useful between "spontaneous variation," and the producer of changed forms, and the environment, as their preserver and destroyer, did not hold in the case of mental progress; as if, in a word, the parallel with Darwinism might no longer obtain, and Spencer might be quite right with his fundamental law of intelligence, which says, "The cohesion between psychical states is proportionate to the frequency with which the relation between the answering external phenomena has been repeated in experience."

But, in spite of all these facts, I have no hesitation whatever in holding firm to the Darwinian distinction even here. I maintain that the facts in question are all drawn from the lower strata of the mind, so to speak,—from the sphere of its least evolved functions, from the region of intelligence which man possesses in common with the brutes. And I can easily show that throughout the whole extent of those mental departments which are highest, which are most characteristically human, Spencer's law is violated at every step; and that as a matter of fact the new conceptions, emotions, and active tendencies which evolve are originally produced in the shape of random images, fancies, accidental out-births of spontaneous variation in the functional activity of the excessively instable human brain, which the outer environment simply confirms or refutes, adopts or rejects, preserves or destroys,—selects, in short, just as it selects morphological and social variations due to molecular accidents of an analogous sort.

It is one of the tritest of truisms that human intelligences of a simple order are very literal. They are slaves of habit, doing what they have been taught without variation; dry, prosaic, and matter-of-fact in their remarks; devoid of humor, except of the coarse physical kind which rejoices in a practical joke; taking the world for granted; and possessing in their faithfulness and honesty the single gift by which they are sometimes able to warm us into admiration. But even this faithfulness seems to have a sort of inorganic ring, and to remind us more of the immutable properties of a piece of inanimate matter than of the steadfastness of a human will capable of alternative choice. When we descend to the brutes, all these peculiarities are intensified. No reader of Schopenhauer can forget his frequent allusions to the *trockener ernst* of dogs and horses, nor to their *ehrlichkeit*. And every noticer of their ways must receive a deep impression of the fatally literal character of the few, simple, and treadmill-like operations of their minds.

But turn to the highest order of minds, and what a change! Instead of thoughts of concrete things patiently following one another in a beaten track of habitual suggestion, we have the most abrupt cross-cuts and transitions from one idea to another, the most rarefied abstractions and discriminations, the most unheard-of combinations of elements, the subtlest associations of analogy; in a word, we seem suddenly introduced into a seething caldron of ideas, where everything is fizzling and bobbing about in a state of bewildering activity, where partnerships can be joined or loosened in an instant, treadmill routine is unknown, and the unexpected seems the only law. According to the idiosyncrasy of the individual, the scintillations will have one character or another. They will be sallies of wit and humor; they will be flashes of poetry and eloquence; they will be constructions of dramatic fiction or of mechanical device, logical or philosophic abstractions, business projects, or scientific hypotheses, with trains of experimental consequences based thereon; they will be musical sounds, or images of plastic beauty or picturesqueness, or visions of moral harmony. But, whatever their differences may be, they will all agree in this,—that their genesis is sudden and, as it were, spontaneous. That is to say, the same premises would not, in the mind of another individual, have engendered just that conclusion; although, when the conclusion is offered to the other individual, he may thoroughly accept and enjoy it, and envy the brilliancy of him to whom it first occurred.

To Professor Jevons is due the great credit of having emphatically pointed out how the genius of discovery depends altogether on the number of these random notions and guesses which visit the investigator's mind. To be fertile in hypotheses is the first requisite, and to be willing to throw them away the moment experience contradicts them is the next. The Baconian method of collating tables of instances may be a useful aid at certain times. But one might as well expect a chemist's note-book to write down the name of the body analyzed, or a weather table to sum itself up into a prediction of probabilities of its own accord, as to hope that the mere fact of mental confrontation with a certain series of facts will be sufficient to make *any* brain conceive their law. The conceiving of the law is a spontaneous variation in the strictest sense of the term. It flashes out of one brain, and no other, because the instability of that brain is such as to tip and upset itself in just that particular direction. But the important thing to notice is that the good flashes and the bad flashes, the triumphant hypotheses and the absurd conceits, are on an exact equality in respect of their origin. Aristotle's absurd Physics and his immortal Logic flow from one source: the forces that produce the one produce the other. When walking along the street, thinking of the blue sky or the fine spring weather, I may either smile at some grotesque whim which occurs to me, or I may suddenly catch an intuition of the solution of a long-unsolved problem, which at that moment was far from my thoughts. Both notions are shaken out of the same reservoir,—the reservoir of a brain in which the reproduction of images in the relations of their outward persistence or frequency has long ceased to be the dominant law. But to the thought, when it is once engendered, the consecration of agreement with outward relations may come. The conceit perishes in a moment, and is forgotten. The scientific hypothesis arouses in me a fever of desire for verification. I read, write, experiment, consult experts. Everything corroborates my notion, which being then published in a book spreads from review to review and from mouth to mouth, till at last there is no doubt I am enshrined in the Pantheon of the great diviners of nature's ways. The environment *preserves* the conception which it was unable to *produce* in any brain less idiosyncratic than my own.

Now, the spontaneous upsettings of brains this way and that at particular moments into particular ideas and combinations are matched by their equally spontaneous permanent tiltings or saggings towards determinate directions. The humorous bent is quite characteristic; the sentimental one equally so. And the personal tone of each mind, which makes it more alive to certain classes of experience than others, more attentive to certain impressions, more open to certain reasons, is equally the result of that invisible and unimaginable play of the forces of growth within the nervous system which, irresponsibly to the environment, makes the brain peculiarly apt to function in a certain way. Here again the selection goes on. The products of the mind with the determined aesthetic bent please or displease the community. We adopt Wordsworth, and grow unsentimental and serene. We are fascinated by Schopenhauer, and learn from him the true luxury of woe. The adopted bent becomes a ferment in the community, and alters its tone. The alteration may be a benefit or a misfortune, for it is (*pace* Mr. Allen) a differentiation from within, which has to run the gauntlet of a larger environment's selective power. Civilized Languedoc, taking the tone of its scholars, poets, princes, and theologians, fell a prey to its rude Catholic environment in the Albigensian crusade. France in 1792, taking the tone of its St. Justs and Marats, plunged into its long career of unstable outward relations. Prussia in 1806, taking the tone of its Humboldts and its Steins, proved itself in the most signal way "adjusted" to its environment in 1872.

Mr. Spencer, in one of the strangest chapters of his Psychology, tries to show the necessary order in which the development of conceptions in the human race occurs. No abstract conception can be developed, according to him, until the outward experiences have reached a certain degree of heterogeneity, definiteness, coherence, and so forth.

Thus the belief in an unchanging order, the belief in *law,* is a belief of which the primitive man is absolutely incapable. . . . Experiences such as he receives furnish but few data for the conception of uniformity, whether as displayed in things or in relations. . . . The daily impressions, which the savage gets yield the notion very imperfectly, and in but few cases. Of all the objects around,—trees, stones, hills, pieces of water, clouds, and so forth,—most differ widely, . . . and few approach complete likeness so nearly as to make discrimination difficult. Even between animals of the same species it rarely happens that, whether alive or dead, they are presented in just the same attitudes. . . . It is only along with a gradual development of the arts . . . that there come frequent experiences of perfectly straight lines admitting of complete apposition, bringing the perceptions of equality and inequality. Still more devoid is savage life of the experiences which generate the conception of the uniformity of succession. The sequences observed from hour to hour and day to day seem anything but uniform; difference is a far more conspicuous trait among them. . . . So that if we contemplate primitive human life as a whole, we see that multiformity of sequence, rather than uniformity, is the notion which it tends to generate. . . . Only as fast as the practice of the arts develops the idea of measure can the consciousness of uniformity become clear. . . . Those conditions furnished by advancing civilization which make possible the notion of uniformity simultaneously make possible the notion of *exactness*. . . . Hence the primitive man has little experience which cultivates the consciousness of what we call *truth*. How closely allied this is to the consciousness which the practice of the arts cultivates is implied even in language. We speak of a true surface as well as a true statement. Exactness describes perfection in a mechanical fit, as well as perfect agreement between the results of calculations.

The whole burden of Mr. Spencer's book is to show the fatal way in which the mind, supposed passive, is moulded by its experiences of "outer relations." In this chapter, the yard-stick, the balance, the chronometer, and other machines and instruments come to figure among the "relations" external to the mind. Surely they are so, after they have been manufactured; but only because of the preservative power of the social environment. Originally all these things and all other institutions were flashes of genius in an individual head, of which the outer environment showed no sign. Adopted by the race and become its heritage, they then supply instigations to new geniuses whom they environ to make new inventions and discoveries; and so the ball of progress rolls. But take out the geniuses, or alter their idiosyncrasies, and what increasing uniformities will the environment show? We defy Mr. Spencer or any one else to reply.

The plain truth is that the "philosophy" of evolution (as distinguished from our special information about particular cases of change) is a metaphysical creed, and nothing else. It is a mood of contemplation, an emotional attitude, rather than a system of thought,—a mood which is old as the world, and which no refutation of any one incarnation of it (such as the Spencerian philosophy) will dispel; the mood of fatalistic pantheism, with intuition of the One and All, which was, and is, and ever shall be, and from whose womb each single thing proceeds. Far be it from us to speak slightingly here of so hoary and mighty a style of looking on the world as this. What we at present call scientific discoveries had nothing to do with bringing it to birth, nor can one easy conceive that they should ever give it its *quietus,* no matter how logically incompatible with its spirit the ultimate phenomenal distinctions which science accumulates should turn out to be. It can laugh at the phenomenal distinctions on which science is based, for it draws its vital breath from a region which—whether above or below—is at least altogether different from that in which science dwells. A critic, however, who cannot disprove the truth of the metaphysic creed, can at least raise his voice in protest against its disguising itself in "scientific" plumes. I think that all who have had the patience to follow me thus far will agree that the spencerian "philosophy" of social and intellectual progress is an obsolete anachronism, reverting to a pre-darwinian type of thought, just as the spencerian philosophy of "Force," effacing all the previous distinctions between actual and potential energy, momentum, work, force, mass, etc., which physicists have with so much agony achieved, carries us back to a pre-galilean age.

FRIEDRICH NIETZSCHE

FRIEDRICH WILHELM NIETZSCHE was born in Saxony on October 15, 1844. He came from a prosperous family of Protestant clergymen. Educated at Naumburg and Pforta, he entered the University of Bonn in 1864 as a student of theology and classical philology, but soon devoted himself exclusively to the latter study.

At the University Nietzsche fell under the influence of the philosophy of Schopenhauer (1788–1860), and he turned away from Christianity. He was appointed to a professorship at the University of Basel when he was twenty-five, and his enthusiasm for Schopenhauer and his love of music soon brought him into touch with Richard Wagner, then living near the Lake of Lucerne. Wagner's ideas and Neitzsche's researches into Greek antiquity resulted in *The Birth of Tragedy* (1871), a work severely condemned by orthodox German classical scholars. In semi-collaboration with Wagner, Nietzsche then published four polemical works (1873–76) which exhorted the Germans to restore themselves to the path of humane and rational development, from which he believed they had been deflected by the victories of 1864, 1866, and 1870, and by the subsequent growth of German jingoism and militarism.

Nietzsche then began to feel estranged from Wagner, believing that Wagner's art was a form of opium for a decadent generation. He also rejected Schopenhauer, finding in him strong religious tendencies which he would no longer accept. Nietzsche was never a strong man physically, and in 1879 he began to suffer from extreme ill health. He was forced to leave his professorship at Basel, receiving a small pension on which he lived in Northern Italy and on the French Riviera. The publication of his most important works followed: *Thus Spake Zarathustra* (1885), *Beyond Good and Evil* (1886) and *The Genealogy of Morals* (1887). His autobiography, *Ecco Homo,* dates from 1888.

Nietzsche was highly critical of the leveling tendencies of democratic society. He gave a new interpretation to Darwinism by regarding evolution as a process in which it is not the morally and spiritually best creatures which survive (as Spencer believed), but only those whose traits run true to a monotonous norm and thus cause the gradual disappearance of things of genuine value and the emergence of a dull mediocrity; without a dramatic breakaway from the past, history would not liberate man from an animal-like bondage to fear and worship of force and success. Nietzsche's entire philosophy—his frequently violent language, his condemnation of Christianity, democracy, and socialism, and his advocacy of radical aristocratic ideals—is a heroic attempt to remedy this condition. He proposed, first, the rejection of ideals, such as humility, protection of the weak, or habits of humdrum industry, when they rest on the sentimental supposition that the mere survival of masses of undistinguished individuals is the paramount good; second, the acceptance of great men performing splendid deeds—"supermen"—as the highest end product of history; and third, the liberation of such men from the opiates of Christianity and philosophic idealism for the sake of achieving this goal. Nietzsche took as the model for his "third morality" the "yea-saying" qualities of the pre-Socratic Greeks, because of their fusion of Dionysian passionate participation in life with Apollonian rational harmony and restraint.

Nietzsche's was a lone voice; he had no reliable followers or disciples in his lifetime. In 1889 he suffered a severe mental breakdown; he died on August 25, 1900, and was buried in the churchyard of his native village. After his death his sister helped make his reputation as an advocate of everything in modern life that Nietzsche himself despised. The following selection is from the 1956 Anchor Book version of *The Genealogy of Morals,* translated by Francis Golffing, and reprinted with the permission of its publisher, Doubleday and Company.

"GOOD AND EVIL," "GOOD AND BAD"

[First Essay]

I

THE ENGLISH psychologists to whom we owe the only attempts that have thus far been made to write a genealogy of morals are by no means posers of riddles, but the riddles they pose are themselves, and being incarnate have one advantage over their books—they are interesting. What are these English psychologists really after? One finds them always, whether intentionally or not, engaged in the same task of pushing into the foreground the nasty part of the psyche, looking for the effective motive forces of human development in the very last place we would wish to have them found, *e.g.,* in the inertia of habit, in forgetfulness, in the blind and fortuitous association of ideas; always in something that is purely passive, automatic, reflexive, molecular, and moreover, profoundly stupid. What drives these psychologists forever in the same direction? A secret, malicious desire to belittle humanity, which they do not acknowledge even to themselves? A pessimistic distrust, the suspiciousness of the soured idealist? Some petty resentment of Christianity (and Plato) which does not rise above the threshold of consciousness? Or could it be a prurient taste for whatever is embarrassing, painfully paradoxical, dubious and absurd in existence? Or is it, perhaps, a kind of stew —a little meanness, a little bitterness, a bit of anti-Christianity, a touch of prurience and desire for condiments? . . . But again, people tell me that these men are simply dull old frogs who hop and creep in and around man as in their own element—as though man were a bog. However, I am reluctant to listen to this, in fact I refuse to believe it; and if I may express a wish where I cannot express a conviction, I do wish wholeheartedly that things may be otherwise with these men—that these microscopic examiners of the soul may be really courageous, magnanimous, and proud animals, who know how to contain their emotions and have trained themselves to subordinate all wishful thinking to the truth—any truth, even a homespun, severe, ugly, obnoxious, un-Christian, unmoral truth. For such truths do exist. . . .

II

. . . . Now it is obvious to me, first of all, that their theory looks for the genesis of the concept *good* in the wrong place: the judgment *good* does not originate with those to whom the good has been done. Rather it was the "good" themselves, that is to say the noble, mighty, highly placed, and high-minded who decreed themselves and their actions to be good, *i.e.,* belonging to the highest rank, in contradistinction to all that was base, low-minded and plebeian. It was only this *pathos of distance* that authorized them to create values and name them—what was utility to them? The notion of utility seems singularly inept to account for such a quick jetting forth of supreme value judgments. Here we come face to face with the exact opposite of that lukewarmness which every scheming prudence, every utilitarian calculus presupposes—and not for a time only, for the rare, exceptional hour, but permanently. The origin of the opposites *good* and *bad* is to be found in the pathos of nobility and distance, representing the dominant temper of a higher, ruling class in relation to a lower, dependent one. (The lordly right of bestowing names is such that one would almost be justified in seeing the origin of language itself as an expression of the rulers' power. They say, "This *is* that or that"; they seal off each thing and action with a sound and thereby take symbolic possession of it.) Such an origin would suggest that there is no *a priori* necessity for associating the word *good* with altruistic deeds, as those moral psychologists are fond of claiming. In fact, it is only after aristocratic values have begun to decline that the egotism-altruism dichotomy takes possession of the human conscience; to use my own terms, it is the herd instinct that now asserts itself. Yet it takes quite a while for this instinct to assume such sway that it can reduce all moral valuations to that dichotomy—as is currently happening throughout Europe, where the prejudice equating the *moral, altruistic* and *disinterested* has assumed the obsessive force of an *idée fixe.*

III

Quite apart from the fact that this hypothesis about the origin of the value judgment *good* is historically untenable, its psychology is intrinsically unsound. Altruistic deeds were originally commended for their usefulness, but this original reason has now been forgotten—so the claim goes. How is such a forgetting conceivable? Has there ever been a point in history at which such deeds lost their usefulness? Quite the contrary, this usefulness has been apparent to every age, a thing that has been emphasized over and over again. Therefore, instead of being forgotten, it must have impressed itself on the consciousness with ever increasing clearness. The opposite theory is far more sensible, though this does not necessarily make it any the truer—the theory held by Herbert Spencer, for example, who considers the concept *good* qualitatively the same as the concepts *useful* or *practical;* so that in the judgments *good* and *bad,* humanity is said to have summed up and sanctioned precisely its unforgotten and unforgettable experiences of the *useful practical* and the *harmful impractical.* According to this theory, the *good* is that which all along has proved itself useful and which therefore may lay the highest claim to be considered valuable. As I have said, the derivation of this theory is suspect, but at least the explanation is self-consistent and psychologically tenable within its limits.

IV

The clue to the correct explanation was furnished me by the question "What does the etymology of the terms for good in various languages tell us?" I discovered that all these terms lead us back to the same conceptual transformation. The basic concept is always *noble* in the hierarchical, class sense, and from this has developed, by historical necessity, the concept *good* embracing nobility of mind, spiritual distinction. This development is strictly parallel to that other which eventually converted the notions *common, plebeian, base* into the notion *bad.* Here we have an important clue to the actual genealogy of morals; that it has not been hit upon earlier is due to the retarding influence which democratic prejudice has had upon all investigation of origins. This holds equally true with regard to the seemingly quite objective areas of natural science and physiology, though I cannot enlarge upon the question now. The amount of damage such prejudice is capable of doing in ethics and history, once it becomes inflamed with hatred, is clearly shown by the case of Buckle. Here we see the plebeian bias of the modern mind, which stems from England, erupt once again on its native soil with all the violence of a muddy volcano and all the vulgar and oversalted eloquence characteristic of volcanoes.

VI

Granting that political supremacy always gives rise to notions of spiritual supremacy, it at first creates no difficulties (though difficulties might arise later) if the ruling caste is also the priestly caste and elects to characterize itself by a term which reminds us of its priestly function. In this context we encounter for the first time concepts of *pure* and *impure* opposing each other as signs of class, and here, too, *good* and *bad* as terms no longer referring to class, develop before long. The reader should be cautioned, however, against taking pure and impure in too large or profound or symbolic a sense: all the ideas of ancient man were understood in a sense much more crude, narrow, superficial and non-symbolic than we are able to imagine today. The pure man was originally one who washed himself, who refused to eat certain foods entailing skin diseases, who did not sleep with the unwashed plebeian women, who held blood in abomination—hardly more than that. At the same time, given the peculiar nature of a priestly aristocracy, it becomes clear why the value opposites would early turn inward and become dangerously exacerbated; and in fact the tension between such opposites has opened abysses between man and man, over which not even an Achilles of free thought would leap without a shudder. There is from the very start something unwholesome about such priestly aristocracies, about their way of life, which is turned away from action and swings between brooding and emotional explosions: a way of life which may be seen as responsible for the morbidity and neurasthenia of priests of all periods. Yet are we not right in maintaining that the cures which they have developed for their morbidities have proved a hundred times more dangerous than the ills themselves? Humanity is still suffering from the aftereffects of those priestly cures. Think, for example, of certain forms of diet (abstinence from meat), fasting, sexual continence, escape "into the desert"; think further of the whole anti-sensual metaphysics of the priests, conducive to inertia and false refinement; of the self-hypnosis encouraged by the example of fakirs and Brahmans, where a glass knob and an *idée fixe* take the place of the god. And at last, supervening on all this, comes utter satiety, together with its radical remedy, nothingness—or God, for the desire for a mystical union with God is nothing other than the Buddhist's desire to sink himself in nirvana. Among the priests everything becomes more dangerous, not cures and specifics alone but also arrogance, vindictiveness, acumen, profligacy, love, the desire for power, disease. In all fairness it should be added, however, that only on this soil, the precarious soil of priestly existence, has man been able to develop into an interesting creature; that only here has the human mind grown both profound and evil; and it is in these two respects, after all, that man has proved his superiority over the rest of creation. . . .

VII

. . . . Human history would be a dull and stupid thing without the intelligence furnished by its impotents. Let us begin with the most striking example. Whatever else has been done to damage the powerful and great of this earth seems trivial compared with what the Jews have done, that priestly people who succeeded in avenging themselves on their enemies and oppressors by radically inverting all their values, that is, by an act of the most spiritual vengeance. This was a strategy entirely appropriate to a priestly people in whom vindictiveness had gone most deeply underground. It was the Jew who, with frightening consistency, dared to invert the aristocratic value equations good/noble/powerful/beautiful/happy/favored-of-the-gods and maintain, with the furious hatred of the underprivileged and impotent, that "only the poor, the powerless, are good; only the suffering, sick, and ugly, truly blessed. But you noble and mighty ones of the earth will be, to all eternity, the evil, the cruel, the avaricious, the godless, and thus the cursed and damned!" . . . We know who has fallen heir to this Jewish inversion of values. . . . In reference to the grand and unspeakably disastrous initiative which the Jews have launched by this most radical of all declarations of war, I wish to repeat a statement I made in a different context (*Beyond Good and Evil*), to wit, that it was the Jews who started the slave revolt in morals; a revolt with two millennia of history behind it, which we have lost sight of today simply because it has triumphed so completely.

X

The slave revolt in morals begins by rancor turning creative and giving birth to values—the rancor of beings who, deprived of the direct outlet of action, compensate by an imaginary vengeance. All truly noble morality grows out of triumphant self-affirmation. Slave ethics, on the other hand, begins by saying *no* to an "outside," an "other," a non-self, and that *no* is its creative act. This reversal of direction of the evaluating look, this invariable looking outward instead of inward, is a fundamental feature of rancor. Slave ethics requires for its inception a sphere different from and hostile to its own. Physiologically speaking, it requires an outside stimulus in order to act at all; all its action is reaction. The opposite is true of aristocratic valuations: such values grow and act spontaneously, seeking out their contraries only in order to affirm themselves even more gratefully and delightedly. Here the negative concepts, *humble, base, bad,* are late, pallid counterparts of the positive, intense and passionate credo, "We noble, good, beautiful, happy ones." Aristocratic valuations may go amiss and do violence to reality, but this happens only with regard to spheres which they do not know well, or from the knowledge of which they austerely guard themselves: the aristocrat will, on occasion, misjudge a sphere which he holds in contempt, the sphere of the common man, the people. On the other hand we should remember that the emotion of contempt, of looking down, provided that it falsifies at all, is as nothing compared with the falsification which suppressed hatred, impotent vindictiveness, effects upon its opponent, though only in effigy. There is in all contempt too much casualness and nonchalance, too much blinking of facts and impatience, and too much inborn gaiety for it ever to make of its object a downright caricature and monster. . . .

[Second Essay]

VI

It is in the sphere of contracts and legal obligations that the moral universe of guilt, conscience, and duty ("sacred" duty) took its inception. Those beginnings were liberally sprinkled with blood, as are the beginnings of everything great on earth. (And may we not say that ethics has never lost its reek of blood and torture—not even in Kant, whose categorical imperative smacks of cruelty?) It was then that the sinister knitting together of the two ideas *guilt* and *pain* first occurred, which by now have become quite inextricable. Let us ask once more: in what sense could pain constitute repayment of a debt? In the sense that to make someone suffer was a supreme pleasure. In exchange for the damage he had incurred, including his displeasure, the creditor received an extraordinary amount of pleasure; something which he prized the more highly the more it disaccorded with his social rank. I am merely throwing this out as a suggestion, for it is difficult, and embarrassing as well, to get to the bottom of such underground developments. To introduce crudely the concept of vengeance at this point would obscure matters rather than clarify them, since the idea of vengeance leads us straight back to our original problem: how can the infliction of pain provide satisfaction? The delicacy—even more, the *tartufferie*—of domestic animals like ourselves shrinks from imagining clearly to what extent cruelty constituted the collective delight of older mankind, how much it was an ingredient of all their joys, or how naïvely they manifested their cruelty, how they considered disinterested malevolence (Spinoza's *sympathia malevolens*) a normal trait, something to which one's conscience could assent heartily. Close observation will spot numerous survivals of this oldest and most thorough human delight in our own culture. In both *Daybreak* and *Beyond Good and Evil* I have pointed to that progressive sublimation and apotheosis of cruelty which not only characterizes the whole history of higher culture, but in a sense constitutes it. Not so very long ago, a royal wedding or great public celebration would have been incomplete without executions, tortures, or *autos da fé;* a noble household without some person whose office it was to serve as a butt for everyone's malice and cruel teasing. (Perhaps the reader will recall Don Quixote's sojourn at the court of the Duchess. *Don Quixote* leaves a bitter taste in our mouths today; we almost quail in reading it. This would have seemed very strange to Cervantes and to his contemporaries, who read the work with the clearest conscience in the world, thought it the funniest of books, and almost died laughing over it.) To behold suffering gives pleasure, but to cause another to suffer affords an even greater pleasure. This severe statement expresses an old, powerful, human, all too human sentiment—though the monkeys too might endorse it, for it is reported that they heralded and preluded man in the devising of bizarre cruelties. There is no feast without cruelty, as man's entire history attests. Punishment, too, has its festive features.

XVI

I can no longer postpone giving tentative expression to my own hypothesis concerning the origin of "bad conscience." It is one that may fall rather strangely on our ears and that requires close meditation. I take bad conscience to be a deep-seated malady to which man succumbed under the pressure of the most profound transformation he ever underwent—the one that made him once and for all a sociable and pacific creature. Just as happened in the case of those sea creatures who were forced to become land animals in order to survive, these semi-animals, happily adapted to the wilderness, to war, free roaming, and adventure, were forced to change their nature. Of a sudden they found all their instincts devalued, unhinged. They must walk on legs and carry themselves, where before the water had carried them: a terrible heaviness weighed upon them. They felt inapt for the simplest manipulations, for in this new, unknown world they could no longer count on the guidance of their unconscious drives. They were forced to think, deduce, calculate, weigh cause and effect—unhappy people, reduced to their weakest, most fallible organ, their consciousness! I doubt that there has ever been on earth such a feeling of misery, such a leaden discomfort. It was not that those old instincts had abruptly ceased making their demands; but now their satisfaction was rare and difficult. For the most part they had to depend on new, covert satisfactions. All instincts that are not allowed free play turn inward. This is what

I call man's interiorization; it alone provides the soil for the growth of what is later called man's *soul*. Man's interior world, originally meager and tenuous, was expanding in every dimension, in proportion as the outward discharge of his feelings was curtailed. The formidable bulwarks by means of which the polity protected itself against the ancient instincts of freedom (punishment was one of the strongest of these bulwarks) caused those wild, extravagant instincts to turn in upon man. Hostility, cruelty, the delight in persecution, raids, excitement, destruction all turned against their begetter. Lacking external enemies and resistances, and confined within an oppressive narrowness and regularity, man began rending, persecuting, terrifying himself, like a wild beast hurling itself against the bars of its cage. This languisher, devoured by nostalgia for the desert, who had to turn *himself* into an adventure, a torture chamber, an insecure and dangerous wilderness—this fool, this pining and desperate prisoner, became the inventor of "bad conscience." Also the generator of the greatest and most disastrous of maladies, of which humanity has not to this day been cured: his sickness of himself, brought on by the violent severance from his animal past, by his sudden leap and fall into new layers and conditions of existence, by his declaration of war against the old instincts that had hitherto been the foundation of his power, his joy, and his awesomeness. Let me hasten to add that the phenomenon of an animal soul turning in upon itself, taking arms against itself, was so novel, profound, mysterious, contradictory, and pregnant with possibility, that the whole complexion of the universe was changed thereby. This spectacle (and the end of it is not yet in sight) required a divine audience to do it justice. It was a spectacle too sublime and paradoxical to pass unnoticed on some trivial planet. Henceforth man was to figure among the most unexpected and breathtaking throws in the game of dice played by Heraclitus' great "child," be he called Zeus or chance. Man now aroused an interest, a suspense, a hope, almost a conviction—as though in him something were heralded, as though he were not a goal but a way, an interlude, a bridge, a great promise.

XVIII

We should guard against taking too dim a view of this phenomenon simply because it is both ugly and painful. After all, the same will to power which in those violent artists and organizers created polities, in the "labyrinth of the heart"—more pettily, to be sure, and in inverse direction—created negative ideals and humanity's bad conscience. Except that now the material upon which this great natural force was employed was man himself, his old animal self—and not, as in that grander and more spectacular phenomenon—his fellow man. This secret violation of the self, this artist's cruelty, this urge to impose on recalcitrant matter a form, a will, a distinction, a feeling of contradiction and contempt, this sinister task of a soul divided against itself, which makes itself suffer for the pleasure of suffering, this most energetic "bad conscience"—has it not given birth to a wealth of strange beauty and affirmation? Has it not given birth to beauty itself? Would beauty exist if ugliness had not first taken cognizance of itself, not said to itself, "I am ugly"? This hint will serve, at any rate, to solve the riddle of why contradictory terms such as *selflessness, self-denial, self-sacrifice* may intimate an ideal, a beauty. Nor will the reader doubt henceforth that the *joy* felt by the self-denying, self-sacrificing, selfless person was from the very start a *cruel* joy.—So much for the origin of altruism as a moral value. Bad conscience, the desire for self-mortification, is the wellspring of all altruistic values.

XXII

By now the reader will have guessed what has really been happening behind all these façades. Man, with his need for self-torture, his sublimated cruelty resulting from the cooping up of his animal nature within a polity, invented bad conscience in order to hurt himself, after the blocking of the more natural outlet of his cruelty. Then this guilt-ridden man seized upon religion in order to exacerbate his self-torment to the utmost. The thought of being in God's debt became his new instrument of torture. He focused in God the last of the opposites he could find to his true and inveterate animal instincts, making these a sin against God (hostility, rebellion against the "Lord," the "Father," the "Creator"). He stretched himself upon the contradiction "God" and "Devil" as on a rack. He projected all his denials of self, nature, naturalness out of himself as affirmations, as true being, embodiment, reality, as God (the divine Judge and Executioner), as transcendence, as eternity, as endless torture, as hell, as the infinitude of guilt and punishment. In such psychological cruelty we see an insanity of the *will* that is without parallel: man's will to find himself guilty, and unredeemably so; his will to believe that he might be punished to all eternity without ever expunging his guilt; his will to poison the very foundation of things with the problem of guilt and punishment and thus to cut off once and for all his escape from this labyrinth of obsession; his will to erect an ideal (God's holiness) in order to assure himself of his own absolute unworthiness. What a mad, unhappy animal is man! What strange notions occur to him; what perversities, what paroxysms of nonsense, what bestialities of idea burst from him, the moment he is prevented ever so little from being a beast of action! . . . All this is exceedingly curious and interesting, but dyed with such a dark, somber, enervating sadness that one must resolutely tear away one's gaze. Here, no doubt, is sickness, the most terrible sickness that has wasted man thus far. And if one is still able to hear—but how few these days have ears to hear it!—in this night of torment and absurdity the cry *love* ring out, the cry of rapt longing, of redemption in love, he must turn away with a shudder of invincible horror. . . . Man harbors too much horror; the earth has been a lunatic asylum for too long. . . .

XXIV

It is clear that I am concluding this essay with three unanswered questions. It may occur to some reader to ask me, "Are you constructing an ideal or destroying one?" I would ask him, in turn, whether he ever reflected upon the price that had to be paid for the introduction of every new ideal on earth? On how much of reality, in each instance, had to be slandered and misconceived, how much of falsehood ennobled, how many consciences disturbed, how many gods sacrificed? For the raising of an altar requires the breaking of an altar: this is a law—let anyone who can prove me wrong. We moderns have a millennial heritage of conscience-vivisection and cruelty to the animals in ourselves. This is our most ancient habit, our most consummate artistry perhaps, in any case our greatest refinement, our special fare. Man has looked for so long with an evil eye upon his natural inclinations that they have finally become inseparable from "bad conscience." A converse effort can be imagined, but who has the strength for it? It would consist of associating all the *unnatural* inclinations—the longing for what is unworldly, opposed to the senses, to instinct, to nature, to the animal in us, all the anti-biological and earth-calumniating ideals—with bad conscience. To whom, today, may such hopes and pretensions address themselves? The *good* man, in particular, would be on the other side; and of course all the comfortable, resigned, vain, moony, weary people. Does anything give greater offense and separate one more thoroughly from others than to betray something of the strictness and dignity with which one treats oneself? But how kind and accommodating the world becomes the moment we act like all the rest and let ourselves go! To accomplish that aim, different minds are needed than are likely to appear in this age of ours: minds strengthened by struggles and victories, for whom conquest, adventure, danger, even pain, have become second nature. Minds accustomed to the keen atmosphere of high altitudes, to wintry walks, to ice and mountains in every sense. Minds possessed of a sublime kind of malice, of that self-assured recklessness which is a sign of strong health. What is needed, in short, is just superb health. Is such health still possible today?

But at some future time, a time stronger than our effete, self-doubting present, the true Redeemer will come, whose surging creativity will not let him rest in any shelter or hiding place, whose solitude will be misinterpreted as a flight from reality, whereas it will in fact be a dwelling *on*, a dwelling *in* reality —so that when he comes forth into the light he may bring with him the redemption of that reality from the curse placed upon it by a lapsed ideal. This man of the future, who will deliver us both from a lapsed ideal and from all that this ideal has spawned—violent loathing, the will to extinction, nihilism —this great and decisive stroke of midday, who will make the will free once more and restore to the earth its aim, and to man his hope; this anti-Christ and anti-nihilist, conqueror of both God and Unbeing—*one day he must come*. . . .

[*Third Essay*]

XIII

But let us return to our argument. The kind of inner split we have found in the ascetic, who pits "life against life," is nonsense, not only in psychological terms, but also physiologically speaking. Such a split can only be *apparent;* it must be a kind of provisional expression, a formula, an adaptation, a psychological misunderstanding of something for which terms have been lacking to designate its true nature. A mere stopgap to fill a hiatus in human understanding. Let me state what I consider to be the actual situation. The ascetic ideal arises from the protective and curative instinct of a life that is degenerating and yet fighting tooth and nail for its preservation. It points to a partial physiological blocking and exhaustion, against which the deepest vital instincts, still intact, are battling doggedly and resourcefully. The ascetic ideal is one of their weapons. The situation, then, is exactly the opposite from what the worshipers of that ideal believe it to be. Life employs asceticism in its desperate struggle against death; the ascetic ideal is a dodge for the preservation of life. The ubiquitousness and power of that ideal, especially wherever men have adopted civilized forms of life, should impress upon us one great, palpable fact: the persistent morbidity of civilized man, his biological struggle against death, or to put it more exactly, against *taedium vitae,* exhaustion, the longing for "the end." The ascetic priest is an incarnation of the wish to be different, to be elsewhere; he is that wish, raised to its highest power, its most passionate intensity. And it is precisely the intensity of his wishing that forges the fetter binding him to this earth. At the same time he becomes an instrument for bettering the human condition, since by this intensity he is enabled to maintain in life the vast flock of defeated, disgruntled sufferers and self-tormentors, whom he leads instinctively like a shepherd. In other words, the ascetic priest, seemingly life's enemy and great negator, is in truth one of the major conserving and affirmative forces. . . . But what about the sources of man's morbidity? For certainly man is sicker, less secure, less stable, less firmly anchored than any other animal; he is the *sick* animal. But has he not also been more daring, more defiant, more inventive than all the other animals together?—man, the great experimenter on himself, eternally unsatisfied, vying with the gods, the beasts, and with nature for final supremacy; man, unconquered to this day, still unrealized, so agitated by his own teeming energy that his future digs like spurs into the flesh of every present moment. . . . How could such a brave and resourceful animal but be the most precarious, the most profoundly sick of all the sick beasts of the earth? There have been many times when man has clearly had enough; there have been whole epidemics of "fed-upness" (for example, around 1348, the time of the Dance of Death) but even this tedium, this weariness, this satiety breaks from him with such vehemence that at once it forges a new fetter to existence. As if by magic, his negations produce a wealth of tenderer affirmations. When this master of destruction, of self-destruction, wounds himself, it is that very wound that forces him to live.

XXIII

The ascetic ideal has corrupted not only health and taste, but a good many things besides—if I were to try to enumerate them all there would never be an end. But my purpose here is not to show what the ideal has effected but only what is signifies, suggests, what lies behind it, beneath it, and hidden within it; the things it has expressed, however vaguely and provisionally. It was only with this purpose in view that I afforded my reader a rapid view of its tremendous consequences, some of which have been disastrous. I wanted to prepare him for the last and, to me, most terrible aspect of the question "What does the ascetic ideal signify? What is the meaning of its incredible *power?* Why have people yielded to it to such an extent? Why have they not resisted it more firmly?" The ascetic ideal expresses a *will:* where do we find a contrary ideal expressing a contrary will? The goal of the ascetic ideal is so universal that, compared with it, all other human interests appear narrow and petty. It orients epochs, nations, individuals inexorably toward that one goal, permitting no alternative interpretation or goal. It rejects, denies, affirms, confirms exclusively in terms of its own interpretation—and has there ever been a system of interpretations more consistently reasoned out? It submits to no other power but believes in its absolute superiority, convinced that no power exists on earth but receives meaning and value from it. . . . Where do we find the antithesis to this closed system? Why are we unable to find it? . . . People say to me that such a counter-ideal exists, that not only has it waged a long, successful battle against asceticism but to all intents and purposes triumphed over it. The whole body of modern scholarship is cited in support of this—that modern scholarship which, as a truly realistic philosophy, clearly believes only in itself, has the courage of its convictions, and has managed splendidly thus far to get along without God, transcendence and restrictive virtues. But such noisy propaganda talk quite fails to impress me. These trumpeters of the "real" are poor musicians. Their voices do not arise out of any authentic depths, the depths of a scholarly conscience—for the scholarly conscience today is an abyss. In the mouths of such trumpeters the word *scholarship* is impudence, indeed blasphemy. The case is exactly the opposite of what is claimed here: scholarship today has neither faith in itself nor an ideal beyond itself, and wherever it is still passion, love, ardor, suffering, it represents not the opposite of the ascetic ideal but, in fact, its noblest and latest form. Does this sound strange to you? There are plenty of decent, modest, hard-working scholars amongst us, who seem perfectly content with their little niche and for this reason proclaim, rather immodestly, that everyone should be content with things as they are these days—especially in the humanities and in science, where so much that is useful remains to be done. I quite agree. I would be the last to want to spoil the pleasure these honest workers take in their work, for I like what they are doing. And yet the fact that people work very hard at their disciplines and are content in their work in no way proves that learning as a whole today has an aim, an ideal, a passionate belief. As I have just said, the reverse is true. Wherever it is not simply the most recent manifestation of the ascetic ideal (and those are rare, noble, special cases, much too special to affect the general verdict), learning today is a hiding place for all manner of maladjustment, lukewarmness, self-depreciation, guilty conscience. Its restless activity thinly veils a lack of ideals, the want of a great love, dissatisfaction with a continence imposed on it from without. How much does learning hide these days, or, at least, how much does it wish to hide! The solidity of our best scholars, their automatic industry, their heads smoking night and day, their very skill and competence: all these qualities betoken more often than not a desire to hide and suppress something. Haven't we all grown familiar with learning as a drug? Scholars are naturally pained by such a view, as everyone knows to his cost who has had close contact with them. A chance remark will hurt them to the quick. We exasperate our learned friends at the very moment we try to honor them; we unleash their fury merely because we are too insensitive to guess that we have before us sufferers unwilling to admit their suffering to themselves, stupefied and unconscious men, mortally afraid of regaining their consciousness. . . .

XXIV

Let us now look at those special cases I mentioned a moment ago, those few idealists still surviving among the philosophers, scholars, and scientists of today. Is it perhaps among them that we must look for the effective antagonists of the ascetic ideal? This is, in fact, what these "unbelievers" (for they are agnostics, all of them) believe themselves to be. Such faith as remains to them is invested in their conviction that they oppose the ascetic ideal. Whenever that issue arises they turn solemn, and their words and gestures become impassioned. But does that prove that what they believe is true? We whose business it is to *inquire* have gradually grown suspicious of all believers. Our mistrust has trained us to reason in a way diametrically opposed to the traditional one: wherever we find strength of faith too prominent, we are led to infer a lack of demonstrability, even something improbable, in the matter to be believed. We have no intention of denying that man is saved by faith, but for this very reason we deny that faith proves anything. A strong, saving faith casts suspicion on the object of that faith; so far from establishing its "truth," it establishes a certain probability—of deception. How does all this apply to our case?—These proud solitaries, absolutely intransigent in their insistence on intellectual precision, these hard, strict, continent, heroic minds, all these wan atheists, Antichrists, immoralists, nihilists, sceptics, suspenders of judgment, embodying whatever remains of intellectual conscience today— are they really as free from the ascetic ideal as they imagine themselves to be? I would tell them something which they cannot see because they are too close to themselves: it is they, precisely, who today represent the ascetic ideal; it is they who are its most subtle exponents, its scouts and advance guard, its most dangerous and elusive *temptation*. If I have ever solved a riddle aright, I would wager that this is a sound guess! These men are a long way from being *free* spirits, because they still believe in truth. . . . When the Christian crusaders in the East happened upon the invincible Society of Assassins, that order of free spirits *par excellence,* whose lower ranks observed an obedience stricter than that of any monastic order, they must have got some hint of the slogan reserved for the highest ranks, which ran, "Nothing is true; everything is permitted." Here we have real freedom, for the notion of truth itself has been disposed of. Has any Christian freethinker ever dared to follow out the labyrinthine consequences of this slogan? Has any of them ever truly experienced the Minotaur inhabiting that maze? I have my doubts. In fact I know none has. Nothing could be more foreign to our intransigents than true freedom and detachment; they are securely tied to their belief in truth—

more securely than anyone else. I know all these things only too well: the venerable "philosopher's continence" which such a faith imposes, the intellectual stoicism which in the end renounces denial quite as strictly as it does affirmation, the desire to stop short at the brute fact, the fatalism of *petits faits* (with which French scholarship nowadays tries to gain an advantage over German), the renunciation of all exegesis (that is to say of all those violations, adjustments, abridgments, omissions, substitutions, which among them constitute the business of interpretation). These things, taken together, spell asceticism every bit as much as does the reunuciation of sensuality; they are, in fact, but a special mode of such renunciation. As for the absolute will to truth which begets such abstinence, it is nothing other than a belief in the ascetic ideal in its most radical form, though an unconscious one. It is the belief in a metaphysical value, in that absolute value of "the true" which stems from the ascetic ideal and stands or falls with it. Strictly speaking, there is no such thing as a science without assumptions; the very notion of such a science is unthinkable, absurd. A philosophy, a "faith" is always needed to give science a direction, a meaning, a limit, a *raison d'être*. (Whoever wants to invert the procedure, that is, put philosophy on a "strictly scientific basis" must first stand not only philosophy but truth itself on its head: the worst breach of etiquette imaginable in the case of two such venerable females.) To quote from a book of my own, *The Gay Science:* "The truthful man (using "truth" in that audacious sense science presupposes) is led to assume a world which is totally other than that of life, nature and history. Does this not mean that he is forced to deny this world of ours? . . . The faith on which our belief in science rests is still a metaphysical faith. Even we students of today, who are atheists and anti-metaphysicians, light our torches at the flame of a millennial faith: the Christian faith, which was also the faith of Plato, that God is truth, and truth divine. . . . But what if this equation becomes less and less credible, if the only things that may still be viewed as divine are error, blindness, and lies; if God himself turns out to be our *longest* lie?" Here let us pause and take thought. It appears that today inquiry itself stands in need of justification (by which I do not mean to say that such justification can be found). In this connection let us glance at both the oldest and the most recent philosophers: to a man they lack all awareness that the will to truth itself needs to be justified. There is a gap here in every philosophy—how are we to explain it? By the fact that the ascetic ideal has so far governed all philosophy; that truth was premised as Being, as God, as supreme sanction; that truth was not allowed to be called in question. But once we withhold our faith from the God of the ascetic ideal a new problem poses itself, the problem of the value of truth. The will to truth must be scrutinized; our business now is tentatively to question the will to truth. . . .

XXV

. . . . Simply examine all those epochs in a nation's history when the scholar assumes a prominent position: those are always the crepuscular times of fatigue and decline; the times of reckless health, instinctual security, confidence in the future, are over. It does not augur well for a culture when the mandarins are in the saddle, any more than does the advent of democracy, of arbitration courts in place of wars, of equal rights for women, of a religion of pity—to mention but a few of the symptoms of declining vitality. (Inquiry seen as a problem; what does inquiry signify: cf. my preface to *The Birth of Tragedy*.) Let us honestly face the fact that inquiry is the best ally of the ascetic ideal, precisely because it is the least conscious, least spontaneous, most secret of allies. All through history the "poor in spirit" and the scholarly antagonists of the ideal have played the same game (one must beware of viewing the latter as the "spiritually rich." This they are not, rather they are the hectic consumptives of the spirit.) As for their famous victories, there have doubtless been such—but victories over what? The ascetic ideal has always emerged unscathed. The only thing inquiry has accomplished has been to raze wall after wall of outer fortifications which the ascetic ideal had succeeded in building around itself, to the detriment of its looks. Or does anyone seriously believe that the defeat of, say, theological astronomy spelled the defeat of the ideal? Does anyone believe that man has grown less hungry for a transcendental solution to life's riddle simply because life has become more casual, peripheral, expendable, in the visible order of things? Has not man's determination to belittle himself developed apace precisely since Copernicus? Alas, his belief that he was unique and irreplaceable in the hierarchy of beings had been shattered for good: he had become an animal, quite literally and without reservations; he, who, according to his earlier belief, had been almost God ("child of God," "God's own image"). Ever since Copernicus man has been rolling down an incline, faster and faster, away from the center— whither? Into the void? Into the "piercing sense of his emptiness"? But has not this been precisely the most direct route to his old ideal? All science (and by no means astronomy alone, concerning whose humiliating and discrediting effect Kant has left us a remarkable confession—"It destroys my importance") all science, natural as well as *unnatural* (by which I mean the self-scrutiny of the "knower") is now determined to talk man out of his former respect for himself, as though that respect had been nothing but a bizarre presumption.

We might even say that man's hard-won self-contempt has brought with it its own special brand of pride, an austere form of stoic *ataraxia,* his last and most serious claim to a sense of respect (for in disrespecting we show that we still maintain a *sense* of respect). Can this really be called opposition to the ascetic ideal? Does anyone seriously maintain today (as theologians did for a while) that Kant's "victory" over the conceptual apparatus of dogmatic theology (God, soul, freedom, immortality) has hurt that ideal? (I leave out of account the question whether Kant himself intended anything of the sort.) But it is certainly true that, since Kant, transcendentalists of every persuasion have had *carte blanche;* they have become emancipated from theology; Kant has indicated to them the secret path whereon, without interference and in keeping with scholarly decorum, they may gratify their hearts' desires. Similarly, does anybody now hold it against the agnostics, those admirers of mystery and the unknown, that they worship the question mark itself as their god? (Xaver Doudan once wrote of the ravages worked by *l'habitude d'admirer l'inintelligible au lieu de rester tout simplement dans l'inconnu.* He thought that the ancients were innocent of that habit.) Assuming that whatever man apprehends not only fails to satisfy his wishes but, indeed, contradicts and confounds them, what a divine expedient to make our intellect, rather than our appetites, responsible for this state of affairs! "There is no true intellection; consequently there must be a God"—what a newfangled syllogistic refinement! what a triumph of the ascetic ideal!

XXVI

Do, perhaps, our modern writers on history reflect a sounder attitude, and one that inspires greater confidence? Their major claim is to be a mirror of events; they reject teleology; they no longer want to "prove" anything; they disdain to act the part of judges (and in this they show a measure of good taste); they neither affirm nor deny, they simply ascertain, describe. . . . All this is very ascetic but even more nihilistic, let us be frank about it! The modern historian has a sad, hard, but determined stare, a stare that looks *beyond,* like that of a lonely arctic explorer (so as not to have to look into the matter, perhaps, or not to have to look back?) There is nothing here but snow; all life is hushed. The last crows whose voices are still heard are "What for?" "In vain," and *"nada."* Nothing thrives any longer except, perhaps, Czarist metapolitics and Tolstoian *pity.* But there is another kind of historian today, perhaps even more modern—an epicurean, philandering kind, who ogles life as much as he does the ascetic ideal, who wears the word "artist" like a kid glove, and who has entirely engrossed the praise of contemplation. How we regret even ascetics and wintry landscapes once these clever fops come in view! No thank you! The devil take that whole contemplative tribe! I would much rather roam with the historical nihilists through their cold, gloomy fogs. In fact, if I were put to the choice, I might even prefer to listen to an entirely a-historical, anti-historical fellow, like that Dühring, whose music now intoxicates a newly emerging group of "simple souls," the anarchic fringe of our educated proletariat. Our calm, contemplative historians are a hundred times worse than that. I can think of nothing as nauseating as such an "objective" armchair, such a perfumed epicure of history, half priest, half satyr, *à la Renan,* who by his falsetto voice betrays what is missing, in what place the cruel Fates have applied their surgical shears. This outrages my taste, and my patience as well. Let him keep his patience who has nothing to lose here. As for me, such a sight makes me furious, such "spectators" embitter me against the spectacle more than the spectacle itself —meaning history, of course—and put me willy-nilly into an anacreontic mood. Nature, who gave the bull his horns, the lion his fangs, gave me a foot—for what? . . . For crushing, by Anacreon, and not simply for running away! For crushing the rotten armchairs, the craven complacency, the prurient eunuchdom that paws over history, the ogling of ascetic ideals, the hypocritical "fairness" of impotence. I have great respect for the ascetic ideal so long as it really believes in itself and is not merely a masquerade. But I have no patience with those coquettish dung beetles who are so eager to smell of the infinite that, before long, the infinite comes to smell of dung. I have no patience with mummies who try to mimic life, with worn-out, used-up people who swathe themselves in wisdom so as to appear "objective," with histrionic agitators who wear magic hoods on their straw heads, with ambitious artists who try to pass for ascetics and priests yet are, at bottom, only tragic buffoons. And I am equally out of patience with those newest speculators in idealism called anti-Semites, who parade as Christian-Aryan worthies and endeavor to stir up all the asinine elements of the nation by that cheapest of propaganda tricks, a moral attitude. (The ease with which any wretched imposture succeeds in present-day Germany may be attributed to the progressive stultification of the German mind. The reason for this general spread of inanity may be found in a diet composed entirely of newspapers, politics, beer, and Wagner's music. Our national vanity and hemmed-in situation and the shaking palsy of current ideas have each done their bit to prepare us for such a diet.) Europe today is extremely rich and inventive in stimulants; in fact, it depends entirely on stimulants and distilled spirits. This may explain the prevalence of counterfeit ideals, those most rarefied distillations of the spirit, as well as the stale quasi-alcoholic fumes one breathes wherever one goes. I wonder how many cargoes of fake idealism, fake heroism, and fake eloquence, how many tons of compassion liqueur (brand: *La Religion de la Souffrance*), how many stilts of "virtuous indignation" for the use of the intellectually flat-footed, how many comedians of Christian morality Europe would have to export today in order to clear its atmosphere. . . . Obviously such overproduction opens up splendid commercial possibilities: a good business could be done in small ideal-idols and the "idealists" that go with them— I hope someone sufficiently enterprising will take up the suggestion. The opportunity to "idealize" the entire globe is in our hands! But why speak of enterprise here at all? The only things needed are the hands, ingenuous, very ingenuous hands. . . .

XXVII

. . . . The one thing I hope I have made clear here is that even at the highest intellectual level the ascetic ideal is still being subverted. Great is the number of those who travesty or counterfeit it—let us be on our guard against them; whilst in all places where a strict, potent, scrupulous spirit still survives every trace of idealism seems to have vanished. The popular term for such abstinence is *atheism*—but the term does scant justice to the will to truth which motivates its votaries. Yet that will, that *residual* ideal, constitutes, believe me, the ideal itself in its strictest and most sublimated form, absolutely esoteric, divested of all trappings: the essence, not the residue. Honest and intransigent atheism (the only air breathed today by the élite of this world) is thus not opposed to asceticism, all appearances to the contrary. Rather it is one of the last evolutionary phases of that ideal, one of its natural and logical consequences. It is the catastrophe, inspiring of respect, of a discipline in truth that has lasted for two millennia and which now prohibits the lie implicit in monotheistic belief. (The same evolution has gone on in India, quite independently of our own, thus affording substantiating proof. There the identical ideal has compelled the identical conclusion. The decisive phase was reached five centuries before the Christian era, with Buddha or, more accurately, with the Sankhya philosophy, later popularized by the Buddha and codified into a religion.) What is it, in truth, that has triumphed over the Christian God? The answer may be found in my *Gay Science*: "The Christian ethics with its key notion, ever more strictly applied, of truthfulness; the casuistic finesse of the Christian conscience, translated and sublimated into the scholarly conscience, into intellectual integrity to be maintained at all costs; the interpretation of nature as a proof of God's beneficent care; the interpretation of history to the glory of divine providence, as perpetual testimony of a moral order and moral ends; the interpretation of individual experience as preordained, purposely arranged for the salvation of the soul—all these are now things of the past: they revolt our consciences as being indecent, dishonest, cowardly, effeminate. It is this rigor, if anything, that makes us good Europeans and the heirs of Europe's longest, most courageous self-conquest." All great things perish of their own accord, by an act of self-cancellation: so the law of life decrees. In the end it is always the legislator himself who must heed the command *patere legem, quam ipse tulisti.* Thus Christianity as dogma perished by its own ethics, and in the same way Christianity as ethics must perish; we are standing on the threshold of this event. After drawing a whole series of conclusions, Christian truthfulness must now draw its strongest conclusion, the one by which it shall do away with itself. This will be accomplished by Christianity's asking itself, "What does all will to truth signify?" Here I touch once more on my problem, on our problem, my unknown friends (for I do not yet know whether I have any friends among you): what would our existence amount to were it not for this, that the will to truth has been forced to examine itself? It is by this dawning self-consciousness of the will to truth that ethics must now perish. This is the great spectacle of a hundred acts that will occupy Europe for the next two centuries, the most terrible and problematical but also the most hopeful of spectacles. . . .

BERTRAND RUSSELL

BERTRAND ARTHUR WILLIAM RUSSELL was born in 1872. His grandfather was Lord John Russell and his godfather John Stuart Mill. He was left an orphan at the age of three, and was raised by his grandmother at Pembroke Lodge, where he studied under private tutors. In 1890 Russell entered Trinity College, Cambridge, where he took first class honors in philosophy. He was elected a fellow of Trinity in 1895, although he did not go directly into residence. After a short term as attaché in 1894 at the British embassy in Paris, he traveled to Germany, where he spent some months studying social democracy; he published his study of *German Social Democracy* in 1896.

Russell visited the Mathematical Congress at Paris in 1900 with his friend Alfred North Whitehead. Impressed with the work of the Italian mathematicians, Russell began his own studies, and in 1903 published *The Principles of Mathematics*. The first volume of the extraordinary work, *Principia Mathematica,* written with Whitehead's collaboration, was published in 1910. That year he returned to Trinity as a lecturer.

During the First World War Russell was a pacifist and a leader in the "No Conscription" society. His activities during this period brought him into serious conflict with the authorities: he was fined, lost his post at Trinity, was refused a passport to go to America to teach at Harvard, and eventually was imprisoned for six months because of a pacifist article he published. While in prison, he wrote his *Introduction to Mathematical Philosophy* (1919).

In the years after the war his travels were as wide as the range of his writing. His contributions to modern study in logic, mathematics, and the theory of knowledge have been great achievements but he has been protean in his interests and a voluminous and always controversial writer on politics and ethics. His famous skepticism and hatred of dogma have their most notable expression in this early essay, which first appeared in the *Independent Review* for December, 1903.

A FREE MAN'S WORSHIP

To DR. FAUSTUS in his study Mephistopheles told the history of Creation, saying:

"The endless praises of the choirs of angels had begun to grow wearisome; for, after all, did he not deserve their praise? Had he not given them endless joy? Would it not be more amusing to obtain undeserved praise, to be worshipped by beings whom he had tortured? He smiled inwardly, and resolved that the great drama should be performed.

"For countless ages the hot nebula whirled aimlessly through space. At length it began to take shape, the central mass threw off planets, the planets cooled, boiling seas and burning mountains heaved and tossed, from black masses of cloud hot sheets of rain deluged the barely solid crust. And now the first germ of life grew in the depths of the ocean, and developed rapidly in the fructifying warmth into vast forest trees, huge ferns springing from the damp mould, sea monsters breeding, fighting, devouring and passing away. And from the monsters, as the play unfolded itself, Man was born, with the power of thought, the knowledge of good and evil, and the cruel thirst for worship. And Man saw that all is passing in this mad, monstrous world, that all is struggling to snatch, at any cost, a few brief moments of life before Death's inexorable decree. And Man said: 'There is a hidden purpose, could we but fathom it, and the purpose is good; for we must reverence something, and in the visible world there is nothing worthy of reverence.' And Man stood aside from the struggle, resolving that God intended harmony to come out of chaos by human efforts. And when he followed the instincts which God had transmitted to him from his ancestry of beasts of prey, he called it Sin, and asked God to forgive him. But he doubted whether he could be justly forgiven, until he invented a divine Plan by which God's wrath was to have been appeased. And seeing the present was bad, he made it yet worse, that thereby the future might be better. And he gave God thanks for the strength that enabled him to forgo even the joys that were possible. And God smiled; and when he saw that Man had become perfect in renunciation and worship, he sent another sun through the sky, which crashed into Man's sun; and all returned again to nebula.

" 'Yes,' he murmured, 'it was a good play; I will have it performed again.' "

Such, in outline, but even more purposeless, more void of meaning, is the world which Science presents for our belief. Amid such a world, if anywhere, our ideals henceforward must find a home. That Man is the product of causes which had no prevision of the end that they were achieving; that his origin, his growth, his hopes and fears, his loves and his beliefs, are but the outcome of accidental collocations of atoms; that no fire, no heroism, no intensity of thought and feeling, can preserve an individual life beyond the grave; that all the labours of the ages, all the devotion, all the inspiration, all the noonday brightness of human genius, are destined to extinction in the vast death of the solar system, and that the whole temple of Man's achievement must inevitably be buried beneath the debris of a universe in ruins—all these things, if not quite beyond dispute, are yet so nearly certain, that no philosophy which rejects them can hope to stand. Only within the scaffolding of these truths, only on the firm foundation of unyielding despair, can the soul's habitation henceforth be safely built.

How, in such an alien and inhuman world, can so powerless a creature as Man preserve his aspirations untarnished? A strange mystery it is that Nature, omnipotent but blind, in the revolutions of her secular hurryings through the abysses of space, has brought forth at last a child, subject still to her power, but gifted with sight, with knowledge of good and evil, with the capacity of judging all the works of his unthinking Mother. In spite of Death, the mark and seal of the parental control, Man is yet free, during his brief years, to examine, to criticise, to know, and in imagination to create. To him alone, in the world with which he is acquainted, this freedom belongs; and in this lies his superiority to the resistless forces that control his outward life.

The savage, like ourselves, feels the oppression of his impotence before the powers of Nature; but having in himself nothing that he respects more than Power, he is willing to prostrate himself before his gods, without inquiring whether they are worthy of his worship. Pathetic and very terrible is the long history of cruelty and torture, of degradation and human sacrifice, endured in the hope of placating the jealous gods: surely, the trembling believer thinks, when what is most precious has been freely given, their lust for blood must be appeased, and more will not be required. The religion of Moloch—as such creeds may be generically called—is in essence the cringing submission of the slave, who dares not, even in his heart, allow the thought that his master deserves no adulation. Since the independence of ideals is not yet acknowledged, Power may be freely worshipped, and receive an unlimited respect, despite its wanton infliction of pain.

But, gradually, as morality grows bolder, the claim of the ideal world begins to be felt; and worship, if it is not to cease, must be given to gods of another kind than those created by the savage. Some, though they feel the demands of the ideal, will still consciously reject them, still urging that naked Power is worthy of worship. Such is the attitude inculcated in God's answer to Job out of the whirlwind: the divine power and knowledge are paraded, but of the divine goodness there is no hint. Such also is the attitude of those who, in our own day, base their morality upon the struggle for survival, maintaining that the survivors are necessarily the fittest. But others, not content with an answer so repugnant to the moral sense, will adopt the position which we have become accustomed to regard as specially religious, maintaining that, in some hidden manner, the world of fact is really harmonious with the world of ideals. Thus Man creates God, all-powerful and all-good, the mystic unity of what is and what should be.

But the world of fact, after all, is not good; and, in submitting our judgment to it, there is an element of slavishness from which our thoughts must be purged. For in all things it is well to exalt the dignity of Man, by freeing him as far as possible from the tyranny of non-human Power. When we have realised that Power is largely bad, that man, with his knowledge of good and evil, is but a helpless atom in a world which has no such knowledge, the choice is again presented to us: Shall we worship Force, or shall we worship Goodness? Shall our God exist and be evil, or shall he be recognised as the creation of our own conscience?

The answer to this question is very momentous, and affects profoundly our whole morality. The worship of Force, to which Carlyle and Nietzsche and the creed of Militarism have accustomed us, is the result of failure to maintain our own ideals against a hostile universe: it is itself a prostrate submission to evil, a sacrifice of our best to Moloch. If strength indeed is to be respected, let us rather respect the strength of those who refuse that false "recognition of facts" which fails to recognise that facts are often bad. Let us admit that, in the world we know, there are many things that would be better otherwise, and that the ideals to which we do and must adhere are not realised in the realm of matter. Let us preserve our respect for truth, for beauty, for the ideal of perfection which life does not permit us to attain, though none of these things meet with the approval of the unconscious universe. If Power is bad, as it seems to be, let us reject it from our hearts. In this lies Man's true freedom: in determination to worship only the God created by our own love of the good, to respect only the heaven which inspires the insight of our best moments. In action, in desire, we must submit perpetually to the tyranny of outside forces; but in thought, in aspiration, we are free, free from our fellowmen, free from the petty planet on which our bodies impotently crawl, free even, while we live, from the tyranny of death. Let us learn, then, that energy of faith which enables us to live constantly in the vision of the good; and let us descend, in action, into the world of fact, with that vision always before us.

When first the opposition of fact and ideal grows fully visible, a spirit of fiery revolt, of fierce hatred of the gods, seems necessary to the assertion of freedom. To defy with Promethean constancy a hostile universe, to keep its evil always in view, always actively hated, to refuse no pain that the malice of Power can invent, appears to be the duty of all who will not bow before the inevitable. But indignation is still a bondage, for it compels our thoughts to be occupied with an evil world; and in the fierceness of desire from which rebellion springs there is a kind of self-assertion which it is necessary for the wise to overcome. Indignation is a submission of our thoughts, but not of our desires; the Stoic freedom in which wisdom consists is found in the submission of our desires, but not of our thoughts. From the submission of our desires springs the virtue of resignation; from the freedom of our thoughts springs the whole world of art and philosophy, and the vision of beauty by which, at last, we half reconquer the reluctant world. But the vision of beauty is possible only to unfettered contemplation, to thoughts not weighted by the load of eager wishes; and thus Freedom comes only to those who no longer ask of life that it shall yield them any of those personal goods that are subject to the mutations of Time.

Although the necessity of renunciation is evidence of the existence of evil, yet Christianity, in preaching it, has shown a wisdom exceeding that of the Promethean philosophy of rebellion. It must be admitted that, of the things we desire, some, though they prove impossible, are yet real goods; others, however, as ardently longed for, do not form part of a fully purified ideal. The belief that what must be renounced is bad, though sometimes false, is far less often false than untamed passion supposes; and the creed of religion, by providing a reason for proving that it is never false, has been the means of purifying our hopes by the discovery of many austere truths.

But there is in resignation a further good element: even real goods, when they are unattainable, ought not to be fretfully desired. To every man comes, sooner or later, the great renunciation. For the young, there is nothing un-attainable; a good thing desired with the whole force of a passionate will, and yet impossible, is to them not credible. Yet, by death, by illness, by poverty, or by the voice of duty, we must learn, each one of us, that the world was not made for us, and that, however beautiful may be the things we crave, Fate may nevertheless forbid them. It is the part of courage, when misfortune comes, to bear without repining the ruin of our hopes, to turn away our thoughts from vain regrets. This degree of submission to Power is not only just and right: it is the very gate of wisdom.

But passive renunciation is not the whole of wisdom; for not by renuncia-tion alone can we build a temple for the worship of our own ideals. Haunting foreshadowings of the temple appear in the realm of imagination, in music, in architecture, in the untroubled kingdom of reason, and in the golden sun-set magic of lyrics, where beauty shines and glows, remote from the touch of sorrow, remote from the fear of change, remote from the failures and dis-enchantments of the world of fact. In the contemplation of these things the vision of heaven will shape itself in our hearts, giving at once a touchstone to judge the world about us, and an inspiration by which to fashion to our needs whatever is not incapable of serving as a stone in the sacred temple.

Except for those rare spirits that are born without sin, there is a cavern of darkness to be traversed before that temple can be entered. The gate of the cavern is despair, and its floor is paved with the gravestones of abandoned hopes. There Self must die; there the eagerness, the greed of untamed desire must be slain, for only so can the soul be freed from the empire of Fate. But out of the cavern the Gate of Renunciation leads again to the daylight of wisdom, by whose radiance a new insight, a new joy, a new tenderness, shine forth to gladden the pilgrim's heart.

When, without the bitterness of impotent rebellion, we have learnt both to resign ourselves to the outward rule of Fate and to recognise that the non-human world is unworthy of our worship, it becomes possible at last so to transform and refashion the unconscious universe, so to transmute it in the crucible of imagination, that a new image of shining gold replaces the old idol of clay. In all the multiform facts of the world—in the visual shapes of trees and mountains and clouds, in the events of the life of man, even in the very omnipotence of Death—the insight of creative idealism can find the reflection of a beauty which its own thoughts first made. In this way mind asserts its subtle mastery over the thoughtless forces of Nature. The more evil the material with which it deals, the more thwarting to untrained desire, the greater is its achievement in inducing the reluctant rock to yield up its hidden treasures, the prouder its victory in compelling the opposing forces to swell the pageant of its triumph. Of all the arts, Tragedy is the proudest, the most triumphant; for it builds its shining citadel in the very centre of the enemy's country, on the very summit of his highest mountain; from its impregnable watchtowers, his camps and arsenals, his columns and forts, are all revealed; within its walls the free life continues, while the legions of Death and Pain and Despair, and all the servile captains of tyrant Fate, afford the burghers of that dauntless city new spectacles of beauty. Happy those sacred ramparts, thrice happy the dwellers on that all-seeing eminence. Honour to those brave warriors who, through countless ages of warfare, have preserved for us the priceless heritage of liberty, and have kept undefiled by sacrilegious invaders the home of the unsubdued.

But the beauty of Tragedy does but make visible a quality which, in more or less obvious shapes, is present always and everywhere in life. In the spectacle of Death, in the endurance of intolerable pain, and in the irrevocableness of a vanished past, there is a sacredness, an overpowering awe, a feeling of the vastness, the depth, the inexhaustible mystery of existence, in which, as by some strange marriage of pain, the sufferer is bound to the world by bonds of sorrow. In these moments of insight, we lose all eagerness of temporary desire, all struggling and striving for petty ends, all care for the little trivial things that, to a superficial view, make up the common life of day by day; we see, surrounding the narrow raft illuminated by the flickering light of human comradeship, the dark ocean on whose rolling waves we toss for a brief hour; from the great night without, a chill blast breaks in upon our refuge; all the loneliness of humanity amid hostile forces is concentrated upon the individual soul, which must struggle alone, with what of courage it can command, against the whole weight of a universe that cares nothing for its hopes and fears. Victory, in this struggle with the powers of darkness, is the true baptism into the glorious company of heroes, the true initiation into the overmastering beauty of human existence. From that awful encounter of the soul with the outer world, enunciation, wisdom, and charity are born; and with their birth a new life begins. To take into the inmost shrine of the soul the irresistible forces whose puppets we seem to be—Death and change, the irrevocableness of the past, and the powerlessness of man before the blind hurry of the universe from vanity to vanity—to feel these things and know them is to conquer them.

This is the reason why the Past has such magical power. The beauty of its motionless and silent pictures is like the enchanted purity of late autumn, when the leaves, though one breath would make them fall, still glow against the sky in golden glory. The Past does not change or strive; like Duncan, after life's fitful fever it sleeps well; what was eager and grasping, what was petty and transitory, has faded away, the things that were beautiful and eternal shine out of it like stars in the night. Its beauty, to a soul not worthy of it, is unendurable; but to a soul which has conquered Fate it is the key of religion.

The life of Man, viewed outwardly, is but a small thing in comparison with the forces of Nature. The slave is doomed to worship Time and Fate and Death, because they are greater than anything he finds in himself, and because all his thoughts are of things which they devour. But, great as they are, to think of them greatly, to feel their passionless splendour, is greater still. And such thought makes us free men; we no longer bow before the inevitable in Oriental subjection, but we absorb it, and make it a part of ourselves. To abandon the struggle for private happiness, to expel all eagerness of temporary desire, to burn with passion for eternal things—this is emancipation, and this is the free man's worship. And this liberation is effected by a contemplation of Fate; for Fate itself is subdued by the mind which leaves nothing to be purged by the purifying fire of Time.

United with his fellow-men by the strongest of all ties, the tie of a common doom, the free man finds that a new vision is with him always, shedding over every daily task the light of love. The life of Man is a long march through the night, surrounded by invisible foes, tortured by weariness and pain, toward a goal that few can hope to reach, and where none may tarry long. One by one, as they march, our comrades vanish from our sight, seized by the silent orders of omnipotent Death. Very brief is the time in which we can help them, in which their happiness or misery is decided. Be it ours to shed sunshine on their path, to lighten their sorrows by the balm of sympathy, to give them the pure joy of a never-tiring affection, to strengthen failing courage, to instil faith in hours of despair. Let us not weigh in grudging scales their merits and demerits, but let us think only of their need—of the sorrows, the difficulties, perhaps the blindnesses, that make the misery of their lives; let us remember that they are fellow-sufferers in the same darkness, actors in the same tragedy with ourselves. And so, when their day is over, when their good and their evil have become eternal by the immortality of the past, be it ours to feel that, where they suffered, where they failed, no deed of ours was the cause; but wherever a spark of the divine fire kindled in their hearts, we were ready with encouragement, with sympathy, with brave words in which high courage glowed.

Brief and powerless is Man's life; on him and all his race the slow, sure doom falls pitiless and dark. Blind to good and evil, reckless of destruction, omnipotent matter rolls on its relentless way; for Man, condemned to-day to lose his dearest, to-morrow himself to pass through the gate of darkness, it remains only to cherish, ere yet the blow falls, the lofty thoughts that ennoble his little day; disdaining the coward terrors of the slave of Fate, to worship at the shrine that his own hands have built; undismayed by the empire of chance, to preserve a mind free from the wanton tyranny that rules his outward life; proudly defiant of the irresistible forces that tolerate, for a moment, his knowledge and his condemnation, to sustain alone, a weary but unyielding Atlas, the world that his own ideals have fashioned despite the trampling march of unconscious power.

GEORGE SANTAYANA

G EORGE SANTAYANA, though generally acknowledged as one of the leading philosophers of the twentieth century, has had few disciples. His thinking is an unusual combination of penetrating analysis, historical insight, and distinctively poetic expression. In his person, he was an essentially solitary figure. Born in 1863, and brought here as a child from Spain, he early acquired a mastery of the English language. He taught at Harvard from 1889 to 1912, and then retired to Europe, ultimately Italy (where he died in 1952), in order to spend the remainder of his life in leisurely contemplation and in the atmosphere of an older tradition which he had always preferred to the more turbulent American scene. Yet it was in America that his finest work, *The Life of Reason* in five volumes (1905-6), was conceived and produced. This enterprise sought to define and champion reason, exhibiting it as embedded in the most elemental human activities and as attaining its fruition in the institutions—the "ideal societies"—of religion, art, and science.

In the many books that subsequently flowed from his pen (including a novel, *The Last Puritan,* in 1936) Santayana tried to elaborate in various ways—and in such various ways that he inevitably incurred the charge of inconsistency— the principal theme of his thinking: on the one hand, that human values and ideals are natural products of a material and mechanical universe, and on the other hand, that such a universe can be understood as giving rise to the marvel of these values and ideals. Santayana almost alone outspokenly defended naturalism at a time when (the turn of the century) it was far more widely felt than it is now that naturalism must lack richness and imaginativeness as a world view. To Santayana the true worth of a human institution like religion lies not in the hopes and dogmas which it offers but in the moral values which it can achieve. Religion cannot pretend to pronounce literal truths, but it can serve as the great symbolizer of the ideals of man. It must cease to be a "false physics" and must become conscious of what, in spite of itself, its true function has always been, dramatically and poetically to celebrate the good. Thus the notion of "God" is not to be interpreted as designating a magical power or a miraculous and incomprehensible creator, but as a symbol of the highest goals of human aspiration.

Santayana always extolled Catholicism for its high appeals to the religious imagination and as rich in symbolism and mythology. The result of this particular preference was a conception of institutional religion ultimately unacceptable both to Catholics and to philosophic naturalists, as well as to others for whom the religious attitude has meant a repudiation of the framework of historical religion. One wit has tried to sum up Santayana's religious viewpoint as asserting that "there is no God, and Mary is his mother."

Santayana's philosophy is unmistakably reflected in his poetry and literary criticism, and it serves as the foundation of his incisive commentaries on life and thought in America, particularly his examination of "the genteel tradition."

It is as a critic of certain tendencies which he felt to be in growing vogue at the dawn of the present century that Santayana speaks in the following selection from *Winds of Doctrine* (New York, Charles Scribner's Sons, 1913). The survey is as much a challenge to the reader's own capacity for appraising his age as it is an opportunity for the reiteration of Santayana's guiding principles.

❦

WINDS OF DOCTRINE

THE INTELLECTUAL TEMPER OF THE AGE

THE PRESENT AGE is a critical one and interesting to live in. The civilisation characteristic of Christendom has not disappeared, yet another civilisation has begun to take its place. We still understand the value of religious faith; we still appreciate the pompous arts of our forefathers; we are brought up on academic architecture, sculpture, painting, poetry, and music. We still love monarchy and aristocracy, together with that picturesque and dutiful order which rested on local institutions, class privileges, and the authority of the family. We may even feel an organic need for all these things, cling to them tenaciously, and dream of rejuvenating them. On the other hand the shell of Christendom is broken. The unconquerable mind of the East, the pagan past, the industrial socialistic future confront it with their equal authority. Our whole life and mind are saturated with the slow upward filtration of a new spirit—that of an emancipated, atheistic, international democracy.

These epithets may make us shudder; but what they describe is something positive and self-justified, something deeply rooted in our animal nature and inspiring to our hearts, something which, like every vital impulse, is pregnant with a morality of its own. In vain do we deprecate it; it has possession of us already through our propensities, fashions, and language. Our very plutocrats and monarchs are at ease only when they are vulgar. Even prelates and missionaries are hardly sincere or conscious of an honest function, save as they devote themselves to social work; for willy-nilly the new spirit has hold of our consciences as well. This spirit is amiable as well as disquieting, liberating as well as barbaric; and a philosopher in our day, conscious both of the old life and of the new, might repeat what Goethe said of his successive love affairs—that it is sweet to see the moon rise while the sun is still mildly shining.

Meantime our bodies in this generation are generally safe, and often comfortable; and for those who can suspend their irrational labours long enough to look about them, the spectacle of the world, if not particularly beautiful or touching, presents a rapid and crowded drama and (what here concerns me most) one unusually intelligible. The nations, parties, and movements that divide the scene have a known history. We are not condemned, as most generations have been, to fight and believe without an inkling of the cause. The past lies before us; the history of everything is published. Every one records his opinion, and loudly proclaims what he wants. In this Babel of ideals few demands are ever literally satisfied; but many evaporate, merge together, and reach an unintended issue, with which they are content. The whole drift of things presents a huge, good-natured comedy to the observer. It stirs not unpleasantly a certain sturdy animality and hearty self-trust which lie at the base of human nature.

A chief characteristic of the situation is that moral confusion is not limited to the world at large, always the scene of profound conflicts, but that it has penetrated to the mind and heart of the average individual. Never perhaps were men so like one another and so divided within themselves. In other ages, even more than at present, different classes of men have stood at different levels of culture, with a magnificent readiness to persecute and to be martyred for their respective principles. These militant believers have been keenly conscious that they had enemies; but their enemies were strangers to them, whom they could think of merely as such, regarding them as blank negative forces, hateful black devils, whose existence might make life difficult but could not confuse the ideal of life. No one sought to understand these enemies of his, nor even to conciliate them, unless under compulsion or out of insidious policy, to convert them against their will; he merely pelted them with blind refutations and clumsy blows. Every one sincerely felt that the right was entirely on his side, a proof that such intelligence as he had moved freely and exclusively within the lines of his faith. The result of this was that his faith was intelligent, I mean, that he understood it, and had a clear, almost instinctive perception of what was compatible or incompatible with it. He defended his walls and he cultivated his garden. His position and his possessions were unmistakable.

When men and minds were so distinct it was possible to describe and to count them. During the Reformation, when external confusion was at its height, you might have ascertained almost statistically what persons and what regions each side snatched from the other; it was not doubtful which was which. The history of their respective victories and defeats could consequently be written. So in the eighteenth century it was easy to perceive how many people Voltaire and Rousseau might be alienating from Bossuet and Fénelon.

But how shall we satisfy ourselves now whether, for instance, Christianity is holding its own? Who can tell what vagary or what compromise may not be calling itself Christianity? A bishop may be a modernist, a chemist may be a mystical theologian, a psychologist may be a believer in ghosts. For science, too, which had promised to supply a new and solid foundation for philosophy, has allowed philosophy rather to undermine its foundation, and is seen eating its own words, through the mouths of some of its accredited spokesmen, and reducing itself to something utterly conventional and insecure. It is characteristic of human nature to be as impatient of ignorance regarding what is not known as lazy in acquiring such knowledge as is at hand; and even those who have not been lazy sometimes take it into their heads to disparage their science and to outdo the professional philosophers in psychological scepticism, in order to plunge with them into the most vapid speculation. Nor is this insecurity about first principles limited to abstract subjects. It reigns in politics as well. Liberalism had been supposed to advocate liberty; but what the advanced parties that still call themselves liberal now advocate is control, control over property, trade, wages, hours of work, meat and drink, amusements, and in a truly advanced country like France control over education and religion; and it is only on the subject of marriage (if we ignore eugenics) that liberalism is growing more and more liberal. Those who speak most of progress measure it by quantity and not by quality; how many people read and write, or how many people there are, or what is the annual value of their trade; whereas true progress would rather lie in reading or writing fewer and better things, and being fewer and better men, and enjoying life more. But the philanthropists are now preparing an absolute subjection of the individual, in soul and body, to the instincts of the majority— the most cruel and unprogressive of masters; and I am not sure that the liberal maxim, "the greatest happiness of the greatest number," has not lost whatever was just or generous in its intent and come to mean the greatest idleness of the largest possible population.

Nationality offers another occasion for strange moral confusion. It had seemed that an age that was levelling and connecting all nations, an age whose real achievements were of international application, was destined to establish the solidarity of mankind as a sort of axiom. The idea of solidarity is indeed often invoked in speeches, and there is an extreme socialistic party that—when a wave of national passion does not carry it the other way—believes in international brotherhood. But even here, black men and yellow men are generally excluded; and in higher circles, where history, literature, and political ambition dominate men's minds, nationalism has become of late an omnivorous all-permeating passion. Local parliaments must be everywhere established, extinct or provincial dialects must be galvanised into national languages, philosophy must be made racial, religion must be fostered where it emphasises nationality and denounced where it transcends it. Man is certainly an animal that, when he lives at all, lives for ideals. Something must be found to occupy his imagination, to raise pleasure and pain into love and hatred, and change the prosaic alternative between comfort and discomfort into the tragic one between happiness and sorrow. Now that the hue of daily adventure is so dull, when religion for the most part is so vague and accommodating, when even war is a vast impersonal business, nationality seems to have slipped into the place of honour. It has become the one eloquent, public, intrepid illusion. Illusion, I mean, when it is taken for an ultimate good or a mystical essence, for of course nationality is a fact. People speak some particular language and are very uncomfortable where another is spoken or where their own is spoken differently. They have habits, judgments, assumptions to which they are wedded, and a society where all this is unheard of shocks them and puts them at a galling disadvantage. To ignorant people the foreigner as such is ridiculous, unless he is superior to them in numbers or prestige, when he becomes hateful. It is natural for a man to like to live at home, and to live long elsewhere without a sense of exile is not good for his moral integrity. It is right to feel a greater kinship and affection for what lies nearest to oneself. But this necessary fact and even duty of nationality is accidental; like age or sex it is a physical fatality which can be made the basis of specific and comely virtues; but it is not an end to pursue or a flag to flaunt or a privilege not balanced by a thousand incapacities. Yet of this distinction our contemporaries tend to make an idol, perhaps because it is the only distinction they feel they have left.

Anomalies of this sort will never be properly understood until people accustom themselves to a theory to which they have always turned a deaf ear, because, though simple and true, it is materialistic: namely, that mind is not the cause of our actions but an effect, collateral with our actions, of bodily growth and organisation. It may therefore easily come about that the thoughts of men, tested by the principles that seem to rule their conduct, may be belated, or irrelevant, or premonitory; for the living organism has many strata, on any of which, at a given moment, activities may exist perfect enough to involve consciousness, yet too weak and isolated to control the organs of outer expression; so that (to speak geologically) our practice may be historic, our manners glacial, and our religion palaeozoic. The ideals of the nineteenth century may be said to have been all belated; the age still yearned with Rousseau or speculated with Kant, while it moved with Darwin, Bismarck, and Nietzsche: and to-day, in the half-educated classes, among the religious or revolutionary

sects, we may observe quite modern methods of work allied with a somewhat antiquated mentality. The whole nineteenth century might well cry
with Faust: "Two souls, alas, dwell in my bosom!" The revolutions it witnessed filled it with horror and made it fall in love romantically with the past
and dote on ruins, because they were ruins; and the best learning and fiction
of the time were historical, inspired by an unprecedented effort to understand
remote forms of life and feeling, to appreciate exotic arts and religions, and
to rethink the blameless thoughts of savages and criminals. This sympathetic
labour and retrospect, however, was far from being merely sentimental; for
the other half of this divided soul was looking ahead. Those same revolutions,
often so destructive, stupid, and bloody, filled it with pride, and prompted it
to invent several incompatible theories concerning a steady and inevitable
progress in the world. In the study of the past, side by side with romantic
sympathy, there was a sort of realistic, scholarly intelligence and an adventurous love of truth; kindness too was often mingled with dramatic curiosity.
The pathologists were usually healers, the philosophers of evolution were
inventors or humanitarians or at least idealists: the historians of art (though
optimism was impossible here) were also guides to taste, quickeners of moral
sensibility, like Ruskin, or enthusiasts for the irresponsibly beautiful, like
Pater and Oscar Wilde. Everywhere in the nineteenth century we find a
double preoccupation with the past and with the future, a longing to know
what all experience might have been hitherto, and on the other hand to hasten
to some wholly different experience, to be contrived immediately with a beating heart and with flying banners. The imagination of the age was intent on
history; its conscience was intent on reform.

Reform! This magic word itself covers a great equivocation. To reform
means to shatter one form and to create another; but the two sides of the act are
not always equally intended nor equally successful. Usually the movement
starts from the mere sense of oppression, and people break down some established form, without any qualms about the capacity of their freed instincts to
generate the new forms that may be needed. So the Reformation, in destroying the traditional order, intended to secure truth, spontaneity, and profuse-
ness of religious forms; the danger of course being that each form might become meagre and the sum of them chaotic. If the accent, however, could only
be laid on the second phase of the transformation, reform might mean the
creation of order where it did not sufficiently appear, so that diffuse life should
be concentrated into a congenial form that should render it strong and self-
conscious. In this sense, if we may trust Mr. Gilbert Murray, it was a great
wave of reform that created Greece, or at least all that was characteristic and
admirable in it—an effort to organise, train, simplify, purify, and make beau-

tiful the chaos of barbaric customs and passions that had preceded. The danger here, a danger to which Greece actually succumbed, is that so refined an organism may be too fragile, not inclusive enough within, and not buttressed strongly enough without against the flux of the uncivilised world. Christianity also, in the first formative centuries of its existence, was an integrating reform of the same sort, on a different scale and in a different sphere; but here too an enslaved rabble within the soul claiming the suffrage, and better equipped intellectual empires rising round about, seem to prove that the harmony which the Christian system made for a moment out of nature and life was partial and insecure. It is a terrible dilemma in the life of reason whether it will sacrifice natural abundance to moral order, or moral order to natural abundance. Whatever compromise we choose proves unstable, and forces us to a new experiment.

Perhaps in the century that has elapsed since the French Revolution the pendulum has had time to swing as far as it will in the direction of negative reform, and may now begin to move towards that sort of reform which is integrating and creative. The veering of the advanced political parties from liberalism to socialism would seem to be a clear indication of this new tendency. It is manifest also in the love of nature, in athletics, in the new woman, and in a friendly medical attitude towards all the passions.

In the fine arts, however, and in religion and philosophy, we are still in full career towards disintegration. It might have been thought that a germ of rational order would by this time have penetrated into fine art and speculation from the prosperous constructive arts that touch the one, and the prosperous natural and mathematical sciences that touch the other. But as yet there is little sign of it. Since the beginning of the nineteenth century painting and sculpture have passed through several phases, representatives of each naturally surviving after the next had appeared. Romanticism, half lurid, half effeminate, yielded to a brutal pursuit of material truth, and a pious preference for modern and humble sentiment. This realism had a romantic vein in it, and studied vice and crime, tedium and despair, with a very genuine horrified sympathy. Some went in for a display of archaeological lore or for exotic *motifs;* others gave all their attention to rediscovering and emphasising abstract problems of execution, the highway of technical tradition having long been abandoned. Beginners are still supposed to study their art, but they have no masters from whom to learn it. Thus, when there seemed to be some danger that art should be drowned in science and history, the artists deftly eluded it by becoming amateurs. One gave himself to religious archaism, another to Japanese composition, a third to barbaric symphonies of colour; sculptors tried to express dramatic climaxes, or inarticulate lyrical passion, such as music might better convey; and the latest whims are apparently to abandon painful observation altogether, to be merely decorative or frankly mystical, and to be satisfied with the childishness of hieroglyphics or the crudity of caricature. The arts are like truant children who think their life will be glorious if they only run away and play for ever; no need is felt of a dominant ideal passion and theme, nor of any moral interest in the interpretation of nature. Artists have no less talent than ever; their taste, their vision, their sentiment are often interesting; they are mighty in their independence and feeble only in their works. . . .

Extremes meet, and the tendency to practical materialism was never wholly absent from the idealism of the moderns. Certainly, the tumid respectability of Anglo-German philosophy had somehow to be left behind; and Darwinian England and Bismarckian Germany had another inspiration as well to guide them, if it could only come to consciousness in the professors. The worship of power is an old religion, and Hegel, to go no farther back, is full of it; but like traditional religion his system qualified its veneration for success by attributing success, in the future at least, to what could really inspire veneration; and such a master in equivocation could have no difficulty in convincing himself that the good must conquer in the end if whatever conquers in the end is the good. Among the pragmatists the worship of power is also optimistic, but it is not to logic that power is attributed. Science, they say, is good as a help to industry, and philosophy is good for correcting whatever in science might disturb religious faith, which in turn is helpful in living. What industry or life are good for it would be unsympathetic to inquire: the stream is mighty, and we must swim with the stream. Concern for survival, however, which seems to be the pragmatic principle in morals, does not afford a remedy for moral anarchy. To take firm hold on life, according to Nietzsche, we should be imperious, poetical, atheistic; but according to William James we should be democratic, concrete, and credulous. It is hard to say whether pragmatism is come to emancipate the individual spirit and make it lord over things, or on the contrary to declare the spirit a mere instrument for the survival of the flesh. In Italy, the mind seems to be raised deliriously into an absolute creator, evoking at will, at each moment, a new past, a new future, a new earth, and a new God. In America, however, the mind is recommended rather as an unpatented device for oiling the engine of the body and making it do double work.

Trustful faith in evolution and a longing for intense life are characteristic of contemporary sentiment; but they do not appear to be consistent with that contempt for the intellect which is no less characteristic of it. Human intelligence is certainly a product, and a late and highly organised product, of evolution; it ought apparently to be as much admired as the eyes of molluscs or the antennae of ants. And if life is better the more intense and concentrated it is, intelligence would seem to be the best form of life. But the degree of intelligence which this age possesses makes it so very uncomfortable that, in this instance, it asks for something less vital, and sighs for what evolution has left behind. In the presence of such cruelly distinct things as astronomy or such cruelly confused things as theology it feels *la nostalgie de la boue*.[1] It was only, M. Bergson tells us, where dead matter oppressed life that life was forced to become intelligence; for this reason intelligence kills whatever it touches; it is the tribute that life pays to death. Life would find it sweet to throw off that painful subjection to circumstance and bloom in some more congenial direction. M. Bergson's own philosophy is an effort to realise this revulsion, to disintegrate intelligence and stimulate sympathetic experience. Its charm lies in the relief which it brings to a stale imagination, an imagination from which religion has vanished and which is kept stretched on the machinery of business and society, or on small half-borrowed passions which we clothe in a mean rhetoric and dot with vulgar pleasures. Finding their intelligence enslaved, our contemporaries suppose that intelligence is essentially servile; instead of freeing it, they try to elude it. Not free enough themselves morally, but bound to the world partly by piety and partly by industrialism, they cannot think of rising to a detached contemplation of earthly things, and of life itself and evolution; they revert rather to sensibility, and seek some by-path of instinct or dramatic sympathy in which to wander. Having no stomach for the ultimate, they burrow downwards towards the primitive. But the longing to be primitive is a disease of culture; it is archaism in morals. To be so preoccupied with vitality is a symptom of anaemia. When life was really vigorous and young, in Homeric times for instance, no one seemed to fear that it might be squeezed out of existence either by the incubus of matter or by the petrifying blight of intelligence. Life was like the light of day, something to use, or to waste, or to enjoy. It was not a thing to worship; and often the chief luxury of living consisted in dealing death about vigorously. Life indeed was loved, and the beauty and pathos of it were felt exquisitely; but its beauty and pathos lay in the divineness of its model and in its own fragility. No one paid it the equivocal compliment of thinking it a substance or a material force. Nobility was not then impossible in sentiment, because there were ideals in life higher and more indestructible than life itself, which life might illustrate and to which it might fitly be sacrificed. Nothing can be meaner than the anxiety to live on, to live on anyhow and in any shape; a spirit with any honour is not willing to live except in its own way, and a spirit with any wisdom is not over-eager to live at all. In those days men recognised im-

---

[1] [*Yearning for mud, that is, the primeval slime.*]

mortal gods and resigned themselves to being mortal. Yet those were the truly vital and instinctive days of the human spirit. Only when vitality is low do people find material things oppressive and ideal things unsubstantial. Now there is more motion than life, and more haste than force; we are driven to distraction by the ticking of the tiresome clocks, material and social, by which we are obliged to regulate our existence. We need ministering angels to fly to us from somewhere, even if it be from the depths of protoplasm. We must bathe in the currents of some non-human vital flood, like consumptives in their last extremity who must bask in the sunshine and breathe the mountain air; and our disease is not without its sophistry to convince us that we were never so well before, or so mightily conscious of being alive.

When chaos has penetrated so far into the moral being of nations they can hardly be expected to produce great men. A great man need not be virtuous, nor his opinions right, but he must have a firm mind, a distinctive, luminous character; if he is to dominate things, something must be dominant in him. We feel him to be great in that he clarifies and brings to expression something which was potential in the rest of us, but which with our burden of flesh and circumstances we were too torpid to utter. The great man is a spontaneous variation in humanity; but not in any direction. A spontaneous variation might be a mere madness or mutilation or monstrosity; in finding the variation admirable we evidently invoke some principle of order to which it conforms. Perhaps it makes explicit what was preformed in us also; as when a poet finds the absolutely right phrase for a feeling, or when nature suddenly astonishes us with a form of absolute beauty. Or perhaps it makes an unprecedented harmony out of things existing before, but jangled and detached. The first man was a great man for this latter reason; having been an ape perplexed and corrupted by his multiplying instincts, he suddenly found a new way of being decent, by harnessing all those instincts together, through memory and imagination, and giving each in turn a measure of its due; which is what we call being rational. It is a new road to happiness, if you have strength enough to castigate a little the various impulses that sway you in turn. Why then is the martyr, who sacrifices everything to one attraction, distinguished from the criminal or the fool, who do the same thing? Evidently because the spirit that in the martyr destroys the body is the very spirit which the body is stifling in the rest of us; and although his private inspiration may be irrational, the tendency of it is not, but reduces the public conscience to act before any one else has had the courage to do so. Greatness is spontaneous; simplicity, trust in some one clear instinct, are essential to it; but the spontaneous variation must be in the direction of some possible sort of order; it must exclude and leave behind what is incapable of being moralised. How,

then, should there be any great heroes, saints, artists, philosophers, or legislators in an age when nobody trusts himself, or feels any confidence in reason,
in an age when the word *dogmatic* is a term of reproach? Greatness has character and severity, it is deep and sane, it is distinct and perfect. For this reason
there is none of it to-day.

There is indeed another kind of greatness, or rather largeness of mind,
which consists in being a synthesis of humanity in its current phases, even if
without prophetic emphasis or direction: the breadth of a Goethe, rather than
the fineness of a Shelley or a Leopardi. But such largeness of mind, not to be
vulgar, must be impartial, comprehensive, Olympian; it would not be greatness if its miscellany were not dominated by a clear genius and if before the
confusion of things the poet or philosopher were not himself delighted, exalted, and by no means confused. Nor does this presume omniscience on his
part. It is not necessary to fathom the ground or the structure of everything
in order to know what to make of it. Stones do not disconcert a builder because he may not happen to know what they are chemically; and so the unsolved problems of life and nature, and the Babel of society, need not disturb
the genial observer, though he may be incapable of unravelling them. He
may set these dark spots down in their places, like so many caves or wells
in a landscape, without feeling bound to scrutinise their depths simply because their depths are obscure. Unexplored they may have a sort of lustre, ex-
plored they might merely make him blind, and it may be a sufficient understanding of them to know that they are not worth investigating. In this way
the most chaotic age and the most motley horrors might be mirrored limpidly
in a great mind, as the Renaissance was mirrored in the works of Raphael and
Shakespeare; but the master's eye itself must be single, his style unmistakable,
his visionary interest in what he depicts frank and supreme. Hence this comprehensive sort of greatness too is impossible in an age when moral confusion
is pervasive, when characters are complex, undecided, troubled by the mere
existence of what is not congenial to them, eager to be not themselves; when,
in a word, thought is weak and the flux of things overwhelms it.

Without great men and without clear convictions this age is nevertheless
very active intellectually; it is studious, empirical, inventive, sympathetic.
Its wisdom consists in a certain contrite openness of mind; it flounders, but at
least in floundering it has gained a sense of possible depths in all directions.
Under these circumstances, some triviality and great confusion in its positive
achievements are not unpromising things, nor even unamiable. These are the
Wanderjahre of faith; it looks smilingly at every new face, which might perhaps be that of a predestined friend; it chases after any engaging stranger; it
even turns up again from time to time at home, full of a new tenderness for all

it had abandoned there. But to settle down would be impossible now. The intellect, the judgment are in abeyance. Life is running turbid and full; and it is no marvel that reason, after vainly supposing that it ruled the world, should abdicate as gracefully as possible, when the world is so obviously the sport of cruder powers—vested interests, tribal passions, stock sentiments, and chance majorities. Having no responsibility laid upon it, reason has become irresponsible. Many critics and philosophers seem to conceive that thinking aloud is itself literature. Sometimes reason tries to lend some moral authority to its present masters, by proving how superior they are to itself; it worships evolution, instinct, novelty, action, as it does in modernism, pragmatism, and the philosophy of M. Bergson. At other times it retires into the freehold of those temperaments whom this world has ostracised, the region of the non-existent, and comforts itself with its indubitable conquests there. This happened earlier to the romanticists . . . although their poetic and political illusions did not suffer them to perceive it. It is happening now, after disillusion, to some radicals and mathematicians like Mr. Bertrand Russell, and to others of us who, perhaps without being mathematicians or even radicals, feel that the sphere of what happens to exist is too alien and accidental to absorb all the play of a free mind, whose function, after it has come to clearness and made its peace with things, is to touch them with its own moral and intellectual light, and to exist for its own sake.

These are but gusts of doctrine; yet they prove that the spirit is not dead in the lull between its seasons of steady blowing. Who knows which of them may not gather force presently and carry the mind of the coming age steadily before it?

A. V. DICEY

ALBERT VENN DICEY (1835–1922), a jurist and scholar of international reputation, taught for twenty-seven years at Oxford. In 1870 his book *On Parties* appeared. Although a keen party politician, Dicey never entered Parliament. But from the time of the Home Rule Bill in 1886 he devoted all of his debating and literary skills to the cause of Liberal Unionism.

In 1879 Dicey's reputation as a legal scholar was established by his treatise on *Domicil,* which he embodied later in a larger book, *The Conflict of Laws.* In 1882 he was appointed as the first Vinerian Professor of English Law, and three years later his classic lectures on the "Law of the Constitution" were published. This work, *Introduction to the Study of the Law of the Constitution,* from which the following selections were taken, has since that date appeared in nine editions. In 1909 Dicey retired from teaching and became professor emeritus.

At the turn of the century Dicey delivered a series of lectures to the students of the Harvard Law School which were published in 1905 under the title, *Lectures on the Relation between Law and Public Opinion in England during the Nineteenth Century.* This remarkable work not only traced the developments of English law in the nineteenth century, but dramatically illustrated the social and political dilemmas of liberalism. Dicey saw the growth of "collectivism" as a reflection of the subtle interrelations among the economic, social, religious, and political issues composing the complex fabric of nineteenth-century society—a world which has directly contributed to the making of our contemporary civilization and its persistent issues.

This selection has been reprinted from A. V. Dicey, *Introduction to the Study of the Law of the Constitution* (Copyright by Macmillan and Company, Ltd., London, 9th ed., 1939) by permission of the publisher and St. Martin's Press, Inc., New York.

INTRODUCTION TO THE STUDY OF THE LAW OF THE CONSTITUTION

Part II

CHAPTER IV: THE RULE OF LAW; ITS NATURE AND GENERAL APPLICATIONS

Two features have at all times since the Norman Conquest characterised the political institutions of England.

The first of these features is the omnipotence or undisputed supremacy throughout the whole country of the central government. This authority of the state or the nation was during the earlier periods of our history represented by the power of the Crown. The King was the source of law and the maintainer of order. The maxim of the courts, *tout fuit in luy et vient de lui al commencement*,[1] was originally the expression of an actual and undoubted fact. This royal supremacy has now passed into [the] sovereignty of Parliament. . . .

The second of these features, which is closely connected with the first, is the rule or supremacy of law. This peculiarity of our polity is well expressed in the old saw of the courts, *"La ley est le plus haute inheritance, que le roy ad; car par la ley il même et toutes ses sujets sont rulés, et si la ley ne fuit; nul roi, et nul inheritance sera."* [2]

This supremacy of the law, or the security given under the English constitution to the rights of individuals looked at from various points of view, forms the subject of . . . this treatise.

Foreign observers of English manners, such for example as Voltaire, de Lolme, de Tocqueville, or Gneist, have been far more struck than have Englishmen themselves with the fact that England is a country governed, as is scarcely any other part of Europe, under the rule of law; and admiration or astonishment at the legality of English habits and feeling is nowhere better expressed than in a curious passage from de Tocqueville's writings, which compares the Switzerland and the England of 1836 in respect of the spirit which pervades their laws and manners.

I am not about . . . to compare Switzerland with the United States, but with Great Britain. When you examine the two countries, or even if you only pass through them, you perceive, in my judgment, the most astonishing differences between them. Take it all in all, England seems to be much more republican than the Helvetic Republic. The principal differences are found in the institutions of the two countries, and especially in their customs (*moeurs*).

1. In almost all the Swiss Cantons liberty of the press is a very recent thing.
2. In almost all of them individual liberty is by no means completely guaranteed, and a man may be arrested administratively and detained in prison without much formality.
3. The courts have not, generally speaking, a perfectly independent position.
4. In all the Cantons trial by jury is unknown.
5. In several Cantons the people were thirty-eight years ago entirely without political rights. Aargau, Thurgau, Tessin, Vaud, and parts of the Cantons of Zurich and Berne were in this condition.

[1] [*All was in him and comes from him at the beginning.*]
[2] [*The law is the highest inheritance that the king has; for he and all his subjects are ruled by the law and if there were no law, neither the king nor the inheritance would be.*]

The preceding observations apply even more strongly to customs than to institutions.

i. In many of the Swiss Cantons the majority of the citizens are quite without taste or desire for *self-government,* and have not acquired the habit of it. In any crisis they interest themselves about their affairs, but you never see in them the thirst for political rights and the craving to take part in public affairs which seem to torment Englishmen throughout their lives.

ii. The Swiss abuse the liberty of the press on account of its being a recent form of liberty, and Swiss newspapers are much more *revolutionary* and much less *practical* than English newspapers.

iii. The Swiss seem still to look upon associations from much the same point of view as the French, that is to say, they consider them as a means of revolution, and not as a slow and sure method for obtaining redress of wrongs. The art of associating and of making use of the right of association is but little understood in Switzerland.

iv. The Swiss do not show the love of justice which is such a strong characteristic of the English. Their courts have no place in the political arrangements of the country, and exert no influence on public opinion. The love of justice, the peaceful and legal introduction of the judge into the domain of politics, are perhaps the most standing characteristics of a free people.

v. Finally, and this really embraces all the rest, the Swiss do not show at bottom that respect for justice, that love of law, that dislike of using force, without which no free nation can exist, which strikes strangers so forcibly in England.

I sum up these impressions in a few words.

Whoever travels in the United States is involuntarily and instinctively so impressed with the fact that the spirit of liberty and the taste for it have pervaded all the habits of the American people, that he cannot conceive of them under any but a Republican government. In the same way it is impossible to think of the English as living under any but a free government. But if violence were to destroy the Republican institutions in most of the Swiss Cantons, it would be by no means certain that after rather a short state of transition the people would not grow accustomed to the loss of liberty. In the United States and in England there seems to be more liberty in the customs than in the laws of the people. In Switzerland there seems to be more liberty in the laws than in the customs of the country.

De Tocqueville's language has a twofold bearing on our present topic. His words point in the clearest manner to the rule, predominance, or supremacy of law as the distinguishing characteristic of English institutions. They further direct attention to the extreme vagueness of a trait of national character which is as noticeable as it is hard to portray. De Tocqueville, we see, is clearly perplexed how to define a feature of English manners of which he at once recognises the existence; he mingles or confuses together the habit of self-government, the love of order, the respect for justice and a legal turn of mind. All these sentiments are intimately allied, but they cannot without confusion be identified with each other. If, however, a critic as acute as de

Tocqueville found a difficulty in describing one of the most marked peculiarities of English life, we may safely conclude that we ourselves, whenever we talk of Englishmen as loving the government of law, or of the supremacy of law as being a characteristic of the English constitution, are using words which, though they possess a real significance, are nevertheless to most persons who employ them full of vagueness and ambiguity. If therefore we are ever to appreciate the full import of the idea denoted by the term "rule, supremacy, or predominance of law," we must first determine precisely what we mean by such expressions when we apply them to the British constitution.

When we say that the supremacy or the rule of law is a characteristic of the English constitution, we generally include under one expression at least three distinct though kindred conceptions.

We mean, in the first place, that no man is punishable or can be lawfully made to suffer in body or goods except for a distinct breach of law established in the ordinary legal manner before the ordinary courts of the land. In this sense the rule of law is contrasted with every system of government based on the exercise by persons in authority of wide, arbitrary, or discretionary powers of constraint.

Modern Englishmen may at first feel some surprise that the "rule of law" (in the sense in which we are now using the term) should be considered as in any way a peculiarity of English institutions, since, at the present day, it may seem to be not so much the property of any one nation as a trait common to every civilised and orderly state. Yet, even if we confine our observation to the existing condition of Europe, we shall soon be convinced that the "rule of law" even in this narrow sense is peculiar to England, or to those countries which, like the United States of America, have inherited English traditions. In almost every continental community the executive exercises far wider discretionary authority in the matter of arrest, of temporary imprisonment, of expulsion from its territory, and the like, than is either legally claimed or in fact exerted by the government in England; and a study of European politics now and again reminds English readers that wherever there is discretion there is room for arbitrariness, and that in a republic no less than under a monarchy discretionary authority on the part of the government must mean insecurity for legal freedom on the part of its subjects.

If, however, we confined our observation to the Europe of today (1908), we might well say that in most European countries the rule of law is now nearly as well established as in England, and that private individuals at any rate who do not meddle in politics have little to fear, as long as they keep the law, either from the Government or from any one else; and we might therefore feel some difficulty in understanding how it ever happened that to foreigners the absence of arbitrary power on the part of the Crown, of the executive, and of every other authority in England, has always seemed a striking feature, we might almost say the essential characteristic, of the English constitution.

Our perplexity is entirely removed by carrying back our minds to the time when the English constitution began to be criticised and admired by foreign thinkers. During the eighteenth century many of the continental governments were far from oppressive, but there was no continental country where men were secure from arbitrary power. The singularity of England was not so much the goodness or the leniency as the legality of the English system of government. When Voltaire came to England—and Voltaire represented the feeling of his age—his predominant sentiment clearly was that he had passed out of the realm of despotism to a land where the laws might be harsh, but where men were ruled by law and not by caprice. He had good reason to know the difference. In 1717 Voltaire was sent to the Bastille for a poem which he had not written, of which he did not know the author, and with the sentiment of which he did not agree. What adds to the oddity, in English eyes, of the whole transaction is that the Regent treated the affair as a sort of joke, and, so to speak, "chaffed" the supposed author of the satire *"I have seen"* on being about to pay a visit to a prison which he "had not seen." In 1725 Voltaire, then the literary hero of his country, was lured off from the table of a Duke, and was thrashed by lackeys in the presence of their noble master; he was unable to obtain either legal or honourable redress, and because he complained of this outrage, paid a second visit to the Bastille. This indeed was the last time in which he was lodged within the walls of a French gaol, but his whole life was a series of contests with arbitrary power, and nothing but his fame, his deftness, his infinite resource, and ultimately his wealth, saved him from penalties far more severe than temporary imprisonment. Moreover, the price at which Voltaire saved his property and his life was after all exile from France. Whoever wants to see how exceptional a phenomenon was that supremacy of law which existed in England during the eighteenth century should read such a book as Morley's *Life of Diderot*. The effort lasting for twenty-two years to get the *Encyclopédie* published was a struggle on the part of all the distinguished literary men in France to obtain utterance for their thoughts. It is hard to say whether the difficulties or the success of the contest bear the strongest witness to the wayward arbitrariness of the French Government.

Royal lawlessness was not peculiar to specially detestable monarchs such

as Louis the Fifteenth: it was inherent in the French system of administration. An idea prevails that Louis the Sixteenth at least was not an arbitrary,
as he assuredly was not a cruel ruler. But it is an error to suppose that up to
1789 anything like the supremacy of law existed under the French monarchy.
The folly, the grievances, and the mystery of the Chevalier d'Eon made as
much noise little more than a century ago as the imposture of the Claimant
in our own day. The memory of these things is not in itself worth reviving.
What does deserve to be kept in remembrance is that in 1778, in the days of
Johnson, of Adam Smith, of Gibbon, of Cowper, of Burke, and of Mansfield,
during the continuance of the American war and within eleven years of the
assembling of the States General, a brave officer and a distinguished diplo-
matist could for some offence still unknown, without trial and without conviction, be condemned to undergo a penance and disgrace which could
hardly be rivalled by the fanciful caprice of the torments inflicted by Oriental
despotism.

Nor let it be imagined that during the latter part of the eighteenth century
the government of France was more arbitrary than that of other countries.
To entertain such a supposition is to misconceive utterly the condition of
the continent. In France, law and public opinion counted for a great deal
more than in Spain, in the petty States of Italy, or in the Principalities of
Germany. All the evils of despotism which attracted the notice of the world
in a great kingdom such as France existed under worse forms in countries
where, just because the evil was so much greater, it attracted the less attention. The power of the French monarch was criticised more severely than
the lawlessness of a score of petty tyrants, not because the French King ruled
more despotically than other crowned heads, but because the French people
appeared from the eminence of the nation to have a special claim to freedom,
and because the ancient kingdom of France was the typical representative of
despotism. This explains the thrill of enthusiasm with which all Europe
greeted the fall of the Bastille. When the fortress was taken, there were not
ten prisoners within its walls; at that very moment hundreds of debtors
languished in English gaols. Yet all England hailed the triumph of the
French populace with a fervour which to Englishmen of the twentieth century is at first sight hardly comprehensible. Reflection makes clear enough
the cause of a feeling which spread through the length and breadth of the
civilised world. The Bastille was the outward and visible sign of lawless
power. Its fall was felt, and felt truly, to herald in for the rest of Europe
that rule of law which already existed in England.

We mean in the second place, when we speak of the "rule of law" as a characteristic of our country, not only that with us no man is above the law, but (what is a different thing) that here every man, whatever be his rank or condition, is subject to the ordinary law of the realm and amenable to the jurisdiction of the ordinary tribunals.

In England the idea of legal equality, or of the universal subjection of all classes to one law administered by the ordinary courts, has been pushed to its utmost limit. With us every official, from the Prime Minister down to a constable or a collector of taxes, is under the same responsibility for every act done without legal justification as any other citizen. The Reports abound with cases in which officials have been brought before the courts, and made, in their personal capacity, liable to punishment, or to the payment of damages, for acts done in their official character but in excess of their lawful authority. A colonial governor, a secretary of state, a military officer, and all subordinates, though carrying out the commands of their official superiors, are as responsible for any act which the law does not authorise as is any private and unofficial person. Officials, such for example as soldiers or clergymen of the Established Church, are, it is true, in England as elsewhere, subject to laws which do not affect the rest of the nation, and are in some instances amenable to tribunals which have no jurisdiction over their fellow-country-men; officials, that is to say, are to a certain extent governed under what may be termed official law. But this fact is in no way inconsistent with the principle that all men are in England subject to the law of the realm; for though a soldier or a clergyman incurs from his position legal liabilities from which other men are exempt, he does not (speaking generally) escape thereby from the duties of an ordinary citizen.

An Englishman naturally imagines that the rule of law (in the sense in which we are now using the term) is a trait common to all civilised societies. But this supposition is erroneous. Most European nations had indeed, by the end of the eighteenth century, passed through that stage of development (from which England emerged before the end of the sixteenth century) when nobles, priests, and others could defy the law. But it is even now far from universally true that in continental countries all persons are subject to one and the same law, or that the courts are supreme throughout the state. If we take France as the type of a continental state, we may assert, with substantial accuracy, that officials—under which word should be included all persons employed in the service of the state—are, or have been, in their official capacity, to some extent exempted from the ordinary law of the land, protected from the jurisdiction of the ordinary tribunals, and subject in certain respects only to official law administered by official bodies.

There remains yet a third and a different sense in which the "rule of law" or the predominance of the legal spirit may be described as a special attribute of English institutions. We may say that the constitution is pervaded by the rule of law on the ground that the general principles of the constitution (as for example the right to personal liberty, or the right of public meeting) are with us the result of judicial decisions determining the rights of private persons in particular cases brought before the courts; whereas under many foreign constitutions the security (such as it is) given to the rights of individuals results, or appears to result, from the general principles of the constitution.

This is one portion at least of the fact vaguely hinted at in the current but misguiding statement that

the constitution has not been made but has "grown." This dictum, if taken literally, is absurd. Political institutions (however the proposition may be at times ignored) are the work of men, owe their origin and their whole existence to human will. Men did not wake up on a summer morning and find them sprung up. Neither do they resemble trees, which, once planted, are "aye growing" while men "are sleeping." In every stage of their existence they are made what they are by human voluntary agency. [J. S. Mill.]

Yet, though this is so, the dogma that the form of a government is a sort of spontaneous growth so closely bound up with the life of a people that we can hardly treat it as a product of human will and energy, does, though in a loose and inaccurate fashion, bring into view the fact that some polities, and among them the English constitution, have not been created at one stroke, and, far from being the result of legislation, in the ordinary sense of that term, are the fruit of contests carried on in the courts on behalf of the rights of individuals. Our constitution, in short, is a judge-made constitution, and it bears on its face all the features, good and bad, of judge-made law.

Hence flow noteworthy distinctions between the constitution of England and the constitutions of most foreign countries.

There is in the English constitution an absence of those declarations or definitions of rights so dear to foreign constitutionalists. Such principles, moreover, as you can discover in the English constitution are, like all maxims established by judicial legislation, mere generalisations drawn either from the decisions or dicta of judges, or from statutes which, being passed to meet special grievances, bear a close resemblance to judicial decisions, and are in effect judgments pronounced by the High Court of Parliament. To put what is really the same thing in a somewhat different shape, the relation of the rights of individuals to the principles of the constitution is not quite the same in countries like Belgium, where the constitution is the result of a legislative act, as it is in England, where the constitution itself is based upon legal decisions. In Belgium, which may be taken as a type of countries possessing a constitution formed by a deliberate act of legislation, you may say with truth that the rights of individuals to personal liberty flow from or are secured by the constitution. In England the right to individual liberty is part of the constitution, because it is secured by the decisions of the courts, extended or confirmed as they are by the Habeas Corpus Acts. If it be allowable to apply the formulas of logic to questions of law, the difference in this matter between the constitution of Belgium and the English constitution may be described by the statement that in Belgium individual rights are deductions drawn from the principles of the constitution, whilst in England the so-called principles of the constitution are inductions or generalisations based upon particular decisions pronounced by the courts as to the rights of given individuals.

This is of course a merely formal difference. Liberty is as well secured in Belgium as in England, and as long as this is so it matters nothing whether we say that individuals are free from all risk of arbitrary arrest, because liberty of person is guaranteed by the constitution, or that the right to personal freedom, or in other words to protection from arbitrary arrest, forms part of the constitution because it is secured by the ordinary law of the land. But though this merely formal distinction is in itself of no moment, provided always that the rights of individuals are really secure, the question whether the right to personal freedom or the right to freedom of worship is likely to be secure does depend a good deal upon the answer to the inquiry whether the persons who consciously or unconsciously build up the constitution of their country begin with definitions or declarations of rights, or with the contrivance of remedies by which rights may be enforced or secured. Now, most foreign constitution-makers have begun with declarations of rights. For this they have often been in nowise to blame. Their course of action has more often than not been forced upon them by the stress of circumstances, and by the consideration that to lay down general principles of law is the proper and natural function of legislators. But any knowledge of history suffices to show that foreign constitutionalists have, while occupied in defining rights, given insufficient attention to the absolute necessity for the provision of adequate remedies by which the rights they proclaimed might be enforced. The Constitution of 1791 proclaimed liberty of conscience, liberty of the press, the right of public meeting, the responsibility of government officials. But there never was a period in the recorded annals of mankind when each and all of these rights were so insecure, one might almost say so completely non-existent, as at the height of the French Revolution. And an observer may well doubt whether a good number of these liberties or rights are even now so well protected under the French Republic as under the English Monarchy. On the other hand, there runs through the English constitution that inseparable connection between the means of enforcing a right and the right to be enforced which is the strength of judicial legislation. The saw, *ubi jus ibi remedium*,[3] becomes from this point of view something much more important than a mere tautologous proposition. In its bearing upon constitutional law, it means that the Englishmen whose labours gradually framed the complicated set of laws and institutions which we call the Constitution, fixed their minds far more intently on providing remedies for the enforcement of particular rights or (what is merely the same thing looked at from the other side) for averting definite wrongs, than upon any declaration of the Rights of Man or of Englishmen. The Habeas Corpus Acts declare no principle and define no rights, but they are for practical purposes worth a hundred constitutional articles guaranteeing individual liberty. Nor let it be supposed that this connection between rights and remedies which depends upon the spirit of law pervading English institutions is inconsistent with the existence of a written constitution, or even with the existence of constitutional declarations of rights. The Constitution of the United States and the constitutions of the separate States are embodied in written or printed documents, and contain declarations of rights.[4] But the statesmen of America have shown unrivalled skill in providing means for giving legal security to the rights declared by American constitutions. The rule of law is as marked a feature of the United States as of England.

The fact, again, that in many foreign countries the rights of individuals, *e.g.* to personal freedom, depend upon the constitution, whilst in England the law of the constitution is little else than a generalisation of the rights

---

[3] [*Where there is a right there is a (legal) remedy.*]

[4] The Petition of Right, and the Bill of Rights, as also the American Declarations of Rights, contain, it may be said, proclamations of general principles which resemble the declarations of rights known to foreign constitutionalists, and especially the celebrated Declaration of the Rights of Man of 1789. But the English and American Declarations on the one hand, and foreign declarations of rights on the other, though bearing an apparent resemblance to each other, are at bottom remarkable rather by way of contrast than of similarity. The Petition of Right and the Bill of Rights are not so much "declarations of rights" in the foreign sense of the term, as judicial condemnations of claims or practices on the part of the Crown, which are thereby pronounced illegal. It will be found that every, or nearly every, clause in the two celebrated documents negatives some distinct claim made and put into force on behalf of the prerogative. No doubt the Declarations contained in the American constitutions have a real similarity to the continental declarations of rights. They are the product of eighteenth-century ideas; they have, however, it is submitted, the distinct purpose of legally controlling the action of the legislature by the Articles of the Constitution. . . .

which the courts secure to individuals, has this important result. The general rights guaranteed by the constitution may be, and in foreign countries constantly are, suspended. They are something extraneous to and independent of the ordinary course of the law. The declaration of the Belgian constitution, that individual liberty is "guaranteed," betrays a way of looking at the rights of individuals very different from the way in which such rights are regarded by English lawyers. We can hardly say that one right is more guaranteed than another. Freedom from arbitrary arrest, the right to express one's opinion on all matters subject to the liability to pay compensation for libellous or to suffer punishment for seditious or blasphemous statements, and the right to enjoy one's own property, seem to Englishmen all to rest upon the same basis, namely, on the law of the land. To say that the "constitution guaranteed" one class of rights more than the other would be to an Englishman an unnatural or a senseless form of speech. In the Belgian constitution the words have a definite meaning. They imply that no law invading personal freedom can be passed without a modification of the constitution made in the special way in which alone the constitution can be legally changed or amended. This, however, is not the point to which our immediate attention should be directed. The matter to be noted is, that where the right to individual freedom is a result deduced from the principles of the constitution, the idea readily occurs that the right is capable of being suspended or taken away. Where, on the other hand, the right to individual freedom is part of the constitution because it is inherent in the ordinary law of the land, the right is one which can hardly be destroyed without a thorough revolution in the institutions and manners of the nation. The so-called "suspension of the Habeas Corpus Act" bears, it is true, a certain similarity to what is called in foreign countries "suspending the constitutional guarantees." But, after all, a statute suspending the Habeas Corpus Act falls very far short of what its popular name seems to imply; and though a serious measure enough, is not, in reality, more than a suspension of one particular remedy for the protection of personal freedom. The Habeas Corpus Act may be suspended and yet Englishmen may enjoy almost all the rights of citizens. The constitution being based on the rule of law, the suspension of the constitution, as far as such a thing can be conceived possible, would mean with us nothing less than a revolution.

That "rule of law," then, which forms a fundamental principle of the constitution, has three meanings, or may be regarded from three different points of view.

It means, in the first place, the absolute supremacy or predominance of regular law as opposed to the influence of arbitrary power, and excludes the existence of arbitrariness, of prerogative, or even of wide discretionary authority on the part of the government. Englishmen are ruled by the law, and by the law alone; a man may with us be punished for a breach of law, but he can be punished for nothing else.

It means, again, equality before the law, or the equal subjection of all classes to the ordinary law of the land administered by the ordinary law courts; the "rule of law" in this sense excludes the idea of any exemption of officials or others from the duty of obedience to the law which governs other citizens or from the jurisdiction of the ordinary tribunals; there can be with us nothing really corresponding to the "administrative law" (*droit administratif*) or the "administrative tribunals" (*tribunaux administratifs*) of France. The notion which lies at the bottom of the "administrative law" known to foreign countries is, that affairs or disputes in which the government or its servants are concerned are beyond the sphere of the civil courts and must be dealt with by special and more or less official bodies. This idea is utterly unknown to the law of England, and indeed is fundamentally inconsistent with our traditions and customs.

The "rule of law," lastly, may be used as a formula for expressing the fact that with us the law of the constitution, the rules which in foreign countries naturally form part of a constitutional code, are not the source but the consequence of the rights of individuals, as defined and enforced by the courts; that, in short, the principles of private law have with us been by the action of the courts and Parliament so extended as to determine the position of the Crown and of its servants; thus the constitution is the result of the ordinary law of the land. . . .

HOUSTON STEWART CHAMBERLAIN

Houston Stewart Chamberlain was born in 1855 at Southsea, England. Although his father was a distinguished British admiral, he was raised in Versailles by his grandmother, after the death of his mother. He returned to England to attend private school and then Cheltenham College, but his education—a period of loneliness and unhappiness for him—was cut short by a severe neurological disorder. Chamberlain spent the next nine years touring and traveling through most of western and central Europe. His guide and companion was a German theologian, who taught him the German language and some appreciation of German culture.

Chamberlain began the study of natural science in 1879, and after receiving his B.A. continued with research in plant biology. His work was interrupted in 1884 by a nervous breakdown, and he spent the next five years in Dresden, studying Kant and deepening his acquaintance with German literature and culture. It was during this period that Chamberlain was deeply influenced by the work of Wagner, and in 1892 he published his first book, in French, *Notes on Lohengrin*. This was followed by a larger and more general appreciation of Wagner that same year; Chamberlain referred to Wagner as "the sun of my life," and his reverence for him was little short of mystical.

In 1899 Chamberlain published his most famous work, *The Foundations of the Nineteenth Century*. The two published volumes were originally meant as an introduction to a larger study which he never completed; nevertheless, they represent the most complete exposition of Chamberlain's ideas. Although racism was not new to European thought and Gobineau before him had already identified the Germanic or Indo-Aryan "race" as the sole bearer of civilization and cultural progress, Chamberlain took the dramatic step of identifying a particular nation as racially superior, and thus entrusted with a spiritual "mission." It was upon the German people that he placed his hopes for the realization of Germanic race-consciousness. Although many German scholars and specialists rejected the book, its racist ideology and appeal to national pride found a wide audience throughout Germany; among the most enthusiastic of Chamberlain's admirers was Kaiser William II.

In 1908 Chamberlain moved to Bayreuth and married Wagner's only daughter, Eva, becoming part of that intimate circle which formed around Wagner's wife Cosima. He regarded the First World War as a great moral crisis; in his *War Essays* he bitterly abused the Allies, especially the British: some of his polemics made even German politicians uncomfortable. He adopted German citizenship in 1915, and after the war became an implacable opponent of the Weimar Republic. From his sick bed he encouraged the efforts of the young Adolph Hitler, whom he met in 1923; there can be no doubt that Chamberlain's pseudo-scientific racism had an impact upon the ideology of National Socialism, and the influence of his magnum opus can be found in the Nazi Alfred Rosenberg's *The Myth of the Twentieth Century* (1943). Chamberlain died in Bayreuth in 1927.

The selection from *The Foundations of the Nineteenth Century* is taken from the translation by John Lees (New York: John Lane Co., 1912).

❧

THE FOUNDATIONS OF THE NINETEENTH CENTURY

Division II: The Heirs

INTRODUCTION

The Chaos. Rome had transferred the centre of gravity of civilisation to the West. This proved to be one of those unconsciously accomplished acts of world-wide importance which no power can undo. The West of Europe, remote from Asia, was to be the focus of all further civilisation and culture. But that happened only gradually. At first it was politics alone which turned ever more and more towards the West and North; intellectually Rome itself long remained very dependent upon the former centre of culture in the East. In the first centuries of our era, with the exception of Rome itself, only what lies South and East of it is intellectually of any importance; Alexandria, Ephesus, Antioch, in fact all Syria, then Greece with Byzantium, as well as Carthage and the other towns of ancient Africa, are the districts where the legacy was taken up and long administered, and the inhabitants of these places then handed it on to later times and other races. And these very countries were at that time, like Rome itself, no longer inhabited by a definite people, but by an inextricable confusion of the most different races and peoples. It was a chaos. And this chaos did not by any means disappear at a later time. In many places this chaotic element was pressed back by the advance of pure races, in others it fell out of the list of those that count through its own weakness and want of character, yet for all that it has beyond doubt maintained itself in the South and East; moreover fresh influx of blood has frequently given it new strength. This is a first point of far-reaching importance. Consider, for example, that all the foundations for the structure of historical Christianity were laid and built up by this mongrel population! With the exception of some Greeks, all of whom, however, with Origenes at their head, disseminated highly unorthodox, directly anti-Jewish doctrines which had no success, one can scarcely even conjecture to what nationality any of the Church fathers actually belonged. The same may be said of the *corpus juris;* here, too, it was the Chaos (according to Hellenic ideas the mother of Erebus and Nox, of darkness and night), to which the task fell of perfecting and transforming the living work of a living people to an international dogma. Under the same influence, art ever more and more lost its personal, freely creative power and became transformed into an hieratically formulary exercise, while the lofty, philosophical speculation of the Hellenes was displaced by its caricature, the cabalistic phantoms of demiurges, angels and daemons—conceptions which could not be designated by a higher name than "airy materialism." We must therefore, to begin with, turn our attention to this Chaos of Peoples.

The Jews. Out of the midst of the chaos towers, like a sharply defined rock amid the formless ocean, one single people, a numerically insignificant people —the Jews. This one race has established as its guiding principle the purity of the blood; it alone possesses, therefore, physiognomy and character. If we contemplate the southern and eastern centres of culture in the world-empire in its downfall, and let no sympathies or antipathies pervert our judgment, we must confess that the Jews were at that time the only people deserving respect. We may well apply to them the words of Goethe, "the faith broad, narrow the thought." In comparison with Rome and still more so with Hellas their intellectual horizon appears so narrow, their mental capacities so limited, that we seem to have before us an entirely new type of being; but the narrowness and want of originality in thought are fully counterbalanced by the power of faith, a faith which might be very simply defined as "faith in self." And since this faith in self included faith in a higher being, it did not lack ethical significance. However poor the Jewish "law" may appear, when compared with the religious creations of the various Indo-European peoples, it possessed a unique advantage in the fallen Roman Empire of that time: it was, in fact, a law; a law which men humbly obeyed, and this very obedience was bound to be of great ethical import in a world of such lawlessness. Here, as everywhere, we shall find that the influence of the Jews— for good and for evil—lies in their character, not in their intellectual achievements. Certain historians of the nineteenth century, even men so intellectually pre-eminent as Count Gobineau, have supported the view that Judaism has always had merely a disintegrating influence upon all peoples. I cannot share this conviction. In truth, where the Jews become very numerous in a strange land, they may make it their object to fulfil the promises of the Prophets and with the best will and conscience to "consume the strange peoples"; did they not say of themselves, even in the lifetime of Moses, that they were "like locusts"? However, we must distinguish between Judaism and the Jews and admit that Judaism as an idea is one of the most conservative ideas in the world. The idea of physical race-unity and race-purity, which is the very essence of Judaism, signifies the recognition of a fundamental physiological fact of life; wherever we observe life, from the hyphomycetes to the noble horse, we see the importance of "race"; Judaism made this law of nature sacred. And this is the reason why it triumphantly prevailed at that critical moment in the history of the world, when a rich legacy was waiting in vain for worthy heirs. It did not further, but rather put a stop to, universal disintegration. The Jewish dogma was like a sharp acid which is poured into a liquid which is being decomposed in order to clear it and keep it from further decomposition. Though this acid may not be to the taste of every one, yet it has played so decisive a part in the history of the epoch of culture to which we belong that we ought to be grateful to the giver: instead of being indignant about it, we shall do better to inform ourselves thoroughly concerning the significance of this "entrance of the Jews into the history of the West," an event which in any case exercised inestimable influence upon our whole culture, and which has not yet reached its full growth.

Another word of explanation. I am speaking of Jews, not of Semites in general; not because I fail to recognise the part played by the latter in the history of the world, but because my task is limited both in respect of time and space. Indeed for many centuries other branches of the Semitic race had founded powerful kingdoms on the South and East coasts of the Mediterranean and had established commercial depots as far as the coasts of the Atlantic Ocean; doubtless they had also been stimulative in other ways, and had spread knowledge and accomplishments of many kinds; but nowhere had there been a close intellectual connection between them and the other inhabitants of future Europe. The Jews first brought this about, not by the millions of Jews who lived in the Diaspora, but first and foremost by the Christian idea. It was only when the Jews crucified Christ that they unconsciously broke the spell which had hitherto isolated them in the pride of ignorance.—At a later time, indeed, a Semitic flood swept once more across the European, Asiatic and African world, a flood such as, but for the destruction of Carthage by Rome, would have swept over Europe a thousand years before, with results which would have been decisive and permanent. But here, too, the Semitic idea—"faith wide, narrow the thought"—proved itself more powerful than its bearers; the Arabs were gradually thrown back and, in contrast to the Jews, not one of them remained on European soil; but where their abstract idolatry had obtained a foothold all possibility of a culture disappeared; the Semitic dogma of materialism, which in this case and in contrast to Christianity had kept itself free of all Aryan admixtures, deprived noble human races of all soul, and excluded them for ever from the "race that strives to reach the light."—Of the Semites only the Jews, as we see, have positively furthered our culture and also shared, as far as their extremely assimilative nature permitted them, in the legacy of antiquity.

The Teutonic Races. The entrance of the Teutonic races into the history of the world forms the counterpart to the spread of this diminutive and yet so influential people. There, too, we see what pure race signifies, at the same time, however, what variety of races is—that great natural principle of many-sidedness, and of dissimilarity of mental gifts, which shallow, venal, ignorant babblers of the present day would fain deny, slavish souls sprung from the chaos of peoples, who feel at ease only in a confused atmosphere of character-lessness and absence of individuality. To this day these two powers—Jews and Teutonic races—stand, wherever the recent spread of the Chaos has not blurred their features, now as friendly, now as hostile, but always as alien forces face to face.

In this book I understand by "Teutonic peoples" the different North-European races, which appear in history as Celts, Teutons (Germanen) and Slavs, and from whom—mostly by indeterminable mingling—the peoples of modern Europe are descended. It is certain that they belonged originally to a single family, as I shall prove in the sixth chapter; but the Teuton in the narrower Tacitean sense of the word has proved himself so intellectually, morally and physically pre-eminent among his kinsmen, that we are entitled to make his name summarily represent the whole family. The Teuton is the soul of our culture. Europe of to-day, with its many branches over the whole world, represents the chequered result of an infinitely manifold mingling of races: what binds us all together and makes an organic unity of us is "Teu-tonic" blood. If we look around, we see that the importance of each nation as a living power to-day is dependent upon the proportion of genuinely Teutonic blood in its population. Only Teutons sit on the thrones of Europe.—What preceded in the history of the world we may regard as Prolegomena; true history, the history which still controls the rhythm of our hearts and circulates in our veins, inspiring us to new hope and new creation, begins at the moment when the Teuton with his masterful hand lays his grip upon the legacy of antiquity.

FOURTH CHAPTER: THE CHAOS

Scientific Confusion. . . . There is perhaps no question about which such absolute ignorance prevails among highly cultured, indeed learned, men, as the question of the essence and the significance of the idea of "race." What are pure races? Whence do they come? Have they any historical importance? Is the idea to be taken in a broad or a narrow sense? Do we know anything on the subject or not? What is the relation of the ideas of race and of nation to one another? I confess that all I have ever read or heard on this subject has been disconnected and contradictory; some specialists among the natural investigators form an exception, but even they very rarely apply their clear and detailed knowledge to the human race. Not a year passes without our being assured at international congresses, by authoritative national economists, ministers, bishops, natural scientists, that there is no difference and no inequality between nations. Teutons, who emphasise the importance of race-relationship, Jews, who do not feel at ease among us and long to get back to their Asiatic home, are by none so slightingly and scornfully spoken of as by men of science. Professor Virchow, for instance, says that the stirrings of consciousness of race among us are only to be explained by the "loss of sound common sense." Moreover, that it is "all a riddle to us, and no one knows what it really means in this age of equal rights." Nevertheless, this learned man closes his address with the expression of a desire for "beautiful self-dependent personalities." As if all history were not there to show us how personality and race are most closely connected, how the nature of the personality is determined by the nature of its race, and the power of the personality dependent upon certain conditions of its blood! And as if the scientific rearing of animals and plants did not afford us an extremely rich and reliable material, whereby we may become acquainted not only with the conditions but with the importance of "race"! Are the so-called (and rightly so-called) "noble" animal races, the draught-horses of Limousin, the American trotter, the Irish hunter, the absolutely reliable sporting dogs, produced by chance and promiscuity? Do we get them by giving the animals equality of rights, by throwing the same food to them and whipping them with the same whip? No, they are produced by artificial selection and strict maintenance of the purity of the race. Horses and especially dogs give us every chance of observing that the intellectual gifts go hand in hand with the physical; this is specially true of the moral qualities: a mongrel is frequently very clever, but never reliable; morally he is always a weed. Continual promiscuity between two pre-eminent animal races leads without exception to the destruction of the pre-eminent characteristics of both. Why should the human race form an exception? A father of the Church might imagine that it does, but is it becoming in a renowned natural investigator to throw the weight of his great influence into the scale of mediaeval ignorance and superstition? Truly one could wish that these scientific authorities of ours, who are so utterly lacking in philosophy, had followed a course of logic under Thomas Aquinas; it could only be beneficial to them. In spite of the broad common foundation, the human races are, in reality, as different from one another in character, qualities, and above all, in the degree of their individual capacities, as greyhound, bulldog, poodle and Newfoundland dog. Inequality is a state towards which nature inclines in all spheres; nothing extraordinary is produced without "specialisation"; in the case of men, as of animals, it is this specialisation that produces noble races; history and ethnology reveal this secret to the dullest eye. . . .

Importance of Race. Nothing is so convincing as the consciousness of the possession of Race. The man who belongs to a distinct, pure race, never loses the sense of it. The guardian angel of his lineage is ever at his side, supporting him where he loses his foothold, warning him like the Socratic Daemon where he is in danger of going astray, compelling obedience, and forcing him to undertakings which, deeming them impossible, he would never have dared to attempt. Weak and erring like all that is human, a man of this stamp recognises himself, as others recognise him, by the sureness of his character, and by the fact that his actions are marked by a certain simple and peculiar greatness, which finds its explanation in his distinctly typical and super-personal qualities. Race lifts a man above himself: it endows him with extraordinary—I might almost say supernatural—powers, so entirely does it distinguish him from the individual who springs from the chaotic jumble of peoples drawn from all parts of the world; and should this man of pure origin be perchance gifted above his fellows, then the fact of Race strengthens and elevates him on every hand, and he becomes a genius towering over the rest of mankind, not because he has been thrown upon the earth like a flaming meteor by a freak of nature, but because he soars heavenward like some strong and stately tree, nourished by thousands and thousands of roots—no solitary individual, but the living sum of untold souls striving for the same goal. He who has eyes to see at once detects Race in animals. It shows itself in the whole habit of the beast, and proclaims itself in a hundred peculiarities which defy analysis: nay more, it proves itself by achievements, for its possession invariably leads to something excessive and out of the common—even to that which is exaggerated and not free from bias. Goethe's dictum, "only that which is extravagant makes greatness," is well known. That is the very quality which a thoroughbred race reared from superior materials bestows upon its individual descendants—something "extravagant"—and, indeed, what we learn from every race-horse, every thoroughbred fox-terrier, every Cochin China fowl, is the very lesson which the history of mankind so eloquently teaches us! Is not the Greek in the fulness of his glory an unparalleled example of this "extravagance"? And do we not see this "extravagance" first make its appearance when immigration from the North has ceased, and the various strong breeds of men, isloated on the peninsula once for all, begin to fuse into a new race, brighter and more brilliant, where, as in Athens, the racial blood flows from many sources—simpler and more resisting where, as in Lacedaemon, even this mixture of blood had been barred out. Is the race not as it were extinguished, as soon as fate wrests the land from its proud exclusiveness and incorporates it in a greater whole? Does not Rome teach us the same lesson? Has not in this case also a special mixture of blood produced an absolutely new race, similar in qualities and capacities to no later one, endowed with exuberant power? And does not victory in this case effect what disaster did in that, but only much more quickly? Like a cataract the stream of strange blood overflooded the almost depopulated Rome and at once the Romans ceased to be. Would one small tribe from among all the Semites have become a world-embracing power had it not made "purity of race" its inflexible fundamental law? In days when so much nonsense is talked concerning this question, let Disraeli teach us that the whole significance of Judaism lies in its purity of race, that this alone gives it power and duration, and just as it has outlived the people of antiquity, so, thanks to its knowledge of this law of nature, will it outlive the constantly mingling races of to-day.

What is the use of detailed scientific investigations as to whether there are distinguishable races? whether race has a worth? how this is possible? and so on. We turn the tables and say: it is evident that there are such races: it is a fact of direct experience that the quality of the race is of vital importance; your province is only to find out the how and the wherefore, not to deny the facts themselves in order to indulge your ignorance. . . .

FIFTH CHAPTER: THE ENTRANCE OF THE JEWS INTO THE HISTORY OF THE WEST

Judaism. One more word in conclusion. My reply to the question, Who is the Jew? has been, in the first place, to point out whence he came, what was his physical foundation, and secondly, to reveal the leading idea of Judaism in its origin and nature. I cannot do more; for the personality belongs to the single individual, and nothing is falser than the widespread procedure of judging a people by individuals. . . .

SIXTH CHAPTER: THE ENTRANCE OF THE GERMANIC PEOPLE INTO THE HISTORY OF THE WORLD

Mon devoir est mon Dieu suprême. —Frederick the Great
(Letter to Voltaire on June 12, 1740)

The entrance of the Jew into European history had, as Herder said, signified the entrance of an alien element—alien to that which Europe had already achieved, alien to all it was still to accomplish; but it was the very reverse with the Germanic peoples. This barbarian, who would rush naked to battle, this savage, who suddenly sprang out of woods and marshes to inspire into a civilised and cultivated world the terrors of a violent conquest won by the strong hand alone, was nevertheless the lawful heir of the Hellene and the Roman, blood of their blood and spirit of their spirit. It was his own property which he, unwitting, snatched from the alien hand. But for him the sun of the Indo-European must have set. The Asiatic and African slave had by assassination wormed his way to the very throne of the Roman Empire, the Syrian mongrel had made himself master of the law, the Jew was using the library at Alexandria to adapt Hellenic philosophy to the Mosaic law, the Egyptian to embalm and bury for boundless ages the fresh bloom of natural science in the ostentatious pyramids of scientific systematisation; soon, too, the beautiful flowers of old Aryan life—Indian thought, Indian poetry—were to be trodden under foot by the savage bloodthirsty Mongolian, and the Bedouin, with his mad delusions bred of the desert, was to reduce to an everlasting wilderness that garden of Eden, Erania,[1] in which for centuries all the symbolism of the world had grown; art had long since vanished; there were nothing but replicas for the rich, and for the poor the circus; accordingly, to use that expression of Schiller which I quoted at the beginning of the first chapter, there were no longer men but only creatures. It was high time for the Saviour to appear. He certainly did not enter into history in the form in which combining, constructive reason, if consulted, would have chosen for the guardian angel, the harbinger of a new day of humanity; but to-day, when a glance back over past centuries teaches us wisdom, we have only one thing to regret, that the Teuton did not destroy with more thoroughness, wherever his victorious arm penetrated, and that as a consequence of his moderation the so-called "Latinising," that is, the fusion with the chaos of peoples, once more gradually robbed wide districts of the one quickening influence of pure blood and unbroken youthful vigour, and at the same time deprived them of the rule of those who possessed the highest talents. At any rate it is only shameful indolence of thought, or disgraceful historical falsehood, that can fail to see in the entrance of the Germanic tribes into the history of the world the rescuing of agonising humanity from the clutches of the everlastingly bestial. . . .

Backward Glance. Freedom and loyalty . . . are the two roots of the Germanic nature, or, if you will, the two pinions that bear it heavenwards. These are not meaningless words, each one of them embraces a wide complex of vivid conceptions, experiences and historical facts. Such a simplification has outwardly only been justified by the fact that we have proved that rich en-

---

[1] [Persia.]

dowments were the inevitable basis of these two things: physical health and strength, great intelligence, luxuriant imagination, untiring impulse to create. And like all true powers of nature, freedom and loyalty flowed into each other: the specifically Germanic loyalty was a manifestation of the most elevated freedom—the maintenance of that freedom, loyalty to our own nature. Here too the specifically Germanic significance of the idea of duty becomes clear. Goethe says in one passage—he is speaking of taste in art, but the remark holds for all spheres: "to maintain courageously our position on the height of our barbarian advantages is our duty." This is Shakespeare's "to thine own self be true!" This is Nelson's signal on the morning of the Battle of Trafalgar "England expects every man to do his duty!" His duty? Loyalty to himself, the maintenance of his barbarian advantages, *i.e.* (as Montesquieu teaches us), of the freedom that is born in him. In contrast to this we behold a man who proclaims as the highest law the destruction of freedom, *i.e.*, of freedom of will, of understanding, of creative work—and who replaces loyalty (which would be meaningless without freedom) by obedience. The individual shall become—as Loyola says word for word in the constitution of his Order—"as it were a corpse which lets itself be turned on any side and never resists the hand laid upon it, or like the staff of an old man which everywhere helps him who holds it, no matter how and where he wishes to employ it." I think it would be impossible to make the contrast to all Aryan thought and feeling more clear than it is in these words: on the one hand sunny, proud, mad delight in creating, men who fearlessly grasp the right hand of the God to whom they pray; on the other a corpse, upon which the "destruction of all independent judgment" is impressed as the first rule in life and for which "cowering slavish fear" is the basis of all religion.

Forward Glance. I sometimes regret that, in a book like this, moralising would be so out of place as to be almost an offence against good taste. When we see those splendid "barbarians" glowing with youth, free, making their entry into history endowed with all those qualities which fit them for the very highest place; when next we realise how they, the conquerors, the true "Freeborn" of Aristotle, contaminate their pure blood by mixture with the impure races of the slave-born; how they accept their schooling from the unworthy descendants of noble progenitors, and force their way with untold toil out of the night of this Chaos towards a new dawn;—then we have to acknowledge the further fact that every day adds new enemies and new dangers to those which already exist—that these new enemies, like the former ones, are received by the Teutons with open arms, that the voice of warning is carelessly laughed at, and that while every enemy of our race, with full consciousness and the perfection of cunning, follows his own designs, we—still great, innocent barbarians—concentrate ourselves upon earthly and heavenly ideals, upon property, discoveries, inventions, brewing, art, metaphysics, love, and heaven knows what else! and with it all there is ever a tinge of the impossible, of that which cannot be brought to perfection, of the world beyond, otherwise we should remain lying idle on our bear-skins! Who could help moralising when he sees how we, without weapons, without defence, unconscious of any danger, go on our way, constantly befooled, ever ready to set a high price on what is foreign and to set small store by what is our own— we, the most learned of all men, and yet ignorant beyond all others of the world around us, the greatest discoverers and yet stricken with chronic blindness! Who could help crying with Ulrich von Hutten: "Oh! unhappy Germany, unhappy by thine own choice! thou that with eyes to see seest not, and with clear understanding understandest not!" But I will not do it. I feel that this is not my business, and to tell the truth this haughty pococurantism is so characteristic a feature that I should regret its loss. The Teuton is no pessimist like the Hindoo, he is no good critic; he really thinks little in comparison with other Aryans; his gifts impel him to act and to feel. To call the Germans a "nation of thinkers" is bitter irony; a nation of soldiers and shopkeepers would certainly be more correct, or of scholars and artists— but of thinkers?—these are thinly sown. Hence it was that Luther went so far as to call the Germans "blind people"; the rest of the Germanic races are the same in scarcely less degree; for analytical thought belongs to seeing, and to that again capacity, time, practice. The Teuton is occupied with other things; he has not yet completed his "entrance into the history of the world"; he must first have taken possession of the whole earth, investigated nature on all sides, made its powers subject to him; he must first have developed the expression of art to a perfection yet unknown, and have collected an enormous store of historical knowledge—then perhaps he will have time to ask himself what is going on immediately around him.

Till then he will continue to walk on the edge of the precipice with the same calmness as on a flowering meadow. That cannot be changed, for this pococurantism is, as I said above, characteristic of the Teuton. The Greeks and the Romans were not unlike this: the former continued to think and invent artistically, the latter to add conquest to conquest without ever becoming conscious of themselves like the Jews, without ever noticing in the least how the course of events was gradually wiping them from off the face of the earth; they did not fall dead like other nations; they descended slowly into Hades full of life to the last, vigorous to the last, in the proud consciousness of victory.

And I, a modest historian, who can neither influence the course of events nor possess the power of looking clearly into the future, must be satisfied if in fulfilling the purpose of this book I have succeeded in showing the distinction between the Germanic and the Non-Germanic. That the Teuton is one of the greatest, perhaps the very greatest power in the history of mankind, no one will wish to deny, but in order to arrive at a correct appreciation of the present time, it behoved us to settle once for all who could and who could not be regarded as Teuton. In the nineteenth century, as in all former centuries, but of course with widely differing grouping and with constantly changing relative power, there stood side by side in Europe these "Heirs"— the chaos of half-breeds, relics of the former Roman Empire, the Germanising of which is falling off—the Jews—and the Germans, whose contamination by mixture with the half-breeds and the descendants of other Non-Aryan races is on the increase. No arguing about "humanity" can alter the fact that this means a struggle. Where the struggle is not waged with cannon-balls, it goes on silently in the heart of society by marriages, by the annihilation of distances which furthers intercourse, by the varying powers of resistance in the different types of mankind, by the shifting of wealth, by the birth of new influences and the disappearance of others, and by many other motive powers. But this struggle, silent though it be, is above all others a struggle for life and death.

JACOB BURCKHARDT

J ACOB CHRISTOPH BURCKHARDT was born in Switzerland in 1818. He received a broad, humanistic education, studying theology at Basel and history under Ranke at Berlin. At Berlin he also attended the lectures of Jacob Grimm and became deeply interested in the history of art. He continued his study of the history of art in Bonn.

In 1845 Burckhardt became editor of the *Basler Zeitung,* a conservative journal. He had little taste for the work, and eagerly seized the first opportunity to leave the paper and journey to Rome. From there he returned to Berlin to resume work on art history at the Academy of Art. The University of Basel offered him a position in 1848, and Burckhardt returned to the academic world, not to abandon his duties at the University until just before his death.

In 1852 Burckhardt published his *Age of Constantine the Great.* In this important work he dealt with the disintegration of ancient culture, not as a "decline and fall" in the manner of Voltaire and Gibbon, but as a precondition for the growth of Christianity and the formation of medieval culture. Three years later he published a comprehensive guide to Italian art from antiquity to the nineteenth century. There followed what was perhaps his most famous work, *The Civilization of the Renaissance in Italy* (1860), a masterpiece of cultural history and an epochal study in intellectual history. His work had a determining influence not only on historical scholarship, but on aesthetic judgment throughout Europe.

Burckhardt taught at the Polytechnique at Zurich in 1855, and three years later was made a professor of history and history of art at Basel. It was there that the young Nietzsche met him, and the two formed a brief but strong relationship.

Burckhardt had hoped to provide in his work a comprehensive study of European culture since antiquity, and with this in mind after 1870 he began work on his *Greek Cultural History,* which remained unfinished at his death. While his contemporaries saw in him a brilliant scholar, the generation after 1918 began to see in Burckhardt a profound critic of his times and his civilization. In his *Weltgeschichtlichen Betrachtungen* (written from 1868 to 1873 but not published until after his death) and in his letters, from which this selection is taken, Burckhardt was severely critical of the abiding optimism of his age. The political and social forces which he saw at work, democracy and materialism, inspired him with both contempt and dread.

After 1866 Burckhardt taught only cultural history at Basel, and in 1893 he retired from academic duties completely. He died four years later. The letters that are reprinted below come from the translation of Alexander Dru, *The Letters of Jacob Burckhardt* (New York: Pantheon Books, 1955).

☙

LETTERS

To Gottfried Kinkel

Berlin, 13 June 1842

. . . . You ask for my views on present-day political philosophy and ethics. This is what I think about it.*

Practically all European peoples have had what is called the historical ground pulled from under their feet, Prussia into the bargain. The complete negation in matters of State, Church, Art and Life, that occurred at the end of last century, precipitated (among the better ones: developed) such an enormous mass of objective knowledge into even moderately active minds that a restoration of the old status, in which the people were really still minors, is quite unthinkable. Just as nowadays Art has lost its naïvety, and the styles of every age are all objectively present, *one beside the other,* so too, with the State; a personal interest in the particularities of his State has had to give place, in the individual, to a conscious idealism that involves free choice. Restorations, however well meant, and however much they seem to offer the only way out, cannot obscure the fact that the nineteenth century began with a *tabula rasa* in relation to everything. I neither praise nor find fault with it, it is simply a fact, and the Princes would do well to face up squarely to the difference between their former and their present position. The frightening accentuation of the rights of the individual consists in this: *cogito* (whether correctly or falsely doesn't matter) *ergo regno.* I still anticipate frightful crises, but mankind will survive them, and Germany will then perhaps attain its golden age. But what, in the meanwhile, is the individual to do? If he is unprejudiced and intelligent the prevailing spiritual currents will help him to form a philosophical postulate, and according to that he must live. There is one thing no revolution can rob him of: his inner truth. One will have to be still more frank, and still more honest than in the past, and perhaps love will found a new Reich on the ruins of the old States. As far as my unimportant self is concerned, I should never think of being an agitator or a revolutionary; a revolution is only lawful when it erupts unconsciously and unsummoned out of the ground. So I shall dedicate myself with all my strength to the advancement of the German spirit, and do what I think right. . . .

P.S. Forgive the grubby paper; and may Frau Directrix too forgive me; my writing-paper is at an end. *Schelling,* so it is said, has miscarried with his *philosophia secunda.* You will be sure to find the most comprehensive review of his doctrine in the *Deutschen Jahrbüchern.* I attended his lectures

* *N.B.* I hammered this out myself.

a couple of times as an outsider during the most turgid of dogmatic discussions, and explained it all to myself as follows: Schelling is a gnostic in the proper sense of the word, like Basilides. Hence all that is sinister, monstrous, formless in this part of his doctrine. I thought that at any moment some monstrous Asiatic God on twelve legs would come waddling in and with twelve arms take six hats off six heads. Little by little even the Berlin students will not be able to put up with his frightful, half-nonsensical, intuitional, contemplational form of expression. It is awful to have to listen to long historical explanations and discussions of the destiny of Messias, epically drawn out, complicated and entirely formless. Anyone who can love Schelling's Christ must have a large heart. *En attendant,* the great world here is interested in Schelling from an orthodox, pietistic, aristocratic standpoint; interested in the way this unfortunate city has of always having sympathies or antipathies without knowing why, simply at a word dropped by a Minister. Such disgusting servility in deed is unknown in Vienna and Munich, that is my opinion. Vale.

To Von Preen

Basle, 3 July 1870

One really gains something from your epistles! Don't for a moment imagine that I am provided with society like yours from any other quarter; I have no other correspondence except with Professor Lübke, and in the evenings I hawk my conversation round the cafés. It is no doubt largely my fault if I prefer to live *par distance* with clever people when I am not assured of real goodness, as I have come across some very curious specimens in my life. It may be that I ought to trust some of them more than I do; but life is short and I haven't time to make experiments. . . .

Like me you find everything in old Europe looking out of the true this year, and what is more judging from an entirely different knowledge of everyday affairs. I really no longer know what can be the value of German culture in making the individual inwardly happy; all those small centres of culture, where the German spirit was sitting pretty *next door* to German philistinism, are being blown sky high with *éclat,* and after all, the chief consequence of centralization is spiritual mediocrity, made most unpleasant by the increasing vexation of "hard work." The latter, reduced to its simplest terms of expression means, in my opinion, roughly this: will anyone who has not got, or does not earn, enough money to cut a figure in a large city kindly cease "existing." If the German spirit can still react from the centre of its truly personal powers against the great violence which is being done to it, if it is capable of opposing that violence with a new art, poetry and religion, then we are saved, but if not, not. I say: religion, because without a super-natural will to counterbalance the whole power and money racket, it can't be done.

During the last few days I have been looking at the two first volumes of *Kritische Gänge,* which contain the quintessential extract of all the discontent and enthusiasm of the years 1840 to 1844. Those years surely seemed to promise more than has since been fulfilled. But what exactly happened? After people had been played about with for two decades and always egged on to will and to want something, suddenly a really first-class "willer" appeared at Sadowa; [1] and since then, exhausted by their former effort of will, they have collapsed at his feet and want what he wants and just thank God that there is someone to give them the direction.

À propos of Sadowa: Did you notice how boldly Ollivier made out that the successful plebiscite was a French Sadowa?

There is something very consoling in the fact that armed with a culture and a life of the mind independent of one's business, one is also a different man in business, and that people guess that there is someone quite different behind the Herr Oberamtmann, who, for all their profane education, they cannot get at. This is where government business and financial business divide sharply, the latter consumes a man entirely, and hardens him to all else. Here, indeed, we still have a class of business men that makes a splendid exception owing to the part they take in life outside their work and yet I see so many individuals who have formally forsworn every kind of reading. They say "with regret" that they have no time, and really just don't feel like it, and what with the present pace of work in business, one can really hardly blame them. Now and then I get an inside view of the life of men in "big business," of the perpetual rush they live in, always standing to attention ready to telegraph, and of their utter inability to stop talking shop even in the evening or—were that possible—to free themselves from the whole business. Now and then one of them says to me: you teachers are lucky, you get holidays. To which I answer: With three or four partners in your business you too could make time for holidays, in rotation; but it's within you, in your souls, that there are no holidays.

You are only making one mistake in your reading: the fact that you are really reading the *Cicerone!* When, with my former insouciance I wrote the book, I little thought that I should be taken so seriously, as so many excellent people have since done. Only recently an American climbed up to my room, in order to develop a complete theory to me, which he linked on to some passage in the *Cicerone* (about the asymmetry of Roman architecture). I

[1] [Bismarck.]

had the greatest trouble imaginable in making it plain to him how entirely divorced I am from art and the literature on the subject. I am delighted that you like the *Cortegiano* and *Galateo,* a complete world of *Courtoisie,* long since departed, and yet it is no longer the Middle Ages, but intelligible to us. I can only enjoy the *Decamerone* if I force myself to enjoy the beauty and limpidity of the style consciously, by reading aloud to myself; the stories are either too long drawn out (compared with our present fashion: telling old stories in brief, just reporting on them); or else, as regards the spicy *genre,* they have been outdone by newer relish. But if you want something really stimulating, get yourself given Vasari's volumes, containing the biographies of Brunellesco, Signorelli, Leonardo, Rafael, Michelangelo, etc.; just skip anything technical that you don't understand; Vasari is the most refreshing reading, one gets such a sense of the very visible growth of the people he is describing.

But if you must know about my reading, well, I am writing this letter between two of Pindar's Olympic Odes, which I have to go through as part of my duties. Here and there, and despite all my admiration, the most disrespectful thoughts occur to me, and from time to time I catch sight of a lot of festive philistines, and Pindar with all his great pathos in pursuit. Pindar had obviously to deal from time to time with boors. But there is a tremendous amount of every sort of thing in these poems that I must know about. It is quite possible that three out of my four weeks' holiday may go on them, as it is no use reading piecemeal, one has got to master the whole Pindaric drapery at one go. Before that I hope to enjoy a week in the Schwarzwald.

To Von Preen

Basle, 20 July 1870

My warmest thanks for your cordial greeting, before the frontier is closed! Under what auspice shall we one day greet one another again? Whatever happens we ought not to forget that it is good for us children of the world to know that, even in tolerable health and in fair circumstances, we live over an abyss, etc.—that is the sermon I preach to myself. And then, as it seems to me, this war, far from originating in specific troubles, really has its roots, justification and inevitability in the depths of the nature of the peoples (which are only human nature raised to a higher power). The last scenes point to a long prelude. In the end L. N. found out what had occurred between A. and W.[2] in Ems, and I don't fancy the Russians were kind enough to tell him. Then up went the *ballon d'essai,* the Gotthard question, in which the French Ministers

[2] [Louis Napoleon, Alexander II, and Wilhelm I.]

played the innocents in a masterly fashion, *doux comme des agneaux*. Upon which the others thought: aha! he doesn't care, and threw out the Candidature for the Spanish Throne. And when they were well out on the *glacis,* he let down the portcullis, and could not be persuaded to raise it again. We now have to go through with the rest. I say *we,* because I don't believe very much in the lasting neutrality of Austria, and ours infallibly collapses with theirs. Your worthy compatriots are rushing their possessions here—very softly, I ask "Why?"

There is one minor historical consolation: how far is a great war followed by a long peace, *i.e.* the clear proclamation of real and lasting powers? I do not want to plead that that is what has been wanting in recent wars, but presuppose a great war, with the resulting lasting peace. But what a horrible price to pay! For only a long destructive war that rouses nations to their very depths (and despite all the wrath, that is still far from being the case) produces that result.

The final end might quite well be an *Imperium Romanum* (only when we are dead, to be sure), and after numerous Assyrians, Medes and Persians. That sort of *Imperium,* as we know, will not be a dynastic one, but a centralized administration with (thanks to its soldiers) a *beata tranquillitas.* In large sections of society the men of today have gradually and unconsciously given up nationality, and really hate every form of diversity. They would readily give up all their individual literatures and cultures, if it had to be so, for the sake of "through sleeping-cars." What I am writing sounds fantastic now, no doubt, and yet it's profoundly true.

O, if only we could avoid the unavoidable with sighs and tears!

To Von Preen

Basle, 27 September 1870

. . . . Since receipt of your letter I have been waiting and waiting to see whether a pause, an armistice, might not give me time to bring some kind of clarity into the whole problem. But events move on. France is to drink the dregs of misery and disorder, before being really allowed to speak. O, my dear friend, where will it all end? Does no one realize that the pestilence from which the conquered are suffering may also infect the victors? This frightful revenge would only be (relatively) justified if Germany were in fact the completely innocent victim of unprovoked attack that she is given out to be. Is the *Landwehr* to go right on to Bordeaux and Bayonne? Logically the whole of France would have to be occupied by a million Germans for many years. I know quite well it will not happen, but that is what one would have to deduce from what has happened hitherto. You know I have always had a mania for prophesying, and have already met with some astonishing rebuffs; but this time I simply must try to picture to myself what seems to be coming. Now supposing that, after the occupation of Paris and possibly of Lyons, the German Army Command were to let the French vote on the government they wanted. A lot would depend on how it was staged; the peasants and a section of the workers would certainly vote for Louis Napoleon again.

There is a new element present in politics that goes deep, and which former victors knew nothing of, or at least they made no conscious use of it. They try to humiliate the vanquished profoundly in his own eyes, so that he should never again really trust himself to achieve anything. It is possible that this aim will be achieved; but whether things will be any better and happier is another matter. What a mistake the poor German nation will make if once home it tries to put its rifle in the corner and devote itself to the arts and the pleasures of peace! In point of fact it will be a matter of military training before everything! And after a time no one will be able to say what they are living for. Then we shall see the Russo-German war in the middle of the picture, and then gradually in the foreground. In the meanwhile, we can both thank Heaven that at least Alsace and Baden are not to be soldered together: it would have produced a fatal mixture. That has been rendered quite impossible owing to the fact that Baden troops were given an essential role in the siege of Strasburg. For I take the liberty of presuming that that was not arranged by mistake. One of two things must happen: Alsace will either become purely Prussian or it remains French. Precisely *because* German dominion in these new *Länder* is so difficult, it can only be administered directly by Prussia, and any intermediary form of guardianship or tutelage under the German Empire would not be feasible. There is one other extraordinary sight to which the world will have to accustom itself: the Protestant House of Hohenzollern as the one effective protector of the Pope, who from now on becomes a subject of the Italian Kingdom.

But enough of Politics! Heaven grant us a tolerably quiet interval. The Philosopher's [3] credit has risen again these last weeks. Living here is one of his faithful, with whom I converse from time to time, as far as I can express myself in his language.[4]

And so, Greetings! We shall have to reorientate ourselves spiritually in more than one respect. Europe without an amusing, decorative France! Phew! And quite a few more things that Europe has forfeited and that have been emphasized for a long time in Renan's work.

---

[3] [Schopenhauer.]   [4] [Nietzsche.]

To Von Preen

Basle, New Year's Eve 1870

. . . . What has not happened in the last three months! Who could have believed that the struggle would have lasted far into a horrible winter, and would still show no sign of ending on the last day of the year? I shall remember the end of this year my whole life long! And not as regards my own, private, fate. The two great intellectual peoples of the continent are in the process of completely sloughing their culture, and a quite enormous amount of all that delighted and interested a man before 1870 will hardly touch the man of 1871—but what a tremendous spectacle, if the new world is born in great suffering.

The change in the German spirit will be as great as in the French; at first the clergy of both confessions will look upon themselves as the heirs of the spiritual disintegration, but something quite different will soon make itself felt, to one side. The shares of the "Philosopher" will rise sharply, whereas Hegel, after this year's jubilee publications, may very possibly make his definitive jubilee retirement.

The worst of all this is not the present war, but the era of wars upon which we have entered, and to this the new mentality will have to adapt itself. O, how much the cultured will have to throw overboard as a spiritual luxury that they have come to love! And how very different from us the coming generation will be. It may well be that, to the young, we shall appear very much as the French *émigrés,* intent on a life of pleasure, appeared to those to whom they fled.

Just think how much of all that has been written up to now is going to die out! What novels and dramas are people going to look at? Are the authors, loved by publisher and public alike, because they met and flattered the needs of the century, indeed, of the year and the month, going to survive? Anything that is to live on must contain a goodly portion of the eternal. And if anything lasting is to be created, it can only be through an overwhelmingly powerful effort of real poetry.

To me, as a teacher of history, a very curious phenomenon has become clear: the sudden devaluation of all mere "events" in the past. From now on in my lectures, I shall only emphasize cultural history, and retain nothing but the quite indispensable external scaffolding. Just think of all the defunct battles in the note-books of all the VV.EE.[5] in their Professional Chairs! Fortunately for me I never went in very much for that kind of thing. But I see I am again talking about myself, when the times may well laugh at all our personal hopes and activities.

[5] [*Viri Eruditissimi.*]

We are hourly expecting a battle in the neighbourhood, somewhere between Besançon and Belfort, and hourly expecting a great decision, who knows where, in France. The position of Switzerland, however strong our determination to maintain a strict neutrality, will not remain what it was, even though peace were signed today. The rest must be left to God.

"Put your house in order," etc., is the wisest thing we can all do, in central Europe. It is going to be different from what it has been.

And with all that I am dreaming of a little tour this summer in Southern Germany, in the course of which I might call on you in Bruchsal. How incurable our optimism. . . .

To Von Preen

Basle, 2 July 1871

Now that the terrible days, under the impression of which your last letter was written, lie a month behind us, what you say gives me once again to think. Yes, petroleum in the cellars of the Louvre and the flames in the other palaces are an expression of what the Philosopher calls "the will to live"; it is the last will and testament of mad fiends desiring to make a great impression on the world; from all that one has read since in intercepted papers, etc., the mainspring of it all was, at bottom, Herostratic. And now they are building schools. Those who arranged those things could all read, write and even compose newspaper articles and other literature. And the ones in Germany who mean to do the same sort of thing are certainly no less "educated." But just look at England, bursting with wealth, and secretly kept in a state of siege by analogous elements! Up till now, for two hundred years, people in England have imagined that every problem could be solved through Freedom, and that one could let opposites correct one another in the free interplay of argument. But what now? The great harm was begun in the last century, mainly through Rousseau, with his doctrine of goodness of human nature. Out of this plebs and educated alike distilled the doctrine of the golden age that was to come quite infallibly, provided people were left alone. The result, as every child knows, was the complete disintegration of the idea of authority in the heads of mortals, whereupon, of course, we periodically fall victim to sheer power. In the meantime, the idea of the natural goodness of man had turned, among the intelligent strata of Europe, into the idea of progress, *i.e.* undisturbed money-making and modern comforts, with philanthropy as a sop to conscience. But the day before yesterday the victorious Prussians found it necessary to declare a state of siege in Königshütte.

The great conceivable salvation would be for this insane optimism, in great and small, to disappear from people's brains. But then our present-day Chris-

tianity is not equal to the task; it has gone in for and got mixed up with optimism for the last two hundred years. A change will and must come, but
after God knows how much suffering. In the meanwhile you are building
schools—at least you can take the responsibility for that before God; while I
instruct my pupils and audience. I make no great secret of my philosophy to
my students; the clever ones understand me, and as at the same time I do
everything in every way I can to honour the real happiness that study and
knowledge give one—however little it may be in itself—I am able to give each
one some degree of consolation.

To Arnold von Salis

Basle, 21 April 1872

. . . . You could perfectly well have kept the Calderon; in fact I do not need
either the Schlegel or the Gries translations at all this summer, and at a word
from you I will send you all five. I have other worries; as the French say:
J'ai d'autres chiens à fouetter. Unfortunately, much more is expected of my
new course of lectures (on the history of Greek culture) than I shall be able
to offer, and my one comfort is that there will be an end to September in anno
1872. Except for the necessary minimum of recreation I sit assiduously at my
last, seeing only one thing: how unpolished and amateurish the whole series
promises to be, although I spend all the scholarly effort I can on it. . . .

Herr B. will tell you in detail all about Nietzsche's lectures (on the work
in our University); he is still in debt to us for the last, from which we awaited
some solutions to the questions and lamentations that he threw out in such a
grand and bold style. But in the meanwhile he has gone to the Waadtland to
recuperate for ten days. He was quite delightful in places, and then again one
heard a note of profound sadness, and I still don't see how the *auditores
humanissimi* are to derive comfort or explanations from it. One thing was
clear: a man of great gifts who possesses everything at first hand, and passes
it on.

What you say about this being a transitional period is felt by all thinking
people about everything. But there is one particular point I want to draw your
attention to: the worries and troubles in store for all spiritual things within
the next few years, resulting from the ever-increasing emphasis on material
things, from the general change in mundane affairs that is bound to follow
on the coming rise in the cost of living (one and a half times), and from the
fact that we are at the beginning of a series of wars, etc. Things have reached
the point at which first-class minds, which ten years ago devolved to scholarship, the Church or the Civil Service are moving over in appreciable numbers
to the *business* party. And as to the extent to which the Universities are feeling the lack of *timber* when they have to stop a gap (that is to say of sufficiently

respected young scholars who are neither deaf nor blind from special research), on that score I have heard quite incredible admissions from a well-informed source.

If I am not mistaken, I told you my fundamental beliefs during the last war: something great, new and liberating must come out of Germany, and what is more *in opposition* to power, wealth and business; it will have to have its martyrs; it must be something which of its very nature will swim above water and survive political, economic and other catastrophies. But what? There you out-question me. It might even be that we too should fail to recognize it if it came into the world.

In the meanwhile let us attend assiduously, and where we are concerned, learn and learn till we bust.

To Von Preen

Basle, 26 April 1872

. . . . I am not being unfair. Bismarck has only taken into his own hands what would have happened in due course without him and in opposition to him. He saw the growing wave of social-democracy would somehow or other bring about a state of naked power, whether through the democrats themselves, or through the Governments, and said: *Ipse faciam,* and embarked on three wars, 1864, 1866, 1870.

But we are only at the beginning. Don't you feel that everything we do now seems more or less amateurish, capricious, and becomes increasingly ridiculous by contrast with the high purposefulness of the military machine worked out to the last details? The latter is bound to become the model of existence. It will be most interesting for you, my dear Sir, to observe how the machinery of State and administration is transformed and militarized; for me—how schools and education are put through the cure, etc. Of all classes, the workers are going to have the strangest time; I have a suspicion that, for the time being, sounds completely mad, and yet I cannot rid myself of it: that the military state will have to turn "industrialist." The accumulations of beings, the mounds of men in the yards and factories cannot be left for all eternity in their need and thirst for riches; a planned and controlled degree of poverty, with promotion and uniforms, starting and ending daily to the roll of drums, that is what ought to come logically. (I know enough history, of course, to know that things do not always work out logically.) Of course, what is done will have to be done well—and then no mercy, whether for those above or those below. In the paper yesterday or the day before the programme of the carpenters' union in Berlin was given, which you will easily find in the Berlin papers. *Lisez et réfléchissez!*

The development of a clever and lasting sovereign power is still in swaddling clothes; it may perhaps wear its *toga virilis* for the first time in Germany. There are still vast uncharted seas to be discovered in this sphere. The Prussian dynasty is so placed that it and its staff can never again be powerful enough. There can be no question of stopping on this path; the salvation of Germany itself is in forging ahead. . . .

To Von Preen

Basle, 17 November 1876

Put forward any idea, and proposal whatsoever in the Conservative's sense, and in practice nothing comes of it; only disintegrating and levelling ideas have any real power. You will find the point we have reached illuminated in the same sense in our *Allgemeine Schweizer Zeitung,* but there is nothing to be done. Our Federal and Cantonal Referendum sometimes frustrates one of the ideas of MM. Homais and company, and for a time they are puzzled what to do, but in itself it is really one more solvent. No amount of uneasiness could any longer plug the source of the ill, which is the leadership of the masses, who are so easily led, and the utter lack of respect shown by Radicalism—not for the old, conservative political forms (since I don't expect piety from it on that score), but for the laws and regulations of their own creation. That's what makes the situation so hopelessly insecure. In the meanwhile duty and policy require that though we may not smile on everything we should at least not look sour-faced. For my part I have long since simplified my outlook by relating every question to the University of Basle and by simply asking whether this or that is good or not good for it. As long as I am neither guilty nor an accomplice of anything that does it harm, I shall be satisfied with the outward course of my life *in globo.* Term has now been going on for four weeks, and the additional public lectures have begun, of which two are behind and two before me. Further, I have been to the Opera six times already, and it's been very good, all things considered. On the 2nd December our simple and beautiful Concert Hall is to be inaugurated with the Ninth Symphony, etc., so I shall see that I get a seat, as the Society in question will almost fill the 1500 seats. Does anyone, nowadays, feel the *Freude, schöner Götterfunken?* Those who do so must be very young. All the same, our Concert Hall is a more pleasing building than your Festhalle, and the programmes it is likely to offer.

To Max Alioth

London, 2 August 1879

I meant to go to the British Museum yesterday but found the Elgin Marbles and almost the whole of the Greek department closed. Thereupon I made my decision at once and went by bus, *outside,* into the thick of the city and looked at St. Paul's and one or two other things; I shall not willingly go again into that crowd unless forced to do so. Then I took my interim fodder in one of the oldest city pubs that I had visited nineteen years ago (The Bell, Old Bailey), and went by Underground to the South Kensington Museum again.

My wonder increased considerably. Where will our history of art lead us, if people go on collecting at the present rate, and nobody tries to take a really general view of it? If I had a year to spend here, I would turn up my sleeves, spit on my hands and do what I could, with the help of others, to formulate as clearly as possible the living law of *forms.* However, I can't change the course of my life for the sake of such splendours. And what good do these great aesthetic incitements do the Londoner, if the look of the town is to be ruined all the same by a colossal horror on purely utilitarian grounds, by comparison with which our new bridge is perfectly innocent! A disgusting, high, straight, cast-iron bridge has been built slap across the main vista of the town, a main-line railway laid across it, and a hideous great round-topped lady's trunk built above it (the main station at Charing Cross). As I strolled in the moonlight yesterday evening, on Waterloo Bridge, and saw how the wonderfully picturesque view of the Houses of Parliament, Westminster Abbey and Lambeth Palace was cut in half, I could have cried. The evening light and the full moon rising made it all the more painful. Further down too, towards London Bridge, there is a similar monstrosity in cast iron, also leading to a colossal terminus. O Lord! what is not going to be sacrificed to the *practical sense* of the nineteenth century! And what will London look like in a hundred years' time, or even in ten years, if more and more of these terrible decisions have to be taken on account of the growing population? I am daily astonished, in the meanwhile, that the crowds don't crush one another to pieces, and that the supply and maintenance is so orderly.

Tomorrow in, I hope, fine weather, to Hampton Court.

Queen Victoria gets off lightly; her face on stamps and coins remains the same as at the beginning of her reign, whereas in truth it must be looking a bit rough.

To Von Preen

Basle, 1 May 1881

In the last few days Radicalism has lurched another step forward all over Switzerland, and unless everything deceives me, there is a European movement at the back of it, and your country will soon experience something of the kind. I feel deep down inside me that something is going to burst out in the West, once Russia has been reduced to confusion by acts of violence. That will be the beginning of the period when every stage of confusion will have to be gone through, until finally a real Power emerges based upon sheer, unlimited violence, and it will take precious little account of the right to vote, the sovereignty of the people, material prosperity, industry, etc. Such is the unavoidable end of the Constitutional State, based on law, once it succumbs to counting hands, and the consequences thereof. You must forgive me, my dear Sir, if I importune you with views which I do not want to make known here.

To Max Alioth

Basle, 10 September 1881

. . . . It is just the same in Italy as in France; the growth of business and material things, and a marked decrease in the political security that goes with such business and the pleasures in question; the good liberals and even those in a radical way of business, may fall on their knees before the leaders of the people and beseech them not to commit any follies. But in order to be re-elected, the leaders of the people, the demagogues, must have the masses on their side, and they in turn demand that something should always be happening, otherwise they don't believe "progress" is going on. One cannot possibly escape from that *cercle vicieux* as long as universal suffrage lasts. One thing after another will have to be sacrificed: positions, possessions, religion, civilized manners, pure scholarship—as long as the masses can put pressure on their *Meneurs,* and as long as some power doesn't shout: Shut up!—and there is not the slightest sign of that for the time being. And (as I lamented long ago to you) that power can really only emerge from the depth of evil, and the effect will be hair-raising.

Today, I begin my classes again in the Pedagogium (four times a week), although I have the right to completely free holidays. But one sets a good example thereby, and the labour is not great. In addition, there are my photographs to be sorted, given to the bookbinder in series, subsequently labelled and finally arranged in portfolios. That has been my autumn occupation on several occasions, a very agreeable little business. Unfortunately the Rector's speech has been foisted on me because Professor Miaskowski has gone to Breslau in the middle of his term as Rector of the University, and with Steffens being ill, I am now the eldest in the faculty concerned. It does not entail much work, but a lot of worry.

To Von Preen

Basle, 13 April 1882

. . . . Stick to your frivolous happiness; I do the same with all my strength, and do not allow the prospect of what is to come (although it's pretty clear) get the better of me. Each and every cheerful mood is a genuine gain, and then you have your sons to translate the things of this world into youth and hopefulness. My circle of friends is limited to cheerful people, for there is nothing to be got from those who have gone sour. Nor do I think that anyone in my neighbourhood could complain that I had damped their spirits; and then, as old people are wont to do, I am really beginning to love solitude (linked to a bit of music).

Everybody has the right to think as they please about the situation, peace or war. There are still, of course, diplomatic secrets on the question, but they are no longer decisive; the danger is in the full light of day, for everyone to see. One principal difference between the present and former years lies in the fact that the Governments of great countries, for example France, are no longer capable of secret negotiations, because the ministries change so often and no form of discretion can be assured. The same is true of Italy; who would dream of trusting or confiding anything to Signor Mancini and his friends?

But the incredible insolence which is spreading everywhere in Russia, far beyond the control of the Cabinet, is very significant. It is not the nihilists who are the most dangerous, but the impertinence of those in high places. I am not surprised that everything points to direct elections with you; parties all over the world are of the opinion that there is perhaps something to be won in that lucky dip, and that anyway there is nothing to be lost, so full steam ahead!—in a mood of despair.

It has long been clear to me that the world is moving towards the alternative between complete democracy and absolute, lawless despotism, and the latter would certainly not be run by the dynasties, who are too soft-hearted, but by supposedly republican Military Commands. Only people do not like to imagine a world whose rulers utterly ignore law, prosperity, enriching work, and industry, credit, etc., and who would rule with utter brutality. But those are the people into whose hands the world is being driven by the competition among all parties for the participation of the masses on any and every question. The *ultima ratio* of many conservatives has been familiar here for a long time: "It's bound to come," as you put it, "and it is useless to resist," referring to complete democratization.

At the same time, the older stratum of workers is quite out of fashion, and people of assured position are more and more seldom found in office—that too is a phenomenon with which we are long familiar, and anyone who wants to see it on a really large scale need only look at France and its present governing personnel.

Your position in local government, my dear Sir, gives you an insight into the real ethos of the times which is entirely wanting to many a "man of the people," and which he would in any case forbid himself. One of the principal phenomena which you emphasize reveals itself as clearly as can be in Switzerland: a flight from the risks of business into the arms of the salary-paying State is manifest in the fact that the moment farming is in a bad way the numbers who want to enter classes for teachers increases. But where on earth is it to end—the enormous luxury of learning side by side with that of teaching? Here in Basle we are now faced again with disbursements of two millions for new school buildings! It's a single chain of related facts: free instruction, compulsory instruction, a maximum of thirty per class, a minimum of so and so many cubic metres per child, too many subjects taught, teachers obliged to have a superficial knowledge of too many subjects, etc. And, naturally, as a result: everyone dissatisfied with everything (as with you), a scramble for higher positions, which are of course very limited in number. Not to mention the absolutely insane insistence upon scholarship that goes on in girls' schools. A town is at the present time a place to which parents without resources want to move simply because there their children are taught all manner of pretentious things. And like many other bankruptcies, the schools will one day go bankrupt, because the whole thing will become impossible; but it may well be accompanied by other disasters, which it is better not to think about. It may even be that the present educational system has reached its peak, and is approaching its decline.

To Von Preen

Basle, 17 March 1888

What you wrote on Kaiser Wilhelm I, about whom you have so much more information and many more personal impressions than many who likewise knew him, was of the greatest interest to me. The mere existence of a man like that is a protest against the view, though the whole world held it, that one can make do with men who are raised up from below, by majorities, by the masses; he was, as you say, the exception. Democracy, to be sure, has no sense for the exception, and when it can't deny it or remove it, hates it from the bottom of its heart. Itself the product of mediocre minds and their envy, Democracy can only use mediocre men as tools, and the ordinary careerist gives it all the guarantees it can desire of common feeling. A new spirit then undoubtedly begins to penetrate down into the masses, and they once again begin to feel an obscure impulse to look for the exceptional, but in this they may be astonishingly badly advised, and capriciously fix on a Boulanger. The parallel happenings in France could be infinitely instructive for Germans if they were in the mood to attend to them. But people are turning from a corpse that is all too historic, to one who is marked for an early death. I can think of no similar situation in the whole of history: in all other cases, when a ruler was succeeded by a man who was dying, little depended on the change, and the world did not, as it does now, feverishly reckon up the probabilities attached to it.

To Von Preen

Baden, Aargau. Hotel Verena-Hof, 24 July 1889

And so you too were destined to join the ranks of those suffering from heart disease. But compared with me you have the advantage of ten years of youth, and will—provided only you are very careful not to work too much—enjoy perfectly good health. For me, on the other hand, the winter season of life has definitely set in, I am easily tired, and must be grateful that eyes and ears hold out, and that I can read with complete comfort. I mean to be back in Basle on the 20th or 22nd at the latest, and all my hopes are fixed upon our meeting again in September. God grant it may be so!

There were special reasons why I decided in favour of Aargau-Baden; I am considerably nearer to an old sister who is very dear to me, and who has been lying between life and death for some time past, and I can get to her in two hours. . . . *Ma parliamo d'altra cosa!* After coffee I crawled along the streets of the town—crawled, so as not to sweat—to a really good bookshop, where one can lay in a stock of "Reclam's Universal Library." There I bought *Roch-holz, Legend of the Aargau,* and must on this occasion confess that myths attract me more and more, and draw me away from history. It was not for nothing that the only book I took with me from Basle was the Greek Pausanias. Bit by bit I am acquiring really mythical eyes, perhaps they are those of an old man once again approaching childhood? I have to laugh when I think that I used to polish off twenty battles and wars, so and so many changes of territory, and whole series of genealogica in a single lecture. Wolfgang will bear me out in this.

Old legends are not my sole concern; like you I recapitulate my own varied past from time to time, only perhaps I have more cause to wonder than you, having made so many foolish decisions and done so many foolish things; who could describe how blind one has been in decisive matters, and the importance one has attached to inessentials, and the degree of emotion! On the whole I really cannot complain, it might all have gone much less well. What we both have in common on our earthly pilgrimage, at least since a certain year, has been the need to be satisfied with the moment through one's work, and what is more a varied and stimulating work. The leaden roller that flattens out so many people has not passed over us.

How the younger generation will survive, and build its nest, is something which, seeing the complete inconstancy of things, one ought really not to worry about too much. The young folk in my family, at any rate, look out on the world just as cheekily as we did in our day, and one of my principles is to conceal my fears for the future entirely from them. The forty-year-olds are of course beginning to notice things for themselves. The picture I have formed of the *terribles simplificateurs* who are going to descend upon poor old Europe is not an agreeable one; and here and there in imagination I can already see the fellows visibly before me, and will describe them to you over a glass of wine when we meet in September. Sometimes I meditate prophetically on how our learning and quisquilian researches will fare when these events are in their very early stages, and culture, in the interval, has only sunk a peg or two. Then, too, I picture to myself something of the lighter side of the great renovation: how the pale fear of death will come over all the careerists and climbers, because once again real naked power is on top and the general *consigne* is: "shut your mouth." In the meanwhile, what is the most grateful task for the moment? Obviously: to amuse people as intensively as possible. We have here a velocipede circus, though only till tonight, which has completely paralysed and emptied two theatres, the operetta in the *Kursaal* and the play at the *Theatre,* to the great aesthetic misery of the local rag. From the point of view of the history of culture, it is not yet quite clear to me how far this sort of display will damage the animal circus, or possibly drive it out of business. Does the spectacle of men perhaps really awaken more interest than the sight of horses? And then consider the minute capital sunk in steel wheels as compared with the purchase of horses, not counting their keep, the vet., hay, straw and oats. Such are the thoughts of my thermal leisure, you will say.

I take part in the social life of the watering-place to the extent that there are several people with whom I have a nodding acquaintance, and converse with my neighbour at the luncheon table, but take the greatest care not to tie myself down in any way for the evenings, and drink my glass of wine by myself. Baden, which is deserted in the Alpine season, is fairly full at the present time.

One of these afternoons I must go to Zürich, where I mean to hire a cab for a couple of hours and take a look at all the new buildings, specially the Quais, the neighbourhood of the Concert Hall, and one or two other things. These things are talked about in Basle, and I must be able to voice my opinion along with the others. But I much prefer to think of Lucerne, where I intend to go for a visit at the end of my cure. O, if only my health allows me to go for a fortnight to Locarno! My finances could stand it, and I should not regret it. I remain here in Baden, as far as I know, till the 12th or 14th August; first of all there are the ritual twenty-one baths to be undergone, and then a couple of days' rest. The real *Bâlois,* by the way, always take twenty-two baths—"just so that one shouldn't have anything to reproach oneself with afterwards."

I don't suppose you know "Goldwändler" by any chance? It is not a tramp or a ghost that wanders about in this district, but a light red wine which grows against the "golden wall" on the steep heights west of the baths. It is an excellent and fairly innocuous wine that the patients can stand, and has been growing there, without any doubt, since Roman times. The place I live in was called *castellum thermarum,* and is mentioned by Tacitus, an honour which Karlsruhe, beautiful Karlsruhe, cannot boast. We in Basle are at least mentioned in Ammianus Marcellinus.

To Von Preen

Basle, 25 March 1890

What times we live in, indeed! Men, interest and things may well come to the fore that will overturn our present antlike existence. Our dear 19th century has so accustomed people to the idea that everything new, however questionable in itself, is justified, that nothing can any longer hinder the process. It is quite incredible how empty-headed and defenceless even thoroughly decent people are when confronted by the spirit of the age. The Parties which have existed up to now seem to me like groups of actors gesticulating in front of the footlights, and illuminated hitherto by a strong light from above—and suddenly caught in their various attitudes and lit from below by a hard red light.

. . . . Everyone reads the papers in his own way; the unrest in Köpenick, for example, made *one* impression upon me which was to say that the rioters followed a strictly military order, which means to say that a sense of duty and the accompanying sense of discipline may be beginning to move over to the other side. The usual rowdyism, which has been latent hitherto, will become more and more prominent, and increasingly difficult to keep down with the methods employed up till now. We had a little example of it here last Saturday among the Germans liable for military service and their defiant and threatening disturbances in the lower town, the like of which have never occurred previously on the same scale.

And in times like these they "shatter" the Chancellor to pieces. Not that he had any medicine in his bag against serious dangers; but it would have been wise, outwardly at least, to do everything possible to preserve whatever looks like authority, or even recalls it. That article may one day become something of a rarity. A troublesome Reichstag can be sent packing, and they will probably be able to govern without it if only for a time. And then, no doubt as a result of some event or other, Ministries will be forced upon the Government by the Parties, and with them you will get unrestrained opportunism, careerists and everything and everybody constantly changing, both personnel and tendencies. In the meanwhile those in the rest of Europe who have had to duck under, or have been elbowed into the gutter by the German Reich, will rise to a more or less courageous and impudent independence. One may, for example, be justifiably curious to see how Italy behaves when, owing to financial crashes, lack of discipline and a failure of authority will have made themselves felt.

All of which is very strange. All the same yesterday we had the last or almost the last sign of good fortune: by a large majority our "people" scotched the Health Insurance Act which the Supreme Council had already accepted out of sheer exhaustion; it had been proposed by the most unruly demagogues and, at the same time, was calculated to promote the despotism of the State over the Private life of individuals in its most extreme form (that is to say, through a Head of Department). Among the whole gang of promoters not one was Bâlois by origin, though one or t'other may have been born here. However, we old Bâlois are quite accustomed to swallowing a good deal of this kind of thing.

To Von Preen

Basle, 25 September 1890

Yes, indeed, Authority is a mystery; how it comes into being is dark, but how it is gambled away is plain enough. The Bund came into being in 1847, after the *Sonderbundkrieg,* and as long as Louis Napoleon ruled in France people behaved fairly legally and tolerably objectively; since then, however, the German *Kulturkampf* has had a completely disintegrating effect upon us and at present we are being carried along on the wave of a general world movement. Individually these waves are called the rise of the world of the workers, the growing danger of World War, revolution imminent in Portugal, and perhaps too in Spain, the McKinley laws in North America, etc. And every month the pulse beat is a little faster. What an easy time the Radicals of the 'thirties had! Their "superficiality combined with ruthless indifference towards the established order" (I entirely endorse your admirable definition) fitted in perfectly with the continued existence of the general situation. Things are different now, and, as you say, our present age of universal unrest will in the future seem relatively calm and undisturbed. "Purely legal questions" have, of course, never existed once whole peoples were set in motion; but this time, to judge by the expression on the world's face, there will be neither Law nor process of Law in any shape or form.

NORMAN ANGELL

NORMAN ANGELL was born in Holbeach, England, on December 26, 1873. He was educated in France and Geneva. As a youth he traveled to America, where he worked as a cowboy, prospector, and journalist in the Western states, returning to England in 1898 as a corresponding journalist for a number of American newspapers. During the next twenty years he managed and edited several newspapers in both France and England.

The Great Illusion, from which the present selection has been made, was published in 1910 and immediately gained for its author an international reputation as a fighter for peace and social justice. It was translated into twenty-two languages and sold over two million copies. It was followed by some thirty books and two thousand articles published by Sir Norman in the course of his active career in international affairs.

During the very World War that he thought unthinkable, Angell served in an ambulance corps, returning to the United States to cooperate with groups working for the League of Nations. In 1919 he attended the meeting of the Second Socialist International at Berne. His two books on peace—*The Economic Chaos and the Peace Treaty* (1919) and *The Fruits of Victory* (1921)—associated him with John Maynard Keynes in opposition to the Versailles Treaty.

From 1928 to 1931 he edited *Foreign Affairs* magazine. At the same time he began a term as Member of Council of the Royal Institute of International Affairs which lasted until 1942. From 1929 to 1933 he served as Labour Member of Parliament for North Bradbury; he was knighted in 1931. In 1933 Sir Norman was awarded the Nobel Peace Prize.

THE GREAT ILLUSION

IT IS GENERALLY ADMITTED that the present rivalry in armaments in Europe—notably such as that now in progress between England and Germany—cannot go on in its present form indefinitely. The net result of each side meeting the efforts of the other with similar efforts is that at the end of a given period the relative position of each is what it was originally, and the enormous sacrifices of both have gone for nothing. If as between England and Germany it is claimed that England is in a position to maintain the lead because she has the money, Germany can retort that she is in a position to maintain the lead because she has the population, which must, in the case of a highly organized European nation, in the end mean money. Meanwhile, neither side can yield to the other, as the one so doing would, it is felt, be placed at the mercy of the other, a situation which neither will accept.

There are two current solutions which are offered as a means of egress from this *impasse*. There is that of the smaller party, regarded in both countries for the most part as one of dreamers and doctrinaires, who hope to solve the problem by a resort to general disarmament, or, at least, a limitation of armament by agreement. And there is that of the larger, which is esteemed the more practical party, of those who are persuaded that the present state of rivalry and recurrent irritation is bound to culminate in an armed conflict, which, by definitely reducing one or other of the parties to a position of manifest inferiority, will settle the thing for at least some time, until after a longer or shorter period a state of relative equilibrium is established, and the whole process will be recommenced *da capo*.

This second solution is, on the whole, accepted as one of the laws of life: one of the hard facts of existence which men of ordinary courage take as all in the day's work. And in every country those favoring the other solution are looked upon either as people who fail to realize the hard facts of the world in which they live, or as people less concerned with the security of their country than with upholding a somewhat emasculate ideal; ready to weaken the defences of their own country on no better assurance than that the prospective enemy will not be so wicked as to attack them. . . .

How deeply the danger is felt even by those who sincerely desire peace and can in no sense be considered Jingoes may be judged by the following from the pen of Mr. Frederic Harrison. I make no apology for giving the quotations at some length. In a letter to the London *Times* he says:

Whenever our Empire and maritime ascendancy are challenged it will be by such an invasion in force as was once designed by Philip and Parma, and again by Napoleon. It is this certainty which compels me to modify the anti-militarist policy which I have consistently maintained for forty years past. . . . To me now it is no question of loss of prestige—no question of the shrinkage of the Empire; it is our existence as a foremost European Power, and even as a thriving nation. . . . If ever our naval defence were broken through, our Navy overwhelmed or even dispersed for a season, and a military occupation of our arsenals, docks, and capital were effected, the ruin would be such as modern history cannot parallel. It would not be the Empire, but Britain that would be destroyed. . . . The occupation by a foreign invader of our arsenals, docks, cities, and capital would be to the Empire what the bursting of the boilers would be to a *Dreadnought*. Capital would disappear with the destruction of credit. . . . A catastrophe so appalling cannot be left to chance, even if the probabilities against its occurring were 50 to 1. But the odds are not 50 to 1. No high authority ventures to assert that a successful invasion of our country is absolutely impossible if it were assisted by extraordinary conditions. And a successful invasion would mean to us the total collapse of our Empire, our trade, and, with trade, the means of feeding forty millions in these islands. If it is asked, "Why does invasion threaten more terrible consequences to us than it does to our neighbors?" the answer is that the British Empire is an anomalous structure, without any real parallel in modern history, except in the history of Portugal, Venice, and Holland, and in ancient history Athens and Carthage. Our Empire presents special conditions both for attack and for destruction. And its destruction by an enemy seated on the Thames would have consequences so awful to contemplate that it cannot be left to be safeguarded by one sole line of defence, however good, and for the present hour however adequate. . . . For more than forty years I have raised my voice against every form of aggression, of Imperial expansion, and Continental militarism. Few men have more earnestly protested against postponing social reforms and the well-being of the people to Imperial conquests and Asiatic and African adventures. I do not go back on a word that I have uttered thereon. But how hollow is all talk about industrial reorganization until we have secured our country against a catastrophe that would involve untold destitution and misery on the people in the mass—which would paralyze industry and raise food to famine prices, whilst closing our factories and our yards!

. . . I think it will be admitted that there is not much chance of misunderstanding the general idea embodied in the passage quoted at the end of the last chapter. Mr. Harrison is especially definite. At the risk of "damnable iteration" I would again recall the fact that he is merely expressing one of the universally accepted axioms of European politics, namely, that a nation's financial and industrial stability, its security in commercial activity—in short, its prosperity and well-being depend, upon its being able to defend itself against the aggression of other nations, who will, if they are able, be tempted to commit such aggression because in so doing they will increase their power, prosperity and well-being, at the cost of the weaker and vanquished.

I have quoted, it is true, largely journalistic authorities because I desire to indicate real public opinion, not merely scholarly opinion. But Mr. Harrison has the support of other scholars of all sorts. Thus Mr. Spenser Wilkinson, Chichele Professor of Military History at Oxford, and a deservedly respected authority on the subject, confirms in almost every point in his various writings the opinions that I have quoted, and gives emphatic confirmation to all that Mr. Frederic Harrison has expressed. In his book, "Britain at Bay," Professor Wilkinson says: "No one thought when in 1888 the American observer, Captain Mahan, published his volume on the influence of sea-power upon history, that other nations beside the British read from that book the lesson that victory at sea carried with it a prosperity and influence and a greatness obtainable by no other means."

Well, it is the object of these pages to show that this all but universal idea, of which Mr. Harrison's letter is a particularly vivid expression, is a gross and desperately dangerous misconception, partaking at times of the nature of an optical illusion, at times of the nature of a superstition—a misconception not only gross and universal, but so profoundly mischievous as to misdirect an immense part of the energies of mankind, and to misdirect them to such a degree that unless we liberate ourselves from the superstition civilization itself will be threatened.

And one of the most extraordinary features of this whole question is that the absolute demonstration of the falsity of this idea, the complete exposure of the illusion which gives it birth, is neither abstruse nor difficult. This demonstration does not repose upon any elaborately constructed theorem, but upon the simple exposition of the political facts of Europe as they exist to-day. These facts, which are incontrovertible, and which I shall elaborate presently, may be summed up in a few simple propositions stated thus:

1. An extent of devastation even approximating to that which Mr. Harrison foreshadows as the result of the conquest of Great Britain, could only be inflicted by an invader as a means of punishment costly to himself, or as the result of an unselfish and expensive desire to inflict misery for the mere joy of inflicting it. Since trade depends upon the existence of natural wealth and a population capable of working it, an invader cannot "utterly destroy it," except by destroying the population, which is not practicable. If he could destroy the population he would thereby destroy his own market, actual or potential, which would be commercially suicidal.[1]

2. If an invasion of Great Britain by Germany did involve, as Mr. Harrison and those who think with him say it would, "the total collapse of the Empire, our trade, and the means of feeding forty millions in these islands . . . the disturbance of capital and destruction of credit," German capital would also be disturbed, because of the internationalization and delicate interdependence of our credit-built finance and industry, and German credit would also collapse, and the only means of restoring it would be for Germany to put an end to the chaos in England by putting an end to the condition which had produced it. Moreover, because of this delicate interdependence of our credit-built finance, the confiscation by an invader of private property, whether stocks, shares, ships, mines, or anything more valuable than jewellery or furniture—anything, in short, which is bound up with the economic life of the people—would so react upon the finance of the invader's country as to make the damage to the invader resulting from the confiscation exceed in value the property confiscated. So that Germany's success in conquest would be a demonstration of the complete economic futility of conquest.

[1] In this self-seeking world, it is not reasonable to assume the existence of an inverted altruism of this kind.

3. For allied reasons, in our day the exaction of tribute from a conquered people has become an economic impossibility; the exaction of a large indemnity so costly directly and indirectly as to be an extremely disadvantageous financial operation.

4. It is a physical and economic impossibility to capture the external or carrying trade of another nation by military conquest. Large navies are impotent to create trade for the nations owning them, and can do nothing to "confine the commercial rivalry" of other nations. Nor can a conqueror destroy the competition of a conquered nation by annexation; his competitors would still compete with him—*i.e.,* if Germany conquered Holland, German merchants would still have to meet the competition of Dutch merchants, and on keener terms than originally, because the Dutch merchants would then be within the German's customs lines; the notion that the trade competition of rivals can be disposed of by conquering those rivals being one of the illustrations of the curious optical illusion which lies behind the misconception dominating this subject.

5. The wealth, prosperity, and well-being of a nation depend in no way upon its political power; otherwise we should find the commercial prosperity and social well-being of the smaller nations, which exercise no political power, manifestly below that of the great nations which control Europe, whereas this is not the case. The populations of States like Switzerland, Holland, Belgium, Denmark, Sweden, are in every way as prosperous as the citizens of States like Germany, Russia, Austria, and France. The wealth *per capita* of the small nations is in many cases in excess of that of the great nations. Not only the question of the security of small States, which, it might be urged, is due to treaties of neutrality, is here involved, but the question of whether political power can be turned in a positive sense to economic advantage.

6. No other nation could gain any advantage by the conquest of the British Colonies, and Great Britain could not suffer material damage by their loss, however much such loss would be regretted on sentimental grounds, and as rendering less easy a certain useful social co-operation between kindred peoples. The use, indeed, of the word "loss" is misleading. Great Britain does not "own" her Colonies. They are, in fact, independent nations in alliance with the Mother Country, to whom they are no source of tribute or economic profit (except as foreign nations are a source of profit), their economic relations being settled, not by the Mother Country, but by the Colonies. Economically, England would gain by their formal separation, since she would be relieved of the cost of their defence. Their "loss" involving, therefore, no change in economic fact (beyond saving the Mother Country the

cost of their defence), could not involve the ruin of the Empire, and the starvation of the Mother Country, as those who commonly treat of such a contingency are apt to aver. As England is not able to exact tribute or economic advantage, it is inconceivable that any other country, necessarily less experienced in colonial management, would be able to succeed where England had failed, especially in view of the past history of the Spanish, Portuguese, French, and British Colonial Empires. This history also demonstrates that the position of British Crown Colonies, in the respect which we are considering, is not sensibly different from that of the self-governing ones. It is *not* to be presumed, therefore, that any European nation, realizing the facts, would attempt the desperately expensive business of the conquest of England for the purpose of making an experiment which all colonial history shows to be doomed to failure.

The foregoing propositions traverse sufficiently the ground covered in the series of those typical statements of policy, both English and German, from which I have quoted. The simple statement of these propositions, based as they are upon the self-evident facts of present-day European politics, sufficiently exposes the nature of those political axioms which I have quoted. But as men even of the calibre of Mr. Harrison normally disregard these self-evident facts, it is necessary to elaborate them at somewhat greater length.

For the purpose of presenting a due parallel to the statement of policy embodied in the quotations made from the London *Times* and Mr. Harrison and others, I have divided the propositions which I desire to demonstrate into seven clauses, but such a division is quite arbitrary, and made only in order to bring about the parallel in question. The whole seven can be put into one, as follows: That as the only possible policy in our day for a conqueror to pursue is to leave the wealth of a territory in the complete possession of the individuals inhabiting that territory, it is a logical fallacy and an optical illusion to regard a nation as increasing its wealth when it increases its territory; because when a province or State is annexed, the population, who are the real and only owners of the wealth therein, are also annexed, and the conqueror gets nothing. The facts of modern history abundantly demonstrate this. When Germany annexed Schleswig-Holstein and Alsatia not a single ordinary German citizen was one *pfennig* the richer. Although England "owns" Canada, the English merchant is driven out of the Canadian markets by the merchant of Switzerland, who does not "own" Canada. Even where territory is not formally annexed, the conqueror is unable to take the wealth of a conquered territory, owing to the delicate interdependence of the financial world (an outcome of our credit and banking systems), which makes the financial and industrial security of the victor dependent upon financial and industrial security in all considerable civilized centres; so that widespread confiscation or destruction of trade and commerce in a conquered territory would react disastrously upon the conqueror. The conqueror is thus reduced to economic impotence, which means that political and military power is economically futile—that is to say, can do nothing for the trade and well-being of the individuals exercising such power. Conversely, armies and navies cannot destroy the trade of rivals, nor can they capture it. The great nations of Europe do not destroy the trade of the small nations for their own benefit, because they cannot; and the Dutch citizen, whose Government possesses no military power, is just as well off as the German citizen, whose Government possesses an army of two million men, and a great deal better off than the Russian, whose Government possesses an army of something like four million. Thus, as a rough-and-ready though incomplete indication of the relative wealth and security of the respective States, the Three per Cents. of powerless Belgium are quoted at 96, and the Three per Cents. of powerful Germany at 82; the Three and a Half per Cents. of the Russian Empire, with its hundred and twenty million souls and its four million army, are quoted at 81, while the Three and a Half per Cents. of Norway, which has not an army at all (or any that need be considered in this discussion), are quoted at 102. All of which carries with it the paradox that the more a nation's wealth is militarily protected the less secure does it become.[2] . . .

There remains a final moral claim for war: that it is a needed moral discipline for nations, the supreme test for the survival of the fittest.

In the first chapter of this section, I have pointed out the importance of this plea in determining the general character of European public opinion, on which alone depends the survival or the disappearance of the militarist regimen. Yet in strict logic there is no need to rebut this claim in detail at all, for only a small fraction of those who believe in it have the courage of their convictions.

The defender of large armaments always justifies his position on the ground that such armaments ensure peace. *Si vis pacem,* etc. As between war and peace he has made his choice, and he has chosen, as the definite object of his endeavors, peace. Having directed his efforts to secure peace, he must accept whatever disadvantages there may lie in that state. He is prepared to admit

[2] This is not the only basis of comparison, of course. Everyone who knows Europe at all is aware of the high standard of comfort in all the small countries—Scandinavia, Holland, Belgium, Switzerland. Mulhall, in "Industries and Wealth of Nations" (p. 391), puts the small States of Europe with France and England at the top of the list, Germany *sixth,* and Russia, territorially and militarily the greatest of all, at the very end. Dr. Bertillon, the French statistician, has made an elaborate calculation of the relative wealth of the individuals of each country. The middle-aged German possesses (on the established average) nine thousand francs ($1800); the Hollander *sixteen thousand* ($3200). (See *Journal,* Paris, August 1, 1910.)

that, of the two states, peace is preferable, and it is peace towards which our efforts should be directed. Having decided on that aim, what utility is there in showing that it is an undesirable one?

We must, as a matter of fact, be honest for our opponent. We must assume that in an alternative, where his action would determine the issue of war or peace, he will allow that action to be influenced by the general consideration that war might make for the moral advantage of his country. More important even than this consideration is that of the general national temper, to which his philosophy, however little in keeping with his professed policy and desire, necessarily gives rise. For these reasons it is worth while to consider in detail the biological case which he presents.

The illusion underlying that case arises from the indiscriminate application of scientific formulae.

Struggle is the law of survival with man, as elsewhere, but it is the struggle of man with the universe, not man with man. Dog does not eat dog—even tigers do not live on one another. Both dogs and tigers live upon their prey.

It is true that as against this it is argued that dogs struggle with one another for the same prey—if the supply of food runs short the weakest dog, or the weakest tiger, starves. But an analogy between this state and one in which co-operation is a direct means of increasing the supply of food, obviously breaks down. If dogs and tigers were groups, organized on the basis of the division of labor, even the weak dogs and tigers could, conceivably, perform functions which would increase the food supply of the group as a whole, and, conceivably, their existence would render the security of that supply greater than would their elimination. If to-day a territory like England supports in comfort, a population of 45,000,000, where in other times rival groups, numbering at most two or three millions, found themselves struggling with one another for a bare subsistence, the greater quantity of food and the greater security of the supply is not due to any process of elimination of Wessex men by Northumbrian men, but is due precisely to the fact that this rivalry has been replaced by common action against their prey, the forces of nature. The obvious facts of the development of communities show that there is a progressive replacement of rivalry by co-operation, and that the vitality of the social organism increases in direct ratio to the efficiency of the co-operation, and to the abandonment of the rivalry, between its parts.

All crude analogies between the processes of plant and animal survival and social survival are vitiated, therefore, by disregarding the dynamic element of conscious cooperation.

That mankind as a whole represents the organism and the planet the en-
nt, to which he is more and more adapting himself, is the only

conclusion that consorts with the facts. If struggle between men is the true reading of the law of life, those facts are absolutely inexplicable, for he is drifting away from conflict, from the use of physical force, and towards co-operation. This much is unchallengeable, as the facts which follow will show.

But in that case, if struggle for extermination of rivals between men is the law of life, mankind is setting at naught the natural law, and must be on the way to extinction.

Happily the natural law in this matter has been misread. The individual in his sociological aspect is not the complete organism. He who attempts to live without association with his fellows dies. Nor is the nation the complete organism. If Britain attempted to live without co-operation with other nations, half the population would starve. The completer the co-operation the greater the vitality; the more imperfect the co-operation the less the vitality. Now, a body, the various parts of which are so interdependent that without co-ordination vitality is reduced or death ensues, must be regarded, in so far as the functions in question are concerned, not as a collection of rival organisms, but as one. This is in accord with what we know of the character of living organisms in their conflict with environment. The higher the organism, the greater the elaboration and interdependence of its part, the greater the need for co-ordination.

If we take this as the reading of the biological law, the whole thing becomes plain; man's irresistible drift away from conflict and towards co-operation is but the completer adaptation of the organism (man) to its environment (the planet, wild nature), resulting in a more intense vitality. . . .

All of us who have had occasion to discuss this subject are familiar with the catch-phrases with which the whole matter is so often dismissed. "You cannot change human nature," "What man always has been during thousands of years, he always will be," are the sort of dicta generally delivered as self-evident propositions that do not need discussion. Or if, in deference to the fact that very profound changes, in which human nature is involved, *have* taken place in the habits of mankind, the statement of the proposition is somewhat less dogmatic, we are given to understand that any serious modification of the tendency to go to war can only be looked for in "thousands of years."

What are the facts? They are these:

That the alleged unchangeability of human nature in this matter is not borne out; that man's pugnacity though not disappearing, is very visibly, under the forces of mechanical and social development, being transformed and diverted from ends that are wasteful and destructive to ends that are less wasteful, which render easier that co-operation between men in the struggle with their environment which is the condition of their survival and advance; that changes which, in the historical period, have been extraordinarily rapid are necessarily quickening—quickening in geometrical rather than in arithmetical ratio.

With very great courtesy, one is impelled to ask those who argue that human nature in all its manifestations must remain unchanged how they interpret history. We have seen man progress from the mere animal fighting with other animals, seizing his food by force, seizing also by force his females, eating his own kind, the sons of the family struggling with the father for the possession of the father's wives; we have seen this incoherent welter of animal struggle at least partly abandoned for settled industry, and partly surviving as a more organized tribal warfare or a more ordered pillaging, like that of the Vikings and the Huns; we have seen even these pillagers abandon in part their pillaging for ordered industry, and in part for the more ceremonial conflict of feudal struggle; we have seen even the feudal conflict abandoned in favor of dynastic and religious and territorial conflict, and then dynastic and religious conflict abandoned. There remains now only the conflict of States, and that, too, at a time when the character and conception of the State is being profoundly modified.

Human nature may not change, whatever that vague phrase may mean; but human nature is a complex factor. It includes numberless motives, many of which are modified in relation to the rest as circumstances change; so that the manifestations of human nature change out of all recognition. Do we mean by the phrase that "human nature does not change" that the feelings of the paleolithic man who ate the bodies of his enemies and of his own children are the same as those of a Herbert Spencer, or even of the modern New Yorker who catches his subway train to business in the morning? If human nature does not change, may we therefore expect the city clerk to brain his mother and serve her up for dinner, or suppose that Lord Roberts or Lord Kitchener is in the habit, while on campaign, of catching the babies of his enemies on spear-heads, or driving his motor-car over the bodies of young girls, like the leaders of the old Northmen in their ox-wagons.

What *do* these phrases mean? These, and many like them, are repeated in a knowing way with an air of great wisdom and profundity by journalists nd writers of repute, and one may find them blatant any day in our news-
rs and reviews; yet the most cursory examination proves them to be
wise nor profound, but simply parrot-like catch-phrases which lack
nse, and fly in the face of facts of everyday experience.
that the facts of the world as they stare us in the face show that,

in our common attitude, we not only overlook the modifications in human nature, which have occurred historically since yesterday—occurred even in our generation—but we also ignore the modification of human nature which mere differences of social habit and custom and outlook effect. Take the duel. Even educated people in Germany, France, and Italy, will tell you that it is "not in human nature" to expect a man of gentle birth to abandon the habit of the duel; the notion that honorable people should ever place their honor at the mercy of whoever may care to insult them is, they assure you, both childish and sordid. With them the matter will not bear discussion.

Yet the great societies which exist in England, North America, Australia—the whole Anglo-Saxon world, in fact—have abandoned the duel, and we cannot lump the whole Anglo-Saxon race as sordid or childish.

That such a change as this, which must have conflicted with human pugnacity in its most insidious form,—pride and personal vanity, the traditions of an aristocratic status, every one of the psychological factors now involved in international conflict—has been effected in our own generation should surely give pause to those who dismiss as chimerical any hope that rationalism will ever dominate the conduct of nations.

Discussing the impossibility of allowing arbitration to cover all causes of difference, Mr. Roosevelt remarked, in justification of large armaments: "We despise a nation, just as we despise a man, who fails to resent an insult." Mr. Roosevelt seems to forget that the duel with us is extinct. Do *we,* the English-speaking people of the world, to whom presumably Mr. Roosevelt must have been referring, despise a man who fails to resent an insult by arms? Would we not, on the contrary, despise the man who should do so? Yet so recent is this charge that it has not yet reached the majority of Europeans.

The vague talk of national honor, as a quality under the especial protection of the soldier, shows, perhaps more clearly than aught else, how much our notions concerning international politics have fallen behind the notions that dominate us in everyday life. When an individual begins to rave about his honor, we may be pretty sure he is about to do some irrational, most likely some disreputable deed. The word is like an oath, serving with its vague yet large meaning to intoxicate the fancy. Its vagueness and elasticity make it possible to regard a given incident, at will, as either harmless or a *casus belli.* Our sense of proportion in these matters approximates to that of the school-boy. The passing jeer of a foreign journalist, a foolish cartoon, is sufficient to start the dogs of war baying up and down the land. We call it "maintaining the national prestige," "enforcing respect," and I know not what other high-sounding name. It amounts to the same thing in the end.

The one distinctive advance in civil society achieved by the Anglo-Saxon world is fairly betokened by the passing away of this old notion of a peculiar possession in the way of honor, which has to be guarded by arms. It stands out as the one clear moral gain of the nineteenth century; and, when we observe the notion resurging in the minds of men, we may reasonably expect to find that it marks one of those reversions in development which so often occur in the realm of mind as well as in that of organic forms.

Two or three generations since, this progress, even among Anglo-Saxons, towards a rational standard of conduct in this matter, as between individuals, would have seemed as unreasonable as do the hopes of international peace in our day. Even to-day the continental officer is as firmly convinced as ever that the maintenance of personal dignity is impossible save by the help of the duel. He will ask in triumph, "What will you do if one of your own order openly insults you? Can you preserve your self-respect by summoning him to the police-court?" And the question is taken as settling the matter offhand.

The survival, where national prestige is concerned, of the standards of the *code duello* is daily brought before us by the rhetoric of the patriots. Our army and our navy, not the good faith of our statesmen, are the "guardians of our national honor." Like the duellist, the patriot would have us believe that a dishonorable act is made honorable if the party suffering by the dishonor be killed. The patriot is careful to withdraw from the operation of possible arbitration all questions which could affect the "National honor." An "insult to the flag" must be "wiped out in blood." Small nations, which in the nature of the case cannot so resent the insults of great empires, have apparently no right to such a possession as "honor." It is the peculiar prerogative of world-wide empires. The patriots who would thus resent "insults to the flag" may well be asked whether they would condemn the conduct of the German lieutenant who kills the unarmed civilian in cold blood "for the honor of the uniform."

It does not seem to have struck the patriot that, as personal dignity and conduct have not suffered but been improved by the abandonment of the principle of the duel, there is little reason to suppose that international conduct, or national dignity, would suffer by a similar change of standards.

The whole philosophy underlying the duel, where personal relations are concerned, excites in our day the infinite derision of all Anglo-Saxons. Yet these same Anglo-Saxons maintain it as rigorously as ever in the relations of States.

Profound as is the change involved in the Anglo-Saxon abandonment of the duel, a still more universal change, affecting still more nearly our psychological impulses, has been effected within a relatively recent historical period.

I refer to the abandonment, by the Governments of Europe, of their right to prescribe the religious belief of their citizens. For hundreds of years, generation after generation, it was regarded as an evident part of a ruler's right and duty to dictate what his subject should believe.

As Lecky has pointed out, the preoccupation which, for numberless generations, was the centre round which all other interests revolved has simply and purely disappeared; coalitions which were once the most serious occupation of statesmen now exist only in the speculations of the expounders of prophecy. Among all the elements of affinity and repulsion that regulate the combinations of nations, dogmatic influences which were once supreme can scarcely be said to exist. There is a change here reaching down into the most fundamental impulses of the human mind. "Until the seventeenth century every mental discussion, which philosophy pronounces to be essential to legitimate research, was almost uniformly branded as a sin, and a large proportion of the most deadly intellectual vices were deliberately inculcated as virtues."

Anyone who argued that the differences between Catholics and Protestants were not such as force could settle, and that the time would come when man would realize this truth, and regard a religious war between European States as a wild and unimaginable anachronism, would have been put down as a futile doctrinaire, completely ignoring the most elementary facts of "unchanging human nature."

There is one striking incident of the religious struggle of States which illustrates vividly the change which has come over the spirit of man. For nearly two hundred years Christians fought the Infidel for the conquest of the Holy Sepulchre. All the nations of Europe joined in this great endeavor. It seemed to be the one thing which could unite them, and for generations, so profound was the impulse which produced the movement, the struggle went on. There is nothing in history, perhaps, quite comparable to it. Suppose that during this struggle one had told a European statesman of that age that the time would come when, assembled in a room, the representatives of a Europe, which had made itself the absolute master of the Infidel, could by a single stroke of the pen secure the Holy Sepulchre for all time to Christendom, but that, having discussed the matter cursorily twenty minutes or so, they would decide that on the whole it was not worth while! Had such a thing been told to a mediaeval statesman, he would certainly have regarded the prophecy as that of a madman. Yet this, of course, is precisely what has taken place.

A glance over the common incidents of Europe's history will show the profound change which has visibly taken place, not only in the minds, but in the hearts of men. Things which even in our stage of civilization would no longer be possible, owing to that change in human nature which the military dogmatist denies, were commonplace incidents with our grandfathers. Indeed, the modifications in the religious attitude just touched on assuredly arise from an emotional as much as from an intellectual change. A theology which could declare that the unborn child would suffer eternal torment in the fires of hell for no crime, other than that of its conception, would be in our day impossible on merely emotional grounds. What was once deemed a mere truism would now be viewed with horror and indignation. Again, as Lecky says, "For a great change has silently swept over Christendom. Without disturbance, an old doctrine has passed away from among the realizations of mankind."

Not only in the religious sphere do we see this progress. In a civilization, which was in many respects an admirable one, it was possible for 400 slaves to be slaughtered because one of them had committed some offence; for a lady of fashion to gratify a momentary caprice by ordering a slave to be crucified; and, a generation or two since, for whole populations to turn torture into a public amusement and a public festival; for kings, historically yesterday, to assist personally at the tortures of persons accused of witchcraft. It is related by Pitcairn, in his "Criminal Trials of Scotland," that James I. of Scotland personally presided over the tortures of one, Dr. Fian, accused of having caused a storm at sea. The bones of the prisoner's legs were broken into small pieces in the boot, and it was the King himself who suggested the following variation and witnessed the execution of it: the nails of both hands were seized by a pair of pincers and torn from the fingers, and into the bleeding stump of each finger two needles were thrust up to their heads!

Does anyone seriously contend that the conditions of modern life have not modified psychology in these matters? Does anyone seriously deny that our wider outlook, which is the result of somewhat larger conceptions and wider reading, has wrought such a change that the repetition of things like these in London, or in Edinburgh, or in Berlin, has become impossible?

Or, is it seriously argued that we may witness a repetition of these events, that we are quite capable at any moment of taking pleasure in burning alive a beautiful child? Does the Catholic or the Protestant really stand in danger of such things from his religious rival? If human nature is unchanged by the progress of ideas, then he does, and Europe's general adoption of religious freedom is a mistake, and each sect should arm against the other in the old way, and the only real hope of religious peace and safety is in the domination of an absolutely universal Church. This was, indeed, the plea of the old inquisitor, just as it is the plea of the *Spectator* to-day, that the only hope of political peace is in the domination of an absolutely universal power:

There is only one way to end war and preparation for war, and that is, as we have said, by a universal monarchy. If we can imagine one country—let us say Russia for the sake of argument—so powerful that she could disarm the rest of the world, and then maintain a force big enough to forbid any Power to invade the rights of any other Power . . . no doubt we should have universal peace.[3]

This dictum recalls one, equally emphatic, once voiced by a colleague of the late Procurator of the Holy Synod in Russia, who said:

There is only one way to ensure religious peace in the State, to compel all in that State to conform to the State religion. Those that will not conform must, in the interests of peace, be driven out.

Mr. Lecky, who of all authors has written most suggestively, perhaps, on the disappearance of religious persecution, has pointed out that the strife between opposing religious bodies arose out of a religious spirit which, though often high-minded and disinterested (he protests with energy against the notion that persecution as a whole was dictated by interested motives), was unpurified by rationalism; and he adds that the irrationality which once characterized the religious sentiment has now been replaced by the irrationality of patriotism. Mr. Lecky says:

If we take a broad view of the course of history, and examine the relations of great bodies of men, we find that religion and patriotism are the chief moral influences to which they have been subjected, and that the separate modifications and mutual interaction of these two agents may almost be said to constitute the moral history of mankind.

Is it to be expected that the rationalization and humanization which have taken place in the more complex domain of religious doctrine and belief will not also take place in the domain of patriotism? More especially, as the same author points out, since it was the necessities of material interest which brought about the reforms in the first domain, and since "not only does interest, as distinct from passion, gain a greater empire with advancing civilization, but passion itself is mainly guided by its power."

Have we not abundant evidence, indeed, that the passion of patriotism, as divorced from material interest, is being modified by the pressure of material interest? Are not the numberless facts of national interdependence, which I have indicated here, pushing inevitably to that result? And are we not

[3] *Spectator*, December 31, 1910.

justified in concluding that, just as the progress of rationalism has made it possible for the various religious groups to live together, to exist side by side without physical conflict; just as there has been in that domain no necessary choice between universal domination or unending strife, so in like manner will the progress of political rationalism mark the evolution of the relationship of political groups; that the struggle for domination will cease because it will be realized that physical domination is futile, and that instead of either universal strife or universal domination there will come, without formal treaties or Holy Alliances, the general determination for each to go his way undisturbed in his political allegiance, as he is now undisturbed in his religious allegiance? . . .

The militarist authorities I have quoted in the preceding chapter admit, therefore, and admit very largely, man's drift, in a sentimental sense, away from war. But that drift, they declare, is degeneration; without those qualities which "war alone," in Mr. Roosevelt's phrase, can develop, man will "rot and decay.". . .

This plea is, of course, directly germane to our subject. To say that the qualities which we associate with war, and nothing else but war, are necessary to assure a nation success in its struggles with other nations is equivalent to saying that those who drift away from war will go down before those whose warlike activity can conserve those qualities essential to survival; and this is but another way of saying that men must always remain warlike if they are to survive, that the warlike nations inherit the earth; that men's pugnacity, therefore, is the outcome of the great natural law of survival, and that a decline of pugnacity marks in any nation a retrogression and not an advance in its struggle for survival. I have already indicated the outlines of the proposition, which leaves no escape from this conclusion. This is the scientific basis of the proposition voiced by the authorities I have quoted—Mr. Roosevelt, Von Moltke, Renan, Nietzsche, and various of the warlike clergy [4]—and it lies at the very bottom of the plea that man's nature, in so far as it touches the tendency of men as a whole to go to war, does not change; that the warlike qualities are a necessary part of human vitality in the struggle for existence; that, in short, all that we know of the law of evolution forbids the conclusion that man will ever lose this warlike pug-

---

[4] See citations, . . . notably Mr. Roosevelt's dictum: "In this world the nation that is trained to a career of unwarlike and isolated ease is bound to go down in the end before other nations which have not lost the manly and adventurous qualities." This view is even emphasized in the speech which Mr. Roosevelt recently delivered at the University of Berlin (See London *Times,* May 13, 1910). "The Roman civilization," declared Mr. Roosevelt—perhaps, as the *Times* remarks, to the surprise of those who have been taught to believe that *latifundia perditere Romam*—"went down primarily because the Roman citizen would not fight, because Rome had lost the fighting edge."

nacity, or that nations will survive other than by the struggle of physical force.

The view is best voiced, perhaps, by Homer Lea, whom I have already quoted. He says, in his "Valor of Ignorance":

As physical vigor represents the strength of man in his struggle for existence, in the same sense military vigor constitutes the strength of nations; ideals, laws, constitutions are but temporary effulgences [P. 11]. The deterioration of the military force and the consequent destruction of the militant spirit have been concurrent with national decay [P. 24]. International disagreements are . . . the result of the primordial conditions that sooner or later cause war. . . . the law of struggle, the law of survival, universal, unalterable . . . to thwart them, to short-cut them, to circumvent them, to cozen, to deny, to scorn, to violate them, is folly such as man's conceit alone makes possible. . . . Arbitration denies the inexorability of natural laws . . . that govern the existence of political entities [Pp. 76, 77]. Laws that govern the militancy of a people are not of man's framing, but follow the primitive ordinances of nature that govern all forms of life, from simple protozoa, awash in the sea, to the empires of man.

I have already indicated the grave misconception which lies at the bottom of the interpretation of the evolutionary law here indicated. What we are concerned with now is to deal with the facts on which this alleged general principle is inductively based. We have seen from the foregoing chapter that man's nature certainly does change; the next step is to show, from the facts of the present-day world, that the warlike qualities do not make for survival, that the warlike nations do not inherit the earth.

Which are the military nations? We generally think of them in Europe as Germany and France, or perhaps also Russia, Austria, and Italy. Admittedly (*vide* all the English and American military pundits and economists) England is the least militarized nation in Europe, the United States perhaps in the world. It is, above all, Germany that appeals to us as the type of the military nation, one in which the stern school of war makes for the preservation of the "manly and adventurous qualities."

The facts want a little closer examination. What is a career of unwarlike ease, in Mr. Roosevelt's phrase? In the last chapter we saw that during the last forty years eight thousand out of sixty million Germans have been engaged in warfare during a trifle over a year, and that against Hottentots or Hereros—a proportion of war days per German to peace days per German which is as one to some hundreds of thousands. So that if we are to take Germany as the type of the military nation, and if we are to accept Mr. Roosevelt's dictum that by war alone can we acquire "those virile qualities necessary to win in the stern strife of actual life," we shall nevertheless be doomed to lose them, for under conditions like those of Germany how many of us can ever see war, or can pretend to fall under its influence? As already pointed out, the men who really give the tone to the German nation, to German life and conduct—that is to say, the majority of adult Germans— have never seen a battle and never will see one. France has done much better. Not only has she seen infinitely more actual fighting, but her population is much more militarized than that of Germany, 50 per cent. more, in fact, since, in order to maintain from a population of forty millions the same effective military force as Germany does with sixty millions, $1\frac{1}{2}$ per cent. of the French population is under arms as against 1 per cent. of the German.

Still more military in organization and in recent practical experience is Russia, and more military than Russia is Turkey, and more military than Turkey as a whole are the semi-independent sections of Turkey, Arabia, and Albania, and then, perhaps, comes Morocco.

On the Western Hemisphere we can draw a like table as to the "warlike, adventurous, manly, and progressive peoples" as compared with the "peaceful, craven, slothful, and decadent." The least warlike of all, the nation which has had the least training in war, the least experience of it, which has been the least purified by it, is Canada. After that comes the United States, and after that the best—(excuse me, I mean, of course, the worst—*i.e.,* the least warlike)—of the Spanish American republics like Brazil and Argentina; while the most warlike of all, and consequently the most "manly and progressive," are the "Sambo" republics, like San Domingo, Nicaragua, Colombia, and Venezuela. They are always fighting. If they cannot manage to get up a fight between one another, the various parties in each republic will fight between themselves. Here we get the real thing. The soldiers do not pass their lives in practising the goose-step, cleaning harness, pipeclaying belts, but in giving and taking hard pounding. Several of these progressive republics have never known a year since they declared their independence from Spain in which they have not had a war. And quite a considerable proportion of the populations spend their lives in fighting. During the first twenty years of Venezuela's independent existence she fought no less than one hundred and twenty important battles, either with her neighbors or with herself, and she has maintained the average pretty well ever since. Every election is a fight—none of your "mouth-fighting," none of your craven talking-shops for them. Good, honest, hard, manly knocks, with anything from one to five thousand dead and wounded left on the field. The presidents of these strenuous republics are not poltroons of politicans, but soldiers —men of blood and iron with a vengeance, men after Mr. Roosevelt's own heart, all following "the good old rule, the simple plan." These are the people who have taken Carlyle's advice to "shut up the talking-shops." *They* fight it out like men; *they* talk with Gatling-guns and Mausers. Oh, they are a very fine, manly, military lot! If fighting makes for survival, they should completely oust from the field Canada and the United States, one of which has never had a real battle for the best part of its hundred years of craven, sordid, peaceful life, and the other of which Homer Lea assures us is surely dying, because of its tendency to avoid fighting.

Mr. Lea does not make any secret of the fact (and if he did, some of his rhetoric would display it) that he is out of sympathy with predominant American ideals. He might emigrate to Venezuela, or Colombia, or Nicaragua. He would be able to prove to each military dictator in turn that, in converting the country into a shambles, far from committing a foul crime for which such dictators should be, and are, held in execration by civilized men the world over, they are, on the contrary, but obeying one of God's commands, in tune with all the immutable laws of the universe. I desire to write in all seriousness, but, to one who happens to have seen at first hand something of the conditions which arise from a real military conception of civilization, it is very difficult. How does Mr. Roosevelt, who declares that "by war alone can we acquire those virile qualities necessary to win in the stern strife of actual life"; how does Von Stengel, who declares that "war is a test of a nation's health, political, physical, and moral"; how do our militarists, who infer that the military state is so much finer than the Cobdenite one of commercial pursuits; how does M. Ernest Renan, who declares that war is the condition of progress, and that under peace we should sink to a degree of degeneracy difficult to realize; and how do the various English clergymen who voice a like philosophy reconcile their creed with military Spanish America? How can they urge that non-military industrialism, which, with all its shortcomings, has on the Western Continent given us Canada and the United States, makes for decadence and degeneration, while militarism and the qualities and instincts that go with it have given us Venezuela and San Domingo? Do we not all recognize that industrialism —Mr. Lea's "gourmandizing and retching" notwithstanding—is the one thing which will save these military republics; that the one condition of their advance is that they shall give up the stupid and sordid gold-braid militarism and turn to honest work?

If ever there was a justification for Herbert Spencer's sweeping generalization that "advance to the highest forms of man and society depends on the decline of militancy and the growth of industrialism," it is to be found in the history of the South and Central American Republics. Indeed, Spanish America at the present moment affords more lessons than we seem to be drawing, and, if militancy makes for advance and survival, it is a most extraordinary thing that all who are in any way concerned with those countries, all who live in them and whose future is wrapped up in them, can never sufficiently express their thankfulness that at last there seems to be a tendency with some of them to get away from the blood and valor nonsense which has been their curse for three centuries, and to exchange the military ideal for the Cobdenite, one of buying cheap and selling dear which excites so much contempt. . . .